FIFTH EDITION

Physiology of Behavior

Neil R. Carlson
University of Massachusetts

Allyn and Bacon

Boston   London   Toronto   Sydney   Tokyo   Singapore

Vice-President, Publisher: Susan Badger
Executive Editor: Laura Pearson
Series Editorial Assistant: Marnie Greenhut
Production Administrator: Cheryl Marconi
Electronic Manuscript Manager: Andrew Walker
Page Layout Artist: Timothy Ries
Editorial-Production Services: Barbara Gracia
Text Designer: The Book Company
Cover Administrator: Linda Dickinson
Cover Designer: Design Ad Cetera
Manufacturing Buyer: Louise Richardson

Copyright © 1994, 1991, 1986, 1981, 1977 by Allyn and Bacon
A Division of Paramount Publishing
160 Gould Street
Needham Heights, MA 02194–2134

Library of Congress Cataloging-in-Publication Data

Carlson, Neil R., 1942–
        Physiology of behavior/Neil R. Carlson.—5th ed.
            p.   cm.
        Includes bibliography references and indexes.
        ISBN 0–205–15436–0
        1. Psychophysiology.   I. Title
        [DNLM: 1. Behavior—physiology.   2. Nervous System—physiology.
    3. Nervous System—anatomy & histology.   4. Psychophysiology.   WL
    102 C284p   1994]
    QP360.C35   1994
    152—dc20
    DNLM/DLC
    for Library of Congress   93–36575
                                                              CIP

FREE COPY: ISBN 0–205–15437–9

Printed in the United States of America

10   9 8 7 6 5 4 3 2   1 98 97 96 95 94 93

For Kerstin and Patrick

CONTENTS

Preface   xiii

Chapter 1   **Introduction**

Philosophical Roots of Physiological Psychology   2
Dualism   2
Monism   4

Biological Roots of Physiological Psychology   5
Experimental Physiology   5
Functionalism: Natural Selection and Evolution   7

Contributions of Modern Psychology   10
The Goals of Research   10
Understanding Self-Awareness: Split Brains   11
The Value of Research with Animals   13
Interim Summary   15

Organization of This Book   16
Outline   16
Some Mechanical Details   17

New Terms   18

Suggested Readings   18

Chapter 2   **Structure and Functions of Cells of the Nervous System   19**

Cells of the Nervous System   20
Neurons   20

Supporting Cells   25
The Blood-Brain Barrier   29
Interim Summary   29

Communication Within a Neuron   30
Measurement of Electrical Potentials of Axons   30
The Membrane Potential:
    Balance of Two Forces   32
The Action Potential   35
Conduction of the Action Potential   37
Interim Summary   39

Neural Communication: An Overview   40
The Rate Law   40
Neural Integration   41
A Simple Reflex   43
Interim Summary   45

New Terms   45

Suggested Readings   46

Chapter 3   **Neural Communication   47**

Synaptic Transmission   48
The Concept of Chemical Transmission   48
Structure of Synapses   49
Release of Transmitter Substance   50
Activation of Receptors   53
Postsynaptic Potentials   54
Termination of the Postsynaptic Potential   56
Autoreceptors   57
Other Types of Synapses   58

v

Nonsynaptic Chemical Communication 58
Interim Summary 60

Transmitter Substances 61
Acetylcholine 61
The Monoamines 62
Amino Acid Transmitter Substances 66
Peptides 67
Lipids 68
Soluble Gases 69
Interim Summary 70

Pharmacology of Synapses 70
Effects on Production of Transmitter
   Substances 70
Effects on Storage and Release of Transmitter
   Substances 71
Effects on Receptors 72
Effects on Reuptake or Destruction of Transmitter
   Substances 72
Interim Summary 73

New Terms 74

Suggested Readings 75

Chapter 4 **Structure of the Nervous System**

Basic Features of the Nervous System 78
An Overview 78
Blood Supply 79
Meninges 81
The Ventricular System and Production of CSF 82
Interim Summary 83

The Central Nervous System 84
Development of the Central Nervous System 84
The Forebrain 88
The Mesencephalon 95
The Hindbrain 97
The Spinal Cord 98
Interim Summary 99

The Peripheral Nervous System 100
Spinal Nerves 100
Cranial Nerves 101
The Autonomic Nervous System 102
Interim Summary 103

New Terms 105

Suggested Readings 106

Chapter 5 **Methods of Physiological Psychology 107**

Neuroanatomical and Neurochemical Techniques 108
Histological Procedures 108
Tracing Neural Connections 110
Tracing Connections in the Human Brain 113
Localization of Neurochemicals 114
Localization of Receptors 116
Measuring Metabolic Activity 116
Study of the Living Human Brain 117
Analyzing Chemicals in the Interstitial Fluid 122
Electron Microscopy 123
Interim Summary 124

Experimental Ablation 124
Evaluating the Behavioral Effects of Brain
   Damage 125
Producing Brain Lesions 125
Stereotaxic Surgery 127

Recording the Brain's Electrical Activity 130
Rationale 130
Electrodes 131
Output Devices 132

Stimulating or Inhibiting Neural Activity 134
Electrical and Chemical Stimulation 134
Microiontophoresis 136
Behavioral Effects of Electrical Brain
   Stimulation 136
Interim Summary 137

New Terms 139

Suggested Readings 139

Chapter 6 **Vision 141**

The Stimulus 142

Anatomy of the Visual System 143

The Eyes   143
Photoreceptors   146
Connections Between Eye and Brain   147
Interim Summary   149

Coding of Visual Information in the Retina   150

Coding of Light and Dark   150
Coding of Color   152
Interim Summary   156

Analysis of Visual Information: Role of the Striate Cortex   157

Anatomy of the Striate Cortex   157
Orientation and Movement   158
Spatial Frequency   158
Texture   160
Retinal Disparity   161
Color   162
Modular Organization of the Striate Cortex   163
Blindsight   165
Interim Summary   165

Analysis of Visual Information: Role of the Visual Association Cortex   166

Two Streams of Visual Analysis   166
Perception of Color   167
Analysis of Form   169
Perception of Movement   175
Perception of Location   177
Interim Summary   179

New Terms   180

Suggested Readings   180

Behavioral Functions of the Auditory System   196
Interim Summary   197

Vestibular System   198

Anatomy of the Vestibular Apparatus   198
The Receptor Cells   199
The Vestibular Pathway   199
Interim Summary   200

Somatosenses   201

The Stimuli   201
Anatomy of the Skin and Its Receptive Organs   202
Detection of Cutaneous Stimulation   203
The Somatosensory Pathways   205
Perception of Pain   206
Interim Summary   211
Gustation   213
The Stimuli   213
Anatomy of the Taste Buds and Gustatory Cells   213
Detection of Gustatory Information   214
The Gustatory Pathway   217
Neural Coding of Taste   218
Interim Summary   218

Olfaction   219

The Stimulus   219
Anatomy of the Olfactory Apparatus   219
Transduction of Olfactory Information   221
Detection of Specific Odors   221
Interim Summary   222

New Terms   223

Suggested Readings   223

Chapter 7   Audition, the Body Senses, and the Chemical Senses   181

Audition   182

The Stimulus   182
Anatomy of the Ear   183
Auditory Hair Cells and the Transduction of Auditory Information   186
The Auditory Pathway   188
Detection of Pitch   191
Detection of Loudness   192
Detection of Timbre   193
Feature Detection in the Auditory System   193

Chapter 8   Control of Movement   225

Muscles   226

Skeletal Muscle   226
Anatomy   226
Smooth Muscle   230
Cardiac Muscle   230
Interim Summary   230

Reflex Control of Movement   230

The Monosynaptic Stretch Reflex   230
The Gamma Motor System   232
Polysynaptic Reflexes   232

Interim Summary 234

Control of Movement by the Brain 235

Organization of Motor Cortex 235
Cortical Control of Movement 237
Deficits of Verbally Controlled Movements:
   The Apraxias 240
The Basal Ganglia 243
The Cerebellum 245
The Reticular Formation 249
Interim Summary 249

New Terms 250

Suggested Readings 251

Chapter 9   **Sleep**   253

A Physiological and Behavioral Description 254

Stages of Sleep 254
Mental Activity During Sleep 258
Interim Summary 259

Why Do We Sleep? 259

Sleep as an Adaptive Response 259
Sleep as a Restorative Process 260
The Functions of REM Sleep 265
Interim Summary 267

Disorders of Sleep 267

Insomnia 267
Problems Associated with REM Sleep 269
Problems Associated with Slow-Wave Sleep 270
Interim Summary 271

Biological Clocks 271

Circadian Rhythms and Zeitgebers 271
Role of the Suprachiasmatic Nucleus 272
Interim Summary 277

**Physiological Mechanisms of Sleep and
Waking** 278

Chemical Control of Sleep 278
Neural Control of Arousal 279
Neural Control of Slow-Wave Sleep 281
Neural Control of REM Sleep 283
Interim Summary 288

New Terms 289

Suggested Readings 290

Chapter 10   **Reproductive
Behavior**   291

Sexual Development 292

Production of Gametes and Fertilization 292
Development of the Sex Organs 292
Sexual Maturation 295
Interim Summary 298

Hormonal Control of Sexual Behavior 298

Hormonal Control of Female Reproductive
   Cycles 298
Hormonal Control of Sexual Behavior of
   Laboratory Animals 299
Organizational Effects of Androgens on Behavior:
   Masculinization and Defeminization 302
Effects of Pheromones 303
Human Sexual Behavior 307
Sexual Orientation 312
Interim Summary 313

Neural Control of Sexual Behavior 315

Males 315
Females 320
Interim Summary 322

Maternal Behavior 324

Maternal Behavior in Rodents 324
Stimuli That Elicit and Maintain Maternal
   Behavior 325
Hormonal Control of Maternal Behavior 327
Neural Control of Maternal Behavior 328
Interim Summary 329

New Terms 330

Suggested Readings 330

Chapter 11   **Emotion and Stress**   331

Emotions as Response Patterns 332

Neural Control of Emotional Response
   Patterns 332
Perception of Stimuli with Emotional
   Significance 337
Interim Summary 344

Expression and Recognition of Emotions 344

Facial Expression of Emotions:
    Innate Responses   345
Neural Basis of Communication of Emotions:
    Studies with Normal Subjects   345
Neural Basis of Communication of Emotions:
    Studies of People with Brain Damage   348
Interim Summary   349

Feelings of Emotions   349

The James-Lange Theory   350
Feedback from Simulated Emotions   351
Interim Summary   351

Aggressive Behavior   352

Nature and Functions of Aggressive Behavior   352
Neural Control of Aggressive Behavior   353
Hormonal Control of Aggressive Behavior   354
Interim Summary   358

Stress   359

Stress and Health   359
Physiology of the Stress Response   359
The Coping Response   362
Stress and Cardiovascular Disease   363
Psychoneuroimmunology   365
Interim Summary   369

New Terms   370

Suggested Readings   370

**Chapter 12   Ingestive Behavior:
Drinking   371**

**The Nature of Physiological Regulatory
Mechanisms   372**

Some Facts About Fluid Balance   373
The Fluid Compartments of the Body   373
The Kidneys   375
Interim Summary   376

Drinking and Salt Appetite   377

Osmometric Thirst   377
Volumetric Thirst   380
Food Related Drinking   382
Salt Appetite   383
Interim Summary   383

**Brain Mechanisms of Thirst and Salt
Appetite   383**

Neural Control of Thirst   384
Neural Control of Salt Appetite   388
Interim Summary   389
Mechanisms of Satiety   389
Drinking   389
Salt Appetite   391
Interim Summary   392

New Terms   393

Suggested Readings   393

**Chapter 13   Ingestive Behavior:
Eating   395**

Some Facts About Metabolism   396

Absorption, Fasting, and the Two Nutrient
    Reservoirs   396
Is Total Body Fat Regulated?   398
Interim Summary   399

What Starts a Meal?   400

Social and Environmental Factors   400
Dietary Selection: Responding to the
    Consequences   401
Depletion of Nutrients   403
Interim Summary   407

What Stops a Meal?   408

Head Factors   408
Gastric Factors   408
Intestinal Factors   409
Liver Factors   411
Long-Term Satiety Factors   412
Interim Summary   413

Brain Mechanisms   414

Brain Stem   414
Hypothalamus   415
Interim Summary   420

Eating Disorders   421

Obesity   421
Anorexia Nervosa/Bulimia Nervosa   427
Interim Summary   428

New Terms   429

Suggested Readings   429

Chapter 14 Learning and Memory: Basic Mechanisms 431

The Nature of Learning 432
Interim Summary 436

Perceptual Learning 437
Visual Learning 437
Auditory Learning 443
Modeling the Brain's Ability to Learn:
Neural Networks 444
Interim Summary 447

Mechanisms of Synaptic Plasticity 447
Induction of Long-Term Potentiation 447
Role of NMDA Receptors 450
Mechanism of Synaptic Strengthening 454
Modulation of Long-Term Potentiation 459
Other Forms of Long-Term Potentiation 460
Role of Long-Term Potentiation in Learning 461
Interim Summary 461

S-R Learning: Classical Conditioning 462
Interim Summary 464

S-R Learning: Instrumental Conditioning 465
Discovery of Reinforcing Brain Stimulation 465
Mechanisms of Reinforcing Brain Stimulation 465
Functions of the Reinforcement System 471
Interim Summary 477

New Terms 478

Suggested Readings 479

Chapter 15 Relational Learning and Amnesia 481

Human Anterograde Amnesia 482
Basic Description 483
Spared Learning Abilities 485
Declarative and Nondeclarative Memories 486
Anterograde Amnesia: Failure of Relational
Learning 488
Anatomy of Anterograde Amnesia 490
Interim Summary 494

Relational Learning in Laboratory Animals 494

Working Memory: Remembering Places
Visited 495
Spatial Perception and Learning 496
Place Cells in the Hippocampal Formation 497
Other Functions of the Hippocampal
Formation 499
Role of Long-Term Potentiation in Hippocampal
Functioning 501
Modulation of Hippocampal Functions by
Acetylcholinergic Neurons 502
A Theory of Hippocampal Functioning 504
Interim Summary 508

New Terms 509

Suggested Readings 509

Chapter 16 Human Communication 511

**Speech Production and Comprehension:
Brain Mechanisms 512**
Lateralization 512
Speech Production 513
Speech Comprehension 517
Prosody: Rhythm, Tone, and Emphasis in
Speech 526
Interim Summary 527

Reading and Writing Disorders 528
Relation to Aphasia 528
Pure Alexia 529
Toward and Understanding of Reading 531
Toward and Understanding of Writing 535
Developmental Dyslexias 537
Interim Summary 539

New Terms 540

Suggested Readings 540

Chapter 17 Mental Disorders: Schizophrenia and the Affective Disorders 541

Schizophrenia 542

Description   542
Heritability   543
Pharmacology of Schizophrenia:
    The Dopamine Hypothesis   545
Schizophrenia as a Neurological Disorder   549
Interim Summary   556

Major Affective Disorders   557

Description   557
Heritability   558
Physiological Treatments   558
Role of Monoamines   560
Evidence for Brain Abnormalities   562
Role of Circadian Rhythms   563
Interim Summary   566

New Terms   567

Suggested Readings   567

Obsessive Compulsive Disorder   573
Interim Summary   576

Autistic Disorder   577

Description   577
Possible Causes   578
Interim Summary   582

Addiction   582

Characteristics of Addictive Substances   583
Genetics of Addiction   590
Interim Summary   593

Concluding Remarks   594

New Terms   595

Suggested Readings   595

Chapter 18   **Mental Disorders:
Anxiety Disorders, Autism,
and Addiction   569**

Anxiety Disorders   570
Panic Disorder   570

Glossary   597

References   627

Name Index   675

Subject Index   686

PREFACE

I wrote the first edition of *Physiology of Behavior* during my first sabbatical leave, at the University of Victoria, on the West Coast of Canada. I managed to finish the book despite the temptations posed by such delightful surroundings. I was also exposed to temptations while working on the present edition; I spent the fall semester of 1992 in Paris. As you can imagine, Paris and the beautiful countryside of France are full of diversions that seem designed to keep a writer away from his or her desk. Nevertheless, I managed to finish this edition, too.

I was able to stay at my desk because of the interesting work that has come out of my colleagues' laboratories. It is their creativity and hard work that gives me something to say. Because there was so much for me to learn, I enjoyed writing this edition just as much as the first one. That is what makes writing new editions interesting—learning something new and then trying to find a way to convey the information to the reader.

In the preface to each of the previous editions I mentioned some of the new research methods that had recently been developed. Investigators are continuing to develop new methods—for example, new staining techniques for specific substances, new imaging methods, new recording methods, and the means for analyzing the release of neurotransmitters and neuromodulators in restricted regions of the brains of freely-moving animals. The methods chapter in this edition reflects the enormous advances made in staining methods—new anterograde and retrograde tracers, dye-coupled antibodies for just about everything, in situ hybridization methods to localize messenger RNA, stains for Fos—and the list continues. Nowadays, as soon as a new method is developed in one laboratory, it is adopted by other laboratories and applied to a wide range of problems. And more and more, researchers are combining techniques that converge upon the solution to a problem. In the past, individuals tended to apply their particular research method to a problem; now they are more likely to use many methods, sometimes in collaboration with other laboratories.

You will notice that the book has a different look. The fourth edition contained several pages in full color, but now the entire book is in full color. In addition, most of the illustrations are new. I prepared many of them myself, using a drawing program on my computer. Most of the others were prepared by an artist, Jay Alexander, who works as a technician in the Psychology Department at the University of Massachusetts. I think the result of our collaboration is a set of clear, consistent, and attractive illustrations.

In this edition, as in the previous ones, I have made some changes to the outline of the book, which readers familiar with the previous edition will discover. Some of these changes were made in response to new directions in research efforts, and some were made in response to suggestions of students and colleagues concerning pedagogy. The first part of the book is concerned with foundations: the history of the field, the structure and functions of neurons, neural communication, neuroanatomy, and research methods. The second part is concerned with inputs and outputs: the sensory systems and the motor system. The third part deals with classes of species-typical behavior: sleep, reproduction, emotional behavior, and ingestion. The chapter on reproductive behavior includes maternal behavior as well as mating. The chapter on emotion includes a discussion of emotional reactions, communication of emotions, feelings of emotions, aggression, and stress. As in the previous edition, ingestive behavior is covered in two chapters—one on drinking and one on eating.

The fourth part of the book deals with learning: the physiology of perceptual learning and stimulus-response learning (including classical and operant conditioning) are discussed in the first chapter, and human amnesia and the role of the hippocampal formation in relational learning are discussed in the second. The final part deals with verbal communication and mental disorders. The latter topic is now covered in two chapters; the first discusses schizophrenia and the affective disorders, and the second discusses the anxiety disorders, autism, and addiction.

Besides updating my discussion of research, I have updated my writing. Writing is a difficult, time-consuming endeavor, and I find that I am still learning how to do it well. I have said this in the preface of every edition of this book, and it is still true. I have worked with copy editors who have ruthlessly marked up my manuscript, showing me how to do it better the next time. I keep thinking, "This time there will be nothing for the copy editor to do," but I am always proved wrong: the amount of red pencil on each page remains constant. But I do think that each time the writing is better organized, smoother, and more coherent.

Good writing means including all steps of a logical discourse. My teaching experience has taught me that an entire lecture can be wasted if the students do not understand all of the "obvious" conclusions of a particular experiment before the next one is described. Unfortunately, puzzled students sometimes write notes feverishly, in an attempt to get the facts down so they can study them—and understand them—later. A roomful of busy, attentive students tends to reinforce the lecturer's behavior. I am sure all my colleagues have been dismayed by a question from a student that reveals a lack of understanding of details long since passed, accom-

panied by quizzical looks from other students that confirm that they too have the same question. Painful experiences such as these have taught me to examine the logical steps between the discussion of one experiment and the next and to make sure they are explicitly stated. A textbook writer must address the students who will read the book, and not simply address colleagues who are already acquainted with much of what he or she will say.

Because research on the physiology of behavior is an interdisciplinary effort, a textbook must provide the student with the background necessary for understanding a variety of approaches. I have been careful to provide enough biological background early in the book so students without a background in physiology can understand what is said later, while students with such a background can benefit from details that are familiar to them.

I designed this text for serious students who are willing to work. In return for their effort, I have endeavored to provide a solid foundation for further study. Those students who will not take subsequent courses in this or related fields should receive the satisfaction of a much better understanding of their own behavior. Also, they will have a greater appreciation for the forthcoming advances in medical practices related to disorders that affect a person's perception, mood, or behavior. I hope that students who carefully read this book will henceforth perceive human behavior in a new light.

ACKNOWLEDGEMENTS

Although I must accept the blame for any shortcomings of the book, I want to thank colleagues who helped me by sending reprints of their work, suggesting topics that I should cover, sending photographs that have been reproduced in this book, and pointing out deficiencies in the previous edition. I thank:

Joachim Bender, Leann L. Birch, Gary G. Blasdel, Jeffrey D. Blaustein, L. Arthur Campfield, George Collier, Geert J. DeVries, Gary H. Duncan, Mark Friedman, Yuri Geinisman, Harvey Grill, Carole M.

Hackney, M.H. Hastings, Luis Hernandez, Bartley G. Hoebel, Suzanne Holroyd, Satya P. Kalra, John S. Kauer, Richard Leblanc, Sarah F. Leibowitz, Leslie S. Lerea, Jerrold S. Meyer, Steven E. Petersen, Joseph Piven, W. Sue Ritter, Kuniyoshi Sakai, Randall R. Sakai, Anton J.W. Scheurink, Thomas R. Scott, Larry R. Squire, Glenn Stanley, Edward G. Stopa, Edward M. Stricker, Simon N. Thornton, William D. Timberlake, George N. Wade, Elizabeth Warrington, Harvey P. Weingarten, and Håkan Widner.

Before I began work on the book, my publisher sent a questionnaire to colleagues who were familiar with the previous edition. Their responses to this questionnaire helped me decide what changes to make in the revision. I thank:

A. Michael Anch, David Asdorian, John Broida, Sam Church, Steve Clark, Linda Enloe, Francis Flynn, Douglas Grimley, Paul C. Koch, Michael Levine, June Millet, Michael Numan, Harold Siegel, Thomas Walsh, Frank M. Webb, Margaret H. White, and Dennis Wright.

Several colleagues have reviewed the manuscript of parts of this book and made suggestions for improving the final drafts. I thank:

Geert J. DeVries, David M. Freed, Fred Helmstetter, James Holland, George Gescheider, Arthur D. Kemp, Joseph E. LeDoux, Sheri Mizumori, Antonio Nuñez, and John Salamone.

Anne (Beth) Powell Anderson, Department of Psychology, Smith College, has prepared a student workbook to accompany this text. We all know how important active participation is in the learning process, and Beth's workbook provides an excellent framework for guiding the student's study behavior. Beth is an outstanding teacher, as her students will attest, and her experience has permitted her to prepare an excellent and useful guide for students.

I also want to thank the people at Allyn and Bacon. Laura Pearson, my editor, provided assistance, support, and encouragement. Dana Hayes and Marnie Greenhut, editorial assistants, helped gather comments and suggestions from colleagues who have read the book. Cheryl Marconi, the production editor, assembled the team that designed and produced the book. Barbara Gracia, of Woodstock Publisher's Services, demonstrated her masterful skills of organization in managing the book's production. She got everything done on time, despite an extremely tight schedule. Few people realize what a difficult, demanding, and time-consuming job a production editor has with a project such as this, with hundreds of illustrations and an author who tends to procrastinate, but I do, and I thank her for all she has done. Joyce Grandy and Carol Beal served as copy editors. Their attention to detail surprised me again and again; they found inconsistencies in my terminology, awkwardness in my prose, and disjunctions in my logical discourse and gave me a chance to fix them before anyone else saw them in print.

I must also thank my wife Mary for her support. Writing is a lonely pursuit, because one must be alone with one's thoughts for many hours of the day. I thank her for giving me the time to read, reflect, and write without feeling that I was neglecting her too much.

I also thank Stylianos Nicolaïdis for giving me an academic home in his laboratory at the Collège de France during the fall semester of 1992. He and his collaborators gave me the opportunity to discuss what I was working on and test my ideas on them. They also let me sit quietly at my desk and tap away at my keyboard.

I was delighted to hear from many students and colleagues who read previous editions of my book, and I hope that the dialogue will continue. Please write to me and tell me what you like and dislike about the book. My address is: Department of Psychology, Tobin Hall, University of Massachusetts, Amherst, Massachusetts 01003. When I write, I like to imagine that I am talking with you, the reader. If you write to me, we can make the conversation a two-way exchange.

CHAPTER 1

Introduction

Philosophical Roots of Physiological Psychology
- Dualism
- Monism

Biological Roots of Physiological Psychology
- Experimental Physiology
- Functionalism: Natural Selection and Evolution

Contributions of Modern Psychology
- The Goals of Research
- Understanding Self-Awareness: Split Brains
- The Value of Research with Animals
  Interim Summary

Organization of This Book
- Outline
- Some Mechanical Details

THE LAST FRONTIER IN THIS WORLD—AND perhaps the greatest one—lies within us. The human nervous system makes possible all that we can do, all that we can know, and all that we can experience. Its complexity is immense, and the task of studying it and understanding it dwarfs all previous explorations our species has undertaken.

Investigation of the physiology of behavior has a long history, with roots in philosophy, biology, and psychology. Philosophers have asked how we perceive and understand reality and have posed the mind-body question, which remains with us still. They have also devised the scientific method—a set of rules that permits us to ask questions about the natural world, with some assurance that we will receive reliable answers. Biologists have devised experimental physiology, which provides the tools we use to investigate the workings of the body. They have also developed the framework needed to integrate findings from diverse species—the principles of natural selection, evolution, and genetics. Psychologists have devised methods of behavioral observation and analysis and have presented many of the theoretical questions that motivate much of the research being performed today.

PHILOSOPHICAL ROOTS OF PHYSIOLOGICAL PSYCHOLOGY

PHILOSOPHY ("LOVE OF WISDOM") ORIGINALLY concerned itself with the basis of human knowledge and thought. Philosophers soon realized that to understand the basis of knowledge, they must understand the nature of reality, which led them to develop "natural philosophy," the predecessor of modern physical and biological science.

One of the most universal human characteristics is curiosity. We want to explain what makes things happen. In ancient times people believed that natural phenomena were caused by animating spirits. All moving objects—animals, the wind and tides, the sun, moon, and stars—were assumed to have spirits that caused them to move. For example, stones fell when they were dropped because their animating spirits wanted to be reunited with Mother Earth.

As our ancestors became more sophisticated and learned more about nature, they abandoned this approach—which we call **animism**—in favor of physical explanations for inanimate moving objects. But they still used spirits to explain human behavior.

From the earliest historical times, people have believed they possess souls. This belief stems from our awareness of our own existence. When we think or act, we feel as though something inside us—our mind or our soul—is thinking or deciding to act. But what is the nature of the human mind? We have a physical body, equipped with muscles that move it and with sensory organs such as eyes and ears that perceive information about the world around us. Within our bodies the nervous system plays a central role, controlling the movements of the muscles and receiving information from the sensory organs. But what role does the mind play? Does it *control* the nervous system? Is it a *part of* the nervous system? Is it physical and tangible, like the rest of the body, or is it a spirit that will always remain hidden?

This puzzle has historically been called the *mind-body question*. Philosophers have been trying to answer it for many centuries, and more recently, scientists have taken up the task. Basically, people have followed two different approaches: dualism and monism. As we shall see, these two approaches reflect very different assumptions about the nature of reality.

Dualism

Early philosophers believed that reality was divided into two categories: the material and the spiritual. According to this belief, humans have physical bodies and nonphysical spirits, or souls. Mind and body are considered to be separate; the body is made of ordinary matter, but the mind is not. This belief is called **dualism.** But if the physical and spiritual aspects of our nature are independent, as this model suggests, then what is the purpose of having both, or in what way are they related? If the body functions independently of the soul, then what does the soul do?

The concept of soul is the cornerstone of religion; philosophers were therefore unwilling to dispense with it. Instead, they suggested that the soul controls the body. Because the eyes and ears—the

FIGURE 1.1

René Descartes (1596–1650), French philosopher and mathematician, at the court of Queen Christina of Sweden. Descartes's particular form of dualism (interactionism) stimulated interest in the relation between mind and body.

(Courtesy of the Granger Collection, New York.)

primary windows to the soul—are located in the head, the probable location of the soul was presumed to be the brain. Moreover, damage to the head can lead to unconsciousness or paralysis, which suggested that the soul moved the body by controlling the operations of the brain.

In the seventeenth century the French philosopher and mathematician René Descartes attempted to explain how the soul could control the body. (See **Figure 1.1.**) Descartes believed that animals other than humans were machines. If we could understand how their parts were put together, we would be able to understand animals completely. The *bodies* of humans were also machines and operated on exactly the same principles. However, unlike other animals, we had a God-given soul. The soul received information about the world through the body's

senses, thought about what it perceived, and made decisions about actions. When it wanted to move the body, it did so by acting on the brain, which in turn moved the muscles.

Descartes formulated the first physiological model of behavior. He based his model on the mechanism that activated the statues in grottoes of the Royal Gardens, just west of Paris. As a young man, he was fascinated by the hidden mechanisms that caused the statues to move and dance when visitors stepped on hidden plates. The statues were moved by hydraulic cylinders powered by water pressure. Descartes believed that the muscles of the body also worked hydraulically. When we exert a force with our limbs, our muscles appear to get larger. Descartes concluded that this enlargement occurred because fluid was pumped into the muscles through the nerves. When nerves are cut, a liquid oozes out; hence the nerves must be hollow.

What is the source of the fluid that gets pumped into the muscles? According to Descartes, it was the *cerebral ventricles*—the hollow, fluid-filled chambers of the brain. He concluded that the mechanism that directed the pressurized fluid into the appropriate nerves was the *pineal body*, a small organ situated on top of the brain stem. The pineal body acted like a little joystick: When it was tilted slightly in various

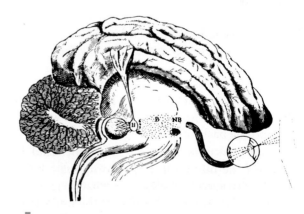

FIGURE 1.2

Descartes's theory. Descartes believed that the soul controlled the movements of the muscles through its influence on the pineal body. His explanation is modeled on the mechanism that animated statues in the Royal Gardens. More recent attempts to explain the physiology of behavior are modeled on newer devices, such as computers.

(Stock Montage.)

directions, it opened pores that permitted fluid to enter the nerves and inflate the muscles. (See *Figure 1.2.*)

Because animals lacked souls, Descartes believed that this model completely explained their behavior. Of course, the details would have to be worked out through further study. Humans, however, possessed souls as well as bodies. The pineal gland, which controlled the movements of the pressurized fluids through the nerves to the muscles, provided the place for the soul to interact with the body. When the soul desired a particular action, it tilted the pineal gland appropriately, and the muscles needed to carry out the action became inflated.

As philosophers have subsequently noted, Descartes's theory contains a built-in contradiction. If the soul or mind is not a part of the physical world, then it cannot exert a force that moves physical objects. Thus, it cannot interact with matter. If the soul or mind possesses material properties that permit it to interact with the body, then it, like the body, is physical. Logically, we cannot have it both ways.

But the spirit of human inquiry is not easily stifled. Some philosophers after Descartes concluded that his conception of the body as a physical machine was correct as far as it went—but that it should go farther. For example, the nineteenth-century British philosopher James Mill agreed that the body was a machine but concluded that the mind was simply a part of that machine. As such, it was subject to the same physical laws as the rest of nature.

Monism

For many years philosophers tried to understand the nature of the human mind by using logic alone. Their lack of success made it clear that mere speculation is futile. If we could answer the mind-body question simply by thinking about it, philosophers would have done so long ago. Physiological psychologists take an empirical, practical, and monistic approach to the study of human nature. **Monism** is the belief that reality consists of a unified whole and, thus, that the mind is a phenomenon produced by the workings of the body. We believe that once we understand how the body works—and, in particu-

lar, how the nervous system works—the mind-body problem will have been solved. What we call "mind" is a consequence of the functioning of the body and its interactions with the environment. The mind-body problem thus exists only as an abstraction. We are convinced that once we understand enough about physiology we will be able to explain how we perceive, how we think, how we remember, and how we act. We will even be able to explain the nature of our own self-awareness. Of course, only time will tell whether this belief is justified.

What can a physiological psychologist say about human self-awareness? We know that it is altered by changes in the structure or chemistry of the brain; therefore, we conclude that consciousness is a physiological function, just like behavior. We can even speculate about the usefulness of self-awareness: Consciousness and the ability to communicate seem to go hand in hand. Species like ours, with our complex social structures and enormous capacity for learning, are well served by our ability to express intentions to one another and to make requests of one another. This communication makes cooperation possible and permits us to establish customs and laws of behavior. Perhaps the ability to make plans and to communicate these plans to others is what was selected for in the evolution of consciousness. Later in this chapter, I will discuss some research that relates to the physiology of consciousness.

The question of human consciousness suggests another issue: *determinism* versus *free will*. Self-awareness seems to bring with it a feeling of control; most people believe their minds choose to make their brains do what they do. They believe that although their environment and their physiology affects them, they are able to act of their own free will. Because a belief in free will implies that the mind is not constrained by physiology, it is a form of dualism. This belief is unacceptable in the laboratory; physiological research is limited to those things that can be measured by physical means—matter and energy. We have no tools that permit us to study nonmaterial entities. In our research we must act like *determinists,* looking for the physical causes of behavior.

Certainly, a belief in determinism is a belief in monism. But in addition, it is a belief that the world is an orderly place where each event is determined by the events that precede it. It is a belief that there are general principles that govern the interactions between matter and energy, and that these principles are responsible for all phenomena, both animate and inanimate. We assume that, in principle, human behavior can be explained down to the last detail by completely understanding its physiology. However, even if we someday discover all there is to know about the physiology of behavior, we will not always be able to predict a particular person's behavior on a particular occasion. In applying the physical laws governing behavior, we would have to know *everything* that is presently going on in a person's body in order to predict what he or she will do next.

From our present perspective this knowledge seems impossible to obtain, which means that for all practical purposes physiological psychology will never take all the mystery out of an individual's behavior. Even physical scientists have to confront the difference between understanding general laws and predicting the behavior of complex systems. For example, although we cannot predict where a feather will fall if we drop it from a tall building during a windstorm, no reasonable person would insist that the landing place is affected by free will on the part of the feather. A determinist would maintain that free will in humans is a myth that is bolstered by two aspects of our nature: the complexity of the human brain, which is far greater than the forces that act on a falling feather, and our own self-awareness, which makes us feel that our minds control our bodies, rather than the reverse.

I am sure that many of you do not agree with the determinist position; you may feel that you are in control of your own behavior, and you can point out—correctly—that I cannot prove otherwise. Fortunately, the issue is a philosophical and religious one that can be divorced from the scientific investigation of the physiology of behavior. If a person believes in his or her own free will, that is fine, as long as he or she *acts* like a determinist in the laboratory. We must limit the scope of our hypotheses to the methods of investigation that we have at hand. Because our techniques are physical, our explanations must also be physical. If organisms do have non-physical minds or souls that control their behavior, the methods of physiological psychology will never detect them.

BIOLOGICAL ROOTS OF PHYSIOLOGICAL PSYCHOLOGY

NOT ALL MODERN PHILOSOPHERS ARE MONISTS, and not all believe that the human mind is based on physiological functioning. Yet scientists who study the physiology of behavior trace their intellectual ancestry to the monistic, deterministic school of philosophy. This school encouraged the development of natural scientists, who first studied living organisms in the world around them and eventually applied their techniques and principles to the study of human behavior.

Although such early natural philosophers as Aristotle speculated about the causes of behavior, René Descartes's physiological model provides a good starting place for a discussion of the biological roots of physiological psychology. His model was wrong, but it was a reasonable hypothesis, considering what was known about the body at the time. Others soon tested its predictions and found them incorrect. For example, experiments showed that the volume of a muscle does not actually increase when it contracts, as it would if it were inflated with fluid. In fact, Luigi Galvani, an eighteenth-century Italian physiologist, found that stimulation of a frog's nerve caused the muscle to which it was attached to contract. The muscle would contract even when the muscle and the nerve attached to it were removed from the rest of the body; thus, pressurized ventricular fluid could obviously not be responsible for the contraction. (Alessandro Volta identified the stimulating event as electricity.) The value of Descartes's physiological model did not lie in whether it was right or wrong; rather, it served to focus the efforts of those who followed him on performing experiments. Thus, knowledge of the physiology of behavior began to accumulate.

Experimental Physiology

One of the most important figures in the development of experimental physiology was Johannes Müller, a nineteenth-century German physiologist. Müller was a forceful advocate of the application of experimental techniques to physiology. Previously, the activities of most natural scientists were limited to observation and classification. Although these activities are essential, Müller insisted that major advances in understanding the workings of the body would be achieved only by experimentally removing or isolating animals' organs, testing their responses to various chemicals, and otherwise altering the environment to see how the organs responded. His most important contribution to the study of the physiology of behavior was his **doctrine of specific nerve energies.** Müller observed that although all nerves carry the same basic message—an electrical impulse—we perceive the messages of different nerves in different ways. For example, messages carried by the optic nerves produce sensations of visual images, and those carried by the auditory nerves produce sensations of sounds. How can different sensations arise from the same basic message?

The answer is that the messages occur in different channels. The portion of the brain that receives messages from the optic nerves interprets the activity as visual stimulation, even if the nerves are actually stimulated mechanically. (For example, when we rub our eyes, we see flashes of light.) Because different parts of the brain receive messages from different nerves, the brain must be functionally divided: Some parts perform some functions, and other parts perform others.

Müller's advocacy of experimentation and the logical deductions from his doctrine of specific nerve energies set the stage for performing experiments directly on the brain. Indeed, Pierre Flourens, a nineteenth-century French physiologist, did just that. Flourens removed various parts of animals' brains and observed their behavior. By seeing what the animal could no longer do, he could infer the function of the missing portion of the brain. This method is called **experimental ablation** (from the Latin *ablatus,* "carried away"). Flourens claimed to have discovered the regions of the brain that control heart rate and breathing, purposeful movements, and visual and auditory reflexes.

Soon after Flourens performed his experiments, Paul Broca, a French surgeon, applied the principle of experimental ablation to the human brain. Of course, he did not intentionally remove parts of human brains to see how they worked. Instead, he observed the behavior of people whose brains had

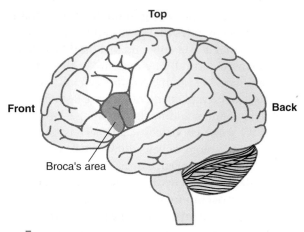

Top

Front

Back

Broca's area

| **FIGURE 1.3**

Broca's area, a region of the brain named for French surgeon Paul Broca. Broca discovered that damage to a part of the left side of the brain disrupted a person's ability to speak.

been damaged by strokes. In 1861 he performed an autopsy on the brain of a man who had had a stroke that caused him to lose the ability to speak. Broca's observations led him to conclude that a portion of the cerebral cortex on the left side of the brain performs functions necessary for speech. (See *Figure 1.3.*) Other physicians soon obtained evidence supporting his conclusions. As you will learn, the physiological basis of speech is not localized in a particular region of the brain. Indeed, speech requires many different functions, which are organized throughout the brain. Nonetheless, the method of experimental ablation remains important to our understanding of the brains of both humans and laboratory animals.

As I mentioned earlier, Luigi Galvani used electricity to demonstrate that muscles contain the source of the energy that powers their contractions. In 1870 the German physiologists Gustav Fritsch and Eduard Hitzig used electrical stimulation as a tool for understanding the physiology of the brain. They applied weak electrical shocks to the exposed surface of a dog's cerebral cortex and observed the effects of the stimulation. They found that stimulation of different portions of a specific region of the cortex caused contraction of specific muscles on the opposite side of the body. We now refer to this region as the primary motor cortex, and we know that nerve cells there communicate directly with those that cause muscular contractions. We also know that other regions of the brain communicate with the primary motor cortex and thus control behaviors. For example, the region that Broca found to be necessary for speech communicates with the portion of the primary motor cortex that controls the muscles of the lips, tongue, and throat, which we use to speak.

One of the most brilliant contributors to nineteenth-century science was the German physicist and physiologist Hermann von Helmholtz. Helmholtz devised a mathematical formulation of the law of conservation of energy, invented the ophthalmoscope (used to examine the retina of the eye), devised an important and influential theory of color vision and color blindness, and studied audition, music, eye movements, geometry, allergies, and the formation of ice. Although Helmholtz had studied under Müller, he opposed Müller's belief that human organs are endowed with a vital nonmaterial force that coordinates their operations. Helmholtz believed, as modern biologists do, that *all* aspects of physiology are mechanistic, subject to experimental investigation.

Helmholtz was the first scientist to attempt to measure the speed of conduction through nerves. Scientists had previously believed that such conduction was identical to the conduction that occurs in wires, traveling at approximately the speed of light. But Helmholtz found that neural conduction was much slower—only about 90 feet per second. This measurement proved that neural conduction was more than a simple electrical message, as we will see in the next chapter.

Twentieth-century developments in experimental physiology include many important inventions, such as sensitive amplifiers to detect weak electrical signals, neurochemical techniques to analyze chemical changes within and between cells, and histological techniques to see cells and their constituents. Because these developments belong to the modern era, they are discussed in detail in subsequent chapters.

Functionalism: Natural Selection and Evolution

In discussing the biological roots of physiological psychology, I have provided a brief history of the

FIGURE 1.4

Charles Darwin (1809-1882). His theory of evolution revolutionized biology and provided the basis for functionalism, a theory that strongly influenced pioneering psychologists.
(North Wind Picture Archives.)

contribution of experimental physiology. Müller's insistence that biology must be an experimental science provided the starting point for an important tradition. However, other biologists continued to observe, classify, and think about what they saw, and some of them arrived at valuable conclusions. The most important of these biologists was Charles Darwin. (See *Figure 1.4*.) Darwin formulated the principle of *natural selection,* which revolutionized biology. He noted that individuals spontaneously undergo structural changes. If these changes produce favorable effects that permit the individual to reproduce more successfully, some of the individual's offspring will inherit the favorable characteristics and will themselves produce more offspring.

Darwin's theory emphasized that all of an organism's characteristics—its structure, its coloration, its behavior—have functional significance. For example, eagles have strong talons and sharp beaks because they permit the birds to catch and eat prey.

Caterpillars that eat green leaves are themselves green because this color makes it difficult for birds to see them against their usual background. Mother mice construct nests because their offspring will be kept warm and out of harm's way. **Functionalism** assumes that characteristics of living organisms perform useful functions, or at least functions that were useful at one time in the history of the species. To understand the physiological basis of various behaviors, we must first understand the significance of these behaviors. We must therefore understand something about the natural history of the species being studied so that the behaviors can be seen in context.

A good example of the functional analysis of an adaptive trait was demonstrated in an experiment by Blest (1957). Certain species of moths and butterflies have spots on their wings that resemble eyes—particularly the eyes of predators such as owls. (See *Figure 1.5.*) These insects normally rely on camouflage for protection; the back of their wings, when folded, are colored like the bark of a tree. However, when a bird approaches, the insect's wings flip open, suddenly displaying the hidden eyespots. The bird then tends to fly away rather than eat the insect. Blest performed an experiment to see whether the eyespots on a moth's or butterfly's wings really disturbed birds that saw them. He placed mealworms

on different backgrounds and counted how many worms the birds ate. Indeed, when the worms were placed on a background that contained eyespots, the birds tended to avoid them.

To understand the workings of a complex piece of machinery, we need to know what its functions are. This principle is just as true for a living organism as it is for a mechanical device. However, an important difference exists between machines and organisms: Machines result from inventors who had a purpose in mind when they designed them, whereas organisms result from a long series of accidents. Thus, strictly speaking, we cannot say that any physiological mechanisms of living organisms have a *purpose.* But they have *functions,* and these we can try to determine. For example, the forelimbs shown in Figure 1.6 are adapted for different uses in different species of animals. (See *Figure 1.6.*)

The cornerstone of evolution is the principle of natural selection. Briefly, here is how the process works for sexually reproducing multicellular animals: Every organism consists of a large number of cells, each of which contains chromosomes. Chromosomes are complex molecules that contain the recipes for producing the proteins that cells need to grow and perform their functions. In essence, the chromosomes contain the blueprints for the construction (that is, the embryological development) of a particular member of a particular species. If these plans are altered, a different organism is produced.

The plans do get altered; mutations occur from time to time. Mutations are accidental changes in the chromosomes of sperms or eggs that join together and develop into new organisms. For example, cosmic radiation might strike a chromosome in a cell of a parental testis or ovary, thus producing a mutation that affects the offspring. Most mutations are deleterious: The offspring either fails to survive or survives with some sort of deficit. However, a small percentage of mutations are beneficial and confer a *selective advantage* to the organism that possesses them. That is, the animal is more likely than those without the mutation to live long enough to reproduce and hence to pass on its chromosomes (with their alteration) to its own offspring. Many different kinds of traits can confer a selective advantage. Examples include resistance to a particular dis-

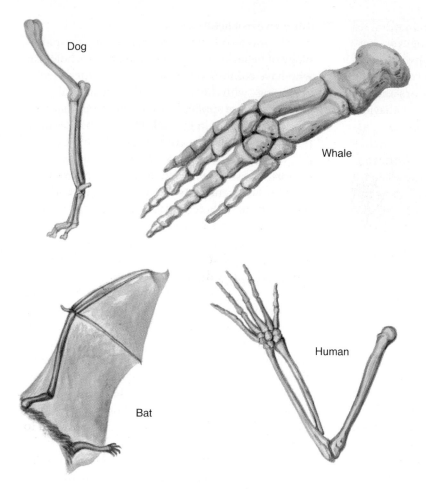

Dog

Whale

Human

Bat

FIGURE 1.6

The humerus bone, shown in red. Through the process of natural selection, this bone has been adapted to suit many different functions.

(Adapted from Moore, R. *Evolution.* New York: Life Nature Library, 1964.)

ease, the ability to digest new kinds of food, more effective weapons for defense or for procurement of prey, and even a more attractive appearance to members of the opposite sex (after all, one must reproduce in order to pass on one's chromosomes).

Naturally, the traits that can be altered by mutations are physical ones; chromosomes make proteins, which affect the structure and chemistry of cells. But the *effects* of these physical alterations can be seen in an animal's behavior. Thus, the process of natural selection can act upon behavior indirectly. For example, if a particular mutation results in changes in the brain that cause a small animal to stop moving and freeze when it perceives a novel stimulus, that animal is more likely to escape undetected when a predator passes nearby. This tendency makes the animal more likely to survive and produce offspring, thus passing on its genes to future generations.

Other mutations are not immediately favorable; but because they do not put their possessors at a disadvantage, they get inherited by at least some members of the species. As a result of thousands of such mutations, the members of a particular species possess a variety of genes and all are at least somewhat different from one another. Different environments provide optimal habitats for different kinds of organisms. When the environment changes, species must adapt or run the risk of becoming extinct. If some members of the species possess assortments of genes that provide characteristics permitting them to adapt to the new environment, their genes will soon dominate and the species will undergo changes. Thus, many mutations that do not cause immediate changes in the genetic composition of a species may at some future time provide the genetic variability that permits at least some individuals to take advantage of environmental changes.

An understanding of the principle of natural selection plays some role in the thinking of every person who undertakes research in physiological psychology. Some researchers explicitly consider the genetic mechanisms of various behaviors and the physiological processes upon which these behaviors depend. Others are concerned with comparative aspects of behavior and its physiological basis; they compare the nervous systems of animals from a variety of species in order to make hypotheses about the evolution of brain structure and the behavioral capacities that correspond to this evolutionary development. But even though many researchers are not directly involved with the problem of evolution, the principle of natural selection guides the thinking of all physiological psychologists. We ask ourselves what the selective advantage of a particular trait might be. We think about how nature might have used a physiological mechanism that already existed to perform more complex functions in more complex organisms. When we entertain hypotheses, we ask ourselves whether a particular explanation makes sense in an evolutionary perspective.

CONTRIBUTIONS OF MODERN PSYCHOLOGY

THE FIELD OF PHYSIOLOGICAL PSYCHOLOGY GREW out of psychology. Indeed, the first textbook of psychology, written by Wilhelm Wundt in the late nineteenth century, was titled *Principles of Physiological Psychology*. In recent years, with the explosion of information in experimental biology, scientists from other disciplines have become prominent contributors to the investigation of the physiology of behavior. The united effort of physiological psychologists, physiologists, and other neuroscientists has come about because of the realization that the ultimate function of the nervous system is *behavior*. Of course, we do things beside move—for example, we perceive, think, and remember. However, the function of perception, thinking, and remembering is that they permit us to engage in behaviors that are responsive to our environment and thus useful to

our own existence.

The modern history of investigating the physiology of behavior has been written by psychologists who have combined the methods of experimental psychology with the methods of experimental physiology and have applied them to the issues that concern psychologists in general. Thus, we have studied perceptual processes, control of movement, sleep and waking, reproductive behaviors, aggressive behaviors, ingestive behaviors, learning, and communication. In recent years we have begun to study the physiology of pathological conditions, such as mental disorders.

The Goals of Research

The goal of all scientists is to explain the phenomena they study. But what do we mean by "explain"? Scientific explanation takes two forms: generalization and reduction. Most psychologists deal with **generalization.** They explain particular instances of behavior as examples of general laws, which they deduce from their experiments. For instance, most psychologists would explain a pathologically strong fear of dogs as an example of classical conditioning. Presumably, the person was frightened earlier in life by a dog. An unpleasant stimulus was paired with the sight of the animal (perhaps the person was knocked down by an exuberant dog or was attacked by a vicious one), and the subsequent sight of dogs evokes the earlier response—fear.

Most physiologists deal with **reduction.** They explain phenomena in terms of simpler phenomena. For example, they may explain the movement of a muscle in terms of the changes in the membranes of muscle cells, the entry of particular chemicals, and the interactions among protein molecules within these cells. Similarly, a molecular biologist would explain these events in terms of forces that bind various molecules together and cause various parts of the molecules to be attracted to one another. In turn, the job of an atomic physicist is to describe matter and energy themselves and to account for the various forces found in nature. Practitioners of each branch of science use reduction to call on more elementary generalizations to explain the phenomena they study.

The task of the physiological psychologist is to explain behavior in physiological terms. But physiological psychologists cannot simply be reductionists. It is not enough to observe behaviors and correlate them with physiological events that occur at the same time. Identical behaviors may occur for different reasons and thus may be initiated by different physiological mechanisms. Therefore, we must understand "psychologically" why a particular behavior occurs before we can understand what physiological events made it occur.

Let me provide a specific example. Mice, like many other mammals, often build nests. Behavioral observations show that mice will build nests under two conditions: when the air temperature is low and when the animal is pregnant. A nonpregnant mouse will not build a nest if the weather is warm, whereas a pregnant mouse will build one regardless of the temperature. The same behavior occurs for different reasons. Thus, it should not be surprising that these behaviors are initiated by different physiological mechanisms, one involving changes in the levels of various hormones in the animal's blood, and another involving nerve cells that detect temperature changes. Nest building can be studied as a behavior related to the process of temperature regulation, or it can be studied in the context of parental behavior.

Sometimes physiological mechanisms can tell us something about psychological processes. This relationship is particularly true of complex phenomena such as language, memory, and mood, which are poorly understood psychologically. For example, damage to a specific part of the brain can cause very specific impairments in a person's language abilities. The nature of these impairments suggests how these abilities are organized. For example, when the damage involves a brain region that is important in analyzing speech sounds, it also produces deficits in spelling. This finding suggests that the ability to recognize a spoken word and the ability to spell it call upon related brain mechanisms. Damage to a different region can make it impossible for a person to read unfamiliar words by sounding them out but does not impair the ability to read words with which this person is already familiar. This finding suggests that reading comprehension can take two routes: one that is related to speech sounds and another that is primarily visual, bypassing acoustic representation.

In practice, the research efforts of physiological psychologists involve both forms of explanation—generalization and reduction. Ideas for experiments are stimulated by the investigator's knowledge both of psychological generalizations about behavior and of physiological mechanisms. A good physiological psychologist must therefore be both a good psychologist and a good physiologist.

Understanding Self-Awareness: Split Brains

I suggested earlier that our self-awareness is related to our ability to communicate verbally with one another. Several chapters will discuss research on problems related to human consciousness, including perception, memory, and verbal communication. But in this chapter I want to introduce you to some research that indicates that awareness is very much a function of the brain. Studies of humans who have undergone a particular surgical procedure demonstrate that when parts of the brain involved with verbal behavior are disconnected from parts that are involved with certain kinds of perceptions, people become unaware of these perceptions. These results suggest that the parts of the brain involved in verbal behavior play a critical role in consciousness.

The surgical procedure is one that has been used for people who have very severe epilepsy that cannot be controlled by drugs. In these individuals, nerve cells in one side of the brain become overactive, and the overactivity is transmitted to the other side of the brain by the corpus callosum. The **corpus callosum** is a large bundle of nerve fibers that connect corresponding parts of one side of the brain with those on the other. Both sides of the brain then engage in wild activity and stimulate each other, causing a generalized epileptic seizure. These seizures can occur many times each day, preventing the patient from leading a normal life. Neurosurgeons discovered that cutting the corpus callosum (the **split-brain operation**) greatly reduced the frequency of the epileptic seizures.

Figure 1.7 shows a drawing of the split-brain operation. We see the brain sliced down the middle, from front to back, dividing it into its two symmet-

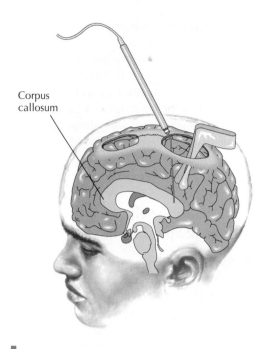

FIGURE 1.7

The split-brain operation.
(Adapted from Gazzaniga, M.S. *Fundamentals of Psychology.* New York: Academic Press, 1973.)

Corpus callosum

rical halves (the **cerebral hemispheres**). The corpus callosum is being cut by the neurosurgeon's special knife. (See ***Figure 1.7.***)

Sperry (1966) and Gazzaniga and his associates (Gazzaniga, 1970; Gazzaniga and LeDoux, 1978) have studied these patients extensively. The two cerebral hemispheres receive sensory information from the opposite sides of the body and control movements of the opposite sides, too. The corpus callosum permits the two hemispheres to share information, so that each side knows what the other side is perceiving and doing. After the split-brain operation is performed, the two hemispheres are disconnected and operate independently; their sensory mechanisms, memories, and motor systems can no longer exchange information. The effects of these disconnections are not obvious to the casual observer, for the simple reason that only one hemisphere—in most people, the left—controls speech. The right hemisphere of an epileptic person with a split brain can understand speech reasonably well, but that hemisphere is poor at reading and spelling and is totally incapable of producing speech.

Because only one side of the brain can talk about what it is experiencing, most observers do not detect the independent operations of the right side of a split brain. Even the patient's left brain has to learn about the independent existence of the right brain. One of the first things that these patients say they notice after the operation is that their left hand seems to have a "mind of its own." For example, patients may find themselves putting down a book held in the left hand, even if they are reading it with great interest. This conflict occurs because the right hemisphere, which controls the left hand, cannot read and therefore finds the book boring. At other times, they surprise themselves by making obscene gestures (with the left hand) when they had not intended to. A psychologist once reported that a man with a split brain attempted to beat his wife with one hand and protect her with the other. Did he *really* want to hurt her? Yes and no, I guess.

One exception to the crossed representation of sensory information is the olfactory system. That is, when a person sniffs a flower through the left nostril, only the left brain receives a sensation of the odor. Thus, if the right nostril of a patient with a split brain is closed, leaving the left nostril open, the patient will accurately identify odors verbally. However, if the odor enters the right nostril, the patient will say that he or she smells nothing. But, in fact, the right hemisphere *has* perceived the odor and *can* identify it. This ability can be demonstrated by asking the patient to smell an odor with the right nostril and then reach for some objects that are hidden from view by a partition. If the patient is asked to use the left hand, controlled by the hemisphere that detected the smell, he or she will select the object that corresponds to the odor—a plastic flower for a floral odor, a toy fish for a fishy odor, a model tree for the odor of pine, and so forth. But the patient fails this test if asked to use the right hand, because the right hand is connected to the left hemisphere, which did not smell the odor. (See ***Figure 1.8.***)

The effects of cutting the corpus callosum reinforce the conclusion that we become conscious of something only if information about it is able to reach the circuits that control speech, which are located in the left hemisphere. If such communication is interrupted, then some kinds of information can never reach consciousness.

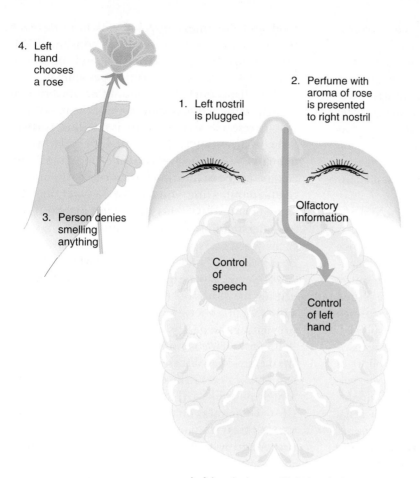

4. Left hand chooses a rose

1. Left nostril is plugged

2. Perfume with aroma of rose is presented to right nostril

3. Person denies smelling anything

Olfactory information

Control of speech

Control of left hand

Left hemisphere   Right hemisphere

FIGURE 1.8

Identification of an object in response to an olfactory stimulus by a person with a split brain.

The Value of Research with Animals

Most of the research that I describe in this book involves experimentation on living animals. Any time we use another species of animals for our own purposes, we should be sure that what we are doing is both humane and worthwhile. I believe that a good case can be made that research on the physiology of behavior qualifies on both counts. Humane treatment is a matter of procedure. We know how to maintain laboratory animals in good health in comfortable, sanitary conditions. We know how to administer anesthetics and analgesics so that animals do not suffer during or after surgery, and we know how to prevent infections with proper surgical procedures and the use of antibiotics. Most industrially developed societies have very strict regulations about the care of animals and also require approval of the procedures to be used in experiments involving animals. There is no excuse for mistreating animals in our care. In fact, the vast majority of laboratory animals *are* treated humanely.

Whether an experiment is *worthwhile* is more difficult to say. We use animals for many purposes. We eat their meat and their eggs and drink their milk; we turn their hides into leather; we extract insulin and other hormones from their organs to treat people with diseases; we train them to do useful work on farms or to entertain us. Even having a pet is a form of exploitation; it is we—not they—who decide that they will live in our homes. The fact is, we have been using other animals throughout the history of our species.

Pet owning causes much more suffering among animals than scientific research does. As Miller

(1983) notes, pet owners are not required to receive permission from a board of experts including a veterinarian to house their pets, nor are they subject to periodic inspections to be sure that their home is clean and sanitary, that their pets have enough space to exercise properly, that their diets are appropriate; but scientific researchers are. Miller also notes that fifty times more dogs and cats are killed by humane societies each year because they have been abandoned by former pet owners than are used in scientific research.

If a person believes that it is wrong to use another animal in any way, regardless of the benefits to humans, there is nothing I can say to convince him or her of the value of scientific research with animals. For this person the issue is closed from the very beginning. Moral absolutes cannot be settled logically; like religious beliefs, they can be accepted or rejected, but they cannot be proved or disproved. Therefore, I will not try to attack or defend absolute moral positions. My arguments in support of scientific research with animals are based on an evaluation of the benefits the research has to humans. (In addition, we should not lose sight of the fact that research with animals often helps *other animals;* procedures used by veterinarians, as well as those used by physicians, come from such research.)

Before I describe the advantages of research with animals, I want to point out that the use of animals in research and teaching is a special target of animal rights activists. Nicholl and Russell (1990) examined twenty-one books written by such activists and calculated the number of pages devoted to concern for different uses of animals. Next, they compared the relative concern the authors showed for these uses to the numbers of animals actually involved in each of these categories. The results indicate that the authors showed relatively little concern for animals used for food, hunting, or furs, or for those killed in pounds; but although only 0.3 percent of the animals are used for research and education, 63.3 percent of the pages were devoted to this use. In terms of pages per million animals used, the authors devoted 0.08 to food, 0.23 to hunting, 1.27 to furs, 1.44 to killing in pounds—and 53.2 to research and education. The authors showed 665 times more concern for research and education compared with

food, and 231 times compared with hunting. Even the use of animals for furs (which consumes two-thirds as many animals as research and education) attracted 41.9 times less attention per animal.

The disproportionate amount of concern that animal rights activists show toward the use of animals in research and education is puzzling, particularly because this is the one *indispensable* use of animals. We *can* survive without eating animals, we *can* live without hunting, we *can* do without furs, but without using animals for research and for training future researchers, we *cannot* make progress in understanding and treating diseases. In not too many years, our scientists will probably have developed a vaccine that will prevent the further spread of AIDS. Some animal rights activists believe that preventing the deaths of laboratory animals in the pursuit of such a vaccine is a more worthy goal than preventing the deaths of millions of humans that will, if a vaccine is not found, occur as a result of the disease. Even diseases we have already conquered would take new victims if drug companies could no longer use animals. If they were deprived of animals, these companies could no longer extract hormones used to treat human diseases, and they could not prepare many of the vaccines we now use to prevent them.

Our species is beset by medical, mental, and behavioral problems, many of which can be solved only through biological research. Let us consider some of the major neurological disorders. Strokes, caused by bleeding or occlusion of a blood vessel within the brain, often leave people partly paralyzed, unable to read or write or communicate verbally with their friends and family. Basic research on the means by which nerve cells communicate with one another has led to important discoveries about the causes of the death of brain cells. This research was not directed toward a specific practical goal; the potential benefits actually came as a surprise to the investigators.

Experiments based on these results have shown that if a blood vessel leading to the brain is blocked for a few minutes, the part of the brain that is nourished by that vessel will die. However, the brain damage can be prevented by first administering a drug that interferes with a particular kind of neural communication. This research is important, because it may lead to medical treatments that can help reduce the brain damage caused by strokes. But it involves operating on a laboratory animal such as a rat and pinching off a blood vessel. (The animals are anesthetized, of course.) Some of the animals will sustain brain damage, and all will be killed so that their brains can be examined. However, I think you will agree that research like this is just as legitimate as using animals for food.

As you will learn later in this book, research with laboratory animals has produced important discoveries about the possible causes or potential treatments of neurological and mental disorders, including Parkinson's disease, schizophrenia, manic-depressive illness, anxiety disorders, obsessive-compulsive disorders, anorexia nervosa, obesity, and drug addictions. Although much progress has been made, these problems are still with us and cause much human suffering. Unless we continue our research with laboratory animals, these problems will not be solved. Some people have suggested that instead of using laboratory animals in our research, we could use tissue cultures or computers. Unfortunately, tissue cultures or computers are not substitutes for living organisms. We have no way to study behavioral problems, such as addictions, in tissue cultures, nor can we program a computer to simulate the workings of an animal's nervous system. (If we could, that would mean we already had all the answers.)

This book will discuss some of the many important discoveries that have helped reduce human suffering. For example, in Chapter 3 you will learn about myasthenia gravis, a disease that produces muscular weakness than can become so severe that the patient cannot eat or breathe without assistance. Research on this problem involved the use of electric fish and rabbits. The discovery of a vaccine for infantile paralysis, an even more serious disease of the nervous system, involved the use of rhesus monkeys. As you will learn in Chapter 3, Parkinson's disease, an incurable, progressive neurological disorder, has been treated for years with a drug called L-DOPA, discovered through animal research. Now, because of research with rats, mice, rabbits, and monkeys, stimulated by the accidental poisoning of several young people with a contaminated batch of synthetic heroin, patients are being treated with a drug that actually slows down the rate of brain degeneration. Researchers have hopes that a drug will be found to prevent the degeneration altogether.

The easiest way to justify research with animals is to point to actual and potential benefits to human health, as I have just done. However, I think that we can also justify this research with a less practical but perhaps equally important argument. One of the traits that characterize our species is a quest for an understanding of our world. For example, astronomers contemplate the universe and try to uncover its mysteries. Even if their discoveries never lead to practical benefits such as better drugs or faster methods of transportation, the fact that they enrich our understanding of the beginning and the fate of our universe justifies their efforts. The pursuit of knowledge is itself a worthwhile endeavor. Surely the attempt to understand the universe within us—our nervous system, which is responsible for all that we are or can be—is also valuable.

INTERIM SUMMARY

The mind-body problem has puzzled philosophers for many centuries. The naive animism of primitive cultures was soon replaced by dualism, which rejected the notion of spirits but retained a belief in a nonmaterial human soul. Modern science has adopted a monistic position—the belief that the world consists of matter and energy and that nonmaterial entities such as minds or souls are not a part of the universe. At the very least, they cannot be studied with the tools available to scientists.

A dualist, René Descartes, proposed a model of the brain based on hydraulically actuated statues. His model stimulated observations that produced important discoveries. The results of Galvani's experiments eventually led to an understanding of the nature of the message transmitted by nerves between the brain and the sensory organs and the muscles. Müller's doctrine of specific nerve energies paved the way for study of the functions of specific parts of the brain, through the methods of experimental ablation and electrical stimulation.

Darwin's theory of evolution, based on the concept of natural selection, provided an important contribution to modern physiological psychology. The theory asserts that we must understand the functions performed by an organ or body part or by a behavior. Through random mutations, changes in an individual's genetic material cause different proteins to be produced, which results in the alteration of some physical characteristics. If the changes confer a selective advantage on the individual, the new genes will be transmitted to more and more members of the species. Even behaviors can evolve, through the selective advantage of alterations in the structure of the nervous system.

All scientists hope to explain natural phenomena. In this context the term *explanation* has two basic meanings: generalization and reduction. Generalization refers to the classification of phenomena according to their essential features so that general laws can be formulated. For example, observing that gravitational attraction is related to the mass of two bodies and to the distance between them helps explain the movement of planets. Reduction refers to the description of phenomena in terms of more basic physical processes. For example, gravitation can be explained in terms of forces and subatomic particles.

Physiological psychologists use both generalization and reduction in explaining behavior. In large part, generalizations use the traditional methods of psychology. Reduction explains behaviors in terms of physiological events within the body—primarily within the nervous system. Thus, physiological psychology builds on the tradition of both experimental psychology and experimental physiology.

Study of the functions of the human nervous system gives us hope that even the most complex mental processes may someday be understood. Cutting the corpus callosum not only splits the brain but also disconnects right-hemisphere brain functions from conscious awareness. For example, when sensory information about a particular object is presented to the right hemisphere of a person with a split brain, the person is not aware of the object but can, nevertheless, indicate by movements of the left hand that the object has been perceived. This phenomenon suggests that conscious awareness involves operations of the verbal mechanisms of the

left hemisphere. Indeed, consciousness may be, in large part, a matter of our "talking to ourselves." Thus, once we understand the language functions of the brain, we may have gone a long way in understanding how the brain can be conscious of its own existence.

Research on the physiology of behavior necessarily involves the use of laboratory animals. It is incumbent on all scientists using these animals to see that they are housed comfortably and treated humanely, and laws have been enacted to ensure that they are. Such research has already produced benefits to humankind and promises to continue to do so in the future.

ORGANIZATION OF THIS BOOK

Outline

The physiology of behavior means, in large part, the role of the nervous system in the control of behavior. Thus, this book begins with the fundamentals of neurophysiology, neurochemistry, neuropharmacology, and neuroanatomy. Chapter 2 describes the cells of the nervous system and explains how neurons send messages along their axons (nerve fibers). Chapter 3 describes communication between neurons, which is almost always accomplished chemically. The release of the chemical transmitter is explained, as well as the effects it has on the cell receiving the message. Because almost all drugs that have behavioral effects produce them by influencing chemical communication between neurons, the effects of these drugs are also covered in Chapter 3. As you will see, beside being used to treat diseases and mental disorders, drugs have become important tools in our attempts to understand the nature of brain mechanisms.

Chapter 4 outlines the anatomy of the brain and its interactions with the endocrine system. A necessary step in understanding how the brain carries out its functions is to determine which neural circuits perform which functions. Thus, in order to understand the results of research in physiological psychology, one must know at least some essentials of neuroanatomy. Chapter 5 describes the basic research methods of physiological psychology, including neuroanatomical methods, experimental ablation methods, electrical-recording methods, electrical stimulation methods, and neurochemical methods.

The second section of the book describes the physiology of perception and movement. Chapter 6 discusses vision, and Chapter 7 discusses the other sensory modalities: audition, the vestibular senses, the somatosenses, gustation, and olfaction. Chapter 8 describes the neural control of movement.

The third section of the book deals with species-typical behaviors, which are of special importance to motivation. Chapter 9 describes the physiology of sleep and waking, including sleep disorders and the control of biological rhythms. Chapter 10 describes the physiology of sexual development and mating behavior. Chapter 11 describes emotions and the physiological causes of the adverse effects of negative emotions on health. Chapter 12 describes the control of drinking and the internal physiological processes related to water balance; Chapter 13 describes eating and metabolism.

The fourth section of the book deals with the physiology of learning and motivation. Chapter 14 deals with the physiology of perceptual learning, stimulus-response learning (classical and instrumental conditioning), and motor learning. Chapter 15 describes research on the role of the hippocampal system in learning and attempts to explain the causes of amnesia that follows damage to this system.

The final section of the book describes the anatomy and physiology of human communication and of disorders of thought and mood. Chapter 16 discusses what we have learned about the neural organization of various types of communication: listening, speaking, reading, and writing. Chapters 17 and 18 describe research on the physiology of mental disorders: schizophrenia, the affective disorders, the anxiety disorders, addiction, and autism.

Some Mechanical Details

Before you begin reading the next chapter, I want to say a few things about the design of the book that may help you with your studies. I have tried to integrate the text and illustrations as closely as possible. In my experience, one of the most annoying aspects of reading some books is not knowing when to look at an illustration. When reading complicated material, I have found that sometimes I look at the figure too soon, before I have read enough to understand it; and sometimes I look at it too late and realize that I could have made more sense out of the text if I had just looked at the figure sooner. Furthermore, after looking at the illustration, I often find it difficult to return to the place where I stopped reading. Therefore, in this book you will find the figure references in boldface italics (like this: *Figure 5.6*), which means "stop reading and look at the figure." I have placed these references in the locations I think will be optimal. If you look away from the text then, you will be assured that you will not be interrupting a line of reasoning in a crucial place and will not have to reread several sentences to get going again. You will find sections like this: "Figure 4.1 shows an alligator and a human. The alligator is certainly laid out in a linear fashion; we can draw a straight line that starts between its eyes and continues down the center of its spinal cord. (See *Figure 4.1*.)" This particular example is a trivial one and will give you no problems no matter when you look at the figure. But in other cases the material is more complex, and you will have less trouble if you know what to look for before you stop reading and examine the illustration.

You will notice that some words in the text are *italicized* and others are printed in **boldface**. Italics mean one of two things: Either the word is being stressed for emphasis and is not a new term, or I am pointing out a new term that I do not think you need to learn. On the other hand, a word in boldface is a new term that you should try to learn. Most of the boldfaced terms in the text are part of the vocabulary of the physiological psychologist. Often, they will be used again in a later chapter. As an aid to your studying, I have included a list of all of the boldfaced terms at the end of each chapter, along with the page number on which the term was first used. Also, the end of the text contains a glossary, which provides definitions for important terms that are used throughout the book. In addition, a comprehensive index at the end of the book provides a list of terms and topics, with page references.

The physiology of behavior is a complex subject, and this book contains many concepts and descriptions of experiments that will be new to you. At the end of each major section I have included an *interim summary,* which provides a place for you to stop and think again about what you have just read, in order to make sure that you understand the direction the discussion has gone. Taken together, these sections provide a detailed summary of the information introduced in the chapter. My students tell me that they review the interim summaries just before taking a test.

 New Terms

Philosophical Roots of Physiological Psychology

animism p. 2

dualism p. 2

monism p. 4

Biologigal Roots of Physiological Phsychology

doctrine of specific nerve
     energies p. 6

experimental ablation p. 6

functionalism p. 8

Contributions of Modern Psychology

generalization p. 10

reduction p. 10

corpus callosum p. 11

split-brain operation p. 11

cerebral hemisphere p. 11

Suggested Readings

Butterfield, H. *The Origins of Modern Science: 1300-1800.* New York: Macmillan, 1959.

Sacks, O. *The Man Who Mistook His Wife for a Hat and Other Clinical Tales.* New York: Harper & Row, 1987.

Schultz, D., and Schultz, S.E. *A History of Modern Psychology,* 4th ed. New York: Academic Press, 1987.

Springer, S.P., and Deutsch, G. *Left Brain, Right Brain,* 3rd ed. New York: W.H. Freeman and Co., 1989.

CHAPTER 2

Structure and Functions of Cells of the Nervous System

Cells of the Nervous System
- Neurons
- Supporting Cells
- The Blood-Brain Barrier
  Interim Summary

Communication Within a Neuron
- Measurement of Electrical Potentials of Axons
- The Membrane Potential: Balance of Two Forces
- The Action Potential
- Conduction of the Action Potential
  Interim Summary

Neural Communication: An Overview
- The Rate Law
- Neural Integration
- A Simple Reflex
  Interim Summary

THE BRAIN IS THE ORGAN THAT MOVES THE muscles. That may sound a bit simplistic, but ultimately, movement—or more accurately, behavior—is the primary function of the nervous system. To make useful movements, the brain must know what is happening outside, in the environment. Thus, the body contains cells that are specialized for detecting environmental events and other cells that are specialized for producing movements. Of course, complex animals such as we do not react automatically to events in our environment; our brains are flexible enough so that we behave in different ways, according to present circumstances and those we experienced in the past. Besides perceiving and acting, we can remember and decide. All these abilities are made possible by the billions of cells found in the nervous system.

This chapter describes the structure and functions of the most important cells of the nervous system. Information, in the form of light, sound waves, odors, tastes, or contact with objects, is gathered from the environment by specialized cells called **sensory neurons**. Movements are accomplished by the contraction of muscles, which are controlled by **motor neurons**. (The term *motor* is used here in its original sense to refer to movement, not to a mechanical engine.) And in between sensory neurons and motor neurons come all the other neurons that do the perceiving, learning, remembering, deciding, and controlling of complex behaviors. How many neurons are there in the human nervous system? I have seen estimates of between 100 and 1000 billion—but no one has counted them yet.

To understand how the nervous system controls behavior, we must first understand its parts—the cells that compose it. Because this chapter deals with cells, you need not be familiar with the structure of the nervous system, which is presented in Chapter 4. However, you need to know that the nervous system consists of two basic divisions, the central nervous system and the peripheral nervous system. The **central nervous system** (CNS) consists of the parts that are encased by the bones of the skull and spinal column: the brain and the spinal cord. The **peripheral nervous system** (PNS) is found outside these bones and consists of the nerves and some of the sensory organs.

CELLS OF THE NERVOUS SYSTEM

THE FIRST PART OF THIS CHAPTER IS DEVOTED TO a description of the most important cells of the nervous system—neurons and their supporting cells—and to the blood-brain barrier, which provides them with chemical isolation from the rest of the body.

Neurons

Basic Structure

The neuron (nerve cell) is the information-processing and information-transmitting element of the nervous system. Neurons come in many shapes and varieties, according to the specialized jobs they perform. Neurons usually have, in one form or another, the following four structures or regions: (1) cell body, or soma; (2) dendrites; (3) axon; and (4) terminal buttons.

Soma. The **soma** (cell body) contains the nucleus and much of the machinery that provides for the life processes of the cell. (See *Figure 2.1.*) Its shape varies considerably in different kinds of neurons.

Dendrites. *Dendron* is the Greek word for tree, and the **dendrites** of the neuron look very much like trees. (See *Figure 2.1.*) Neurons "converse" with one another, and dendrites serve as important recipients of these messages. The messages that pass from neuron to neuron are transmitted across the **synapse**, a junction between the terminal buttons (described later) of the sending cell and a portion of the somatic or dendritic membrane of the receiving cell. (The word *synapse* derives from the Greek *sunaptein*, "to join together.") Communication at a synapse proceeds in only one direction: from the terminal button to the membrane of the other cell.

Axon. The **axon** is a long, slender tube, often covered by a *myelin sheath*. (The myelin sheath is described later.) The axon carries information away from the cell body to the terminal buttons. (See *Figure 2.1.*) The basic message it carries is called an *action potential*. This function is an important one and will be described in more detail later in the chapter.

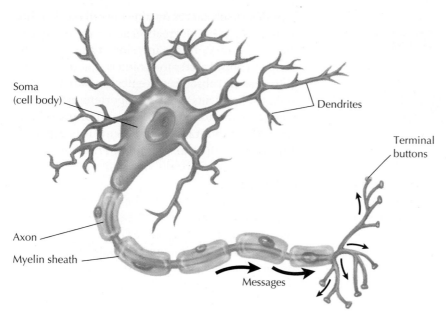

FIGURE 2.1

The principal structures or regions of a multipolar neuron.

Soma
(cell body)

Dendrites

Terminal
buttons

Axon

Myelin sheath

Messages

For now, it suffices to say that it is a brief electrical/chemical event that starts at the end of the axon next to the cell body and travels toward the terminal buttons. The action potential is like a brief pulse; in a given axon, the action potential is always the same size and duration. When it reaches a point where the axon branches, it splits up but does not diminish in size. Each branch receives a *full-strength* action potential

Like dendrites, axons and their branches come in different shapes. In fact, the three principal types of neurons are classified according to the way in which their axons and dendrites leave the soma. The neuron depicted in Figure 2.1 is the most common type found in the central nervous system; it is a **multipolar neuron**. In this type of neuron the somatic membrane gives rise to one axon but to the trunks of many dendritic trees. **Bipolar neurons** give rise to one axon and one dendritic tree, at opposite ends of the soma. (See *Figure 2.2a.*) These neurons are usually sensory; that is, their dendrites detect events occurring in the environment and communicate information about these events to the central nervous system.

The third type of nerve cell is the **unipolar neuron**. It has only one stalk, which leaves the soma and divides into two branches a short distance away. (See *Figure 2.2b.*) Unipolar neurons, like bipolar neurons, transmit information from the environment to the CNS. The arborizations (treelike branches) farther from the CNS are dendrites; the arborizations within the CNS end in terminal buttons. The dendrites of most unipolar neurons detect touch, temperature changes, and other sensory events that affect the skin.

Terminal Buttons. Most axons divide and branch many times. At the ends of the twigs are found little knobs called **terminal buttons,** which have a very special function: When an action potential traveling down the axon reaches the terminal buttons, they secrete a chemical called a **transmitter substance**, also known as a **neurotransmitter.** This chemical (there are many different ones in the CNS) affects the receiving cell. The effect the neurotransmitter produces excites or inhibits the receiving cell and thus helps determine whether this cell will send a message down its axon to the cells with which it communicates. Details of this process will be described later in this chapter and in Chapter 3.

An individual neuron receives information from the terminal buttons of axons of other neurons—and the terminal buttons of *its* axons form synapses with other neurons. A neuron may receive information from dozens or even hundreds of other neurons, each of which can form a large number of

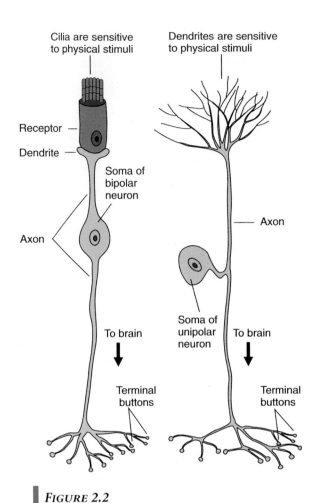

FIGURE 2.2

Neurons. (a) A bipolar neuron, primarily found in sensory systems (for example, vision and audition).(b) A unipolar neuron, found in the somatosensory system (touch, pain, and the like).

synaptic connections with it. Figure 2.3 illustrates the nature of these connections. As you can see, terminal buttons can form synapses on the membrane of the dendrites or the soma. (See **Figure 2.3.**)

Internal Structure

Figure 2.4 illustrates the internal structure of a typical multipolar neuron. (See **Figure 2.4.**) The **membrane** defines the boundary of the cell. The membrane consists of a double layer of lipid (fatlike) molecules. Floating in it are a variety of protein molecules that have special functions. Some pro-

teins detect substances outside the cell (such as hormones) and pass information about the presence of these substances to the interior of the cell. Other proteins control access to the interior of the cell, permitting some substances to enter but barring others. Still other proteins act as transporters, actively carrying certain molecules into or out of the cell. Because the membrane of the neuron is especially important in the transmission of information, its characteristics will be discussed in more detail later in this chapter.

The **nucleus** ("nut") of the cell is round or oval and is covered by the nuclear membrane. The nucleolus and the chromosomes reside here. The **nucleolus** manufactures **ribosomes,** small structures that are involved in protein synthesis. The **chromosomes,** which consist of long strands of **deoxyribonucleic acid** (DNA), contain the organism's genetic information. When they are active, portions of the chromosomes (**genes**) cause production of another complex molecule, **messenger ribonucleic acid** (mRNA). The mRNA leaves the nuclear membrane and attaches to ribosomes, where it causes the production of a particular protein.

Proteins are important in cell functions. As well as providing structure, proteins serve as **enzymes,** which direct the chemical processes of a cell by controlling chemical reactions. Enzymes are special protein molecules that act as catalysts; that is, they cause a chemical reaction to take place without becoming a part of the final product themselves. Because cells contain the constituents needed to synthesize an enormous variety of compounds, the ones that cells actually do produce depend primarily on the particular enzymes that are present. Furthermore, there are enzymes that break molecules apart as well as put them together; the enzymes present in a particular region of a cell thus determine which molecules remain intact. For example,

$$A + B \underset{Y}{\overset{X}{\rightleftharpoons}} AB$$

In this reversible reaction the relative concentrations of enzymes X and Y determine whether the complex substance AB or its constituents, A and B, will pre-

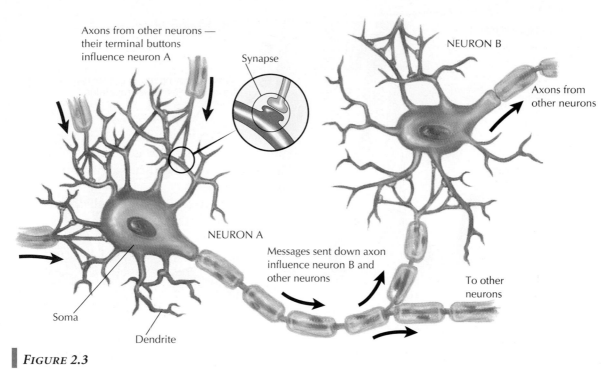

Axons from other neurons — their terminal buttons influence neuron A

Synapse

NEURON B

Axons from other neurons

NEURON A

Messages sent down axon influence neuron B and other neurons

To other neurons

Soma

Dendrite

FIGURE 2.3

An overview of the synaptic connections between neurons.

dominate. Enzyme X makes A and B join together; enzyme Y splits AB apart. (Energy may also be required to make the reactions proceed.)

The bulk of the cell consists of cytoplasm. **Cytoplasm** is complex and varies considerably across types of cells, but it can be most easily characterized as a jellylike, semiliquid substance that fills the space outlined by the membrane. Cytoplasm is not static and inert; it streams and flows. It contains small, specialized structures, just as the body contains specialized organs. The most important of these are described next.

Mitochondria (singular: mitochondrion) are shaped like oval beads and are formed of a double membrane. The inner membrane is wrinkled, and the wrinkles make up a set of shelves (*cristae*) that fill the inside of the bead. Mitochondria perform a vital role in the economy of the cell; many of the biochemical steps involved in the extraction of energy from the breakdown of nutrients take place on the cristae. Most cell biologists believe that many eons ago mitochondria were free-living organisms that came to "infect" larger cells. Because the mitochondria could extract energy more efficiently than

the larger cells, they became useful to them and eventually became a permanent part of the cells. The cell provides mitochondria with nutrients, and the mitochondria provide the cell with a special molecule—**adenosine triphosphate** (ATP)—that it uses as its immediate source of energy.

Endoplasmic reticulum, which serves as a storage reservoir and as a channel for transporting chemicals through the cytoplasm, appears in two forms: rough and smooth. Both types consist of parallel layers of membrane, arranged in pairs, of the sort that encloses the cell. Rough endoplasmic reticulum contains ribosomes. The protein produced by the ribosomes that are attached to the rough endoplasmic reticulum is destined to be transported out of the cell or used in the membrane. Unattached ribosomes are also distributed around the cytoplasm; the unattached variety appears to produce protein for use within the neuron. The smooth endoplasmic reticulum is concerned with the transport of substances around the cytoplasm and provides channels for the segregation of various molecules involved in different cellular processes. Lipid (fatlike) molecules are produced here.

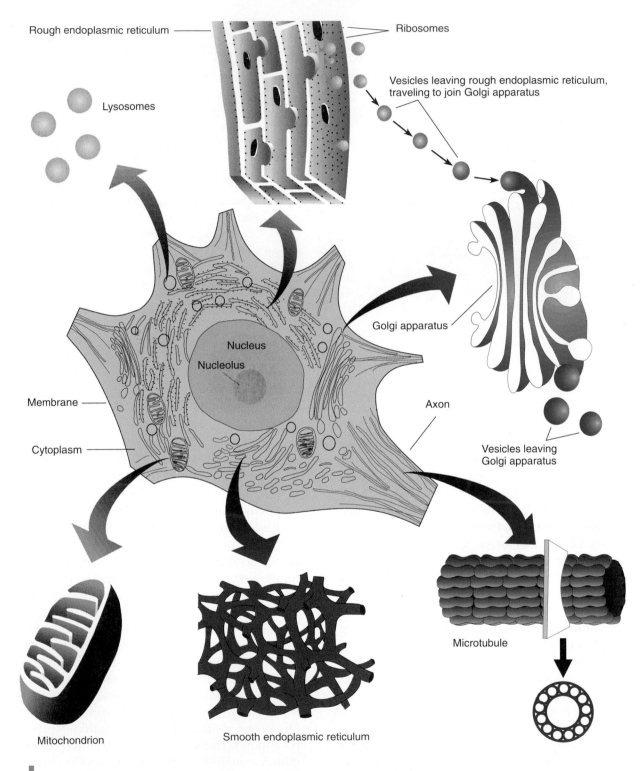

Rough endoplasmic reticulum

Ribosomes

Vesicles leaving rough endoplasmic reticulum, traveling to join Golgi apparatus

Lysosomes

Golgi apparatus

Nucleus

Nucleolus

Membrane

Axon

Cytoplasm

Vesicles leaving Golgi apparatus

Microtubule

Mitochondrion

Smooth endoplasmic reticulum

FIGURE 2.4

The principal internal structures of a multipolar neuron.

The **Golgi apparatus** is a special form of endoplasmic reticulum. Some complex molecules, made up of simpler individual molecules, are assembled here. The Golgi apparatus also serves as a wrapping or packaging agent. For example, secretory cells (such as those that release hormones) wrap their product in a membrane produced by the Golgi apparatus. When the cell secretes its products, it uses a process called **exocytosis** (*exo*, "outside"; *cyto*, "cell"; -*osis*, "process"). Briefly stated, the container migrates to the outer membrane of the cell, fuses with it, and bursts, spilling the product into the fluid surrounding the cell. As we will see, neurons are secretory cells; they communicate with one another by secreting chemicals by this means. Thus, I will describe the process of exocytosis in more detail in Chapter 3. The Golgi apparatus also produces **lysosomes,** small sacs that contain enzymes that break down substances no longer needed by the cell. These products are then recycled or excreted from the cell.

Arranged throughout the neuron are neurofilaments and microtubules. **Neurofilaments** are made of long protein fibers similar to those that provide the motive force in muscles. Located just under the membrane, neurofilaments give cells their particular shape and control the location of proteins that are embedded in the membrane. **Microtubules** are thicker and much longer than neurofilaments and consist of bundles of filaments arranged around a hollow core. They transport substances from place to place within the cell.

Axons can be extremely long, relative to their diameter and the size of the soma. For example, the longest axon in a human stretches from the big toe to a region located in the base of the brain. Because terminal buttons need some items that can be produced only in the soma, there must be a system that can transport these items rapidly and efficiently through the axoplasm (that is, the cytoplasm of the axon). This system is referred to as **axoplasmic transport,** an active process by which substances are propelled along microtubules that run the length of the axon. *Fast* axoplasmic transport moves items from the soma toward the terminal buttons at the rate of several hundred millimeters a day. (In an adult of average height, substances would get from

the brain to the big toe in a little less than a week.) *Slow* axoplasmic transport is only about one percent as fast, but it moves items in either direction.

Supporting Cells

Neurons constitute only about half the volume of the CNS. The rest consists of a variety of supporting cells. Because neurons have a very high rate of metabolism but have no means of storing nutrients, they must constantly be supplied with nutrients and oxygen or they will quickly die. Unlike most other cells of the body, neurons cannot be replaced when they die; we are born with as many as we will ever have. Thus, the role played by the cells that support and protect neurons is very important to our existence.

Glia

The most important supporting cells of the central nervous system are the *neuroglia,* or "nerve glue." **Glia,** (also called *glial cells)* do indeed glue the CNS together, but they do much more than that. Neurons lead a very sheltered existence; they are buffered physically and chemically from the rest of the body by the glial cells. Glial cells surround neurons and hold them in place, controlling their supply of some of the chemicals they need to exchange messages with other neurons; they insulate neurons from one another so that neural messages do not get scrambled; and they even act as housekeepers, destroying and removing the carcasses of neurons that are killed by injury or that die as a result of old age.

There are several types of glial cells, each of which plays a special role in the CNS. The two most important types are *astrocytes* and *oligodendroglia.* **Astrocyte** means "star cell," and this name accurately describes the shape of these cells. Astrocytes (or *astroglia*) provide physical support to neurons and clean up debris within the brain. They produce some chemicals that neurons need to fulfill their functions. In addition, astrocytes help control the chemical composition of the fluid surrounding neurons by actively taking up or releasing substances whose concentrations must be kept within critical levels.

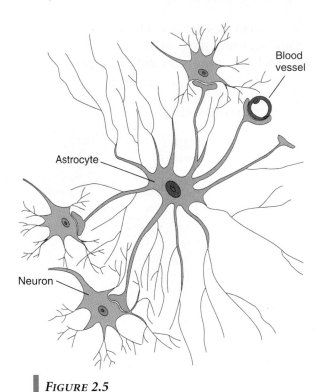

Blood
vessel

Astrocyte

Neuron

FIGURE 2.5

Structure and location of astrocytes, whose processes surround capillaries and neurons of the central nervous system.

Some of the astrocyte's processes (the arms of the star) are wrapped around blood vessels; other processes are wrapped around parts of neurons, so that the somatic and dendritic membranes of neurons are largely surrounded by astrocytes. (See *Figure 2.5.*) This arrangement suggested to the Italian histologist Camillo Golgi (1844–1926) that astrocytes supplied neurons with nutrients from the capillaries and disposed of their waste products (Golgi, 1903). He thought that nutrients passed from capillaries to the cytoplasm of the astrocytes and then through the cytoplasm to the neurons, with waste products following the opposite route. As Figure 2.5 shows, this hypothesis is plausible. However, it has not been confirmed.

Besides having a possible role in transporting chemicals to neurons, astrocytes serve as the matrix that holds neurons in place. These cells also surround and isolate synapses, apparently minimizing the dispersion of transmitter substances that are released by the terminal buttons. Thus, astrocytes provide each synapse with an isolation booth, keeping the neurons' conversations private.

Neurons occasionally die for unknown reasons or are killed by head injury, infection, or stroke. Certain kinds of astrocytes then take up the task of cleaning away the debris. These cells are able to travel around the CNS; they extend and retract their processes *(pseudopodia,* or "false feet") and glide about the way amoebas do. When astrocytes contact a piece of debris from a dead neuron, they push themselves against it, finally engulfing and digesting it. We call this process **phagocytosis** *(phagein,* "to eat"; *kutos,* "cell"). If there is a considerable amount of injured tissue to be cleaned up, astrocytes will divide and produce enough new cells to do the task. Once the dead tissue is broken down, a framework of astrocytes will be left to fill in the vacant area, and a specialized kind of astrocyte will form scar tissue, walling off the area.

Oligodendrocytes are residents of the CNS, and their principal function is to provide support to axons and to produce the **myelin sheath,** which insulates most axons from one another. (Some axons are not myelinated and lack this sheath.) Myelin, 80 percent lipid and 20 percent protein, is produced by the oligodendrocytes in the form of a tube surrounding the axon. This tube does not form a continuous sheath; rather, it consists of a series of segments, each approximately 1 mm long, with a small (1–2 μm) portion of uncoated axon between the segments. (A *micrometer,* abbreviated μm, is one-millionth of a meter, or one thousandth of a millimeter.) The bare portion of axon is called a **node of Ranvier,** after its discoverer. The myelinated axon, then, resembles a string of elongated beads. (Actually, the beads are *very much* elongated—their length is approximately 80 times their width.)

A given oligodendrocyte produces several segments of myelin. During the development of the CNS, oligodendrocytes form processes shaped something like canoe paddles. Each of these paddle-shaped processes then wraps itself many times around a segment of an axon and, while doing so, produces layers of myelin. Each paddle thus becomes a segment of an axon's myelin sheath. (See *Figure 2.6.*)

Unmyelinated axons of the CNS are not actually naked; they are also covered by oligodendrocytes.

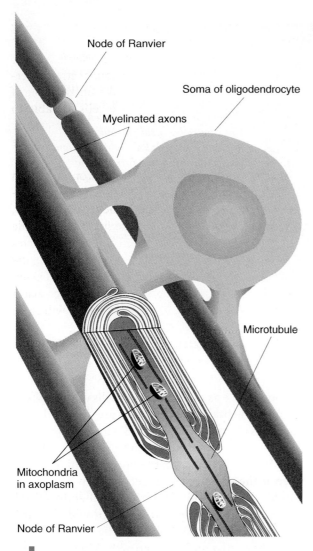

FIGURE 2.6

Oligodendrocytes, which form the myelin that surrounds many axons in the central nervous system. Each cell forms one segment of myelin for several adjacent axons.

However, in this case the glial cells do not manufacture myelin; they simply wrap a process loosely around the axon and hold it in place.

Schwann Cells

In the CNS the oligodendrocytes support axons and produce myelin. In the PNS the **Schwann cells** perform the same functions. Most axons in the PNS are myelinated. The myelin sheath occurs in segments, as it does in the CNS; each segment consists of a single Schwann cell, wrapped many times around the

axon. In the CNS the oligodendrocytes grow a number of paddle-shaped processes that wrap around a number of axons. In the PNS a Schwann cell provides myelin for only one axon, and the entire Schwann cell—not merely a part of it—surrounds the axon. (See *Figure 2.7.*)

Schwann cells also differ from their CNS counterparts, the oligodendrocytes, in an important way. A peripheral nerve consists of a bundle of many myelinated axons, all covered in a sheath of tough, elastic connective tissue. (See *Figure 2.8.*) If damage occurs to such a nerve, Schwann cells aid in the digestion of the dead and dying axons. Then the Schwann cells arrange themselves in a series of cylinders that act as guides for regrowth of the axons. The distal portions of the severed axons die, but the stump of each severed axon grows sprouts, which then spread in all directions. If one of these sprouts encounters a cylinder provided by a Schwann cell, the sprout will grow through the tube quickly (at a rate of up to 3–4 mm a day), while the other, nonproductive sprouts wither away. If the cut ends of the nerve are still located close enough to each other,

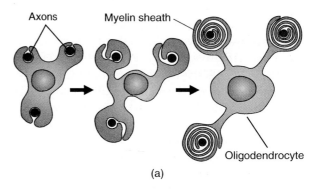

(a)

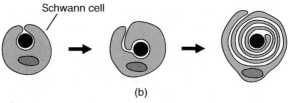

(b)

FIGURE 2.7

Formation of myelin. During development, a process of an oligodendrocyte or an entire Schwann cell tightly wrap itself many times around an individual axon in the peripheral nervous system and form one segment of the myelin sheath.

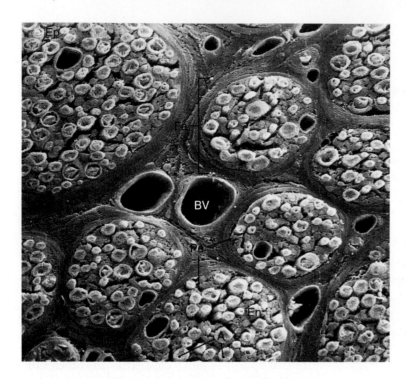

■ *FIGURE 2.8*

A scanning electron photomicrograph of the cut end of a peripheral nerve. Ep = epineurium (the connective tissue surrounding the nerve); Fa = fascicle (bundle of axons); Pe = perineurium (the connective tissue surrounding individual fascicles); En = endoneurium (the connective tissue surrounding single axons); A = axons; BV = blood vessel.

(From Kessel, R.G., and Kardon, R.H. Tissues and Organs: A Text-Atlas of Scanning Electron Microscopy. San Francisco: W.H. Freeman, 1979.)

the axons will reestablish connections with the muscles and sense organs they previously served.

On the other hand, if a section of the nerve is damaged beyond repair, the axons will not be able to find their way to the original sites of innervation. In such cases neurosurgeons can sew the cut ends of the nerve together, if not too much of the nerve has been damaged. (Nerves are flexible and can be stretched a bit.) If too long a section has been lost, and if the nerve was an important one (controlling hand muscles, for example), a piece of nerve about the same size as the lost section can be taken from another part of the body. Because many nerves overlap in the area of tissue they innervate, neurosurgeons have no trouble finding a branch of a nerve that the patient can lose without ill effect. The surgeon, using a special microscope and very delicate instruments, grafts this piece of nerve to the damaged one. Of course, the axons in the excised and transplanted piece of nerve die away, but the tubes produced by the Schwann cells guide the sprouts of the damaged nerve and help them find their way back to the affected muscles, in this case, to the hand muscles.

Unfortunately, the glial cells of the CNS are not as cooperative as the supporting cells of the PNS. If axons in the brain or spinal cord are damaged, new sprouts will form, as in the PNS. However, the budding axons encounter scar tissue produced by the astrocytes, and they cannot penetrate this barrier. Even if the sprouts could get through, the axons would not reestablish their original connections without guidance similar to that provided by the Schwann cells of the PNS. During development, axons have two modes of growth. The first mode causes them to elongate so that they reach their target, which could be as far away as the other end of the brain or spinal cord. Schwann cells provide this signal to injured axons. The second mode causes axons to stop elongating and begin sprouting terminal buttons, because they have reached their target. Liuzzi and Lasek (1987) found that even when astrocytes do not produce scar tissue, they appear to produce a chemical signal that instructs regenerating axons to begin the second mode of growth: to stop elongating and start sprouting terminal buttons. Thus, the difference in the regenerative properties of the CNS and the PNS results from differences in the characteristics of the supporting cells, not from differences in the neurons.

The Blood-Brain Barrier

Over one hundred years ago, Paul Ehrlich discovered that if a blue dye is injected into an animal's bloodstream, all tissues except the brain and spinal cord will be tinted blue. However, if the same dye is injected into the ventricles of the brain, the blue color will spread throughout the CNS (Bradbury, 1979). This experiment demonstrates that a barrier exists between the blood and the fluid that surrounds the cells of the brain—the **blood-brain barrier**.

Some substances can cross the blood-brain barrier; others cannot. Thus, it is *selectively permeable* (*per,* "through"; *meare,* "to pass"). In most of the body the cells that line the capillaries do not fit together absolutely tightly. Small gaps are found between them that permit the free exchange of most substances between the blood plasma and the fluid outside the blood vessels that surrounds the cells. In the central nervous system the capillaries lack these gaps, and thus, many substances cannot leave the blood. Substances that can dissolve in lipids pass through the capillaries easily because they simply dissolve through the membranes of the cells that line the capillaries. Other substances, such as glucose (the primary fuel of the central nervous system), must be actively transported through the capillary walls, carried by special proteins.

The messages that are conveyed from place to place in the nervous system involve movements of substances through the membranes of neurons. If the composition of the fluid that bathes neurons is changed even slightly, the transmission of these messages will be disrupted. Thus, if this fluid is not closely regulated, the brain cannot function normally. The presence of the blood-brain barrier probably makes it easier to regulate the composition of this fluid.

The blood-brain barrier is not uniform throughout the nervous system. In several places the barrier is relatively permeable, allowing substances excluded elsewhere to cross freely. For example, the **area postrema** is a part of the brain that controls vomiting. The blood-brain barrier is much weaker there, permitting neurons in this region to detect the presence of toxic substances in the blood. A poison that enters the circulatory system from the stomach can thus stimulate this area to initiate vomiting. If the organism is lucky, the poison can be expelled from the stomach before it causes too much damage.

||||| *INTERIM SUMMARY*

All organs of the body consist of cells, which contain a quantity of clear cytoplasm, enclosed in a membrane. Embedded in the membrane are protein molecules that have special functions, such as the transport of particular substances into and out of the cell. The cytoplasm contains the nucleus, which contains the genetic information; the nucleolus (located in the nucleus), which manufactures ribosomes; the ribosomes, which serve as sites of protein synthesis; the endoplasmic reticulum, which serves as a storage reservoir and as a channel for transportation of chemicals through the cytoplasm; the Golgi apparatus, which wraps substances that the cell secretes in a membrane; neurofilaments and microtubules, which compose the internal "skeleton" of the cell and provide the motive power for transporting chemicals from place to place; and the mitochondria, which serve as the location for most of the chemical reactions through which the cell extracts energy from nutrients.

Neurons receive messages directly from the environment (for example, sights, sounds, smells, and tastes) or from other neurons. They receive messages from other neurons by means of synapses, junctions between the terminal buttons of the transmitting neurons and the membrane of a dendrite or the soma of the receiving neuron. Terminal buttons are located at the ends of the axons.

Neurons are supported by the glial cells of the central nervous system and the satellite cells of the peripheral nervous system. Within the CNS, astrocytes provide the primary support and also remove debris and form scar tissue in the event of tissue damage. Oligodendrocytes form myelin, the substance that insulates axons, and also support unmyelinated axons. Within the PNS, support and myelin are provided by the Schwann cells.

In most organs, molecules freely diffuse between the blood within the capillaries that serve them and the extracellular fluid that bathes their cells. The molecules pass through gaps between the cells that line the capillaries. The walls of the capillaries of the CNS lack these gaps; consequently, fewer substances can enter or leave the brain across the blood-brain barrier.

COMMUNICATION WITHIN A NEURON

THE DETAILS OF SYNAPTIC TRANSMISSION—THE communication between neurons—will be described in Chapter 3. This section describes the nature of communication *within* a neuron—the way an action potential is sent from the cell body down the axon to the terminal buttons, informing them to release some transmitter substance. As we shall see in this section, an action potential is conducted by means of alterations in the membrane of the axon that permit various chemicals to move between the interior of the axon and the fluid surrounding it. These exchanges produce electrical currents.

Measurement of Electrical Potentials of Axons

Here we will examine the nature of the message that is conducted along the axon. To do so, we obtain an axon that is large enough to work with. Fortunately, nature has provided the neuroscientist with the giant squid axon (the giant axon of a squid, not the axon of a giant squid!). This axon is about 0.5 mm in diameter, which is hundreds of times larger than the largest mammalian axon. (This large axon controls an emergency response: sudden contraction of the mantle, which squirts water through a jet and propels the squid away from a source of danger.) We place an isolated giant squid axon in a dish of seawater, in which it can exist for a day or two.

To measure the electrical charges generated by an axon, we will need to use a pair of electrodes. **Electrodes** are electrical conductors that provide a path for electricity to enter or leave a medium. One of the electrodes is a simple wire that we place in the seawater. The other one, which we use to record the message from the axon, has to be special. Because even a giant squid axon is rather small, we must use a tiny electrode that will record the membrane potential without damaging the axon. To do so, we use a microelectrode.

FIGURE 2.9

Measuring electrical charge. (a) A voltmeter detecting the charge across a membrane of an axon. (b) A light bulb detecting the charge across the terminals of a battery.

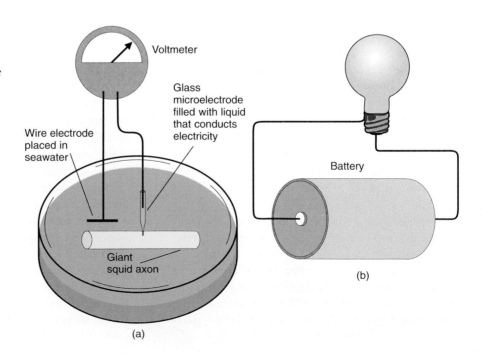

Voltmeter

Glass microelectrode filled with liquid that conducts electricity

Wire electrode placed in seawater

Battery

Giant squid axon

(b)

(a)

A **microelectrode** is simply a very small electrode, and it can be made of metal or glass. In this case we will use one made of thin glass tubing, which is heated and drawn down to an exceedingly fine point, less than a thousandth of a millimeter in diameter. Because glass will not conduct electricity, the glass microelectrode is filled with a liquid that conducts electricity, such as a solution of potassium chloride.

We place the wire electrode in the seawater and insert the microelectrode into the axon. (See *Figure 2.9a.*) As soon as we do so, we discover that the inside of the axon is negatively charged with respect to the outside; the difference in charge being 70 mV (millivolts, or thousandths of a volt). Thus, the inside of the membrane is -70 mV. This electrical charge is called the **membrane potential.** The term *potential* refers to a stored-up source of energy—in this case, electrical energy. For example, a flashlight battery that is not connected to an electrical circuit has a *potential* charge of 1.5 V between its terminals. If we connect a light bulb to the terminals, the potential energy is tapped and converted into radiant energy (light). (See *Figure 2.9b.*) Similarly, if we connect our electrodes—one inside the axon and one outside it—to a very sensitive voltmeter, we will convert the potential energy to movement of the meter's needle. Of course, the potential electrical energy of the axonal membrane is very weak, compared with that of a flashlight battery.

As we shall see, the message that is conducted down the axon consists of a brief change in the membrane potential. However, this change occurs very rapidly—too rapidly for us to see if we were using a voltmeter. Thus, to study the message, we will use an **oscilloscope.** This device, like a voltmeter, measures voltages, but it also produces a record of these voltages, graphing them as a function of time. These graphs are displayed on a screen, much like the one found in a television. The vertical axis represents voltage, and the horizontal axis represents time, going from left to right.

Once we insert our microelectrode into the axon, the oscilloscope draws a straight horizontal line at -70 mV, as long as the axon is not disturbed. This electrical charge across the membrane is called, quite appropriately, the **resting potential.** Now let us disturb the resting potential and see what happens. To do so, we will use another device—an electrical stimulator that allows us to alter the membrane potential at a specific location. (See *Figure 2.10.*) The stimulator can pass current through another microelectrode that we have inserted into the axon. Because the inside of the axon is negative, a positive charge applied to the inside of the membrane produces a **depolarization.** That is, it takes away some of the electrical charge across the membrane near the electrode, reducing the membrane potential.

Let us see what happens to an axon when we artificially change the membrane potential at one point. Figure 2.11 shows a graph drawn by an oscilloscope that has been monitoring the effects of brief depolarizing stimuli. The graphs of the effects of these separate stimuli are superimposed on the same

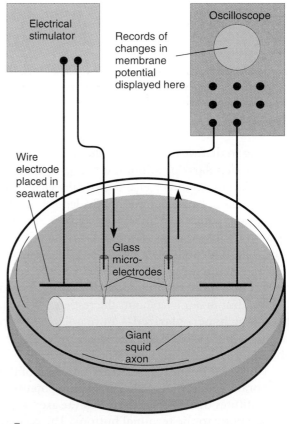

FIGURE 2.10

The means by which an axon can be stimulated while its membrane potential is being recorded.

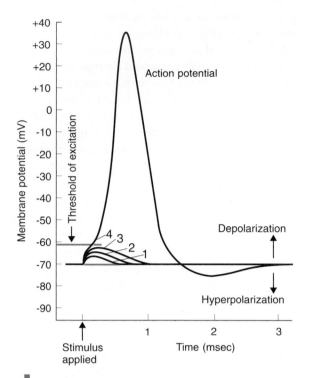

FIGURE 2.11

The results that would be seen on an oscilloscope screen if depolarizing stimuli of varying intensities were delivered to the axon shown in Figure 2.10.

drawing so that we can compare them. We deliver a series of depolarizing stimuli, starting with a very weak stimulus (number 1) and gradually increasing their strength. Each stimulus briefly depolarizes the membrane potential a little more. Finally, after we present depolarization number 4, the membrane potential suddenly reverses itself, so that the inside becomes *positive* (and the outside becomes negative). The membrane potential quickly returns to normal, but first it overshoots the resting potential, becoming **hyperpolarized**—more polarized than normal—for a short time. The whole process takes about 2 msec (milliseconds). (See **Figure 2.11.**)

This phenomenon, a very rapid reversal of the membrane potential, is called the **action potential**. It constitutes the message carried by the axon from the cell body to the terminal buttons. The voltage level that triggers an action potential, which was achieved only by shock number 4, is called the **threshold of excitation.**

The Membrane Potential: Balance of Two Forces

To understand what causes the action potential to occur, we must first understand the reasons for the existence of the membrane potential. As we will see, this electrical charge is the result of a balance between two opposing forces: diffusion and electrostatic pressure.

The Force of Diffusion

When a spoonful of sugar is carefully poured into a container of water, it settles to the bottom. After a time the sugar dissolves, but it remains close to the bottom of the container. After a much longer time (probably several days), the molecules of sugar distribute themselves evenly throughout the water, even if no one stirs the liquid. The process whereby molecules distribute themselves evenly throughout the medium in which they are dissolved is called **diffusion.**

When there are no forces or barriers to prevent diffusion, molecules diffuse from regions of high concentration to regions of low concentration. Molecules are constantly in motion, and their rate of movement is proportional to the temperature. Only at absolute zero [0 K (kelvin) = -273.15°C = -459.7°F] do molecules cease their random movement. At all other temperatures they move about, colliding and veering off in different directions, thus pushing one another away. The result of these collisions in the example of sugar and water is to force sugar molecules upward (and to force water molecules downward), away from the regions in which they are most concentrated.

The Force of Electrostatic Pressure

When some substances are dissolved in water, they split into two parts, each with an opposing electrical charge. Substances with this property are called **electrolytes;** the charged particles into which they decompose are called **ions.** Ions are of two basic types: **Cations** have a positive charge, and **anions** have a negative charge. For example, when sodium chloride (NaCl, table salt) is dissolved in water, many of the molecules split into sodium cations (Na^+) and chloride anions (Cl^-). (I find that the eas-

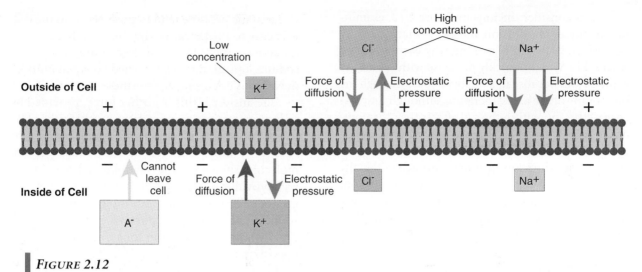

FIGURE 2.12

The relative concentration of some important ions inside and outside the neuron and the forces acting on them.

iest way to keep the terms *cation* and *anion* straight is to think of the cation's plus sign as a cross, and remember the superstition of a black *cat* crossing your path.)

As you have undoubtedly learned, particles with the same kind of charge repel each other (+ repels +, and - repels -), but particles with different charges are attracted to each other (+ and - attract). Thus, anions repel anions, cations repel cations, but anions and cations attract each other. The force exerted by this attraction or repulsion is called **electrostatic pressure.** Just as the force of diffusion moves molecules from regions of high concentration to regions of low concentration, electrostatic pressure moves ions from place to place: Cations are pushed away from regions with an excess of cations, and anions are pushed away from regions with an excess of anions.

Ions in the Extracellular and Intracellular Fluid

The fluid within cells (**intracellular fluid**) and the fluid surrounding them (**extracellular fluid**) contain different ions. The forces of diffusion and electrostatic pressure contributed by these ions give rise to the membrane potential. Because the membrane potential is produced by a balance between the forces of diffusion and electrostatic pressures, understanding what produces this potential requires that we know the concentration of the various ions in the extracellular and intracellular fluids.

There are several important ions in these fluids. I will discuss four of them here: organic anions (symbolized by A^-), chloride ions (Cl^-), sodium ions (Na^+), and potassium ions (K^+). The Latin words for sodium and potassium are *natrium* and *kalium;* hence, they are abbreviated *Na* and *K,* respectively. Organic anions—negatively charged proteins and intermediate products of the cell's metabolic processes—are found only in the intracellular fluid. Although the other three ions are found in both the intracellular and extracellular fluids, K^+ is found predominantly in the intracellular fluid, whereas Na^+ and Cl^- are found predominantly in the extracellular fluid. The sizes of the boxes in Figure 2.12 indicate the relative concentrations of these four ions. (See *Figure 2.12.*) The easiest way to remember which ion is found where is to recall that the fluid that surrounds our cells is similar to seawater, which is predominantly a solution of salt, NaCl. The primitive ancestors of our cells lived in the ocean; thus, the seawater was their extracellular fluid. Our extracellular fluid thus resembles seawater, produced and maintained by regulatory mechanisms that are described in Chapter 12.

Let us consider the ions in Figure 2.12, examining the forces of diffusion and electrostatic pressure exerted on each and reasoning why each is located where it is. We can quickly dispense with A⁻, the organic anion, because it is unable to pass through the membrane of the axon; therefore, although the presence of this ion within the cell affects the other ions, it is located where it is because the membrane is impermeable to it.

The potassium ion K⁺ is concentrated within the axon; thus, the force of diffusion tends to push it out of the cell. The outside of the cell is charged positively with respect to the inside, so electrostatic pressure tends to force the cation inside. Thus, the two opposing forces balance. (See *Figure 2.12.*)

The chloride ion Cl⁻ is in greatest concentration outside the axon. The force of diffusion pushes this ion inward. However, because the inside of the axon is negatively charged, electrostatic pressure pushes the anion outward. Again, two opposing forces balance each other. (See *Figure 2.12.*)

The sodium ion Na⁺ is also in greatest concentration outside the axon, so it, like Cl⁻, is pushed into the cell by the force of diffusion. But unlike chloride, the sodium ion is *positively* charged. Therefore, electrostatic pressure does *not* prevent Na⁺ from entering the cell; the negative charge inside the axon *attracts* Na⁺. (See *Figure 2.12.*)

How can Na⁺ remain in greatest concentration in the extracellular fluid, despite the fact that both forces (diffusion and electrostatic pressure) tend to push it inside? The simplest explanation would be that the membrane is impermeable to Na⁺, as it is to A⁻, the organic anion. This possibility can be tested with the following experiment. A giant squid axon is placed in a dish of seawater containing some radioactive Na⁺, is allowed to sit awhile, and is then removed and washed off. The axon is now radioactive, which shows that Na⁺ *can* pass through the membrane, because some of the radioactive Na⁺ in the seawater found its way into the axon.

Although the axon contains radioactive Na⁺, analysis of its cytoplasm (which can be squeezed out like toothpaste) shows that the concentration of Na⁺ is unchanged. This analysis indicates that although some molecules of Na⁺ entered the axon, an equal number left again, keeping the concentration constant. But as we know, the forces of diffusion and electrostatic pressure tend to push Na⁺ into the cell. It is easy to understand why the axon became radioactive—these forces pushed some radioactive sodium ions in. But what pushed an equal number of Na⁺ ions out again, against these two forces?

The answer is this: Another force, provided by *sodium-potassium pump,* continuously pushes Na⁺ out of the axon. The sodium-potassium pump consists of a large number of individual protein molecules situated in the membrane, driven by energy provided by the mitochondria as they metabolize the cell's nutrients. These molecules, known as **sodium-potassium transporters,** exchange Na⁺ for K⁺, pushing three sodium ions out for every two potassium ions they push in. (See *Figure 2.13.*)

Because the membrane is not very permeable to Na⁺, sodium-potassium transporters very effectively keep the intracellular concentration of Na⁺ low. By transporting K⁺ into the cell, they also increase the intracellular concentration of K⁺ somewhat. The membrane is approximately 100 times more permeable to K⁺ than to Na⁺, so the increase is slight; but as we will see when we study the process of neural inhibition in Chapter 3, it is very impor-

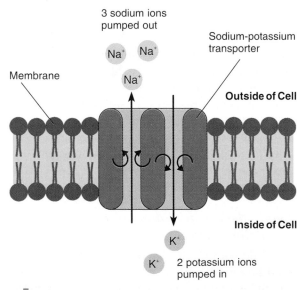

FIGURE 2.13

A sodium-potassium transporter, situated in the cell membrane.

Ions

Protein subunits
of ion channel

Pore of ion channel

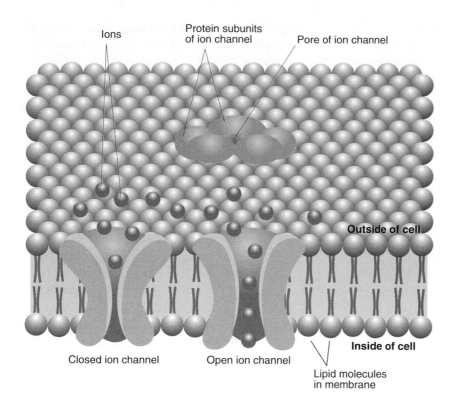

Outside of cell

Inside of cell

Closed ion channel

Open ion channel

Lipid molecules
in membrane

FIGURE 2.14

Ion channels. When they are open, ions can pass through them, entering or leaving the cell.

tant. The transporters that make up the sodium-potassium pump use considerable energy: Up to 40 percent of the neuron's metabolic resources are used to operate them. Neurons, muscle cells, glia—in fact, most cells of the body—have sodium-potassium transporters in their membrane.

The Action Potential

As we saw, the forces of both diffusion and electrostatic pressure tend to push Na^+ into the cell. However, the membrane is not very permeable to this ion, and sodium-potassium transporters continuously pump out Na^+, keeping the intracellular level of Na^+ low. But imagine what would happen if the membrane suddenly became permeable to Na^+. The forces of diffusion and electrostatic pressure would cause Na^+ to rush into the cell. This sudden influx (inflow) of positively charged ions would drastically change the membrane potential. Indeed, experiments have shown that this mechanism is precisely what causes the action potential: A brief drop in the membrane resistance to Na^+ (allowing these ions to rush into the cell) is immediately followed by a tran-

sient drop in the membrane resistance to K^+ (allowing these ions to rush out of the cell).

I said earlier that the membrane consists of a double layer of lipid molecules in which are floating many different kinds of protein molecules. One class of protein molecules provides a way for ions to enter or leave the cells. These molecules constitute **ion channels,** which contain passages ("pores") that can open or close. When an ion channel is open, a particular type of ion can flow through the pore and thus can enter or leave the cell. (See *Figure 2.14.*) Neural membranes contain many thousands of ion channels. For example, the giant squid axon contains from 100 to 600 sodium channels in each square micrometer of membrane. (There are one million square micrometers in a square millimeter; thus, a patch of axonal membrane the size of the lowercase letter "o" would contain several hundred million sodium channels.) The permeability of a membrane to a particular ion at a given moment is determined by the number of ion channels that are open. (By the way, neurobiologists have discovered approximately 75 different types of ion channels, and more will undoubtedly be discovered.)

The following numbered paragraphs describe the movements of ions through the membrane during the action potential. The numbers on the figure correspond to the numbers of the paragraphs that follow. (See *Figure 2.15*.)

1. As soon as the threshold of excitation is reached, the sodium channels in the membrane open and Na$^+$ rushes in, propelled by the forces of diffusion and electrostatic pressure. The opening of these channels is triggered by the depolarization of the membrane potential; they open at the threshold of excitation. Because these channels are opened by changes in the membrane potential, they are called **voltage-dependent ion channels.** The influx of positively charged sodium ions produces a rapid change in the membrane potential, from -70 to +50 mV.

2. The membrane of the axon contains voltage-dependent potassium channels, but these channels are less sensitive than voltage-dependent sodium channels. That is, they require a greater level of depolarization before they begin to open. Thus, they open later than the sodium channels.

3. At about the time the action potential reaches its peak (in approximately 1 msec), the sodium channels close—in fact, they cannot open again until the membrane once more reaches the resting potential. At this time, then, no more Na$^+$ can enter the cell.

4. By now, the voltage-dependent potassium channels in the membrane are open, letting K$^+$ ions move freely through the membrane. At this time, the inside of the axon is now *positively* charged, so K$^+$ is driven out of the cell by diffusion and by electrostatic pressure. This outflow of cations causes the membrane potential to return toward its normal value. As it does so, the potassium channels begin to close again.

5. As the membrane potential returns to normal, the potassium channels close, and no more potassium leaves the cell. The membrane actually overshoots its resting value (-70mV) and only gradually returns to normal. The accumulation of K$^+$ ions outside the membrane causes it to become temporarily hyperpolarized. These extra ions soon diffuse away, and the membrane potential returns to -70 mV. Eventually, sodium-potassium transporters remove the Na$^+$ that leaked in and retrieve the K$^+$ that leaked out.

How much ionic flow is there? When I say "Na$^+$ rushes in," I do not mean that the axoplasm becomes flooded with Na$^+$. Because the drop in membrane resistance to Na$^+$ is so brief, and because diffusion over any appreciable distance takes some time, not too many Na$^+$ molecules flow in, and not too many K$^+$ molecules flow out. At the peak of the action potential a very thin layer of fluid immediately inside the axon becomes full of newly arrived Na$^+$ ions; this amount is indeed enough to reverse the membrane potential. However, not enough time has elapsed for these ions to fill the entire axon. Before that event can take place, the Na$^+$ channels close and K$^+$ starts flowing out.

Experiments have shown that an action potential temporarily increases the number of Na$^+$ ions inside the giant squid axon by 0.0003 percent. Although the concentration just inside the membrane is high, the total number of ions entering the cell is very small, relative to the number already there. On a short-term basis, sodium-potassium transporters are not very important. The few Na$^+$ ions that manage to leak in diffuse into the rest of the axoplasm, and the slight increase in Na$^+$ concentration is

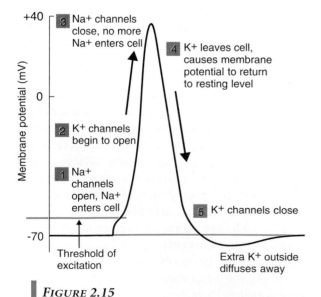

FIGURE 2.15

The movements of ions during the action potential.

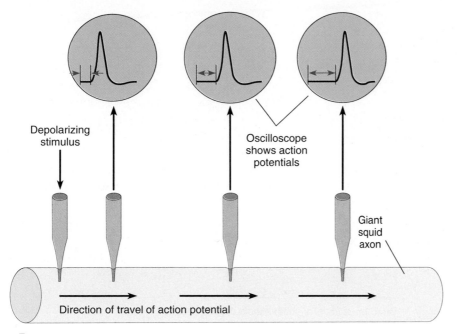

FIGURE 2.16

Conduction of the action potential. When an action potential is triggered, its size remains undiminished as it travels down the axon. The speed of conduction can be calculated from the delay between the stimulus and the action potential.

hardly noticeable. However, sodium-potassium transporters are important on a long-term basis, because in many axons action potentials occur at a very high rate. Without the activity of sodium-potassium transporters the axoplasm would eventually become full of sodium ions, and the axon would no longer be able to function.

Conduction of the Action Potential

Now that we have a basic understanding of the resting membrane potential and the production of the action potential, we can consider the movement of the message down the axon, or *conduction of the action potential.* To study this phenomenon, we again make use of the giant squid axon. We attach an electrical stimulator to an electrode at one end of the axon and place recording electrodes, attached to oscilloscopes, at different distances from the stimulating electrode. Then we apply a depolarizing stimulus to the end of the axon and trigger an action potential. We record the action potential from each of the

electrodes, one after the other. Thus, we see that the action potential is conducted down the axon. As the action potential travels, it remains constant in size. (See *Figure 2.16.*)

This experiment establishes a basic law of axonal conduction: the **all-or-none law.** This law states that an action potential either occurs or does not occur; once it has been triggered, it is transmitted down the axon to its end. An action potential always remains the same size, without growing or diminishing. In fact, the axon will transmit an action potential in either direction, or even in both directions, if it is started in the middle of the axon's length. However, because action potentials in living animals always start at the end attached to the soma, axons normally carry one-way traffic.

Action potentials are not the only kind of electrical signals that occur in neurons. As we shall see in the last section of this chapter, when a message is sent across a synapse, a small electrical signal is produced in the membrane of the neuron that receives the message. To understand this process, and to un-

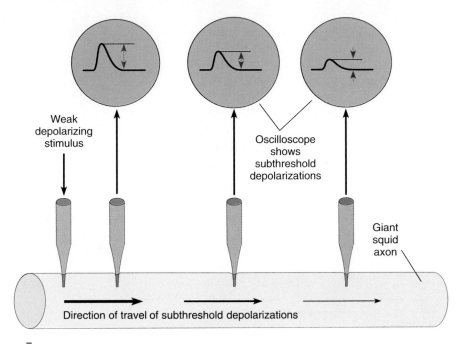

Weak depolarizing stimulus

Oscilloscope shows subthreshold depolarizations

Giant squid axon

Direction of travel of subthreshold depolarizations

FIGURE 2.17

Decremental conduction. When a subthreshold depolariztion is applied to the axon, the disturbance in the membrane potential is largest near the stimulating electrode and gets progressively smaller at distances farther along the axon.

derstand the way that action potentials are conducted in myelinated axons (described later in this section), we must see how such signals other than action potentials are conducted. To do so, we produce a subthreshold depolarization (too small to produce an action potential) at one end of an axon and record its effects from electrodes placed along the axon. We find that the stimulus produces a disturbance in the membrane potential that becomes smaller as it moves away from the point of stimulation. (See *Figure 2.17.*)

The transmission of the small, subthreshold depolarization is *passive*. Neither sodium channels nor potassium channels are opening or closing. The axon is acting like an electrical cable, carrying along the current started at one end. This property of the axon follows laws discovered in the nineteenth century that describe the conduction of electricity through telegraph cables laid along the ocean floor. As a signal passes through a submarine cable, the signal gets smaller because of the electrical characteristics of the cable, including leakage through the

insulator and resistance in the wire. Because the signal decreases in size (decrements), it is referred to as *decremental conduction*. We say that the conduction of a small depolarization by the axon follows the laws that describe the **cable properties** of the axon—the same laws that describe the electrical properties of a submarine cable. And because hyperpolarizations never trigger action potentials, these disturbances, too, are transmitted by means of the passive cable properties of an axon.

Recall that all but the smallest axons in mammalian nervous systems are myelinated; segments of the axons are covered by a myelin sheath produced by the oligodendrocytes of the CNS or the Schwann cells of the PNS. These segments are separated by portions of naked axon, the nodes of Ranvier. Conduction of an action potential in a myelinated axon is somewhat different from conduction in an unmyelinated axon.

Schwann cells (and the oligodendrocytes of the CNS) wrap tightly around the axon, leaving no measurable extracellular fluid between them and the axon. The only place where a myelinated axon comes in contact with the extracellular fluid is at a node of Ranvier, where the axon is naked. In the myelinated areas there can be no inward flow of Na^+ when the sodium channels open, because there *is* no extracellular sodium. How, then, does the "action potential" travel along the area of axonal membrane covered by myelin sheath? You guessed it—by cable properties. The axon passively conducts the electrical disturbance from the action potential to the next node of Ranvier. The disturbance gets smaller, but it is still large enough to trigger an action potential at the node. The action potential gets retriggered, or repeated, at each node of Ranvier and is passed, by means of cable properties of the axon, along the myelinated area to the next node. Such conduction, hopping from node to node, is called **saltatory conduction**, from the Latin *saltare*, "to dance." (See *Figure 2.18*.)

There are two advantages to saltatory conduction. The first one is economic. Energy must be expended by sodium-potassium transporters to get rid of the excess Na^+ that enters the axon during the action potential. Sodium-potassium transporters must be located all along an unmyelinated axon, because Na^+ enters everywhere. But because Na^+ can enter a myelinated axon only at the nodes of Ranvier, much less gets in and, consequently, much less has to be pumped out again. Therefore, a myelinated axon expends much less energy to maintain its sodium balance.

The second advantage to myelin is speed. Conduction of an action potential is faster in a myelinated axon because the transmission between the nodes, which occurs by means of the axon's cable properties, is very fast. Increased speed makes it possible for an animal to react faster and (undoubtedly) to think faster. One of the ways to increase the speed of conduction is to increase size. Because it is so large, the unmyelinated squid axon, with a diameter of 500 μm, achieves a conduction velocity of approximately 35 m/sec (meters per second). However, the same speed is achieved by a myelinated cat axon with a diameter of a mere 6 μm. The fastest myelinated axon, 20 μm in diameter, can conduct action potentials at a speedy 120 m/sec, or 432 km/h. At that speed a signal can get from one end of an axon to the other without much delay.

INTERIM SUMMARY

Neurons communicate by means of synapses. When a message is sent down an axon, the terminal buttons secrete a chemical that has either an excitatory or an inhibitory effect on the neuron with which it communicates. Ultimately, the effects of these exci-

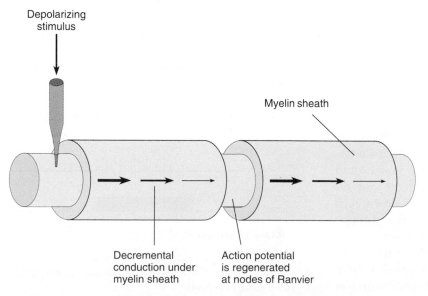

FIGURE 2.18

Saltatory conduction, showing propagation of an action potential down a myelinated axon.

Depolarizing stimulus

Myelin sheath

Decremental conduction under myelin sheath

Action potential is regenerated at nodes of Ranvier

tatory and inhibitory synapses cause behavior, in the form of muscular contraction.

The message conducted down an axon is called an action potential. The membranes of all cells of the body are electrically charged, but only axons can produce action potentials. The resting membrane potential occurs because various ions are located in different concentrations in the fluid inside and outside the cell. The extracellular fluid (like seawater) is rich in Na^+ and Cl^-, and the intracellular fluid is rich in K^+ and various organic anions, designated as A^-.

The cell membrane is freely permeable to water, but its permeability to various ions—in particular, Na^+ and K^+—is regulated by ion channels. When the membrane potential is at its resting value (-70 mV), the gates of the voltage-dependent sodium and potassium channels are closed. The experiment with radioactive seawater showed us that some Na^+ continuously leaks into the axon but is promptly forced out of the cell again by the sodium-potassium transporters (which also pump potassium *into* the axon). When an electrical stimulator depolarizes the membrane potential of the axon so that it reaches the threshold of excitation, voltage-dependent sodium channels open and Na^+ rushes into the cell, driven by the force of diffusion and by electrostatic pressure. The entry of the positively charged ions further reduces the membrane potential and, indeed, causes it to reverse, so that the inside becomes positive. The opening of the sodium channels is temporary; they soon close again. The depolarization of the membrane potential caused by the influx of Na^+ activates voltage-dependent potassium channels, and K^+ leaves the axon, down its concentration gradient. This efflux (outflow) of K^+ quickly brings the membrane potential back to its resting value.

The action potential normally begins at one end of the axon, where the axon attaches to the soma. The action potential travels continuously down unmyelinated axons, remaining constant in size, until it reaches the terminal buttons. (When the axon divides, the action potential continues down each branch.) In myelinated axons, ions can flow through the membrane only at the nodes of Ranvier, because the axons are covered everywhere else with myelin, which isolates them from the extracellular fluid. Thus, the action potential is conducted from one node of Ranvier to the next by means of passive cable properties. When the electrical message reaches a node, voltage-dependent sodium channels open, and the action potential reaches full strength again. This mechanism saves a considerable amount of energy, because sodium-potassium transporters are not needed along the myelinated portions of the axons; and saltatory conduction is also faster.

NEURAL COMMUNICATION: AN OVERVIEW

NOW THAT YOU KNOW ABOUT THE BASIC structure of neurons and the nature of the action potential, it is time to provide an overview of the ways they can interact, gathering sensory information and initiating a behavior. The examples described here will be very simple, but more complex ones will be described in subsequent chapters.

The Rate Law

The strength of a muscular contraction can range from very weak to very forceful, and the strength of a stimulus can range from barely detectable to very

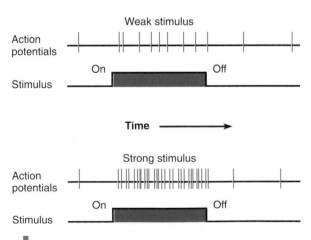

FIGURE 2.19

The rate law. The strength of a stimulus is represented by the rate of firing of an axon. The size of each action potential is always constant.

intense. We know that the occurrence of action potentials in the axons of motor neurons controls the strength of muscular contractions and that their occurrence in sensory neurons represents the intensity of a physical stimulus. But if the action potential is a pulselike, all-or-none event, how can it represent information that varies in a continuous fashion? The answer is simple: A single action potential is not the basic element of information; rather, variable information is represented by an axon's *rate of firing.* (In this context, firing refers to the occurrence of an action potential.) A high rate of firing in the axons of motor neurons causes a strong muscular contraction, and a strong stimulus (such as a bright light) causes a high rate of firing in the axons of sensory neurons that serve the eyes. Thus, the all-or-none law is supplemented by the **rate law**. (See *Figure 2.19.*)

Neural Integration

As we have seen, neurons communicate through synapses. The message transmitted by a particular synapse has one of two effects: excitation or inhibition. Excitatory effects increase the likelihood that the neuron receiving them will send an action potential down its axon; inhibitory effects decrease this likelihood. Thus, the rate at which a given axon fires is determined by the excitatory and inhibitory effects produced at the synaptic connections on the soma and dendrites of the cell to which the axon belongs.

Let us look at the elements of this process. The interaction of the effects of excitatory and inhibitory synapses on a particular neuron is called **neural integration**. (*Integration* means "to make whole," in the sense of combining two functions.) To illustrate this process, we can perform a hypothetical experiment.

We anesthetize an animal and place two microelectrodes in the dendrites of a multipolar neuron in its brain (neuron C). We have chosen this hypothetical animal because the neuron receives synaptic inputs from two neurons (A and B), one inhibitory and one excitatory. One electrode is located near an excitatory synapse and the other is located near an inhibitory synapse. We also place two other microelectrodes in the axons of neurons A and B and attach them to two electrical stimulators, so that we can make these axons fire whenever we want. (See *Figure 2.20.*)

FIGURE 2.20

Measurement of the depolarizations and hyperpolarizations produced by excitatory and inhibitory synapses.

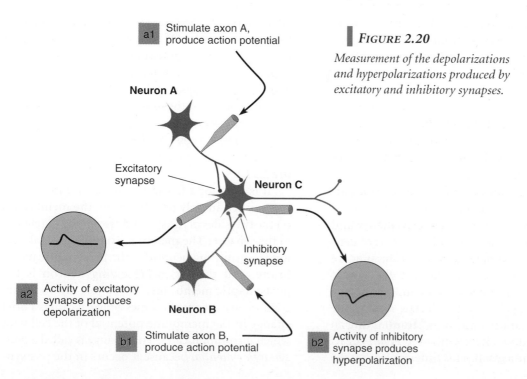

a1 Stimulate axon A, produce action potential

Neuron A

Excitatory synapse

Neuron C

a2 Activity of excitatory synapse produces depolarization

Inhibitory synapse

Neuron B

b1 Stimulate axon B, produce action potential

b2 Activity of inhibitory synapse produces hyperpolarization

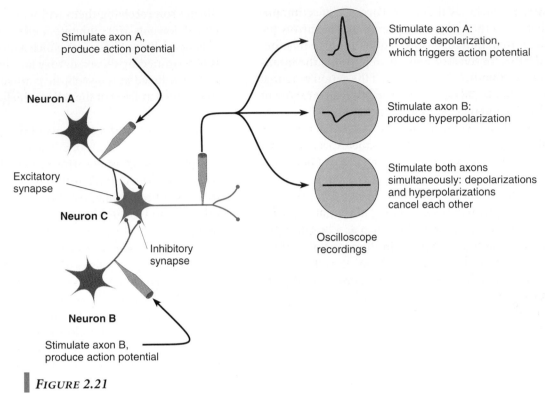

FIGURE 2.21

Neural integration. The effects of excitatory and inhibitory synapses on the production of action potentials in the postsynaptic neuron.

First, we stimulate axon A, one of the incoming axons, and record the membrane potential of neuron C from microelectrode A. We find that the activity of this synapse—an excitatory synapse—produces a brief depolarization. (See boxes a1 and a2 in *Figure 2.20.*) Next, we stimulate axon B and find that the activity of its synaptic connection—an inhibitory one—produces a brief hyperpolarization. (See boxes b1 and b2 in *Figure 2.20.*) Thus, we have just seen that *excitatory* synapses produce *depolarizations* and *inhibitory* synapses produce *hyperpolarizations*.

Now let us look at the effect of excitatory and inhibitory inputs on the activity of the axon of neuron C. Again, we stimulate axon A, but this time we record from a microelectrode placed in the axon of neuron C. After a brief delay the membrane potential of the axon begins to depolarize, reaches the threshold of excitation, and "fires," transmitting an action potential down its length. (See *Figure 2.21.*) Next, we stimulate axon B. This time, we see that the

effect is to *hyperpolarize* the membrane of axon C. (See *Figure 2.21.*) Of course, hyperpolarizations never cause action potentials. Now let us see what happens when we simultaneously stimulate axons A and B. The synapses at the end of axon A cause depolarizations, and those at the end of axon B cause hyperpolarizations. These effects cancel each other; the membrane potential of axon C changes very little, and an action potential is not triggered. (See *Figure 2.21.*)

It is time for a few terms. Because a message is transmitted in only one direction, the membranes on the two sides of the synapse are named in relation to the synapse: The membrane of the terminal button (transmitting neuron) is the **presynaptic membrane**, and that of the receiving neuron is the **postsynaptic membrane.** As you just saw in Figure 2.20, when a synapse becomes active, it causes a brief change in the membrane potential of the cell with which it communicates. This change is called a *postsynaptic potential* because it occurs in the postsynaptic neuron. Hyperpolarizations *inhibit* the production of action potentials; hence hyperpolarizations are called **inhibitory postsynaptic potentials (IPSPs).** Depolarizations *excite* the neuron, making action potentials more likely; hence depolarizations are called **excitatory postsynaptic potentials (EPSPs).** An individual neuron may have tens of thousands of synapses on it. Thus, the rate of firing of its axon at a particular time depends on the relative number of EPSPs and IPSPs that are produced on its membrane.

Note that *neural* inhibition (that is, an inhibitory postsynaptic potential) does not always produce *behavioral* inhibition. For example, suppose a group of neurons inhibits a particular movement. If these neurons are inhibited, they will no longer suppress the behavior. Thus, inhibition of the inhibitory neurons makes the behavior more likely to occur. Of course, the same is true for neural excitation. Neural *excitation* of neurons that *inhibit* a behavior suppresses that behavior. For example, when we are dreaming, a particular set of inhibitory neurons in the brain becomes active and prevents us from get-

ting up and acting out our dreams. (If these neurons are destroyed, people *will* act out their dreams.) Neurons are elements in complex circuits; without knowing the details of these circuits, one cannot predict the effects of the excitation or inhibition of one set of neurons on an organism's behavior.

A Simple Reflex

To appreciate the importance of neural integration, let us examine a simple assembly of three neurons that accomplishes a useful behavior: a withdrawal reflex. In the next two figures (and in subsequent figures that illustrate simple neural circuits) neurons are depicted in short-hand fashion as several-sided stars. The points of these stars represent dendrites, and only one or two terminal buttons are shown at the end of the axon. The first neuron is a sensory receptor that detects painful stimuli. When its dendrites are stimulated by a pinprick, it sends messages down the axon to the terminal buttons, which are located in the spinal cord. (You will recognize this cell as a unipolar neuron; see ***Figure 2.22.***) The ter-

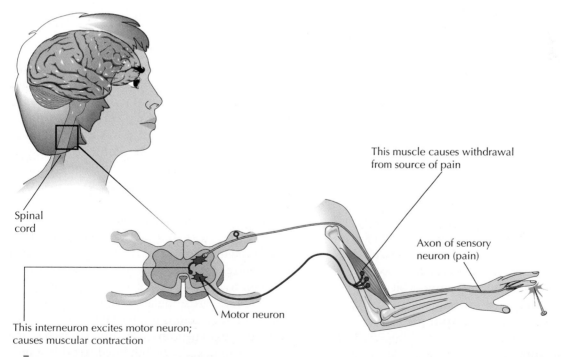

Spinal cord

This muscle causes withdrawal from source of pain

Axon of sensory neuron (pain)

Motor neuron

This interneuron excites motor neuron; causes muscular contraction

FIGURE 2.22

A withdrawal reflex, a simple example of a useful function of the nervous system.

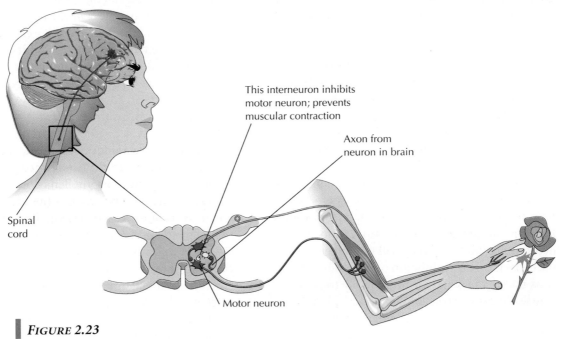

This interneuron inhibits motor neuron; prevents muscular contraction

Axon from neuron in brain

Spinal cord

Motor neuron

FIGURE 2.23

The role of inhibition. Inhibitory signals arising from the brain can prevent the withdrawal reflex from causing the person to drop the rose.

minal buttons of the sensory neuron release a transmitter substance that excites the somatic and dendritic membranes of the second neuron (the *interneuron*), causing it to send messages down its axon. In turn, the terminal buttons of the second neuron release a chemical that excites the third neuron (the motor neuron), which sends messages down its axon. The terminal buttons of the motor neuron synapse with the cells in a muscle. When they release their chemical, the muscle cells contract, causing a part of the body to move. This scheme represents a simplified version of what happens when a pinprick on the end of a finger causes a person to react by reflexively moving his or her arm away from the source of the pain. (See *Figure 2.22.*)

So far, all of the synaptic effects have been excitatory. Now let us complicate matters a bit to see the effect of inhibitory synapses. Suppose you are carrying a bunch of roses from your garden. As you walk, the thorns begin to prick your fingers. The pain receptors stimulate a withdrawal reflex like the one shown in Figure 2.23, which tends to make you open your hand and let go of the roses. However, be-

cause you do not want to drop your flowers, you manage to hold onto them until you have a chance to get a better, less painful grip on them. The message not to drop the roses comes through the axon of a neuron located in the brain. The terminal buttons at the end of this axon form synapses with an inhibitory neuron in the spinal cord. The terminal buttons of the inhibitory neuron release a chemical that inhibits the activity of the motor neuron. Thus, messages from the brain prevent the withdrawal reflex from operating. (See *Figure 2.23.*)

Of course, reflexes are more complicated than this description, and the mechanisms that inhibit them are even more so. And thousands of neurons are involved in this process. The five neurons shown in this figure represent many others: Dozens of sensory neurons detect the prick of the thorn, hundreds of interneurons are stimulated by their activity, hundreds of motor neurons produce the contraction—and thousands of neurons in the brain must become active if the reflex is to be inhibited. Yet this simple model, demonstrating one example of the importance of excitation and inhibition, provides an overview of the process of neural communication, which is described in more detail in this chapter and the next.

 ## INTERIM SUMMARY

Because an action potential of a given axon is an all-or-none phenomenon, neurons represent intensity by their rate of firing. Synapses consist of junctions between the terminal buttons of one neuron and the membrane—usually the somatic or dendritic membrane—of another. When an action potential is transmitted down an axon, the terminal buttons at the end release a transmitter substance, a chemical that produces either depolarizations (EPSPs) or hyperpolarizations (IPSPs) of the post-synaptic membrane. The rate of firing of the axon of the postsynaptic cell is determined by the relative activity of the excitatory and inhibitory synapses on the membrane of its dendrites and soma—a phenomenon known as neural integration.

The importance of neural integration is illustrated by a simple withdrawal reflex, which consists of three sets of neurons: sensory neurons, interneurons, and motor neurons. This reflex can be suppressed when neurons in the brain activate inhibitory interneurons that form synapses with the motor neurons.

New Terms

sensory neuron p. 20

motor neuron p. 20

central nervous system p. 20

peripheral nervous system p. 20

Cells of the Nervous System

soma p. 20

dendrite p. 20

synapse p. 20

axon p. 20

multipolar neuron p. 21

bipolar neuron p. 21

unipolar neuron p. 21

terminal button p. 21

transmitter substance p. 21

neurotransmitter p. 21

membrane p. 22

nucleus p. 22

nucleolus (*new CLEE o lus*) p. 22

ribosome (*RY bo soam*) p. 22

chromosome p. 22

deoxyribonucleic acid (*DEE ox ee RY bo new CLAY ik*) p. 22

gene p. 22

messenger ribonucleic acid p. 22

enzyme p. 22

cytoplasm p. 23

mitochondria p. 23

adenosine triphosphate (*ah DEN o seen*) p. 23

endoplasmic reticulum p. 23

Golgi apparatus (*GOAL jee*) p. 25

exocytosis (*EX o sy TOE sis*) p. 25

lysosome (*LIGH so soam*) p. 25

neurofilament p. 25

microtubule p. 25

axoplasmic transport p. 25

glia (*GLEE ah*) p. 25

astrocyte p. 25

phagocytosis (*FAGG o sy TOE sis*) p. 26

oligodendrocyte (*oh li go DEN droh site*) p. 26

myelin sheath (*MY a lin*) p. 26

node of Ranvier (*RAW vee ay*) p. 26

Schwann cell p. 27

blood-brain barrier p. 29

area postrema (*poss TREE ma*) p. 29

Communication Within a Neuron

electrode p. 30

microelectrode p. 31

membrane potential p. 31

oscilloscope p. 31

resting potential p. 31

depolarization p. 31

hyperpolarization p. 32

action potential p. 32

threshold of excitation p. 32

diffusion p. 32

electrolyte p. 32

ion p. 32

cation (*CAT aye un*) p. 32

anion p. 32

electrostatic pressure p. 33

intracellular fluid p. 33

extracellular fluid p. 33

sodium-potassium transporter p. 34

ion channel p. 35

voltage-dependent ion
    channel p. 36

all-or-none law p. 37

cable properties p. 38

saltatory conduction p. 39

Neural Communication:
an Overview

rate law p. 41

neural integration p. 41

presynaptic membrane p. 42

postsynaptic membrane p. 42

inhibitory postsynaptic potential
    (IPSP) p. 43

excitatory postsynaptic potential
    (EPSP) p. 43

Suggested Readings

Kandel, E.R., and Schwartz, J.H., and Jessell, T.M. *Principles of Neural Science,* 3rd ed. Norwalk, Conn.: Appleton & Lange, 1992.

Nicholls, J.G., Martin, A.R., Wallace, B.G., and Kuffler, S.W. *From Neuron to Brain,* 3rd ed. Sunderland, Mass.: Sinauer Associates, 1992.

Shepherd, G.M. *Neurobiology,* 2nd ed. New York: Oxford University Press, 1988.

CHAPTER 3

Neural Communication

Synaptic Transmission
- The Concept of Chemical Transmission
- Structure of Synapses
- Release of Transmitter Substance
- Activation of Receptors
- Postsynaptic Potentials
- Termination of the Postsynaptic Potential
- Autoreceptors
- Other Types of Synapses
- Nonsynaptic Chemical Communication
  Interim Summary

Transmitter Substances
- Acetylcholine
- The Monoamines
- Amino Acid Transmitter Substances
- Peptides
- Lipids
- Soluble Gases
  Interim Summary

Pharmacology of Synapses
- Effects on Production of Transmitter Substances
- Effects on Storage and Release of Transmitter Substances
- Effects on Receptors
- Effects on Reuptake or Destruction of Transmitter Substance
  Interim Summary

CHAPTER 2 DISCUSSED THE RESTING membrane potential and described how a small decrease in this potential triggers an action potential that is conducted down the axon to the terminal buttons. It also discussed the concept of neural integration—the way that the activity of excitatory and inhibitory synapses controls the rate at which a neuron fires. This chapter discusses the nature of communication among neurons and the ways in which drugs facilitate or interfere with this communication.

SYNAPTIC TRANSMISSION

AS WE SAW IN CHAPTER 2, NEURONS COMMUNIcate by means of synapses, and the medium used for these one-way conversations is the chemical released by terminal buttons. These chemicals, called *transmitter substances* (or *neurotransmitters),* diffuse across the fluid-filled gap between the terminal buttons and the membranes of the neurons with which they form synapses. The transmitter substances produce postsynaptic potentials—brief depolarizations or hyperpolarizations—which increase or decrease the rate of firing of the axon of the postsynaptic neuron.

This section begins with a discussion of the communication of information by means of chemicals. Next, it describes the structure of synapses and details the steps involved in the process of synaptic transmission, from release of the transmitter substance to termination of the postsynaptic potential.

The Concept of Chemical Transmission

Chemicals are used to transmit information within an organism and even between them. These chemicals—transmitter substances, neuromodulators, hormones, and pheromones—control the behavior of cells, organs, or entire animals. All these methods of transmission require the presence of cells that release the chemical and specialized protein molecules (receptors) that detect their presence.

These methods differ primarily in the distance between the cell that secretes the chemical and the receptors that detect its presence.

Transmitter substances (often called *neurotransmitters)* are released by terminal buttons of neurons and are detected by receptors in the membrane of another cell located a very short distance away. The communication at each synapse is private. Neuromodulators travel farther and are dispersed more widely than are neurotransmitters. **Neuromodulators,** too, are released by terminal buttons but are secreted in larger amounts and diffuse for longer distances, modulating the activity of many neurons in a particular part of the brain. Most neuromodulators are composed of proteinlike molecules called *peptides*, which are described later in this chapter.

Hormones are produced in cells located in special organs called **endocrine glands** (from the Greek *endo-*, "within" and *krinein,* "to secrete"). The secretory cells of endocrine glands release their hormones into the extracellular fluid. The hormones are then distributed to the rest of the body through the bloodstream. Hormones affect the activity of cells (including neurons) by stimulating receptors located either on the surface of their membrane or deep within their nuclei. (Both types are described later in this chapter.) Some of the neurons located in the brain contain such receptors, and hormones are able to affect behavior by stimulating the receptors and changing the activity of these neurons. For example, a sex hormone, testosterone, increases the aggressiveness of most male mammals.

Neurotransmitters, neuromodulators, and hormones exert their effects on cells by attaching to a particular region of a receptor molecule called the **binding site.** A molecule of the transmitter fits into the binding site the way a key fits into a lock; the shape of the binding site and the shape of the molecule of the transmitter substance are complementary. (A chemical that attaches to a binding site is called a **ligand,** from *ligare,* "to bind.") Natural ligands are neurotransmitters, neuromodulators, or hormones. But other chemicals found in nature (primarily in plants or in the poisonous venoms of animals) can serve as ligands, attaching to the binding sites of particular receptors. In addition, artificial ligands can be produced in the laboratory. These chemicals are discussed in the section of this chapter that deals with drugs and their effects.

Pheromones are chemicals that are released into the environment through sweat, urine, or the secretions of specialized glands. The odor of these chemicals is detected by receptors in the noses of other animals. Most pheromones affect the reproductive behavior or physiology of other members of the same species. For example, pheromones can attract potential mates, arouse them sexually, inhibit their aggression, and alter the activity of their endocrine system. These interesting chemicals are discussed in more detail in Chapter 10.

This chapter will deal mostly with synaptic transmission, which is the private communication between a terminal button and the membrane of another cell. However, you should bear in mind that the same principles are seen in chemical communication over longer distances, and probably all of these forms of communication evolved from a common mechanism.

Structure of Synapses

As you have already learned, synapses are junctions between the terminal buttons at the ends of the axonal branches of one neuron and the membrane of another. As Figure 3.1 shows, these membranes are separated by a small gap, which varies in size from synapse to synapse but is usually around 200 Å wide. (An ångström, Å, is one ten-millionth of a millimeter.) The space, called the **synaptic cleft,** contains extracellular fluid, through which the transmitter substance diffuses. (See *Figure 3.1.*)

As you may have noticed in Figure 3.1, three prominent structures are located in the cytoplasm of the terminal button: mitochondria, synaptic vesicles, and a Golgi apparatus. The presence of mitochondria implies that the terminal button needs energy to perform its functions. **Synaptic vesicles** are small, rounded objects in the shape of spheres or ovoids. (The term *vesicle* means "little bladder.")

FIGURE 3.1

Details of a synapse.

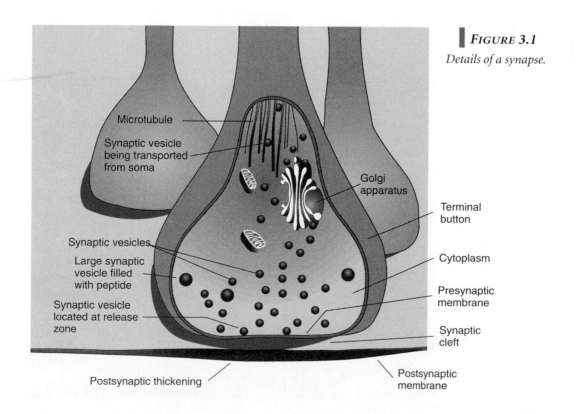

Microtubule

Synaptic vesicle being transported from soma

Golgi apparatus

Terminal button

Cytoplasm

Presynaptic membrane

Synaptic cleft

Synaptic vesicles

Large synaptic vesicle filled with peptide

Synaptic vesicle located at release zone

Postsynaptic thickening

Postsynaptic membrane

Many terminal buttons contain two types of synaptic vesicles, large and small. Small synaptic vesicles (found in all terminal buttons) contain molecules of the transmitter substance. These vesicles are found in greatest numbers around the part of the presynaptic membrane that faces the synaptic cleft—next to the **release zone**, the region from which transmitter substance is released. Large synaptic vesicles are found scattered throughout the terminal button. These vesicles contain one of a number of different neuropeptides, the functions of which are described later in this chapter. (See *Figure 3.1.*)

Small synaptic vesicles are produced in the terminal buttons by the Golgi apparatus, the cell's packaging system. As we will shall see, the Golgi apparatus, also serves as a recycling center, making synaptic vesicles out of the membrane of old vesicles that have expelled their contents into the synaptic cleft. In contrast, large synaptic vesicles are produced in the soma and transported through the axoplasm to the terminal buttons.

In an electron micrograph the postsynaptic membrane under the terminal button appears somewhat thicker than the membrane elsewhere. As we will see, this thickening is caused by the presence of receptors—specialized protein molecules that detect the presence of transmitter substances in the synaptic cleft. (See *Figure 3.1.*)

Release of Transmitter Substance

When action potentials are conducted down an axon (and down all of its branches), something happens inside all of the terminal buttons: A number of small synaptic vesicles located just inside the postsynaptic membrane attach themselves to the membrane and then break open, spilling their contents into the synaptic cleft.

Heuser and colleagues (Heuser, 1977; Heuser et al., 1979) obtained photomicrographs that illustrate this process. Because the release of transmitter substance is a very rapid event, taking only a few milliseconds to occur, special procedures are needed to stop the action so that the details can be studied. The experimenters electrically stimulated the nerve attached to an isolated frog muscle and then dropped the muscle against a block of pure copper that had been cooled to 4 K (approximately -453°F). Contact with the supercooled metal froze the outer layer of tissue in 2 milliseconds or less. The ice held the components of the terminal buttons in place until they could be chemically stabilized and examined

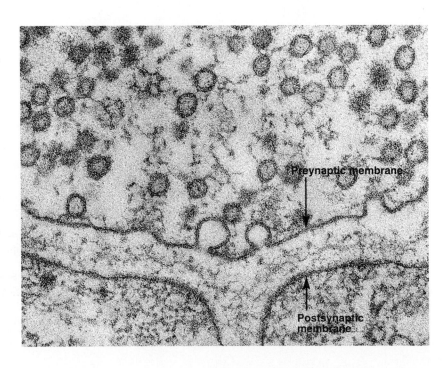

FIGURE 3.2

A photograph from an electron microscope, showing a cross section of a synapse. The omega-shaped figures are synaptic vesicles fusing with the presynaptic membranes of terminal buttons that form synapses with frog muscle.

(From Heuser, J.E., in *Society for Neuroscience Symposia, Vol. II,* edited by W.M. Cowan and J.A. Ferrendelli. Bethesda, Md.: Society for Neuroscience, © 1977, Society for Neuroscience. Photomicrograph prduced by Dr. John E. Heuser of Washington University School of Medicine, St. Louis, Mo.)

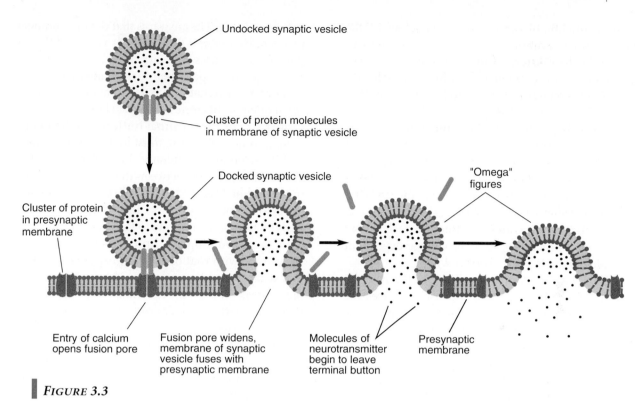

Undocked synaptic vesicle

Cluster of protein molecules in membrane of synaptic vesicle

Docked synaptic vesicle

"Omega" figures

Cluster of protein in presynaptic membrane

Entry of calcium opens fusion pore

Fusion pore widens, membrane of synaptic vesicle fuses with presynaptic membrane

Molecules of neurotransmitter begin to leave terminal button

Presynaptic membrane

FIGURE 3.3

Release of neurotransmitter. An action potential opens calcium channels. Calcium ions enter and bind with the protein embedded in the membrane of synaptic vesicles docked at the release zone. The fusion pores open and the transmitter substance is released into the synaptic cleft. The membrane of the vesicles fuses with that of the terminal button.

with an electron microscope. Figure 3.2 shows a portion of the synapse in cross section; note the vesicles that appear to be fused with the presynaptic membrane, forming the shape of an omega (Ω). (See *Figure 3.2*.)

How does an action potential cause synaptic vesicles to release the transmitter substance? Based on experiments with secretory cells in a variety of different species, Almers (1990) suggested the following model. Some synaptic vesicles are "docked" against the presynaptic membrane, ready to release their transmitter substance into the synaptic cleft. Docking is accomplished when clusters of protein molecules attach to protein molecules located in the presynaptic membrane. (See *Figure 3.3*.)

The release zone of the presynaptic membrane contains voltage-dependent calcium channels. When the membrane of the terminal button is depolarized by an arriving action potential, the cal-

cium channels open. Like sodium ions, calcium ions (Ca^{2+}) are located in highest concentration in the extracellular fluid. Thus, when the voltage-dependent calcium channels open, Ca^{2+} flows into the cell, propelled by electrostatic pressure and the force of diffusion. The entry of Ca^{2+} is an essential step; if neurons are placed in a solution that contains no calcium ions, an action potential no longer causes the release of the transmitter substance. (Calcium transporters, similar in operation to sodium-potassium transporters, later remove the intracellular Ca^{2+}.)

As we will see later in this chapter and in subsequent chapters of this book, the calcium ion plays many important roles in biological processes within cells. The calcium ion can bind with various types of proteins, changing their characteristics. According to Almers, the calcium that enters the terminal button binds with the clusters of protein molecules that join the membrane of the synaptic vesicles with the presynaptic membrane. This event makes the segments of the clusters of protein molecules move apart, producing a *fusion pore*—a hole through both membranes that enables them to fuse together. (See **Figure 3.3.**)

Figure 3.4 shows two photomicrographs of the presynaptic membrane, before and after the fusion pores have opened. We see the face of the presynaptic membrane as it would be viewed from the postsynaptic membrane. As you can see, the synaptic vesicles are aligned in a row along the release zone. The small bumps arranged in lines on each side of the synaptic vesicles appear to be voltage-dependent calcium channels. (See **Figure 3.4.**)

What happens to the membrane of the synaptic vesicles after they have broken open and released the transmitter substance they contain? Every time some transmitter substance is released the membrane of the terminal button gains the membrane of the synaptic vesicles that fuse with it and becomes slightly larger. Obviously, this process cannot go on indefinitely, or else the terminal buttons would get enormously big. The answer is that the membrane is recycled. Heuser and Reese (1973) proposed that as the synaptic vesicles fuse with the presynaptic membrane and burst open, their membrane becomes incorporated into that of the terminal button, which consequently becomes larger. Therefore, if the proper size of the terminal button is to be maintained, some membrane must be removed. Heuser and Reese obtained evidence that suggested that at the point of junction between the axon and the terminal button, little buds of membrane pinch off into the cytoplasm, in a process called **pinocytosis**. The buds of membrane migrate to the cisternae and fuse with them, pooling the lipid molecules in their membrane with that of the Golgi apparatus. Then new synaptic vesicles are produced as beads of membrane break off from the cisternae. These vesicles are then filled with molecules of transmitter substance and transported toward the presynaptic membrane. (See **Figure 3.5.**)

In their experiment Heuser and Reese used a chemical with the unlikely name **horseradish peroxidase**. As we will see, this enzyme, extracted from

│ FIGURE 3.4

Photomicrographs of the release of neurotransmitter by a terminal button that forms a synapse with a frog muscle. The views are of the surface of the fusion zone of the terminal button. Top: Just prior to release. The two rows of dots are probably calcium channels. Bottom: During release. The larger circles are holes in the presynaptic membrane, revealing the contents of the synaptic vesicles that have fused with it.

(From Heuser, J., and Reese, T. *Journal of Cell Biology*, 1981, *88*, 564–580.)

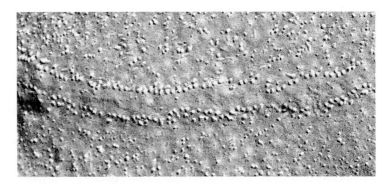

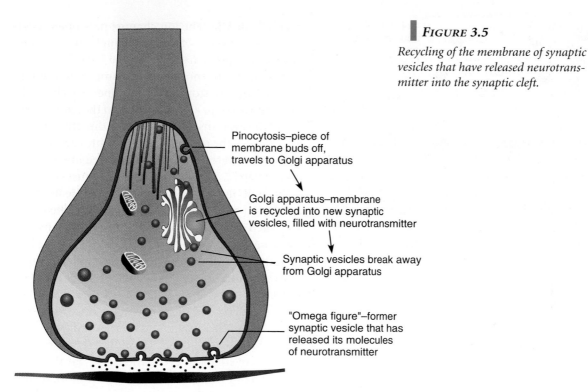

Pinocytosis–piece of membrane buds off, travels to Golgi apparatus

Golgi apparatus–membrane is recycled into new synaptic vesicles, filled with neurotransmitter

Synaptic vesicles break away from Golgi apparatus

"Omega figure"–former synaptic vesicle that has released its molecules of neurotransmitter

the horseradish plant, is useful to neurochemists and neuroanatomists. Heuser and Reese placed a frog muscle and its attached nerve in a solution of horseradish peroxidase and electrically stimulated the nerve, causing the axons to fire. Shortly thereafter, they removed the muscle and nerve from the solution and treated them with chemicals that react with horseradish peroxidase, producing black spots that are visible under a microscope wherever the chemical is present in the tissue. When they chemically treated and examined the nerve tissue soon after placing it in the horseradish peroxidase solution, they found black spots inside small vesicles in the cytoplasm near the junction of the axon and terminal button. When they waited a longer time before chemically treating the tissue, they found black spots in the cisternae. When they waited even longer, they found these spots in the synaptic vesicles themselves. The results indicate that the horseradish peroxidase, which was taken into the cell with a bit of extracellular fluid when buds pinched off the axonal membrane during pinocytosis, was transported to the cisternae and then into the newly made synaptic vesicles.

Activation of Receptors

How do molecules of the transmitter substance produce a depolarization or hyperpolarization in the postsynaptic membrane? They do so by diffusing across the synaptic cleft and attaching to the binding sites of special protein molecules attached to the postsynaptic membrane, called **postsynaptic receptors.** Once binding occurs, the postsynaptic receptors open one or more **neurotransmitter- dependent ion channels,** which permit the passage of specific ions into or out of the cell. Thus, the presence of the transmitter substance in the synaptic cleft allows particular ions to pass through the membrane, changing the local membrane potential.

Neurotransmitters open ion channels by at least two different methods, direct and indirect. The direct method is simpler, so I shall describe it first. Figure 3.6 illustrates a neurotransmitter-dependent ion channel that is equipped with its own binding site. When a molecule of the appropriate neurotransmitter attaches to it, the ion channel opens. The formal name for this combination receptor/ion channel is an **ionotropic receptor.** (See *Figure 3.6.*)

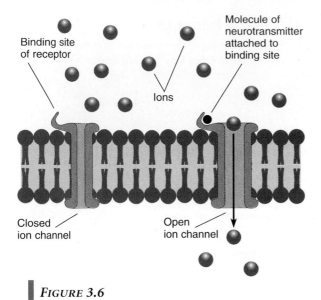

FIGURE 3.6

Ionotropic receptors. The ion channel opens when a molecule of neurotransmitter attaches to the binding site.

The ionotropic receptor was first discovered in the organ that produces electrical current in *Torpedo*, the electric ray, where it occurs in great number. (The electric ray is a fish that generates a powerful electrical current, not some kind of Star Wars weapon.) These receptors, which are sensitive to a transmitter substance called *acetylcholine*, contain sodium channels. When these channels are open, sodium ions enter the cell.

The indirect method is more complicated. Most receptors do not open ion gates directly but instead start a chain of chemical events. These receptors are called **metabotropic receptors** because they involve steps that require that the cell expend energy. Metabotropic receptors are located in close proximity to another protein attached to the membrane—a **G protein.** Figure 3.7(a) shows the simplest type of metabotropic receptor. (See *Figure 3.7*, and note that the numbers in the color squares correspond to the numbers in the description that follows.) When a molecule of the transmitter substance binds with the receptor (step 1), the receptor activates a G protein situated nearby (step 2). An inactive G protein consists of three subunits. When it is activated, the α subunit breaks away from the others and attaches to a special binding site of an ion

channel (step 3). The ion channel now opens (step 4), permitting ions to pass through the channel, producing a postsynaptic potential (step 5).

Figure 3.7(b) shows a more complicated system by which metabotropic receptors open ion channels. The first two steps are the same as in the simpler system. However, instead of binding directly with an ion channel, the α subunit of the G protein attaches to—and activates—an enzyme situated in the membrane (step 3). The activated enzyme causes the production of one of several different chemicals in the cytoplasm of the cell. Generically, these chemicals are called **second messengers** (the neurotransmitter being the first messenger). The second messenger then initiates another series of chemical steps that causes the ion channel to open. (See steps 1–6, *Figure 3.7b.*)

The first second messenger to be discovered was *cyclic AMP*, a chemical that is synthesized from ATP. Since then, several other second messengers have been discovered, but cyclic AMP is by far the most common of them. As you will see later in this chapter, second messengers play an important role in both synaptic and nonsynaptic communication. And they can do more than open ion channels; for example, they can travel to the nucleus or other parts of the cell and initiate biochemical changes.

Most of the information that has been learned about the activity of single ion channels has been gained through a technique known as the **patch clamp** method. A micropipette with a rather wide tip is placed against the membrane of a neuron. Then suction is applied gently, pulling the cell membrane partly into the tip of the micropipette. Often, an individual ion channel can be isolated this way, and the electrical signals it produces can be recorded. (See *Figure 3.8.*)

Postsynaptic Potentials

Because postsynaptic potentials can be either depolarizing (excitatory) or hyperpolarizing (inhibitory), the alterations in membrane permeability must be caused by the movement of particular species of ions. As shown in Figure 3.9, there are four major types of neurotransmitter-dependent ion channels in the postsynaptic membrane: sodium (Na^+), potassium (K^+), chloride (Cl^-), and calcium

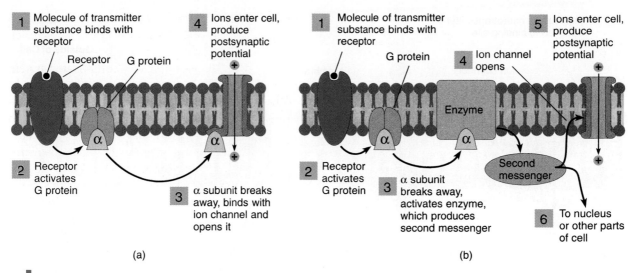

1 Molecule of transmitter substance binds with receptor

Receptor | G protein

2 Receptor activates G protein

3 α subunit breaks away, binds with ion channel and opens it

4 Ions enter cell, produce postsynaptic potential

(a)

1 Molecule of transmitter substance binds with receptor

G protein

4 Ion channel opens

Enzyme

2 Receptor activates G protein

3 α subunit breaks away, activates enzyme, which produces second messenger

Second messenger

5 Ions enter cell, produce postsynaptic potential

6 To nucleus or other parts of cell

(b)

FIGURE 3.7

Metabotropic receptors. (a) The ion channel is opened directly by the α subunit of an activated G protein. (b) The α subunit of the G protein activates an enzyme, which produces a second messenger that opens the ion channel.

(Ca^{2+}). Although the figure depicts only directly activated (ionotropic) ion channels, you should realize that most ion channels are activated indirectly, by metabotropic receptors coupled to G proteins.

The neurotransmitter-dependent sodium channel is the most important source of excitatory postsynaptic potentials. As we saw in Chapter 2, sodium-potassium transporters keep sodium outside the cell, waiting for the forces of diffusion and electrostatic pressure to push it in. Obviously, when sodium channels are opened, the result is a depolarization—an EPSP. (See **Figure 3.9a.**)

We also saw in Chapter 2 that sodium-potassium transporters maintain a small surplus of potassium ions inside the cell. If potassium channels open, some of these cations will follow this gradient and leave the cell. Because K^+ is positively charged, its efflux will hyperpolarize the membrane, producing an IPSP. (See **Figure 3.9b.**)

At many synapses inhibitory transmitter substances open the chloride channels, instead of (or in addition to) potassium channels. The effect of opening chloride channels depends on the membrane potential of the neuron. If the membrane is at the resting potential, nothing happens, because (as we saw in Chapter 2) the forces of diffusion and

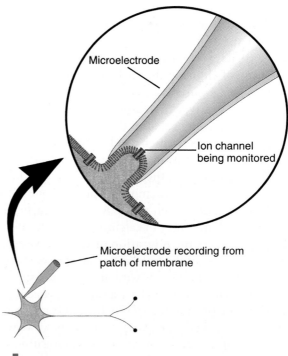

Microelectrode

Ion channel being monitored

Microelectrode recording from patch of membrane

FIGURE 3.8

The patch-clamp technique for recording the effects of a single ion channel.

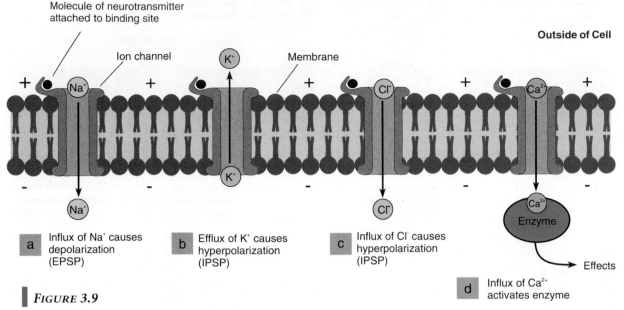

FIGURE 3.9

Ionic movements during postsynaptic potentials.

electrostatic pressure balance perfectly for the chloride ion. However, if the membrane potential has already been depolarized by the activity of excitatory synapses located nearby, then the opening of chloride channels will permit Cl⁻ to leave the cell. The efflux of anions will bring the membrane potential back to its normal resting condition. Thus, the opening of chloride channels serves to neutralize EPSPs. (See *Figure 3.9c.*)

The fourth type of neurotransmitter-dependent ion channel is the calcium channel. Calcium ions (Ca^{2+}), being positively charged and being located in highest concentration outside the cell, act like sodium ions; that is, the opening of calcium channels depolarizes the membrane, producing EPSPs. But calcium does even more. As we saw earlier in this chapter, the entry of calcium into the terminal button triggers the migration of synaptic vesicles and the release of the transmitter substance. *Postsynaptically*, calcium binds with and activates special enzymes. These enzymes have a variety of effects, including the production of biochemical and structural changes in the postsynaptic neuron. As we will see in Chapter 15, one of the ways that learning affects the connections between neurons involves changes in dendritic spines initiated by the opening of calcium channels. (See *Figure 3.9d.*)

Termination of the Postsynaptic Potential

Postsynaptic potentials are brief depolarizations or hyperpolarizations caused by the activation of postsynaptic receptors with molecules of a transmitter substance. They are kept brief by two mechanisms: reuptake and enzymatic deactivation.

The postsynaptic potentials produced by almost all transmitter substances are terminated by **reuptake.** This process is simply an extremely rapid removal of transmitter substance from the synaptic cleft by the terminal button. The transmitter substance does not return in the vesicles that get pinched off the membrane of the terminal button. Instead, the membrane contains special carrier molecules that draw on the cell's energy reserves to force molecules of the transmitter substance from the synaptic cleft directly into the cytoplasm—just as sodium-potassium transporters move Na⁺ and K⁺ across the membrane. When an action potential arrives, the terminal buttons release a small amount of transmitter substance into the synaptic cleft and then take it back, giving the postsynaptic receptors only a brief exposure to the transmitter substance. (See *Figure 3.10.*)

Enzymatic deactivation is accomplished by an enzyme that destroys the transmitter molecule. As far as we know, postsynaptic potentials are terminated in this way for only one transmitter substance—**acetylcholine** (ACh). Transmission at synapses on muscle fibers and at some synapses between neurons is mediated by ACh. Postsynaptic potentials produced by ACh are short-lived because the postsynaptic membrane at these synapses contains an enzyme called **acetylcholinesterase** (AChE). AChE destroys ACh by cleaving it into its constituents—choline and acetate. Because neither of these substances is capable of activating postsynaptic receptors, the postsynaptic potential is terminated once the molecules of ACh are broken apart. AChE is an extremely energetic destroyer of ACh; one molecule of AChE will chop apart more than five thousand molecules of ACh each second.

Autoreceptors

Postsynaptic receptors detect the presence of a transmitter substance in the synaptic cleft and initiate excitatory or inhibitory postsynaptic potentials. But the postsynaptic membrane is not the only location of receptors that respond to transmitter substances.

Many neurons also possess receptors that respond to the transmitter substance that *they* release, called **autoreceptors.**

Autoreceptors can be located on the membrane of any part of the cell, but in this discussion we will consider those located on the terminal button. As far as we know, autoreceptors do not control ion channels. Thus, when stimulated by a molecule of the appropriate transmitter substance, autoreceptors do not produce changes in the membrane potential. Instead, they regulate internal processes, including the synthesis and release of the transmitter substance. (As you may have guessed, autoreceptors are metabotropic; the control they exert on these processes is accomplished through G proteins and second messengers.) In most cases the effects of autoreceptor activation are inhibitory; that is, the presence of the transmitter substance in the extracellular fluid in the vicinity of the neuron causes a decrease in the rate of synthesis or release of the transmitter substance. Most investigators believe that autoreceptors are part of a regulatory system that controls the amount of transmitter substance released. If too much substance is released, the autoreceptors shut down production; if not enough substance is released, the rate of production goes up.

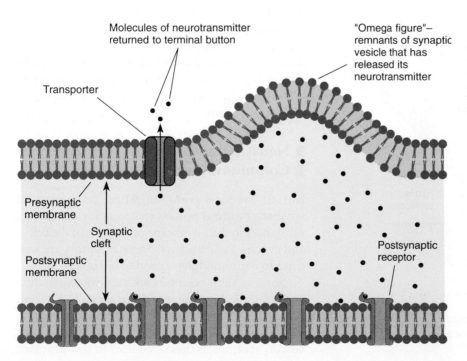

Molecules of neurotransmitter returned to terminal button

Transporter

"Omega figure"– remnants of synaptic vesicle that has released its neurotransmitter

Presynaptic membrane

Synaptic cleft

Postsynaptic membrane

Postsynaptic receptor

FIGURE 3.10

Reuptake. Molecules of a neurotransmitter that has been released into the synaptic cleft are transported back into the terminal button.

Other Types of Synapses

So far, the discussion of synaptic activity has referred only to the effects of postsynaptic excitation or inhibition. These effects occur at **axosomatic synapses** or **axodendritic synapses** (synapses between the terminal buttons of axons with somatic or dendritic membrane, respectively). Other kinds of synapses exist as well.

A junction between a terminal button and an axon of another cell (usually on or near the terminal button) is referred to as an **axoaxonic synapse.** This type of synapse does not contribute directly to neural integration, as do the axosomatic and axodendritic synapses discussed in the previous section. Instead, axoaxonic synapses alter the amount of transmitter substance released by the terminal buttons of the postsynaptic axon. They can produce presynaptic modulation: presynaptic inhibition or presynaptic facilitation.

As you know, the release of a transmitter substance by a terminal button is initiated by an action potential. Normally, a particular terminal button releases a fixed amount of transmitter substance each time an action potential arrives. However, the release of transmitter substance can be modulated by the activity of axoaxonic synapses. If the activity of the axoaxonic synapse decreases the release of the transmitter substance, the effect is called **presynaptic inhibition**. If it increases the release, it is called **presynaptic facilitation.** (See *Figure 3.11.*)

Many very small neurons have extremely short processes and apparently lack axons. These neurons form **dendrodendritic synapses,** or synapses between dendrites. Because these neurons lack long axonal processes, they do not transmit information from place to place within the brain. Most investigators believe that they perform regulatory functions, perhaps helping to organize the activity of groups of neurons. Because these neurons are so small, they are difficult to study; thus, little is known about their function.

Some larger neurons, as well, form dendrodendritic synapses. Some of these synapses are chemical, indicated by the presence of synaptic vesicles in one of the juxtaposed dendrites and a postsynaptic thickening in the membrane of the other. Other synapses are *electrical*; the membranes meet and almost touch, forming a **gap junction.** The membranes on both sides of a gap junction contain channels that permit ions to diffuse from one cell to another. Thus, changes in the membrane potential of one neuron induce changes in the membrane of the other. (See *Figure 3.12.*) Although most gap junctions in vertebrate synapses are dendrodendritic, axosomatic and axodendritic gap junctions also occur. Gap junctions are common in invertebrates; their function in the vertebrate nervous system is not known.

Nonsynaptic Chemical Communication

Not all chemical communication takes place at synapses. Neurons possess receptors for a variety of substances in the membrane of all parts of the cell—and even in their nucleus. These receptors are sensitive to neuromodulators and to hormones.

Some of these receptors are ionotropic in nature and contain binding sites for several different molecules, including both neurotransmitters and neuromodulators. (The best known example, the $GABA_A$ receptor, is described later in this chapter.)

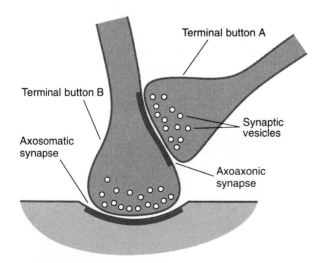

FIGURE 3.11

An axoaxonic synapse. The activity of terminal button A can increase or decrease the amount of neurotransmitter released by terminal button B.

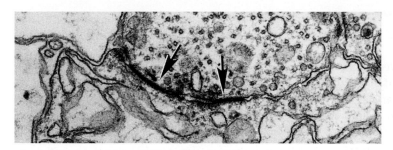

FIGURE 3.12

A gap junction, which permits direct electrical coupling between the membranes of adjacent neurons.
(From Bennett, M.V.L., and Pappas, G.D. *The Journal of Neuroscience,* 1983, *3,* 748–761.)

But most of the receptors found in the membrane are metabotropic—coupled to a G protein that generates a second messenger that produces changes in the cell's physiological processes.

First, let us consider receptors for hormones. Endocrine glands produce two classes of hormones: peptides and steroids. **Peptides** are chains of amino acids that are linked together by special chemical links called *peptide bonds* (hence their name). For example, insulin and the hormones of the pituitary gland are peptides. Peptides exert their effects on target cells by stimulating metabotropic receptors located in the membrane. The second messenger that is generated travels to the nucleus of the cell, where it initiates changes in the cell's physiological processes.

Steroids consist of very small fat-soluble molecules. (*Steroid* derives from *stereos,* "solid," and *oleum,* "oil." They are synthesized from chole*sterol.*) Examples of steroid hormones include the sex hormones secreted by the ovaries and testes and the hormones secreted by the adrenal cortex. Because steroid hormones are soluble in lipids, they pass easily through the cell membrane. They travel to the nucleus, where they attach themselves to receptors located there. The receptors, stimulated by the hormone, then direct the machinery of the cell to alter its protein production. (See ***Figure 3.13.***)

In the past few years, investigators have discovered the presence of steroid receptors in terminal buttons and around the postsynaptic membrane of some neurons. These steroid receptors influence synaptic transmission, and they do so rapidly. (Some of their effects are described in Chapter 10.) Exactly how these steroid receptors work is still not known.

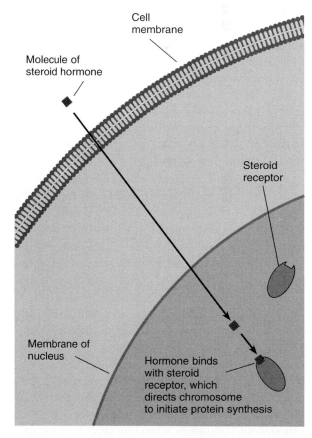

Cell membrane

Molecule of steroid hormone

Steroid receptor

Membrane of nucleus

Hormone binds with steroid receptor, which directs chromosome to initiate protein synthesis

FIGURE 3.13

Action of steroid hormones. Steroid hormones affect their target cells by means of specialized receptors in the nucleus. Once a receptor binds with a molecule of a steroid hormone, it causes genetic mechanisms to initiate protein synthesis.

||||| INTERIM SUMMARY

Chemical communication takes place between a cell that secretes a chemical and one that contains receptors for that chemical. The communication can involve neurotransmitters, neuromodulators, hormones, or pheromones; the distance varies from the space that separates the presynaptic and postsynaptic membrane to the space that separates two individual organisms. Neurotransmitters, neuromodulators, and hormones act on cells by attaching to the binding sites of receptors and initiating chemical changes in these cells.

Synapses consist of junctions between the terminal buttons of one neuron and the membrane—usually the somatic or dendritic membrane—of another. The terminal button contains synaptic vesicles. Most terminal buttons contain two sizes of vesicles, the smaller of which are found in greatest numbers around the release zone of the presynaptic membrane. When an action potential is transmitted down an axon, the depolarization opens voltage-dependent calcium channels, which permit CA^{2+} to enter. The calcium ions bind with the clusters of protein molecules in the membranes of synaptic vesicles already docked at the release zone. The protein clusters spread apart, causing the vesicles to break open and fuse their membrane with that of the terminal button, thus releasing transmitter substance. The extra membrane pinches off into the cytoplasm and travels to the cisternae, where it is recycled in the production of new vesicles.

When postsynaptic receptors are activated by molecules of a transmitter substance, they open neurotransmitter-dependent ion channels. Ionotropic receptors do so directly, and metabotropic receptors do so with G proteins (and often second messengers) as intermediaries. Peptide hormones also exert their effects by activating receptors coupled to G proteins, but steroid hormones stimulate receptors located within the nucleus of their target cells.

The activation of postsynaptic receptors by molecules of a transmitter substance causes neurotransmitter-dependent ion channels to open, resulting in postsynaptic potentials. Ionotropic receptors contain ion channels, which are directly opened when a ligand attaches to the binding site. Metabotropic receptors are linked to G proteins, which, when activated, open ion channels—usually by producing a member of a category of chemicals called second messengers.

The nature of the postsynaptic potential depends on the type of ion channel that is opened by the postsynaptic receptors at a particular synapse. Excitatory postsynaptic potentials occur when Na^+ enters the cell. Inhibitory postsynaptic potentials are produced by the opening of K^+ channels or Cl^- channels. The entry of Ca^{2+} produces EPSPs, but more importantly, it activates special enzymes that cause physiological changes in the postsynaptic cell.

Postsynaptic potentials normally are brief. They are terminated by two means. Acetylcholine is deactivated by the enzyme acetylcholinesterase. In all other cases (as far as we know) molecules of the transmitter substance are removed from the synaptic cleft by means of carriers located in the presynaptic membrane, which transport the molecules back into the cytoplasm. This retrieval process is called reuptake.

The presynaptic membrane, as well as the postsynaptic membrane, contains receptors that detect the presence of a transmitter substance. Presynaptic receptors, also called autoreceptors, monitor the quantity of transmitter substance that a neuron releases and, apparently, regulate the amount that is synthesized or released.

Axosomatic and axodendritic synapses are not the only kinds found in the nervous system. Axoaxonic synapses produce presynaptic inhibition by depolarizing the membrane of a terminal button enough so that an action potential, if it occurs, produces a smaller change in the polarization of the membrane. The result of this effect is to cause the terminal button to release a smaller quantity of its transmitter substance. Dendrodendritic synapses also exist, but their role in neural communication is not yet understood.

Nonsynaptic chemical transmission is similar to synaptic transmission. Peptide neuromodulators and hormones activate metabotropic peptide receptors located in the membrane; their effects are mediated through the production of second messengers. Steroid hormones enter the nucleus, where they bind with receptors capable of altering the synthesis of proteins that regulate the cell's physiological processes. These hormones also bind with receptors located outside the nucleus, but less is known about their functions.

TRANSMITTER SUBSTANCES

BECAUSE TRANSMITTER SUBSTANCES HAVE TWO general effects on the postsynaptic membrane—depolarization (EPSP) or hyperpolarization (IPSP)—one might expect that there would be two kinds of transmitter substances, excitatory and inhibitory. Instead, there are many different kinds. Although some do appear to be exclusively excitatory or inhibitory, others can produce either excitation or inhibition, depending on the nature of the ion channels that are controlled by the postsynaptic receptors. The most-studied classes of transmitter substances include *acetylcholine, monoamines, amino acids,* and *peptides.* This section will describe the production of transmitter substances, briefly summarize their role in behavior, and discuss their interactions with drugs.

Acetylcholine

The transmitter substance that is released at synapses on skeletal muscles is acetylcholine (ACh). (These synapses are said to be *acetylcholinergic. Ergon* is the Greek word for "work.") ACh is also found in the ganglia of the autonomic nervous system and at the target organs of the parasympathetic branch of the autonomic nervous system (discussed in more detail in Chapter 4). Because ACh is found outside the central nervous system in locations that are easy to study, this transmitter substance has received much attention from neuroscientists. The fact that ACh has an excitatory effect on the membrane of skeletal muscle fibers and an inhibitory effect on the membrane of muscle fibers in the heart illustrates an important principle: *The effect that a transmitter substance has on the postsynaptic membrane is not determined by the chemical itself but by the nature of the postsynaptic receptors it stimulates.*

ACh receptors on skeletal muscle fibers control sodium ion channels and produce depolarizations (excitations); ACh receptors on cardiac muscle fibers control potassium ion channels and produce hyperpolarizations (inhibition).

ACh is also found in the brain. Apparently, ACh is involved in learning and remembering and in controlling the stage of sleep in which dreams occur—topics discussed in later chapters. ACh is composed of two components: *choline*, a substance derived from the breakdown of lipids, and *acetate*, the cation found in vinegar, also called acetic acid. Acetate cannot be attached directly to the choline; instead, it is transferred from a molecule of *Acetyl CoA*. **CoA** (coenzyme A) is a complex molecule, consisting in part of the vitamin pantothenic acid (one of the B vitamins). CoA is produced by the mitochondria, and it takes part in many reactions in the body. **Acetyl CoA** is simply CoA with an acetate ion attached to it. ACh is produced by the following reaction: In the presence of the enzyme **choline acetyltransferase**, the acetate ion is transferred from the CoA molecule to the choline molecule, yielding a molecule of ACh and one of ordinary CoA. (See *Figure 3.14.*)

A simple analogy illustrates the role of coenzymes in chemical reactions. Think of acetate as a hot dog and choline as a bun. The task of the person (enzyme) who operates the hot dog vending stand is to put a hot dog into the bun (make acetyl-

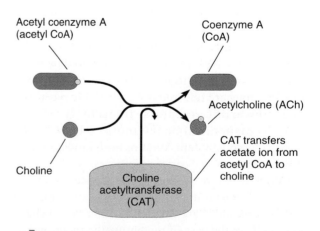

FIGURE 3.14

The biosynthesis of acetylcholine.

choline). To do so, the vendor needs a fork (coenzyme) to remove the hot dog from the boiling water. The vendor inserts the fork into the hot dog (attaches acetate to CoA) and transfers the hot dog from fork to bun.

You will recall that after being released by the terminal button, ACh is deactivated by the enzyme acetylcholinesterase (AChE), which is present in the postsynaptic membrane. The deactivation produces choline and acetate from ACh. Because the amount of choline that is picked up by the soma from the general circulation and then sent to the terminal buttons by means of axoplasmic flow is not sufficient to keep up with the loss of choline by an active synapse, choline must be recycled. After ACh is destroyed by the AChE in the postsynaptic membrane, the choline is returned to the terminal buttons by means of reuptake. There, it is converted back into ACh. This process has an efficiency of 50 percent; that is, half of the choline is retrieved and recycled. (See *Figure 3.15*.)

Sometimes, too much ACh is produced—more than can be stored in the synaptic vesicles. For this reason, AChE is also present in the cytoplasm of the terminal buttons. This AChE cannot destroy the ACh that is stored in the vesicles, but it can—and does—destroy any transmitter substance produced by the cell that exceeds the storage capacity of the synaptic vesicles.

There are two different types of ACh receptors—one ionotropic and one metabotropic. These receptors were identified when investigators discovered that different drugs activated or inhibited them. The ionotropic ACh receptor is stimulated by nicotine (a poison found in tobacco leaves), and the metabotropic ACh receptor is stimulated by muscarine (a poison found in mushrooms). Consequently, they are referred to as **nicotinic receptors** and **muscarinic receptors,** respectively. Muscle fibers contain nicotinic receptors exclusively; the central nervous system contains both kinds, but primarily contains muscarinic receptors.

Why are there several types of receptors for a particular transmitter substance? One answer is that different receptors are coupled to different ion channels, and (in the case of metabotropic receptors) to different G proteins that have different physiological effects. Ionotropic receptors produce very rapid—

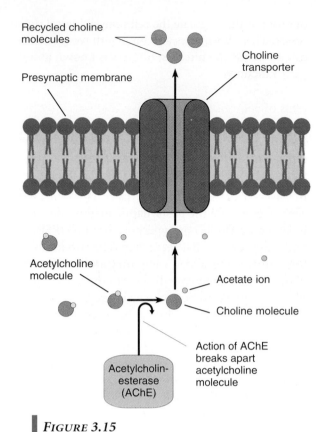

FIGURE 3.15

The destruction of acetylcholine by acetylcholinesterase and the reuptake of choline.

and usually very short-lived—postsynaptic potentials. Metabotropic receptors usually produce slower—and longer-lived—postsynaptic potentials and may also induce changes in the physiological processes in the interior of the cell. Finally, some receptors contain binding sites that are sensitive to the presence of neuromodulators. Thus, a single neurotransmitter can have a variety of effects in different locations in the nervous system.

The Monoamines

Epinephrine, norepinephrine, dopamine, and serotonin are four chemicals that belong to a family of compounds called **monoamines.** Because the molecular structures of these substances are similar, some drugs affect the activity of all of them, to some degree. The first three—epinephrine, norepinephrine, and dopamine—belong to a subclass of monoamines called **catecholamines.** It is worthwhile learning the terms in Table 3.1, because they will be used many times in the rest of this book. (See *Table 3.1.*)

The monoamines are produced by several systems of neurons in the brain. Most of these systems consist of a relatively small number of cell bodies located in the back of the brain, whose axons branch repeatedly and give rise to an enormous number of terminal buttons distributed throughout many regions of the brain. Monoaminergic neurons do not appear to transmit specific information (such as the presence of particular stimuli), but they serve to modulate the function of widespread regions of the brain. Thus, they act as volume controls, increasing or decreasing the activities of particular brain functions.

Dopamine

The first catecholamine, **dopamine** (DA), produces both excitatory and inhibitory postsynaptic potentials, depending on the postsynaptic receptor. Dopamine is one of the more interesting neurotransmitters because it has been implicated in several important functions, including movement, attention, and learning; thus, it is discussed in Chapters 8 and 14.

The synthesis of the catecholamines is somewhat more complicated than that of ACh, but each step is a simple one. The precursor molecule is modified slightly, step by step, until it achieves its final shape. Each step is controlled by a different enzyme, which causes a small part to be added or taken off. The precursor for both of the catecholamine transmitter

substances (dopamine and norepinephrine) is *tyrosine*, an essential amino acid that we must obtain from our diet. Tyrosine receives a hydroxyl group (OH—an oxygen atom and a hydrogen atom) and becomes L-**DOPA** (L-3,4-dihydroxyphenylalanine). The enzyme that adds the hydroxyl group is called *tyrosine hydroxylase.* L-DOPA then loses a carboxyl group (COOH—one carbon atom, two oxygen atoms, and one hydrogen atom) through the activity of the enzyme *DOPA decarboxylase* and becomes dopamine. Finally, the enzyme *dopamine ß-hydroxylase* attaches a hydroxyl group to dopamine, which becomes norepinephrine. These reactions are shown in *Figure 3.16.*

Just as the AChE in the terminal buttons of acetylcholinergic neurons destroys the ACh in excess of the amount that can be stored in the synaptic vesicles, the production of the catecholamines is regulated by an enzyme called **monoamine oxidase** (MAO). This enzyme is also found in the blood, where it deactivates amines that are present in foods such as chocolate and cheese; without such deactivation these amines could cause dangerous increases in blood pressure.

Degeneration of dopaminergic neurons that connect two parts of the brain's motor system causes **Parkinson's disease,** a movement disorder characterized by tremors, rigidity of the limbs, poor balance, and difficulty in initiating movements. The cell bodies of these neurons are located in a region of the brain called the *substantia nigra* ("black substance"). This region is normally stained black with melanin, the substance that gives color to skin. This compound is produced by the breakdown of dopamine. (The brain damage that causes Parkinson's disease was discovered by pathologists who observed that the substantia nigra of a deceased person who had had this disorder was pale rather than black.) People with Parkinson's disease are given L-DOPA, a drug that stimulates the production of dopamine, thus causing more dopamine to be released by the surviving dopaminergic neurons. As a consequence, the patients' symptoms are alleviated.

Dopamine has been implicated as a transmitter substance that might be involved in schizophrenia, a serious mental disorder that includes hallucinations, delusions, and disruption of normal, logical thought processes. Drugs that block the activity of dopamin-

---

TABLE 3.1

Classification of the Monoamine Transmitter Substances

Monoamines

Catecholamines	Indolamines
Dopamine	Serotonin
Norepinephrine	
Epinephrine	

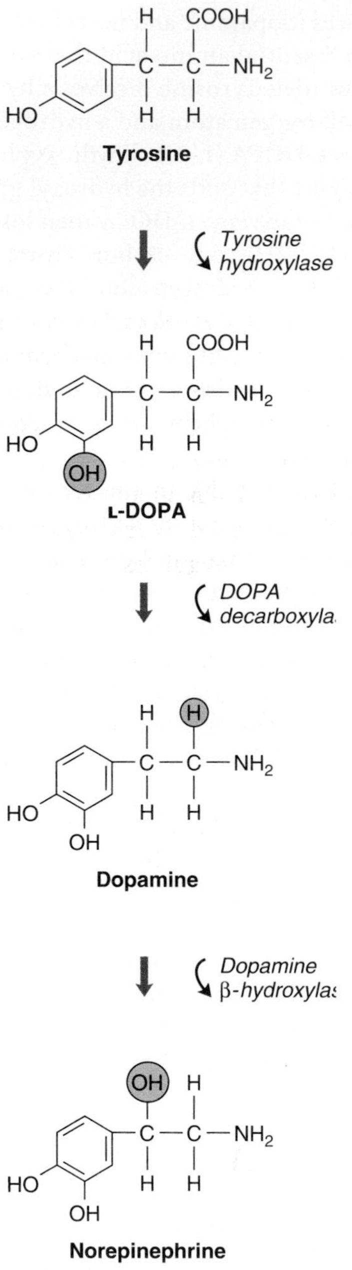

H   COOH

C — C — NH$_2$

H   H

HO

Tyrosine

↓ 〔 *Tyrosine hydroxylase*

H   COOH

C — C — NH$_2$

H   H

HO

(OH)

L-DOPA

↓ 〔 *DOPA decarboxyla*

H   (H)

C — C — NH$_2$

H   H

HO

OH

Dopamine

↓ 〔 *Dopamine β-hydroxylas*

(OH)   H

C — C — NH$_2$

H   H

HO

OH

Norepinephrine

FIGURE 3.16

Biosynthesis of the catecholamines.

ergic neurons alleviate these symptoms; hence investigators have speculated that schizophrenia is produced by overactivity of these neurons. In fact, symptoms of schizophrenia are an occasional side effect of L-DOPA in patients with Parkinson's disease. Fortunately, these symptoms can usually be

eliminated by reducing the drug dosage. The physiology of schizophrenia is discussed in Chapter 17.

At least five types of dopamine receptors have been identified, all metabotropic. Of these, two are most important: *D1 dopamine receptors* and *D2 dopamine receptors.* It appears that D1 receptors are exclusively postsynaptic, whereas D2 receptors are found both presynaptically and postsynaptically in the brain. Stimulation of D1 receptors increases the production of the second messenger cyclic AMP, whereas stimulation of D2 receptors decreases it.

Most neurons that release catecholamines do not do so through terminal buttons on the ends of axonal branches. Instead, they usually release them through **axonal varicosities,** beadlike swellings of the axonal branches. These varicosities give the axonal branches of catecholaminergic neurons the appearance of beaded chains. Figure 3.17 shows a portion of a dendrite equipped with *spines*, which form synapses with nondopaminergic terminals. The varicosities of a branch of a dopaminergic axon form synapses with the base of the spines or the dendritic shaft. (See *Figure 3.17.*)

Norepinephrine

Because **norepinephrine** (NE), like ACh, is found in neurons in the autonomic nervous system, this neurotransmitter has received much experimental attention. I should note that *Adrenalin* and *epinephrine* are synonymous, as are *noradrenalin* and *norepinephrine.* **Epinephrine** is a hormone produced by the adrenal medulla, the central core of the

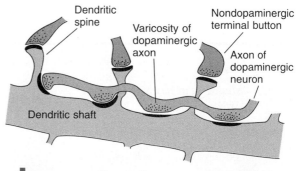

FIGURE 3.17

Axonal varicosities. Dopaminergic and noradrenergic axons release their neurotransmitters through varicosities rather than terminal buttons.

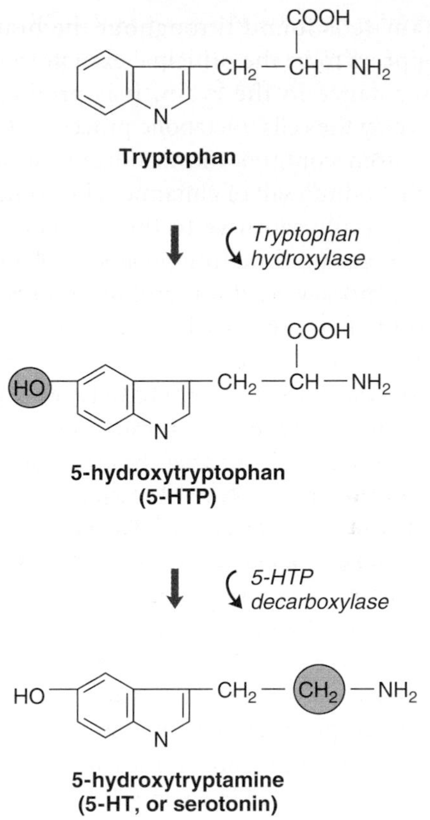

COOH
|
CH$_2$—CH—NH$_2$

Tryptophan

↓ Tryptophan
hydroxylase

COOH
|
(HO) CH$_2$—CH—NH$_2$

**5-hydroxytryptophan
(5-HTP)**

↓ 5-HTP
decarboxylase

HO CH$_2$—(CH$_2$)—NH$_2$

**5-hydroxytryptamine
(5-HT, or serotonin)**

FIGURE 3.18

Biosynthesis of serotonin (5-hydroxytryptamine, or 5-HT).

adrenal glands, which are small endocrine glands located above the kidneys. Epinephrine also serves as a transmitter substance in the brain, but it is of minor importance, compared with norepinephrine. *Ad renal* is Latin for "toward kidney." In Greek, one would say *epi nephron* ("upon the kidney"), hence the term *epinephrine.* The latter term has been adopted by pharmacologists, probably because the word *Adrenalin* was appropriated by a drug company as a proprietary name; therefore, to be consistent with general usage, I will refer to the transmitter substance as *norepinephrine.* The accepted adjectival form is *noradrenergic;* I suppose that *norepinephrinergic* never caught on because it is too difficult to pronounce.

Noradrenergic neurons in the brain are primarily involved in control of alertness and wakefulness; a small group of neurons located in the back part of the brain sends axons to widespread regions of the rest of the brain. Noradrenergic synapses in the cen-

tral nervous system produce inhibitory postsynaptic potentials. By contrast, at the target organs of the sympathetic nervous system (discussed in Chapter 4), norepinephrine usually has an excitatory effect.

We have already seen the biosynthetic pathway for norepinephrine in Figure 3.16; this transmitter is produced from dopamine. Most transmitter substances are synthesized in the cytoplasm of the terminal button and then stored in newly formed synaptic vesicles. However, for norepinephrine the final step of synthesis occurs inside the vesicles themselves. The vesicles are first filled with dopamine. Then, the dopamine is converted to norepinephrine through the action of dopamine ß-hydroxylase. Excess norepinephrine in the terminal buttons is destroyed by monoamine oxidase, the same enzyme that regulates dopamine.

There are several types of noradrenergic receptors, identified by their differing sensitivities to various drugs. Actually, these receptors are usually called *adrenergic* receptors, rather than *noradrenergic* receptors, because they are sensitive to epinephrine (Adrenalin) as well as norepinephrine. Neurons in the central nervous system contain ß$_1$- and ß$_2$-*adrenergic receptors* and α$_1$- and α$_2$-*adrenergic receptors.* All four kinds of receptors are also found in various organs of the body besides the brain and are responsible for the effects of the catecholamines when they act as hormones. All of these receptors are coupled to G proteins that generate the second messenger cyclic AMP.

Serotonin

The third monoamine transmitter substance, **serotonin** (also called **5-HT,** or 5-hydroxytryptamine), has also received much experimental attention. At most synapses, serotonin produces inhibitory postsynaptic potentials. In addition, its behavioral effects are also generally inhibitory. Serotonin plays a role in the regulation of mood; in the control of eating; in the control of sleep and arousal; and in the regulation of pain. Serotonergic neurons are involved somehow in the control of dreaming. In fact, the drug LSD appears to produce hallucinations by interfering with the activity of serotonergic synapses; the drug appears to produce dreaming while the person is awake.

The precursor for serotonin is the amino acid *tryptophan*. The enzyme *tryptophan hydroxylase* adds a hydroxyl group, producing *5-HTP* (5-hydroxytryptophan). The enzyme *5-HTP decarboxylase* removes a carboxyl group from 5-HTP, and the result is 5-HT (serotonin). (See *Figure 3.18.*)

Investigators have identified at least seven different types of serotonin receptors: 5-HT$_{1A-1D}$ and 5-HT$_{2-4}$. Of these, the 5-HT$_2$ receptors appear to be found exclusively in postsynaptic membranes, whereas the others are found both presynaptically and postsynaptically. Except for the 5-HT$_3$ receptor, all 5-HT receptors are metabotropic.

Amino Acid Transmitter Substances

So far, all of the transmitter substances I have described are synthesized within neurons: acetylcholine from choline, the catecholamines from the amino acid tyrosine, and serotonin from the amino acid tryptophan. Some neurons secrete simple amino acids as transmitter substances. Because amino acids are used for protein synthesis by all cells of the brain, it is difficult to prove that a particular amino acid is a transmitter substance. However, investigators suspect that at least eight amino acids may serve as transmitter substances in the mammalian central nervous system (CNS). Three of them are especially important because they appear to be the most common transmitter substances in the CNS: glutamic acid, gamma-aminobutyric acid (GABA), and glycine.

Glutamic Acid

Because **glutamic acid** (often called *glutamate)* and gamma-aminobutyric acid (GABA) are found in very simple organisms, many investigators believe that these neurotransmitters are the first to have evolved. Besides producing postsynaptic potentials by activating postsynaptic receptors, they also have direct excitatory effects (glutamic acid) and inhibitory effects (GABA) on axons; they raise or lower the threshold of excitation, thus affecting the rate at which action potentials occur. These direct effects suggest that these substances had a general modulating role even before the evolutionary development of specific receptor molecules.

Glutamate is found throughout the brain. In fact, it appears to be the principal excitatory transmitter substance in the brain. It is produced in abundance by the cells' metabolic processes. Oriental food often contains monosodium glutamate (MSG), the sodium salt of glutamic acid. Some people are especially sensitive to the effects of MSG and experience mild neurological symptoms, including temporary dizziness and numbness, after eating food that contains large amounts of the chemical.

Investigators have discovered five types of glutamate receptors. Three of these receptors are ionotropic, and are named after the artificial ligands that stimulate them: the *NMDA receptor,* the *AMPA receptor,* and the *kainate receptor.* The other two glutamate receptors—*metabotropic 1* and *metabotropic 2*—are (obviously!) metabotropic. Because the NMDA receptor has some special characteristics (it contains an ion channel that is both voltage- and neurotransmitter-dependent) and appears to be responsible for producing some of the synaptic changes that are responsible for learning; it will be discussed in more detail in Chapter 14.

GABA

GABA (gamma-aminobutyric acid) is produced from glutamic acid by the action of an enzyme (GAD, or glutamic acid decarboxylase) that removes a carboxyl group. GABA is an inhibitory transmitter substance, and it appears to have a widespread distribution throughout the brain and spinal cord. Two GABA receptors have been identified: GABA$_A$ and GABA$_B$. The GABA$_A$ receptor is ionotropic and controls a chloride channel; the GABA$_B$ receptor is metabotropic and controls a potassium channel.

As you know, neurons in the brain are greatly interconnected. Without the activity of inhibitory synapses these interconnections would make the brain unstable. That is, through excitatory synapses, neurons would excite their neighbors, which would then excite *their* neighbors, which would then excite the originally active neurons, and so on, until most of the neurons in the brain would be firing uncontrollably. In fact, this event does sometimes occur, and we refer to it as a *seizure. (Epilepsy* is a neurological disorder characterized by the presence of seizures.) Normally, an inhibitory influence is supplied by GABA-secreting neurons, which are present in large numbers in the brain. Some investigators believe that one of the causes of epilepsy is an abnormality in the biochemistry of GABA-secreting neurons.

GABA$_A$ receptors are complex; they contain binding sites for at least three different transmitter substances and neuromodulators. The primary binding site is, of course, for GABA. A second site binds with a class of tranquilizing drugs called the **benzodiazepines.** These drugs include diazepam (Valium) and chlordiazepoxide (Librium), which are used to reduce anxiety, promote sleep, reduce seizure activity, and produce muscle relaxation. The third site binds to barbiturates and alcohol. When either of these two secondary binding sites is activated, the effects of GABA on the chloride channel are enhanced. Thus, because GABA is an inhibitory neurotransmitter, the net effect of the benzodiazepines, the barbiturates, and alcohol is to increase neural inhibition.

Although the brain does not produce Valium or barbiturates, it is unlikely that the existence of the benzodiazepine and barbiturate/alcohol binding sites is coincidental. Perhaps some neurons in the brain produce neuromodulators that cause a stress reaction (or reduce it) by activating or blocking these receptors. In fact, two possible candidate ligands for the benzodiazepine binding site have been found in the brain; one compound blocks the receptor and the other appears to stimulate it. More research is needed to find out whether one or both of these chemicals actually serve as neuromodulators in the brain.

Glycine

The amino acid **glycine** appears to be the inhibitory neurotransmitter in the spinal cord and lower portions of the brain. Little is known about its biosynthetic pathway; there are several possible routes, but not enough is known to decide how neurons produce glycine. The bacteria that cause tetanus (lockjaw) release a chemical that blocks the activity of glycine synapses; the removal of the inhibitory effect of these synapses causes muscles to contract continuously.

Peptides

Recent studies have discovered that the neurons of the central nervous system release a large variety of peptides. As we saw earlier in this chapter, peptides consist of two or more amino acids, linked together by peptide bonds. Like proteins, peptides are synthesized by the ribosomes according to instructions contained on the chromosomes in the nucleus.

Several different peptides are released by neurons. Although most peptides appear to serve as neuromodulators, some act as neurotransmitters. One of the most important family of peptides is the **endogenous opioids.** (*Endogenous* means "produced from within"; *opioid* means "like opium.") Several years ago it became clear that opiates (drugs such as opium, morphine, and heroin) reduce pain because they have direct effects on the brain. Pert, Snowman, and Snyder (1974) discovered that neurons in a localized region of the brain contain specialized receptors that respond to opiates. Then, soon after the discovery of the opioid receptor, other neuroscientists discovered the natural ligands for these receptors (Terenius and Wahlström, 1975; Hughes et al., 1975), which they called **enkephalins** (from the Greek word *enkephalos,* "in the head"). We now know that the enkephalins are only two members of a family of endogenous opiate peptides, all of which are synthesized from one of three large peptides that serve as precursors. In addition, we know that there are at least three different types of opioid receptors: μ (mu), ∂ (delta), and k (kappa).

Several different neural systems are activated when opiate receptors are stimulated. One type produces analgesia, another inhibits species-typical defensive responses such as fleeing and hiding, and another stimulates a system of neurons involved in reinforcement ("reward"). The last effect explains why opiates are often abused. The situations that cause neurons to secrete endogenous opioids are discussed in Chapter 7, and the brain mechanisms of opiate addiction are discussed in Chapter 18.

Because the synthesis of peptides takes place in the soma, vesicles containing these chemicals must be delivered to the terminal buttons by axoplasmic flow. Peptides are released from all parts of the terminal button, not just from the active zone; thus, only a portion of the molecules are released into the synaptic cleft. The rest presumably act on receptors belonging to other cells in the vicinity. Once they are released, peptides are deactivated by enzymes, and are not returned to the terminal buttons and recycled. All of the peptides that have been studied so far are produced from a small number of precursor molecules. These precursors are large peptides that are broken into pieces by special enzymes; a particular neuron manufactures the enzymes that it needs to break the precursor apart in the right places. The pieces of the precursor that a particular neuron uses are stored in synaptic vesicles, and the other ones are destroyed.

As we saw earlier, many terminal buttons contain two different types of synaptic vesicles, each filled with a different substance. These terminal buttons release peptides in conjunction with a "classical" neurotransmitter (one of those I just described). The primary reason for the co-release of peptides is their ability to regulate the sensitivity of presynaptic or postsynaptic receptors to the neurotransmitter. For example, the terminal buttons of the salivary nerve of the cat (which control the secretion of saliva) release both acetylcholine and a peptide called VIP. When the axons fire at a low rate, only ACh is released and only a little saliva is secreted. At a higher rate, both ACh and VIP are secreted and the VIP dramatically increases the sensitivity of the muscarinic receptors in the salivary gland to ACh; thus, much saliva is released. Table 3.2 lists some peptides that are known to be released along with the "classical" transmitter substances. (See *Table 3.2*.)

Several peptide hormones are also found in the brain, where they serve as neurotransmitters or neuromodulators. In some cases, the peripheral and the central peptide perform related functions (Panksepp, 1991). For example, outside the nervous system the hormone angiotensin acts directly on the kidneys and blood vessels to produce effects that help the body cope with the loss of fluid, and inside the nervous system circuits of neurons that use angiotensin as a neurotransmitter perform similar functions.

TABLE 3.2

Peptides Known to Be Released with Transmitter Substances

Transmitter Substance	Peptide
Acetylcholine	Vasoactive intestinal peptide (VIP)
Dopamine	Cholecystokinin (CCK) Neurotensin
Epinephrine	Neuropeptide Y Neurotensin
GABA	Somatostatin
Norepinephrine	Enkephalin Somatostatin Neuorpeptide Y Neurotensin
Oxytocin	Enkephalin
Serotonin	Enkephalin Substance P Thyroid hormone releasing hormone (TRH)
Vasopressin	Cholecystokinin (CCK) Dynorphin

Note: Several peptides (such as cholecystokinin) were first discovered in other organs; thus, their names do not reflect their function in the brain.

Source: Adapted from Cooper, J.R., Bloom, F.E., and Roth, R.H., *The Biochemical Basis of Neuropharmacology,* 5th ed. New York: Oxford University Press, 1986.

Lipids

Various substances derived from lipids can serve to transmit messages within or between cells. One of them appears to be the natural ligand for the THC receptor, which is responsible for the physiological effects of the active ingredient in marijuana.

Matsuda et al. (1990) discovered that THC (tetrahydrocannibal, the active ingredient of marijuana) stimulates specific receptors, which are present in specific regions of the brain. (See *Figure 3.19*.) THC produces analgesia and sedation, stimulates appetite, reduces nausea caused by drugs used

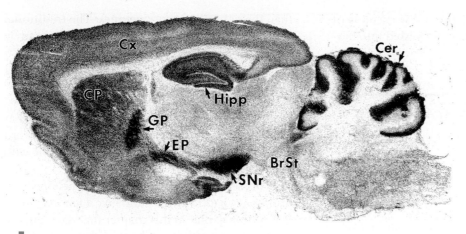

An autoradiogram of a rat brain that has been incubated in a solution containing a radioactive ligand for THC receptors. The receptors are indicated by dark areas. (Autoradiography is described in Chapter 5.) (Br St = brain stem, Cer = cerebellum, CP = caudate nucleus/putamen, Cx = cortex, EP = entopeduncular nucleus, GP = globus pallidus, Hipp = hippocampus, SNr = substantia nigra.)
(Courtesy of Miles Herkenham, National Institute of Mental Health, Bethesda, Md.)

to treat cancer, relieves asthma attacks, decreases pressure within the eyes in patients with glaucoma, and reduces the symptoms of certain motor disorders. On the other hand, THC interferes with concentration and memory, alters visual and auditory perception, and distorts perceptions of the passage of time. Devane et al. (1992) discovered the natural ligand for the THC receptor: a lipidlike substance that they named *anandamide,* from the Sanskrit word *ananda,* or "bliss." Researchers have not yet found how it is released or what physiological functions it performs. Perhaps, now that the receptor and endogenous ligand have been discovered, it will be possible to develop drugs that have the therapeutic effects of THC but not its adverse effects on cognition.

Soluble Gases

Recently, investigators have discovered that neurons use at least two simple, soluble gases—nitric oxide and carbon monoxide—to communicate with one another. One of these, nitric oxide (NO), has re-

ceived the most attention. Nitric oxide (not to be confused with nitrous oxide, or laughing gas) is a soluble gas that is produced by the activity of an enzyme found in certain neurons. Researchers have found that NO is used as a messenger in many parts of the body; for example, it is involved in the control of the muscles in the wall of the intestines, it dilates blood vessels in regions of the brain that become metabolically active, and it stimulates the changes in blood vessels that produce penile erections (Culotta and Koshland, 1992). As we will see in Chapter 14, it may also play a role in the establishment of neural changes that are produced by learning.

All of the neurotransmitters discussed so far (with the possible exception of anandamide) are stored in synaptic vesicles and released by terminal buttons. Nitric oxide is produced in several regions of a nerve cell—including dendrites—and is released as soon as it is produced. More accurately, it diffuses out of the cell as soon as it is produced. It does not activate membrane-bound receptors, but enters neighboring cells, where it activates an enzyme responsible for the production of a second messenger, cyclic GMP. Within a few seconds of being produced, nitric oxide is converted into biologically inactive compounds.

|||||| INTERIM SUMMARY

The nervous system contains a variety of transmitter substances, each of which interacts with a specialized receptor. Those that have received the most study are acetylcholine and the monoamines: dopamine, norepinephrine, and 5-hydroxytryptamine (serotonin). The synthesis of these transmitter substances is controlled by a series of enzymes. Several amino acids also serve as transmitter substances, the most important of which are glutamic acid (glutamate), GABA, and glycine. Glutamate serves as an excitatory transmitter substance; the others serve as inhibitory transmitter substances. Peptide transmitter substances consist of chains of amino acids. Like proteins, peptides are synthesized at the ribosomes according to sequences coded for by the chromosomes. The best known class of peptides in the nervous system includes the endogenous opioids, whose effects are mimicked by drugs such as opium and heroin. One lipid appears to serve as a chemical messenger: anandamide, the endogenous ligand for the THC (marijuana) receptor. In addition, two soluble gases—nitric oxide and carbon monoxide—can diffuse out of the cell in which they are produced and trigger the production of a second messenger in adjacent cells.

PHARMACOLOGY OF SYNAPSES

THROUGHOUT THE HISTORY OF OUR SPECIES, people have discovered that plants (and a few animals) produce chemicals that act on synapses. Some of these chemicals have been used for their pleasurable effects; others have been used to treat illness, reduce pain, or poison other animals (or enemies). More recently, scientists have learned to produce completely artificial drugs with potencies far greater than the naturally occurring ones. The traditional uses of drugs remain, but in addition, they can be used in research laboratories to investigate the operations of the nervous system. Drugs that affect synaptic transmission are classified into two general categories. Those that block or inhibit the postsynaptic effects are called **antagonists.** Those that facilitate them are called **agonists.** (The Greek word *agon* means "contest." Thus, an *agonist* is one who takes part in the contest.)

This section will describe the basic effects of drugs on synaptic activity and give a few examples. Recall from earlier in this chapter that the sequence of synaptic activity goes like this: Transmitter substances are synthesized and stored in synaptic vesicles. When axons fire, the transmitter substances are released into the synaptic cleft, where they activate postsynaptic receptors (and perhaps presynaptic receptors, too). So that their effects are brief, they are destroyed by an enzyme or taken back by carrier molecules into the terminal button to be recycled. The discussion of the effects of drugs in this section follows the same basic sequence. All of the effects I will describe are summarized in Figure 3.20.

▌ Effects on Production of Transmitter Substances

The first step is the synthesis of the transmitter substance from its precursors. In some cases the rate of synthesis and release of a neurotransmitter is increased when a precursor is administered; in these cases the precursor itself serves as an agonist. As we saw, L-DOPA serves as a dopamine agonist. (See step 1 in *Figure 3.20.*)

The steps in the synthesis of transmitter substances are controlled by enzymes. Therefore, if a drug inactivates one of these enzymes, it will prevent the transmitter substance from being produced. For example, the drug **PCPA** (parachlorophenylalanine) blocks the enzyme tryptophan hydroxylase, which prevents synthesis of serotonin. Thus, PCPA is a serotonin antagonist. (See step 2 in *Figure 3.20.*) PCPA is sometimes used to block the activity of a tumor composed of cells that secrete serotonin.

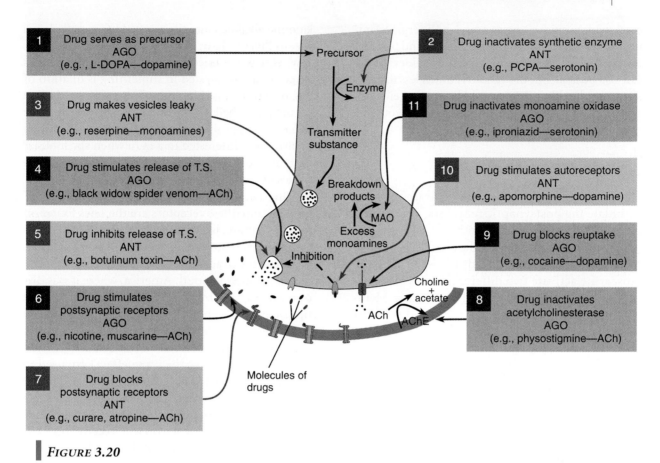

1 Drug serves as precursor
AGO
(e.g., L-DOPA—dopamine)

2 Drug inactivates synthetic enzyme
ANT
(e.g., PCPA—serotonin)

3 Drug makes vesicles leaky
ANT
(e.g., reserpine—monoamines)

11 Drug inactivates monoamine oxidase
AGO
(e.g., iproniazid—serotonin)

4 Drug stimulates release of T.S.
AGO
(e.g., black widow spider venom—ACh)

10 Drug stimulates autoreceptors
ANT
(e.g., apomorphine—dopamine)

5 Drug inhibits release of T.S.
ANT
(e.g., botulinum toxin—ACh)

9 Drug blocks reuptake
AGO
(e.g., cocaine—dopamine)

6 Drug stimulates
postsynaptic receptors
AGO
(e.g., nicotine, muscarine—ACh)

8 Drug inactivates
acetylcholinesterase
AGO
(e.g., physostigmine—ACh)

7 Drug blocks
postsynaptic receptors
ANT
(e.g., curare, atropine—ACh)

Precursor · Enzyme · Transmitter substance · Breakdown products · MAO · Excess monoamines · Inhibition · Choline + acetate · ACh · AChE · Molecules of drugs

FIGURE 3.20

A summary of the ways that drugs can affect the synaptic transmission (AGO = agonist; ANT = antagonist). Agonist drugs are marked in blue; antagonist drugs are marked in red.

Effects on Storage and Release of Transmitter Substances

Transmitter substances are stored in synaptic vesicles, which are transported to the presynaptic membrane, where the chemicals are released. One drug, **reserpine,** prevents the storage of the monoamines in synaptic vesicles by making their membranes become leaky. The transmitter substances leak out of the synaptic vesicles and thus remain in the cytoplasm of the terminal button, where they are destroyed by MAO; hence, nothing is released when the vesicles eventually rupture against the presynaptic membrane. Reserpine, then, is a monoamine antagonist. (See step 3 in *Figure 3.20.*) The drug, which comes from the root of a shrub, was discovered over three thousand years ago in India, where it was found to be useful in treating snakebite and seemed to have a calming effect. Pieces of the root are still sold in markets in rural areas of India. In Western medicine, reserpine is sometimes used to treat high blood pressure.

Some drugs act as antagonists by preventing the release of transmitter substances from the terminal button; for example, **botulinum toxin,** produced by bacteria that can grow in improperly canned food, prevents the release of ACh. This drug is an extremely potent poison; someone once calculated that a teaspoonful of pure botulinum toxin could kill the world's entire human population. Other drugs act as agonists by stimulating the release of a neurotransmitter. For example, the venom of the black widow spider causes acetylcholinergic terminal buttons to release ACh. (See steps 4 and 5 in *Figure 3.20.*) The effects of black widow spider venom can also be fatal, but the venom is much less toxic. In fact, most healthy adults would have to receive several bites, but infants or frail old people would be more susceptible.

Effects on Receptors

Once the transmitter substance is released, it must stimulate the postsynaptic receptors. Some drugs serve as agonists by binding with and activating the receptors directly, mimicking the effects of the transmitter substance. As you already know, nicotine and muscarine activate two different classes of acetylcholine receptor: nicotinic and muscarinic. Members of another category of drugs bind with the postsynaptic receptors but do *not* activate them. Because these drugs occupy the receptors without activating them, they prevent the transmitter substance from exerting its effect and hence act as antagonists. These drugs are called **receptor blockers.** By analogy, a key that fits into a lock but does not turn it prevents it from opening, because the proper key cannot enter the lock as long as it is occupied. (See steps 6 and 7 in *Figure 3.20.*)

As you certainly know, nicotine is found in tobacco, which comes from a plant with the Latin name *Nicotiniana tabacum.* Nicotine is a very potent poison; the amount found in a single cigarette could constitute a fatal dose if it were extracted and injected into a person. (Most nicotine in a cigarette is destroyed by the heat of combustion.) Muscarine, found in the poison mushroom *Amanita muscaria,* is also fatal in low doses.

Just as two different drugs stimulate the two classes of acetylcholine receptors, two different drugs *block* them. Both were discovered in nature long ago, and both are used by modern medicine. The first, **atropine,** blocks muscarinic receptors. The drug is named after *Atropos,* the Greek fate who cut the thread of life (which a sufficient dose of atropine will certainly do). Atropine is one of several *belladonna alkaloids* extracted from a plant called the "deadly nightshade," and therein lies a tale. Many years ago, women who wanted to increase their attractiveness to men put drops containing bel-

ladonna alkaloids into their eyes. In fact, *belladonna* means "pretty lady." Why was the drug used this way? One of the unconscious responses that occurs when we are interested in something is dilation of our pupils. By blocking the effects of acetylcholine on the pupil, belladonna alkaloids such as atropine make the pupils dilate. This change makes a woman appear more interested in a man when she looks at him, and, of course, this apparent sign of interest makes him regard her as more attractive.

Another drug, **curare,** blocks nicotinic receptors. Because these receptors are the ones found on muscles, curare, like botulinum toxin, causes paralysis. However, the effects of curare are much faster. The drug is extracted from several different species of plants found in South America, where it was discovered long ago by people who used it to coat the tips of arrows and darts. Within minutes of being struck by one of these points, an animal collapses, ceases breathing, and dies. Nowadays, curare (and other drugs that have the same effect) are used to paralyze people who are to undergo surgery so that their muscles will relax completely and not contract when they are cut with a scalpel. An anesthetic must also be used, because a person who receives only curare will remain perfectly conscious and sensitive to pain, even though paralyzed. And, of course, a respirator must be used to supply air to the lungs.

As we saw earlier in this chapter, the presynaptic membranes of some neurons possess autoreceptors, which apparently regulate the amount of transmitter substance that is released. Because stimulation of these receptors causes less transmitter substance to be released, drugs that selectively activate them, but do not activate the postsynaptic receptors, act as antagonists. For example, low doses of **apomorphine** stimulate dopaminergic autoreceptors and thus inhibit dopamine release. (See step 8 in *Figure 3.20.*)

Effects on Reuptake or Destruction of Transmitter Substance

The next step after stimulation of the postsynaptic receptor is termination of the postsynaptic potential; molecules of the transmitter substance are destroyed by an enzyme or taken back into the terminal button through the process of reuptake. Drugs can interfere with either of these processes;

because they prolong the presence of the transmitter substance in the synaptic cleft (and hence in a location where they can stimulate postsynaptic receptors), both types serve as *agonists*. The postsynaptic activity of transmitter substances is terminated by active uptake mechanisms in the terminal button. Drugs that block or retard the reuptake process permit molecules of the transmitter substance to remain in the synaptic cleft for a longer time, where they produce a prolonged postsynaptic potential. Similarly, a drug that deactivates the enzyme acetylcholinesterase (AChE) permits acetylcholine to remain intact longer than usual. (See steps 9 and 10 in *Figure 3.20.*)

Cocaine is a particularly potent catecholamine agonist because it retards the reuptake of norepinephrine and (especially) dopamine. As we shall see in Chapter 18, the effect of cocaine on dopaminergic synapses explains why this drug is often abused. The transporter molecule responsible for dopamine reuptake contains a cocaine binding site. (Why it does is not yet understood.) When cocaine binds with this site, the channel through the transporter is blocked; the transporter becomes inactive and no longer carries dopamine into the terminal button. (See *Figure 3.21.*)

Drugs that deactivate or inhibit AChE are used for several purposes. Some are used as insecticides. These drugs readily kill insects but not humans and other mammals, because our blood contains enzymes that destroy them. (Insects lack the enzyme.) Other AChE inhibitors are used medically. For example, a hereditary disorder called *myasthenia gravis* is caused by a disorder in which a person's immune system begins attacking the protein molecules that serve as nicotinic acetylcholine receptors, located in muscles. The person becomes weaker and weaker as the muscles become less responsive to the neurotransmitter. If given an AChE inhibitor such as **physostigmine,** the person regains strength, because the acetylcholine that is released has a more prolonged effect on the remaining receptors.

As we saw earlier in this chapter, monoamine oxidase is present in the terminal buttons of monoaminergic synapses, where it regulates the production of the transmitter substance by destroying any extra quantities that the cell produces. Drugs that inactivate MAO allow an increased amount of neurotransmitter to be released when the axon fires. An example of a MAO inhibitor is **iproniazid,** which selectively blocks the particular form of MAO that destroys serotonin; thus, it is a serotonin agonist. (See step 11 in *Figure 3.20.*)

As I mentioned earlier, drugs that affect synapses find many uses: chemicals that give pleasure, poisons, antidotes to poisons, and treatments for illnesses and mental disorders. Especially important to the topic of this book, they serve as tools to help neuroscientists investigate the functions of the nervous system. You will encounter many of them in subsequent pages.

⦀ INTERIM SUMMARY

The process of synaptic transmission entails the synthesis of the transmitter substance, its storage in synaptic vesicles, its release into the synaptic cleft, its interaction with postsynaptic receptors, and the consequent opening of ion channels in the postsynaptic membrane. The effects of the transmitter substance are then terminated by enzymatic deactivation (in the case of acetylcholine) or reuptake into the terminal button.

Each of the steps necessary for synaptic transmission can be interfered with by drugs, and a few

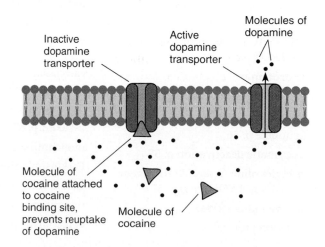

FIGURE 3.21

The effects of cocaine on the activity of the dopamine transporter.

can be stimulated. Thus, drugs can increase the pool of available precursor, block a biosynthetic enzyme, prevent the storage of transmitter substance in the synaptic vesicles, stimulate or block the release of the transmitter substance, stimulate or block postsynaptic receptors, retard reuptake, or deactivate enzymes that destroy the transmitter substance postsynapti-cally (acetylcholinesterase) or presynaptically (monoamine oxidase). Drugs have been used to treat neurological and psychiatric disorders, and as we will see throughout the rest of this book, they have served as important tools for investigating the functions of various classes of neurons.

 New Terms

Synaptic Transmission

neuromodulator p. 48

endocrine gland p. 48

binding site p. 48

ligand *(LIGH gand)* p. 48

pheromone *(FAIR o moan)* p. 49

synaptic cleft p. 49

synaptic vesicle p. 49

release zone p. 50

pinocytosis *(PEE no sy TOE sis)* p. 52

horseradish peroxidase p. 52

postsynaptic receptor p. 53

neurotransmitter-dependent ion channel p. 53

ionotropic receptor *(eye on o TROE pic)* p. 53

metabotropic receptor *(me tab o TROE pic)* p. 54

G protein p. 54

second messenger p. 54

patch clamp p. 54

reuptake p. 56

enzymatic deactivation p. 57

acetylcholine *(a set il KOH leen or ass a teel KOH leen)* p. 57

acetylcholinesterase p. 57

autoreceptor p. 57

axosomatic synapse p. 58

axodendritic synapse p. 58

axoaxonic synapse p. 58

presynaptic inhibition p. 58

presynaptic facilitation p. 58

dendrodendritic synapse p. 58

gap junction p. 58

peptide p. 59

steroid *(STEER oid)* p. 59

Transmitter Substances

CoA p. 61

acetyl CoA p. 61

choline acetyltransferase p. 61

nicotinic receptor p. 62

muscarinic receptor *(muss ka RIN ic)* p. 62

monoamine *(MAHN o a meen)* p. 62

catecholamine *(cat a KOHL a meen)* p. 63

dopamine p. 63

L-DOPA p. 63

monoamine oxidase p. 63

Parkinson's disease p. 63

axonal varicosity p. 64

norepinephrine p. 64

epinephrine p. 64

serotonin (5-HT) p. 65

glutamic acid p. 66

GABA p. 66

benzodiazepine *(ben zoe dy AZZ a peen)* p. 67

glycine *(GLY seen)* p. 67

endogenous opioids *(en DODGE en us OH pee oydz)* p. 67

enkephalin *(en KEFF a lin)* p. 67

Pharmacology of Synapses

antagonist p. 70

agonist p. 70

PCPA p. 70

reserpine *(ree SUR peen)* p. 71

botulinum toxin *(bot you LIN um)* p. 71

receptor blocker p. 72

atropine *(AT ro peen)* p. 72

curare *(kew RAHR ee)* p. 72

apomorphine *(ap o MORE feen)* p. 72

cocaine p. 73

physostigmine *(FY so STIG meen)* p. 73

iproniazid *(ipp ro NY a zid)* p. 73

Suggested Readings

Cooper, J.R., Bloom, F.E., and Roth, R.H. *The Biochemical Basis of Neuropharmacology,* 6th ed. New York: Oxford University Press, 1991.

Hall, Z.W. *An Introduction to Molecular Neurobiology.* Sunderland, Mass.: Sinauer Associates, 1992.

Kandel, E.R., Schwartz, J.H., and Jessell, T.M. *Principles of Neural Science,* 3rd ed. Norwalk, Conn.: Appleton & Lange, 1992

Nicholls, J.G., Martin, A.R., Wallace, B.G., and Kuffler, S.W. *From Neuron to Brain,* 3rd ed. Sunderland, Mass.: Sinauer Associates, 1992.

Shepherd, G.M. *Neurobiology,* 2nd ed. New York: Oxford University Press, 1988.

CHAPTER 4

Structure of the Nervous System

Basic Features of the Nervous System
- An Overview
- Blood Supply
- Meninges
- The Ventricular System and Production of CSF
  Interim Summary

The Central Nervous System
- Development of the Central Nervous System
- The Forebrain
- The Mesencephalon
- The Hindbrain
- The Spinal Cord
  Interim Summary

The Peripheral Nervous System
- Spinal Nerves
- Cranial Nerves
- The Autonomic Nervous System
  Interim Summary

The goal of neuroscience research is to understand how the brain works. To understand the results of this research, you must be acquainted with the basic structure of the nervous system. The number of terms introduced in this chapter is kept to a minimum (but as you will see, the minimum is still a rather large number). With the framework you will receive from this chapter, you should have no trouble learning the material presented in subsequent chapters.

BASIC FEATURES OF THE NERVOUS SYSTEM

Before beginning a description of the nervous system, I want to discuss the terms used to describe it. The gross anatomy of the brain was described long ago, and everything that could be seen without the aid of a microscope was given a name. Early anatomists named most brain structures according to their similarity to commonplace objects: amygdala, or "almond-shaped object"; hippocampus, or "sea horse"; genu, or "knee"; cortex, or "bark"; pons, or "bridge"; uncus, or "hook," to give a few examples. Throughout this book I will translate the names of anatomical terms as I introduce them because the translation makes the terms more memorable. For example, knowing that *cortex* means "bark" (like the bark of a tree) will help you remember that the cortex is the outer layer of the brain.

When describing features of a structure as complex as the brain, we need to use terms denoting directions. Directions in the nervous system are normally described relative to the **neuraxis,** an imaginary line drawn through the spinal cord up to the front of the brain. For simplicity's sake, let us consider an animal with a straight neuraxis. Figure 4.1 shows an alligator and a human. This alligator is certainly laid out in a linear fashion; we can draw a straight line that starts between its eyes and continues down the center of its spinal cord. (See *Figure 4.1.*) The front end is **anterior,** and the tail is **posterior.** The terms **rostral** (toward the beak) and **caudal** (toward the tail) are also employed, especially when referring specifically to the brain. The top of the head and the back are part of the **dorsal** surface, while the **ventral** (front) surface faces the ground. These directions are somewhat more complicated in the human; because we stand upright, our neuraxis bends, so that the top of the head is perpendicular to the back. The frontal views of the alligator and the human illustrate the terms **lateral** and **medial,** toward the side and toward the midline, respectively. (See *Figure 4.1.*)

Two other useful terms are *ipsilateral* and *contralateral*. **Ipsilateral** refers to structures on the same side of the body. Thus, if we say that the olfactory bulb sends axons to the *ipsilateral* hemisphere, we mean that the left olfactory bulb sends axons to the left hemisphere and the right olfactory bulb sends axons to the right hemisphere. **Contralateral** refers to structures on opposite sides of the body. If we say that a particular region of the left cerebral cortex controls movements of the *contralateral* hand, we mean that the region controls movements of the right hand.

To see what is in the nervous system, we have to cut it open; to be able to convey information about what we find, we slice it in a standard way. Figure 4.2 shows a human nervous system. We can slice the nervous system in three ways:

1. Transversely, like a salami, giving us **cross sections** (also known as **frontal sections**)

2. Parallel to the ground, giving us **horizontal sections**

3. Perpendicular to the ground and parallel to the neuraxis, giving us **sagittal sections**

Note that because of our upright posture, cross sections of the spinal cord are actually parallel to the ground. (See *Figure 4.2.*)

An Overview

The nervous system consists of the brain and spinal cord, which make up the **central nervous system** (CNS), and the cranial nerves, spinal nerves, and peripheral ganglia, which constitute the **peripheral nervous system** (PNS). The CNS is encased in bone: The brain is covered by the skull, and the spinal cord is encased by the vertebral column.

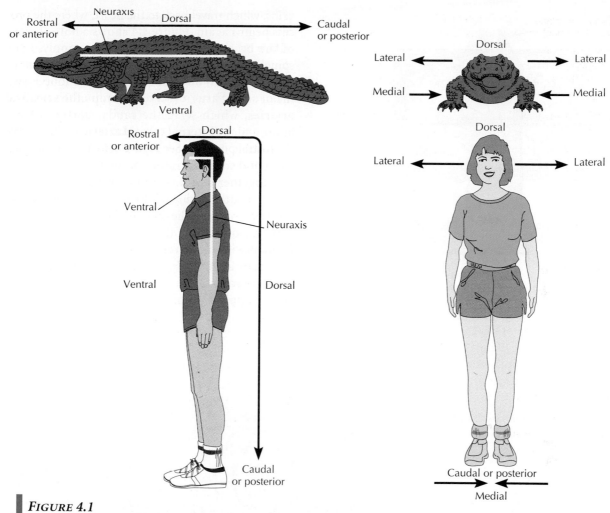

FIGURE 4.1

Side and frontal views of an alligator and a human, showing the terms used to denote anatomical directions.

Figure 4.3 illustrates the relation of the brain and spinal cord to the head and neck of a human. Do not be concerned with unfamiliar labels on this figure; these structures will be described later. (See *Figure 4.3*.) The brain is a large mass of neurons, glia, and other supporting cells. It is the most protected organ of the body, encased in a tough, bony skull and floating in a pool of cerebrospinal fluid. The brain receives a copious supply of blood and is chemically guarded by the blood-brain barrier.

Blood Supply

The brain receives approximately 20 percent of the blood flow from the heart, and it receives it continu-ously. Other parts of the body, such as the skeletal muscles or digestive system, receive varying quanti-ties of blood, depending on their needs, relative to those of other regions. But the brain always receives its share. The brain cannot store its fuel (primarily glucose), nor can it temporarily extract energy with-out oxygen, as the muscles can; therefore, a consistent blood supply is essential. A 1-second interruption of the blood flow to the brain uses up much of the dis-solved oxygen; a 6-second interruption produces un-consciousness. Permanent damage occurs within a few minutes.

Circulation of blood in the body proceeds from large arteries to small arteries to capillaries. The cap-illaries then drain into small veins and then to large

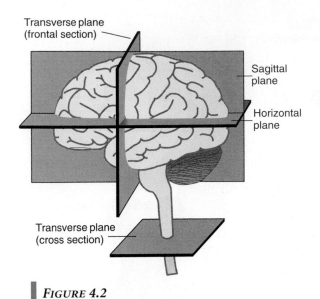

FIGURE 4.2

Planes of section as they pertain to the human central nervous system.

veins, which travel back to the heart, where the process begins again. Figure 4.4 shows a bottom view of the brain and its major arterial supply. (The spinal cord has been cut off, as have the left half of the cerebellum and the left temporal lobe.) Two major sets of arteries serve the brain: the **vertebral arteries,** which serve the caudal portion of the brain, and the **internal carotid arteries,** which serve the rostral portion. (See *Figure 4.4.*) You can see that the blood supply is rather peculiar; major arteries join together and then separate again. Normally, there is a little mixing of blood from the rostral and caudal arterial supplies and, in the case of the rostral supply, from that of the right and left sides of the brain. But if a blood vessel becomes blocked (for example, by a blood clot), blood flow can follow alternative routes, reducing the probability of loss of blood supply and subsequent destruction of brain tissue.

FIGURE 4.3

The relation of the brain and spinal cord to the head and neck.

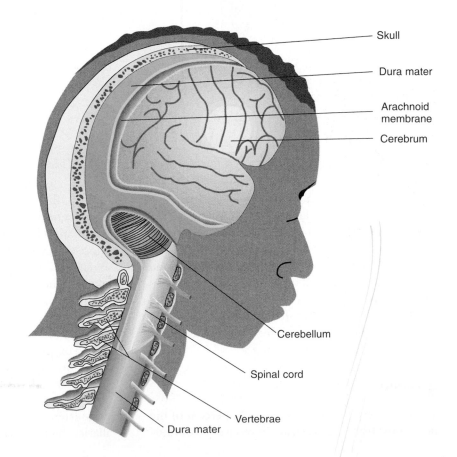

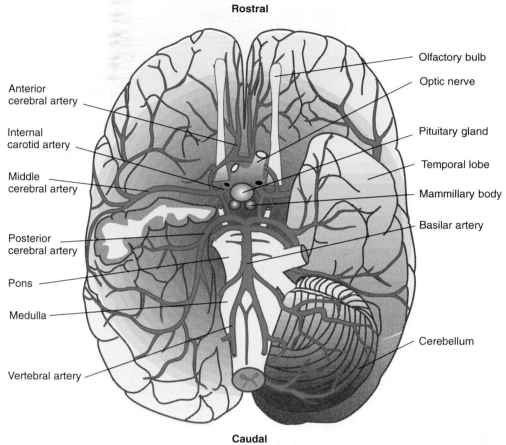

Rostral

Olfactory bulb

Optic nerve

Pituitary gland

Temporal lobe

Mammillary body

Basilar artery

Cerebellum

Anterior
cerebral artery

Internal
carotid artery

Middle
cerebral artery

Posterior
cerebral artery

Pons

Medulla

Vertebral artery

Caudal

FIGURE 4.4

Arterial blood supply to the brain, viewed from beneath.

Meninges

The entire nervous system—brain, spinal cord, cranial and spinal nerves, and autonomic ganglia—is covered by tough connective tissue. The protective sheaths around the brain and spinal cord are referred to as the **meninges** (singular: *meninx*). The meninges consist of three layers, which are shown in Figure 4.5. The outer layer is thick, tough, and flexible but unstretchable; its name, **dura mater,** means "hard mother." The middle layer of the meninges, the **arachnoid membrane,** gets its name from the weblike appearance of the *arachnoid trabeculae* that protrude from it (from the Greek *arachne,* meaning "spider"; *trabecula* means "track"). The arachnoid membrane, soft and spongy, lies be-

neath the dura mater. Closely attached to the brain and spinal cord, and following every surface convolution, is the **pia mater** ("pious mother"). The smaller surface blood vessels of the brain and spinal cord are contained within this layer. Between the pia mater and arachnoid membrane is a gap called the **subarachnoid space.** This space is filled with a liquid called **cerebrospinal fluid** (CSF). (See *Figure 4.5.*)

The peripheral nervous system (PNS) is covered with two layers of meninges. The middle layer (arachnoid membrane), with its associated pool of CSF, covers only the brain and spinal cord. Outside the central nervous system, the outer and inner layers (dura mater and pia mater) fuse and form a sheath that covers the spinal and cranial nerves and the autonomic ganglia.

The meninges: dura mater, arachnoid membrane, and pia mater.

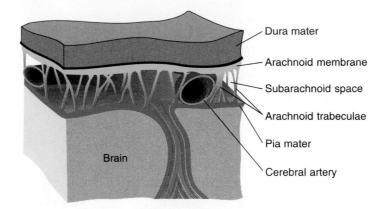

In the first edition of this book I said that I did not know why the outer and inner layers of the meninges were referred to as "mothers." I received a letter from medical historians at the Department of Anatomy at UCLA that explained the name. (Sometimes, it pays to proclaim one's ignorance.) A tenth-century Persian physician, Ali ibn Abbas, used the Arabic term *al umm* to refer to the meninges. The term literally means "mother" but was used to designate any swaddling material, because Arabic lacked a specific term for the word *membrane.* The tough outer membrane was called *al umm al djafiya,* and the soft inner one was called *al umm al rigiga.* When the writings of Ali ibn Abbas were translated into Latin during the eleventh century, the translator, who was probably not familiar with the structure of the meninges, made a literal translation of *al umm.* He referred to the membranes as the "hard mother" and the "pious mother" (*pious* in the sense of "delicate"), rather than use a more appropriate Latin word.

The Ventricular System and Production of CSF

The brain is very soft and jellylike. The considerable weight of a human brain (approximately 1400 g), along with its delicate construction, necessitates that it be protected from shock. A human brain cannot even support its own weight well; it is difficult to remove and handle a fresh brain from a recently deceased human without damaging it.

Fortunately, the intact brain within a living human is well protected. It floats in a bath of CSF contained within the subarachnoid space. Because the brain is completely immersed in liquid, its net weight is reduced to approximately 80 g; thus, pressure on the base of the brain is considerably diminished. The CSF surrounding the brain and spinal cord also reduces the shock to the central nervous system that would be caused by sudden head movement.

The brain contains a series of hollow, interconnected chambers called **ventricles,** which are filled with CSF. (See *Figure 4.6.*) The largest chambers are the **lateral ventricles,** which are connected to the **third ventricle.** The third ventricle is located at the midline of the brain; its walls divide the surrounding part of the brain into symmetrical halves. A bridge of neural tissue called the *massa intermedia* crosses through the middle of the third ventricle and serves as a convenient reference point. The **cerebral aqueduct,** a long tube, connects the third ventricle to the **fourth ventricle.** The lateral ventricles constitute the first and second ventricles, but they are never referred to as such. (See *Figure 4.6.*)

Cerebrospinal fluid is extracted from the blood and resembles blood plasma in its composition. CSF is manufactured by special tissue with an especially rich blood supply called the **choroid plexus,** which protrudes into all four of the ventricles. Circulation of CSF begins in the lateral ventricles, flows into the third ventricle, then flows through the cerebral aqueduct into the fourth ventricle. From there, it flows through a set of openings into the subarachnoid space, which encases the entire central nervous system. Finally, the fluid is reabsorbed into the blood supply.

The total volume of CSF is approximately 125 milliliters (ml), and the half-life (the time it takes for half of the CSF present in the ventricular system to be replaced by fresh fluid) is about 3 hours. Therefore, the choroid plexus produces this amount several times each day.

Occasionally, the flow of CSF is interrupted at some point in its route of passage. For example, a brain tumor growing in the midbrain may push against the cerebral aqueduct, blocking its flow. This occlusion results in greatly increased pressure within the ventricles, because the choroid plexus continues to produce CSF. The walls of the ventricles then expand and produce a condition known as **hydrocephalus** (literally, "water-head"). If the obstruction remains, and if nothing is done to reverse the increased intracerebral pressure, blood vessels will be occluded and permanent—perhaps fatal—brain damage will occur. Fortunately, a surgeon can usually operate on the person, drilling a hole through the skull and inserting a plastic tube into one of the ventricles. The tube is then placed beneath the skin and connected to a pressure relief valve that is implanted in the abdominal cavity. When the pressure in the ventricles becomes excessive, the valve permits the CSF to escape into the abdomen, where eventually it is reabsorbed into the blood supply.

▏▏▏▏ INTERIM SUMMARY

Anatomists have adopted a set of terms to describe the locations of parts of the body. *Anterior* is toward the head, *posterior* is toward the tail, *lateral* is toward the side, *medial* is toward the middle, *dorsal* is toward the back, and *ventral* is toward the front surface of the body. In the special case of the nervous system, *rostral* means toward the beak (or nose) and *caudal* means toward the tail. *Ipsilateral* means "same side," and *contralateral* means "other side." A cross section (or frontal section) slices the nervous system like a salami, a horizontal section slices it parallel to the ground, and a sagittal section slices it perpendicular to the ground, parallel to the neuraxis.

The central nervous system consists of the brain and spinal cord, and the peripheral nervous system consists of the spinal and cranial nerves and peripheral ganglia. The CNS is covered with the meninges:

▏ *FIGURE 4.6*

The ventricular system of the brain.

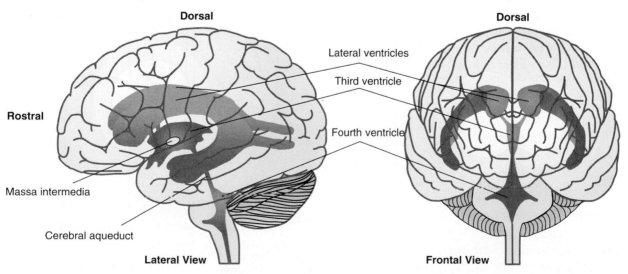

dura mater, arachnoid membrane, and pia mater. The space under the arachnoid membrane is filled with cerebrospinal fluid, in which the brain floats. The PNS is covered with only the dura mater and pia mater. Cerebrospinal fluid is produced in the choroid plexus of the lateral, third, and fourth ventricles. It flows from the two lateral ventricles into the third ventricle, through the cerebral aqueduct into the fourth ventricle, then into the subarachnoid space, and finally back into the blood supply. If the flow of CSF is blocked by a tumor or other obstruction, the result is hydrocephalus: enlargement of the ventricles and subsequent brain damage.

THE CENTRAL NERVOUS SYSTEM

ALTHOUGH THE BRAIN IS EXCEEDINGLY COMPLIcated, an understanding of the basic features of brain development makes it easier to learn and remember the location of the most important struc-

tures. With that end in mind, I introduce these features here in the context of development of the central nervous system.

Development of the Central Nervous System

The central nervous system begins its existence early in embryonic life as a hollow tube, and it maintains this basic shape even after it is fully developed. During development, parts of the tube elongate, pockets and folds form, and the tissue around the tube becomes thicker. The cells that give rise to neurons are found on the inner surface of the tube. These cells divide and produce neurons, which then migrate in a radial direction, away from the center. Their final location is guided by both physical and chemical factors. Physical guidance is provided by radially oriented glial cells; the newly born neurons migrate along the processes of these cells. Chemical guidance attracts particular types of neurons to particular locations, where they come to rest. (See *Figure 4.7.*)

FIGURE 4.7

A cross section through the nervous system early in its development. Radially oriented glial cells help guide the migration of newly formed neurons. (Adapted from Bloom, F.E., and Lazerson, A. Brain, Mind, and Behavior, 2nd ed. New York: W.H. Freeman, 1988.)

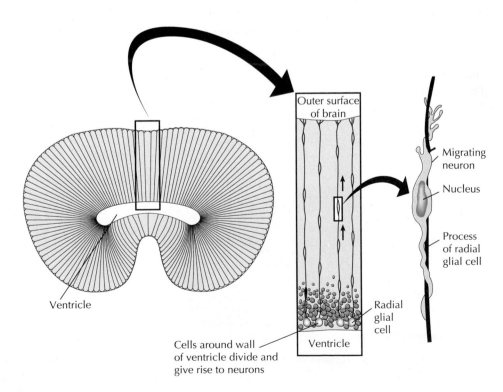

Outer surface of brain

Migrating neuron

Nucleus

Process of radial glial cell

Radial glial cell

Ventricle

Ventricle

Cells around wall of ventricle divide and give rise to neurons

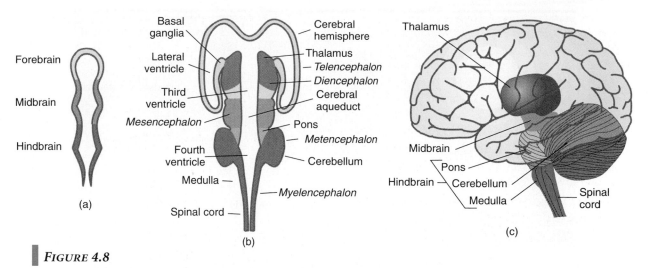

FIGURE 4.8

An outline of brain development, showing its relation to the ventricles. Parts (a) and (b) are horizontal sections through the developing brain; part (c) is a side view. (a) Early development. (b) Mid development. (c) Late development, near time of birth.

(Adapted from Gardner, E. *Fundamentals of Neurology*, 6th ed. Philadelphia: Saunders, 1975.)

Early in development the central nervous system contains three interconnected chambers. These chambers become ventricles, and the tissue that surrounds them become the three major parts of the brain: the forebrain, the midbrain, and the hindbrain. (See *Figure 4.8a.*) Later, the rostral chamber divides into three separate chambers, which become the two lateral ventricles and the third ventricle. The region around the lateral ventricles becomes the telencephalon ("end brain"), and the region around the third ventricle becomes the diencephalon ("interbrain"). (See *Figure 4.8b.*) In its final form the chamber inside the midbrain (mesencephalon) becomes narrow, forming the cerebral aqueduct, and two structures develop in the hindbrain: the metencephalon ("afterbrain") and the myelencephalon ("marrowbrain"). (See *Figure 4.8c.*)

Table 4.1 summarizes the terms I have introduced here and mentions some of the major structures found in each part of the brain. These structures will be described in the remainder of the chapter. (See *Table 4.1.*)

Once neurons have migrated to their final locations where they collect in groups, they begin forming connections with other groups of neurons. They grow dendrites, which receive the terminal buttons from the axons of other neurons, and they grow axons of their own. Like neural migration, axonal growth is guided by physical and chemical factors. Once the growing ends of the axons (the *growth cones*) reach their targets, they form numerous branches. Each of these branches finds a vacant place on the membrane of the appropriate type of postsynaptic cell, grows a terminal button, and establishes a synaptic connection. (Apparently, different types of cells secrete different chemicals, which attract different types of axons.) Of course, the establishment of a synaptic connection also requires efforts on the part of the postsynaptic cell; this cell must contribute its parts of the synapse, including the postsynaptic receptors. The chemical signals that the cells exchange in order to tell one another to establish these connections are not yet known.

The layer of cells surrounding the neural tube gives rise to many more neurons than are needed. In fact, the neurons that are produced must compete in order to survive. The axons of approximately 50 percent of these neurons do not find vacant postsynaptic cells of the right type with which to form synaptic connections—so they die. This phenomenon, too, involves a chemical signal; when a presynaptic neuron establishes synaptic connec-

	TABLE 4.1		
	Anatomical Subdivisions of the Brain		
Major division	**Ventricle**	**Subdivision**	**Principal structures**
Forebrain	Lateral	Telencephalon	Cerebral cortex Basal ganglia Limbic system
	Third	Diencephalon	Thalamus Hypothalamus
Midbrain	Cerebral aqueduct	Mesencephalon	Tectum Tegmentum
Hindbrain	Fourth	Metencephalon	Cerebellum Pons
		Myelencephalon	Medulla oblongata

tions, it receives a signal from the postsynaptic cell that permits it to survive. Those neurons that come too late do not find any available space and thus do not receive this life-sustaining signal. This scheme may seem wasteful, but apparently the evolutionary process found that the safest strategy was to produce too many neurons and let them fight to establish synaptic connections, rather than try to produce exactly the right number of each type of neuron.

During development, thousands of different pathways develop in the brain. These pathways—groups of axons that connect one brain region with another—seem to be specified genetically. And within many of these pathways, the connections are orderly and systematic. For example, the axons of sensory neurons from the skin form orderly connections in the brain; axons from the little finger form synapses in one region, those of the ring finger form synapses in a neighboring region, and so on. In fact, the surface of the body is "mapped" on the surface of the brain. Similarly, the surface of the retina of the eye is "mapped" on another region of the surface of the brain.

What guides the orderly connections of individual axons in a particular pathway? What process assures that neurons located next to each other in the retina will form synapses on adjacent neurons in their target region in the brain? Each human optic nerve contains approximately one million axons. Is each developing axon guided individually?

Research has shown that the answer is no. Years of study have revealed that the establishment of orderly synaptic connections in the brain's sensory system is controlled by neural activity (Kandel and O'Dell, 1993). Let us consider the development of the connections of the retina with one of its target regions. At first, the axons branch and form synaptic connections indiscriminately with neurons in the target region. (See *Figure 4.9a.*) But then, a critical period begins. During this phase of development, some synapses are stabilized. These synapses remain and become permanent. Other synapses are weeded out—the terminal buttons dissolve, and the branches of the axon to which they are attached retract. The terminal buttons that disappear are replaced by others; the axons that remain sprout new branches that grow new terminal buttons. (See *Figure 4.9b,c.*)

The rule that determines which synapses remain and which do not is a very simple one: The survivors are those synapses whose activity is correlated with that of their neighbors. What determines whether the activity of terminal buttons is correlated? In the case of the visual system, it is the relative location on the retina of the cell body that gives rise to them. Terminal buttons that belong to neighboring retinal cells are likely to fire at the same time. When the eye is exposed to visual stimuli, patterns of light and dark fall on the retina. Two neurons located side-by-side will have very similar activity, because they will probably both be located in a region of light or shadow. In contrast, the activity of two neurons from distant regions of the retina is likely to be uncorrelated; sometimes one will be in light while the other in shadow, sometimes both will be in light, and so on. Thus, terminal buttons located on the same cell as those that come from neighboring retinal cells are the ones that survive.

How do we know that this story is true? If action potentials in the axons of the optic nerves are blocked with drugs during the critical period, the synaptic connections remain haphazard—none of the synapses are weeded out. The same effect is produced by raising the animal in the dark or by simultaneously stimulating all the neurons in the retina by raising the animal in a featureless environment and exposing it to flashes of light. And what mechanism is responsible for weeding out terminal buttons whose activity is not correlated with that of their neighbors? In many parts of the brain, that process involves a special postsynaptic receptor—the *NMDA receptor.* The ion channel of the NMDA receptor opens only if two conditions are met: The postsynaptic membrane must be adequately depolarized, and the terminal button must release the transmitter substance. These two conditions are met only when the terminal button *and* its neighbors are active. A single terminal button acting alone produces very little depolarization in the postsynaptic membrane. But when several terminal buttons are active at the same time, the postsynaptic membrane depolarizes sufficiently, and each of the active terminal buttons receives a chemical signal from the postsynaptic neuron that helps keep it alive. This signal is released when the ion channel in the NMDA receptor opens, allowing calcium ions to enter. The calcium activates enzymes that are responsible for producing the signal. (See *Figure 4.10.*)

As we shall see later, the mechanism I have just described is useful not only during development. Later in life, it is responsible for changes in synaptic strength that enable learning to take place. Thus, the development of the nervous system and the formation of memories follow similar principles.

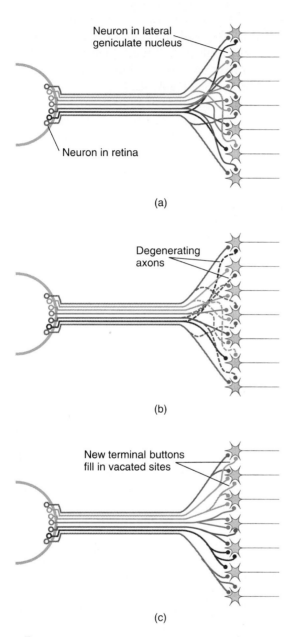

(a)

(b)

(c)

| FIGURE 4.9

Development of orderly connections from the retina to one of its target regions. (a) Initially, the synaptic connections are indiscriminate. (b) Terminal buttons that are not located near terminal buttons belonging to neighboring neurons in the retina disappear. (c) The axons of the remaining terminal buttons establish new synapses to fill in the vacated spaces.

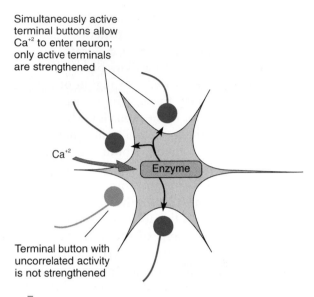

Simultaneously active terminal buttons allow Ca⁺² to enter neuron; only active terminals are strengthened

Ca⁺²

Enzyme

Terminal button with uncorrelated activity is not strengthened

FIGURE 4.10

The mechanism that determines whether the activity of terminal buttons is correlated with that of their neighbors.

The Forebrain

As we saw, the **forebrain** surrounds the rostral end of the neural tube. Its two major components are the telencephalon and the diencephalon.

Telencephalon

The telencephalon includes most of the two symmetrical cerebral hemispheres that comprise the cerebrum. The cerebral hemispheres are covered by the cerebral cortex and contain the limbic system and the basal ganglia. The latter two sets of structures are primarily in the **subcortical regions** of the brain—those located deep within it, beneath the cerebral cortex.

Cerebral Cortex. *Cortex* means "bark," and the **cerebral cortex** surrounds the cerebral hemispheres like the bark of a tree. In humans the cerebral cortex is greatly convoluted; these convolutions, consisting of **sulci** (small grooves), **fissures** (large grooves), and **gyri** (bulges between adjacent sulci or fissures), greatly enlarge the surface area of the cortex, compared with a smooth brain of the same size. In fact, two-thirds of the surface of the cortex is hidden in the grooves; thus, the presence of gyri

and sulci triples the area of the cerebral cortex. The total surface area is approximately 2360 cm² (2.5 ft²), and the thickness is approximately 3 mm. The cerebral cortex consists mostly of glia and the cell bodies, dendrites, and interconnecting axons of neurons. Because cells predominate, giving the cerebral cortex a grayish brown appearance, it is referred to as *gray matter*. (See *Figure 4.11.*) Beneath the cerebral cortex run millions of axons that connect the neurons of the cerebral cortex with those located elsewhere in the brain. The large concentration of myelin gives this tissue an opaque white appearance—hence the term *white matter*.

The surface of the cerebral hemispheres is divided into four lobes, named after the bones of the skull that overlie them. The **frontal lobe, parietal lobe, temporal lobe,** and **occipital lobe** are visible on the lateral surface and are shown in Figure 4.12. The **central sulcus** divides the frontal lobe from the parietal lobe, and the **lateral fissure** divides the temporal lobe from the overlying frontal and parietal lobes. (See *Figure 4.12.*)

Figure 4.13 shows a *midsagittal* view of the brain. The brain (and part of the spinal cord) has been sliced down the middle, dividing it into its two symmetrical halves. The left half has been removed, so we see the inner surface of the right half. The cerebral cortex that covers most of the surface of the cerebral hemispheres is called the **neocortex** ("new" cortex, because it is of relatively recent evolutionary origin). Another form of cerebral cortex, the **limbic cortex,** is located around the edge of the cerebral hemispheres (*limbus* means "border"). The **cingulate gyrus,** an important region of the limbic cortex, can be seen in this figure. (See *Figure 4.13.*)

Figure 4.13 also shows the **corpus callosum,** which is the largest **commissure** (cross-hemisphere connection) in the brain. The corpus callosum consists of axons that connect the cortex of the two cerebral hemispheres. The axons unite geographically similar regions of the two cerebral cortices. To slice the brain into its two symmetrical halves, one must slice through the middle of the corpus callosum. (Recall that I described the split-brain operation, in which the corpus callosum is severed, in Chapter 1.) (See *Figure 4.13.*)

The frontal lobes are specialized for the planning, execution, and control of movements. The

FRONT

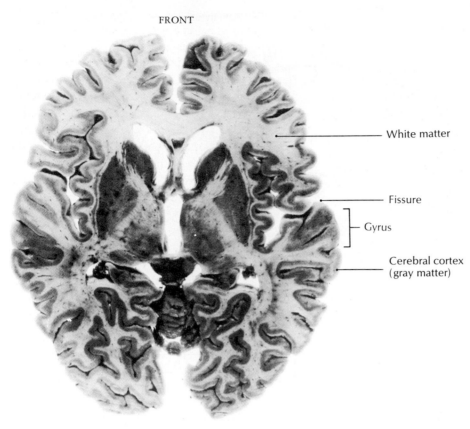

White matter

Fissure

Gyrus

Cerebral cortex
(gray matter)

BACK

(Photograph from *Structure of the Human Brain: A Photographic Atlas,* Second Edition, by
Stephen J. DeArmond, Madelaine M. Fusco, and Maynard M. Dewey. Copyright © 1976 by
Oxford University Press, Inc. Reprinted by permission.)

FIGURE 4.11

A photograph of a slice of a human brain showing fissures and gyri and the layer of cerebral cortex that follows these convolutions.

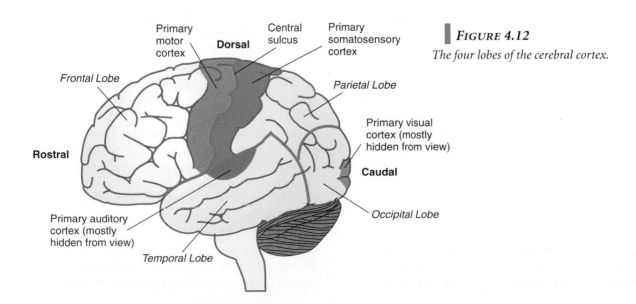

Primary
motor
cortex

Central
sulcus

Primary
somatosensory
cortex

Dorsal

Frontal Lobe

Parietal Lobe

Primary visual
cortex (mostly
hidden from view)

Rostral

Caudal

Occipital Lobe

Primary auditory
cortex (mostly
hidden from view)

Temporal Lobe

FIGURE 4.12

The four lobes of the cerebral cortex.

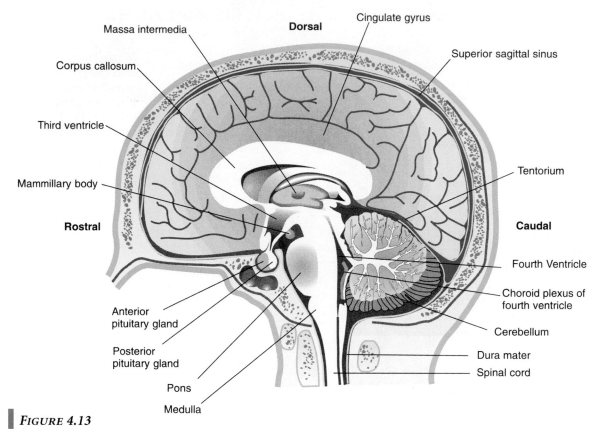

FIGURE 4.13

A midsagittal view of the brain and part of the spinal cord.

primary motor cortex, immediately rostral to the central sulcus, contains neurons that participate in the control of movement. (See *Figure 4.14.*) If an experimenter places a wire on the surface of the primary motor cortex and stimulates the neurons there with a weak electrical current, the current will cause movement of a particular part of the body. Moving the wire to a different spot causes a different part of the body to move. Because the cerebral hemispheres are connected with the *opposite* sides of the body, stimulation of the right primary motor cortex moves parts of the left side of the body, and stimulation of the left cortex moves the right side.

The posterior lobes of the brain (the parietal, temporal, and occipital lobes) are specialized for perception. The **primary somatosensory cortex** lies immediately caudal to the central sulcus, right behind the primary motor cortex. This region of cerebral cortex receives information about the somatosenses ("body senses": touch, pressure, temperature, and pain). Again, the connections are crossed; sensory receptors in the right side of the body send information to the left side of the brain, and those in the left side send it to the right. The **primary visual cortex** lies at the back of the occipital lobes along the calcarine fissure, mostly hidden between the two cerebral hemispheres. As its name implies, it receives visual information. The **primary auditory cortex** lies in the temporal lobes, mostly hidden in the lateral fissure. (See *Figure 4.14.*)

The rest of the neocortex is referred to as **association cortex.** The association cortex in the frontal lobes is involved in the planning of movements; thus, neurons there control the activity of those in the primary motor cortex, which in turn control muscle movements. The association cortex in the posterior lobes receives information from the primary sensory areas and is involved in perception and memories. The primary somatosensory cortex sends information to the somatosensory association cortex, the primary visual cortex sends information to the visual association cortex, and the primary auditory cortex sends information to the auditory association cortex. (See *Figure 4.14.*)

If people sustain damage to the somatosensory association cortex, their deficits are related to somatosensation and to the environment in general; for example, they may have difficulty perceiving the shapes of objects that they can touch but not see, they may be unable to name parts of their bodies, or they may have trouble drawing maps or following them. People who sustain damage to the visual association cortex will not become blind; but they may be unable to recognize objects by sight, although they can often recognize them if they feel them with their hands. People who sustain damage to the auditory association cortex may have difficulty perceiving speech or even producing meaningful speech of their own. People who sustain damage to regions of the association cortex at the junction of the three posterior lobes, where the somatosensory, visual, and auditory functions overlap, may have difficulty reading or writing.

Limbic System. A neuroanatomist, Papez (1937), suggested that a set of interconnected brain structures formed a circuit whose primary function was motivation and emotion. This system included several regions of the limbic cortex (already described) and a set of interconnected structures surrounding the core of the forebrain. A physiologist, MacLean (1949), expanded the system to include other structures and coined the term **limbic system.** Besides the limbic cortex, the most important parts of the limbic system are the **hippocampus** ("sea horse") and the **amygdala** ("almond"), located next to the lateral ventricle in the temporal lobe. (See *Figure 4.15.*)

MacLean noted that the evolution of this system, which includes the first and simplest form of cerebral cortex, appears to have coincided with the development of emotional responses. As you will see in Chapter 15, we now know that parts of the limbic

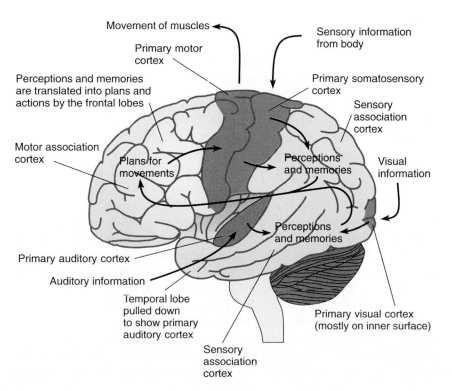

Movement of muscles

Primary motor cortex

Perceptions and memories are translated into plans and actions by the frontal lobes

Motor association cortex

Plans for movements

Primary auditory cortex

Auditory information

Temporal lobe pulled down to show primary auditory cortex

Sensory association cortex

Sensory information from body

Primary somatosensory cortex

Sensory association cortex

Perceptions and memories

Visual information

Perceptions and memories

Primary visual cortex (mostly on inner surface)

FIGURE 4.14

The relation between primary sensory and motor cortex and association cortex.

FIGURE 4.15

The major components of the lymbic system.

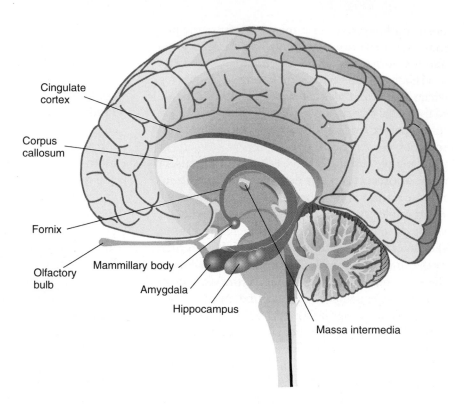

Cingulate cortex

Corpus callosum

Fornix

Olfactory bulb

Mammillary body

Amygdala

Hippocampus

Massa intermedia

system (notably, the hippocampal formation and the region of limbic cortex that surrounds it) are involved in learning and memory rather than emotional behavior. However, the rest of the limbic system does seem to do what Papez and MacLean hypothesized.

Basal Ganglia. The **basal ganglia** are a collection of subcortical nuclei in the forebrain, which lie beneath the anterior portion of the lateral ventricles. (See ***Figure 4.16.***) The basal ganglia are involved in the control of movement. For example, Parkinson's disease is caused by degeneration of dopaminergic neurons located in the midbrain that send axons to parts of the basal ganglia. This disease consists of weakness, tremors, rigidity of the limbs, poor balance, and difficulty in initiating movements.

The amygdala, considered by some anatomists to be part of the basal ganglia, is located within the temporal lobe near its rostral tip. As we already saw, the amygdala is an important component of the limbic system. As we will see in later chapters, the amygdala plays an important role in emotional behavior, including aggression, defense, and reproduction.

Diencephalon

The second major division of the forebrain, the **diencephalon,** is situated between the telencephalon and the mesencephalon; it surrounds the third ventricle. (See ***Figure 4.17.***) Its two most important structures are the thalamus and hypothalamus.

Thalamus. The **thalamus** (from the Greek *thalamos,* "inner chamber") comprises the dorsal part of the diencephalon. It is a large structure with two lobes, connected by a bridge of gray matter called the *massa intermedia,* which pierces the middle of the third ventricle. (See ***Figure 4.17.***) The massa intermedia is probably not an important structure, because it is absent in the brains of some apparently normal people. However, it serves as a useful reference point when looking at diagrams of the brain; it appears in Figures 4.13, 4.15, 4.17, 4.18, and 4.19.

Most neural input to the cerebral cortex is received from the thalamus; indeed, much of the cortical surface can be divided into regions that receive projections from specific parts of the thalamus. **Projection fibers** are sets of axons that arise from cell bodies located in one region of the brain and synapse on neurons located within another region (that is, they *project to* these regions).

The thalamus is divided into several **nuclei,** which are groups of neurons of similar shape. Some of these nuclei receive sensory information from the sensory systems. The neurons in these nuclei then relay the sensory information to specific sensory projection areas of the cerebral cortex. For example, the **lateral geniculate nucleus** receives information from the eye and sends axons to the primary visual cortex, and the **medial geniculate nucleus** receives information from the inner ear and sends axons to the primary auditory cortex. Other thalamic nuclei project to specific regions of the cerebral cortex, but they do not relay primary sensory information. For example, the **ventrolateral nucleus** receives information from the cerebellum and projects to the primary motor cortex. (See *Figure 4.18.*)

Hypothalamus. As its name implies, the **hypothalamus** lies at the base of the brain, under the thalamus. Although the hypothalamus is a relatively small structure, it is an important one. It controls

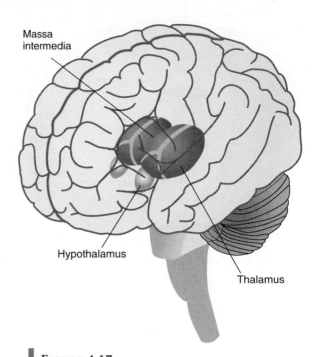

FIGURE 4.17

The location of the human diencephalon, which includes the thalamus and hypothalamus.

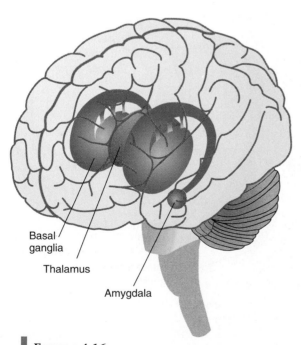

FIGURE 4.16

The location of the basal ganglia in a human brain.

the autonomic nervous system and the endocrine system and organizes behaviors related to survival of the species—the so-called four F's: fighting, feeding, fleeing, and mating.

The hypothalamus is situated on both sides of the inferior portion of the third ventricle. The hypothalamus is a very complex structure, containing many nuclei and fiber tracts. Figure 4.19 indicates its location and size. Note that the pituitary gland is attached to the base of the hypothalamus via the pituitary stalk. Just in front of the pituitary stalk is the **optic chiasm,** the place where half of the axons in the optic nerves (from the eyes) cross from one side of the brain to the other. (See *Figure 4.19.*) The role of the hypothalamus in the control of the four F's (and other behaviors, such as drinking and sleeping) will be considered in several chapters later in this book.

Much of the endocrine system is controlled by hormones produced by cells in the hypothalamus. A special system of blood vessels directly connects the hypothalamus with the **anterior pituitary gland.**

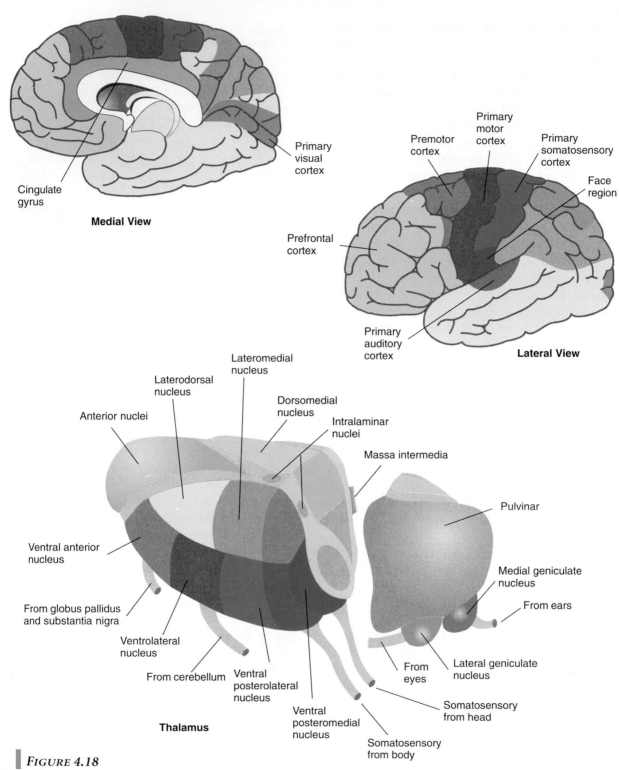

FIGURE 4.18

Some of the nuclei and cortical projection regions of the thalamus.

(Adapted from Netter, F. H. *The CIBA Collection of Medical Illustrations. Vol. I: Nervous System. Part I: Anatomy and Physiology.* Summit, N. J.: CIBA Pharmaceutical Products Co., 1983.)

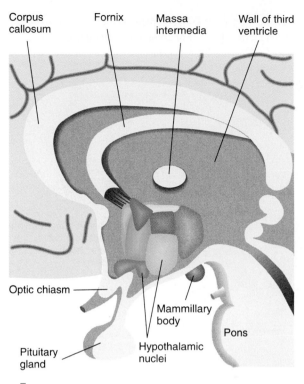

Corpus callosum — Fornix — Massa intermedia — Wall of third ventricle

Optic chiasm

Mammillary body

Pons

Pituitary gland

Hypothalamic nuclei

FIGURE 4.19

The regions of the hypothalamus in a human brain.

(See *Figure 4.20.*) The hypothalamic hormones are secreted by specialized neurons called **neurosecretory cells,** located near the base of the pituitary stalk. These hormones stimulate the anterior pituitary gland to secrete its hormones. For example, *gonadotropin-releasing hormone* causes the anterior pituitary gland to secrete the *gonadotropic hormones,* which play a role in reproductive physiology and behavior.

Most of the hormones secreted by the anterior pituitary gland control other endocrine glands. Because of this function, the anterior pituitary gland has been called the body's "master gland." For example, the gonadotropic hormones stimulate the gonads (ovaries and testes) to release male or female sex hormones. These hormones affect cells throughout the body, including some in the brain. Two other anterior pituitary hormones—prolactin and somatotropic hormone (growth hormone)—do not control other glands but act as the final messenger. The behavioral effects of many of the anterior pituitary hormones are discussed in later chapters.

The hypothalamus also produces the hormones of the **posterior pituitary gland** and controls their secretion. These hormones include oxytocin, which stimulates ejection of milk and uterine contractions at the time of childbirth, and vasopressin, which regulates urine output by the kidneys. They are produced by neurons in the hypothalamus whose axons travel down the pituitary stalk and terminate in the posterior pituitary gland. The hormones are carried in vesicles through the axoplasm of these neurons and collect in the terminal buttons in the posterior pituitary gland. When these axons fire, the hormone contained within their terminal buttons is liberated and enters the circulatory system.

The Mesencephalon

The **midbrain** (also called the **mesencephalon**) surrounds the cerebral aqueduct and consists of two major parts: the tectum and the tegmentum.

Tectum

The **tectum** ("roof") is located in the dorsal portion of the mesencephalon. Its principal structures are the **superior colliculi** and **inferior colliculi,** which appear as four bumps on the surface of the **brain stem.** The brain stem includes the diencephalon, midbrain, and hindbrain, and it is so called because it looks just like that—a stem. (See *Figure 4.21.*) The inferior colliculi are a part of the auditory system. The superior colliculi are part of the visual system. In mammals they are primarily involved in visual reflexes and reactions to moving stimuli.

Tegmentum

The **tegmentum** ("covering") consists of the portion of the mesencephalon beneath the tectum. It includes the rostral end of the reticular formation, several nuclei controlling eye movements, the periaqueductal gray matter, the red nucleus, the substantia nigra, and the ventral tegmental area. (See *Figure 4.22.*)

The **reticular formation** is a large structure consisting of many nuclei (over ninety in all). It is also characterized by a diffuse, interconnected network of neurons with complex dendritic and axonal processes. (Indeed, *reticulum* means "little net" ; early

FIGURE 4.20

The pituitary gland. Hormones released by the neurosecretory cells in the hypothalamus enter capillaries and are conveyed to the anterior pituitary gland, where they control its secretion of hormones. The hormones of the posterior pituitary gland are produced in the hypothalamus and transported there in vesicles through axons.

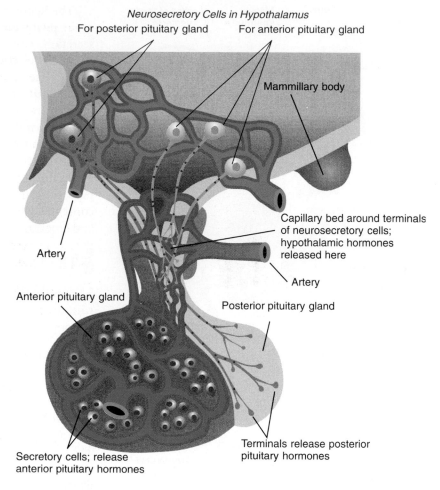

Neurosecretory Cells in Hypothalamus
For posterior pituitary gland   For anterior pituitary gland

Mammillary body

Capillary bed around terminals of neurosecretory cells; hypothalamic hormones released here

Artery

Artery

Anterior pituitary gland

Posterior pituitary gland

Terminals release posterior pituitary hormones

Secretory cells; release anterior pituitary hormones

anatomists were struck by the netlike appearance of the reticular formation.) The reticular formation occupies the core of the brain stem, from the lower border of the medulla to the upper border of the midbrain. (See *Figure 4.22.*) The reticular formation receives sensory information by means of various pathways and projects axons to the cerebral cortex, thalamus, and spinal cord. It plays a role in sleep and arousal, attention, muscle tonus, movement, and various vital reflexes. Its functions will be described more fully in later chapters.

The **periaqueductal gray matter** is so called because it consists mostly of cell bodies of neurons ("gray matter," as contrasted with the "white matter" of axon bundles) that surround the cerebral aqueduct as it travels from the third to the fourth ventricle. The periaqueductal gray matter contains neural circuits that control sequences of movements that constitute species-typical behaviors, such as fighting and mating. As we will see in Chapter 7, opiates such as morphine decrease an organism's sensitivity to pain by stimulating receptors on neurons located in this region.

The **red nucleus** and **substantia nigra** ("black substance") are important components of the motor system. A bundle of axons that arises from the red nucleus constitutes one of the two major fiber systems that bring motor information from the brain to the spinal cord. The substantia nigra contains dopamine-secreting neurons that project to the caudate nucleus. As we have seen, degeneration of these neurons causes Parkinson's disease.

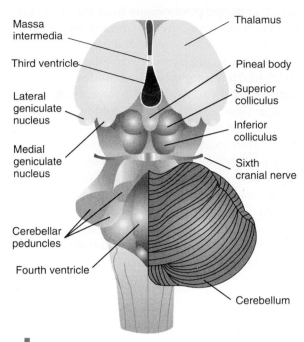

FIGURE 4.21

The attachment of the cerebellum to the human brain stem. Only the right cerebellar hemisphere is shown; the left has been removed to show its site of attachment to the pons.

The Hindbrain

The **hindbrain,** which surrounds the fourth ventricle, consists of two major divisions: the metencephalon and the myelencephalon.

Metencephalon

The metencephalon consists of the cerebellum and the pons.

Cerebellum. The **cerebellum** ("little brain") resembles a miniature version of the cerebrum. It is covered by **cerebellar cortex** and has a set of **deep cerebellar nuclei** that project to its cortex and receive projections from it, just as the thalamic nuclei connect with the cerebral cortex. Figure 4.21 shows the brain stem with the cerebellum dissected away on one side to illustrate the superior, middle, and inferior **cerebellar peduncles** ("little feet"), bundles of

white matter that connect the cerebellum to the pons. (See *Figure 4.21.*)

Damage to the cerebellum impairs standing, walking, or performance of coordinated movements. (A virtuoso pianist or other performing musician owes much to his or her cerebellum.) The cerebellum receives visual, auditory, vestibular, and somatosensory information, and it also receives information about individual muscle movements being directed by the brain. The cerebellum integrates this information and modifies the motor outflow, exerting a coordinating and smoothing effect on the movements. Cerebellar damage results in jerky, poorly coordinated, exaggerated movements; extensive cerebellar damage makes it impossible even to stand.

Pons. The **pons,** a large bulge in the brain stem, lies between the mesencephalon and medulla oblongata, immediately ventral to the cerebellum. (*Pons* means "bridge," but it does not really look like one. See *Figure 4.13.*) The pons contains, in its core, a portion of the reticular formation, including some nuclei that appear to be important in sleep and arousal.

Myelencephalon

The myelencephalon contains one major structure, the **medulla oblongata** (literally, "oblong marrow"),

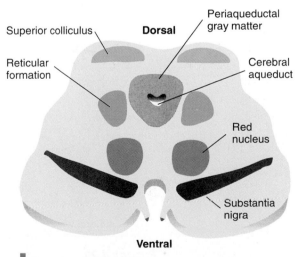

FIGURE 4.22

A cross section through the human tegmentum.

usually just called the *medulla.* This structure is the most caudal portion of the brain stem; its lower border is the rostral end of the spinal cord. (See *Figure 4.13.*) The medulla contains part of the reticular formation, including nuclei that control vital functions such as regulation of the cardiovascular system, respiration, and skeletal muscle tonus.

The Spinal Cord

The **spinal cord** is a long, conical structure, approximately as thick as our little finger. The principal function of the spinal cord is to distribute motor fibers to the effector organs of the body (glands and muscles) and to collect somatosensory information to be passed on to the brain. The spinal cord also has a certain degree of autonomy from the brain; various reflexive control circuits (some of which are described in Chapter 8) are located there.

The spinal cord is protected by the vertebral column, which is composed of twenty-four individual vertebrae of the *cervical* (neck), *thoracic* (chest), and *lumbar* (lower back) regions, and the fused vertebrae making up the *sacral* and *coccygeal* portions of the column (located in the pelvic region). The spinal cord passes through a hole in each of the vertebrae (the *spinal foramens*). **Figure 4.23** illustrates the divisions and structures of the spinal cord and vertebral column. Note that the spinal cord is only about two-thirds as long as the vertebral column; the rest of the space is filled by a mass of **spinal roots** composing the **cauda equina** ("mare's tail").

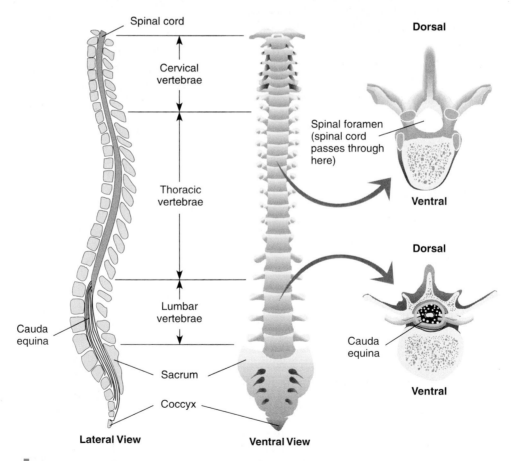

FIGURE 4.23

The human spinal column, with details showing the anatomy of the vertebrae and the relation between the spinal cord and spinal column.

Early in embryological development the vertebral column and spinal cord are the same length. As development progresses, the vertebral column grows faster than the spinal cord. This differential growth rate causes the spinal roots to be displaced downward; the most caudal roots travel the farthest before they emerge through openings between the vertebrae and thus compose the cauda equina. To produce the **caudal block** sometimes used in pelvic surgery or childbirth, a local anesthetic can be injected into the CSF contained within the sac of dura mater surrounding the cauda equina. The drug blocks conduction in the axons of the cauda equina.

Small bundles of fibers emerge from the spinal cord in two straight lines along its dorsolateral and ventrolateral surfaces. Groups of these bundles fuse together and become the thirty-one paired sets of **dorsal roots** and **ventral roots.** The dorsal and ventral roots join together as they pass through the intervertebral foramens and become spinal nerves. Figure 4.24 illustrates a cross section of the spinal column taken between two adjacent vertebrae, showing the junction of the dorsal and ventral roots in the intervertebral foramens. (See *Figure 4.24.*)

The spinal cord, like the brain, consists of white matter and gray matter. Unlike the brain's, its white matter (consisting of ascending and descending bundles of myelinated axons) is on the outside; the gray matter (mostly neural cell bodies and short, unmyelinated axons) is on the inside.

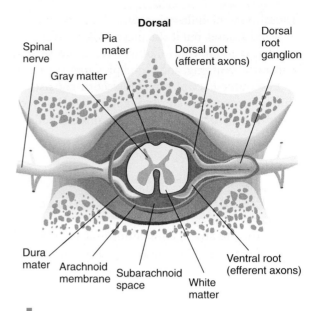

▌ *FIGURE 4.24*

A cross section through a vertebra, showing the spinal cord, dorsal and ventral roots, and spinal nerves.

||||||| *INTERIM SUMMARY*

The central nervous system consists of three major divisions, organized around the three chambers of the tube that develops early in embryonic life: the forebrain, the midbrain, and the hindbrain. The development of the CNS is illustrated in Figure 4.9, and Table 4.1 outlines the major divisions and subdivisions of the brain.

The forebrain, which surrounds the lateral and third ventricles, consists of the telencephalon and diencephalon. The telencephalon contains the cerebral cortex, the limbic system, and the basal ganglia. The cerebral cortex is organized into the frontal, parietal, temporal, and occipital lobes. The central sulcus divides the frontal lobe, which deals specifically with movement and the planning of movement, from the other three lobes, which deal primarily with perceiving and learning. The limbic system, which includes the limbic cortex, the hippocampus, and the amygdala, is involved in emotion, motivation, and learning. The basal ganglia participate in the control of movement. The diencephalon consists of the thalamus, which directs information to and from the cerebral cortex, and the hypothalamus, which controls the endocrine system and modulates species-typical behaviors.

The midbrain, which surrounds the cerebral aqueduct, consists of the tectum and tegmentum. The tectum is involved in audition and the control of visual reflexes and reactions to moving stimuli. The tegmentum contains the reticular formation, which is important in sleep, arousal, and movement; the periaqueductal gray matter, which controls various species-typical behaviors; and the red nucleus and the substantia nigra, both parts of the motor system. The hindbrain, which surrounds the fourth ventricle, contains the cerebellum, the pons, and the medulla. The cerebellum plays an important role in integrating and coordinating movements. The pons contains some nuclei that are important in sleep and arousal. The medulla oblongata, too, is involved in sleep and arousal, but it also plays a role in control of movement and in control of vital functions such as heart rate, breathing, and blood pressure.

The outer part of the spinal cord consists of white matter: axons conveying information up or down. The central gray matter contains cell bodies.

THE PERIPHERAL NERVOUS SYSTEM

The brain and spinal cord communicate with the rest of the body via the cranial nerves and spinal nerves. These nerves are part of the peripheral nervous system, which conveys sensory information to the central nervous system and conveys messages from the central nervous system to the body's muscles and glands.

Spinal Nerves

The **spinal nerves** begin at the junction of the dorsal and ventral roots of the spinal cord. The nerves leave the vertebral column and travel to the muscles or sensory receptors they innervate, branching repeatedly as they go. Branches of spinal nerves often follow blood vessels, especially those branches that innervate skeletal muscles. *Figure 4.25* is a dorsal view of a human, showing a few branches of the spinal nerves.

Now let us consider the pathways by which sensory information enters the spinal cord and motor information leaves it. The cell bodies of all axons that bring sensory information into the brain and spinal cord are located outside the CNS. (The sole exception is the visual system; the retina of the eye is actually a part of the brain.) These incoming axons are referred to as **afferent axons** because they "bear toward" the CNS. The cell bodies that give rise to the axons that bring somatosensory information to the spinal cord reside in the **dorsal root ganglia,** rounded swellings of the dorsal root. (See *Figure 4.24.*) These neurons are of the unipolar type (described in Chapter 2). The axonal stalk divides close to the cell body, sending one limb into the spinal

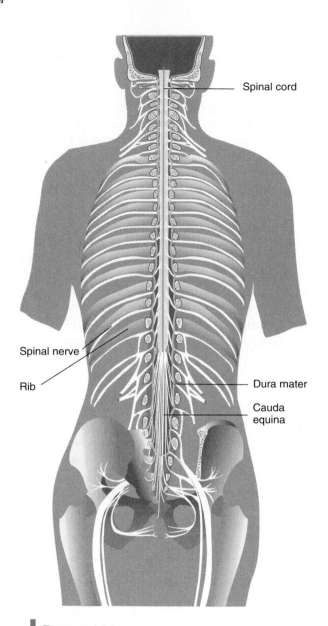

Spinal cord

Spinal nerve

Rib

Dura mater

Cauda equina

FIGURE 4.25

A dorsal view of the human spinal cord and some of the principal spinal nerves.

cord and the other limb out to the sensory organ. Note that all of the axons in the dorsal root convey somatosensory information.

Cell bodies that give rise to the ventral root are located within the gray matter of the spinal cord. The axons of these multipolar neurons leave the spinal cord via a ventral root, which joins a dorsal root to make a spinal nerve. The axons that leave the spinal cord through the ventral roots control muscles and glands. They are referred to as **efferent axons** because they "bear away from" the CNS.

Cranial Nerves

Twelve pairs of **cranial nerves** leave the ventral surface of the brain. Most of these nerves serve sensory and motor functions of the head and neck region. One of them, the *tenth,* or **vagus nerve,** regulates the functions of organs in the thoracic and abdominal cavities. It is called the *vagus* ("wandering") nerve because its branches wander throughout the thoracic and abdominal cavities. (The word *vagabond*

has the same root.) Figure 4.26 presents a view of the base of the brain and illustrates the cranial nerves and the structures they serve. Note that efferent (motor) fibers are drawn as solid lines and that afferent (sensory) fibers are drawn as broken lines. (See *Figure 4.26* and *Table 4.2.*)

As I mentioned in the previous section, cell bodies of sensory nerve fibers that enter the brain and spinal cord (except for the visual system) are located outside the central nervous system. Somatosensory information (and the sense of taste) is received, via the cranial nerves, from unipolar neurons. Auditory, vestibular, and visual information is received via fibers of bipolar neurons (described in Chapter 2).

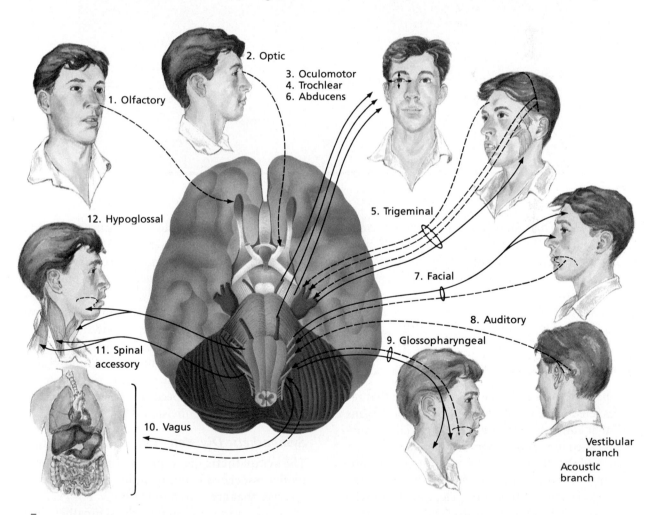

FIGURE 4.26

The twelve pairs of cranial nerves and the regions they serve. Solid lines denote axons that control muscles or glands; broken lines denote sensory axons.

TABLE 4.2

The Cranial Nerves and Their Functions

Number	Name	Function*
1	Olfactory	Olfaction (smell) S
2	Optic	Vision S
3	Occulomotor	Eye movements, control of pupil and lens, tears MP
4	Trochlear	Eye movements M
5	Trigeminal	Facial sensations, chewing SM
6	Abducens	Eye movements M
7	Facial	Facial muscles, salivary glands, taste SMP
8	Auditory	Acoustic branch: audition S Vestibular branch: balance S
9	Glossopharyngeal	Throat muscles, salivary glands, taste SMP
10	Vagus	Parasympathetic control of internal organs, sensation from internal organs, taste SMP
11	Spinal accessory	Head and neck muscles M
12	Hypoglossal	Tongue and neck muscles M

* S, sensory; M, motor; P, parasympathetic functions.

Olfactory information is received via the **olfactory bulbs,** which receive information from the olfactory receptors in the nose. The olfactory bulbs are complex structures containing a considerable amount of neural circuitry; actually, they are part of the brain. Sensory mechanisms are described in more detail in Chapters 6 and 7.

The Autonomic Nervous System

The part of the peripheral nervous system that receives sensory information from the sensory organs and that controls movements of the skeletal muscles is called the **somatic nervous system.** The other branch of the peripheral nervous system—the **autonomic nervous system** (ANS)—is concerned with regulation of smooth muscle, cardiac muscle, and glands. (*Autonomic* means "self-governing.") Smooth muscle is found in the skin (associated with hair follicles), in blood vessels, in the eyes (controlling pupil size and accommodation of the lens), and

in the walls and sphincters of the gut, gallbladder, and urinary bladder. Merely describing the organs innervated by the autonomic nervous system suggests the function of this system: regulation of "vegetative processes" in the body.

The ANS consists of two anatomically separate systems, the *sympathetic division* and the *parasympathetic division*. With few exceptions, organs of the body are innervated by both of these subdivisions, and each has a different effect. For example, the sympathetic division speeds the heart rate, whereas the parasympathetic division slows it.

Sympathetic Division of the ANS

The **sympathetic division** is most involved in activities associated with expenditure of energy from reserves that are stored in the body. For example, when an organism is excited, the sympathetic nervous system increases blood flow to skeletal muscles, stimulates the secretion of epinephrine (resulting in increased heart rate and a rise in blood sugar level), and causes piloerection (erection of fur in mammals that have it and production of "goose bumps" in humans).

The cell bodies of sympathetic motor neurons are located in the gray matter of the thoracic and lumbar regions of the spinal cord (hence the sympathetic nervous system is also known as the *thoracolumbar system*). The fibers of these neurons exit via the ventral roots. After joining the spinal nerves, the fibers branch off and pass into **spinal sympathetic ganglia** (not to be confused with the dorsal root ganglia). Figure 4.27 shows the relation of these ganglia to the spinal cord. Note that the various spinal sympathetic ganglia are connected to the neighboring ganglia above and below, thus forming the **sympathetic chain.** (See *Figure 4.27.*)

The axons that leave the spinal cord through the ventral root are part of the **preganglionic neurons.** With one exception, all sympathetic preganglionic axons enter the ganglia of the sympathetic chain, but not all of them synapse there. (The exception is the medulla of the adrenal gland, described in the following paragraph.) Some axons leave and travel to one of the other sympathetic ganglia, located among the internal organs. All sympathetic preganglionic axons form synapses with neurons located in one of the ganglia. The neurons with which they form synapses are called **postganglionic neurons.** In turn, the postganglionic neurons send axons to the target organs, such as the intestines, stomach, kidneys, or sweat glands. (See *Figure 4.27.*)

The sympathetic nervous system controls the **adrenal medulla,** a set of cells located in the center of the adrenal gland. The adrenal medulla closely resembles a sympathetic ganglion. It is innervated by preganglionic axons, and its secretory cells are very similar to postganglionic sympathetic neurons. These cells secrete epinephrine and norepinephrine when they are stimulated. These hormones function chiefly as an adjunct to the direct neural effects of sympathetic activity; for example, they increase blood flow to the muscles and cause stored nutrients to be broken down into glucose within skeletal muscle cells, thus increasing the energy available to these cells.

All synapses within the sympathetic ganglia are acetylcholinergic; the terminal buttons on the target organs, belonging to the postganglionic axons, are noradrenergic. (An exception to this rule is provided by the sweat glands, which are innervated by acetylcholinergic terminal buttons.)

Parasympathetic Division of the ANS

The **parasympathetic division** of the autonomic nervous system supports activities that are involved with increases in the body's supply of stored energy. These activities include salivation, gastric and intestinal motility, secretion of digestive juices, and increased blood flow to the gastrointestinal system.

Cell bodies that give rise to preganglionic axons in the parasympathetic nervous system are located in two regions: the nuclei of some of the cranial nerves (especially the vagus nerve) and the intermediate horn of the gray matter in the sacral region of the spinal cord. Thus, the parasympathetic division of the ANS has often been referred to as the *craniosacral system.* Parasympathetic ganglia are located in the immediate vicinity of the target organs; the postganglionic fibers are therefore relatively short. The terminal buttons of both preganglionic and postganglionic neurons in the parasympathetic nervous system secrete acetylcholine.

⦀ INTERIM SUMMARY

The spinal nerves and the cranial nerves convey sensory axons into the central nervous system and motor axons out from it. Spinal nerves are formed by the junctions of the dorsal roots, which contain incoming (afferent) axons, and the ventral roots, which contain outgoing (efferent) axons. The autonomic nervous system consists of two divisions: the sympathetic division, which controls activities that occur during excitement or exertion, such as increased heart rate; and the parasympathetic division, which controls activities that occur during relaxation, such as decreased heart rate and increased activity of the digestive system. The pathways of the autonomic nervous system contain preganglionic axons, from the brain or spinal cord to the sympathetic or parasympathetic ganglia, and postganglionic axons, from the ganglia to the target organ. The adrenal medulla, which secretes epinephrine and norepinephrine, is controlled by axons of the sympathetic nervous system.

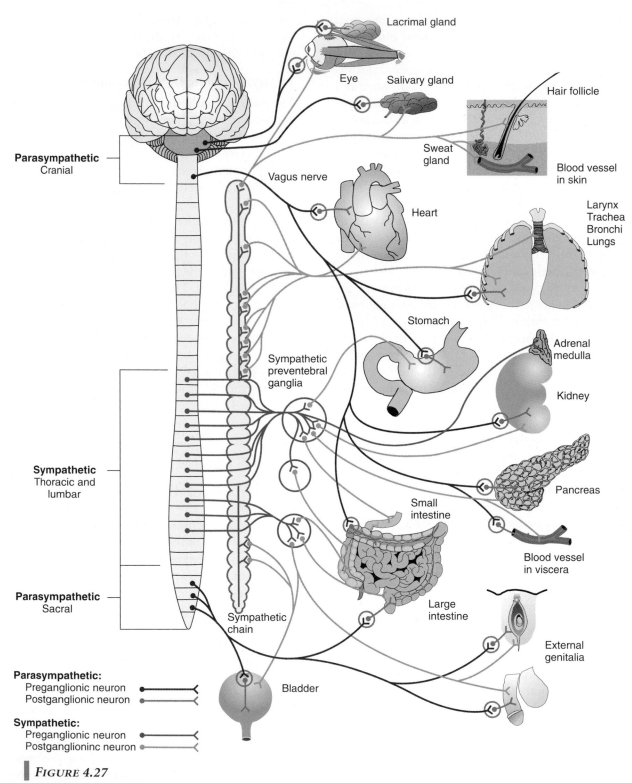

Parasympathetic
Cranial

Lacrimal gland

Eye   Salivary gland

Hair follicle

Sweat gland

Blood vessel in skin

Vagus nerve

Heart

Larynx
Trachea
Bronchi
Lungs

Stomach

Adrenal medulla

Kidney

Sympathetic preventebral ganglia

Pancreas

Small intestine

Blood vessel in viscera

Sympathetic
Thoracic and lumbar

Large intestine

Parasympathetic
Sacral

Sympathetic chain

External genitalia

Parasympathetic:
  Preganglionic neuron
  Postganglionic neuron

Bladder

Sympathetic:
  Preganglionic neuron
  Postganglioninc neuron

FIGURE 4.27

The autonomic nervous system and the target organs it serves.

New Terms

Basic Features of the Nervous System

neuraxis p. 78

anterior p. 78

posterior p. 78

rostral p. 78

caudal p. 78

dorsal p. 78

ventral p. 78

lateral p. 78

medial p. 78

ipsilateral p. 78

contralateral p. 78

cross section p. 78

frontal section p. 78

horizontal section p. 78

sagittal section (*SAJ i tul*) p. 78

central nervous system p. 78

peripheral nervous system p. 78

vertebral artery (*ver TEE brul*) p. 80

internal carotid artery p. 80

meninges (*men IN jees*) p. 81

dura mater p. 81

arachnoid membrane (*a RAK noyd*) p. 81

pia mater p. 81

subarachnoid space p. 81

cerebrospinal fluid p. 81

ventricle (*VEN trik ul*) p. 82

cerebral aqueduct p. 82

fourth ventricle p. 82

choroid plexus p. 82

hydrocephalus p. 83

The Central Nervous System

forebrain p. 88

subcortical region p. 88

cerebral cortex p. 88

sulcus (plural: sulci) (*SUL kus, SUL sigh*) p. 88

fissure p. 88

gyrus (plural: gyri) (*JY russ*) p. 88

frontal lobe p. 88

parietal lobe (*pa RY i tul*) p. 88

temporal lobe (*TEM por ul*) p. 88

occipital lobe (*ok SIP i tul*) p. 88

central sulcus p. 88

lateral fissure p. 88

neocortex p. 88

limbic cortex p. 88

cingulate gyrus (*SING yew lett*) p. 88

corpus callosum (*ka LOH sum*) p. 88

commissure (*KAHM i sher*) p. 88

primary motor cortex p. 90

primary somatosensory cortex p. 90

primary visual cortex p. 90

primary auditory cortex p. 90

association cortex p. 90

limbic system p. 91

hippocampus p. 91

amygdala (*a MIG da la*) p. 91

basal ganglia p. 92

diencephalon (*dy en SEFF a lahn*) p. 92

thalamus p. 92

projection fiber p. 92

nuclei p. 93

lateral geniculate nucleus p. 93

medial geniculate nucleus p. 93

ventrolateral nucleus p. 93

hypothalamus p. 93

optic chiasm (*KY az'm*) p. 93

anterior pituitary gland p. 93

neurosecretory cell p. 95

posterior pituitary gland p. 95

midbrain p. 95

mesencephalon (*mezz en SEFF a lahn*) p. 95

tectum p. 95

superior colliculi p. 95

inferior colliculi p. 95

brain stem p. 95

tegmentum p. 95

reticular formation p. 95

periaqueductal gray matter p. 96

red nucleus p. 96

substantia nigra p. 96

hindbrain p. 97

cerebellum p. 97

cerebellar cortex p. 97

deep cerebellar nuclei p. 97

cerebellar peduncle (*PEE dun kul*) p. 97

pons p. 97

medulla oblongata (*me DOO la*) p. 97

spinal cord p. 98

spinal root p. 98

cauda equina (*ee KWIGH na*) p. 98

caudal block p. 99

dorsal root p. 99

ventral root p. 99

The Peripheral Nervous System

spinal nerve p. 100

afferent axon p. 100

dorsal root ganglia p. 100

efferent axon (*EFF ur ent or EE fair ent*) p. 101

cranial nerve p. 101

vagus nerve p. 101

olfactory bulb p. 102

somatic nervous system p. 102

autonomic nervous system p. 102

sympathetic division p. 102

spinal sympathetic ganglia p. 103

sympathetic chain p. 103

preganglionic neuron p. 103

postganglionic neuron p. 103

adrenal medulla p. 103

parasympathetic division p. 103

parasympathetic division p. 103

Suggested Readings

Brodal, A. Neurological Anatomy in Relation to Clinical Medicine. Oxford: Oxford University Press, 1981.

Diamond, M.C., Scheibel, A.B., and Elson, L.M. *The Human Brain Coloring Book.* New York: Barnes & Noble, 1985.

Gluhbegovic, N., and Williams, T.H. *The Human Brain: A Photographic Guide.* New York: Harper & Row, 1980.

Haines, D.E. *Neuroanatomy: An Atlas of Structures, Sec-tions, and Systems,* 3rd ed. Baltimore: Urban and Schwarzenberg, 1991.

Nauta, W.J.H., and Feirtag, M. *Fundamental Neu-roanatomy.* New York: W.H. Freeman, 1986.

Netter, F.H. *The CIBA Collection of Medical Illustrations. Vol. 1: Nervous System. Part 1: Anatomy and Physiology.* Summit, N.J.: CIBA Pharmaceutical Products Co., 1983.

CHAPTER 5

Methods of Physiological Psychology

Neuroanatomical and Neurochemical Techniques
- Histological Procedures
- Tracing Neural Connections
- Tracing Connections in the Human Brain
- Localization of Neurochemicals
- Localization of Receptors
- Measuring Metabolic Activity
- Study of the Living Human Brain
- Analyzing Chemicals in the Interstitial Fluid
- Electron Microscopy
  Interim Summary

Experimental Ablation
- Evaluating the Behavioral Effects of Brain Damage
- Producing Brain Lesions
- Stereotaxic Surgery

Recording the Brain's Electrical Activity
- Rationale
- Electrodes
- Output Devices

Stimulating or Inhibiting Neural Activity
- Electrical and Chemical Stimulation
- Microiontophoresis
- Behavioral Effects of Electrical Brain Stimulation
  Interim Summary

STUDY OF THE PHYSIOLOGY OF BEHAVIOR involves the efforts of scientists in many disciplines, including physiology, neuroanatomy, biochemistry, psychology, endocrinology, and histology. To pursue a research project in physiological psychology requires competence in many experimental techniques. Because different procedures often produce contradictory results, investigators must be familiar with the advantages and limitations of the methods they employ. Scientific investigation entails a process of asking questions of nature. The method that is used frames the question. Often we receive a puzzling answer, only to realize later that we were not asking the question we thought we were. As we will see, the best conclusions about the physiology of behavior are made by comparing the results of studies that approach the problem with different methods. The use of two or more different methods to study a particular problem is called **converging operations.** I will have more to say about this topic in the interim summary at the end of this chapter, after I have described the individual methods.

NEUROANATOMICAL AND NEURO-CHEMICAL TECHNIQUES

IF WE WANT TO KNOW HOW THE BRAIN WORKS, we have to know something about its anatomy and chemistry. Neuroanatomical techniques provide us information about the structure of the brain, and neurochemical techniques tell us about the chemical reactions that take place there.

Histological Procedures

The gross anatomy of the brain was described long ago, and everything that could be identified was given a name. As we saw in Chapter 4, many of these names, such as amygdala ("almond") or hippocampus ("sea horse"), described the general shape of the structures. Detailed anatomical information about the brain requires more than dissection and simple observation; it requires the use of various *histological* (tissue-preparing) techniques. As we have seen, the brain consists of many billions of neurons and

glial cells, the nerve cells forming distinct nuclei and fiber bundles. We cannot possibly see the details of cell structure and connections between neurons by gross examination of the brain. And even a microscope is useless without fixation, sectioning, and staining of the neural tissue.

Fixation

If we hope to study the tissue in the form it had at the time of the organism's death, we must destroy the autolytic enzymes (*autolytic* means "self-dissolving"), which will otherwise turn the tissue into shapeless mush. The tissue must also be preserved to prevent its decomposition by bacteria or molds. To achieve both of these objectives, we place the neural tissue in a **fixative.** The most commonly used fixative is **formalin,** an aqueous solution of formaldehyde, a gas. Formalin halts autolysis, hardens the very soft and fragile brain, and kills any microorganisms that might destroy it.

Before the brain is fixed (that is, put into a fixative solution), it is usually perfused. **Perfusion** of tissue (literally, "a pouring through") entails removal of the blood and its replacement with another fluid. The animal's brain is perfused because better histological results are obtained when there is no blood present in the tissue. The animal whose brain is to be studied is humanely killed with an overdose of a general anesthetic. Blood vessels are opened so that the blood can be drained from them and replaced with a dilute salt solution. The brain is removed from the skull and placed in a jar containing the fixative.

Once the brain has been fixed, the investigator must slice it into thin sections and stain various cellular structures in order to see anatomical details. Some procedures require that the tissue be stained before being sliced, but the techniques that physiological psychologists most commonly use call for sectioning first and then staining. Therefore, I will describe the procedures in that order.

Sectioning

A **microtome** is used to slice neural tissue. This device (literally, "that which slices small") is an instrument capable of slicing tissue into very thin sections. Sections prepared for examination under a light microscope are typically 10 to 80 μm in thickness; those prepared for the electron microscope are generally cut at less than l μm. Electron microscopy will be discussed later in this chapter.

A microtome contains three parts: a knife, a platform on which to mount the tissue, and a mechanism that advances the knife (or the platform) the correct amount after each slice, so that another section can be cut. Figure 5.1 shows a microtome. The knife holder slides forward on an oiled rail and takes a section off the top of the tissue mounted on the platform. The platform automatically rises by a predetermined amount as the knife and holder are pushed back. (See *Figure 5.1.*)

Slicing brain tissue is not quite as simple as it might at first appear. As I mentioned, raw neural tissue is very soft. Fixation in formalin will harden the brain somewhat, but it is still too soft to cut. Either of two techniques can be used to make the tissue hard enough to cut thinly: *freezing* or *embedding*.

Freezing is simplest. The tissue is chilled with a refrigeration device. Often the brain is first soaked in a sucrose (table sugar) solution, which minimizes tissue damage by preventing the formation of large ice crystals as the brain freezes. The temperature of the brain must be carefully regulated; if the block of brain tissue is too cold, the tissue will shatter into little fragments. If it is too warm, a layer of tissue will be torn off rather than sliced off.

A brain can also be embedded in materials that are of sliceable consistency at room temperature, such as paraffin or nitrocellulose. Paraffin comes in various grades, according to the room temperature at which it can best be sliced. The brain is first soaked in a solvent for paraffin (such as xylene) and is then soaked in successively stronger solutions of paraffin that are kept melted in an oven. The brain is then placed in a small container of liquid paraffin, which is allowed to cool and harden. The entire block is sliced, the paraffin providing the physical support for the tissue.

After the tissue is cut, the slices are usually mounted on glass microscope slides with an agent such as albumin (protein extracted from egg whites). The slides are dried and heated, making the albumin insoluble and cementing the tissue sections to the glass. The tissue can then be stained by putting the entire slide into various chemical solutions. The stained and mounted sections are covered

FIGURE 5.1

A microtome.

with a mounting medium, and a very thin glass coverslip is placed over the sections. The mounting medium (which is thick and resinous) gradually dries out, keeping the coverslip in position.

Staining

If you looked at an unstained section of brain tissue under a microscope, you would be able to see the outlines of some large cellular masses and the more prominent fiber bundles. However, no fine details would be revealed. For this reason, the study of microscopic neuroanatomy requires special histological stains. Three basic types of stains are used for neural tissue: those that reveal cell bodies by interacting with the contents of the cytoplasm, those that selectively color myelin sheaths, and those that stain the cell membrane (of the entire cell or just the axons). In addition, stains have been found that selectively color certain chemicals in the brain, including transmitter substances.

Cell-Body Stains. In the late nineteenth century Franz Nissl, a German neurologist, discovered that methylene blue, a dye derived from the distillation of coal tar, would stain the cell bodies of brain tissue. The material that takes up the dye, known as the **Nissl substance,** consists of RNA, DNA, and associated proteins located in the nucleus and scattered, in the form of granules, in the cytoplasm. Many dyes can be used to stain cell bodies, but the most frequently used is cresyl violet. The dyes were not developed for histological purposes but were originally manufactured for use in dyeing cloth.

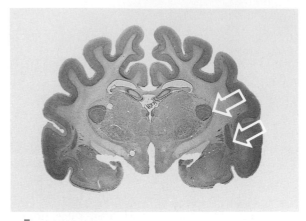

FIGURE 5.2

A frontal section of a cat brain, stained with cresyl violet, a cell-body stain. The arrowheads point to nuclei, or groups of cell bodies.

(Histological material courtesy of Mary Carlson.)

The discovery of cell-body stains (also called *Nissl stains*) made it possible to identify nuclear masses in the brain. Figure 5.2 shows a frontal section of a cat brain stained with cresyl violet. Note that you can observe fiber bundles by their lighter appearance; they do not take up the stain. (See *Figure 5.2.*) The stain is not selective for *neural* cell bodies; all cells are stained, neurons and glia alike. It is up to the investigators to determine which is which—by size, shape, and location.

Myelin Stains. **Myelin stains** color myelin sheaths. These stains make it possible to identify fiber bundles. (What is light in Figure 5.2 is dark in Figure 5.3.) However, pathways of single fibers cannot be traced. There is simply too much intermingling of the individual fibers. (See *Figure 5.3.*)

Membrane Stains. **Membrane stains** contain salts of various heavy metals, such as silver, uranium, or osmium, that interact with the somatic, dendritic, and axonal membranes. The **Golgi-Cox stain** (which uses silver) is highly selective, staining only a fraction of the neurons in a given region. Why this happens is not known, and this selectivity undoubtedly gives a biased view of the neurons that populate the region. But the selective staining makes it possible to observe the axonal and dendritic branches of individual neurons and to trace details of synaptic interconnections. Figure 5.4 shows the appearance

of individual neurons of the cerebral cortex stained by a new modification of the Golgi-Cox stain. Note the individual neurons and their interconnecting processes. The large cells in the center are oligodendroglia, providing myelin sheaths for the bundles of fibers running horizontally. (See *Figure 5.4.*)

Tracing Neural Connections

The central nervous system contains many billions of neurons, most of which are gathered together in thousands of distinct regions of cerebral cortex or subcortical discrete nuclei. These structures are interconnected by incredibly complex systems of axons. The neuroanatomist's problem is to trace these connections and find out which nuclei are connected to which others and what route is taken by the interconnecting fibers. This problem cannot be resolved by means of histological procedures that stain all neurons, such as cell-body, membrane, or myelin stains. If we look closely at a brain that has been prepared by these means, we see only a tangled mass of neurons. In recent years, very precise methods have been developed so that specific axons being investigated will stand out from all the others.

Tracing Efferent Axons

Suppose an investigator is interested in a particular nucleus in the brain and wants to know what other parts of the brain receive information from the

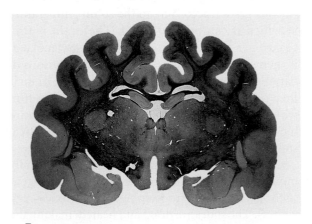

FIGURE 5.3

A frontal section of a cat brain, stained with a myelin stain.

(Histological material courtesy of Mary Carlson.)

FIGURE 5.4

A section of cortex of a cat brain, stained by a modified Golgi-Cox method.

(Histological material courtesy of D.N. Spinelli and J.K Lane.)

nucleus. That is, he or she wants to know to what regions the efferent axons of neurons located in this nucleus go. **Anterograde labeling methods** will supply the answer. *Anterograde* means "moving forward." Anterograde labeling methods employ chemicals that are taken up by dendrites or cell bodies and are transported through the axons toward the terminal buttons.

Over the years, neuroscientists have developed several different methods for tracing the pathways followed by efferent axons. A recently developed method is replacing earlier ones, so I will devote my discussion to this method. Cell biologists have discovered that a family of proteins produced by plants bind with specific complex molecules present in

cells of the immune system. These proteins, called *lectins,* have also found a use in tracing neural pathways. A particular lectin produced by the kidney bean, **PHA-L** (*phaseolus vulgaris leukoagglutinin*), is used to identify efferent axons.

To discover the destination of the efferent axons of neurons located within a particular nucleus, the experimenter injects a minute quantity of PHA-L into that nucleus. The molecules of PHA-L are taken up by dendrites and are transported through the soma to the axon, where they travel by means of fast axoplasmic transport to the terminal buttons. Within a few days, the cells are filled in their entirety with molecules of PHA-L: dendrites, soma, axons and all their branches, and terminal buttons. Then, the experimenter kills the animal, slices the brain, and mounts the sections on microscope slides. A special *immunocytochemical* method is used to make the molecules of PHA-L visible, and the slides are examined under a microscope. (See *Figure 5.5.*)

Immunocytochemical methods take advantage of the immune reaction. The body's immune system has the ability to produce antibodies in response to antigens. *Antigens* are proteins (or peptides), such as those found on the surface of bacteria or viruses. *Antibodies,* which are also proteins, are produced by white blood cells to destroy invading microorganisms. Antibodies are either secreted by white blood cells, or they are located on their surface, in the way neurotransmitter receptors are located on the surface of neurons. When the antigens present on the surface of an invading microorganism come into contact with the antibodies that recognize them, the antibodies trigger an attack on the invader by the white blood cells.

Cell biologists have developed methods for producing antibodies to any peptide or protein. The antibody molecules are attached to various types of dye molecules. Some of these dyes react with other chemicals and stain the tissue a brown color. Others are fluorescent; they emit visible light when they are exposed to ultraviolet light. To determine where the peptide or protein (the antigen) is located in the brain, the investigator places fresh slices of brain tissue in a solution that contains the antibody/dye molecules. The antibodies attach themselves to their antigen. When the investigator examines the slices with a microscope (under ultraviolet light in the

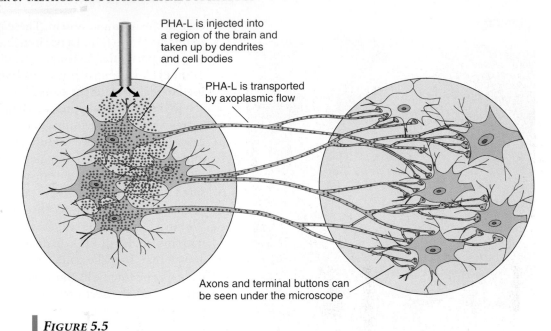

PHA-L is injected into
a region of the brain and
taken up by dendrites
and cell bodies

PHA-L is transported
by axoplasmic flow

Axons and terminal buttons can
be seen under the microscope

FIGURE 5.5

The rationale for the use of PHA-L to trace efferent axons.

case of fluorescent dyes), he or she can see which parts of the brain—even which individual neurons—contain the antigen.

Figure 5.6 shows how PHA-L can be used to identify the efferents of a particular region of the brain. Molecules of this chemical were injected into a nucleus of the forebrain, the *bed nucleus of the stria terminalis* (BNST). Two days later, after the PHA-L had been taken up by the neurons in this region and transported to the ends of their axons, the animal was killed. Slices of the brain were treated with an antibody to PHA-L, attached to a dye that stains the tissue a brown color. Figure 5.6a shows the site of the injection; as you can see, the lectin fills nearby cell bodies and dendrites. (See *Figure 5.6a.*) Figure 5.6b shows a photomicrograph of a portion of the contralateral BNST. As you can see, this region contains some labeled axons and terminal buttons, which proves that some neurons in each BNST communicate with their counterparts on the opposite side of the brain. (See *Figure 5.6.*)

Tracing Afferent Axons

Suppose an investigator wants to know what other parts of the brain provide input to a particular nucleus. The location of the cells whose terminal

buttons form synapses in that nucleus can be revealed through **retrograde labeling methods.** *Retrograde* means "moving backward." Retrograde labeling methods employ chemicals that are taken up by terminal buttons and are carried back through the axons toward the cell bodies.

The method for identifying the afferent inputs to a particular region of the brain is similar to the method used for identifying its efferents. First, a small quantity of a chemical is injected into the region. The chemical is taken up by the terminal buttons and is transported back to the cell body, by means of retrograde axoplasmic transport. Then the animal is killed, the brain is sliced, and special methods are used to show the location of the chemical.

Several different chemicals are currently used as retrograde labels. The most commonly used method uses a dye called **fluorogold.** Molecules of fluorogold are easily visualized in slices of brain tissue; they fluoresce when illuminated with ultraviolet light. Figure 5.7 illustrates the use of the fluorogold as a retrograde tracer. The chemical was injected into the lateral septum, where it was taken up by terminal buttons. The dye was carried back, by retrograde axoplasmic flow, to cell bodies located in the BNST, shown in the photomicrograph. The results

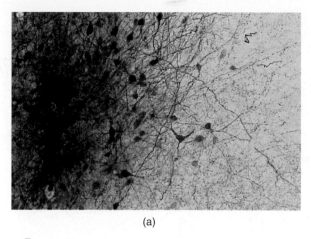

(a)

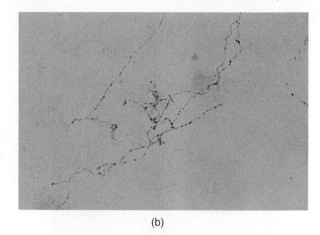

(b)

FIGURE 5.6

An anterograde labeling method. PHA-L was injected into the bed nucleus of the stria terminalis (BNST), where it was taken up by dendrites and carried through the cells' axons to their terminal buttons. (a) The injection site. (b) Labeled axons and terminal buttons in the contralateral BNST.

(Courtesy of Geert DeVries, University of Massachusetts.)

indicate that the lateral septum receives input from the BNST. (See *Figure 5.7.*)

Together, anterograde and retrograde labeling methods permit investigators to discover the source of the inputs to a particular part of the brain and the locations to which that region sends axons. Thus, these techniques help to provide us with a "wiring diagram" of the brain.

Tracing Connections in the Human Brain

The methods of tracing efferent and afferent connections that I just described require that chemicals be injected into the brain of a living animal. Obviously, these methods are not suitable for studying the human brain. Until recently, no method was available for studying detailed connections of the human brain. Now, researchers are able to trace at least some axons in the human brain using **DiI,** a fluorescent carbocyanine dye. After a person dies, the brain is removed and fixed with a formalin solution. Crystals of DiI are placed in the fiber tract being investigated. Molecules of the chemical dissolve in the lipid membranes of the remnants of the axons and travel, through simple diffusion, to the

ends of the axons. When the tissue is examined under ultraviolet light, the chemical fluoresces bright red, revealing the location of the axons. (See *Figure 5.8.*)

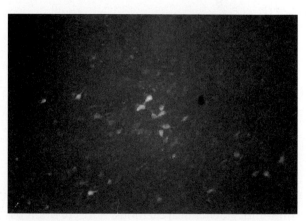

FIGURE 5.7

A retrograde tracing method. Fluorogold was injected in the lateral septum, where it was taken up by terminal buttons and transported back through the axons to their cell bodies. The photograph shows these cell bodies, located in the BNST.

(Courtesy of Hussein Al-Shamma, University of Massachusetts.)

FIGURE 5.8

Axons in the human brain, stained by DiI. These axons travel from the retina to a nucleus in the hypothalamus that plays a role in daily rhythms of behavior and hormone secretion.

(From Friedman, D.I., Johnson, J.K., Chorsky, R.L., and Stopa, E.G. *Brain Research,* 1991, *560,* 297-302. Reprinted with permission.)

Localization of Neurochemicals

To understand the detailed circuitry of the brain, we need to know the location of neurons that produce and secrete particular neurochemicals, including neurotransmitters and neuromodulators. There are three basic ways of localizing neurochemicals in the brain: localizing the *chemicals* themselves, localizing the *enzymes* that produce them, and localizing the *messenger RNA* involved in their synthesis.

Peptides can be localized directly by means of immunocytochemical methods. Slices of brain tissue are exposed to an antibody for the peptide, linked to a dye (usually, a fluorescent dye). The slices are then examined under a microscope using ultraviolet light. For example, Figure 5.9 shows the location of axons in the hypothalamus that contain vasopressin, a peptide neurotransmitter. Two sets of axons are shown. One set, which form a cluster around the third ventricle at the base of the brain, show up as a rusty color. The other set, scattered through the lateral septum, look like strands of gold fibers. (See **Figure 5.9.**)

If the chemical in question is not a peptide, then it is often possible to localize the enzyme that produces it. For example, the synthesis of norepinephrine is made possible by the enzyme dopamine-ß-hydroxylase. Thus, neurons that contain this enzyme almost certainly secrete norepinephrine. Figure 5.10 shows dopaminergic neurons in the pons that have been identified by means of immunocytochemistry; the

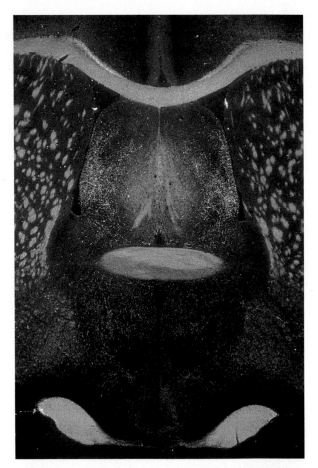

FIGURE 5.9

Localization of a peptide by means of immunocytochemistry. The photomicrograph shows a frontal section through the rat forebrain. The gold- and rust-colored fibers are axons and terminal buttons that contain vasopressin, a peptide neurotransmitter.

(Courtesy of Geert DeVries, University of Massachusetts.)

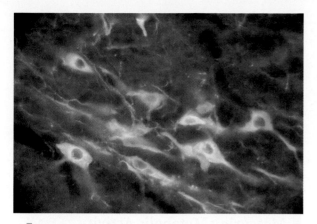

FIGURE 5.10

Localization of an enzyme responsible for the synthesis of a neurotransmitter, revealed by immunocytochemistry. The photomicrograph shows a section through the subcoerulear cell group, located in the pons. The green neurons contain dopamine-ß-hydroxylase, which implies that they produce (and thus secrete) dopamine.

(Courtesy of Paul Sawchenko, Salk Institute.)

brain tissue was exposed to an antibody to dopamine-ß-hydroxylase attached to a fluorescent dye. (See *Figure 5.10.*)

Another indirect way to localize a substance uses a technique known as **in situ hybridization:** All peptides and proteins (which includes all enzymes, of course) are synthesized according to information contained on the chromosomes. When a particular protein is to be produced, the necessary information is copied from a chromosome onto a piece of messenger RNA, which then leaves the nucleus and travels to a ribosome, where protein synthesis takes place. The recipe for the protein is coded as a particular sequence of nucleotide bases that make up the messenger RNA. If this code is known (and in most cases it is), molecular biologists can synthesize a piece of radioactive RNA that contains a sequence of nucleotide bases complementary to the sequence on the messenger RNA. Slices of brain tissue are exposed to the radioactive RNA, which sticks to molecules of the appropriate messenger RNA. Then, the investigator uses a procedure called *autoradiography* to reveal the location of the messenger RNA and, by inference, the location of the protein whose synthesis the RNA initiates.

Autoradiography can be translated roughly as "writing with one's own radiation." Sections of the brain are mounted on microscope slides and are exposed to a solution containing a radioactive antibody for the peptide. The slides are rinsed off, leaving molecules of radioactive RNA in the cells that contain the complementary messenger RNA. The slides are then taken into a darkroom, where they are coated with a photographic emulsion (the substance found on photographic film). Several weeks later, the slides, with their coatings of emulsion, are developed, just like photographic film. The molecules of radioactive RNA show themselves as spots of silver grains in the developed emulsion because the radioactivity exposes the emulsion, just as X-rays or light will do.

Figure 5.11 explains the in situ hybridization method graphically, and Figure 5.12 shows the location of the messenger RNA responsible for the synthesis of a peptide, vasopressin, as revealed by this method. Side lighting of the microscope slide makes the silver grains in the photographic emulsion show up as white spots. (See *Figures 5.11* and *5.12.*)

A very useful property of these methods of localizing neurochemicals is that they can be combined

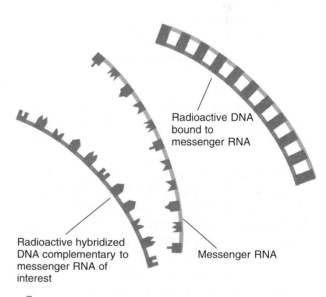

Radioactive DNA bound to messenger RNA

Radioactive hybridized DNA complementary to messenger RNA of interest

Messenger RNA

FIGURE 5.11

An explanation of the use of in situ hybridization to localize messenger RNA that is responsible for the synthesis of a particular protein or peptide.

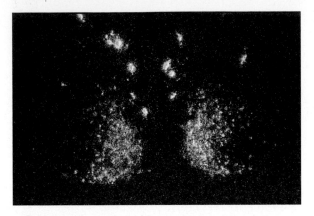

FIGURE 5.12

In situ hybridization. The tissue was exposed to radioactive RNA that binds with the messenger RNA responsible for the synthesis of vasopressin, a peptide. The location of the radioactive RNA, revealed by means of autoradiography, shows up as white spots. The labeled neurons are located in a pair of nuclei in the hypothalamus.

(Courtesy of Geert DeVries, University of Massachusetts.)

with anterograde or retrograde tracers. Thus, investigators not only can determine where particular axons go to or come from, but they can also determine what neurotransmitters these axons secrete or what kind of receptors they contain. This method is called **double labeling.** Figure 5.13 shows a group of neurons in the periaqueductal gray matter. The cells that appear brown have been stained with an immunocytochemical method that reveals the presence of estrogen receptors. The terminal buttons that appear to form synapses with these neurons have been stained with PHA-L, which was injected into the ventrolateral nucleus of the hypothalamus, a region involved in sexual behavior of female rodents. These results tell us that neurons in the periaqueductal gray matter that are sensitive to estrogens (female sex hormones) also receive input from the ventrolateral nucleus of the hypothalamus. (See *Figure 5.13.*)

Localization of Receptors

As we saw in Chapter 3, neurotransmitters, neuromodulators, and hormones convey their messages to their target cells by binding with receptors. The loca-

tion of these receptors can be determined by means of autoradiography. First, slices of brain tissue are exposed to a solution containing a radioactive ligand for a particular receptor. Next, the slices are rinsed, so that the only radioactivity remaining in the slices is that of the molecules of the ligand bound to their receptors. Autoradiographic methods are used to localize the radioactive ligand. Figure 5.14 shows an autoradiograph of a horizontal section of a rat brain that has been exposed to a radioactive ligand for opiate receptors. (See *Figure 5.14.*)

Measuring Metabolic Activity

If the neural activity of a particular region of the brain increases, the metabolic rate increases, too, largely as a result of increased operation of ion pumps in the membrane of the cells in that region. This increased metabolic rate can be measured. The experimenter injects radioactive **2-deoxyglucose** (2-DG) into the animal and permits the radioactive compound to be taken into cells. This chemical is a

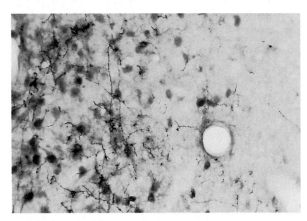

FIGURE 5.13

Double labeling, using immunocytochemistry and anterograde tracing. The photomicrograph shows a slice through the periaqueductal gray matter of a guinea pig. The tissue has been treated with an antibody to estradiol receptor protein; a dye label attached to the antibody makes the cells that contain these receptors show up as brown. The purple-colored axons and terminal buttons are labeled with PHA-L, which was injected into the ventrolateral nucleus of the hypothalamus.

(Courtesy of Kirsten Nielsen Ricciardi, University of Massachusetts.)

metabolic rate. Chapter 9 describes these nuclei and their function. (See *Figure 5.15.*)

Another method of identifying active regions of the brain capitalizes on the fact that when neurons are activated (for example, by the terminal buttons that form synapses with them), particular genes in the nucleus are turned on and particular proteins are produced. These proteins then bind with the chromosomes in the nucleus. Exactly what they do is not yet known; the important fact is their presence indicates that the cell has just been activated. The most important of these proteins is called **Fos**. Immunocytochemical techniques can be used to localize the Fos protein itself, or in situ hybridization techniques can be used to localize the messenger RNA responsible for its synthesis. Figure 5.16 shows neurons in the medial amygdala of a female rat that has just mated; the presence of the dark spots indicates the presence of Fos. Thus, these neurons appear to be activated by physical stimulation of the genitals. (See *Figure 5.16.*)

Study of the Living Human Brain

Advances in X-ray techniques and computers have led to the development of several methods for studying the anatomy of the living brain. The first to be developed was called **computerized tomography** (*tomos,* "cut"; *graphein,* "to write"). This procedure,

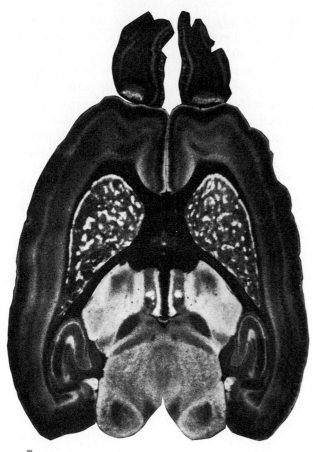

FIGURE 5.14

An autoradiogram of a rat brain (horizontal section, rostral is at top) that has been incubated in a solution containing a radioactive ligand for opiate receptors. The receptors are indicated by white areas.

(From Herkenham, M.A., and Pert, C.B. *Journal of Neuroscience,* 1982, *2,* 1129-1149. Reprinted by permission of the *Journal of Neuroscience.*)

form of glucose that is transported into neurons just like normal glucose. Thus, the most active cells, which use glucose at the highest rate, will take up the highest concentrations of radioactive 2-DG. But unlike normal glucose, 2-DG cannot be metabolized, so it stays in the cell. The experimenter then kills the animal, removes the brain, slices it, and prepares it for autoradiography. The most active regions of the brain contain the most radioactivity, showing this radioactivity in the form of dark spots in the developed emulsion. Figure 5.15 shows an autoradiograph of a slice of a rat brain; the dark spots at the bottom (indicated by the arrow) are nuclei of the hypothalamus with an especially high

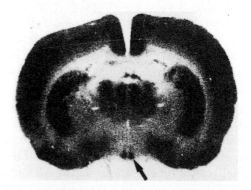

FIGURE 5.15

A 2-DG autoradiogram of a rat brain (frontal section, dorsal is at top), showing especially high regions of activity in the pair of nuclei in the hypothalamus, at the base of the brain.

(From Schwartz, W.J., and Gainer, H. *Science,* 1977, *197,* 1089-1091.)

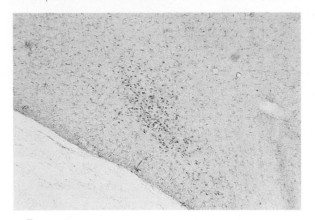

FIGURE 5.16

Localization of Fos protein. The photomicrograph shows a frontal section of the brain of a female rat, taken through the medial amygdala. The green fluorescence indicates the presence of Fos protein, localized by means of immunocyto-chemistry. The synthesis of Fos protein was stimulated by permitting the animal to engage in copulatory behavior.
(Courtesy of Marc Tetel, University of Massachusetts.)

usually referred to as a *CT scan,* works as follows: The patient's head is placed in a large doughnut-shaped ring. The ring contains an X-ray tube and, directly opposite it (on the other side of the patient's head), an X-ray detector. The X-ray beam passes through the patient's head, and the amount of radioactivity that gets through it is measured by the detector. The X-ray emitter and detector scan the head from front to back. They are then moved around the ring by a few degrees, and the transmission of radioactivity is measured again. The process is repeated until the brain has been scanned from all angles. (See **Figure 5.17.**)

The computer takes the information and plots a two-dimensional picture of a horizontal section of the brain. The patient's head is then moved up or down through the ring, and a scan is taken of another section of the brain. Figure 5.18 shows a series of these scans taken through the head of a patient who sustained a stroke that damaged portions of the right parietal and occipital lobes. (See **Figure 5.18.**)

Computerized tomography has been used extensively in the diagnosis of various pathological conditions of the brain, including tumors, blood clots,

hydrocephalus, and degenerative diseases such as multiple sclerosis. The benefits to the patient are obvious; often a CT scan can tell the physician whether brain surgery is necessary. The technique is also of considerable importance to neuropsychologists, who try to infer brain functions by studying the behavioral capacities of people who have sustained brain damage by disease or physical injury. The CT scan enables neuropsychologists to determine the approximate location of the lesion.

An even more detailed picture of what is inside a person's head is provided by a process called **magnetic resonance imaging** (MRI). The MRI scanner resembles a CT scanner, but it does not use X-rays. Instead, it passes an extremely strong magnetic field through the patient's head. When a person's body is placed in a strong magnetic field, the nuclei of some molecules in the body spin with a particular orientation. If a radio frequency wave is then passed through the body, these nuclei emit radio waves of their own. Different molecules emit energy at different frequencies. The MRI scanner is tuned to detect the radiation from hydrogen molecules. Because these molecules are present in different concentrations in different tissues, the scanner can use the

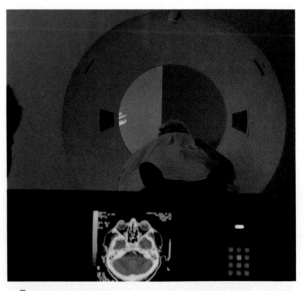

FIGURE 5.17

A computerized tomography (CT) scanner.
(Photo Researchers, Inc.)

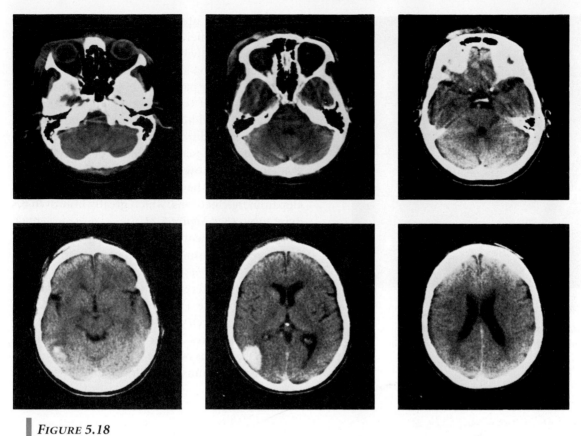

FIGURE 5.18

A series of CT scans from a patient with a lesion in the right occipital-parietal area (scan 2 row 2). The lesion appears white because it was accompanied by bleeding; blood absorbs more radiation than the surrounding brain tissue. Rostral is up, caudal is down; left and right are reversed. Scan 1 row 1 shows a section through the eyes and the base of the brain.
(Courtesy of J.McA. Jones, Good Samaritan Hospital, Portland, Oregon.)

information to prepare pictures of slices of the brain. Unlike CT scans, which are limited to the horizontal plane, MRI scans can be taken in the sagittal or frontal planes, as well. (See *Figure 5.19.*)

Another technique, **positron emission tomography** (PET), permits investigators to assess the amount of metabolic activity in various parts of the brain. First, the patient receives an injection of radioactive 2-DG. As we saw earlier in this chapter, 2-DG is a form of sugar that enters and accumulates in the most active cells. (Eventually, the chemical is broken down and leaves the cells. The dose given to humans is harmless.) The person's head is placed in a PET scanner—a machine that looks something like a CT scanner. As the radioactive isotopes decay,

they emit subatomic particles called positrons. A series of detectors in the PET scanner are able to determine where these subatomic particles came from, and a computer uses this information to produce a picture of a slice of the brain, showing the activity level of various regions in that slice. (See *Figure 5.20.*)

Although PET scanners are very expensive machines (they require an atom-splitting cyclotron to produce short-lived radioactive isotopes), they are also very versatile. They can be used to localize *any* radioactive substance that emits positrons. For example, Figure 5.21 shows PET scans of the brain of a patient who was given an injection of radioactive L-DOPA one hour before each scan was made.

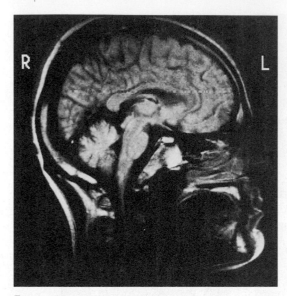

FIGURE 5.19

A midsagittal MRI scan of a human brain.

(Image provided courtesy of Philips Medical Systems, Inc.)

L-DOPA is taken up by the terminals of dopaminergic neurons, where it is converted to dopamine; thus, the radioactivity shown in the scans indicates the presence of dopamine-secreting terminals in the basal ganglia. The patient had injected himself with an illicit drug that was contaminated with a chemical that destroyed his dopaminergic neurons. As a result, he suffered from severe parkinsonism. (This phenomenon is described in more detail in Chapter 8.) The scans show the amount of radioactivity before and after he received a transplant of fetal dopaminergic neurons, which greatly improved his symptoms. (See *Figure 5.21.*)

The development of computers capable of calculating and presenting detailed color graphics displays has made it possible to combine images obtained by different techniques in remarkable ways. For example, Figure 5.22 shows a side view of the head of a seven-year-old girl who had almost continuous seizures. The source of the seizure activity in the brain was near the part of the motor cortex that controls the muscles responsible for speech and

FIGURE 5.20

PET scans of a human brain (horizontal sections). The top row shows three scans from a person at rest. The bottom row shows three scans from the same person while clenching and unclenching his right fist. The scans show increased uptake of radioactive 2-deoxyglucose in regions of the brain that are devoted to the control of movement, which indicates increased metabolic rate in these areas. Different computer-generated colors indicate different rates of uptake of 2-DG, as shown in the scale at the right.

(Courtesy of the Brookhaven National Laboratory and the State University of New York, Stony Brook.)

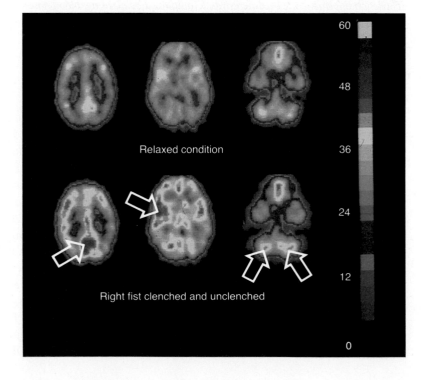

FIGURE 5.21

PET scans showing uptake of radioactive L-DOPA in the basal ganglia of a patient with parkinsonian symptoms induced by a toxic chemical before and after receiving a transplant of fetal dopaminergic neurons. The scan labeled "Mar 88" was taken prior to surgery; the other scans were taken four and thirteen months after surgery. The increased uptake of L-DOPA indicates that the fetal transplant was secreting dopamine.

(From Widner, H., Tetrud, J., Rehncrona, S., Snow, B., Brundin, P., Gustavii, B., Björklund, A., Lindvall, O., and Langston, J.W. *New England Journal of Medicine,* 1992, *327,* 1556-1563. Reprinted by permission of the New England Journal of Medicine.)

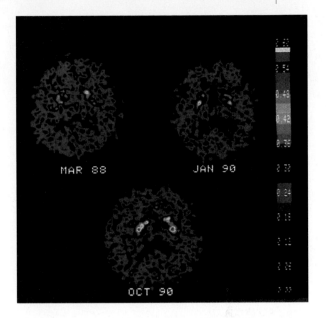

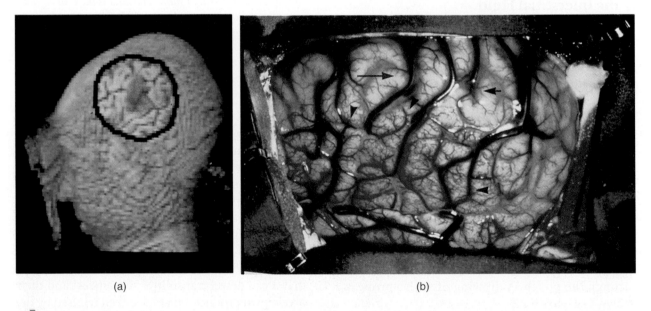

(a) (b)

FIGURE 5.22

Seizure focus. (a) A computer display of a composite scan of the head of a seven-year-old girl, made from a series of PET and MRI scans. The purple spot shows the seizure focus, whose metabolic activity is higher than the rest of the brain. (b) A photograph of the surface of the skull made during surgery. Long arrows point to the primary motor cortex; short arrows point to the primary somatosensory cortex; arrowheads point to the seizure focus. You can see that the large blood vessels are smaller in this region but that the small blood vessels contained within the pia mater are dilated.

(From Levin, D.N., Hu, X., Tan, K.K., Galhotra, S., Pelizzari, C.A., Chen, G.T.Y., Beck, R.N., Chen, C.-T., Cooper, M.D., Mullan, J.F., Hekmatpanah, J., and Spire, J.-P. *Radiology,* 1989, *172,* 783-789.)

respiration, and consequently, she was unable to talk and had great difficulty breathing. The seizures could not be controlled by medication, so removal of the abnormal brain tissue was the only recourse. Because this abnormal tissue was so close to Broca's area, it was important to identify its location precisely so that a minimum of brain tissue could be removed. The image shown in the photograph was derived from a series of PET and MRI scans, presented in three dimensions, showing the area of abnormal metabolic activity. Next to it is a photograph of the same area made during the operation. As you can see, the neurosurgeon knew what to expect even before the skull was opened. (See *Figure 5.22.*) The operation was successful, by the way; the seizures stopped, and the girl was able to breathe without assistance.

Analyzing Chemicals in the Interstitial Fluid

Sometimes, an investigator wants to know how much of a particular compound is present in a particular region of the brain. For example, the investigator might suspect that a particular drug increases the release of a particular transmitter substance in that region. To see whether it does, he or she would use a procedure called **microdialysis.** *Dialysis* is a process in which substances are separated by means of an artificial membrane that is permeable to some molecules but not others. A microdialysis probe consists of a small metal tube that introduces a solution into a section of dialysis tubing—a piece of artificial membrane shaped in the form of a cylinder. Another small metal tube leads the solution away after it has circulated through the pouch. A drawing of such a probe is shown in *Figure 5.23.*

The tip of the probe is placed in the animal's brain in the location of interest. A small amount of a solution similar to extracellular fluid is pumped through one of the small metal tubes into the dialysis tubing. The fluid circulates through the dialysis tubing and passes through the second metal tube, where it is collected in a miniature vial attached to a holder mounted on the animal's head. As the fluid passes through the dialysis tubing, it collects

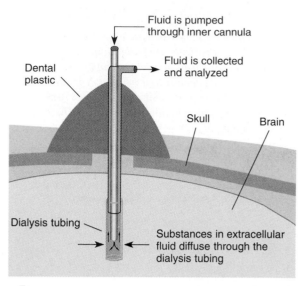

FIGURE 5.23

Microdialysis. A salt solution is slowly infused into the microdialysis tube, where it picks up molecules that diffuse in from the extracellular fluid. The fluid is then collected in a small vial attached to the animal's head and is analyzed by high-performance liquid chromatography (HPLC).

molecules from the extracellular fluid of the brain, which are pushed across the membrane by the force of diffusion. Every few minutes, the vial is removed so that its contents can be analyzed, and a clean vial is put in its place.

The solution that has passed through the dialysis tubing is analyzed by an extremely sensitive analytical method called *high-performance liquid chromatography* (HPLC). This method is so sensitive that it can detect transmitter substances (and their breakdown products) that have been released by the terminal buttons and have escaped from the synaptic cleft into the rest of the extracellular fluid. (Remember that most of the transmitter substance that is released is taken back into the terminal buttons.) As we shall see in Chapter 18, experiments using microdialysis have shown that many addictive drugs, including cocaine, alcohol, and nicotine, cause the release of dopamine in a particular region of the brain.

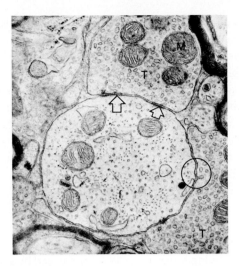

Figure 5.24

An electron photomicrograph of a section through an axo-dendritic synapse. Two synaptic regions are indicated by arrows, and a circle points out a region of pinocytosis in an adjacent terminal button, presumably representing recycling of vesicular membrane. T = terminal button; f = microfilaments; M = mitochondrion.

(From Rockel, A.J., and Jones, E.G. *Journal of Comparative Neurology*, 1973, *147*, 61-92.)

Electron Microscopy

The light microscope is limited in its ability to resolve extremely small details. Because of the nature of light itself, magnification of more than approximately 1500 times does not add any detail. To see such small anatomical structures as synaptic vesicles and details of cell organelles, investigators must use an electron microscope. A beam of electrons is passed through the tissue to be examined. A shadow of the tissue is then cast upon a sheet of photographic film, which is exposed by the electrons. Electron photomicrographs produced in this way can provide information about structural details on the order of a few ångström units. (See *Figure 5.24*.)

A **scanning electron microscope** provides less magnification than a standard one, which transmits the electron beam through the tissue. However, it shows objects in three dimensions. The microscope scans the tissue with a moving beam of electrons. The information received from the reflection of the beam is used to produce a remarkably detailed three-dimensional view. (See *Figure 5.25*.)

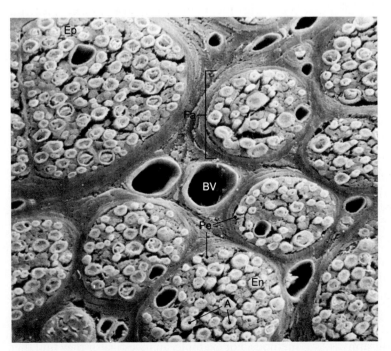

Figure 5.25

A scanning electron photomicrograph of the cut end of a peripheral nerve. Ep = epineurium (the connective tissue surrounding the nerve); Fa = fascicle (bundle of axons); Pe = perineurium (the connective tissue surrounding individual fascicles); En = endoneurium (the connective tissue surrounding single axons); A = axons; BV = blood vessel.

(From Kessel, R.G., and Kardon, R.H. *Tissues and Organs: A Text-Atlas of Scanning Electron Microscopy.* San Francisco: W.H. Freeman, 1979.)

⫼ INTERIM SUMMARY

For an examination of the details of the nervous system, the brain is perfused and the tissue is preserved in a fixative such as formalin, is hardened by freezing or soaking in paraffin or nitrocellulose, and is then sliced by a microtome. Cell-body stains, myelin stains, or membrane stains reveal what their names imply. Tracing tracts involves the use of even more special techniques. Efferent axons can be traced by injecting molecules of PHA-L into a region of the brain. This anterograde tracer is taken up by dendrites and transported down the axons to the terminal buttons. Later, the brain is removed and sliced, and the tissue is exposed to an antibody to PHA-L, attached to a fluorescent dye. The tissue is illuminated with ultraviolet light and examined under a microscope. (The use of antibodies to localize proteins or peptides is called immunocytochemistry.) Afferent axons are traced by injecting retrograde tracers, such as wheat-germ agglutinin, fluorogold, or rhodamine beads. These substances are taken up by terminal buttons and transported back to the cell bodies. Their presence is revealed by means of immunocytochemistry.

Study of neural connections in the human brain is much more difficult because tract tracing methods require injection of chemicals into the living brain. A recently developed method, using a dye called DiI, permits at least some axons to be identified.

Chemicals produced by cells in the brain can be localized directly, or the enzymes or messenger responsible for their production can be localized. Immunocytochemical methods can be used to localize peptides and proteins, which includes enzymes, of course. Messenger RNA can be localized by the method of in situ hybridization. The tissue is exposed to a solution containing strands of radioactive RNA that contains a sequence of bases complementary to that of the messenger RNA. The radioactive RNA is localized by means of autoradiography. In a darkroom, the tissue is coated with a photographic emulsion. After a sufficient amount of time, the emulsion is developed; the molecules of the radioactive RNA show up as black spots. Receptors can also be localized with autoradiography.

Slices of brain tissue are exposed to molecules of a radioactive ligand, which bind with the receptors.

Metabolic activity in specific regions of the brain can be measured by injecting the animal with radioactive 2-DG, a form of glucose that enters metabolically active cells and remains there. The radioactivity is localized by autoradiography. Another method of measuring neural activity takes advantage of the fact that when neurons are stimulated by their synaptic inputs, they begin to synthesize a particular protein, called Fos. Fos protein can be localized by means of immunocytochemistry, or its messenger RNA can be localized through in situ hybridization methods.

The living human brain can be studied by several means. CT scanners use X-rays to construct images of horizontal sections through the brain. MRI scanners use a combination of a magnetic field and radio waves to construct even more detailed images in any plane. PET scanners can be used to reveal the metabolic rate of different regions of the brain after a person has received an injection of radioactive 2-DG. PET scans can also localize receptors; the subject is given an injection of a radioactive ligand.

The secretions of cells in a particular region of the brain can be analyzed by placing a microdialysis probe in the brain and analyzing the substances that the fluid picks up from the brain. Electron microscopy reveals details of the contents of cells, including internal structures and processes such as dendrites, axons, and terminal buttons. A scanning electron microscope shows the detailed three-dimensional anatomy of small structures such as nerves and sensory organs.

EXPERIMENTAL ABLATION

ONE OF THE MOST IMPORTANT RESEARCH methods used to investigate brain functions involves destroying part of the brain and evaluating the animal's subsequent behavior. This technique is not as glamorous as many of the more recently devised techniques, but it often serves as the final test that confirms or disproves conclusions made by other methods. For example, an investigator may find that neurons in a particular part of the brain become active when the animal performs a particular behavior. This finding suggests that the structure may be at least partly responsible for that behavior. If the animal no longer performs the behavior after the structure is destroyed, we become more confident of our conclusion about the structure's responsibility for the behavior. However, if the animal still performs the behavior, we know that the structure is not necessary for its performance. It may still play a role, but not an essential one. In this situation, then, the principle of converging operations (studying a problem by two or more different methods) can be put to use.

Evaluating the Behavioral Effects of Brain Damage

A *lesion* literally refers to a wound or injury, and when a physiological psychologist destroys part of the brain, he or she usually refers to the damage as a brain lesion. The rationale for lesion studies is that the function of an area of the brain can be inferred from the behavioral capacity that is missing from the animal's repertoire after the area is destroyed. For example, if an animal can no longer see after part of the brain is destroyed, we can conclude that the destroyed area plays some role in vision.

However, we must be very careful in interpreting the effects of brain lesions. For example, how do we ascertain that the lesioned animal is blind? Does it bump into objects, or fail to run through a maze toward the light that signals the location of food, or no longer constrict its pupils to light? An animal could bump into objects because of deficits in motor coordination, it could have lost its memory for the maze problem, or it could see quite well but could have lost its visual reflexes. The experimenter must be clever enough to ask the right question, especially when studying complex processes such as hunger, attention, or memory. Even when studying simpler processes, people can be fooled. For years people thought that the albino rat was blind. (It isn't.) Think about it: How would you test to see whether a rat can see? Remember that rats have vibrissae (whiskers) that can be used to detect a wall before bumping into it or the edge of a table before walking off it. They can also find their way around a room by following odor trails.

The interpretation of lesion studies is also complicated by the fact that all regions of the brain are interconnected, and no single part is wholly responsible for any one function. When a nucleus is destroyed, the lesion may also sever axons passing through the area. If a structure normally inhibits another, the observed changes in behavior might really be caused by disinhibition of that second structure. Also, we very often see a partial recovery of function some time after part of a brain is damaged. It is impossible to say whether this recovery results from a "taking over" of the function of the damaged structure by some other brain region or from repair of temporarily injured synapses. In later chapters we will see examples of the difficulty that occurs when trying to infer the role of a brain region from the behavior of an animal lacking that region.

I should also note that histological evaluation must be made of each animal's brain lesion. Brain lesions often miss the mark, and one must verify the precise location of the brain damage after testing the animal behaviorally. The investigator may have intended to destroy structure X but occasionally missed, destroying nearby structure Y in some animals instead. After the behavioral observations are completed, the animals are killed, and the investigator slices and stains the animals' brains to see where the damage is. Only the data collected from the animals in which structure X was destroyed are included in the analysis. (Sometimes, interesting results are obtained accidentally; the investigator may find that structure Y is even more important than structure X to the function being studied.)

Producing Brain Lesions

It is easy to destroy parts of the dorsal surface of the cerebral or cerebellar cortex; the animal is anesthetized, the scalp is cut, part of the skull is removed, and the cortex is brought into view. Then a suction device is used to aspirate the brain tissue. To accomplish this tissue removal, the dura mater is cut away and a glass pipette is placed on the surface of the brain. A vacuum pump attached to the pipette is used to suck away brain tissue. With practice, it is quite easy to aspirate the cortical gray matter, stopping at the underlying layer of white matter, which has a much tougher consistency.

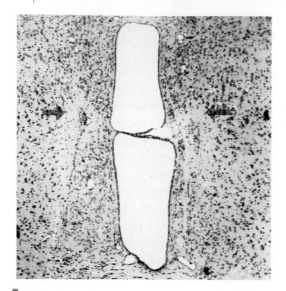

FIGURE 5.26

Radio frequency lesion. The arrows point to very small lesions produced by passing radio frequency current through the tips of stainless steel electrodes placed in the medial preoptic nucleus of a rat brain. (Frontal section, cell-body stain.)

(From Turkenburg, J.L., Swaab, D.F., Endert, E., Louwerse, A.L., and van de Poll, N.E. *Brain Research Bulletin*, 1988, *21*, 215-224.)

Subcortical brain lesions are usually produced by passing electrical current through a stainless steel wire that is electrically insulated with paint or varnish except for a portion of the tip. The investigator guides the wire stereotaxically, so that its end reaches the appropriate location, and then turns on the lesion-making device. (Stereotaxic surgery is described in the next subsection.) Two kinds of electrical current can be used. Direct-current (DC) devices create lesions by initiating chemical reactions whose products destroy the cells in the vicinity of the electrode tip. Radio frequency (RF) lesion-making devices produce alternating current of a very high frequency. This current does not stimulate neural tissue, nor does it cause chemical reactions. Instead, it destroys nearby cells with the heat produced by the passage of the current through the tissue, which offers electrical resistance. (See **Figure 5.26**.)

Radio frequency lesions have a distinct advantage over DC lesions: No metal ions are left in the damaged tissue. In contrast, when DC lesions are produced, some of the electrode is left behind in the brain, because ions of metal are carried away by the electrical current. These ions can affect the surviving neurons in the vicinity of the lesion and alter the behavior of the animal (King and Frohman, 1986).

Lesions produced by means of radio frequency or direct current destroy everything in the vicinity of the electrode tip, including neuron cell bodies and the axons of neurons that pass through the region. A more selective method of producing brain lesions employs a neurotoxin ("nerve poison"), such as *kainic acid* or *ibotenic acid*. When these chemicals are injected through a cannula into a region of the brain, they destroy cell bodies in the vicinity but spare axons that are passing nearby. (See **Figure 5.27**.) This selectivity permits the investigator to determine whether the behavioral effects of destroying a particular brain structure occur because the cells there are killed or because the axons that pass nearby are severed. For example, RF lesions of a region of the pons abolish a particular form of sleep; thus, investigators believed that this region was involved in the production of this stage of sleep. But later studies showed that when kainic acid was used to destroy the neurons located there, the animals' sleep was *not* affected. Thus, the sleep-altering effects of RF lesions must be caused by destroying the axons that pass through the area, not the cell bodies that reside there.

Even more specific methods of lesion production are available. For example, the drug **6-hydroxy-dopamine** (6-HD) resembles the catecholamines norepinephrine and dopamine. You will recall that the postsynaptic effects of most neurotransmitters are terminated by reuptake; the terminal button releases the neurotransmitter, then retrieves it. Because 6-HD resembles the catecholamines, it is taken up by the axons of neurons that secrete dopamine or norepinephrine. Once inside, the chemical poisons and kills the neurons. Thus, 6-HD can be injected directly into particular regions of the brain to kill specific populations of neurons that use one of these transmitter substances. If the investigator uses the proper concentration of 6-HD, only catecholamine-secreting neurons will be damaged.

Most of the time, investigators produce permanent brain lesions, but sometimes it is advantageous

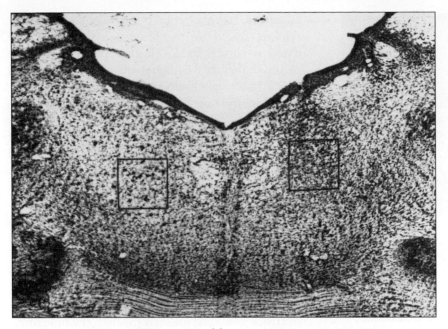

(a)

FIGURE 5.27

Neurotoxic lesion. Ibotenic acid was injected into one side of the pontine reticular formation of a cat brain. (a) Frontal section. The arrows show the path followed by the metal cannula that was used to inject the neurotoxin. The two photographs in parts b and c show the brain tissue in more detail (indicated by black squares here). (b) Damaged tissue. Only glial cells can be seen. (c) Normal tissue. Large neurons and small glial cells can be seen.

(From Suzuki, S.S., Siegel, J.M., and Wu, M.-F. *Brain Research*, 1989, *484*, 78-93.)

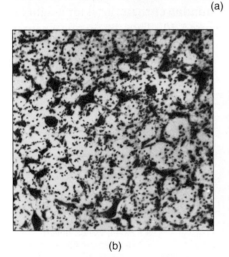

(b)

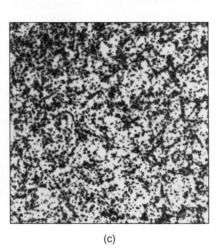

(c)

to disrupt the activity of a particular region of the brain temporarily. The easiest way to do so is to inject a local anesthetic into the appropriate part of the brain. The anesthetic blocks action potentials in axons entering or leaving that region, thus effectively producing a temporary lesion. Temporary lesions can also be produced by cooling brain tissue enough to slowly suppress neural activity. Figure 5.28 shows a device called a *cryode,* which can be used to produce temporary lesions of a region of the cerebral cortex of the monkey brain. The device consists of a series of stainless steel tubes through which a chilled liquid can be circulated. It is implanted between the skull and the surface of the brain. (See *Figure 5.28.*)

Stereotaxic Surgery

If an investigator wants to place a wire or a cannula into a particular part of the brain, he or she will do so by means of stereotaxic surgery. This procedure permits the insertion of an object into the depths of the brain without serious damage to the overlying tissue.

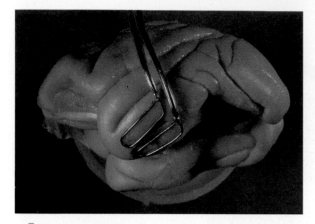

FIGURE 5.28

A cryode, a device that produces temporary lesions of the cerebral cortex. The device is surgically implanted between the skull and the brain, and the temporary lesion can be produced while the animal is awake and alert. A chilled liquid is circulated through the stainless steel tubes. The cryode shown in the photograph was placed against a region of the visual association cortex of the left hemisphere of a monkey brain.

(Courtesy of James Horel, SUNY Upstate Medical Center.)

Stereotaxis literally means "solid arrangement"; more specifically, it refers to the ability to locate objects in space. A stereotaxic apparatus permits the investigator to locate brain structures that are hidden from view. This device contains a holder that fixes the animal's head in a standard position and a carrier that moves an electrode or a cannula through measured distances in all three axes of space. However, to perform stereotaxic surgery, one must first study a stereotaxic atlas, so I will describe the atlas first.

The Stereotaxic Atlas

No two brains of animals of a given species are completely identical, but there is enough similarity among individuals to predict the location of a particular brain structure, relative to external features of the head. For instance, a particular thalamic nucleus of a rat might be so many millimeters ventral, anterior, and lateral to a point formed by the junction of several bones of the skull. Figure 5.29 shows two views of a rat skull: a drawing of the dorsal surface and, beneath it, a midsagittal view. (See *Figure 5.29.*) The junction of the coronal and sagit-

tal *sutures* (seams between adjacent bones of the skull) is labeled **bregma.** If the animal's skull is oriented as shown in the illustration, a particular region of the brain occupies a fairly constant location in space, relative to bregma. Not all atlases use bregma as the reference point, but this reference is the easiest to describe.

A **stereotaxic atlas** contains pages that correspond to frontal sections taken at various distances anterior and posterior to bregma (or another reference point). For example, the page shown in Figure 5.30 contains a drawing of a slice of the brain located 0.6 mm anterior to bregma. If we wanted to place the tip of a wire in the structure labeled F (the fornix), we would have to drill a hole through the skull 0.6 mm anterior to bregma (because the structure shows up on the 0.6-mm page) and 1.0 mm lateral to the midline. (See *Figures 5.29* and *5.30.*) The electrode would be lowered through the hole until the tip was 7.0 mm lower than the skull height at bregma. (See *Figure 5.30.*) Thus, by finding a neural

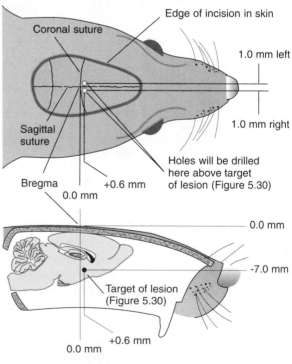

FIGURE 5.29

Relation of the skull sutures to a rat's brain, and the stereotaxic coordinates for an electrode placement.

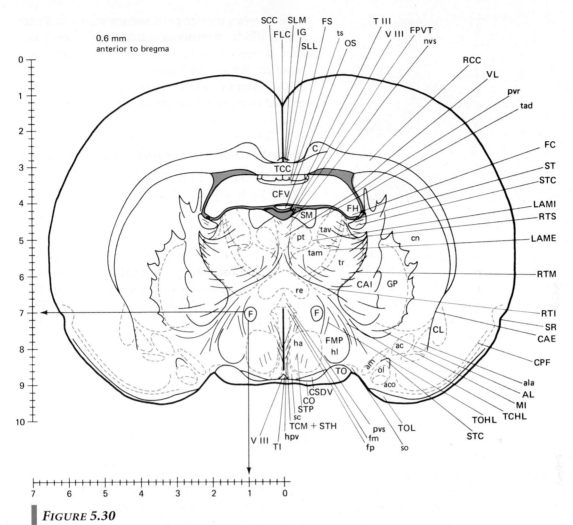

FIGURE 5.30

A page from a stereotaxic atlas of the rat brain. The scale on the side and bottom of the figure (From König, J.F.R., and Klippel, R.A. *The Rat Brain: A Stereotaxic Atlas of the Forebrain and Lower Parts of has been modified to be consistent with my description of bregma as a reference point. the Brain Stem.* Copyright 1963 by the Williams & Wilkins Co., Baltimore.)

structure (which we cannot see in our animal) on one of the pages of a stereotaxic atlas, we can determine the structure's location relative to bregma (which we can see). I should note that, because of variations in different strains and ages of animals, the atlas gives only an approximate location. It is always necessary to try out a new set of coordinates, slice and stain the animal's brain, see where the lesion was made, correct the numbers, and try again.

There are human stereotaxic atlases, by the way. Sometimes, a neurosurgeon produces subcortical lesions (for example, to reduce severe tremors caused by Parkinson's disease). Usually, the surgeon uses multiple landmarks and verifies the location of the wire (or other device) inserted into the brain by taking X-rays before producing a brain lesion.

The Stereotaxic Apparatus

A **stereotaxic apparatus** operates on simple principles. The device includes a head holder, which holds the animal's skull in the proper orientation, a holder for the electrode, and a calibrated mechanism that moves the electrode holder in measured distances along the three axes: anterior-posterior, dorsal-ven-

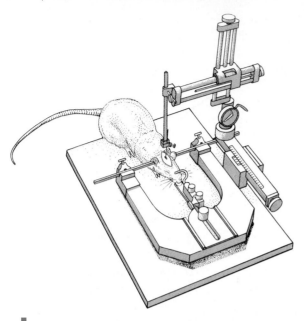

FIGURE 5.31

A stereotaxic apparatus for performing brain surgery on rats.

tral, and lateral-medial. Figure 5.31 illustrates a stereotaxic apparatus designed for small animals; various head holders can be used to outfit this device for such diverse species as rats, mice, hamsters, pigeons, and turtles. (See *Figure 5.31.*)

Once the investigator has obtained the stereotaxic coordinates, he or she anesthetizes the animal, places it in the apparatus, and cuts the scalp open. This cut exposes the skull so that the cannula or electrode can be placed with its tip on bregma. The investigator measures the location of bregma along each of the axes and moves the cannula or electrode the proper distance along the anterior-posterior and lateral-medial axes to a point just above the target. He or she then drills a hole through the skull just below the cannula or electrode and lowers the device into the brain by the proper amount. Now the tip of the cannula or electrode is in the correct position in the brain and the investigator is ready to produce the lesion.

Of course, stereotaxic surgery may be used for purposes other than lesion production. Wires placed in the brain may be used to stimulate neurons as well as destroy them, and drugs can be injected that stimulate neurons or block specific receptors. Can-

nulas or wires may be permanently implanted with acrylic plastic, a procedure that will be described later in this chapter. In all cases, once surgery is complete, the wound is sewed together, and the animal is taken out of the stereotaxic apparatus and allowed to recover from the anesthetic.

RECORDING THE BRAIN'S ELECTRICAL ACTIVITY

Rationale

Axons produce action potentials, and terminal buttons elicit postsynaptic potentials in the membrane of the cells with which they form synapses. These electrical events can be recorded (as we have already seen), and changes in the electrical activity of a particular region can be used to determine whether that region plays a role in various behaviors. For example, recordings can be made during stimulus presentations, decision making, or motor activities. The rationale is sound; but as we will see, electrical recordings of neural activity, especially of those electrical events that might be correlated with complex behaviors, are difficult to interpret.

Recordings can be made chronically, over an extended period of time after the animal recovers from surgery, or acutely, for a relatively short period of time during which the animal is kept anesthetized. Acute recordings, made while the animal is anesthetized, are usually restricted to studies of sensory pathways. Acute recordings seldom involve behavioral observations, since the behavioral capacity of an anesthetized animal is limited, to say the least.

Chronic electrodes can be implanted in the brain with the aid of a stereotaxic apparatus, and an electrical socket attached to the electrodes can be cemented to the animal's skull by means of an acrylic plastic that is normally used for making dental plates. Then, after recovery from surgery, the animal can be "plugged in" to the recording system. (See *Figure 5.32.*)

Electrical recordings can be taken through very small electrodes that detect the activity of one neuron (or just a few neurons) or through large elec-

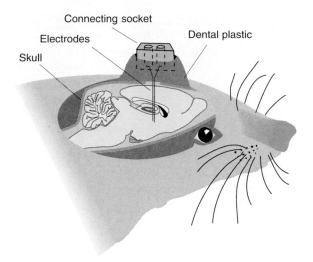

FIGURE 5.32

A permanently attached set of electrodes, with a connecting socket cemented to the skull.

trodes that respond to the electrical activity of large populations of neurons. In either case the electrical signal detected by the electrode is quite small and must be amplified. A biological amplifier works just like the amplifiers in a stereo system, converting the weak signals recorded at the brain (about as weak as those produced by a phonograph cartridge) into stronger ones, large enough to be displayed on the appropriate device. Output devices vary considerably. Their basic purpose is to convert the raw data (amplified electrical signals from the brain) into a form we can perceive—usually a visual display.

Electrodes

Depending on the type of electrical signal he or she wishes to detect, the investigator constructs or purchases special electrodes. Although these electrodes come in many forms, they can be classified into two basic types: microelectrodes and macroelectrodes.

Microelectrodes have a very fine tip, small enough to record the electrical activity of individual neurons. This technique is usually called **single-unit recording** (a unit refers to an individual neuron). Microelectrodes can be constructed of fine metal wires or glass tubes. Metal electrodes are sharpened by etching them in an acid solution. Current is passed through a fine wire as it is moved in

and out of the solution. The tip erodes away, leaving a very fine, sharp point. The wire (usually of tungsten or stainless steel) is then insulated with a special varnish. The very end of the tip is so sharp that it does not retain insulation and thus can record electrical signals.

As we already saw in Chapter 2, electrodes can also be constructed of fine glass tubes. Glass tubes have an interesting property. If they are heated until soft, and if the ends are pulled apart, the softened glass will stretch into a very fine filament. However, no matter how thin the filament becomes, it will still have a hole running through it. To construct glass microelectrodes, the investigator heats the middle of a length of capillary tubing (glass with an outside diameter of approximately 1 mm) and then pulls the ends sharply apart. The glass tube is drawn out finer and finer, until the tube snaps apart. The result is two microelectrodes, as shown in **Figure 5.33.** (These devices are usually produced with the aid of a special machine, called a *microelectrode puller.*) Glass will not conduct electricity, so the microelectrode is filled with a conducting liquid, such as a solution of potassium chloride. Glass microelectrodes were used to provide the data concerning axonal conduction and synaptic transmission described in Chapters 2 and 3.

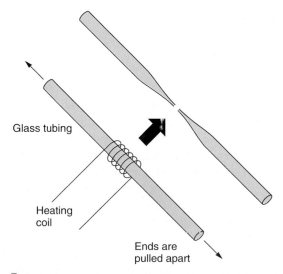

FIGURE 5.33

Microelectrodes produced by heating the center portion of a length of glass capillary tubing and pulling the ends apart.

Macroelectrodes, which record the activity of a very large number of neurons, are not nearly so difficult to make or to use. They can be constructed from a variety of materials: Stainless steel or platinum wires, insulated except for the tip, can be inserted into the brain or placed on top of it. Small balls of metal can be placed on the surface of the brain. Wires can be attached to screws that are driven into holes in the skull. Flat disks of silver or gold can be attached to the scalp with an electrically conductive paste. (The last type of electrode is used for recordings of the electrical activity from the human head, discussed later in this chapter.)

Macroelectrodes do not detect the activity of individual neurons; rather, the records obtained with these devices represent the postsynaptic potentials of many thousands—or millions—of cells in the area of the electrode. Recordings taken from the scalp, especially, represent the electrical activity of an enormous number of neurons.

Output Devices

After being amplified, electrical signals from the nervous system must be displayed so that we can see them and measure them. Obviously, we cannot directly observe the electrical activity from an amplifier; just as a sound system is useless without speakers or headphones, so a biological amplifier is useless without an output device.

Oscilloscope

In Chapter 2, I described the basic principle of an *oscilloscope,* a device that plots electrical potentials as a function of time. To illustrate the use of an oscilloscope for the recording of single-unit activity, consider the procedure shown in Figure 5.34. A light is flashed in front of the cat, and at the same time, the dot on the oscilloscope is started across the screen, moving from left to right. Thus, the vertical axis represents the electrical signal from a neuron and the horizontal axis represents time. Suppose we record from a cell in the visual cortex that responds to a light flash by giving a burst of action potentials. If we move the beam slowly, we will see the record of this event on the face of the oscilloscope as vertical lines superimposed on a horizontal one. If we move the beam rapidly, we will see the shapes of the individual

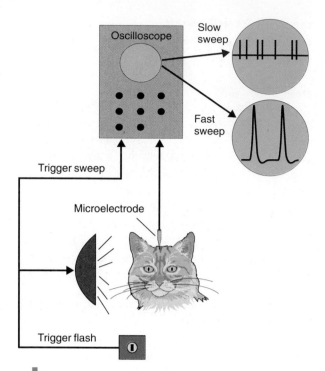

FIGURE 5.34

The means by which the responses of single units to a flash of light can be recorded.

action potentials. (See ***Figure 5.34.***) You might wonder how the illustrated display can be seen; after all, the display consists of a moving dot, and I have shown a continuous line. The explanation is that most oscilloscope screens exhibit *persistence;* as the dot moves, it leaves a trace of its pathway behind, which slowly fades away.

When recording single-unit activity, the investigator usually also attaches the output of the amplifier to a loudspeaker. When an investigator lowers a microelectrode through the brain, he or she must stop before the optimal recording point, to allow the brain tissue, which has been pushed down by the progress of the electrode, to spring back up. If the electrode goes down too far, the cell will probably be injured or killed by the electrode when the tissue moves up. Therefore, the investigator must detect the firing of a cell as soon as possible, so that he or she can stop moving the electrode before damage is done. Our ears are much more efficient than our eyes in extracting the faint signal of a firing neuron from the random background noise. We can hear the ticking, snapping sound of single-unit activity from the loudspeaker long before we can see the action potentials on the face of the oscilloscope. Our auditory system does an excellent job of extracting signal from noise.

Oscilloscopes are also ideal for the display of evoked potentials. **Evoked potentials** are electrical changes in the brain that are *evoked* by a stimulus, such as a sound or a flash of light. They are recordings made through macroelectrodes and should not be confused with *action* potentials, which occur in single axons. When a stimulus is presented to an organism, a series of electrical events is initiated at the receptor organ. This activity is conducted into the brain, where it propagates through sensory pathways. If a macroelectrode is placed in or near one of these pathways, it will detect the electrical activity evoked by the stimulus. For example, we might place a scalp electrode on the back of a person's head and present a flash of light, while simultaneously triggering the sweep of an oscilloscope. Figure 5.35 shows such an experiment, along with the evoked potential from the visual cortex, recorded through the skull and scalp. (See ***Figure 5.35.***)

Ink-Writing Oscillograph

Oscilloscopes are most useful in the display of phasic activity, such as an evoked potential, that occurs during a relatively brief period of time. If neural activity is continuously recorded and displayed on an oscilloscope screen, it will be seen as a series of successive sweeps of the beam, presenting a rather

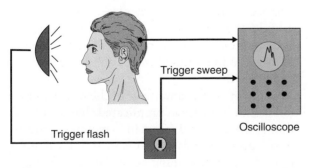

FIGURE 5.35

The means by which electrical potentials in the brain, evoked by a flash of light, can be recorded from the human scalp.

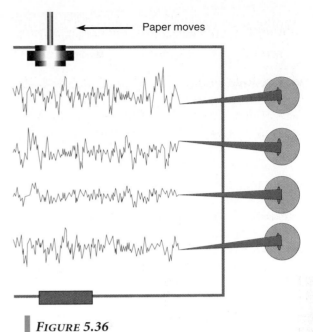

FIGURE 5.36

A record from an ink-writing oscillograph.

confusing picture. A much better device for such a purpose is the ink-writing oscillograph (often called a *polygraph*).

The time base of the polygraph is provided by a mechanism that moves a very long strip of paper past a series of pens. Essentially, the pens are the pointers of large voltmeters, moving up and down in response to the electrical signal sent to them by the biological amplifiers. Figure 5.36 illustrates a record of electrical activity recorded from macroelectrodes attached to various locations on a person's scalp. (See ***Figure 5.36.***) Such records are called **electroencephalograms** (EEGs), or "writings of electricity from the head." They can be used to diagnose epilepsy or brain tumors, or to study the stages of sleep and wakefulness, which are associated with characteristic patterns of electrical activity. I should note that many modern polygraphs do not use ink; they print electrostatically or with heated pens on specially treated paper, or they are collected by a computer and displayed on a video screen. Nevertheless, their principle of operation is the same.

Figure 5.37 shows the EEG recorded from the hippocampus of a rat during sleep and during the performance of various behaviors while awake. You

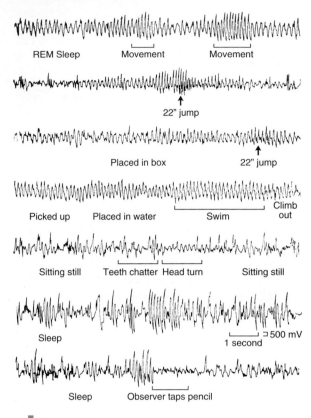

FIGURE 5.37

EEG activity from the rat hippocampus, recorded during various behaviors.

(From Whishaw, I.Q., and Vanderwolf, C.H. *Behavioral Biology*, 1973, 8, 461-484.)

will see that the pattern of activity changes drastically during different behaviors. (See *Figure 5.37*.)

Computers

Electrophysiological data are often stored in computers, which can also be used to display the data. A computer can convert the analog signal (one that can continuously vary, like the EEG) received from the biological amplifier into a series of numbers (digital values). Figure 5.38 illustrates how an evoked potential can be represented by a series of digital values. Each point represents the voltage of the analog signal at successive millisecond intervals. The values were obtained from a rat's brain through screws attached to the skull, were stored in a computer, and were then displayed on the screen of an oscilloscope. (See *Figure 5.38*.)

A computer can do more than display the data; it can perform many kinds of analyses as well. For example, it can compute the delay between the presentation of a stimulus and the occurrence of an evoked potential, or it can count the number of action potentials that a stimulus produces in a single unit.

STIMULATING OR INHIBITING NEURAL ACTIVITY

NEURAL ACTIVITY CAN BE ELICITED BY ELECTRIcal or chemical stimulation of the brain; it can also be inhibited through the use of drugs.

Electrical and Chemical Stimulation

Electrical stimulation simply involves passing an electrical current through a wire inserted into the brain. Chemical stimulation is usually accomplished by injecting a small amount of an excitatory amino acid such as kainic acid or glutamic acid into the brain. As you learned in Chapter 3, the principal excitatory transmitter substance in the brain is glutamic acid, and both of these substances stimulate glutamate receptors, thus activating the neurons on which these receptors are located.

Injections of chemicals into the brain can be done chronically, so that the animal's behavior can be observed several times. A metal cannula (a guide cannula) is placed in an animal's brain and its top is cemented to the skull. At a later date a smaller cannula of measured length is placed inside the guide cannula, and a chemical is injected into the brain while the animal moves about freely. (See *Figure 5.39*.)

The principal disadvantage of chemical stimulation is that it is more complicated than electrical stimulation; chemical stimulation requires cannulas, tubes, special pumps or syringes, and sterile solutions of excitatory amino acids. However, it has a distinct advantage over electrical stimulation: It activates cell bodies but not axons. Because only cell bodies (and their dendrites, of course) contain glutamate receptors, we can be assured that an injection

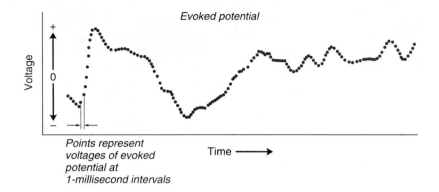

of an excitatory amino acid into a particular region of the brain excites the cells there but not the axons that happen to pass through the region. Thus, the effects of chemical stimulation are more localized than the effects of electrical stimulation.

You may have noticed that I just said that kainic acid, which I described earlier as a neurotoxin, can be used to stimulate neurons. These two uses are not really contradictory. In fact, kainic acid kills neurons by stimulating them to death, through a phenomenon called *excitotoxicity.* Thus, large doses of a concentrated solution kill neurons, whereas small doses of a dilute solution simply stimulate them.

Drugs such as kainic acid stimulate all neurons

that they reach, because, as far as we know, all neurons have at least some receptors for excitatory amino acids. As we saw in Chapter 3, pharmacologists have discovered a wide variety of drugs that have a wide variety of effects on synaptic transmission. For example, some drugs stimulate particular postsynaptic receptors, others block them, others prevent reuptake, and still others inhibit enzymes that destroy transmitter substances. These drugs can be injected directly into the brain, where they can affect synaptic transmission in localized regions. Thus, investigators can study the behavioral effects of stimulating or blocking the activity of particular types of synapses in particular regions of the brain.

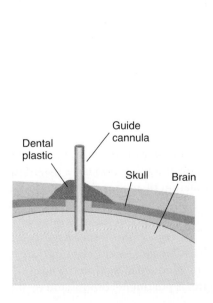

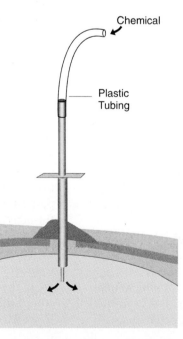

FIGURE 5.39

An intracranial cannula. A guide cannula is permanently attached to the skull, and at a later time a thinner cannula can be inserted through the guide cannula into the brain. Chemicals can be infused into the brain through this device.

Microiontophoresis

When drugs are injected into the brain through cannulas, the chemicals diffuse over a region that involves hundreds (or thousands) of neurons. Sometimes, we want to study the effect of chemicals on the activity of a single cell. To do that we use a technique known as *microiontophoresis.*

When transmitter substances bind with postsynaptic receptors, ion channels open, producing excitatory or inhibitory postsynaptic potentials. These potentials increase or decrease the cell's firing rate. To determine the effects of transmitter substances (or drugs that stimulate or block particular receptors) on the activity of an individual neuron, an investigator uses a **multi-barreled micropipette.** This device consists of two or more glass microelectrodes (also called *micropipettes*), bundled together so that their tips are close to one another.

Figure 5.40 illustrates a seven-barreled micropipette glued to a recording microelectrode. Each of the seven micropipettes can be filled with transmitter substances, neuromodulators, hormones, or drugs. The pH (acid-base balance) of the solutions in the micropipettes is adjusted so that the chemicals ionize. Then when an electrical current is passed through one of the micropipettes, some molecules of the substance will be discharged. The injection of extremely small quantities of a chemical this way is called **microiontophoresis** (*iontophoresis* means "ion carrying," from *pherein,* "to bear or carry"). (See *Figure 5.40.*)

The recording microelectrode detects the neural activity of the cell that is being exposed to one of the chemicals placed in the micropipettes—for example, a particular transmitter substance. If the neuron changes its firing rate when some of the hormone is ejected from the micropipette, we can conclude that the neuron contains receptors for that transmitter substance.

Behavioral Effects of Electrical Brain Stimulation

Stimulation of the brain of a freely moving animal often produces behavioral changes. For example, hypothalamic stimulation can elicit behaviors such

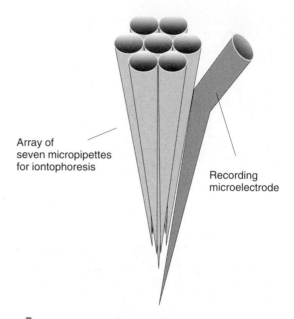

Array of seven micropipettes for iontophoresis

Recording microelectrode

FIGURE 5.40

Microiontophoresis. Molecules of different chemicals are carried out of the seven micropipettes by an electrical current. The recording microelectrode records the activity of the neuron and determines whether it responds to the chemical.

as feeding, drinking, grooming, attack, or escape, which suggests that the hypothalamus is involved in their control. Stimulation of the caudate nucleus often halts ongoing behavior, which suggests that this structure is involved in motor inhibition. Brain stimulation can serve as a signal for a learned task or can even serve as a rewarding or punishing event, as we will see in Chapter 14.

There are problems in interpreting the significance of the effects of brain stimulation, especially when it is produced with electricity. An electrical stimulus (usually a series of pulses) can never duplicate the natural neural processes that go on in the brain. The normal interplay of spatial and temporal patterns of excitation and inhibition is destroyed by the artificial stimulation of an area. Electrical brain stimulation is probably as natural as attaching ropes to the arms of the members of an orchestra and then shaking all the ropes simultaneously to see what they can play. In fact, local stimulation is sometimes used to produce a "temporary lesion," by which the region is put out of commission by the meaningless artificial stimulation. The surprising finding is that stimulation so often *does* produce orderly changes in behavior.

One of the more interesting uses of electrical stimulation of the brain was developed by the late Wilder Penfield (see Penfield and Jasper, 1954) to treat focal-seizure disorders. These problems are produced by localized regions of neural tissue that periodically irritate the surrounding areas, triggering epileptic seizures (wild, sustained firing of cerebral neurons, resulting in some behavioral disruption). If severe cases of focal epilepsy do not respond to medication, surgical excision of the focus may be necessary. The focus is identified by means of EEG recordings before surgery and is confirmed by EEG recordings during surgery, after the brain is exposed. (As we saw in an earlier section, it can also be identified by special imaging techniques.)

Patients undergoing open-head surgery first have their heads shaved. Then a local anesthetic is administered to the scalp along the line that will be followed by the incision. A general anesthetic is not used, because the method requires that the patient be awake and conscious during surgery. The surgeon cuts the scalp and saws through the skull under the cut so that a piece of skull can then be removed. Next, the surgeon cuts and folds back the dura mater, exposing the brain itself.

When removing an epileptic focus, the surgeon wants to cut away all the abnormal tissue, while sparing neural tissue that performs important functions, such as the comprehension and production of speech. For this reason, Penfield first stimulated parts of the brain to determine which regions he could safely remove, before removing the seizure focus. Penfield touched the tip of a metal electrode to various parts of the brain and observed the effects of stimulation on the patient's behavior. For example, stimulation of the primary motor cortex produced movement, and stimulation of the primary auditory cortex elicited reports of the presence of buzzing noises. Stimulation of portions of the temporal lobe and frontal lobe stopped the patient's ongoing speech and disrupted the ability to understand what the surgeon and his associates were saying.

After the surgeon removes the region of the brain that contains the seizure focus, the dura mater is sewn back together and the skull is replaced.

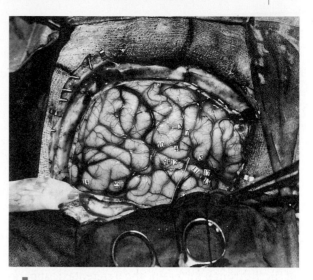

FIGURE 5.41

The appearance of the cortical surface of a conscious patient whose brain has been stimulated. The points of stimulation are indicated by the numbered tags placed there by the surgeon.

(From Case M.M., in Wilder Penfield, *The Mystery of the Mind: A Critical Study of Consciousness and the Human Brain,* with Discussions by William Feindel, Charles Hendel, and Charles Symonds. Copyright © 1975 by Princeton University Press. Figure 4, p. 24 reprinted by permission of Princeton University Press.)

Besides giving patients relief from their epileptic attacks, the procedure provided Penfield with interesting data. As he stimulated various parts of the brain, he noted the effect and placed a sterile piece of paper, on which a number was written, on the point stimulated. When various points had been stimulated, Penfield photographed the exposed brain with its numbered locations before removing the slips of paper and proceeding with the surgery. After the operation, he could then compare the recorded notes with the photograph of the patient's brain, showing the location of the points of stimulation. (See **Figure 5.41.**)

INTERIM SUMMARY

Brain lesions can be produced electrically, by passing direct current or radio frequency current through a metal electrode that is insulated except for the tip. Radio frequency lesions are better, because no metal ions are left in the brain. Brain lesions can also be produced chemically, by injecting an excitatory amino acid such as kainic acid or ibotenic acid, which stimulates neurons so much that they die. These lesions spare axons that happen to be passing through the region. Some neurotoxins will destroy only particular kinds of neurons; for example, 6-HD kills catecholaminergic neurons. After brain lesions are made, their location and extent must be verified through histological examination. Temporary lesions can also be produced by injecting a local anesthetic into the brain or by cooling the cerebral cortex.

Stereotaxic surgery involves the use of a stereotaxic atlas, which contains drawings or photographs of slices through the brain, and a stereotaxic apparatus, a device that permits the investigator to position the tip of an electrode or cannula in a precise point in space. Usually, junctions between the bones of the skull are used as reference points to locate the desired target.

Electrical recordings can be made through macroelectrodes, which record the postsynaptic activity of a large number of neurons in a particular region, or through microelectrodes, which record postsynaptic potentials or action potentials of individual neurons. Oscilloscopes, ink-writing oscillographs, or computers are used to display the data. Of course, computers can analyze the data as well as display them.

The brain can be stimulated electrically, through a metal electrode, or chemically, by infusing a dilute solution of an excitatory amino acid that activates glutamate receptors. Even human brains can be stimulated during neurosurgery. Microiontophoresis permits an investigator to infuse small quantities of neurotransmitters, neuromodulators, hormones, or drugs in the vicinity of a neuron and record its response to the chemical.

In this chapter I referred to the strategy of converging operations. The results of any single research method are not definitive; each method has its limitations and ambiguities. Yet when several methods all yield the same conclusion—when their results *converge*—we can be much more confident that the conclusion is correct.

Let me give an example. Investigators have determined that the sexual behavior of female rats is stimulated by estradiol. Suppose we wanted to know about the location of the estradiol-sensitive neurons in the brain. I already described the use of autoradiography to determine which neurons selectively take up this hormone. These neurons are located in several parts of the brain, but particularly in the ventromedial nucleus of the hypothalamus. Consider what other methods, already described in this chapter, could be used to confirm these results. We might use stereotaxic surgery to destroy the ventromedial nucleus, predicting that the lesion would abolish the behavioral effects of estradiol on female sexual behavior. (We might want to destroy the nucleus with a neurotoxin such as kainic acid to be sure that the effects are not caused by destroying axons that pass through the region.) We might record the activity of these neurons while we infused estradiol into the region with a micropipette, expecting that their activity would change. We might administer a small amount of estradiol directly into the ventromedial nucleus with a small cannula, predicting that the hormone would stimulate sexual behavior. If these experiments produced consistent results, we might decide to investigate the connections of the neurons in the ventromedial hypothalamus with neurons elsewhere in the brain. To do so, we would inject PHA-L into this region to see where the axons of these neurons terminated. We would then make lesions in *those* regions to see whether they affected sexual behavior. And so on.

As we will see in Chapter 10, these studies *have* been performed, and the results were pretty much as predicted. The rest of this book describes the efforts that have been made to understand the physiology of behavior. The quest involves many different methods, all devoted to a common goal. This chapter has introduced you to the most important methods used in neuroscience research, so you should have no trouble understanding the experiments described in later chapters of the book. I hope that you have also learned enough so that you will be able to understand the rationale behind most experimental procedures you might read about in scientific journals or other books.

New Terms

converging operations p. 108

Neuroanatomical and Neuro-chemical Techniques

fixative p. 108

formalin p. 108

perfusion p. 108

microtome p. 108

Nissl substance p. 109

myelin stain p. 110

membrane stain p. 110

Golgi-Cox stain p. 110

anterograde labeling method p. 111

PHA-L p. 111

immunocytochemical method p. 111

retrograde labeling method p. 112

fluorogold p. 112

DiI (*dye EYE*) p. 113

in situ hybridization p. 115

autoradiography p. 115

double labeling p. 116

2-deoxyglucose p. 116

Fos (*fahs*) p. 117

computerized tomo-graphy p. 117

magnetic resonance imaging p. 118

positron emission tomography p. 119

microdialysis p. 122

scanning electron microscope p. 123

Experimental Ablation

6-hydroxydopamine p. 126

bregma p. 128

stereotaxic atlas p. 128

stereotaxic apparatus p. 129

Recording the Brain's Electrical Activity

microelectrode p. 131

single-unit recording p. 131

macroelectrode p. 132

evoked potential p. 133

electroencephalogram p. 133

Stimulating or Inhibiting Neural Activity

multi-barreled micro-pipette p. 136

microiontophoresis (*MY kro eye on toe for EE sis*) p. 136

Suggested Readings

Laboratory Manuals:

Webster, W.G. *Principles of Research Methodology in Physiological Psychology.* New York: Harper & Row, 1975.

Wellman, P. *Laboratory Exercises in Physiological Psychology.* Boston: Allyn and Bacon, 1986.

Stereotaxic Atlases:

Koenig, J.F.R., and Klippel, R.A. *The Rat Brain: A Stereotaxic Atlas of the Forebrain and Lower Parts of the Brain Stem.* Baltimore: Williams & Wilkins, 1963.

Paxinos, G., and Watson, C. *The Rat Brain in Stereotaxic Coordinates,* 2nd ed. Sydney: Academic Press, 1986.

Slotnick, B.M., and Leonard, C.M. *A Stereotaxic Atlas of the Albino Mouse Forebrain.* Rockville, Md.: Public Health Service, 1975. (U.S. Government Printing Office Stock Number 017-024-00491-0.)

Snider, R.S., and Niemer, W.T. *A Stereotaxic Atlas of the Cat Brain.* Chicago: University of Chicago Press, 1961.

Swanson, L.W. *Brain Maps: Structure of the Rat Brain.* Amsterdam: Elsevier, 1992.

Histological Methods:

Heimer, L., and Záborsky, L. *Neuroanatomical Tract-Tracing Methods 2: Recent Progress.* New York: Plenum Press, 1989.

CHAPTER 6

Vision

The Stimulus

Anatomy of the Visual System
- The Eyes
- Photoreceptors
- Connections Between Eye and Brain
  Interim Summary

Coding of Visual Information in the Retina
- Coding of Light and Dark
- Coding of Color
  Interim Summary

Analysis of Visual Information: Role of the Striate Cortex
- Anatomy of the Striate Cortex
- Orientation and Movement
- Spatial Frequency
- Texture
- Retinal Disparity
- Color
- Modular Organization of the Striate Cortex
- Blindsight
  Interim Summary

Analysis of Visual Information: Role of the Visual Association Cortex
- Two Streams of Visual Analysis
- Perception of Color
- Analysis of Form
- Perception of Movement
- Perception of Location
  Interim Summary

As we saw in Chapter 4, the brain performs two major functions: It controls the movements of the muscles, producing useful behaviors, and it regulates the body's internal environment. To perform both these tasks, the brain must be informed about what is happening both in the external environment and within the body. Such information is received by the sensory systems. This chapter and the next are devoted to a discussion of the ways in which sensory organs detect changes in the environment and the ways in which the brain interprets neural signals from these organs.

People often say that we have five senses: sight, hearing, smell, taste, and touch. Actually, we have more than five, but even experts disagree about how the lines between the various categories should be drawn. Certainly, we should add the vestibular senses; as well as providing us with auditory information, the inner ear supplies information about head orientation and movement. The sense of touch (or, more accurately, *somatosensation*) detects changes in pressure, warmth, cold, vibration, limb position, and events that damage tissue (that is, produce pain). Everyone agrees that we can detect these stimuli; the issue is whether or not they are detected by separate senses.

This chapter considers vision, the sensory modality that receives the most attention from psychologists, anatomists, and physiologists. One reason for this attention derives from the fascinating complexity of the sensory organs of vision and the relatively large proportion of the brain that is devoted to the analysis of visual information. Another reason, I am sure, is that vision is so important to us as individuals. A natural fascination with such a rich source of information about the world leads to curiosity about how this sensory modality works. Chapter 7 deals with the other sensory modalities: audition, the somatosenses, the vestibular senses, gustation, and olfaction.

THE STIMULUS

As we all know, our eyes detect the presence of light. For humans, light is a narrow band of the spectrum of electromagnetic radiation. Electromagnetic radiation with a wavelength of between 380 and 760 nm (a nanometer, nm, is one-billionth of a meter) is visible to us. (See *Figure 6.1.*) Other animals can detect different ranges of electromagnetic radiation. For example, honeybees can detect differences in ultraviolet radiation reflected by flowers that appear white to us. The range of wavelengths we call *light* is not qualitatively different from the rest of the electromagnetic spectrum; it is simply the part of the continuum that we humans can see.

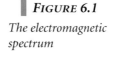

FIGURE 6.1

The electromagnetic spectrum

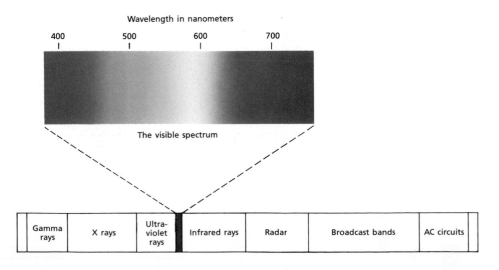

Increasing saturation ──────────▶

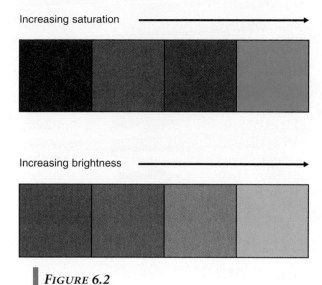

Increasing brightness ──────────▶

FIGURE 6.2

Examples of colors with the same dominant wavelength (hue), but different levels of saturations or brightness.

The perceived color of light is determined by three dimensions: *hue, saturation,* and *brightness.* Light travels at a constant speed of approximately 300,000 kilometers (186,000 miles) per second. Thus, if the frequency of oscillation of the wave varies, the distance between the peaks of the waves will similarly vary, but in inverse fashion. Slower oscillations lead to longer wavelengths, and faster ones to shorter wavelengths. Wavelength determines the first of the three perceptual dimensions of light: **hue.** The visible spectrum displays the range of hues that our eyes can detect.

Light can also vary in intensity, which corresponds to the second perceptual dimension of light: **brightness.** If the intensity of the electromagnetic radiation is increased, the apparent brightness increases, too. The third dimension, **saturation,** refers to the relative purity of the light that is being perceived. If all the radiation is of one wavelength, the perceived color is pure, or fully saturated. Conversely, if the radiation contains all wavelengths, it produces no sensation of hue—it appears white. Colors with intermediate amounts of saturation consist of different mixtures of wavelengths. Figure 6.2 shows some color samples, all with the same hue but with different levels of brightness and saturation. (See *Figure 6.2.*)

ANATOMY OF THE VISUAL SYSTEM

FOR AN INDIVIDUAL TO SEE, AN IMAGE MUST BE focused on the retina, the inner lining of the eye. This image causes changes in the electrical activity of millions of neurons in the retina, which results in messages being sent through the optic nerves to the rest of the brain. (I said "the rest" because the retina is actually part of the brain; it and the optic nerve are in the central—not peripheral—nervous system.) This section describes the anatomy of the eyes, the photoreceptors in the retina that detect the presence of light, and the connections between the retina and the brain.

The Eyes

The eyes are suspended in the *orbits*, bony pockets in the front of the skull. They are held in place and moved by six extraocular muscles attached to the tough, white outer coat of the eye called the *sclera.* (See *Figure 6.3.*) Normally, we cannot look behind our eyeballs and see these muscles because their attachments to the eyes are hidden by the *conjunctiva.* These mucous membranes line the eyelid and fold back to attach to the eye (thus preventing a contact lens that has slipped off the cornea from "falling behind the eye"). Figure 6.4 illustrates the external and internal anatomy of the eye. (See *Figure 6.4.)*

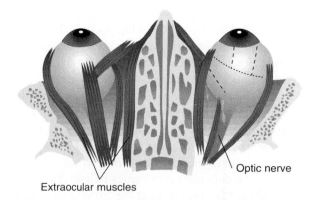

Extraocular muscles

Optic nerve

FIGURE 6.3

The extraocular muscles, which move the eyes.

FIGURE 6.4

The human eye.

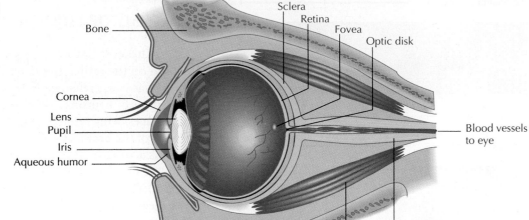

The eyes make three types of movements: vergence movements, saccadic movements, and pursuit movements. **Vergence movements** are cooperative movements that keep both eyes fixed upon the same target—or, more precisely, that keep the image of the target object on corresponding parts of the two retinas. If you hold up a finger in front of your face, look at it, and then bring your finger closer to your face, your eyes will make vergence movements toward your nose. If you then look at an object on the other side of the room, your eyes will rotate outward, and you will see two separate blurry images of your finger.

When you scan the scene in front of you, your gaze does not roam slowly and steadily across its features. Instead, your eyes make jerky **saccadic movements**—you shift your gaze abruptly from one point to another. When you read a line in this book, your eyes stop several times, moving very quickly between each stop. You cannot consciously control the speed of movement between stops; during each *saccade* the eyes move as fast as they can. Only by performing a **pursuit movement**—say, by looking at your finger while you move it around—can you make your eyes move more slowly.

The outer layer of most of the eye, the sclera, is opaque and does not permit entry of light. However, the cornea, the outer layer at the front of the eye, is transparent and admits light. The amount of light that enters is regulated by the size of the pupil, which

is an opening in the iris, the pigmented ring of muscles situated behind the cornea. The lens, situated immediately behind the iris, consists of a series of transparent, onionlike layers. Its shape can be altered by contraction of the ciliary muscles. These changes in shape permit the eye to focus images of near or distant objects on the retina—a process called **accommodation.**

After passing through the lens, light traverses the main part of the eye, which contains the *vitreous humor.* Vitreous humor ("glassy liquid") is a clear, gelatinous substance that gives the eye its bulk. After passing through the vitreous humor, light falls on the **retina,** the interior lining of the back of the eye. In the retina are located the receptor cells, the **rods** and **cones** (named for their shapes), collectively known as **photoreceptors.** The human retina contains approximately 120 million rods and 6 million cones. Although they are greatly outnumbered by rods, cones provide us with most of the information about our environment. In particular, they are responsible for our daytime vision. They provide us with information about small features in the environment and thus are the source of vision of the highest sharpness, or *acuity* (from *acus,* "needle"). The **fovea,** or central region of the retina, which mediates our most acute vision, contains only cones. Cones are also responsible for color vision—our ability to discriminate light of different wavelengths. Although rods do not detect different colors and

Optic disk
(Blind spot)

Fovea

FIGURE 6.5

A test for the blind spot. With your left eye closed, look at the + with your right eye and move the page nearer and farther from you. When the page is about 20 cm from your face, the blue circle disappears, because its image falls on the blind spot of your right eye.

provide vision of poor acuity, they are more sensitive to light. In a very dimly lighted environment we use our rod vision; therefore, in dim light we are color-blind and lack foveal vision. You have probably noticed, while out on a dark night, that looking directly at a dim, distant light (i.e, placing the image of the light on the fovea) causes it to disappear.

Another feature of the retina is the **optic disk**, where the axons conveying visual information gather together and leave the eye through the optic nerve. The optic disk produces a *blind spot*, because no receptors are located there. We do not normally perceive our blind spots, but their presence can be demonstrated. If you have not found yours, you may want to try the exercise described in *Figure 6.5.*

Close examination of the retina shows that it consists of several layers of neuron cell bodies, their axons and dendrites, and the photoreceptors. Fig-

ure 6.6 illustrates a cross section through the primate retina, which is divided into three main layers: the photoreceptive layer, the bipolar cell layer, and the ganglion cell layer. Note that the photoreceptors are at the *back* of the retina; light must pass through the overlying layers to get to them. Fortunately, these layers are transparent. (See *Figure 6.6.*)

The photoreceptors form synapses with **bipolar cells**, neurons whose two arms connect the shallowest and deepest layers of the retina. In turn, these neurons form synapses with the **ganglion cells**, neurons whose axons travel through the optic nerves (the second cranial nerves) and carry visual information into the brain. In addition, the retina contains **horizontal cells** and **amacrine cells,** both of which transmit information in a direction parallel to the surface of the retina and thus combine messages from adjacent photoreceptors. (See *Figure 6.6.*)

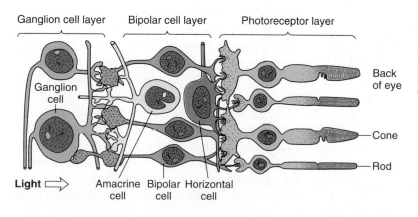

Ganglion cell layer   Bipolar cell layer   Photoreceptor layer

Ganglion
cell

Back
of eye

Cone

Rod

Light

Amacrine
cell

Bipolar
cell

Horizontal
cell

FIGURE 6.6

Details of retinal circuitry.

(Adapted from Dowling, J.E., and Boycott, B.B. *Proceedings of the Royal Society of London,* B., 1966, *166,* 80–111.)

Photoreceptors

Figure 6.7 shows a drawing of a rod and a cone. Note that each photoreceptor consists of an outer segment connected by a cilium to the inner segment, which contains the nucleus. (See *Figure 6.7.*) The outer segment contains several hundred **lamellae,** or thin plates of membrane. (*Lamella* is the diminutive form of *lamina,* "thin layer.")

The first step in the chain of events that leads to visual perception involves a special chemical called a photopigment. (The steps of this process were discovered by George Wald, who received a Nobel prize for his work in 1967.) **Photopigments** are special molecules embedded in the membrane of the lamellae; a single human rod contains approximately 10 million of them. The molecules consist of two parts: an **opsin** (a protein) and **retinal** (a lipid). There are several forms of opsin; for example, the photopigment of human rods, **rhodopsin,** consists of *rod opsin* plus retinal. (*Rhod-* refers to the Greek *rhodon,* "rose," not to *rod.* Before it is bleached by the action

of light, rhodopsin has a pinkish hue.) Retinal is synthesized from vitamin A, which explains why carrots, rich in this vitamin, are said to be good for your eyesight.

When a molecule of rhodopsin is exposed to light, it breaks into its two constituents, rod opsin and retinal. When that happens, the rod opsin changes from its rosy color to a pale yellow; hence, we say that the light *bleaches* the photopigment. The splitting of the photopigment causes a change in the membrane potential of the photoreceptor called the **receptor potential,** which changes the rate at which the photoreceptor releases its transmitter substance. The membrane of photoreceptors is different from that of other neurons—it contains ion channels that are normally *open.* These ion channels admit anions; thus, the resting membrane potential is less polarized than that of other neurons, and the receptor potential is a *hyperpolarization.* Also unlike other neurons, photoreceptors continuously release their neurotransmitter. When light causes a molecule of the photopigment to split, the sodium channels in the outer membrane of the photoreceptor close. Because anions can no longer enter the cell, the membrane then becomes more polarized, and the transmitter substance is no longer released. (See *Figure 6.8.*)

In the vertebrate retina, photoreceptors provide input to both bipolar cells and horizontal cells. Figure 6.9 shows the neural circuitry from a photoreceptor to a ganglion cell. The circuitry is much simplified and omits the horizontal cells and amacrine cells. The first two types of cells in the circuit—photoreceptors and bipolar cells—do not produce action potentials. Instead, their release of transmitter substance is regulated by the value of their membrane potential; depolarizations increase the release, and hyperpolarizations decrease it. The circles indicate what would be seen on an oscilloscope screen recording changes in the cells' membrane potentials in response to a spot of light shining on the photoreceptor.

The hyperpolarizing effect of light on the membranes of photoreceptors is shown in the right graph. The hyperpolarization *reduces* the release of transmitter substance by the photoreceptor. Because the transmitter substance normally hyperpolarizes the dendrites of the bipolar cell, a *reduction* in its

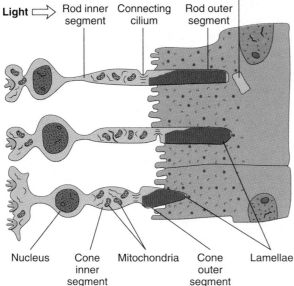

Fragment detached from rod outer segment during normal loss and regeneration of lamellae

Light — Rod inner segment — Connecting cilium — Rod outer segment — Nucleus — Cone inner segment — Mitochondria — Cone outer segment — Lamellae

FIGURE 6.7

Photoreceptors.
(Redrawn from Young, R.W. Visual cells, *Scientific American,* October 1970.)

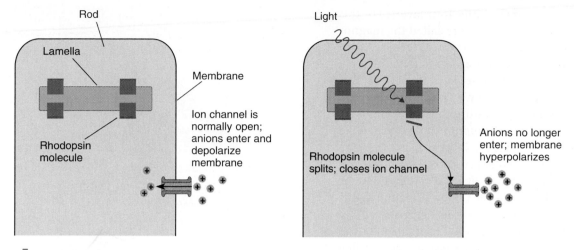

FIGURE 6.8

Transduction. A hypothetical explanation for the production of receptor potentials in photoreceptors.

release causes the membrane of the bipolar cell to *depolarize*. Thus, light hyperpolarizes the photoreceptor and depolarizes the bipolar cell. (See *Figure 6.9.*) The depolarization causes the bipolar cell to release more transmitter substance, which depolarizes the membrane of the ganglion cell, causing it to increase its rate of firing. Thus, light shining on the photoreceptor causes excitation of the ganglion cell.

The circuit shown in Figure 6.9 illustrates a ganglion cell whose firing rate increases in response to light. As we will see, other ganglion cells *decrease* their firing rate in response to light. These neurons are connected to bipolar cells that form different types of synapses with the photoreceptors. The

functions of these two types of circuits is discussed later, in a section entitled "Coding of Visual Information in the Retina."

Connections Between Eye and Brain

The axons of the retinal ganglion cells bring information to the rest of the brain. They ascend through the optic nerves and reach the **dorsal lateral geniculate nucleus** of the thalamus. This nucleus receives its name from its resemblance to a bent knee (*genu* means "knee"). It contains six layers of neurons, each of which receives input from only one eye. The neurons in the two inner layers contain cell bodies

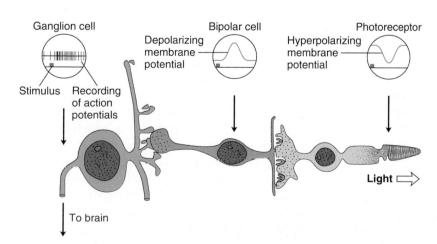

FIGURE 6.9

Neural circuitry in the retina. Light striking a photoreceptor produces a hyperpolarization, so the photoreceptor releases less *transmitter substance. Because the transmitter substance normally hyperpolarizes the membrane of the bipolar cell, the reduction causes a* depolarization. *This depolarization causes the bipolar cell to release* more *transmitter substance, which excites the ganglion cell.*

(Adapted from Dowling, J.E., in *The Neurosciences: Fourth Study Program,* edited by F.O. Schmitt and F.G. Worden. Cambridge, Mass.: MIT Press, 1979.)

larger than those in the outer four layers. For this reason, the inner two layers are called the **magnocellular layers** and the outer four layers are called the **parvocellular layers** (*parvo-* refers to the small size of the cells). As we will see later, these two sets of layers belong to different systems, which are responsible for the analysis of different types of visual information. They receive input from different types of retinal ganglion cells. (See *Figure 6.10*.)

The neurons in the dorsal lateral geniculate nucleus send their axons via the optic radiations to the primary visual cortex—the region surrounding the **calcarine fissure** (*calcarine* means "spur-shaped"), a horizontal fissure located in the medial and posterior occipital lobe. The primary visual cortex is often

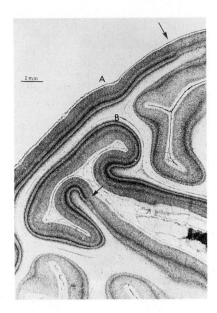

│ FIGURE 6.11

A photomicrograph of a cross section through the striate cortex of a rhesus macaque monkey. The ends of the striate cortex are shown by arrows.

(From Hubel, D.H., and Wiesel, T.N. *Proceedings of the Royal Society of London, B.*, 1977, *198*, 1–59.)

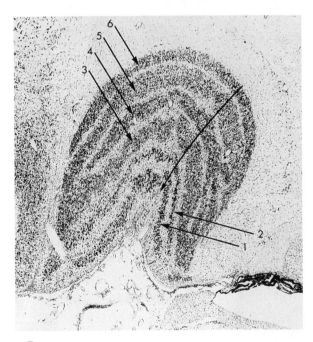

│ FIGURE 6.10

A photomicrograph of a section through the right lateral geniculate nucleus of a rhesus monkey (cresyl violet stain). Layers 1, 4, and 6 receive input from the contralateral (left) eye, and layers 2, 3, and 5 receive input from the ipsilateral (right) eye. Layers 1 and 2 are the magnocellular layers; layers 3–6 are the parvocellular layers. The receptive fields of all six layers are in almost perfect registration; cells located along the line of the unlabeled arrow have receptive fields centered on the same point.

(From Hubel, D.H., Wiesel, T.N., and Le Vay, S. *Philosophical Transactions of the Royal Society of London, B.*, 1977, *278*, 131–163.)

called the **striate cortex** because it contains a dark-staining layer *(striation)* of cells. (See *Figure 6.11*.)

Figure 6.12 shows a diagrammatical view of a horizontal section of the human brain. The optic nerves join together at the base of the brain to form the X-shaped **optic chiasm** *(khiasma* means "cross"). There, axons from ganglion cells serving the inner halves of the retina (the nasal sides) cross through the chiasm and ascend to the dorsal lateral geniculate nucleus of the opposite side of the brain. The axons from the outer halves of the retina (the temporal sides) remain on the same side of the brain. The lens inverts the image of the world projected on the retina (and similarly reverses left and right). Therefore, because the axons from the nasal halves of the retinas cross to the other side of the brain, each hemisphere receives information from the contralateral half (opposite side) of the visual scene. That is, if a person looks straight ahead, the right hemisphere receives information from the left half of the visual field, and the left hemisphere receives information from the right. (See *Figure 6.12*.)

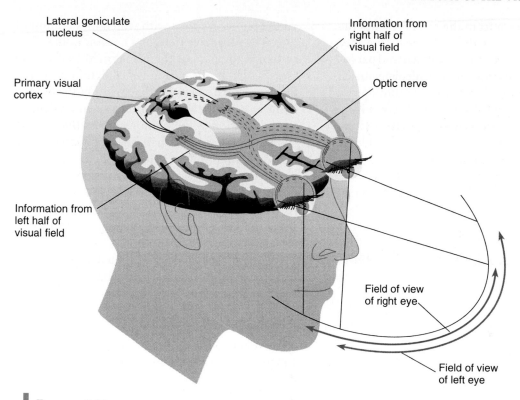

Lateral geniculate nucleus

Information from right half of visual field

Primary visual cortex

Optic nerve

Information from left half of visual field

Field of view of right eye

Field of view of left eye

FIGURE 6.12

The primary visual pathway.

Besides the primary retino-geniculo-cortical pathway, there are several other pathways taken by fibers from the retina. For example, one pathway to the hypothalamus synchronizes an animal's activity cycles to the 24-hour rhythms of day and night. (We will study this system in Chapter 9.) Other pathways, especially those that travel to the optic tectum and the pretectal nuclei, coordinate eye movements, control the muscles of the iris and lens, and help direct our attention to sudden movements in the periphery of our visual field.

||||| INTERIM SUMMARY

Light consists of electromagnetic radiation, similar to radio waves but of a different frequency and wavelength. Color can vary in three perceptual dimensions: hue, brightness, and saturation, which correspond, respectively, to the physical dimensions of wavelength, intensity, and purity.

The photoreceptors in the retina—the rods and the cones—detect light. Muscles move the eyes so that images of the environment fall on the retina. Accommodation is accomplished by the ciliary muscles, which change the shape of the lens. Photoreceptors communicate through synapses with bipolar cells, which communicate through synapses with ganglion cells. Horizontal cells and amacrine cells combine messages from adjacent photoreceptors.

When light strikes a molecule of photopigment in a photoreceptor, the retinal molecule detaches from the opsin molecule. This detachment initiates a series of chemical reactions that closes sodium channels and produces the receptor potential—hyperpolarization of the photoreceptor membrane. As a result, the rate of firing of the ganglion cell changes, signaling the detection of light. Because different types of cones contain different types of opsins, they are most sensitive to light of different wavelengths. This fact provides the basis for color vision.

Visual information from the retina reaches the striate cortex surrounding the calcarine fissure after being relayed through the magnocellular and parvocellular layers of the dorsal lateral geniculate nuclei. Several other regions of the brain, including the hypothalamus and the tectum, also receive visual information. These regions help regulate activity during the day/night cycle, coordinate eye and head movements, control attention to visual stimuli, and regulate the size of the pupils.

CODING OF VISUAL INFORMATION IN THE RETINA

THIS SECTION DESCRIBES THE WAY IN WHICH CELLS of the retina encode information they receive from the photoreceptors.

Coding of Light and Dark

One of the most important methods for studying the physiology of the visual system is the use of microelectrodes to record the electrical activity of single neurons. As we saw in the previous section, some ganglion cells become excited when light falls on the photoreceptors with which they communicate. The **receptive field** of a neuron in the visual system is the part of the visual field that neuron "sees"—that is, the part in which light must fall for the neuron to be stimulated. Obviously, the location of the receptive field of a particular neuron depends on the location of the photoreceptors that provide it with visual information. If a neuron receives information from photoreceptors located in the fovea, its receptive field will be at the fixation point—the point at which the eye is looking. If the neuron receives information from photoreceptors located in the periphery of the retina, its receptive field will be located off to one side.

At the periphery of the retina many individual receptors converge on a single ganglion cell, bringing information from a relatively large area of the retina—and hence a relatively large area of the visual field. However, foveal vision is more direct, with approximately equal numbers of ganglion cells and cones. These receptor-to-axon relationships explain the fact that our foveal (central) vision is very acute, but our peripheral vision is much less precise. (See *Figure 6.13.*)

Over sixty years go, Hartline (1938) discovered that the frog retina contained three types of ganglion cells. ON cells responded with an excitatory burst when the retina was illuminated, OFF cells re-

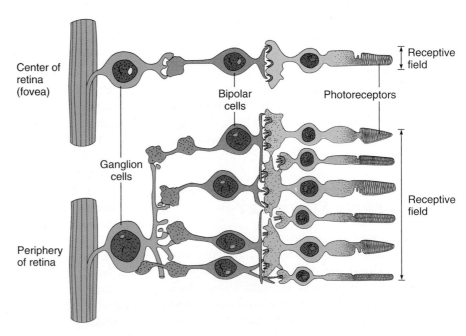

FIGURE 6.13

Central versus peripheral acuity. Ganglion cells in the fovea receive input from a smaller number of photoreceptors than in the periphery and hence provide more acute visual information.

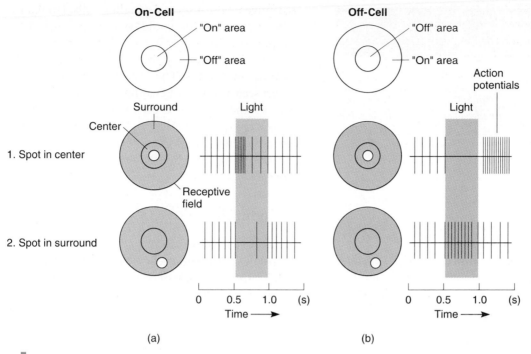

Responses of ON and OFF ganglion cells to stimuli presented in the center or the surround of the receptive field.
(Adapted from Kuffler, S.W. *Cold Spring Harbor Symposium for Quantitative Biology,* 1952, *17,* 281–292.)

sponded when the light was turned off, and ON/OFF cells responded briefly when the light went on and again when it went off. Kuffler (1952, 1953), recording from ganglion cells in the retina of the cat, discovered that their receptive field consists of a roughly circular center, surrounded by a ring. Stimulation of the center or surrounding fields had contrary effects: ON cells were excited by light falling in the central field (*center*) and were inhibited by light falling in the surrounding field (*surround*), whereas OFF cells responded in the opposite manner. ON/OFF ganglion cells receive information from both types of bipolar cells. In the primate retina, these ON/OFF cells project primarily to the superior colliculus (Schiller and Malpeli, 1977); thus, they do not appear to play a direct role in form perception. (See *Figure 6.14.*)

Figure 6.14 also illustrates a rebound effect that occurs when the light is turned off again. Neurons whose firing is inhibited while the light is on will show a brief burst of excitation when it is turned off.

In contrast, neurons whose firing is increased will show a brief period of inhibition when the light is turned off. (See *Figure 6.14.*)

The two major categories of ganglion cells (ON and OFF) and the organization of their receptive fields into contrasting center and surround provide useful information to the rest of the visual system. Let us consider the two types of ganglion cells first. As Schiller (1992) notes, ganglion cells normally fire at a relatively low rate. Then, when the level of illumination in the center of their receptive field increases or decreases (for example, when an object moves or the eye makes a saccade), they signal the change. In particular, ON cells signal increases and OFF cells signal decreases—but both signal them by an increased rate of firing. Such a system is particularly efficient. Theoretically, a single type of ganglion cell could fire at an intermediate rate and signal changes in the level of illumination by increases or decreases in rate of firing. However, in this case the average rate of firing of the one million

FIGURE 6.15

Enhancement of contrast. Although each gray square is of uniform darkness, the right edge of each square looks somewhat lighter and the left edge looks somewhat darker. This effect appears to be caused by the opponent center-surround arrangement of the receptive fields of the retinal ganglion cells.

axons in each optic nerve would have to be much higher.

Several studies have shown that ON cells and OFF cells do, indeed, signal different kinds of information. Schiller, Sandell, and Maunsell (1986) injected APB (2-amino-4-phosphonobutyrate), a drug that selectively blocks synaptic transmission in ON bipolar cells, into the retinas of monkeys. They found that the animals were less able to detect spots that were made brighter than the background but had no difficulty detecting spots slightly darker than the background. In addition, Dolan and Schiller (1989) found that an injection of APB completely blocked vision in very dim light, which is normally mediated by rods. Thus, rod bipolar cells must all be of the ON type. (If you think about it, that arrangement makes sense; in very dim light we are more likely to see brighter objects against a dark background than dark objects against a light background.)

The second characteristic of the receptive fields of ganglion cells—their center-surround organization—enhances our ability to detect the outlines of objects even when the contrast between the object and the background is low. Figure 6.15 illustrates this phenomenon. This figure shows six gray squares, arranged in order of brightness. The right side of each square looks darker than the left side, which makes the borders between the squares stand out. But these exaggerated borders do not exist in the drawing; they are added by our visual system because of the center-surround organization of the retinal ganglion cells. (See *Figure 6.15.*)

Figure 6.16 explains how this phenomenon works. We see the centers and surrounds of the

receptive fields of several ganglion cells. (In reality, these receptive fields would be overlapping, but the simplified arrangement is easier to understand. This example also includes only ON cells—again, for the sake of simplicity.) The image of the edge of an object seen against a slightly lighter background falls across some of these receptive fields. The cells whose centers are located in the brighter region but whose surrounds are located at least partially in the darker region will have the highest rate of firing. (See *Figure 6.16.*)

Coding of Color

So far, we have been examining the monochromatic properties of ganglion cells—that is, their responses to light and dark. But, of course, objects in our environment selectively absorb some wavelengths of light and reflect others, which, to our eyes, gives

All of the surrounds of the ON cells whose receptive fields fall within the lighter gray are evenly illuminated; this illumination partially inhibits the firing of these cells.

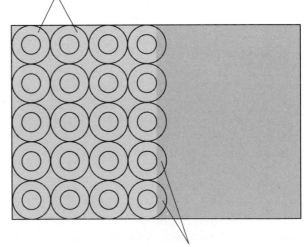

A portion of the inhibitory surrounds of the ON cells near the border receives less illumination; thus, these cells have the highest rate of firing.

FIGURE 6.16

A schematic explanation of the phenomenon shown in Figure 6.15. Only ON cells are shown; OFF cells are responsible for the darker appearance of the left side of the darker square.

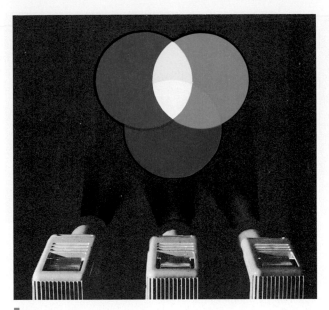

FIGURE 6.17

Additive color mixing and paint mixing. When blue, red, and green light of the proper intensity are all shone together, the result is white light. When red, blue, and yellow paints are mixed together, the result is a dark gray.
(Photo courtesy of GATF.)

them different colors. Although monochromatic (black-and-white) vision is perfectly adequate for most purposes, color vision gives us, for example, the ability to distinguish ripe fruit from unripe fruit and makes it more difficult for other animals to hide themselves by means of camouflage (Mollon, 1989).

Color Mixing

Various theories of color vision have been proposed for many years—long before it was possible to disprove or validate them by physiological means. In 1802 Thomas Young, a British physicist and physician, proposed that the eye detected different colors because it contained three types of receptors, each sensitive to a single hue. His theory was referred to as the *trichromatic* (three-color) *theory*. It was suggested by the fact that for a human observer any color can be reproduced by mixing various quantities of three colors judiciously selected from different points along the spectrum.

I must emphasize that *color mixing* is different from *pigment mixing*. If we combine yellow and blue pigments (as when we mix paints), the resulting

mixture is green. Color mixing refers to the addition of two or more light sources. If we shine a beam of red light and a beam of bluish green light together on a white screen, we will see yellow light. If we mix yellow and blue light, we get white light. When white appears on a color television screen, it actually consists of tiny dots of red, blue, and green light. (See *Figures 6.17* and *6.18*.)

Another fact of color perception suggested to a German physiologist, Ewald Hering (1905/1965), that hue might be represented in the visual system as *opponent colors*. Humans have long regarded yellow, blue, red, and green as primary colors. (Black and white are primary, too, but we perceive them as colorless.) All other colors can be described as mixtures of these primary colors. The trichromatic system cannot explain why *yellow* is included in this group. In addition, some colors appear to blend, whereas others do not. For example, one can speak of a bluish green or a yellowish green, and orange appears to have both red and yellow qualities. Purple resembles both red and blue. But try to imagine a reddish green or a bluish yellow. It is impossible;

(a)   (b)

FIGURE 6.18

Color coding. The television screen demonstrates—in reverse—the principle of color coding by the three types of cones in the retina. (a) A small white rectangle shown in the middle of the screen. (b) An enlargement of the same white rectangle. Note that the screen displays only red, blue, and green spots of light. At a distance these colors blend and produce white light.

these colors seem to be opposite to each other. Again, these facts are not explained by the trichromatic theory. As we shall see in the following section, the visual system uses both trichromatic and opponent-color systems to encode information related to color.

Photoreceptors: Trichromatic Coding

Physiological investigations of retinal photoreceptors in higher primates have found that Young was right: Three different types of photoreceptors (three different types of cones) are responsible for color vision. Investigators have studied the absorption characteristics of individual photoreceptors, determining the amount of light of different wavelengths that is absorbed by the photopigments. These characteristics are controlled by the particular opsin a photoreceptor contains; different opsins absorb particular wavelengths more readily. Figure 6.19 shows the absorption characteristics of the four types of photoreceptors in the human retina: rods and the three types of cones. (See *Figure 6.19.*)

The peak sensitivities of the three types of cones are approximately 420 nm (blue-violet), 530 nm (green), and 560 nm (yellow-green). The peak sensitivity of the short-wavelength cone is actually 440

nm in the intact eye, because the lens absorbs some short-wavelength light. For convenience, the short-, medium-, and long-wavelength cones are traditionally called "blue," "green," and "red" cones, respectively. The retina contains approximately equal numbers of "red" and "green" cones but a much smaller number of "blue" cones (approximately 8 percent of the total).

Genetic defects in color vision appear to result from anomalies in one or more of the three types of cones (Boynton, 1979; Nathans et al., 1986). The first two kinds of defective color vision described here involve genes on the X chromosome; thus, because males have only one X chromosome, they are much more likely to have this disorder. (Females are likely to have a normal gene on one of their X chromosomes, which compensates for the defective one.) People with **protanopia** ("first-color defect") confuse red and green. They see the world in shades of yellow and blue; both red and green look yellowish to them. Their visual acuity is normal, which suggests that their retinas do not lack "red" or "green" cones. This fact, and their sensitivity to lights of different wavelengths, suggests that their "red" cones are filled with "green" cone opsin. People with **deuteranopia** ("second-color defect") also confuse red and green and also have normal visual acuity. Their "green" cones appear to be filled with "red" cone opsin.

Tritanopia ("third-color defect") is rare, affecting fewer than 1 in 10,000 people. This disorder involves a faulty gene that is not located on an X chromosome; thus, it is equally prevalent in males and females. People with tritanopia have difficulty with hues of short wavelengths and see the world in greens and reds. To them, a clear blue sky is a bright green, and yellow looks pink. Their retinas appear to lack "blue" cones. Because the retina contains so few of these cones, their absence does not noticeably affect visual acuity.

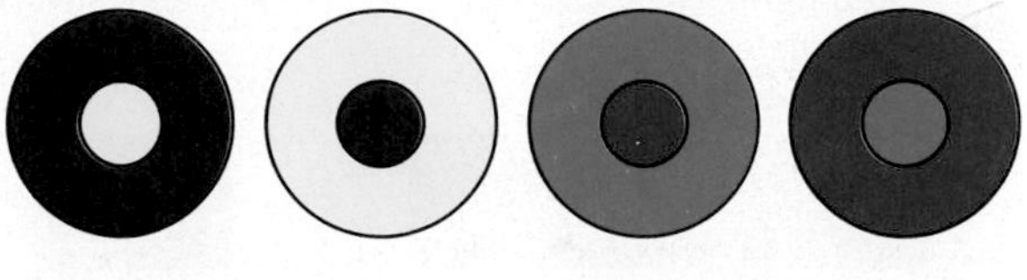

Retinal Ganglion Cells: Opponent-Process Coding

At the level of the retinal ganglion cell, the three-color code gets translated into an opponent-color system. Daw (1968) and Gouras (1968) found that these neurons respond specifically to pairs of primary colors, with red opposing green and blue opposing yellow. Thus, the retina contains two kinds of color-sensitive ganglion cells: *red-green* and *yellow-blue*. Most color-sensitive ganglion cells respond

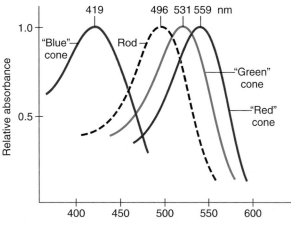

| Yellow on, blue off | Blue on, yellow off | Red on, green off | Green on, red off |

FIGURE 6.20

Receptive fields of color-sensitive ganglion cells. When a region of the receptive field is illuminated with the color shown, the cell's rate of firing increases. When a region is illuminated with the complementary color, the cell's rate of firing decreases.

FIGURE 6.19

Relative absorbance of light of various wavelengths by rods and the three types of cones in the human retina.

(From Dartnall, H.J.A., Bowmaker, J.K., and Mollon, J.D. Human visual pigments: Microspectrophotometric results from the eyes of seven persons. *Proceedings of the Royal Society of London, B.*, 1983, *220*, 115–130.)

in a center-surround fashion. For example, a cell might be excited by red and inhibited by green in the center of their receptive field, while showing the opposite response in the surrounding ring. (See **Figure 6.20**.) Other ganglion cells that receive input from cones do not respond differentially to different wavelengths but simply encode relative brightness in the center and surround. These cells serve as "black-and-white" detectors.

The response characteristics of retinal ganglion cells to light of different wavelengths are obviously determined by the particular circuits that connect the three types of cones with the two types of ganglion cells. These circuits involve different types of bipolar cells, amacrine cells, and horizontal cells.

Figure 6.21 helps explain how particular hues are detected by the "red," "green," and "blue" cones and translated into excitation or inhibition of the red-green and yellow-blue ganglion cells. The diagram does not show the actual neural circuitry, which includes the retinal neurons that connect the cones with the ganglion cells. The arrows refer merely to the effects of the light falling on the retina. Detection and coding of pure red, green, or blue light is the easiest to understand. For example, red light excites "red" cones, which causes the excitation of red-green ganglion cells. (See **Figure 6.21a**.) Green light excites "green" cones, which causes the *inhibition* of red-green cells. (See **Figure 6.21b**.) But consider the effect of yellow light. Because the wavelength that produces the sensation of yellow is intermediate between red and green, it will stimulate both "red" and "green" cones about equally. Yellow-blue gan-

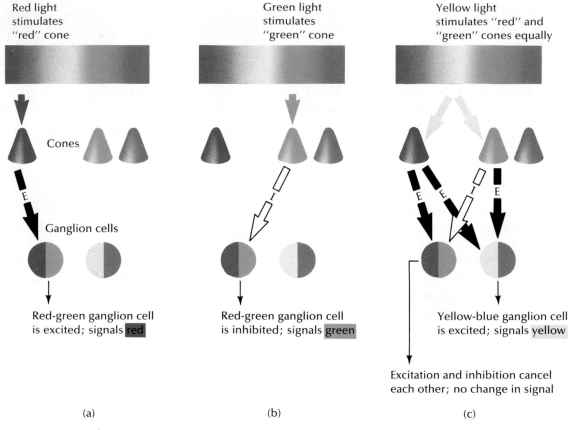

FIGURE 6.21

Color coding in the retina. (a) Red light stimulating a "red" cone, which causes excitation of a red-green ganglion cell. (b) Green light stimulating a "green" cone, which causes inhibition of a red-green ganglion cell. (c) Yellow light stimulating "red" and "green" cones equally but not affecting "blue" cones. The stimulation of "red" and "green" cones causes excitation of a yellow-blue ganglion cell. The arrows labeled E and I represent neural circuitry within the retina that translates excitation of a cone into excitation or inhibition of a ganglion cell. For clarity, only some of the circuits are shown.

glion cells are excited by both "red" and "green" cones, so their rate of firing increases. However, red-green ganglion cells are excited by red and inhibited by green, so their firing rate does not change. The brain detects an increased firing rate from the axons of yellow-blue ganglion cells, which it interprets as yellow. (See *Figure 6.21c.*)

The opponent-color system employed by the ganglion cells explains why we cannot perceive a reddish green or a bluish yellow: An axon that signals red or green (or yellow or blue) can either increase or decrease its rate of firing; it cannot do both at the

same time. A reddish green would have to be signaled by a ganglion cell firing slowly and rapidly at the same time, which is obviously impossible.

INTERIM SUMMARY

Recordings of the electrical activity of single neurons in the retina indicate that each ganglion cell receives information from several photoreceptors—fewer in the fovea, and many more in the periphery. The receptive field of most retinal ganglion cells consists of two concentric circles, becoming excited when light falls in one region and becoming inhibited when it falls in the other. This arrangement enhances the ability of the nervous system to detect contrasts in brightness. ON cells are excited by light in the center, and OFF cells are excited by light in the surround. ON cells detect light objects against dark backgrounds; OFF cells detect dark objects against light backgrounds.

Color vision occurs as a result of information provided by three types of cones, each of which is sensitive to light of a certain wavelength: long, medium, or short. Most color-sensitive ganglion cells respond in an opposing center-surround fashion to the pairs of primary colors: red and green, and blue and yellow.

The absorption characteristics of the cones are determined by the particular opsin that their photopigment contains. Most forms of defective color vision appear to be caused by alterations in cone opsins. The "red" cones of people with protanopia are filled with "green" cone opsin, and the "green" cones of people with deuteranopia are filled with "red" cone opsin. The retinas of people with tritanopia appear to lack "blue" cones.

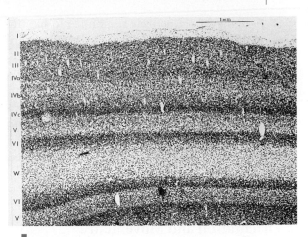

FIGURE 6.22

A photomicrograph of a small section of striate cortex, showing the six principal layers. The letter W refers to the white matter that underlies the visual cortex; beneath the white matter is layer VI of the striate cortex on the opposite side of the gyrus.

(From Hubel, D.H., and Wiesel, T.N. *Proceedings of the Royal Society of London, B.,* 1977, *198,* 1–59. Reprinted with permission.)

ANALYSIS OF VISUAL INFORMATION: ROLE OF THE STRIATE CORTEX

THE RETINAL GANGLION CELLS ENCODE INFORMAtion about the relative amounts of light falling on the center and surround of their receptive field and, in many cases, about the wavelength of that light. The striate cortex and visual association cortex perform additional processing of this information, which it then transmits to the visual association cortex.

Anatomy of the Striate Cortex

The striate cortex consists of six principal layers (and several sublayers), arranged in bands parallel to the surface. These layers contain the nuclei of cell bodies and dendritic trees that show up as bands of light or dark in sections of tissue that have been dyed with a cell-body stain. (See *Figure 6.22.*)

In primates, information from the dorsal lateral geniculate nucleus enters the middle layer (layer IV_c) of the striate cortex. From there, it is relayed upward and downward, to be analyzed by circuits of neurons in different layers.

If we consider the striate cortex as a whole—if we imagine that we remove it and spread it out on a flat surface—we find that it contains a map of the contralateral half of the visual field. (Remember that each side of the brain sees the opposite side of the visual field.) The map is distorted; approximately 25 percent of the striate cortex is devoted to the analysis of information from the fovea, which represents a small part of the visual field. (The area of the visual field seen by the fovea is approximately the size of a large grape held at arm's length.)

The pioneering studies of David Hubel and Torsten Wiesel at Harvard University during the 1960s began a revolution in the study of the physiology of visual perception (see Hubel and Wiesel, 1977, 1979). Hubel and Wiesel discovered that neurons in the visual cortex did not simply respond to spots of light; they selectively responded to specific *features* of the visual world. That is, the neural circuitry within the visual cortex combines information from several sources (for example, from axons carrying information received from several different ganglion cells) in such a way as to detect features that are larger than the receptive field of a single ganglion cell. The following subsections describe the visual characteristics that researchers have studied so far: orientation and movement, spatial frequency, texture, retinal disparity, and color.

Orientation and Movement

Most neurons in the striate cortex are sensitive to *orientation*. That is, if a line is positioned in the cell's receptive field and rotated around its center, the cell will respond only when the line is in a particular position—a particular orientation. (See *Figure 6.23.*) Some neurons respond best to a vertical line, some to a horizontal line, and some to a line oriented somewhere in between.

Some orientation-sensitive neurons have receptive fields organized in an opponent fashion. Hubel and Wiesel referred to them as **simple cells.** For example, a line of a particular orientation (say, a dark 45-degree line against a white background) might excite a cell if placed in the center of the receptive field but inhibit it if moved away from the center. (See *Figure 6.24a.*) Another type of neuron,

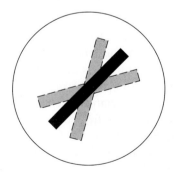

FIGURE 6.23

Orientation sensitivity. An orientation-sensitive neuron in the striate cortex will become active only when a line of a particular orientation appears within its receptive field. For example, the neuron might respond to the black bar, but not to either of the gray bars.

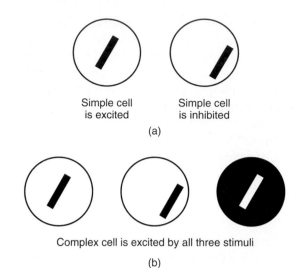

Simple cell is excited   Simple cell is inhibited

(a)

Complex cell is excited by all three stimuli

(b)

FIGURE 6.24

Response characteristics of neurons to orientation in the primary visual cortex. (a) Simple cell. (b) Complex cell.

which the researchers referred to as a **complex cell,** also responded best to a line of a particular orientation but did not show an inhibitory surround; that is, it continued to respond while the line was moved within the receptive field. In fact, many complex cells increased their rate of firing when the line was moved perpendicular to its angle of orientation; thus, they also served as movement detectors. In addition, complex cells responded equally well to white lines against black backgrounds and black lines against white backgrounds. (See *Figure 6.24b.*)

Spatial Frequency

Although the early studies by Hubel and Wiesel suggested that neurons in the primary visual cortex detected lines and edges, subsequent research found that they actually responded best to sine-wave gratings (De Valois, Albrecht, and Thorell, 1978). Figure 6.25 compares a sine-wave grating with a more familiar square-wave grating. A square-wave grating consists of a simple set of rectangular bars that vary in brightness; the brightness along the length of a line perpendicular to them would vary in a stepwise (square-wave) fashion. (See *Figure 6.25a.*) A **sine-wave grating** looks like a series of fuzzy, unfocused parallel bars. Along any line perpendicular to the long axis of the grating, the brightness varies according to a sine-wave function. (See *Figure 6.25b.*)

A sine-wave grating is designated by its spatial frequency. We are accustomed to the expression of frequencies (for example, of sound waves or radio waves) in terms of time or distance (such as cycles per second or cycles per meter). But because the image of a stimulus on the retina varies in size according to how close it is to the eye, the visual angle is generally used instead of the physical distance between adjacent cycles. Thus, the **spatial frequency** of a sine-wave grating is its variation in brightness measured in cycles per degree of visual angle. (See *Figure 6.26.*)

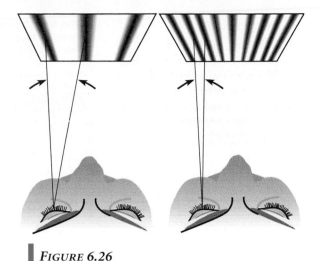

FIGURE 6.26

The concepts of visual angle and spatial frequency. Angles are drawn between the sine waves, with the apex at the viewer's eye. The visual angle between adjacent sine waves is smaller when the waves are closer together.

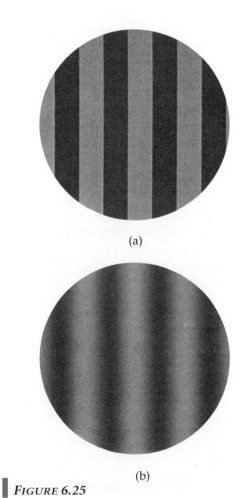

(a)

(b)

FIGURE 6.25

Parallel gratings. (a) Square-wave grating. (b) Sine-wave grating.

(From De Valois, R.L., and De Valois, K.K. *Spatial Vision.* New York: Oxford University Press, 1988.)

Most neurons in the striate cortex respond best when a sine-wave grating of a particular spatial frequency is placed in the appropriate part of the visual field. Different neurons detect different spatial frequencies. For orientation-sensitive neurons the grating must be aligned at the appropriate angle of orientation. Albrecht (1978) mapped the shapes of receptive fields of simple cells by observing their response while moving a very thin flickering line of the appropriate orientation through their receptive fields. He found that many of them had multiple inhibitory and excitatory regions surrounding the center. The profile of the excitatory and inhibitory regions of such neurons looked like a modulated sine wave—precisely what would be needed to detect a few cycles of a sine-wave grating. (See *Figure 6.27.*) In most cases a neuron's receptive field is large enough to include between 1.5 and 3.5 cycles of the grating (De Valois, Thorell, and Albrecht, 1985).

What is the point of having neural circuits that analyze spatial frequency? A complete answer requires some rather complicated mathematics, so I will give a simplified one here. (If you are interested, you can consult De Valois and De Valois, 1988.) Consider the types of information provided by high and low spatial frequencies. Small objects, details within a large object, and large objects with sharp

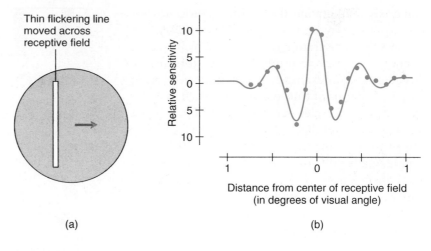

FIGURE 6.27

The experiment by Albrecht, 1978. (a) The stimulus presented to the animal. (b) The response of a simple cell in the primary visual cortex.

(Adapted from De Valois, R.L., and De Valois, K.K. *Spatial Vision.* New York: Oxford University Press, 1988.)

edges provide a signal rich in high frequencies; whereas large areas of light and dark are represented by low frequencies. An image that is deficient in high-frequency information looks fuzzy and out of focus, like the image seen by a nearsighted person who is not wearing corrective lenses. This image still provides much information about forms and objects in the environment; thus, the most important visual information is that contained in *low spatial frequencies.* When low-frequency information is removed, the shapes of images are very difficult to perceive. (We will see the more primitive magnocellular system provides low-frequency information.)

Many experiments have confirmed that the concept of spatial frequency plays a central role in visual perception, and mathematical models have shown that the information present in a scene can be represented very efficiently if it is first encoded in terms of spatial frequency. Thus, the brain probably represents the information in a similar way. Here I will describe just one example to help show the validity of the concept. Look at the two pictures in *Figure 6.28.* You can see that the picture on the right looks much more like the face of Abraham Lincoln than the one on the left. And yet both pictures contain the same information. The creators of the pictures, Harmon and Julesz (1973), used a computer to construct the figure on the left, which consists of a series of squares, each representing the average brightness of a portion of a picture of Lincoln. The one on the right is simply a transformation of the first one in which high frequencies have been removed. Sharp

edges contain high spatial frequencies, so the transformation eliminates them. In the case of the picture on the left, these frequencies have nothing to do with the information contained in the original picture; thus, they can be seen as visual "noise." The filtration process (accomplished by a computer) removes this noise—and makes the image much clearer to the human visual system. Presumably, the high frequencies produced by the edges of the squares in the left figure stimulate neurons in the striate cortex that are tuned to high spatial frequencies. When the visual association cortex receives this noisy information, it has difficulty perceiving the underlying form.

If you want to watch the effect of filtering the extraneous high-frequency noise, try the following demonstration. Put the book down and look at the pictures in Figure 6.28 from across the room. The distance "erases" the high frequencies, because they exceed the resolving power of the eye, and the two pictures look identical. Now walk toward the book, focusing on the left figure. As you get closer, the higher frequencies reappear and this face gets harder and harder to recognize. (See *Figure 6.28.*)

Texture

Recently, von der Heydt, Peterhans, and Dürstler (1992) discovered a new class of neurons in the monkey striate cortex. These neurons respond to "periodic patterns." They do not respond when single lines, bars, or edges are placed in their receptive

FIGURE 6.28

Spatial filtering. Both pictures contain the same amount of low-frequency information, but extraneous high-frequency information has been filtered from the picture on the right. If you look at the pictures from across the room, they look identical.

(From Harmon, L.D., and Julesz, B. *Science,* 1973, *180,* 1191–1197. Copyright 1973 by the American Association for the Advancement of Science.)

fields, but they do respond vigorously when a grating (square-wave, sine-wave, or thin-line) of a particular spatial frequency and orientation is presented there. To provide a reliable response, these cells require a minimum of 2–7 alternating dark and light bars. They are not spatial-frequency analyzers like the ones I just described. The proof of this fact is difficult to convey in a few words, because it requires an understanding of the underlying mathematics. Those of you who would like to know more should consult the article.

These neurons showed extreme sensitivity to deviations from their optimal frequency and orientation. Figure 6.29 shows three square-wave gratings. The middle one produced the optimal response in a particular neuron in the striate cortex. The one on the left, which has a slightly higher spatial frequency, produced only half as much excitation. The one on the right, which is rotated slightly counterclockwise, also produced only half as much excitation. (See *Figure 6.29.*)

Von der Heydt and his colleagues estimate that approximately 4 million periodic-pattern-selective cells serve the central four degrees of vision in the monkey striate cortex. They suggest that the function provided by these cells is perception of surfaces. Most surfaces (especially those found in nature) have a rough texture, and many of them contain a repeating pattern. For example, tree trunks, grasslands, boulders, leaves of bushes and trees, pebble-strewn ground—even a close-up view of the fur of another animal—contain periodic patterns that potentially could be detected by these cells. These cells could help us discriminate surfaces that differ only in terms of their texture, and could help us determine their orientation. As Figure 6.30 shows, texture gradients provide an important cue for perception of distance. (See *Figure 6.30.*)

Retinal Disparity

We perceive depth by many means, most of which involve cues that can be detected monocularly, by one eye alone. For example, perspective, relative retinal size, loss of detail through the effects of atmospheric haze, and relative apparent movement of retinal images as we move our heads all contribute to depth perception and do not require binocular vision. However, binocular vision provides a vivid perception of depth through the pro-

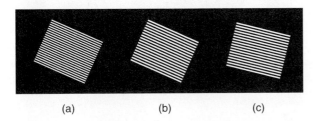

(a)   (b)   (c)

FIGURE 6.29

Sensitivity of a "texture" cell. The center stimulus (b) produced the highest rate of firing. The firing rate decreased by 50 percent when the spatial frequency of the grating was slightly higher (a) or the grating was rotated slightly (c).

(Adapted from von der Heydt, R., Peterhans, E., and Duersteler, M.R. *Journal of Neuroscience,* 1992, *12,* 1416–1434.)

FIGURE 6.30

Texture cues. Variations in texture can produce an appearance of distance. (Nancy Sheehan.)

cess of stereoscopic vision, or *stereopsis.* If you have used a stereoscope (such as a View Master) or have seen a three-dimensional movie, you know what I mean. Stereopsis is particularly important in the visual guidance of fine movements of the hands and fingers, such as we use when we thread a needle.

Most neurons in the striate cortex are *binocular*—that is, they respond to visual stimulation of either eye. Many of these binocular cells, especially those found in a layer that receives information from the magnocellular system, have response patterns that appear to contribute to the perception of depth (Poggio and Poggio, 1984). In most cases the cells respond most vigorously when each eye sees a stimulus in a slightly *different* location. That is, the neurons respond to **retinal disparity,** a stimulus that produces images on slightly different parts of the retina of each eye. This is exactly the information that is needed for stereopsis; each eye sees a three-dimensional scene slightly differently, and the presence of retinal disparity indicates differences in the distance of objects from the observer.

Color

In the striate cortex, information from color-sensitive ganglion cells is transmitted, through the parvocellular layers of the dorsal lateral geniculate nucleus, to a special group of cells grouped together in blobs. (Yes, that is really what they are officially called.) Blobs were discovered by Wong-Riley (1978), who found that a stain for cytochrome oxidase, an enzyme present in mitochondria, showed a patchy distribution. Subsequent research with the stain (Horton and Hubel, 1980; Humphrey and Hendrickson, 1980) revealed the presence of a polka-dot pattern of dark columns extending through layers 2 and 3 and (more faintly) layers 5 and 6. The columns are oval in cross section, approximately 150 x 200 μm in diameter and spaced at 0.5-mm intervals (Fitzpatrick, Itoh, and Diamond, 1983; Livingstone and Hubel, 1987).

Figure 6.31 shows a photomicrograph of a slice through a macaque monkey's visual cortex that has been flattened out and stained for the mitochondrial enzyme. You can clearly see the blobs within the striate cortex. Because the curvature of the cortex pre-

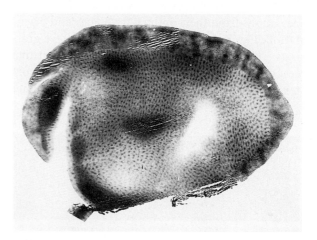

FIGURE 6.31

A photomicrograph of a slice through the primary visual cortex of a macaque monkey, parallel to the surface. The dark spots are the blobs, colored by a stain for cytochrome oxidase.

(From Hubel, D.H., and Livingstone, M.S. *Journal of Neuroscience,* 1989, *7,* 3378–3415. Reprinted by permission of the *Journal of Neuroscience.*

vents it from being perfectly flattened, some of the tissue is missing in the center of the slice. (See *Figure 6.31.*)

To summarize, neurons in the striate cortex respond to several different features of a visual stimulus, including orientation, movement, spatial frequency, texture, retinal disparity, and color. Now let us turn our attention to the way this information is organized within the striate cortex.

Modular Organization of the Striate Cortex

Most investigators believe that the brain is organized in modules, which probably range in size from a hundred thousand to a few million neurons. Each module receives information from other modules, performs some calculations, and then passes the results to other modules. In recent years investigators have been learning the characteristics of the modules that are found in the visual cortex (De Valois and De Valois, 1988; Livingstone and Hubel, 1988).

The striate cortex is divided into approximately 2500 modules, each approximately 0.5 x 0.7 mm and containing approximately 150,000 neurons. The neurons in each module are devoted to the analysis of various features contained in one very small portion of the visual field. Collectively, these modules receive information from the entire visual field, the individual modules serving like the tiles in a mosaic mural. Input from the parvocellular and magnocellular layers of the dorsal lateral geniculate nucleus is received by different sublayers of the striate cortex: The parvocellular input is received by layer 4Cß, whereas the magnocellular input is received by layer 4Cα.

The modules actually consist of two segments, each surrounding a blob. As we saw in the previous subsections, although the neurons in a given module respond to information from approximately the same part of the visual field, those located within the blobs have a special function: They are sensitive to color but ignore the other features (Livingstone and Hubel, 1982). Outside the blob, neurons show sensitivity to orientation, movement, spatial frequency, and binocular disparity—but not to color. Each half of the module receives input from only one eye, but

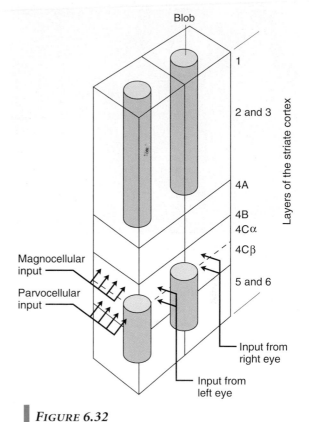

FIGURE 6.32

One of the modules of the primary visual cortex.

because most neurons in the striate cortex are binocular, the circuitry within the module obviously combines the information from both eyes. (See *Figure 6.32.*)

For several years investigators have realized that the striate cortex is organized in a regular fashion—that the modules are strung together so that cells responsive to particular directions are aligned in one dimension and cells responsive to one eye or another are arranged in another dimension. They also realized that the architecture of the striate cortex was not like a checkerboard, with the borders of the modules following perfectly straight lines. Blasdel (1992a, 1992b) developed an ingenious technique to visualize just how the modules are arranged. He operated on monkeys, removing part of their skull and placing a glass window over the striate cortex. The window was equipped with a fitting that permitted him to inject a voltage-sensitive dye—a dye that changes its color according to the strength of an electrical field that passes through it.

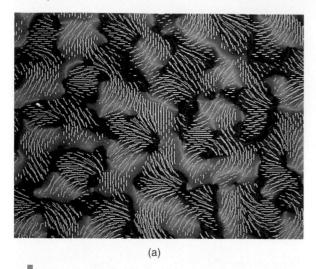

(a)

(b)

FIGURE 6.33

Modular organization of the striate cortex. (a) Distribution of directionally sensitive cells. The white lines indicate the directional sensitivity, which is encoded by color. (b) Relation between directional sensitivity and ocular dominance. The white lines indicate the location of cells that respond exclusively to one eye. Note that the color bands are roughly perpendicular to the white lines.

(From Blasdel, G.G., *Journal of Neuroscience*, 1992, *12*, 3139–3161. Reprinted by permission.)

After the animals recovered from the surgery, Blasdel injected the dye, which spread across the surface of the striate cortex. Then he showed the animals visual stimuli designed to excite neurons that were sensitive to particular features. If a large number of neurons in a particular region were sensitive to that feature, their excitation would change the color of the dye covering that region. Blasdel presented patterns containing lines of different orientations to identify cells that responded to particular orientations, and presented stimuli monocularly to identify cells that received direct input from either the right or the left eye. During the presentation of the stimuli he used a sensitive video camera to record the pattern of color changes in the dye and analyzed these patterns with a computer.

Figure 6.33 shows some of his results. The colors shown on the figure were produced by the computer and do not represent the actual color of the dye on the surface of the cortex; and they do *not* represent the sensitivity of cortical neurons to different wavelengths. Instead, the colors represent the orientation sensitivity of the cortical neurons. Neurons in a region colored red are sensitive to horizontal lines; those in a region colored orange are sensitive to a line rotated counterclockwise by 30 degrees; and so on for yellow, green, blue, and violet. You will notice that this sequence of colors corresponds to a circular arrangement of hues in the visual spectrum, as shown in Figure 6.1. Figure 6.33(a) shows how orientation sensitivity (indicated by white lines) is coded by color; as you will see, the red regions contain neurons sensitive to horizontal lines, the green regions contain neurons sensitive to vertical lines, and so on. (See *Figure 6.33a.*)

Figure 6.33(b) shows the relation between orientation sensitivity and *ocular dominance*—that is, the degree to which a cell responds to only one eye. The white lines indicate the location of cells that respond exclusively to one eye; thus, cells that respond equally well to stimuli presented to either eye are located midway between these lines. As you will see, the "rainbows" are lined up along the channels defined by the white lines, which means that changes in orientation sensitivity run at right angles to changes in ocular dominance. The blobs, which receive information from only one eye and which contain neurons that are not sensitive to orientation, are located at regular intervals along these white lines. (See *Figure 6.33b*.)

How does spatial frequency fit into this organization? One study (Silverman et al., 1989) suggests that sensitivity to spatial frequency varies with distance from the blobs. However, another study (Born and Tootell, 1991) suggests that spatial frequency is not organized systematically. Thus, the issue seems to be unresolved at present. The spatial arrangement of the newly discovered grating cells in the striate cortex has not yet been investigated.

Blindsight

Visual perception depends on the integrity of the connections between the retina and the striate cortex. Thus, damage to the eyes, optic nerves, optic tracts, lateral geniculate nucleus, optic radiations, or primary visual cortex itself results in loss of vision in particular portions of the visual field or in complete blindness if the damage is total. However, an interesting phenomenon is seen in people with damage to the optic radiations or primary visual cortex.

It has long been recognized that damage to the optic radiations or primary visual cortex on one side of the brain causes blindness in the contralateral visual field. That is, if the right side of the brain is damaged, the patient will be blind to everything located to the left when he or she looks straight ahead. However, Weiskrantz and his colleagues (Weiskrantz et al., 1974; Weiskrantz, 1987) found that if an object is placed in the patient's blind field and the patient is asked to reach for it, he or she will be able to do so rather accurately. The patients are surprised to find their hands repeatedly coming in contact with an object in what appears to them as darkness; they say that they see nothing there. The patient is also sensitive to movement and, to a certain extent, the orientation of objects in the blind field.

This phenomenon, called **blindsight,** may depend on the connections that the visual association cortex receives from the superior colliculus and from the dorsal lateral geniculate nucleus (Cower and Stoerig, 1991). The role of these connections in the intact brain is not known. Most of the inputs to the visual association cortex come directly from the striate cortex, and these connections are obviously necessary for normal visual perception.

Besides telling us something about the functions of the various parts of the visual system, the phenomenon of blindsight also shows that visual information can control behavior without producing a conscious sensation. Although the superior colliculi send visual information to parts of the brain that guide hand movements, they do not appear to send them to parts of the brain responsible for conscious awareness. Perhaps that connection is a more recent evolutionary development. I will have more to say about this topic in Chapters 15 and 16, which discuss memory and communication.

INTERIM SUMMARY

THE STRIATE CORTEX CONSISTS OF SIX LAYERS AND several sublayers. Visual information is received from the magnocellular and parvocellular layers of the dorsal lateral geniculate nucleus. The magnocellular system is more primitive, color-blind, and sensitive to movement, depth, and small differences in brightness, and the parvocellular system is more recent, color-sensitive, and able to discriminate finer details.

The striate cortex is organized into modules, each surrounding a pair of blobs, which are revealed by a stain for cytochrome oxidase, an enzyme found in mitochondria. Each half of a module receives information from one eye; but because information is shared, most of the neurons respond to input to both eyes. The neurons in the blobs are sensitive to color, whereas those between the blobs are sensitive to sine-wave gratings of different spatial frequencies and orientations and to retinal disparity and movement. Some cells are specifically sensitive to orientation and frequency of gratings and probably are involved in detecting the texture of surfaces.

Damage to the visual system up to the striate cortex produces blindness in all or part of the visual field. However, damage limited to the striate cortex or to the optic radiations leading to them produces a syndrome called blindsight. People with blindsight deny seeing anything in the blind part of their visual field but can nevertheless point to objects located there and discriminate their size and orientation. They are also sensitive to movement. However, although their behavior can be affected by objects in their blind field, they have no conscious awareness of the presence of these objects. Their ability to respond to visual stimuli apparently depends on efferent connections from the superior colliculus and lateral geniculate nucleus to the visual association cortex.

ANALYSIS OF VISUAL INFORMATION: ROLE OF THE VISUAL ASSOCIATION CORTEX

ALTHOUGH THE STRIATE CORTEX IS NECESSARY FOR visual perception, perception of objects and of the totality of the visual scene does not take place there. Each module of the striate cortex sees only what is happening in one tiny part of the visual field. Thus, for us to perceive objects and entire visual scenes, the information from these individual modules must be combined. That combination takes place in the visual association cortex.

Two Streams of Visual Analysis

Visual information received from the striate cortex is analyzed in the visual association cortex. Based on their own research and on a review of the literature, Ungerleider and Mishkin (1982) concluded that the visual association cortex contains two streams of analysis. Subsequent anatomical studies have confirmed this conclusion (Baizer, Ungerleider, and Desimone, 1991). Both streams begin in the striate cortex, but they begin to diverge in the extrastriate cortex. One stream turns downward, ending in the cortex of the inferior temporal lobe. The other turns upward, ending in the cortex of the posterior parietal lobe. The ventral stream recognizes *what* an object is, and the dorsal stream recognizes *where* the object is located. Figure 6.34 shows these two streams, drawn on a lateral view of a rhesus monkey brain. (See *Figure 6.34.*)

The parvocellular and magnocellular systems provide different kinds of information (Livingstone and Hubel, 1987). The magnocellular system is found in all mammals, whereas the parvocellular system is found only in primates. These two systems receive information from different types of ganglion cells, which are connected to different types of bipolar cells and photoreceptors. Only the cells in the parvocellular system receive information about wavelength from cones; thus, this system analyzes information concerning color. Cells in this system also show high spatial resolution and low temporal resolution; that is, they are able to detect very fine details, but their response is slow and prolonged. In contrast, neurons in the magnocellular system are color-blind, are not able to detect fine details, and respond very briefly to a visual stimulus. And although they appear to be responsible for vision of lower acuity, these neurons are able to detect smaller contrasts between light and dark. They are especially sensitive to movement.

At one time, researchers believed that the dorsal stream received its information from the magnocellular system and the ventral stream received its information from the parvocellular system. But more recent research has shown that both systems contribute information to both streams (Maunsell, 1992). The dorsal stream receives mostly magnocellular input, but the ventral stream receives approximately equal input from both systems.

Neurons in the striate cortex send axons to the **extrastriate cortex,** the region of the visual association cortex that surrounds the striate cortex (Zeki and Shipp, 1988). The primate extrastriate cortex (sometimes called the prestriate cortex or circumstriate cortex) consists of several regions, each of which contains one or more independent maps of the visual field. Each region is specialized, containing neurons that respond to a particular feature of visual information, such as orientation, movement, spatial frequency, retinal disparity, or color. So far, investigators have identified 25 distinct regions and subregions of visual cortex, arranged hierarchically (Van Essen, Anderson, and Felleman, 1992). Most of the information passes up the hierarchy; each region receives information from regions located beneath it in the hierarchy, analyzes the information, and passes the results on to "higher" regions for further analysis. Some information is also transmitted in the opposite direction, but axons that descend the hierarchy are much less numerous than those that ascend it. Unfortunately, we do not yet know the

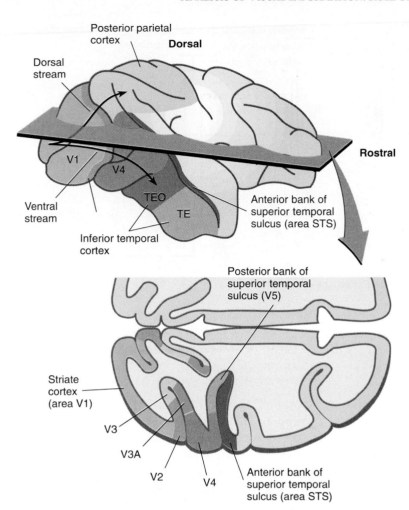

FIGURE 6.34

Areas of visual cortex in the rhesus monkey brain.
(Adapted from Zeki, S.M. *Journal of Physiology,* 1978, *277,* 227–244.)

functions of all of these regions, and further research will undoubtedly discover still more regions and still more interconnections.

Figure 6.35 presents a diagram of some of the more important regions of the visual cortex and their interconnections. Although some connections go from "higher" regions to "lower" ones, only the connections that ascend the hierarchy are shown. In subsequent sections I will specifically discuss the functions of areas V4, V5, TEO, TE, STS, and the posterior parietal cortex. (See **Figure 6.35.**)

Perception of Color

As we saw earlier, neurons within the blobs in the striate cortex respond to colors. Like the ganglion cells in the retina (and the parvocellular neurons in the dorsal lateral geniculate nucleus), these neurons respond in opponent fashion. This information is analyzed by the regions of the visual association cortex that constitute the ventral stream.

Studies with Laboratory Animals

In the monkey brain, neurons in the blobs send information about color to a specific subarea of the extrastriate cortex. Zeki (1980) found that neurons in this subarea (called *V4*) also respond selectively to colors, but their response characteristics are much more complex. Unlike the neurons we have encountered so far, these neurons respond to a variety of wavelengths, not just those that correspond to red, green, yellow, and blue.

The perceived color of a stimulus is influenced by the surrounding scene (Land, 1974). For exam-

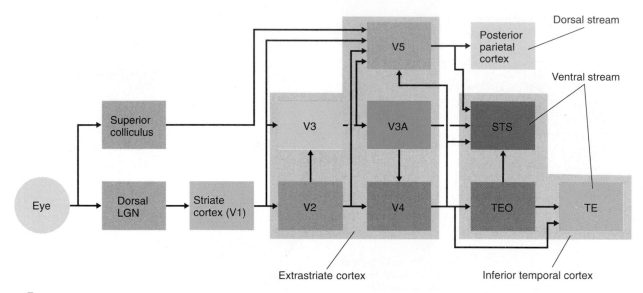

| **FIGURE 6.35**

Interconnections of areas of visual cortex in the rhesus monkey brain. This diagram is greatly simplified; only the major areas and the most important connections are shown. The colors correspond to those shown in Figure 6.34.

ple, the appearance of the colors of objects remains much the same whether we observe them under artificial light, under an overcast sky, or at noon on a cloudless day. This phenomenon is known as **color constancy**. Our visual system does not simply respond according to the wavelength of the light reflected by objects in each part of the visual field; instead, it compensates for the source of the light. This compensation appears to be made by simultaneously comparing the color composition of each point in the visual field with the average color of the entire scene. If the scene contains a particularly high level of long-wavelength light (as it would if an object were illuminated by the light of a setting sun), then some long-wavelength light is "subtracted out" of the perception of each point in the scene.

Schein and Desimone (1990) performed a careful study of the response characteristics of neurons in region V4 of the monkey extrastriate cortex. They found that these neurons responded to specific colors and that some responded to colored bars of specific orientation. They also had a rather unusual secondary receptive field—a large region surrounding the primary field. When stimuli were presented in the secondary receptive field, the neuron did not

respond. However, stimuli presented there could suppress the neuron's response to a stimulus presented in the primary field. For example, if a cell would fire when a red spot was presented in the primary field, it would fire at a slower rate (or not at all) when a red stimulus was presented in the surrounding secondary field. In other words, these cells responded to particular wavelengths of light but subtracted out the amount of that wavelength that was present in the background. As Schein and Desimone point out, this subtraction could serve as the basis for color constancy.

Studies with Humans

Lesions of a restricted region of the human extrastriate cortex can cause complete loss of color vision without disrupting visual acuity; the patients describe their vision as resembling a black-and-white film (Damasio et al., 1980). The condition is known as **achromatopsia** ("vision without color"). If the brain damage is unilateral, people will lose color vision in only half of the visual field. In addition, they cannot even imagine colors or remember the colors or objects they saw before their brain damage occurred. It seems likely that these lesions destroyed the part of the human extrastriate cortex that corresponds to area V4 of the monkey brain—or perhaps to a subregion of this area.

Zeki et al. (1991) used a PET scanner to measure regional cerebral blood flow in normal human subjects. They had subjects inhale air containing minute quantities of radioactive carbon dioxide. At the same time, they showed the subjects a plain gray stimulus or a multicolored pattern made up of rectangles of different sizes. While the subjects examined the stimuli, the investigators took PET scans that revealed the regional blood flow throughout the brain—a measure that correlated with the rate of metabolic activity. They found that both stimuli increased the metabolic activity of the striate cortex and the region of the extrastriate cortex that surrounds it (region V2). The colored stimulus activated a specific region of the extrastriate cortex: the lingual and fusiform gyri. Thus, the extrastriate cortex of the human brain, like that of the rhesus monkey, contains a specific region devoted to the analysis of color. The region of the lingual and fusiform gyri appears to be homologous to area V4 in the monkey brain. (See *Figure 6.36.*)

Of course, perception of colors is useless in itself. The function of our ability to perceive different colors is to help us perceive different objects in our environment. Thus, to perceive and understand what is in front of us, we must have information about color combined with other forms of information. Some people with brain damage lose the ability to perceive shapes but can still perceive colors (Zeki, 1992). They can identify the colors of objects in their visual field, but they cannot say what these objects are. Functionally, they are blind.

Analysis of Form

The analysis of form by the visual cortex begins with neurons in the striate cortex that are sensitive to orientation and spatial frequency. These neurons send information to several regions of the extrastriate cortex, including V3, V3A, and V4. (Note that area V4 is involved in form perception, not just in the analysis of color.) These regions analyze the information and send it along the ventral stream toward the temporal neocortex.

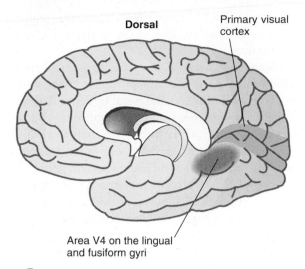

FIGURE 6.36

A medial view of the human brain showing the location of the lingual and fusiform gyri.

Studies with Laboratory Animals

In primates the recognition of visual patterns and identification of particular objects takes place in the **inferior temporal cortex,** located on the ventral part of the temporal lobe. This region of visual association cortex is located at the end of the ventral stream. It is here that analyses of form and color are put together and perceptions of three-dimensional objects and backgrounds are achieved. The inferior temporal cortex consists of two major regions, areas TE and TEO. (Refer to *Figures 6.34* and *6.35.*)

The receptive fields of neurons in area TEO are quite variable in size, but generally they are larger than those of neurons in area V4 and smaller than those of neurons in area TE (Boussaoud, Desimone, and Ungerleider, 1991). Their primary inputs come from area V4 and their primary outputs go to area TE, which suggests that "the neural coding of visual objects in TEO is based on object features that are more global than those in V4, but not quite as global as those in TE" (Boussaoud et al., 1991, p. 574). Lesions of TEO make it almost impossible for monkeys to learn a task that requires them to discriminate between two simple two-dimensional patterns differing in form, size, orientation, color, or brightness (Iwai and Mishkin, 1969; Gross, 1973; Dean, 1982; Ungerleider and Mishkin, 1982; Mishkin,

Ungerleider, and Macko, 1983). Thus, this region serves as an essential link in the analysis of visual information.

Neurons in area TE have the largest receptive fields of all, often encompassing the entire contralateral half of the visual field. In general, these neurons respond best to three-dimensional objects (or photographs of them) rather than to simple stimuli such as spots, lines, or sine-wave gratings. They continue to respond even when these stimuli are moved to a different location or are placed against a different background. They appear to participate in the recognition of objects rather than the analysis of specific features. Tanaka and his colleagues (see Tanaka, 1992) investigated the response characteristics of these neurons. First, they located a single neuron with a microelectrode and then presented a large number of three-dimensional items, such as toy animals, plants, and "junk" objects, until they found one that produced the best response. Then they used a computerized system to present a series of simplified versions of the picture to find the simplest pattern that would still excite the cell. Figure 6.37 illustrates this procedure. The cell responded when the tiger's head was presented, and continued to respond to successively simplified patterns. The cell was activated by a pair of black rectangles superimposed on a white square, but not by either of the two components of this stimulus. (See *Figure 6.37.*)

Obviously, the fact that the cell responded to the tiger's face does not mean that it was a "tiger's face analyzer." As Tanaka observed, no single cell could recognize a complex stimulus found in nature.

Instead, particular stimuli would be represented by the activity of a large group of cells, each sensitive to slightly different patterns. It is the *pattern* of activity in circuits of neurons in area TE that represents the perception of particular objects.

Lesions of area TE produce only slight deficits in monkeys' ability to perform simple visual discriminations, whereas lesions of TEO produce severe deficits. Thus, even after area TE is gone, the efferent connections of TEO with motor mechanisms elsewhere in the brain obviously provide enough information about forms and shapes for the animals to respond appropriately. However, when area TE is destroyed, animals lose much of their visual flexibility. That is, they can learn to recognize a particular two-dimensional stimulus, but they can no longer recognize it when it changes in size or is presented against a different background (Iwai, Osawa, and Umitsu, 1979). In addition, they are unable to learn to recognize particular three-dimensional objects (Mishkin, 1966, 1982).

Several studies have found neurons in the temporal lobe that are specifically excited by the sight of another face—either that of another monkey or that of a human. For example, Desimone et al. (1984) found neurons that specifically responded to full-face views and others that specifically responded to profiles. Most of these face-sensitive cells are located in area TE and in the cortex that lines the anterior bank of the superior temporal sulcus (area STS). (Refer to *Figures 6.34* and *6.35.*)

Face-sensitive cells continue to respond even when the images of the faces that are being presented are blurred or changed in color, size, or dis-

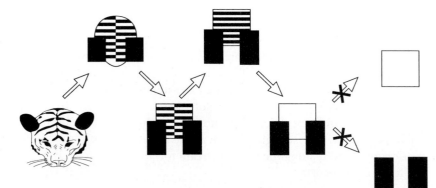

FIGURE 6.37

An analysis of the response characteristics of a neuron in area TE. The cell responded vigorously to the tiger's face, and also to the four simplified patterns selected by the computer. It did not respond to the white square or the two black rectangles presented alone.

(From Tanaka, K. *Current Opinion in Neurobiology*, 1992, 2, 502–505.)

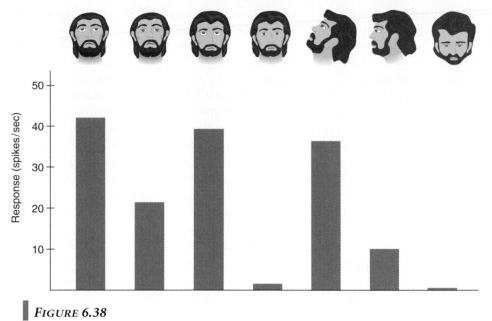

Responses of a single neuron in the cortex lining the superior temporal sulcus of a monkey's brain. The cell fired most vigorously when the monkey was presented a photograph of a face looking up.

(From Perret, D. I., Harries, M. H., Mistlin, A. J., Hiatanen, J. K., Benson, P. J., Bevan, R., Thomas, S., Oram, M.W., Ortega, J., and Brierley, K. *International Journal of Comparative Psychology,* 1990, *4,* 25–55.)

tance (Rolls and Baylis, 1986). In addition, most of these neurons are sensitive to differences between faces, suggesting that the circuits of which they are a part are responsible for a monkey's ability to recognize particular individuals. Thus, these neurons participate in *learning* to perceive particular visual stimuli.

Perrett and his colleagues (see Perrett et al., 1992) have discovered an interesting function performed by circuits of neurons in the superior temporal sulcus: directing the animal's attention to important stimuli. They found that some face-sensitive cells responded only when the eyes or the face was oriented in a particular direction. For example, Figure 6.38 shows the activity level of a neuron that responded when a human face was looking up. (See *Figure 6.38.*)

The neocortex that lines the superior temporal sulcus seems to be specifically involved in detecting social signals about the location of important stimuli, and not in the general recognition of faces. Lesions of this region disrupt monkeys' ability to

discriminate the direction of another animal's gaze, but they do not impair their ability to recognize other animals' faces (Campbell et al., 1990; Heywood and Cowey, 1992). As we will see in the last section of this chapter, the parietal lobe—the endpoint of the ventral stream of visual analysis—is concerned with perceiving the location of objects in space. Presumably, the connections that exist between the superior temporal sulcus and the parietal cortex enable the orientation of another animal's gaze to direct one's attention to a particular location in space (Harries and Perrett, 1991).

Studies with Humans

Damage to the human visual association cortex can cause a category of deficits known as **visual agnosia**. *Agnosia* ("failure to know") refers to an inability to perceive or identify a stimulus by means of a particular sensory modality, even though its details can be detected by means of that modality and the person retains relatively normal intellectual capacity. *Apperceptive* visual agnosias are failures in high-level perception, whereas *associative* visual agnosias are disconnections between these perceptions and verbal systems. The distinction will be described in more detail later in this section.

People with visual agnosia cannot identify common objects by sight, even though they have relatively normal visual acuity (Warrington and James, 1988). In some cases they can read small print but fail to recognize a common object, such as a wristwatch. However, if they are permitted to hold the object (say, the wristwatch), they can immediately recognize it by touch and say what it is. Thus, they have not lost their memory for the object or forgotten how to say its name.

Apperceptive Visual Agnosia. People with **apperceptive visual agnosia** may have normal visual acuity, but they cannot successfully recognize objects visually by their shape. For example, a brain-damaged patient studied by Benson and Greenberg (1969) was initially believed to be blind but was subsequently observed to navigate his wheelchair around the halls of the hospital. Testing revealed that his visual fields were full (there were no blind spots other than ones we all have) and that he could pick up threads placed on a sheet of white paper. He could discriminate among stimuli that differed in size, brightness, or hue but could not distinguish those that differed only in shape.

Corbetta et al. (1991) obtained evidence that perception of shape, color, and movement involves different regions of the visual cortex. They had subjects look at a display containing 30 colored rectangles, all moving in the same direction. The display was presented for 0.4 sec, then the screen went blank for 0.2 sec, and then another set of rectangles was displayed for 0.4 sec. The rectangles sometimes changed in shape, color, or speed of movement between the first and second presentation, and sometimes they remained the same. The subjects were asked to say whether they detected a change. On some trials, the subjects were told to pay attention to a particular attribute: shape, color, or speed of movement.

The investigators used a PET scanner to measure regional cerebral activation while the subjects were performing the discrimination tasks. They found that paying attention to shape, color, or speed of movement caused activation of different brain regions. (The stimuli were counterbalanced so that the same set of displays were presented during each condition.) Figure 6.39 shows their results. As you can see, paying attention to either shape or color increased the activity around the collateral sulcus in the left ventromedial occipito-temporal region, but the color condition produced additional activation in a slightly more dorsal region. (The collateral sulcus is located adjacent to the fusiform gyrus, which Zeki and his colleagues identified as the region homologous to area V4 in the rhesus monkey brain.) In addition, paying attention to color activated the left dorsolateral extrastriate cortex, and paying attention to shape activated neurons in the vicinity of the superior temporal sulcus of the right superior temporal lobe. Paying attention to speed of movement increased the activity of the left parietal cortex, near its junction with the temporal and occipital lobes. (See *Figure 6.39.*)

A common symptom of apperceptive visual agnosia is **prosopagnosia,** an inability to recognize particular faces (*prosopon* means "face"). That is, the patients can recognize that they are looking at a face, but they cannot say whose face it is—even if it belongs to a relative or close friend. They still remember who these people are and will usually recognize them when they hear their voice. Prosopagnosia is a subtle deficit that can occur even when a person has no apparent difficulty recognizing common objects visually. Some investigators have speculated that facial recognition is mediated by special circuits in the brain that are devoted to the specific analysis of facial features. Others argue that the distinction between prosopagnosia and visual agnosia for common objects is quantitative, not qualitative; that is, visual agnosia for common objects is simply a more severe deficit, caused by more extensive damage to the relevant parts of the visual association cortex. Alexander and Albert (1983) note that although prosopagnosia can occur without visual-object agnosia, all patients with visual-object agnosia also have prosopagnosia.

Damasio, Damasio, and Van Hoesen (1982) describe three patients with prosopagnosia who could recognize common objects but had difficulty discriminating between particular objects of the same class. For example, none of them could recog-

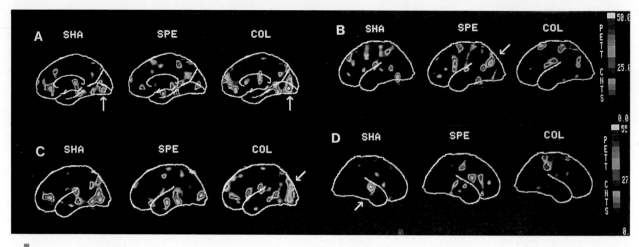

FIGURE 6.39

Computer-generated drawings of the results of PET scans. The arrows indicate regions of the brain that were activated the most. The three-letter abbreviations above each scan indicate the stimulus dimension to which the subject was paying attention. Abbreviations: SHA, shape; SPE, speed of movement; COL, color.

(From Corbetta, M., Miezin, F.M., Dobmeyer, S., Shulman, G.L., and Petersen, S.E. *Journal of Neuroscience,* 1991, *11,* 2383–2402.)

nize their own car, although they could tell a car from other types of motorized vehicles. One of them could find her own car in a parking lot only by reading all the license plates until she found her own. Another patient, a farmer, could no longer recognize his cows (Bornstein, Stroka, and Munitz, 1969). Sergent and Signoret (1990) studied three patients with prosopagnosia who could recognize drawings of objects presented as we normally see them but who could not recognize them when they were presented from unusual viewpoints. For example, they could recognize a drawing of a side view of a coffee cup but could not recognize a drawing of a coffee cup viewed from above. These results suggest that prosopagnosia is simply a relatively mild form of visual agnosia; faces are particularly complex stimuli, and even a mild agnosia will make it difficult for a person to recognize them.

Sergent, Ohta, and MacDonald (1992) used a PET scanner to measure regional cerebral blood flow while subjects identified photographs of particular faces, identified categories of common objects, or discriminated between simple sine-wave gratings of different orientations. All tasks increased the activity in the striate cortex and part of the extras-

triate cortex of both hemispheres. In addition, the face identification task specifically activated the right lingual and fusiform gyri. All tasks also increased activity in other brain regions outside the visual association cortex, but these regions are probably not involved directly in visual perception.

Lesion studies also suggest that the right hemisphere may be more important than the left in the perception of faces. Although most cases of prosopagnosia involve bilateral damage, some cases have been produced by right-hemisphere damage (Sergent and Villemure, 1989). However, no cases of prosopagnosia that include only left-hemisphere damage have been reported in right-handed people.

As we saw in the previous subsection, the cortex that lines the superior temporal sulcus of the monkey brain contains neurons that respond specifically to faces (and to the direction of their gaze), but damage to this region does not impair the animal's ability to perceive faces. Obviously, people can easily see where other people are looking, and perceiving the direction of other people's gazes certainly provides useful information. Campbell et al. (1990) described a patient who could not recognize faces but could perceive the direction in which they were gazing, and Perrett et al. (1988) described a patient who could do exactly the opposite—recognize faces but not direction of gaze. Thus, the ability to recognize gaze direction and identify particular faces appears to require different circuits of neurons.

Associative Visual Agnosia.   A person with apperceptive agnosia who cannot recognize common objects also cannot draw them or copy other people's drawings; thus, we properly speak of a deficit in perception. However, people with an **associative visual agnosia** appear to be able to perceive normally but cannot name what they have seen. In fact, they seem to be *unaware* of these perceptions. For example, a patient studied by Ratcliff and Newcombe (1982) could copy a drawing of an anchor (better than I could have done). Thus, he could perceive the shape of the anchor. However, he could not recognize either the sample or the copy that he had just drawn. When asked on another occasion to draw (not copy) a picture of an anchor, he could not do so. Even though he could copy a real image of an anchor, the word *anchor* failed to produce a mental image of one. (See ***Figure 6.40.***) When asked (on yet another occasion) to define *anchor,* he said, "a brake for ships," so we can conclude that he knew what the word meant.

Associative agnosia also extends to prosopagnosia. For example, Sergent and Signoret (1992) reported the case of a patient who could match photos of different views of the same face but could not identify the faces—even when they were pictures of the patient herself. The lesion seems to have affected the ability to identify faces without severely damaging perceptual analysis.

Associative visual agnosia appears to involve difficulty in transferring visual information to verbal mechanisms. That is, the person perceives the object well enough to draw it (or to match it with similar stimuli), but his or her verbal mechanisms do not receive the necessary information to produce the appropriate word. David Margolin and I studied a man who had sustained brain damage from an inflammatory disease that affected his cerebral blood vessels. (The damage was diffuse, so we could not make any conclusions about the anatomy of his disorder.) Suffering from an apparent visual

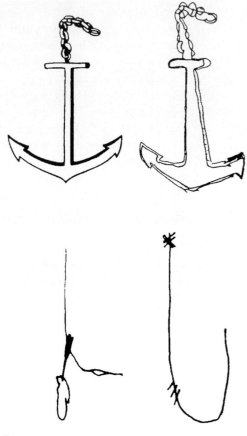

FIGURE 6.40

Associative visual agnosia. The patient successfully copied an anchor (top) *but failed on two attempts to comply with a request to "draw an anchor"* (bottom).

(From Ratcliff, G., and Newcombe, F., in *Normality and Pathology in Cognitive Functions,* edited by A.W. Ellis. London: Academic Press, 1982.)

agnosia, he failed to identify most pictures of objects. However, he sometimes made unintentional gestures when studying a picture that gave him enough of a clue that he could identify it. For example, on one occasion while puzzling over a picture of a cow, he started making movements with both hands that were unmistakably ones he would make if he were milking a cow. He looked at his hands and said, "Oh, a cow!" (He was a farmer, by the way.)

We might speculate that his perceptual mechanisms, in the visual association cortex, were relatively normal but that connections between these mechanisms and the speech mechanisms of the left hemisphere were disrupted. However, the connections between the perceptual mechanisms and the motor mechanisms of the frontal lobe were spared, permitting him to make appropriate movements when looking at some pictures. In fact, a particularly observant and conscientious speech therapist helped the patient learn how to read by these means. She taught him the manual alphabet used by deaf people, in which letters are represented by particular hand and finger movements. (This system is commonly called *finger spelling.*) He could then look at individual letters of words he could not read, make the appropriate movements, observe the sequence of letters that he spelled, and decode the word.

Recent studies suggest that associative visual agnosia is best explained as a disruption of connections between the ventral stream of the visual cortex from the brain's verbal mechanisms without damage to the connections between these mechanisms and the dorsal stream. I will say more about these studies in the next subsection.

Perception of Movement

We need not only to know what things are, but also where they are and where they are going. Without the ability to perceive the direction and velocity of movement of objects, we would have no way to predict where they will be. We would be unable to catch them (or avoid letting them catch us). This section examines the perception of movement; the final section examines the perception of location.

Studies with Laboratory Animals

One of the regions of the extrastriate cortex—area V5, also known as area MT—contains neurons that respond to movement. Damage to this region severely disrupts a monkey's ability to perceive moving stimuli (Siegel and Andersen, 1986). Area V5 receives input directly from the striate cortex and from areas V2, V3, and V4. It also receives input from the superior colliculus—directly and from projections relayed through the pulvinar, a nucleus of the thalamus (not shown). (Refer to *Figures 6.34* and *6.35.*)

The input from the superior colliculus contributes in some way to the movement sensitivity of neurons in area V5. Rodman, Gross, and Albright (1989, 1990) found that destruction of the striate cortex or the superior colliculus alone does not eliminate the movement sensitivity of V5 neurons, but destruction of both areas does. The roles played by these two sources of input are not yet known. Clearly, both inputs provide useful information; Seagraves et al. (1987) found that monkeys still could detect movement after lesions of the striate cortex but had difficulty estimating its rate.

Albright, Desimone, and Gross (1984) mapped the characteristics of movement-sensitive neurons in area V5. They found that all V5 neurons responded better to moving stimuli than to stationary ones and that most of them gave the same response regardless of the color or shape of the test stimulus. Most neurons showed directional sensitivity; that is, they responded only to movements in a particular direction. They also found that, like the striate cortex, area V5 is divided into rectangular modules. Along the long axis of a module are neurons with directional sensitivities that vary systematically, in a clockwise or counterclockwise fashion.

As we saw in Chapter 5, no single method permits us to be certain that a particular region of the brain is directly involved in a particular function. But if several different methods provide compatible results, we can have more confidence that our conclusions are correct. As you have seen, most experiments investigating the neural basis of visual perception involve recording neural activity (of single units or of regions of the brain) or examining the behavioral effects of destruction of particular brain regions. Salzman et al. (1992) developed an additional approach that permitted them to alter the neural activity of particular neurons to see whether this alteration would affect the animal's perception. If it did, we could be reasonably confident that the activity of these neurons is at least partly responsible for the perception.

Salzman and his colleagues operated on monkeys, attaching a device to their skulls that permitted them to record, without causing discomfort, the activity of single units in area V5 while the animal was awake. Later, they presented the monkeys with a computer-controlled video display that contained an array of randomly located dots. Varying proportions of these dots (from 0 percent to 100 percent) moved in a particular direction. Under the 0 percent (no movement) condition, the dots moved randomly in a display resembling the "snow" seen on the screen of a television tuned between channels. Under the 100 percent condition, the display showed a set of dots all streaming in one direction. The animals' task was to indicate whether they detected coherent movement in the display by directing their gaze toward one of two small lights. Correct responses were rewarded with a small sip of water or fruit juice.

The investigators moved the microelectrode until they found a cluster of neurons that responded to movement in a particular direction. (As we just saw, area V5 is organized in modules, and neurons responsive to movements in a particular direction are clustered together.) Next, they adjusted the display so that it fell on the receptive field of this cluster of neurons and adjusted the proportion of the dots moving in the same direction so that the animals made correct responses on approximately half of the trials. Then, on some of the trials, the researchers applied a weak electrical current through the microelectrode. They found that the stimulation affected the animals' perception; during the stimulation the animals became more likely to perceive movement in the preferred direction of the cluster of neurons.

So far this discussion has been confined to movement of objects in the visual field. But if an animal moves its eyes, its head, or its whole body, the image on the retina will move even if everything within the animal's visual field remains stable. Often, of course, *both* kinds of movements will occur at the same time. The problem for the visual system is to determine which of these images are produced by movements of objects in the environment and which are produced by the animals own eye, head, and body movements.

To illustrate this problem, think about how the page of this book looks as you read it. If we could make a videotape of one of your retinas, we would see that the image of the page projected there is in constant movement as your eyes make several saccades along a line and then snap back to the beginning of the next line. And yet, the page seems perfectly still to you. On the other hand, if you look at a single point on the page (say, a period at the end of a sentence) and then move the page around while

following it with your eyes, you perceive the book as moving, even though the image on your retina remains relatively stable. (Try it.) And then think about the images on your retina while you are driving in busy traffic, constantly moving your eyes around to keep track of your own location and that of other cars moving in different directions at different speeds.

Little is known about how the visual system solves this very complicated problem. One subcortical brain structure has been implicated: the **pulvinar**. This large thalamic nucleus is one of the regions of the brain that has enlarged in size (relative to the rest of the brain) during the evolution of our species. Anatomical evidence and the results of single-unit recording suggest that it plays a role in our ability to compensate for the effects of our own movements on movements of images on the retina (Robinson and Petersen, 1992). The pulvinar receives inputs from the lateral geniculate nucleus and the superior colliculus and has reciprocal connections with all regions of the visual cortex. Some neurons in the pulvinar fire immediately after an eye movement, even when it is made in the dark. Other neurons respond to movements of retinal images, but not to those produced by eye movements (Robinson et al., 1991). Thus, the pulvinar is informed about eye movements and about movements of the visual image.

The pulvinar receives information about eye movements from the superior colliculus, which is interconnected with the brain stem nuclei that control the eye muscles, and it receives information about visual images from the striate cortex. Presumably, the pulvinar puts this information together and helps the visual association cortex "subtract out" eye movements from movements of the retinal image. Whether the pulvinar is also involved in compensating for head and body movements is not known.

Studies with Humans

Bilateral damage to parts of the visual association cortex of the human brain can produce an agnosia for movement. For example, Zihl et al. (1991) reported the case of a woman with bilateral lesions of the lateral occipital cortex and middle temporal gyrus and the underlying white matter. The woman had an almost total loss of movement perception. She was unable to cross a street without traffic lights, because she could not judge the speed at which cars were moving. Although she could perceive movements, she found moving objects very unpleasant to look at. For example, while talking with another person, she avoided looking at the person's mouth because she found its movements very disturbing. When the investigators asked her to try to detect movements of a visual target in the laboratory, she said, "First the target is completely at rest. Then it suddenly jumps upwards and downwards" (p. 2244). She was able to see that the target was constantly changing its position, but she was unaware of any sensation of movement.

As we saw in the previous subsection, area V5 is the one region of the monkey brain that is most important for perception of movement. Two studies using PET scanners (Corbetta et al., 1990; Zeki et al., 1991) suggest that the region of the human brain that performs this function is located near the junction of the occipital, temporal, and parietal lobes.

Perception of movement can even help us perceive three-dimensional forms. Johansson (1973) demonstrated just how much information we can derive from movement. He dressed actors in black and attached small lights to several points on their bodies, such as their wrists, elbows, shoulders, hips, knees, and feet. He made movies of the actors in a darkened room while they were performing various behaviors, such as walking, running, jumping, limping, doing push-ups, and dancing with a partner who was also equipped with lights. Even though observers who watched the films could see only a pattern of moving lights against a dark background, they could readily perceive the pattern as belonging to a moving human and could identify the behavior the actor was performing. Subsequent studies (Kozlowski and Cutting, 1977; Barclay, Cutting, and Kozlowski, 1978) showed that people could even tell, with reasonable accuracy, the sex of the actor wearing the lights. The cues appeared to be supplied by the relative amounts of movement of the shoulders and hips as the person walked.

Often, people with visual agnosia can still perceive *actions* (such as someone pretending to stir something in a bowl or deal out some playing cards)

even though they cannot recognize objects by sight. They may be able to recognize friends by the way they walk, even though they cannot recognize their faces. Presumably, their lesions damage the ventral stream of the visual association cortex but leave area V5 and its efferent connections with the rest of the brain intact.

Perception of Location

As we just saw, all subareas of the extrastriate cortex send information to the inferior temporal cortex, the region in which object perception appears to take place. In addition, three subareas of the extrastriate cortex—those involved with color, orientation, and movement—send information through area V5 to the parietal cortex. (Refer to *Figures 6.34* and *6.35*.) The parietal lobe is involved in spatial perception, and it is through these connections that it receives its visual input. Damage to the parietal lobes disrupts performance on a variety of tasks that require perceiving and remembering the locations of objects (Ungerleider and Mishkin, 1982).

A particularly interesting phenomenon called **Balint's syndrome** occurs in people with bilateral damage to the parieto-occipital region—the region bordering the parietal lobe and occipital lobe (Balint, 1909; Damasio, 1985). Balint's syndrome consists of three major symptoms: optic ataxia, ocular apraxia, and simultanagnosia. All three symptoms are related to spatial perception.

Optic ataxia is a deficit in reaching for objects under visual guidance (*ataxia* comes from the Greek word for "disorderly"). A person with Balint's syndrome might be able to perceive and recognize a particular object, but when he or she tries to reach for it, the movement is often misdirected. **Ocular apraxia** (literally "without visual action") is a deficit of visual scanning. If a person with Balint's syndrome looks around a room filled with objects, he or she will see an occasional item and will be able to perceive it normally. However, the patient will not be able to maintain fixation; his or her eyes will begin to wander and another object will come into view for a time. The person is unable to make a systematic scan of the contents of the room and will not be able to perceive the location of the objects he or she sees. If an object moves, or if a light flashes, the person may report seeing something but will not be able to make an eye movement that directs the gaze toward the target.

Simultanagnosia is the most interesting of the three symptoms (Rizzo and Robin, 1990). As I just mentioned, if the gaze of a person with Balint's syndrome happens to fall on an object, he or she will perceive it. But *only one object* will be perceived at a time. For example, if an examiner holds either a comb or a pen in front of a patient's eyes, the patient will recognize the object. But if the examiner holds a pen and a comb together (for example, so that they form the legs of an X), the patient will see either the comb or the pen, but not both. The existence of simultanagnosia means that perception of separate objects takes place at least somewhat independently, even when the outlines of the objects overlap in the visual field.

Goodale and Milner (1992) suggest that the primary function of the dorsal stream of the visual cortex is to guide actions rather than simply to perceive spatial locations. As Ungerleider and Mishkin (1982) originally put it, the ventral and dorsal streams tell us "what" and "where." Goodale and Milner suggest that the better terms are *"what"* and *"how."* First, they note that the visual cortex of the parietal lobe is extensively connected to regions of the frontal lobe involved in controlling eye movements, reaching movements of the limbs, and grasping movements of the hands and fingers (Cavada and Goldman-Rakic, 1989; Gentilucci and Rizzolatti, 1990). Second, they note that the optic ataxia and ocular apraxia of Balint's syndrome, which are caused by bilateral damage to the dorsal stream, are deficits in visually guided movements. They cite the case of a person with such lesions who had no difficulty recognizing line drawings (that is, the ventral stream was intact), but who had trouble picking up objects (Jakobson et al., 1991). The patient could easily perceive the difference in the size of wooden blocks set out before her, but she failed to adjust the distance between her thumb and forefinger to the size of the block she was about to pick up. In contrast, Milner et al. (1991) studied a patient with profound visual agnosia who could not distinguish between wooden blocks of different sizes, but who *did* adjust the distance between her thumb and forefinger when she picked them up.

Goodale and Milner's conclusion seems a reasonable one. Of course, the dorsal stream is involved in perception of the location of objects space—but then, if its primary role is to direct movements, it *must* be involved in location of these objects, or else how could it direct movements toward them? In addition, it must contain information about the size and shape of objects, or else how could it control the distance between thumb and forefinger?

I mentioned earlier that I would attempt to explain associative visual agnosia as a disruption of the connections between the ventral stream and the brain's verbal mechanisms. As we saw, people with associative agnosia cannot verbally identify visually presented objects or pictures of them, but they can copy them and sometimes they can make hand movements that enable them to guess what the object is. Sirigu, Duhamel, and Poncet (1991) reported the case of a patient with bilateral lesions of the anterior temporal cortex who was able to copy drawings of objects but was unable to name them. However, he was able to say or demonstrate *what to do* with these objects. For example, he said, "You open on one side, stick something on it, close it, and it stays in. I can tell you how it works, but I don't see its exact use" (p. 2555). And what had the investigators shown him? A safety pin. When they showed him a picture of a jackhammer, he acted as if he were holding one, and made shaking movements. What was it for? "Probably to make holes . . . in the wall . . . when you want to hang a picture" (p. 2566).

It is important to realize that the patient recognized *what to do* with objects he saw, not *what they were used for.* He was able to describe or mime behaviors, not functions. Certainly, one would not use a jackhammer to hang a picture on the wall. Consider what he said when shown a pair of pliers: "It is used manually, when you pull apart here [points to handle] it opens up at the other end." So far, so good. But then he went on to say, "Perhaps to hold several pieces of paper together" (p. 2566). When shown an iron, he said "You hold it in one hand, and move it back and forth horizontally." He then mimed the action, as if he were pressing some clothes on an ironing board. "Maybe you can spread glue evenly with it" (p. 2566).

Even though the patient could not identify most objects visually, he accurately answered questions about their physical properties, such as "Which one would feel the heaviest?" or "Which one would feel the coldest?" The fact that he could answer these questions (and could mime what to do with them) indicates that the circuits responsible for visual form perception (those in the ventral stream) were relatively intact, but that they were no longer connected to the circuits responsible for speech (and for consciousness). His dorsal stream and its connections with speech mechanisms were undamaged, and it was apparently through these connections that he was able to describe how to use the objects. This interpretation is consistent with Goodale and Milner's conclusion that the ventral stream is primarily occupied with controlling movements, not simply perceiving the location of objects.

||||| INTERIM SUMMARY

The visual cortex consists of the striate cortex, the extrastriate cortex (also called the prestrite or circumstriate cortex), and the visual association cortex of the inferior temporal lobe and the posterior parietal lobe. There are at least 25 different subregions of the visual cortex, arranged in a hierarchical fashion. The extrastriate cortex receives information from the striate cortex and from the superior colliculus. The color-sensitive cells in the blobs in the striate cortex send information to area V4 of the extrastriate cortex. Damage to the human extrastriate cortex (presumably, damage to area V4) can cause achromatopsia, a loss of color vision.

The visual cortex is organized into two streams. The ventral stream, which ends with the inferior temporal cortex, is involved with perception of objects. Lesions of area TEO disrupt perception of simple two-dimensional patterns, whereas lesions of TE disrupt perception of more complex, three-dimensional objects. Also, single neurons in TE respond best to complex stimuli, and continue to do so even if the object is moved to a different location or placed against a different background. The dorsal stream, which ends with the posterior parietal cortex, is involved with perception of location, movement, and control of eye and hand move-ments. Damage to area V5 or to the posterior parietal cortex disrupts an animal's ability to perceive movement or the spatial location of objects. Microstimulation of clusters of neurons in area V5 can alter a monkey's perception of movement. The pulvinar, a thalamic nucleus that receives information about eye movements from the superior colliculus and information about movement of retinal images from the visual cortex, appears to inform the visual cortex about which movements are caused by eye movements and which are caused by movements in the environment.

PET studies indicate that specific regions of the cortex are involved in perception of form, movement, and color, and these studies will undoubtedly enable us to discover the correspondences between the anatomy of the human visual system and that of laboratory animals. Studies with humans who have sustained damage to the visual association cortex have discovered two basic forms of visual agnosia. Apperceptive visual agnosia involves difficulty in perceiving the shapes of objects, even though the fine details can often be detected. Prosopagnosia, failure to recognize faces, has traditionally been regarded as a separate disorder, but it probably represents a mild form of apperceptive visual agnosia. The second basic form of visual agnosia, associative visual agnosia, is characterized by relatively good object perception (shown by the fact that the patients can copy drawings of objects) but the inability to recognize what is perceived. This disorder is probably caused by damage to axons that connect the visual association cortex with regions of the brain that are important for verbalization and thinking in words. Some patients with this disorder can describe or mime actions appropriate to the objects they see but cannot recognize.

Damage to the human visual association cortex corresponding to area V5 disrupts perception of movement. Sometimes people with visual agnosia caused by damage to the ventral system can still perceive the meanings of actions or recognize friends by the way they walk, which indicates that the dorsal stream of their visual cortex is largely intact. Balint's syndrome, which is caused by bilateral damage to the parieto-occipital region (the dorsal stream), includes the symptoms of optic ataxia, ocular apraxia, and simultanagnosia.

New Terms

The Stimulus

hue p. 143

brightness p. 143

saturation p. 143

Anatomy of the Visual System

vergence movement p. 144

saccadic movement *(suh KAD ik)* p. 144

pursuit movement p. 144

accommodation p. 144

retina p. 144

rod p. 144

cone p. 144

photoreceptor p. 144

fovea *(FOE vee a)* p. 144

optic disk p. 145

bipolar cell p. 145

ganglion cell p. 145

horizontal cell p. 145

amacrine cell *(AMM a krin)* p. 145

lamella p. 146

photopigment p. 146

opsin *(OPP sin)* p. 146

retinal *(RETT i nahl)* p. 146

rhodopsin *(roh DOPP sin)* p. 146

receptor potential p. 146

dorsal lateral geniculate nucleus p. 147

magnocellular layer p. 148

parvocellular layer p. 148

calcarine fissure *(KAL ka rine)* p. 148

striate cortex *(STRY ate)* p. 148

optic chiasm p. 148

Coding of Visual Information in the Retina

receptive field p. 150

protanopia *(pro tan OWE pee a)* p. 154

deuteranopia *(dew ter an OWE pee a)* p. 154

tritanopia *(try tan OEW pee a)* p. 155

Analysis of Visual Information: Role of the Striate Cortex

simple cell p. 158

complex cell p. 158

sine-wave grating p. 158

spatial frequency p. 159

retinal disparity p. 162

blob p. 162

blindsight p. 165

Analysis of Visual Iformation: Role of the Visual Association Cortex

extrastriate cortex p. 166

color constancy p. 168

achromatopsia *(ay krohm a TOP see a)* p. 168

inferior temporal cortex p. 169

visual agnosia *(ag NO zha)* p. 171

apperceptive visual agnosia p. 172

prosopagnosia *(prah soh pag NO zha)* p. 172

associative visual agnosia p. 174

pulvinar *(PULL vi nar)* p. 176

Balint's syndrome p. 177

optic ataxia *(ay TACK see a)* p. 177

ocular apraxia *(ay PRAK see a)* p. 177

simultanagnosia *(sime ul tane ag NO zha)*. p. 178

Suggested Readings

De Valois, R.L., and De Valois, K.K. *Spatial Vision.* New York: Oxford University Press, 1988.

Land, M.F., and Fernald, R.D. The evolution of eyes. *Annual Review of Neuroscience,* 1992, *15,* 1–30.

Lund, J.S. Anatomical organization of macaque monkey striate visual cortex. *Annual Review of Neuroscience,* 1988, *11,* 253–288.

Miyashita, Y. Inferior temporal cortex: Where visual perception meets memory. *Annual Review of Neuroscience,* 1993, *16,* 245–264.

Merigan, W.H., and Maunsell, J.H.R. How parallel are the primate visual pathways? *Annual Review of Neuroscience,* 1993, *16,* 369–402.

Rodieck, R.W. The primate retina. In *Comparative Primate Biology. Volume 4: Neurosciences,* edited by H.D. Steklis and J. Erwin. New York: A.R. Liss, 1988.

Valberg, A., and Lee, B.B. *From Pigments to Perception.* New York: Plenum Press, 1991.

Yau, K.-W., and Baylor, D.A. Cyclic GMP-activated conductance of retinal photoreceptor cells. *Annual Review of Neuroscience,* 1989, *12,* 289–328.

Zeki, S. The visual image in mind and brain. *Scientific American,* 1992, *267(3),* 69–76.

CHAPTER 7

Audition, the Body Senses, and the Chemical Senses

Audition
- The Stimulus
- Anatomy of the Ear
- Auditory Hair Cells and the Transduction of Auditory Information
- The Auditory Pathway
- Detection of Pitch
- Detection of Loudness
- Detection of Timbre
- Feature Detection in the Auditory System
- Behavioral Functions of the Auditory System
  Interim Summary

Vestibular System
- Anatomy of the Vestibular Apparatus
- The Receptor Cells
- The Vestibular Pathway
  Interim Summary

Somatosenses
- The Stimuli
- Anatomy of the Skin and Its Receptive Organs
- Detection of Cutaneous Stimulation
- The Somatosensory Pathways
- Perception of Pain
  Interim Summary

Gustation
- The Stimuli
- Anatomy of the Taste Buds and Gustatory Cells
- Detection of Gustatory Information
- The Gustatory Pathway
- Neural Coding of Taste
  Interim Summary

Olfaction
- The Stimulus
- Anatomy of the Olfactory Apparatus
- Transduction of Olfactory Information
- Detection of Specific Odors
  Interim Summary

ONE CHAPTER WAS DEVOTED TO VISION, but the rest of the sensory modalities must share a chapter. This unequal allocation of space reflects the relative importance of vision to our species and the relative amount of research that has been devoted to it. People often say that we have five senses: sight, hearing, smell, taste, and touch. Actually, we have more than five. For example, besides providing us with auditory information, the inner ear supplies information about head orientation and movement. And the sense of touch (more accurately, *somatosensation*) detects changes in pressure, warmth, cold, vibration, limb position, and events that damage tissue (that is, produce pain).

This chapter is divided into five major sections, which discuss audition, the vestibular system, the somatosenses, gustation, and olfaction.

AUDITION

FOR MOST PEOPLE, AUDITION IS THE SECOND MOST important sense. The value of verbal communication makes it even more important than vision in some respects; for example, a blind person can join others in conversation far more easily than a deaf person can. Acoustic stimuli also provide information about things that are hidden from view, and our ears work just as well in the dark. This section describes the nature of the stimulus, the sensory receptors, the brain mechanisms devoted to audition, and some of the details of the physiology of auditory perception.

The Stimulus

We hear sounds, which are produced by objects that vibrate and set the molecules of the air into motion. When an object vibrates, its movements cause the air surrounding it alternately to condense and rarefy (pull apart), producing waves that travel away from the object at approximately 700 miles per hour. If the vibration ranges between approximately 30 and 20,000 times per second, these waves will stimulate receptive cells in our ears and will be perceived as sounds.

In Chapter 6 we saw that light has three perceptual dimensions—hue, brightness, and saturation—which correspond to three physical dimensions. Similarly, sounds vary in their pitch, loudness, and timbre. The perceived **pitch** of an auditory stimulus is determined by the frequency of vibration, which is measured in **hertz** (Hz), or cycles per second. (The term honors Heinrich Hertz, a nineteenth-century German physicist.) **Loudness** is a function of intensity—the degree to which the condensations and rarefactions of air differ from each other. More vigorous vibrations of an object produce more intense sound waves and, hence, louder ones. **Timbre** provides information about the nature of the particular sound—for example, the sound of an oboe or a train whistle. Most natural acoustic stimuli are complex, consisting of several different frequencies of vibration. The particular mixture determines the sound's timbre. (See *Figure 7.1.*)

The eye is a *synthetic* organ (literally, "a putting together"). When two different wavelengths of light are mixed, we perceive a single color. For example,

FIGURE 7.1

The physical and perceptual dimensions of sound waves.

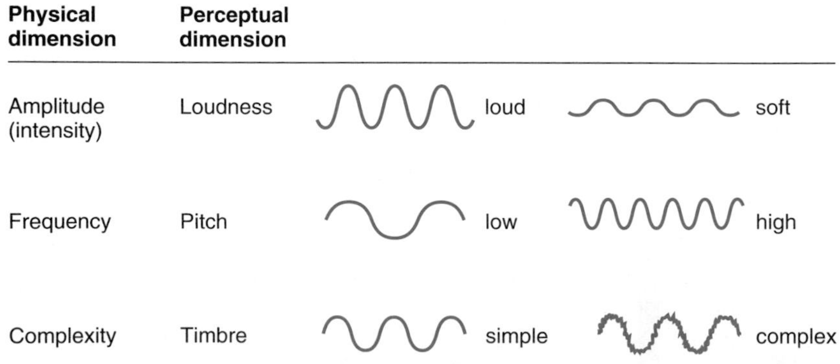

Physical dimension	Perceptual dimension				
Amplitude (intensity)	Loudness	∿	loud	∿	soft
Frequency	Pitch	∿	low	∿	high
Complexity	Timbre	∿	simple	∿	complex

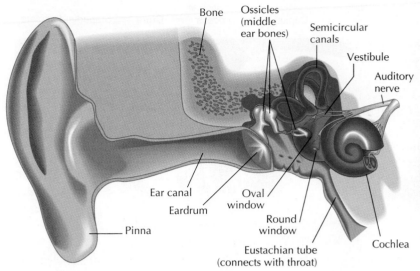
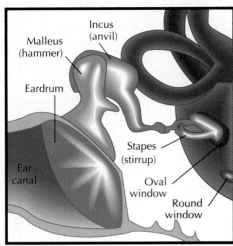

FIGURE 7.2

The auditory apparatus.

when we see a mixture of red and bluish green light, we perceive pure yellow light and cannot detect either of the two constituents. In contrast, the ear is an *analytical* organ (from *analuein,* "to undo"). When two different frequencies of sound waves are mixed, we do not perceive an intermediate tone; instead, we hear both original tones. As we will see, the ability of our auditory system to detect the individual component frequencies of a complex tone gives us the capacity to identify the nature of particular sounds, such as those of different musical instruments.

Anatomy of the Ear

Figure 7.2 shows a section through the ear and auditory canal and illustrates the apparatus of the middle and inner ear. (See *Figure 7.2.*) Sound is funneled via the *pinna* (external ear) through the *external auditory canal* to the **tympanic membrane** (eardrum), which vibrates with the sound. We are not good at moving our ears, but by orienting our heads we can modify the sound that finally reaches the receptors.

The *middle ear* consists of a hollow region behind the tympanic membrane, approximately 2 ml in volume. It contains the bones of the middle ear, called the **ossicles,** which are set into vibration by the tympanic membrane. The **malleus** (hammer) connects with the tympanic membrane and transmits vibrations via the **incus** (anvil) and **stapes** (stirrup) to the **cochlea,** the structure that contains the receptors. The baseplate of the stapes presses against the membrane behind the **oval window,** the opening in the bony process surrounding the cochlea. (See *Figures 7.2* and *7.3.*)

The cochlea is part of the *inner ear.* It is filled with fluid; therefore, sounds transmitted through the air must be transferred into a liquid medium. This process normally is very inefficient—99.9 percent of the energy of airborne sound would be reflected away if the air impinged directly against the oval window of the cochlea. (If you have ever swum underwater, you have probably noted how quiet it is there; most of the sound arising in the air is reflected off the surface of the water.) The chain of ossicles serves as an extremely efficient means of energy transmission. The bones provide a mechanical advantage, with the baseplate of the stapes making smaller but more forceful excursions against the oval window than the tympanic membrane makes against the malleus.

The name *cochlea* comes from the Greek word *kokhlos,* or "land snail." It is indeed snail-shaped, consisting of two and three-quarters turns of a grad-

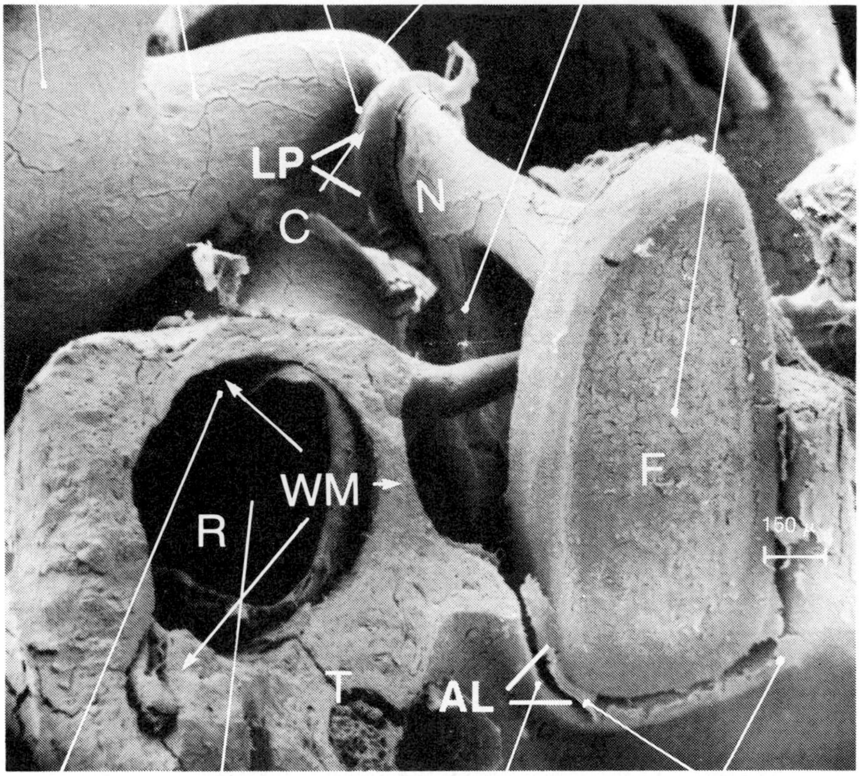

FIGURE 7.3

A scanning electron micrograph of the stapes and the round window.

(Reproduced from R. G. Kessel and R. H. Kardon, *Tissues and Organs: A Text-Atlas of Scanning Electron Microscopy.* W. H. Freeman, 1979. Reprinted with permission.)

Incus — Inferior process — Capital — Lenticular process — Crura — Stapedial footplate

Round window membrane — Round window — Boundary of oval window — Annular ligament

ually tapering cylinder. The cochlea is divided longitudinally into three sections—the *scala vestibuli* ("vestibular stairway"), the *scala media* ("middle stairway"), and the *scala tympani* ("tympanic stairway"), as shown in *Figure 7.4.* The receptive organ, known as the **organ of Corti,** consists of the *basilar membrane,* the *hair cells,* and the *tectorial membrane.* The auditory receptor cells are called **hair cells,** and they are anchored, via rodlike **Deiters's cells,** to the **basilar membrane.** The cilia of the hair cells pass through the *reticular membrane,* and the ends of some of them attach to the fairly rigid **tectorial membrane,** which projects overhead like a shelf. (See *Figure 7.4.*) Sound waves cause the basilar membrane to move relative to the tectorial membrane, which bends the cilia of the hair cells. This bending produces receptor potentials.

Georg von Békésy—in a lifetime of brilliant studies on the cochleas of various animals, from human cadavers to elephants—found that the vibratory energy exerted on the oval window causes the basilar membrane to bend (von Békésy, 1960). Because of the physical characteristics of the basilar membrane, the portion that bends the most is determined by the frequency of the sound: High-frequency sounds cause the end nearest the oval window to bend.

Figure 7.5 shows this process in a cochlea that has been partially straightened out. If the cochlea were a closed system, no vibration would be transmitted through the oval window, because liquids are essentially incompressible. However, there is a membrane-covered opening, the **round window,** which allows the fluid inside the cochlea to move back and forth. The baseplate of the stapes vibrates against the

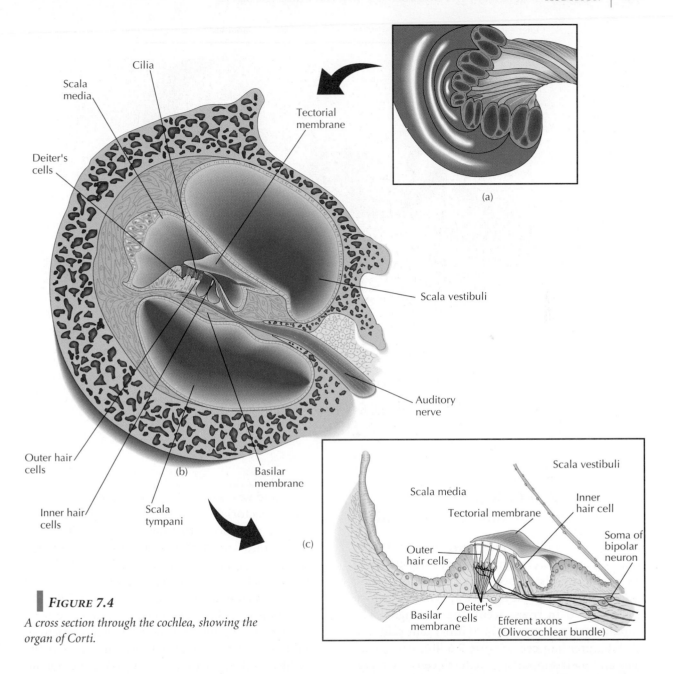

Scala media

Cilia

Tectorial membrane

Scala vestibuli

Deiter's cells

Auditory nerve

(a)

(b)

Outer hair cells

Inner hair cells

Scala tympani

Basilar membrane

Scala media

Scala vestibuli

Tectorial membrane

Inner hair cell

Outer hair cells

Soma of bipolar neuron

Basilar membrane

Deiter's cells

Efferent axons (Olivocochlear bundle)

(c)

| FIGURE 7.4

A cross section through the cochlea, showing the organ of Corti.

membrane behind the oval window and introduces sound waves of high or low frequency into the cochlea. The vibrations cause part of the basilar membrane to flex back and forth. Pressure changes in the fluid underneath the basilar membrane are transmitted to the membrane of the round window, which moves in and out in a manner opposite to the movements of the oval window. That is, when the baseplate of the stapes pushes in, the membrane behind the round window bulges out. (See *Figure 7.5.*)

Some people suffer from a middle ear disease that causes the bone to grow over the round window. Because their basilar membrane cannot easily flex back and forth, these people have a severe hearing loss. However, their hearing can be restored by a surgical procedure called *fenestration* ("window making"), in which a tiny hole is drilled in the bone where the round window should be.

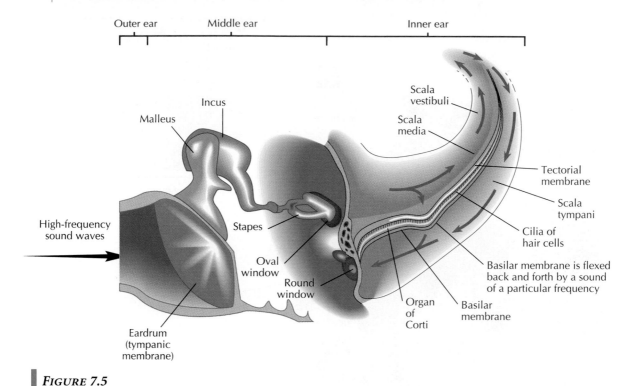

Figure 7.5

Stimulation of the organ of Corti. Sound waves transmitted through the oval window deform a portion of the basilar membrane.

Auditory Hair Cells and the Transduction of Auditory Information

Two types of auditory receptors, *inner* and *outer* auditory hair cells, lie on the inside and outside of the cochlear coils, respectively. Hair cells contain **cilia** ("eyelashes"), fine hairlike appendages, which are arranged in rows, according to height. The human cochlea contains 3400 inner hair cells and 12,000 outer hair cells. Figure 7.6 illustrates these cells and their supporting Deiters's cells. (See *Figure 7.6.*) The hair cells form synapses with dendrites of neurons that give rise to the auditory nerve axons. Figure 7.7 shows the actual appearance of the inner and outer hair cells and the reticular membrane in a photograph taken by means of a scanning electron microscope, which shows excellent three-dimensional detail. Note the three rows of outer hair cells on the right and the single row of inner hair cells on the left. (See *Figure 7.7.*)

Sound waves cause both the basilar membrane and the tectorial membrane to flex up and down. Because the fulcra (turning points) of these two membranes are located in different places, and because the tips of the outer hair cells are attached to the tectorial membrane, the vibrations bend the cilia in one direction or the other. (See *Figure 7.8.*) The cilia of the inner hair cells do not touch the overlying tectorial membrane, but the relative movement of the two membranes causes the fluid within the cochlea to flow past them and makes them bend back and forth, too.

Cilia contain actin filaments, which make them stiff and rigid (Flock, 1977). Adjacent cilia are linked to each other in two places: at their tip, and partway down from the top (labeled *lateral contact* in Figure 7.9). Thus, movement of the bundle of cilia in the direction of the tallest of them stretches the linking fibers, whereas movement in the opposite direction relaxes them. (See *Figure 7.9.*)

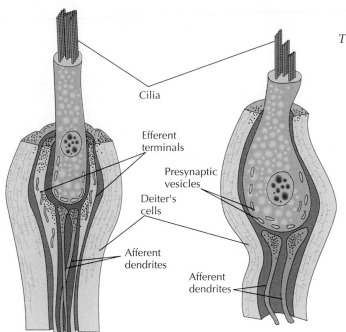

Cilia

Efferent
terminals

Presynaptic
vesicles

Deiter's
cells

Afferent
dendrites

Afferent
dendrites

The bending of the bundle of cilia causes receptor potentials. The resting potential of an auditory hair cell is approximately -60 mV. Each cilium contains three to seven ion channels, located near the tips (Holton and Hudspeth, 1986; Howard and Hudspeth, 1988). When the bundle is straight, approximately 20 percent of the ion channels are open. When the bundle moves toward the tallest one, the increased tension on the connecting fibers

pulls more ion channels open, the flow of K^+ into the cilium increases, and the membrane depolarizes. As a result, the release of neurotransmitter by the hair cell increases. When the bundle moves in the opposite direction, the relaxation of the fibers allows the opened ion channels to close. The influx of K^+ decreases, the membrane hyperpolarizes, and the release of neurotransmitter decreases. (See **Figure 7.10.**)

Reticular membrane

Hair cell

Cilia of inner hair cells   Cilia of outer hair cells

FIGURE 7.7

A scanning electron photomicrograph of a portion of the organ of Corti, showing the cilia of the inner and outer hair cells.

(Photomicrograph courtesy of I. Hunter-Duvar, The Hospital for Sick Children, Toronto, Ontario.)

Hackney et al. (1992) found the exact location of the ion channels in the auditory hair cells. They prepared an antibody against a similar ion channel found in kidneys, and used immunocytochemical methods to stain the hair cell ion channels. As Figure 7.11 shows, these ion channels are located in the membrane of the cilia just below the tip links. (See *Figure 7.11.*)

Auditory hair cells can be damaged when the ear is exposed to excessively loud sounds, causing a permanent hearing loss. Although hair cells in fish, birds, and amphibians can apparently regenerate, there is no evidence that such regeneration occurs in mammals (Corwin and Warchol, 1991).

The Auditory Pathway

Connections with the Cochlear Nerve

The organ of Corti sends auditory information to the brain by means of the **cochlear nerve,** a branch of the auditory nerve (eighth cranial nerve). The neurons that give rise to the afferent axons that travel through this nerve are of the bipolar type. Their cell bodies reside in the *cochlear nerve ganglion.* (This ganglion is also called the *spiral ganglion,* because it consists of clumps of cell bodies arranged in a spiral caused by the curling of the cochlea.) These neurons have axonal processes, capable of sustaining action potentials, that protrude from both ends of the soma. The end of one process acts like a dendrite, responding with excitatory postsynaptic potentials when the transmitter substance is released by the auditory hair cells. The excitatory postsynaptic potentials trigger action potentials in the auditory nerve axons, which form synapses with neurons in the medulla. (Refer to *Figure 7.4c.*)

Each cochlear nerve contains approximately 50,000 afferent axons. The dendrites of approximately 95 percent of these axons form synapses with the inner hair cells. Most afferent fibers make contact with only one inner hair cell, but each inner hair cell forms synapses with approximately 20 fibers (Spoendlin, 1973; Keithley and Schreiber, 1987). The axons that receive information from the inner hair cells are thick and myelinated. The other 5 percent of the sensory fibers in the cochlear nerve form

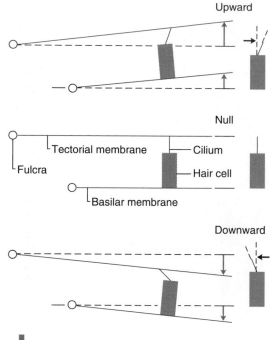

FIGURE 7.8

A schematic explanation of the fact that vibrations of the basilar membrane cause bending of the cilia of the hair cells.

(Adapted from Gulick, W.L., Gescheider, G.A., and Frisina, R.D. *Hearing: Physiological Acoustics, Neural Coding, and Psychoacoustics.* New York: Oxford University Press, 1989.)

synapses with the much more numerous outer hair cells, and these axons are thin and unmyelinated. Thus, although the inner hair cells represent only 22 percent of the total number of receptive cells, their connections with auditory nerves suggest that they are of primary importance in the transmission of auditory information to the central nervous system.

Physiological and behavioral studies confirm the inferences made from the synaptic connections of the two types of hair cells: The inner hair cells are necessary for normal hearing. In fact, Deol and Gluecksohn-Waelsch (1979) found that a mutant strain of mice whose cochleas contain *only* outer hair cells apparently cannot hear at all. Most investigators currently believe that the outer hair cells are primarily *effector* cells, involved in altering the mechanical characteristics of the basilar membrane and thus influencing the effects of sound vibrations on the inner hair cells. I will discuss this possibility in the section on place coding of pitch.

The cochlear nerve contains efferent axons as well as afferent ones. The source of the efferent axons is the superior olivary complex, a group of nuclei in the medulla; thus, the efferent fibers con-

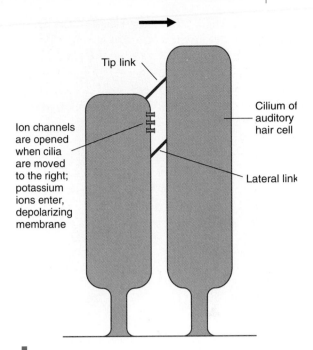

FIGURE 7.10

Transduction. Tension on the links between adjacent cilia opens ion channels, resulting in entry of potassium ions, which depolarizes the membrane potential.

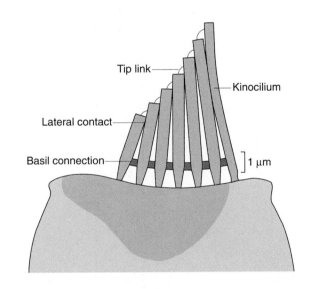

(a)

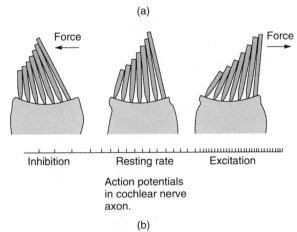

(b)

FIGURE 7.9

Cilia of auditory hair cells. (a) Their appearance. (b) Transduction. Movement of the bundle stretches or relaxes tension on the links between the tips of adjacent cilia and changes the rate of firing of the afferent axon.

(Adapted from Howard, J., Roberts, W.M., and Hudspeth, A.J. *Annual Review of Biophysics and Biophysical Chemistry*, 1988, *17*, 99–124.)

stitute the **olivocochlear bundle.** The fibers form synapses directly on outer hair cells and on the dendrites that serve the inner hair cells. (Refer to *Figures 7.4c* and *7.6.*) The transmitter substance at the afferent synapses appears to be an excitatory amino acid such as glutamate or aspartate. The efferent terminal buttons secrete acetylcholine, which appears to have an inhibitory effect on the hair cells.

The Central Auditory System

The anatomy of the auditory system is more complicated than that of the visual system. Rather than give a detailed verbal description of the pathways, I will refer you to *Figure 7.12.* Note that axons enter the **cochlear nucleus** of the medulla and synapse there. Most of the neurons in the cochlear nucleus send axons to the **superior olivary complex,** also located in the medulla. Neurons there project axons through a large bundle of axons called the **lateral lemniscus** to the inferior colliculus, located in the

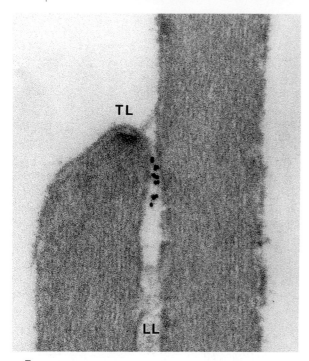

FIGURE 7.11

An electron photomicrograph of a section through two cilia of a guinea pig auditory hair cell. The ion channels, stained by means of immunocytochemistry, show up as dark patches located just below the tip of the shorter cilium. TL, tip link; LL, lateral link.

(From Hackney, C.M., Furness, D.N., Benos, D.J., Woodley, J., and Barratt, J. *Proceedings of the Royal Society of London [B]*, 1992, *248*, 215–221. Reprinted with permission.)

resented most medially in the auditory cortex, and the *apical* end is represented most laterally there. Because, as we will see, different parts of the basilar membrane respond best to different frequencies of sound, this relationship between cortex and basilar membrane is referred to as **tonotopic representation** (*tonos* means "tone" and *topos* means "place").

Neurons in the primary auditory cortex send axons to the auditory association cortex. In Chapter 4, we saw that the primary auditory cortex lies hidden on the inside of the lateral fissure, and that the auditory association cortex lies on the superior part of the temporal lobe.

dorsal midbrain. Neurons there project to the medial geniculate nucleus of the thalamus, which sends axons to the auditory cortex of the temporal lobe. As you can see, there are many synapses along the way to complicate the story. Each hemisphere receives information from both ears but primarily from the contralateral one. And auditory information is relayed to the cerebellum and reticular formation as well.

If we unrolled the basilar membrane into a flat strip and followed afferent axons serving successive points along its length, we would reach successive points in the nuclei of the auditory system and ultimately successive points along the surface of the primary auditory cortex. The *basal* end of the basilar membrane (the end toward the oval window) is rep-

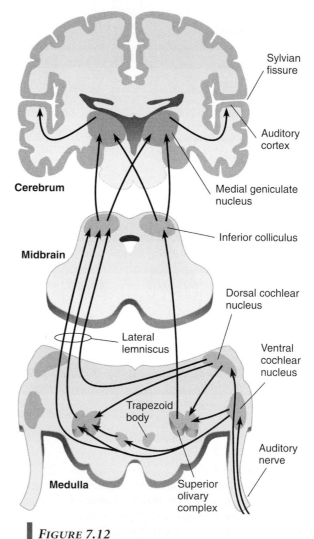

FIGURE 7.12

The pathway of the auditory system.

Detection of Pitch

As we have seen, the perceptual dimension of pitch corresponds to the physical dimension of frequency. The cochlea detects frequency by two means: moderate to high frequencies by place coding and low frequencies by rate coding. These two types of coding are described next.

Place Coding

The work of von Békésy has shown us that because of the mechanical construction of the cochlea and basilar membrane, acoustic stimuli of different frequencies cause different parts of the basilar membrane to flex back and forth. Figure 7.13 illustrates the amount of deformation along the length of the basilar membrane produced by stimulation with tones of various frequencies. Note that higher frequencies produce more displacement at the basal end of the membrane (the end closest to the stapes). (See *Figure 7.13.*)

These results suggest that at least some frequencies of sound waves are detected by means of a **place code**. In this context a code represents a means by which neurons can represent information. Thus, if neurons at one end of the basilar membrane are excited by higher frequencies and those at the other end by lower frequencies, we can say that the frequency of the sound is *coded* by the particular neurons that are active. In turn, the firing of particular axons in the cochlear nerve tells the brain about the presence of particular frequencies of sound.

Evidence for place coding of pitch comes from several sources. High doses of the antibiotic drugs kanamycin and neomycin produce degeneration of the auditory hair cells. Damage to auditory hair cells begins at the basal end of the cochlea and progresses toward the apical end; this pattern can be verified by killing experimental animals after dosing them with the antibiotic for varying amounts of time. Longer exposures to the drug are associated with increased progress of hair cell damage down the basilar membrane. Stebbins et al. (1969) found that the progressive death of hair cells induced by an antibiotic closely parallels a progressive hearing loss: The highest frequencies are the first to go, and the lowest are the last.

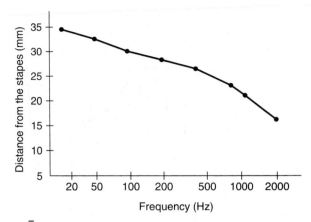

FIGURE 7.13

Anatomical coding of pitch. Stimuli of different frequencies maximally deform different regions of the basilar membrane.

(From von Békésy, G. *Journal of the Acoustical Society of America*, 1949, *21*, 233–245.)

The work of von Békésy indicated that although the basilar membrane codes for frequency along its length, the coding was not very specific. His studies, and those of investigators who followed him, indicated that a given frequency causes a large region of the basilar membrane to be deformed. This finding contrasted with the observation that people can detect changes in frequency of only 2 or 3 Hz.

An experiment by Katsuki (1961) also suggested that the selectivity of the basilar membrane is much greater than Békésy's observations indicated. Katsuki made recordings from single axons in the cochlear nerve and prepared some **auditory tuning curves.** The data were collected as follows: The investigator located an axon with a microelectrode and presented tones of various frequencies and intensities. For each cell he plotted points that corresponded to the least intense tone that gave a response at a given frequency. The V shapes indicate that at higher intensities (the top of the V-shaped curves), a given axon responds to a wider range of frequencies. At low intensities (the bottom of the V-shaped curves) a given axon responds to a very limited range of frequencies. (See *Figure 7.14.*) The tuning curves of neurons in the cochlear nerve, which receive input from the hair cells, indicated a high degree of selectivity.

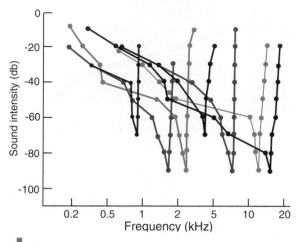

FIGURE 7.14

Tuning curves of single units in the cochlear nerve. dB = decibel; kHz = kilohertz (1000 Hz).

(From Katsuki, Y. in *Sensory Communication*, edited by W.A. Rosenblith. Copyright 1961 by MIT Press.)

The reason for this discrepancy is now clear. Because of technical limitations, von Békésy had to observe the cochleas of animals that were no longer living or, at best, cochleas that had been damaged by the procedure necessary to make the measurements. More recently, investigators have used much more sensitive—and less damaging—procedures to observe movements of the basilar membrane in response to different frequencies of sound. It appears that the point of maximum vibration of the basilar membrane to a particular frequency is very precisely localized—but only when the cells in the organ of Corti are alive and healthy (Evans, 1992; Ruggero, 1992).

The fact that the tuning characteristics of the basilar membrane change when the cells in the organ of Corti die suggests that these cells somehow affect the mechanical properties of the basilar membrane. We now know that the outer hair cells are responsible for this selective tuning, but we do not understand yet exactly how they accomplish this feat. As I mentioned earlier, outer hair cells are not only sensory transducers but are also contractile elements, like muscle fibers. When these cells are exposed to an electrical current, or when acetylcholine is placed on them, they contract by up to 10 percent of their length (Brownell et al., 1985; Zen-

ner, Zimmermann, and Schmitt, 1985). Because the tips of their cilia are embedded in the tectorial membrane, contraction would affect the mechanical characteristics of the basilar membrane—and consequently, the response properties of the inner hair cells. Kemp (1978) discovered that when brief sounds are presented to a normal cochlea, it produces a sound itself, which can be detected with a microphone. Presumably, this sound is produced by contraction of the outer hair cells. Most investigators believe that the signals that cause contraction of the outer hair cells come partly from the olivocochlear bundle and partly from local circuits of neurons within the organ of Corti.

Rate Coding

We have seen that the frequency of a sound can be detected by place coding. However, the lowest frequencies do not appear to be accounted for in this manner. Kiang (1965) was unable to find any cells that responded best to frequencies of less than 200 Hz. How, then, can animals distinguish low frequencies? It appears that lower frequencies are detected by neurons that fire in synchrony to the movements of the apical end of the basilar membrane. Thus, lower frequencies are detected by means of **rate coding**.

Miller and Taylor (1948) provided good evidence that pitch can be encoded by synchronized firing of the auditory hair cells. These investigators presented **white noise** (sound containing all frequencies, similar to the hissing sound you hear between FM radio stations) to human observers. When the investigators rapidly switched the white noise on and off, the observers reported that they heard a tone corresponding to the frequency of pulsation. The white noise, containing all frequencies, stimulated the entire length of the basilar membrane, so the frequency that was detected could not be coded for by place. The only frequency-specific information the auditory system could have had was the firing rate of cochlear nerve axons.

Detection of Loudness

The cochlea is an extremely sensitive organ. Wilska (1935) used an ingenious procedure to estimate the smallest vibration needed to produce a perceptible sound. He glued a small wooden rod to a volunteer's tympanic membrane (temporarily, of course) and made the rod vibrate longitudinally by means of an electromagnetic coil that could be energized with alternating current. He could vary the frequency and intensity of the current, which consequently changed the perceived pitch and loudness of the stimulus. He found that subjects could detect a sound even when the eardrum was vibrated over a distance less than the diameter of a hydrogen atom—showing that the auditory system is very sensitive. Thus, in very quiet environments a young, healthy ear is limited in its ability to detect sounds in the air by the masking noise of blood rushing through the cranial blood vessels, rather than by the sensitivity of the auditory system itself. More recent studies using modern instruments (reviewed by Hudspeth, 1983) have essentially confirmed Wilska's measurements. The softest sounds that can be detected appear to move the tip of the hair cells between 1 and 100 picometers (pm; trillionths of a meter). They achieve their maximum response when the tips are moved 100 nm (Corwin and Warchol, 1991).

The axons of the cochlear nerve appear to inform the brain of the loudness of a stimulus by altering their rate of firing. More intense vibrations produce a more intense shearing force on the cilia of the auditory hair cells, presumably causing them to release more transmitter substance, resulting in a higher rate of firing by the cochlear nerve axons. This explanation seems simple for the axons involved in place coding of pitch; in this case pitch is signaled by which neurons fire, and loudness is signaled by their rate of firing. However, the neurons that signal lower frequencies do so by their rate of firing. If they fire more frequently, they signal a higher pitch. Therefore, most investigators believe that the loudness of low-frequency sounds is signaled by the *number* of axons that are active at a given time.

Detection of Timbre

Although laboratory investigations of the auditory system often employ pure sine waves as stimuli, these waves are seldom encountered outside the laboratory. Instead, we hear sounds with a rich mix-
ture of frequencies—sounds of complex timbre. For example, consider the sound of a clarinet playing a particular note. If we hear it, we can easily say that it is a clarinet and not a flute or a violin. The reason we can do so is that these three instruments produce sounds of different timbre, which our auditory system can distinguish.

Figure 7.15 shows the waveform from a clarinet playing a steady note (*top*). The shape of the waveform repeats itself regularly at the **fundamental frequency,** which corresponds to the perceived pitch of the note. A Fourier analysis of the waveform shows that it actually consists of a series of sine waves that includes the fundamental frequency and many **overtones,** multiples of the fundamental frequency. Different instruments produce overtones with different intensities. (See *Figure 7.15*.) Electronic synthesizers simulate the sounds of real instruments by producing a series of overtones of the proper intensities, mixing them, and passing them through a loudspeaker.

When the basilar membrane is stimulated by the sound of a clarinet, different portions respond to each of the overtones. This response produces a unique anatomically coded pattern of activity in the cochlear nerve, which is subsequently identified by the auditory system of the brain. Just how this analysis is done is not known and probably will not be known for many years. When you consider that we can listen to an orchestra and identify several instruments that are playing simultaneously, you can appreciate the complexity of the analysis performed by the auditory system.

Feature Detection in the Auditory System

So far, I have discussed coding of pitch, loudness, and timbre only (the last of which is actually a complex frequency analysis). The auditory system also responds to other qualities of acoustic stimuli. For example, our ears are very good at determining whether the source of a sound is to the right or left of us. (To discriminate front from back, we merely turn our heads, transforming the discrimination into a left-right decision.) Two separate physiological mechanisms detect the location of sound sources: We use phase differences for low frequen-

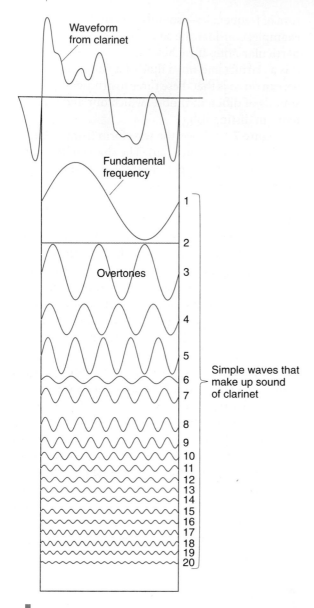

FIGURE 7.15

The shape of a sound wave from a clarinet (top) and the individual frequencies into which it can be analyzed.

(Reprinted from *Stereo Review*, copyright © 1977 by Diamandis Communications Inc.)

Localization by Means of Arrival Time and Phase Differences

If we are blindfolded, we can still determine with rather good accuracy the location of a stimulus that emits a click. We do so because neurons respond selectively to different *arrival times* of the sound waves at the left and right ears. If the source of the click is to the right or left of the midline, the sound pressure wave will reach one ear sooner and initiate action potentials there first. Only if the stimulus is straight ahead will the ears be stimulated simultaneously. Many neurons in the auditory system respond to sounds presented to either ear. Some of these neurons, especially those in the superior olivary complex of the medulla, respond according to the difference in arrival times of sound waves produced by clicks presented *binaurally* (that is, to both ears). Their response rates reflect differences as small as a fraction of a millisecond.

Of course, we can hear continuous sounds as well as clicks, and we can also perceive the location of their source. We detect the source of continuous low-pitched sounds by means of phase differences. **Phase differences** refer to the simultaneous arrival, at each ear, of different portions (phases) of the oscillating sound wave. For example, if we assume that sound travels at 700 miles per hour through the

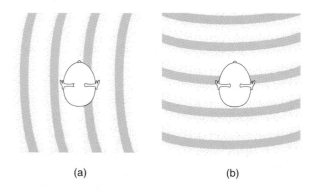

(a)   (b)

FIGURE 7.16

Phase differences. (a) Source of a 1000-Hz tone is located to the right. The pressure waves on each eardrum are out of phase; one eardrum is pushed in, while the other is pushed out. (b) Source of a 1000-Hz tone is located to the front or back of the head. The eardrums vibrate in phase.

cies (less than approximately 3000 Hz) and intensity differences for higher frequencies. Stevens and Newman (1936) found that localization is worst at approximately 3000 Hz, presumably because both mechanisms are rather inefficient at that frequency.

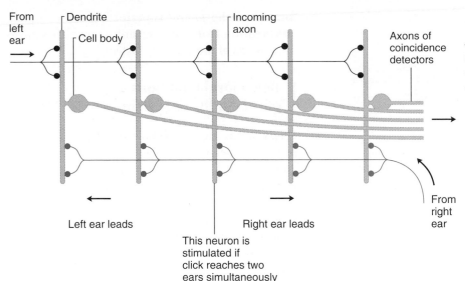

From
left
ear

Dendrite

Cell body

Incoming
axon

Axons of
coincidence
detectors

Left ear leads

Right ear leads

This neuron is
stimulated if
click reaches two
ears simultaneously

From
right
ear

FIGURE 7.17

A model of a coincidence detector that can determine differences in arrival times at each ear of an auditory stimulus.

air, adjacent cycles of a 1000-Hz tone are 12.3 inches apart. Thus, if the source of the sound is located to one side of the head, one eardrum is pulled out while the other is pushed in. The movement of the eardrums will reverse, or be 180° *out of phase.* If the source were located directly in front of the head, the movements would be perfectly in phase (0° out of phase). (See **Figure 7.16.**) Because some auditory neurons respond only when the eardrums (and thus the bending of the basilar membrane) are at least somewhat out of phase, neurons in the superior olivary complex in the brain are able to use the information they provide to detect the source of a continuous sound.

A possible mechanism to explain the ability of the nervous system to detect very short delays in the arrival times of two signals was first proposed by Jeffress (1948). He suggested that neurons received information from two sets of axons coming from the two ears. Each neuron served as a *coincidence detector;* it responded only if it received signals simultaneously from synapses belonging to both sets of axons. If a signal reached the two ears simultaneously, neurons in the middle of the array would fire. If, however, the signal reached one ear before the other, then neurons farther away from the "early" ear would be stimulated. (See **Figure 7.17.**)

In fact, that is exactly how the mechanism works. Carr and Konishi (1989; 1990) obtained anatomical

evidence in support of Jeffress's hypothesis from the brain of the barn owl, a nocturnal bird that can detect very accurately the source of a sound (such as that made by an unfortunate mouse). Figure 7.18 shows a drawing of the distribution of the branches of two axons, one from each ear, projecting to the nucleus laminaris, the barn owl analog of the mammalian medial superior olive. As you can see, axons from the ipsilateral and contralateral ears penetrate the nucleus from opposite directions; therefore, dorsally located neurons within the nucleus are stimulated by sounds that first reach the contralateral ear. (Compare **Figures 7.17** and **7.18.**) Carr and Konishi recorded from single units within the nucleus and found that the response characteristics of the neurons located there were perfectly consistent with these anatomical facts.

Localization by Means of Intensity Differences

The auditory system cannot readily detect binaural phase differences of high-frequency stimuli; the differences in phases of such rapid sine waves are just too short to be measured by the neurons. However, high-frequency stimuli that occur to the right or left of the midline stimulate the ears unequally. The head absorbs high frequencies, producing a "sonic shadow," so that the ear opposite the source of the sound receives less intense stimulation. Some neu-

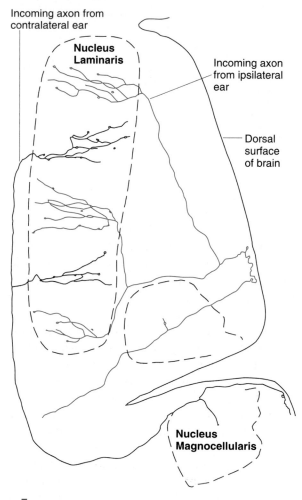

Incoming axon from
contralateral ear

**Nucleus
Laminaris**

Incoming axon
from ipsilateral
ear

Dorsal
surface
of brain

**Nucleus
Magnocellularis**

FIGURE 7.18

Evidence for a coincidence detector in the brain of a barn owl. Compare the branches of the axons with those of Figure 7.17. The drawing was prepared from microscopic examination of sections of stained tissue.

(Adapted from Carr, C.E., and Konishi, M. *Proceedings of the National Academy of Sciences, USA,* 1989, *85,* 8311–8315.)

rons in the auditory system respond differentially to binaural stimuli of different intensity in each ear, which means that they provide information that can be used to detect the source of tones of high frequency.

The neurons that detect binaural differences in loudness are located in the superior olivary complex. But whereas neurons that detect binaural differences in phase or arrival time are located in the *medial* superior olivary complex, these neurons are

located in the *lateral* superior olivary complex. Information from both sets of neurons is sent to other levels of the auditory system.

Behavioral Functions of the Auditory System

Hearing has three primary functions: to detect sounds, to determine the location of their sources, and to recognize the identity of these sources—and thus their meaning and relevance to us (Heffner and Heffner, 1990c; Yost, 1991). Let us consider the third function, recognizing the identity of a sound source. Unless you are in a completely silent location, pay attention to what you can hear. Right now, I am sitting in an office and can hear the sound of a fan in a computer, the tapping of the keys as I write this, the footsteps of someone passing outside the door, the voice of some people talking in the hallway. How can I recognize these sources? The axons in my cochlear nerve contain a constantly changing pattern of activity corresponding to the constantly changing mixture of frequencies that strike my eardrums. Somehow, the auditory system of my brain recognizes particular patterns that belong to particular sources, and I perceive each of them as independent entities.

The task of the auditory system in identifying sound sources, then, is one of *pattern recognition.* The auditory system must recognize that particular patterns of constantly changing activity belong to different sound sources. And few patterns are simple mixtures of fixed frequencies. For example, when a clarinet plays notes of different pitches, different patterns of activity are produced in our cochlear nerve—and yet we recognize each of the notes as belonging to a clarinet. Needless to say, we are far from understanding how this pattern recognition works.

Although the subcortical components of the auditory system are often referred to as "relay nuclei," it is clear that these nuclei do much more than passively transmit information from the cochlear nerve to the auditory cortex. For example, as we saw earlier in this chapter, the superior olivary complex contains circuits that analyze the location of sound sources according to arrival time (or phase differences) and intensity differences.

Pattern recognition, however, appears to be accomplished by circuits of neurons in the neocortex. We know a little bit about the types of analyses that the auditory cortex accomplishes. Various studies (Whitfield and Evans, 1965; Saitoh, Maruyama, and Kudoh, 1981) have found neurons in the auditory cortex that respond only to the onset or cessation of a sound (or to both), to changes in pitch or intensity (sometimes only to changes in one direction), or to complex stimuli that contain a variety of frequencies. Winter and Funkenstein (1971) found neurons in the auditory cortex of the squirrel monkey that responded specifically to the vocalizations made by members of this species. McKenna, Weinberger, and Diamond (1989) found that when they presented a series of different tones, some neurons in the primary auditory cortex responded to a particular frequency only in a particular context; for example, they would respond if the tone were the last in a series but not if it were the first. Sutter and Schreiner (1991) found neurons that responded best to a combination of two or more tones of particular frequencies. Thus, neurons in the auditory cortex encode rather complex features. Because data are scanty so far, we have no real conception of the coding mechanism that the brain uses for these changes or even of precisely what features are coded.

Bilateral lesions of the auditory cortex in monkeys causes an almost total hearing loss, which eventually shows some recovery (Heffner and Heffner, 1990a). The animals' ability to localize sounds is severely disrupted; they can eventually learn to discriminate a sound coming from the left or right or from one coming from the center, but they are unable to walk toward the source of the sound. Thus, their sound localizing ability does not translate into useful behavior (Heffner and Heffner, 1990b). In addition, lesions of the left auditory cortex disrupt the animals' ability to discriminate the vocalizations made by other members of this species.

As we saw in the previous chapter, lesions of the visual association cortex in humans can produce visual agnosias. Similarly, lesions of the auditory association cortex can produce auditory agnosias, the inability to comprehend the meaning of sounds. If the lesion occurs in the left hemisphere, the person will sustain a particular form of language disor-der. If it occurs in the right hemisphere, the person will be unable to recognize the nature or location of nonspeech sounds. Because of the importance of audition to language, these topics are discussed in much more detail in Chapter 16.

INTERIM SUMMARY

The receptive organ for audition is the organ of Corti, located on the basilar membrane. When sound strikes the tympanic membrane, it sets the ossicles into motion, and the baseplate of the stapes pushes against the membrane behind the oval window. Pressure changes thus applied to the fluid within the cochlea cause a portion of the basilar membrane to flex, causing the basilar membrane to move laterally with respect to the tectorial membrane that overhangs it. This movement pulls directly on the cilia of the outer hair cells and causes movements in the fluid within the cochlea, which, in turn, causes the cilia of the outer hair cells to wave back and forth. These mechanical forces open potassium channels in the tips of the hair cells and thus produce receptor potentials.

The hair cells form synapses with the dendrites of the bipolar neurons whose axons give rise to the cochlear branch of the eighth cranial nerve. The central auditory system involves several brain stem nuclei, including the cochlear nuclei, superior olivary complexes, and inferior colliculi. The medial geniculate nucleus relays auditory information to the primary auditory cortex on the medial surface of the temporal lobe.

Pitch is encoded by two means. High-frequency sounds cause the base of the basilar membrane (near the oval window) to flex; lower-frequency sounds cause the apex (opposite end) to flex. Because high and low frequencies thus stimulate different groups of auditory hair cells, frequency is encoded anatomically. The lowest frequencies cause the apex of the basilar membrane to flex back and forth in time with the acoustic vibrations. Possibly, the outer hair cells act as motive elements as well as sensory transducers, contracting in response to activity of the efferent axons and modifying the mechanical properties of the basilar membrane.

The auditory system is analytical in its operation. That is, it can discriminate between sounds with different timbres by detecting the individual overtones that constitute the sounds and producing unique patterns of neural firing in the auditory system.

Left-right localization is performed by analyzing binaural differences in arrival time, in phase relations, and in intensity. The location of sources of brief sounds (such as clicks) and sounds of frequencies below approximately 3000 Hz is detected by neurons in the lateral superior olivary complex, which respond most vigorously when one ear receives the click first, or when the phase of a sine wave received by one ear leads that received by the other. The location of sources of high-frequency sounds is detected by neurons in the medial superior olivary complex, which respond most vigorously when one organ of Corti is stimulated more intensely than the other.

To recognize the source of sounds, the auditory system must recognize the constantly changing patterns of activity received from the axons in the cochlear nerve. Studies have found neurons in the auditory cortex that respond to complex stimuli, such as ascending or descending pitches, series of tones, combinations of two or more tones, or even species-specific vocalizations. Bilateral lesions of the auditory cortex of monkeys produce severe impairments in hearing, and lesions of the left auditory cortex impair the ability to discriminate the vocalizations of other monkeys.

VESTIBULAR SYSTEM

THE VESTIBULAR SYSTEM HAS TWO COMPONENTS: the vestibular sacs and the semicircular canals. They represent the second and third components of the *bony labyrinths* of the inner ear. (We just studied the first component, the cochlea.) The **vestibular sacs** respond to the force of gravity and inform the brain about the head's orientation. The **semicircular canals** respond to angular acceleration—changes in the rotation of the head—but not to steady rotation.

They also respond (but rather weakly) to changes in position or to linear acceleration.

The functions of the vestibular system include balance, maintenance of the head in an upright position, and adjustment of eye movement to compensate for head movements. Vestibular stimulation does not produce any readily definable sensation; certain low-frequency stimulation of the vestibular sacs can produce nausea, and stimulation of the semicircular canals can produce dizziness and rhythmic eye movements (*nystagmus*). However, we are not directly aware of the information received from these organs. This section describes the vestibular system: the vestibular apparatus, the receptor cells, and the vestibular pathway in the brain.

Anatomy of the Vestibular Apparatus

Figure 7.19 shows the bony labyrinths, which include the cochlea, the semicircular canals, and the two vestibular sacs: the **utricle** ("little pouch") and the **saccule** ("little sack"). (See *Figure 7.19.*) The semicircular canals approximate the three major planes of the head: sagittal, transverse, and horizontal. Receptors in each canal respond maximally to angular acceleration in one plane. Figure 7.20 shows cross sections through one semicircular canal. The semicircular canal consists of a membranous canal floating within a bony one; the membranous canal contains a fluid called *endolymph* and floats within a

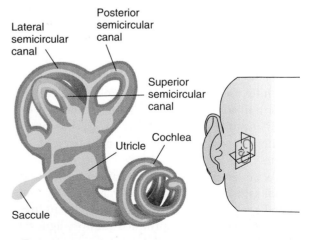

Lateral semicircular canal
Posterior semicircular canal
Superior semicircular canal
Cochlea
Utricle
Saccule

FIGURE 7.19

The bony labyrinths of the inner ear.

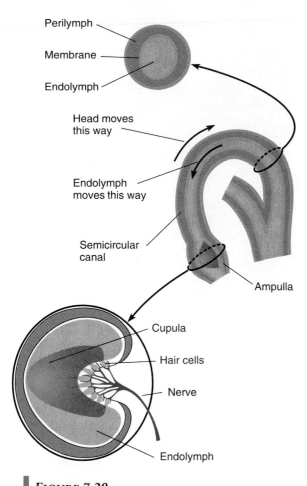

Perilymph

Membrane

Endolymph

Head moves
this way

Endolymph
moves this way

Semicircular
canal

Ampulla

Cupula

Hair cells

Nerve

Endolymph

| *FIGURE 7.20*

Cross sections through one semicircular canal.

fluid called *perilymph.* An enlargement called the **ampulla** contains the organ in which the sensory receptors reside. The sensory receptors are hair cells similar to those found in the cochlea. Their cilia are embedded in a gelatinous mass called the **cupula,** which blocks part of the ampulla. (See *Figure 7.20.*)

To explain the effects of angular acceleration on the semicircular canals, I will first describe an "experiment." If we place a glass of water on the exact center of a turntable and then start the turntable spinning, the water in the glass will, at first, remain stationary (the glass will move with respect to the water it contains). Eventually, however, the water will begin rotating with the container. If we then stop the turntable, the water will continue spinning for a while, because of its inertia.

The semicircular canals operate on the same principle. The endolymph within these canals, like the water in the glass, resists movement when the head begins to rotate. This inertial resistance pushes the endolymph against the cupula, causing it to bend, until the fluid begins to move at the same speed as the head. If the head rotation is then stopped, the endolymph, still circulating through the canal, pushes the cupula the other way. Angular acceleration is thus translated into bending of the cupula, which exerts a shearing force on the cilia of the hair cells. (Of course, unlike the glass of water in my example, we do not normally spin around in circles; the semicircular canals measure very slight and very brief rotations of the head.)

The vestibular sacs (the utricle and saccule) work very differently. These organs are roughly circular, and each contains a patch of receptive tissue. The receptive tissue is located on the "floor" of the utricle and on the "wall" of the saccule when the head is in an upright position. The receptive tissue, like that of the semicircular canals and cochlea, contains hair cells. The cilia of these receptors are embedded in an overlying gelatinous mass, which contains something rather unusual: *otoconia,* which are small crystals of calcium carbonate. (See *Figure 7.21.*) The weight of the crystals causes the gelatinous mass to shift in position as the orientation of the head changes. Thus, movement produces a shearing force on the cilia of the receptive hair cells.

| The Receptor Cells

The hair cells of the semicircular canal and vestibular sacs are similar in appearance. Each hair cell contains several cilia, graduated in length from short to long. Figure 7.22 shows two views of a hair cell of a bullfrog saccule made by a scanning electron microscope. (See *Figure 7.22.*)

| The Vestibular Pathway

The vestibular and cochlear nerves constitute the two branches of the eighth cranial nerve (auditory nerve). The bipolar cell bodies that give rise to the afferent axons of the vestibular nerve are located in the **vestibular ganglion,** which appears as a nodule on the vestibular nerve.

FIGURE 7.21

The receptive tissue of the utricle and saccule.

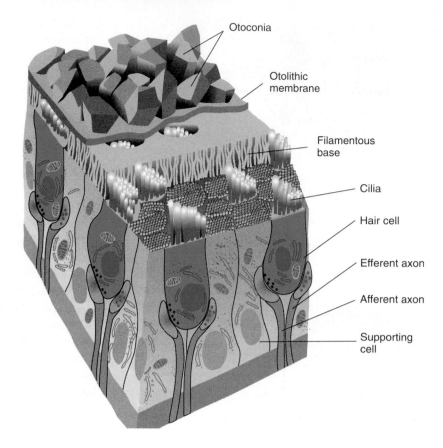

Otoconia

Otolithic membrane

Filamentous base

Cilia

Hair cell

Efferent axon

Afferent axon

Supporting cell

Most of the axons of the vestibular nerve synapse within the vestibular nuclei in the medulla, but some axons travel directly to the cerebellum. Neurons of the vestibular nuclei send their axons to the cerebellum, spinal cord, medulla, and pons. There also appear to be vestibular projections to the temporal cortex, but the precise pathways have not been determined. Most investigators believe that the cortical projections are responsible for feelings of dizziness; the activity of projections to the lower brain stem can produce the nausea and vomiting that accompany motion sickness. Projections to brain stem nuclei controlling neck muscles are clearly involved in maintaining an upright position of the head.

Perhaps the most interesting connections are those to the cranial nerve nuclei (third, fourth, and sixth) that control the eye muscles. As we walk or (especially) run, the head is jarred quite a bit. The vestibular system exerts direct control on eye movement, to compensate for the sudden head movements. This process, called the *vestibulo-ocular reflex*, maintains a fairly steady retinal image. Test this reflex yourself: Look at a distant object and hit yourself (gently) on the side of the head. Note that your image of the world jumps a bit, but not too much. People who have suffered vestibular damage, and who lack the vestibulo-ocular reflex, have difficulty seeing anything while walking or running. Everything becomes a blur of movement.

INTERIM SUMMARY

The semicircular canals are filled with fluid. When the head begins rotating or comes to rest after rotation, inertia causes the fluid to push the cupula to one side or the other. This movement exerts a shearing force on the cupula, the organ containing the vestibular hair cells. The vestibular sacs contain a patch of receptive tissue that contains hair cells whose cilia are embedded in a gelatinous mass. The

(a)   (b)

FIGURE 7.22

(a) Oblique view of a normal bundle of vestibular hair cells. (b) Top view of a bundle of hair cells from which the longest has been detached.

(From Hudspeth, A.J., and Jacobs, R. *Proceedings of the National Academy of Sciences, USA*, 1979, *76*, 1506–1509.)

weight of the otoconia in the gelatinous mass shifts when the head tilts, causing a shearing force on some of the cilia of the hair cells.

Each hair cell contains one long cilium and several shorter ones. These cells form synapses with dendrites of bipolar neurons whose axons travel through the vestibular nerve. The receptors also receive efferent terminal buttons from neurons located in the cerebellum and medulla, but the function of these connections is not known. Vestibular information is received by the vestibular nuclei in the medulla, which relay it on to the cerebellum, spinal cord, medulla, pons, and temporal cortex. These pathways are responsible for control of posture, head movements, eye movements, and the puzzling phenomenon of motion sickness.

SOMATOSENSES

THE SOMATOSENSES PROVIDE INFORMATION about what is happening on the surface of our body and inside it. The **cutaneous senses** (skin senses) include several submodalities commonly referred to as *touch*. **Kinesthesia** provides information about body position and movement and arises from receptors in joints, tendons, and muscles. The muscle receptors are discussed in this section and in Chapter 8. The **organic senses** arise from receptors in and around the internal organs, providing us with unpleasant sensations, such as stomachaches or gall-

bladder attacks, or pleasurable ones, such as those provided by a warm drink on a cold winter day. Because the cutaneous senses are the most studied of the somatosenses, both perceptually and physiologically, I will devote most of my discussion to them.

The Stimuli

The cutaneous senses respond to several different types of stimuli: pressure, vibration, heating, cooling, and events that cause tissue damage (and hence, pain). Feelings of pressure are caused by mechanical deformation of the skin. Vibration is produced in the laboratory or clinic by tuning forks or mechanical devices, but it more commonly occurs when we move our fingers across a rough surface. Thus, we use vibration sensitivity to judge an object's roughness. Obviously, sensations of warmth and coolness are produced by objects that change skin temperature from normal. Sensations of pain can be caused by many different types of stimuli, but it appears that most cause at least some tissue damage.

Kinesthesia is provided by stretch receptors in skeletal muscles that report changes in muscle length to the central nervous system and by stretch receptors in tendons that measure the force being exerted by the muscles. Receptors within joints between adjacent bones respond to the magnitude and direction of limb movement. The muscle length detectors (sensory endings on the *intrafusal muscle fibers*) do not give rise to conscious sensations; their information is used to control movement. These receptors will be discussed separately in Chapter 8.

Organic sensitivity is provided by receptors in the linings of muscles, outer layers of the gastrointestinal system and other internal organs, and linings of the abdominal and thoracic cavities. Many of these tissues are sensitive only to stretch and do not report sensations when cut, burned, or crushed. In addition, the stomach and esophagus are responsive to heat and cold and to some chemicals.

Anatomy of the Skin and Its Receptive Organs

The skin is a complex and vital organ of the body—one that we tend to take for granted. We cannot survive without it; extensive skin burns are fatal. Our cells, which must be bathed by a warm fluid, are protected from the hostile environment by the skin's outer layers. The skin participates in thermoregulation by producing sweat, thus cooling the body, or by restricting its circulation of blood, thus conserving heat. Its appearance varies widely across the body, from mucous membrane to hairy skin to the smooth, hairless skin of the palms and the soles of the feet.

Skin consists of subcutaneous tissue, dermis, and epidermis and contains various receptors scattered throughout these layers. Figure 7.23 shows cross sections through hairy and **glabrous skin** (hairless skin, such as we have on our fingertips and palms). Hairy skin contains unencapsulated (free) nerve endings and **Ruffini corpuscles**, which respond to low-frequency vibration. Free nerve endings are found just below the surface of the skin, in a basketwork around the base of hair follicles and around the emergence of hair shafts from the skin. (See *Figure 7.23.*)

Glabrous skin contains a more complex mixture of free nerve endings and axons that terminate within specialized end organs (Iggo and Andres, 1982). The increased complexity probably reflects the fact that we use the palms of our hands and the inside surfaces of our fingers to explore the environment actively: We use them to hold and touch objects. In contrast, the rest of our body most often contacts the environment passively; that is, other things come in contact with it.

Pacinian corpuscles are the largest sensory end organs in the body. Their size, approximately 0.5 x 1.0 mm, makes them visible to the naked eye. They are found in glabrous skin and in the external genitalia, mammary glands, and various internal organs. These receptors consist of up to seventy onionlike layers wrapped around the terminal button of a single myelinated axon. They are sensitive to touch,

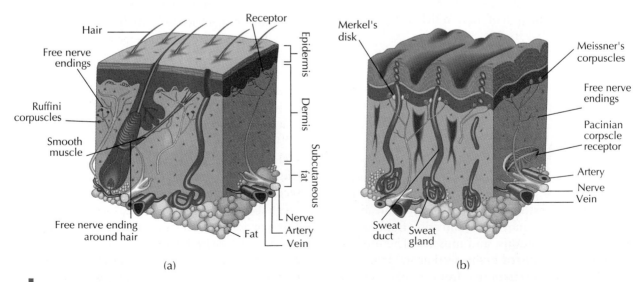

(a)   (b)

FIGURE 7.23

Sensory receptors. (a) In hairy skin. (b) In glabrous (hairless) skin.

particularly to high-frequency vibration. **Meissner's corpuscles** are found in *papillae* ("nipples"), small elevations of the dermis that project up into the epidermis. These end organs are innervated by between two and six axons. They respond to low-frequency vibration. **Merkel's disks**, which also respond to indentation of the skin, are found at the base of the epidermis, in the same general locations as Meissner's corpuscles, adjacent to sweat ducts. (See *Figure 7.23.*)

Detection of Cutaneous Stimulation

The three most important qualities of cutaneous stimulation are touch, temperature, and pain. These qualities are described in the sections that follow.

Touch

Sensitivity to pressure and vibration is caused by movement of the skin. The best-studied receptor is the Pacinian corpuscle, which primarily detects vibration. When the corpuscle is bent relative to the axon, the membrane becomes depolarized. If the threshold of excitation is exceeded, an action potential is produced at the first node of Ranvier. Loewenstein and Mendelson (1965) have shown that the layers of the corpuscle alter the mechanical characteristics of the organ, so the axon responds briefly when the intact organ is bent and again when it is released. Thus, this receptor is sensitive to vibration but not to steady pressure.

The bending of the tip of the nerve ending in a Pacinian corpuscle appears to produce a receptor potential by opening ion channels in the membrane. These channels appear to be anchored to protein filaments beneath the membrane and have long carbohydrate chains attached to them. When a mechanical stimulus changes the shape of the nerve ending, tension is exerted on the carbohydrate chains, pulling the channel open. (See *Figure 7.24.*) Most investigators believe that the encapsulated endings serve only to modify the physical stimulus transduced by the axons that enter them.

Adaptation. Investigators have known for a long time that a moderate, constant stimulus applied to the skin fails to produce any sensation after it has been present for a while. For example, we not only

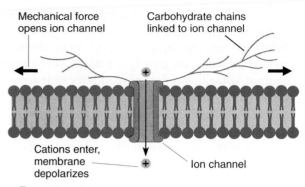

FIGURE 7.24

A hypothetical explanation of transduction of somatosensory information. Mechanical force on carbohydrate chains linked to ion channels opens the channels, permitting the entry of anions, which depolarizes the membrane potential.

ignore the pressure of a wristwatch, but we cannot feel it at all if we keep our arm still (assuming that the band is not painfully tight). Physiological studies have shown that the reason for the lack of sensation is the absence of receptor firing; the receptors adapt to a constant stimulus.

This adaptation is not caused by "fatigue" of physical or chemical processes within the receptor. Instead, adaptation occurs because of the physical construction of the skin and the cutaneous sensory organs. Nafe and Wagoner (1941) recorded the sensations reported by human subjects as a stimulus weight gradually moved downward, deforming the skin. Pressure was reported until the weight finally stopped moving. When the weight was increased, pressure was reported until downward movement stopped again. Pressure sensations were also briefly recorded when the weight was removed, while the surface of the skin regained its normal shape. (You may have noticed that when you first take your hat off, it feels as if you were still wearing it.)

Responsiveness to Moving Stimuli. A moderate, constant, nondamaging stimulus is rarely of any importance to an organism, so this adaptation mechanism is useful. Our cutaneous senses are used much more often to analyze shapes and textures of stimulus objects moving with respect to the surface of the skin. Sometimes, the object itself moves; but more often, we do the moving ourselves.

If I placed an object in your palm and asked you to keep your hand still, you would have a great deal of difficulty recognizing the object by touch alone. If I said you could now move your hand, you would manipulate the object, letting its surface slide across your palm and the pads of your fingers. You would be able to describe its three-dimensional shape, hardness, texture, slipperiness, and so on. Obviously, your motor system must cooperate, and you need kinesthetic sensation from your muscles and joints, besides the cutaneous information. If you squeeze the object and feel a lot of well-localized pressure in return, it is hard. If you feel a less intense, more diffuse pressure in return, it is soft. If it produces vibrations as it moves over the ridges on your fingers, it is rough. If very little effort is needed to move the object while pressing it against your skin, it is slippery. If it does not produce vibrations as it moves across your skin, but moves in a jerky fashion, and if it takes effort to remove your fingers from its surface, it is sticky. Thus, our somatosenses work dynamically with the motor system to provide useful information about the nature of objects that come in contact with our skin.

Temperature

Feelings of warmth and coolness are relative, not absolute (except at the extremes). There is a temperature level that, for a particular region of skin, will produce a sensation of temperature neutrality—neither warmth nor coolness. This neutral point is not an absolute value but depends on the prior history of thermal stimulation of that area. If the temperature of a region of skin is raised by a few degrees, the initial feeling of warmth is replaced by one of neutrality. If the skin temperature is lowered to its initial value, it now feels cool. Thus, increases in temperature lower the sensitivity of warmth receptors and raise the sensitivity of cold receptors. The converse holds for decreases in skin temperature. This adaptation to ambient temperature can be demonstrated easily by placing one hand in a bucket of warm water and the other in a bucket of cool water until some adaptation has taken place. If you then simultaneously immerse both hands in water at room temperature, it will feel warm to one hand and cool to the other.

Thermal receptors are difficult to study, because changes in temperature alter the metabolic activity, and also the rate of axonal firing, of a variety of cells. For example, a receptor that responds to pressure might produce varying amounts of activity in response to the same mechanical stimulus, depending upon the temperature. Nevertheless, most investigators agree that changes in temperature are detected by free nerve endings and that warmth and coolness are detected by different populations of receptors (Sinclair, 1981). The transduction of temperature changes into the rate of axonal firing has not yet been explained.

An ingenious experiment by Bazett et al. (1932) showed long ago that receptors for warmth and cold lie at different depths in the skin. The investigators lifted the prepuce (foreskin) of uncircumcised males with dull fishhooks. They applied thermal stimuli on one side of the folded skin and recorded the rate at which the temperature changes were transmitted through the skin by placing small temperature sensors on the opposite side. They then correlated these observations with verbal reports of warmth and coolness. The investigators concluded that cold receptors were close to the skin and that warmth receptors were located deeper in the tissue. (This experiment shows the extremities to which scientists will go to obtain information—pun intended.)

Pain

The story of pain is quite different from that of temperature and pressure; the analysis of this sensation is extremely difficult. It is obvious that our awareness of pain and our emotional reaction to it are controlled by mechanisms within the brain. For example, we can have a tooth removed painlessly while under hypnosis, which has no effect on the stimulation of pain receptors. Stimuli that produce pain also tend to trigger species-typical escape and withdrawal responses. Subjectively, these stimuli *hurt,* and we try hard to avoid them. However, sometimes we are better off ignoring pain and getting on with other tasks. In fact, our brains possess mechanisms that can reduce pain, largely through the activity of special opiatelike peptides. These mechanisms are described in more detail in a later section of this chapter.

Most investigators identify pain reception with the networks of free nerve endings in the skin. Pain appears to be produced by a variety of procedures. Intense mechanical stimulation activates a class of high-threshold receptors that produce a sensation of pain. However, most painful stimuli cause tissue damage, suggesting that pain is also caused by the release of a chemical by injured cells (Besson et al., 1982). When cells are damaged, they very rapidly synthesize a **prostaglandin,** a category of hormones first discovered in the prostate gland. This chemical sensitizes free nerve endings to another chemical, histamine, which is also released by damaged cells. (The analgesic effect of aspirin occurs by virtue of the fact that it interferes with the synthesis of prostaglandins.)

The Somatosensory Pathways

Somatosensory axons from the skin, muscles, or internal organs enter the central nervous system via spinal nerves. Those located in the face and head primarily enter through the trigeminal nerve (fifth cranial nerve). The cell bodies of the unipolar neurons are located in the dorsal root ganglia and cranial nerve ganglia. Axons that convey precisely localized information, such as fine touch, ascend through the *dorsal columns* in the white matter of the spinal cord to nuclei in the lower medulla. From there, axons cross the brain and ascend through the *medial lemniscus* to the *ventral posterior nuclei of the thalamus,* the relay nuclei for somatosensation. Axons from the thalamus project to the primary somatosensory cortex, which in turn sends axons to the secondary somatosensory cortex. In contrast, axons that convey poorly localized information, such as pain or temperature, form synapses with other neurons as soon as they enter the spinal cord. The axons of these neurons cross to the other side of the spinal cord and ascend through the *spinothalamic tract* to the ventral posterior nuclei of the thalamus. (See *Figure 7.25.*)

Recall from Chapter 6 that the primary visual cortex contains columns of cells, each of which responds to particular features, such as orientation, ocular dominance, or spatial frequency. Within these columns are blobs that contain cells that

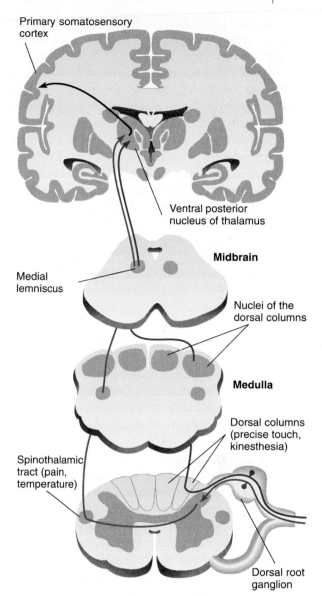

FIGURE 7.25

The somatosensory pathways from the spinal cord to the somatosensory cortex. Note that precisely localized information (such as fine touch) and imprecisely localized information (such as pain and temperature) are transmitted by different pathways.

respond to particular colors. The somatosensory cortex also has a columnar arrangement; in fact, cortical columns were discovered there by Mountcastle (1957) before they were found in the visual and auditory cortex. Within a column, neurons respond to a particular type of stimulus (for example, temperature or pressure) applied to a particular part of the body.

Dykes (1983) has reviewed research indicating that the primary and secondary somatosensory cortical areas are divided into at least five (and perhaps as many as ten) different maps of the body surface. Within each map, cells respond to a particular submodality of somatosensory receptors. So far, separate areas have been identified that respond to slowly adapting cutaneous receptors, rapidly adapting cutaneous receptors, receptors that detect changes in muscle length, receptors located in the joints, and Pacinian corpuscles.

As you learned in Chapter 6, the extrastriate cortex consists of several subareas, each of which contains an independent representation of the visual field. For example, one area responds specifically to color and form, and another responds to movement. The somatosensory cortex appears to follow a similar scheme: Each cortical map of the body contains neurons that respond to a specific submodality of stimulation. Undoubtedly, further investigations will provide more accurate functional maps of the cortical subareas of both of these sensory systems.

Perception of Pain

Pain is a curious phenomenon. It is more than a mere sensation; it can be defined only by some sort of withdrawal reaction or, in humans, by verbal report. Pain can be modified by opiates, by hypnosis, by the administration of pharmacologically inert sugar pills, by emotions, and even by other forms of stimulation, such as acupuncture. Recent research efforts have made remarkable progress in discovering the physiological bases of these phenomena.

We might reasonably ask *why* we experience pain. In most cases pain serves a constructive role. For example, people who have congenital insensitivity to pain suffer an abnormally large number of injuries, such as cuts and burns. One woman did not make the shifts in posture that we normally do when our joints start to ache. As a consequence, she suffered damage to the spine that ultimately resulted in death. Other people have died from ruptured appendixes and ensuing abdominal infections that

they did not feel (Sternbach, 1968). I am sure that a person who is passing a kidney stone would not find much comfort in the fact that pain does more good than ill; but pain is, nevertheless, very important to our existence.

Some environmental events diminish the perception of pain. For example, Beecher (1959) noted that wounded American soldiers back from the battle at Anzio, Italy, during World War II reported that they felt no pain from their wounds—they did not even want medication. It would appear that their perception of pain was diminished by the relief they felt from surviving such an ordeal. There are other instances in which people still report the perception of pain but are not bothered by it. Some tranquilizers have this effect.

Physiological evidence provides a clear distinction between the perception and tolerance of pain. Mark, Ervin, and Yakovlev (1962) made stereotaxically placed lesions in the thalamus in an attempt to relieve the pain of patients suffering from the advanced stages of cancer. Damage to different parts of the thalamus either abolished cutaneous pain or deep pain or eliminated the emotional component of pain—the patients still felt the pain, but it no longer bothered them. As we shall see in Chapter 11, damage to the prefrontal cortex also reduces emotional reactions to pain.

Because patients rarely report pain sensations when the cerebral cortex is electrically stimulated during surgery (Adams and Victor, 1989), investigators have concluded that the neocortex does not play a role in pain perception. However, some patients with seizure disorders caused by a focus in the somatosensory cortex report sensations of pain just before a seizure occurs (Young, Barr, and Blume, 1986), and lesions of this region can reduce the perceived intensity of painful stimuli (White and Sweet, 1969). Talbot et al. (1991) used a PET scanner to determine whether any regions of the cerebral cortex were activated by painful stimuli in humans. They attached a device to people's forearms that could produce either painless sensations of warmth or painful sensations of heat. They adjusted the level of the painful stimulus so that it was tolerable and not produce emotional reactions. They used the computer associated with the PET scanner to sub-

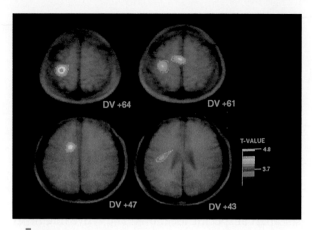

FIGURE 7.26

PET scans showing cortical activation produced by a painful stimulus applied to the forearm. The scans are an average of eight subjects, and the response to a warm stimulus has been subtracted out.

(From Talbot, J.E., Marrett, S., Evans, A.C., Meyer, E., Bushnell, M.C., and Duncan, G.H. *Science,* 1991, *251,* 1355–1358. Copyright 1991 by the American Association for the Advancement of Science.)

tract out neural activity produced by warmth from that produced by pain, so that the resulting images indicated the location of neural activity specifically produced by sensations of pain.

Figure 7.26 shows the results of Talbot and colleagues. The pain sensations activated four regions of the cerebral cortex: one in the primary somatosensory cortex (point 3), another in the secondary somatosensory cortex (point 2), and two more in the anterior cingulate cortex (points 1 and 4). (See *Figure 7.26.*) As we will see in Chapter 11, the cingulate cortex is involved in emotional reactions—including those provoked by painful stimuli. However, the patients showed no signs of autonomic arousal and reported that the pain sensations did not disturb them, and the activated regions in the cingulate cortex were contralateral to the arm that was stimulated. The authors conclude the activation of the anterior cingulate cortex does not reflect emotional arousal but appears to indicate that this region receives specific input concerning painful stimuli from the somatosensory system.

A particularly interesting form of pain sensation occurs after a limb has been amputated. After the limb is gone, up to 70 percent of amputees report that they feel as though the missing limb still existed and that it often hurts. This phenomenon is referred to as the **phantom limb** (Melzak, 1992). People with phantom limbs report that the limb feels very real, and they often say that if they try to reach out with it, it feels as though it were responding. Sometimes, they perceive it as sticking out, and they may feel compelled to avoid knocking it against the side of a doorframe or sleeping in a position that would make it come between them and the mattress. People have reported all sorts of sensations in phantom limbs, including pain, pressure, warmth, cold, wetness, itching, sweatiness, and prickliness.

The classic explanation for phantom limbs has been activity of the sensory axons belonging to the amputated limb. Presumably, this activity is interpreted by the nervous system as coming from the missing limb. When nerves are cut and connections cannot be reestablished between the proximal and distal portions, the cut ends of the proximal portions form nodules known as *neuromas.* The treatment for phantom pain has been to cut the nerves above these neuromas, to cut the dorsal roots that bring the afferent information from these nerves into the spinal cord, or to make lesions in somatosensory pathways in the spinal cord, thalamus, or cerebral cortex. Sometimes these procedures work for a while, but often the pain returns.

Melzak suggests that the phantom limb sensation is inherent in the organization of the parietal cortex. As we saw in Chapter 4, the parietal cortex is involved in our awareness of our own bodies. Indeed, people with lesions of the parietal lobe (especially in the right hemisphere) have been known to push their own leg out of bed, believing that it actually belongs to someone else. Melzak reports some people born with missing limbs nevertheless experience phantom limb sensations, which would suggest that our brains are genetically programmed to provide sensations for all four limbs.

The Endogenous Opiates

For many years investigators have known that perception of pain can be modified by environmental stimuli. Recent work, beginning in the 1970s, has revealed the existence of neural circuits whose activity can produce **analgesia,** a decreased sensitivity to pain (from *an,* "not," and *algos,* "pain"). A variety of environmental stimuli can activate these analgesia-producing circuits. An important component of these mechanisms is a class of neuromodulators called the **endogenous opiates** or, more simply, **opioids.** (*Endogenous* means "produced from within.")

Discovery of Opiate Receptors. As you know, opiates such as morphine produce analgesia. Several years ago, it became clear that they did so by means of direct effects on the brain. In particular, microinjections of morphine into the periaqueductal gray matter of the midbrain produce analgesia, whereas injections into many other regions are ineffective (Tsou and Jang, 1964; Herz et al., 1970). Pert, Snowman, and Snyder (1974) discovered that neurons in the brain contain specialized receptors that respond to opiates. They homogenized the brains of rats and extracted portions of cell membranes. They incubated the membranes with radioactive naloxone and dihydromorphine, rinsed them, and found that the membranes became radioactive. (**Naloxone** is a drug that reverses the effects of opiates, and dihydromorphine is a synthetic opiate.) The finding that these two drugs both bind with molecules in fragments of postsynaptic neural membrane is strong evidence for the existence of specific opiate receptors. Naloxone blocks the effects of opiates by binding with, but not activating, the receptors.

Classes of Opiatelike Peptides. Of course, nature did not put opiate receptors in the brain for the amusement of neuroscientists. If there are receptors in the brain, then the brain must produce its own chemicals to occupy these receptors. And, in fact, it does. Terenius and Wahlström (1975) reported the existence of a substance in human cerebrospinal fluid that had a specific affinity for opiate receptors that had been extracted from rat brain. They called this chemical *morphinelike factor.*

Hughes et al. (1975) found that the brain produces two morphinelike factors, which they identified as very small peptide chains, each containing five amino acids. They gave them the name **enkephalin** (from the Greek *kephale,* "head"). They synthesized these substances and found that the arti-

ficial compounds acted as potent opiates. The two enkephalins (labeled *Leu*-enkephalin and *Met*-enkephalin) were found to bind with opiate receptors even more effectively than morphine.

We now know that Leu- and Met-enkephalin, which contain the amino acid leucine or methionine, respectively, are only two members of a family of endogenous opiate peptides (opioids), all of which are synthesized from one of three large peptides that serve as precursors. Cells that produce one of the endogenous opiates synthesize them and also synthesize specialized enzymes that cut the precursor apart at specific locations. The active fragments are stored in vesicles, and the unneeded ones are destroyed. The first, *Pro-opiomelanocortin,* gives rise to several hormones found in the pituitary gland, only one of which serves an opiatelike function (**ß-endorphin**). The second precursor, *Pro-enkephalin,* gives rise only to enkephalins, of which there are several types. The third precursor, *Pro-dynorphin,* gives rise to several different kinds of **dynorphins,** another class of opiates that are active in the brain.

Besides producing several different opiates, the brain contains several different types of opiate receptors (Akil et al., 1984; Cooper, Bloom, and Roth, 1987). Like the nicotinic and muscarinic acetylcholine receptors, these receptors have been defined by the categories of chemicals that bind to them. The μ (mu) receptor is found in the neural pathways mediating pain. (Naloxone blocks these receptors.) The ∂ (delta) receptor is found in the limbic system and may play a role in regulation of mood. The κ (kappa) receptor is found in the cerebral cortex and may be involved with the sedative effects of the opiates. The σ (sigma) receptor is found in the hippocampus, and the ε (epsilon) receptor is found in the basal forebrain, in and around the hypothalamus.

The Anatomy of Opiate-Induced Analgesia

Electrical stimulation of particular locations within the brain can cause analgesia, which can even be profound enough to serve as an anesthetic for surgery in rats (Reynolds, 1969). The most effective locations appear to be within the periaqueductal gray matter and in the rostroventral medulla. For example, Mayer and Liebeskind (1974) reported that electrical stimulation of the periaqueductal gray matter produced analgesia in rats equivalent to that produced by at least 10 milligrams of morphine per kilogram of body weight, which is a large dose. The rats did not react to stimuli that normally would be painful. The technique has even found an application in reducing severe, chronic pain in humans: Electrodes are surgically implanted in the periaqueductal gray matter or in the somatosensory relay nuclei of the thalamus. They are then attached to a coil of wire implanted beneath the surface of the skin. When the patient places a small transmitter unit against this part of the skin and pushes a button, a mild electrical current is passed through the electrodes (Kumar, Wyant, and Nath, 1990).

Analgesic brain stimulation apparently triggers the neural mechanisms that reduce pain. These mechanisms are normally stimulated through more natural means, which will be discussed later in this section. We now know that the periaqueductal gray matter and the rostroventral medulla are two components of a pain-attenuating circuit. Activity of this circuit inhibits the firing of neurons in the dorsal horn of the spinal cord gray matter, whose axons give rise to the spinothalamic tract. Thus, this activity directly diminishes the signal that gives rise to sensations of pain.

Basbaum and Fields (1978) summarized their work and that of others and proposed a neural cir-cuit that mediates opiate-induced analgesia. A more recent review (Basbaum and Fields, 1984) elaborated (and complicated) their original model. Basically, they propose the following: Endogenous opiates (released by environmental stimuli or administered as a drug) stimulate opiate receptors on neurons in the periaqueductal gray matter. As we have already seen, electrical stimulation of this region or microinjection of opiates into it produces analgesia. In addition, microinjection of naloxone into the periaqueductal gray matter blocks the analgesic effect of the systemic injection of opiates (Yeung and Rudy, 1980), and administration of morphine increases the neural activity in this region (Criswell and Rogers, 1978; Urca and Nahin, 1978). The relevant receptor type appears to be the μ receptor (Smith et al., 1988). Because the effect of opiates appears to be inhibitory (Nicoll, Alger, and Nicoll, 1980), Basbaum and Fields propose that the neurons that contain opiate receptors are themselves inhibitory interneurons. Thus, the administration of opiates activates the neurons on which these interneurons synapse. (See *Figure 7.27.*)

Neurons in the periaqueductal gray matter send axons to the rostroventral medulla, especially to the **nucleus raphe magnus.** The terminal buttons of these neurons appear to release an excitatory peptide transmitter substance called *neurotensin* (Beitz,

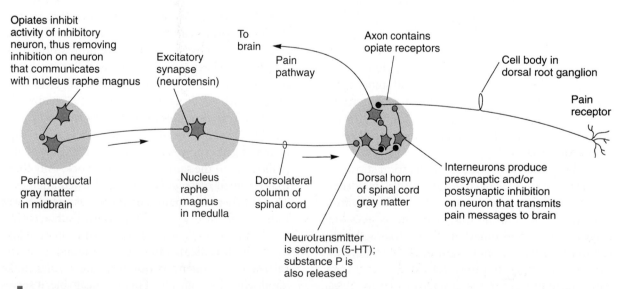

Opiates inhibit activity of inhibitory neuron, thus removing inhibition on neuron that communicates with nucleus raphe magnus

Excitatory synapse (neurotensin)

To brain

Pain pathway

Axon contains opiate receptors

Cell body in dorsal root ganglion

Pain receptor

Periaqueductal gray matter in midbrain

Nucleus raphe magnus in medulla

Dorsolateral column of spinal cord

Dorsal horn of spinal cord gray matter

Interneurons produce presynaptic and/or postsynaptic inhibition on neuron that transmits pain messages to brain

Neurotransmitter is serotonin (5-HT); substance P is also released

FIGURE 7.27

The neural circuit that mediates opiate-induced analgesia, as hypothesized by Basbaum and Fields (1978).

1982b). Fang, Moreau, and Fields (1987) found that microinjections of neurotensin into the nucleus raphe magnus cause analgesia, strongly suggesting that this portion of the pathway is, indeed, mediated by neurons that secrete this peptide. (See *Figure 7.27.*)

The neurons in the nucleus raphe magnus send axons through the **dorsolateral columns** to the dorsal horn of the spinal cord gray matter. If these tracts are destroyed, injections of morphine no longer produce analgesia. The raphe neurons secrete serotonin; thus, administration of PCPA (which prevents the biosynthesis of serotonin) also abolishes morphine-produced analgesia.

The neural circuitry within the dorsal gray matter of the spinal cord is not well understood. Basbaum and Fields (1984) review evidence that suggests that the inhibitory effects of the descending serotonergic neurons may be mediated by means of either presynaptic or postsynaptic inhibition, probably involving one or two interneurons that use various neurotransmitters. To further complicate matters, the raphe neurons that project to the spinal cord appear to release a peptide (substance P) along with serotonin, and the incoming pain-receptive axons in this area contain opiate receptors. Thus, endogenous opiates may mediate presynaptic inhibition there. (See *Figure 7.27.*)

The periaqueductal gray matter receives inputs from the frontal cortex, amygdala, and hypothalamus (Beitz, 1982a; Mantyh, 1983). These inputs permit learning and emotional reactions to affect an animal's responsiveness to pain. In addition, pain-responsive regions of the brain stem and spinal cord also send axons to the periaqueductal gray matter, which may account for the fact that painful stimulation can itself diminish further sensitivity to pain (Gebhardt, 1982).

Analgesia that is produced by electrical stimulation of the brain is partly, but not completely, mediated by endogenous opiates. Akil, Mayer, and Liebeskind (1976) found that naloxone reduces the analgesic effect of stimulation of the periaqueductal gray matter but does not completely eliminate it. This finding suggested that there are at least two brain mechanisms for analgesia: one that involves the release of endogenous opiates and one that does

not. Indeed, Nichols, Thorn, and Berntson (1989) found that an injection of naloxone (which blocks μ receptors) would block analgesia produced by stimulation of the *ventral* but not the *dorsal* periaqueductal gray matter, so these two systems are both anatomically and biochemically distinct.

Biological Significance of Analgesia

It appears that a considerable amount of neural circuitry is devoted to reducing the intensity of pain. What functions do these circuits perform? When an animal encounters a noxious stimulus, it usually stops what it is doing and engages in withdrawal or escape behaviors. Obviously, these responses are quite appropriate. However, they are sometimes counterproductive. For example, if an animal sustains a wound that causes chronic pain, a tendency to engage in withdrawal responses will interfere with its performance of everyday activities, such as obtaining food. Thus, chronic, unavoidable pain would best be diminished.

Another useful function of analgesia is the suppression of pain during important behaviors such as fighting or mating. For example, males fighting for access to females during mating season will fail to pass on their genes if pain elicits withdrawal responses that interfere with fighting. As we will see, these conditions *do* diminish pain.

First, let us consider the effects of unavoidable pain. Several experiments have shown that analgesia can be produced by the application of painful stimuli or even by the pre sence of nonpainful stimuli that have been paired with painful ones (that is, through classically conditioned analgesia). For example, Maier, Drugan, and Grau (1982) administered inescapable shocks to rats' tails or administered shocks that the animals could learn to escape by making a response. Although both groups of animals received the same amount of shock, only those that received *inescapable* shocks showed analgesia. That is, when their pain sensitivity was tested, it was found to be lower than that of control subjects. The analgesia was abolished by administration of naloxone, which indicates that it was mediated by the release of endogenous opiates. The results make good sense, biologically. If pain is escapable, it serves to motivate the animal to make appropriate responses. If it occurs whatever the animal does, then a reduction in pain sensitivity is in the animal's best interest. Defeat by another animal of the same species or exposure to the sound or smell of a predator all have been reported to produce analgesia (Lester and Fanselow, 1985; Kavaliers, 1988; Hendrie, 1991).

Fanselow (1979) found that a well-known behavioral phenomenon is related to pain-induced analgesia. Normally, animals prefer signaled foot shock to nonsignaled foot shock. That is, a shock that is preceded by the sound of a buzzer is preferred to a sudden foot shock that comes out of the blue. The preference for signaled foot shock is eliminated by naloxone injections; then the rats no longer care whether the shocks come with a warning. Presumably, the warning stimulus causes endogenous opiates to be secreted, which makes signaled shock less painful than nonsignaled shock.

Pain can be reduced by stimulating regions other than those that hurt. For example, people often rub or scratch the area around a wound, in an apparent attempt to diminish the severity of the pain. And as you know, acupuncturists insert needles into various parts of the body to reduce pain. The needle is usually then rotated, thus stimulating axons and nerve endings in the vicinity. Often, the region that is stimulated is far removed from the region that becomes less sensitive to pain.

Several experimental studies have shown that acupuncture does, indeed, produce analgesia (Mann et al., 1973; Gaw, Chang, and Shaw, 1975). Mayer, Price, Rafii, and Barber (1976) reported that the analgesic effects of acupuncture could be blocked by naloxone. However, when pain was reduced by hypnotic suggestion, naloxone had no effect. Thus, acupuncture, but not hypnosis, appears to cause analgesia through the release of endogenous opiates.

Although pain reduction produced by acupuncture may be more effective if a person believes that it will work, belief in its efficacy is not the only reason this procedure works. Many studies have demonstrated that acupuncture reduces the reaction of laboratory animals to pain, where "belief" can certainly not be an issue. Lee and Beitz (1992) reported that acupuncture that was able to reduce an animal's sensitivity to painful stimuli also reduced the production of Fos protein in somatosensory neurons in the dorsal horn of the spinal cord. (You will recall from Chapter 5 that the production of Fos protein in neurons indicates that they have been activated.)

There is evidence that engaging in behaviors that are important to survival also reduces sensitivity to pain. For example, Komisaruk and Larsson (1971) found that gentle probing of a rat's vagina with a glass rod produced analgesia. Such probing also increases the activity of neurons in the periaqueductal gray matter and decreases the responsiveness of neurons in the ventrobasal thalamus to painful stimulation (Komisaruk and Steinman, 1987). The phenomenon also occurs in humans; Whipple and Komisaruk (1988) found that self-administered vaginal stimulation reduces sensitivity to painful stimuli but not to neutral tactile stimuli. Presumably, copulation triggers analgesic mechanisms. The adaptive significance of this phenomenon is clear: Painful stimuli encountered during the course of copulation are less likely to cause the behavior to be interrupted; thus, the chances of pregnancy are increased.

Pain can also be reduced, at least in some people, by administering a **placebo,** or pharmacologically inert substance. (The term *placebo* comes from *placere,* which means "to please." The physician pleases an anxious patient by giving him or her an innocuous substance.) The pain reduction seems to be mediated by endogenous opiates, because it is blocked by naloxone (Levine, Gordon, and Fields, 1979). Somehow, when some patients take a medication that they think will reduce pain, it does so *pharmacologically,* by triggering the release of endogenous opiates. This pharmacological effect is eliminated by the opiate receptor-blocker naloxone. Thus, for some people a placebo is not pharmacologically "inert." The placebo effect is probably mediated through the connections of the frontal cortex with the periaqueductal gray matter.

‖‖‖ INTERIM SUMMARY

Cutaneous sensory information is provided by specialized receptors in the skin. Pacinian corpuscles provide information about vibration. Ruffini corpuscles, similar to Pacinian corpuscles but considerably smaller, respond to low-frequency vibration, usually referred to as "flutter." Meissner's corpuscles, found in papillae and innervated by several axons, respond to mechanical stimuli. Merkel's disks, also found in papillae, consist of single, flattened dendritic endings next to specialized epithelial cells. These receptors respond to mechanical stimulation. Painful stimuli are detected primarily by free nerve endings.

Our somatosensory system is most sensitive to changes in mechanical stimuli. Unless the skin is moving, we do not detect nonpainful stimuli, because the receptors adapt to constant mechanical pressure. Temperature receptors also adapt; moderate changes in skin temperature are soon perceived as "neutral," and deviations above or below this temperature are perceived as warmth or coolness.

Precise, well-localized somatosensory information is conveyed by a pathway through the dorsal columns and their nuclei and the medial lemniscus, connecting the dorsal column nuclei with the ventral posterior nuclei of the thalamus. Information about pain and temperature ascends the spinal cord through the spinothalamic system. Organic sensibility reaches the central nervous system by means of axons that travel through nerves of the autonomic nervous systems.

The neurons in the primary somatosensory cortex are topographically arranged, according to the part of the body from which they receive sensory information (somatotopic representation). Columns within the somatosensory cortex respond to a particular type of stimulus from a particular region of the body. Recent studies have shown that different types of somatosensory receptors send their information to separate areas of the somatosensory cortex.

Pain perception is not a simple function of stimulation of pain receptors; it is a complex phenomenon that can be modified by experience and the immediate environment. Lesion studies have shown that pain perception involves nuclei of the thalamus, and that a person's emotional response to pain involves the limbic system and the prefrontal cortex. A PET study with humans indicates that painful stimulation activates neurons in the primary and secondary somatosensory cortex and two regions within the anterior cingulate cortex. The phantom limb phenomenon, which often is accompanied by phantom pain, appears to be inherent in the organization of the parietal lobe.

Just as we have mechanisms to perceive pain, we have mechanisms to reduce it—to produce analgesia. Under the appropriate circumstances neurons in the periaqueductal gray matter are stimulated through synaptic connections with the frontal cortex, amygdala, and hypothalamus. In addition, some neurosecretory cells in the brain release enkephalins, a class of endogenous opiates. These neuromodulators activate receptors on neurons in the periaqueductal gray matter and provide additional stimulation of neurons in this region. Connections from the periaqueductal gray matter to the nucleus raphe magnus of the medulla activate serotonergic neurons located there. These neurons send axons through the dorsolateral columns to the dorsal horn of the spinal cord gray matter, where they cause either presynaptic or postsynaptic inhibition of neurons whose axons transmit pain information to the brain. In humans, chronic pain is sometimes treated by implanting electrodes in the periaqueductal gray matter or the thalamus and permitting the patients to stimulate the brain through these electrodes when the pain becomes severe.

Analgesia occurs when it is important for an animal to continue a behavior that would tend to be inhibited by pain—for example, mating or fighting. In addition, inescapable pain activates brain mechanisms that produce analgesia, but escapable pain does not. This distinction makes sense: If the pain is escapable, its sensation should not be blunted but should serve to motivate the animal's efforts to escape. Because the endogenous opiates are found in several regions of the brain that are apparently not involved in pain perception, these neuromodulators undoubtedly serve functions besides analgesia. The fact that many people have chosen to self-administer opiates extracted from the opium poppy attests to its potency as a reinforcer of behavior.

Analgesia can also be produced by stimulating regions other than those that hurt, which is the basis for acupuncture. This phenomenon can be demonstrated in laboratory animals. The administration of placebos can also produce analgesia. Because this effect is blocked by naloxone, it must involve the release of endogenous opiates.

GUSTATION

THE STIMULI WE HAVE ENCOUNTERED SO FAR produce receptor potentials by imparting physical energy: thermal, photic (involving light), or kinetic. However, the stimuli received by the last two senses to be studied, gustation and olfaction, interact with their receptors chemically. This section discusses the first of them: gustation.

The Stimuli

Gustation is clearly related to eating; this sense modality helps us determine the nature of things we put in our mouths. For a substance to be tasted, molecules of it must dissolve in the saliva and stimulate the taste receptors on the tongue. Tastes of different substances vary, but much less than we generally realize. There are only four qualities of taste: *bitterness, sourness, sweetness,* and *saltiness.* Flavor, as opposed to taste, is a composite of olfaction and gustation. Much of the flavor of a steak depends on its odor; to an *anosmic* person (one who lacks the sense of smell) or to a person whose nostrils are stopped up, an onion tastes like an apple, and a steak tastes like salty cardboard.

Most vertebrates possess gustatory systems that respond to all four taste qualities. (An exception is the cat family; lions, tigers, leopards, and house cats do not detect sweetness.) Clearly, sweetness receptors are food detectors. Most sweet-tasting foods, such as fruits and some vegetables, are safe to eat (Ramirez, 1990). Saltiness receptors detect the presence of sodium chloride. In some environments inadequate amounts of this mineral are obtained from the usual source of food, so sodium chloride detectors help the animal detect its presence. Injuries that cause bleeding deplete an organism of its supply of sodium rapidly, so the ability to find it quickly can be critical.

Most species of animals will readily ingest substances that taste sweet or taste somewhat salty. However, they will tend to avoid substances that taste sour or bitter. Because of bacterial activity, many foods become acidic when they spoil. The acidity tastes sour and causes an avoidance reaction. (Of course, we have learned to make highly pre-ferred mixtures of sweet and sour, such as lemonade.) Bitterness is almost universally avoided and cannot easily be improved by adding some sweetness. Many plants produce poisonous alkaloids, which protect them from being eaten by animals. Alkaloids taste bitter; thus, the bitterness receptor undoubtedly serves to warn animals away from these chemicals.

Anatomy of the Taste Buds and Gustatory Cells

The tongue, palate, pharynx, and larynx contain approximately 10,000 taste buds. Most of these receptive organs are arranged around *papillae,* small protuberances of the tongue. *Fungiform papillae,* located on the anterior two-thirds of the tongue, contain up to eight taste buds, along with receptors for pressure, touch, and temperature. *Foliate papillae* consist of up to eight parallel folds along each edge of the back of the tongue. Approximately 1300 taste buds are located in these folds. *Circumvallate papillae,* arranged in an inverted V on the posterior third of the tongue, contain approximately 250 taste buds. They are shaped like little plateaus surrounded by moatlike trenches. Taste buds consist of groups of 20–50 receptor cells, arranged somewhat like the segments of an orange. Cilia are located at the end of each cell and project through the opening of the taste bud (the pore) into the saliva that coats the tongue. Tight junctions between adjacent taste cells prevent substances in the saliva from diffusing freely into the taste bud itself. Figure 7.28 shows the appearance of a circumvallate papilla; a cross section through the surrounding trench contains a taste bud. (See *Figure 7.28.*)

Taste buds that respond to the different taste qualities have different distributions on the tongue. The tip of the tongue is most sensitive to sweetness and saltiness, the sides are most sensitive to sourness, and the back of the tongue, throat, and soft palate are most sensitive to bitterness. This distribution explains why saccharin, an artificial sweetener, tastes both sweet and bitter to some people, producing a sensation of sweetness on the front of the tongue when it is first tasted and then a sensation of bitterness in the back of the mouth when it is swallowed.

FIGURE 7.28

(a) A taste bud. (b) Papillae on the surface of the tongue.

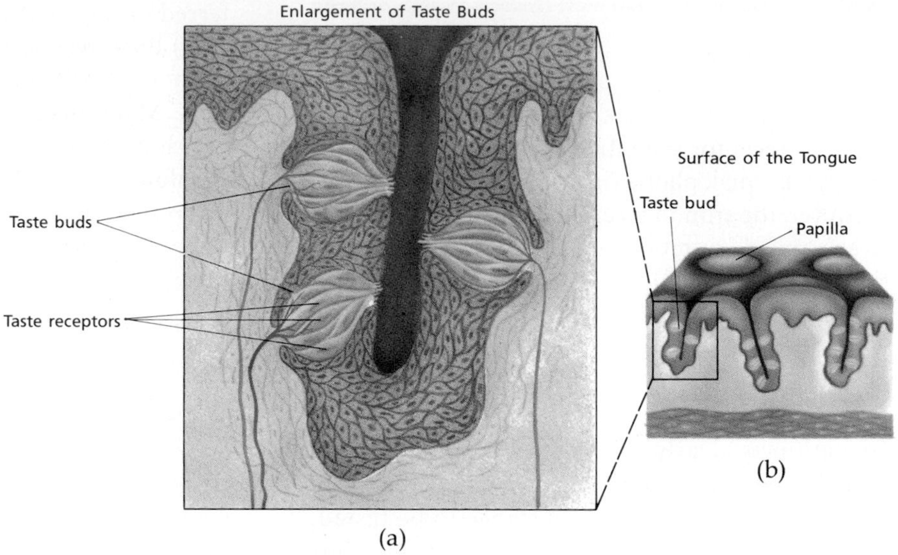

Enlargement of Taste Buds

Taste buds

Taste receptors

Surface of the Tongue

Taste bud

Papilla

(b)

(a)

Taste receptors form synapses with dendrites of sensory neurons that convey gustatory information to the brain. The receptors have a life span of only ten days. They quickly wear out, being directly exposed to a rather hostile environment. As they degenerate, they are replaced by newly developed cells; the afferent dendrite is passed on to the new cell (Beidler, 1970). The presence of vesicles within the cytoplasm of the receptor cell around the synaptic region suggests that transmission at this synapse is chemical.

Detection of Gustatory Information

It seems most likely that transduction of taste is similar to the chemical transmission that takes place at synapses: The tasted molecule binds with the receptor and produces changes in membrane permeability that cause receptor potentials. Different substances bind with different types of receptors, producing different taste sensations.

To taste salty, a substance must ionize. Although the best stimulus for saltiness receptors is sodium chloride (NaCl), a variety of salts containing metallic cations (such as Na^+, K^+, and Li^+) with a halogen or other small anion (such as Cl^-, Br^-, SO_4^{2-}, or NO_3^-) taste salty. The receptor for saltiness seems to be a simple sodium channel. When present in the saliva, sodium enters the taste cell and depolarizes it,

triggering action potentials that cause the cell to release transmitter substance (Avenet and Lindemann, 1989; Kinnamon and Cummings, 1992). The best evidence that sodium channels are involved is the fact that amiloride, a drug that is known to block sodium channels, prevents sodium chloride from activating taste cells and blocks sensations of saltiness (Schiffman, Lockhead, and Maes, 1983). (See *Figure 7.29a.*)

Until recently, investigators have been puzzled by the *anion effect*. If detection of saltiness is accomplished by sodium channels, then the anion associated with the sodium ion should have no effect on the saltiness of a compound—and yet, sodium salts with large anions, such as sodium acetate, taste much less salty than those with small anions, such as sodium chloride. Ye, Heck, and DeSimone (1991) discovered the cause of this effect. There are tight junctions between adjacent taste cells that prevent substances in the saliva from diffusing freely into the taste bud itself. The investigators hypothesized that some anions, but not others, might be able to pass through the tight junction. They measured the membrane potential across this junction and found that their hypothesis was confirmed. When sodium chloride was put on the tongue, both sodium and chloride ions passed through the tight junction. Because equal numbers of anions and cations entered the interstitial fluid within the taste bud,

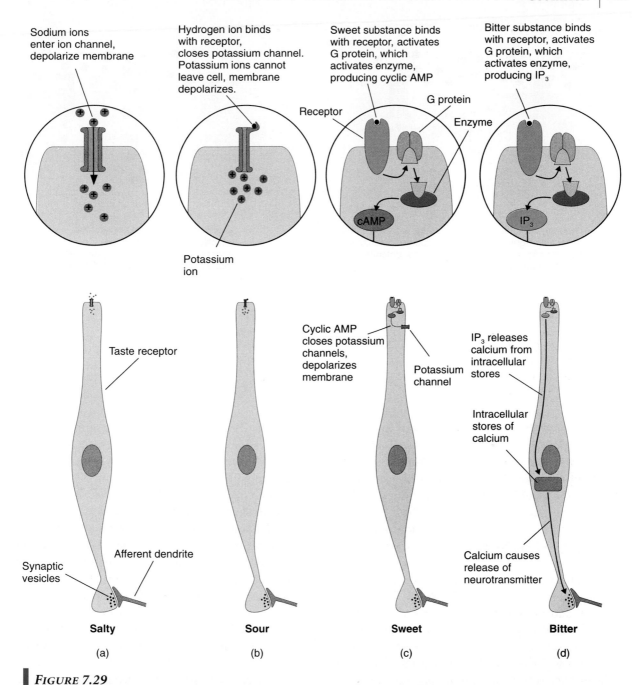

Sodium ions enter ion channel, depolarize membrane

Hydrogen ion binds with receptor, closes potassium channel. Potassium ions cannot leave cell, membrane depolarizes.

Sweet substance binds with receptor, activates G protein, which activates enzyme, producing cyclic AMP

Bitter substance binds with receptor, activates G protein, which activates enzyme, producing IP$_3$

Receptor

G protein

Enzyme

cAMP

IP$_3$

Potassium ion

Taste receptor

Cyclic AMP closes potassium channels, depolarizes membrane

Potassium channel

IP$_3$ releases calcium from intracellular stores

Intracellular stores of calcium

Calcium causes release of neurotransmitter

Synaptic vesicles

Afferent dendrite

Salty

(a)

Sour

(b)

Sweet

(c)

Bitter

(d)

FIGURE 7.29

Transduction of taste information. (a) Salty taste. (b) Sour taste. (c) Sweet taste. (d) Bitter taste.

there was no net change in the membrane potential. (See ***Figure 7.30a.***) However, when sodium acetate was put on the tongue, the sodium ions passed easily through the tight junction, but very few of the larger acetate ions managed to get through. As a result, the membrane of the taste cell

located within the taste bud became hyperpolarized, which inhibited the formation of action potentials. (See ***Figure 7.30b.***)

Sourness receptors appear to respond to the hydrogen ions present in acidic solutions. However, because the sourness of a particular acid is not sim-

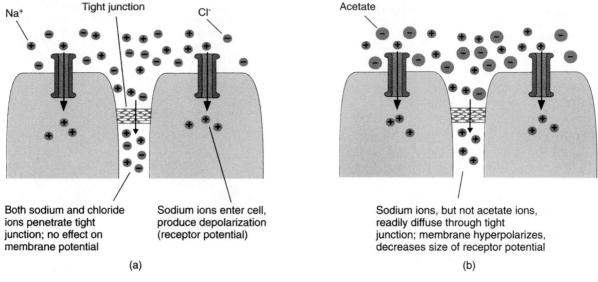

Both sodium and chloride ions penetrate tight junction; no effect on membrane potential

Sodium ions enter cell, produce depolarization (receptor potential)

(a)

Sodium ions, but not acetate ions, readily diffuse through tight junction; membrane hyperpolarizes, decreases size of receptor potential

(b)

FIGURE 7.30

An explanation of the anion effect. (a) Response to sodium chloride. (b) Response to sodium acetate.
(Adapted from Ye, Q., Heck, G.L., and DeSimone, J.A. *Science,* 1991, *254,* 724–726.)

ply a function of the concentration of hydrogen ions, the anions must have an effect, as well. The reason for this anion effect is not yet known. Kinnamon, Dionne, and Beam (1988) suggest that sourness is detected by sites on potassium channels in the membrane of taste cell cilia. These channels are normally open, permitting K^+ to flow out of the cell. Hydrogen ions bind with these sites and close the channels. Their closure prevents this outward current and depolarizes the membrane, producing action potentials. (See *Figure 7.29b.*)

Bitter and sweet substances are more difficult to characterize. The typical stimulus for bitterness is a plant alkaloid such as quinine; for sweetness it is a sugar such as glucose or fructose. The fact that some molecules elicit both sensations suggests that bitterness and sweetness receptors may be similar. For example, the Seville orange rind contains a glycoside (complex sugar) that tastes extremely bitter; the addition of a hydrogen ion to the molecule makes it taste intensely sweet (Horowitz and Gentili, 1974). Some amino acids taste sweet. Indeed, the commercial sweetener aspartame consists simply of two amino acids, aspartate and phenylalanine.

The detection of sweetness and bitterness appears to involve G proteins and second messengers. Most molecules that taste sweet have a hydrogen ion situated 0.3 nm away from a site that will accept a hydrogen ion. Presumably, the sweetness receptor has sites that match these. The G protein coupled to these receptors activates an enzyme that catalyzes the synthesis of cyclic AMP. This second messenger closes potassium channels located on the body of the taste cell. These channels, like those in the ciliary membrane of cells sensitive to sourness, are normally open. Their closure depolarizes the cell and produces action potentials (Avenet, Hoffman, and Lindemann, 1988; Striem et al., 1989). (See *Figure 7.29c.*)

The characteristics of molecules that cause bitterness are not yet known. The bitterness receptors are coupled with G proteins that activate an enzyme that catalyzes the production of a second messenger known as IP_3. This molecule causes calcium ions to be released into the cytoplasm from storage sites located within the cell. The calcium then activates the release of the transmitter substance. Unlike all other forms of sensory transduction, the membrane potential is not changed, and action potentials do not occur (Akabas, Dodd, and Al-Awqati, 1988; Hwang et al., 1990; Kinnamon and Cummings, 1992). (See *Figure 7.29d.*)

Researchers have proposed two other taste qualities: umami and carbohydrates. **Umami,** a Japanese word that means "good taste," refers to the taste of monosodium glutamate (MSG), a substance often used as a flavor enhancer in Oriental cuisine (Kurihara, 1987; Scott and Plata-Salaman, 1991). There is good evidence that the umami receptor exists in several species, but the existence of this taste quality is still not universally accepted in humans. Presumably, the umami receptor is used to detect the presence of amino acids, the building blocks of proteins. (Glutamate is an amino acid found in all proteins.) Even though MSG is used as a flavor enhancer, it has no effects on the responses of taste cells to sweet, salty, bitter, or sour compounds (Yoshii, Yokouchi, and Kurihara, 1986). Some studies suggest that monkeys and rodents can taste complex carbohydrates (Feigin, Sclafani, and Sunday, 1987; Sunderland and Sclafani, 1988), but further research is needed to be certain.

The Gustatory Pathway

Gustatory information is transmitted through cranial nerves 7, 9, and 10. Information from the anterior part of the tongue travels through the **chorda tympani,** a branch of the seventh cranial nerve (facial nerve). Taste receptors in the posterior part of the tongue send information through the lingual (tongue) branch of the ninth cranial nerve (glossopharyngeal nerve); the tenth cranial nerve (vagus nerve) carries information from receptors of the palate and epiglottis. The chorda tympani gets its name because it passes through the middle ear just beneath the tympanic membrane. Because of its convenient location, it is accessible to a recording or stimulating electrode. Investigators have even recorded from this nerve during the course of human ear operations.

The first relay station for taste is the **nucleus of the solitary tract,** located in the medulla. In primates the taste-sensitive neurons of this nucleus send their axons to the ventral posteromedial thalamic nucleus, a nucleus that also receives somatosensory information received from the trigeminal nerve (Beckstead, Morse, and Norgren, 1980). Thalamic taste-sensitive neurons send their axons to the primary gustatory cortex, which is located in the frontal insular and opercular cortex (Pritchard et al., 1986). Unlike most other sense modalities, taste is ipsilaterally represented in the brain. (See *Figure 7.31.*)

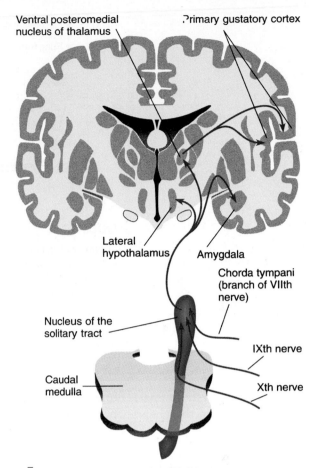

FIGURE 7.31
Neural pathways of the gustatory system.

Gustatory information also reaches the amygdala and the hypothalamus and adjacent basal forebrain (Nauta, 1964; Russchen, Amaral, and Price, 1986). Many investigators believe that the hypothalamic pathway plays a role in mediating the reinforcing effects of sweet and salty tastes. In fact, some neurons in the hypothalamus respond to sweet

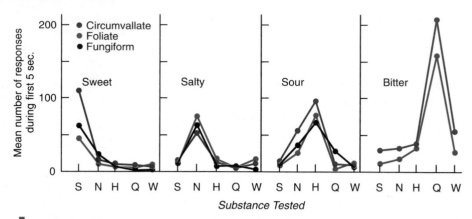

| **FIGURE 7.32**

Mean number of responses recorded from axons in rat chorda tympani and glos-sopharyngeal nerve during the first 5 seconds after the application of sugar (S), NaCl (N), HCl (H), quinine (Q), and water (W). The response characteristics of the axons are categorized as sweet, salty, sour, or bitter.

(From Nowlis, G.H., and Frank, M., in *Olfaction and Taste 6*, edited by J. Le Magnen and P. MacLeod. Washington, D.C.: Information Retrieval, 1977.)

stimuli only when the animal is hungry (Rolls et al., 1986). I will discuss this phenomenon in more detail in Chapter 13.

Neural Coding of Taste

Almost all fibers in the chorda tympani respond to more than one taste quality, and many respond to changes in temperature, as well. Most show a preference for one of the four qualities (sweet, salty, sour, or bitter). Figure 7.32 shows the average responses of fibers in the rat chorda tympani and glossopharyngeal nerve to sucrose (S), NaCl (N), HCl (H), quinine (Q), and water (W), as recorded by Nowlis and Frank (1977). (See *Figure 7.32.*)

Scott and his colleagues (Scott et al., 1991; Smith-Swintosky, Plata-Salaman, and Scott, 1991) operated on monkeys, attaching devices that permitted them to record the activity of single neurons in the gustatory cortex while the animals were awake and alert. They found that slightly over 3 percent of the cells they found responded to taste. Others responded to movement of the mouth or to various somatosensory stimuli. Many cells did not respond to any of the stimuli that the investigators tried.

Although the distribution of the taste-sensitive neurons in the nucleus of the solitary tract and the gustatory thalamus resembles that found on the surface of the tongue (Beckstead, Morse, and Norgren, 1980; Scott et al., 1986), their distribution in the gustatory cortex appears to be unsystematic. However, the investigators did find clusters of neurons with similar response characteristics, which suggests that like other regions of sensory cortex, the gustatory cortex may be organized in columns. They found two major groups of taste-sensitive neurons, sweet and salty. They found cells responsive to sour and bitter also, but the responses were less distinct. They note that the minimum concentrations of salty, sweet, sour, and bitter substances that produced responses in these neurons were very close to the minimum concentrations of these substances that human subjects can detect.

||||| INTERIM SUMMARY

Taste receptors detect only four sensory qualities: bitterness, sourness, sweetness, and saltiness. Bitter foods often contain plant alkaloids, many of which are poisonous. Sour foods have usually undergone bacterial fermentation, which can produce toxins. On the other hand, sweet foods (such as fruits) are usually nutritious and safe to eat, and salty foods contain an essential cation, sodium. The fact that people in affluent cultures today tend to ingest excessive amounts of sweet and salty foods suggests that stimulation of these neurons is naturally reinforcing.

Saltiness receptors appear to be simple sodium channels. The anion effect is explained by the fact that large anions cannot penetrate the tight junction at the outer ends of the taste cells. Sourness receptors appear to detect the presence of hydrogen ions, which closes potassium channels and depolarizes the membrane of the cell. Sweetness receptors are coupled to G proteins that increase the level of cyclic AMP, which closes potassium channels. The G proteins coupled to bitterness receptors cause calcium ions to be released from storage sites within the cell, which causes the release of the transmitter substance. Two other tastes, for the glutamate contained in proteins (umami) and for carbohydrate, may also exist.

Gustatory information from the anterior part of the tongue travels through the chorda tympani, a branch of the facial nerve that passes beneath the eardrum on its way to the brain. The posterior part of the tongue sends gustatory information through the glossopharyngeal nerve, and the palate and epiglottis send gustatory information through the vagus nerve. Gustatory information is received by the nucleus of the solitary tract (located in the medulla) and is relayed to the thalamic taste area, to the primary gustatory cortex of the opercular and insular cortex, and then to the orbitofrontal cortex, amygdala, hypothalamus, and basal forebrain.

OLFACTION

OLFACTION, THE SECOND CHEMICAL SENSE, HELPS us identify food and avoid food that has spoiled and is unfit to eat. It helps the members of many species to track prey or detect predators and to identify friends, foes, and receptive mates. For humans, olfaction is the most enigmatic of all sensory modalities. Odors have a peculiar ability to evoke memories, often vague ones that seem to have occurred in the distant past—a phenomenon vividly described by Marcel Proust in his book *Remembrance of Things Past.* Although people can discriminate among many thousands of different odors, we lack a good vocabulary to describe them. It is relatively easy to describe sights we have seen or sounds we have heard, but the description of an odor is difficult. At best, we can say it smells like something else. Thus, the olfactory system appears to be specialized for *identifying things,* not for analyzing particular qualities.

The Stimulus

The stimulus for odor consists of volatile substances having a molecular weight in the range of approximately 15 to 300. Almost all odorous compounds are organic. However, many substances that meet these criteria have no odor at all, and we do not yet know why.

Anatomy of the Olfactory Apparatus

Our 50 million olfactory receptors reside within two patches of mucous membrane (**olfactory epithelium**), each having an area of about 1 square inch. The olfactory epithelium is located at the top of the nasal cavity, as shown in *Figure 7.33.* Less than 10 percent of the air that enters the nostrils reaches the olfactory epithelium; a sniff is needed to sweep air upward into the nasal cavity so that it reaches the olfactory receptors.

The inset in Figure 7.33 illustrates a group of olfactory receptor cells, along with their supporting cells. (See *inset, Figure 7.33.*) Olfactory receptor cells are bipolar neurons whose cell bodies lie within the olfactory mucosa that lines the *cribriform plate,* a bone at the base of the rostral part of the brain. There is a constant turnover of olfactory receptor cells, as there is of gustatory receptor cells; their life cycle is approximately 60 days. The cells send a process toward the surface of the mucosa, which divides into 10 to 20 cilia that penetrate the layer of mucus. Odorous molecules must dissolve in the mucus and stimulate receptor molecules on the olfactory cilia.

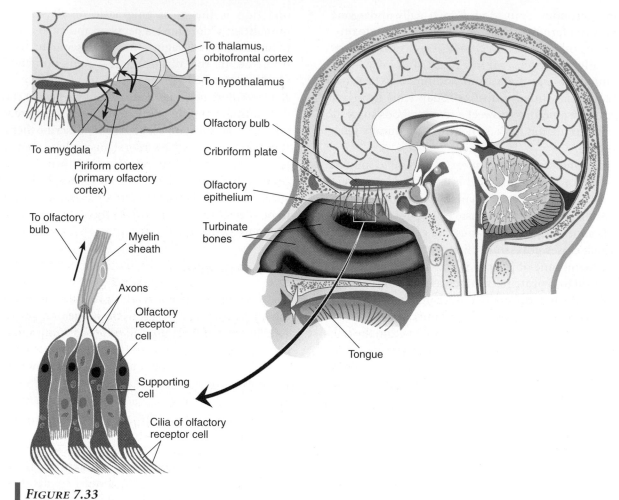

FIGURE 7.33

The olfactory system.

The axons of olfactory receptor cells enter the skull through small holes in the cribriform ("perforated") plate. The olfactory mucosa also contains free nerve endings of trigeminal nerve axons; these nerve endings presumably mediate sensations of pain that can be produced by sniffing some irritating chemicals, such as ammonia.

The **olfactory bulbs** lie at the base of the brain on the ends of the stalklike olfactory tracts. The axons of the olfactory receptors terminate in the olfactory bulbs, where they synapse with dendrites of **mitral cells** (named for their resemblance to a bishop's miter). These synapses take place in the complex axonal and dendritic arborizations called **olfactory glomeruli** (from *glomus,* "ball"). There are approximately ten thousand glomeruli, each of which receives input from a bundle of approximately one thousand axons. The axons of the mitral cells travel to the rest of the brain through the olfactory tracts. Some of these axons synapse in the brain; whereas others cross the brain, enter the other olfactory nerve, and synapse in the contralateral olfactory bulb.

Olfactory tract axons project directly to the primary olfactory cortex, which is on the pyriform cortex, a part of the limbic lobe. (See **Figure 7.33.**) The pyriform cortex projects to the hypothalamus and to the dorsomedial thalamus, which projects to the orbitofrontal cortex (Cain, 1988). As you may recall, the orbitofrontal cortex also receives gustatory information; thus, it may be involved in the combining of taste and olfaction into flavor. The hypothalamus also receives a considerable amount of olfactory information, which is probably important for the acceptance or rejection of food and for the olfactory control of reproductive processes seen in many species of mammals.

Most mammals have another organ that responds to olfactory stimuli: the *vomeronasal organ*. Because it plays an important role in animals' responses to odors that affect reproductive physiology and behavior, its structure and function are described in Chapter 10.

Efferent fibers from several locations in the brain enter the olfactory bulbs. The synapses of these fibers appear to be inhibitory, but their role in the processing of olfactory information is a mystery. However, the brain controls the effects of olfactory stimuli in a more obvious way: We can sniff the air, maximizing the exposure of our olfactory epithelium to the odor molecules, or we can pinch our nostrils and breathe through the mouth, thus producing minimal olfactory stimulation.

Transduction of Olfactory Information

Olfactory cilia contain receptors that are stimulated by odor molecules. Jones and Reed (1989) identified a particular G protein, which they called G_{olf} This protein is able to activate an enzyme that catalyzes the synthesis of cyclic AMP, which, in turn, can open sodium channels and depolarize the membrane of the olfactory cell (Bakalyar and Reed, 1991; Firestein, Zufall, and Shepherd, 1991; Kaupp, 1991). Recently, Menco et al. (1992) used immunocytochemical methods to confirm that G_{olf} is present where it was presumed to be: in the distal portions of olfactory cilia.

Buck and Axel (1991) used molecular genetics techniques and discovered a family of genes that code for what is almost certainly the olfactory receptor protein. These proteins contain a sequence common to all receptors linked with G proteins. There are probably several hundred receptors, each sensitive to different odorants.

Detection of Specific Odors

Because the family of olfactory receptors was not discovered until recently, we still know little about the way in which different odors are detected and coded. Undoubtedly, particular odors are coded by patterns of activity of different receptors. Even if there turn out to be several hundred different receptors, this number is too small for each odorous substance to be detected by its own receptor. Some investigators estimate that we can distinguish between many thousands of different odors, and chemists synthesize many new substances with new odors every year.

Cain (1988) notes that although most odors are produced by mixtures of many different chemicals, we identify odors as belonging to particular objects. For example, the smells of coffee, fried bacon, and cigarette smoke are each made of up to several hundred different types of molecules. Although each of these odors is a mixture, we recognize them as being unique—we do not detect the individual components. This fact suggests that olfaction, like vision, is synthetic. (You will recall that we perceive a mixture of red light and bluish green light as pure yellow light; we do not perceive either of the components.) However, if the smells of coffee, fried bacon, and cigarette smoke are mixed together, we still recognize all three odors; thus, the olfactory system also has the characteristics of an analytic sensory modality, like audition. Obviously, these apparently contradictory facts will have to be resolved somehow.

Recordings in more central levels of the olfactory system show that neural responses tend to be finely tuned to particular odors. For example, Tanabe et al. (1974) and Tanabe, Iino, and Takagi (1975) found that neurons in the olfactory area of the orbitofrontal cortex of monkeys were more selective. Of the 40 cells from which they recorded, half responded to only one odor, and decreasing numbers responded to two, three, or four different odors. None responded to more than five odors. The nature of the coding system is unknown.

Kauer (1988) used a voltage-sensitive dye to investigate the pattern of responses of neurons in the olfactory bulb to various odors. He found that dif-

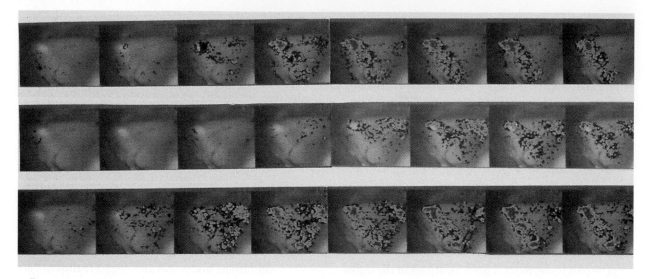

FIGURE 7.34

Computer-generated patterns of activity in the olfactory bulb of the salamander, obtained from recordings of changes in density of a voltage-sensitive dye. Each horizontal row shows successive frames of activity, 33 ms apart, taken after the presentation of the odorous substance.

(From Kauer, J.S. *Nature*, 1988, *331*, 166–168. Reprinted with permission.)

ferent odors produced different patterns of responses and that these patterns changed across time. Figure 7.34 presents the responses of the olfactory bulbs to three different odors. Each response is shown in six time frames, each taken 33 ms apart; thus, they can be read from left to right, like frames of a movie. The colors, which indicate different voltages, are supplied by the computer. (See *Figure 7.34*.) His results suggest that odor quality may be represented by spatial and temporal patterns of activity of neurons in the olfactory system. Only further research will reveal whether this procedure can be used to identify categories of olfactory qualities.

||||| INTERIM SUMMARY

The olfactory receptors consist of bipolar neurons located in the olfactory epithelium that lines the roof of the nasal sinuses, on the bone that underlies the frontal lobes. The receptors send processes toward the surface of the mucosa, which divide into cilia. The membranes of these cilia appear to contain receptors that detect aromatic molecules dissolved in the air that sweeps past the olfactory mucosa. The axons of the olfactory receptors pass through the perforations of the cribriform plate and form synapses with the dendrites of the mitral cells of the olfactory bulbs. These neurons send axons through the olfactory tracts to the brain, principally to the amygdala, the ventral frontal neocortex, and the limbic cortex. Some axons travel to the thalamic taste area and may be responsible for at least some of the convergence of olfactory and gustatory information into the perception of flavor.

Aromatic molecules produce membrane potentials by interacting with a newly discovered family of receptor molecules, which may number in the hundreds. These receptors are coupled to a special G protein, G_{olf}. This protein catalyzes the synthesis of cyclic AMP, which opens sodium channels and depolarizes the membrane. A study with a voltage-sensitive dye shows that different odors produce different sequences of excitation in different regions of the olfactory bulbs, but we do not yet know whether these results imply the existence of a spatial code or what its rules are.

New Terms

Audition

pitch p. 182

hertz (Hz) p. 182

loudness p. 182

timbre (*TIM ber* or *TAMM ber*) p. 182

tympanic membrane p. 183

ossicle (*AHSS i kul*) p. 183

malleus p. 183

incus p. 183

stapes (*STAY peez*) p. 183

cochlea (*COCK lee uh*) p. 183

oval window p. 183

organ of Corti p. 184

hair cell p. 184

Deiters's cell (*DYE terz*) p. 184

basilar membrane (*BAZZ i ler*) p. 184

tectorial membrane (*tek TORR ee ul*) p. 184

round window p. 184

cilia p. 186

cochlear nerve p. 188

olivocochlear bundle p. 189

cochlear nucleus p. 189

superior olivary complex p. 189

lateral lemniscus p. 189

tonotopic representation (*tonn oh TOP ik*) p. 190

place code p. 191

auditory tuning curve p. 191

rate coding p. 192

white noise p. 192

fundamental frequency p. 193

overtone p. 193

phase difference p. 194

Vestibular System

vestibular sac p. 198

semicircular canal p. 198

utricle (*YOU trih kul*) p. 198

saccule (*SAK yule*) p. 198

ampulla (*am PULL uh*) p. 199

cupula (*KEW pew luh*) p. 199

vestibular ganglion p. 200

Somatosenses

cutaneous sense (*kw TANE ee us*) p. 201

kinesthesia p. 201

organic sense p. 201

glabrous skin (*GLAB russ*) p. 202

Ruffini corpuscle p. 202

Pacinian corpuscle (*pa CHIN ee un*) p. 202

Meissner's corpuscle p. 203

Merkel's disk p. 203

prostaglandin p. 205

phantom limb p. 207

analgesia (*an ul JEE zya*) p. 208

endogenous opiate (*en DODJ en us*) p. 208

opioid (*OH pee oid*) p. 208

naloxone (*nuh LOX own*) p. 208

enkephalin (*en KEFF a linn*) p. 208

ß-endorphin (*en DORF in*) p. 208

dynorphin p. 208

nucleus raphe magnus p. 209

dorsolateral column p. 210

placebo p. 211

Gustation

umami (*oo mah mee*) p. 217

chorda tympani p. 217

nucleus of the solitary tract p. 217

Olfaction

olfactory epithelium p. 219

olfactory bulb p.220

mitral cell p. 220

olfactory glomeruli (*glow MARE you lee*) p. 220

Suggested Readings

Audition

Ashmore, J.F. The electrophysiology of hair cells. *Annual Review of Physiology,* 1991, *53,* 465–476.

Corwin, J.T., and Warchol, M.E. Auditory hair cells: Structure, function, development, and regeneration. *Annual Review of Neuroscience,* 1991, *14,* 301–333.

Edelman, G.M., Gall, W.E., and Cowan, W.M. *Auditory Functions.* New York: John Wiley & Sons, 1988.

Gulick, W.L., Gescheider, G.A., and Frisina, R.D. *Hearing: Physiological Acoustics, Neural Coding, and Psychoacoustics.* New York: Oxford University Press, 1989.

Somatosenses

Basbaum, A.I., and Fields, H.L. Endogenous pain control systems: Brainstem spinal pathways and endorphin circuitry. *Annual Review of Neuroscience,* 1984, *7,* 309–338.

Dubner, R., and Bennett, G.J. Spinal and trigeminal mechanisms of nociception. *Annual Review of Neuroscience,* 1983, *6,* 381–418.

Iggo, A., and Andres, K.H. Morphology of cutaneous receptors. *Annual Review of Neuroscience,* 1982, *5,* 1–32.

Melzak, R. Phantom limbs. *Scientific American,* 1992, *266(4),* 120–126.

Olfaction and Gustation

Bruch, R.C., Kalinoski, D.L., and Kare, M.R. Biochemistry of vertebrate olfaction and taste. *Annual Review of Nutrition,* 1988, *8,* 21–42.

Finger, T.E., and Silver, W.L. *Neurobiology of Taste and Smell.* New York: Wiley-Interscience, 1987.

Getchell, T.V. *Smell and Taste in Health and Disease.* New York: Raven Press, 1991.

Halász, N. *The Vertebrate Olfactory System.* Budapest, Akadèmiai Kiadó, 1990.

Kinnamon, S.C., and Cummings, T.A. Chemosensory transduction mechanisms in taste. *Annual Review of Physiology,* 1992, *54,* 715–731.

Roper, S.D. The cell biology of vertebrate taste receptors. *Annual Review of Neuroscience,* 1989, *12,* 329–354.

CHAPTER 8

Control of Movement

Muscles
- Skeletal Muscle
- Smooth Muscle
- Cardiac Muscle
  Interim Summary

Reflex Control of Movement
- The Monosynaptic Stretch Reflex
- The Gamma Motor System
- Polysynaptic Reflexes
  Interim Summary

Control of Movement by the Brain
- Organization of Motor Cortex
- Cortical Control of Movement
- Deficits of Verbally Controlled
  Movements: The Apraxias
- The Basal Ganglia
- The Cerebellum
- The Reticular Formation
  Interim Summary

S O FAR, I HAVE DESCRIBED THE NATURE OF
neural communication, the basic structure
of the nervous system, and the physiology of perception. Now it is time to consider the ultimate
function of the nervous system: control of behavior. The brain is the organ that moves the muscles. It
does many other things, but all of them are secondary to making our bodies move. This chapter
describes the principles of muscular contraction,
some reflex circuitry within the spinal cord, and the
means by which the brain initiates behaviors. The
rest of the book describes the physiology of particular categories of behaviors and the ways in which
our behaviors can be modified by experience.

MUSCLES

MAMMALS HAVE THREE TYPES OF MUSCLES: SKELE-
tal muscle, smooth muscle, and cardiac muscle.

Skeletal Muscle

Skeletal muscles are the ones that move us (our
skeletons) around and thus are responsible for our
behavior. Most of them are attached to bones at each
end and move the bones when they contract.
(Exceptions include eye muscles and some abdominal muscles, which are attached to bone at one end
only.) Muscles are fastened to bones via *tendons,*
strong bands of connective tissue. Several different
classes of movement can be accomplished by the
skeletal muscles, but I will refer principally to two of
them: flexion and extension. Contraction of a flexor
muscle produces **flexion,** the drawing in of a limb.
Extension, which is the opposite movement, is produced by contraction of extensor muscles. These are
the so-called *antigravity muscles*—the ones we use to
stand up. When a four-legged animal lifts a paw, the
movement is one of flexion. Putting it back down is
one of extension. Sometimes, people say they "flex"
their muscles. This is an incorrect use of the term.
Muscles *contract;* limbs *flex.* Bodybuilders show off
their arm muscles by simultaneously contracting the
flexor and extensor muscles of that limb.

Anatomy

The detailed structure of a skeletal muscle is shown
in *Figure 8.1.* As you can see, it consists of two
types of muscle fibers. The **extrafusal muscle
fibers** are served by axons of the **alpha motor neurons.** Contraction of these fibers provides the muscle's motive force. The **intrafusal muscle fibers** are
specialized sensory organs that are served by two
axons, one sensory and one motor. These organs
are also called *muscle spindles* because of their
shape. In fact, the Latin word *fusus* means "spindle"; hence *intrafusal* muscle fibers are found
within the spindles, and *extrafusal* muscle fibers
are found outside them.

The central region (*capsule*) of the intrafusal
muscle fiber contains sensory endings that are sensitive to stretch applied to the muscle fiber. Actually, there are two types of intrafusal muscle fibers,
but for simplicity's sake only one kind is shown
here. The efferent axon of the **gamma motor neuron** causes the intrafusal muscle fiber to contract;
however, this contraction contributes an insubstan-
tial amount of force. As we will see, the function of
this contraction is to modify the sensitivity of the
fiber's afferent ending to stretch.

A single myelinated axon of an alpha motor neuron serves several extrafusal muscle fibers. In primates the number of muscle fibers served by a single
axon varies considerably, depending on the preci-
sion with which the muscle can be controlled. In
muscles that move the fingers or eyes the ratio can
be less than one to ten; in muscles that move the leg
it can be one to several hundred. An alpha motor
neuron, its axon, and associated extrafusal muscle
fibers constitute a **motor unit.**

A single muscle fiber consists of a bundle of
myofibrils, each of which consists of overlapping
strands of **actin** and **myosin.** Note the small protrusions on the myosin filaments; these structures
(*myosin cross bridges*) are the motile elements that
interact with the actin filaments and produce muscular contractions. (See *Figure 8.1.*) The regions in
which the actin and myosin filaments overlap produce dark stripes, or *striations;* hence skeletal muscle is often referred to as **striated muscle.**

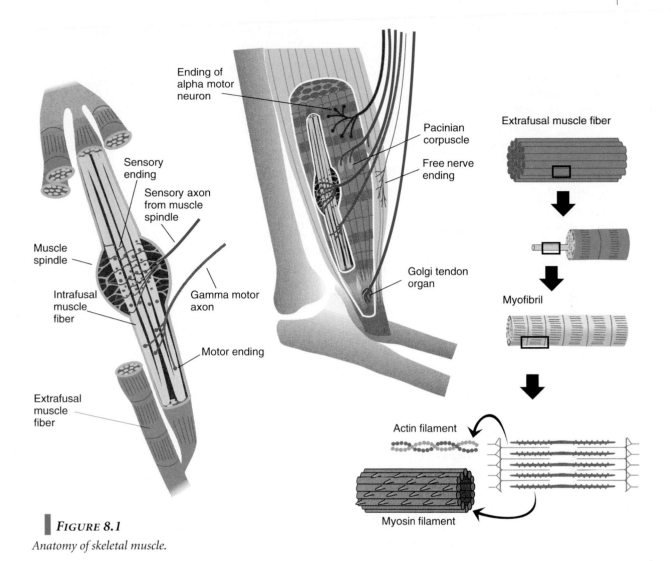

| **FIGURE 8.1**

Anatomy of skeletal muscle.

The Physical Basis of Muscular Contraction

The synapse between the terminal button of an efferent neuron and the membrane of a muscle fiber is called a **neuromuscular junction.** The terminal buttons of the neurons synapse on **motor endplates,** located in grooves along the surface of the muscle fibers. When an axon fires, acetylcholine is liberated by the terminal buttons and produces a depolarization of the postsynaptic membrane (**endplate potential**). The endplate potential is much larger than an excitatory postsynaptic potential in synapses between neurons; an endplate potential *always* causes the muscle fiber to fire, propagating the potential along its length. This action potential induces a contraction, or *twitch,* of the muscle fiber.

The depolarization of a muscle fiber opens the gates of voltage-dependent calcium channels, permitting calcium ions to enter the cytoplasm. This event triggers the contraction. Calcium acts as a cofactor that permits the myofibrils to extract energy from the ATP that is present in the cytoplasm. The myosin cross bridges alternately attach to the actin strands, bend in one direction, detach themselves, bend back, reattach to the actin at a

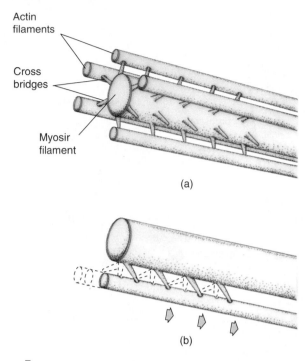

Actin filaments

Cross bridges

Myosir filament

(a)

(b)

FIGURE 8.2

The mechanism by which muscles contract. (a) Location of the myosin cross bridges. (b) The myosin cross bridges performing "rowing" movements, which cause the actin and myosin filaments to move relative to each other.

(Adapted from Anthony, C.P., and Kolthoff, N.J. *Textbook of Anatomy and Physiology,* 8th edition. St. Louis: C.V. Mosby, 1971.)

point farther down the strand, and so on. Thus, the cross bridges "row" along the actin filaments. Figure 8.2 illustrates this rowing sequence and shows how this sequence results in shortening the muscle fiber. (See *Figure 8.2.*)

A single impulse of a motor neuron produces a single twitch of a muscle fiber. The physical effects of the twitch last considerably longer than will the action potential, because of the elasticity of the muscle and the time required to rid the cell of calcium. (Like sodium, calcium is actively extruded by a pump situated in the membrane.) Figure 8.3 shows how the physical effects of a series of action potentials can overlap, causing a sustained contraction by the muscle fiber. A single motor unit in a leg muscle of a cat can raise a 100-gram weight, which attests to the remarkable strength of the contractile mechanism. (See *Figure 8.3.*)

As you know from your own experience, muscular contraction is not an all-or-nothing phenomenon, as are the twitches of the constituent muscle fibers. Obviously, strength of muscular contraction is determined by the average rate of firing of the various motor units. If, at a given moment, many units are firing, the contraction will be forceful. If few are firing, the contraction will be weak.

Sensory Feedback from Muscles

As we saw, the intrafusal muscle fibers contain sensory endings that are sensitive to stretch. The intrafusal muscle fibers are arranged in parallel with the extrafusal muscle fibers. Therefore, they are stretched when the muscle lengthens and are relaxed when it shortens. Thus, even though these afferent neurons are *stretch receptors,* they serve as *muscle length detectors.* This distinction is important. Stretch receptors are also located within the tendons, in the **Golgi tendon organ** (GTO). These

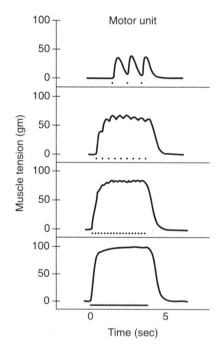

FIGURE 8.3

Action potentials and contractions. A rapid succession of action potentials can cause a muscle fiber to produce a sustained contraction. Each dot represents an individual action potential.

[Adapted from Devanandan, M.S., Eccles, R.M., and Westerman, R.A. *Journal of Physiology (London),* 1965, *178,* 359–367.]

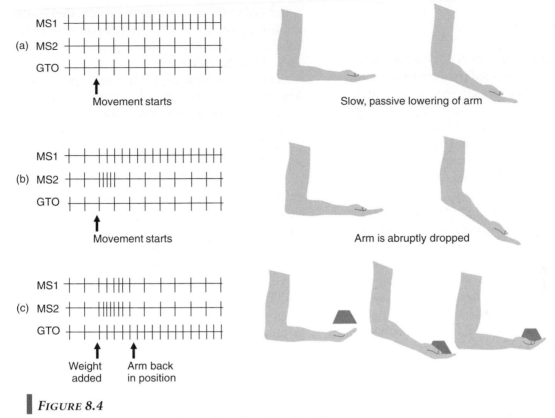

| *FIGURE 8.4*

Effects of arm movements on the firing of muscle and tendon afferent axons.
(a) Slow passive extension of the arm. (b) Rapid extension of the arm.
(c) Addition of a weight to an arm held in a horizontal position. MS₁ and MS₂ are
two types of muscle spindles; GTO is an afferent fiber from the Golgi tendon organ.

receptors detect the total amount of stretch exerted by the muscle, through its tendons, on the bones to which the muscle is attached. The stretch receptors of the Golgi tendon organ encode the degree of stretch by the rate of firing. They respond not to a muscle's length but to how hard it is pulling. In contrast, the receptors on intrafusal muscle fibers detect muscle length, not tension.

Figure 8.4 shows the response of afferent axons of the muscle spindles and Golgi tendon organ to various types of movements. Figure 8.4a shows the effects of passive lengthening of muscles, the kind of movement that would be seen if your forearm, held in a completely relaxed fashion, were slowly lowered by someone who was supporting it. The rate of firing of one type of muscle spindle afferent neuron (MS_1) increases, while the activity of the

afferent of the Golgi tendon organ remains unchanged. (See *Figure 8.4a.*) Figure 8.4b shows the results when the arm is dropped quickly; note that this time the second type of muscle spindle afferent neuron (MS_2) fires a rapid burst of impulses. This fiber, then, signals rapid changes in muscle length. (See *Figure 8.4b.*) Figure 8.4c shows what would happen if a weight were suddenly dropped into your hand while your forearm was held parallel to the ground. Neurons MS_1 and MS_2 (especially MS_2, which responds to rapid changes in muscle length) briefly fire, because your arm lowers briefly and then comes back to the original position. The Golgi tendon organ, monitoring the strength of contraction, fires in proportion to the stress on the muscle, so it increases its rate of firing as soon as the weight is added. (See *Figure 8.4c.*)

Smooth Muscle

Our bodies contain two types of **smooth muscle,** both of which are controlled by the autonomic nervous system. *Multiunit smooth muscles* are found in large arteries, around hair follicles (where they produce *piloerection,* or fluffing of fur), and in the eye (controlling lens adjustment and pupillary dilation). This type of smooth muscle is normally inactive, but it will contract in response to neural stimulation or to certain hormones. In contrast, *single-unit smooth muscles* normally contract in a rhythmical fashion. Some of these cells spontaneously produce *pacemaker potentials,* which we can regard as self-initiated excitatory postsynaptic potentials. These slow potentials elicit action potentials, which are propagated by adjacent smooth muscle fibers, causing a wave of muscular contraction. The efferent nerve supply (and various hormones) can modulate the rhythmical rate, increasing or decreasing it. Single-unit smooth muscles are found chiefly in the gastrointestinal system, uterus, and small blood vessels.

Cardiac Muscle

As its name implies, **cardiac muscle** is found in the heart. This type of muscle looks somewhat like striated muscle but acts like single-unit smooth muscle. The heart beats regularly, even if it is denervated. Neural activity and certain hormones (especially the catecholamines) serve to modulate the heart rate. A group of cells in the *pacemaker* of the heart are rhythmically active and initiate the contractions of cardiac muscle that constitute the heartbeat.

||||| *INTERIM SUMMARY*

Our bodies possess skeletal muscle, smooth muscle, and cardiac muscle. Skeletal muscles contain extrafusal muscle fibers, which provide the force of contraction. The alpha motor neurons form synapses with the extrafusal muscle fibers and control their contraction. Skeletal muscles also contain intrafusal muscle fibers, which detect changes in muscle length. The length of the intrafusal muscle fiber, and hence its sensitivity to increases in muscle length, is controlled by the gamma motor neuron. Besides the intrafusal muscle fibers, the muscles contain stretch receptors in the Golgi tendon organs, located at the ends of the muscles.

The force of muscular contraction is provided by long protein molecules called actin and myosin, arranged in overlapping parallel arrays. When an action potential, initiated by the synapse at the motor endplate, causes Ca^{2+} to enter the muscle fiber, the myofibrils extract energy from ATP and cause a twitch of the muscle fiber, producing a ratchetlike "rowing" movement of the myosin cross bridges.

Smooth muscle is controlled by the autonomic nervous system through direct neural connections and indirectly through the endocrine system. Multiunit smooth muscles contract only in response to neural or hormonal stimulation. In contrast, single-unit smooth muscles normally contract rhythmically, but their rate is controlled by the autonomic nervous system. Cardiac muscle also contracts spontaneously, and its rate of contraction, too, is influenced by the autonomic nervous system.

REFLEX CONTROL OF MOVEMENT

ALTHOUGH BEHAVIORS ARE CONTROLLED BY THE brain, the spinal cord possesses a certain degree of autonomy. Particular kinds of somatosensory stimuli can elicit rapid responses through neural connections located within the spinal cord. These reflexes constitute the simplest level of motor integration.

The Monosynaptic Stretch Reflex

The activity of the simplest functional neural pathway in the body is easy to demonstrate. Sit on a surface high enough to allow your legs to dangle freely and have someone lightly tap your patellar tendon, just below the kneecap. This stimulus briefly stretches your quadriceps muscle, on the top of your thigh. The stretch causes the muscle to contract, which makes your leg kick forward. (I am sure few of you will bother with this demonstration, because you are already familiar with it; most physical examinations include a test of this reflex.) The time inter-

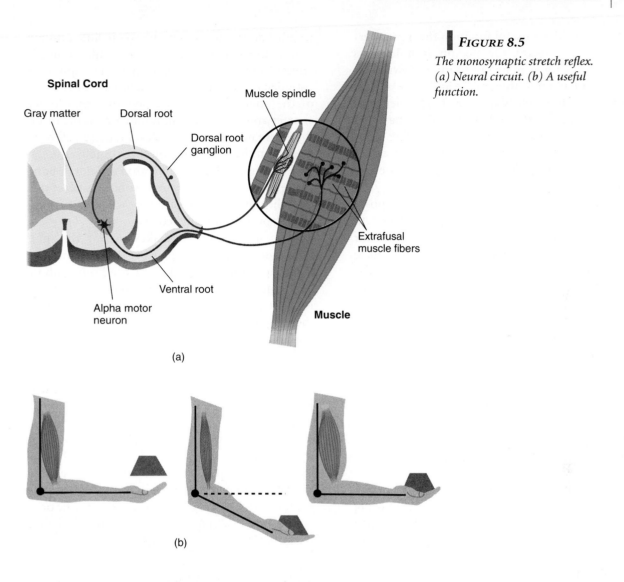

FIGURE 8.5
*The monosynaptic stretch reflex.
(a) Neural circuit. (b) A useful
function.*

Spinal Cord

Gray matter

Dorsal root

Dorsal root
ganglion

Muscle spindle

Extrafusal
muscle fibers

Ventral root

Alpha motor
neuron

Muscle

(a)

(b)

val between the tendon tap and the start of the leg
extension is about 50 milliseconds. That interval is
too short for the involvement of the brain; it would
take considerably longer for sensory information to
be relayed to the brain and for motor information to
be relayed back. For example, suppose a person is
asked to move his or her leg as quickly as possible
after being *touched* on the knee. This response
would not be reflexive but would involve sensory
and motor mechanisms of the brain. In this case the
interval between the stimulus and the start of the
response would be several times greater than the
time required for the patellar reflex.

Obviously, the patellar reflex as such has no utility; no selective advantage is bestowed upon animals

that kick a limb when a tendon is tapped. However,
if a more natural stimulus is applied, the utility of
this mechanism becomes apparent. Figure 8.5 shows
the effects of placing a weight in a person's hand.
This time I have included a piece of the spinal cord,
with its roots, to show the neural circuit that com-
poses the **monosynaptic stretch reflex.** First, follow the circuit: Starting at the muscle spindle,
afferent impulses are conducted to terminal buttons
in the gray matter of the spinal cord. These terminal buttons synapse on an alpha motor neuron that
innervates the extrafusal muscle fibers of the same
muscle. Only one synapse is encountered along the
route from receptor to effector—hence the term
monosynaptic. (See **Figure 8.5.**)

Now consider a useful function this reflex performs. If the weight the person is holding is increased, the forearm begins to move down. This movement lengthens the muscle and increases the firing rate of the muscle spindle afferent neurons, whose terminal buttons then stimulate the alpha motor neurons, increasing their rate of firing. Consequently, the strength of the muscular contraction increases, and the arm pulls the weight up. (See *Figure 8.5.*)

Another important role played by the monosynaptic stretch reflex is control of posture. In order to stand, we must keep our center of gravity above our feet, or we will fall. As we stand, we tend to oscillate back and forth, and from side to side. Our vestibular sacs and our visual system play an important role in the maintenance of posture. However, these systems are aided by the activity of the monosynaptic stretch reflex. For example, consider what happens when a person begins to lean forward. The large calf muscle (gastrocnemius) is stretched, and this stretching elicits compensatory muscular contraction that pushes the toes down, thus restoring upright posture. (See *Figure 8.6.*)

The Gamma Motor System

The muscle spindles are very sensitive to changes in muscle length; they will increase their rate of firing when the muscle is lengthened by a very small amount. The interesting thing is that this detection mechanism is adjustable. Remember that the ends of the intrafusal muscle fibers can be contracted by activity of the associated efferent axons of the gamma motor neurons; their rate of firing determines the degree of contraction. When the muscle spindles are relaxed, they are relatively insensitive to stretch. However, when the gamma motor neurons are active, they become shorter and hence become much more sensitive to changes in muscle length. This property of adjustable sensitivity simplifies the role of the brain in controlling movement. The more control that can occur in the spinal cord, the fewer messages must be sent to and from the brain.

We already saw that the afferent axons of the muscle spindle help maintain limb position even when the load carried by the limb is altered. Efferent control of the muscle spindles permits these muscle length detectors to assist in changes in limb position, as well. Consider a single muscle spindle. When its efferent axon is completely silent, the spindle is completely relaxed and extended. As the firing rate of the efferent axon increases, the spindle gets shorter and shorter. If, simultaneously, the rest of the entire muscle also gets shorter, there will be no stretch on the central region that contains the sensory endings, and the afferent axon will not respond. However, if the muscle spindle contracts faster than does the muscle as a whole, there will be a considerable amount of afferent activity.

The motor system makes use of this phenomenon in the following way: When commands from the brain are issued to move a limb, both the alpha motor neurons and the gamma motor neurons are activated. The alpha motor neurons start the muscle contracting. If there is little resistance, both the extrafusal and the intrafusal muscle fibers will contract at approximately the same rate, and little activity will be seen from the afferent axons of the muscle spindle. However, if the limb meets with resistance, the intrafusal muscle fibers will shorten more than the extrafusal muscle fibers, and hence sensory axons will begin to fire and cause the monosynaptic stretch reflex to strengthen the contraction. Thus, the brain makes use of the gamma motor system in moving the limbs. By establishing a rate of firing in the *gamma motor system*, the brain controls the length of the muscle spindles and, indirectly, the length of the entire muscle.

Polysynaptic Reflexes

The monosynaptic stretch reflex is the only spinal reflex we know of that involves only one synapse. All others are *polysynaptic*. Examples include relatively simple ones, like limb withdrawal in response to pain, and relatively complex ones, like the ejaculation of semen. Spinal reflexes do not exist in isolation; they are normally controlled by the brain. For example, Chapter 2 described how inhibition from the brain can prevent a person from dropping a bunch of roses with thorns, even though the painful stimuli received by the fingers serve to cause reflexive extension of the fingers. This section will describe some general principles by which polysynaptic spinal reflexes operate.

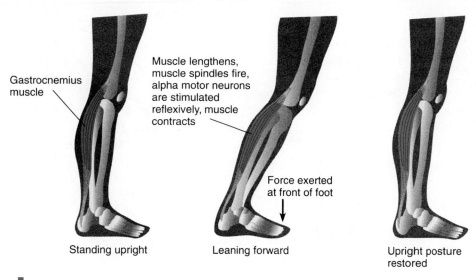

Gastrocnemius muscle

Muscle lengthens, muscle spindles fire, alpha motor neurons are stimulated reflexively, muscle contracts

Force exerted at front of foot

Standing upright

Leaning forward

Upright posture restored

FIGURE 8.6

The role of the monosynaptic stretch reflex in postural control.

Before I begin the discussion, I should mention that the simple circuit diagrams used here (including the one you just looked at in Figure 8.6) are much too simple. Reflex circuits are typically shown as a single chain of neurons, but in reality most reflexes involve thousands of neurons. Each axon usually synapses on many neurons, and each neuron receives synapses from many different axons.

As we previously saw, the afferent axons from the Golgi tendon organ serve as detectors of muscle stretch. There are two populations of afferent axons from the Golgi tendon organ, with different sensitivities to stretch. The more sensitive afferent axons tell the brain how hard the muscle is pulling. The less sensitive ones have an additional function. Their terminal buttons synapse on spinal cord interneurons—neurons that reside entirely within the gray matter of the spinal cord and serve to interconnect other spinal neurons. These interneurons synapse on the alpha motor neurons serving the same muscle. The terminal buttons liberate glycine and hence produce inhibitory postsynaptic potentials on the motor neurons. (See *Figure 8.7.*) The function of this reflex pathway is to decrease the strength of muscular contraction when there is danger of damage to the tendons or bones to which the muscles are attached. Weight lifters can lift heavier weights if their Golgi tendon organs are deactivated with injections of a local anesthetic, but they run the risk of pulling the tendon away from the bone or even breaking the bone.

The discovery of the inhibitory Golgi tendon organ reflex provided the first real evidence of neural inhibition, long before the synaptic mechanisms were understood. A **decerebrate** cat, whose brain stem has been cut through, exhibits a phenomenon known as **decerebrate rigidity.** The animal's back is arched, and its legs are extended stiffly from its body. This rigidity results from excitation originating in the caudal reticular formation, which greatly facilitates all stretch reflexes, especially of extensor muscles, by increasing the activity of the gamma motor system. Rostral to the brain stem transection is an inhibitory region of the reticular formation, which normally counterbalances the excitatory one. The transection removes the inhibitory influence, leaving only the excitatory one. If you attempt to flex the outstretched leg of a decerebrate cat, you will meet with increasing resistance, which suddenly melts away, allowing the limb to flex. It almost feels as though you were closing the blade of a pocketknife—hence the term **clasp-knife reflex.** The sudden release is, of course, mediated by activation of the Golgi tendon organ reflex.

Even the monosynaptic stretch reflex serves as the basis of polysynaptic reflexes. Muscles are

■ **FIGURE 8.7**

Polysynaptic inhibitory reflex. Input from the Golgi tendon organ can cause inhibitory postsynaptic potentials to occur on the alpha motor neuron.

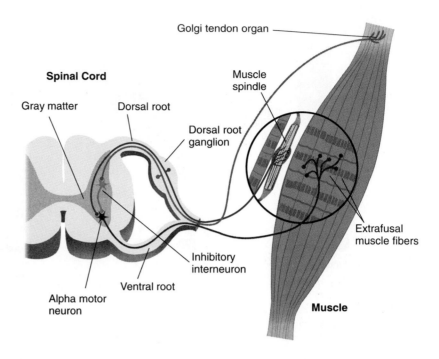

arranged in opposing pairs. The **agonist** moves the limb in the direction being studied, and because muscles cannot push back, the **antagonist** muscle must move the limb back in the opposite direction. Consider this finding: When a stretch reflex is elicited in the agonist, it contracts quickly, thus causing the antagonist to lengthen. It would appear, then, that the antagonist is presented with a stimulus that should elicit *its* stretch reflex. And yet the antagonist relaxes instead. Let us see why.

In addition to sending terminal buttons to the alpha motor neuron and to the brain, afferent axons of the muscle spindles also synapse on inhibitory interneurons. The terminal buttons of these interneurons synapse on the alpha motor neurons that innervate the antagonistic muscle. (See *Figure 8.8.*) Thus, a stretch reflex excites the agonist and *inhibits the antagonist,* so that the limb can move in the direction controlled by the stimulated muscle.

||||| **INTERIM SUMMARY**

Reflexes are simple circuits of sensory neurons, interneurons (usually), and efferent neurons that

control simple responses to particular stimuli. In the monosynaptic stretch reflex the terminal buttons of axons that receive sensory information from the intrafusal muscle fibers synapse with alpha motor neurons that innervate the same muscle. Thus, a sudden lengthening of the muscle causes the muscle to contract. By setting the length of the intrafusal muscle fibers, and hence their sensitivity to increases in muscle length, the motor system of the brain can control limb position. Changes in a weight being held that cause the limb to move will be quickly compensated for by means of the monosynaptic stretch reflex.

Polysynaptic reflexes contain at least one interneuron between the sensory neuron and the motor neuron. For example, when a strong muscular contraction threatens to damage muscles or limbs, the increased rate of firing of the afferent axons of Golgi tendon organs stimulates inhibitory interneurons, which inhibit the alpha motor neurons of those muscles. And when the afferent axons of intrafusal muscle fibers fire, they excite inhibitory interneurons that slow the rate of firing of the alpha motor neurons that serve the antagonistic muscles, causing the antagonist to relax and the agonist to contract.

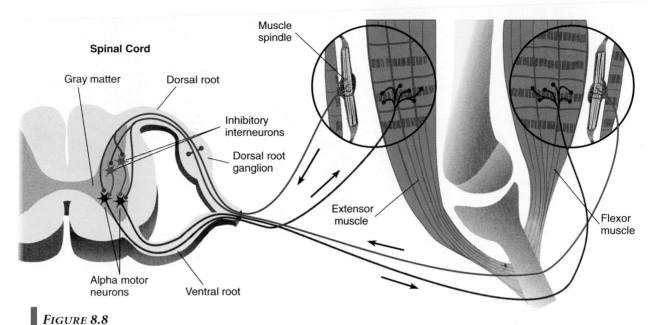

FIGURE 8.8

Secondary reflexes. Firing of the muscle spindle causes excitation on the alpha motor neuron of the agonist and inhibition on the antagonist.

CONTROL OF MOVEMENT BY THE BRAIN

MOVEMENTS CAN BE INITIATED BY SEVERAL means. For example, rapid stretch of a muscle triggers the monosynaptic stretch reflex, a stumble triggers righting reflexes, and the rapid approach of an object toward the face causes a startle response, a complex reflex consisting of movements of several muscle groups. Other stimuli initiate sequences of movements that we have previously learned. For example, the presence of food causes eating, and the sight of a loved one evokes a hug and a kiss. Because there is no single cause of behavior, we cannot find a single starting point in our search for the neural mechanisms that control movement.

The brain and spinal cord include several different motor systems, each of which can simultaneously control particular kinds of movements. For example, a person can walk and talk with a friend simultaneously. While doing so, he or she can gesture with the hands to emphasize a point, scratch an itch, brush away a fly, wipe sweat off his or her forehead, and so on. Walking, postural adjustments, talking, movement of the arms, and movements of the fingers all involve different specialized motor systems.

Organization of Motor Cortex

The primary motor cortex lies on the precentral gyrus, just rostral to the central sulcus. Stimulation studies (including those in awake humans) have shown that the activation of neurons located in particular parts of the primary motor cortex causes movements of particular parts of the body. Figure 8.9 shows a *motor homunculus* based on the observations of Penfield and Rasmussen (1950). Note that a disproportionate amount of cortical area is devoted to movements of the fingers and muscles used for speech. (See *Figure 8.9*.)

The principal cortical input to the primary motor cortex is the frontal association cortex,

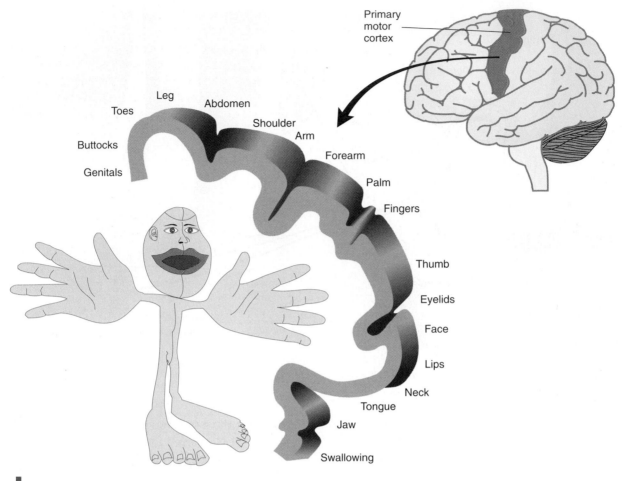

FIGURE 8.9

A motor homunculus. Stimulation of various regions of the primary motor cortex causes movement in muscles of various parts of the body.

located rostral to it. Lesion studies (some of which I will describe later in this chapter) indicate that the planning of most complex behaviors takes place here. These plans are executed by the primary motor cortex, which directly controls particular movements. In turn, the frontal association cortex receives axons from association areas of the occipital, temporal, and parietal cortex. As we saw, the occipital and temporal lobes contain the visual association cortex, and the temporal lobe also contains the auditory association cortex. And as we will see later, the association cortex of the parietal lobes is responsible for a person's perception of space. Thus, the frontal association cortex receives information about the environment (including memories previ-

ously acquired by means of vision, audition, and somatosensation) from the posterior lobes and uses this information to plan movements. Because the parietal lobes contain spatial information, the pathway from them to the frontal lobes is especially important in controlling both locomotion and arm and hand movements. After all, meaningful locomotion requires us to know where we are, and meaningful movements of our arms and hands require us to know where objects are located in space. (See **Figure 8.10.**)

The primary motor cortex also receives projections from the adjacent primary somatosensory cortex, located just across the central sulcus. The connections between these two areas are quite spe-

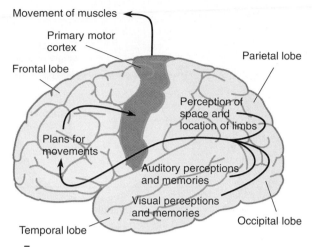

FIGURE 8.10

Cortical control of movement. The posterior association cortex is involved with perceptions and memories, and the frontal association cortex is involved with plans for movement.

cific: Neurons in the primary somatosensory cortex that respond to stimuli applied to a particular part of the body send axons to neurons in the primary motor cortex that move muscles in the same part of the body. For example, Asanuma and Rosén (1972) and Rosén and Asanuma (1972) found that somatosensory neurons that respond to a touch on the back of the thumb send axons to motor neurons that cause thumb extension, and somatosensory neurons that respond to a touch on the ball of the thumb send axons to motor neurons that cause thumb flexion. This organization appears to provide rapid feedback to the motor system during manipulation of objects.

Evidence that supports this suggestion was obtained by Evarts (1974), who recorded the activity of single neurons in the precentral gyrus of monkeys. He trained his subjects to move a lever back and forth by means of wrist flexions and extensions. When the monkeys made the movements in the correct amount of time, they received a squirt of grape juice, a drink they appeared to enjoy. Figure 8.11 shows the experimental preparation as well as the relationship between lever movement and the firing of a cortical neuron. Note that the firing of this neuron is nicely related to the movement, with the rate increasing during flexion. (See **Figure 8.11.**) Evarts

trained monkeys to produce a hand movement in response to a flash of a light or to a tactile stimulus delivered through the handle. He found that neurons in the motor cortex began firing 100 msec after a visual stimulus but responded as soon as 25 msec after a tactile stimulus. These results confirm the conclusion that hand and finger movements are controlled by somatosensory feedback received by neurons in the postcentral gyrus.

Cortical Control of Movement

Neurons in the primary motor cortex control movements by four different pathways. They directly control the corticospinal and corticobulbar pathways and indirectly control two sets of pathways that originate in the brain stem, which will be described later in this section.

The **corticospinal pathway** consists of axons of cortical neurons that terminate in the gray matter of the spinal cord. The largest concentration of cell bodies responsible for these axons is located in the primary motor cortex, but neurons in the parietal and temporal lobes also send axons through the corticospinal pathway. The axons leave the cortex and travel through subcortical white matter to the ventral midbrain, where they enter the cerebral peduncles. They leave the peduncles in the medulla and join the **pyramidal tracts,** so-called because of their shape. At the level of the caudal medulla, most of the fibers decussate (cross over) and descend through the contralateral spinal cord, forming the **lateral corticospinal tract.** The rest of the fibers descend through the ipsilateral spinal cord, forming the **ventral corticospinal tract.** (See light and dark blue lines in **Figure 8.12.**)

Most of the axons in the lateral corticospinal tract originate in the regions of the primary motor cortex that control the distal parts of the limbs: the arms, hands, and fingers and the lower legs, feet, and toes. They form synapses, directly or via interneurons, with motor neurons in the gray matter of the spinal cord—in the lateral part of the ventral horn. These motor neurons control muscles of the distal limbs, including those that move the arms, hands, and fingers. (See light blue lines in **Figure 8.12.**)

The axons in the ventral corticospinal tract originate in the upper leg and trunk regions of the pri-

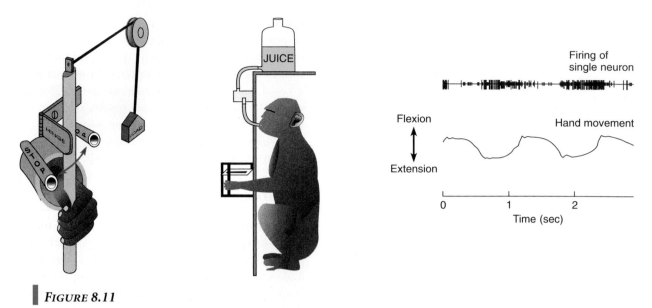

Figure 8.11

The relation between firing of single neurons in the motor cortex and hand movements. The single-unit records are redrawn from the original data and are therefore only approximate representations.

(Redrawn from Evarts, E.V. *Journal of Neurophysiology,* 1968, *31,* 14–27.)

mary motor cortex. They descend to the appropriate region of the spinal cord and divide, sending terminal buttons into both sides of the gray matter. They control motor neurons that move the muscles of the upper legs and trunk. (See dark blue lines in *Figure 8.12.*)

Lawrence and Kuypers (1968a) cut both pyramidal tracts in monkeys in order to assess their motor functions. Within six to ten hours after recovery from the anesthesia, the animals were able to sit upright, but their arms hung loosely from their shoulders. Within a day they could stand, hold the cage bars with their hands, and even climb a little. By six weeks the monkeys could walk and climb rapidly. Thus, posture and locomotion were not disturbed. However, the animals' manual dexterity was poor. They could reach for objects and grasp them, but they used their fingers together as though they were wearing mittens; they could not manipulate their fingers independently to pick up small pieces of food. And once they had grasped food with their hand, they had difficulty releasing their grip. They usually had to use their mouth to pry their hand open. In contrast, they had no difficulty releasing their grip when they were climbing the bars of their cage.

The results confirm what we would predict from the anatomical connections: The corticospinal pathway controls hand and finger movements and is indispensable for moving the fingers independently when reaching and manipulating. Postural adjustments of the trunk and use of the limbs for reaching and locomotion are unaffected; therefore, these types of movements are controlled by other systems. Because the monkeys had difficulty releasing their grasp when they picked up objects but had no trouble doing so when climbing the walls of the cage, we can conclude that the same behavior (opening the hand) is controlled by different brain mechanisms in different contexts.

The **corticobulbar pathway** projects to the medulla (sometimes called the *bulb*). This pathway is similar to the corticospinal pathway, except that it terminates in the motor nuclei of the fifth, seventh, tenth, and twelfth cranial nerves (the trigeminal, facial, vagus, and hypoglossal nerves). (In this context, *bulb* refers to the medulla.) These nerves control movements of the face and tongue. (See green lines in *Figure 8.12.*)

Two sets of pathways originate in the brain stem and terminate in the spinal cord gray matter: the ventromedial pathways and the rubrospinal tract.

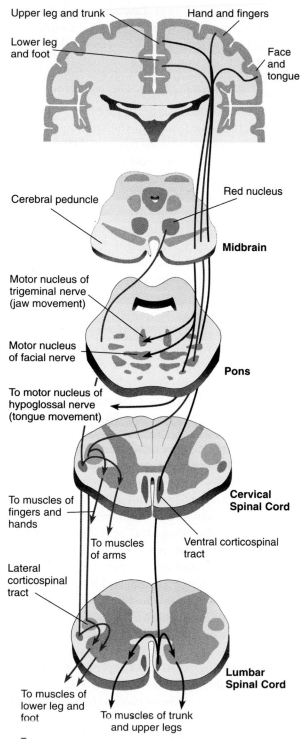

Upper leg and trunk

Lower leg and foot

Hand and fingers

Face and tongue

Cerebral peduncle

Red nucleus

Midbrain

Motor nucleus of trigeminal nerve (jaw movement)

Motor nucleus of facial nerve

Pons

To motor nucleus of hypoglossal nerve (tongue movement)

To muscles of fingers and hands

To muscles of arms

Ventral corticospinal tract

Cervical Spinal Cord

Lateral corticospinal tract

To muscles of lower leg and foot

To muscles of trunk and upper legs

Lumbar Spinal Cord

FIGURE 8.12

The corticospinal pathways (dark and light blue lines), corticobulbar pathway (green lines), and rubrospinal tract (red lines).

Through indirect connections the primary motor cortex can affect the activity of both sets of pathways. The **rubrospinal tract** originates in the red nucleus (*nucleus ruber*) of the midbrain. The red nucleus receives its most important inputs from the motor cortex and cerebellum. Axons of the rubrospinal tracts terminate on motor neurons in the spinal cord that control movements of forelimb and hindlimb muscles. (They do not control the muscles that move the fingers.) (See red lines in *Figure 8.12*.)

Lawrence and Kuypers (1968b) destroyed the rubrospinal tract *unilaterally* in some of the animals that had previously received bilateral lesions of the pyramidal tract. The rubrospinal tract lesion severely affected the animals' use of the ipsilateral arm. The arm tended to hang straight from the shoulder, with hand and fingers extended. If they could reach food only with the affected arm, they made a raking movement with the arm as a whole, bending their elbow and wrist as the food approached their mouth. The arm movement was accompanied by movements of the trunk. The monkeys did not hold the food with their hand, even with the mittenlike grasp that is produced by pyramidal tract lesions. The animals managed to hold onto cage bars with their affected hand, but the grip was weaker.

Lawrence and Kuypers concluded that the rubrospinal system controls independent movements of the forearms and hands—that is, movements that are independent of trunk movements. This control overlaps with that of the pyramidal system but does not include independent movements of the fingers.

The second set of pathways originating in the brain stem—the **ventromedial pathways**—includes the **vestibulospinal tracts,** the **tectospinal tracts,** and the **reticulospinal tracts.** Neurons of all three of these tracts control motor neurons in the ventromedial part of the spinal cord gray matter. Thus, they primarily control movements of the trunk and proximal limb muscles. The cell bodies of neurons of the vestibulospinal tracts are located in the vestibular nuclei. As you might expect, this system plays a role in the control of posture. The cell bodies of neurons in the tectospinal tracts are located in the superior colliculus and are involved in coordinating head and

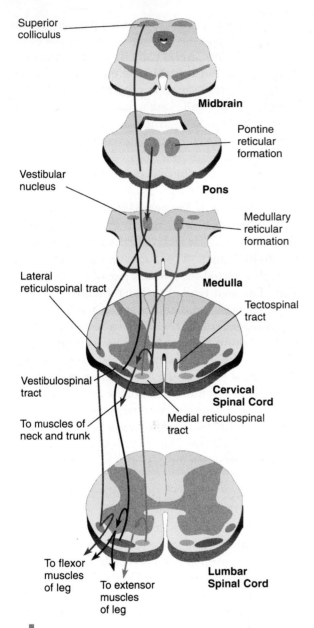

FIGURE 8.13

The ventromedial pathways.

trunk movements with eye movements. The cell bodies of neurons of the reticulospinal tracts are located in many nuclei in the brain stem and midbrain reticular formation. These neurons control several automatic functions, such as muscle tonus, respiration, coughing, and sneezing; but they are also involved in behaviors under direct neocortical control, such as walking. (See *Figure 8.13.*)

You will recall that Lawrence and Kuypers (1968a) found no deficits in postural movements after they had destroyed both the right and left pyramidal tracts. Presumably, the animals maintained their control of posture through the ventromedial pathways. Another study confirmed this speculation. Lawrence and Kuypers (1968b) cut the ventromedial fibers of some of the animals that had previously received bilateral pyramidal tract lesions. These animals showed severe impairments in posture. After a long recovery period they could eventually stand with great difficulty but could not take more than a few steps without falling. When they reached for food, their upper arms hung at their sides. Thus, we can conclude that the ventromedial pathways control the muscles of the trunk and proximal limbs, with supplementary control of the trunk muscles coming from the ventral corticospinal tract.

Table 8.1 summarizes the names of these pathways, their locations, and the muscle groups they control. (See *Table 8.1.*)

Deficits of Verbally Controlled Movements: The Apraxias

Damage to the corpus callosum, frontal lobe, or parietal lobe of the human brain produces a category of deficits called **apraxia.** Literally, the term means "without action," but apraxia differs from paralysis or weakness that occurs when motor structures such as the precentral gyrus, basal ganglia, brain stem, or spinal cord are damaged. Apraxia is the "inability to properly execute a learned skilled movement" (Heilman, Rothi, and Kertesz, 1983, p. 381). Neuropsychological studies of the apraxias have provided information about the way skilled behaviors are organized and initiated.

There are four major types of apraxia, two of which I will discuss in this chapter. *Limb apraxia* refers to problems with movements of the arms, hands, and fingers. *Oral apraxia* refers to problems with movements of the muscles used in speech. *Apraxic agraphia* refers to a particular type of writing deficit. *Constructional apraxia* refers to difficulty in drawing or constructing objects. Because of their relation to language, I will describe oral apraxia and the agraphias in Chapter 16.

TABLE 8.1			
Major motor pathways			
	Origin	**Termination**	**Muscle Groups**
Corticospinal Pathways			
Lateral corticospinal tract	Finger, hand, and arm region of motor cortex	Spinal cord	Fingers, hands, and arms
Ventral corticospinal tract	Trunk and upper leg region of motor cortex	Spinal cord	Trunk and upper legs
Corticobulbar Pathway	Face region of motor cortex	Cranial nerve nuclei: 5, 7, 10, and 12	Face and tongue
Ventromedial Pathways			
Vestibulospinal tract	Vestibular nuclei	Spinal cord	Trunk and legs
Tectospinal tract	Superior colliculi	Spinal cord	Neck and trunk
Lateral reticulospinal tract	Medullary reticular formation	Spinal cord	Flexor muscles of legs
Medial reticulospinal tract	Pontine reticular formation	Spinal cord	Extensor muscles of legs
Rubrospinal Tract	Red nucleus	Spinal cord	Hands (not fingers), lower arms, feet, and lower legs

Limb Apraxia

Limb apraxia is characterized by movement of the wrong part of the limb, incorrect movement of the correct part, or correct movements but in the incorrect sequence. It is assessed by asking patients to perform movements. The most difficult ones involve pantomiming particular acts. For example, the examiner may ask the patient, "Pretend you have a key in your hand and open a door with it." In response, a patient with limb apraxia may wave his wrist back and forth rather than rotate it, or rotate his wrist first and then pretend to insert the key. Or if asked to pretend she is brushing her teeth, a patient may use her finger as though it were a toothbrush, rather than pretend to hold a toothbrush in her hand.

To perform behaviors on verbal command without having a real object to manipulate, a person must comprehend the command and be able to imagine the missing article as well as to make the proper movements; therefore, these requests are the most difficult to carry out. Somewhat easier are tasks that involve imitating behaviors performed by the experimenter. Sometimes, a patient who cannot mime the use of a key can copy the examiner's hand movements. The easiest tasks involve the actual use of objects. For example, the examiner may give the patient a door key and ask him or her to demonstrate its use. If the brain lesion makes it impossible for the patient to understand speech, then the examiner cannot assess the ability to perform behaviors upon verbal command. In this case the examiner can only measure the patient's ability to imitate movements or use actual objects. (See Heilman, Rothi, and Kertesz, 1983, for a review.)

Limb apraxia can be caused by three types of lesions. **Callosal apraxia** is apraxia of the left limb that is caused by damage to the anterior corpus callosum. The explanation for the deficit is the following: When a person hears a verbal request to perform a movement, the meaning of the speech is analyzed by circuits in the posterior left hemisphere (discussed in Chapter 16). A neural command to make the movement is conveyed through long transcortical axons to the prefrontal area. There, the command activates neural circuits that contain the memory of the movements that constitute the behavior. This information is transmitted through the corpus callosum to the right prefrontal cortex, and from there to the right precentral gyrus. Neurons in this area control the individual movements. Damage to the anterior corpus callosum prevents communication between the left and right premotor areas, regions of the motor association cortex just rostral to the precentral gyrus. Thus, the right arm can perform the requested movement, but the left arm cannot. (See lesion A in *Figure 8.14*.)

A similar form of limb apraxia is caused by damage to the anterior left hemisphere, sometimes called **sympathetic apraxia.** The damage causes a primary motor impairment of the right arm and hand: full or partial paralysis. As with anterior callosal lesions, the damage also causes apraxia of the left arm. The term *sympathetic* was originally adopted because the clumsiness of the left hand appeared to be a "sympathetic" response to the paralysis of the right one. (See lesion B in *Figure 8.14*.)

The third form of limb apraxia is **left parietal apraxia,** caused by lesions of the posterior left hemisphere. These lesions involve both limbs. The posterior parietal lobe contains areas of association cortex that receive information from the surrounding sensory association cortex of the occipital, temporal, and anterior parietal lobes. (See lesion C in *Figure 8.14*.)

From the effects of parietal lobe lesions in humans and monkeys, Mountcastle et al. (1975) suggest that this region contains a sensory representation of the surrounding environment and keeps track of the location of objects in the environment and the location of the organism's body parts in relation to them. Because the right parietal lobe is especially important for perception of three-dimensional space, information about location of objects external to the person is probably supplied from this region. According to Mountcastle and his colleagues, the left parietal region serves as a "command apparatus for the operation of the limbs, hands, and eyes within immediate extrapersonal space." For example, when a person hears a command to reach for a particular object, the left auditory association cortex decodes the meaning of the request and passes it on to the left parietal association cortex. Using information received from the right parietal association cortex about the spatial

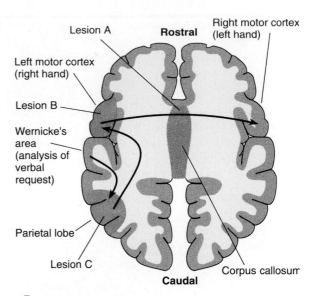

FIGURE 8.14

Apraxias. Lesion A causes callosal apraxia of the left limb, lesion B causes sympathetic apraxia of the right limb, and lesion C causes left parietal apraxia of both limbs.

location of the object, neural circuits in the left parietal association cortex assess the relative location of the person's hand and the object and send information about the starting and ending coordinates to the left premotor cortex. There, the sequence of muscular contractions necessary to perform the movement is organized, and this sequence is executed through the primary motor cortex and its connections with the spinal cord and subcortical motor systems. (See *Figure 8.15*.)

Constructional Apraxia

Constructional apraxia is caused by lesions of the right hemisphere, particularly the right parietal lobe. People with this disorder do not have difficulty making most types of skilled movements with their arms and hands. They have no trouble using objects properly, imitating their use, or pretending to use them. However, they have trouble drawing pictures or assembling objects from elements such as toy building blocks.

The primary deficit in constructional apraxia appears to involve the ability to perceive and imagine geometrical relations. Because of this deficit, a person cannot draw a picture, say, of a cube, because he or she cannot imagine what the lines and angles

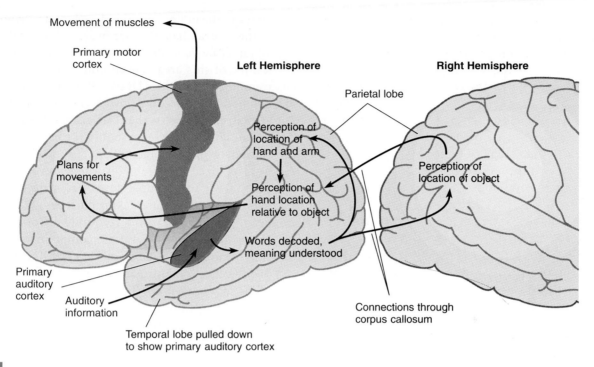

FIGURE 8.15

The "command apparatus" of the left parietal lobe.

of a cube look like, not because of difficulty controlling the movements of his or her arm and hand. (See *Figure 8.16.*) Besides being unable to draw accurately, a person with constructional apraxia invariably has trouble with other tasks involving spatial perception, such as following a map.

The Basal Ganglia

The basal ganglia constitute an important component of the motor system. We know they are important because their destruction by disease or injury causes severe motor deficits. The motor nuclei of the basal ganglia include the caudate nucleus, putamen, and globus pallidus. The basal ganglia receive most of its input from the primary motor cortex and the substantia nigra, and sends its outputs back to the primary motor cortex and the substantia nigra, and to the vestibular nucleus and reticular formation via the *pedunculopontine nucleus.* Through these connections the basal ganglia influence movements under the control of the primary motor cortex and

exert some control over the ventromedial system. (See *Figure 8.17.*)

We already saw in Chapter 3 that degeneration of the nigrostriatal bundle, the dopaminergic pathway from the substantia nigra of the midbrain to the caudate nucleus and putamen (the *neostriatum*), causes Parkinson's disease. The primary disorder is slowness of movement and difficulty in stopping one behavior and starting another. These deficits are seen in all muscle groups—those controlling fingers, hands, arms, and trunk. For example, once a person with Parkinson's disease is seated, he or she finds it difficult to arise. Once the person begins walking, he or she has difficulty stopping. Thus, a person with Parkinson's disease cannot easily pace back and forth across a room. Reaching for an object can be accurate, but the movement usually begins only after a considerable delay. Writing is slow and labored, and as it progresses, the letters get smaller and smaller. Postural movements are impaired. If someone bumps into a normal person who is standing, he or she will quickly move to restore balance—for example, by taking a step in the direction of the

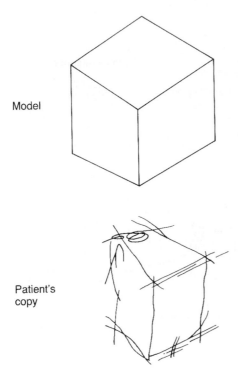

Model

Patient's
copy

▌ *FIGURE 8.16*

*Attempt to copy a cube by a patient with constructional
apraxia caused by a lesion of the right parietal lobe.*
(From *Fundamentals of Human Neuropsychology,* by B. Kolb and
I.Q. Whishaw. W.H. Freeman and Company. Copyright © 1980.)

impending fall or by reaching out with the arms to
grasp onto a piece of furniture. However, a person
with Parkinson's disease fails to do so and simply
falls. A person with this disorder is even unlikely to
put out his or her arms to break the fall.

Parkinson's disease also produces a resting
tremor—vibratory movements of the arms and
hands that diminish somewhat when the individual
makes purposeful movements. The tremor is
accompanied by rigidity; the joints appear stiff.
However, the tremor and rigidity are not the cause
of the slow movements. Although the slowness
appears to be caused by degeneration of the nigrostriatal bundle, the rigidity and tremor probably
occur because of damage to neurons in other pathways. Indeed, experimental studies with laboratory
animals have found that damage to the substantia
nigra produces hypoactivity but not tremors. The
tremors probably originate in a feedback circuit
consisting of a loop of neurons from the ventral tha-

lamus to the motor cortex and back again. Neurons
in the ventral thalamus fire in synchrony with the
vibratory movements of the tremor, and stereotaxic
lesions of this area can eliminate or reduce the
tremor and rigidity (Dray, 1980). However, the
lesions do not affect the slowness of movement.

Research suggests that Parkinson's disease may
be caused by toxins—present in the environment,
caused by faulty metabolism, or produced by
unrecognized infectious disorders. Several years
ago, a few young people developed symptoms of
Parkinson's disease after taking illicit drugs that had
been prepared in "underground" laboratories.
Unfortunately, the drugs were contaminated with
small amounts of a chemical called MPTP, which
had the effect of destroying dopaminergic neurons
of the substantia nigra (Langston et al., 1983). Further investigation showed that the damage occurs
when enzymes present in dopaminergic neurons
convert MPTP into an extremely toxic compound
called MPP^+. Studies with laboratory animals
revealed that injections of a drug that inhibits MAO
(the enzyme that breaks down the monoamines,
including dopamine) protects against the damage
caused by MPTP (Langston et al., 1984). Presumably, MAO is responsible for converting MPTP into
MPP^+. In fact, a more recent clinical trial with
deprenyl, a MAO inhibitor, was so encouraging that
many patients with Parkinson's disease are now
receiving the drug (Tetrud and Langston, 1989). If
the drug retards the rate of degeneration of
dopaminergic neurons, it will be the most important discovery since L-DOPA for the treatment of
this disorder.

Another basal ganglia disease, **Huntington's
chorea,** is caused by degeneration of the caudate
nucleus and putamen, especially of GABAergic and
acetylcholinergic neurons. (See ***Figures 8.18*** and
8.19.) Whereas Parkinson's disease causes a poverty
of movements, Huntington's chorea causes uncontrollable ones, especially jerky limb movements.
(*Chorea* derives from the Greek *khoros,* meaning
"dance.") The movements of Huntington's chorea
look like fragments of purposeful movements but
occur involuntarily. The disease is hereditary; it is
caused by a dominant gene on chromosome 4. It is
progressive and eventually causes death.

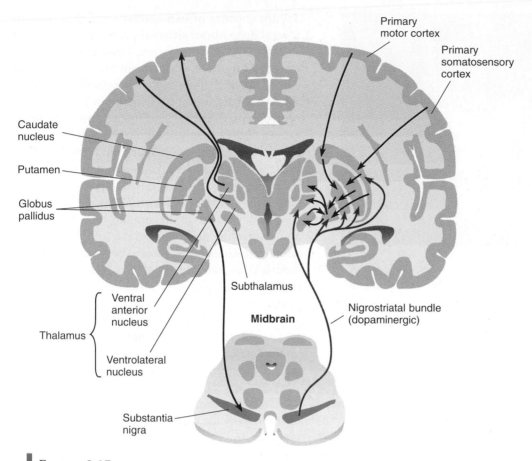

Primary
motor cortex

Primary
somatosensory
cortex

Caudate
nucleus

Putamen

Globus
pallidus

Subthalamus

Midbrain

Ventral
anterior
nucleus

Nigrostriatal bundle
(dopaminergic)

Thalamus

Ventrolateral
nucleus

Substantia
nigra

FIGURE 8.17

Some important interconnections of the basal ganglia.

A complete description of these two syndromes is much more complicated than my brief outline, but we can easily see that the basal ganglia can either inhibit or facilitate movements. Mainly on the basis of clinical observations of patients with motor disorders, Kornhuber (1974) suggests that the basal ganglia may play a special role in the control of slow, smooth movements. DeLong (1974) obtained some electrophysiological evidence that supports Kornhuber's hypothesis. He found that a majority of the neurons in the putamen fire before and during slow movements but not before and during rapid ones.

Damage to the caudate nucleus or putamen generally causes symptoms of *release;* patients exhibit rigidity (excessive muscular contraction) or uncontrollable movements of the limbs or facial muscles. Damage to the globus pallidus or ventral thalamus

generally causes symptoms of *deficiency,* such as **akinesia** (lack of movement) or mutism (failure to talk). Thus, the caudate nucleus and putamen appear to be inhibitory in function, and the globus pallidus and ventral thalamus appear to be excitatory. In Parkinson's disease the slowness of movement probably occurs because degeneration of the nigrostriatal bundle disrupts an inhibitory input to the caudate nucleus. Loss of inhibition increases the inhibitory function of the caudate nucleus, and movements become slower.

The Cerebellum

The cerebellum is an important part of the motor system. When it is damaged, people's movements become jerky, erratic, and uncoordinated. The cere-

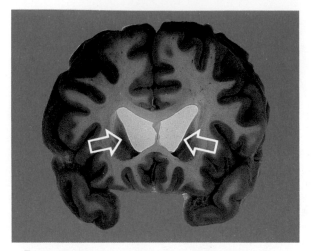

FIGURE 8.18

A slice through the brain of a person who had Huntington's chorea. The arrowheads indicate the location of the caudate nuclei, which are severely degenerated. As a consequence of the degeneration, the lateral ventricles (open spaces in the middle of the slice) have enlarged. Compare the caudate nuclei and lateral ventricles here with those shown in Figure 8.19.

(Courtesy of Anthony D'Agostino, Good Samaritan Hospital, Portland, Oregon.)

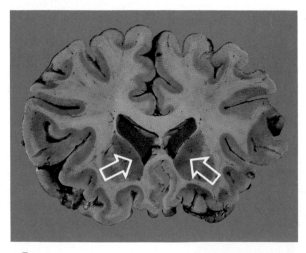

FIGURE 8.19

A slice through a normal human brain, showing the normal appearance of the caudate nuclei (arrowheads) and lateral ventricles.

(Courtesy of Harvard Medical School/Betty G. Martindale.)

bellum consists of two hemispheres that contain several deep nuclei situated beneath the wrinkled and folded cerebellar cortex. Thus, the cerebellum resembles the cerebrum in miniature. The medial part of the cerebellum is phylogenetically older than the lateral part, and it participates in control of the ventromedial system. The **flocculonodular lobe,** located at the caudal end of the cerebellum, receives input from the vestibular system and projects axons to the vestibular nucleus. You will not be surprised to learn that this system is involved in postural reflexes. (See green lines in *Figure 8.20.*) The **vermis** ("worm"), located on the midline, receives auditory and visual information from the tectum and cutaneous and kinesthetic information from the spinal cord. It sends its outputs to the **fastigial nucleus** (one of the set of deep cerebellar nuclei). Neurons in the fastigial nucleus send axons to the vestibular nucleus and to motor nuclei in the reticular formation. Thus, these neurons influence behavior through the vestibulospinal and reticulospinal tracts, two of the three ventromedial pathways. (See blue lines in *Figure 8.20.*)

The rest of the cerebellar cortex receives most of its input from the cerebral cortex, including the primary motor cortex and association cortex. This input is relayed to the cerebellar cortex through the pontine tegmental reticular nucleus. The intermediate zone of the cerebellar cortex projects to the **interposed nuclei,** which in turn project to the red nucleus. Thus, the intermediate zone influences the control of the rubrospinal system over arm and hand movements. The interposed nuclei also send outputs to the ventrolateral thalamic nucleus. (See red lines, *Figure 8.20.*)

The lateral zone of the cerebellum is involved in the control of independent limb movements, especially rapid, skilled movements. Such movements are initiated by neurons in the frontal association cortex, which control neurons in the primary motor cortex. But although the frontal cortex can plan and initiate movements, it does not contain the neural circuitry needed to calculate the complex, closely timed sequences of muscular contractions that are needed for rapid, skilled movements. That task falls to the lateral zone of the cerebellum.

Both the frontal association cortex and the primary motor cortex send information about

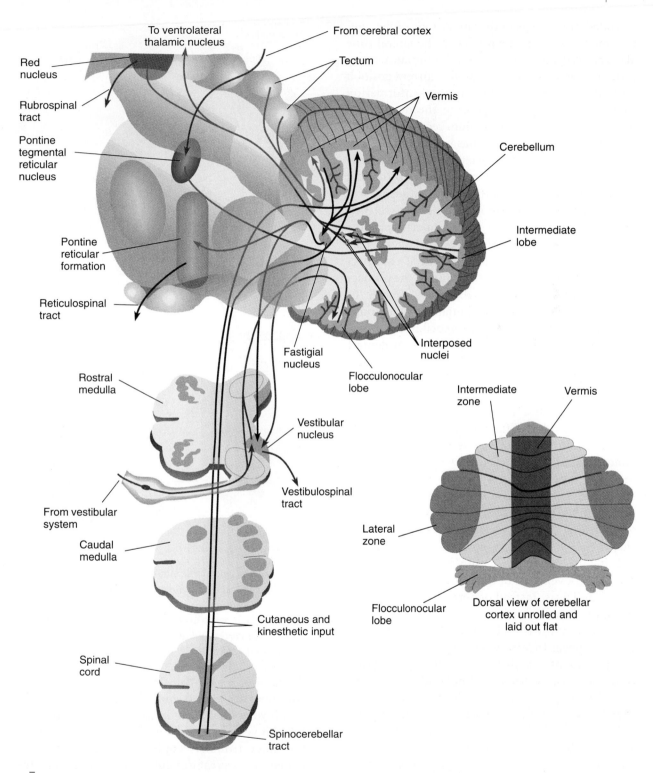

FIGURE 8.20

Inputs and outputs of three systems of the cerebellum: the flocculonodular lobe (green lines), the vermis (blue lines), and the intermediate zone of the cerebellar cortex (red lines).

intended movements to the lateral zone of the cerebellum via the **pontine nucleus.** The lateral zone also receives information from the somatosensory system, which informs it about the current position and rate of movement of the limbs—information that is necessary for computing the details of a movement. When the cerebellum receives information that the motor cortex has begun to initiate a movement, it computes the contribution that various muscles will have to make to perform that movement. The results of this computation are sent to the **dentate nucleus,** another of the deep cerebellar nuclei. Neurons in the dentate nucleus pass the information on to the ventrolateral thalamus, which projects to the primary motor cortex. The projection from the ventrolateral thalamus to the primary motor cortex enables the cerebellum to modify the ongoing movement that was initiated by the frontal cortex. The lateral zone of the cerebellum also sends efferents to the red nucleus (again, via the dentate nucleus); thus, it helps control independent limb movements through this system as well. (See *Figure 8.21.*)

In humans, lesions of different regions of the cerebellum produce different symptoms. Damage to the flocculonodular lobe or vermis causes disturbances in posture and balance. Damage to the intermediate zone produces deficits in movements controlled by the rubrospinal system. The principal symptom of this damage is limb rigidity. Damage to the lateral zone causes weakness and *decomposition of movement.* For example, if a person attempts to bring the hand to the mouth, he or she will make separate movements of the joints of the shoulder, elbow, and wrist instead of performing simultaneous smooth movements.

Lesions of the lateral zone of the cerebellar cortex also appear to impair the timing of rapid *ballistic* movements. Ballistic (literally, "throwing") movements occur too fast to be modified by feedback. The sequence of muscular movements must then be programmed in advance, and the individual muscles must be activated at the proper times. You might like to try this common neurological test. Have a friend place his or her finger in front of your face, about three-quarters of an arm's length away. While your friend slowly moves his or her finger around to serve as a moving target, alternately touch

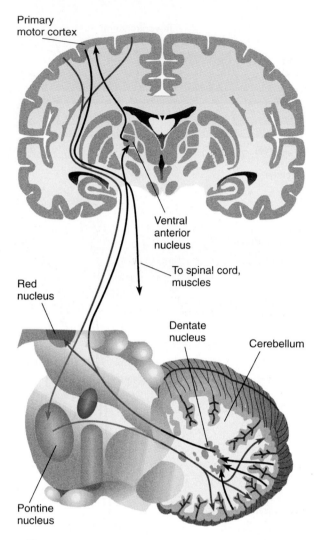

│ FIGURE 8.21

Inputs and outputs of the lateral zone of the cerebellar cortex. This zone receives information about impending movements from the frontal lobes and helps smooth and integrate the movements through its connections to the primary motor cortex and red nucleus through the dentate nucleus and ventral thalamus.

your nose and your friend's finger as rapidly as you can. If your cerebellum is normal, you can successfully hit your nose and your friend's finger without too much trouble. People with lateral cerebellar damage have great difficulty; they tend to miss the examiner's hand and poke themselves in the eye. (I have often wondered why neurologists do not adopt a less dangerous test.)

When we make rapid, aimed movements, we cannot rely on feedback to stop the movement when we reach the target. By the time we perceive that our finger has reached the proper place, it is too late to stop the movement, and we will overshoot the target if we try to stop it then. Instead of relying on feedback, the movement appears to be timed. We estimate the distance between our hand and the target, and our cerebellum calculates the amount of time that the muscles will have to be turned on. After the proper amount of time the cerebellum briefly turns on antagonistic muscles to stop the movement. In fact, Kornhuber (1974) suggests that one of the primary functions of the cerebellum is timing the duration of rapid movements. Obviously, learning must play a role in controlling such movements.

The cerebellum also appears to integrate successive *sequences* of movements that must be performed one after the other. For example, Holmes (1939) reported that one of his patients said, "The movements of my left arm are done subconsciously, but I have to think out each movement of the right [affected] arm. I come to a dead stop in turning and have to think before I start again." Thach (1978) obtained experimental evidence that corroborates this role. He found that many neurons in the dentate nuclei (which receive inputs from the lateral zone of the cerebellar cortex) showed response patterns that predicted the *next* movement in a sequence rather than the one that was currently taking place. Presumably, the cerebellum was planning these movements.

The Reticular Formation

The reticular formation consists of a large number of nuclei located in the core of the medulla, pons, and midbrain. The reticular formation controls the activity of the gamma motor system and hence regulates muscle tonus. In addition, the pons and medulla contain several nuclei with specific motor functions. For example, different locations in the medulla control automatic or semiautomatic responses such as respiration, sneezing, coughing, and vomiting. As we saw, the ventromedial pathways originate in the superior colliculi, vestibular nuclei, and reticular formation. Thus, the reticular formation plays a role in the control of posture.

The reticular formation also plays a role in locomotion. Stimulation of the **mesencephalic locomotor region,** located ventral to the inferior colliculus, causes a cat to make pacing movements (Shik and Orlovsky, 1976). The mesencephalic locomotor region does not send fibers directly to the spinal cord but apparently controls the activity of reticulospinal tract neurons.

Other motor functions of the reticular formation are also being discovered. Siegel and McGinty (1977) recorded from thirty-five single neurons in the reticular formation of unanesthetized, freely moving cats. Thirty-two of these neurons responded during *specific* movements of the head, tongue, facial muscles, ears, forepaw, or shoulder. The specific nature of the relations suggests that the neurons play some role in controlling the movements. For example, one neuron responded when the tongue moved out and to the left. The function of these neurons and the range of movements they control are not yet known.

||||| INTERIM SUMMARY

The motor systems of the brain are complex. (Having read this section, you do not need me to tell you that.) A good way to review the systems is through an example. While following my description, you might want to look at Table 8.1 and Figures 8.12 and 8.13 again. Suppose you see, out of the corner of your eye, that something is moving. You quickly turn your head and eyes toward the source of the movement and discover that a vase of flowers on a table someone has just bumped is ready to fall. You quickly reach forward, grab it, and restore it to a stable upright position. (For simplicity's sake, I will assume that you are right-handed.)

The rapid movement of your head and eyes is controlled by mechanisms that involve the superior colliculi and nearby nuclei. The head movement and corresponding movement of the trunk are mediated by the tectospinal tract. You perceive the tipping vase because of the activity of neurons in your visual association cortex. Your visual association cortex also contributes information about depth to your right parietal lobe, whose association cortex determines the exact spatial location of the vase. Your left parietal lobe uses the spatial information, together with its own record of the location of your hand, to compute the path your hand must travel to intercept the vase. The information is relayed to your left frontal lobe, where the motor association cortex starts the movement. Because the movement will have to be a ballistic one, the cerebellum controls its timing, based on information it receives from the association cortex of the frontal and parietal lobes. Your hand stops just as it touches the vase, and connections between the somatosensory cortex and the primary motor cortex initiate a reflex that closes your hand around the vase.

The movement of your hand is controlled through a cooperation between the corticospinal, rubrospinal, and ventromedial pathways. Even before your hand moves, the ventral corticospinal tract and the ventromedial pathways (vestibulospinal and reticulospinal system, largely under the influence of the basal ganglia) begin adjusting your posture so that you will not fall forward when you suddenly reach in front of you. Depending on how

far forward you will have to reach, the reticulospinal tract may even cause one leg to step forward in order to take your weight. The rubrospinal tract controls the muscles of your upper arm, and the lateral corticospinal tract controls your finger and hand movements. Perhaps you say, triumphantly, "I got it!" The corticobulbar pathway, under the control of speech mechanisms in the left hemisphere, causes the muscles of your vocal apparatus to say these words.

A person with apraxia will have difficulty making controlled movements of the limb in response to a verbal request. Most cases of apraxia are produced by lesions of the left parietal lobe, which sends information about the requested movement to the left frontal association cortex. This region directly controls movement of the right limb by activating neurons in the left primary motor cortex and indirectly controls movement of the left limb by sending information to the right frontal association cortex. Damage to the left frontal association cortex or its connections with the right hemisphere also produce apraxia.

New Terms

Muscles

skeletal muscle p. 226

flexion p. 226

extension p. 226

extrafusal muscle fiber p. 226

alpha motor neuron p. 226

intrafusal muscle fiber p. 226

gamma motor neuron p. 226

motor unit p. 226

myofibril p. 226

actin p. 226

myosin p. 226

striated muscle p. 226

neuromuscular junction p. 227

motor endplate p. 227

endplate potential p. 227

Golgi tendon organ p. 228

smooth muscle p. 230

cardiac muscle p. 230

Reflex Control of Movement

monosynaptic stretch reflex p. 231

decerebrate p. 233

decerebrate rigidity p. 233

clasp-knife reflex p. 233

agonist p. 234

antagonist p. 234

Control of Movement by the Brain

corticospinal pathway p. 237

pyramidal tract p. 237

lateral corticospinal tract p. 237

ventral corticospinal tract p. 237

corticobulbar pathway p. 238

rubrospinal tract p. 239

ventromedial pathway p. 239

vestibulospinal tract p. 239

tectospinal tract p. 239

reticulospinal tract p. 239

apraxia p. 240

callosal apraxia p. 241

sympathetic apraxia p. 242

left parietal apraxia p. 242

constructional apraxia p. 242

Huntington's chorea p. 244

akinesia p. 245

flocculonodular lobe p. 246

vermis p. 246

fastigial nucleus p. 246

interposed nuclei p. 246

pontine nucleus p. 248

dentate nucleus p. 248

mesencephalic locomotor region p. 249

Suggested Readings

Kandel, E.R., Schwartz, J.H., and Jessell, T.M. *Principles of Neural Science,* 3rd ed. Norwalk, Conn.: Appleton & Lange, 1992

Kolb, B., and Whishaw, I.Q. *Fundamentals of Human Neuropsychology,* 3rd ed. New York: W.H. Freeman, 1989.

Nicholls, J.G., Martin, A.R., Wallace, B.G., and Kuffler, S.W. *From Neuron to Brain,* 3rd ed. Sunderland, Mass.: Sinauer Associates, 1992.

Schneider, J.S., and Lidsky, T.I. *Basal Ganglia and Behavior: Sensory Aspects and Motor Functioning.* Bern: Hans Huber, 1987.

Shepherd, G.M. *Neurobiology,* 2nd ed. New York: Oxford University Press, 1988.

CHAPTER 9

Sleep

A Physiological and Behavioral Description
- Stages of Sleep
- Mental Activity During Sleep
Interim Summary

Why Do We Sleep?
- Sleep as an Adaptive Response
- Sleep as a Restorative Process
- The Functions of REM Sleep
Interim Summary

Disorders of Sleep
- Insomnia
- Problems Associated with REM Sleep
- Problems Associated with Slow-Wave Sleep
Interim Summary

Biological Clocks
- Circadian Rhythms and Zeitgebers
- Role of the Suprachiasmatic Nucleus
Interim Summary

Physiological Mechanisms of Sleep and Waking
- Chemical Control of Sleep
- Neural Control of Arousal
- Neural Control of Slow-Wave Sleep
- Neural Control of REM Sleep
Interim Summary

Why do we sleep? Why do we spend at least one-third of our lives doing something that provides most of us with only a few fleeting memories? I will attempt to answer this question in several ways. In the first part of this chapter I will describe what is known about the phenomenon of sleep: How much do we sleep? What do we do while asleep? What happens if we do not get enough sleep? What factors affect the duration and quality of sleep? Does sleep perform a restorative function? How effective are sleeping medications? What do we know about sleepwalking and other sleep-related disorders? In the second part of the chapter I will discuss the mechanism that controls daily rhythms of sleep and activity. In the third I will describe the search for the chemicals and the neural circuits that control sleep and wakefulness.

A PHYSIOLOGICAL AND BEHAVIORAL DESCRIPTION

SLEEP IS A BEHAVIOR. THAT STATEMENT MAY SEEM peculiar, because we usually think of behaviors as activities that involve movements, such as walking or talking. Movements do occur during sleep, but except for the rapid eye movements that accompany a particular stage, sleep is not distinguished by movement. What characterizes sleep is that the insistent urge of sleepiness forces us to seek out a quiet, comfortable place, lie down, and remain there for several hours. Because we remember very little about what happens while we sleep, we tend to think of sleep more as a state of consciousness than as a behavior. The change in consciousness is undeniable, but it should not prevent us from noticing the behavioral changes.

Stages of Sleep

The best research on human sleep is conducted in a sleep laboratory. A sleep laboratory, which is usually located at a university or medical center, consists of one or several small bedrooms adjacent to an observation room, where the experimenter spends the night (trying to stay awake). The experimenter prepares the sleeper for electrophysiological measurements by attaching electrodes to the scalp to monitor the electroencephalogram (EEG) and to the chin to monitor muscle activity, recorded as the **electromyogram** (EMG). Electrodes attached around the eyes monitor eye movements, recorded as the **electro-oculogram** (EOG). In addition, other electrodes and transducing devices can be used to monitor autonomic measures such as heart rate, respiration, and skin conductance. Wires from the electrodes are bundled together in a "ponytail," which is then plugged into a junction box at the head of the bed. (See **Figure 9.1**.)

FIGURE 9.1

A subject prepared for a night's sleep in a sleep laboratory. Philippe Platilly/Science Source/Photo Researchers, Inc.)

During wakefulness the EEG of a normal person shows two basic patterns of activity: *alpha activity* and *beta activity*. **Alpha activity** consists of regular, medium-frequency waves of 8–12 Hz. The brain produces this activity when a person is resting quietly, not particularly aroused or excited and not engaged in strenuous mental activity (such as problem solving). Although alpha waves sometimes occur when a person's eyes are open, they are much more prevalent when the eyes are closed. The other type of waking EEG pattern, **beta activity,** consists of irregular, mostly low-amplitude waves of 13–30 Hz. This activity occurs when a person is alert and attentive to events in the environment or is thinking actively. (See *Figure 9.2.*)

What is the significance of these two types of waveforms? As we saw in Chapter 5, the EEG is a recording of the summed postsynaptic activity of cerebral neurons (mostly, neurons in the cerebral cortex). Therefore, a low-frequency, high-voltage EEG (alpha activity, as opposed to beta activity) reflects neural **synchrony.** These waves are produced by a regular, synchronized pattern of activity in a large number of neurons. The activity of the individual neurons is analogous to a large number of people chanting the same words together (speaking *synchronously*). Similarly, beta activity is referred to as **desynchrony;** it is like a large number of people broken into many small groups, each carrying on an individual conversation.

The analogy helps explain why desynchrony is generally assumed to represent activation, whereas synchrony reflects a resting or depressed state. A group of people who are all chanting the same message will process very little information; only one message is being produced. On the other hand, a desynchronized group will process and transmit many different messages. The alert, waking state of the brain is more like the desynchronized group of people, with much information processing going on. During synchrony the neurons of the resting brain (especially the cortex) quietly murmur the same message in unison.

Let us look at a typical night's sleep of a female college student on her third night in the laboratory. (Of course, we would obtain similar results from a male, with one exception, which is noted later.) The

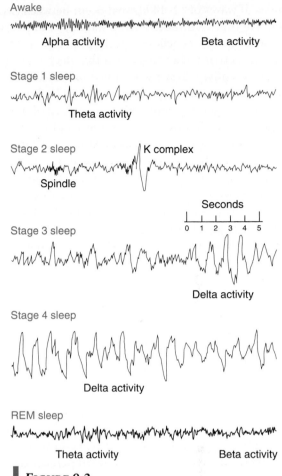

FIGURE 9.2

An EEG recording of the stages of sleep.
(From Horne, J.A. *Why We Sleep: The Functions of Sleep in Humans and Other Mammals.* Oxford, England: Oxford University Press, 1988. Copyright 1988 Oxford University Press. By permission of the Oxford University Press.)

experimenter attaches the electrodes, turns the lights off, and closes the door. Our subject becomes drowsy and soon enters stage 1 sleep, marked by the presence of some **theta activity** (3.5–7.5 Hz). This stage is actually a transition between sleep and wakefulness; if we watch our volunteer's eyelids, we will see that from time to time they slowly open and close and that her eyes roll upward and downward. (See *Figure 9.2.*) About 10 minutes later she enters stage 2 sleep. The EEG during this stage is generally irregular but contains periods of theta activity, *sleep spindles,* and *K complexes.* Sleep spindles are short bursts of waves of 12–14 Hz that occur between two and five times a minute during stages 1–4 of sleep. Some investigators believe that sleep spindles represent the activity of a mechanism that decreases the brain's sensitivity to sensory input and thus keep the person asleep (Silverstein and Levy, 1976; Bowersox, Kaitin, and Dement, 1985). The sleep of older people contains fewer sleep spindles and is generally accompanied by more awakenings during the night. K complexes are sudden, sharp waveforms, which, unlike sleep spindles, are usually found only during stage 2 sleep. They spontaneously occur at the rate of approximately one per minute but often can be triggered by noises. Some investigators believe that they, too, represent mechanisms involved in keeping the person asleep (Halasz, Pal, and Rajna, 1985). (See *Figure 9.2.*)

The subject is sleeping soundly now; but if awakened, she might report that she has not been asleep. This phenomenon often is reported by nurses who awaken loudly snoring patients early in the night (probably to give them a sleeping pill) and find that the patients insist they were lying there awake all the time. About 15 minutes later the subject enters stage 3 sleep, signaled by the occurrence of high-amplitude **delta activity** (less than 3.5 Hz). (See *Figure 9.2.*) The distinction between stage 3 and stage 4 is not clear-cut; stage 3 contains 20–50 percent delta activity, and stage 4 contains more than 50 percent.

About 90 minutes after the beginning of sleep (and about 45 minutes after the onset of stage 4 sleep), we notice an abrupt change in a number of physiological measures recorded from our subject. The EEG suddenly becomes mostly desynchronized, with a sprinkling of theta waves, very similar to the record obtained during stage 1 sleep. (See *Figure 9.2.*) We also note that her eyes are rapidly darting back and forth beneath her closed eyelids. We can see this activity in the EOG, recorded from electrodes attached to the skin around her eyes, or we can observe the eye movements directly. The cornea produces a bulge in the closed eyelids that can be seen to move about. We also see that the EMG becomes silent; there is a profound loss of muscle tonus. In fact, physiological studies have shown that, aside from occasional twitching, a person actually becomes paralyzed during REM sleep.

This peculiar stage of sleep is quite distinct from the quiet sleep we saw earlier. It is usually referred to as **REM sleep** (for the *r*apid *e*ye *m*ovements that characterize it). It has also been called *paradoxical sleep,* because of the presence of beta activity, which is usually seen during wakefulness or stage 1 sleep. The term *paradoxical* merely reflects people's surprise at observing an unexpected phenomenon, but the years since its first discovery (reported by Aserinsky and Kleitman in 1955) have blunted the surprise value.

At this point, I should introduce some terminology. Stages 1–4 are usually referred to as **non-REM sleep.** Stages 3 and 4 are referred to as **slow-wave sleep,** because of the presence of delta activity. As we will see, research has focused on the role of REM sleep and of slow-wave sleep; most investigators believe that the other stages of non-REM sleep, stages 1 and 2, are less important than the others. (As we shall see, when people are sleep deprived, they make up most of their slow-wave sleep and REM sleep, but not their stage 1 and stage 2 sleep.) By some criteria, stage 4 is the deepest stage of sleep; only loud noises will cause a person to awaken, and when awakened, the person acts groggy and confused. During REM sleep a person may not react to noises, but he or she is easily aroused by meaningful stimuli, such as the sound of his or her name. Also, when awakened from REM sleep, a person appears alert and attentive.

If we arouse our volunteer during REM sleep and ask her what was going on, she will almost certainly report that she had been dreaming. The dreams of REM sleep tend to be narrative in form; there is a storylike progression of events. If we wake her during slow-wave sleep and ask, "Were you dreaming?" she will most likely say, "No." However, if we question her more carefully, she might report the presence of a thought, an image, or some emotion. I will return to this issue later.

During the rest of the night our subject's sleep alternates between periods of REM and non-REM sleep. Each cycle is approximately 90 minutes long, containing a 20- to 30-minute bout of REM sleep. Thus, an 8-hour sleep will contain four or five periods of REM sleep. **Figure 9.3** shows a graph of a typical night's sleep. The *x*-axis indicates the EEG

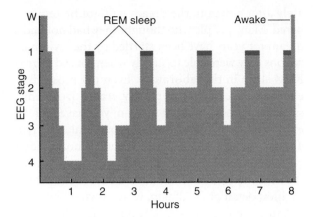

FIGURE 9.3

A typical pattern of the stages of sleep during a single night.
(From Hartmann, E. *The Biology of Dreaming,* 1967. Courtesy of
Charles C Thomas, Publisher, Springfield, Illinois.)

activity that is being recorded; thus REM sleep and
stage 1 sleep are placed on the same line because
similar patterns of EEG activity occur at these times.
Note that most slow-wave sleep (stages 3 and 4)
occurs during the first half of the night. Subsequent
bouts of non-REM sleep contain more and more
stage 2 sleep, and bouts of REM sleep (the colored
horizontal bars) become more prolonged.

The fact that REM sleep occurs at regular 90-
minute intervals suggests that a brain mechanism
alternately causes REM and slow-wave sleep. Normally, a period of slow-wave sleep must precede
REM sleep. In addition, there seems to be a refractory period after each occurrence of REM sleep, during which time REM sleep cannot take place again.
In fact, the cyclical nature of REM sleep appears to
be controlled by a "clock" in the brain that also controls an activity cycle that continues through waking. The first suggestion that a 90-minute activity
cycle occurs throughout the day came from the
observation that infants who are fed on demand
show regular feeding patterns (Kleitman, 1961).
Later studies found 90-minute cycles of rest and
activity, including such activities as eating, drinking,
smoking, heart rate, oxygen consumption, stomach
motility, urine production, and performance on
various tasks that make demands upon a person's
ability to pay attention. Kleitman termed this phenomenon the **basic rest-activity cycle (BRAC).** (See

Kleitman, 1982, for a review.) As we will see later in
this chapter, an internal "clock" in the medulla
causes regular changes in activity and alertness during the day and controls periods of slow-wave and
REM sleep at night.

Several investigators have suggested that the eye
movements made during REM sleep are related to
the visual imagery that occurs while we dream. Roffwarg et al. (1962) recorded the eye movements of
subjects during REM sleep and then awakened them
and asked them to describe what had been happening in their dreams. They found that the eye movements were similar to what would have been
expected if the subjects had actually been watching
these events. Miyauchi, Takino, and Azakami (1990)
recorded the EEG of sleeping subjects and found
that a particular wave accompanied eye movements
during REM sleep. This wave was also seen when
waking subjects scanned a scene—but it was *not*
seen when they simply made eye movements in a
dark room. Thus, the EEG wave is not produced by
eye movements themselves, but may actually indicate that the subjects had been scanning a visual
image during a dream.

During REM sleep we become paralyzed; most
of our spinal and cranial motor neurons are strongly
inhibited. (Obviously, the ones that control respiration and eye movements are spared.) At the same
time, the brain is very active. Cerebral blood flow
and oxygen consumption are accelerated. In addition, a male's penis will become at least partially
erect, and a female's vaginal secretions will increase.
However, Fisher, Gross, and Zuch (1965) found that
in males, genital changes do not signify that the person is experiencing a dream with sexual content. (Of
course, people can have dreams with frank sexual
content. In males some dreams culminate in ejaculation—the so-called nocturnal emissions, or "wet
dreams." Females, too, sometimes experience
orgasm during sleep.)

The fact that penile erections occur during REM
sleep, independent of sexual arousal, has been used
clinically to assess the causes of impotence (Karacan,
Salis, and Williams, 1978). A subject sleeps in the
laboratory with a device attached to his penis that
measures its circumference. If penile enlargement
occurs during REM sleep, then his failure to obtain

an erection during attempts at intercourse is not caused by physiological problems such as nerve damage or a circulatory disorder. Often, once a man finds out that he is physiologically capable of achieving an erection, the knowledge is therapeutic in itself. (A neurologist told me that there is a less expensive way to gather the same data. The patient obtains a strip of postage stamps, moistens them, and applies them around his penis before going to bed. In the morning he checks to see whether the perforations are broken.)

The important differences between REM and slow-wave sleep are listed in *Table 9.1.*

Mental Activity During Sleep

Although sleep is a period during which we do not respond very much to the environment, it is incorrect to refer to sleep as a state of unconsciousness. During sleep our consciousness is certainly different from consciousness while awake, but we *are* conscious. In the morning we usually forget what we experienced while asleep, and in retrospect we recall a period of "unconsciousness." However, when experimenters wake sleeping subjects, the reports that the subjects give make it clear that they were conscious.

Some people insist that they never dream. They are wrong; everyone dreams. What does happen, however, is that most dreams are subsequently forgotten. Unless a person awakens during or immedi-

ately after a dream, the dream will not be remembered. Many people who thought they had not had a dream for years have been startled by the vivid narrations they were able to supply when roused during REM sleep in the laboratory. Even the most vivid experiences can be completely erased from consciousness. I am sure that many of you have had the experience of waking during a particularly vivid dream. You decide to tell your friends about it, and you start to review what you will say. As you do so, the memory just slips away. You can't remember the slightest detail of the dream, which was so vivid and real just a few seconds ago. You may feel that if you could remember just one thing about it, everything would come back. Understanding this phenomenon would probably help us understand the more general issue of learning and forgetting.

Madsen et al. (1991) found that the rate of cerebral blood flow in the human brain during REM sleep was high in the visual association cortex but low in the inferior frontal cortex. As we shall see in Chapter 11, the inferior frontal cortex is involved in making plans and keeping track of the organization of events in time. As Madsen and his colleagues note, dreams are characterized by good visual images (undoubtedly involving the visual association cortex), but they are poorly organized with respect to time; for example, past, present, and future are often interchanged (Hobson, 1988). And as Melges (1982) put it, "the dreamer often has no feeling of striving for long-term goals but rather is carried along by the flow of time by circumstances that crop up in an unpredictable way." This quote could just as well be describing the daily life of a person whose inferior frontal cortex has been damaged.

Although narrative, storylike dreaming occurs during REM sleep, mental activity can also accompany slow-wave sleep. Some of the most terrifying nightmares occur during slow-wave sleep, especially in stage 4 sleep (Fisher et al., 1970). If people are awakened from slow-wave sleep, they are unlikely to report a storylike dream. Instead, they often report a situation, such as being crushed or suffocated, or simply a feeling of fear or dread. This common sensation is reflected in the terms that some languages use for describing what we call a *nightmare*. For example, in French the word is *cauchemar,* or "pressing devil." Figure 9.4 shows a victim of a

TABLE 9.1	
Principal charcteristics of REM and slow-wave sleep	
REM Sleep	**Slow-Wave Sleep**
EEG desynchrony	EEG synchrony
Lack of muscle tonus	Moderate muscle tonus
Rapid eye movements	Slow or absent eye movment
Penile erection or vaginal secretion	Lack of genital activity
PGO waves	Lack of PGO waves
Narrative-type dreams	Static Dreams

| *FIGURE 9.4*

The Nightmare, 1781, by Henry Fuseli, Swiss, 1741–1825.

(Gift of Mr. and Mrs. Bert L. Smokler and Mr. and Mrs. Lawrence A. Fleischman, Acc. No. 55.5. Courtesy of The Detroit Institute of Arts.)

nightmare (undoubtedly in the throes of stage 4 slow-wave sleep) being squashed by an *incubus* (from the Latin *incubare,* "to lie upon"). (See *Figure 9.4.*)

‖‖‖ *INTERIM SUMMARY*

Sleep is generally regarded as a state, but it is, nevertheless, a behavior. As we will see later in this chapter, we do not sleep because our brains "run down"; instead, active brain mechanisms cause us to engage in the behavior of sleep. The stages of non-REM sleep, stages 1 through 4, are defined by EEG activity. Slow-wave sleep (stages 3 and 4) are the two deepest stages. Alertness consists of desynchronized beta activity (13–30 Hz); relaxation and drowsiness consist of alpha activity (8–12 Hz); stage 1 sleep consists of alternating periods of alpha activity, irregular fast activity, and theta activity (3.5–7.5 Hz); the EEG of stage 2 sleep lacks alpha activity but contains sleep spindles (short periods of 12–14 Hz activity) and occasional K complexes; stage 3 sleep consists of 20–50 percent delta activity (less than 3.5 Hz); and stage 4 sleep consists of more than 50 percent delta activity. About 90 minutes after the beginning of sleep, people enter REM sleep. Cycles of REM and slow-wave sleep alternate with a period of approximately 90 minutes.

WHY DO WE SLEEP?

WE ALL KNOW HOW INSISTENT THE URGE TO SLEEP can be and how uncomfortable we feel when we have to resist it and stay awake. With the exception of the effects of severe pain and the need to breathe, sleepiness is probably the most insistent drive. People can commit suicide by refusing to eat or drink, but even the most stoical person cannot indefinitely defy the urge to sleep. Sleep will come, sooner or later, no matter how hard a person tries to stay awake. However, despite the insistent nature of sleepiness, researchers have not yet found a simple answer to the question posed in the title of this section. The two major hypotheses that have been proposed are discussed next.

‖ Sleep as an Adaptive Response

Sleep is a universal phenomenon among vertebrates. As far as we know, all mammals and birds sleep (Durie, 1981). Reptiles also sleep, and fish and amphibians enter periods of quiescence that probably can be called sleep. However, only warm-blooded vertebrates (mammals and birds) exhibit unequivocal REM sleep, with EEG signs of desynchrony along with rapid eye movements. (Obviously, birds such as flamingos, which sleep while perched on one leg, do not lose tone in the muscles they use to remain standing.) Thus, REM sleep appears to be of recent phylogenetic origin. This special form of sleep will be discussed separately, in a later section.

Some investigators believe that the best way to understand sleep is to see it as a useful behavior that we have inherited from our ancestors. For example, Webb (1975, 1982) suggests that sleep might not have special restorative properties but might simply be a behavior that keeps an animal out of harm's way when there is nothing important to do. We can imagine that our primitive ancestors benefited from irresistible periods of sleep that kept them from stumbling around in the dark, when predators were harder to see, when food was difficult to find, and when injuries were more likely to occur.

Many animals obtain food during only part of the day-night cycle. These animals profit from a period of inactivity, during which less energy is expended. In fact, animals who have safe hiding places (for example, rabbits) sleep a lot, unless they are very small and need to eat much of the time (for example, shrews). Large predators such as lions can sleep safely wherever and whenever they choose, and indeed, they sleep many hours of the day. In contrast, large animals who are preyed upon and have no place to hide (for example, cattle) sleep very little. Presumably, they must remain awake to be alert for predators.

An argument *against* the suggestion that sleep serves merely as an adaptive response is the fact that sleep is found in some species of mammals that would seem to be better off without it. For example, the Indus dolphin (*Platanista indi*) lives in the muddy waters of the Indus estuary in Pakistan (Pilleri, 1979). Over the years it has become blind, presumably because vision is not useful in the animal's environment. (It has an excellent sonar system, which it uses to navigate and find prey.) However, despite the dangers caused by sleeping, sleep has not disappeared. The Indus dolphin never stops swimming; doing so would result in injury, because of the dangerous currents and the vast quantities of debris carried by the river during the monsoon season. Pilleri captured two dolphins and studied their habits. He found that they slept a total of 7 hours a day, in naps of 4–60 seconds each. If sleep were simply an

adaptive response, why was it not eliminated (as vision was) through the process of natural selection?

Some other species of marine mammals have developed an extraordinary pattern of sleep: The cerebral hemispheres take turns sleeping, presumably because that strategy always permits at least one hemisphere to be alert. The bottlenose dolphin (*Tursiops truncatus*) and the porpoise (*Phocoena phocoena*) both sleep this way (Mukhametov, 1984). Figure 9.5 shows the EEG records from the two hemispheres; note that slow-wave sleep occurs independently in the left and right hemispheres. (See *Figure 9.5*.)

Undoubtedly, sleep *does* serve as a useful behavior. The fact that sleeping time varies with environmental factors suggests that sleep is not simply a response to physiological need. But its presence in all species of mammals and birds suggests a certain amount of sleep is physiologically necessary.

Sleep as a Restorative Process

Most investigators believe that sleep accomplishes some sort of restoration from the effects of wear and tear that occur during wakefulness. However, until recently, evidence for this hypothesis was very thin, indeed. In fact, sleep does not seem to be necessary for keeping the body in good condition (at least, in our own species). However, it *does* appear to be needed to keep the brain functioning normally. (For convenience, I will talk about the "body" and the "brain" in the following section, even though we both know that the brain is a part of the body.)

Effects of Sleep Deprivation

When we are forced to miss a night's sleep, we become very sleepy. The fact that sleepiness is so motivating suggests that sleep is a necessity of life. If so, it should be possible to deprive people or laboratory animals of sleep and see what capacities are disrupted. We should then be able to infer the role that sleep plays. However, the results of sleep deprivation studies have not revealed as much as investigators had originally hoped.

Studies with Humans. There is a distinct difference between sleepiness and tiredness. We might want to rest after playing tennis or after having a vig-

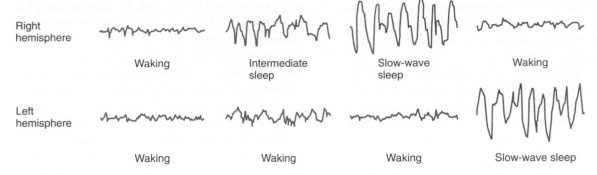

FIGURE 9.5

Sleep in a dolphin. The two hemispheres sleep independently, presumably so that the animal remains behaviorally alert.

(Adapted from Mukhametov, L.M., in *Sleep Mechanisms*, edited by A.A. Borbély and J.L. Valatx. Munich: Springer-Verlag, 1984.)

orous swim, but that feeling is quite different from the sleepiness we feel at the end of a day—a sleepiness that occurs even if we have been relatively inactive. What we should do, therefore, to study the role of sleep (as opposed to the restorative function of rest) is to have our subjects rest without sleeping. Unfortunately, that is not possible. When Kleitman first began studying sleep in the early 1920s, he hoped to have subjects undress and lie quietly in bed. They would remain awake so that he could observe the effects of "pure" sleep deprivation. It did not work. People cannot stay awake without engaging in physical activity, no matter how hard they try. So Kleitman had to accept that because his subjects could stay awake only by being active, they were rest-deprived as well as sleep-deprived.

Deprivation studies have not obtained persuasive evidence that sleep is needed to keep the body functioning normally. Horne (1978) reviewed over fifty experiments in which humans had been deprived of sleep. He reported that most of them found that sleep deprivation did not interfere with people's ability to perform physical exercise. In addition, they found no evidence of a physiological stress response to sleep deprivation. If people encounter stressful situations that cause illness or damage to various organ systems, changes can be seen in such physiological measures as blood levels of cortisol and epinephrine. (The physiology of stress is described in more detail in Chapter 11.) Generally, these changes did not occur.

Sleep deprivation produces other signs of impaired cerebral functioning. For example, most studies have found that after a few days of sleep deprivation, people begin to report perceptual distortions or even hallucinations. For example, Morris, Williams, and Lubin (1960) reported that sleep-deprived subjects made statements such as, "The floor seems wavy," "That black mark looked like it was changing into different rock formations," or "I thought steam was rising from the floor, so I tested my eyes to check whether it was real." The effects on a subject without a history of mental illness are never particularly severe—the subjects will realize that the perceptual distortions and hallucinations are not real—but they do suggest that sleep deprivation adversely affects cerebral functioning.

What happens to sleep-deprived subjects after they are permitted to sleep again? Most of them sleep longer the next night or two, but they never regain all of the sleep they lost. In one remarkable case a 17-year-old boy stayed awake for 264 hours so that he could obtain a place in the *Guinness Book of World Records* (Gulevich, Dement, and Johnson, 1966). After his ordeal the boy slept for a little less than 15 hours and awoke feeling fine. He slept slightly more than 10 hours the second night and just under 9 hours the third. Almost 67 hours were never made up. However, percentage of recovery was not equal for all stages of sleep. Only 7 percent of stages 1 and 2 were made up, but 68 percent of stage 4 slow-wave sleep and 53 percent of REM sleep were made up. Other studies (for example, Kales et al., 1970) have found similar results, which suggests that stage 4 sleep and REM sleep are more important than the other stages.

As I mentioned earlier, REM sleep will be discussed later. But what do we know about slow-wave sleep? What happens then that is so important? Both cerebral metabolic rate and cerebral blood flow decline during slow-wave sleep, falling to about 75 percent of the waking level during stage 4 sleep (Sakai et al., 1979; Buchsbaum et al., 1989). In particular, the regions marked by the highest amounts of delta waves decline the most. As we know from behavioral observation, people are unreactive to all but intense stimuli during slow-wave sleep and, if awakened, act groggy and confused—as if their cerebral cortex has been shut down and has not yet resumed its functioning. These observations suggest that during stage 4 sleep the brain is, indeed, resting.

Studies with Laboratory Animals. Until recently, sleep deprivation studies with animals have provided us with little insight into the role of sleep. Because animals cannot be "persuaded" to stay awake, it is especially difficult to separate the effects of sleep deprivation from those caused by the method used to keep the animals awake. We can ask a human volunteer to try to stay awake and can expect some cooperation. He or she will say, "I'm getting sleepy—help me to stay awake." However, animals are interested only in getting to sleep and must constantly be stimulated—and hence, stressed. Rechtschaffen and his colleagues (Rechtschaffen et al., 1983, 1989) devised a procedure that was designed to control for the effects of forced exercise that are necessary to keep an animal from sleeping. They constructed a circular platform on which two rats lived, each restrained in a plastic cage. When the platform was rotated by an electrical motor, the rats were forced to walk to avoid falling into a pool of water. (See *Figure 9.6.*)

The investigators employed a *yoked-control* procedure to deprive one rat of sleep but force both members of the pair to exercise an equal amount of time. They used a computer to record the EEGs and EMGs of both rats so that they could detect both slow-wave and REM sleep. One rat served as the experimental (sleep-deprived) animal, and the other

served as the yoked control. As soon as the EEG record indicated that the experimental animal was falling asleep, the computer turned on the motor that rotated the disk, forcing both animals to exercise. Because the platform rotated whenever the experimental animal started to sleep, the procedure reduced the experimental animal's total sleep time by 87 percent. However, the sleep time of the yoked-control rat was reduced by only 31 percent.

Sleep deprivation had serious effects. The control animals remained in perfect health. However, the experimental animals looked sick and apparently stopped grooming their fur. They became weak and uncoordinated and lost their ability to regulate their body temperature. Although they began eating much more food than normal, their metabolic rate became so high that they continued to lose weight.

The effects of sleep deprivation are less drastic in humans than in rats. Several hypotheses could account for this difference. Perhaps human sleep deprivation studies have just not continued long enough to cause serious harm. The human body is much larger than that of a rat, and changes in metabolic rate would take much longer to affect body weight. Or perhaps (as Horne, 1988, suggests) the procedures used to keep humans and rats awake cause different amounts of stress. A human in a sleep deprivation study knows that he or she is being watched carefully by the experimenters and that no serious harm will occur. The subject also knows that even though the experience is somewhat of an ordeal, it will soon be over, and he or she will be able to sleep again. In contrast, the rat knows only that its environment has suddenly become very hostile; it has no way of knowing whether the ordeal will end. In a similar situation perhaps a person would suffer ill effects, also. (In fact, sleep deprivation was an important component of the brainwashing techniques used to persuade captured American servicemen to change their political beliefs during the Korean War.)

Effects of Exercise on Sleep

Sleep deprivation studies with humans suggest that the brain may need slow-wave sleep in order to recover from the day's activities but that the rest of the body does not. Another way to determine

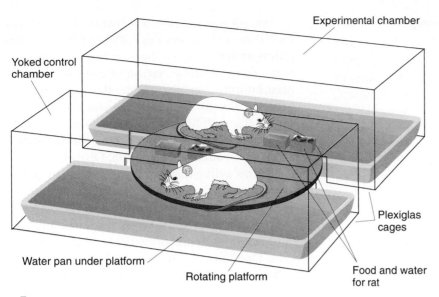

Experimental chamber

Yoked control chamber

Plexiglas cages

Water pan under platform

Rotating platform

Food and water for rat

FIGURE 9.6

The apparatus used to deprive rats of sleep. Whenever one of the pair of rats in the experimental chambers fell asleep, the turntable was rotated until the animal was awake for 6 seconds.

(Redrawn from Rechtschaffen, A., Gilliland, M.A., Bergmann, B.M., and Winter, J.B. *Science*, 1983, *221*, 182–184.)

whether sleep is needed for restoration of physiological functioning is to look at the effects of daytime activity on nighttime sleep. If the function of sleep is to repair the effects of activity during waking hours, then we should expect that sleep and exercise are related. That is, we should sleep more after a day of vigorous exercise than after a day spent quietly at an office desk.

In fact, the relation between sleep and exercise is not very compelling. For example, Ryback and Lewis (1971) found no changes in slow-wave or REM sleep of healthy subjects who spent six weeks resting in bed. If sleep repairs wear and tear, we would expect these people to sleep less. Adey, Bors, and Porter (1968) studied the sleep of *completely* immobile quadriplegics and paraplegics and found only a small decrease in slow-wave sleep as compared with uninjured people.

Horne (1981, 1988) reported that some studies have found that exercise increases slow-wave sleep but others have not. He noted that an important factor seems to be the climate in which the exercise occurs. If the temperature and the humidity are high, the exercise is likely to increase slow-wave sleep. Horne suggested that the important variable might be whether the exercise succeeded in heating the body.

To test this hypothesis, Horne and Moore (1985) had subjects exercise on a treadmill. Some subjects were cooled by electric fans, and their skin was periodically sprayed with water. Their body temperature rose only 1°C. That night, the slow-wave sleep of the "hot exercised" subjects rose by 25 percent, whereas that of the "cool exercised" subjects was unchanged. Horne (1988) now believes that the increased body temperature itself is not the significant factor but that an increase in brain temperature is. Perhaps, he says, an increase in brain temperature raises its metabolic rate and hence its demand for more slow-wave sleep. A preliminary study suggests that this hypothesis may have some merit. Horne and Harley (1988) warmed subjects' heads and faces with a hair dryer, which raised their brain temperature by an estimated 1°C. Four of the six subjects showed an increase in slow-wave sleep the next night. Clearly, further research is needed.

Effects of Mental Activity on Sleep

If slow-wave sleep permits the brain to rest and recover from its daily activity, then we might expect that increased cerebral activity would cause an increase in slow-wave sleep. Indeed, as we just saw, that is precisely the way that Horne interprets the effects of increased body temperature. First of all, tasks that demand alertness and mental activity *do* increase glucose metabolism in the brain, as measured by a PET scanner (Roland, 1984). The most significant increases are seen in the frontal lobes, where delta activity is most intense during slow-wave sleep.

In an ingenious study Horne and Minard (1985) found a way to increase mental activity without affecting physical activity and without causing stress. The investigators told subjects to show up for an experiment in which they were supposed to take some tests designed to test reading skills. In fact, when the subjects turned up, they were told that the plans had been changed. They were invited for a day out, at the expense of the experimenters. (Not surprisingly, the subjects willingly accepted.) They spent the day visiting an art exhibition, a shopping center, a museum, an amusement park, a zoo, and an interesting mansion. After a scenic drive through the countryside they watched a movie in a local theater. They were driven from place to place and certainly did not become overheated by exercise. After the movie they returned to the sleep laboratory. They said they were tired, and they readily fell asleep. Their sleep duration was normal, and they awoke feeling refreshed. However, their slow-wave sleep—particularly stage 4 sleep—was increased.

Does Physical Restoration Occur During Sleep?

The evidence that I have reviewed so far suggests that slow-wave sleep is not necessary for restoration of the body but that it may be necessary for restoration of the brain. I have discussed the effects of sleep deprivation and the effects of physical and mental activity on sleep. One other approach remains: to see whether physiological changes occur during sleep that suggest that restoration and repair takes place at that time.

Investigators who believe that the body repairs itself during sleep point to evidence for restorative processes during sleep. The most important finding is the fact that the secretion of growth hormone occurs during sleep, shortly after the first occurrence of delta activity in slow-wave sleep (Takahashi, 1979). (Growth hormone is, of course, important for stimulating children's growth, but it also has functions in adults.) In addition, Obál et al. (1991) found that a drug that inhibits the release of growth hormone also suppressed sleep in rats. The sleep-dependent secretion of growth hormone is significant, because this hormone increases the ability of amino acids, the constituents of proteins, to enter cells. Undoubtedly, protein synthesis is an important aspect of restoration of body tissue, because proteins are relatively fragile and must constantly be renewed and replaced.

However, as Horne (1988) points out, growth hormone facilitates protein synthesis only if amino acids are freely available, and that is the case for only about 5 hours after a meal. After that time the amino acids have become incorporated into protein, have been oxidized, or have been converted into fats and stored in the body's adipose tissue. Most people eat several hours before going to bed, so during most of the night the pool of available amino acids is low.

Perhaps for some species, such as the rat, sleep provides the sole opportunity for tissue restoration. When rats are awake, they are actively doing something: foraging for food, seeking sexual partners, grooming, eating, drinking, or otherwise keeping occupied. The only time that they really rest is when they are asleep. However, we humans are able to rest during the day. We are capable of sitting quietly (as I am doing now, and as you will be doing when you read this chapter). In fact, our metabolic rate is only about 9 percent lower during sleep than it is during quiet wakefulness (Reich, Geyer, and Karnovsky, 1972). Thus, we probably do not sleep for physical rest as much as for the opportunity it gives our brain to rest.

As we saw earlier, PET scans and studies of cerebral blood flow have shown that the metabolic rate of the human brain is, indeed, substantially lower during slow-wave sleep. In addition, Ramm and Smith (1990) found that the rate of protein synthesis in the brains of rats increased during slow-wave sleep, which could indicate that the brain is restoring itself as well as resting.

The Functions of REM Sleep

Clearly, REM sleep is a time of intense physiological activity. The eyes dart about rapidly, the heart rate shows sudden accelerations and decelerations, breathing becomes irregular, and the brain becomes more active. It would be unreasonable to expect that REM sleep has the same functions as slow-wave sleep. An early report on the effects of REM sleep deprivation (Dement, 1960) observed that as the deprivation progressed, subjects had to be awakened from REM sleep more frequently; the "pressure" to enter REM sleep built up. Furthermore, after several days of REM sleep deprivation, subjects would show a **rebound phenomenon** when permitted to sleep normally; they spent a much greater-than-normal percentage of the recovery night in REM sleep. This rebound suggests that there is a need for a certain amount of REM sleep—that REM sleep is controlled by a regulatory mechanism. If selective deprivation causes a deficiency in REM sleep, the deficiency is made up later, when uninterrupted sleep is permitted.

How have investigators explained the occurrence of REM sleep? The similarities between REM sleep and waking have led some investigators to suggest that REM sleep permits an animal to become more sensitive to its environment and avoid being surprised by predators (Snyder, 1966). (You will recall that during REM sleep humans are more sensitive to meaningful stimuli, such as the sound of their name.) Others have suggested that REM sleep has a special role in learning. Some investigators suggest that memories of events of the previous day—especially those dealing with emotionally related information—are consolidated and integrated with existing memories (Greenberg and Pearlman, 1974); others have suggested that this time is utilized to accomplish the opposite function—to flush useless information from memory, to prevent the storage of useless clutter (Newman and Evans, 1965; Crick and Mitchison, 1983). Another investigator (Jouvet, 1980) suggests that REM sleep helps integrate

learned and instinctive behaviors—it provides a time to modify the neural circuits controlling species-typical behaviors according to the experience gained in the past day. The fact that the sleep of infants consists mainly of REM sleep has suggested to others that this stage is associated with brain development (Roffwarg, Muzio, and Dement, 1966). The association could go either way; brain development could cause REM sleep (perhaps to tidy up after spurts of neural growth), or REM sleep could be setting the stage for brain growth to occur.

As you can see, many hypotheses have been advanced to explain the rather puzzling phenomenon of REM sleep. In the previous paragraph I mentioned four categories: *vigilance, learning* (either consolidation or flushing), *species-typical reprogramming,* and *brain development.* It is probably safe to say that when there are so many hypothetical explanations for a phenomenon, we do not know very much about its causes. So far, none of the hypotheses have been either unambiguously supported or proved wrong. REM sleep deprivation, imposed after a session of training, does impair learning—especially of complicated tasks—but the effect is not very large (McGrath and Cohen, 1978; Smith, 1985). Similarly, a training session does increase REM sleep—especially early in the sleep period. Thus, the learning hypothesis receives a certain amount of support. The vigilance and reprogramming hypotheses have not been developed enough to make specific predictions that can be tested experimentally. The developmental hypothesis is supported by the fact that infant animals born with well-developed brains (such as guinea pigs) spend proportionally less time in REM sleep than infant animals born with less-developed brains (such as rats, cats, or humans). But then, why do adults have REM sleep?

Studies with laboratory animals suggest that REM sleep performs functions that facilitate learning. Experiments have shown that when animals are deprived of REM sleep after participating in a training session, they learn the task more slowly; thus, REM sleep deprivation retards memory formation. In addition, when animals learn a new task the amount of time they spend in REM sleep increases, as if the learning increases the need for this stage of sleep. For example, Bloch, Hennevin, and Leconte

(1977) gave rats daily training trials in a complex maze. They found that the experience enhanced subsequent REM sleep. Moreover, daily performance was related to subsequent REM sleep. The lower curve in Figure 9.7 shows REM sleep as a percentage of total sleep. The upper curve illustrates the animals' performance in the maze. You can see that the largest increase in running speed (possibly representing the largest increase in learning) was accompanied by the largest amount of REM sleep. Also note that once the task was well learned (after day 6), REM sleep declined back to baseline levels. (See *Figure 9.7*.)

In contrast to the studies with laboratory animals, studies with human subjects show that REM sleep deprivation has only a small effect on a person's ability to learn or to remember what was previously learned. But several studies have found that learning can affect the amount of REM sleep that a person obtains. For example, several studies have found that retarded children engage in less REM sleep than normal children and that intellectually gifted children engage in more (Dujardin, Guerrien, and Leconte, 1990). In addition, Smith and Lapp (1987) found that REM sleep of college students increased during exam time, when they presumably were spending more time learning new information.

A few studies suggest that learning related to emotionally significant material may be affected by REM sleep deprivation. Greenberg, Pillard, and Pearlman (1972) had subjects view a film that generally produces anxiety in the observers (a particularly gruesome circumcision rite performed with stone knives by members of a remote South Sea Island tribe). Normally, people who see the film twice show less anxiety during the second viewing. The investigators found that subjects who were permitted to engage in REM sleep between the first and second viewings of the film showed less anxiety the second time than subjects who were deprived of REM sleep. In addition, Breger, Hunter, and Lane (1971) found that the dream content of subjects viewing the film was affected by the anxiety-producing material. Taken together, the studies suggest that REM sleep (and perhaps the dreaming that occurs then) somehow assists people to come to grips with newly learned information that has emo-

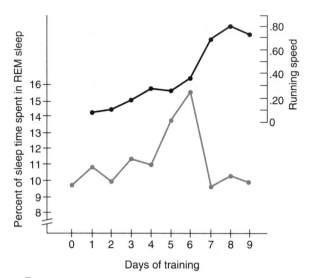

FIGURE 9.7

Percentage of sleep time spent in REM sleep (lower curve) as a function of maze-learning performance (upper curve).

(From Bloch, V., Hennevin, E., and Leconte, P., in *Neurobiology of Sleep and Memory,* edited by R.R. Drucker-Colín and J.L. McGaugh. New York: Academic Press, 1978.)

tional consequences. As we all know, things generally seem less disturbing after a good night's sleep.

Some studies with animals also suggest that REM sleep may be related to emotional stress. Rampin et al. (1991) immobilized rats for 2 hours by placing them in a small plastic tube. Although such treatment is harmless and painless, the animals struggle and show signs of distress. During the next 10 hours, the stressed rats spent 92 percent more time in REM sleep than control rats that were handled gently for 2 hours or simply left in their cages. The results could mean (but certainly do not prove) that REM sleep helps repair the effects of stress. The authors suggest that the increased REM sleep may have been triggered by a stress-related hormone. (Stress-related hormones are discussed in more detail in Chapter 11.)

The calming effect of REM sleep appears to be contradicted by a puzzling phenomenon. The symptoms of people with severe, psychotic depression are *reduced* when they are deprived of REM sleep. In addition, treatments that reduce the symptoms of depression, such as antidepressant drugs and electroconvulsive therapy, also suppress REM sleep. (These results will be discussed in more detail in Chapter 17.) If REM sleep helps people assimilate emotionally relevant information, why should REM sleep deprivation relieve the symptoms of people who are suffering from a serious emotional disorder? Unfortunately, we do not have an answer for this question yet.

A particularly interesting case of brain damage suggests that whatever the functions of REM sleep may be, they do not appear to be necessary for survival. Lavie et al. (1984) reported that a 33-year-old man whose head was injured by shrapnel at age 20 engaged in almost no REM sleep. In the sleep laboratory the man slept an average of 4.5 hours. On three of eight nights he engaged in no REM sleep; the average on the other five nights was approximately 6 minutes. The pieces of metal damaged the pons, left temporal lobe, and left thalamus. As we shall see later in this chapter, the pons seems to be the part of the brain that controls REM sleep. The almost complete lack of REM sleep did not appear to cause serious side effects. After receiving his injury, the man completed high school, attended law school, and began practicing law. (I have a feeling that I could work in a lawyer joke here, but I think I'll refrain.)

⫿⫿⫿ *INTERIM SUMMARY*

The two principal explanations for sleep are that sleep serves as an adaptive response or that it provides a period of restoration. The fact that a species' degree of safety and rate of metabolism are related to the amount of sleep it engages in supports the adaptive hypothesis, but the fact that all vertebrates sleep, including some that would seem to be better off without it, does not.

The effects of several days of sleep deprivation are not devastating to humans; the primary finding is intense sleepiness, difficulty performing tasks that require prolonged concentration, and perceptual distortions and (sometimes) mild hallucinations. These effects suggest that sleep deprivation does impair cerebral functioning. Deep slow-wave sleep

appears to be the most important stage, and perhaps its function is to permit the brain (but not necessarily the rest of the body) to recuperate. Animals who are sleep-deprived eventually die, but we cannot be sure that the stress is caused by lack of sleep or by the procedure needed to keep them awake.

Exercise can increase the amount of slow-wave sleep a person receives, but the effect appears to occur only if the brain temperature rises; the effect can be abolished by cooling the person during exercise or induced by warming the head. Perhaps, then, the fundamental cause is an increase in brain metabolism. Growth hormone normally is secreted only during slow-wave sleep, but the significance of this phenomenon is uncertain, given the fact that the blood level of amino acids during sleep is normally low in humans.

The function of REM sleep is even less understood than that of slow-wave sleep. It may promote vigilance, learning, species-typical reprogramming, or brain development. So far, the evidence is inconclusive, although several studies have shown a modest relation between REM sleep and learning.

DISORDERS OF SLEEP

Insomnia

Insomnia is a problem that is said to affect at least 20 percent of the population at some time (Raybin and Detre, 1969). At the onset I must emphasize that there is no single definition of insomnia that can apply to all people. The amount of sleep that individuals require is quite variable. A short sleeper may feel fine with 5 hours; a long sleeper may still feel unrefreshed after 10 hours of sleep. Insomnia must be defined in relation to a person's particular sleep needs. Some short sleepers have sought medical assistance because they thought that they were supposed to get more sleep, even though they felt fine. These people should be reassured that whatever amount of sleep seems to be enough *is* enough. Meddis, Pearson, and Langford (1973) reported the case of a 70-year-old woman who slept approximately 1 hour each day (documented by sessions in a sleep laboratory). She felt fine and was of the opinion that most people "wasted much time" in bed.

Ironically, the most important cause of insomnia seems to be sleeping medication. Insomnia is not a disease that can be corrected with a medicine, in the way that diabetes can be treated with insulin. Insomnia is a symptom. If it is caused by pain or discomfort, the physical ailment that leads to the sleeplessness should be treated. If it is secondary to personal problems or psychological disorders, these problems should be dealt with directly. Patients who receive a sleeping medication develop a tolerance to the drug and suffer rebound symptoms if it is withdrawn (Weitzman, 1981). That is, the drug loses its effectiveness, so the patient requests larger doses from the physician. If the patient attempts to sleep without the accustomed medication or even takes a smaller dose one night, he or she is likely to experience a withdrawal effect: a severe disturbance of sleep. The patient becomes convinced that the insomnia is even worse than before and turns to more medication for relief. This common syndrome is called **drug dependency insomnia.** Kales et al. (1979) found that withdrawal of some sleeping medications produced a rebound insomnia after the drugs were used for as few as three nights.

Most patients who receive a prescription for a sleeping medication are given one on the basis of their own description of their symptoms. That is, they tell their physician that they sleep very little at night, and the drug is prescribed on the basis of this testimony. Very few patients are observed during a night's sleep in a sleep laboratory; thus, insomnia is one of the few medical problems that physicians treat without having direct clinical evidence for its existence. But studies on the sleep of people who complain of insomnia show that most of them grossly underestimate the amount of time they actually sleep. The U.S. Institute of Medicine (1979) found that most insomniacs, even without sleeping medication, fall asleep in less than 30 minutes and sleep for at least 6 hours. *With* sleeping medication they obtained less than a 15-minute reduction in falling asleep, and their sleep length was increased by only about 30 minutes. Given the unfortunate side effects, sleeping medication does not seem to be worthwhile.

Some people suffer from an interesting, but unfortunate, form of "pseudoinsomnia": They dream that they are awake. They do not dream that they are running around in some Alice-in-Wonderland fantasy but that they are lying in bed, trying unsuccessfully to fall asleep. In the morning their memories are of a night of insomnia, and they feel as unrefreshed as if they had really been awake.

Another form of insomnia—a true one, not a pseudoinsomnia—is caused by the inability to sleep and breathe at the same time. Patients with this disorder, called **sleep apnea,** fall asleep and then cease to breathe. (Nearly all people, especially people who snore, have occasional episodes of sleep apnea, but not to the extent that it interferes with sleep.) During a period of sleep apnea the level of carbon dioxide in the blood stimulates chemoreceptors (neurons that detect the presence of certain chemicals), and the person wakes up, gasping for air. The oxygen level of the blood returns to normal, the person falls asleep, and the whole cycle begins again. Fortunately, many cases of sleep apnea are caused by an obstruction of the airway that can be corrected surgically or relieved by a device that attaches to the sleeper's face and provides pressurized air that keeps the airway open (Sher, 1990; Westbrook, 1990).

Occasionally, infants are found dead in their cribs without any apparent signs of illness, victims of *sudden infant death syndrome (SIDS)*. Many investigators believe that one of the principal causes of SIDS is sleep apnea; in these cases, however, the infants are *not* awakened by a high level of carbon dioxide in the blood.

Evidence suggests that a susceptibility to SIDS is inherited; parents and siblings of some infants who have died of SIDS do not respond normally to increases in carbon dioxide (Kelly et al., 1980; Schiffman et al., 1980). Often infants who die of SIDS show signs of a low-grade illness, which may increase the tissue need for oxygen while simultaneously depressing respiratory mechanisms. Many infants' lives have been saved by monitoring devices that sound an alarm when a susceptible infant stops breathing during sleep, thus waking the parents in time for them to revive the child.

Problems Associated with REM Sleep

Narcolepsy (*narke* means "numbness," and *lepsis* means "seizure") is a neurological disorder characterized by sleep (or some of its components) at inappropriate times. The symptoms can be described in terms of what we know about the phenomena of sleep. The primary symptom of narcolepsy is the **sleep attack**. The narcoleptic sleep attack is an overwhelming urge to sleep that can happen at any time but occurs most often under monotonous, boring conditions. Sleep (which appears to be entirely normal) usually lasts for 2 to 5 minutes. The person usually wakes up feeling refreshed.

Another symptom of narcolepsy—in fact, the most striking one—is **cataplexy** (from *kata*, "down," and *plexis*, "stroke"). During a cataplectic attack a person will suddenly wilt and fall like a sack of flour. The person will lie there, *fully conscious,* for a few seconds to several minutes. What apparently happens is that one of the phenomena of REM sleep—muscular paralysis—occurs at an inappropriate time. You will recall that the EMG indicates a loss of muscle tonus during REM sleep. As we will see later, this loss of tonus is caused by massive inhibition of motor neurons. When muscular paralysis occurs during waking, the victim of a cataplectic attack falls as suddenly as if a switch had been thrown.

Cataplexy is quite different from a narcoleptic sleep attack; cataplexy is usually precipitated by strong emotion or by sudden physical effort, especially if the patient is caught unawares. Laughter, anger, or trying to catch a suddenly thrown object can trigger a cataplectic attack. Common situations that bring on cataplexy are attempting to discipline one's children or making love (an awkward time to become paralyzed!).

REM sleep paralysis sometimes intrudes into waking, but at a time that does not present any physical danger—just before or just after normal sleep, when a person is already lying down. This symptom of narcolepsy is referred to as **sleep paralysis,** an inability to move just before the onset of sleep or upon waking in the morning. A person can be snapped out of sleep paralysis by being touched or by hearing someone call his or her name. Some-

times, the mental components of REM sleep intrude into sleep paralysis; that is, the person dreams while lying awake, paralyzed. These episodes, called **hypnagogic hallucinations,** are often alarming or even terrifying. (The term *hypnagogic* comes from the Greek words *hupnos,* "sleep," and *agogos,* "leading.")

Almost certainly, narcolepsy is produced by a brain abnormality that causes the neural mechanisms responsible for various aspects of REM sleep to become active at inappropriate times. Indeed, Rechtschaffen et al. (1963) found that narcoleptic patients generally skip the slow-wave sleep that normally begins a night's sleep; instead, they go directly into REM sleep from waking. This finding suggests that in the brains of narcoleptics, the neural mechanisms that produce REM sleep are poorly controlled.

Narcolepsy appears to be a genetic disorder. Kessler, Guilleminault, and Dement (1974) found that relatives of narcoleptic patients are sixty times more likely to have this disorder themselves, as compared with people from the general population; and almost all narcoleptics have a particular antigen, called HLA-DR2, in their blood (Juji et al., 1984). Researchers have even successfully bred dogs that are afflicted with narcolepsy. (See *Figure 9.8.*) The dogs show evidence of biochemical abnormalities in regions of the brain that control REM sleep (Miller et al., 1990; Nishino et al., 1991). (These regions will be discussed later in this chapter.)

The symptoms of narcolepsy can be successfully treated with drugs, which suggests that the disorder may result from abnormalities in neurotransmitter synthesis, release, or reuptake or receptor sensitivity (Aldrich, 1990). Sleep attacks are diminished by stimulants such as amphetamine, a catecholamine agonist; and the REM sleep phenomena (cataplexy, sleep paralysis, and hypnagogic hallucinations) can be alleviated by imipramine, which facilitates both serotonergic and catecholaminergic activity. Often, the drugs are given together.

A few years ago, Schenck et al. (1986) reported the existence of an interesting disorder. The formal name is *REM sleep behavioral disorder,* but a better name is **REM without atonia.** (*Atonia* refers to the lack of muscular activity seen during paralysis.) As you now know, REM sleep is accompanied by paral-

(a)

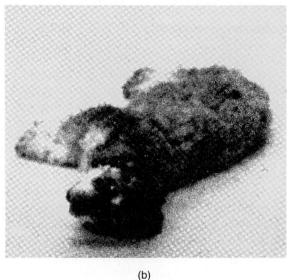

(b)

FIGURE 9.8

Dogs bred for vulnerability to cataplexy. (a) Attack beginning. (b) Attack complete; recovery is beginning.

(Sleep Disorder Clinic, Stanford University.)

ysis. Despite the fact that the motor cortex and subcortical motor systems are extremely active (McCarley and Hobson, 1979), people are unable to move at this time. The fact that they are dreaming suggests the possibility that but for the paralysis, they would act out their dreams. Indeed, they would. The behavior of people who exhibit REM without atonia corresponds with the contents of their dreams. Consider the following case:

> I was a halfback playing football, and after the quarterback received the ball from the center he lateraled it sideways to me and I'm supposed to go around end and cut back over tackle and—this is very vivid—as I cut back over tackle there is this big 280-pound tackle waiting, so I, according to football rules, was to give him my shoulder and bounce him out of the way . . . when I came to I was standing in front of our dresser and I had [gotten up out of bed and run and] knocked lamps, mirrors and everything off the dresser, hit my head against the wall and my knee against the dresser. (Schenck et al., 1986, p. 294)

As we shall see later in this chapter, the neural circuitry responsible for the paralysis that accompanies REM sleep has been discovered in studies with laboratory animals. In humans, REM without atonia seems to be produced by damage to the brain stem—apparently to the same regions (Culebras and Moore, 1989). The symptoms of REM without atonia are the opposite of those of cataplexy; that is, rather than exhibit paralysis outside REM sleep, patients with REM without atonia *fail* to exhibit paralysis *during* REM sleep. In fact, the drugs used to treat the symptoms of cataplexy will aggravate the symptoms of REM without atonia (Schenck and Mahowald, 1992).

Problems Associated with Slow-Wave Sleep

Some maladaptive behaviors occur during slow-wave sleep, especially during its deepest phase, stage 4. These behaviors include bedwetting *(nocturnal enuresis)*, sleepwalking *(somnambulism)*, and night terrors *(pavor nocturnus)*. All three events occur most frequently in children. Often bedwetting can be cured by training methods, such as having a special electronic circuit ring a bell when the first few drops of urine are detected in the bed sheet (a few drops usually precede the ensuing flood). Night terrors consist of anguished screams, trembling, a rapid pulse, and usually no memory for what caused the terror. Night terrors and somnambulism usually cure themselves as the child gets older. Neither of these phenomena is related to REM sleep; a sleep-walking person is *not* acting out a dream. Most authorities firmly advise that the best treatment for these two disorders is no treatment at all. There is no evidence that they are associated (at least in childhood) with mental disorders or personality variables.

||||| INTERIM SUMMARY

Although many people believe that they have insomnia—that they do not obtain as much sleep as they would like—insomnia is not a disease. Insomnia can be caused by depression, pain, illness, or even excited anticipation of a pleasurable event. Far too many people receive sleeping medications, which often lead to a condition called drug dependency insomnia. Sometimes, insomnia is caused by sleep apnea, which can often be corrected surgically. When sleep apnea occurs in infants, it can lead to sudden infant death; hence the respiration rate of susceptible infants should be monitored electronically until they are old enough to be past danger.

Narcolepsy is characterized by four symptoms. *Sleep attacks* consist of overwhelming urges to sleep for a few minutes. *Cataplexy* is sudden paralysis, during which the person remains conscious. *Sleep paralysis* is similar to cataplexy, but it occurs just before sleep or upon waking. *Hypnagogic hallucinations* are dreams that occur during periods of sleep paralysis, just before a night's sleep. Sleep attacks are treated with stimulants such as amphetamine, and the other symptoms are treated with drugs such as imipramine. Studies with narcoleptic dogs suggest that the disorder may involve biochemical abnormalities in the brain. Another disorder associated with REM sleep, REM without atonia, occurs because of damage to brain stem mechanisms that produce paralysis during REM sleep.

During slow-wave sleep, especially during stage 4, some people are afflicted by bedwetting (nocturnal enuresis), sleepwalking (somnambulism), or night terrors (pavor nocturnus). These problems are most common in children, who usually out-grow them. Only if they occur in adults do they suggest the existence of a physical or psychological disorder.

BIOLOGICAL CLOCKS

MUCH OF OUR BEHAVIOR FOLLOWS REGULAR rhythms. For example, we saw that the stages of sleep are organized around a 90-minute cycle of REM and slow-wave sleep. The same rhythm continues during the day as the basic rest-activity cycle (BRAC). And, of course, our daily pattern of sleep and waking follows a 24-hour cycle. In recent years investigators have learned much about the neural mechanisms responsible for these rhythms.

Circadian Rhythms and Zeitgebers

Daily rhythms in behavior and physiological processes are found throughout the plant and animal world. These cycles are generally called **circadian rhythms.** (*Circa* means "about," and *dies* means "day"; therefore, a circadian rhythm is one that varies on a cycle of approximately 24 hours.) Some of these rhythms are passive responses to changes in illumination. However, other rhythms are controlled by mechanisms within the organism—by "internal clocks." For example, Figure 9.9 shows the activity of a rat during various conditions of illumination. Each horizontal line represents 24 hours. Vertical tick marks represent the animal's activity in a running wheel. The upper portion of the figure shows the activity of the rat during a normal day-night cycle, with alternating 12-hour periods of light and dark. Notice that the animal is active during the night, which is normal for a rat. (See *Figure 9.9.*)

Next, the dark-light cycle was shifted by 6 hours; the animal's activity cycle quickly followed the change. (See *Figure 9.9.*) Finally, dim lights were left on continuously. The cyclical pattern in the rat's activity remained. Because there were no cycles in the rat's environment, the source of rhythmicity must be located within the animal; that is, the animal must contain an internal, biological clock. You can see that the rat's clock was not set precisely to 24 hours; when the illumination was held constant, the clock ran a

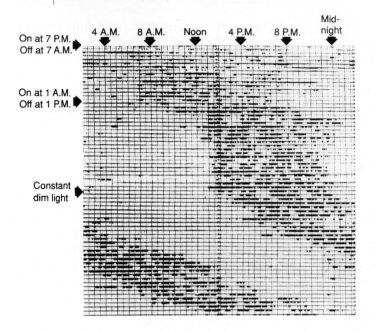

On at 7 P.M.
Off at 7 A.M.

On at 1 A.M.
Off at 1 P.M.

Constant
dim light

4 A.M.   8 A.M.   Noon   4 P.M.   8 P.M.   Midnight

FIGURE 9.9

Wheel-running activity of a rat. Note that the animal's activity occurs at "night" (that is, during the 12 hours the light is off) and that the active period is reset when the light period is changed. When the animal is maintained in constant dim illumination, it displays a free-running activity cycle of approximately 25 hours.

(From Groblewski, T.A., Nuñez, A., and Gold, R.M. Paper presented at the meeting of the Eastern Psychological Association, April 1980.)

bit slow. The animal began its bout of activity almost 1 hour later each day. (See **Figure 9.9**.)

The phenomenon illustrated in Figure 9.9 is typical of the circadian rhythms shown by many species. A free-running clock, with a cycle a little longer than 24 hours, controls some biological functions—in this case, motor activity. Regular daily variation in the level of illumination (that is, sunlight and darkness) normally keeps the clock adjusted to 24 hours. In the parlance of scientists who study circadian rhythms, light serves as a **zeitgeber** (German for "time giver"); it synchronizes the endogenous rhythm. Studies with many species of animals have shown that if they are maintained in constant darkness, a brief flash of light will reset their internal clock, advancing or retarding it, depending upon when the light flash occurs (Aschoff, 1979).

Like other animals, humans exhibit circadian rhythms. Our normal period of inactivity begins several hours after the start of the dark portion of the day-night cycle and persists for a variable amount of time into the light portion. Without the benefits of modern civilization we would probably go to sleep earlier and get up earlier than we do; we use artificial lights to delay our bedtime and window shades to extend our time for sleep. Under constant illumination our biological clocks will run free, gaining or losing time like a watch that runs too slow or too fast. Different people have different cycle lengths, but most people in that situation will begin to live a "day" that is approximately 25 hours long. This works out quite well, because the morning light simply resets the clock.

Role of the Suprachiasmatic Nucleus

Researchers working independently in two laboratories (Moore and Eichler, 1972; Stephan and Zucker, 1972) discovered that the primary biological clock of the rat is located in the **suprachiasmatic nucleus** (SCN) of the hypothalamus; they found that lesions disrupted circadian rhythms of wheel running, drinking, and hormonal secretion. The SCN also provides the primary control over the timing of sleep cycles. Rats are nocturnal animals; they sleep during the day and forage and feed at night. Lesions of the SCN abolish this pattern; sleep occurs in bouts randomly dispersed throughout both day and night (Ibuka and Kawamura, 1975; Stephan and Nuñez, 1977). However, rats with SCN lesions still obtain the same amount of sleep that normal animals do. The lesions disrupt the circadian pattern but do not affect the total amount of sleep.

Figure 9.10 shows the suprachiasmatic nuclei in a transverse section through the hypothalamus of a mouse; they appear as two clusters of dark-staining neurons at the base of the brain, just above the optic chiasm. (See *Figure 9.10.*) The suprachiasmatic nuclei of the rat consist of approximately ten thousand small neurons, tightly packed into a volume of between 0.1 and 0.3 mm^3 (Meijer and Rietveld, 1989). The dendrites of these neurons form synapses with one another—a phenomenon that is found only in this part of the hypothalamus and that undoubtedly relates to the special function of these nuclei. A group of neurons is found clustered around the capillaries that serve the SCN. These neurons contain a large amount of rough endoplasmic reticulum, which suggests that they may be neurosecretory cells (Card, Riley, and Moore, 1980; Moore, Card, and Riley, 1980). Thus, some of the control that the SCN exerts over other parts of the brain may be accomplished by the secretion of neuromodulators.

Because light is the primary zeitgeber for most mammals' activity cycles, one would expect that the SCN receives fibers from the visual system. Indeed, autoradiographic techniques have revealed a direct projection of fibers from the retina to the SCN (Hendrickson, Wagoner, and Cowan, 1972). If you look carefully at **Figure 9.10**, you can see small dark spots within the optic chiasm, just ventral and medial to the base of the SCN; these are cell bodies of oligodendroglia that serve axons that enter the SCN and provide information from the retina.

As we saw earlier, pulses of light reset an animal's circadian rhythms. So do pulses of electrical stimulation delivered directly to the SCN; presumably, these pulses simulate the effects of light (Rusak and Groos, 1982). Light pulses that reset an animal's circadian rhythms also trigger the production of Fos protein in the SCN, which indicates that the light initiates a period of neural activity (Rusak et al., 1990, 1992). (The significance of the Fos protein was discussed in Chapter 5.) The administration of a drug that blocks glutamate receptors suppresses the behavioral response to light pulses and abolishes the production of Fos protein in all but a small region of the SCN; thus, the input to the SCN from the retina appears to involve the release of an excitatory amino acid (Abe, Rusak, and Robertson, 1991; Vindlacheruvu et al., 1992). (See *Figure 9.11.*) In fact, an injection of glutamic acid directly into the SCN causes a shift in the timing of circadian rhythms, just as pulses of light or electrical stimulation do (Meijer, van der Zee, and Dietz, 1988).

The SCN also receives visual input indirectly, from the *intergeniculate leaflet* and the *ventral lateral geniculate nucleus* (Card and Moore, 1982; Morin, Blanchard, and Moore, 1992). (You will recall from Chapter 6 that the *dorsal* lateral geniculate nucleus sends visual information to the striate cortex.) The input from the thalamus is mediated by a transmitter substance called **neuropeptide Y**. The geniculohypothalamic pathways appear to play a role in the effects of light on the SCN; electrical stimulation of

FIGURE 9.10

A frontal section through a mouse brain, showing the location and appearance of the suprachiasmatic nuclei. Cresyl violet stain.

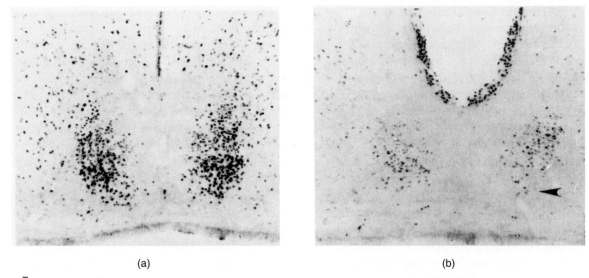

(a)   (b)

FIGURE 9.11

A frontal section through the suprachiasmatic nuclei of two hamster brains stained for the Fos protein. The animals received an injection into the third ventricle 10 minutes before being presented with a pulse of light. (a) Control animal, who received an injection of a placebo. (b) Experimental animal, who received an injection of a drug that blocks glutamate receptors.

(From Vindlacheruvu, R.R., Ebling, F.J.P., Maywood, E.S., and Hastings, M.H. *European Journal of Neuroscience,* 1992, *4,* 673–679. Reprinted with permission of Oxford University Press.)

the intergeniculate leaflet or microinfusion of neuropeptide Y directly into the SCN shifts the timing of circadian rhythms (Albers and Ferris, 1984; Rusak, Meijer, and Harrington, 1989). Damage to the geniculohypothalamic pathways reduces, but does not abolish, the effects of changes in the light-dark cycle on an animal's circadian rhythms (Harrington and Rusak, 1986). Thus, the direct pathway from the retina to the SCN and the indirect pathway through the thalamus both mediate the effects of light as a zeitgeber. Undoubtedly, there are some differences in their functions, but they have not yet been discovered.

How does the SCN control drinking, eating, sleep cycles, and hormone secretion? Neurons of the SCN project caudally to the midbrain and to other hypothalamic nuclei, dorsally to other diencephalic regions, and rostrally to other hypothalamic nuclei and to the septum. If all of these connections are severed by large semicircular knife cuts around most of the SCN, circadian rhythms are disrupted (Meijer and Rietveld, 1989).

We cannot say that the SCN controls all the physiological and behavioral rhythms by means of direct neural connections. For one thing, knife cuts do not simply sever axons; they also cut blood vessels and interrupt patterns of blood flow. In addition, several pieces of evidence suggest that some of the control of the SCN over the rest of the brain may be mediated by the secretion of neuromodulators. Lehman et al. (1987) destroyed the SCN and then transplanted in their place a new set of suprachiasmatic nuclei obtained from donor animals. The grafts succeeded in reestablishing circadian rhythms, even though very few efferent connections were observed. Ralph et al. (1990) found that such transplants could establish circadian rhythms in motor activity within six or seven days. Thus, either the SCN needs very few connections with the rest of the brain to exert its control over activity cycles or that control is mediated through the secretion of neuromodulators.

Although experimental studies obviously have not been done, it appears likely that the primary

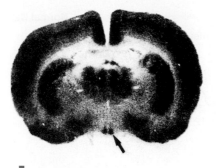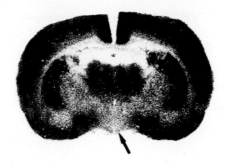

FIGURE 9.12

Autoradiographs of transverse sections through the brains of rats that had been injected with carbon 14-labeled 2-deoxyglucose during the day (left) and the night (right). The dark region at the base of the brain (arrows) indicates increased metabolic activity of the suprachiasmatic nuclei.

(From Schwartz, W.J., and Gainer, H. *Science*, 1977, *197*, 1089–1091. Reprinted with permission.)

biological clock that controls human sleep and waking cycles is also located in the SCN. Humans certainly have circadian rhythms, and these rhythms are affected by exposure to light—even ordinary room light (Czeisler et al., 1989). Anatomical studies clearly show that humans have suprachiasmatic nuclei (Lydic et al., 1980), and a study using the carbocyanine dye, DiI, found that human brains contain a pathway from the retina to the SCN (Friedman et al., 1991). (DiI was described in Chapter 5.) In addition, brain tumors that damage the region of the SCN have been reported to produce disorders in sleep-waking cycles (Fulton and Bailey, 1929). Of course, these tumors damage a wide area of the hypothalamus, and we cannot be sure that the SCN damage is critical.

The Nature of the Clock

All clocks must have a time base. Mechanical clocks use flywheels or pendulums; electronic clocks use quartz crystals. The SCN, too, must contain a physiological mechanism that parses time into units. So far, we do not know what this mechanism is.

Several studies have demonstrated circadian rhythms in the activity of the suprachiasmatic nucleus. A study by Schwartz and Gainer (1977) nicely demonstrated day-night fluctuations in the activity of the SCN. These investigators injected rats with radioactive 2-deoxyglucose (2-DG). As you will recall, this chemical is structurally similar to ordinary glucose; thus, it is taken up by cells that are metabolically active. However, it cannot be utilized, nor can it leave the cell. Therefore, metabolically active cells will accumulate radioactivity. (This technique was also used in a study on the visual mechanisms of the cerebral cortex, reported in Chapter 6.)

The investigators injected some rats with radioactive 2-DG during the day and injected others at night. The animals were then killed, and autoradiographs of cross sections through the brain were prepared. Figure 9.12 shows photographs of two of these cross sections. Note the evidence of radioactivity (and hence a high metabolic rate) in the SCN of the brain that was injected during the day (*left*). (See *Figure 9.12.*)

Schwartz and his colleagues (Schwartz et al., 1983) found a similar pattern of activity in the SCN of squirrel monkeys, which are diurnal animals (active during the day). These results suggest that it is not differences in the SCN that determine whether an animal is nocturnal or diurnal but differences elsewhere in the brain. The SCN keeps track of day and night, but it is up to mechanisms located elsewhere to determine when the animal is to be awake or asleep.

Several studies have succeeded in keeping pieces of brain tissue containing the suprachiasmatic nucleus alive in a culture medium. These studies

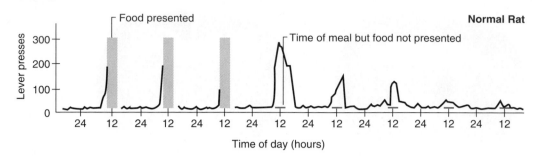

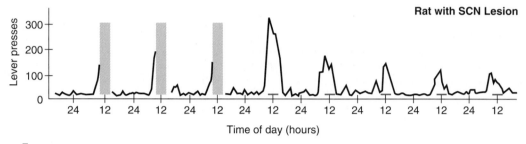

FIGURE 9.13

Anticipation of a meal. After being fed at the same time each day, both a normal rat (top) and a rat with bilateral SCN lesions (bottom) increase their lever-press-ing activity at the customary time for feeding.

(From Boulos, Z., Rosenwasser, A.M., and Terman, M. *Behavioral Brain Research,* 1980, *1,* 39–65. Reprinted with permission.)

have shown that the activity of single neurons in these slices show circadian rhythms in their rate of action potentials and their levels of Fos protein (Bos and Mirmiran, 1990; Prosser and Gillette, 1991). These studies indicate that the SCN contains all that is necessary for generating the "ticks" of the daily clock and that neural and chemical communication with the rest of the brain is unnecessary.

The "ticking" of the biological clock within the SCN could involve interactions of circuits of neu-rons, or it could be intrinsic to individual neurons themselves. Evidence suggests the latter—that each neuron contains a clock. Moore and Bernstein (1989) studied the prenatal and postnatal develop-ment of the SCN in the rat. Previous reports (Rep-pert and Schwartz, 1984) had shown that circadian rhythms in glucose metabolism are found in these nuclei prenatally, as early as the nineteenth day after conception. However, Moore and Bernstein found that at this time, the SCN contains fewer than one synapse per neuron, which seems to indicate that the neurons are "ticking" independently. In addition,

Schwartz, Gross, and Morton (1987) found that continuous infusion of TTX (tetrodotoxin), a drug that prevents action potentials by blocking voltage-dependent sodium channels, abolishes circadian rhythms. However, the drug does not appear to stop the "ticking" of the individual cells; when the infu-sions are stopped, the animals' circadian rhythms continued as if the clock had been running the whole time.

Evidence for Other Biological Clocks

The SCN is not the only biological clock in the mammalian nervous system. For example, the basic rest-activity cycle (which controls the occurrence of REM sleep) is considerably shorter than 24 hours; in humans, it has a 90-minute period.

Animals who are fed on a regular daily schedule will soon become active just before the feeding time. This anticipation obviously depends upon some internal clock, because it occurs in the absence of environmental cues. Boulos, Rosenwasser, and Ter-man (1980) found that rats showed this anticipation even after their SCN was destroyed; therefore, another clock must be able to perform this function. (See *Figure 9.13.*)

Although the SCN has an intrinsic rhythm of approximately 24 hours, it plays a role in much longer rhythms. Male hamsters show annual rhythms of testosterone secretion, which appear to be based upon the amount of light that occurs each day. Their breeding season begins as the day length increases and ends when it decreases. Lesions of the SCN abolish these annual breeding cycles; the animals' testes then secrete testosterone all year (Rusak and Morin, 1976). Possibly, the lesions disrupt these annual cycles because they destroy the 24-hour clock against which the daily light period is measured to determine the season. That is, if the light period is considerably shorter than 12 hours, the season is winter; if it is considerably longer than 12 hours, the season is summer.

The control of seasonal rhythms involves another part of the brain: the **pineal gland** (Morin and Dark, 1992). This structure sits on top of the midbrain, just in front of the cerebellum. (See *Figure 9.14.*) The pineal gland secretes a hormone celled **melatonin,** so named because it has the ability in certain animals (primarily fish, reptiles, and amphibians) to turn the skin temporarily dark. (The dark color is produced by a chemical known as *melanin.*) In mammals, melatonin controls seasonal rhythms. Neurons in the SCN make synaptic connections with neurons in the *paraventricular nucleus of the hypothalamus* (the PVN). The axons of these neurons travel all the way to the spinal cord, where they form synapses with preganglionic neurons of the sympathetic nervous system. The postganglionic neurons innervate the pineal gland and control the secretion of melatonin.

In response to input from the SCN, the pineal gland secretes melatonin during the night. This melatonin acts back on various structures in the brain (including the SCN) and controls hormones, physiological processes, and behaviors that show seasonal variations; during long nights a large amount of melatonin is secreted, and the animals go into the winter phase of their cycle. Lesions of the SCN, the paraventricular nucleus (PVN), or the pineal gland disrupt seasonal rhythms that are controlled by day length—and so do knife cuts that

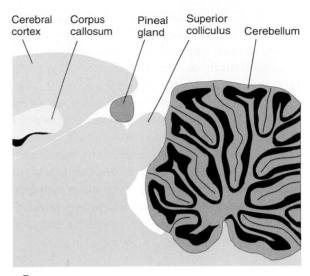

FIGURE 9.14

The pineal gland, located on the dorsal surface of the midbrain.

(Adapted from Paxinos, G., and Watson, C. *The Rat Brain in Stereotaxic Coordinates.* Sydney: Academic Press, 1982.)

interrupt the neural connection between the SCN and the PVN, which indicates that this is one function of the SCN that is not mediated by the release of a chemical. Furthermore, transplants of fetal suprachiasmatic nuclei will not restore seasonal rhythms, because the transplanted tissue does not establish neural connections with the PVN (Ralph and Lehman, 1991).

Much progress has been made in the investigation of the neural mechanisms of biological rhythms during the past few years. The unanswered questions concern the nature of the physiological processes that provide the underlying rhythm, the location of biological clocks other than the SCN, and the means by which these clocks influence cyclic behaviors such as sleep and waking.

INTERIM SUMMARY

Our daily lives are characterized by cycles in physical activity, sleep, body temperature, secretion of hormones, and many other physiological changes. Circadian rhythms—those with a period of approximately one day—are controlled by biological clocks in the brain. The principal biological clock appears to be located in the suprachiasmatic nuclei of the hypothalamus; lesions of these nuclei disrupt most circadian rhythms, and the activity of neurons located there correlates with the day-night cycle. Light serves as a zeitgeber for most circadian rhythms. That is, the biological clocks tend to run a bit slow, with a period of approximately 25 hours. The sight of sunlight in the morning is conveyed from the retina to the SCN, resetting the clock to the start of a new cycle. We do not know how biological clocks keep time, although we do know that individual neurons, rather than circuits of neurons, are responsible for the "ticks."

PHYSIOLOGICAL MECHANISMS OF SLEEP AND WAKING

SO FAR, I HAVE DISCUSSED THE NATURE OF SLEEP, its functions, problems associated with it, and the control of biological rhythms. Now it is time to examine what researchers have discovered about the physiological mechanisms that are responsible for the behavior of sleep, and for its counterpart, alert wakefulness. But before I do so, I must emphasize that sleep does not occur simply because neurons get tired and begin to fire more slowly. Like other behaviors, sleep occurs when certain neural circuits become *active*.

Chemical Control of Sleep

As we have seen, sleep is *regulated;* that is, if an organism is deprived of slow-wave sleep or REM sleep, the organism will make up at least part of the missed sleep when permitted to do so. In addition, the amount of slow-wave sleep that a person obtains during a daytime nap is deducted from the amount of slow-wave sleep he or she obtains the next night (Karacan et al., 1970). These facts suggests that some physiological mechanism monitors the amount of sleep that an organism receives. What might this mechanism be?

The most obvious explanation would be that the body produces either *sleep-promoting substances* during wakefulness or *wakefulness-promoting* substances during sleep. For example, a sleep-promoting substance might accumulate in the blood during wakefulness and be destroyed during sleep. The longer someone is awake, the longer he or she has to sleep in order to deactivate this substance. Obviously, because slow-wave sleep and REM sleep are mostly independent of each other, there would have to be two substances, one for each stage of sleep. Alternatively, sleep could be regulated by a *wakefulness-promoting* substance. This substance would be used up during wakefulness and be manufactured only during sleep. A *decline* in the blood level of this substance would cause sleepiness.

Evidence suggests that these hypotheses are false. De Andres et al. (1976) attached a second head to a dog and found that the two brains slept independently. If sleep and wakefulness were controlled by factors present in the blood, one would expect that the sleep cycles of the two brains would be synchronized. (Of course, the second head was neurally isolated from the rest of the body and had no control of the animal's behavior.) But perhaps the strongest evidence against a hypothetical blood-borne sleep-promoting (or wakefulness-promoting) substance comes from the sleep of dolphins and porpoises. As we saw earlier, the cerebral hemispheres of these animals sleep at different times (Mukhametov, 1984). If their sleep were controlled by *blood-borne* chemicals, the hemispheres should sleep at the same time.

These observations suggest that if sleep is controlled by chemicals, these chemicals are produced within the brain and remain there. As we saw, evidence seems to support the hypothesis that slow-wave sleep serves as a period of rest and recuperation for the cerebral hemispheres. Perhaps chemicals produced by the brain serve as neuromodulators, activating neural circuits responsible for sleep (or deactivating circuits necessary for wakefulness).

In a fifty-two-page article that cites over four hundred papers, Borbély and Tobler (1989) report that the search for sleep-promoting substances within the brain has not yet yielded unambiguous results. But we should not conclude that because a sleep-promoting (or wakefulness-promoting) substance has not yet been unambiguously identified means that there is none to be found; after all, there are undoubtedly many thousands of chemicals present in the fluid that bathes the cells of the brain. The fact that sleep is regulated means that *something* has to keep track of the sleep debt, and I find it difficult to imagine what that something would be if it were not a chemical. Perhaps it is a chemical that accumulates *inside* individual neurons in the brain; if so, it will probably take some time before investigators succeed in identifying it.

Neural Control of Arousal

As we have seen, sleep is not a unitary condition but consists of several different stages with very different characteristics. Wakefulness, too, is nonuniform; sometimes we are alert and attentive, and sometimes we fail to notice much about what is happening around us. Of course, sleepiness has an effect on wakefulness; if we are fighting to stay awake, the struggle might impair our ability to concentrate on other things. But everyday observations suggest that even when we are not sleepy, our alertness can vary. For example, when we observe something very interesting (or frightening, or simply surprising), we feel ourselves become more activated and aware of our surroundings.

Experimental evidence suggests that the brain stem contains circuits of neurons that can increase an animal's level of alertness and activation—what is commonly referred to as *arousal.* In 1949 Moruzzi and Magoun found that electrical stimulation of the brain stem reticular formation produced arousal. The reticular formation, which occupies the central core of the brain stem, receives collateral axons from ascending sensory pathways. Presumably, sensory input, the event that normally produces arousal, activates the reticular formation by means of these collateral axons. The activated reticular formation then arouses the cerebral cortex by means of two pathways (Jones, 1990). The dorsal pathway projects to the medial thalamus, which in turn projects to the cerebral cortex; and the ventral pathway projects to the lateral hypothalamus, basal ganglia, and basal forebrain region. One part of the basal forebrain

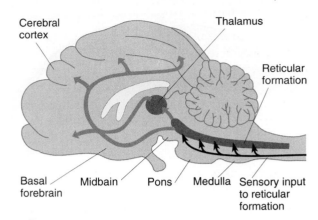

FIGURE 9.15

A midsagittal view of a cat brain, showing the reticular formation and its hypothesized role in arousal.

region projects extensively to the cerebral cortex, and another part projects to the hippocampus. (See *Figure 9.15.*)

What neurotransmitters are involved in arousal? Investigators have long known that catecholamine agonists such as amphetamine produce arousal and sleeplessness. These effects appear to be primarily mediated by the noradrenergic system of the **locus coeruleus,** located in the dorsal pons. Neurons of the locus coeruleus send axons that branch widely, releasing norepinephrine (from axonal varicosities) throughout the neocortex, hippocampus, thalamus, cerebellar cortex, pons, and medulla; thus, they potentially affect widespread and important regions of the brain. (See *Figure 9.16.*)

Aston-Jones and Bloom (1981a) recorded from noradrenergic neurons of the locus coeruleus across the sleep-waking cycle in unrestrained rats. As Figure 9.17 shows, these neurons exhibited a close relation to behavioral arousal. Note the decline in firing rate before and during sleep and the abrupt increase when the animal wakes. The rate of firing of neurons in the locus coeruleus falls almost to zero during REM sleep and increases dramatically when the animal wakes. As we shall see later in this chapter, these facts suggest that these neurons (along with serotonergic neurons) play a role in controlling REM sleep. (See *Figure 9.17.*)

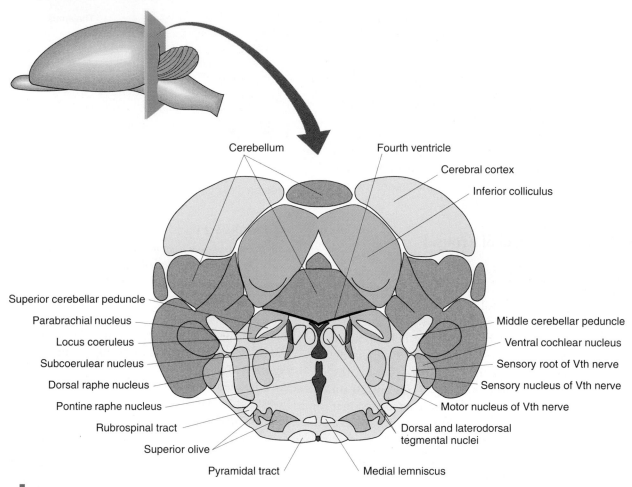

Cerebellum

Fourth ventricle

Cerebral cortex

Inferior colliculus

Superior cerebellar peduncle

Parabrachial nucleus

Locus coeruleus

Subcoerulear nucleus

Dorsal raphe nucleus

Pontine raphe nucleus

Rubrospinal tract

Superior olive

Pyramidal tract

Middle cerebellar peduncle

Ventral cochlear nucleus

Sensory root of Vth nerve

Sensory nucleus of Vth nerve

Motor nucleus of Vth nerve

Dorsal and laterodorsal tegmental nuclei

Medial lemniscus

FIGURE 9.16

The locus coeruleus, the location of the cell bodies of most of the brain's noradrenergic neurons.
(Adapted from Paxinos, G., and Watson, C. *The Rat Brain in Stereotaxic Coordinates.* Sydney: Academic Press, 1982.)

Aston-Jones and Bloom (1981a, 1981b) found that although sudden environmental stimuli presented during sleep or quiet wakefulness increased the activity of noradrenergic neurons, the firing rate of these neurons was very low while the animals were grooming or drinking sweetened water—activities that are accompanied by a high level of arousal. The authors suggested that the activity of noradrenergic neurons showed a better correlation with *vigilance* than with arousal. That is, at times when the animals were sensitive to external stimuli, the neurons were found to be firing at a high rate. While an animal is grooming or drinking, it is certainly aroused and busy, but it is not paying much attention to external stimuli.

Aston-Jones et al. (1986) used neuroanatomical methods to study the afferent connections of the locus coeruleus, and to their surprise, they found only two significant inputs: a nucleus in the ventrolateral medulla and another in the dorsomedial medulla. Ennis and Aston-Jones (1986, 1988) found that one input excited neurons in the locus coeruleus, while the other inhibited them. Obviously, the next step will be to investigate the sources of input to *these* regions.

Although norepinephrine was the first neuro-

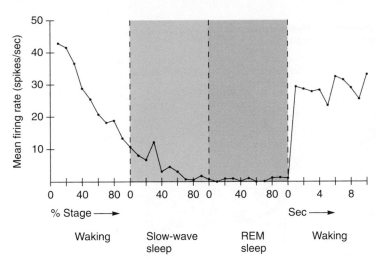

FIGURE 9.17

Activity of noradrenergic neurons in the locus coeruleus of freely moving cats during various stages of sleep and waking.

(From Aston-Jones, G., and Bloom, F.E. *The Journal of Neuroscience*, 1981, *1*, 876–886. Copyright 1981, The Society for Neuroscience.)

transmitter suspected to play a role in arousal and wakefulness, acetylcholine now appears to be even more important. Many of axons that travel from the reticular formation to the thalamus and the basal forebrain are acetylcholinergic (Jones, 1990). Researchers have long known that acetylcholinergic antagonists decrease EEG signs of cortical arousal, and that acetylcholinergic agonists increase them (Vanderwolf, 1992). Day, Damsma, and Fibiger (1991) used microdialysis probes to measure the release of acetylcholine in the striatum, hippocampus, and frontal cortex—three regions whose activity is closely related to an animal's alertness and behavioral arousal. They found that the levels of ACh in these regions were closely related to the animals' level of motor activity.

A third neurotransmitter, serotonin (5-HT), also appears to play a role in alert wakefulness. Almost all of the brain's serotonergic neurons are found in the **raphe nuclei,** which are located in the medullary and pontine regions of the reticular formation. (See *Figure 9.18.*) The axons of these neurons project to many parts of the brain, including the thalamus, hypothalamus, basal ganglia, hippocampus, and neocortex. Stimulation of the raphe nuclei causes locomotion and cortical arousal (as measured by the EEG), whereas PCPA, a drug that prevents the synthesis of serotonin, reduces cortical arousal (Peck and Vanderwolf, 1991). Unlike noradrenergic neurons, which increase their rate of firing during stressful situations, serotonergic neurons do *not* respond to external stimuli that produce pain or

induce a stress response (Jacobs, Wilkinson, and Fornal, 1990).

Figure 9.19 shows the activity of serotonergic neurons, recorded by Trulson and Jacobs (1979). As you can see, these neurons were most active during waking. Their firing rate declined during slow-wave sleep and became virtually zero during REM sleep. However, once the period of REM sleep ended, the neurons temporarily became very active again. (See *Figure 9.19.*)

In summary, three systems of neurons play important roles in alert wakefulness: noradrenergic, acetylcholinergic, and serotonergic. The functions performed by these three systems of neurons are undoubtedly different; for example, noradrenergic neurons may be more important for vigilance and attention, and serotonergic and acetylcholinergic neurons may be more important for behavioral activation. But the exact nature of these functions is still poorly understood.

Neural Control of Slow-Wave Sleep

Although researchers have made considerable progress in identifying the neural circuits responsible for REM sleep (discussed in the final section of this chapter), less is known about the neural control of slow-wave sleep.

Although sleep is a behavior that involves most of the brain, one region seems to be particularly important: the **basal forebrain region,** located just rostral to the hypothalamus. Nauta (1946) found

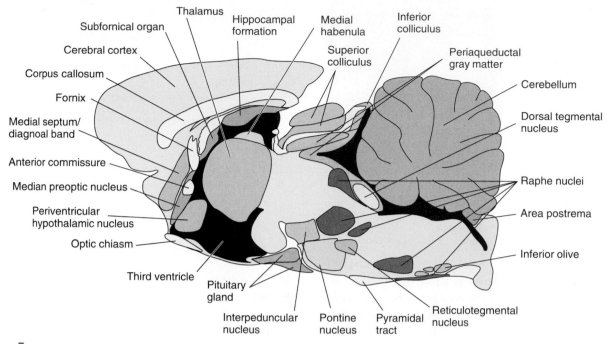

FIGURE 9.18

A midsagittal section through a rat brain, showing the location of the raphe nuclei, which contain the
cell bodies of most of the brain's serotonergic neurons.
(Adapted from Paxinos, G., and Watson, C. *The Rat Brain in Stereotaxic Coordinates.* Sydney: Academic Press, 1982.)

that destruction of this area produced total insomnia in rats. The animals subsequently fell into a
coma and died; the average survival time was only
three days. McGinty and Sterman (1968) found that
cats reacted somewhat differently; the animals did
not become sleepless until several days after the
lesion was made. Two of the cats, whose sleep was
totally suppressed, died within ten days. Infusions of
kainic acid into the basal forebrain region, which
destroys cell bodies without damaging axons passing
through the region, also suppresses sleep (Szymusiak and McGinty, 1986b).

The effects of the lesion experiments are corroborated by the effects of electrical stimulation of the
basal forebrain region. Sterman and Clemente
(1962a, 1962b) found that electrical stimulation of
this region produced signs of drowsiness in the
behavior and the EEG of unanesthetized, freely
moving cats. The average latency period between the
stimulation and the changes in the EEG was 30 seconds, but sometimes the effect was immediate. The
animals often subsequently fell asleep. In addition,

a recording study by Szymusiak and McGinty
(1986a) found that many neurons in the basal forebrain changed their rate of firing when the animals
fell asleep.

One part of the basal forebrain, the **preoptic
area,** contains neurons that are involved in temperature regulation. Some of these neurons are directly
sensitive to changes in brain temperature, and some
receive information from thermosensors located
in the skin. Warming of the preoptic area, like electrical stimulation, produces drowsiness and sleep
(Roberts and Robinson, 1969; Benedek et al., 1982).
Thus, a more "natural" stimulation mimics the
effects of electrical stimulation. The excessive sleepiness that accompanies a fever may be produced by
this mechanism. And perhaps the connections
between the preoptic area and thermosensors in the
skin account for the drowsiness and lassitude we feel
on a hot day.

As we saw earlier in this chapter, the most likely
function of slow-wave sleep is to permit the brain
to rest. As Horne and his colleagues showed, when

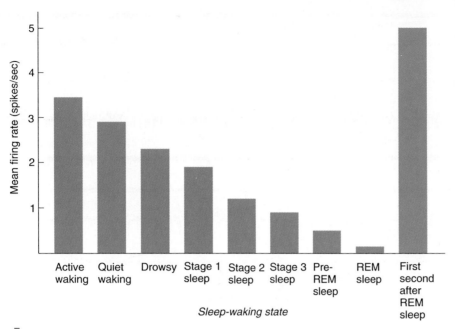

Activity of serotonergic (5-HT-secreting) neurons in the dorsal raphe nuclei of freely moving cats during various stages of sleep and waking.

(Adapted from Trulson, M.E., and Jacobs, B.L. *Brain Research,* 1979, *163,* 135–150. Redrawn with permission.)

people's brains are warmed during the day, they engage in more sleep the following night. McGinty and Szymusiak (1990a) describe evidence linking brain temperature, the preoptic area, and sleep. For example, we already saw that the cerebral hemispheres of dolphins take turns sleeping. Kolvalzon and Mukhametov (1982) found that the temperature of the sleeping hemisphere was always lower than that of the awake one. The injection of prostaglandins into the preoptic area raises body temperature and increases slow-wave sleep (Hayaishi, 1988), while drugs that inhibit the synthesis of prostaglandins (such as aspirin or indomethacin) lower body temperature and reduce slow-wave sleep (Naito et al., 1988). In addition, neurons in the preoptic area that become active when the region is artificially warmed also become active when the animal falls sleep (McGinty and Szymusiak, 1990b).

McGinty and Szymusiak note that brain functioning is closely related to temperature. For example, people's alertness throughout the day is closely related to their body temperature (Czeisler et al.,

1980). The researchers suggest that the modern mammalian brain (and that of birds, which are also warm-blooded) operates at a temperature that is near the upper limit; just a few more degrees causes malfunctioning, confusion, seizures, and irreparable damage. Thus, they suggest that slow-wave sleep is part of a mechanism designed to cool the brain periodically by suppressing the animal's behavior and lowering the brain's metabolic rate.

Neural Control of REM Sleep

As we saw earlier in this chapter, REM sleep consists of desynchronized EEG activity, muscular paralysis, rapid eye movements, and (in humans, at least) increased genital activity. The rate of cerebral metabolism is as high as it is during waking (Maquet et al., 1990) and, were it not for the state of paralysis, the level of *physical* activity would also be high. In laboratory animals, REM sleep also includes *PGO waves.* **PGO waves** (for *p*ons, *g*eniculate, and *o*ccipital) are the first manifestation of REM sleep. They

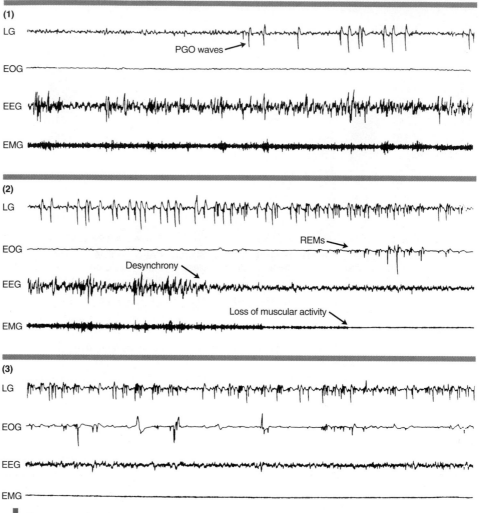

FIGURE 9.20

Onset of REM sleep in a cat. The arrows indicate the onset of PGO waves, EEG desynchrony, loss of muscular activity, and rapid eye movements. LG = lateral geniculate nucleus; EOG = electro-oculogram (eye movements).

(Adapted from Steriade, M., Paré, D., Bouhassira, D., Deschênes, M., and Oakson, G. *Journal of Neuroscience,* 1989, *9,* 2215–2229. Redrawn by permission of the Journal of Neuroscience.)

consist of brief, phasic bursts of electrical activity that originate in the pons and are propagated to the lateral geniculate nuclei and then to the primary visual (occipital) cortex. They can be seen only when electrodes are placed directly into the brain, so they have not been recorded in humans. It seems likely, however, that they occur in our species, too. Figure 9.20 shows the typical onset of REM sleep, recorded in a cat. The first sign of an impending bout of REM sleep is the presence of PGO waves—in this case, recorded from electrodes implanted in the lateral geniculate nucleus. Next, the EEG becomes desynchronized, and then muscular activity ceases and rapid eye movements commence. (See *Figure 9.20.*)

As we shall see, REM sleep is controlled by mechanisms located within the brain stem, primarily within the pons. The executive mechanism (whose activity turns on the various components of

REM sleep) consists of neurons that secrete acetylcholine. This mechanism is normally inhibited by the serotonergic neurons of the raphe nuclei and the noradrenergic neurons of the locus coeruleus.

Acetylcholine

Drugs that excite acetylcholinergic synapses facilitate REM sleep. Stoyva and Metcalf (1968) found that people who have been exposed to organophosphate insecticides, which act as acetylcholine agonists, spend an increased time in REM sleep. In a controlled experiment with human subjects, Sitaram, Moore, and Gillin (1978) found that an ACh agonist (arecoline) shortened the interval between periods of REM sleep, and a cholinergic antagonist (scopolamine) lengthened it.

Jasper and Tessier (1969) analyzed the levels of acetylcholine that had been released by terminal buttons in the cat cerebral cortex. They found that the levels of ACh were highest during waking and REM sleep and were lowest during slow-wave sleep. Using 2-DG autoradiography in cats, Lydic et al. (1991) found that the rate of glucose metabolism was elevated in those regions of the brain that contain ACh-secreting neurons or that receive input from the axons of these neurons. As we saw earlier in this chapter, acetylcholinergic neurons play an important role in cerebral activation during alert wakefulness. The findings I just cited suggest that these neurons are also responsible for the cerebral activation seen during REM sleep.

The brain contains several acetylcholinergic pathways. The one that plays the most central role in REM sleep is found in the dorsolateral pons, primarily in the *pedunculopontine tegmental nucleus* (PPT) and *laterodorsal tegmental nucleus* (LDT) (Jones and Beaudet, 1987). The axons of these neurons form a part of the reticular activating system. They project to several regions of the forebrain, including the thalamus, basal ganglia, basal forebrain region, hippocampus, hypothalamus, and cingulate cortex, and to several brain stem regions involved with visual functions (Cornwall, Cooper, and Phillipson, 1990). Cornwall and his colleagues note that the pattern of outputs suggests that this system is involved in controlling visual attention. Given the importance of visual imagery in dreams, this conclusion seems quite reasonable.

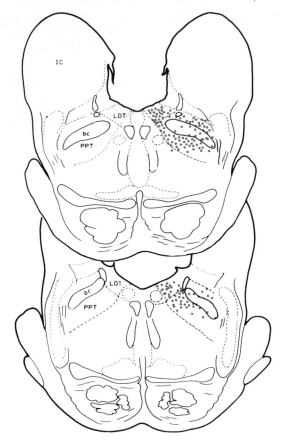

FIGURE 9.21

Acetylcholinergic neurons in the brain stem of the cat (colored circles) as revealed by a stain for choline acetyltransferase. LDT = lateral tegmental nucleus; PPT = pedunculopontine tegmental nucleus; bc = brachium conjunctivum, IC = inferior colliculus.

(Adapted from Jones, B.E., and Beaudet, A. *Journal of Comparative Neurology,* 1987, *261,* 15–32. Reprinted with permission.)

If a small amount of an acetylcholinergic agonist is infused into the dorsolateral pons, the animal will exhibit PGO waves alone, muscular paralysis alone, or all the signs of REM sleep, depending on the location of the infusion (Katayama et al., 1986; Callaway et al., 1987). Figure 9.21 contains two drawings through the brain stem of a cat, prepared by Jones and Beaudet (1987). The location of acetylcholinergic cell bodies is shown by colored circles. As you can see by comparing the labels on the left side with the filled circles on the right, most of these neurons are found in the LDT and the PPT. (See **Figure 9.21.**)

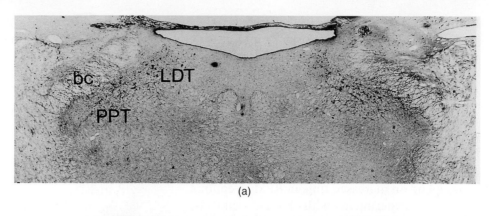

(a)

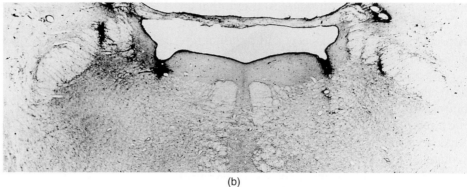

(b)

▌ FIGURE 9.22

Destruction of acetylcholine-secreting neurons in the pons. (a) A section through the pons of an intact brain. (b) A section through the pons after infusions of kainic acid. Acetylcholine-secreting neurons show up as black spots in (a). LDT = lateral tegmental nucleus; PPT = pedunculopontine tegmental nucleus; bc = brachium conjunctivum.

(From Jones, B.E., and Webster, H.H. *Brain Research*, 1988, *451*, 13–32. Reprinted with permission.)

Several studies (for example, El Mansari, Sakai, and Jouvet, 1989; Steriade et al., 1990; Kayama, Ohta, and Jodo, 1992) have shown that the activity of single neurons in the LDT–PPT is related to the sleep cycle. Some neurons fire at a high rate only during REM sleep, some fire at a high rate during active wakefulness and during REM sleep, some show bursts of activity just before and during PGO waves, some show bursts of activity during the transition between sleep and waking or between slow-wave and REM sleep, and some cease firing during REM sleep. However, most of the cells in the dorsolateral pons belong to the first two categories, firing at a high rate during REM sleep or during both REM sleep and active wakefulness. Presumably, the activity of these acetylcholinergic cells is what produces REM sleep.

Webster and Jones (1988) made lesions of the dorsolateral pons by infusing kainic acid into this region. They found that REM sleep was drastically reduced. The amount of REM sleep that remained was directly related to the number of cholinergic neurons that were spared. Figure 9.22(a) contains a photomicrograph through the pons of a normal cat, and part (b) that of a cat with a kainic acid lesion. Acetylcholinergic neurons show up as black granules. As you can see, very few of them remain in the cat with the lesion. (See **Figure 9.22.**)

If the acetylcholinergic neurons in the dorsolateral pons are responsible for the onset of REM sleep, how do they control each of its components, cortical desynchrony, PGO waves, rapid eye movements, and muscular paralysis? As we saw, the dorsolateral pons is an integral part of the reticular activating system, and its ascending axons produce arousal and cortical desynchrony. PGO waves are controlled by connections between the pons and the lateral geniculate nucleus (Sakai and Jouvet, 1980). Webster and Jones (1988) suggest that the control of rapid eye movements may be achieved by projections from the dorsolateral pons to the tectum.

The last of the REM-related phenomenon, muscular paralysis, is particularly interesting. As we saw earlier, some patients with lesions in the brain stem fail to become paralyzed during REM sleep and thus act out their dreams. (As you will recall, the phenomenon is called *REM without atonia.*) The same thing happens—that is, assuming that cats dream—when a lesion is placed just caudal to the acetylcholinergic neurons of the dorsolateral pons. Jouvet (1972) described this phenomenon:

> To a naive observer, the cat, which is standing, looks awake since it may attack unknown enemies, play with an absent mouse, or display flight behavior. There are orienting movements of the head or eyes toward imaginary stimuli, although the animal does not respond to visual or auditory stimuli. These extraordinary episodes . . . are a good argument that "dreaming" occurs during [REM sleep] in the cat. (Jouvet, 1972, pp. 236–237)

Jouvet's lesions destroyed the axons of neurons responsible for the muscular paralysis that occurs during REM sleep. These axons belong to a group of acetylcholinergic neurons found in the **subcoerulear nucleus,** which is located just adjacent to the locus coeruleus. These axons travel caudally to the **magnocellular nucleus,** located in the medial medulla (Sakai, 1980). Neurons in the magnocellular nucleus send axons to the spinal cord, where they form inhibitory synapses with motor neurons (Morales, Boxer, and Chase, 1987).

There is good evidence that this pathway is responsible for the atonia that accompanies REM sleep. Shouse and Siegel (1992) found that lesions of the subcoerulear nucleus had no effect on REM sleep itself but abolished the atonia that accompanies it. Kanamori, Sakai, and Jouvet (1980) recorded

from single neurons in the magnocellular nucleus in unrestrained cats and found that they became active during REM sleep. Sakai (1980) found that electrical stimulation of this nucleus caused paralysis in awake cats, and Schenkel and Siegel (1989) found that lesions produced REM without atonia. Fort et al. (1990) found that the magnocellular nucleus contains glycine-secreting neurons, and this inhibitory transmitter substance is undoubtedly responsible for the inhibition of the motor neurons located in the spinal cord.

The fact that our brains contain an elaborate mechanism whose sole function is to keep us paralyzed while we dream—that is, to prevent us from acting out our dreams—suggests that the motor components of dreams are as important as the sensory components. Perhaps the practice our motor system gets during REM sleep helps us improve our performance of behaviors we have learned that day. The inhibition of the motor neurons in the spinal cord prevents the movements being practiced from actually occurring, with the exception of a few harmless twitches of the hands and feet.

As we saw earlier, when an animal (including a member of our own species) is deprived of REM sleep, it shows a rebound effect when the period of deprivation ends. Mallick, Siegel, and Fahringer (1989) placed recording electrodes next to "REM-on" neurons in the dorsolateral pons—that is, those that become active during REM sleep. They found that short-term REM sleep deprivation increased the activity of these neurons, even while the cats were awake. They suggested that this activity might represent the "REM pressure" that is responsible for the rebound effect. Of course, the experiment does not reveal *why* REM sleep deprivation makes these neurons become more active. When we find the answer to that question, we will learn more about the functions of REM sleep.

One of the factors (but certainly not the only one) that stimulates REM sleep is temperature. As we saw, brain temperature falls during slow-wave sleep; in fact, this fall in temperature may even be one of the major functions of this phase of sleep. The fall in temperature appears to stimulate neurons responsible for REM sleep; normal animals will not enter REM sleep if their brain temperature is artificially kept high, and a decerebrate cat—which no

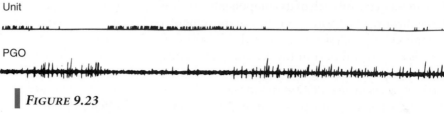

FIGURE 9.23

Activity of a single unit in the dorsal raphe nucleus. Note that the activity is inversely related to the occurrence of PGO waves, the first sign of REM sleep. (Adapted from Lydic, R., McCarley, R.W., and Hobson, J.A. *Brain Research*, 1983, *274*, 365–370. Redrawn with permission.)

longer can regulate its body temperature—will display REM sleep when its temperature is lowered (Jouvet, 1975). The increased brain activity that occurs during REM sleep causes a rise in brain temperature, which then falls again during the subsequent period of slow-wave sleep.

Serotonin and Norepinephrine

As you will recall from the earlier discussion of narcolepsy, serotonergic and noradrenergic agonists have inhibitory effects on REM sleep. In addition, the rate of activity in the serotonergic neurons of the raphe nuclei and the noradrenergic neurons of the locus coeruleus are at their very lowest levels during sleep. The patterns of firing of noradrenergic neurons of the locus coeruleus and the serotonergic neurons of the raphe nuclei were already presented in Figures 9.17 and 9.19.

Figure 9.23 shows the very close linkage between the activity of a single unit in the dorsal raphe nucleus and the occurrence of PGO waves, the first manifestation of REM sleep (Lydic, McCarley, and Hobson, 1983). Note that the PGO waves occur only when the serotonergic neuron is silent. (See **Figure 9.23.**)

The evidence I have just cited strongly suggests that inhibitory effects of the locus coeruleus and the dorsal raphe nuclei normally prevent REM sleep from occurring and that the event that triggers a bout of REM sleep is a decrease of activity in these nuclei. In fact, infusion of a noradrenergic antagonist directly into the rostrolateral pons causes an increase in REM sleep (Denlinger, Patarca, and Hobson, 1988), and stimulation of the dorsal raphe nucleus inhibits it (Jacobs, Asher, and Dement, 1973). Acetylcholinergic neurons in the dorsolateral pons receive both serotonergic and noradrenergic inputs (Sakai, 1985).

So far we have seen that REM sleep occurs when acetylcholinergic neurons in the dorsolateral pons become active. That event occurs when serotonergic and noradrenergic neurons in the raphe nuclei and the locus coeruleus become silent. (See **Figure 9.24.**) But what makes these neurons become silent? And is there an excitatory input to the dorsolateral pons as well as the inhibitory ones that *increases* at the beginning of REM sleep? Where is the pacemaker that controls the regular cycles of REM and slow-wave sleep, and how is this pacemaker connected to the acetylcholinergic neurons in the dorsolateral pons? Are rises and falls in brain temperature partly responsible for these cycles? Research efforts will probably find answers to some of these questions in the next few years.

INTERIM SUMMARY

The fact that the amount of sleep is regulated suggests that sleep-promoting substances (produced during wakefulness) or wakefulness-promoting substances (produced during sleep) may exist. The sleeping pattern of the dolphin brain and studies with artificial or natural Siamese twins suggest that such substances do not accumulate in the blood. They may accumulate in the brain, but so far, attempts to find them have not been successful. The release of a growth hormone (a hormone that pro-

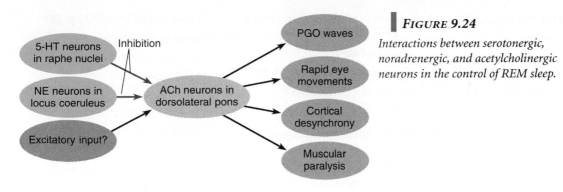

FIGURE 9.24

Interactions between serotonergic, noradrenergic, and acetylcholinergic neurons in the control of REM sleep.

motes protein synthesis) occurs primarily during slow-wave sleep, and a drug that disrupts the release of this hormone also disrupts slow-wave sleep. In addition, the rate of protein synthesis in the brain is increased during slow-wave sleep.

Three systems of neurons appear to be important for alert, active wakefulness: the acetylcholinergic system of the pons, the noradrenergic system of the locus coeruleus, and the serotonergic system of the raphe nuclei. The particular roles played by each system are still not understood.

Slow-wave sleep occurs when neurons in the basal forebrain become active. These neurons are also involved in temperature regulation, leading some investigators to suggest that an important function of slow-wave sleep is to lower brain temperature (and permit the brain to rest). REM sleep occurs when the activity of acetylcholinergic neurons in the dorsolateral pons increases; some of these neurons control PGO waves, some initiate cor-

tical arousal, and others produce rapid eye movements. Atonia (muscular paralysis that prevents our acting out our dreams) is produced by a group of acetylcholinergic neurons located in the subcoerulear nucleus that activate neurons in the magnocellular nucleus of the medulla, which in turn produce inhibition of motor neurons in the spinal cord. REM sleep, too, is related to temperature; it occurs only after the brain temperature has been lowered by a period of slow-wave sleep.

The noradrenergic neurons of the locus coeruleus and the serotonergic neurons of the raphe nuclei have inhibitory effects on the acetylcholinergic neurons of the pons that are responsible for REM sleep. Bouts of REM sleep begin only after the activity of the noradrenergic and serotonergic neurons ceases; whether this event is the only one to trigger REM sleep or whether direct excitation of acetylcholinergic neurons also occurs is not yet known.

New Terms

A Physiological and Behavioral Description

electromyogram (*MY oh gram*) p. 254

electro-oculogram (*AH kew loh gram*) p. 254

alpha activity p. 255

beta activity p. 255

synchrony p. 255

desynchrony p. 255

theta activity p. 255

delta activity p. 256

REM sleep p. 256

non-REM sleep p. 256

slow-wave sleep p. 256

basic rest-activity cycle (BRAC) p. 257

Why Do We Sleep?

rebound phenomenon p. 265

Disorders of Sleep

drug dependency insomnia p. 268

sleep apnea (*APP nee a*) p. 268

narcolepsy (*NAHR ko lep see*) p. 269

sleep attack p. 269

cataplexy (*KAT a plex ee*) p. 269

sleep paralysis p. 269

hypnagogic hallucination (*hip na GAH jik*) p. 269

REM without atonia (*ay TONE ee a*) p. 269

Biological Clocks

circadian rhythm (*sur KAY dee un or sur ka DEE un*) p. 271

zeitgeber (*TSITE gay ber*) p. 272

suprachiasmatic nucleus (*soo pra ky az MAT ik*) p. 272

neuropeptide Y p. 273

pineal gland (*py NEE ul*) p. 277

melatonin (*mell a TONE in*) p. 277

Physiological Mechanisms of Sleep and Waking

locus coeruleus (*sa ROO lee us*) p. 279

raphe nuclei (*ruh FAY*) p. 281

basal forebrain region p. 281

preoptic area p. 282

PGO wave p. 283

subcoerulear nucleus (*sub sa ROO lee ur*) p. 287

magnocellular nucleus p. 287

Suggested Readings

Cohen, D.B. *Sleep and Dreaming: Origins, Nature and Functions.* Oxford: Pergamon Press, 1979.

Hastings, J.W., Rusak, B., and Boulos, Z. Circadian rhythms: The physiology of biological timing. In *Neural and Integrative Animal Physiology,* edited by C.L. Prosser. New York: Wiley-Liss, 1991.

Horne, J. *Why We Sleep: The Functions of Sleep in Humans and Other Mammals.* Oxford: Oxford University Press, 1988.

Kryger, M.H., Roth, T., and Dement, W.C. *Principles and Practices of Sleep Disorders in Medicine.* New York: W.B. Saunders Co., 1989.

Mancia, M., and Marini, G. *The Diencephalon and Sleep.* New York: Raven Press, 1990.

Webb, W. *Sleep: The Gentle Tyrant,* 2nd ed. Bolton, Mass.: Anker Publishing Co., 1992.

CHAPTER 10

Reproductive Behavior

Sexual Development
- Production of Gametes and Fertilization
- Development of the Sex Organs
- Sexual Maturation
  Interim Summary

Hormonal Control of Sexual Behavior
- Hormonal Control of Female Reproductive Cycles
- Hormonal Control of Sexual Behavior of Laboratory Animals
- Organizational Effects of Androgens on Behavior: Masculinization and Defeminization
- Effects of Pheromones
- Human Sexual Behavior
- Sexual Orientation
  Interim Summary

Neural Control of Sexual Behavior
- Males
- Females
  Interim Summary

Maternal Behavior
- Maternal Behavior in Rodents
- Stimuli That Elicit and Maintain Maternal Behavior
- Hormonal Control of Maternal Behavior
- Neural Control of Maternal Behavior
  Interim Summary

REPRODUCTIVE BEHAVIORS CONSTITUTE the most important category of social behaviors, because without them, most species would not survive. These behaviors—which include courting, mating, parental behavior, and most forms of aggressive behaviors—are the most striking categories of **sexually dimorphic behaviors**, that is, behaviors that differ in males and females (*di* + *morphous*, "two forms"). As you will see, hormones present both before and after birth play a very special role in the development and control of sexually dimorphic behaviors.

This chapter describes male and female sexual development and then discusses the neural and hormonal control of two sexually dimorphic behaviors most important to reproduction: sexual behavior and maternal behavior.

SEXUAL DEVELOPMENT

A PERSON'S CHROMOSOMAL SEX IS DETERMINED AT the time of fertilization. However, this event is merely the first in a series of steps that culminate in the development of a male or female. This section considers the major features of sexual development.

Production of Gametes and Fertilization

All cells of the human body (other than sperms or ova) contain twenty-three pairs of chromosomes, including a pair of sex chromosomes. The genetic information that programs the development of a human is contained in the DNA that constitutes these chromosomes. We pride ourselves on our ability to miniaturize computer circuits on silicon chips; but that accomplishment looks primitive when we consider that the blueprint for a human being is too small to be seen by the naked eye.

The production of **gametes** (ova and sperms; *gamein* means "to marry") entails a special form of cell division. This process produces cells that contain one member of each of the twenty-three pairs of chromosomes. The development of a human begins at the time of fertilization, when a single sperm and ovum join, sharing their twenty-three single chromosomes to reconstitute the twenty-three pairs.

A person's genetic sex is determined by the father's sperm at the time of fertilization. Twenty-two of the pairs of chromosomes determine the organism's physical development independent of its sex. The last pair consists of two **sex chromosomes,** which determine whether the offspring will be a boy or a girl.

There are two types of sex chromosomes: **X chromosomes** and **Y chromosomes.** Females have two X chromosomes (XX); thus, all the ova that a woman produces will contain an X chromosome. Males have an X and a Y chromosome (XY). When a man's sex chromosomes divide, half the sperms contain an X chromosome and the other half a Y chromosome. A Y-bearing sperm produces an XY-fertilized ovum and, therefore, a male. An X-bearing sperm produces an XX-fertilized ovum and, therefore, a female. (See *Figure 10.1.*)

Development of the Sex Organs

Men and women differ in many ways: Their bodies are different, parts of their brains are different, and their reproductive behaviors are different. Are all these differences encoded on the tiny Y chromosome, the sole piece of genetic material that distinguishes males from females? The answer is no. The X chromosome and the twenty-two nonsex chromosomes found in the cells of both males and females contain all the information needed to develop the bodies of either sex. Exposure to sex hormones, both before and after birth, is responsible for our sexual dimorphism. What the Y chromosome does control is the development of the glands that produce the male sex hormones.

There are three general categories of sex organs: the gonads, the internal sex organs, and the external genitalia. The **gonads**—testes or ovaries—are the first to develop. Gonads (from the Greek *gonos,* "procreation") have a dual function: They produce ova or sperms, and they secrete hormones. Through the fourth week of prenatal development, male and female fetuses are identical. Both sexes have a pair of identical undifferentiated gonads, which can develop into either testes or ovaries. The factor that

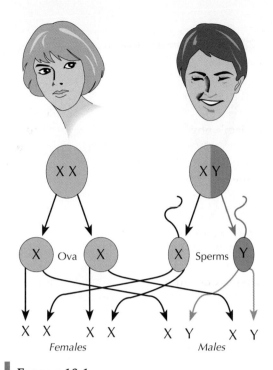

FIGURE 10.1

Determination of gender. The gender of the offspring depends on whether the sperm cell that fertilizes the ovum carries an X or a Y chromosome.

controls their development appears to be a single gene on the Y chromosome called *SRY.* This gene produces an enzyme called *testis-determining factor,* which causes the undifferentiated gonads to become testes. If the gene is not present, they become ovaries. In fact, if this gene is inserted into one of the X chromosomes of a female (XX) embryonic mouse, the animal will develop as a male (Koopman et al., 1991).

Once the gonads have developed, a series of events is set into action that determines the individual's gender. These events are directed by hormones, which affect sexual development in two ways. During prenatal development these hormones have **organizational effects,** which influence the development of a person's sex organs and brain. These effects are permanent; once a particular path is followed in the course of development, there is no going back. The second role of sex hormones is their **activational effect.** These effects occur later in life, after the sex organs have developed. For example,

hormones activate the production of sperms, make erection and ejaculation possible, and induce ovulation. Because the bodies of adult males and females have been organized differently, sex hormones will have different activational effects in the two sexes.

The internal sex organs are *bisexual;* that is, all embryos contain the precursors for both female and male sex organs. However, during the third month of gestation only one of these precursors develops; the other withers away. The precursor of the internal female sex organs, which develops into the *fimbriae* and *Fallopian tubes,* the *uterus,* and the *inner two-thirds of the vagina,* is called the **Müllerian system.** The precursor of the internal male sex organs, which develops into the *epididymis, vas deferens, seminal vesicles,* and *prostate,* is called the **Wolffian system.** (These systems were named after their discoverers, Müller and Wolff. See *Figure 10.2.*)

The gender of the internal sex organs of a fetus is determined by the presence or absence of hormones secreted by the testes. That is, if these hormones are present, the Wolffian system develops. If they are not, the Müllerian system develops. The Müllerian (female) system needs no hormonal stimulus from the gonads to develop; it just normally does so. In contrast, the cells of the Wolffian (male) system do not develop unless they are stimulated by a hormone. Thus, testes secrete two types of hormones. The first, a peptide hormone called **Müllerian-inhibiting hormone,** does exactly what its name says: It prevents the Müllerian system from developing. It therefore has a **defeminizing effect.** The second, a set of steroid hormones called **androgens,** stimulates the development of the Wolffian system. (This class of hormone is also aptly named: *andros* means "man," and *gennan* means "to produce.") Androgens have a **masculinizing effect.**

Two different androgens are responsible for masculinization. The first, **testosterone,** is secreted by the testes—and gets its name from these glands. An enzyme called 5-α *reductase* converts testosterone into another androgen, known as **dihydrotestosterone.**

As you will recall from Chapter 3, hormones exert their effects on target cells by stimulating the appropriate hormone receptor. Thus, the precursor of the male internal sex organs—the Wolffian system—contains androgen receptors that are coupled

Development of the internal sex organs.

(Adapted from Corning, H.K. *Lehrbuch der Entwicklungsgeschichte des Menschen.* Munich: J.F. Bergman, 1921.)

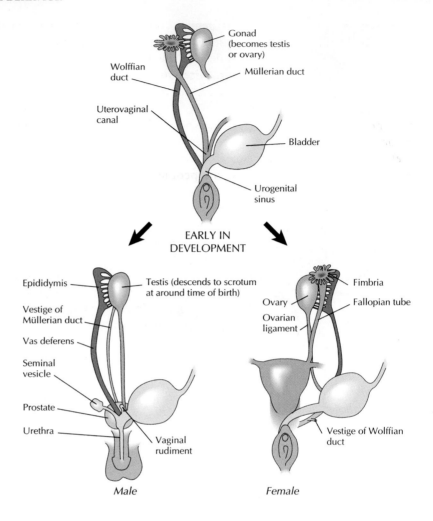

to cellular mechanisms that promote growth and division. When molecules of testosterone bind with these receptors, the epididymis, vas deferens, and prostate develop and grow. In contrast, the cells of the Müllerian system contain receptors for Müllerian-inhibiting hormone that somehow *prevent* growth and division. Thus, Müllerian-inhibiting hormone prevents the development of the female internal sex organs.

Experiments with laboratory animals have shown that ovaries are not necessary for the development of the Müllerian system. This finding has led to the dictum "Nature's impulse is to create a female." A genetic anomaly shows that this statement is true for humans, too. People with **Turner's syndrome** have only one sex chromosome: an X chromosome. (Thus, instead of having XX cells, they have X0

cells—0 indicating a missing sex chromosome.) In most cases, the existing X chromosome comes from the mother, which means that the cause of the disorder lies with a defective sperm (Knebelmann et al., 1991). Because a Y chromosome is not present, testes do not develop. In addition, because two X chromosomes are needed to produce ovaries, these glands are not produced, either. Even though people with Turner's syndrome have no gonads at all, they develop into females, with normal female internal sex organs and external genitalia—which proves that fetuses do not need ovaries to develop as females. Of course, they cannot bear children, because without ovaries they cannot produce ova.

The external genitalia are the visible sex organs, including the penis and scrotum in males and the labia, clitoris, and outer part of the vagina in females. As we just saw, the external genitalia do not need to be stimulated by female sex hormones to become female; they just naturally develop that way. However, masculine development requires the presence of androgens—in particular, the presence of dihydrotestosterone (Josso et al., 1991). Thus, the gender of a person's external genitalia is determined by the presence or absence of testes—or, more precisely, by the presence or absence of the androgens they secrete. This fact explains why people with Turner's syndrome have female external genitalia even though they lack ovaries. (See *Figure 10.3.*)

Figure 10.4 summarizes the factors that control the development of the gonads, internal sex organs, and genitalia. (See *Figure 10.4.*)

Sexual Maturation

The *primary* sex characteristics include the gonads, internal sex organs, and external genitalia. These organs are present at birth. The *secondary* sex char-

acteristics, such as enlarged breasts and widened hips or a beard and deep voice, do not appear until puberty. Without seeing genitals, we must guess the sex of a prepubescent child from his or her haircut and clothing; the bodies of young boys and girls are rather similar. However, at puberty the gonads are stimulated to produce their hormones, and these hormones cause the person to mature sexually. The onset of puberty occurs when cells in the hypothalamus secrete **gonadotropin-releasing hormones** (GnRH), which stimulate the production and release of two **gonadotropic hormones** by the anterior pituitary gland. The gonadotropic ("gonad-turning") hormones stimulate the gonads to produce *their* hormones, which are ultimately responsible for sexual maturation. (See *Figure 10.5.*)

The two gonadotropic hormones are **follicle-stimulating hormone** (FSH) and **luteinizing hormone** (LH), named for the effects they produce in the female (production of a *follicle* and its subsequent *luteinization,* to be described in the next sec-

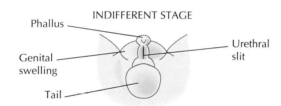

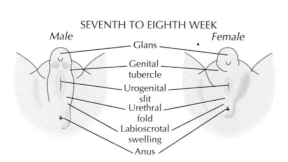

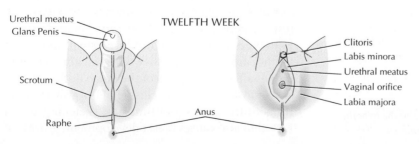

FIGURE 10.3

Development of the external genitalia.
(Adapted from Spaulding, M.H., in *Contributions to Embryology,* Vol. 13. Washington, D.C.: Carnegie Institute of Washington, 1921.)

FIGURE 10.4

Hormonal control of masculinization and defeminization of the internal sex organs and external genitalia.

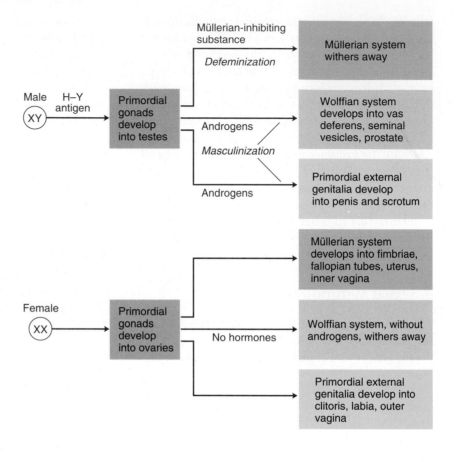

FIGURE 10.5

Sexual maturation. Puberty is initiated when the hypothalamus secretes gonadotropin-releasing hormones.

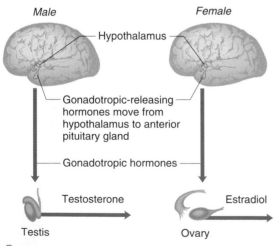

tion of this chapter). However, the same hormones are produced in the male, where they stimulate the testes to produce sperms and to secrete testosterone. If male and female pituitary glands are exchanged in rats, the ovaries and testes respond perfectly to the hormones secreted by the new glands (Harris and Jacobsohn, 1951–1952).

In response to the gonadotropic hormones (usually called *gonadotropins*), the gonads secrete sex steroid hormones. The ovaries produce **estradiol,** one of a class of hormones known as **estrogens.** The testes chiefly produce *testosterone* (an androgen). Both types of glands also produce a small amount of the hormones of the other sex. The gonadal hormones affect many parts of the body. Both estradiol and testosterone initiate closure of the growing portions of the bones and thus halt skeletal growth. Estradiol also causes breast development, growth of

TABLE 10.1

Classification of sex hormones

Class	Principal Hormones in Humans (Where Produced)	Examples of Effects
Androgens	Testosterone (testes)	Development of Wolffian system; production of sperms, growth of facial, pubic, and axillary hair; muscular development; enlargement of larynx; inhibition of bone growth; sex drive in men (and women?)
	Dihydrotestosterone (produced from testosterone by action of 5-α reductase)	Maturation of male external genitalia
	Androstenedione (adrenal glands)	In women, growth of pubic and axillary hair; less important than testosterone in men
Estrogens	Estradiol (ovaries)	Maturation of female genitalia; growth of breasts; alterations in fat deposits; growth of uterine lining; inhibition of bone growth; sex drive in women (?)
Gestagens	Progesterone (ovaries)	Maintenance of uterine lining
Hypothalamic hormones	Gonadotrophin-releasing hormone (hypothalamus)	Secretion of gonadotropins
Gonadotropins	Follicle-stimulating hormone (anterior pituitary)	Development of ovarian follicle
	Luteinizing hormone (anterior pituitary)	Ovulation; development of corpus luteum
Other hormones	Prolactin (posterior pituitary)	Milk production; male refractory period (?)
	Oxytocin (posterior pituitary)	Milk ejection; orgasm; male refractory period (?); social bonding (?)

the lining of the uterus, changes in the deposition of body fat, and maturation of the female genitalia. Testosterone stimulates growth of facial, axillary (underarm), and pubic hair; lowers the voice; alters the hairline on the head (often causing baldness later in life); stimulates muscular development; and causes genital growth. This description leaves out two of the female secondary characteristics: axillary and pubic hair. These characteristics are produced not by estrogens but rather by androgens secreted by the cortex of the adrenal glands. Even a male who is castrated (whose testes are removed) before puberty will grow axillary and pubic hair, stimulated by his own adrenal androgens. A list of the principal sex hormones and examples of their effects are presented in Table 10.1. Note that some of these effects are discussed later in this chapter. (See *Table 10.1.*)

The bipotentiality of some of the secondary sex characteristics remains throughout life. If a man is treated with an estrogen (for example, to control an androgen-dependent tumor), he will grow breasts, and his facial hair will become finer and softer. However, his voice will remain low, because the enlargement of the larynx is permanent. Conversely, a woman who receives high levels of an androgen (usually from a tumor that secretes androstenedione) will grow a beard, and her voice will become lower.

‖‖‖‖ INTERIM SUMMARY

Gender is determined by the sex chromosomes: XX produces a female, and XY produces a male. Males are produced by the action of the SRY gene on the Y chromosome that contains the code for the production of the testis-determining protein, which causes the primitive gonads to become testes. The testes secrete two kinds of hormones that cause a male to develop. Testosterone (an androgen) stimulates the development of the Wolffian system (masculinization), and Müllerian-inhibiting hormone suppresses the development of the Müllerian system (defeminization). The external genitalia develop from common precursors. In the absence of gonadal hormones the precursors develop the female form; in the presence of androgens (primarily dihydrotestosterone, which derives from testosterone through the action of 5-α reductase), they develop the male form (masculinization). By default, the body is female ("Nature's impulse . . ."); only by the actions of testicular hormones does it become male. Masculinization and defeminization are referred to as *organizational* effects of hormones; *activational* effects occur after development is complete. A person with Turner's syndrome (X0) fails to develop gonads but nevertheless develops female internal sex organs and external genitalia.

Sexual maturity occurs when the hypothalamus begins secreting gonadotropin-releasing hormone, which stimulates the secretion of follicle-stimulating hormone and luteinizing hormone by the anterior pituitary gland. These hormones stimulate the gonads to secrete their hormones, thus causing the genitals to mature and the body to develop the secondary sex characteristics (activational effects).

HORMONAL CONTROL OF SEXUAL BEHAVIOR

WE HAVE SEEN THAT HORMONES ARE RESPONSIBLE for sexual dimorphism in the structure of the body and its organs. Hormones have organizational and activational effects on the internal sex organs, geni-

tals, and secondary sex characteristics. Naturally, all of these effects influence a person's behavior. Simply having the physique and genitals of a man or a woman exerts a powerful effect. But hormones do more than give us masculine or feminine bodies; they also affect behavior by interacting directly with the nervous system. Androgens present during prenatal development affect the development of the nervous system. In addition, both male and female sex hormones have activational effects on the adult nervous system, influencing physiological processes and behavior. This section considers some of these hormonal effects.

Hormonal Control of Female Reproductive Cycles

The reproductive cycle of female primates is called a **menstrual cycle** (from *mensis*, meaning "month"). Females of other species of mammals also have reproductive cycles, called **estrous cycles.** *Estrus* means "gadfly"; when a female rat is in estrus, her hormonal condition goads her to act differently than she does at other times. (For that matter, it goads male rats to act differently, too.) The primary feature that distinguishes menstrual cycles from estrous cycles is the monthly growth and loss of the lining of the uterus. The other features are approximately the same—except that the estrous cycle of rats takes four days.

Menstrual cycles and estrous cycles consist of a sequence of events that are controlled by hormonal secretions of the pituitary gland and ovaries. These glands interact, the secretions of one affecting those of the other. A cycle begins with the secretion of gonadotropins by the anterior pituitary gland. These hormones (especially FSH) stimulate the growth of **ovarian follicles,** small spheres of epithelial cells surrounding each ovum. Women normally produce one ovarian follicle each month; if two are produced and fertilized, dizygotic (fraternal) twins will develop. As ovarian follicles mature, they secrete estradiol, which causes the growth of the lining of the uterus in preparation for implantation of the ovum, should it be fertilized by a sperm. Feedback from the increasing level of estradiol eventually triggers the release of a surge of LH by the anterior pituitary gland. (See *Figure 10.6.*)

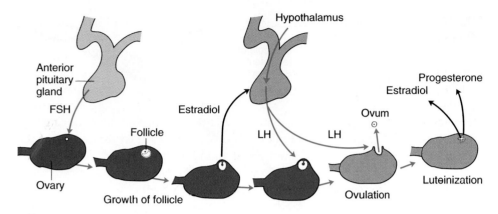

FIGURE 10.6

Neuroendocrine control of the menstrual cycle.

The LH surge causes *ovulation:* The ovarian follicle ruptures, releasing the ovum. Under the continued influence of LH the ruptured ovarian follicle becomes a **corpus luteum** ("yellow body"), which produces estradiol and **progesterone.** (See *Figure 10.6.*) The latter hormone promotes pregnancy *(gestation).* It maintains the lining of the uterus, and it inhibits the ovaries from producing another follicle. Meanwhile, the ovum enters one of the Fallopian tubes and begins its progress toward the uterus. If it meets sperm cells during its travel down the Fallopian tube and becomes fertilized, it begins to divide, and several days later it attaches itself to the uterine wall.

If the ovum is not fertilized, or if it is fertilized too late to develop sufficiently by the time it gets to the uterus, the corpus luteum will stop producing estradiol and progesterone, and then the lining of the walls of the uterus will slough off. At this point menstruation will commence.

Hormonal Control of Sexual Behavior of Laboratory Animals

The interactions between sex hormones and development of the human brain are difficult to study. We must turn to two sources of information: experiments with animals and various developmental disorders in humans, which serve as nature's own "experiments." Let us first consider the evidence gathered from research with laboratory animals.

Males

Male sexual behavior is quite varied, although the essential features of *intromission* (entry of the penis into the female's vagina), *pelvic thrusting* (rhythmic movement of the hindquarters, causing genital friction), and *ejaculation* (discharge of semen) are characteristic of all male mammals. Humans, of course, have invented all kinds of copulatory and noncopulatory sexual behavior. For example, the pelvic movements leading to ejaculation may be performed by the woman, and sex play can lead to orgasm without intromission.

The sexual behavior of rats has been studied more than that of any other laboratory animal. When a male rat encounters a receptive female, he will spend some time nuzzling her and sniffing and licking her genitals, mount her, and engage in pelvic thrusting. He will mount her several times, achieving intromission on most of the mountings. After eight to fifteen intromissions approximately 1 minute apart (each lasting only about one-quarter of a second), the male will ejaculate.

After ejaculating, the male refrains from sexual activity for a period of time (minutes, in the rat). Most mammals will return to copulate again and again, showing a longer pause, called a **refractory period,** after each ejaculation. (The term comes from the Latin *refringere,* "to break off.") An interesting phenomenon occurs in some mammals. If a male, after finally becoming "exhausted" by repeated copulation with the same female, is presented with a new female, he begins to respond quickly—often as fast as he did in his initial contact with the first female. Successive introductions of new females can keep up his performance for prolonged periods of time. This phenomenon is undoubtedly important in species in which a single male inseminates all the females in his harem. Species with approximately equal numbers of reproductively active males and females are less likely to act this way.

The phenomenon I have just described, also seen in roosters, is usually called the **Coolidge effect.** The following story is reputed to be true, but I cannot vouch for that fact. (If it is not true, it ought to be.) The late former U.S. president Calvin Coolidge and his wife were touring a farm, when Mrs. Coolidge asked the farmer whether the continuous and vigorous sexual activity among the flock of hens was the work of just one rooster. The reply was yes. "You might point that out to Mr. Coolidge," she said. The president then asked the farmer whether a different hen was involved each time. The answer, again, was yes. "You might point that out to Mrs. Coolidge," he said.

Sexual behavior of male rodents depends on testosterone, a fact that has long been recognized (Bermant and Davidson, 1974). If a male rat is castrated (that is, if his testes are removed), his sexual activity eventually ceases. However, the behavior can be reinstated by injections of testosterone. I will describe the neural basis of this activational effect later in this chapter.

As we saw earlier, testosterone can be converted, through the action of 5α reductase, to dihydrotestosterone, which is responsible for some of the masculinization that occurs during prenatal development. Testosterone can be converted into yet another hormone: estradiol. The process, called **aromatization,** is accomplished by an enzyme called an *aromatase.* (In chemistry an *aromatic compound* is one that contains a particular six-carbon ring.) Many cells of the brain contain aromatase; when molecules of testosterone enter them, they are converted into estradiol. The molecules of estradiol travel to the nucleus, bind with estrogen receptors, and trigger their physiological effects. (See *Figure 10.7.*)

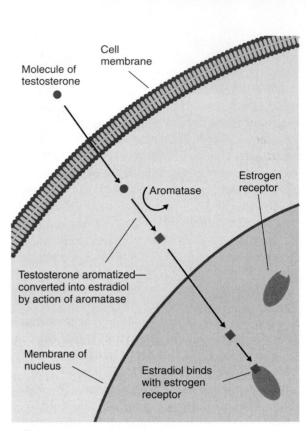

FIGURE 10.7

Aromatization. In some cells the effects of testosterone are carried out by an estrogen. Testosterone is aromatized into estradiol, which activates estrogen receptors in the nucleus.

At least some of the activational effects of testosterone on male sexual behavior are produced by the action of aromatized testosterone (that is, estradiol) on estrogen receptors. Bonsall, Clancy, and Michael (1992) found that a drug that blocks aromatase (the enzyme that converts testosterone to estrogen) decreased (but did not abolish) the sexual behavior of adult male rats.

Other hormones play a role in male sexual behavior. **Oxytocin** is a hormone produced by the posterior pituitary gland that contracts the milk ducts—and thus causes milk ejection in lactating females. It is also produced in males, where it obviously plays no role in lactation. Oxytocin is released at the time of orgasm in both males and females and appears to contribute to the contractions of the smooth muscle in the male ejaculatory system and of the vagina and uterus (Carter, 1992c). The effects of this hormonal release can easily be seen in lactating women, who often eject some milk at the time of orgasm. Because this hormone is secreted at the end of copulation, some investigators believe that this hormone plays a role in sexual satiety and, perhaps in some species, in social bonding of the sex partners (Carter, 1992b). As we shall see later in this chapter, oxytocin also serves as a neurotransmitter or neuromodulator in the brain, where it may have facilitatory effects on sexual behavior.

The refractory period that occurs after an ejaculation may be produced by another hormone, perhaps in conjunction with oxytocin. **Prolactin,** a hormone secreted by the anterior pituitary gland, stimulates milk production by the mammary glands. Like oxytocin, prolactin is released by male rats after ejaculation (Oaknin et al., 1989). In addition, prolactin has an inhibitory effect on male sexual behavior. For example, Doherty, Baum, and Todd (1986) transplanted a pituitary gland into males rats, which causes their blood level of prolactin to increase dramatically. Although the hormone had no effect on the animals' ability to attain penile erections, it severely depressed mounting behavior and intromissions. Possibly, then, both the oxytocin and prolactin that are secreted during ejaculation inhibit further sexual activity during the refractory period.

Females

The mammalian female is generally described as being the passive participant in copulation. It is true that in many species the female's role during mounting and intromission is merely to assume a posture that exposes her genitals to the male. This behavior is called the **lordosis** response (from the Greek *lordos,* meaning "bent backward"). The female will also move her tail away (if she has one) and stand rigidly enough to support the weight of the male.

The behavior of a female laboratory animal in initiating copulation is often very active, however. Certainly, if copulation with a nonestrous rodent is attempted, she will either actively flee or rebuff the male. But when she is in a receptive state, she will often approach the male, nuzzle him, sniff his geni-

tals, and show behaviors characteristic of her species. For example, a female rat will exhibit quick, short, hopping movements and rapid ear wiggling, which most male rats find irresistible (McClintock and Adler, 1978).

Sexual behavior of female rodents depends on the gonadal hormones present during estrus: estradiol and progesterone. In rats, estradiol increases about 40 hours before the female becomes receptive; just before receptivity occurs, the corpus luteum begins secreting large quantities of progesterone (Feder, 1981). Ovariectomized rats (rats whose ovaries have been removed) are not sexually receptive. Although sexual receptivity can be produced in ovariectomized rodents by administering large doses of estradiol alone, the most effective treatment duplicates the normal sequence of hormones: a small amount of estradiol, followed by progesterone. Progesterone alone is ineffective; thus, the estradiol "primes" its effectiveness. Priming with estradiol takes about 16–24 hours, after which an injection of progesterone produces receptive behaviors within an hour (Takahashi, 1990). The neural mechanisms that are responsible for these effects will be described later in this chapter.

The sequence of estradiol followed by progesterone has three effects on female rats: It increases their receptivity, their proceptivity, and their attractiveness. *Receptivity* refers to their ability and willingness to copulate—to accept the advances of a male by holding still and displaying lordosis when he attempts to mount her. *Proceptivity* refers to a female's eagerness to copulate, as shown by the fact that she seeks out a male and engages in behaviors that tend to arouse his sexual interest. *Attractiveness* refers to physiological and behavioral changes that affect the male. The male rat (along with many other male mammals) is most responsive to females who are in estrus ("in heat"). Males will ignore a female whose ovaries have been removed, but injections of estradiol and progesterone will restore her sex appeal (and also change her behavior toward the male). The stimuli that arouse a male rat's sexual interest include her odor and her behavior. In some species, visible changes, such as the swollen sex skin in the genital region of a female monkey, also affect sex appeal.

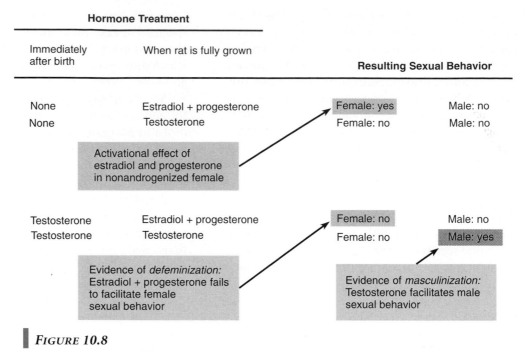

FIGURE 10.8

Organizational effects of testosterone. Around the time of birth, testosterone masculinizes and defeminizes rodents' sexual behavior.

Organizational Effects of Androgens on Behavior: Masculinization and Defeminization

The dictum "Nature's impulse is to create a female" applies to sexual behavior as well as to sex organs. That is, if a rodent brain is *not* exposed to androgens during a critical period of development, the animal will engage in female sexual behavior as an adult (if then given estradiol and progesterone). Fortunately for experimenters, this critical time comes shortly after birth for rats and for several other species of rodents, who are born in a rather immature condition. Thus, if a male rat is castrated immediately after birth, permitted to grow to adulthood, and then given injections of estradiol and progesterone, it will respond to the presence of another male by arching its back and presenting its hindquarters. In other words, it will act as if it were a female (Blaustein and Olster, 1989).

In contrast, if a rodent brain is exposed to androgens during development, two phenomena occur: behavioral defeminization and behavioral masculinization. *Behavioral defeminization* refers to the organizational effect of androgens that prevents the animal from displaying female sexual behavior in adulthood. As we shall see later, this effect is accomplished by suppressing the development of neural circuits controlling female sexual behavior. For example, if a female rodent is ovariectomized and given an injection of testosterone immediately after birth, she will *not* respond to a male rat when, as an adult, she is given injections of estradiol and progesterone. *Behavioral masculinization* refers to the organizational effect of androgens that enables animals to engage in male sexual behavior in adulthood. This effect is accomplished by stimulating the development of neural circuits controlling male sexual behavior. For example, if the female rodent in my previous example is given testosterone in adulthood, rather than estradiol and progesterone, she will mount and attempt to copulate with a receptive female. (See Breedlove, 1992, and Carter, 1992b, for references to specific studies.) (See *Figure 10.8.*)

The two organizational effects of androgens on the brain—behavioral masculinization and behavioral defeminization—are, of course, stimulated by testosterone, but some of these effects involve estradiol receptors. As you will recall, the enzyme aromatase, which is present in some cells, converts testosterone into estradiol, which then stimulates estrogen receptors located in the nucleus. It appears that behavioral defeminization is largely accomplished by the stimulation of estrogen receptors, whereas some aspects of behavioral masculinization are accomplished by the direct effects of testosterone on androgen receptors and others by the indirect effects of aromatized testosterone on estrogen receptors (see Brand et al., 1991, for specific references).

You might wonder why *all* fetuses do not become defeminized and at least partly androgenized; after all, the fetuses are exposed to their mother's estradiol. The answer to this question is interesting. The blood of fetuses contains a substance called α-*fetoprotein,* which binds with estradiol and inactivates it (Breedlove, 1992). This means that the only estradiol that has organizational effects is that which is produced *inside* the cell by the action of aromatase on molecules of testosterone.

Research by Moore and her colleagues (reviewed by Moore, 1987) indicates that some of the masculinizing and defeminizing effects of androgens are indirect. As we will see in a later section female rats spend a considerable amount of time licking the genital region of their offspring. This behavior is very useful, because it stimulates urination and permits the mother to ingest the water and minerals that are released so they can be recycled in her milk.

Moore and her colleagues discovered that mothers spent much more time licking their male offspring and wondered whether this licking could have any effects on the sexual behavior of these offspring later in life. Indeed, it did. First, the experimenters found that androgens were responsible for the presence of an odor in the male pups' urine, which was attractive to the mothers. Next, they found that if they destroyed the mothers' ability to smell the odor, the mothers failed to give the males special attention—and that these males showed decreases in their sexual behavior in adulthood. But if the experimenters stroked the genitals of the male pups with a small brush each day, the animals showed normal sexual behavior when they grew up. Thus, at least some of the organizational effects of androgens are accomplished through an intermediary—the infant's mother.

Effects of Pheromones

Hormones transmit messages from one part of the body (the secreting gland) to another (the target tissue). Another class of chemicals, called **pheromones,** carries messages from one animal to another. These chemicals, like hormones, affect reproductive behavior. Karlson and Luscher (1959) coined the term, from the Greek *pherein,* "to carry," and *horman,* "to excite." Pheromones are released by one animal and directly affect the physiology or behavior of another. Most pheromones are detected by means of olfaction, but some are ingested or absorbed through the skin.

Pheromones can affect reproductive physiology or behavior. First, let us consider the effects on reproductive physiology. When groups of female mice are housed together, their estrous cycles slow down and eventually stop. This phenomenon is known as the **Lee–Boot effect** (van der Lee and Boot, 1955). If groups of females are exposed to the odor of a male (or of his urine), they begin cycling again, and their cycles tend to be synchronized. This phenomenon is known as the **Whitten effect** (Whitten, 1959). The **Vandenbergh effect** (Vandenbergh, Whitsett, and Lombardi, 1975) is the acceleration of the onset of puberty in a female rodent caused by the odor of a male. Both the Whitten effect and the Vandenbergh effect are caused by a pheromone present only in the urine of intact adult males; the urine of a juvenile or castrated male has no effect. Thus, the production of the pheromone requires the presence of testosterone.

The **Bruce effect** (Bruce, 1960a, 1960b) is a particularly interesting phenomenon: When a recently impregnated female mouse encounters a normal male mouse other than the one with which she mated, the pregnancy is very likely to fail. This effect, too, is caused by a substance secreted in the urine of intact males—but not of males that have been castrated. Thus, a male mouse that encounters a pregnant female is able to destroy the genetic material of another male and subsequently impreg-

| *FIGURE 10.9*

The rodent accessory olfactory system.
(Adapted from Wysocki, C.J. *Neuroscience* & *Biobehavioral Reviews*, 1979, *3*, 301–341.)

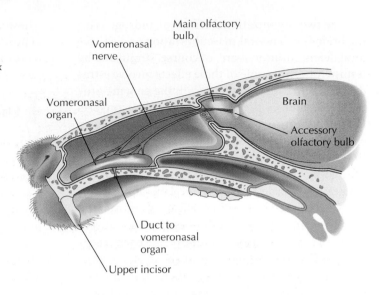

nate the female himself. And this phenomenon is advantageous even from the female's point of view. The fact that the new male has managed to take over the old male's territory indicates that he is probably healthier and more vigorous—and therefore his genes will contribute to the formation of offspring more likely to survive.

As you learned in Chapter 7, detection of odors is accomplished by the olfactory bulbs, which constitute the primary olfactory system. However, the four effects that pheromones have on reproductive cycles appear to be mediated by another organ—the **vomeronasal organ**—which consists of a small group of sensory receptors arranged around a pouch connected by a duct to the nasal passage. The vomeronasal organ, which is present in all orders of mammals except for cetaceans (whales and dolphins), projects to the **accessory olfactory bulb,** located immediately behind the olfactory bulb (Wysocki, 1979). (See *Figure 10.9.*) The vomeronasal organ probably does not detect airborne molecules, as the olfactory bulbs do, but instead is sensitive to nonvolatile compounds found in urine or other substances. In fact, stimulation of a nerve that serves the nasal region of the hamster causes fluid to be pumped into the vomeronasal organ, which exposes the receptors to substances that may be present (Meredith and O'Connell, 1979). This pump is activated whenever the animal encounters a novel stimulus (Meredith, 1987).

Removal of the accessory olfactory bulb disrupts the Lee–Boot effect, the Whitten effect, the Vandenbergh effect, and the Bruce effect; thus, this organ is essential for these phenomena (Halpern, 1987). The accessory olfactory bulb sends axons to the **medial nucleus of the amygdala,** which in turn projects to the preoptic area and anterior hypothalamus and to the ventromedial nucleus of the hypothalamus. (As you learned in Chapter 7, so does the main olfactory bulb.) Thus, the neural circuit responsible for the effects of these pheromones appears to involve these regions. As we shall see, the preoptic area, the medial amygdala, and the ventromedial nucleus of the hypothalamus all play important roles in reproductive behavior. (See *Figure 10.10.*)

The Bruce effect involves learning; the female obviously learns to recognize the odor of the male with which she mates, because his odor will not cause her to abort if she encounters it later. This learning appears to involve the activity of a set of noradrenergic axons that enter the olfactory bulbs and form synapses with neurons in both the main and accessory olfactory bulbs. Keverne and de la Riva (1982) found that after these axons had been destroyed with infusions of 6-hydroxydopamine (6-HD), a female mouse would not learn to recognize the odor of the male that mated with her; *his* odor would cause her to abort.

It is possible that the stimuli associated with copulation trigger the noradrenergic mechanism and "imprint" the odor of the male on the female, ensuring that she will not abort if she later encounters his odor. Indeed, Rosser and Keverne (1985) found that vaginal stimulation increases the activity in the noradrenergic axons that serve the olfactory bulbs. As other studies have shown (Gray, Freeman, and Skinner, 1986; Leon, 1987), the release of norepinephrine in the olfactory bulbs is necessary for olfactory learning.

Pheromones also have some effects on the reproductive physiology of males. For example, when male mice encounter a novel female (or her urine), their blood level of testosterone increases. This effect is abolished by lesions of the vomeronasal organ (Wysocki, Katz, and Bernhard, 1983). (See *Figure 10.11.*)

Besides having effects on reproductive physiology, some pheromones directly affect behavior. For example, pheromones present in the vaginal secretions of female hamsters stimulate sexual behavior in males. Males are attracted to the secretions of females, and they sniff and lick the female's genitals before copulating. In fact, there may be two categories of pheromones, one detected by the vomeronasal organ and another detected by the olfactory epithelium; mating behavior of male hamsters is disrupted only if *both* systems are interrupted (Powers and Winans, 1975; Winans and Powers, 1977). As we saw, both the primary and accessory olfactory systems send fibers to the medial nucleus of the amygdala. Lehman and Winans (1982) found that lesions of the medial

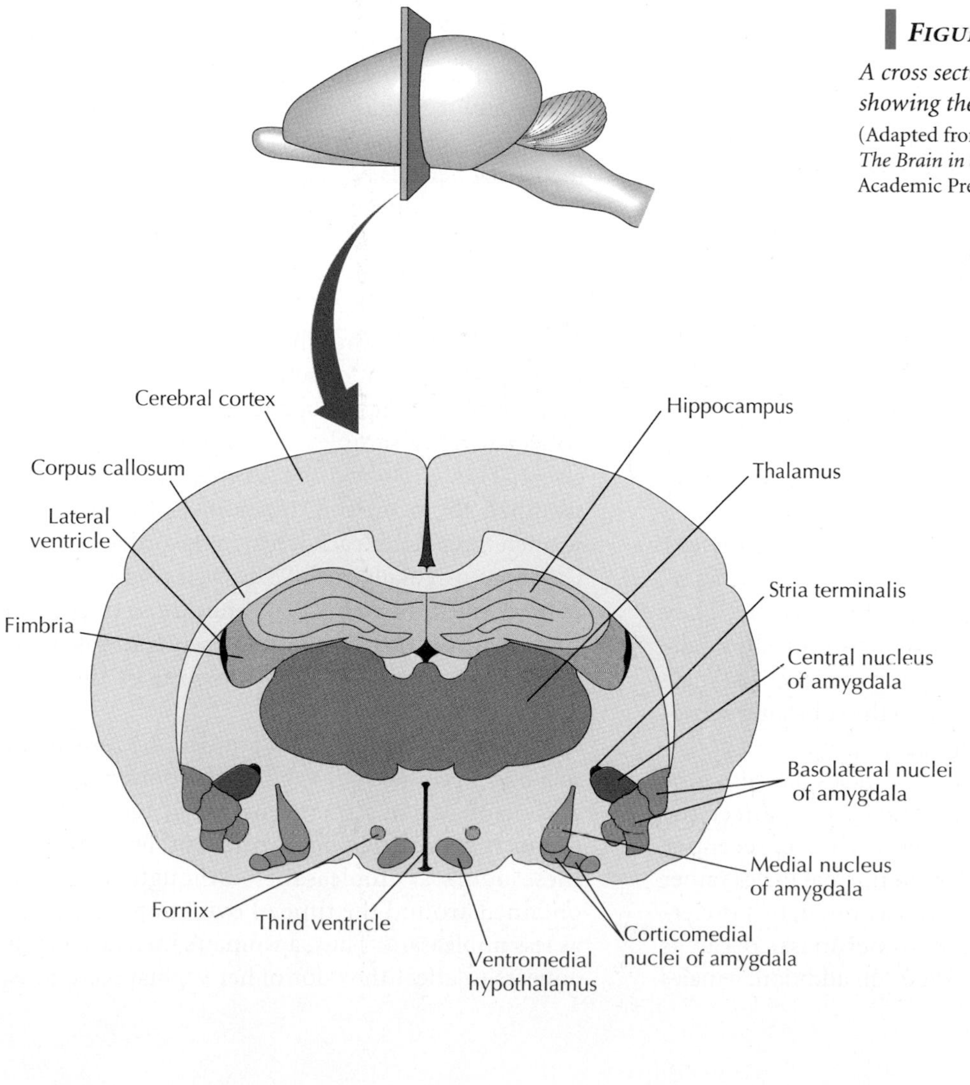

FIGURE 10.10

A cross section through the rat brain showing the location of the amygdala. (Adapted from Paxinos, G., and Watson, C. *The Brain in Stereotaxic Coordinates.* Sydney: Academic Press, 1982.

Cerebral cortex
Corpus callosum
Lateral ventricle
Fimbria
Fornix
Third ventricle
Ventromedial hypothalamus
Hippocampus
Thalamus
Stria terminalis
Central nucleus of amygdala
Basolateral nuclei of amygdala
Medial nucleus of amygdala
Corticomedial nuclei of amygdala

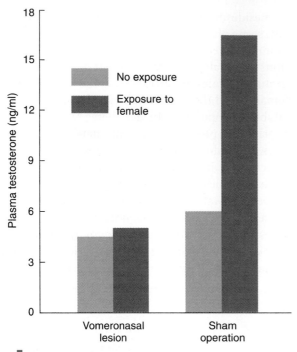

FIGURE 10.11.

Effects of destruction of the vomeronasal system on testosterone secretion stimulated by the presence of a female mouse.

(Adapted from Wysocki, C.J., Katz, Y., and Bernhard, R. *Biology of Reproduction*, 1983, *4*, 2230–2236.)

amygdala abolished the sexual behavior of male hamsters. Thus, the amygdala is part of the system that mediates the effects of pheromones on the sexual behavior of male hamsters.

Singer and his colleagues (Singer et al., 1986; Singer, 1991) succeeded in isolating and analyzing the molecular structure of a sex-attractant pheromone in the vaginal discharge of female hamsters, a protein that they named *aphrodisin*. They tested the effectiveness of this pheromone by swabbing it on the hindquarters of an anesthetized male hamster; test males who sniffed the substance subsequently attempted to mount the animal.

Some evidence suggests that males may also produce sex-attractant pheromones that affect the behavior of females. If given a choice, receptive female rats prefer to be close to normal males rather than to males that have been castrated; this preference disappears after the vomeronasal organ is destroyed (Romero et al., 1990). In addition, females who mate briefly with a series of males become more and more receptive. Rajendren, Dudley, and Moss (1990) found that this increased receptivity, too, is abolished by destruction of the vomeronasal organ.

It appears that at least some pheromone-related phenomena occur in humans. In the past, most investigators believed that the human nose did not contain a vomeronasal organ, and thus they assumed that all effects of pheromones on humans involved the main olfactory system. However, a recent study suggests that we do have such an organ. Two plastic surgeons, Garcia-Velasco and Mondragon (1991), examined the olfactory mucosae of 1000 patients during surgical reconstructions of their noses, and they reported finding vomeronasal organs in virtually every case. So far, no one has obtained evidence that the human vomeronasal organ actually has some physiological functions.

McClintock (1971) studied the menstrual cycles of women attending an all-female college. She found that women who spent a large amount of time together tended to have synchronized cycles—their menstrual periods began within a day or two of one another. In addition, women who regularly spent some time in the presence of men tended to have shorter cycles than those who rarely spent time with (smelled?) men.

Russell, Switz, and Thompson (1977) obtained direct evidence that olfactory stimuli can synchronize women's menstrual cycles. The investigators collected daily samples of a woman's underarm sweat. They dissolved the samples in alcohol and swabbed them on the upper lips of a group of women three times each week, in the order in which they were originally taken. The cycles of the women who received the extract (but not those of control subjects whose lips were swabbed with pure alcohol) began to synchronize with the cycle of the odor donor.

Some investigators have studied the possibility that odors produced by vaginal secretions may affect a woman's sexual attractiveness. Doty et al. (1975) found, however, that both males and females rated these odors as unpleasant—although secretions obtained around the time of ovulation were rated as less unpleasant. Thus, a woman's menstrual cycle appears to affect the odor of her vaginal secretions, but there is no direct evidence that these changes increase her sexual attractiveness.

Cowley and Brookshank (1991) obtained some interesting evidence that suggests that pheromones may affect the social behavior of humans. They asked male and female college students to wear necklaces overnight and to keep a record of their social interactions the following day. Some of the necklaces contained *androstenol,* a substance found in human underarm sweat—especially that of males. Other necklaces contained an inert control substance. The investigators found that the androstenol had no effect on the social interactions of male subjects, but that female subjects engaged in more social exchanges with men. Thus, exposure to a substance normally produced by men has at least a small effect on women's tendency to engage in social interactions with men. The phenomenon is probably mediated by the main olfactory bulbs, because activation of the vomeronasal organ appears to require direct contact with chemicals dissolved in liquids.

Although there is currently only scanty evidence that pheromones play a role in sexual attraction in higher primates, the familiar odor of a sex partner may have a positive effect on sexual arousal. We are not generally conscious of the fact, but we can identify other people on the basis of olfactory cues. For example, a study by Russell (1976) found that people were able to distinguish by odor between T-shirts that they had worn and those previously worn by other people. They could also tell whether the unknown owner of a T-shirt was male or female. Thus, it is likely that men and women can *learn* to be attracted by their partners' characteristic odors, just as they can learn to be attracted by the sound of their voice. In an instance like this, the odors are serving simply as sensory cues, not as pheromones.

Human Sexual Behavior

Human sexual behavior, like that of other mammals, is influenced by the activational effects of gonadal hormones. But as we will see in the following sections, the effects are different. Men and women are more similar in their responses to sex hormones than are males and females of other species. Because some of the activational effects depend on prior organizational effects, the organizational effects are discussed first.

Organizational Effects of Prenatal Androgens

A myth that should be dispelled immediately is that men and women would exchange their behavioral roles if their hormonal balances were reversed (subject, of course, to anatomical differences). Nothing of the sort would happen. Castrating a heterosexual man and giving him female sex hormones would not make him suddenly become interested in males as sex partners. His body would change and he would lose the ability to have sexual intercourse, but his sexual orientation would not change. Similarly, removing a heterosexual woman's ovaries and giving her testosterone would not make her lose her sexual interest in men or make her want to engage in sexual activity with other women. She would not even lose her sex drive (although men might be turned off by her beard and husky voice). In fact, she may become even *more* interested in sex than she was before.

As we shall see later in this chapter, prenatal androgenization does affect development of the human brain; there are parts of the brain that differ in men and women. Thus, androgens may have defeminizing and masculinizing effects on human sexual behavior, just as they do in other mammals. However, the data we have so far are not conclusive. Even if prenatal androgenization does influence human sexual behavior, the effect is certainly different from the effect that occurs in laboratory animals. The most important reason for this difference is that, unlike rodents, human males and females do not exhibit rigidly different sexual behaviors. That statement might sound foolish to you. "Of course," you say to yourself, "men and women have different sexual behavior." But think about what men and women do, in contrast to other mammals. Male rats mount, intromit, and perform pelvic thrusts. Female rats arch their backs, move their tails, and stand still. Their copulatory behaviors are very stereotyped and very different. All males basically copulate the same way, and so do all females.

Human sexual behavior is much less stereotyped. The behavior of humans during sexual intercourse shares an important element with other species, namely, the movement of the penis in the vagina. However, this movement can be accomplished by the man, the woman, or both of them. There is no single pattern of movements that all humans are obliged to follow in order to copulate; human sexual activity comes in a variety of forms. Except for the obvious effects of anatomical differences, we cannot characterize particular sets of movements as exclusively "male" or "female."

What *does* distinguish between heterosexual men and women is *the gender of their preferred sex partner.* Heterosexual men prefer women, and heterosexual women prefer men. (Bisexual men and women are attracted to people of both sexes.) A person's sexual orientation is defined not by the particular behaviors he or she performs but by the gender of the partner with whom he or she performs them. Therefore, if the brain of a human fetus is altered by exposure to testosterone, we would not expect this alteration to affect particular *behaviors.* Rather, we might expect it to affect whether the person is sexually attracted to men or to women. This possibility will be explored in the next section and later in this chapter when I discuss sexual orientation.

Prenatal Androgenization of Human Females. Evidence suggests that prenatal androgenization can affect human social behavior and sexual orientation, as well as anatomy. In a disorder known as the **adrenogenital syndrome,** the adrenal glands secrete abnormal amounts of androgens. (Note that the word is *adreno*genital, because of the involvement of the adrenal glands, not *andro*genital.) The secretion of androgens begins prenatally; thus, the syndrome causes prenatal androgenization. Boys born with adrenogenital syndrome develop normally; the extra androgen does not seem to have significant effects. However, a girl with adrenogenital syndrome will be born with an enlarged clitoris, and her labia may be partly fused together. (As Figure 10.3 shows, the scrotum and labia develop from the same tissue in the fetus.) If the masculinization of the genitals is pronounced, surgery will be performed to correct them. In any event, once the syndrome is identified, the person will be given a synthetic hormone that suppresses the abnormal secretion of androgens.

Money, Schwartz, and Lewis (1984) studied thirty young women with a history of adrenogenital syndrome. They had all been born with enlarged clitorises and partly fused labia, which led to the diagnosis. (A few mild cases were not diagnosed for several years.) Once the diagnosis was made, they were treated with drugs that suppress the secretion of adrenal androgens and, if necessary, genital surgery was performed. Money and his colleagues asked the young women to describe their sexual orientation. Thirty-seven percent of the women described themselves as bisexual or homosexual, 40 percent said they were exclusively heterosexual, and 23 percent refused to talk about their sex lives. If the noncommittal women are excluded from the sample, the percentage of homo- or bisexuality rises to 48 percent.

The Kinsey report on sexuality in women (Kinsey et al., 1953) reported that approximately 10 percent of American women had had some sexual contact with another woman by the age of twenty; in the sample of androgenized women the percentage was at least four times as high. The results therefore suggest that the exposure of a female fetus to an abnormally high level of androgens does affect sexual orientation. A plausible explanation is that the effect takes place in the brain, but we must remember that the androgens also affect the genitals; possibly, the changes in the genitals played a role in shaping the development of the girls' sexual orientation. If the differences seen in sexual orientation *were* caused by effects of the prenatal androgens on brain development, then we could reasonably conclude that androgens have this effect in males, too. That is, these results support the hypothesis that male sexual orientation is at least partly determined by masculinizing (and defeminizing) effects of androgens on the human brain.

Because controlled experiments cannot be performed on humans, some investigators have turned to our close relatives to see whether prenatal androgenization has enduring behavioral effects. Goy, Bercovitch, and McBrair (1988) administered injections of testosterone to pregnant monkeys. The testosterone entered the blood supply of the fetuses and masculinized them. Female infants that had been androgenized during early fetal development were born with masculinized genitals; the genitals of those that had been androgenized later were normal. *Both* groups showed differences in their sociosexual interactions with peers, displaying a higher proportion of malelike behavior than normal females did.

For example, even as young adults, the group with normal genitals continued to mount their peers significantly more than normal females did. The results suggest that genital changes cannot account for all the behavioral effects of prenatal androgenization in primates. Whether *human* primates share these characteristics is, of course, another question.

Failure of Androgenization. Nature has performed the equivalent of a prenatal castration experiment in humans (Money and Ehrhardt, 1972; Ris-Stalpers et al., 1990). Some people are insensitive to androgens; they have **androgen insensitivity syndrome,** one of the more aptly named disorders. The cause of androgen insensitivity syndrome is a genetic mutation that prevents the formation of functioning androgen receptors. (The gene for the androgen receptor is located on the X chromosome.) The primitive gonads of a genetic male fetus with androgen insensitivity syndrome become testes and secrete Müllerian-inhibiting substance and androgens. However, only the Müllerian-inhibiting substance has an effect on development. Because the cells of the body cannot respond to the androgens, the person develops female external genitalia. The Müllerian-inhibiting substance prevents the female internal sex organs from developing, though; the uterus fails to develop and the vagina is shallow. (Incidentally, androgen insensitivity syndrome occurs in several species, including rats.)

If an individual with this syndrome is raised as a girl, all is well. Normally, the testes are removed because they often become cancerous; but if they are not, the body will become feminized at the time of puberty by the small amounts of estradiol produced by the testes. (If the testes are removed, the person will be given estradiol.) At adulthood the individual will function sexually as a woman, although surgical lengthening of the vagina may be necessary. Women with this syndrome report average sex drives, including normal frequency of orgasm in intercourse. Most marry and lead normal sex lives. Of course, lacking a uterus and ovaries, they cannot have children. (See *Figure 10.12.*)

During the Summer Olympics of 1992, a heated controversy arose over the use of sex testing of female athletes. One of the effects of androgens is to increase the size and strength of skeletal muscles;

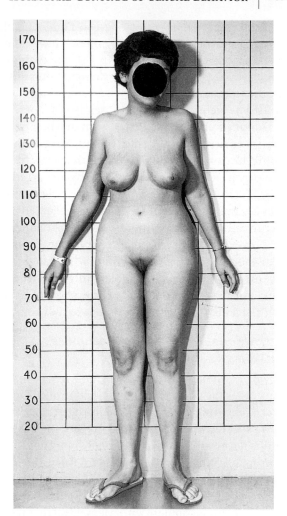

FIGURE 10.12

An XY female displaying androgen insensitivity syndrome. The absence of pubic hair can be explained by the person's insensitivity to androstenedione.

(From Money, J., and Ehrhardt, A.A. *Man & Woman, Boy & Girl.* Copyright 1973 by The Johns Hopkins University Press, Baltimore, Maryland. By permission.)

thus, men generally have greater physical strength than women. In the past, men have occasionally disguised themselves as women and have competed in women's events, in the hopes that they would have a better chance of winning a medal. To prevent such deception, the officials decided to take a sample of cells from all women athletes and examine their chromosomes; only those with the XX genotype would be accepted as women. (As you undoubtedly know, both men and women athletes have taken anabolic steroids, which are simply synthetic androgens, to increase their muscular strength—but this is another matter.)

But as we just saw, genetic sex is not a perfect indicator of phenotypic sex. A woman with androgen insensitivity syndrome and an XY genotype would be disqualified from Olympic competition in women's events—and, in fact, this occurred in 1992. Such disqualification is manifestly unjust, because the only reason for separating women and men in athletic competition is the effect of androgens on muscular development. But because women with androgen insensitivity syndrome lack androgen receptors, androgens have absolutely no effect on their muscles! (As you can see, there would be no point at all in their taking anabolic steroids.)

Activational Effects of Sex Hormones on Women's Sexual Behavior

As we saw, the sexual behavior of most female mammals other than higher primates is controlled by the ovarian hormones estradiol and progesterone. (In some species, such as cats and rabbits, only estradiol is necessary.) As Wallen (1990) points out, the ovarian hormones not only control the *willingness* (or even eagerness) of an estrous female to mate, but they control her *ability* to mate, as well. That is, a male rat cannot copulate with a female rat that is not in estrus. Even if he would overpower her and mount her, her lordosis response would not occur, and he would be unable to achieve intromission. (The neural control of the lordosis response and the effects of ovarian hormones on it are described later in this chapter.)

In higher primates (including our own species), the ability to mate is not controlled by ovarian hormones. There are no physical barriers to sexual intercourse during any part of the menstrual cycle. If a woman or other female primate consents to sexual activity at any time (or is forced to submit by a male), intercourse can certainly take place.

This difference between females with estrous cycles and menstrual cycles has obscured the effects of ovarian hormones on the sexual behavior of female primates. Most studies have reported that fluctuations in the level of the ovarian hormones

have only a minor effect on women's sexual interest (Adams, Gold, and Burt, 1978; Morris et al., 1987). However, as Wallen (1990) points out, these studies have almost all involved married women who live with their husbands. In stable, monogamous relationships in which the partners are together on a daily basis, sexual activity can be instigated by either of them. Normally, a husband does not force his wife to have intercourse with him, but even if she is not interested in engaging in sexual activity at that moment, she may find that she wants to do so because of her affection for him. In fact, a study of lesbian couples showed a significant increase in sexual interest and activity during the middle portions of women's menstrual cycles (Matteo and Rissman, 1984).

Several studies have found that the sexual behavior of female monkeys is only poorly related to their menstrual cycles. However, most of these studies were carried out with small numbers of monkeys living in small cages. Thus, intercourse was as likely to be instigated by a male as by the female. Wallen et al. (1986) observed female monkeys who were housed in large groups in large cages, in a situation in which a female could seek out a sex partner if she wanted one, but could avoid sexual contact if she preferred. Figure 10.13 contrasts the results of these two types of studies; note that the sexual activity of females housed in large-group situations closely corresponded with their cycles of ovarian hormones. (See *Figure 10.13.*)

These results pose an interesting question. If all of a woman's sexual encounters were initiated by her, without regard to her partner's desires, would we find as strong an effect of ovarian hormones as Wallen and her colleagues found in monkeys? As Alexander et al. (1990) showed, women taking oral contraceptives (which prevent the normal cycles in secretion of ovarian hormones) were less likely to show fluctuations in sexual interest during the menstrual cycle. In any event, the more recent results with monkeys indicate that the possibility remains that ovarian hormones *do* have a significant effect on a woman's sexual desire.

A possible difference between higher primates and animals with estrous cycles is their reaction to androgens. Persky et al. (1978) studied the sexual activity and blood levels of various hormones in

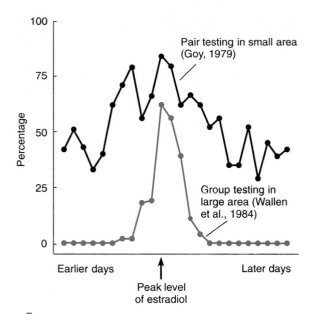

FIGURE 10.13

Percentage of tests in which ejaculations occurred in the course of a female monkey's menstrual cycle.
(Adapted from Wallen, K. *Neuroscience and Biobehavioral Reviews*, 1990, *14*, 233–241; after Goy, 1979 and Wallen et al., 1984.)

married couples over a period of three menstrual cycles. They found that the frequency of intercourse over the entire cycle was at least moderately correlated with the wife's peak testosterone level, which occurs around the time of ovulation. In addition, the wives reported more sexual gratification when their testosterone levels were high.

Although experiments with humans are not possible, research on the effects of hormones on female sexual behavior has been performed with rhesus macaques, a common species of laboratory monkey. In general, results have confirmed a role for androgens in the sexual behavior of this species. Everitt, Herbert, and Hamer (1972) found that removal of the adrenal glands (which secrete some androgens) decreased the sexual interest of female rhesus macaques who had previously been ovariectomized. The effect was seen most strikingly in the animals' soliciting behavior, or proceptivity. Removal of the adrenal glands had a much smaller effect on the animals' willingness to engage in sexual activity with a male who initiates the behavior. Administration of testosterone reinstituted these behaviors to normal levels.

Finally, oxytocin may play a role in a woman's sexual response. As we saw earlier in this chapter, oxytocin appears to stimulate contractions of the uterus and vagina that accompany orgasm, and some investigators have suggested that the pleasant "afterglow" that follows sexual intercourse may involve the action of oxytocin. Whether this hormone actually plays a role in pair-bonding in humans has yet to be established. I find it difficult to imagine how this question could be addressed through scientific study.

Activational Effects of Sex Hormones in Men

Although women and female rodents appear to differ in their behavioral responsiveness to sex hormones, men and male rodents (and other mammals, for that matter) resemble each other in their behavioral responsiveness to testosterone. With normal levels they can be potent and fertile; without testosterone, sperm production ceases and, sooner or later, so does sexual activity. Some investigators have said that the sexual activity of humans is "emancipated" from the effects of hormones. In one sense this is true. Men who have been castrated for medical reasons do report a continuing interest in sexual activity with their wives. Even if sexual activity no longer takes the form of intercourse, other types of sexual contact can occur.

The decline of sexual activity after castration is quite variable. As reported by Money and Ehrhardt (1972), some men lose potency immediately, whereas others show a slow, gradual decline over several years. Perhaps at least some of the variability is a function of prior experience; practice not only may "make perfect" but may also forestall a decline in function. Although there is no direct evidence with respect to this possibility in humans, Rosenblatt and Aronson (1958a, 1958b) found that high levels of sexual activity before castration substantially prolonged subsequent potency in male cats. In addition, there are other sources of androgens besides the testes that may supply at least small amounts of male sex hormones: the adrenal glands, the prostate gland, and even fat tissue (Carter, 1992a).

Testosterone not only affects sexual activity but also is affected by it—or even by thinking about it. A scientist stationed on a remote island (Anonymous,

1970) removed his beard with an electrical shaver each day and weighed the clippings. Just before he left for visits to the mainland (and to the company of a female companion), his beard began growing faster. Because rate of beard growth is related to androgen levels, the effect indicates that his anticipation of sexual activity stimulated testosterone production. Confirming these results, Hellhammer, Hubert, and Schurmeyer (1985) found that watching an erotic film increased men's testosterone level.

As we saw earlier in this chapter, oxytocin and prolactin may play a role in male sexual behavior. Both hormones are secreted during orgasm, and both may be at least partly responsible for the refractory period. In addition, oxytocin may even contribute to the "afterglow" that is usually experienced by both partners after making love.

Sexual Orientation

What controls a person's sexual orientation—the gender of the preferred sex partner? Many humans (especially males) who are essentially heterosexual engage in homosexual episodes sometime during their lives. Although many animals occasionally engage in sexual activity with a member of the same sex, *exclusive* homosexuality appears to occur only in humans (Ehrhardt and Meyer-Bahlburg, 1981). Animals of other species, if they are not exclusively heterosexual, are likely to be bisexual, engaging in sexual activity with members of both sexes. In contrast, the number of men and women who describe themselves as exclusively homosexual exceeds the number who describe themselves as bisexual.

Some investigators believe that homosexuality is a result of childhood experiences, especially interactions between the child and parents. A large-scale study of several hundred male and female homosexuals reported by Bell, Weinberg, and Hammersmith (1981) attempted to assess the effects of these factors. The researchers found no evidence that homosexuals had been raised by domineering mothers or submissive fathers, as some clinicians had suggested. The best predictor of adult homosexuality was a self-report of homosexual feelings, which usually preceded homosexual activity by three years. The investigators concluded that their data did not support social explanations for homo-

sexuality but were consistent with the possibility that homosexuality is at least partly biologically determined.

If homosexuality does have a physiological cause, it certainly is not variations in the levels of sex hormones during adulthood. Many studies have examined the levels of sex steroids in male homosexuals (Meyer-Bahlburg, 1984), and the vast majority of them found these levels to be normal. A few studies suggest that about 30 percent of female homosexuals have elevated levels of testosterone (but still lower than those found in men). Whether these differences are related to a biological cause of lesbianism or whether differences in lifestyles may increase the secretion of testosterone is not yet known.

A more likely biological cause of homosexuality is a subtle difference in brain structure caused by differences in the degree of prenatal androgenization. As we saw earlier in this chapter, men and women do not differ from one another so much in their sexual *behavior* as in the gender of their sex partners. The same comparison is true for heterosexual and homosexual people; the gender of their partner, not the kind of sexual activity they engage in, distinguishes them. Therefore, if prenatal androgenization influences human brain development, the effects are likely to be seen in a person's choice of sex partner, not in the form of his or her sexual behavior. Perhaps, then, the brains of male homosexuals are neither masculinized nor defeminized, those of female homosexuals are masculinized and defeminized, and those of bisexuals are masculinized but not defeminized. Of course, these are *speculations* that so far cannot be supported by human data; they are not *conclusions*. They should be regarded as suggestions to guide future research.

Several studies have examined the brains of deceased heterosexual and homosexual men and heterosexual women. So far, three have found differences in the size of different subregions of the brain: the suprachiasmatic nucleus, the sexually dimorphic nucleus, and the anterior commissure (Swaab and Hofman, 1990; LeVay, 1991; Allen and Gorski, 1992). You are already familiar with the suprachiasmatic nucleus from Chapter 9; the sexually dimorphic nucleus will be described later; and the anterior commissure is a fiber bundle that interconnects parts of the left and right temporal lobes. The suprachiasmatic nucleus was found to be larger in homosexual men and smaller in heterosexual men and women; the sexually dimorphic nucleus was found to be larger in heterosexual men and smaller in homosexual men and heterosexual women; and the anterior commissure was found to be larger in homosexual men and heterosexual women and smaller in heterosexual men. Obviously, the differences did not follow a simple pattern.

We cannot necessarily conclude that any of the brain regions I just mentioned are directly involved in people's sexual orientation, but the results do suggest the following: The brains of heterosexual women, heterosexual men, and homosexual men may have been exposed to different patterns of hormones prenatally. The *real* differences—if indeed sexual orientation is determined by prenatal androgenization—may lie elsewhere in the brain, but at least we have an indication that differences do exist. There remains also the possibility that a person's lifestyle may affect the structure of parts of his or her brain; thus, the differences mentioned in the previous paragraph could be the *result* of people's sexual orientation rather than the cause. In any event, more research must be done on this subject.

A study performed with laboratory animals suggests that prenatal stress can alter normal patterns of adult sexual behavior. Ward (1972) subjected pregnant rats to periods of stress by confining them and exposing them to a bright light, which suppresses androgen production in male fetuses. The male rats born to the stressed mothers were less likely than control subjects to display male sexual behavior and were more likely to display female sexual behavior when they were given injections of estradiol and progesterone. Another study (Ward and Stehm, 1991) found that the play behavior of juvenile male rats whose mothers were stressed while pregnant resembled that of females more than that of males—that is, the animals showed less rough-and-tumble play. Thus, the behavioral effects caused by prenatal stress are not restricted to changes in sexual behavior.

Other studies have shown that besides having behavioral effects, prenatal stress reduces the size of the sexually dimorphic nucleus, which normally is larger in males than in females—the same nucleus that is found to be smaller in homosexual men (Anderson et al., 1986). Although we cannot assume that prenatal stress in humans and laboratory animals has similar effects on the brain and behavior, the results of these studies are consistent with the hypothesis that male homosexuality may be related to events that reduce prenatal androgenization.

Another factor that may play a role in sexual orientation is heredity. Twin studies take advantage of the fact that identical twins have identical genes, whereas the genetic similarity between fraternal twins is, on the average, 50 percent. Bailey and Pillard (1991) studied pairs of male twins in which at least one member identified himself as homosexual. If both twins are homosexual, they are said to be *concordant* for this trait. If only one is homosexual, the twins are said to be *discordant*. Thus, if homosexuality has a genetic basis, the percentage of monozygotic twins concordant for homosexuality should be higher than that for dizygotic twins. And this is exactly what Bailey and Pillard found; the concordance rate was 52 percent for identical twins and only 22 percent for fraternal twins.

To summarize, evidence suggests that two biological factors—prenatal hormonal exposure and heredity—may affect a person's sexual orientation. These research findings certainly contradict the suggestion that a person's sexual orientation is a moral issue. It appears that homosexuals are no more responsible for their sexual orientation than heterosexuals are. Ernulf, Innala, and Whitam (1989) found that people who believed that homosexuals were "born that way" expressed more positive attitudes toward them than people who believed that they "chose to be" or "learned to be" that way. Thus, we can hope that research on the origins of homosexuality will reduce prejudice based on a person's sexual orientation. The question, "Why does someone become homosexual?" will probably be answered when we find out why someone becomes *heterosexual.*

INTERIM SUMMARY

Sexual behaviors are controlled by the organizational and activational effects of hormones. The female reproductive cycle (menstrual cycle or estrous cycle) begins with the maturation of one or more ovarian follicles, which occurs in response to the secretion of FSH by the anterior pituitary gland. As the ovarian follicle matures, it secretes estradiol, which causes the lining of the uterus to develop. When estradiol reaches a critical level, it causes the pituitary gland to secrete a surge of LH, triggering ovulation. The empty ovarian follicle becomes a corpus luteum, under the continued influence of LH, and secretes estradiol and progesterone. If pregnancy does not occur, the corpus luteum dies and stops producing hormones, and menstruation begins.

The sexual behavior of males of all mammalian species appears to depend on the presence of androgens. Oxytocin has a facilitatory effect on erection and ejaculation, whereas prolactin has a generally inhibitory effect. Both hormones may be involved in the male refractory period, and oxytocin in particular may be involved in social bonding. The proceptivity, receptivity, and attractiveness of female mammals other than primates depend primarily on estradiol and progesterone. In particular, estradiol has a priming effect on the subsequent appearance of progesterone. Oxytocin also may facilitate social bonding in females.

In most mammals female sexual behavior is the norm, just as the female body and female sex organs are the norm. That is, unless prenatal androgens masculinize and defeminize the animal's brain, its sexual behavior will be feminine. Behavioral masculinization refers to the androgen-stimulated development of neural circuits that respond to testosterone in adulthood, producing male sexual behavior. Behavioral defeminization refers to the inhibitory effects of androgens on the development of neural circuits that respond to estradiol and progesterone in adulthood, producing female sexual behavior. Behavioral defeminization is caused by intracellular estradiol, derived from testosterone through the action of aromatase.

Some organizational effects of androgens are indirect. Androgens render the urine of male rat pups more attractive to their mothers, who spend more time licking their anogenital region. This tactile stimulation contributes to their behavioral masculinization.

Pheromones can affect sexual physiology and behavior. Odorants present in the urine of female mice affect their estrous cycles, lengthening and eventually stopping them (Lee–Boot effect). Odorants present in the urine of male mice abolish these effects and cause the females' cycles to become synchronized (Whitten effect). (Phenomena similar to the Lee–Boot effect and the Whitten effect also occur in women.) Odorants can also accelerate the onset of puberty in females (Vandenbergh effect). In addition, the odor of the urine from a male other than the one that impregnated the female mouse will cause her to abort (Bruce effect). The Bruce effect involves learning the odor of the male that impregnates the female, and the activity of a noradrenergic input to the olfactory bulb (triggered by vaginal stimulation) is involved in this learning. Finally, odorants in the urine of female mice stimulate the release of testosterone in male mice.

In the hamster the attractiveness of an estrous female to the male derives in part from chemicals present in her vaginal secretions, detected by the olfactory epithelium and vomeronasal organ. Connections between the olfactory system and the amygdala appear to be important in stimulating male sexual behavior. One sex-attractant chemical, a protein named aphrodisin, has been isolated from the urine of female hamsters.

Males appear to produce pheromones that affect female behavior. Female rats prefer to be near intact adult males rather than those whose testes have been removed, and contact with several males increases their level of sexual arousal; both phenomena disappear after removal of the vomeronasal system. The search for sex attractant pheromones in humans has so far been fruitless, although we may well recognize our sex partners by their odors. One study does suggest that exposure to androstenol, a substance present in male underarm sweat, may increase a woman's tendency to engage in social interchanges with men.

The behavioral effects of prenatal androgenization in humans, if any, are not well understood. Studies of prenatally androgenized girls suggest that organizational effects may well influence the development of sexual orientation; androgenization appears to increase the incidence of homosexuality. If androgens cannot act (as they cannot in cases of androgen insensitivity syndrome), then the person's anatomy and behavior are feminine. Testosterone has an activational effect on the sexual behavior of men, just as it does on the behavior of other male mammals. Women do not require estradiol or progesterone in order to experience sexual interest or to engage in sexual behavior. However, these hormones may affect the quality and intensity of their sex drive, and studies comparing the sexual behavior of female monkeys housed in small groups with those housed in large groups in large cages suggest that the sexual proceptivity may be related to ovarian hormones even in higher primates. In addition, androgens may have an activational effect on women's sex drives.

Sexual orientation (that is, heterosexuality or homosexuality) may be influenced by prenatal androgenization. So far, researchers have obtained evidence that suggests that the sizes of three brain regions are related to a man's sexual orientation, and studies with rats have shown that events that cause stress during pregnancy can interfere with defeminization of the sexual behavior of the male offspring. In addition, twin studies suggest that heredity may play a role in sexual orientation in males.

NEURAL CONTROL OF SEXUAL BEHAVIOR

THE CONTROL OF SEXUAL BEHAVIOR—AT LEAST IN laboratory animals—involves different brain mechanisms in males and females. This section describes these mechanisms.

Males

Spinal Mechanisms

Some sexual responses are controlled by neural circuits contained within the spinal cord. For example, genital stimulation can elicit sexual movements and postures in female cats and rats even after their spinal cord is transected below the brain (Beach, 1967; Hart, 1969). In male dogs with spinal cord transections genital stimulation can produce erection and ejaculation (Hart, 1967). Thus, the brain is not required for these reflexes.

In humans, too, erection and ejaculation are controlled by spinal reflexes. Men with spinal damage have become fathers when their wives have been artificially inseminated with semen obtained by mechanical stimulation (Hart, 1978). Because the spinal damage prevents sensory information from reaching the brain, these men do not experience an orgasm; thus, they are unaware of the erection and ejaculation unless they see it happening. However, they do occasionally experience a "phantom erection" along with an orgasm (Money, 1960; Comarr, 1970). Nothing happens to their genitals or internal sex organs, but the spontaneous activity of various brain mechanisms gives rise to feelings of arousal and orgasm.

Evidence obtained by Chung, McVary, and McKenna (1988) suggests that, at least in the rat, the ejaculatory reflex does not depend on androgens. They found that an ejaculatory response could be triggered by gentle, rhythmic stimulation of the end of the urethra with a small catheter that had been placed inside it. Castration had no effect on the magnitude of the response, although it did reduce the size of penile erections. The investigators also found that a similar response could be produced in female rats (intact or ovariectomized), shown by rhythmic contractions of the vagina. The results suggest that male and female "orgasmic" responses are controlled by similar mechanisms. (The word *orgasmic* is in quotation marks, because we have no way of determining how rats feel.)

Although there may be more similarities in the sexual reflexes of males and females than had previously been suspected, Breedlove and Arnold (1980, 1983) discovered striking sex differences in the size of a nucleus in the ventral horn of the lumbar region of the spinal cord of rats. This structure, called the **spinal nucleus of the bulbocavernosus** (SNB), contains motor neurons whose axons innervate the bulbocavernosus muscle, which is attached to the base of the penis and is involved in sexual activity. Although the muscle is not present in female rats, it is present in both sexes in humans. (It is usually called the *sphincter vaginae* in women.)

Breedlove et al. (1982) found that if female rats were injected with testosterone on the second day after birth, the spinal nucleus of the bulbocavernosus would develop. Conversely, if male rats were

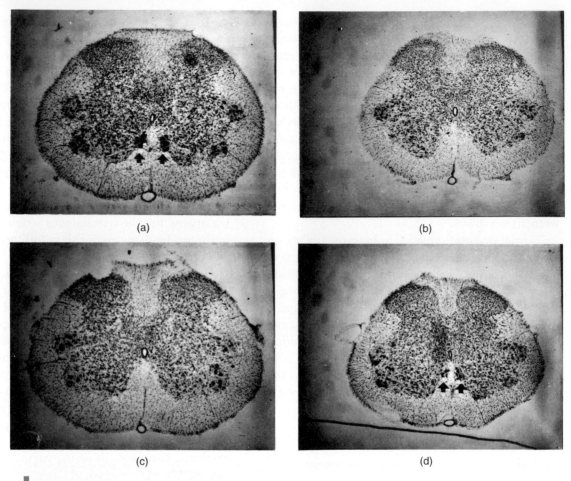

FIGURE 10.14

Photomicrographs of sections of the rat spinal cord through the region of the spinal nucleus of the bulbocavernosus. (a) Normal male. (b) Normal female. (c) Castrated male treated with an antiandrogen prenatally. (d) Androgenized female.

(From Breedlove, S.M., and Arnold, A. *Journal of Neuroscience*, 1983, *3*, 417–423; 424–432. © 1983, Society for Neuroscience.)

treated prenatally by injecting the pregnant females with drugs that inhibit the effects of androgens and were then castrated postnatally, the SNB would not develop. Figure 10.14 shows photomicrographs of sections of the rat spinal cord. The nuclei (*arrows*) are present in normal males (top left) and androgenized females but not in normal females or nonandrogenized males. (See *Figure 10.14.*)

Arnold and his colleagues found that the effect of androgens is to prevent cell death (Arnold and Jordan, 1988). During most of prenatal development, the SNB has similar numbers of neurons in males and females. Then, a day or two before birth, the number of neurons in the female SNB begins to decline. In the absence of androgens, by ten days of age, the number has fallen to about one-third of that found in males.

As we saw earlier in this chapter, Moore and her colleagues have found that in rats, some of the masculinizing and defeminizing effects of androgens on behavior are indirect. That is, androgens make the urine of infant male pups more attractive to the mothers, who spend more time licking their anogenital region, which affects their behavior in adulthood. Moore, Dou, and Juraska (1992) found that this licking also affects the development of the structure of the nervous system. They found that when they destroyed the mothers' sense of smell so that they spent less time licking their male offspring, the animals showed 11 percent fewer neurons in the SNB. Thus, although androgens have direct effects on the survival of these motor neurons, tactile stimuli delivered by the mother reinforce these effects.

Brain Mechanisms

The **medial preoptic area** (MPA), located just rostral to the hypothalamus, is the forebrain region most critical for male sexual behavior. (As we will see later in this chapter and in Chapter 11, it is also critical for other sexually dimorphic behavior, including maternal behavior and territorial aggression.) Electrical stimulation of this region elicits male copulatory behavior (Malsbury, 1971), and the act of copulation increases the metabolic activity of the MPA and induces the production of Fos protein (Oaknin et al., 1989; Robertson et al., 1991).

Destruction of the MPA permanently abolishes male sexual behavior (Heimer and Larsson, 1966/1967). (See *Figure 10.15.*)

Androgens exert their activational effects on neurons in the medial preoptic area. If a male rat is castrated in adulthood, its sexual behavior will cease. However, the behavior can be reinstated by implanting a small amount of testosterone directly into the medial preoptic area (Davidson, 1980). This region has been shown to contain a high concentration of androgen receptors in the male rat brain—more than five times as many as are found in females (Roselli, Handa, and Resko, 1989).

Androgens also are responsible for sexual dimorphisms in brain structure. Gorski et al. (1978) discovered a nucleus within the MPA of the rat that is three to seven times larger in males than in females. This area is called (appropriately enough) the **sexually dimorphic nucleus** (SDN) of the preoptic area. The size of this nucleus is controlled by the amount of androgens present during fetal development. According to Rhees, Shryne, and Gorski (1990a,

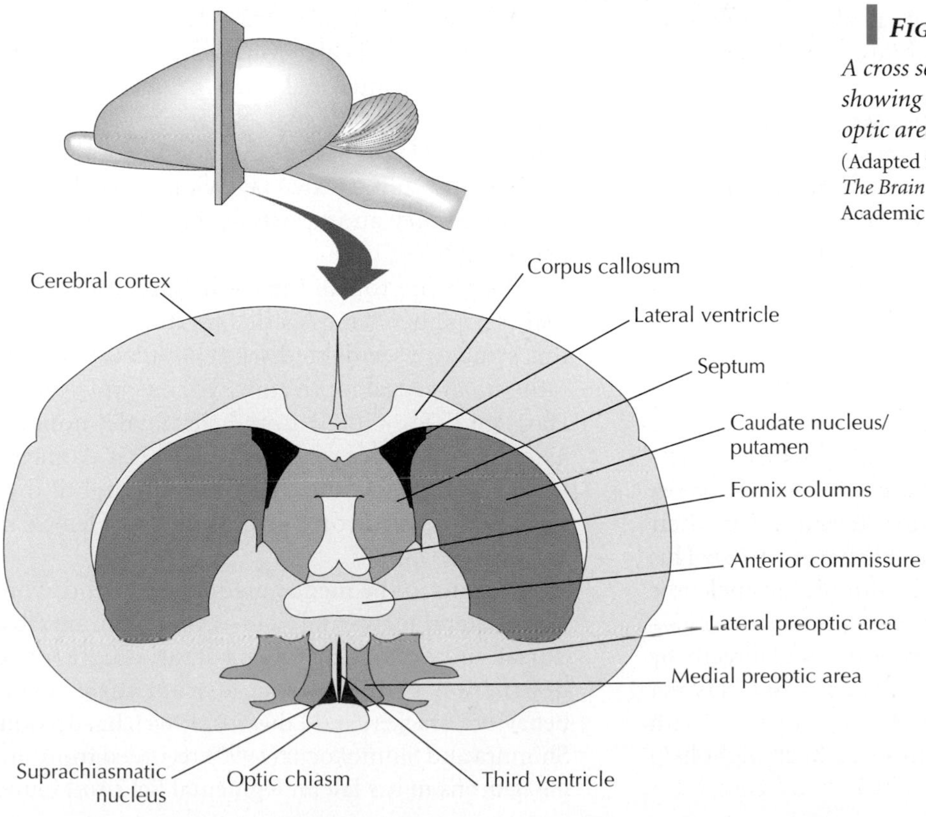

FIGURE 10.15

A cross section through the rat brain showing the location of the medial preoptic area.
(Adapted from Paxinos, G., and Watson, C. *The Brain in Stereotaxic Coordinates.* Sydney: Academic Press, 1982.)

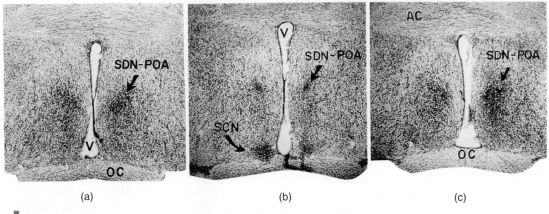

(a)   (b)   (c)

FIGURE 10.16

Photomicrographs of sections through the preoptic area of the rat brain. (a) Normal male. (b) Normal female. (c) Androgenized female. SDN-POA = sexually dimorphic nucleus of the preoptic area; OC = optic chiasm; V = third ventricle; SCN = suprachiasmatic nucleus; AC = anterior commissure.

(From Gorski, R.A., in *Neuroendocrine Perspectives,* Vol. 2, edited by E.E. Müller and R.M. MacLeod. Amsterdam: Elsevier-North Holland, 1983.)

1990b), the critical period for androgenization of the SDN appears to start on the 18th day of gestation and end once the animals are five days old. (Normally, rats are born on the 22nd day of gestation.) (See *Figure 10.16.*)

Masculinization of the sexually dimorphic nucleus appears to be accomplished by aromatized testosterone—that is, by testosterone that has been converted to estradiol within the cell (Breedlove, 1992). This fact has some interesting implications. First, it means that, in rats with androgen insensitivity syndrome, the sexually dimorphic nucleus is masculinized, because estrogen receptors, not androgen receptors, are required for this process. But studies have found that women with androgen insensitivity syndrome are almost exclusively heterosexual (that is, they are attracted to men as sex partners) and are especially "feminine" in their social behavior (Money and Ehrhardt, 1972). This means that either the sexually dimorphic nucleus is irrelevant to sexual orientation in humans, or else—unlike rats—the nucleus is masculinized directly by testosterone. So far as I know, no one has yet reported any studies on the brains of people with androgen insensitivity syndrome, which might help clarify this issue.

In the section on sexual orientation I mentioned that Anderson et al. (1986) found that prenatal stress reduced the size of the SDN in male rats. These investigators also found that volume of the SDN in an individual male rat was directly related to the animal's level of sexual activity. In addition, De Jonge et al. (1989) found that lesions of the SDN decrease masculine sexual behavior. Thus, the SDN appears to play an important role in male sexual behavior.

The precise role of the medial preoptic area in male sexual behavior is still a mystery. Damage to this structure seems to disrupt copulatory ability rather than sexual motivation. For example, Slimp, Hart, and Goy (1975) found that male monkeys whose medial preoptic areas had been damaged would no longer copulate with a female, but they would often masturbate while watching a female in an adjacent cage.

Neurons in the medial preoptic area send axons to the lateral tegmental field of the midbrain (just dorsal and medial to the substantia nigra), and destruction of these axons disrupt male sexual behavior (Brackett and Edwards, 1984). In addition, Shimura and Shimokochi (1990) recorded from single neurons in the lateral tegmental field and found that the activity of virtually all neurons increased during various aspects of copulatory behavior. For example, some increased their firing rate only when the male achieved intromission. These results suggest that the medial preoptic area exerts its effect by controlling motor mechanisms in the midbrain.

Other parts of the brain play a role in sexual behavior, too. As we saw earlier in this chapter, the medial amygdala receives information from the olfactory bulbs and the vomeronasal organ, and damage to this region disrupts many of the effects produced by pheromones. One region within the medial amygdala (which contains an especially high concentration of androgen receptors) is 85 percent larger in male rats than in female rats (Hines, Allen, and Gorski, 1992). In addition, destruction of the medial amygdala disrupts the sexual behavior of male rats. De Jonge et al. (1992) found that the rats with these lesions took longer to mount receptive females and to ejaculate. They also found that pre-exposure to receptive females that could be seen and smelled but not touched—which excites normal rats—did not enhance their sexual behavior. (See *Figure 10.17.*)

In humans, temporal lobe dysfunctions are often correlated with decreased sex drives. (The temporal lobes contain the amygdala, but the hippocampus and the temporal neocortex may also be involved.) For example, seizures that originate from localized, irritative lesions of the temporal lobes are often associated with lack of interest in sexual activity (Blumer and Walker, 1975; Morrell, 1991). Usually, if the seizures are successfully treated by medication or by surgical removal of the affected tissue, the person attains normal sexual interest.

Several neurotransmitters appear to affect male sexual behavior. As we saw earlier, oxytocin, a hormone secreted by the posterior pituitary gland, may play a role in ejaculation and its aftereffects. Oxytocin is also a transmitter substance in the brain (Arletti, Benelli, and Bertolini, 1992). Several studies (see Argiolas and Gessa, 1991) have shown that injections of oxytocin into the brains of male rats increase the likelihood of penile erections. Arletti, Benelli, and Bertolini (1992) found that intracerebral injections of this hormone had no effect on mounting behavior, but caused the rats to ejaculate sooner; thus, the role of this hormone in sexual

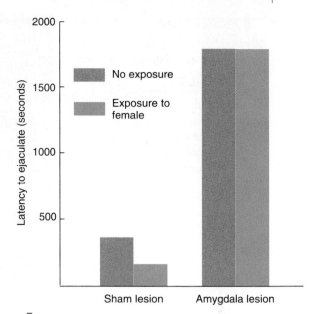

FIGURE 10.17.

Effects of lesions of the medial amygdala on ejaculation latency of male rats after exposure to a receptive female. (Adapted from De Jonge, F.H., Oldenburger, W.P., Louwerse, A.L., and Van de Poll, N.E. *Physiology and Behavior,* 1992, *52,* 327–332.)

behavior appears to be limited to its effects on erection and ejaculation.

Another peptide hormone secreted by the posterior pituitary gland, **vasopressin,** serves as a transmitter substance in the brain. (As we shall see in Chapter 12, vasopressin is involved in control of kidney function.) As De Vries and his colleagues have discovered (see De Vries, 1990), the amount of vasopressin in the brain correlates very nicely with male sexual behavior. As you know, when a male is castrated, its sexual performance declines. This decline is reflected in a decrease in brain vasopressin. (See *Figure 10.18.*) If the animals are given drugs that stimulate vasopressin receptors in the brain, their sexual behavior declines more slowly. And when testosterone is administered to rats that were castrated several weeks earlier, sexual activity and brain vasopressin both return at the same time.

Several studies have shown that the activity of dopaminergic synapses in the MPA is essential for male sexual behavior; microinjection of a dopamine antagonist there disrupts copulation and pursuit of females, whereas microinjection of a dopamine ago-

FIGURE 10.18

Photomicrographs of frontal sections through half of the septum of two rats, arranged side by side for comparison. The bright yellow fibers are vasopressin-containing axons, stained by means of immunocytochemistry. (a) The brain of a male castrated three months previously. The loss of testosterone has caused the vasopressin-containing axons to disappear. (b) The brain of a normal male.

(Courtesy of Geert DeVries, University of Massachusetts.)

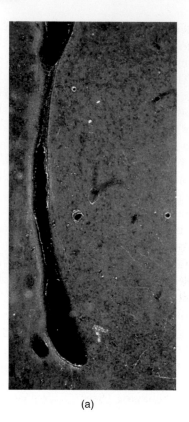

(a) (b)

nist facilitates erections and increases the rate of intromissions (Warner et al., 1991; Bitran and Hull, 1987). Finally, several studies have found that serotonin has inhibitory effects on male sexual behavior. In general, serotonergic antagonists facilitate male sexual behavior (Gorzalka, Mendelson, and Watson, 1990). Watson and Gorzalka (1990) obtained behavioral evidence that suggests that the level of serotonin receptors (in particular, 5-HT$_2$ receptors) is elevated in male rats that fail to copulate with females, or who copulate only poorly.

Females

The one part of the brain that is most critical for performance of female sexual behavior is the **ventromedial nucleus of the hypothalamus** (VMH). Female rats with bilateral lesions of the ventromedial nuclei will not display lordosis, even if they are treated with estradiol and progesterone. In fact, when trapped in a corner by a male rat, they will attack him (Pfaff and Sakuma, 1979). Conversely, electrical stimulation of the ventromedial nucleus

facilitates female sexual behavior (Pfaff and Sakuma, 1979). The critical region appears to be the anterior third of the VMH (Richmond and Clemens, 1988). (See **Figure 10.19.**)

As we saw earlier, sexual behavior of female rats is activated by a priming dose of estradiol, followed by progesterone. Injections of these hormones directly into the VMH will stimulate sexual behavior even in females whose ovaries have been removed (Rubin and Barfield, 1980; Pleim and Barfield, 1988). Thus, these hormones exert their effects on behavior by activating neurons in this nucleus.

Rose (1990) recorded from single neurons in the ventromedial hypothalamus of freely moving female hamsters and found that injections of progesterone (following estradiol pretreatment) increased the activity level of these neurons, particularly when the animals were displaying lordosis.

The mechanism by which estrogen primes a female's sensitivity to progesterone appears to be simple: Estradiol increases the production of progesterone receptors. Blaustein and Feder (1979) administered estradiol to ovariectomized guinea pigs and found a 150 percent increase in the number of progesterone receptors in the hypothalamus. Presumably, the estradiol activates genetic mechanisms in the nucleus that are responsible for the production of progesterone receptors.

Figure 10.20 shows two slices through the hypothalamus of ovariectomized guinea pigs, stained for progesterone receptors. One of the animals had previously received a priming dose of estradiol; the other had not. You probably will not need to read the figure caption to see which is which. (See *Figure 10.20.*)

The neurons of the ventromedial nucleus send axons to the **periaqueductal gray matter** (PAG) of the midbrain, which surrounds the cerebral aqueduct. This region, too, has been implicated in female sexual behavior; Sakuma and Pfaff (1979a, 1979b)

found that electrical stimulation of the PAG facilitates lordosis in female rats and that lesions there disrupt it. In addition, Hennessey et al. (1990) found that lesions that disconnect the VMH from the PAG abolish female sexual behavior. Finally, Sakuma and Pfaff (1980a, 1980b) found that estradiol treatment or electrical stimulation of the ventromedial nuclei increased the firing rate of neurons in the PAG.

The neurons of the periaqueductal gray matter send axons to the reticular formation of the medulla, and cells there send axons to the spinal cord. It seems likely that this pathway is the final link between the hormone-sensitive neurons in the ventromedial nucleus of the hypothalamus and the muscles that are responsible for the lordosis response.

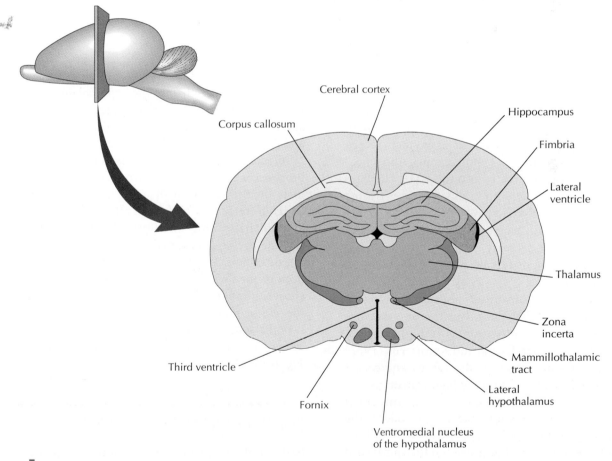

FIGURE 10.19

A cross section through the rat brain showing the location of the ventromedial nucleus of the hypothalamus.
(Adapted from Paxinos, G., and Watson, C. *The Brain in Stereotaxic Coordinates.* Sydney: Academic Press, 1982.)

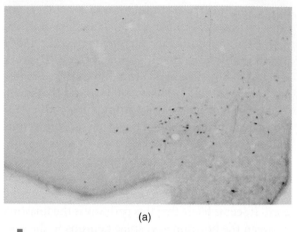

(a)

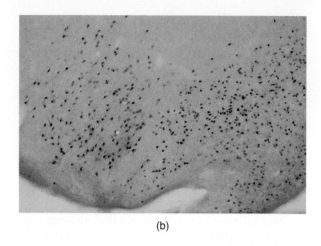

(b)

FIGURE 10.20

Photomicrographs of sections through the arcuate nucleus of ovariectomized guinea pigs, stained for progesterone receptors. (a) No priming. (b) After receiving a priming dose of estradiol.
(Courtesy of Joanne Turcotte and Jeffrey Blaustein, University of Massachusetts.)

As we saw earlier, oxytocin serves both as a hormone and a neurotransmitter or neuromodulator. Schumacher et al. (1990) found that injections of progesterone in female rats previously primed with estradiol increased the number of oxytocin receptors in the ventromedial hypothalamus. Also, injections of oxytocin directly into the VMH facilitate lordosis—but only after the animal has been treated with estradiol and progesterone (Schumacher et al., 1989). Finally, intracerebral injections of an oxytocin antagonist decrease both receptive and proceptive behavior of female rats (Witt and Insel, 1991).

Several neurotransmitters appear to play a role in female sexual behavior, but the one that has received the most attention is norepinephrine. Crowley, Rodriguez-Sierra, and Komisaruk (1977) found that stimulation of the vagina and cervix increased the activity of noradrenergic neurons. (As we saw in the section on pheromones, this effect enables a female mouse to remember the odor of the male that inseminated her.) Damage either to the noradrenergic axons that project to the spinal cord or to those that project to the forebrain decrease lordosis (Hansen and Ross, 1983; Hansen, Stanfield, and Everitt, 1980). Injection of norepinephrine or an NE agonist directly into the hypothalamus facilitates estrous behavior, whereas injection of an NE antagonist inhibits it (Fernandez-Guasti, Larsson, and Beyer, 1985; Crowley, Nock, and Feder, 1978).

Figure 10.21 shows the effects of estradiol, then progesterone, and then the introduction of an active male on the secretion of norepinephrine in the VMH of freely moving female rats, as measured by microdialysis (Vathy and Etgen, 1989). As you can see, the presence of a male provokes a very large release of norepinephrine, but only in rats that have been primed with estradiol and progesterone. The effect seems to be specific to sexual activity, because the release of norepinephrine in another part of the hypothalamus, which does not appear to be involved in female sexual behavior, was *not* increased. (See *Figure 10.21.*)

INTERIM SUMMARY

Sexual reflexes such as sexual posturing, erection, and ejaculation are organized in the spinal cord. The "orgasmic" reflex appears to be similar in males and

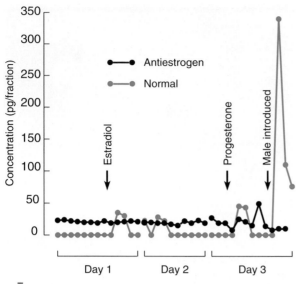

FIGURE 10.21

Norepinephrine concentration in the ventromedial hypothalamus of female rats, measured by microdialysis. One rat was given a priming dose of estradiol, then progesterone, and then a male was introduced. The other rat received an antiestrogenic drug along with the estradiol, which blocked its behavioral effects and prevented the release of norepinephrine.

(Adapted from Vathy, I.U., and Etgen, A.M. *Journal of Neuroendocrinology,* 1989, *1,* 383–388.)

females and does not depend on an organizational effect of androgens. The spinal cord contains at least one sexually dimorphic region, the spinal nucleus of the bulbocavernosus (SNB), whose size is controlled by prenatal androgens. In rats, at least part of the masculinization of this nucleus is a result of tactile stimulation delivered by the animal's mother.

In laboratory animals, different brain mechanisms control male and female sexual behavior. The medial preoptic area is the forebrain region most critical for male sexual behavior. Stimulating this area produces copulatory behavior; destroying it permanently abolishes the behavior. Neurons in the MPA contain testosterone receptors. Copulatory activity causes an increase in the metabolic activity of this region. Implantation of testosterone directly into the MPA reinstates copulatory behavior that

was previously abolished by castration in adulthood. Neurons in the MPA send their axons to various regions, including the lateral tegmental field, where lesions also disrupt male sexual behavior.

The sexually dimorphic nucleus, located in the medial preoptic area, develops only if an animal is exposed to androgens early in life. This nucleus is found in humans, as well. The size of the SDN (part of the MPA) is reduced by prenatal stress and correlates with an animal's level of sexual behavior; its destruction impairs such behavior. The temporal lobes, too, appear to play a role in sexual interest; damage to the medial amygdala (which receives input from both the main and accessory olfactory systems), disrupts male sexual behavior. In humans, sexual dysfunctions are associated with seizure activity originating in the temporal lobes.

The activity of dopamine in the MPA is related to male sexual activity. In addition, the level of vasopressin, a hormone secreted by the posterior pituitary gland that also serves as a neurotransmitter, is correlated with male sexual activity. Axons with terminal buttons secreting this neurotransmitter disappear after castration and reappear after the animal is given testosterone. A third neurotransmitter, serotonin, appears to have an inhibitory effect on male sexual behavior.

The most important forebrain region for female sexual behavior is the ventromedial nucleus of the hypothalamus (VMH). Its destruction abolishes copulatory behavior, and its stimulation facilitates this behavior. Both estradiol and progesterone exert their facilitating effects on female sexual behavior in this region, and studies have confirmed the existence of progesterone and estrogen receptors there. The priming effect of estradiol is caused by an increase in progesterone receptors in the VMH. The steroid-sensitive neurons of the VMH send axons to the periaqueductal gray matter of the midbrain; presumably, neurons in the midbrain, through their connections with the medullary reticular formation, control the particular responses that constitute female sexual behavior.

Two neurotransmitters, oxytocin and norepinephrine, appear to facilitate female sexual behavior. Both substances are released by vaginal stimulation, and both appear to act in the VMH.

MATERNAL BEHAVIOR

IN MOST MAMMALIAN SPECIES, REPRODUCTIVE behavior takes place after the offspring are born as well as at the time they are conceived. This section examines the role of hormones in the initiation and maintenance of maternal behavior and the role of the neural circuits that are responsible for their expression. Most of the research has involved rodents; less is known about the neural and endocrine bases of maternal behavior in primates.

In focusing on maternal behavior, I do not deny the existence of paternal behavior, but male parental behavior is most prominent in higher primates such as humans—and we know little about the neurological basis of human parental behavior. Most male rodents do not show parental behavior except under special circumstances. There are, of course, other classes of animals (for example, many species of fish) in which the male takes care of the young, and in many species of birds the task of caring for the offspring is shared equally. However, neural mechanisms of parental behavior have not received much study in these species.

This section describes both nurturing behaviors and defensive behaviors directed against other animals that might threaten a female's offspring.

Maternal Behavior in Rodents

The final test of the fitness of an animal's genes is the number of offspring that survive to a reproductive age. Just as the process of natural selection favors reproductively competent animals, it favors those that care adequately for their young (if their young in fact require care). Rat and mouse pups certainly do; they cannot survive without a mother who attends to their needs.

At birth, rats and mice resemble fetuses. The infants are blind (their eyes are still shut), and they can only helplessly wriggle. They are poikilothermous ("cold-blooded"); their brain is not yet developed enough to regulate body temperature. They even lack the ability to release their own urine and feces spontaneously and must be helped to do so by their mother. As we will see shortly, this phenomenon actually serves a useful function.

FIGURE 10.22

A mouse's brood nest. Beside it is a length of the kind of rope the mouse used to construct it.

During gestation, female rats and mice build nests. The form this structure takes depends on the material available for its construction. In the laboratory the animals are usually given strips of paper or lengths of rope or twine. A good *brood nest*, as it is called, is shown in Figure 10.22. This nest is made of hemp rope; a piece of the rope is shown below the nest. The mouse laboriously shredded the rope and then wove an enclosed nest, with a small hole for access to the interior. (See *Figure 10.22.*)

At the time of *parturition* (delivery of offspring) the female begins to groom and lick the area around the vagina. As a pup begins to emerge, she assists the uterine contractions by pulling the pup out with her teeth. She then eats the placenta and umbilical cord and cleans off the fetal membranes—a quite delicate operation. (A newborn pup looks like it is sealed in very thin plastic wrap.) After all the pups are born and cleaned up, the mother will probably nurse them. Milk is usually present very near the time of birth.

FIGURE 10.23

A female mouse carrying one of her pups.

Periodically, the mother licks the pups' anogenital region, stimulating reflexive urination and defecation. Friedman and Bruno (1976) have shown the utility of this mechanism. They noted that a lactating female rat produces approximately 48 grams (g) of milk on the tenth day of lactation. This milk contains approximately 35 milliliters (ml) of water. The experimenters injected some of the pups with tritiated (radioactive) water and later found radioactivity in the mother and in the littermates. They calculated that a lactating rat normally consumes 21 ml of water in the urine of her young, thus recycling approximately two-thirds of the water she gives to the pups in the form of milk. The water, traded back and forth between mother and young, serves as a vehicle for the nutrients—fats, protein, and sugar—contained in milk. Because each day the milk production of a lactating rat is approximately 14 percent of her body weight (for a human weighing 120 lb, that would be around 2 gal), the recycling is extremely useful, especially when the availability of water is a problem.

Besides cleaning, nursing, and purging her offspring, a female rodent will retrieve pups if they leave or are removed from the nest. The mother will even construct another nest in a new location and move her litter there, should the conditions at the old site become unfavorable (for example, when an inconsiderate experimenter puts a heat lamp over it). The way a female rodent picks up her pup is quite consistent: She gingerly grasps the animal by the back, managing not to injure it with her very sharp teeth. (1 can personally attest to the ease with which these teeth can penetrate skin.) She then carries the pup with a characteristic prancing walk, her head held high. (See *Figure 10.23.*) The pup is brought back to the nest and is left there. The female then leaves the nest again to search for another pup. She continues to retrieve pups until she finds no more; she does not count her pups and stop retrieving when they are all back. A mouse or rat will usually accept all the pups she is offered, if they are young enough. I once observed two lactating female mice with nests in corners of the same cage, diagonally opposite each other. I disturbed their nests, which triggered a long bout of retrieving, during which each mother stole youngsters from the other's nest. The mothers kept up their exchange for a long time, passing each other in the middle of the cage.

Maternal behavior begins to wane as the pups become more active and begin to look like adults. At around sixteen to eighteen days of age they are able to get about easily by themselves and begin to obtain their own food. The mother ceases to retrieve them when they leave the nest and will eventually run away from them if they attempt to nurse.

Stimuli That Elicit and Maintain Maternal Behavior

As we saw earlier in this chapter, most sexually dimorphic behaviors are controlled by the organizational and activational effects of sex hormones. Maternal behavior is somewhat different in this respect. First, there is no evidence that organizational effects of hormones play a role; as we will see, under the proper conditions even males will take care of infants. (Obviously, they cannot provide them with milk.) Second, although maternal behavior is affected by hormones, it is not *controlled* by them.

Most virgin female rats will begin to retrieve and care for young pups after having infants placed with them for several days (Wiesner and Sheard, 1933). And once the rats are sensitized, they will thereafter take care of pups as soon as they encounter them; sensitization lasts for a lifetime.

Olfaction plays an important role in sensitization—at least, in species such as the rat. A virgin female rat does not normally approach a rat pup; in fact, when she encounters one, she retreats from the pup as if she were repelled by the pup's odor. Fleming and Rosenblatt (1974) confirmed that the avoidance is, indeed, based on smell. They rinsed the olfactory mucosa of virgin female rats with zinc sulfate, which temporarily eliminates olfactory sensitivity. The treatment abolished the animals' natural aversion to the pups, and soon they started taking care of them. Thus, sensitization involves overcoming a natural aversion to the odor of pups.

Fleming et al. (1979) found that cutting the vomeronasal nerve, which disrupts the accessory olfactory system, also facilitates the responsiveness of virgin females to pups. Thus, both the primary and the accessory olfactory systems play a role in olfactory control of maternal behavior. You will recall that both the primary and accessory olfactory systems project to the medial amygdala. Fleming, Vaccarino, and Luebke (1980) found that lesions of the medial amygdala also facilitated responsiveness, as did lesions of the **stria terminalis,** a fiber bundle that connects the medial amygdala with various forebrain regions, including the medial preoptic area. (Refer to *Figure 10.10*.) (As we will see, the medial preoptic area is essential for maternal behavior.) Note that lesions of the amygdala or stria terminalis do not abolish the sense of smell; they only abolish the animals' aversion to the smell of pups.

The most important sense modality in the *initiation* of maternal behavior in rodents appears to be olfaction. However, other sense modalities are involved in its control. For example, mouse, rat, and hamster pups emit at least two different kinds of ultrasonic calls (Noirot, 1972). These sounds cannot be heard by humans; they have to be translated into lower frequencies by a special device (a "bat detector") in order to be perceived by the experimenter. Of course, the mother can hear these calls. When a pup gets cold (as it would if it were removed from the nest), it emits a characteristic call that brings the mother out of her nest. The sound is so effective that female mice have been observed to chew the cover off a loudspeaker that is transmitting a recording of this call. Once out of the nest, the female uses olfactory cues as well as auditory ones to find the pups; she can find a buried, anesthetized baby mouse that is unable to make any noise. The second call is made in response to rough handling. When a mother hears this sound, she stops what she is doing. Typically, it is she who is administering the rough handling, and the distress call makes her stop. This mechanism undoubtedly plays an important role in training mother mice to handle pups properly.

Stern (1989a, 1989b) reviews experimental findings that indicate that tactile stimuli also play an important role in the maintenance and control of maternal behavior. She notes that most maternal behaviors include the use of the mouth: nuzzling, licking, and carrying pups; building and repairing nests; attacking and biting intruders. Many of these behaviors are initiated by somatosensory information received by the region around the mouth as the mother sniffs the pups and nuzzles them with her mouth. For example, when the region around the mouth (the *perioral region*) is desensitized by cutting nerves or injecting a local anesthetic, female rats are less likely to lick their pups, retrieve them, build or repair a nest, or attack an intruder. Tactile feedback from the pups against the mother's ventral surface is important, too. When the regions around pups' mouths are anesthetized so that they cannot root against their mother, she will not show the crouching posture that is necessary for nursing. She will, however, retrieve them and lick them.

Stern suggests that both distal and proximal cues interact to produce the entire complement of maternal behavior. Distal cues (the sight, sound, and odor of pups) attract the mother to them and arouse contact-seeking behaviors. These behaviors lead to perioral contact, which triggers nuzzling, licking, and hovering. The proximity of the mother leads the pups to root against her ventral surface, which stimulates a crouching posture that presents her nipples to them. (See *Figure 10.24*.)

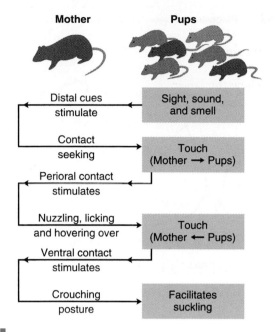

Mother   **Pups**

Distal cues stimulate → Sight, sound, and smell

Contact seeking → Touch (Mother → Pups)

Perioral contact stimulates

Nuzzling, licking and hovering over → Touch (Mother ← Pups)

Ventral contact stimulates

Crouching posture → Facilitates suckling

FIGURE 10.24

A proposed model of sensory regulation of the maternal behavior of a female rat.

(Redrawn from Stern, J.M., in *Ethoexperimental Approaches to the Study of Behavior,* edited by D.C. Blanchard, S. Parmigiani, and P.F. Brain. The Hague: Nijhoff Publishing Co., 1989.)

Hormonal Control of Maternal Behavior

As we have just seen, hormones are not essential for the activation of maternal behavior; mere exposure to pups will accomplish that. (Of course, hormones are necessary for milk production.) However, many aspects of maternal behavior are facilitated by hormones. Nest-building behavior is facilitated by progesterone, the principal hormone of pregnancy. Lisk, Pretlow, and Friedman (1969) found that nonpregnant female mice built brood nests after a pellet of progesterone was implanted under the skin. The pellet slowly dissolved, maintaining a continuously high level of progesterone. The enhanced nest building was suppressed by the administration of estradiol. After parturition, mothers continue to maintain their nests, and they construct new nests if necessary, even though their blood level of proges-

terone is very low then. Voci and Carlson (1973) found that hypothalamic implants of prolactin as well as progesterone facilitated nest building in mice. Presumably, nest building can be facilitated by either hormone: progesterone during pregnancy and prolactin after parturition. (Prolactin, produced by the anterior pituitary gland, is responsible for milk production.)

Although pregnant female rats will not immediately care for foster pups that are given to them during pregnancy, they will do so as soon as their pups are born. A female rodent's responsiveness to her offspring appears to be triggered by the hormones present during pregnancy. Figure 10.25 shows the levels of the three hormones that have been implicated in maternal behavior: estradiol, progesterone, and prolactin. Note that just before parturition the level of estradiol begins rising, then the level of progesterone falls dramatically, followed by a sharp increase in prolactin. (See *Figure 10.25.*) If ovariectomized virgin female rats are given estradiol and progesterone in a pattern that duplicates this sequence, the time it takes to sensitize their maternal behavior is drastically reduced (Moltz, Lubin, Leon, and Numan, 1970; Bridges, 1984). Prolactin is not necessary.

Fleming et al. (1989) found that the administration of progesterone and estradiol had effects similar to those produced by sensitization. First, the hormone-treated rats became less timid in a strange environment that contained novel odors. Second, the animals spent more time near a jar containing some bedding material removed from a nest containing a lactating female and her pups. These effects may be the ones that occur during sensitization: The animal is no longer repelled by (frightened by?) the strange odor of pups and, indeed, comes to prefer the smell. In addition, Fleming and Sarker (1990) found that sensitization produces stronger long-term effects if the animal is first primed with estradiol and progesterone.

Another hormone present during lactation—prolactin—may also have stimulating effects on maternal behavior; and its effects, like those of estradiol, may be exerted in the medial preoptic area. Bridges et al. (1990) infused minute quantities of prolactin into the lateral ventricles or directly into

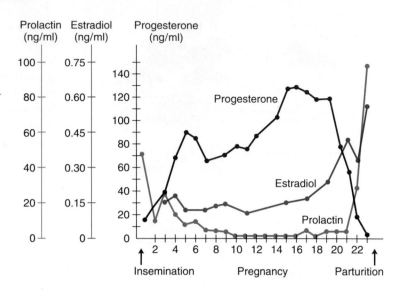

FIGURE 10.25

Blood levels of progesterone, estradiol, and prolactin in pregnant rats.

(From Rosenblatt, J.S., Siegel, H.I., and Mayer, A.D. *Advances in the Study of Behavior*, 1979, *10*, 225–310.)

the MPA of virgin female rats. They found that the animals quickly began taking care of pups. The stimulating effect occurred only if the animals were first given a series of injections of progesterone and estradiol; thus, the maternal behavior of normal females may depend on an interaction between several hormones.

Neural Control of Maternal Behavior

The most critical brain region responsible for maternal behavior appears to be the medial preoptic area, located in the forebrain. Numan (1974) found that lesions of the MPA disrupted both nest building and pup care. The mothers simply ignored their offspring. However, female sexual behavior was unaffected by these lesions. Male sexual behavior is also disrupted by lesions of the MPA. It would be interesting to see whether transplants of fetal hypothalamic tissue would reinstate maternal behavior, as they reinstate male sexual behavior.

As you learned earlier, in the discussion of the neural basis of male sexual behavior, the MPA sends axons to the midbrain. Numan and his colleagues found that the pathway critical for maternal behavior runs from the MPA to the **ventral tegmental area** (VTA) of the midbrain. Numan and Smith

(1984) found that lesions that interrupted this pathway disrupted maternal behavior. However, a later study (Numan and Numan, 1991) found that lesions of the ventral tegmental area made by injecting an excitatory amino acid (which kills cell bodies but spares axons that are passing through the region) did not disrupt maternal behavior. But knife cuts caudal to the VTA did; thus, the critical axons pass through the VTA and synapse farther back in the brain stem. Where they do so is not yet known.

The medial preoptic area appears to be the place where estradiol affects maternal behavior. The MPA contains estrogen receptors (Pfaff and Keiner, 1973). Giordano et al. (1989) found that the concentration of estrogen receptors in the MPA increases during pregnancy and appears to reflect the priming effect produced by the sequence of hormones that occurs during pregnancy. In addition, direct implants of estradiol in the MPA facilitate maternal behavior (Numan, Rosenblatt, and Komisaruk, 1977), whereas injections of an antiestrogen chemical in the MPA block it (Adieh, Mayer, and Rosenblatt, 1987).

As we just saw, zinc sulfate treatment (which abolishes olfactory sensitivity), lesions of the medial amygdala, or lesions of the stria terminalis (which connects the medial amygdala with the medial pre-

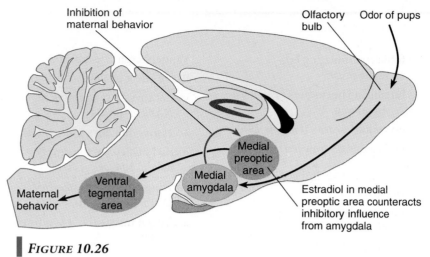

FIGURE 10.26

A possible explanation of the facilitating effects of estradiol on maternal behavior.

optic area) all facilitate maternal behavior in virgin female rats by eliminating the inhibitory effects caused by the odor of pups. Perhaps the stimulating effect of estradiol on the medial preoptic area works in a similar fashion, removing the inhibitory influence of the amygdala. (See *Figure 10.26.*)

INTERIM SUMMARY

Many species must care for their offspring. Among rodents, this duty falls to the mother, who must build a nest, deliver her own pups, clean them, keep them warm, nurse them, and retrieve them if they are moved out of the nest. They must even induce their pups' urination and defecation, and their ingestion of the urine recycles water, which is often a scarce commodity.

Exposure to young pups stimulates maternal behavior within a few days. Apparently, the odor of pups elicits handling and licking, whereas the sound of their distress calls elicits nest building. Unsensitized virgin female rats appear to be repelled by the odor of pups, but deafferentation of the olfactory system with zinc sulfate abolishes this aversion and causes the animals to begin caring for pups more

quickly. The inhibitory effect of the odor of pups may be mediated by the accessory olfactory system; cutting the vomeronasal nerve facilitates maternal behavior. Both components of the olfactory system project to the medial amygdala. Lesions of the medial amygdala or the stria terminalis also facilitate maternal responsiveness. Therefore, the inhibitory effects of olfaction on maternal behavior may be mediated by the pathway from the olfactory system to the medial amygdala to the medial preoptic area, via the stria terminalis.

Nest building appears to be facilitated by progesterone during pregnancy and by prolactin during the lactation period. Injections of progesterone and estradiol that duplicate the sequence that occurs during pregnancy facilitate maternal behavior, and so does injection of prolactin directly into the brain.

The medial preoptic area is the most important forebrain structure for maternal behavior, and the ventral tegmental area of the midbrain is the most important brain stem structure. Neurons in the medial preoptic area send axons caudally through the ventral tegmental area toward more caudal regions of the brain stem. If these connections are interrupted bilaterally, rats cease providing maternal care of offspring.

New Terms

sexually dimorphic behavior p. 292

Sexual Development

gamete *(GAMM eet)* p. 292

sex chromosome p. 292

X chromosome p. 292

Y chromosome p. 292

gonad (rhymes with *MOAN ad)* p. 292

organizational effect (of hormone) p. 293

activational effect (of hormone) p. 293

Müllerian system p. 293

Wolffian system p. 293

Müllerian-inhibiting hormone p. 293

defeminizing effect p. 293

androgen *(AN dro jen)* p. 293

masculinizing effect p. 293

testosterone *(tess TAHSS ter own)* p. 293

dihydrotestosterone *(dy hy dro tess TAHSS ter own)* p. 293

Turner's syndrome p. 294

gonadotropin-releasing hormone *(go NAD oh trow pin)* p. 295

gonadotropic hormone p. 295

follicle-stimulating hormone p. 295

luteinizing hormone *(LEW tee a nize ing)* p. 295

estradiol *(ess tra DI ahl)* p. 296

estrogen *(ESS trow jen)* p. 296

Hormonal Control of Sexual Behavior

menstrual cycle *(MEN strew al)* p. 299

estrous cycle p. 299

ovarian follicle p. 299

corpus luteum *(LEW tee um)* p. 299

progesterone *(pro JESS ter own)* p. 299

refractory period *(ree FRAK to ree)* p. 299

Coolidge effect p. 300

aromatization *(AIR oh mat i ZAY shun)* p. 300

oxytocin *(ox ee TOW sin)* p. 300

prolactin p. 301

lordosis p. 301

pheromone *(FAIR oh moan)* p. 303

Lee–Boot effect p. 303

Whitten effect p. 303

Vandenbergh effect p. 303

Bruce effect p. 303

vomeronasal organ *(voah mer oh NAY zul)* p. 304

accessory olfactory bulb p. 304

medial nucleus of the amygdala p. 304

adrenogenital syndrome *(ah DREE no JEN i tal)* p. 308

androgen insensitivity syndrome p. 309

Neural Control of Sexual Behavior

spinal nucleus of the bulbocavernosus *(bul boah kav er NO sis)* p. 315

medial preoptic area p. 317

sexually dimorphic nucleus p. 317

vasopressin *(vay zo PRESS in)* p. 319

ventromedial nucleus of the hypothalamus p. 320

periaqueductal gray matter p. 321

Maternal Behavior

stria terminalis *(STREE a ter mi NAL is)* p. 326

ventral tegmental area p. 328

Suggested Readings

Becker, J.B., Breedlove, S.M., and Crews, D. *Behavioral Endocrinology.* Cambridge, Mass.: MIT Press, 1992.

Gerall, A.A., Moltz, H., and Ward, I.I. *Handbook of Behavioral Neurobiology. Vol. 11:* Sexual Differentiation. New York: Plenum Press, 1992.

Knobil, E., and Neill, J. *The Physiology of Reproduction.* New York: Raven Press, 1988.

Krasnegor, N.A., and Bridges, R.S. *Mammalian Parenting: Biochemical, Neurobiological, and Behavioral Determinants.* New York: Oxford University Press, 1990.

Rosen, R.C., and Beck, J.G. *Patterns of Sexual Arousal.* New York: Guilford Press, 1988.

CHAPTER 11

Emotion and Stress

Emotions as Response Patterns
- Neural Control of Emotional Response Patterns
- Perception of Stimuli with Emotional Significance
Interim Summary

Expression and Recognition of Emotions
- Facial Expression of Emotions: Innate Responses
- Neural Basis of Communication of Emotions: Studies with Normal Subjects
- Neural Basis of Communication of Emotions: Studies of People with Brain Damage
Interim Summary

Feelings of Emotions
- The James-Lange Theory
- Feedback from Simulated Emotions
Interim Summary

Aggressive Behavior
- Nature and Functions of Aggressive Behavior
- Neural Control of Aggressive Behavior
- Hormonal Control of Aggressive Behavior
Interim Summary

Stress
- Stress and Health
- Physiology of the Stress Response
- The Coping Response
- Stress and Cardiovascular Disease
- Psychoneuroimmunology
Interim Summary

THE WORD *EMOTION* CAN MEAN SEVERAL
things. Most of the time, it refers to positive or negative feelings that are produced by particular situations. For example, being treated
unfairly makes us angry, seeing someone suffer
makes us sad, and being close to a loved one makes
us feel happy. Emotions consist of patterns of physiological responses and species-typical behaviors. In
humans these responses are accompanied by feelings. In fact, most of us use the word *emotion* to
refer to the feelings, not to the behaviors. But it is
behavior, and not private experience, that has consequences for survival and reproduction. Thus, the
useful purposes served by emotional behaviors are
what guided the evolution of our brain. The feelings
that accompany these behaviors came rather late in
the game.

This chapter is divided into five major parts. The
first considers the patterns of behavioral and physiological responses that constitute emotions. It
describes the nature of these response patterns, their
neural control, and the perception of situations that
give rise to emotions; and it includes a discussion
of prefrontal lobotomy and other types of psychosurgery. The second section describes the communication of emotions—their expression and
recognition. The third section examines the nature
of the feelings that accompany emotions. The fourth
section considers the neural and hormonal control
of aggressive and defensive behaviors. Finally, the
fifth section considers the harmful aspects of negative emotional reactions—the physiology of stress.

EMOTIONS AS RESPONSE PATTERNS

AN EMOTIONAL RESPONSE CONSISTS OF THREE
types of components: behavioral, autonomic, and
hormonal. The *behavioral* component consists of
muscular movements that are appropriate to the situation that elicits them. For example, a dog defending its territory against an intruder first adopts an
aggressive posture, growls, and shows its teeth. If the
intruder does not leave, the defender runs toward it
and attacks. *Autonomic* responses facilitate the
behaviors and provide quick mobilization of energy

for vigorous movement. In this example the activity of the sympathetic branch increases while that
of the parasympathetic branch decreases. As a consequence, the dog's heart rate increases, and changes
in the size of blood vessels shunt the circulation of
blood away from the digestive organs toward the
muscles. *Hormonal* responses reinforce the autonomic responses. The two hormones secreted by
the adrenal medulla—epinephrine and norepinephrine—further increase blood flow to the muscles and cause nutrients stored in the muscles to be
converted into glucose. In addition, the adrenal cortex secretes steroid hormones, which also help make
glucose available to the muscles.

This section discusses research on the control of
overt emotional behaviors and the autonomic and
hormonal responses that accompany them. Special
behaviors that serve to communicate emotional
states to other animals, such as the threat gestures
that precede an actual attack and the smiles and
frowns used by humans, will be discussed in the second section of the chapter. As you will see, the first
and last sections concentrate on *negative* emotions.
Most of the research on the physiology of emotions
has been confined to fear and anxiety and their consequence—stress. The physiology of behaviors associated with positive emotions—such as lovemaking,
caring for one's offspring, enjoying a good meal or
a cool drink of water (or an alcoholic beverage)—
are described in other chapters, but not in the specific context of emotions.

Neural Control of Emotional Response Patterns

As we will see later in this chapter, stimulation of
various parts of the brain can induce an animal to
attack another one or can cause it to make vigorous
attempts to escape. In other words, the stimulation
can produce the behaviors associated with anger or
fear. The overt behaviors, the autonomic responses,
and the hormonal secretions associated with these
emotional reactions are controlled by separate neural systems. The *integration* of these responses
appears to be controlled by the amygdala.

The amygdala plays a special role in physiological and behavioral reactions to objects and situations that have special biological significance, such

as those that warn of pain or other unpleasant consequences or signify the presence of food, water, salt, potential mates or rivals, or infants in need of care. Researchers in several different laboratories have shown that single neurons in various nuclei of the amygdala become active when emotionally relevant stimuli are presented. For example, these neurons are excited by such stimuli as the sight of a device that has been used to squirt either a bad-tasting or a sweet solution into the animal's mouth, the sound of another animal's vocalization, the sound of the opening of the laboratory door, the smell of smoke, or the sight of another animal's face (O'Keefe and Bouma, 1969; Jacobs and McGinty, 1972; Rolls, 1982; Leonard et al., 1985). And as we have already seen in Chapter 10, the amygdala is involved in the effects of pheromones on reproductive physiology and behavior (including maternal behavior). This section describes research on the role of the amygdala in organizing emotional responses produced by aversive stimuli.

The amygdala (or more precisely, the *amygdaloid complex*) is located within the temporal lobes. It consists of several groups of nuclei, each with different inputs and outputs—and with different functions. (Refer to *Figure 10.10.*) According to Turner and Herkenham (1991), the major divisions of the amygdala are the *corticomedial group,* the *lateral-basomedial group,* the *central nucleus,* and the *basolateral group.* The **corticomedial group** consists of several nuclei that receive sensory information about the presence of pheromones and relay the information to the medial basal forebrain and to the hypothalamus. The regions that receive this information include the medial preoptic area and the ventromedial nucleus of the hypothalamus, both of which were discussed in Chapter 10. The **lateral-basomedial group** of nuclei receive other types of sensory information and relay it to the same regions as the corticomedial group. The **central nucleus** is the one that will most concern us in this chapter. It receives all forms of sensory information, received from the primary sensory cortex, association cortex, and thalamus, relayed to it by the **basolateral group**. It projects to regions of the hypothalamus, midbrain, pons, and medulla that are responsible for the expression of the various components of emotional responses.

The central nucleus of the amygdala is the single most important part of the brain for the expression of emotional responses provoked by aversive stimuli. When threatening stimuli are presented, the neural activity of the central nucleus increases, and the production of Fos protein increases (Pascoe and Kapp, 1985; Campeau et al., 1991). Damage to the central nucleus (or to the basolateral group, which provide it with sensory information) reduces or abolishes a wide range of emotional behaviors and physiological responses. After this region has been destroyed, animals no longer show signs of fear when confronted with stimuli that have been paired with aversive events. They also act more tamely when handled by humans, their blood levels of stress hormones are lower, and they are less likely to develop ulcers or other forms of stress-induced illnesses (Coover, Murison, and Jellestad, 1992; Davis, 1992b; LeDoux, 1992). In contrast, when the central amygdala is stimulated by means of electricity or by an injection of an excitatory amino acid, the animal shows physiological and behavioral signs of fear and agitation (Davis, 1992b), and long-term stimulation of the central nucleus produces stress-induced illnesses such as gastric ulcers (Henke, 1982). These observations suggest that the autonomic and endocrine responses controlled by the central nucleus are among those responsible for the harmful effects of long-term stress, which are discussed in the final section of this chapter.

As we saw earlier, neurons in the central nucleus of the amygdala send axons to regions of the brain that are responsible for the expression of the various components of emotional responses. Rather than describe each of these regions and the responses they control, I will refer you to Figure 11.1, which summarizes them. (See *Figure 11.1.*)

The central amygdala is particularly important for aversive emotional learning. There are a few stimuli that automatically produce fear reactions—for example, loud unexpected noises, the approach of large animals, heights, or (for some species) specific sounds or odors. But even more importantly, we can *learn* that a particular situation is dangerous or threatening. Once the learning has taken place, we will become frightened when we encounter that situation—our heart rate and blood pressure will increase, our muscles will become more tense, our

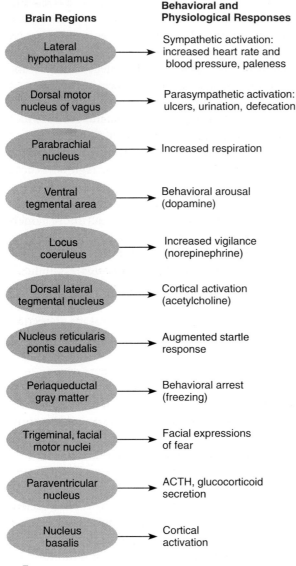

Brain Regions

Behavioral and Physiological Responses

Lateral hypothalamus → Sympathetic activation: increased heart rate and blood pressure, paleness

Dorsal motor nucleus of vagus → Parasympathetic activation: ulcers, urination, defecation

Parabrachial nucleus → Increased respiration

Ventral tegmental area → Behavioral arousal (dopamine)

Locus coeruleus → Increased vigilance (norepinephrine)

Dorsal lateral tegmental nucleus → Cortical activation (acetylcholine)

Nucleus reticularis pontis caudalis → Augmented startle response

Periaqueductal gray matter → Behavioral arrest (freezing)

Trigeminal, facial motor nuclei → Facial expressions of fear

Paraventricular nucleus → ACTH, glucocorticoid secretion

Nucleus basalis → Cortical activation

FIGURE 11.1

Some important brain regions that receive input from the central nucleus of the amygdala and the emotional responses controlled by these regions.

(Adapted from Davis, M. *Trends in Pharmacological Sciences*, 1992, *13*, 35-41.)

adrenal glands will secrete epinephrine, and we will proceed cautiously, alert and ready to respond.

The type of learning I just described involves the development of a **conditioned emotional response.** The word *conditioned* refers to a process called *classical conditioning*, which is described in more detail in Chapter 14. Briefly, classical conditioning occurs when a neutral stimulus is regularly followed by a stimulus that automatically evokes a response. For example, if a dog regularly hears a bell ring just before it receives some food that makes it salivate, it will begin salivating as soon as it hears the sound of the bell. (You probably already know that this phenomenon was discovered by Ivan Pavlov.)

A conditioned emotional response is one that is produced by a neutral stimulus that has been paired with an emotion-producing stimulus. For example, a painful stimulus (such as an electrical shock) applied to an animal's paw will elicit a specific defensive reflex: The animal will move its leg in a way that withdraws its paw from the source of the pain. In addition, the painful stimulus will also elicit responses controlled by the autonomic nervous system: The animal's pupils will dilate, its heart rate and blood pressure will increase, it will breathe faster, and so on. The stimulus will also cause some stress-related hormones to be secreted. And depending on the animal's species and the nature of the aversive stimulus, it may run away or it may stop moving and "freeze" in place.

If an animal learns to make a specific response that avoids contact with the aversive stimulus (or at least minimizes its painful effect), most of the nonspecific "emotional" responses will eventually disappear. That is, if the animal learns a successful **coping response,** the emotional responses will no longer occur. For example, if an animal learns to retract its paw every time a warning stimulus occurs, thus avoiding a painful stimulus, the responses it showed earlier—the increased heart rate, blood pressure, and breathing—will no longer be seen. The situation is under control and no longer provokes an emotional reaction. In contrast, if an aversive stimulus follows a warning stimulus *no matter what the animal does,* the animal will continue to display a conditioned emotional response. You can imagine your own emotional response to the buzzing sound of a flying wasp if on several occasions you were stung after hearing this sound, even though you tried to get away from the wasp.

Several laboratories have investigated the role of the central nucleus of the amygdala in the development of classically conditioned emotional responses. For example, LeDoux and his colleagues

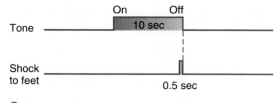

FIGURE 11.2

The procedure used to produce conditioned emotional responses.

have studied these responses in rats by pairing an auditory stimulus with a brief electrical shock delivered to the feet (LeDoux, 1992). In their studies they presented an 800-Hz tone for 10 sec, and then they delivered a brief (0.5 sec) shock to the floor on which the animals were standing. (See *Figure 11.2*.) By itself, the shock produces an *unconditional* emotional response: The animal jumps into the air, its heart rate and blood pressure increase, its breathing becomes more rapid, and its adrenal glands secrete catecholamines and steroid stress hormones. The experimenters presented several pairings of the two stimuli, which established classical conditioning.

The investigators tested conditioned emotional responses the next day by presenting the 800-Hz tone several times and measuring the animals' blood pressure and heart rate and observing its behavior. (This time, they did not present the shock.) When the rats heard the tone, they showed the same type of physiological responses as they did when they were shocked the previous day. In addition, they showed behavioral arrest—a species-typical defensive response called *freezing*. That is, the animals acted as if they were expecting to receive a shock.

LeDoux and his colleagues have shown that the central nucleus is necessary for the development of a conditioned emotional response (LeDoux, 1987). If this nucleus is destroyed, conditioning does not take place. In addition, LeDoux et al. (1988) destroyed two regions that receive projections from the central nucleus: the lateral hypothalamus and the caudal periaqueductal gray matter. They found that lesions of the lateral hypothalamus interfered with the change in blood pressure, whereas lesions of the periaqueductal gray matter interfered with the freezing response. Thus, two different mecha-

nisms, both under the control of the central nucleus of the amygdala, are responsible for the autonomic and behavioral components of conditioned emotional responses. (As you saw in Figure 11.1, activation of the central nucleus produces many other responses, but not all of them have been studied in this situation.)

Although most of the experiments investigating the role of the central nucleus of the amygdala in conditioned emotional responses have used auditory stimuli, results from studies using stimuli of other sensory modalities are consistent with the ones I have reviewed. For example, lesions of the central nucleus disrupt conditioned responses evoked by visual or olfactory stimuli that have been paired with a foot shock, and they make an animal act less timid in a strange environment (Hitchcock and Davis, 1986; Sananes and Campbell, 1989; Grijalva et al., 1990). (By the way, timidity in a strange environment is a useful trait; animals that enter an unfamiliar place boldly and heedlessly may find something waiting for them that will end their opportunity to contribute to the gene pool.)

Another behavioral measure of fear has received considerable attention: the augmented startle response. When an animal hears a sudden, loud noise, its muscles suddenly contract. An especially strong response may even cause a four-footed animal such as a rat to jump into the air. The magnitude of the startle response is strongly modulated by fear. For example, if a rat is placed in a chamber in which it previously received electrical shocks, a sudden noise makes it jump much more than it otherwise would. In fact, an animal's "jumpiness" is an excellent indication of its level of fear.

Davis and his colleagues (see Davis, 1992a, 1992b) have investigated the neural circuits responsible for this phenomenon. They measured the startle response by placing a rat in a cage equipped with pressure transducers that provided an electrical signal any time the floor of the cage was jostled. Thus, when an animal made a sudden movement, the pressure transducers would send a signal that could be analyzed electronically. The investigators produced a conditioned fear to light by turning on a light and then shocking the animal. The next day, they placed the rat in the apparatus and measured

Training: light and shock paired

Testing: noise-alone trial

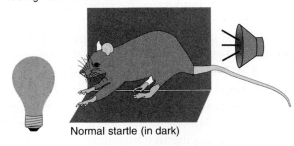

Normal startle (in dark)

Testing: light + noise trial

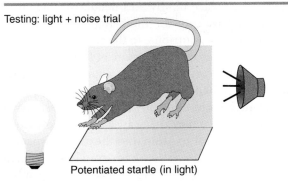

Potentiated startle (in light)

FIGURE 11.3

The method used by Davis and his colleagues to investigate the augmented startle response.

(Adapted from Davis, M. *Trends in Pharmacological Sciences,* 1992, *13*, 35-41.)

the magnitude of its startle response to a sudden sound—in the dark and then with the light on. Clearly, the light provoked fear; the animals were more "jumpy" when it was on than when it was off. (See *Figure 11.3.*)

The first step in the investigation was to trace the pathway from the ear to the muscles. The researchers found that the first relay is in the auditory system, in the *ventral cochlear nucleus.* The next relay is in the *ventral nucleus of the lateral lemniscus,* the next in the *nucleus reticularis pontis caudalis,*

which projects directly to motor neurons in the spinal cord that are directly responsible for the muscular contractions. Davis and his colleagues found that the augmentation of the startle response was accomplished by a connection between the central nucleus of the amygdala and the nucleus reticularis pontis caudalis—usually referred to as the *rpc.* The central nucleus receives both visual information (light) and somatosensory information (foot shock). The pairing of these two stimuli causes changes to take place in this nucleus—changes that are responsible for classical conditioning. Then when the visual stimulus is presented by itself, the central nucleus becomes active and, through its efferent connections, raises the level of excitation of neurons in the rpc. This increased excitation augments the startle response. (See *Figure 11.4.*)

Research on the details of the physical changes responsible for classical conditioning—including the role of the central nucleus of the amygdala—has provided some interesting information about the physiology of learning and memory. This research will be discussed in more detail in Chapter 14.

Some of the effects of anxiolytic (anxiety-reducing) drugs appear to be produced through the central nucleus. The basolateral nucleus, which projects to the central nucleus, contains a high concentration of benzodiazepine receptors, and the central nucleus itself contains a high concentration of opiate receptors. The infusion of either opiates or benzodiazepines into the amygdala decreases both the learning and the expression of conditioned emotional responses (Davis, 1992a). However, Yadin et al. (1991) found that even after the amygdala is destroyed, benzodiazepines still have some anxiolytic effect; thus, the amygdala is not responsible for all of the effects of these drugs. And as we will see in Chapter 18, opiates have effects on many different parts of the brain.

As we shall also see in Chapter 18, some evidence suggests that increased activity of the neural mechanisms described in this section are associated with a fairly common category of psychological disorders—the *anxiety disorders.* Whether the primary cause of the increased anxiety lies within these circuits or elsewhere in the brain (or in the patient's environment and past history) has yet to be determined.

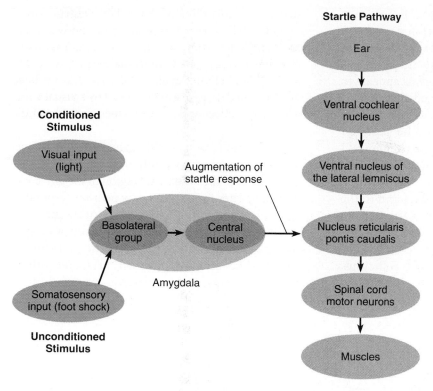

Startle Pathway

FIGURE 11.4

The neural circuits responsible for an auditory startle response and for its augmentation by conditioned aversive stimuli.

(Adapted from Davis, M., *Trends in Pharmacological Sciences,* 1992, *13*, 35-41.)

Finally, as we shall see in Chapter 13, the amygdala is involved in behaviors associated with another negative emotion—disgust. When an animal (including a member of our own species) becomes nauseated as a result of eating tainted food (or receiving an injection of a nausea-inducing drug by an experimenter), the animal develops an aversion to the flavor of the last thing it ate or drank prior to the nausea. This form of learning is abolished by lesions of the basolateral amygdala.

Perception of Stimuli with Emotional Significance

As we have seen, the amygdala (particularly the central nucleus) plays a critical role in producing emotional responses to aversive stimuli. When it is activated, it elicits a pattern of behavioral, autonomic, and hormonal responses through its connections with critical regions of the hypothalamus, midbrain, pons, and medulla. But the amygdala does not decide by itself to produce an emotional response. The amygdala is simply the push button (so to speak) attached to the neural circuits that con-

trol these responses. The activation of the amygdala occurs when a threatening stimulus is detected; thus, the next question to ask is, "What parts of the brain are responsible for detecting these threatening stimuli and activating the central nucleus of the amygdala?" Several kinds of stimuli, from the very simple to the very complex, can produce emotional reactions. Thus, several different neural mechanisms are undoubtedly involved in producing these reactions. In the next section we will look at mechanisms located in three parts of the brain: the thalamus, the sensory association cortex, and the orbitofrontal cortex.

Simple Stimuli: The Thalamus

Most emotional reactions, especially those associated with defensive or aggressive behaviors, have been around for a long time. That is, they emerged early in the evolutionary process and thus involve some of the older parts of the brain. The detection of a simple stimulus can also be accomplished by phylogenetically ancient parts of the brain; it does not require the presence of the newer brain structures, such as the neocortex. In fact, lesions of the primary auditory cortex do not disrupt the learning or expression of a conditioned emotional response involving a simple auditory stimulus, but lesions of the thalamus do (LeDoux, Sakaguchi, and Reis, 1984). The critical part of the thalamus appears to lie in a region ventrolateral to the medial geniculate nucleus—an area that includes the *medial division of the medial geniculate nucleus* and the *posterior intralaminar thalamic nucleus*. For convenience, I will refer to this region as the MGM/PIN. (See **Figure 11.5**.)

As you will recall from Chapters 4 and 6, the medial geniculate nucleus of the thalamus relays auditory information to the primary auditory cortex. However, the MGM/PIN, which receives auditory information from the inferior colliculus, projects this information only to other subcortical

structures—including the amygdala. Destruction of the MGM/PIN or the connections between the MGM/PIN and the amygdala prevents rats from learning a conditioned emotional responses (Iwata et al., 1986; LeDoux et al., 1986). The lesions have no effect on defensive learning cued by a visual stimulus, so the effect appears to be specific to the auditory system.

Bordi and LeDoux (1992) investigated the effects of different auditory stimuli on the activity of single neurons in the basolateral region of the amygdala of the rat. They found that many neurons responded to stimuli containing a wide range of frequencies, such as clicks or white noise (basically, a hissing sound). Others responded to specific frequencies, which were always above 10 kHz. Yet others responded only to very intense noises. Sounds

FIGURE 11.5

The medial division of the medial geniculate nucleus (MGM) and the posterior intralaminar thalamic nucleus (PIN), parts of the thalamus that receive information from the auditory system and project to subcortical regions, including the amygdala.

(Adapted from Paxinos, G., and Watson, C. *The Rat Brain in Stereotaxic Coordinates.* Sydney: Academic Press, 1982.)

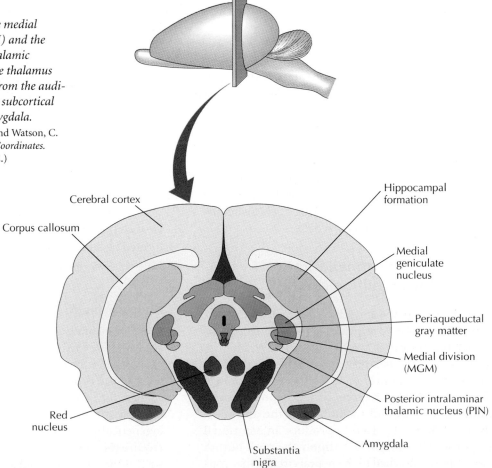

important to a rat, such as rustling noises made by the approach of a predator or the ultrasonic calls made by a frightened rat, would appear to activate these neurons—as would very loud noises, which often indicate the presence of something dangerous. Blanchard et al. (1991) found that when rats are exposed to a predator, they emit an ultrasonic call, which presumably alerts and frightens other rats who hear it.

Just as one region of the thalamus can detect simple auditory stimuli that warn of dangers and activate the amygdala, another region can perform the same function for simple visual stimuli. Rosen et al. (1992) found that lesions of the ventral lateral geniculate nucleus (the part of the lateral geniculate nucleus that does *not* project to the visual cortex) blocked the classically conditioned augmentation of the startle response. Removal of all the primary and secondary visual cortex had no effect; thus, information about simple visual stimuli appears to reach the central nucleus of the amygdala directly from the thalamus.

Complex Stimuli: Sensory Association Cortex

Although a few emotional reactions seen in humans are produced by simple stimuli (such as the buzzing sound of a wasp or the rustling sound of someone approaching through the woods), most of them involve more complex stimuli—for example, the sight of a particular person with whom we have had unpleasant encounters. For these reactions to occur, we must first recognize the individual, and such recognition involves the visual association cortex. Similarly, recognition of a particular person's voice involves the auditory association cortex, and comprehension of the meaning of his or her words requires even more of the brain's resources.

The amygdala receives information from the inferior temporal cortex and the cortex at the very end of the temporal lobe—the *temporal pole*. These regions receive information from the visual, auditory, and somatosensory association cortex; thus, the amygdala is informed about all that is happening around the individual. As I mentioned earlier in this chapter, several studies have shown that individual neurons in the amygdala become active when an animal perceives complex stimuli with emotional significance. The information concerning these stimuli is received through the inputs from the temporal cortex.

A study by Downer (1961) showed the importance of these connections. Downer operated on a monkey, destroying the amygdala on the left side of the brain and cutting the corpus callosum, anterior commissure, and the optic chiasm. Cutting the corpus callosum and the anterior commissure prevented visual information received by one side of the brain from reaching the other. (The anterior commissure is a bundle of axons that interconnects the right and left temporal lobes.) Cutting the optic chiasm meant that visual information received by the left eye went only to the left hemisphere, and information received by the right eye went only to the right hemisphere.

The monkey was an aggressive and emotional animal. Before the surgery, it would become enraged when it saw a human and would try to attack. (As we saw in Chapter 6, the recognition of complex visual stimuli such as the presence of a human being is accomplished by the visual association cortex.) Afterward, it was still aggressive and emotional, but only under certain conditions. If it was touched anywhere, it would react violently and try to attack. If it saw a person with its right eye, it would do the same. However, if its right eye were covered, it remained calm and passive. It would even approach the experimenter and take raisins from his hand. Its left eye was not blind; the monkey could still perceive visual stimuli when only this eye was open. However, these stimuli just did not evoke an emotional response. (See *Figure 11.6.*)

As we will see in Chapter 15, the hippocampal formation is involved in recognizing contextual information, including information about particular events and places. (The hippocampal formation receives the information it requires to recognize these events and places from the sensory association cortex.) The basolateral region of the amygdala receives information from the hippocampus as well as from the thalamus and neocortex, and this connection appears to inform the amygdala when the animal has encountered a dangerous situation. Phillips and LeDoux (1992) found that hippocampal lesions had no effect on rats' ability to acquire a conditioned emotional response to a tone. However, the animals showed no signs of fear when they were

FIGURE 11.6.

The experiment by Downer (1962). Visual information did not provoke an aggressive response unless it reached the intact amygdala on the right side of the monkey's brain.

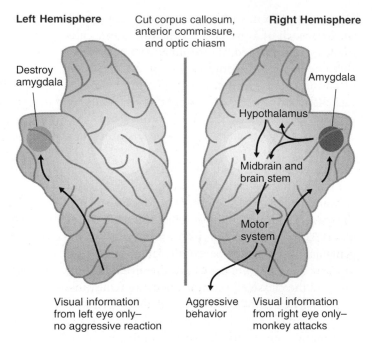

placed in the apparatus where they had previously received several foot shocks. Presumably, the damage to the hippocampal formation impaired the animals' ability to recognize the apparatus as a place they had been shocked, but it did not impair the ability of a simple auditory stimulus, acting through the thalamus, to trigger emotional reactions controlled by the amygdala.

Social Situations: The Orbitofrontal Cortex

We humans are capable of reacting emotionally to very complex situations, especially those involving other people. Perceiving the meaning of social situations is obviously more complex than perceiving individual stimuli. The analysis of social situations involves much more than sensory analysis; it involves experiences and memories, inferences and judgments. In fact, the skills involved include some of the most complex ones we possess. These skills are not localized in any one part of the cerebral cortex, although research does suggest that the right hemisphere is more important than the left. But one region of the brain—the orbitofrontal cortex—plays a special role.

The **orbitofrontal cortex** is located at the base of the frontal lobes. It covers the part of the brain just above the *orbits*—the bones that form the eye sock-

ets—hence the term *orbitofrontal*. (See **Figure 11.7.**) The orbitofrontal cortex receives direct inputs from the dorsomedial thalamus, from the temporal cortex, and from the ventral tegmental area. It also receives indirect inputs from the amygdala and from the olfactory system. Its outputs go to several brain regions, including the cingulate cortex, hippocampal formation, temporal cortex, lateral hypothalamus, and amygdala. Finally, it communicates with other parts of the frontal lobes. Thus, its inputs provide it with information about what is happening in the environment and what plans are being made by the rest of the frontal lobes, and its outputs permit it to affect a variety of behaviors and physiological responses, including emotional responses organized by the amygdala.

The fact that the orbitofrontal cortex plays an important role in emotional behavior is shown by the effects of damage to this region. The first—and most famous—case comes from the mid-1800s. Phineas Gage, a dynamite worker, was using a steel rod to ram a charge of dynamite into a hole drilled in solid rock. Suddenly, the charge exploded and sent the rod into his cheek, through his brain, and out the top of his head. (See **Figure 11.8.**) He survived, but he was a different man. Before his injury he was serious, industrious, and energetic. Afterward, he became childish, irresponsible, and thoughtless of others. He was unable to make or carry out plans, and his actions appeared to be capricious and whimsical. His accident largely destroyed the orbitofrontal cortex.

Over the succeeding years physicians reported several cases similar to that of Phineas Gage. In general, damage to the orbitofrontal cortex reduced people's inhibitions and self-concern; they became indifferent to the consequences of their actions. Although they remained sensitive to noxious stimuli, the pain no longer bothered them—it no longer produced an emotional reaction. Then in 1935 the report of an experiment with a chimpanzee triggered events whose repercussions are still felt today.

Jacobsen, Wolf, and Jackson (1935) tested some chimpanzees on a behavioral task that requires the animal to remain quiet and remember the location of food that the experimenter has placed behind a screen. One animal, Becky, displayed a violent emotional reaction whenever she made an error while performing this task. "[When] the experimenter lowered . . . the opaque door to exclude the animal's view of the cups, she immediately flew into a temper tantrum, rolled on the floor, defecated and urinated. After a few such reactions during the training period, the animal would make no further

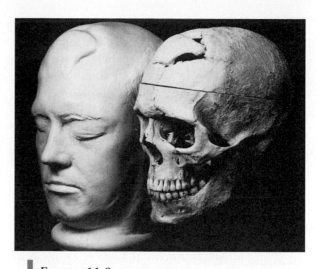

| **FIGURE 11.8.**

A bust and skull of Phineas Gage. The steel rod entered his left cheek and exited through his left forehead.
(From Warren Museum, Harvard Medical School. Reprinted with permission.)

responses. . . ." After the chimpanzee's frontal lobes were removed, it became a model of good comportment. It "offered its usual friendly greeting, and eagerly ran from its living quarters to the transfer cage, and in turn went properly to the experimental cage. . . . If the animal made a mistake, it showed no evidence of emotional disturbance but quietly awaited the loading of the cups for the next trial" (Jacobsen, Wolf, and Jackson, 1935, pp. 9-10).

These findings were reported at a scientific meeting in 1935, which was attended by Egas Moniz, a Portuguese neuropsychiatrist. He heard the report by Jacobsen and his colleagues and also one by Brickner (1936), which indicated that radical removal of the frontal lobes in a human patient (performed because of a tumor) did not appear to produce intellectual impairment—thus, people could presumably get along without their frontal lobes. These two reports suggested to Moniz that "if frontal-lobe removal . . . eliminates frustrational behavior, why would it not be feasible to relieve anxiety states in man by surgical means?" (Fulton, 1949, pp. 63-64). In fact, Moniz persuaded a neurosurgeon to do so, and approximately one hundred operations were eventually performed under his supervision. (In 1949 Moniz received the Nobel Prize for the development of this procedure.)

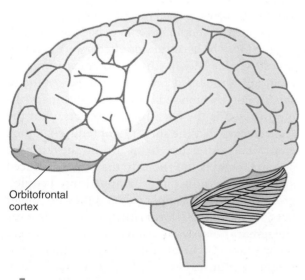

Orbitofrontal cortex

| **FIGURE 11.7.**

The orbitofrontal cortex.

Two paragraphs ago, I wrote that the repercussions of the 1935 meeting are still felt today. Since that time tens of thousands of people have received prefrontal lobotomies, primarily to reduce symptoms of emotional distress, and many of these people are still alive. At first, the procedure was welcomed by the medical community because it provided their patients with relief from emotional anguish. Only after many years were careful studies performed on the side effects of the procedure. These studies showed that although patients did perform well on standard tests of intellectual ability, they showed serious changes in personality, becoming irresponsible and childish. They also lost the ability to carry out plans and most were unemployable. And although pathological emotional reactions were eliminated, so were normal ones. Because of these findings, and because of the discovery of drugs and therapeutic methods that relieve the patients' symptoms without producing such drastic side effects, neurosurgeons eventually abandoned the prefrontal lobotomy procedure (Valenstein, 1986).

I should point out that the prefrontal lobotomies performed under Moniz's supervision, and by the neurosurgeons who followed, were not as drastic as the surgery performed by Jacobsen and his colleagues on Becky, the chimpanzee. In fact, no brain tissue was removed. Instead, the surgeons introduced various kinds of cutting devices into the frontal lobes and severed white matter (bundles of axons). One rather gruesome procedure did not even require an operating room; it could be performed in a physician's office. A *transorbital leucotome,* shaped like an ice pick, was introduced into the brain by passing it beneath the upper eyelid until the point reached the orbital bone above the eye. The instrument was hit with a mallet, driving it through the bone into the brain. The end was then swept back and forth so that it cut through the white matter. The patient often left the office within an hour. (See *Figure 11.9.*)

Many physicians objected to the "ice pick" procedure because it was done blind (that is, the surgeon could not see just where the blade of the leucotome was located) and because it produced more damage than was necessary. Also, the fact that it was so easy and left no external signs other than a pair of black eyes may have tempted its practitioners

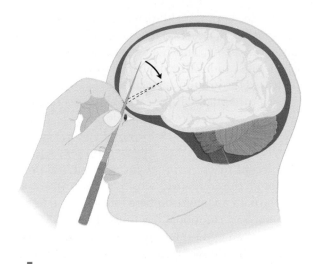

▌ FIGURE 11.9.

"Ice pick" prefrontal lobotomy. The sharp metal rod is inserted under the eyelid and just above the eye, so that it pierces the skull and enters the base of the frontal lobe.
[Adapted from Freeman, W. *Proceedings of the Royal Society of Medicine,* 1949, *42(suppl.),* 8-12.]

to perform it too casually. In fact, at least twenty-five hundred patients received this form of surgery (Valenstein, 1986).

What we know today about the effects of prefrontal lobotomy—whether done transorbitally or by more conventional means—tells us that such radical surgery should never have been performed. For too long the harmful side effects were ignored. (As we will see later in Chapter 18, neurosurgeons eventually developed a much restricted version of this surgery, which reduces the symptoms without producing the harmful side effects.) But the fact remains that the surgery *did* reduce people's emotional suffering, or it would never have become so popular. Primarily, the surgery reduced anxiety, obsessions, and compulsions. People's groundless fears disappeared, and they no longer felt compelled to perform rituals to ward off some (imaginary) disastrous events. Before the surgery the world was a threatening place, and their emotional responses and behavior caused them anguish and made shambles of their lives. After surgery their cares disappeared and they could function more normally.

In one extraordinary case a patient performed his own psychosurgery. Solyom, Turnbull, and Wilensky (1987) reported the case of a young man with a serious obsessive compulsive disorder whose ritual hand washing and other behaviors made it impossible for him to continue his schooling or lead a normal life. (This disorder is described in more detail in Chapter 18.) Finding that his life was no longer worthwhile, he decided to end it. He placed the muzzle of a .22-caliber rifle in his mouth and pulled the trigger. The bullet entered the base of the brain and damaged the frontal lobes. He survived, and he was amazed to find that his compulsion was gone. Fortunately, the damage did not disrupt his ability to make or execute plans; he went back to school and completed his education and now has a job. His IQ was unchanged. Ordinary surgery would have been less hazardous and messy, but it could hardly have been more successful.

All types of prefrontal lobotomies disrupted the functions of the frontal lobes (primarily the orbitofrontal cortex) by severing connections between this area and the rest of the brain. Some procedures approached the frontal lobes from the base of the brain, primarily cutting their connections with the diencephalon and temporal lobes. Other procedures approached the frontal lobes from above and disconnected the orbitofrontal cortex from the cingulate gyrus. In either case the patients' emotional distress was usually reduced.

What, exactly, does the orbitofrontal cortex do? One possibility is that it is involved in assessing the personal consequences of what is presently happening. However, this analysis does not appear to be correct. People whose orbitofrontal cortex has been damaged by disease or accident are still able to accurately assess the significance of particular situations, but only in a *theoretical* sense. For example, Eslinger and Damasio (1985) found that a patient with bilateral damage of the orbitofrontal cortex (produced by a benign tumor, which was successfully removed) displayed excellent social judgment. When he was given hypothetical situations that required him to make decisions about what the people involved should do—situations involving moral, ethical, or practical dilemmas—he always gave sensible answers and justified them with carefully reasoned logic. However, his own life was a different matter.

He frittered away his life's savings on investments that his family and friends pointed out were bound to fail. He lost one job after another because of his irresponsibility. He became unable to distinguish between trivial decisions and important ones, spending hours trying to decide where to have dinner but failing to use good judgment in situations that concerned his occupation and family life. (His wife finally left him and sued for divorce.) As the authors noted, "He had learned and used normal patterns of social behavior before his brain lesion, and although he could recall such patterns when he was questioned about their applicability, *real-life situations failed to evoke them*" (p. 1737). Thus, it appears that the orbitofrontal cortex is not directly involved in making judgments and conclusions about events (these occur elsewhere in the brain) but in translating these judgments into appropriate feelings and behaviors.

In performing prefrontal lobotomies, neurosurgeons have made two different approaches toward the frontal lobes. The ventral connections with the diencephalon and temporal lobes presumably bring environmental information to the orbitofrontal cortex, tell it about emotionally relevant activity of the amygdala, and permit it to influence the amygdala, in turn. The dorsal connections with the cingulate gyrus presumably provide a way for the orbitofrontal cortex to influence both behavior and the autonomic nervous system.

The cingulate gyrus deserves some discussion. The cortex that covers this gyrus is an important part of the limbic system. It appears to provide an interface between the decision-making processes of the frontal cortex, the emotional functions of the limbic system, and the brain mechanisms controlling movement. It communicates (in both directions) with the rest of the limbic system, as well as with other regions of the frontal cortex. Electrical stimulation of the cingulate gyrus in humans can produce feelings of either positive or negative emotions (Talairach et al., 1973). Damage to this region leads to **akinetic mutism,** a syndrome accurately described by its name—the patient stops talking and moving (Amyes and Nielsen, 1955). If the damage is severe, the patient dies. Thus, the cingulate gyrus plays an excitatory role in emotions and in motivated behavior in general.

||||| INTERIM SUMMARY

The word *emotion* refers to behaviors, physiological responses, and feelings. This section has discussed emotional response patterns, which consist of behaviors that deal with particular situations and physiological responses (both autonomic and hormonal) that support the behaviors. The amygdala organizes behavioral, autonomic, and hormonal responses to a variety of situations, including those that produce fear, anger, or disgust. In addition, it is involved in the effects of odors and pheromones on sexual and maternal behavior. It receives inputs from the olfactory system, the association cortex of the temporal lobe, the frontal cortex, and the rest of the limbic system. Its outputs go to the frontal cortex, hypothalamus, hippocampal formation, and brain stem nuclei that control autonomic functions and some species-typical behaviors. Damage to specific brain regions that receive these outputs will abolish particular components of emotional response patterns. Stimulation of the amygdala leads to emotional responses, and its destruction disrupts them. Electrical recordings of single neurons in the amygdala indicate that some of them respond when the animal perceives particular stimuli with emotional significance.

Emotional reactions to simple stimuli can be accomplished by subcortical mechanisms. For example, conditioned emotional responses to simple auditory stimuli occur when the central nucleus of the amygdala receives auditory information from the medial division of the medial geniculate nucleus; input from the auditory cortex is unnecessary. Similarly, conditioned emotional responses to simple visual stimuli are controlled by connections between the ventral lateral geniculate nucleus. Emotional reactions to more complex situations require input from the neocortex. For complex visual stimuli this input is provided by the inferotemporal cortex and the temporal pole.

The orbitofrontal cortex plays an important role in emotional reactions. People with orbitofrontal lesions are able to explain the implications of complex social situations but are unable to respond appropriately when these situations concern *them*. Thus, this region does not appear to be necessary for making judgments about the personal significance of social situations, but it does appear to be necessary for translating these judgments into actions and emotional responses. The orbitofrontal cortex receives information from other regions of the frontal lobes, from the temporal pole, and from the amygdala and other parts of the limbic system via the mediodorsal nucleus of the thalamus. It produces emotional reactions through its connections with the amygdala and the cingulate gyrus.

The cingulate gyrus is involved in the activation of behavior—what we might refer to as motivation. Damage to the cingulate gyrus produces akinetic mutism and, if the damage is severe, causes death. Electrical stimulation produces feelings of both positive and negative emotions. Its outputs include the rest of the limbic system and most of the frontal cortex.

Between the late 1930s and the late 1950s many people received prefrontal lobotomies, which involved cutting the white matter in the ventromedial frontal lobes. Although the operations affected many parts of the frontal lobes, the most important region was probably the orbitofrontal cortex. The surgery did often relieve emotional anguish and the suffering caused by pain, but it also made people become largely indifferent to the social consequences of their own behavior and to the feelings of others, and it interfered with their ability to make and execute plans. Prefrontal lobotomies are no longer performed.

EXPRESSION AND RECOGNITION OF EMOTIONS

The previous section described emotions as organized responses (behavioral, autonomic, and hormonal) that prepare an animal to deal with existing situations in the environment, such as events that pose a threat to the organism. For our earliest pre-mammalian ancestors, that is undoubtedly all there was to emotions. But over time other responses, with new functions, evolved. Many species of animals (including our own) communicate their emotions to others by means of postural changes and facial expressions. These expressions serve useful social functions; they tell other individuals how we feel and—more to the point—what we are likely to do. For example, they warn a rival that we are angry or tell friends that we are sad and would like some comfort and reassurance. In many species they indicate that a danger may be present or that something interesting seems to be happening. This section examines such expression and communication of emotions.

Facial Expression of Emotions: Innate Responses

Charles Darwin (1872/1965) suggested that human expressions of emotion have evolved from similar expressions in other animals. He said that emotional expressions are innate, unlearned responses consisting of a complex set of movements, principally of the facial muscles. Thus, a man's sneer and a wolf's snarl are biologically determined response patterns, both controlled by innate brain mechanisms, just as coughing and sneezing are. (Of course, men can sneer and wolves can snarl for quite different reasons.) Some of these movements resemble the behaviors themselves and may have evolved from them. For example, a snarl shows one's teeth and can be seen as an anticipation of biting.

Darwin obtained evidence for his conclusion that emotional expressions were innate by observing his own children and by corresponding with people living in various isolated cultures around the world. He reasoned that if people all over the world, no matter how isolated, show the same facial expressions of emotion, then these expressions must be inherited instead of learned. The logical argument goes like this: When groups of people are isolated for many years, they develop different languages. Thus, we can say that the words people use are arbitrary; there is no biological basis for using particular words to represent particular concepts. However, if facial expressions are inherited, then they should take approximately the same form in people from all cultures, despite their isolation from one another. And Darwin did, indeed, find that people in different cultures used the same patterns of movement of facial muscles to express a particular emotional state.

Research by Ekman and his colleagues (Ekman and Friesen, 1971; Ekman, 1980) tends to confirm Darwin's hypothesis that facial expression of emotion uses an innate, species-typical repertoire of movements of facial muscles (Darwin, 1872/1965). For example, Ekman and Friesen (1971) studied the ability of members of an isolated tribe of people in New Guinea to recognize facial expressions of emotion produced by westerners. They had no trouble doing so and themselves produced facial expressions that westerners readily recognized. Figure 11.10 shows four photographs taken from videotapes of a man from this tribe reacting to stories designed to evoke facial expressions of sadness, disgust, happiness, and anger. I am sure that you will have no trouble recognizing which is which. (See *Figure 11.10.*)

Because the same facial expressions were used by people who had not previously been exposed to each other, Ekman and Friesen concluded that the expressions were unlearned behavior patterns. In contrast, different cultures use different words to express particular concepts; production of these words does not involve innate responses but must be learned.

Investigators have not yet determined whether other means of communicating emotions, such as tone of voice or hand movements, are learned or are at least partly innate. However, as we will see, some progress has been made in studying the anatomical basis of expressing and recognizing emotions.

Neural Basis of Communication of Emotions: Studies with Normal Subjects

Effective communication is a two-way process. That is, the ability to display one's emotional state by changes in expression is useful only if other people are able to recognize them. In fact, Kraut and Johnston (1979) observed people in circumstances that would be likely to make them happy and found that they were more likely to smile when other people were present than when they were alone. Jones et al. (1991) found that even ten-month-old children showed this tendency. Evidence indicates that recognizing other people's emotional expressions and producing our own expressions involve particular neural mechanisms.

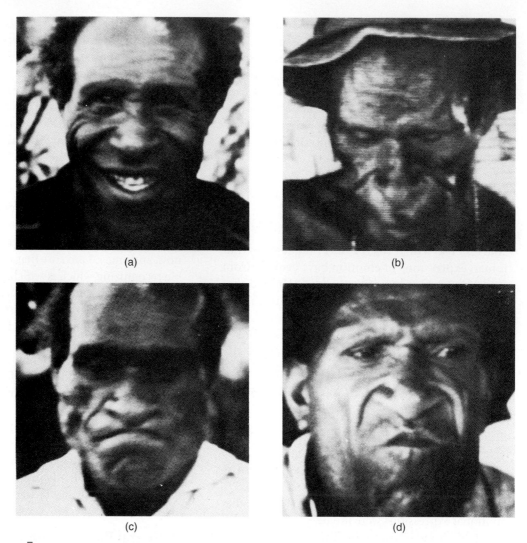

FIGURE 11.10

A member of an isolated New Guinea tribe, studied by Ekman and Friesen, making faces when told stories. (a) "Your friend has come and you are happy." (b) "Your child had died." (c) "You are angry and about to fight." (d) "You see a dead pig that has been lying there a long time."

(From Ekman, P. *The Face of Man: Expressions of Universal Emotions in a New Guinea Village.* New York: Garland STPM Press, 1980. Reprinted with permission)

Recognition of Other People's Emotions

We recognize other people's feelings by means of vision and audition—seeing their facial expressions and hearing their tone of voice and choice of words. Several studies by Bryden, Ley, and colleagues have found that the right hemisphere plays a more important role than the left hemisphere in comprehension of emotion. The rationale for these studies is that each hemisphere directly receives information from the contralateral part of the environment. For example, when a person looks directly ahead, visual stimuli to the left of the fixation point (seen with *both* eyes) are transmitted to the right hemisphere, and stimuli to the right are transmitted to the left hemisphere. Of course, the hemispheres exchange information by means of the corpus callosum, but it appears that this transcommissural information is not as precise and detailed as information that is directly received. Similarly, although each hemisphere receives auditory information from both ears, the contralateral projections are richer than the ipsilateral ones. Thus, when stimuli are presented to the left visual field or left ear, the right hemisphere receives more specific information than the left hemisphere does.

In studies of hemispherical differences in visual recognition, stimuli are usually presented with a *tachistoscope* (literally, "seen most swiftly"), which flashes an image in a specific part of the visual field so fast that the subject does not have time to move his or her eyes. Many studies (reviewed by Bryden and Ley, 1983) have shown that the left hemisphere is better than the right at recognizing words or letter strings. Knowing what you do about the verbal functions of the left hemisphere, this finding will come as no surprise to you. However, when a person is required to discriminate among different faces or detect differences in the tilt of lines presented to one side of the visual field, the right hemisphere performs better than the left.

Ley and Bryden (1979) prepared cartoon drawings of five different people, each displaying one of five facial expressions, ranging from negative to neutral to positive. (See *Figure 11.11.*) Using a tachistoscope, they showed these drawings briefly in the right or left visual field, one at a time. After each presentation they showed the same face or a different one in the center of the visual field (to both hemispheres) and asked the subjects to say whether the same emotion was presented. When the experimenters showed the subjects neutral or mild expressions, the hemispheres performed approximately the same. However, when the experimenters showed the subjects strong expressions, the right hemisphere judged them more accurately.

Ley and Bryden (1982) also investigated perception of tone of voice. They simultaneously presented different verbal messages with a different (happy,

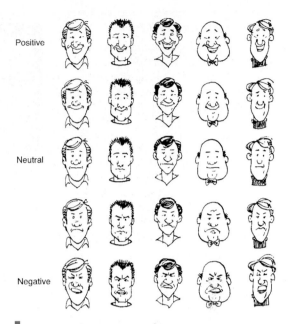

FIGURE 11.11

The faces and expressions used as stimuli in the study by Ley and Bryden.

(From Ley, R.G., and Bryden, M.P. *Brain and Language*, 1979, *7*, 127-138. Reprinted with permission.)

neutral, or sad) tone of voice to each ear and asked the subjects to attend to the message presented to one ear and report on its verbal content and emotion. Most of the subjects more accurately detected the verbal content of the message when it was presented to the left hemisphere and more accurately detected the emotional tone of the voice when it was presented to the right hemisphere. The results suggested that when a message is heard, the right hemisphere assesses the emotional expression of the voice, while the left hemisphere assesses the meaning of the words.

Expression of Emotion

When people show emotions with their facial muscles, the left side of the face usually makes a more intense expression. For example, Sackheim and Gur (1978) cut photographs of people who were posing emotions into right and left halves, prepared mirror images of each of them, and pasted them together. They found that the left halves were more expressive than the right ones. (See *Figure 11.12.*)

▌FIGURE 11.12

An example of a stimulus used by Sackheim and Gur (1978). (a) Original photo. (b) Composite of the right side of the man's face. (c) Composite of the left side of the man's face.

(Reprinted from *Neuropsychologia, 16*, H.A. Sackheim and R.C. Gur. Lateral asymmetry in intensity of emotional expression, 473–482. Copyright 1978, reprinted with kind permission from Pergamon Press Ltd.)

(a)   (b)   (c)

Because motor control is contralateral, the results suggest that the right hemisphere is more expressive than the left.

Moscovitch and Olds (1982) made more natural observations of people in restaurants and parks and found that the left side of their faces appeared to make stronger expressions of emotions. They confirmed these results in the laboratory by analyzing videotapes of people telling sad or humorous stories.

▌Neural Basis of Communication of Emotions: Studies of People with Brain Damage

Facial expressions of emotion appear to be organized in the brain stem but controlled by the frontal lobes. The best evidence for this proposition comes from a syndrome known as *pseudobulbar palsy.* Damage to the medulla (also known as the *bulb*) can cause a paralysis of the facial region known as *bulbar palsy.* The face muscles that are involved simply will not move. **Pseudobulbar palsy** resembles this disorder but is caused by damage to the pathway between the motor cortex of the frontal lobes and the cranial nerve nuclei of the lower pons and medulla that control the facial muscles. People with pseudobulbar palsy cannot make voluntary movements of the facial muscles, but they can still show *automatic* movements such as yawning, coughing, and clearing the throat. More to the point, they can still smile, frown, laugh, and cry. Thus, voluntarily curling the ends of one's lips upward involves different brain mechanisms than making a genuine smile.

Recognition of Other People's Emotions

Observations of people with brain damage suggest that the right hemisphere plays a special role in both recognition and expression of emotion. Damage to the right hemisphere (especially to the caudal part) appears to impair the recognition of emotions being expressed by other people. For example, Heilman, Scholes, and Watson (1975) presented patients who had unilateral lesions of the temporal-parietal region with sentences with neutral content (such as *The boy went to the store*), said in a happy, sad, angry, or indifferent tone of voice. Patients with right-hemisphere damage judged the emotion being expressed less accurately. Heilman, Watson, and Bowers (1983) recorded an interesting case of a man with a disorder called *pure word deafness* (Chapter 16). The man could not comprehend the meaning of speech but had no difficulty identifying the emotion being expressed by its intonation. This case demonstrates that comprehension of words and recognition of tone of voice are independent functions.

Visual recognition of emotions, as well as auditory recognition, also appears to be more of a right-hemisphere function than a left-hemisphere function. DeKosky et al. (1980) found that right-hemisphere damage, more than left-hemisphere damage, disrupted patients' ability to discriminate among different facial expressions of emotion. In addition, Bowers and Heilman (1981) reported the case of a patient with a large tumor of the posterior right hemisphere who could accurately distinguish among faces of different people but not among different emotional expressions. In contrast, he had no trouble recognizing the emotional content of voices.

Thus, although recognition of different faces and recognition of different expressions are both primarily right-hemisphere tasks, their anatomical basis differs.

Blonder, Bowers, and Heilman (1991) found that patients with right-hemisphere lesions had no difficulty making emotional judgments but were severely impaired in judging the emotions conveyed by facial expressions or hand gestures. Patients with left-hemisphere lesions had no difficulty with these tasks. For example, none of the subjects had difficulty identifying the emotion that would be evoked by the situations described in sentences like *After you drink the water, you see the sign* (fear) or *Your house seems empty without her* (sadness). However, patients with right-hemisphere damage had difficulty recognizing the emotions depicted by sentences like *He scowled, Tears fell from her eyes,* or *He shook his fist.* In addition, Bowers et al. (1991) found that patients with right-hemisphere damage had difficulty producing or describing mental images of facial expressions of emotions. Subjects were asked to imagine the face of someone who was very happy (or very sad, angry, or afraid). Then they were asked questions about the facial expression—for example, *Do the eyes look twinkly? Is the brow raised? Are the corners of the lips raised up?* People with right-hemisphere damage had trouble answering these questions but could easily answer questions about nonemotional images, such as *What's higher off the ground, a horse's knee or the top of its tail?* or *What number from one to ten does a peanut look like?* or *What's bigger, a thimble or a pencil eraser?*

Expression of Emotion

Left-hemisphere lesions do not usually impair vocal expressions of emotion. For example, a person with Wernicke's aphasia (described in Chapter 16) usually modulates his or her voice according to mood, even though the words he or she says make no sense. However, right-hemisphere lesions do impair expression of emotion, both facially and by tone of voice.

Buck and Duffy (1980) found deficits in emotional expression in people with right-hemisphere brain damage. The investigators showed slides designed to elicit expressions of emotions to patients with damage to the right or left hemisphere. For example, when they showed a picture of a starving child and a crying woman, they found that people with right-hemisphere damage showed fewer facial expressions of emotion.

⦚⦚⦚ *INTERIM SUMMARY*

We (and members of other species) communicate our emotions primarily through facial gestures. Darwin believed that such expressions of emotion were innate—that these muscular movements were inherited behavioral patterns. Ekman and his colleagues performed cross-cultural studies with members of an isolated tribe in New Guinea. Their results supported Darwin's hypothesis.

Facial expression of emotions (and other stereotyped behaviors such as laughing and crying) are controlled by neural circuits in the brain stem. The best evidence for this conclusion comes from pseudobulbar palsy, caused by damage to the outputs of the motor cortex. People with this disorder cannot make voluntary movements of their facial muscles, but events in the environment can still elicit laughing and crying and facial gestures of emotion.

Expression and comprehension of emotions involve the right hemisphere more than the left. Studies with normal people have shown that people can judge facial expressions or tone of voice better when the information is presented to the right hemisphere than when it is presented to the left hemisphere. In addition, the left halves of people's faces tend to be more expressive than the right halves.

Damage to the right hemisphere is more likely to produce deficits in expression and comprehension of emotions conveyed by tone of voice or by facial expression than is damage to the left hemisphere. In addition, people with right-hemisphere lesions show fewer facial expressions of emotion.

FEELINGS OF EMOTIONS

SO FAR, WE HAVE EXAMINED TWO ASPECTS OF emotions: the organization of patterns of responses that deal with the situation that provokes the emotion, and the communication of emotional states with other members of the species. The final aspect of emotion to be examined in this chapter is the subjective component—feelings of emotion.

The James-Lange Theory

William James (1842-1910), an American psychologist, and Carl Lange (1834-1900), a Danish physiologist, independently suggested similar for emotion, which most people refer to collectively as the **James-Lange theory** (James, 1884; Lange, 1887). Basically, the theory states that emotion-producing situations elicit an appropriate set of physiological responses, such as trembling, sweating, and increased heart rate. The situations also elicit behaviors, such as clenching of the fists or fighting. The brain receives sensory feedback from the muscles and from the organs that produce these responses, and it is this feedback that constitutes our feeling of emotion.

James says that our own emotional feelings are based on what we find ourselves doing and on the sensory feedback we receive from the activity of our muscles and internal organs. Thus, when we find ourselves trembling and feel queasy, we experience fear. Where feelings of emotions are concerned, we are self-observers. Thus, the two aspects of emotions reported in the first two sections of this chapter (patterns of emotional responses and expressions of emotions) give rise to the third—feelings. (See *Figure 11.13*.)

James's description of the process of emotion might strike you as being at odds with your own experience. Many people think that they experience emotions directly, internally. They consider the outward manifestations of emotions to be secondary events. But have you ever found yourself in an unpleasant confrontation with someone else and discovered that you were trembling, even though you did not think that you were so bothered by the encounter? Or did you ever find yourself blushing in response to some public remark that was made about you? Or did you ever find tears coming to your eyes while watching a film that you did not think was affecting you? What would you conclude about your emotional states in situations like these?

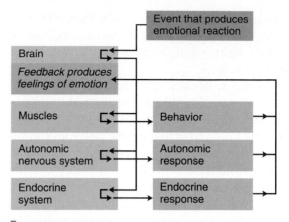

FIGURE 11.13

A diagrammatic representation of the James-Lange theory of emotion. An event in the environment triggers behavioral, autonomic, and endocrine responses. Feedback from these responses produces feelings of emotions.

Would you ignore the evidence from your own physiological reactions?

The suggestion that we experience our emotions indirectly, through feedback from emotional behaviors and autonomic reactions, receives some support from neuroanatomy. As we saw earlier in this chapter, the limbic system seems to play the most important role in controlling emotional reactions. There are few direct connections between the limbic system and the parts of the brain that are involved in language. As we will see in Chapter 16, the brain's verbal mechanisms appear to be responsible for our self-awareness; thus, indirect feedback through the thalamus and the sensory cortex may provide the richest source of information about our own emotional responses.

Hohman (1966) collected data from humans that directly tested James's hypothesis. He questioned people who had suffered damage to the spinal cord about how intense their emotional feelings were. If feedback is important, one would expect that emotional feelings would be less intense if the injury were high (that is, close to the brain) than if it were low, because a high spinal cord injury would make the person become insensitive to a larger part of the body. This result is precisely what Hohman found:

The higher the injury, the less intense the feeling was. As one of Hohman's subjects said:

> I sit around and build things up in my mind, and I worry a lot, but it's not much but the power of thought. I was at home alone in bed one day and dropped a cigarette where I couldn't reach it. I finally managed to scrounge around and put it out. I could have burned up right there, but the funny thing is, I didn't get all shook up about it. I just didn't feel afraid at all, like you would suppose. (Hohman, 1966, pp. 150-151)

Feedback from Simulated Emotions

James stressed the importance of two aspects of emotional responses, emotional behaviors and autonomic responses. As we saw earlier in this chapter, a particular set of muscles—those of the face—helps us communicate our emotional state to other people. Several experiments suggest that feedback from the contraction of facial muscles can affect people's moods and even alter the activity of the autonomic nervous system.

Ekman and his colleagues (Ekman, Levenson, and Friesen, 1983; Levenson, Ekman, and Friesen, 1990) asked subjects to move particular facial muscles to simulate the emotional expressions of fear, anger, surprise, disgust, sadness, and happiness. They did not tell the subjects what emotion they were trying to make them produce but only what movements they should make. For example, to simulate fear, they told the subjects to "Raise your brows. While holding them raised pull your brows together. Now raise your upper eyelids and tighten the lower eyelids. Now stretch your lips horizontally." (These movements produce a facial expression of fear.) While the subjects made the expressions, the investigators monitored several physiological responses controlled by the autonomic nervous system.

The simulated expressions *did* alter the activity of the autonomic nervous system. Different facial expressions produced somewhat different patterns of activity. For example, anger increased heart rate and skin temperature, fear increased heart rate but decreased skin temperature, and happiness decreased heart rate without affecting skin temperature.

Why should a particular pattern of movements of the facial muscles cause changes in mood or in the activity of the autonomic nervous system? Perhaps the connection is a result of experience; in other words, perhaps the occurrence of particular facial movements along with changes in the autonomic nervous system leads to classical conditioning, so that feedback from the facial movements becomes capable of eliciting the autonomic response—and a change in perceived emotion. Or perhaps the connection is innate. The adaptive value of emotional expressions is that they communicate feelings and intentions to others. One of the ways we communicate feelings may be through imitation.

When people see someone expressing an emotion, they tend to imitate the expression. This tendency to imitate appears to be innate. Field et al. (1982) had adults make facial expressions in front of infants. The infants' own facial expressions were videotaped and were subsequently rated by people who did not know what expressions were being displayed by the adults. Field and her colleagues found that even newborn babies (with an average age of 36 hours) tended to imitate the expressions they saw. Clearly, the effect occurs too early in life to be a result of learning. Figure 11.14 shows three photographs of the adult expressions and the expressions they elicited in a baby. Can you look at them yourself without changing your own expression, at least a little? (See *Figure 11.14.*)

Perhaps imitation provides one of the channels by which organisms communicate their emotions. For example, if we see someone looking sad, we tend to assume a sad expression ourselves. The feedback from our own expression helps put us in the other person's place and makes us more likely to respond with solace or assistance. And perhaps one of the reasons we derive pleasure from making someone else smile is that their smile makes *us* smile and feel happy.

||||| INTERIM SUMMARY

From the earliest times people recognized that emotions were accompanied by feelings that seemed to come from inside the body, which probably pro-

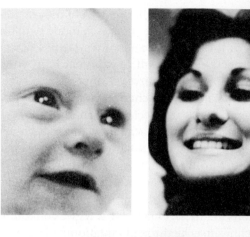

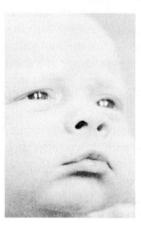 

FIGURE 11.14

Photographs of happy, sad, and surprised faces posed by an adult, and the responses made by the infant.

(From Field, T., in *Development of Nonverbal Behavior in Children*, edited by R.S. Feldman. New York: Springer-Verlag, 1982. Reprinted with permission.)

vided the impetus for developing physiological theories of emotion. James and Lange suggested that the physiological and behavioral reactions to emotion-producing situations were perceived by people as states of emotion, and that emotional states were not the *causes* of these reactions. Hohman's study of people with spinal cord damage supported the James-Lange theory; people who could not feel the reactions from most of their body said that they no longer experienced intense emotional states.

Ekman and his colleagues have shown that even simulating an emotional expression causes changes in the activity of the autonomic nervous system. Perhaps feedback from these changes explains why an emotion can be "contagious": We see someone smile with pleasure, we ourselves imitate their smile, and the internal feedback makes us feel at least somewhat happier.

AGGRESSIVE BEHAVIOR

ALMOST ALL SPECIES OF ANIMALS ENGAGE IN aggressive behaviors, which involve threatening gestures or actual attack directed toward another animal. Aggressive behaviors are species-typical; that is, the patterns of movements (for example, posturing, biting, striking, and hissing) are organized by neural circuits whose development is largely programmed by an animal's genes. Most aggressive behaviors are related to reproduction. For example, aggressive behaviors that gain access to mates, defend territory needed to attract mates or to provide a site for building a nest, or defend offspring against intruders can all be regarded as reproductive behaviors.

Aggressive behavior can take different forms and can be provoked by different situations. In this section I will first describe aggressive behaviors and their neural organization. Then I will discuss the situations that provoke these behaviors and the role that hormones play in regulating their occurrence.

Nature and Functions of Aggressive Behavior

In cats and rodents (the species most often studied in the laboratory), aggressive behavior takes three basic forms: *offense, defense,* and *predation* (Adams, 1986). **Offensive behaviors** include physical assaults of one animal on another. When threatened or attacked, an animal often exhibits **defensive behaviors.** Defensive behaviors can consist of actual attacks, or they may simply involve **threat behaviors,** which consist of postures or gestures that warn the adversary to leave or it will become the target of an attack. The threatened animal might show **submissive behaviors,** which indicate that it will not challenge the other animal.

In the natural environment most animals display far more threats than actual attacks. Threat behaviors are useful in reinforcing social hierarchies in organized groups of animals or in warning intruders away from an animal's territory. They have the advantage of not involving actual fighting, which can harm one or both of the combatants. **Predation** is the attack of a member of one species on that of another, usually because the latter serves as food for the former. While engaged in either offensive or defensive behaviors, the animals appear to be extremely aroused and excited, and the activity of their autonomic nervous system is high. In contrast, predatory behaviors are much more "cold-blooded"; they consist of an efficient bite to the neck and are not accompanied by a high level of autonomic activation.

Neural Control of Aggressive Behavior

As we shall see in this section, the three major types of aggressive behavior—offense, defense, and predation—are controlled by different brain mechanisms. The neural control of aggressive behavior is hierarchical. That is, the particular muscular movements an animal makes in attacking or defending itself are programmed by neural circuits in the brain stem. Whether an animal attacks depends on many factors, including the nature of the eliciting stimuli in the environment and the animal's previous experience. The activity of the brain stem circuits appears to be controlled by the hypothalamus and the limbic system (especially the amygdala), which also influence many other species-typical behaviors. And, of course, the activity of the limbic system is controlled by perceptual systems that detect the status of the environment, including the presence of other animals.

First, let us consider offensive behavior. Adams (1986) made lesions in the ventral tegmental area (VTA) of rats and tested the animals' offensive, defensive, and predatory behavior. Offensive behavior was tested by introducing an adult male rat into the subjects' home cage and observing whether they showed the typical sideways posture and a bite-and-kick attack. Defense was tested by placing the subjects with another male in a cage with an electrified grid floor and seeing whether the animal assumed an upright posture and "boxed" with the other rat. Finally, predation was tested by placing a mouse in the animal's cage. The lesions disrupted only offensive attack; predation and defensive behavior were unaffected. The anterior hypothalamus, the lateral septum, and the medial amygdala all have excitatory effects on offensive attack, but these effects appear to be directed toward the VTA. Adams et al. (1993) found that the injection of an excitatory drug into the anterior hypothalamus elicited an offensive attack. (The investigators injected *picrotoxin*, a drug that blocks GABA receptors and thus produces excitation by removing the inhibitory effects of GABAergic synapses.)

Offensive attack is facilitated by vasopressin, a peptide found in neural circuits that play a role in reproductive behaviors. Koolhaas et al. (1990) found that an injection of vasopressin into the medial amygdala increased offensive behavior in rats. Ferris et al. (1990) found that an injection of vasopressin into another part of the limbic system—the lateral septum—increased dominance behavior in hamsters. The effect of this injection was abolished by a lesion of the anterior hypothalamus ipsilateral to the injection site but not contralateral to it. Thus, the effect seems to involve a connection between the septum and the hypothalamus.

In general, increased activity of serotonergic synapses inhibits offensive attack. For this reason, some clinicians have used serotonergic drugs to treat violent behavior in humans. Destruction of serotonergic axons in the forebrain facilitates offensive attack, presumably by removing an inhibitory effect (Vergnes et al., 1988). Raleigh et al. (1991) found that serotonergic drugs could affect the social status of primates. They removed the dominant male from each of several groups of vervet monkeys and treated the top two remaining males with serotonergic drugs: One received an agonist and the other received an antagonist. The monkeys who received the serotonin agonist became dominant, while the status of those who received the antagonist declined.

Several studies (see Kruk, 1991) have found that 5-HT$_{1A}$ receptors are responsible for the inhibitory effect of serotonin. At least some of these receptors appear to be located in the medial amygdala; in a study with rats Pucilowski, Plaznik, and Kostowski (1985) found that an injection of serotonergic agonists into the medial amygdala reduced offensive attack.

The other aggressive behaviors, defensive attack and predation, appear to be controlled by neurons in the periaqueductal gray matter (PAG). These behaviors have primarily been studied in cats. Stimulation of different parts of the PAG with electricity or excitatory amino acids produces defensive behavior, predatory behavior, flight, or immobility (Shaikh, Barrett, and Siegel, 1987; Zhang, Bandler, and Carrive, 1990). Flight and immobility are not aggressive behaviors, but they are clearly related to aggression, because they often occur in response to threat gestures from another animal.

Both the hypothalamus and the amygdala appear to modulate defense. Lu, Shaikh, and Siegel (1992) implanted metal cannulas into the PAG and found locations where electrical stimulation would produce defensive behaviors. Then they injected fluorogold into these regions and waited six days for the retrograde tracer to be taken up by terminal buttons and carried back to their cells of origin. They found labeled cells in the medial hypothalamus—in a location where electrical stimulation can produce defensive behavior. An immunocytochemical study found that these neurons used glutamate as their transmitter substance. Thus, an excitatory connection between the medial hypothalamus and the PAG is involved in the elicitation of defensive behavior.

Evidence that the amygdala plays a role in defensive behavior comes from the fact that lesions of the amygdala have a taming effect on animals. For example, as we saw earlier in this chapter, an amygdala lesion eliminated the defensive attack of a particularly wild rhesus monkey against human handlers. In addition, Adamec (1991) found that cats who were particularly defensive when presented with threatening stimuli showed higher levels of neural activity in the amygdala. Cats who were not bothered by the threatening stimuli showed much less neural activity.

As we saw, predation can be elicited by stimulation of the PAG. Lesions of the PAG abolish the killing bite of a predator, but they do not prevent the animal from stalking and lunging toward the prey (Waldbillig, 1979). Predation can also be elicited by stimulation of the lateral hypothalamus (Flynn et al., 1970; Panksepp, 1971); thus, different sets of neurons in the hypothalamus have facilitatory effects on all three forms of aggression.

Hormonal Control of Aggressive Behavior

With the exception of self-defense and predatory aggression, most instances of aggressive behavior are in some way related to reproduction. For example, males of some species establish territories that attract females during the breeding season. To do so, they must defend them against the intrusion of other males. Even in species in which breeding does not depend on the establishment of a territory, males may compete for access to females, which also involves aggressive behavior. Females, too, often compete with other females for space in which to build nests or dens in which to rear their offspring, and they will defend their offspring against the intrusion of other animals. As you learned in Chapter 10, most reproductive behaviors are controlled by the organizational and activational effects of hormones; thus, we should not be surprised that most forms of aggressive behavior are, like mating, affected by hormones.

Aggression in Males

Adult males of many species fight for territory or access to females. In laboratory rodents androgen secretion occurs prenatally, decreases, and then increases again at the time of puberty. Intermale aggressiveness also begins around the time of puberty, which suggests that the behavior is controlled by neural circuits that are stimulated by androgens. Indeed, many years ago Beeman (1947) found that castration reduced aggressiveness and that injections of testosterone reinstated it.

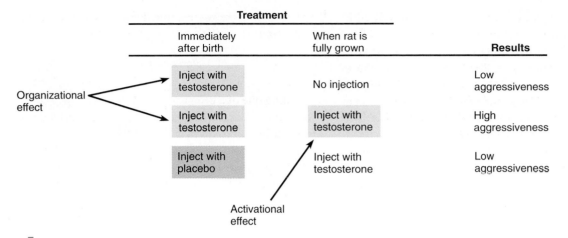

	Treatment		
	Immediately after birth	When rat is fully grown	Results
Organizational effect	Inject with testosterone	No injection	Low aggressiveness
Organizational effect	Inject with testosterone	Inject with testosterone	High aggressiveness
	Inject with placebo	Inject with testosterone	Low aggressiveness

Activational effect

FIGURE 11.15

Organizational and activational effects of testosterone on social aggression.

In Chapter 10 we saw that early androgenization has an *organizational effect.* The secretion of androgens early in development modifies the developing brain, making neural circuits that control male sexual behavior become more responsive to testosterone. Similarly, early androgenization has an organizational effect that stimulates the development of testosterone-sensitive neural circuits that facilitate intermale aggression. (See *Figure 11.15.*)

We also saw in Chapter 10 that androgens stimulate male sexual behavior by interacting with androgen receptors in neurons located in the medial preoptic area (MPA). This region also appears to be important in mediating the effects of androgens on intermale aggression. Bean and Conner (1978) found that implanting testosterone in the MPA reinstated intermale aggression in castrated male rats. Presumably, the testosterone directly activated the behavior by stimulating the androgen-sensitive neurons located there. The medial preoptic area, then, appears to be involved in several behaviors related to reproduction: male sexual behavior, maternal behavior, and intermale aggression.

Aggression in Females

Two adult female rodents that meet in a neutral territory are less likely than males to fight. But aggression between females, like aggression between males, appears to be facilitated by testosterone. Van de Poll et al. (1988) ovariectomized female rats and

then gave them daily injections of testosterone, estradiol, or a placebo for fourteen days. The animals were then placed in a test cage and an unfamiliar female was introduced. As Figure 11.16 shows, testosterone increased aggressiveness, whereas estradiol decreased it. (See *Figure 11.16.*)

Androgens have an organizational effect on the aggressiveness of females, and a certain amount of prenatal androgenization appears to occur naturally.

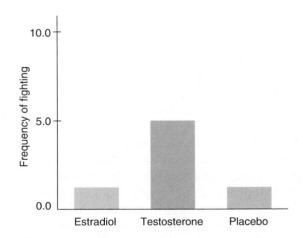

FIGURE 11.16

Effects of estradiol and testosterone on interfemale aggression in rats.

(Adapted from van de Poll, N.E., Taminiau, M.S., Endert, E., and Louwerse, A.L. *International Journal of Neuroscience*, 1988, *41*, 271-286.)

Most rodent fetuses share their mother's uterus with brothers and sisters, arranged in a row like peas in a pod. A female mouse may have zero, one, or two brothers adjacent to her. Researchers refer to these females as 0M, 1M, or 2M, respectively. (See *Figure 11.17*.) Being next to a male fetus has an effect on a female's blood levels of androgens prenatally. Vom Saal and Bronson (1980) found that females located between two males had significantly higher levels of testosterone in their blood than females located between two females (or between a female and the end of the uterus). When they are tested as adults, 2M females are more likely to exhibit interfemale aggressiveness.

Females of some primate species (for example, rhesus monkeys and baboons) are more likely to engage in fights around the time of ovulation (Carpenter, 1942; Saayman, 1971). This phenomenon is probably caused by their increased sexual interest and consequent proximity to males. As Carpenter noted, "She actively approaches males and must overcome their usual resistance to close association, hence she becomes an object of attacks by them" (p. 136). Another period of fighting occurs just before menstruation (Sassenrath, Powell, and Hendrickx, 1973; Mallow, 1979). During this time females tend to attack other females.

Researchers have studied the possibility that irritability and aggressiveness may increase in women just before the time of menstruation, as it does in some other primate species. Floody (1983) reviewed the literature on the so-called *premenstrual syndrome* (PMS). Almost all studies that observed actual aggressiveness, primarily of women in institutions, found decreases around the time of ovulation and increases just before menstruation. Clearly, the changes in irritability are not universal; some women experience little or no mood shift before menstruation. And even if changes in mood occur, most women do not actually become aggressive. Although women with a history of criminal behavior (such as those in prison) may indeed exhibit premenstrual aggressiveness, emotionally stable women may fail to show even a small increase in aggressiveness (Persky, 1974). Depending on their history and temperament, different people respond differently to similar physiological changes.

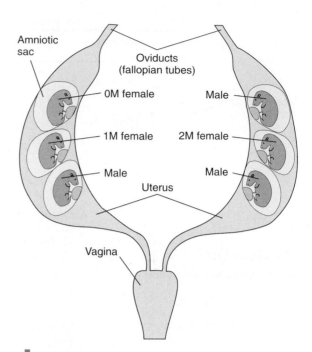

FIGURE 11.17

0M, 1M, and 2M female mouse fetuses.
(Adapted from vom Saal, F.S., in *Hormones and Aggressive Behavior*, edited by B.B. Svare. New York: Plenum Press, 1983.)

Effects of Androgens on Human Aggressive Behavior

Boys are generally more aggressive than girls. Clearly, Western society tolerates assertiveness and aggressive behavior from boys more than girls. Without doubt, the way we treat boys and girls and the models we expose them to play important roles in sex differences in aggressiveness in our species. The question is not whether socialization has an effect (it does) but whether biological influences, such as exposure to androgens, have an effect, too.

Prenatal androgenization increases aggressive behavior in all species that have been studied, including primates. Therefore, if androgens did not affect aggressive behavior in humans, our species would be exceptional. Boys' testosterone levels begin to increase during the early teens, at which time aggressive behavior and intermale fighting also increase (Mazur, 1983). Of course, boys' social status changes during puberty, and their testosterone affects their muscles as well as their brains; so we cannot be sure that the effect is hormonally produced or, if it is, that it is mediated by the brain.

Males of many species can be gentled by castration. In the past, authorities have attempted to suppress sex-related aggression by castrating convicted male sex offenders. Investigators have reported that both heterosexual and homosexual aggressive attacks disappear, along with the offender's sex drive (Hawke, 1951; Sturup, 1961; Laschet, 1973). However, the studies typically lack appropriate control groups and do not always measure aggressive behavior directly. Because the studies with castrated males were not performed with the appropriate double-blind controls, we cannot conclude that testosterone was the responsible agent for the increase in aggressive behavior.

Some cases of aggressiveness, especially sexual assault, have been treated with drugs that block androgen receptors and thus prevent androgens from exerting their normal effects. The rationale is based on animal research indicating that androgens promote male sexual behavior and intermale aggression. Clearly, treatment with drugs is preferable to castration, because the effects are not irreversible. However, the efficacy of treatment with antiandrogens has yet to be established conclusively (Bain, 1987).

Another way to determine whether androgens affect aggressiveness in humans is to examine the testosterone levels of people who exhibit varying levels of aggressive behavior. However, even though this approach poses fewer ethical problems, it presents methodological ones. First, let me review some evidence. Dabbs et al. (1987) measured the testosterone levels of male prison inmates and found a significant correlation with several measures of violence, including the nature of the crime for which they were convicted, infractions of prison rules, and ratings of "toughness" by their peers. These relations are seen in female prison inmates, too; Dabbs et al. (1988) found that women prisoners who showed unprovoked violence and had several prior convictions also showed higher levels of testosterone. (As we saw earlier, testosterone increases interfemale aggression in laboratory animals as well.)

But we must remember that *correlation* does not necessarily indicate *causation*. A person's environ-

ment can affect his or her testosterone level. For example, losing a tennis match or a wrestling competition causes a fall in blood levels of testosterone (Mazur and Lamb, 1980; Elias, 1981). In a very elaborate study Jeffcoate et al. (1986) found that the blood levels of a group of five men confined on a boat for fourteen days changed as they established a dominance-aggression ranking among themselves: The higher the rank, the higher the testosterone level. Thus, we cannot be sure in any correlational study that high testosterone levels *cause* people to become dominant or violent; perhaps their success in establishing a position of dominance increases their testosterone levels relative to those of the people they dominate.

A few studies have looked at the behavioral effects of administering androgens. Because of ethical concerns, people cannot be given androgen supplements merely to see whether they become more aggressive. First, excessive amounts of androgens have deleterious effects on a person's health. Second, it would be wrong to subject innocent people to possible harm from the aggressive behavior of someone who receives androgens while participating in an experiment. Thus, the only evidence we have comes from case studies in which a person with abnormally low levels of testosterone is given the hormone to replace what would normally be present. For example, O'Carroll and Bancroft (1985) reported the case of an institutionalized, mentally retarded man who had lost his testes when he was seven years old. When he received an injection of testosterone, he became violent.

As everyone knows, some athletes take anabolic steroids in order to increase their muscle mass and strength and, supposedly, to increase their competitiveness. Anabolic steroids include natural androgens and synthetic hormones with androgenic effects. Thus, we might expect that these hormones would increase aggressiveness. Indeed, several studies have found exactly that. For example, Yates, Perry, and Murray (1992) found that male weight lifters who were taking anabolic steroids were more aggressive and hostile than those who were not. But as the authors note, we cannot be certain that the steroid is responsible for the increased aggressiveness; it could simply be that the men who were

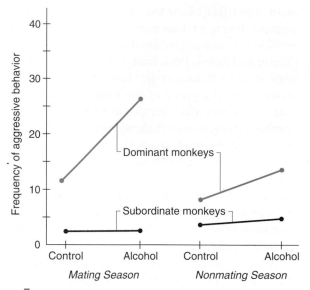

FIGURE 11.18

Effect of alcohol intake on frequency of aggressive behavior of dominant and subordinate male squirrel monkeys during the mating season and the nonmating season.

(Based on data from Winslow, J.T., and Miczek, J.A. *Psychopharmacologia*, 1988, *95*, 92-98.)

already more competitive and aggressive were the ones who chose to take the steroids.

An interesting set of experiments with another species of primates may have some relevance to human aggression. As you undoubtedly know, alcohol intake is often associated with aggression in humans. Alcohol increases intermale aggression in dominant male squirrel monkeys, but only during the mating season, when their blood level of testosterone is two to three times higher than during the nonmating season (Winslow and Miczek, 1985, 1988). Alcohol does *not* increase the aggressive behavior of subordinate monkeys at any time of the year. These studies suggest that the effects of alcohol interact with both social status and with testosterone. (See *Figure 11.18.*) This suggestion was confirmed by Winslow, Ellingoe, and Miczek (1988), who tested monkeys during the nonmating season. They found that alcohol increased the aggressive behavior of dominant monkeys if they were also given injections of testosterone. However, these treatments were ineffective in subordinate monkeys, who had presumably learned not to be aggressive. The next step will

be to find the neural mechanisms that are responsible for these interactions.

INTERIM SUMMARY

Aggressive behaviors are species-typical and serve useful functions most of the time. Their primary forms are offense, defense, and predation. In addition, animals may exhibit threat or submissive behaviors, which may avoid an actual fight.

The ventral tegmental area of the midbrain appears to be involved in the control of offensive behavior; lesions there abolish this behavior without affecting defense or predation. The periaqueductal gray matter appears to be involved in defensive behavior and predation and also in flight behavior and immobility, which are possible responses to attack by another animal. The midbrain mechanisms are modulated by the hypothalamus, septum, and amygdala. Electrical or chemical stimulation of the anterior hypothalamus facilitates offense, as does injection of vasopressin in the medial amygdala or septum. Offensive behavior is inhibited by the activity of serotonergic synapses—perhaps those located in the medial amygdala. Stimulation of the medial hypothalamus produces defensive behavior, and lesions and recording studies suggest that the amygdala is also involved. Predation can be elicited by stimulation of the lateral hypothalamus.

Because many aggressive behaviors are related to reproduction, they are influenced by hormones, especially sex steroid hormones. Androgens primarily affect offensive attack; they are not necessary for defensive behaviors, which are shown by females as well as males. In males androgens have organizational and activational effects on offensive attack, just as they have on male sexual behavior. The effects of androgens on intermale aggression appear to be mediated by the medial preoptic area.

Females who have been slightly androgenized (2M females) are more likely to attack other females. Female primates are most likely to fight around the time of ovulation, perhaps because their increased sexual interest brings them closer to males. Although some women report irritability just before menstruation, the phenomenon is not universal.

Androgens apparently promote aggressive behavior in humans, but this topic is more difficult to study in our species than in laboratory animals. Differences in testosterone levels have been observed in criminals with a history of violence, but we cannot be sure whether higher androgen levels promote violence or whether successful aggression increases androgen levels. Studies with monkeys suggest that testosterone and alcohol have synergistic effects, particularly in dominant animals. (*Synergy,* from a Greek word meaning "working together," refers to combinations of factors that are more effective than the sum of their individual actions.) Perhaps these effects are related to our observations that some men with a history of violent behavior become more aggressive when they drink.

STRESS

Aversive stimuli can produce more than negative emotional responses; they can also harm people's health. Many of these harmful effects are produced not by the stimuli themselves but by our reactions to them. Thus, the expression of negative emotions can have adverse effects on ourselves as well as the people with whom we interact. Walter Cannon, the physiologist who criticized the James-Lange theory, introduced the term **stress** to refer to the physiological reaction caused by the perception of aversive or threatening situations. This section discusses the stress response and its effects on health.

Stress and Health

First, I need to say a few words about terminology. The word *stress* was borrowed from engineering, where it refers to the action of physical forces of mechanical structures. The word can be a noun or a verb; and the noun can refer to situations or the animal's response to them. Because of this potential confusion, I will refer to "stressful" stimuli and situations as **stressors** and to the animal's reaction as a **stress response.** The word *stress* will refer to the general process (as in the title to this subsection).

Stress definitely can be hazardous to one's health. Some disease conditions, such as peptic ulcers, are often caused by the physiological responses that accompany negative emotions. Other disorders, such as heart attacks, strokes, asthma, menstrual problems, headaches, and skin rashes, can occur in the absence of stress but are aggravated by it. As we saw in the first section of this chapter, emotional responses evolved because they are useful and adaptive. Why, then, can they harm our health?

The answer to this question appears to be that our emotional responses are designed primarily to cope with short-term events. The physiological responses that accompany the negative emotions prepare us to threaten rivals or fight them, or to run away from dangerous situations. Walter Cannon introduced the phrase **fight-or-flight response** to refer to the physiological reactions that prepare us for the strenuous efforts required by fighting or running away. Normally, once we have bluffed or fought with an adversary or run away from a dangerous situation, the threat is over and our physiological condition can return to normal. The fact that the physiological responses may have adverse long-term effects on our health is unimportant as long as the responses are brief. But sometimes, the threatening situations are continuous rather than episodic, producing a more or less continuous stress response.

There is no doubt about the deleterious effects of stress on health. For example, survivors of concentration camps, who were obviously subjected to long-term stress, have generally poorer health later in life than other people of the same age (Cohen, 1953). Drivers of subway trains that injure or kill people are more likely to suffer from illnesses several months later (Theorell et al., 1992). Air traffic controllers—especially those who work at busy airports where the danger of collisions is greatest—show a greater incidence of high blood pressure, which gets worse as they grow older (Cobb and Rose, 1973). (See *Figure 11.19.*) They also are more likely to suffer from ulcers or diabetes.

Physiology of the Stress Response

As we saw earlier in this chapter, emotions consist of behavioral, autonomic, and endocrine responses. The latter two components—the autonomic and endocrine responses—are the ones that can have adverse effects on health. (Well, I guess the behav-

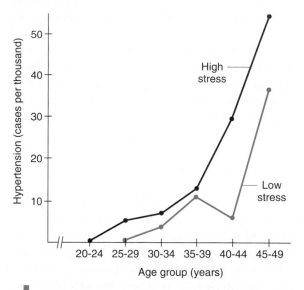

FIGURE 11.19

Incidence of hypertension in various age groups of air traffic controllers at high-stress and low-stress airports.
(Based on data from Cobb and Rose, 1973.)

ioral components can, too, if a person rashly gets into a fight with someone much bigger and stronger.) Because threatening situations generally call for vigorous activity, the autonomic and endocrine responses that accompany them are catabolic in nature; that is, they help mobilize the body's energy resources. The sympathetic branch of the autonomic nervous system is active, and the adrenal glands secrete epinephrine, norepinephrine, and steroid stress hormones. Because the effects of sympathetic activity are similar to those of the adrenal hormones, I will limit my discussion to the hormonal responses.

Epinephrine affects glucose metabolism, causing the nutrients stored in muscles to become available to provide energy for strenuous exercise. Along with norepinephrine, the hormone also increases blood flow to the muscles by increasing the output of the heart. In doing so, it also increases blood pressure, which, over the long term, contributes to cardiovascular disease.

Besides serving as a stress hormone, norepinephrine is (as you know) secreted in the brain as a neurotransmitter. Some of the behavioral and physiological responses produced by aversive stimuli appear to be mediated by noradrenergic neurons.

For example, microdialysis studies have found that stressful situations increase the release of norepinephrine in the hypothalamus, frontal cortex, and lateral basal forebrain (Yokoo et al. 1990; Cenci et al. 1992). Montero, Fuentes, and Fernandez-Tome (1990) found that destruction of the noradrenergic axons that ascend from the brain stem to the forebrain prevented the rise in blood pressure that is normally produced by social isolation stress. Presumably, the release of norepinephrine in the brain is produced by a pathway from the central nucleus of the amygdala to the norepinephrine-secreting regions of the brain stem (Wallace, Magnuson, and Gray, 1992).

The other stress-related hormone is *cortisol*, a steroid secreted by the adrenal cortex. Cortisol is called a **glucocorticoid** because it has profound effects on glucose metabolism. (Aldosterone, the other steroid secreted by the adrenal cortex, is called a *mineralocorticoid* because of its effects on sodium metabolism, which are described in Chapter 12.) In addition, glucocorticoids help break down protein and convert it to glucose, help make fats available for energy, increase blood flow, and stimulate behavioral responsiveness—presumably by affecting the brain. They decrease the sensitivity of the gonads to luteinizing hormone (LH), which suppresses the secretion of the sex steroid hormones. In fact, Singer and Zumoff (1992) found that the blood level of testosterone in male hospital residents was severely depressed, presumably because of the stressful work schedule they are obliged to follow. Glucocorticoids have other physiological effects, too, some of which are only poorly understood. Almost every cell in the body contains glucocorticoid receptors, which means that few of them are unaffected by these hormones.

The secretion of glucocorticoids is controlled by neurons in the paraventricular nucleus of the hypothalamus (PVN), whose axons terminate in the median eminence, where the hypothalamic capillaries of the portal blood supply to the anterior pituitary gland are located. (The pituitary portal blood supply was described in Chapter 4.) The neurons of the PVN secrete a peptide called **corticotropin-releasing factor** (CRF), which stimulates the anterior pituitary gland to secrete **adrenocorticotropic hormone** (ACTH). ACTH enters the general circu-

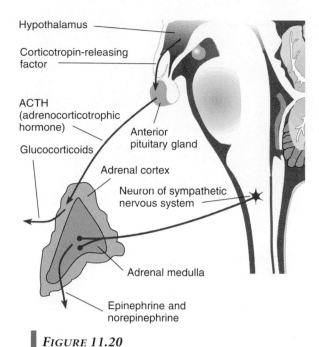

Hypothalamus

Corticotropin-releasing factor

ACTH (adrenocorticotrophic hormone)

Glucocorticoids

Anterior pituitary gland

Adrenal cortex

Neuron of sympathetic nervous system

Adrenal medulla

Epinephrine and norepinephrine

FIGURE 11.20

Control of the secretion of glucocorticoids by the adrenal cortex and of catecholamines by the adrenal medulla.

lation and stimulates the adrenal cortex to secrete glucocorticoids. (See *Figure 11.20.*)

CRF is also secreted within the brain, where it serves as a neuromodulator/neurotransmitter—especially in regions of the limbic system involved in emotional responses, such as the periaqueductal gray matter, the locus coeruleus, and the central nucleus of the amygdala. The physiological and behavioral effects produced by an injection of CRF into the brain are similar to those produced by aversive situations; thus, some elements of the stress response appear to be produced by the release of CRF in the brain (Dunn and Berridge, 1990; Liang et al., 1992).

The secretion of glucocorticoids does more than help an animal react to a stressful situation—it helps it survive. If a rat's adrenal glands are removed, it becomes much more susceptible to the effects of stress. In fact, a stressful situation that a normal rat would take in its stride may kill one whose adrenal glands have been removed. And physicians know that if an adrenalectomized human is subjected to stressors, he or she must be given additional amounts of glucocorticoid (Tyrell and Baxter, 1981).

A pioneer in the study of stress, Hans Selye, suggested that most of the harmful effects of stress were produced by the prolonged secretion of glucocorticoids (Selye, 1976). Although the short-term effects of glucocorticoids are essential, the long-term effects are damaging. These effects include increased blood pressure, damage to muscle tissue, steroid diabetes, infertility, inhibition of growth, inhibition of the inflammatory responses, and suppression of the immune system. High blood pressure can lead to heart attacks and stroke. Inhibition of growth in children subjected to prolonged stress prevents them from attaining their full height. Inhibition of the inflammatory response makes it more difficult for the body to heal itself after an injury, and suppression of the immune system makes an individual vulnerable to infections and (perhaps) cancer.

Several lines of research suggest that stress is related to aging in at least two ways. First, older organisms, even when they are perfectly healthy, do not tolerate stress as well as younger ones (Shock, 1977). Second, stress may accelerate the aging process (Selye and Tuchweber, 1976). Sapolsky and his colleagues have investigated one rather serious long-term effect of stress: brain damage. As you will learn in Chapter 15, the hippocampal formation plays a crucial role in learning and memory, and evidence suggests that one of the causes of memory loss that occurs with aging is degeneration of this brain structure. Research with animals has shown that long-term exposure to glucocorticoids destroys neurons located in a particular region (the CA1 field) of the hippocampal formation. The hormone appears to destroy the neurons by making them more susceptible to potentially harmful events, such as decreased blood flow, which often occurs as a result of the aging process. The primary effect of the hormone is to lower the ability of the neurons in the hippocampus to utilize glucose, so that when the blood flow decreases, their metabolism falls and they begin to die (Sapolsky, 1986; Sapolsky, Krey, and McEwen, 1986). Perhaps, then, the stressors to which people are subjected throughout their lives increases the likelihood of memory problems as they grow older.

Uno et al. (1989) found that if stress is intense enough, it can even cause brain damage in young primates. The investigators studied a colony of

FIGURE 11.21

Photomicrographs showing brain damage caused by stress. (a) Section through the hippocampus of a normal monkey. (b) Section through the hippocampus of a monkey of low social status subjected to stress. Compare the regions between the arrowheads, normally filled with large pyramidal cells.

(From Uno, H., Tarara, R., Else, J.G., Suleman, M.A., and Sapolsky, R.M. *Journal of Neuroscience*, 1989, *9*, 1706-1711. Reprinted by permission of the *Journal of Neuroscience*.)

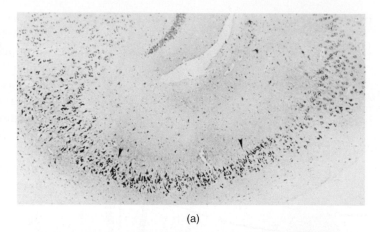

(a)

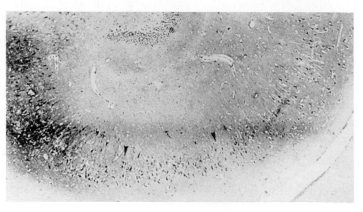

(b)

vervet monkeys housed in a primate center in Kenya. They found that some monkeys died, apparently from stress. Vervet monkeys have a hierarchical society, and monkeys near the bottom of the hierarchy are picked on by the others; thus, they are almost continuously subjected to stress. (Ours is not the only species with social structures that cause a stress reaction in some of its members.) The deceased monkeys had gastric ulcers and enlarged adrenal glands, which are signs of chronic stress. And as Figure 11.21 shows, neurons in the CA1 field of their hippocampal formation were completely destroyed. (See **Figure 11.21.**) Severe stress appears to cause brain damage in humans as well; Jensen, Genefke, and Hyldebrandt (1982) found evidence of brain degeneration in CT scans of people who had been subjected to torture.

As we saw in Chapter 10, prenatal stress tends to inhibit androgenization of the fetuses. That is, when a pregnant female is exposed to stressors, the behav-

ior and brain structure of her male offspring appear less masculinized and defeminized than control animals. Prenatal stress also appears to produce long-term effects on animals' stress reactions; Takahashi, Turner, and Kalin (1992) found that rats whose mothers had been stressed reacted more strongly when they were presented with stressful stimuli during adulthood.

The Coping Response

As we have seen, many of the harmful effects of long-term stress are caused by our own reactions—primarily the secretion of stress hormones. Some events that cause stress responses, such as prolonged exertion or extreme cold, cause damage directly. These stressors will affect everyone; their severity will depend on each person's physical capacity. The effects of other stressors, such as situations that cause fear or anxiety, depend on people's perceptions and emotional reactivity. That is, because of individual differences in temperament or experience with a particular situation, some people may find a situation stressful and others may not. In these cases it is the perception that counts.

One of the most important variables that determines whether an aversive stimulus will cause a stress reaction is the degree to which the situation can be controlled. As I mentioned earlier in this chapter, when an animal can learn a coping response that avoids contact with an aversive stimulus or decreases its severity, its emotional response will disappear. Weiss (1968) found that rats who learned to minimize (but not completely avoid) shocks by making a response whenever they heard a warning tone developed fewer stomach ulcers than rats who had no control over the shocks. The effect was not caused by the pain itself, because both groups of animals received exactly the same number of shocks. Thus, being able to exert some control over an aversive situation reduces an animal's stress response. Humans react similarly. Situations that permit some control are less likely to produce signs of stress than those in which other people (or machines) control the situation (Gatchel, Baum, and Krantz, 1989). Perhaps this phenomenon explains why some people like to have a magic charm or other "security blanket" with them in stressful situations. Perhaps even the *illusion* of control can be reassuring.

Personality variables also affect people's reactions to potential stressors. Some people are simply not bothered by situations that others perceive to be stressful. Both humans and laboratory animals show genetic differences in susceptibility to stressors, such as the tendency to develop peptic ulcers (Glavin et al., 1991).

Stress and Cardiovascular Disease

One of the most important causes of death is cardiovascular diseases—diseases of the heart and the blood vessels. Cardiovascular diseases can cause heart attacks and strokes; heart attacks occur when the blood vessels that serve the heart become blocked, while strokes involve the blood vessels in the brain. The two most important risk factors in cardiovascular disease are high blood pressure and a high level of cholesterol in the blood.

The degree to which people react to potential stressors may affect the likelihood that they will suffer from cardiovascular disease. For example, Wood et al. (1984) examined the blood pressure of people who had been subjected to a *cold pressor test* in 1934, when they were children. The cold pressor test reveals how people's blood pressure reacts to the stress caused by their hand being placed in a container of ice water for 1 minute. Wood and his colleagues found that 70 percent of the subjects who hyperreacted to the cold pressor test when they were children had high blood pressure, compared with 19 percent of those who showed little reaction to the test.

A study with monkeys showed that individual differences in emotional reactivity are a risk factor for cardiovascular disease. Manuck et al. (1983, 1986) fed a high-cholesterol diet to a group of monkeys, which increases the likelihood of their developing coronary artery disease. They measured the animals' emotional reactivity by threatening to capture the animals. (Monkeys avoid contact with humans, and they perceive being captured as a stressful situation.) Those animals who showed the strongest negative reactions eventually developed the highest rates of coronary artery disease. Presumably, these animals reacted more strongly to all types of stressors, and their reactions had detrimental effects on their health.

Apparently, at least some of the differences in emotional reactivity displayed by individual animals are caused by genetic differences in brain chemistry and function. Eilam et al. (1991) transplanted some tissue from the hypothalamus of genetically hypertensive rats into normal rats and found that the blood pressure of the recipient rats increased by an average of 31 percent. (Transplants of hypothalamic tissue from normotensive rats did not increase recipients' blood pressure.) (See *Figure 11.22.*)

Friedman and Rosenman (1959) identified a behavior pattern that appeared to be related to a person's susceptibility to cardiovascular disease. They characterized the disease-prone **type A pattern** as one of excessive competitive drive, impatience, hostility, fast movements, and rapid speech. People with the **type B pattern** were less competitive, less hostile, more patient, and more easygoing and tolerant, and they moved and talked more slowly; they were also less likely to suffer from cardiovascular

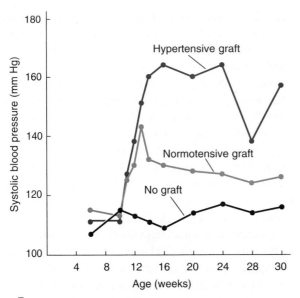

FIGURE 11.22

Systolic blood pressure in normal rats, rats with grafts of hypothalamic tissue from normal rats, and rats with grafts from genetically hypertensive rats.

(Adapted from Eilam, R., Malach, R., Bergmann, F., and Segal, M. *Journal of Neuroscience*, 1991, *11*, 401-411.)

disease. Friedman and Rosenman developed a questionnaire that distinguished these two types of people. The test is rather interesting, because the person who administers it is not a passive participant. The interviewer asks questions in an abrupt, impatient manner, interrupting the subject if he or she takes too much time to answer a question. The point of such behavior is to try to elicit type A behavior from the subject.

Researchers have devoted much attention to the relation between the type A personality and cardiovascular disease. The Western Collaborative Group Study (Rosenman et al., 1975), which studied 3154 healthy men for eight and one-half years, found that the type A behavior pattern was associated with twice the rate of coronary artery disease. Results such as these led an independent review panel to classify the type A behavior pattern as a risk factor for this disease (Review Panel, 1981). However, since then many contradictory results have been obtained. For example, one large study found that although people classified as type A were more likely to have

a heart attack, the long-term survival rate after having a heart attack was higher for type A patients than for type B patients (Ragland and Brand, 1988). In this case it would seem better to be type A, at least after having a nonfatal heart attack. Other studies have failed to find a difference in cardiovascular disease in people with type A and type B personalities (Dimsdale, 1988).

Williams et al. (1980) suggested that one aspect of the type A personality—hostility—is of particular importance in cardiovascular disease. Several subsequent studies carried out in the early to mid-1980s confirmed that hostility was an important risk factor, but more recent studies have not. For example, Helmer, Ragland, and Syme (1991) studied 118 men who underwent angiography (X-ray inspection of the buildup of atherosclerotic plaque in the arteries of the heart that can ultimately cause a heart attack). They found no relation between either of two measures of hostility and the degree of coronary artery disease.

Although the relation between cardiovascular disease and hostility or the type A behavior pattern is unclear, several studies found that personality variables are related to particular risk factors. For example, Howard, Cunningham, and Rechnitzer (1976) found that people who exhibited extreme type A behavior were more likely to smoke and to have high blood pressure and high blood levels of cholesterol. Weidner et al. (1987) confirmed the high level of cholesterol in a sample of men and women with the type A behavior pattern, and Irvine et al. (1991) confirmed the association between type A behavior and high blood pressure. Lombardo and Carreno (1987) found that type A smokers held the smoke in their lungs longer, leading to a high level of carbon monoxide in their blood.

What are we to conclude? Most investigators believe that personality variables *are* involved in susceptibility to heart attack but that we need a better definition of just what these variables are. In addition, it is possible that different personality variables are associated with different risk factors, which make it difficult to tease out the relevant variables. Personality factors certainly play an important role in cardiovascular disease, but at present the precise nature of this role is uncertain. This topic is important and clearly merits further research.

Psychoneuroimmunology

As we have seen, long-term stress can be harmful to one's health and can even result in brain damage. The most important cause of these effects is elevated levels of glucocorticoids, but the high blood pressure caused by epinephrine and norepinephrine also plays a contributing role. In addition, the stress response can impair the functions of the immune system, which protects us from assault from viruses, microbes, fungi, and other types of parasites. Study of the interactions between the immune system and behavior (mediated by the nervous system, of course) is called **psychoneuroimmunology.** This new field is described in the following section.

The Immune System

The immune system is one of the most complex systems of the body. Its function is to protect us from infection; and because infectious organisms have developed devious tricks through the process of evolution, our immune system has evolved devious tricks of its own. The description I provide here is abbreviated and simplified, but it presents some of the important elements of the system.

The immune system derives from white blood cells that develop in the bone marrow and in the thymus gland. Some of the cells roam through the blood or lymphatic system; others reside permanently in one place. The immune reaction occurs when the body is invaded by foreign organisms, including bacteria, fungi, and viruses. Two types of reactions occur, *nonspecific* and *specific*. One nonspecific reaction, called the *inflammatory reaction,* occurs early, in response to tissue damage produced by an invading organism. The damaged tissue secretes substances that increase the local blood circulation and make capillaries leak fluids, which causes the region to become inflamed. The secretions also attract phagocytic white blood cells that destroy both the invading cells and the debris produced by the breakdown of the body's own cells. Another nonspecific reaction occurs when a virus infects a cell. The infection causes the cell to release a peptide called *interferon,* which suppresses the ability of viruses to reproduce. In addition, **natural killer cells** continuously prowl through tissue; when they encounter a cell that has been infected by a virus or that has become transformed into a cancer cell, they engulf and destroy it. Thus, natural killer cells constitute our first defense against the development of malignant tumors.

The immune system produces two types of specific immune reactions: *chemically mediated* and *cell-mediated.* Chemically mediated immune reactions involve antibodies. Infectious microorganisms have unique proteins on their surfaces, called **antigens.** These proteins serve as the invaders' calling cards, identifying them to the immune system. Through exposure to the microorganisms, the immune system learns to recognize these proteins. (I will not try to explain the mechanism by which this learning takes place.) The result of this learning is the development of special lines of cells that produce specific **antibodies**—proteins that recognize antigens and help kill the invading microorganism. One type of antibody is released into the circulation by **B-lymphocytes,** which receive their name from the fact that they develop in bone marrow. These antibodies, called **immunoglobulins,** are chains of protein. Each type of immunoglobulin (there are five of them) is identical except for one end, which contains a unique receptor. A particular receptor binds with a particular antigen, just as a molecule of a hormone or neurotransmitter binds with its receptor. When the appropriate line of B-lymphocytes detects the presence of an invading bacterium, the cells release their antibodies, which bind with the antigens present on the surface of the invading microorganisms. The antigens either kill the invaders directly or attract other white blood cells, which then destroy them. (See *Figure 11.23a.*)

The other type of defense by the immune system—cell-mediated immune reactions—is produced by **T-lymphocytes,** which originally develop in the thymus gland. These cells also produce antibodies, but the antibodies remain attached to the outside of their membrane. T-lymphocytes primarily defend the body against fungi, viruses, and multicellular parasites. When antigens bind with their surface antibodies, the cells either directly kill the invaders or signal other white blood cells to come and kill them. (See *Figure 11.23b.*)

The reactions illustrated in Figure 11.23 are much simplified; actually, both chemically mediated

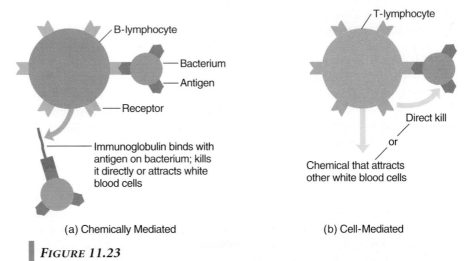

(a) Chemically Mediated

(b) Cell-Mediated

FIGURE 11.23

Immune reactions. (a) Chemically mediated reaction. The B-lymphocyte detects an antigen on a bacterium and releases a specific immunoglobulin. (b) Cell-mediated reaction. The T-lymphocyte detects an antigen on a bacterium and kills it directly or releases a chemical that attracts other white blood cells.

and cell-mediated immune reactions involve several different types of cells. The communication between these cells is accomplished by **cytokines,** chemicals that stimulate cell division. The cytokines released by certain white blood cells when an invading microorganism is detected (principally *interleukin-1* and *interleukin-2*) cause other white blood cells to proliferate and direct an attack against the invader. The primary way that glucocorticoids suppress specific immune responses is by interfering with the messages conveyed by the cytokines (Sapolsky, 1992).

Although the immune system normally protects us, it can cause us harm, too. Allergic reactions occur when an antigen causes cells of the immune system to overreact, releasing a particular immunoglobulin that produces a localized inflammatory response. The chemicals released during this reaction can enter the general circulation and cause life-threatening complications. Obviously, allergic responses are harmful, and why they occur is unknown. The immune system can do something else that harms the body—it can attack its cells. **Autoimmune diseases** occur when the immune system becomes sensitized to a protein present in the body and attacks the tissue that contains this pro-

tein. Exactly what causes the protein to be so targeted is not known. What is known is that autoimmune diseases often follow viral or bacterial infections. Presumably, in learning to recognize antigens that belong to the infectious agent, the immune system develops a line of cells that treat one of the body's own proteins as foreign. Some common autoimmune diseases include rheumatoid arthritis, diabetes mellitus, lupus, and multiple sclerosis. As we shall see in Chapter 17, some researchers even believe that schizophrenia is caused by an autoimmune dysfunction.

Neural Control of the Immune System

As we will see in the next subsection, the stress response can increase the likelihood of infectious diseases, and it can also aggravate autoimmune diseases. It may even affect the growth of cancers. What is the physiological explanation for these effects? One answer, and probably the most important one, is that stress increases the secretion of glucocorticoids, and as we saw, these hormones directly suppress the activity of the immune system.

A direct relation between stress and the immune system was demonstrated by Kiecolt-Glaser et al. (1987). These investigators found that caregivers of family members with Alzheimer's disease—who certainly underwent considerable stress—showed weaker immune systems, based on several different laboratory tests. Bereavement, another source of stress, also suppresses the immune system. Schleifer et al. (1983) tested the husbands of women with breast cancer and found that their immune response was lower after their wives died. (See *Figure 11.24.*) Knapp et al. (1992) even found that when healthy subjects imagined themselves reliving unpleasant emotional experiences, the immune response measured in samples of their blood was decreased.

Several studies indicate that the suppression of the immune response by stress is largely mediated by glucocorticoids. For example, in a study with rats Keller et al. (1983) found that the stress of inescapable shock decreased the number of lymphocytes (B-cells, T-cells, and natural killer cells) found in the blood. This effect was abolished by removal of the adrenal glands; thus, it appears to have been caused by the release of glucocorticoids triggered by the stress response. (See *Figure 11.25a.*) However, the same authors found that adrenalectomy did *not* abolish the effects of stress on another type of immune response: stimulation of lymphocytes by an antigen. (See *Figure 11.25b.*) Thus, not all the effects of stress on the immune system are mediated by glucocorticoids; there must be other mechanisms as well.

Because the secretion of glucocorticoids is controlled by the brain (through its secretion of CRF), the brain is obviously responsible for the suppressing effect of these hormones on the immune system. Neurons in the central nucleus of the amygdala send axons to CRF-secreting neurons in the paraventricular nucleus of the hypothalamus; thus, we can reasonably expect that the mechanism responsible for negative emotional responses is also responsible for the stress response and the immunosuppression that accompanies it. Several studies have shown that stress increases the activity of neurons in brain regions that have been shown to play a role in emotional responses, including the central nucleus of the amygdala and the PVN (Sharp et al., 1991; Imaki et al., 1992).

Some of the stress-induced immunosuppression that does not involve the secretion of glucocorticoids may be under direct neural control. The bone

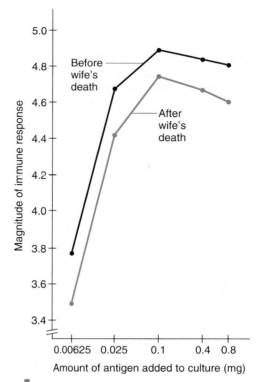

FIGURE 11.24

Stimulation of white blood cell (lymphocyte) production by an antigen in blood of husbands before and after their wifes' death.

(Adapted from Schleifer, S.J., Keller, S.E., Camerino, M., Thornton, J.C., and Stein, M. *Journal of the American Medical Association,* 1983, *250,* 374-377.)

marrow, the thymus gland, and the lymph nodes all receive neural input. Although researchers have not yet obtained direct proof that this input modulates immune function, it would be surprising if it did not. In addition, the immune system appears to be sensitive to chemicals produced by the nervous system. The best evidence comes from studies with the opioids produced by the brain. Shavit et al. (1984) found that inescapable intermittent shock produced both analgesia (decreased sensitivity to pain) and suppression of the production of natural killer cells. These effects both seem to have been mediated by endogenous opioids, because both effects were abolished when the experimenters administered a drug that blocks opiate receptors. Shavit et al. (1986) found that natural killer cell activity could be suppressed by injecting morphine directly into the

FIGURE 11.25

Effects of removal of rats' adrenal glands on the suppression of the immune system by inescapable shocks. (a) Number of white blood cells (lymphocytes) found in the blood. (b) Stimulation of lymphocyte production after exposure to an antigen.

(Based on data from Keller, Weiss, Schleifer, Miller, and Stein, 1983.)

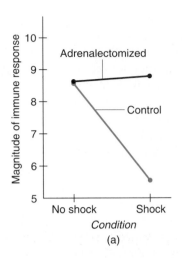
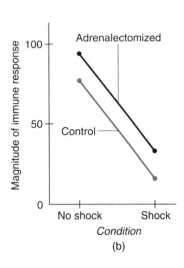

(a)   (b)

Stress and Infectious Diseases

brain; thus, the effect of the opiates appears to take place in the brain. The mechanism by which the brain affects the natural killer cells is not yet known.

Often when a married person dies, his or her spouse dies soon afterward, frequently of an infection. In fact, a wide variety of stress-producing events in a person's life can increase the susceptibility to illness. For example, Glaser et al. (1987) found that medical students were more likely to contract acute infections—and to show evidence of suppression of the immune system—during the time that final examinations were given. In addition, autoimmune diseases often get worse when a person is subjected to stress, as Feigenbaum, Masi, and Kaplan (1979) found for rheumatoid arthritis. In a laboratory study Rogers et al. (1980) found that when rats were stressed by handling them or exposing them to a cat, they developed a more severe case of an artificially induced autoimmune disease. Lehman et al. (1991) found that the incidence of diabetes in a strain of rats susceptible to this autoimmune disease was considerably higher when the animals were subjected to moderate chronic stress.

Stone, Reed, and Neale (1987) attempted to see whether stressful events in people's daily lives might predispose them to upper respiratory infection. If a person is exposed to a microorganism that might cause such a disease, the symptoms do not occur for several days; that is, there is an incubation period between exposure and signs of the actual illness. Thus, the authors reasoned that if stressful events suppressed the immune system, one might expect to see a higher likelihood of respiratory infections several days after such stress. To test their hypothesis, they asked volunteers to keep a daily record of desirable and undesirable events in their lives over a twelve-week period. The volunteers also kept a daily record of any discomfort or symptoms of illness.

The results were as predicted: During the three-to-five-day period just before showing symptoms of an upper respiratory infection, people experienced an increased number of undesirable events and a decreased number of desirable events in their lives. (See **Figure 11.26.**) Stone et al. (1987) suggest that the effect is caused by decreased production of a particular immunoglobulin that is present in the secretions of mucous membranes, including those in the nose, mouth, throat, and lungs. This immunoglobulin serves as the first defense against infectious microorganisms that enter the nose or mouth. They found that this immunoglobulin (known as IgA) is associated with mood; when a subject is unhappy or depressed, its levels are lower than normal. The results suggest that the stress caused by undesirable events may, by suppressing the production of IgA, lead to a rise in the likelihood of upper respiratory infections.

The results of the study by Stone and his colleagues were confirmed by an experiment by Cohen, Tyrrell, and Smith (1991). The investigators found

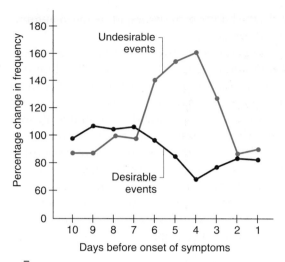

FIGURE 11.26

Mean percentage change in frequency of undesirable and desirable events during the ten-day period preceding the onset of symptoms of upper respiratory infections.

(Based on data from Stone, A.A., Reed, B.R., and Neale, J.M. *Journal of Human Stress*, 1987, *13*, 70-74.)

that subjects who were given nasal drops containing cold viruses were much more likely to develop colds if they reported stressful experiences during the past year and if they said they felt threatened, out of control, or overwhelmed by events. (See *Figure 11.27*.)

||||| INTERIM SUMMARY

People's emotional reactions to aversive stimuli can harm their health. The stress response, which Cannon called the fight-or-flight response, is useful as a short-term response to threatening stimuli but is harmful in the long term. This response includes increased activity of the sympathetic branch of the autonomic nervous system and increased secretion of hormones by the adrenal gland: epinephrine, norepinephrine, and glucocorticoids.

Although increased levels of epinephrine and norepinephrine can raise blood pressure, most of the harm to health comes from glucocorticoids. Prolonged exposure to high levels of these hormones can increase blood pressure, damage muscle tissue,

lead to infertility, inhibit growth, inhibit the inflammatory response, and suppress the immune system. It can also damage the hippocampus, and some investigators believe glucocorticoids accelerate the aging process.

Because the harm of most forms of stress comes from our own response to it, individual differences in personality variables can alter the effects of stressful situations. The most important variable is the nature of a person's coping response. Research on the type A behavior pattern suggests that some of these variables—in particular, hostility—can predict the likelihood of cardiovascular disease. However, the research findings are mixed, and some suggest that health-related behaviors may be more important than patterns of emotional reactions. Investigators hope that research on this topic will foster the development of training methods to teach people behavior patterns that will reduce the incidence of the disease.

Psychoneuroimmunology is a new field of study that investigates interactions between behavior and the immune system, mediated by the nervous system. The immune system consists of several types

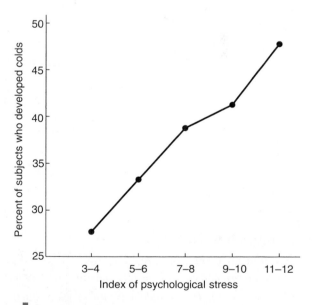

FIGURE 11.27

Percent of subjects with colds as a function of an index of psychological stress.

(Adapted from Cohen, S., Tyrrell, D.A.J., and Smith, A.P. New England Journal of Medicine, 1991, 325, 606-612.)

of white blood cells that produce both nonspecific and specific responses to invading microorganisms. The nonspecific responses include the inflammatory response, the antiviral effect of interferon, and the action of natural killer cells against viruses and cancer cells. The specific responses include chemically mediated and cell-mediated responses. Chemically mediated responses are carried out by B-lymphocytes, which release antibodies that bind with the antigens on microorganisms and kill them directly or target them for attack by other white blood cells. Cell-mediated responses are carried out by T-lymphocytes, whose antibodies remain attached to their membranes. The immune system can produce harm when it triggers an allergic reaction or when it attacks the body's own tissues, in so-called autoimmune diseases.

A wide variety of stressful situations have been shown to increase people's susceptibility to infectious diseases. Animal research suggests that stress can even encourage the growth of malignant tumors, and that allergies and autoimmune diseases can be exacerbated by stress. The most important mechanism by which stress impairs immune function is the increased blood levels of glucocorticoids. In addition, the neural input to the bone marrow, lymph nodes, and thymus gland may also play a role; and the endogenous opioids appear to suppress the activity of natural killer cells.

New Terms

Emotions as Response Patterns

corticomedial group p. 333

lateral-basomedial group p. 333

central nucleus p. 333

basolateral group p. 333

conditioned emotional response p. 334

coping response p. 334

orbitofrontal cortex p. 340

akinetic mutism p. 343

Expression and Recognition of Emotions

pseudobulbar palsy (*soo doh BUL bur*) p. 348

Feelings of Emotions

James-Lange theory p. 350

Aggresive Behavior

offensive behavior p. 353

defensive behavior p. 353

threat behavior p. 353

submissive behavior p. 353

predation p. 353

Stress

stress p. 359

stressor p. 359

stress response p. 359

fight-or-flight response p. 359

glucocorticoid p. 360

corticortopin-releasing factor (CRF) p. 360

adrenocorticotropic hormone (ACTH) p. 360

type A pattern p. 363

type B pattern p. 363

psychoneuroimmunology p. 365

natural killer cell p. 365

antigen p. 365

antibody p. 365

B-lymphocyte p. 365

immunoglobulin p. 365

T-lymphocyte p. 365

cytokine p. 366

autoimmune disease p. 366

Suggested Readings

Ader, R., Felten, D.L., and Cohen, N. (eds.). *Psychoneuroimmunology*, 2nd ed. San Diego: Academic Press, 1990.

Aggleton, J. (ed.). *The Amygdala: Neurobiological Aspects of Emotion, Memory, and Mental Dysfunction.* New York: Wiley-Liss, 1992.

Brown, M.R., Koob, G.F., and Rivier, C. (eds.). *Stress: Neurobiology and Neuroendocrinology.* New York: Dekker, 1990.

McNaughton, Neil. *Biology and Emotion.* Cambridge, England: Cambridge University Press, 1989.

Stein, N.L., Leventhal, B., and Trabasso, T. (eds.). *Psychological and Biological Approaches to Emotion.* Hillsdale, N.J.: Lawrence Erlbaum Associates, 1990.

CHAPTER 12

Ingestive Behavior: Drinking

The Nature of Physiological Regulatory Mechanisms

Some Facts About Fluid Balance
• The Fluid Compartments of the Body
• The Kidneys
Interim Summary

Drinking and Salt Appetite
• Osmometric Thirst
• Volumetric Thirst
• Food-Related Drinking
• Salt Appetite
Interim Summary

Brain Mechanisms of Thirst and Salt Appetite
• Neural Control of Thirst
• Neural Control of Salt Appetite
Interim Summary

Mechanisms of Satiety
• Drinking
• Salt Appetite
Interim Summary

As the French physiologist Claude Bernard (1813–1878) said, "The constancy of the internal milieu is a necessary condition for a free life." This famous quote succinctly says what organisms must do to be able to exist in environments hostile to the living cells that compose them (that is, to live a "free life"): They must regulate the nature of the internal fluid that bathes their cells.

The physiological characteristics of the cells that constitute our bodies evolved long ago, when these cells floated freely in the ocean. In essence, what the evolutionary process has accomplished is the ability to make our own seawater for bathing our cells, to add to this seawater the oxygen and nutrients that our cells need, and to remove from it waste products that would otherwise poison them. To perform these functions, we have digestive, respiratory, circulatory, and excretory systems. We also have the behaviors necessary for finding and ingesting food and water.

Regulation of the fluid that bathes our cells is part of a process called **homeostasis** ("similar standing"). This chapter discusses the means by which we mammals achieve homeostatic control of the vital characteristics of our extracellular fluid through our **ingestive behavior:** intake of food, water, and minerals such as sodium. First, we will examine the general nature of regulatory mechanisms; then we will consider our drinking and eating behavior.

THE NATURE OF PHYSIOLOGICAL REGULATORY MECHANISMS

A physiological regulatory mechanism is one that maintains the constancy of some internal characteristic of the organism in the face of external variability—for example, keeping body temperature constant despite changes in the ambient temperature. A regulatory mechanism contains four essential features: the **system variable** (the characteristic to be regulated), a **set point** (the optimal value of the system variable), a **detector** that moni-

tors the value of the system variable, and a **correctional mechanism** that restores the system variable to the set point.

An example of a regulatory system is a room whose temperature is regulated by a thermostatically controlled heater. The system variable is the air temperature of the room, and the detector for this variable is a thermostat. This device can be adjusted so that contacts of a switch will be closed when the temperature falls below a preset value (the set point). Closure of the contacts turns on the correctional mechanism—the coils of the heater. (See *Figure 12.1.*)

If the room cools below the set point of the thermostat, the thermostat turns the heater on, which warms the room. The rise in room temperature causes the thermostat to turn the heater off. Because the activity of the correctional mechanism (heat production) feeds back to the thermostat and causes it to turn the heater off, this process is called **negative feedback.** Negative feedback is an essential characteristic of all regulatory systems.

This chapter and Chapter 13 consider regulatory systems that involve ingestive behaviors: drinking and eating. These behaviors are correctional mechanisms that replenish the body's depleted stores of water or nutrients. Because of the delay between ingestion and replenishment of the depleted stores, ingestive behaviors are controlled by **satiety mechanisms** as well as by detectors that monitor the system variables. Satiety mechanisms are required because of the physiology of our digestive system. For example, suppose you exercise in a hot, dry environment and lose body water. The loss of water causes internal detectors to initiate the correctional mechanism—drinking. You quickly drink a glass or two of water and then stop. What stops your ingestive behavior? The water is still in your digestive system, not yet in the fluid surrounding your cells, where it is needed. Therefore, although drinking was initiated by detectors that measure your body's need for water, *it was stopped by other means.* There must be a satiety mechanism that says, in effect, "Stop—this water, when absorbed by the digestive system into the blood, will eventually replenish the body's need." Satiety mechanisms monitor the activity of the correctional mechanism (in this case, drinking), not the system variables themselves.

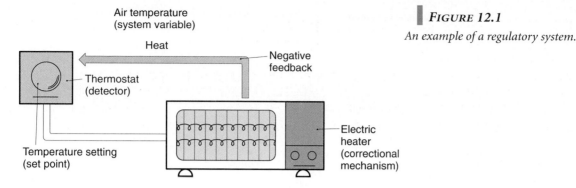

FIGURE 12.1

An example of a regulatory system.

When a sufficient amount of drinking occurs, the satiety mechanisms stop further drinking *in anticipation* of the replenishment that will occur later. (See *Figure 12.2.*)

SOME FACTS ABOUT FLUID BALANCE

BEFORE YOU CAN UNDERSTAND THE PHYSIOLOGICAL control of drinking, you must know something about the fluid compartments of the body and their relations with one another. And to understand these facts, you must also know something about the functions of the kidney.

The Fluid Compartments of the Body

The body contains four major fluid compartments: one compartment of intracellular fluid and three compartments of extracellular fluid. Approximately two-thirds of the body's water is contained in the **intracellular fluid**—the fluid portion of the cytoplasm of cells. The rest is **extracellular fluid,** which includes the **intravascular fluid** (the blood plasma), the cerebrospinal fluid, and the **interstitial fluid.** *Interstitial* means "standing between"; indeed, the interstitial fluid stands between our cells—it is the "seawater" that bathes them. For the purposes of this chapter I will ignore the cerebrospinal fluid and concentrate on the other three compartments. (See *Figure 12.3.*)

The fluid compartments are separated by semipermeable barriers, which permit the passage of some substances but not others. The walls of the capillaries separate the intravascular fluid (blood plasma) from the interstitial fluid, and the cell membranes separate the interstitial fluid from the intracellular fluid. The volume of the intracellular fluid is controlled by the concentration of solutes in the interstitial fluid. (*Solutes* are the solid substances dissolved in a solution.) Normally, the interstitial fluid is **isotonic** (from *isos,* "same," and *tonos,* "tension") with the intracellular fluid. That is, the concentration of solutes in the cells and in the interstitial fluid that bathes them is balanced, so that water does not tend to move into or out of the cells. If the interstitial fluid loses water (becomes more concentrated, or **hypertonic**), water will then diffuse out of the cells. On the other hand, if the interstitial fluid gains water (becomes more dilute, or **hypotonic**), water will diffuse into the cells. Either condition endangers cells; a loss of water deprives them of the ability to perform many chemical reactions, and a gain of water can cause their membrane to rupture. Thus, the concentration of the interstitial fluid must be regulated closely.

The volume of the blood plasma must be closely regulated because of the mechanics of the operation of the heart. If the blood volume becomes too high, blood pressure can reach dangerously high levels. If the blood volume becomes too low, the heart can no longer pump the blood effectively; and if the volume is not restored, heart failure will result. This condition is called **hypovolemia,** literally "low volume of the blood" (*-emia* comes from the Greek *haima,* "blood"). The vascular system of the body can make some adjustments for loss of blood volume by contracting the muscles present in the walls

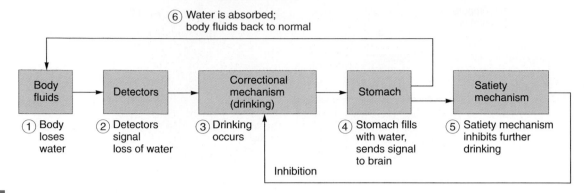

FIGURE 12.2

An outline of the system that controls drinking.

of the smaller veins and arteries, thereby presenting a smaller space for the blood to fill, but this correctional mechanism has definite limits.

The volume of the interstitial fluid need not be regulated closely. The most important reason is that when the volumes of the intracellular and intravascular fluid compartments are kept within normal limits, the volume of the interstitial fluid will automatically stay within its normal limits. Only in certain pathological conditions—such as capillary damage, heart failure, or a very low level of protein in the blood—will the volume of the interstitial fluid become abnormally high. (There is no way for it to become abnormally low without the other fluid compartments becoming abnormal.) However, although the *volume* of the interstitial fluid is normally not a matter of concern, its *tonicity* (solute concentration) must be closely regulated, because this variable is what determines whether water diffuses into cells or out of them.

As we will see, the intracellular fluid and the blood volume are monitored by two different sets of receptors. A single set of receptors would not work, because it is possible for one of these fluid compartments to be changed without affecting the other. For example, a loss of blood (obviously) reduces the volume of the intravascular fluid, but it has no effect on the volume of the intracellular fluid. On the other hand, a salty meal will increase the solute concentration of the interstitial fluid and draw water out of the cells. These cells will remain dehydrated even after the kidney has gotten rid of the excess sodium (and water to flush it away) and

restored the blood volume back to normal. Thus, the body needs a set of receptors measuring blood volume and another measuring cell volume.

Just as there are two sets of receptors, there are two sets of correctional mechanisms. One set involves the ingestion and excretion of water, and the other involves the ingestion and excretion of sodium. Obviously, the excretions of water and sodium are accomplished by the kidney, and the ingestion of these substances is accomplished by the behavior of eating salt (or foods containing salt) and drinking water.

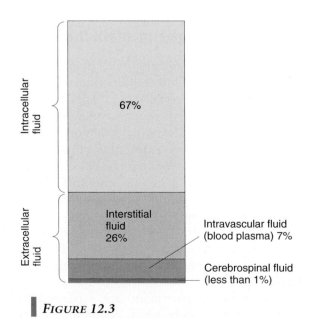

FIGURE 12.3

The relative size of the body's fluid compartments.

Most of the time, we drink more water than our body needs, and the excess is excreted by the kidneys. Similarly, we ingest more sodium than we need, and the kidneys get rid of this surplus, too. Thus, if we want to understand the means of regulating our water and sodium balance, we must understand what the kidneys do and how they are controlled.

The Kidneys

A human kidney consists of approximately a million functional units called **nephrons.** Each nephron extracts fluid from the blood and carries it, through collecting ducts, to the **ureter.** The ureter, in turn, connects the kidney to the urinary bladder, where urine is stored until it can be released at a convenient time. (This behavior, which physiologists politely refer to as *micturition,* from the Latin word for "urinate," has absolutely nothing to do with regulation. Once the urine is in the bladder, it is out of the body as far as the three fluid compartments are concerned.) (See *Figure 12.4.*)

The kidneys control the amount of water and sodium that the body excretes, which controls both the volume and the concentration (tonicity) of the extracellular fluid. If we drink a large amount of water and must get rid of the excess, our kidneys pass a large quantity of urine to the bladder. Similarly, if we eat salty food and must get rid of the excess sodium, our kidneys extract the sodium from our blood and pass it on to the bladder. However, if the organism has lost water through evaporation, the kidneys conserve water, producing the minimum quantity of urine. In addition, if the body becomes deficient in sodium, the kidneys will begin to excrete a very small amount of this mineral in the urine.

The amounts of sodium and water that the kidneys excrete are controlled by two hormones: aldosterone and vasopressin. Sodium excretion is controlled by **aldosterone,** a steroid hormone secreted by the adrenal cortex. High levels of aldosterone cause the kidneys to retain sodium in the body—to pass very little sodium on to the bladder. Thus, if the body contains too much sodium, the level of aldosterone secretion falls and sodium is excreted in the urine. If too little salt is present, a

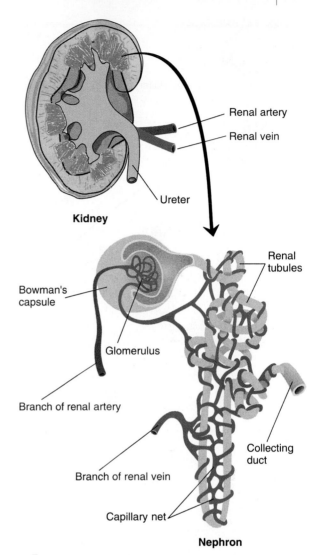

Renal artery

Renal vein

Ureter

Kidney

Renal tubules

Bowman's capsule

Glomerulus

Branch of renal artery

Branch of renal vein

Capillary net

Collecting duct

Nephron

FIGURE 12.4

Anatomy of the kidney and an individual nephron.
(Adapted from Orians, G.H. *The Study of Life.* Boston: Allyn and Bacon, 1973.)

high aldosterone level causes it to be conserved. (See *Figure 12.5.*)

The excretion of water by the kidneys is controlled by a hormone called **vasopressin.** The name of this hormone does not describe its primary function with respect to control of fluid homeostasis, which is to instruct the kidneys how much water to retain. High levels of vasopressin will cause the kidneys to retain as much water as possible, only excreting as much as is needed to rid the body of the waste

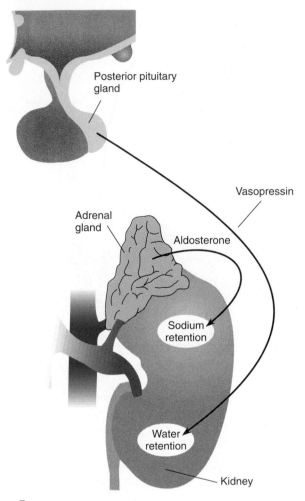

Posterior pituitary gland

Vasopressin

Adrenal gland

Aldosterone

Sodium retention

Water retention

Kidney

❙ *Figure 12.5*

Hormonal control of the kidney. Aldosterone, secreted by the cortex of the adrenal gland, causes sodium retention by the kidney. Vasopressin, secreted by the posterior pituitary gland, causes water retention.

products of metabolism. The term *vasopressin* refers to its ability under certain circumstances to cause blood vessels to contract (*vas* means "vessel" in Latin). A more descriptive term is *antidiuretic hormone*. (*Diuresis* comes from the Greek *dia*, "through," and *ouron*, "urine"; thus, *anti*diuretic hormone reduces the production of urine.) Nevertheless, vasopressin is the name that most physiologists use.

Vasopressin is a peptide hormone secreted by the posterior pituitary gland. It is produced in the cell

bodies of neurons located in two nuclei of the hypothalamus: the **supraoptic nucleus** and the **paraventricular nucleus.** The hormone is stored in vesicles and travels through axons to the posterior pituitary gland, where it collects in the terminal buttons. When the neurons in the supraoptic and paraventricular nuclei become active, their terminal buttons release vasopressin, which enters the blood supply. Thus, the production, storage, and release of vasopressin is exactly like that of any peptide transmitter substance, except that it affects receptors in another part of the body, not in a membrane across a synaptic cleft.

If we drink more water than our body needs, the posterior pituitary gland reduces its secretion of vasopressin, and the kidneys excrete the excess water. If we become dehydrated, the posterior pituitary gland increases vasopressin secretion, and the kidneys excrete a minimum amount of water. (See **Figure 12.5.**)

The importance of vasopressin in the retention of water is demonstrated by the disease produced by the lack of this hormone: **diabetes insipidus**. The term literally means "a tasteless passing through," because the urine of a person with diabetes insipidus is so dilute that it has little taste. People with untreated diabetes insipidus will excrete approximately 25 liters (over 6.5 gallons) of water each day, which means that they will have to stay close to a bathroom and a source of water. The treatment is, of course, vasopressin—administered in the form of a nasal spray, which is absorbed into the bloodstream.

So far, I have been talking only about system variables and correctional mechanisms. What about detectors? It turns out that the detectors that control the secretion of aldosterone and vasopressin (and thus control the excretion of sodium and water by the kidneys) also control the intake of water and salt. Thus, I will discuss them in the next section.

⦀ **Interim Summary**

A regulatory system contains four features: a system variable (the variable that is regulated), a set point (the optimal value of the system variable), a detector to measure the system variable, and a correctional mechanism to change it. Physiological regulatory systems, such as control of body fluids and nutrients, require a satiety mechanism to anticipate the effects of the correctional mechanism, because the changes brought about by eating and drinking occur only after a considerable period of time.

The body contains three major fluid compartments: the intracellular fluid, the interstitial fluid, and the intravascular fluid. Sodium and water can pass easily between the intravascular fluid and the interstitial fluid, but sodium cannot penetrate the cell membrane. The solute concentration of the interstitial fluid must be closely regulated. If it becomes hypertonic, cells lose water; if it becomes hypotonic, they gain water. The volume of the intravascular fluid (blood plasma) must also be kept within bounds.

The kidneys regulate the excretion of water and sodium; in the process of excreting water, waste products are carried away by the urine. Aldosterone, a steroid hormone released by the adrenal cortex, causes sodium retention. Vasopressin, a peptide hormone produced by the supraoptic and paraventricular nuclei and released by the posterior pituitary gland, causes water retention.

DRINKING AND SALT APPETITE

AS WE JUST SAW, FOR OUR BODIES TO FUNCTION properly, the volume of two fluid compartments—intracellular and intravascular—must be regulated. Most of the time we ingest more water and sodium than we need, and the kidneys excrete the excess. However, if the levels of water or sodium fall too low, correctional mechanisms—drinking of water or ingestion of sodium—are activated. Everyone is familiar with the sensation of thirst, which occurs when we need to ingest water. However, a salt appetite is much more rare, because it is difficult for people *not* to get enough sodium in their diet, even if they do not put extra salt on their food. Nevertheless, the mechanisms to increase sodium intake exist, even though they are seldom called upon in members of our species.

Because loss of water from either the intracellular or intravascular fluid compartments stimulates

drinking, researchers have adopted the terms *osmometric thirst* and *volumetric thirst* to describe them (Fitzsimons, 1972; Epstein, 1973). The term *volumetric* is clear—it refers to the metering (measuring) of the volume of the blood plasma. The term *osmometric* requires more explanation, which I will provide in the next section. The term *thirst* means different things in different circumstances. Its original definition referred to a sensation that people say they have when they are dehydrated. Here I use it in a descriptive sense. Because we do not know how experimental animals feel, *thirst* simply means a tendency to seek water and to ingest it.

Osmometric Thirst

Osmometric thirst occurs when the tonicity (solute concentration) of the interstitial fluid increases. This event draws water out of the cells, and they shrink in volume. The term *osmometric* refers to the fact that the detectors are actually responding to (metering) differences in the concentration of their own intracellular fluid and that of the interstitial fluid that surrounds them. *Osmosis* is the movement of water through a semipermeable membrane, from a region of low solute concentration to one of high solute concentration.

Verney (1947) first hypothesized that the brain contained neurons that respond to changes in the solute concentration of the interstitial fluid. He called these neurons **osmoreceptors.** He found that an infusion of hypertonic sodium chloride into a dog's carotid artery would stimulate the secretion of vasopressin and thus cause the kidneys to decrease their excretion of water. Figure 12.6 shows how the injection caused an almost immediate decrease in the production of urine. (See *Figure 12.6.*)

Verney hypothesized that osmoreceptors were neurons whose firing rate was affected by their level of hydration. That is, if the interstitial fluid surrounding them became more concentrated, they would lose water through osmosis. The shrinkage would cause them to alter their firing rate, which would send signals to the neurons that control the rate of vasopressin secretion. (See *Figure 12.7.*) As we will see, more recent studies have confirmed that osmoreceptors do exist and that they can initiate drinking as well as vasopressin secretion.

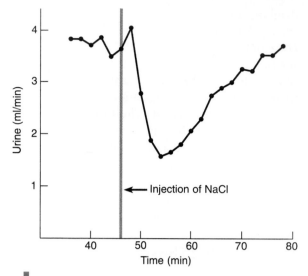

← Injection of NaCl

FIGURE 12.6

Effects of an injection of hypertonic saline solution into a dog's carotid artery. The solution removed water from cells in the brain and caused the posterior pituitary gland to secrete vasopressin. The hormone caused water to be retained by the kidneys, reducing the flow of urine.
(From Verney, E.G. *Proceedings of the Royal Society of London, B.*, 1947, *135*, 25–106.)

Before I discuss the evidence concerning the existence and location of osmoreceptors, I want to say more about the conditions that cause osmometric thirst. Our bodies lose water continuously, primarily through evaporation. Each breath exposes the moist inner surfaces of the respiratory system to the air; thus, each breath causes the loss of a small amount of water. In addition, our skin is not completely waterproof; some water finds its way through the layers of the skin and evaporates from the surface. The moisture lost through evaporation is, of course, pure distilled water. (Sweating loses water, too; but because it loses salt along with the water, it produces a sodium need as well.) When we lose water through evaporation, we lose it from all fluid compartments, intracellular, interstitial, and intravascular. Thus, normal dehydration produces both *osmometric* and *volumetric* thirst.

Figure 12.8 illustrates how the loss of water through evaporation depletes both the intracellular and intravascular fluid compartments. For the sake of simplicity, only a few cells are shown, and the volume of the interstitial fluid is greatly exaggerated. Water is lost directly from the interstitial fluid, which becomes slightly more concentrated than either the intracellular or the intravascular fluid. Thus, water is drawn from both the cells and the blood plasma. When enough water is lost from the cells, the secretion of vasopressin will be stimulated, and urine production will diminish. And eventually, the loss of water from the cells and the blood plasma will be great enough that both osmometric and volumetric thirst will be produced. (See *Figure 12.8.*)

If evaporation were the only way that the distribution of water in the three fluid compartments could be disturbed, then we would not need two kinds of detectors to stimulate thirst; a set of osmoreceptors would be sufficient. However, it is possible to incur a loss of intracellular fluid without losing intravascular fluid. (And as we shall see in the next section, the opposite condition is possible, too.)

The most common way to incur a loss of just intracellular fluid is to eat a salty meal. The salt is absorbed from the digestive system into the blood plasma; hence the blood plasma becomes hypertonic. This condition draws water from the interstitial fluid, which makes this compartment become hypertonic, too, and thus causes water to diffuse out of the cells. As the blood plasma increases in volume, the kidneys begin excreting large amounts of both sodium and water. Eventually, the excess sodium is excreted, along with the water that was taken from the interstitial and intracellular fluid.

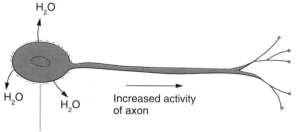

H_2O

H_2O H_2O Increased activity of axon

Increased solute concentration causes osmoreceptor to lose water and shrink in size

FIGURE 12.7

A hypothetical explanation of the workings of an osmoreceptor.

Skin

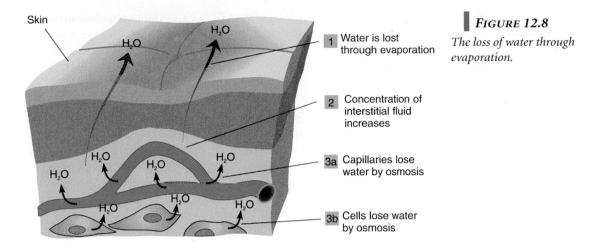

1 Water is lost through evaporation

2 Concentration of interstitial fluid increases

3a Capillaries lose water by osmosis

3b Cells lose water by osmosis

FIGURE 12.8

The loss of water through evaporation.

The net result is a loss of water from the cells. *At no time did the volume of the blood plasma fall;* in fact, it was temporarily higher than normal, which is what triggered the excretion of sodium and water by the kidneys.

As we saw earlier, Verney hypothesized that the loss of water by the cells of the body is the stimulus that produces osmometric thirst. Fitzsimons (1972) obtained evidence that supports Verney's hypothesis by demonstrating that the stimulus for osmometric thirst is not simply a change in the solute concentration of the interstitial fluid but the *effect* that these changes have on the water content of the cells. Fitzsimons removed the kidneys of a group of rats to prevent the kidneys from eliminating water or any of the substances he administered to the animals. Next, he injected the animals with hypertonic solutions of substances that can enter cells (such as glucose and urea) or substances that cannot (such as sodium chloride, sodium sulfate, and sucrose—table sugar). All of the substances that he injected would increase the solute concentration of the interstitial fluid. However, only the substances that *cannot* enter cells would draw water from them. For example, an increased concentration of urea in the interstitial fluid has no effect on cells because the urea freely diffuses into them, and a concentration gradient is not set up.

In fact, the only animals that drank excessively were those that received substances that could not enter the cells and hence drew water from them; thus, cell dehydration is the stimulus for osmomet-ric thirst. In addition, Fitzsimons found that an injection of urea produced a small amount of drinking. The reason for this effect is that urea passes slowly through the blood-brain barrier. Therefore, an injection of urea produces a slight, and temporary, increase in the solute concentration of the blood plasma relative to that of the brain, which causes water to diffuse from the brain into the intravascular fluid. Thus, urea produces a temporary dehydration of the brain. The fact that *brain* dehydration produces drinking suggests that the osmoreceptors that produce thirst are located there. (I will return to this finding later.)

Fitzsimons was not the first to obtain evidence that osmoreceptors that produce thirst were located in the brain. Andersson (1953) found that injections of hypertonic saline solution into the rostrolateral hypothalamus produced drinking but not vasopressin release, whereas injections into caudal hypothalamic regions stimulated vasopressin secretion but not thirst. Thus, different sets of receptors appear to mediate drinking and vasopressin release in response to hypertonicity.

The location of the osmoreceptors that control drinking is not yet settled. An extensive mapping study by Peck and Blass (1975) suggested that the osmoreceptors that stimulate thirst in rats are located in the medial portion of the lateral preoptic area. They found that injections of hypertonic sucrose in this region produced drinking. In addition, Blass and Epstein (1971) found that when a rat was made thirsty by giving it a subcutaneous injection of hypertonic saline, drinking could be inhibited by injecting water into the preoptic area. Presumably, the water turned off the signal for thirst at the detectors. (This manipulation was similar to what would happen if we heated the thermostat in a cold room; we would "fool" the thermostat and cause it to turn off the furnace.)

A more recent study failed to confirm these findings. Andrews et al. (1992) used special minipumps to continuously infuse small quantities of hypertonic and hypotonic solutions bilaterally into the preoptic area. They found that the infusions had variable effects on the rats' drinking: Sometimes infusions of hypertonic saline would *reduce* the animals' drinking and infusions of water would *increase* it. Also, several studies (for example, Coburn and Stricker, 1978) have found that rats still show osmometric thirst after the lateral preoptic area has been destroyed.

So where are the osmoreceptors? Most researchers now believe that they are located more medially, in the region that borders the anteroventral tip of the third ventricle (the *AV3V*). Buggy et al. (1979) found that injections of hypertonic saline directly into the AV3V produced drinking, whereas injections into the lateral preoptic area did not. In some species (such as the dog) the osmoreceptors may be located in a specialized *circumventricular organ* located just rostral to the AV3V. The brain contains several circumventricular organs—specialized regions with rich blood supplies located along the ventricular system. You are already familiar with two of these: the area postrema and the pineal gland (discussed in Chapters 2 and 9). You will learn about two more in this chapter: the OVLT and the SFO. (Refer to *Figure 12.10.*)

The **OVLT** (if you really want to know, that stands for the *organum vasculosum of the lamina terminalis*), like the other circumventricular organs, is located on the *blood* side of the blood-brain barrier. That means that substances dissolved in the blood pass easily into the interstitial fluid within this organ. (The importance of this fact will become apparent soon.) Thrasher and Keil (1987) found that after the OVLT was destroyed, dogs no longer drank when given injections of hypertonic saline—nor did they show increases in vasopressin secretion. However, studies by Johnson and his colleagues (see Johnson and Edwards, 1990) found that in rats,

lesions of the OVLT alone did not abolish osmometric drinking; the lesions had to include additional brain tissue around the AV3V. Thus, although some of the osmoreceptors in the rat brain may be located in the OVLT, others are located in the medial preoptic area.

As we saw earlier, when rats are given an injection of urea, they show a small amount of osmometric thirst, presumably because the urea temporarily dehydrates the brain. But urea does not dehydrate any of the tissue *outside* the blood-brain barrier, which includes the OVLT. Thus, Johnson and Edwards must be right—some of the osmoreceptors must be located *inside* the blood-brain barrier.

Volumetric Thirst

Volumetric thirst occurs when the volume of the blood plasma—the intravascular volume—decreases. When we lose water through evaporation, we lose it from all three fluid compartments, intracellular, interstitial, and intravascular. Thus, evaporation produces both volumetric thirst and osmometric thirst. If evaporation were the only way that our body lost fluids, we would not need to have drinking mechanisms controlled by detectors that monitor blood volume. However, it is possible to incur a loss in intravascular volume without affecting the interstitial compartment.

Loss of blood is the most obvious cause of pure volumetric thirst. From the earliest recorded history, reports of battles note that the wounded survivors called out for water. (More prosaically, vomiting or diarrhea rids the body of isotonic fluid and hence lowers the volume of the intravascular fluid.) Thus, volumetric thirst provides a second line of defense against a loss of water should the osmometric system be damaged, and it provides the means for the loss of isotonic fluid to instigate drinking. In addition, because hypovolemia involves a loss of sodium as well as water (that is, the sodium that was contained in the isotonic fluid that was lost), hypovolemia leads to a salt appetite.

The easiest way to produce hypovolemia in experimental animals such as rats would be to remove some of their blood. A less drastic procedure is to inject a **colloid** into the animal's abdominal cavity or under the loose skin of the back (Fitzsimons, 1961). Colloids are gluelike substances (from the Greek *kolla,* "glue") made of large molecules that cannot cross cell membranes. Thus, they stay in the abdominal cavity or in the space under the skin. Because the solution of molecules is hypertonic, it draws extracellular fluid out of tissue. The fluid that leaves the blood plasma is isotonic; as water molecules move down the concentration gradient produced by the colloid, they draw sodium chloride with them. Initially, the water comes from the interstitial fluid; but as the volume of this fluid space decreases, the pressure of the blood causes fluid from the blood plasma to begin to fill the vacant space. Fluid does *not* leave the cells, because the solute concentration of the interstitial fluid remains stable. Within an hour the posterior pituitary gland begins to release vasopressin, and urine volume drops. At about the same time the animal begins to drink, and it continues to do so until most of the volume of fluid stolen from the extracellular fluid has been replaced.

Let us look at a specific experiment that produced volumetric thirst. Fitzsimons (1961) injected a colloid called *polyethylene glycol* into the abdominal cavity of rats and later drained the fluid that accumulated, ridding the body of the colloid along with the water and sodium chloride it had drawn from the extracellular fluid. The loss of fluid caused a considerable thirst; the animals drank water copiously. The next day, he presented the rats with both water and a hypertonic 1.8 percent saline solution, which rats normally refuse to drink. This time, the rats avidly consumed the saline solution. Why did they do so? Because the procedure had removed both water and salt, they needed both substances to restore their fluid compartments to normal. Thus, the loss of salt induced a strong **salt appetite.**

What detectors are responsible for initiating volumetric thirst and a salt appetite? In fact, there are at least two sets of receptors: one in the kidneys, and one in the heart and large blood vessels.

The Renin-Angiotensin System

The kidneys contain cells that are able to detect decreases in flow of blood to the kidneys. The primary cause of a reduced flow of blood is a loss of blood volume; thus, these cells detect the presence of

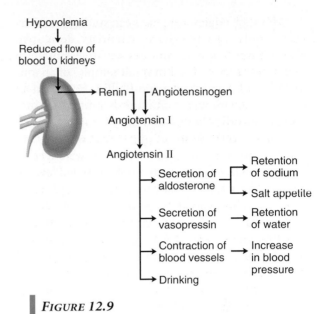

FIGURE 12.9

Detection of hypovolemia by the kidney and the renin-angiotensin system.

hypovolemia. When the flow of blood to the kidneys decreases, these cells secrete an enzyme called **renin.** Renin enters the blood, where it catalyzes the conversion of a protein called **angiotensinogen** into a hormone called **angiotensin.** (In fact, there are two forms of angiotensin. Angiotensinogen becomes angiotensin I, which is quickly converted by an enzyme to angiotensin II. The active form is angiotensin II, which I shall abbreviate as *AII*.)

Angiotensin II has several physiological effects: It stimulates the adrenal cortex to secrete aldosterone, it stimulates the posterior pituitary gland to secrete vasopressin, and it increases blood pressure by causing the muscles in the small arteries to contract. (Recall that the presence of aldosterone inhibits the kidneys from excreting sodium, and the presence of vasopressin inhibits them from excreting water.) In addition, AII has two behavioral effects: It initiates drinking, and (through its stimulation of aldosterone) it produces a salt appetite. Therefore, a reduction in the flow of blood to the kidneys causes water and sodium to be retained by the body, helps compensate for their loss by reducing the size of the blood vessels, and encourages the animal to find and ingest both water and salt. (See *Figure 12.9.*)

Although angiotensin has been studied for many years, only recently have scientists developed radioimmunoassay techniques sensitive enough to measure the level of AII in small samples of an animal's blood. Van Eekelen and Phillips (1988), in an experiment with rats, continuously infused AII into a vein, periodically sampled blood from an artery, and analyzed the amount of AII that was present. They found that the animals, which were free to move around, did not drink until the blood level of AII reached a level of approximately 450 pg/ml. (A *picogram,* abbreviated *pg,* is a trillionth of a gram, or 10^{-12}. The prefix *pico-* comes from the Italian word *piccolo,* "small.") A blood level of AII of 450 pg/ml occurs normally when a rat has been deprived of water for approximately 48 hours. Thus, it is possible that the ability of the renin-angiotensin system to produce drinking is important only in emergencies.

Baroreceptors

The second set of receptors for volumetric thirst lies within the heart. Physiologists had long known that the atria of the heart (the parts that receive blood from the veins) contain sensory neurons that detect stretch. The atria are filled passively with blood being returned from the body by the veins. The more blood that is present, the fuller the atria become just before each contraction of the heart. Thus, when the volume of the blood plasma falls, the stretch receptors within the atria will detect the change. These receptors occupy the best possible location to detect the presence of hypovolemia.

Fitzsimons and Moore-Gillon (1980) showed that information from the atrial baroreceptors can stimulate thirst. They operated on dogs, placing a small balloon in the inferior vena cava, the vein that brings blood from most of the body (excluding the head and arms) to the heart. When the balloon was inflated, it reduced the flow of blood to the heart and thus lowered the amount of blood that entered the right atrium. Within 30 minutes the dogs began to drink. The effect occurred even when the investigators administered **saralasin,** a drug that blocks angiotensin receptors; thus, it was not produced by secretion of renin by the kidneys. In another experiment Moore-Gillon and Fitzsimons (1982)

implanted a small balloon in the junction between one of the large veins from the lungs and the left atrium of the heart. (They removed the part of the lung served by the vein so that inflating the balloon had no effect on the flow of blood into the heart.) Inflation of the balloon directly stimulated stretch receptors in the left atrium—and reduced the amount of water that the animals drank. Finally, Quillen, Keil, and Reid (1990) found that when the nerves connecting the atrial baroreceptors with the brain were cut, the animals drank much less water when the blood flow to their heart was temporarily reduced.

Food-Related Drinking

Although research on the physiology of drinking has generally focused on drinking caused by need (that is, by hypovolemia or by cellular dehydration), most drinking occurs *in anticipation* of actual need, during meals (de Castro, 1988; Kraly, 1990). For two reasons, eating produces a need for water. First, eating causes water to be diverted from the rest of the body into the stomach and small intestine, where it is needed for the digestive process (Lepkovsky et al., 1957). Second, once food is absorbed (especially salty food or food rich in amino acids), it increases the solute concentration of the blood plasma and thus induces an osmometric thirst. But animals do not wait until they need the water; they drink it with their meal. Fitzsimons and Le Magnen (1969) found that when rats were switched from a high-carbohydrate diet to a high-protein diet, they increased their water intake. At first, they drank most of the water *after* the meal, when the osmotic demands were being felt. However, within a few days the animals began drinking more water with the meals. They apparently learned the association of the new diet with subsequent thirst and drank in anticipation of that thirst.

According to research by Kraly and his colleagues, food-related drinking appears to involve angiotensin. The movement of water into the digestive system during and after a meal causes hypovolemia (Nose, Morita, Yawata, and Norimoto, 1986). As we just saw, hypovolemia stimulates the kidneys to secrete renin, which results in increased blood levels of angiotensin II. Kraly and Corneilson (1990) found that when they prevented the synthesis of angiotensin II with captopril (a drug that blocks the enzyme responsible for converting angiotensin I to angiotensin II), rats drank less water with their meals.

Food-related drinking also involves histamine, a compound that serves as a transmitter substance in the brain and as a hormonelike messenger in the rest of the body. When an animal eats, cells in the stomach release histamine. If, prior to eating a meal, a rat is given drugs that block histamine receptors, the animal will drink much less water with that meal (Kraly and Specht, 1984). In addition, an injection of histamine will itself cause drinking (Kraly, 1983). Kraly and Corneilson (1990) suggest that thirst provoked by histamine may involve angiotensin. They note that the secretion of renin is controlled by histamine receptors on cells in the kidney (Radke et al., 1986), and they found that blocking the synthesis of angiotensin II with captopril abolished the stimulating effect of histamine on drinking. Perhaps, then, the entry of food into the stomach causes the release of histamine, which stimulates the secretion of renin by the kidneys. The renin catalyzes the synthesis of angiotensin, which activates drinking mechanisms in the brain.

Salt Appetite

You will recall from Chapter 7 that the tongue contains four types of taste receptors, which provide the sensations of sweetness, bitterness, sourness, and saltiness. As we have seen, the reason our tongue has receptors that specifically detect the presence of sodium chloride is that this mineral plays a vital role in maintaining our fluid balance. A fall in the body's level of sodium makes it impossible to maintain the intravascular fluid at its proper level.

The primary stimulus for a salt appetite is the presence of aldosterone, whose secretion is under the control of angiotensin. When an animal becomes hypovolemic, the blood flow to the kidneys decreases, renin is secreted, angiotensin is produced, and the adrenal glands begin secreting aldosterone. The aldosterone acts directly on the brain, as we will see in the next section.

INTERIM SUMMARY

Osmometric thirst occurs when the interstitial fluid becomes hypertonic, drawing water out of cells. This event, which can be caused by evaporation of water from the body or by ingestion of a salty meal, is detected by osmoreceptors in the region of the anteroventral third ventricle (the AV3V). The receptors are located both in OVLT, a circumventricular organ, and in adjacent regions of the brain. Activation of the osmoreceptors increases vasopressin secretion and stimulates drinking.

Volumetric thirst occurs along with osmometric thirst when the body loses fluid through evaporation. Pure volumetric thirst is caused by the loss of blood, vomiting, and diarrhea, or through experimental manipulations such as the injection of a colloid. One stimulus for volumetric thirst is provided by a fall in blood flow to the kidneys, which triggers the secretion of renin. Renin converts plasma angiotensinogen to angiotensin I, which becomes AII. AII then stimulates the secretion of aldosterone (which conserves salt, needed to keep up the plasma volume), increases blood pressure, and causes drinking. Aldosterone also produces a sodium appetite. Volumetric drinking can also be stimulated by a set of baroreceptors in the atria of the heart that sends messages to the brain.

Much drinking occurs with meals, in anticipation of the need for water produced by the digestive process and the addition of solutes to the body's fluid compartments. The hypovolemia that accompanies a meal induces drinking through the release of AII, which may be triggered by the release of histamine by cells in the stomach.

BRAIN MECHANISMS OF THIRST AND SALT APPETITE

AS WE SAW, THE OSMORECEPTORS RESPONSIBLE for thirst appear to be located in the preoptic area and the anterior hypothalamus. The regions that play an important role in volumetric drinking and salt appetite also appear to be located in the fore-brain. However, the picture of the neural circuitry that has been obtained so far is still fuzzy; at best, we can say that some structures have been implicated in the physiological and behavioral control of fluid balance, but the exact roles these structures play is still uncertain.

Neural Control of Thirst

The Circumventricular System

As we saw earlier in this chapter, the brain region around the anteroventral third ventricle (including the OVLT) contains the osmoreceptors that stimulate thirst and vasopressin secretion. The entire region around the anterior third ventricle—dorsal as well as ventral—seems to be the part of the brain where osmometric and volumetric signals are integrated and drinking, salt appetite, and vasopressin secretion are controlled.

As you have already learned, the osmoreceptors that initiate drinking and vasopressin secretion are located in the OVLT and (in some species, at least) in the brain tissue around the AV3V. This region also appears to receive information from the baroreceptors located in the atria of the heart. Sensory information received from the internal organs (and from the taste buds, as well) is received by a nucleus in the medulla: the **nucleus of the solitary tract.** The nucleus of the solitary tract sends efferent axons to many parts of the brain, including the region around the AV3V (see Johnson and Edwards, 1990).

Thornton, de Beaurepaire, and Nicolaïdis (1984) recorded the activity of single neurons in the region just in front of the AV3V, in rats. They found that the neurons were sensitive to changes in blood pressure that occurred spontaneously or were induced by temporary removal of small amounts of blood from a vein. Possibly, these neurons receive information via the nucleus of the solitary tract from stretch receptors located in the atria of the heart, and they may be part of a neural circuit responsible for volumetric thirst.

The region of the AV3V seems to play a critical role in fluid regulation in humans, as well. For example, McIver et al. (1991) report that brain damage that includes this region can cause both diabetes

insipidus and *adipsia*—lack of drinking. The patients report no sensation of thirst, even after they are given an injection of hypertonic saline. To survive, they must deliberately drink water at regular intervals each day, even though they feel no need to do so.

Another thirst signal, angiotensin, is a peptide composed of eight amino acids. As far as we know, all peptides that directly affect behavior do so by interacting with specific receptors in neural membranes. Therefore, researchers hypothesized that the brain contains neurons that initiate thirst when they detect the presence of angiotensin. Because angiotensin does not cross the blood-brain barrier, a likely site of action would be one of the circumventricular organs. Angiotensin could leave the capillaries in one of these organs, enter the interstitial fluid, and stimulate angiotensin receptors.

Although all of the circumventricular organs contain AII receptors, one of them, the **subfornical organ (SFO)**, appears to be the site at which blood angiotensin acts to produce thirst. This structure gets its name from its location, just below the commissure of the ventral fornix. (See *Figure 12.10.*)

Evidence clearly indicates that the subfornical organ is the site of action of angiotensin. Simpson, Epstein, and Camardo (1978) found that very low doses of angiotensin injected directly into the SFO caused drinking and that destruction of the SFO or injection of saralasin, which blocks AII receptors, abolished the drinking response to injections of angiotensin into the blood. Phillips and Felix (1976) found that microiontophoretic injections of angiotensin into the SFO increased the firing rate of single neurons located there. Kadekaro et al. (1989) found that an intravenous injection of AII caused the metabolic activity of the SFO to increase, even when the axons connecting the SFO with the rest of the brain had been cut. (They used the technique of 2-DG autoradiography, described in Chapter 5, to assess metabolic activity.) Thus, AII directly activates the neurons of the SFO.

The subfornical organ, whose primary role is to detect the presence of a hormone in the blood, has few neural inputs but sends axons to several parts of the brain. As Miselis, Weiss, and Shapiro (1987) note, the outputs of the SFO fall into three categories: endocrine, autonomic, and behavioral. As we

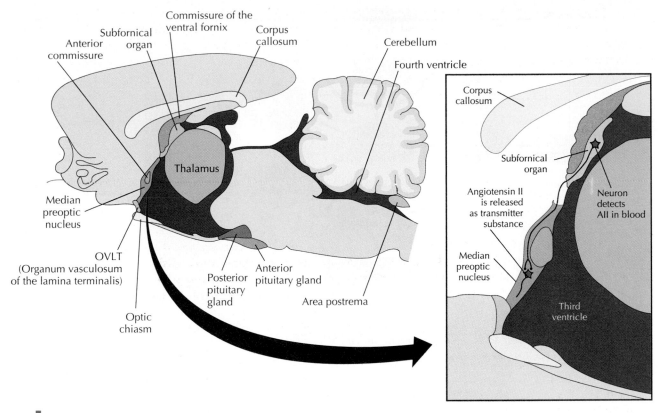

FIGURE 12.10

A sagittal section of the rat brain, showing the location of the circumventricular organs. Inset: A hypothetical circuit connecting the subfornical organ with the median preoptic nucleus.

saw earlier, angiotensin has four major effects: It stimulates aldosterone secretion, it stimulates vasopressin secretion, it increases blood pressure, and it causes drinking.

The first of these effects, aldosterone secretion, occurs directly in the adrenal cortex. The other three involve the brain. The *endocrine outputs* of the SFO include axons that project to the neurons in the supraoptic and paraventricular nuclei that are responsible for production and secretion of the posterior pituitary hormones, vasopressin and oxytocin. (The reason for the connection with the vasopressin neurons is obvious, but the function of the connection with the oxytocin neurons is still not understood.) The *autonomic outputs* include axons that project to the cells of the paraventricular nucleus and other parts of the hypothalamus, which in turn send axons to brain stem nuclei that control

the sympathetic and parasympathetic nervous system. This system is responsible for the effects of angiotensin on blood pressure. The most important *behavioral outputs,* which control drinking, are probably those to a region of the basal forebrain just in front of the ventral portion of the anterior third ventricle.

Let us consider the behavioral outputs of the SFO—the efferent connections that are responsible for its effects on drinking. Lind, Thunhorst, and Johnson (1984) found that lesions of the ventral stalk of the SFO, which destroys its efferent connections, abolished the drinking response that is produced by injecting AII into a vein. Thus, the thirst produced by the renin-angiotensin system is mediated by efferent axons of the SFO that pass through the ventral stalk. However, these lesions had only a small effect on the drinking response that is pro-

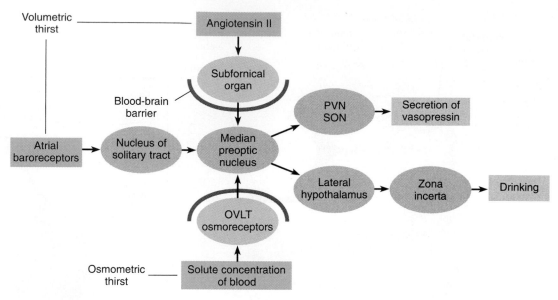

FIGURE 12.11

Neural circuitry concerned with the control of drinking. Not all connections are shown, and some connections may be indirect. PVN = paraventricular nucleus; SON = supraoptic nucleus.
(Adapted from Thrasher, T.N. *Acta Physiologica Scandanivica*, 1989, *136*, 141–150.)

duced by injecting AII into the third ventricle. These results indicate that angiotensin receptors located elsewhere in the brain are capable of stimulating drinking.

Many of these receptors are located in the **median preoptic nucleus** (not to be confused with the *medial* preoptic nucleus), which is shaped like half a doughnut, wrapped around the front of the anterior commissure, a fiber bundle that connects the amygdala and anterior temporal lobe. (See inset, *Figure 12.10.*) The median preoptic nucleus is on the *brain* side of the blood-brain barrier; thus, its AII receptors are never exposed to angiotensin present in the blood. Only when angiotensin is injected directly into the third ventricle can it reach them.

If angiotensin cannot get from the blood to the median preoptic nucleus, what is the point of having AII receptors there? Lind and Johnson (1982) proposed the following answer: When neurons in the SFO are stimulated by the presence of angiotensin in the blood, a message is sent down their axons to the neurons in the median preoptic nucleus. The terminal buttons of these axons release angiotensin *as a transmitter substance.* Thus, the AII receptors in the

median preoptic nucleus are not there to detect the presence of a hormone; instead, they are postsynaptic receptors for a peptide transmitter substance that just happens to be a hormone, too.

There is considerable evidence to support Lind and Johnson's hypothesis. For example, after the median preoptic nucleus has been destroyed, injections of AII into the blood or the third ventricle have no effect on drinking (Johnson and Cunningham, 1987). In addition, Nelson and Johnson (1985) prepared a vertical slice of the rat brain, parallel to the midline, and placed the slice in a liquid medium that kept the cells alive for a while. They electrically stimulated neurons in the SFO and found that single neurons in the median preoptic nucleus responded to this stimulation. The responses of the neurons in the median preoptic nucleus were abolished by the application of saralasin, the drug that blocks AII receptors. (See inset, *Figure 12.10.*)

Based on these findings, and on other research that I will describe shortly, Thrasher and his colleagues (see Thrasher, 1989) suggest that the region in front of the third ventricle acts as an integrating system for most or all of the stimuli for osmometric and volumetric thirst. As we have already seen, the OVLT contains osmoreceptors and the SFO contains receptors that detect angiotensin present in the blood. Both circumventricular organs communicate with the median preoptic nucleus. In addition, the median preoptic nucleus receives information from the atrial baroreceptors via the nucleus of the solitary tract, located in the medulla. This nucleus integrates the information and, through its efferent connections with other parts of the brain, controls both drinking and the secretion of vasopressin. (The roles of the lateral hypothalamus and the zona incerta are described later.) (See *Figure 12.11.*)

As we have already seen, lesions of the SFO disrupt angiotensin-induced drinking and lesions of the OVLT (and the surrounding region of the AV3V) disrupt osmometric drinking. Neurotoxic lesions of the median preoptic nucleus (which spare axons passing through the region) almost totally abolish drinking in response to injections of angiotensin or hypertonic saline (Cunningham et al., 1992). (See *Figure 12.12.*) However, the lesions did not completely abolish drinking; thus, we cannot conclude that *all* signals for drinking are routed through the median preoptic nucleus. In fact, it is unlikely that the evolutionary process would have entrusted such an important function to a single brain structure. Undoubtedly, there is some redundancy in the control of water intake.

Although the region anterior to the third ventricle has been shown to be important for osmometric and volumetric thirst, we do not yet know the brain mechanisms responsible for meal-associated drinking. Similarly, we do not know whether the satiety signals for drinking (discussed in the final section of this chapter) are routed through this region.

The Lateral Hypothalamus and Zona Incerta

The control of osmometric and volumetric drinking, initiated by the median preoptic area, involves other brain structures. Many years ago, investigators discovered that lesions of the lateral hypothalamus abolished drinking behavior. (As we will see in Chapter 13, the lesions also abolished eating and other behaviors.) Eventually, through careful nursing, the animals began drinking again, but only during meals (Teitelbaum and Epstein, 1964). In other

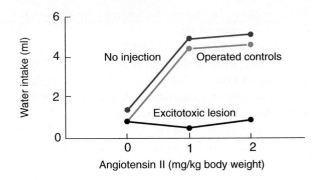

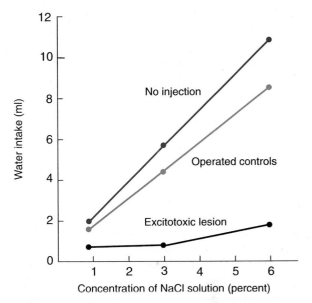

FIGURE 12.12

The effects of lesions of the median preoptic nucleus on drinking produced by injections of angiotensin II and a hypertonic saline solution.

(Adapted from Cunningham, T.J., Beltz, T., Johnson, R.F., and Johnson, A.K. *Brain Research,* 1992, *580,* 325–330.)

words, lesions of the hypothalamus disrupt osmometric and volumetric thirst, but do not disrupt meal-associated drinking.

Another structure involved in osmometric drinking is the **zona incerta.** This region is an oblong extension of the midbrain reticular formation; its posterior end is in the midbrain, between the substantia nigra and the ventral tegmental area, and its anterior end is in the diencephalon, just lateral and dorsal to the paraventricular nuclei of the hypothalamus. It receives input from several forebrain regions, including the lateral hypothalamus. (Refer to *Figure 10.19.*)

Huang and Mogenson (1972) found that electrical stimulation of the rostral zona incerta elicited drinking in rats, indicating that this region is connected to motor mechanisms responsible for drinking behavior. Walsh and Grossman (1978) found that lesions of the zona incerta caused a profound deficit in osmometric drinking; injections of hypertonic sodium chloride did not induce drinking. In addition, rats with these lesions did not drink when they were given an injection of angiotensin, either, but they *did* drink if they were given an injection of polyethylene glycol. Thus, damage to the zona incerta also disrupts the hormonal stimulus for volumetric thirst but not the neural one that originates in the atrial baroreceptors.

Mok and Mogenson (1986) recorded from single neurons in the zona incerta. They found that injections of hypertonic saline, hypertonic sucrose, or distilled water into the basal forebrain anterior to the third ventricle changed the firing rate of these neurons. In addition, Czech and Stein (1992) found that injections of angiotensin into a cerebral ventricle increased the metabolic activity of several regions, including the lateral hypothalamus and the zona incerta. Then, when the animal began drinking, the metabolic activity of these regions returned to normal levels.

The zona incerta sends axons to many brain structures involved in movement, including the basal ganglia, the brain stem reticular formation, the red nucleus, the periaqueductal gray matter, and the ventral horn of the spinal cord (Ricardo, 1981). Thus, the zona incerta appears to be in an excellent position to influence drinking behavior.

Neural Control of Salt Appetite

We already saw that a sodium deficiency stimulates a salt appetite through the action of aldosterone. That is, the sodium deficiency causes hypovolemia, which stimulates the secretion of renin, and the increased blood level of angiotensin that results stimulates the adrenal glands to secrete aldosterone.

Aldosterone appears to exert its behavioral effects by stimulating receptors in the medial nucleus of the amygdala. First, the medial nucleus

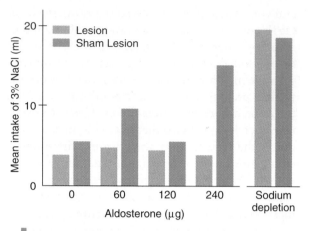

FIGURE 12.13

Effects of lesions of the medial amygdala on salt intake of rats produced by aldosterone or sodium depletion.
(Adapted from Schulkin, J., Marini, J., and Epstein, A.N. *Behavioral Neuroscience*, 1989, *103*, 178–185.)

contains aldosterone receptors (Coirini et al., 1985). In addition, Schulkin, Marini, and Epstein (1989) found that lesions of the medial region of the amygdala specifically abolished the effects of aldosterone on salt intake. However, when the investigators induced a sodium deficiency (by feeding the animals a sodium-free diet and giving them an injection of furosemide, a drug that causes the kidneys to excrete sodium), the rats ingested a normal amount of a sodium chloride solution. Thus, aldosterone cannot be the sole stimulus for salt appetite. (See *Figure 12.13.*)

Besides aldosterone, there are two possible signals for salt appetite: angiotensin and the atrial baroreceptors. Let us first consider angiotensin. This hormone stimulates the production of aldosterone in the first place. Perhaps it also stimulates salt appetite, just as it stimulates drinking through its effects on the SFO. However, the evidence we have at present indicates that an increased level of AII in the blood does not stimulate salt appetite. Sakai, Chow, and Epstein (1990) found that injections of AII that were sufficient to cause drinking had no effect on salt appetite. In addition, injections of sarile, a drug that blocks angiotensin receptors, had no effect on sodium appetite produced by a sodium deficiency—even though the drug did block thirst produced by an injection of AII. Several studies (for example, Fitts and Masson, 1990) have shown that injections of AII directly into the brain can produce sodium appetite, but this effect simply means that the angiotensin is acting locally—as a transmitter substance—just as it does for thirst.

So far, there is no direct evidence that the other signal of hypovolemia—the atrial baroreceptors—can produce a sodium appetite. As we saw in Figure 12.13, lesions of the medial amygdala block sodium appetite produced by aldosterone but not that produced by a sodium deficiency. If, as Sakai and his colleagues have shown, angiotensin is not responsible for this appetite, then the source of the appetite must be the atrial baroreceptors. But many scientists have found that predictions that "must be true" turn out to be false. We need further evidence.

As we saw in the previous subsection, the zona incerta plays a critical role in osmometric drinking and drinking stimulated by angiotensin. It also appears to play a role in the development of salt appetite. Grossman and Grossman (1978) found that when a hypertonic sodium chloride solution is presented to sodium-depleted rats with lesions of the zona incerta, the animals will consume much less salt than a normal animal will. Conversely, electrical stimulation of parts of the zona incerta will induce salt intake (Gentil, Mogenson, and Stevenson, 1971). Thus, the stimulation of aldosterone receptors in the medial amygdala must be communicated to the neurons in the zona incerta.

‖‖‖ *INTERIM SUMMARY*

Volumetric thirst stimulated by AII involves another circumventricular organ: the subfornical organ. Volumetric thirst stimulated by the atrial stretch receptor system reaches the AV3V region via a relay in the nucleus of the solitary tract. Neurons in the SFO, the AV3V region, and the OVLT (which, you will remember, contains osmoreceptors) all send axons to the median preoptic nucleus.

Neurons in the median preoptic nucleus stimulate the secretion of vasopressin through their connections with the supraoptic and paraventricular nuclei. They stimulate drinking through their connections with the lateral hypothalamus and the zona

incerta. The zona incerta sends axons to many parts of the brain involved in motor control.

The medial amygdala appears to be involved in sodium appetite induced by aldosterone, but another mechanism (perhaps the atrial baroreceptors) must also exist. The zona incerta is involved in sodium appetite as well as in drinking; lesions there decrease salt intake, whereas stimulation increases it.

MECHANISMS OF SATIETY

As I explained in the first part of this chapter, an anticipatory mechanism, which we call satiety, is needed to stop drinking even before the system variables (cellular dehydration or hypovolemia) have been restored. In this section I will consider satiety produced by drinking and satiety caused by ingestion of sodium chloride.

‖ Drinking

Normally, when a thirsty animal is given the opportunity to drink, it will rapidly drink enough water to restore its loss and then stop. In most cases satiety occurs before substantial amounts of water are absorbed from the digestive system. For example, a dog consumes the water it needs within 2 to 3 minutes (Adolph, 1939). However, replenishment of the water previously lost from the blood plasma does not begin for 10 to 12 minutes and is not completed until 40 to 45 minutes (Ramsay, Rolls, and Wood, 1977). Perhaps receptors in the mouth and throat are responsible for satiety.

Receptors in the mouth and throat *do* influence the amount of water an organism drinks, but their effects are secondary to those of receptors located farther along the digestive system. Receptors in the digestive system send a signal to the brain that water has been received and is therefore making progress along the way to absorption. Miller, Sampliner, and Woodrow (1957) allowed thirsty rats to drink 14 ml of water or administered it directly into the stomach through a tube that had been placed there previously. At various times after the preload the rats were permitted to drink. As Figure 12.14 shows, rats

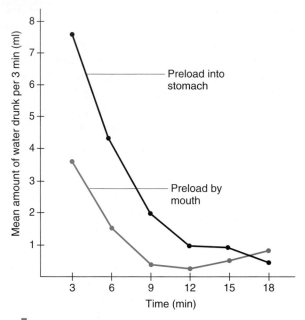

FIGURE 12.14

Effects of receiving 14 ml of water by mouth or through a tube inserted into the stomach on subsequent drinking of thirsty rats.

(From Miller, N.E., Sampliner, R.I., and Woodrow, P. *Journal of Comparative and Physiological Psychology,* 1957, *50,* 1–5. Copyright 1957 by the American Psychological Association. Reprinted with permission of the author.)

who received the 14-ml preload by mouth drank less than those that received it directly into the stomach. In other words, water placed directly into the stomach is less satiating than water that gets there after being tasted and swallowed. Thus, receptors in the mouth and throat play a role in satiety. (See **Figure 12.14.**)

It is clear, however, that satiety produced by receptors in the mouth and throat does not last long. Many studies, dating from Bernard (1856), have shown that when water that an animal drinks is not allowed to reach the stomach, an animal may pause for a while the first time it drinks but will soon resume drinking and will continue to do so until it is exhausted. These experiments used a surgical procedure called an **esophageal fistula.** (A *fistula* is an abnormal or artificial opening between one hollow organ and another or between a hollow organ and the outside of the body.) An esophageal fistula causes water that is swallowed to fall to the ground.

(After the animal's behavior has been tested, the experimenter puts water directly into its stomach.)

Hall (1973) and Hall and Blass (1977) obtained evidence that receptors in the stomach are less important for satiety than those of the duodenum or liver. They prepared a noose out of fine fishing line, passed it around the **pylorus,** the junction of the small intestine with the stomach, and threaded the line through a plastic tube. They brought the end of the tube through the rat's skin and fastened it to the top of the rat's head. The experimenters could tighten and loosen the noose without disturbing the rats. (See **Figure 12.15.**) When the experimenters tightened the noose, the pylorus closed, and contents of the stomach could not enter the intestine. When water could not leave the stomach, thirsty rats drank *more* water than when the noose was open. These results suggest that signals from the small intestine or liver are important in satiety; the noose prevented water from reaching them, thus preventing these signals from being sent.

Before I say more about these potential signals, I should describe two important parts of the body to you: the small intestine and the liver. The first part of the small intestine, which receives food and water from the stomach, is called the **duodenum.** The original Greek name for this part of the gut was *dodekadaktulon,* or "twelve fingers long." In fact, the duodenum is twelve finger *widths* long. The walls of the duodenum contain receptors, some of which may communicate with the brain through the nerves that serve the intestine. The liver is the first organ to receive substances from the digestive system. It receives them through the *hepatic portal system,* a special vascular system. (The adjective *hepatic* refers to the liver.) Water and nutrients enter the blood supply through capillaries located in the small intestine. These capillaries collect into larger and larger veins and finally into the **hepatic portal vein,** which travels to the liver and branches into capillaries again. (See **Figure 12.16.**)

At present, I know of no evidence that indicates that receptors in the duodenum are involved in satiety, although they well may be. However, there is good evidence that the liver plays such a role. Kozlowski and Drzewiecki (1973) obtained evidence supporting this hypothesis. They infused small quantities of water into the hepatic portal vein,

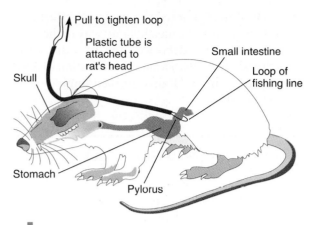

FIGURE 12.15

The procedure used by Hall and Blass (1977) to prevent water from leaving the stomach.

which conveys blood from the intestine to the liver. Thus, this vein carries substances absorbed from the intestines—including water. The infusions inhibited osmometric drinking initiated by injections of hypertonic saline. (Control infusions of the same amount of water in the jugular vein had no effect.) More recently, Kobashi and Adachi (1992) found that infusions of water into the hepatic portal vein suppressed drinking in rats that had been made thirsty by 24 hours of water deprivation. Infusions of hypertonic saline did not increase drinking; thus, the osmoreceptors in the liver are responsible for satiation of thirst, but not for the induction of thirst. In addition, Smith and Jerome (1983) found that when they cut the branch of the vagus nerve that connects the liver to the brain, thirsty rats drank more water than normal. Presumably, the increase occurred because the operation interrupted the communication of inhibitory signals from the liver to the brain.

Salt Appetite

Satiety associated with salt intake has received less attention than satiety associated with drinking, but some general conclusions can be made. First, although an animal identifies the presence of sodium in the diet by tasting it, receptors in the mouth do not appear to play a role in satiety; a sodium-deficient rat will continue to drink a con-

centrated salt solution if a gastric fistula allows it to escape from the stomach (Mook, 1969). In addition, stomach or duodenal receptors do not appear to be important; an injection of a salt solution directly into the stomach of a sodium-deficient rat does not have an immediate effect on salt appetite, although it will inhibit sodium intake after a delay of several hours (Wolf, Schulkin, and Simson, 1984).

Tordoff, Schulkin, and Friedman (1987) obtained evidence that suggests that sodium receptors in the liver contribute to the satiation of a sodium appetite. The investigators placed catheters into rats' hepatic portal vein and jugular vein. Thus, they were able to make injections into the veins while the rats were moving around freely. They induced a sodium deficiency in order to provoke a sodium appetite. They found that an injection of a hypertonic sodium chloride solution into the hepatic portal vein, which directly enters the liver, reduced the amount of salt solution that an animal would drink. Thus, the experiment provides evidence that the liver detects the presence of sodium in

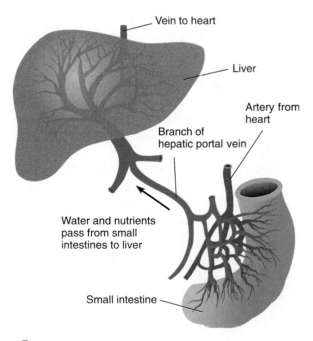

FIGURE 12.16

The hepatic portal blood supply. The liver receives water, minerals, and nutrients from the digestive system through this system.

the blood it receives from the digestive system and sends a satiety signal to the brain.

Another satiety signal for salt appetite comes from a hormone secreted in what might seem to be an unlikely place: the atria of the heart. As we saw earlier, the atria of the heart provide a perfect location to detect a fall in blood volume. Similarly, they provide a perfect location to detect a *rise* in blood volume.

De Bold and his colleagues discovered that a hormone, **atrial natriuretic peptide** (ANP), is secreted by the atria of the heart (De Bold et al., 1981; De Bold, 1985). The term *natriuretic* (not the easiest word to pronounce) comes from the fact that the hormone promotes the excretion of sodium (in Latin, *natrium*) by the kidneys. ANP appears to be an emergency backup system that helps prevent disastrously high volumes of blood plasma. The hormone is secreted when the atria are stretched more than usual by the presence of too much fluid in the blood plasma. Because plasma volume is largely controlled by the sodium concentration, eliminating sodium is obviously a useful response. But ANP does more than produce sodium excretion; it also increases the excretion of water, inhibits the secretion of renin, vasopressin, and aldosterone, and inhibits both drinking and sodium appetite. (See Tarjan, Denton, and Weisinger, 1988, for a review.) ANP receptors are found in the adrenal medulla, the pituitary gland, and the brain; presumably, these sites are responsible for the effects of the hormone on the endocrine system and on behavior (Quirion, 1989).

Some of the inhibitory effect of ANP on drinking appears to be exerted in the subfornical organ, which contains ANP receptors (Quirion et al., 1984). Nermo-Lindquist et al. (1990) found that injection of ANP blocked the excitatory effect that angiotensin has on the metabolic activity of the SFO. The injection also decreased the rat's drinking. Ehrlich and Fitts (1990) found that injection of ANP directly into the SFO also blocked angiotensin-induced drinking.

||||| INTERIM SUMMARY

Although receptors in the mouth and throat play a role in anticipatory satiety produced by drinking, the most important detectors appear to be in the duodenum or liver; when the pylorus is held shut, an animal drinks more than when it is open. Water infused into the hepatic portal vein will inhibit osmometric drinking, and water-deprived rats will drink more water if the hepatic branch of the vagus nerve is cut. Thus, osmoreceptors in the liver appear to play a role in satiety for drinking.

Although receptors on the tongue detect the presence of salt for a sodium-depleted animal, their stimulation does not produce satiety; that occurs only when the salt solution is permitted to accumulate in the stomach. Here, too, osmoreceptors in the liver play a role; an infusion of hypertonic sodium chloride into the hepatic portal vein reduces the intake of a sodium chloride solution by a sodium-depleted rat.

The atria of the heart secrete a peptide hormone, atrial natriuretic peptide, that is secreted in response to significant increases in blood volume. ANP stimulates sodium excretion by the kidneys and inhibits the secretion of renin, vasopressin, and aldosterone, and inhibits sodium appetite and drinking. At lease some of the inhibitory effects of ANP are exerted in the SFO.

New Terms

homeostasis *(home ee oh STAY sis)* p. 372

ingestive behavior *(in JESS tiv)* p. 372

The Nature of Physiological Regulatory Mechanisms

system variable p. 372

set point p. 372

detector p. 372

correctional mechanism p. 372

negative feedback p. 372

satiety mechanism p. 372

Some Facts About Fluid Balance

intracellular fluid p. 373

extracellular fluid p. 373

intravascular fluid p. 373

interstitial fluid p. 373

isotonic p. 373

hypertonic p. 373

hypotonic p. 373

hypovolemia (hy poh voh LEE mee a) p. 373

nephron p. 375

ureter *(YOUR eh ter)* p. 375

aldosterone *(al DAHS ter own)* p. 375

vasopressin *(vay zo PRESS in)* p. 375

supraoptic nucleus *(sue pra OP tik)* p. 376

paraventricular nucleus p. 376

diabetes insipidus *(in SIPP i duss)* p. 376

Drinking and Salt Appetite

osmometric thirst p. 377

osmoreceptor p. 377

OVLT *(organum vasculosum of the lamina terminalis)* p. 380

volumetric thirst p. 380

colloid *(KALH oyd)* p. 380

salt appetite p. 381

renin *(REE nin)* p. 381

angiotensinogen *(ann gee oh ten SIN oh jen)* p. 381

angiotensin *(ann gee oh TEN sin)* p. 381

saralasin *(sair a LAY sin)* p. 382

Brain Mechanisms of Thirst and Salt Appetite

nucleus of the solitary tract p. 384

subfornical organ *(SFO)* p. 384

median preoptic nucleus p. 386

zona incerta *(in SIR ta)* p. 387

Mechanisms of Satiety

esophageal fistula *(ee soff a JEE ul FISS tew la)* p. 390

pylorus *(pie LORR us)* p. 390

duodenum *(dew oh DEE num)* p. 390

hepatic portal vein p. 390

atrial natriuretic peptide *(nay tree ur ETT ik)* p. 392

Suggested Readings

De Caro, G., Epstein, A.N., and Massi, M. *The Physiology of Thirst and Sodium Appetite.* New York: Plenum Publishing Co., 1986.

Gross, P. *Circumventricular Organs and Body Fluids. Vol. III.* Boca Raton, Fla.: CRC Press, 1987.

Johnson, A.K., and Edwards, G.L. The neuroendocrinology of thirst: Afferent signaling and mechanisms of central integration. *Current Topics in Neuroendocrinology,* 1990, *10,* 149-190.

Stricker, E.M. *Handbook of Behavioral Neurobiology. Vol. 10. Neurobiology of Food and Fluid Intake.* New York: Plenum Press, 1990.

CHAPTER 13

Ingestive Behavior: Eating

Some Facts about Metabolism
- Absorption, Fasting, and the Two Nutrient Reservoirs
- Is Total Body Fat Regulated?
  Interim Summary

What Starts a Meal?
- Social and Environmental Factors
- Dietary Selection: Responding to the Consequences
- Depletion of Nutrients
  Interim Summary

What Stops a Meal?
- Head Factors
- Gastric Factors
- Intestinal Factors
- Liver Factors
- Long-Term Satiety Factors
  Interim Summary

Brain Mechanisms
- Brain Stem
- Hypothalamus
  Interim Summary

Eating Disorders
- Obesity
- Anorexia Nervosa/Bulimia Nervosa
  Interim Summary

CLEARLY, EATING IS ONE OF THE MOST important things we do—and it can also be one of the most pleasurable. Much of what an animal learns to do is motivated by the constant struggle to obtain food; thus, the need to ingest undoubtedly shaped the evolutionary development of our own species. After having read Chapter 12, in which you saw that the signals that cause thirst are well understood, you may be surprised to learn that we still are not sure just what the system variables for hunger are. Control of ingestive behavior is even more complicated than the control of drinking and sodium intake. We can achieve water balance by the intake of two ingredients: water and sodium chloride. When we eat, we must obtain adequate amounts of carbohydrates, fats, amino acids, vitamins, and minerals other than sodium. Thus, our food-ingestive behaviors are more complex, and so are the physiological mechanisms that control them.

This chapter describes research on the control of eating: metabolism, regulation of body weight, the environmental and physiological factors that begin and stop a meal, and the neural mechanisms that monitor the nutritional state of our bodies and control our ingestive behavior. It also describes the most serious eating disorders, obesity and anorexia nervosa. Despite all the effort that has gone into understanding the physiology of ingestive behavior, these disorders are still difficult to treat. Our best hope of finding effective treatments is achieving a better understanding of the physiology of metabolism and ingestive behavior.

SOME FACTS ABOUT METABOLISM

AS YOU SAW IN CHAPTER 12, YOU MUST KNOW something about the fluid compartments of the body and the functions of the kidney in order to understand the physiology of drinking. Thus, you will not be surprised that this chapter begins with a discussion of metabolism. Your first inclination may be to skip over this section; but if you do so, you will find that you will not understand experiments that are described later. For example, the sys-

tem variables that cause an animal to seek food and eat it are obviously related to the animal's metabolism. This section will discuss only as much about this subject as you will need to understand these experiments.

Absorption, Fasting, and the Two Nutrient Reservoirs

When we eat, we incorporate into our own bodies molecules that were once part of other living organisms, plant and animal. We ingest these molecules for two reasons: to construct and maintain our own organs and to obtain energy for muscular movements and for keeping our bodies warm. In other words, we need both building blocks and fuel. Although food used for building blocks is essential, I will discuss only the food used for fuel, because most of the molecules we eat get "burned" to provide energy for movement and heating.

In order to stay alive, our cells must be supplied with fuel and oxygen. Obviously, fuel comes from the digestive tract, and its presence there is a result of eating. But the digestive tract is sometimes empty; in fact, most of us wake up in the morning in that condition. So there has to be a reservoir that stores nutrients to keep the cells of the body nourished when the gut is empty. Indeed, there are two reservoirs—one short-term and the other long-term. The short-term reservoir stores carbohydrates, and the long-term reservoir stores fats.

The short-term reservoir is located in the cells of the liver and the muscles, and it is filled with a complex, insoluble carbohydrate called **glycogen.** I will consider only the most important of these locations—the liver. Cells in the liver convert glucose (a simple, soluble carbohydrate) into glycogen and store the glycogen. They are stimulated to do so by the presence of **insulin,** a peptide hormone produced by the pancreas. Thus, when glucose and insulin are present in the blood, some of the glucose is used as a fuel, and some of it is stored as glycogen. Later, when all of the food has been absorbed from the digestive tract, the level of glucose in the blood begins to fall.

The fall in glucose is detected by cells in the brain, which cause an increase in the activity of sympathetic axons that innervate the pancreas. This

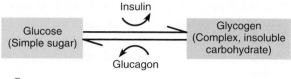

FIGURE 13.1

Effects of insulin and glucagon on glucose and glycogen.

activity inhibits the secretion of insulin and causes another set of cells of the pancreas to begin secreting a different peptide hormone, **glucagon.** The effect of glucagon is opposite that of insulin; it stimulates the conversion of glycogen into glucose. (Unfortunately, the terms *glucose, glycogen,* and *glucagon* are similar enough that it is easy to confuse them. Even worse, you will soon encounter another one, *glycerol.*) (See ***Figure 13.1.***) Thus, the liver soaks up excess glucose and stores it as glycogen when plenty of glucose is available, and it releases glucose from its reservoir when the digestive tract becomes empty and the level of glucose in the blood begins to fall.

The carbohydrate reservoir in the liver is primarily reserved for the central nervous system (CNS). When you wake in the morning, your brain is being fed by your liver, which is in the process of converting glycogen to glucose and releasing it into the blood. The glucose reaches the CNS, where it is absorbed and metabolized by the neurons and the glia. This process can continue for a few hours, until all of the carbohydrate reservoir in the liver is used up. (The average liver holds approximately 300 calories of carbohydrate.) Usually, we eat some food before this reservoir gets depleted, which permits us to refill it. But if we do not eat, the CNS has to start living on the products of the long-term reservoir.

Our long-term reservoir consists of adipose tissue (fat tissue). This reservoir is filled with fats, or, more precisely, with **triglycerides.** Triglycerides are complex molecules that contain **glycerol** (a soluble carbohydrate, also called *glycerine*) combined with three **fatty acids** (stearic acid, oleic acid, and palmitic acid). Adipose tissue is found beneath the skin and in various locations in the abdominal cavity. It consists of cells capable of absorbing nutrients from the blood, converting them to triglycerides, and storing them. They can expand in size enormously; in fact, the primary physical differ-

ence between an obese person and a person of normal weight is the size of their fat cells, which is determined by the amount of triglycerides that these cells contain.

The long-term fat reservoir is obviously what keeps us alive when we are fasting. As we begin to use the contents of our short-term carbohydrate reservoir, fat cells start converting triglycerides into fuels that the cells can use and releasing these fuels into the bloodstream. As we just saw, when we wake in the morning with an empty digestive tract, our brain (in fact, all of the central nervous system) is living on glucose released by the liver. But what about the other cells of the body? They are living on fatty acids, sparing the glucose for the brain. As you will recall from Chapter 4, the sympathetic nervous system is primarily involved in the breakdown and utilization of stored nutrients. When the digestive system is empty, there is an increase in the activity of the sympathetic axons that innervate adipose tissue, the pancreas, and the adrenal medulla. All three effects (direct neural stimulation, secretion of glucagon, and secretion of catecholamines) cause triglycerides in the long-term fat reservoir to be broken down into glycerol and fatty acids. The fatty acids can be directly metabolized by cells in all of the body *except the brain,* which needs glucose. That leaves glycerol. The liver takes up glycerol and converts it to glucose. That glucose, too, is available to the brain.

You may be asking *why* the cells of the rest of the body treat the brain so kindly, letting it consume almost all the glucose that the liver releases from its carbohydrate reservoir and constructs from glycerol. The answer is simple: Insulin has several other functions besides causing glucose to be converted to glycogen. One of these functions is the control of the entry of glucose into cells. Glucose easily dissolves in water, but it will not dissolve in fats. Cell membranes are made of lipids (fatlike substances); thus, glucose cannot directly pass through them. In order for glucose to be taken into a cell, it must be transported there by *glucose transporters*—protein molecules situated in the membrane similar to those responsible for the reuptake of transmitter substances. Glucose transporters contain insulin receptors, which control their activity; only when insulin binds with these receptors can glucose be transported into the cell. But the cells of the nervous system are an exception to this rule. Their glucose transporters do not contain insulin receptors; thus, these cells can absorb glucose *even when insulin is not present.*

Figure 13.2 reviews what I have said so far about the metabolism that takes place while the digestive tract is empty, which physiologists refer to as the **fasting phase** of metabolism. A fall in the blood glucose level causes the pancreas to stop secreting insulin and to start secreting glucagon. The absence of insulin means that most of the cells of the body can no longer use glucose; thus, all the glucose present in the blood is reserved for the central nervous system. The presence of glucagon instructs the liver to start drawing on the short-term carbohydrate reservoir—to start converting its glycogen into glucose. The presence of glucagon, along with increased activity of the sympathetic nervous system, instructs fat cells to start drawing on the long-term fat reservoir—to start breaking down triglycerides into fatty acids and glycerol. Most of the body lives on the fatty acids, and the glycerol, which is converted into glucose by the liver, gets used by the brain. (See *Figure 13.2.*)

The phase of metabolism that occurs when food is present in the digestive tract is called the **absorptive phase.** Now that you understand the fasting phase, this one is simple. Suppose that we eat a balanced meal of carbohydrates, proteins, and fats. The carbohydrates are broken down into glucose and the proteins are broken down into amino acids. The fats basically remain as fats. Let us consider each of these three nutrients.

1. As we start absorbing the nutrients, the level of glucose in the blood rises. This rise is detected by cells in the brain, which causes the activity of the sympathetic nervous system to decrease and the activity of the parasympathetic nervous system to increase. This change tells the pancreas to stop secreting glucagon and to begin secreting insulin. The insulin permits all the cells of the body to use glucose as a fuel. Extra glucose is converted into glycogen, which fills the short-term carbohydrate reservoir. If some glucose is left over, fat cells absorb it and convert it to triglycerides.

2. A small proportion of the amino acids received from the digestive tract are used as building blocks to construct proteins and peptides; the rest are converted to fats and stored in adipose tissue.

3. Fats are not used at this time; they are simply stored in adipose tissue. (See *Figure 13.2.*)

Is Total Body Fat Regulated?

No one questions the fact that body fluids are regulated, but some people have suggested that body weight (or, more accurately, total body fat) might not be. The reason for this suggestion is easy to see: Many people are obese, and some of those who are not say that they have to make a real effort to remain thin. If total body fat is truly regulated, then we might expect that people should get hungry only when they need to eat and should stop eating when they have eaten enough. But obviously, we sometimes eat when we are not really hungry, and we continue to eat even when we have had enough.

There are several reasons to explain the apparent failure of the body to regulate weight. First, as we shall see, some of the eating habits imposed on us by our society interfere with regulatory mechanisms that evolved in different types of environments. Second, regulation is not as bad as it may seem. The fact that many people show visible fat in their abdomens or in their hips and thighs does not mean that their body weights are not regulated; it may only mean that the amount of fat that is normal for them is higher than what we find aesthetically pleasing nowadays. The purpose of fat is to provide a reservoir that can be drawn upon in time of need. In the past (and in the present, in some parts of the world), the supply of food was (is) unreliable. When certain plants were in season, when the fish were running in the river, or when migratory animals were passing through the region, there was plenty to eat. At other times people ate very little and made up the difference by living off their fat. If they had *not* stored fat during the good seasons, they would have died during times when food was harder to find.

As we will see in the section on eating disorders near the end of this chapter, heredity plays an important role in determining a person's body size

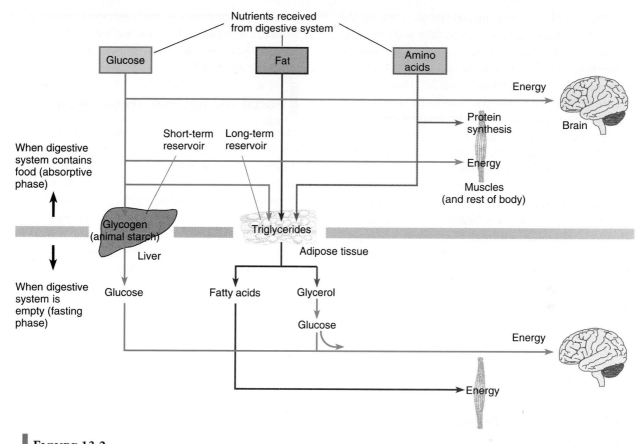

FIGURE 13.2

Metabolic pathways during the fasting phase and absorptive phase of metabolism.

and shape. Primarily because of genetic differences, some people are just naturally fatter than others. In other words, people's "set points" can vary. The reasons for these differences and their implications for control of total body fat will be discussed later.

Perhaps the best evidence that there are some controls over total body fat comes from studies that indicate that changes in diet cause compensatory changes in behavior or in metabolism. For example, if animals are given a diet with fewer calories, they soon eat more of it; whereas if they are given a richer diet, they begin to eat less. People respond this way too; Foltin et al. (1990) found that when they varied the number of calories in people's lunches (by changing either the carbohydrate or the fat content), the subjects altered the amount of food they ate the rest of the day, keeping the intake of calories relatively constant. In addition, if animals

are force-fed through a tube placed in their stomach so that they become fat, they will subsequently reduce their food intake until their weight returns to normal levels (Hoebel and Teitelbaum, 1966; Steffens, 1975).

INTERIM SUMMARY

Metabolism consists of two phases. During the absorptive phase we receive glucose, amino acids, and fats from the intestines. The blood level of insulin is high, which permits all cells to metabolize glucose. In addition, the liver and the muscles convert glucose to glycogen, which replenishes the short-term reservoir. Excess carbohydrates and amino acids are converted to fats, and fats are placed into the long-term reservoir in the adipose tissue.

During the fasting phase the activity of the parasympathetic nervous system falls and the activity of the sympathetic nervous system increases. In response, the level of insulin falls, and the level of glucagon and the adrenal catecholamines rises. These events cause liver glycogen to be converted to glucose and triglycerides to be broken down into glycerol and fatty acids. In the absence of insulin only the central nervous system can use the glucose available in the blood; the rest of the body lives on fatty acids. Glycerol is converted to glucose by the liver, and the glucose is metabolized by the brain.

Body weight (or, more likely, quantity of adipose tissue) is regulated, although the amount of fat people's bodies contain can vary widely. Both people and laboratory animals will eat less of a rich diet and more of a diet low in calories, and they will change their food intake if their metabolic requirements change.

WHAT STARTS A MEAL?

THE HEADING TO THIS SECTION IS A VERY SIMPLE question, but the answer is complex. The short answer, I suppose, is that we still are not sure, but that will not stop me from writing more. In fact, many factors start a meal, including the presence of appetizing food, the company of people who are eating, or the words "It's time to eat!" More fundamentally, there must be some sort of signal that tells the brain that the supply of nutrients has gotten low and that it is time to begin looking for, and ingesting, some food. This section considers all of these factors.

Before I begin, I will point out that the physiological signals that cause a meal to begin are different from the ones that cause it to end. As I said in the discussion of regulatory systems at the beginning of this chapter, there is a considerable delay between the act of eating (the correctional mechanism) and a change in the system variable. We may start eating because the supply of nutrients has fallen below a certain level, but we certainly do not stop eating because the level of those nutrients has been restored to normal. In fact, we stop eating long before that happens, because digestion takes several hours. Thus, the signals for hunger and satiety are sure to be different.

Social and Environmental Factors

Most people, if they were asked why they eat, would say that they do so because they get hungry. By that, they probably mean that something happens inside their body that provides a sensation that makes them want to eat. In other words, we tend to think of eating as something provoked by physiological factors. But often we eat because of habit or because of some stimuli present in our environment. These stimuli include a clock indicating that it is time to eat, the sight of a plate of food, the smell of food cooking in the kitchen, or the presence of other people sitting around the table. Many studies have shown that eating can be classically conditioned in both humans and laboratory animals. For example, Weingarten (1983) presented hungry rats with a buzzer and a light (CS$^+$) followed by food six times a day for eleven days. Another stimulus, a tone (CS$^-$), was turned on intermittently between meals. During test days following the training, he periodically turned on the CS$^+$ and the CS$^-$ and observed the animals' eating behavior. The rats began eating within 5 seconds after the CS$^+$ was presented, even when they were satiated, but did not react to the CS$^-$. (See *Figure 13.3*.) Birch et al. (1989) observed a similar phenomenon in nursery school children. Thus, it seems reasonable to suppose that stimuli naturally associated with eating can provoke a meal.

One of the most important variables affecting appetite is the meal schedule. We tend to take our meals at fixed times: soon after waking, at midday, and in the evening. This custom makes it difficult for us to adjust the timing of our meals, as other animals can do. What we do instead is adjust the *size* of our meals. If we have eaten recently or if the previous meal was large, we tend to eat a smaller meal (Jiang and Hunt, 1983; de Castro et al., 1986). Other animals tend to be less schedule-bound. For example, when a rat is free to eat whenever it wants, the size of the meal is primarily determined by external factors, such as the taste and texture of the food. However, the *time* of the next meal is related to the size of the one just eaten; that is, if a rat eats a large meal, it waits longer until the next one (Le Magnen and Tallon, 1963, 1966). The difference between our pattern and that of animals such as rats seems to be caused by our habit of eating at fixed times. If people live in isolation, away from cues that indicate the time of day, their meal patterns resemble those of rats: The bigger the meal, the longer the wait until the next one (Bernstein, 1981).

The presence of other people is yet another factor that strongly affects our eating behavior. De Castro and de Castro (1989) asked people to keep diaries that listed all the food they ate during a seven-day period and the number of other people who were present while they were eating. The investigators found that the amount of food eaten was directly related to the number of other people who were present—the more people present, the more the subjects ate. In addition, the correlation that is normally seen between the time since the previous meal and the size of the present meal was observed only when the subjects ate alone; when other people were present, the correlation was abolished. Thus, social factors can overcome the effects of metabolic factors.

Dietary Selection: Responding to the Consequences

Animals need to obtain a variety of different nutrients: carbohydrates, fats, essential amino acids, minerals, and various chemicals that the body cannot make, which we call vitamins. Some animals can get along well eating only one type of food. For example, the physiology of a koala is perfectly suited to a diet of eucalyptus leaves, and that of a giant panda to bamboo shoots. Predators can count on their prey to get a balanced diet and, by eating them, obtain all the nutrients, vitamins, and minerals they need. But animals that eat only one type of food will be limited by the distribution of their food; you will not find koalas where there are not eucalyptus trees, nor giant pandas where there are not bamboo forests. Similarly, predators are utterly dependent on their prey.

It is probably not a coincidence that two of the most successful species on earth, humans and rats,

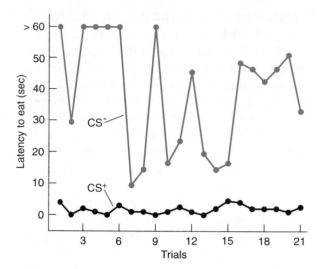

FIGURE 13.3

Classical conditioning of eating; results of the study by Weingarten (1983).

are omnivores. (Please excuse the comparison.) Omnivores ("all-devouring creatures") are liberated from dependency on a particular type of food. However, as always, with freedom comes responsibility. The metabolism of omnivores is such that no single food will provide all essential nutrients. Thus, it is advantageous to eat many different kinds of foods. As we shall see, we tend to do that, naturally. But in some situations, when the foods available at a particular time and place lack an essential nutrient, such as a vitamin or mineral, the animal must make special efforts to find a food that supplies what is needed. In addition, omnivores are exposed to foods that may contain toxic substances. All plants produce chemicals designed by the evolutionary process to poison animals (primarily insects) that might eat them. Most of these poisons are harmless to mammals, but some are not. In addition, food that has been infected with various types of bacteria or molds can become toxic. Thus, omnivores must learn to avoid foods that might cause harm.

Let us consider the tendency to obtain a varied diet. Most of us find a meal that consists of moderate quantities of several different foods to be more interesting than a huge platter of only one food. If we eat a single food, we soon become tired of it, a phenomenon that has been labeled **sensory-specific**

satiety. Le Magnen (1956) demonstrated this phenomenon elegantly. He fed rats a diet to which he could add a flavoring. He let the rats eat one flavor for 30 minutes. By that time they had pretty much stopped eating. He replaced the dish with a second flavor, and the rats began eating again. He presented a total of four different flavors (of the same basic food, remember) and found that the rats would eat a meal that was two to three times larger than a 2-hour meal consisting of a single course. Rolls et al. (1981) observed the same phenomenon in humans; they found that people would eat a larger meal when they were offered four types of sandwich fillings or four different flavors of yogurt. Obviously, the phenomenon of sensory-specific satiety encourages the consumption of a varied diet.

Of course, it is not enough simply to get a varied diet. Foods differ in their ability to provide needed calories and specific nutrients. Omnivores are able to learn about the consequences of eating different kinds of food. For example, Sclafani and Nissenbaum (1988) showed that rats can learn which flavors provide them with calories. The investigators gave rats flavored water to drink. On some days the water was cherry-flavored; on other days it was grape-flavored. The rats drank the flavored water from a special drinking tube that permitted the experimenters to detect each lick that the animals took. As the animals drank the flavored water, an automatic pump delivered either water or a nutritive starch solution into their stomachs, through tubes that had been previously placed there. For each rat a particular flavor was paired with the injection of the starch solution. After four days of training the rats were permitted to chose between the two flavors. They overwhelmingly chose the flavor that had been paired with the starch infusions; thus, rats are able to learn which flavor is associated with the delivery of a nutritive substance to their stomach. (See *Figure 13.4.*)

As we saw in Chapter 7, most mammals come provided with specialized receptors that detect substances that are possibly poisonous. Our tongue contains receptors that detect alkaloids and acids (the bitterness and sourness detectors), many of which are poisonous. Thus, we tend to reject bitter or sour tastes. (As we shall see, this tendency is controlled by mechanisms in the brain stem; thus, it is

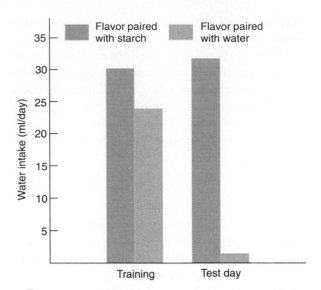

FIGURE 13.4

Preference for a flavor paired with an infusion of starch into the stomach; results of the study by Sclafani and Nissenbaum (1988).

undoubtedly a very primitive reaction.) But taste tells us about the nature of food only when it is in the mouth, so taste provides us with a limited range of information. Much more information is provided by the olfactory system. Although there are many odors that almost everyone finds disgusting, such as the smell of rotten meat (you'll be able to think of some others), studies with infants suggest that there are no odors that are innately repulsive (Engen, 1974, 1982.) Thus, they appear to be learned. Some, undoubtedly, are learned socially. We see that our parents find an odor disgusting, and we learn to do so, too. But others are learned by direct experience of the consequences of ingestion.

If an animal encounters a particular food, eats it, becomes sick, and survives, the animal will avoid eating that food afterward. That is, the animal will have formed a **conditioned flavor aversion.** The aversion can be formed simply on the basis of taste; but more often, olfaction is also involved, because flavor is a composite of taste and olfaction. The phenomenon was first experimentally demonstrated by Garcia and Koelling (1966). The investigators let rats taste some saccharin and then injected them with lithium chloride, which produces nausea. (Rats cannot vomit, but their behavior indicates that lithium chloride makes them feel ill.) Afterward, the rats refused to drink saccharin. Other studies have shown that conditioned aversions can readily be formed to the complex flavors of particular foods, which are the composites of odors and tastes.

If a rat encounters a new and potentially interesting food, it only takes a small nibble of the food. If the food contained something toxic, and if it survives its subsequent illness, it will never eat that food again. But if it does *not* get ill, it will take a larger meal the next time; it acts as if it has learned that the food is safe. Humans, too, can form conditioned flavor aversions. These aversions can sometimes occur by chance. A friend of mine often took trips on airplanes with her parents when she was a child. Unfortunately, she usually got airsick. Just before takeoff, her mother would give her some spearmint-flavored chewing gum to help relieve the pressure on her eardrums that would occur when the plane ascended. Yes, she developed a conditioned flavor aversion to spearmint gum. In fact, the odor of the gum still makes her feel nauseated. A more serious problem is encountered by patients undergoing chemotherapy for cancer. The drugs they are given often cause nausea, and the patients can form an aversion to the foods they eat during the course of therapy (Bernstein, 1978).

Rozin and Kalat (1971) describe an interesting phenomenon: Conditioned flavor aversions can motivate an animal to find a nutrient that it needs. As we saw in Chapter 12, if a rat is fed a food that is deficient in sodium, it will develop a sodium appetite and will seek foods that contain sodium, which it is able to taste. This tendency need not be learned; it is innate. However, rats (and humans) cannot innately recognize the flavor of vital ingredients of the diet, such as vitamins or minerals other than sodium. If a rat is fed a food that is deficient in a particular vitamin, such as thiamine, it will become ill. Its illness will cause the formation of a conditioned aversion to that food. If it is offered another, it will eat it; and if it gets well after eating that food (because it contains the ingredient lacking in its diet), it will learn to prefer that food over the old one.

Thus, we omnivores are endowed with some innate tendencies and with the ability to learn from our experience with particular foods. These ten-dencies and abilities permit us to obtain the nutrients we need from an enormous variety of food-stuffs, while avoiding foods that could be dangerous to us. Later in this chapter, I will discuss the physiology of sensory-specific satiety and conditioned flavor aversions.

Depletion of Nutrients

Most of the time, we begin a meal because it is time to eat. But the motivation to eat can also be stimulated by metabolic factors. If we skip several meals, we get hungrier and hungrier; presumably, we do so because of physiological signals indicating the loss of nutrients from our long-term reservoir. And as we saw in the previous section, if clocks and dinner bells are not present, we eat soon after a small meal but wait longer after a large one. These facts suggest that hunger is inversely related to the amount of nutrients left over from previous meals.

Most investigators believe that the physiological signal that stimulates eating is a fall in level of metabolic fuels available to cells. As you learned earlier in this chapter, during the absorptive phase of metabolism we live on food that is being absorbed from the digestive tract. After that, we start drawing on our nutrient reservoirs: The brain lives on glucose and the rest of the body lives on fatty acids. Although the metabolic needs of the cells of the body are being met, the fact is that we are taking fuel out of our long-term reservoir. And this withdrawal may provide the signal that it is time to eat.

The Glucostatic Hypothesis

What might the nature of this signal be? For several reasons the most obvious candidate is the level of glucose in the blood. To begin with, glucose is the primary fuel during the absorptive phase of metabolism; thus, when it is plentiful, the animal does not need to eat. In addition, a drop in the level of blood glucose is the event that inhibits the secretion of insulin and stimulates sympathetic activity, thus triggering the fasting phase of metabolism. If a fall in blood glucose is responsible for the fasting phase of metabolism, perhaps it is responsible for hunger, too. Finally, because the brain controls eating, it seems reasonable that hunger might be triggered by a decrease in the brain's primary fuel.

The hypothesis that the metabolic signal for hunger is a fall in blood glucose is called the **glucostatic hypothesis** (Mayer, 1955). A *glucostat* is assumed to be a neuron that measures blood glucose the way a thermostat measures temperature. The glucostatic hypothesis suggests that the firing rate of glucostats is related to the level of glucose in the interstitial fluid. A fall in the level of glucose produces a signal in these neurons that stimulates food seeking and eating.

A drop in the level of glucose in the blood usually causes hunger. For example, a large injection of insulin causes liver cells and fat cells to take up glucose and store it away, thus producing a dramatic decrease in blood glucose level. The effect of this decrease is intense hunger. But normally, regulatory mechanisms keep the level of blood glucose within rather close limits. When an animal fasts for a long time, the breakdown of triglycerides (and, eventually, amino acids) produces enough glucose to maintain a normal level of blood glucose. Severe hypoglycemia (low blood glucose level), such as that caused by a large injection of insulin, may cause hunger by turning on a mechanism that operates only during emergencies.

Louis-Sylvestre and Le Magnen (1980) devised a procedure that permitted them to continuously analyze the level of glucose in a rat's blood. They withdrew 15 μl of blood each minute from a catheter implanted in a rat's jugular vein and replaced it with an equal amount of blood from a donor rat; thus, the subject's blood volume was not reduced. They found that the blood glucose level fell slightly several minutes before each meal.

Campfield and Smith (1990) review a series of experiments investigating this phenomenon. Figure 13.5 shows the shape of the decline in blood glucose that precedes most meals. The glucose level falls and then rises again; the meal begins approximately 5 min after the lowest point. (See *Figure 13.5.*)

Campfield and his colleagues obtained evidence that the fall in blood glucose just before a spontaneous meal is not just *related* to the onset of a meal, it is the *cause* of it. If they injected a very small amount of glucose into the rats' veins when they detected a decline in the blood glucose level, the predicted meal was postponed. It was as if the injection removed the hunger signal. However, if they infused some glucose while the level of blood glucose had passed its low point and was rising again, the rats did eat. (See *Figure 13.5.*)

What causes the level of blood glucose to suddenly fall? It seems unlikely that the animals suddenly run out of some nutrient. Campfield and his colleagues found that even if the rats were prevented from eating, their blood glucose level returned to normal, so obviously their bodies contain enough nutrients to maintain a normal blood glucose level. In fact, the cause of the fall seems to be a brief, 50 percent rise in insulin secretion, which occurs just before the change in the blood glucose level. An injection of carbamyl-ß-methylcholine, an acetylcholine agonist that does not cross the blood-brain barrier, produces a similar surge in insulin secre-

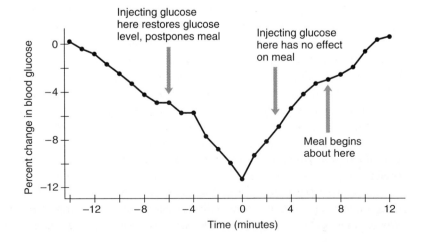

FIGURE 13.5

Blood glucose level before, during, and after a spontaneous meal of a rat.

(Adapted from Campfield, L.A., and Smith, F.A., in Handbook of Behavioral Neurobiology, Vol. 10, Neurobiology of Food and Fluid Intake, edited by E.M. Stricker. New York: Plenum Press, 1990.)

tion—with a subsequent fall in glucose and the onset of a meal. Thus, according to Campfield and his colleagues, a signal from the brain to the pancreas begins a chain of events that triggers the start of a meal. But if the brain is the source of the command for the pancreas to secrete a pulse of insulin, then we must ask what causes the brain to transmit this command. So far, this question is unanswered.

Beyond the Glucostatic Hypothesis

As we just saw, a drastic fall in the level of blood glucose resulting from an injection of insulin produces hunger. In addition, a naturally occurring fall in blood glucose level also stimulates eating, but this fall appears to be the consequence of a signal originating in the brain. In any event, although glucose may provide an important physiological signal for hunger, it does not provide the only one. After all, our cells can use other nutrients besides glucose.

When we stimulate hunger by injecting an animal with insulin and lowering the level of glucose in the blood, we are causing **glucoprivation;** that is, we are depriving the cells of glucose. Glucoprivation can also be caused by injecting an animal with 2-deoxyglucose (2-DG). You are already familiar with this chemical, because I have described several experiments that used radioactive 2-DG in conjunction with PET scanners or autoradiography to study the metabolic rate of different parts of the brain. When (nonradioactive) 2-DG is given in large doses, it interferes with glucose metabolism by competing with glucose for access to the mechanism that transports glucose through the cell membrane and for access to the enzymes that metabolize glucose. (A similar chemical, 5-TG, has the same effect.) Hunger can also be produced by causing **lipoprivation**— depriving cells of lipids. More precisely, they are deprived of the ability to metabolize fatty acids through injection of *methyl palmoxirate* (MP) or *mercaptoacetate* (MA).

Glucose and fatty acids are only two of the three major nutrients. However, less is known about the importance of amino acids in the body's metabolism. One of the problems in studying the role of amino acids in hunger is that they are essential for protein synthesis. Thus, a diet low in amino acids interferes with many biological processes. Similarly, a diet that is very high in amino acids pro-

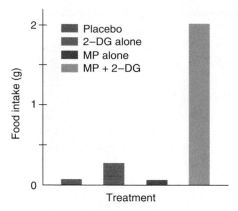

FIGURE 13.6

Effects of lipoprivation (MP treatment) and glucoprivation (2-DG treatment) on food intake of rats. Intake is stimulated much more when both fatty acid and carbohydrate metabolism are impaired.

(Adapted from Friedman, M.I., Tordoff, M.G., and Ramirez, I. *Brain Research Bulletin*, 1986, *17*, 855–859.)

duces toxic waste products. Thus, experimental manipulations in the amino acid content of diets cause effects unrelated to energy metabolism. For that reason experimenters have concentrated on carbohydrates and lipids.

Severe glucoprivation or severe lipoprivation causes hunger. However, Friedman, Tordoff, and Ramirez (1986) found that *moderate* glucoprivation or *moderate* lipoprivation alone has only a small effect on eating; but when they are combined, an animal eats much more. They administered moderate doses of 2-DG or MP separately or together; only when they were given together did the animals eat large quantities of food. (See *Figure 13.6.*) Presumably, when the metabolism of only one fuel was reduced, the rats simply relied more heavily on the other fuel. The investigators also found that if rats were fed a diet high in fats but low in carbohydrates, treatment with MP alone caused food intake to increase. With no carbohydrates for the animals to fall back on, a treatment that interferes with fatty acid metabolism is enough to stimulate eating.

What is the nature of the detectors responsible for measuring the level of metabolic fuels, and where are they located? Are there two sets of receptors, one responsible for glucoprivic hunger and another for lipoprivic hunger? The evidence obtained so far suggests that there are several differ-

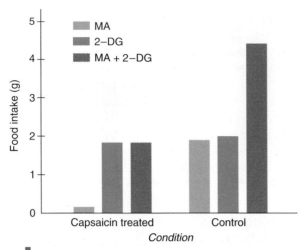

FIGURE 13.7

Effects of capsaicin-induced damage to unmyelinated peripheral axons on glucoprivic hunger (MA treatment) and lipoprivic hunger (2-DG treatment). Only lipoprivic hunger is affected.

(Based on data from Ritter, S., and Taylor, J.S. *American Journal of Physiology*, 1989, *256*, R1232–R1239.)

ent sets of receptors—some located in the brain, and some located in the liver and other internal organs. Some of these receptors appear to respond to the level of glucose available to cells, others to the amount of fatty acids, and still others may respond to the presence of any available metabolic fuel.

Ritter and her colleagues (reviewed by Ritter et al., 1992) have obtained evidence that two different sets of receptors are responsible for glucoprivic and lipoprivic hunger. Ritter and Taylor (1989) administered **capsaicin,** a neurotoxin found in red peppers, to rats. This drug destroys fine-diameter unmyelinated axons of the peripheral nervous system, many of which convey sensory information from the internal organs to the brain. The capsaicin blocked lipoprivic hunger but did not affect glucoprivic hunger. After this treatment the rats increased their food intake when they were given injections of 2-DG but not when they were given MA; nor were injections of both substances more effective than injections of 2-DG alone. (See *Figure 13.7.*)

Ritter and Taylor (1990) found lipoprivic hunger (but not glucoprivic hunger) was also abolished by cutting the vagus nerve as it entered the abdominal cavity. Thus, the receptors that detect low availability of fatty acids seem to be located in the abdominal cavity and send their information to the brain through small diameter, unmyelinated axons.

At least some of the receptors responsible for glucoprivic feeding seem to be located in the hindbrain. Ritter, Slusser, and Stone (1981) injected some silicone grease into the cerebral aqueduct, which blocked communication between the third and fourth ventricles. Next, they injected 5-TG into either the third ventricle or the fourth ventricle. Injections into the fourth ventricle stimulated eating, but injections into the third ventricle (located in the middle of the hypothalamus) had no effect. Presumably, the 5-TG diffused out of the fourth ventricle into the surrounding brain tissue and inhibited glucose metabolism in neurons in the hindbrain.

As you will recall from Chapter 12, the liver contains osmoreceptors that play a role in thirst. As several studies have shown (for example, Niijima, 1969, 1982), the liver contains glucose-sensitive receptors that send information to the brain through afferent fibers in the vagus nerve. These receptors appear to provide "hunger" signals; they fire at a high rate when the level of nutrients in the hepatic portal blood is low and fire at a low rate when the nutrient level is high. A study by Novin, VanderWeele, and Rezek (1973) suggested that receptors in the liver can stimulate glucoprivic hunger; when these cells are deprived of nutrients, they cause eating. The investigators infused 2-DG into the hepatic portal vein. (Because the animals had been eating a high-carbohydrate, low-fat diet, the 2-DG effectively starved the cells of the liver.) They found that the intraportal infusions of 2-DG caused immediate eating. The effect appeared to be mediated by the neural connections between the liver and the brain, because it was largely eliminated by cutting the vagus nerve.

Tordoff, Rawson, and Friedman (1991) obtained even more convincing evidence that receptors in the liver serve as the source of a hunger signal. They found that an injection of 2,5-AM (2,5-anhydro-D-mannitol), which interferes with liver metabolism, caused rats to eat. A study with radioactive 2,5-AM showed that this drug does not cross the blood-brain barrier, so its effects could not have occurred there. In addition, when the investigators cut the branch of the vagus nerve that serves the liver, the effect of the drug was abolished.

Rawson et al. (1993) believe that the receptors in the liver do not detect the presence or absence of a specific nutrient in the blood but, instead, simply signal their own metabolic rate. For example, people with untreated diabetes are typically hungry even though their blood level of glucose is very high. Because these people lack insulin, the glucose in their blood cannot enter cells and be metabolized. Thus, the cells starve in the midst of plenty.

Rawson and her colleagues showed that 2,5-AM decreased the production of ATP in liver cells, which indicates a decrease in energy production. Another drug, *L-ethionine*, which also suppresses the production of ATP in the liver, also induces hunger (Rawson et al., 1992). These results are consistent with the *ischymetric hypothesis* of hunger (from the Greek word *ischis,* "power") proposed by Nicolaïdis (1974, 1987). Nicolaïdis suggested that some neurons serve as witnesses that testify to the rest of the nervous system about the level of nutrients available to them. The firing rate of their axons is very sensitive to the cells' metabolic rate. If the level of fuels falls (or if drugs interfere with their rate of energy production), their metabolic rate falls too, and the change in the firing rate of their axons tells other neurons that it is time to start thinking about the next meal.

In any case, it is clear that no single set of receptors is solely responsible for the information the brain uses to control eating. For example, Tordoff, Hopfenbeck, and Novin (1982) found that cutting the hepatic branch of the vagus nerve, which prevents hunger signals originating in the liver from reaching the brain, had little effect on an animal's day-to-day eating. In addition, capsaicin injections, which interfere with lipoprivic feeding, do not lead to long-term disturbances in the control of feeding (Ritter, 1992). Apparently, the control of metabolism and ingestive behavior is just too important to entrust to one mechanism.

⁞⁞⁞⁞⁞ INTERIM SUMMARY

Many stimuli, environmental and physiological, can initiate a meal. Stimuli associated with eating—such as clocks pointing to lunchtime or dinnertime, the smell or sight of food, or (especially) the taste of food—increase appetite. The size of a meal taken by a rat (or a person living in isolation) determines the interval until the next one. In contrast, most people eat at relatively fixed times but vary their intake according to how much (or when) they ate the previous meal. The presence of other people tends to increase our meal and removes the controlling effect of the previous meal.

Omnivores are naturally attracted to sweet tastes and avoid sour or bitter ones. The phenomenon of sensory-specific satiety encourages omnivores to eat a varied diet. In addition, they can learn to avoid (form an aversion to) the flavors of foods that make them ill. If they eat a diet that lacks an essential ingredient, their illness produces an aversion to their present diet and motivates them to seek another. If that diet cures them, they learn to prefer it.

The glucostatic hypothesis suggests that the primary physiological signal for hunger is a fall in the level of blood glucose. Continuous measurements of blood glucose level indicate that meals are preceded by a brief fall in this fuel, but the phenomenon appears to be caused by a transient hypersecretion of insulin. The cause of the insulin secretion is not known.

Studies with inhibitors of the metabolism of glucose and fatty acids indicate that both of these nutrients are involved; that is, animals will eat in response to both glucoprivation and lipoprivation. Studies with capsaicin indicate that the signal for lipoprivic eating is detected by receptors in or around organs in the abdominal cavity and transmitted through unmyelinated afferent axons of the vagus nerve. Glucoprivic eating can be stimulated by interfering with glucose metabolism in the region surrounding the fourth ventricle.

Receptors in the liver, too, are able to provide a glucoprivic signal to the brain. Apparently, the signal is not simply provided by glucose-sensitive neurons; inhibition of the oxidation of metabolic fuels and the production of ATP by the liver, resulting from an injection of 2,5-AM into the hepatic portal vein, causes eating to take place.

No single set of receptors is solely responsible for the control of food intake; although vagotomy (cutting the vagus nerve) or capsaicin abolish an animal's response to a sudden, drastic fall in the availability of fatty acids, this treatment does not disrupt day-to-day eating.

WHAT STOPS A MEAL?

AS WE SAW, THE SIGNALS THAT STOP A MEAL ARE different from those that start it. However, these two types of signals interact. If a meal is started when there is not much physiological need for nutrients (that is, when the nutrient reservoirs are well stocked), then the meal will be a small one. If, however, a meal is started after a long fast, when the nutrient reservoirs are somewhat depleted, the meal will be a large one. In other words, if the hunger signal is moderate, than a moderate satiety signal will stop the meal. If the hunger signal is strong, than only a strong satiety signal will stop it.

The search for these signals that stop a meal follows the pathway traveled by ingested food: the eyes, nose, and mouth; the stomach; the duodenum; and the liver. Each of these locations can potentially provide a signal to the brain that indicates that food has been ingested and is progressing on the way toward absorption. To discover the nature of the detectors in these locations and their effects on behavior, experimenters "trick" the organism by taking food out of the digestive system, placing food there, or surgically disconnecting receptors along the digestive tract from the brain.

Head Factors

The term *head factors* refers to several sets of receptors located in the head: the eyes, the nose, the tongue, and the throat. Information about the appearance, odor, taste, texture, and temperature of food has some automatic effects on food intake, but most of the effects involve learning. Simply eating does not produce long-lasting satiety; an animal with a gastric fistula (a tube placed in the stomach that drains ingested food out of the stomach before it can be digested) will eat indefinitely.

Undoubtedly, the most important role of head factors in satiety is the fact that taste and odor of food can serve as stimuli that permit animals to learn about the caloric contents of different foods. Thus, animals can learn to adjust their intake according to the caloric value of what they are eating. For example, Mather, Nicolaïdis, and Booth (1978) found that rats learned to eat less of a food with a particular flavor when the eating of that food was accompanied by intravenous infusions of glucose, which supplied extra calories.

Gastric Factors

Although most people associate feelings of hunger with "hunger pangs" in the stomach and feelings of satiety with an impression of gastric fullness, the stomach is not necessary for feelings of hunger. Humans whose stomachs have been removed because of cancer or the presence of large ulcers still periodically get hungry (Ingelfinger, 1944). Of necessity, these people eat frequent, small meals; in fact, a large meal causes nausea and discomfort, apparently because the duodenum quickly fills up. (As you will recall from Chapter 12, the duodenum is the part of the small intestine that attaches to the stomach.) However, although the stomach may not be especially important in producing hunger, it does appear to play an important role in satiety.

The stomach apparently contains receptors that can detect the presence of nutrients. Davis and Campbell (1973) allowed rats to eat their fill, and shortly thereafter, they removed food from the rats' stomachs through an implanted tube. When the rats were permitted to eat again, they ate almost exactly the same amount of food that had been taken out. This finding suggests that animals are able to monitor the amount of food in their stomachs.

Deutsch and Gonzalez (1980) confirmed and extended these findings. They operated on rats and attached an inflatable cuff around the pylorus— something that looked like a miniature blood pressure cuff. The cuff could be inflated by remote control, which would cause it to compress the pylorus, preventing the stomach from emptying. (As we saw in Chapter 12, Hall and Blass used a similar device, in which a noose of fishing line could be tightened to prevent water from leaving the stomach.) With their device Deutsch and Gonzalez could confine food to the stomach, eliminating the possi-

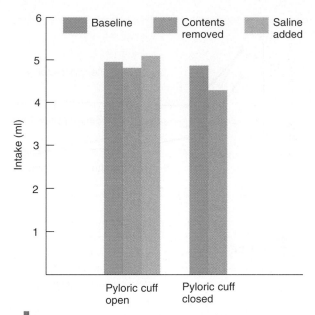

FIGURE 13.8

Evidence for a gastric satiety signal. Eating is provoked by the removal of food from the rat's stomachs.

(Based on data from Deutsch, J.A., and Gonzalez, M.F. *Behavioral and Neural Biology*, 1980, *31*, 113–116.)

ble influence of receptors in the intestine or liver. After observations were made, the cuff could be deflated so that the stomach would empty normally.

Each day, the investigators inflated the pyloric cuff and gave the rats a 30-min opportunity to drink a commercial high-calorie liquid diet. Because the rats had not eaten for 15 h, they readily consumed the liquid diet. After the meal the investigators removed 5 ml of the stomach's contents through an implanted tube. On some days they replaced the contents with a saline solution, and on others they let the rats eat without intervention. The rats adjusted their food intake perfectly, compensating for the calories that were removed but ignoring the added nonnutritive saline solution. (See *Figure 13.8*.) The results indicate that animals can monitor the total amount of nutrients received by the stomach. They do not do so simply by measuring the volume of the food there, because they are not fooled by the infusion of a saline solution. And the detection takes place in the stomach, not the intestine, because the pyloric cuff keeps all the food in the stomach. (Of course, there could be detectors in the intestines, as well.)

Deutsch (1983) found that signals from the stomach could control food intake *only when the animal was familiar with the food it was eating.* If the rat ate familiar food, it would eat the amount required to replace any food removed by the experimenter. However, if a novel flavor was added to the food, the animal did *not* compensate for the food that was removed. After several days experience with the new flavor, the animals began compensating again. Thus, it appears that rats use feedback from the metabolic consequences of a particular food to calibrate the signal the brain receives from the stomach. The flavor of the food identifies it, and that tells the brain how to handle the signal coming from the stomach. Oral and olfactory signals are necessary for an animal to learn how to use gastric signals.

How are the signals transmitted from the stomach to the brain? The most likely route would be the branch of the vagus nerve that innervates the stomach. Indeed, the vagus nerve does convey emergency signals from stretch receptors in the walls of the stomach. Gonzalez and Deutsch (1981) equipped rats with pyloric cuffs and found that the animals would stop eating when they injected a large amount of saline into their stomach. Almost certainly, this inhibitory effect is not satiety but simply discomfort; the rats' stomachs were simply too full to accept any food. When the animals' vagus nerves were severed, though, an injection of saline into the stomach would *not* inhibit eating.

Although the emergency signal from the stomach's stretch receptors is conveyed neurally, the signal from the stomach's nutrient receptors to the brain appears to be conveyed hormonally. Gonzalez and Deutsch found that even after the rats' vagus nerves were severed, the animals would increase their food intake to compensate for food that the experimenters had removed from their stomachs. Thus, essential information about nutrients in the stomach is not conveyed to the brain through the vagus nerve. Instead, the information is presumably transmitted by one of the hormones known to be secreted by cells in the walls of the stomach.

Intestinal Factors

After food reaches the stomach, it is mixed with hydrochloric acid and pepsin, an enzyme that breaks proteins into their constituent amino acids. As digestion proceeds, food is gradually introduced into the duodenum. There, the food is mixed with bile and pancreatic enzymes, which continue the digestive process. The duodenum controls the rate of stomach emptying by secreting a peptide hormone called **cholecystokinin** (CCK). This hormone receives its name from the fact that it causes the gallbladder (cholecyst) to contract, injecting bile into the duodenum. (Bile breaks down fats into small particles so that they can be absorbed from the intestines.) CCK is secreted in response to the presence of fats, which are detected by receptors in the walls of the duodenum. In addition to stimulating contraction of the gallbladder, CCK causes the pylorus to contract and inhibits gastric contractions, thus keeping the stomach from giving it more food.

Obviously, the blood level of CCK must be related to the amount of nutrients (particularly fats) that the duodenum receives from the stomach. Thus, this hormone could potentially provide a satiety signal to the brain, telling it that the duodenum was receiving food from the stomach. In fact, many studies have indeed found that injections of CCK suppress eating (Gibbs, Young, and Smith, 1973; Smith, Gibbs, and Kulkosky, 1982). Because CCK cannot cross the blood-brain barrier, its site of actions must be either outside the central nervous system or in one of the circumventricular organs (like that of angiotensin).

In fact, CCK seems to act peripherally. Smith, Gibbs, and Kulkosky (1982) reported that the inhibitory effect of CCK on food intake was abolished by cutting the gastric branch of the vagus nerve, which disconnects the stomach from the brain. Evidence suggests that the pylorus, a region rich in CCK receptors, may be an important site of action. Moran et al. (1989) removed rats' pyloruses, attaching the stomach directly to the cut end of the duodenum. After the surgery the suppressive effect of CCK on the animals' eating was significantly decreased. However, by 2–3 months after the surgery the junction between the stomach and the duodenum had grown new CCK receptors, and the hormone again suppressed food intake. (See *Figure 13.9.*)

The suppressive effect of CCK on eating is well established. However, several investigators have

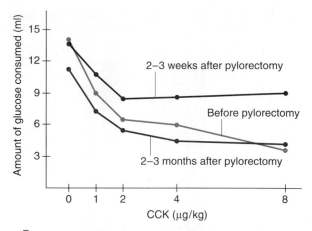

FIGURE 13.9.

Effects of cholecystokinin (CCK) on the amount of glucose consumed by rats before and after removal of the pyloric region.

(Based on data from Moran, Shnayder, Hostetler, and McHugh, 1989.)

questioned whether the suppression is caused by *aversion* or by *satiety*. That is, CCK might simply make the animals feel nauseated, so they stop eating. Deutsch and Hardy (1977) found that when an injection of CCK was paired with a particular flavor, rats formed a conditioned aversion to that flavor. In addition, Moore and Deutsch (1985) found that an injection of an *antiemetic* drug (one that suppresses nausea and vomiting) diminished the inhibitory effect of CCK on eating. Also, Bowers et al. (1992) found that rats who received low doses of CCK after drinking sweetened condensed milk from a drinking spout in their home cage would later not only avoid drinking the milk but also bury the drinking spout with the bedding material—a response that rats make when they encounter something that appears to be dangerous. Finally, Stricker and his colleagues (McCann, Verbalis, and Stricker, 1989; Stricker and Verbalis, 1991) found that several chemicals known to produce nausea, including lithium chloride, copper sulfate, and apomorphine, cause a release of oxytocin by the posterior pituitary gland; thus, they consider oxytocin release an indicator of malaise. They found that injections of CCK, too, cause a release of oxytocin. Satiety produced by eating a normal meal does *not* cause the release of oxytocin.

Although investigators still disagree about whether CCK serves as an intestinal satiety signal, it is clear that the presence of food in the intestine does inhibit eating. Studies have shown that afferent axons arising from the duodenum are sensitive to the presence of glucose, amino acids, and fatty acids (Ritter et al., 1992). These axons may transmit a satiety signal to the brain. Greenberg, Smith, and Gibbs (1990) attached gastric fistulas to a group of rats so that when the animals drank a liquid diet, it would drain out of their stomachs. Under these conditions the animals will eat for a long time, because food does not accumulate in the digestive system. (This behavior is referred to as **sham feeding,** because it is an imitation of the real thing.) The researchers infused *Intralipid*, a commercial mixture of lipids and fatty acids, into the rats' duodenums. The infusion inhibited the sham feeding, which indicates the presence of a duodenal satiety signal. When the researchers added a local anesthetic to the liquid diet, the infusion was much less effective in reducing sham feeding. Thus, the signal seems to arise from nutrient detectors located inside the duodenum. In support of this conclusion Greenberg et al. (1991) found that the satiating effect of an injection of radioactively labeled Intralipid into the duodenum occurred before radioactivity was seen in the blood of the hepatic portal vein. Thus, the satiating effect occurred before digestion had taken place.

Liver Factors

Satiety produced by head factors and gastric factors is anticipatory; that is, these factors predict that the food in the digestive system will, when absorbed, eventually restore the system variables that cause hunger. Food in the mouth or stomach does not restore the body's store of nutrients. Not until nutrients are absorbed from the intestines are the internal system variables that cause hunger returned to normal. The last stage of satiety appears to occur in the liver, which is the first organ to learn that food is finally being received from the intestines.

Over twenty years ago, Russek (1971) noted that although intravenous (IV) injections of glucose had little effect on food intake, **intraperitoneal (IP)** injections (that is, into the abdominal cavity) suppressed eating. Russek realized that most of the glu-

cose injected into the abdominal cavity is taken up by the liver and stored as glycogen. The fact that the glucose injected intraperitoneally probably got no farther than the liver but nevertheless inhibited eating suggested to him that the liver might contain detectors that were sensitive to glucose. Perhaps these detectors send signals to the brain that activate mechanisms that control eating.

To test this hypothesis, Russek attached two chronic cannulas in a dog, one in the hepatic portal vein and another in the jugular vein, located in the neck. Injection in the jugular vein introduces a substance into the general circulation. By the time the substance reaches the liver, it is already diluted by the blood. In contrast, injection in the hepatic portal vein introduces a substance directly into the liver. Russek found that an injection of glucose into the hepatic portal vein produced long-lasting satiety, whereas a similar injection into the jugular vein had no effect on food intake. Since then, many other studies (for example, Novin et al., 1983) have confirmed these results.

Tordoff and Friedman (1988) demonstrated that this effect seems to be localized in the liver. They infused small amounts of two nutrients, glucose and fructose, into the hepatic portal vein. The amounts they used were similar to those that are produced when a meal is being digested. Both nutrients reduced the amount of food that the rats ate. Almost certainly, the signal was detected by the liver. First, neither the glucose nor the fructose increased the animals' blood level of glucose, free fatty acids, glycerol, or ketones; thus, the infusions did not provide a signal that could be detected directly by nutrient receptors in the brain. Second, fructose cannot cross the blood-brain barrier and is metabolized very poorly by cells in the rest of the body (Park et al., 1957; Van den Berghe, 1978). However, fructose can readily be metabolized by the liver. Therefore, the results strongly suggest that when the liver receives nutrients from the intestines, it sends a signal to the brain that produces satiety. (More accurately, the signal *continues* the satiety that was already started by signals arising from the stomach and duodenum.)

Of course, we cannot necessarily conclude that a treatment produces *satiety* just because it inhibits eating. (As we saw, the researchers disagree about whether the suppression of food intake produced by CCK should be called satiety.) However, the effects of infusions of nutrients into the hepatic portal vein do not appear to be aversive. Tordoff and Friedman (1986) infused either a saline solution or a solution of glucose into the hepatic portal blood supply of rats while the animals were eating. The two solutions were randomly paired with two non-nutritive flavors added to their food: chicken or chocolate. As expected, the glucose suppressed eating. But later, when the rats were permitted to choose between the two flavors of food, they preferred the one associated with the glucose infusion. Thus, not only is the infusion not aversive, but it is also actually reinforcing. And as we saw earlier, Sclafani and Nissenbaum (1988) found that an infusion of starch into the stomach produced a preference for a flavor associated with the infusion; thus, the brain interprets the signals from the stomach and the liver not simply as satiety signals but as signals that a beneficial event has occurred.

Long-Term Satiety Factors

So far, I have discussed satiety factors arising from a meal. But as we saw in the first section of this chapter, total body fat appears to be regulated over a long-term basis. If an animal is force-fed so that it becomes fatter than normal, it will reduce its food intake once it is permitted to choose how much to eat. And if an animal is put on a diet that reduces its body weight, gastric satiety factors become much less effective (Cabanac and Lafrance, 1991). Thus, signals arising from the long-term nutrient reservoir may either suppress hunger signals or augment satiety signals.

Koopmans (1985) demonstrated the interaction between long-term and short-term signals in the control of food intake. He operated on pairs of rats, surgically producing "Siamese twins." He attached them side by side and connected their intestines in such a way that much of the food that one rat ate was actually absorbed by the other rat. The animals exchanged very little blood, so their nutrient reservoirs did not mix. (See *Figure 13.10.*) (The rats were genetically identical members of an inbred strain, so there was no problem with tissue rejection.) The rat that received the extra nutrients from its partner

began eating much less, and the donor began eating much more. Although satiety signals arising from the stomachs and duodenums of both rats were unaffected by the surgery, signals arising from the depletion of the animals' long-term nutrient reservoirs were obviously able to override these signals.

What, exactly, is the system variable that permits the body weight of most organisms to remain relatively stable? It seems highly unlikely that body *weight* itself is regulated—this variable would have to be measured by detectors in the soles of our feet or (for those of us who are sedentary) in the skin of our buttocks. What is more likely is that some variable related to body fat is regulated. As we saw earlier, the basic difference between obese and nonobese people is the amount of fat stored in their adipose tissue. Perhaps fat tissue provides a signal to the brain that indicates how much of it there is. If so, the signal is almost certainly some sort of chemical, because cutting the nerves that serve the fat tissue in an animal's body does not affect its total body fat.

As you might expect, several investigators have tried to identify a chemical signal that is produced by adipose tissue. Davis et al. (1969, 1971) found that when rats received an injection of blood taken from sated rats, they ate less than they normally would. Blood taken from hungry rats had no effect on food intake. Hulsey and Martin (1992) overfed rats by injecting food into their stomachs. They removed the fat tissue from these rats and were able to extract a protein that they called *adipose satiety factor*. When this protein was injected into normally fed rats, it suppressed their food intake for over 12 hours. Bender (1992) extracted a peptide with similar properties from the blood of pigs. Further studies will have to be performed to determine whether any of these substances actually do tell the brain how much fat the body possesses.

Some investigators believe that the signal from fat deposits to the brain may involve insulin. Several studies have shown that small quantities of insulin are found in cerebrospinal fluid (CSF) and that the level of the hormone is proportional to the animal's total body fat (Woods, Decke, and Vasselli, 1974; Bernstein et al., 1975; Woods et al., 1985). Exactly how body fat affects CSF insulin levels is not clear; some researchers believe that the hormone

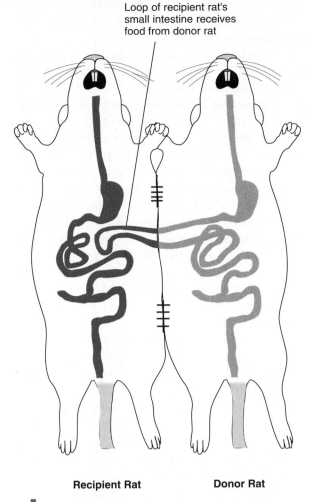

Loop of recipient rat's small intestine receives food from donor rat

Recipient Rat　　　**Donor Rat**

❙ FIGURE 13.10

A surgical preparation used by Koopmans (1985) to cause most of the nutrients eaten by one rat to be absorbed in the body of its partner.

gains access to the brain through the circumventricular organs, such as the area postrema and the subfornical organ. Once the insulin is in the CSF, it can diffuse into the brain tissue itself. Others believe that insulin may be produced directly in the brain in response to some as yet undiscovered signals.

In any event, many studies have shown that the presence of insulin in the brain inhibits food intake. For example, McGowan, Andrews, and Grossman (1992) continuously infused very small quantities of insulin or antibodies to insulin directly into the ventromedial hypothalamus for one week. They found that the insulin infusions lowered body weight and suppressed feeding during the night (when rats normally eat), whereas the infusions of insulin antibodies increased both body weight and feeding. The effects of the hormone and its antibody on body weight could not be accounted for simply by the changes in food intake; thus, insulin in the brain appears to affect metabolism as well as behavior.

‖‖ INTERIM SUMMARY

Because of the long delay between swallowing food and digesting it, the regulation of food intake requires a satiety mechanism; without it, we would overeat and damage our stomachs. The feedback produced by tasting, smelling, and swallowing food provides the first satiety signal, but unless this signal is followed by feedback from the stomach indicating that food has arrived there, the animal will eat again. The stomach contains nutrient detectors that tell the brain how much food has been received. If some food is removed from the stomach, the animal eats enough to replace it, even if the experimenter tries to fool the animal by injecting an equal volume of a saline solution. However, the signal from the stomach must be calibrated; the animal must have eaten the food before in order to learn what its nutritional value is. Although an emergency signal from stretch receptors in the walls of the stomach is carried to the brain by the vagus nerve, the information about the nutrient content seems to be conveyed by means of a hormone.

Signals originating in the intestines may also produce satiety. Several investigators have suggested that cholecystokinin, released by the duodenum when it receives fat-rich food from the stomach, provides a satiety signal. The inhibitory effect of CCK on eating appears to be mediated by receptors in the pylorus and transmitted to the brain via the vagus nerve. However, studies have shown that CCK has an aversive effect. The duodenum also appears to contain nutrient detectors that send a satiety signal to the brain without the intermediate of a hormone; infusion of a mixture of lipids and fatty acids suppresses sham feeding.

Another satiety signal comes from the liver, which detects nutrients' being received from the intestines. Infusion of glucose or fructose (which does not cross the blood-brain barrier) directly into the hepatic portal vein suppresses food intake of hungry animals. The signal from the liver does not appear to be aversive; it can even be used to reinforce the consumption of a particular flavor.

Signals arising from nutrient reservoirs affect food intake on a long-term basis. Force-feeding facilitates satiety, and starvation inhibits it. A study with surgically produced "Siamese twins" showed that long-term food intake is influenced by the quantity of nutrients actually received from the digestive system. Fat tissue may provide a signal to the brain that inhibits food intake. This signal may come from the adipose tissue itself, or the information may be conveyed indirectly through increased levels of insulin, some of which makes its way to the hypothalamus.

BRAIN MECHANISMS

ALTHOUGH HUNGER AND SATIETY SIGNALS ORIGI- nate in the digestive system and in the body's nutrient reservoirs, the target of these signals is the brain. This section looks at some of the research on brain mechanisms of food intake and metabolism.

Brain Stem

Ingestive behaviors are phylogenetically ancient; obviously, all our ancestors ate and drank or died. Thus, we should expect that the basic ingestive behaviors of chewing and swallowing are programmed by phylogenetically ancient brain circuits. Indeed, studies have shown that these behaviors can be performed by decerebrate rats, whose brains were transected between the diencephalon and the midbrain (Norgren and Grill, 1982; Grill and Kaplan, 1992). Of course, they cannot approach and eat food; the experimenters must place food, in liquid form, into their mouths. Decerebrate animals can distinguish between different tastes; they drink and swallow sweet or slightly salty liquids and spit out bitter ones. They even respond to hunger and satiety signals. They drink more sucrose after having been

deprived of food for 24 hours, and they drink less of it if some sucrose is first injected directly into their stomachs.

As you learned in Chapter 7, gustatory information reaches the brain through three cranial nerves (the seventh, ninth, and tenth). The first synapse is in the nucleus of the solitary tract (NST), which is situated in the dorsal medulla. This nucleus (and the adjacent area postrema) also receives information from the internal organs, including the stomach, duodenum, and liver; thus, it is in a position to monitor hunger and satiety signals. In fact, Giza, Scott, and VanderWeele (1992) found that intravenous injections of glucose or glucagon, which produce satiety, decreased the response of neurons in the NST to the application of glucose on the tongue. These results suggest that the excitatory effect of the sweet taste of glucose is decreased by satiety signals, and that the interaction between these signals takes place in the NST.

Ritter and Taylor (1990) found that lesions of the NST and the area postrema (NST/AP) abolish both glucoprivic and lipoprivic feeding. (See *Figure 13.11.*) Besides receiving information from abdominal organs, the NST/AP may also contain nutrient-sensitive receptors, or at least receive information

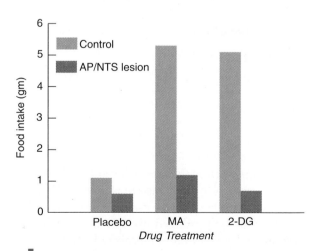

FIGURE 13.11

Effects of lesions of the nucleus of the solitary tract and adjacent area postrema on glucoprivic hunger (MA treatment) and lipoprivic hunger (2-DG treatment).

(Based on data from Ritter, S., and Taylor, J.S. *American Journal of Physiology,* 1990, *258,* R1395–R1401.)

from such receptors elsewhere in the brain stem. As we saw earlier, Ritter, et al. (1981) found that brain stem glucoprivation caused by an injection of 5-TG into the fourth ventricle produces eating.

Hypothalamus

Discoveries made in the 1940s and 1950s focused the attention of researchers interested in ingestive behavior on two regions of the hypothalamus: the lateral area and the ventromedial nucleus. For many years investigators believed that these two regions controlled hunger and satiety, respectively; one was the accelerator, and the other was the brake. The basic findings were these: After the lateral hypothalamus was destroyed, animals stopped eating or drinking (Anand and Brobeck, 1951; Teitelbaum and Stellar, 1954). Electrical stimulation of the same region would produce eating, drinking, or both behaviors. Conversely, lesions of the ventromedial hypothalamus produced overeating that led to gross obesity, whereas electrical stimulation suppressed eating (Hetherington and Ranson, 1942). The story was too simple, of course. Although both the lateral and the ventromedial hypothalamus participate in the control of food intake, both regions appear to play both excitatory and inhibitory roles.

Medial Hypothalamus

One of the most striking effects of a localized brain lesion is the overeating and obesity that is produced by a lesion of the ventromedial hypothalamus (VMH). The most plausible explanation for a lesion causing an increase in eating is that it damages satiety mechanisms in the brain, and this explanation was accepted for many years. However, the *VMH syndrome* (the set of behaviors that accompany these lesions) turns out to be much more complex than a loss of inhibitory control of eating. Animals with VMH lesions are "finicky"; they will not overeat if some quinine is added to their diet (Ferguson and Keesey, 1975.) If given a choice of different diets, animals with VMH lesions will primarily overeat carbohydrates (Sclafani and Aravich, 1983). And in addition to affecting behavior, VMH lesions disrupt the control of the autonomic nervous system. In particular, they cause an increase in parasympathetic activity of the vagus nerve, which stimulates

the secretion of insulin and inhibits the secretion of glucagon and adrenal catecholamines (Weingarten, Chang, and McDonald, 1985). Thus, the liver and adipose tissue of an animal with a VMH lesion are unable to release their nutrients during the fasting phase of metabolism; although the nutrient reservoirs are full, their contents are inaccessible. Consequently, the animal *has* to eat to keep up the supply of nutrients in its blood.

The VMH syndrome is complex anatomically as well as behaviorally. In fact, VMH lesions destroy not only the ventromedial hypothalamus but also axons that connect the paraventricular nucleus of the hypothalamus (PVN) with structures in the brain stem. Kirchgessner and Sclafani (1988) found that the destination of the axons from cells in the VMH and the PVN seems to be the nucleus of the solitary tract and the dorsal motor nucleus of the vagus. As we just saw, the nucleus of the solitary tract receives nutrient-related information from the tongue, stomach, duodenum, and liver; thus, changes in its activity could affect an animal's intake of food. The dorsal motor nucleus of the vagus nerve controls the activity of the parasympathetic axons that stimulate insulin secretion; thus, the increased insulin secretion produced by VMH lesions may be caused by disruption of this pathway.

Much of the research interest in the VMH syndrome in recent years has focused on the role of the paraventricular nucleus. (See ***Figure 13.12.***) You learned in Chapter 12 that the PVN is involved in control of the posterior pituitary gland. This nucleus also appears to play an important role in food intake—in particular, carbohydrate intake. Rats, being nocturnal animals, generally sleep and fast during the day; then, when night comes, they take their first big meal. This meal tends to be high in carbohydrates, which are the most easily digested and metabolized nutrients; later meals are higher in fats and protein (Leibowitz, Weiss, and Shor-Posner, 1988). This carbohydrate appetite appears to be under the control of neurons in the paraventricular nucleus.

Several neurotransmitters and neuromodulators have excitatory or inhibitory effects on eating when injected into the PVN. Norepinephrine (NE) stimulates the intake of carbohydrates and serotonin (5-HT) inhibits it. In addition, galanin (a peptide) stimulates the intake of fats.

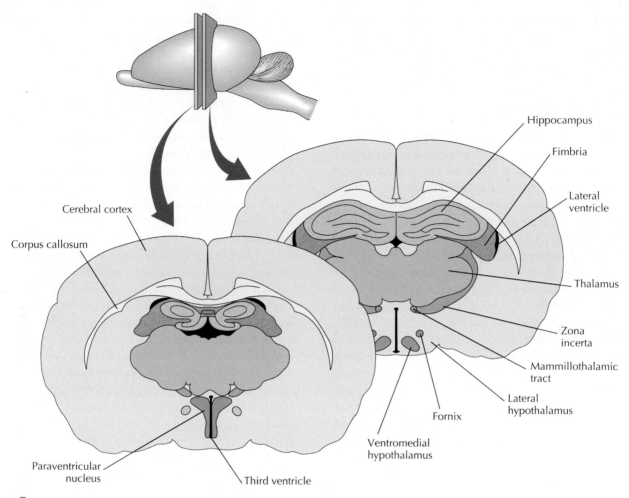

FIGURE 13.12

Cross sections through the rat brain, showing the location of regions of the hypothalamus that play a role in the control of eating and metabolism.

(Adapted from Paxinos, G., and Watson, C. *The Brain in Stereotaxic Coordinates.* Sydney: Academic Press, 1982.)

First, let us consider the role of norepinephrine. Leibowitz et al. (1985) found that microinfusion of NE into the PVN stimulates eating, especially of carbohydrates. (See *Figure 13.13.*) In fact, if clonidine (a drug that stimulates adrenergic α_2 receptors) is continuously infused into the PVN, the animal will overeat and get fat; and if AMPT (a drug that blocks the synthesis of NE) is infused, the animal will undereat and lose weight (Yee et al., 1987). Lesions of the PVN or destruction of the noradrenergic axons that enter it disrupts an animal's ability to regulate its carbohydrate intake (Shor-Posner et al.,

1986, 1987). It is not clear whether the effects of NE stimulate eating directly or whether they do so indirectly, by increasing the secretion of insulin by the pancreas. Sawchenko, Gold, and Leibowitz (1981) found that after they cut the branch of the vagus nerve that serves the pancreas, animals showed a smaller intake of food when they put NE in the PVN, which suggests that at least part of the effect may be caused by hormonal changes.

The level of NE release is correlated with an animal's eating habits. Stanley et al. (1989) placed a microdialysis probe in the paraventricular nucleus of rats and recorded the level of extracellular NE across the sleep-waking cycle. The investigators found that the level of NE showed a sharp rise just after the onset of the dark phase of the light cycle, at about the time when the animals ate their first meal. (See *Figure 13.14*.)

So far, little is known about the control of NE secretion in the PVN. As we saw in Chapter 9 ("Sleep"), the locus coeruleus, the primary source of the noradrenergic axons to the PVN, is itself controlled by two regions of the medulla. Perhaps the activity of the noradrenergic neurons is regulated by signals from nutrient detectors in the brain stem and liver, by taste signals from the tongue, and by information from the suprachiasmatic nucleus that the active period of the light-dark cycle has begun.

The release of another transmitter substance, 5-HT, has an effect opposite that of NE: It *inhibits* the eating of carbohydrates. The inhibitory effects of 5-HT are not precisely localized; Leibowitz, Weiss, and Suh (1990) found that injections of 5-HT into the PVN, VMH, and suprachiasmatic nucleus (SCN) all suppressed carbohydrate intake. This effect occurred only if the neurotransmitter was injected early in the dark part of the day-night cycle, when rats normally eat a high-carbohydrate meal. Perhaps, the authors suggest, the 5-HT interferes with

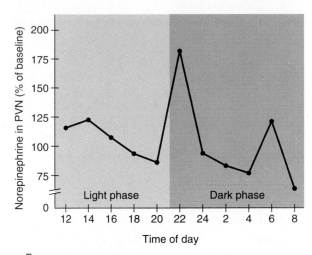

FIGURE 13.14

Extracellular norepinephrine levels in the paraventricular nucleus during the light and dark phases of the day-night cycle, as measured by microdialysis.

(Adapted from Stanley, B.G., Schwartz, D.H., Hernandez, L., Hoebel, B.G., and Leibowitz, S.F. *Life Sciences*, 1989, *45*, 275–282.)

a signal that originates in the SCN, which (as you learned in Chapter 9) serves as the circadian pacemaker.

Drugs that destroy serotonergic neurons, inhibit the synthesis of 5-HT, or block 5-HT receptors have the opposite effect of 5-HT: They *increase* food intake, especially carbohydrates (Breisch, Zemlan, and Hoebel, 1976; Saller and Stricker, 1976; Stallone and Nicolaïdis, 1989). A 5-HT agonist, *fenfluramine,* is commonly used to suppress appetite in obese people who are trying to lose weight. This drug appears to exert its effects by facilitating the effects of 5-HT in the hypothalamus.

Weiss et al. (1991) suggest that 5-HT plays a role in satiety for carbohydrates. They propose that the level of serotonin in the medial hypothalamus gradually increases during a high-carbohydrate meal, which suppresses further carbohydrate intake and shifts the animal's preference toward other macronutrients. While this hypothesis seems quite reasonable, a study by Schwartz, Hernandez, and Hoebel (1990) suggests that we need more evidence before we can accept it. These investigators implanted microdialysis probes in the medial and lateral hypothalamus of rats and measured the amount of 5-HT in the interstitial fluid. They put

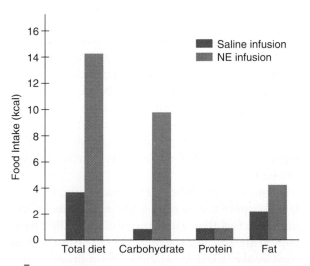

FIGURE 13.13

Effects of infusion of norepinephrine into the paraventricular nucleus on intake of carbohydrate, protein, and fat.

(Adapted from Leibowitz, S.F., Weiss, G.F., Yee, F., and Tretter, J.B. *Brain Research Bulletin*, 1985, *14*, 561–567.)

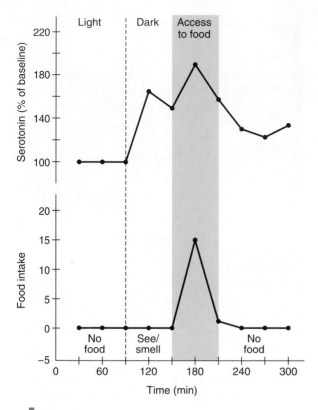

FIGURE 13.15

Extracellular serotonin (5-HT) in the lateral hypothalamus before and during the first meal during the dark portion of the day-night cycle, as measured by microdialysis. (Adapted from Schwartz, D.H., Hernandez, L., and Hoebel, B.G. *Brain Research Bulletin*, 1990, *25*, 797–802.)

the rats on a 14-hour fast and then placed a dish of food beneath the cage floor, where the animals could see and smell it. One hour later, they placed the container in the cage and permitted the animals to eat. Surprisingly, even the sight and smell of the food triggered the release of serotonin. (See *Figure 13.15.*) If the only role of serotonergic terminals in the hypothalamus 5-HT was that of satiety, we would not expect the level of 5-HT to rise until after the animals had consumed at least part of their meals. This discrepancy has not yet been explained.

Galanin, a peptide found in the brain, is colocalized with norepinephrine in terminal buttons in the hypothalamus (Melander et al., 1987). Thus, these two substances are released together. Infusion of galanin into the PVN produces eating. In particular, when rats that receive such an infusion are per-

mitted to choose among carbohydrates, fats, and proteins, they choose to eat fats (Tempel, Leibowitz, and Leibowitz, 1988). Infusion of galanin also alters the secretion of insulin and corticosterone, which indicates that it has metabolic as well as behavioral effects (Tempel and Leibowitz, 1990). Little is known so far about the conditions under which galanin is released or the mechanisms responsible for this release.

Lateral Hypothalamus

For approximately two decades after the discovery that lesions of the lateral hypothalamus abolished eating behavior, most investigators subscribed to the hypothesis that this region was a "feeding center." (Refer to *Figure 13.12.*) During the 1970s researchers finally began to pay attention to the fact that rats with these lesions have other types of behavioral impairments. In fact, they hardly move at all and pay little attention to stimuli around them. Stricker and Zigmond (1976) reviewed the existing evidence and concluded that the behavioral effects of lateral hypothalamic lesions, including the suppression of eating, were produced by damage to dopaminergic axons of the nigrostriatal bundle that passes through this region, which is known to play a role in the control of movement. However, subsequent research showed that neurotoxic lesions of the lateral hypothalamus made with ibotenic acid, which kills cells while sparing axons passing through the region, produces a long-lasting decrease in food intake and body weight (Winn, Tarbuck, and Dunnett, 1984; Dunnett, Lane, and Winn, 1985). The lesions did not affect dopamine levels in the forebrain. Thus, the neurons of the lateral hypothalamus, as well as the axons passing through this region, appear to play a role in the control of ingestive behavior.

Another piece of evidence indicating that the lateral hypothalamus plays a role in ingestive behavior is the fact that a neuromodulator called **neuropeptide Y** is an extremely potent stimulator of food intake (Clark et al., 1984). An infusion of this substance into the hypothalamus causes eating. Early studies suggested that the site of action of this compound was the paraventricular nucleus (which suggests that this discussion should have been included in the previous section), but subsequent experiments indicated a more lateral site of action. Stanley et al. (1993) used very fine metal cannulas to infuse extremely small quantities (10 nanoliters) of neuropeptide Y into various regions of the hypothalamus. They found that although infusions into many regions (including the PVN) produced eating, the most effective site was in the midlateral hypothalamus, in the region just medial to the fornix. (Refer to **Figure 13.12.**)

Neuropeptide Y produces ravenous, almost frantic eating. Rats who receive an infusion of this peptide will work very hard, pressing a lever many times for each morsel of food; they will eat food made bitter with quinine; and they will continue to drink milk even when doing so means that they receive an electric shock to their tongue (Flood and Morley, 1991; Jewett et al., 1992). The potency of this peptide suggests that it plays an important role in the control of food intake.

Neuropeptide Y is found in neurons that project from the various regions of the brain stem to the hypothalamus, colocalized with both epinephrine and norepinephrine (Sawchenko et al.,1985). Just how neuropeptide Y interacts with these catecholamines is not known, but drugs that block adrenergic α_2 receptors decrease eating produced by hypothalamic infusions of neuropeptide Y (Clark et al., 1988). Neuropeptide Y appears to be related to metabolic signals for eating; Sahu, Kalra, and Kalra (1988) found that hypothalamic levels of neuropeptide Y are increased by food deprivation and lowered by eating, and Stanley et al. (1992) found that injections of neuropeptide Y antibodies into the brain suppressed eating caused by food deprivation. This last finding, in particular, provides strong evidence that normal food intake is at least partially stimulated by neuropeptide Y.

As we saw in Chapter 12, another peptide, angiotensin, produces a variety of effects, including contraction of blood vessels, secretion of aldosterone, and thirst. These effects all serve a common purpose: increasing blood volume and maintaining normal blood pressure during a period of hypovolemia. Neuropeptide Y may also have multiple effects. Besides stimulating eating, neuropeptide Y appears to reduce energy expenditure (Egawa, Yoshimatsu, and Bray, 1991). It also suppresses ovulation by suppressing gonadotropin release, and it inhibits sexual behavior (Clark, Kalra, and Kalra, 1985). As Wade and his colleagues have shown (Wade and Schneider, 1992), when the level of available nutrients falls below a certain level in females of many species, they stop ovulating, which prevents them from becoming pregnant. Pregnancy is a costly enterprise, because the female must feed her fetuses as well as herself. The fact the neuropeptide Y suppresses both ovulation and sexual behavior as well as stimulating hunger suggests that the peptide, like angiotensin, may be responsible for effects with a common purpose.

Some neurons in the hypothalamus act as glucoreceptors; that is, they change their firing rate when glucose is infused in their vicinity. Most of these glucose-sensitive neurons are located in the lateral hypothalamus (Oomura, 1976). Himmi, Boyer, and Orsini (1988) found that many neurons in the lateral hypothalamus change their firing rate in response to spontaneous fluctuations in the level of glucose in the blood supply to the brain or in fluctuations produced by glucose infusions. These neurons may be involved in the control of eating, in the control of hormones that regulate metabolism, or both.

Rolls and his colleagues (see Rolls, 1986) have studied the response characteristics of single neurons in the lateral hypothalamus and substantia innominata (a nearby region in the basal forebrain). Burton, Rolls, and Mora (1976) found that some neurons located there respond to either the sight or taste of food, but they do so *only if the animal is hungry.* These neurons may be involved in the motivational aspects of eating. In support of this suggestion Rolls et al. (1986) found that the firing rate of these neurons was related to sensory-specific satiety. For example, one neuron showed a high rate of firing when the monkey was shown a peanut, a banana, an orange, or a syringe that was used to squirt a glucose solution into its mouth. The animal was then given repeated drinks of the glucose solution. At first it drank the solution enthusiastically, but after a while acceptance turned to rejection. At the same time the neuron responded less and less when the monkey was shown the syringe. However, the neuron still responded to the sight of a peanut, an orange, or a banana. The monkey was then allowed to eat all the bananas it wanted. The neuron stopped

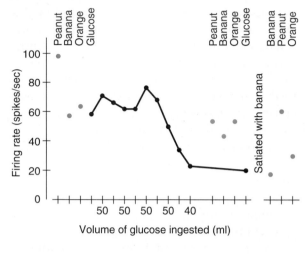

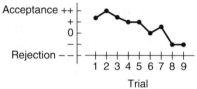

FIGURE 13.16

Sensory-specific satiety. The graph plots the firing rate of a single neuron in a monkey's lateral hypothalamus when the animal is shown various foods. The smaller graph at the bottom indicates ratings of the monkey's acceptance or rejection of the glucose solution, presented nine times.

(Adapted from Rolls, E.T., Murzi, E., Yaxley, S., Thorpe, S.J., and Simpson, S.J. *Brain Research*, 1986, *368*, 79–86.)

responding to the sight of the banana, but it still responded to the sight of the peanut. It pretty much stopped responding to the sight of an orange, too, but perhaps after drinking 440 milliliters of a glucose solution and eating all the banana one wants, an orange provides less of a flavor contrast than a peanut does. (See *Figure 13.16.*)

⦀ INTERIM SUMMARY

The brain stem contains neural circuits that are able to control acceptance or rejection of sweet or bitter foods and can even be modulated by satiation or physiological hunger signals, such as a decrease in glucose metabolism or the presence of food in the digestive system. The nucleus of the solitary tract

and area postrema (NST/AP) receive signals from the tongue, stomach, small intestine, and liver; these signals interact and help control food intake. Lesions of the NST/AP disrupt both glucoprivic and lipoprivic eating.

Lesions of the ventromedial hypothalamus produce overeating and obesity, and electrical or chemical stimulation of this area inhibits eating. However, this region is not a simple "satiety center." The lesions make an animal finicky and increase the secretion of insulin (thus forcing the animal to eat more). Some (perhaps most) of the VMH syndrome is caused by damage to fibers from the ventromedial hypothalamus and PVN to the nucleus of the solitary tract and the dorsal motor nucleus of the vagus. This damage increases fat storage as well as eating.

The first meal of the active portion of the dark-light cycle tends to be high in carbohydrates. It is preceded by a large increase in norepinephrine in the PVN. In addition, when NE is infused into the PVN, the animal eats—especially carbohydrates. The response may be a result of changes in the activity of the autonomic nervous system as well as direct stimulation of circuits that control eating.

Another transmitter substance, 5-HT, has an inhibitory effect on eating in the PVN. Although investigators suggest that 5-HT is involved in satiety, it appears to be secreted even before a meal is consumed. The most common appetite suppressant, fenfluramine, is a 5-HT agonist. Infusions of galanin, a neuropeptide colocalized with NE, increases fat intake and alters metabolism through its effects on the endocrine system.

Lesions of the lateral hypothalamus abolish eating (along with many other behaviors), and stimulation elicits it. Although many of the behavioral effects involve dopamine-secreting axons that pass through this region, experiments with neurotoxic lesions indicate that the lateral hypothalamus, by itself, plays an excitatory role in eating. Neuropeptide Y may be a "hunger peptide." Fasting causes this substance to be secreted in the lateral hypothalamus, and eating reduces its secretion. When neuropeptide Y is infused into the midlateral hypothalamus, it stimulates vigorous eating. It also suppresses sexual behavior and stops ovulation—responses that occur when food is scarce. The lat-

TABLE 13.1

Neurochemicals That Affect Eating When Injected into the Hypothalamus

Neurochemical	Site of action	Effect
Norepinephrine (NE)	Paraventricular nucleus	Stimulates carbohydrate intake
Serotonin (5-HT)	Paraventricular nucleus	Inhibits carbohydrate intake
Galanin	Lateral hypothalamus	Stimulates fat intake
Neuropeptide Y	Lateral hypothalamus	Stimulates ravenous eating; effect suppressed by α_2 blockers

eral hypothalamus contains glucose receptors and neurons whose firing rate increases when food-related stimuli are presented and the animal is hungry. Studies with sensory-specific satiety show that the activity of these neurons is closely tied to food-related motivation.

Table 13.1. summarizes the substances mentioned in this section, their effects, and their probable sites of action.

EATING DISORDERS

UNFORTUNATELY, SOME PEOPLE ARE SUSCEPTIBLE to eating disorders. Some people grow obese, even though our society regards this condition as unattractive and even though obese people tend to have more health problems—and to die sooner—than people of normal weight. Other people (especially young women) can become obsessed with losing weight, eating little and increasing their activity level until their body weight becomes extremely low—often fatally so. Others manage to keep from losing or gaining weight, but often lose control of the intake, eating enormous amounts of food and then taking strong laxatives or forcing themselves to vomit. Has what we have learned about the physiology of appetite helped us understand these conditions?

Obesity

Obesity is a widespread problem that can have serious medical consequences. In the United States approximately 34 million people are overweight, 12.5 million of them severely so (Kuczmarski, 1992).

Possible Causes

There are undoubtedly many causes of obesity, including learning and innate or acquired differences in metabolism. The behavior of eating, like most other behaviors, is subject to modification through learning. Unfortunately, many aspects of modern, industrialized societies tend to weaken physiological controls over eating. For example, as children we learn to eat what is put on our plates; indeed, many children are praised for eating all that they have been given and punished for failing to do so. As Birch et al. (1987) showed, the effect of this kind of training can be to make children less sensitive to the nutrient content of their diet. As we get older, our metabolic requirements decrease; and if we continue to eat as we did when we were younger, we tend to accumulate fat. The inhibitory signals associated with food consumption are certainly not absolute; they can be overridden by habit or by the simple pleasure of ingesting good-tasting food. In fact, the arrangement of meals into courses followed by dessert inhibits the development of sensory-specific satiety and encourages increased food intake.

Obesity is extremely difficult to treat; the enormous financial success of diet books, fat farms, and weight reduction programs attests to the trouble people have losing weight. More precisely, many programs help people lose weight initially, but then the weight is quickly regained. Kramer et al. (1989) reported that four to five years after participating in a fifteen-week behavioral weight loss program, fewer than 3 percent of the participants managed to maintain the weight loss they had achieved during the program.

Many psychological variables have been suggested as causes of obesity, including field dependence, lack of impulse control, poor ability to delay gratification, and maladaptive eating styles (primarily eating too fast). However, in a review of the literature Rodin, Schank, and Striegel-Moore (1989) found that none of these suggestions have received empirical support. Rodin and her colleagues also found that unhappiness and depression seem to be the *effects* of obesity, not its causes, and that dieting behavior seems to make the problem worse. (As we shall see later in this section, repeated bouts of weight loss and gain may make subsequent weight loss more difficult to achieve.)

One reason that many people have so much difficulty losing weight is that metabolic factors appear to play an important role in obesity. In fact, a good case can be made that obesity is most often not an *eating disorder* (despite the title of this section), but a *metabolic disorder*. Rodin and her colleagues found that most studies comparing the amounts of food eaten by obese people and people of normal weight failed to show a significant difference. But unfortunately, we cannot take all these studies at face value. Lichtman et al. (1992) studied a group of obese people who had a history of *diet resistance*—difficulty in losing weight even on a reduced-calorie diet. The investigators made direct measurements of these people's actual intake and physical activity during a fourteen-day stay in a controlled environment and compared these measurements with self-reports. They found the subjects underreported their actual intake by an average of 47 percent and overreported their physical activity by 51 percent. The subjects were surprised and distressed to learn afterward that their reported figures were so far off the mark;

apparently, they were not intentionally trying to deceive the investigators.

Almost all excess body weight is carried in the form of fat. Normally, we carry a certain amount of fat in our long-term nutrient reservoir, making deposits and withdrawals each day during the absorptive and fasting phases of metabolism but keeping the total amount stable. Obesity occurs when deposits exceed withdrawals. We expend energy in two basic ways: through exercise (muscular activity) and through the production of heat. Actually, *most* of our energy expenditure is in the form of heat production; according to Calles-Escandon and Horton (1992), 70–85 percent of a person's energy expenditure is made through their resting metabolism and the energy needed to digest and assimilate food. Physical activity accounts for a small proportion of energy expenditure.

Although many weight loss programs emphasize exercise as well as restriction of caloric intake, most studies have found that exercise does not facilitate weight loss (Calles-Escandon and Horton, 1992; Sweeney et al., 1993). As Segal and Pi-Sunyer (1989) noted, if food intake were kept constant, an obese person would have to increase his or her activity level tremendously in order to lower body weight. Of course, exercise brings with it many benefits, such as cardiovascular fitness and a sense of well-being, so it is a worthwhile endeavor for people of all body weights.

Just as cars differ in their fuel efficiency, so do people. Rose and Williams (1961) studied pairs of people who were matched for weight, height, age, and activity. Some of these matched pairs differed by a factor of two in the number of calories they ate each day. People with an efficient metabolism have calories left over to deposit in the long-term nutrient reservoir; thus, they have difficulty keeping this reservoir from growing. In contrast, people with an inefficient metabolism can eat large meals without getting fat. Thus, whereas a fuel-efficient automobile is desirable, a fuel-efficient body runs the risk of becoming obese.

Nonobese people respond to overeating very differently from obese people. For example, Sims and Horton (1968) enlisted the participation of some prison inmates in an experiment to determine the effects of overeating on body weight. The subjects, men of normal weight, were fed varied and tasty meals several times a day and were asked to eat all they could. Some participants ate up to 8000 calories a day, an enormous quantity for relatively sedentary people. Their weight gain was rather modest, and at the end of the experiment, when the subjects were permitted to select their own diet, they quickly returned to their normal weights.

Differences in body weight (perhaps reflecting differences in metabolism) appear to have a hereditary basis. Price and Gottesman (1991) reported on twin studies indicating that between 40 and 60 percent of the variability in body fat is due to genetic differences. Bouchard (1989, 1991) concluded that heredity probably plays a role in people's resting metabolic rate, in the amount of heat produced by the body after a meal, in the energy expended during exercise, and in the likelihood that ingested calories will be stored as fat. And the environment in which people are raised apparently has no significant effect on their body weight as adults; Stunkard et al. (1986) found that the body weight of a sample of people who had been adopted as infants was highly correlated with their *biological* parents but not with their *adoptive* parents. Sørensen et al. (1989) came to similar conclusions in a study comparing adopted people with their full and half siblings, with whom they had not been raised.

Why are there genetic differences in metabolic efficiency? James and Trayhurn (1981) suggest that under some environmental conditions metabolic efficiency is advantageous. That is, in places where food is only intermittently available in sufficient quantities, being able to stay alive on small amounts of food and to store up extra nutrients in the form of fat when food becomes available for a while is a highly adaptive trait. Therefore, people's metabolic rates may reflect the nature of the environment experienced by their ancestors. For example, physically active lactating women in Gambia manage to maintain their weight on only 1500 calories per day (Whitehead et al., 1978). This efficiency allows people to survive in environments in which food is scarce. However, in a society that produces an abundance of food, an inefficient metabolism is a definite advantage.

An animal model of obesity—the genetically obese Zucker rat—has suggested some leads for researchers interested in understanding the causes of obesity. Zucker rats possess a pair of defective genes that lead to their condition (Zucker and Zucker, 1961). They have a chronically high level of insulin in their blood and show various other endocrine changes. Many investigators believe the obesity of the Zucker rat is caused by abnormalities in the brain. For example, the level of neuropeptide Y in the hypothalamus is abnormally high (Beck et al., 1990). (As we saw earlier in this chapter, infusions of neuropeptide Y cause ravenous eating and may affect metabolism, as well.) Evidence for increased hypothalamic neuropeptide Y is seen early in the life of a Zucker rat, even before its obesity develops (Beck et al, 1991; Sanacora, Finkelstein, and White, 1992). Thus, the overabundance of this peptide may be a cause of the obesity. Whether human obesity may be linked to disregulation of hypothalamic neuropeptide Y is not known.

Another factor—this one nonhereditary—can influence people's metabolism. Many obese people diet and then relapse, thus undergoing large changes in body weight. Some investigators have suggested that starvation causes the body's metabolism to become more efficient. For example, Brownell et al. (1986) fed rats a diet that made them become obese and then restricted their food intake until their body weights returned to normal. Then they made the rats fat again and reduced their food intake again. The first time, the rats became fat within 46 days and returned to normal within 21 days. The second time, they became fat in only 14 days but required 46 days to lose the excess weight. Clearly, the experience of gaining and losing large amounts of body weight altered the animals' metabolic efficiency.

Steen, Oppliger, and Brownell (1988) obtained evidence that the same phenomenon (which we can call the "yo-yo" effect) takes place in humans. They measured the resting metabolic rate in two groups of high school wrestlers: those who fasted just before a meet and binged afterward, and those who did not. (The motive for fasting just before a match is to qualify for a lower-weight group, where the competition is presumably less challenging.) The investigators found that wrestlers who fasted and binged had a resting metabolic rate 14 percent lower than those who did not. Possibly, these people will have difficulty maintaining a normal body weight as they get older.

In normal animals overeating causes a rise in metabolic rate, which partly compensates for the increased intake of calories. Rothwell and Stock (1979) fed rats a very palatable diet consisting of supermarket "junk" foods such as potato chips and cookies, which caused them to increase their daily caloric intake greatly. Despite an average caloric increase of 80 percent, weight gain was only 27 percent higher than that of control animals. For this effect to occur, the animals would have had to increase their energy expenditure by approximately 100 percent. Indeed, their resting oxygen consumption was consistently higher than that of control animals. However, the increase was probably not caused by an increase in physical activity, because the animals were housed in pairs in small cages, and they would have had to walk 6 kilometers per day to expend this much energy.

This phenomenon occurs in humans, as well. Welle, Nair, and Campbell (1989) had human subjects overeat by 1600 calories per day for ten days. At the end of that time their metabolic rate had increased by 22 percent. Even a single meal—or stimuli associated with eating—can cause a rise in metabolic rate. LeBlanc and Cabanac (1989) placed human subjects in a chamber so that they could continuously monitor their oxygen consumption and, thereby, calculate their metabolic rate. They found that eating a sugar pie or tasting it, chewing it, and spitting it out again caused an increase in metabolic rate. Even when the subjects simply went through the motions of eating—moving their hands to their mouths and making chewing and swallowing motions—their metabolic rates increased slightly. (See *Figure 13.17*.)

What are the physiological differences between people with efficient and inefficient metabolisms? So far, no one knows for sure. Research with laboratory animals has focused on specialized adipose cells that convert calories of food directly into heat. These cells are especially important for hibernating animals, who must warm up before they can wake in the spring. Heat production by this tissue is called **nonshivering thermogenesis** (*thermo*, "heat"; *gene-*

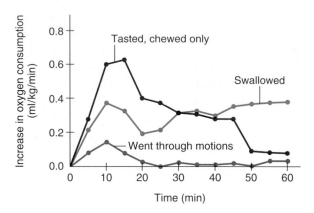

FIGURE 13.17

Effects of eating a sugar pie, tasting and chewing it only, or simply going through the motions on metabolic rate of human subjects, as measured by oxygen consumption.
(Adapted from LeBlanc, J., and Cabanac, M. *Physiology and Behavior*, 1989, 46, 479–482.)

sis, "creation"). These specialized fat cells are rich in mitochondria, which serve as sites of fuel breakdown and heat production (Nichols, 1979). The mitochondria give the fat a brown appearance, which gives this tissue the name **brown adipose tissue.** (The fat tissue that comprises the body's long-term nutrient reservoir is called *white* adipose tissue.)

In rats, feeding-induced thermogenesis appears to be mediated primarily by the activity of the brown adipose tissue. For example, Glick, Teague, and Bray (1981) found that a single meal increased the metabolism of brown adipose tissue by up to 200 percent. Studies have shown that the brown adipose tissue of an obese strain of rats does not respond to a meal (Triandafillou and Himms-Hagen, 1983); thus, at least one form of genetic obesity is accompanied by deficient meal-induced thermogenesis.

The excitatory effect of a meal on the metabolic activity of brown adipose tissue is controlled by the medial hypothalamus. After the medial hypothalamus has been surgically destroyed, a meal no longer produces a rise in the temperature of the brown adipose tissue (Hogan, Himms-Hagen, and Coscina, 1985). Stimulation of several regions in the ventromedial hypothalamus, including the PVN, increase the temperature of brown adipose tissue (Freeman and Wellman, 1987; Amir 1990a, 1990b).

Does this phenomenon play a role in the development of obesity in humans? Although humans do possess some brown adipose tissue, investigators disagree about its role in meal-induced thermogenesis and obesity (Himms-Hagen, 1980; Blaza, 1983). Clearly, metabolic differences are an important cause of human obesity, but the sources of these differences are not yet known.

Treatment of Obesity

Whatever the cause of obesity, the metabolic fact of life is this: If calories in exceed calories out, then body fat will increase. Because it is difficult to increase the "calories out" side of the equation enough to bring an obese person's weight back to normal, most treatments for obesity attempt to reduce the "calories in." The extraordinary difficulty that obese people have in reducing caloric intake for a sustained period of time (that is, for the rest of their lives) has led to the development of some extraordinary means. In this section I shall describe mechanical, surgical, and pharmacological methods that have been devised to make obese people eat less.

In order to eat, we must open our mouths. This obvious fact led to the development of jaw wiring, a procedure in which wires are attached to a person's teeth in order to keep the jaw from opening. The patient is not left to starve; he or she is given a liquid diet to sip through a straw. Of course, there is no guarantee that a person will ingest fewer calories each day simply because he or she is deprived of the opportunity to chew. In fact, Munro et al. (1987) reported that some of their patients managed to *gain* weight on a liquid diet. However, many patients do manage to lose weight. Unfortunately, almost all of them regain it once the wires are removed, and many become even more obese than they were when they started out.

To reduce the recidivism rate, some therapists have fastened a nylon cord around the waist of their patients after they had lost weight through a jaw-wiring procedure. The ends of the cord were fused together so that the cord could not be removed without cutting it. Unfortunately, about half of the patients did just that.

Surgeons have also become involved in trying to help obese people lose weight. The procedures they have developed either reduce the amount of food that can be eaten during a meal or interfere with absorption of calories from the intestines. Surgery has been aimed at the stomach, the small intestine, or both.

The most common surgical procedure for reducing food intake has been to make the person's stomach smaller. Early procedures actually removed some of the stomach, but more recent methods have stapled part of it shut or have put bands around it so that it can expand only a limited amount—a procedure known as *gastroplasty* (literally, "a reshaping of the stomach"). Ideally, gastroplasty should result in a feeling of satiety after the ingestion of a small amount of food. But in fact, the surgery usually produces *nimiety*, or an aversive feeling of overfullness (from the Latin *nimius,* "excessive"). The meal stops not because the patients feel satisfied but because they feel so uncomfortable that they cannot go on.

Surgeons have developed several procedures that reduce the absorption of food from the intestines. All of these procedures rearrange the intestines so that food takes a shorter path to the large intestine, leaving less time for nutrients to be absorbed. The unabsorbed nutrients are evacuated from the body, of course, so it should come as no surprise that diarrhea and flatulence (excessive intestinal gas) are commonly associated with these procedures. Many types of intestinal bypass operations do not simply interfere with absorption—they also reduce food intake by producing nimiety. After some surgical procedures relatively undigested food is dumped into regions of the intestines that normally receive only well-digested food, and the result is a feeling of discomfort.

Besides producing diarrhea and flatulence, intestinal bypass surgery can produce undesirable side effects such as bacterial overgrowth and production of toxins in a bypassed segment of intestine; deficiencies of iron, vitamin B_{12}, vitamin B_1, or protein; and abnormalities in calcium metabolism. A severe vitamin B_1 (thiamine) deficiency can damage the nervous system; as you will learn in Chapter 15, the result can be a permanent memory loss. Of course, if a patient's condition is carefully monitored by a physician after receiving the surgery, these complications can be avoided or corrected; but not all patients cooperate with their physicians for postsurgical care.

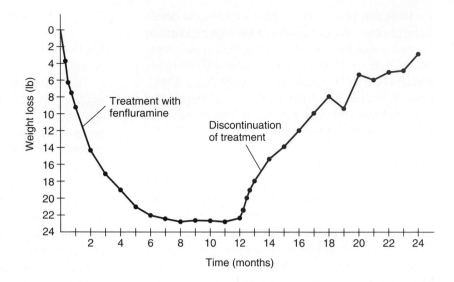

FIGURE 13.18

Mean weight change during twelve months of treatment with fenfluramine.

(Adapted from Bray, 1992; after Hudson, K.D. *Journal of the Royal College of General Practitioner,* 1977, *27,* 497–501.)

In order to avoid the necessity of surgery, some therapists have tried putting balloons in people's stomachs and then inflating them to reduce the amount of food they will hold. The results have not been entirely successful; as Kral (1989) noted, "After a brief period of extraordinary financial success for the gastroenterologists placing the balloons, the 'Gastric Bubble' has been taken off the market in the United States, largely because of proven lack of efficacy and the realization that chronic balloon placement is not tolerated by the gastric mucosa" (p. 254).

A less drastic form of therapy for obesity—drug treatment—shows some promise. As we saw earlier in this chapter, the stimulation of 5-HT receptors in the PVN suppresses eating. A review by Bray (1992) concludes that serotonin agonists can be of benefit in weight loss programs. Figure 13.18 shows the effects of *fenfluramine,* a drug that specifically inhibits the reuptake of serotonin, on the body weight of a group of 176 patients. As you can see, the patients showed a stable weight loss during the twelve months they took the drug but then largely regained their weight after they discontinued it. (See *Figure 13.18.*)

As Bray notes, regulatory agencies are reluctant to endorse the long-term use of drugs to treat obesity, which is most assuredly a chronic problem. Certainly, drugs such as fenfluramine do not *cure* obesity; but then many drugs in common use do not cure the conditions they are used for. For example, glaucoma is treated by pilocaprine and ulcers are treated by cymetadine. If these drugs are discontinued, the glaucoma and the ulcers will recur. But according to Bray, physicians have been disciplined by regulatory boards for prescribing appetite-suppressing drugs for more than a few weeks. He suggests that this double standard is based on the common belief that obesity results from a failure of will—that people could lose weight if they would only push themselves away from the table sooner.

The variety of methods—surgical, mechanical, behavioral, and pharmacological—that therapists and surgeons have developed to treat obesity attests to the tenacity of the problem. The basic difficulty, beyond that caused by having an efficient metabolism, is that eating is pleasurable and satiety signals are easy to ignore or override. Despite the fact that relatively little success has been seen until now, I am personally optimistic about what the future may hold. I think that if we learn more about the physiology of hunger signals, satiety signals, and the reinforcement provided by eating, we will be able to develop safe and effective drugs that attenuate the signals that encourage us to eat and strengthen those that encourage us to stop eating. Of course, we will also have to overcome our prejudices against the long-term use of these drugs.

Anorexia Nervosa/Bulimia Nervosa

Most people, if they have an eating problem, tend to overeat. However, some people, especially young adolescent women, have the opposite problem: They eat too little, even to the point of starvation. This disorder is called **anorexia nervosa.** Another eating disorder, **bulimia nervosa,** is characterized by a loss of control of food intake. (The term *bulimia* comes from the Greek *bous,* "ox," and *limos,* "hunger.") People with bulimia nervosa periodically gorge themselves with food, especially dessert or snack food, and especially in the afternoon or evening. These binges are usually followed by self-induced vomiting or the use of laxatives, along with feelings of depression and guilt (Mawson, 1974; Halmi, 1978). With this combination of binging and purging, the net nutrient intake (and consequently, the body weight) of bulimics can vary; Weltzin et al. (1991) report that 44 percent of bulimics undereat, 37 percent eat a normal amount, and 44 percent overeat. Episodes of bulimia are seen in some patients with anorexia nervosa.

The literal meaning of the word *anorexia* suggests a loss of appetite, but people with this disorder are usually interested in—even preoccupied with—food. They may enjoy preparing meals for others to consume, collect recipes, and even hoard food that they do not eat. Broberg and Bernstein (1989) presented anorexic and lean (but nonanorexic) young women with a warm, appetizing cinnamon roll. They cut the roll and said that they could eat it if they wanted. For the next 10 minutes the experimenters withdrew blood samples and analyzed the insulin content. They found that both groups of subjects showed an increase in insulin level; surprisingly, the increase was even higher in the anorexic subjects. Thus, we cannot conclude that anorexics are simply unresponsive to food. (See *Figure 13.19.*) Incidentally, as you might expect, the normal subjects ate the roll, but the anorexics did not, saying that they were not hungry.

Although anorexics may not be oblivious to the effects of food, they express an intense fear of becoming obese, which continues even if they become dangerously thin. Many exercise by cycling,

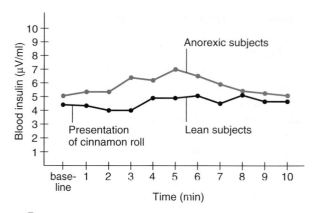

FIGURE 13.19

Effects of the sight and smell of a warm cinnamon roll on insulin secretion in anorexic women and thin, nonanorexic women.

(Adapted from Broberg, D.J., and Bernstein, I.L. *Physiology and Behavior,* 1989, *45,* 871–874.)

running, or almost constant walking and pacing. Studies with animals suggest that the increased activity may be a result of the fasting. When rats are deprived of food, they will spend more and more time running in a wheel if one is available, even though doing so means that the animals will lose weight faster (Routtenberg, 1968). Some investigators believe that the exercise stimulates the breakdown of lipids into fatty acids and glycerol and thus actually reduces feelings of hunger. Wilckens, Schweiger, and Pirke (1992) found that deprivation-induced wheel running can be inhibited by drugs that stimulate 5-HT$_{1C}$ receptors.

The fact that anorexia nervosa is seen primarily in young women has prompted both biological and social explanations. Most psychologists favor the latter, concluding that the emphasis our society places on slimness—especially in women—is responsible for this disorder. However, the success of therapy is not especially encouraging; Ratnasuriya et al. (1991) reported that twenty years later, only 29 percent of a group of patients treated for anorexia nervosa showed a good recovery. Almost 15 percent of the patients had died of suicide or complications of the disease. Many anorexics suffer from osteoporosis, and bone fractures are common. When the weight loss becomes severe enough, they cease menstruating. Two disturbing reports (Artmann, et al., 1985; Lankenau et al., 1985) indicate that CT scans revealed enlarged ventricles and widened sulci, which indicates loss of brain tissue. The widened sulci, but not the enlarged ventricles, apparently return to normal after recovery.

There is good evidence, primarily from twin studies, that hereditary factors play an important role in the development of anorexia (Russell and Treasure, 1989). The existence of hereditary factors suggests that abnormalities in physiological mechanisms may be involved. As you might suspect, many investigators have suggested that anorexia and bulimia may be caused by biochemical or structural abnormalities in the brain mechanisms that control metabolism or eating. In a review of the literature Fava et al. (1989) reported that studies have found evidence for changes in NE, 5-HT, and opioids in people with anorexia nervosa, and changes in NE and 5-HT in people with bulimia nervosa. Studies have reported changes in endocrine levels of anorexic patients, but these changes are probably effects of the disorder, not causes. In most cases, when a patient recovers, the endocrine system returns to normal.

Some investigators have suggested that neuropeptide Y may play a role in anorexia. Kaye et al. (1990) found elevated levels of neuropeptide Y in the cerebrospinal fluid of severely underweight anorexics. However, once the patients regained their normal weights, the levels of the peptide returned to normal. The investigators suggest that the increased level of neuropeptide Y is a response to the loss of weight and at least partly accounts for the obsession with food that is typical in anorexia. In addition, the peptide may be responsible for the absence of menstruation in these patients. (You will recall that neuropeptide Y suppresses ovulation in laboratory animals.)

We cannot rule out the possibility that some biochemical disturbance in brain functions related to metabolism or food intake underlie anorexia nervosa. Measurements of neurotransmitters, neuromodulators, and their metabolites in the cerebrospinal fluid is a crude and indirect indication of the release and activity of these substances in the brain. Unfortunately, we do not have a good animal model of anorexia to study in the laboratory.

Researchers have tried to treat anorexia nervosa with many drugs that increase appetite in non-anorexics or in laboratory animals—for example, antipsychotic medications, drugs that stimulate adrenergic α_2 receptors, L-DOPA, and THC (the active ingredient in marijuana). Unfortunately, none of these drugs have shown themselves to be helpful (Mitchell, 1989). One study (Halmi et al., 1986) found that cyproheptadine, an antihistaminergic drug that also has an antiserotonergic effect, may speed the recovery of anorexics. The drug only aided patients who did not exhibit bulimia; the drug actually interfered with the recovery of those who did exhibit bulimia. These results have not yet been confirmed by other investigators. And in any event, the fact that anorexics are usually obsessed with food (and show high levels of neuropeptide Y in their CSF) suggests that the disorder is not caused by the absence of hunger. Researchers have had better luck with bulimia nervosa; several studies suggest that serotonin agonists such as fenfluramine (also used to treat obesity) may aid in the treatment of this disorder (Kennedy and Goldbloom, 1991).

Anorexia nervosa is a serious condition; understanding its causes is more than an academic matter. We can hope that research on the biological and social control of feeding and metabolism will help us understand this puzzling and dangerous disorder.

‖‖‖ INTERIM SUMMARY

Two sets of eating disorders, obesity and anorexia/bulimia nervosa, present serious health problems. Although environmental effects, such as learning to eat everything on the plate and arranging food in appetizing courses, may contribute to overeating, the most important cause appears to be an efficient metabolism, which permits fat to accumulate easily. Metabolic rates are controlled by hereditary and environmental factors. Adoption studies find no evidence that a person's early environment has an effect on his or her body weight in adulthood. Studies with the obese Zucker rat suggests that biochemical abnormalities in the hypothalamus, including hypersecretion of neuropeptide Y, may play a role in obesity. Ironically, dieting—especially repeated bouts of weight changes—may promote an increase in metabolic efficiency and make further weight loss more difficult to achieve. The "yo-yo" effect has been demonstrated both in rats and humans.

When we overeat, our metabolic rate goes up, which helps burn off some of the additional calories. In rats the most important furnace for these calories is the brown adipose tissue, whose activity is regulated by the VMH through its control of the sympathetic axons. However, the physiological causes of the differences in people's metabolism are not yet known.

Researchers have tried many mechanical, surgical, and pharmacological treatments for obesity, but no panacea has yet been found. The best hope probably comes from drugs; specific serotonin agonists suppress eating and decrease body weight, but so far

the medical community has been reluctant to use such drugs on a long-term basis. Anorexia nervosa is a serious—even life-threatening—disorder. Although anorexic patients avoid eating, they often remain preoccupied with food, and their insulin level rises when they are presented with an appetizing stimulus. Bulimia nervosa (sometimes associated with anorexia) consists of periodic binging and purging.

Researchers are beginning to study possible abnormalities in the regulation of transmitter substances and neuropeptides that seem to play a role in normal control of feeding to see whether medical treatments can be discovered. So far, no useful drugs have been found to treat anorexia nervosa; but fenfluramine, a serotonin agonist also used to treat obesity, may help suppress episodes of bulimia.

New Terms

Some Facts About Metabolism

glycogen *(GLY ko jen)* p. 396

insulin p. 396

glucagon *(GLOO ka gahn)* p. 397

triglyceride *(try GLISS er ide)* p. 397

glycerol *(GLISS er all)* p. 397

fatty acid p. 397

fasting phase p. 398

absorptive phase p. 398

What Starts a Meal?

sensory-specific satiety p. 401

conditioned flavor aversion p. 402

glucostatic hypothesis p. 404

glucoprivation p. 405

lipoprivation p. 405

capsaicin *(kap SAY sin)* p. 406

What Stops a Meal?

cholecystokinin *(coal i sis toe KY nin)* p. 410

sham feeding p. 411

intraperitoneal (IP) *(in tra pair i toe NEE ul)* p. 411

Brain Mechanisms

galanin *(GAL a nin)* p. 418

neuropeptide Y p. 418

Eating Disorders

nonshivering thermogenesis p. 424

brown adipose tissue p. 424

anorexia nervosa p. 427

bulimia nervosa p. 427

Suggested Readings

Friedman, M.I., Tordoff, M.G., and Kare, M.R. *Chemical Senses. Vol. 4: Appetite and Nutrition.* New York: Dekker, 1991.

Keesey, R.E., and Powley, T.L. The regulation of body weight. *Annual Review of Psychology,* 1986, *37,* 109-134.

Le Magnen, J. *Neurobiology of Feeding and Nutrition.* San Diego: Academic Press, 1992.

Ritter, R.C., Ritter, S., and Barnes, C.D. *Feeding Behavior: Neural and Humoral Controls.* New York: Academic Press, 1986.

Stricker, E.M. *Handbook of Behavioral Neurobiology. Vol. 10. Neurobiology of Food and Fluid Intake.* New York: Plenum Press, 1990.

Walsh, B.T. *Eating Disorders.* Washington, D.C.: American Psychiatric Press, 1988.

Winick, M. *Control of Appetite.* New York: John Wiley & Sons, 1988.

CHAPTER 14

Learning and Memory: Basic Mechanisms

The Nature of Learning
Interim Summary

Perceptual Learning
• Visual Learning
• Auditory Learning
• Modeling the Brain's Ability to Learn:
  Neural Networks
  Interim Summary

Mechanisms of Synaptic Plasticity
• Induction of Long-Term Potentiation
• Role of NMDA Receptors
• Mechanism of Synaptic Strengthening
• Modulation of Long-Term Potentiation
• Other Forms of Long-Term Potentiation
• Role of Long-Term Potentiation in Learning
  Interim Summary

S-R Learning: Classical Conditioning
Interim Summary

S-R Learning: Instrumental Conditioning
• Discovery of Reinforcing Brain
  Stimulation
• Mechanisms of Reinforcing Brain
  Stimulation
• Functions of the Reinforcement System
  Interim Summary

EXPERIENCES CHANGE US; ENCOUNTERS with our environment alter our behavior by modifying our nervous system. As many investigators have said, an understanding of the physiology of memory is the ultimate challenge to neuroscience research. The brain is complex, and so is learning and remembering. Although the individual changes that occur within the cells of the brain may be relatively simple, the brain consists of many billions of neurons. Therefore, isolating and identifying the particular changes that are responsible for a particular memory is exceedingly difficult. Similarly, although the elements of a particular learning task may be simple, its implications for an organism may be complex. The behavior that the investigator observes and measures may be only one of many that change as a result of an experience. However, despite the difficulties, the long years of work finally seem to be paying off. New approaches and new methods have evolved from old ones, and real progress has been made in understanding the anatomy and physiology of learning and remembering.

THE NATURE OF LEARNING

LEARNING REFERS TO THE PROCESS BY WHICH experiences change our nervous system and, hence, our behavior. We refer to these changes as *memories.* Although it is convenient to describe memories as if they were notes placed in filing cabinets, this is certainly not the way experiences are reflected within the brain. Experiences are not "stored"; rather, they change the way we perceive, perform, think, and plan. They do so by physically changing the structure of the nervous system, altering neural circuits that participate in perceiving, performing, thinking, and planning.

The primary function of the ability to learn is to develop behaviors that are adapted to an ever-changing environment. The ability to learn permits us to find food when we are hungry, warmth when we are cold, companions when we are lonely. It also permits us to avoid objects or situations that might harm us. However, the fact that the ultimate function of learning is a useful change in behavior does not mean that learning takes place only in the parts of the brain that control movement. Learning can take at least four basic forms: perceptual learning, stimulus-response learning, motor learning, and relational learning. This chapter discusses the first three forms, and Chapter 15 discusses relational learning.

Perceptual learning is the ability to learn to recognize stimuli that have been seen before. The primary function of this type of learning is the ability to identify and categorize objects (including other members of our own species) and situations. Unless we have learned to recognize something, we cannot learn how we should behave with respect to it—we will not profit from our experiences with it, and profiting from experience is what learning is all about.

Each of our sensory systems is capable of perceptual learning. We can learn to recognize objects by their visual appearance, the sounds they make, how they feel, or how they smell. We can recognize people by the shape of their faces, the movements they make when they walk, or the sound of their voices. When we hear people talk, we can recognize the words they are saying and, perhaps, their emotional state. As we shall see, perceptual learning appears to be accomplished primarily by changes in the sensory association cortex. That is, learning to recognize complex visual stimuli involves changes in the visual association cortex, learning to recognize complex auditory stimuli involves changes in the auditory association cortex, and so on. (Very simple stimuli, such as changes in brightness, do not require the neocortex; learning that involves these stimuli can be accomplished by subcortical components of the sensory systems.)

Stimulus-response learning is the ability to learn to perform a particular behavior when a particular stimulus is present. Thus, it involves the establishment of connections between circuits involved in perception with those involved in movement. The behavior could be an automatic response such as a defensive reflex, or it could be a complicated sequence of movements that was learned previously. Stimulus-response learning includes two major categories of learning that psychologists have studied extensively: *classical conditioning* and *instrumental conditioning.*

The child watches the balloon grow large
(neutral stimulus) until it bursts (US), which
causes a defensive startle reaction (UR).

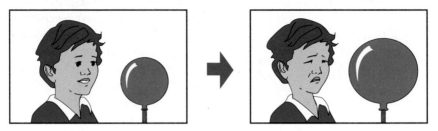

After the child's first experience with a bursting
balloon, the mere sight of an inflating balloon
(CS) elicits a defensive reaction (CR).

FIGURE 14.1

The process of classical conditioning.

Classical conditioning is a form of learning in which an unimportant stimulus acquires the properties of an important one. It involves an *association between two stimuli*. A stimulus that previously had little effect on behavior becomes able to evoke a reflexive, species-typical behavior. For example, we flinch when we see a balloon being overinflated near our face. The flinch is a species-typical defensive reaction that serves to protect our eyes. Normally, this reaction occurs when we hear a loud noise, when something rapidly approaches our face, or when our eyes or the skin around them is touched; we do not have to learn to make this response. We respond this way when we see an overinflated balloon because of our prior experience with bursting balloons. Sometime in the past, probably when we were children, an overinflated balloon burst near our face, and the blast of air elicited a defensive flinch. Through classical conditioning the stimulus that preceded the blast of air—the sight of an overinflated balloon—became an elicitor of flinching.

The names that have been assigned to the stimuli and responses that constitute classical condition-ing are shown in Figure 14.1. I will use these terms again in this chapter, so it is worth your while learning them now, if they are not already familiar to you. The blast of air, the original eliciting stimulus, is called the **unconditional stimulus** (US): It unconditionally elicits the species-typical response. The response of flinching is itself called the **unconditional response** (UR). After a few experiences with bursting balloons, the sight of the inflated balloon— the **conditional stimulus** (CS)—comes to elicit flinching, which is now called the **conditional response** (CR): The response is conditional on the pairing of the conditional and unconditional stimuli. (See *Figure 14.1.*)

Classical conditioning occurs when a neutral stimulus is followed by one that automatically elicits a response. It enables organisms to learn to make species-typical responses under new conditions. Thus, classical conditioning serves to prepare an organism for a forthcoming event. For example, a warning signal can permit the organism to defend itself against harm; stimuli associated with a potential mate can cause it to make a response that serves

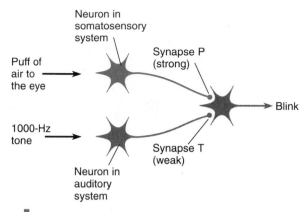

FIGURE 14.2

A simple neural model of classical conditioning. When the 1000-Hz tone is presented just before the puff of air to the eye, synapse T is strengthened.

as a sexual display; and stimuli associated with food can cause secretion of saliva, digestive juices, and insulin. In addition (and perhaps even more importantly), classical conditioning establishes neutral stimuli as conditioned reinforcers or punishers—but more about that later.

When classical conditioning takes place, what kinds of changes occur in the brain? Figure 14.2 shows a simplified neural circuit that could account for this type of learning. I will use a simple example: the defensive eyeblink response of a rabbit. A small puff of air aimed at the eye can trigger this reflex; thus, a puff of air serves as a US. The CS is a 1000-Hz tone. For the sake of simplicity, we will assume that the US is detected by a single neuron in the somatosensory system, and the CS is detected by a single neuron in the auditory system. We will also assume that the response—the eyeblink—is controlled by a single neuron in the motor system. (See *Figure 14.2.*)

Now let us see how the circuits works. If we present a 1000-Hz tone, we find that the animal makes no reaction, because the synapse connecting the tone-sensitive neuron with the neuron in the motor system is weak. However, if we present a puff of air to the eye, the eye blinks. This reaction occurs because nature has provided the animal with a strong synapse between the somatosensory neuron and the motor neuron that causes a blink (synapse P, for "puff"). To establish classical conditioning, we

first present the 1000-Hz tone and then almost immediately follow it with a puff of air. After we repeat these pairs of stimuli several times, we find that we can dispense with the air puff; the 1000-Hz tone produces the blink all by itself.

Over forty years ago, Hebb proposed a rule that might explain how neurons are changed by experience in a way that would cause changes in behavior (Hebb, 1949). The **Hebb rule** says that if a synapse repeatedly becomes active at about the same time that the postsynaptic neuron fires, changes will take place in the structure or chemistry of the synapse that will strengthen it. How would the Hebb rule apply to our circuit? If the 1000-Hz tone is presented first, then weak synapse T (for "tone") becomes active. If the puff is presented immediately afterward, then strong synapse P becomes active and makes the motor neuron fire. The act of firing then strengthens any synapse with the motor neuron *that has just been active.* Of course, this means synapse T. After several pairings of the two stimuli, and after several increments of strengthening, synapse T becomes strong enough to cause the motor neuron to fire by itself. Learning has occurred. (See *Figure 14.2.*)

Obviously, the rabbit's auditory system contains more than one neuron, and so does its motor system. Neurons in the auditory system have connections with all kinds of neurons in the motor system—with neurons that control ear wiggling, nose twitching, running, sniffing, chewing, and other things rabbits can do. But before learning takes place, all of these connections are weak; hearing a 1000-Hz tone produces so little activation of the neurons in the motor system that the animal does not make an overt response. (Of course, the noise may startle the animal, but this response usually disappears after the tone is presented a few times.) Of all the thousands of synapses in the motor system that become activated by the 1000-Hz tone, only those located on neurons that have just fired will become strengthened. If the US has just been presented and the animal has just blinked, most of the recently activated cells will be those controlling eyeblinks—and only synapses on these cells will be strengthened.

When Hebb formulated his rule, he was unable to determine whether it was true or false. Now, finally, enough progress has been made in labora-

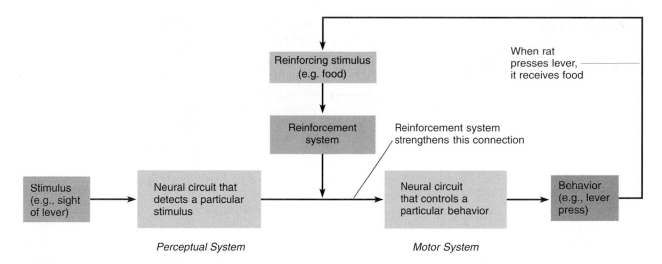

FIGURE 14.3

A simple neural model of instrumental conditioning.

tory techniques that the strength of individual synapses can be determined, and investigators are studying the physiological bases of learning. We will see the results of some of these approaches later in this chapter in a section entitled "Mechanisms of Synaptic Plasticity."

The second major class of stimulus-response learning is **instrumental conditioning** (also called *operant conditioning*). Whereas classical conditioning involves automatic, species-typical responses, instrumental conditioning involves behaviors that have been learned. And whereas classical conditioning involves an association between two stimuli, instrumental conditioning involves an *association between a response and a stimulus*. Instrumental conditioning is a more flexible form of learning. It permits an organism to adjust its behavior according to the consequences of that behavior. That is, when a behavior is followed by favorable consequences, the behavior tends to occur more frequently; when it is followed by unfavorable consequences, it tends to occur less frequently. Collectively, "favorable consequences" are referred to as **reinforcing stimuli**, and "unfavorable consequences" are referred to as **punishing stimuli**. For example, a response that enables a hungry organism to find food will be reinforced, and a response that causes pain will be punished. (Psychologists often refer to these terms as *reinforcers* and *punishers*.)

Let us consider the process of reinforcement. Briefly stated, reinforcement causes changes in an animal's nervous system that increase the likelihood that a particular stimulus will elicit a particular response. For example, when a hungry rat is first put in an operant chamber (a "Skinner box"), it is not very likely to press the lever mounted on a wall. However, if it does press the lever, and if it receives a piece of food immediately afterward, the likelihood of making another response increases. Put another way, reinforcement causes the sight of the lever to serve as the stimulus that elicits the lever-pressing response. It is not accurate to say simply that a particular behavior becomes more frequent. If no lever is present, a rat that has learned to press one will not wave its paw around in the air. The *sight of a lever* is needed to produce the response. Thus, the process of reinforcement strengthens a connection between neural circuits involved in perception (the sight of the lever) and those involved in movement (the act of lever pressing). As we will see later in this chapter, the brain contains a reinforcement mechanism that controls this process. (See *Figure 14.3.*)

The third major category of learning, *motor learning*, is actually a special form of stimulus-response learning; for that reason I will not discuss it separately. For simplicity's sake, we can think of perceptual learning as the establishment of changes within the sensory systems of the brain, stimulus-

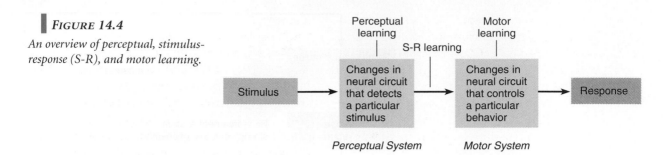

FIGURE 14.4

An overview of perceptual, stimulus-response (S-R), and motor learning.

response learning as the establishment of connections between sensory systems and motor systems, and motor learning as the establishment of changes within motor systems. But in fact, motor learning cannot occur without sensory guidance from the environment. Thus, it is actually a special form of stimulus-response learning. For example, most skilled movements involve interactions with objects: bicycles, pinball machines, knitting needles, and so on. Even skilled movements we make by ourselves, such as solitary dance steps, involve feedback from the joints, muscles, vestibular apparatus, eyes, and contact between the feet and the floor. Motor learning differs from other forms of learning primarily in the degree to which new forms of behavior are learned; the more novel the behavior, the more the neural circuits in the motor systems of the brain must be modified. (See **Figure 14.4**.)

The three forms of learning I have described so far consist primarily of changes in one sensory system, between one sensory system and the motor system, or in the motor system. But obviously, learning is usually more complex than that. The fourth form of learning involves learning the *relations* among individual stimuli. For example, a somewhat more complex form of perceptual learning involves connections between different areas of the association cortex. When we hear the sound of a cat meowing in the dark, we can imagine what a cat looks like and what it would feel like if we stroked its fur. Thus, the neural circuits in the auditory association cortex that recognize the meow are somehow connected to the appropriate circuits in the visual association cortex and the somatosensory association cortex. These interconnections, too, are accomplished as a result of learning.

Spatial learning—perception of spatial location—also involves learning about the relations among many stimuli. For example, consider what we must learn in order to become familiar with the contents of a room. First, we must learn to recognize each of the objects. Then, in addition, we must learn the relative locations of the objects with respect to each other. As a result, when we find ourselves located in a particular place in the room, our perceptions of these objects and their locations relative to us tell us exactly where we are.

Other types of relational learning are even more complex. *Episodic learning*—remembering sequences of events (episodes) that we witness—requires us to keep track not only of individual stimuli but also of the order in which they occur. *Observational learning*—learning by watching and imitating other people—requires us to remember what someone else does, the situation in which the behavior is performed, and the relation between the other person's movements and our own. As we will see in Chapter 15, a special system that involves the hippocampus and associated structures appears to perform coordinating functions that are necessary for many types of learning that go beyond single regions of the cerebral cortex.

‖‖‖ INTERIM SUMMARY

Learning produces changes in the way we perceive, act, think, and feel. It does so by producing changes in the nervous system in the circuits responsible for perception, in those responsible for the control of movement, and in connections between the two.

Perceptual learning consists primarily of changes in perceptual systems that make it possible for us to recognize stimuli so that we can respond to them appropriately. Stimulus-response learning consists of connections between perceptual and motor systems. The most important forms are classical and instrumental conditioning. Classical conditioning occurs when a neutral stimulus is followed by an unconditional stimulus (US) that naturally elicits an unconditional response (UR). After this pairing, the neutral stimulus becomes a conditional stimulus (CS); it now elicits the conditional response (CR) by itself.

Instrumental conditioning occurs when a response is followed by a reinforcing stimulus, such as a drink of water for a thirsty animal. The reinforcing stimulus increases the likelihood that the other stimuli present when the response was made will evoke the response. Both forms of stimulus-response learning may occur as a result of strengthened synaptic connections, as described by the Hebb rule.

Motor learning, although it may primarily involve changes within neural circuits that control movement, is guided by sensory stimuli; thus, it is actually a form of stimulus-response learning. Relational learning, the most complex form of learning, is described in Chapter 15. It includes the ability to recognize objects through more than one sensory modality, to recognize the relative location of objects in the environment, and to remember the sequence in which events occurred during particular episodes.

PERCEPTUAL LEARNING

LEARNING ENABLES US TO ADAPT TO OUR ENVIronment and to respond to changes in it. In particular, it provides us with the ability to perform an appropriate behavior in an appropriate situation. Situations can be as simple as the sound of a buzzer or as complex as the social interactions of a group of people. The first part of learning involves learning to perceive.

Perceptual learning involves learning *about* things, not *what to do* when they are present. (Learning what to do is discussed in the next section of this chapter.) Perceptual learning can involve learning to recognize entirely new stimuli, or it can involve learning to recognize changes or variations in familiar stimuli. For example, if a friend gets a new hairstyle or replaces glasses with contact lenses, our visual memory of that person changes. We also learn that particular stimuli are found in particular locations or contexts or in the presence of other stimuli. We can even learn and remember particular *episodes:* sequences of events taking place at a particular time and place. These more complex forms of perceptual learning will be discussed in Chapter 15, which is devoted to relational learning.

Simple perceptual learning—learning to recognize particular stimuli or categories of stimuli—appears to take place in appropriate regions of sensory association cortex. That is, learning to recognize particular sounds takes place in the auditory association cortex; learning to recognize particular objects by sight takes place in the visual association cortex; and so on. *Very* simple perceptual learning can even be accomplished subcortically, presumably by mechanisms we inherited from our remote ancestors. This section describes research on visual and auditory learning that illustrates some of the progress that has been made in understanding this topic.

Visual Learning

In mammals with large and complex brains objects are recognized visually by circuits of neurons in the visual association cortex. As we saw in Chapter 6, the primary visual cortex receives information from the lateral geniculate nucleus of the thalamus. Within the primary visual cortex individual modules of neurons analyze information from restricted regions of the visual scene that pertain to movement, orientation, color, binocular disparity, and spatial frequency. Information about each of these attributes is collected in subregions of the extrastriate cortex, which surrounds the primary visual cortex (striate cortex). For example, specific regions are devoted to the analysis of form, color, and movement.

After analyzing particular attributes of the visual scene, the subregions of the extrastriate cortex send the results of their analysis to the inferior temporal cortex, where the information is combined, producing neural activity that corresponds to the perception of particular three-dimensional objects. (See *Figure 14.5.*)

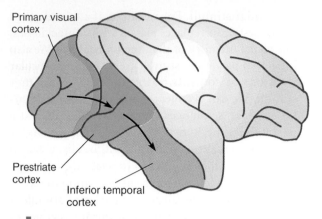

Primary visual cortex

Prestriate cortex

Inferior temporal cortex

| **FIGURE 14.5**

The major divisions of the visual cortex of the rhesus monkey. The arrows indicate the primary direction of the flow of information.

Many studies have shown that lesions that damage the inferior temporal cortex disrupt monkeys' ability to discriminate between different visual stimuli. Mishkin (1966) showed that if visual information were prevented from reaching the inferior temporal cortex, monkeys lost the ability to distinguish between different visual patterns. First, he removed the striate cortex on one side of the brain and tested the animals' ability to discriminate between visual patterns. They performed well. Next, he removed the contralateral inferior temporal cortex; again, no deficit. Finally, he cut the corpus callosum, which isolated the remaining inferior temporal cortex from the remaining primary visual cortex. This time, the animals could no longer perform the visual discrimination task. Therefore, we can conclude that the inferior temporal cortex is necessary for visual pattern discrimination and that it must receive information from the primary visual cortex. (See *Figure 14.6.*)

Presumably, learning to recognize a particular visual stimulus is accomplished by changes in synaptic connections in the inferior temporal cortex that establish new neural circuits. (Research on the nature of these circuits and the synaptic changes they involve are described later in this chapter.) At a later time, when the same pattern of activity is received from the extrastriate cortex, these circuits become active again. This activity constitutes the

recognition of the stimulus—the "readout" of the visual memory, so to speak.

Several studies have found that when familiar visual stimuli are presented, different sets of neurons in the inferior temporal cortex do indeed become active. For example, Fuster and Jervey (1981) trained monkeys on a **delayed matching-to-sample task.** This task requires that the animal remember a particular stimulus for a period of time. The investigators turned on a colored light (yellow, green, red, or blue) behind a translucent disk (the *sample stimulus*), turned it off, and, after a delay interval, turned on yellow, green, red, and blue lights behind four other disks (the *matching stimuli*). (See *Figure 14.7.*) If the monkey pressed the disk whose color matched the one it had just seen, it received a piece of food.

While the monkeys were performing this task, the experimenters recorded the activity of single neurons in the inferior temporal cortex. Some neurons responded selectively to color: to yellow, red, green, or blue. Presumably, they became active because the *circuits* of neurons of which they were a part became active. It is these circuits, not individual neurons, that recognize particular stimuli. In addition, many of these neurons remained active during the delay interval. For example, Figure 14.8 shows data from a neuron that responded to red light, but not to green light, during a 16-second delay interval. The horizontal lines above each graph represent individual trials; vertical tick marks represent action potentials. The graphs beneath the horizontal lines are sums of the individual trials, showing the total responses during successive intervals. As you can see, when the sample stimulus consisted of a red light, the neuron became active—and remained active even after the sample stimulus went off. (See *Figure 14.8.*) Under normal conditions a stimulus causes a neuron to respond briefly. Thus, the sustained response during the delay interval suggests that the neuron part of a circuit that is involved in remembering that a red light was presented.

More recently, Fuster (1990) modified the delayed matching-to-sample task slightly, placing a pattern in the middle of the sample disk. The shape of the pattern indicated whether the animal should remember the color of the disk or the pattern. Fuster found some color-sensitive neurons in the inferior

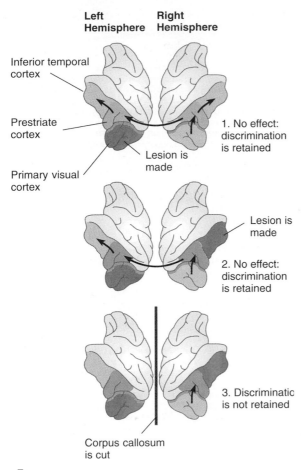

Left Hemisphere   Right Hemisphere

Inferior temporal cortex

Prestriate cortex

Primary visual cortex

Lesion is made

1. No effect: discrimination is retained

Lesion is made

2. No effect: discrimination is retained

3. Discriminatio is not retained

Corpus callosum is cut

FIGURE 14.6

The procedure used by Mishkin (1966). Not all of the control groups used in the experiment are shown here.

(Adapted from Mishkin, M., in *Frontiers in Physiological Psychology,* edited by R.W. Russell. New York: Academic Press, 1966.)

on a visual delayed matching-to-sample task. Once the monkeys had learned the task, they electrically stimulated the cortex through the electrodes from time to time while the animals were performing. When they administered the stimulation during the delay interval, just before they showed the monkeys the matching stimuli, the animals performed poorly on that trial. It was as if the stimulation had disrupted the normal activity in the cortex and erased the memory of the stimulus the monkeys had just seen.

So far, researchers do not have recording techniques sensitive enough to show changes in the responses of single neurons before and after an animal learns to recognize a particular stimulus. For one thing, perceptual learning takes place very fast; a monkey can often remember a particular stimulus after having seen it just once. For another thing, because of the natural variability of the response of a single neuron, we need to compare average response rates on several trials before and after learning—

temporal cortex that became active if the pattern indicated that the animal should remember the color—but not if it should remember the pattern, instead. These results provide even more support for the suggestion that visual memories are maintained in the inferior temporal cortex.

Several studies (for example, Mishkin, 1982) have shown that lesions of the inferior temporal cortex disrupt an animal's ability to remember a stimulus that it has just seen. So does temporary disruption of neural activity in this region. Kovner and Stamm (1972) implanted electrodes in the inferior temporal cortex of monkeys and trained them

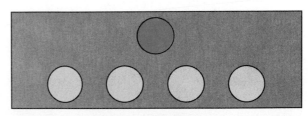

Sample stimulus

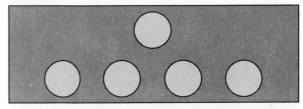

Delay interval

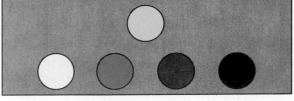

Matching stimuli

FIGURE 14.7

The delayed matching-to-sample procedure used by Fuster and Jervey (1981).

Figure 14.8

Responses of a single unit during the presentation of the sample stimulus, the delay interval, and the presentation of matching stimuli in the experiment outlined in Figure 14.7.

(From Fuster, J.M., in *Conditioning: Representation of Involved Neural Functions,* edited by C.D. Woody. New York: Plenum Press, 1982. Reprinted with permission.)

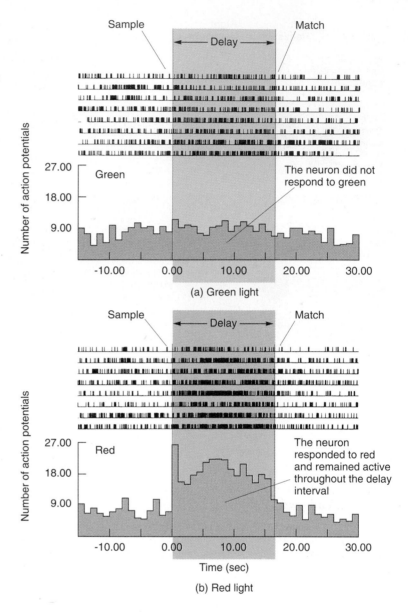

but if learning occurs in one trial, we can never obtain a "before-learning" average. Sakai and Miyashita (1991) therefore used a different method to see whether visual learning modified neural circuits. They recorded the responses of single neurons in the inferior temporal cortex to pairs of visual stimuli. The stimuli were generated by a computer, and the pairs were made randomly. As you can see in Figure 14.9, the members of the pairs do not particularly resemble each other. (See **Figure 14.9.**)

The task went like this: The monkeys were briefly shown one member of the pair. Then after a delay period of 4 seconds, they were shown two stimuli: the other member of the pair and a stimulus from another pair. If the animal touched the correct stimulus, it received a sip of fruit juice. After the training the investigators found neurons in the inferior temporal cortex that responded selectively to some, but not all, of the stimuli. And if a neuron responded to one member of a pair, it was likely to respond to the other member, too. For example, the neuron whose activity is shown in Figure 14.10 responded to only two stimuli: 12 and 12^1. If a particular neuron responds to only two of twenty-four

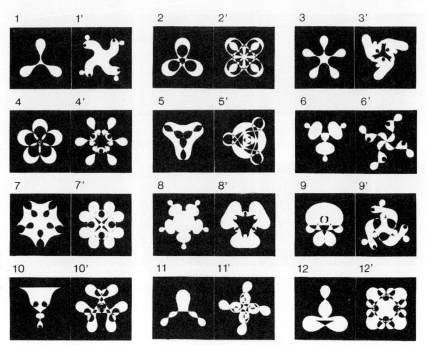

FIGURE 14.9

The twelve pairs of stimuli used in the experiment by Sakai and Miyashita (1991).

(From Sakai, K., and Miyashita, Y. *Nature,* 1991, *354,* 152–155. Reprinted with permission.)

different stimuli, the likelihood of these two stimuli being members of the same pair is only one in twenty-three. (See ***Figure 14.10.***)

Sakai and Miyashita observed another interesting result. Like Fuster and Jervey, they found that many neurons continued to respond during the delay interval, as if the neuron were part of a circuit that "remembered" the sample stimulus. And the presentation of *either* stimulus could activate this circuit—even in cases in which a particular neuron responded to only one of the two members of a pair. The results suggest that when stimuli are paired, the neural circuits responsible for recognizing them become linked together; perception of either stimulus activates both circuits. Presumably, the same thing happens when familiar stimuli undergo changes—as when your friend gets a new hairstyle.

As we saw in Chapter 6, some neurons in the inferior temporal cortex show remarkable specificity in their response characteristics, which suggests that they are part of circuits that detect the presence of specific stimuli. For example, neurons located near the superior temporal sulcus become active when the animal is shown pictures of faces. Baylis, Rolls, and Leonard (1985) found that most of these neurons are sensitive to *particular* faces. Rolls and Baylis

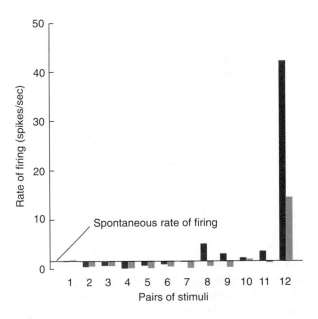

FIGURE 14.10

The responses of a single neuron in the inferior temporal cortex to each member of the twelve pairs of stimuli shown in Figure 14.9.

(Adapted from Sakai, K., and Miyashita, Y. *Nature,* 1991, *354,* 152–155.)

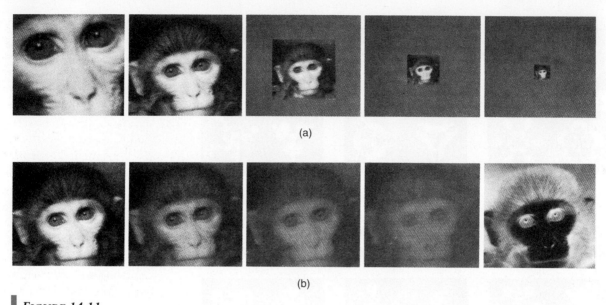

(a)

(b)

FIGURE 14.11

Examples of photographs of faces that produced similar responses in face-sensitive neurons in the inferior temporal cortex. (a) Faces of different sizes. (b) Faces of reduced and reversed contrast.
(From Rolls, E.T., and Baylis, G.C. *Experimental Brain Research,* 1986, *65,* 38–48. Reprinted with permission.)

(1986) found that the responses of some of these neurons remain constant even if the picture is blurred or changed in color, size, or distance. (See **Figure 14.11.**)

Rolls et al. (1989) found that as monkeys became familiar with particular faces, the response characteristics of some face-sensitive neurons in the inferior temporal cortex changed. They presented monkeys with pictures of human and monkey faces on the screen of a video monitor. They found that many cells showed changes in their response characteristic when new faces were shown to the monkey. For example, in one experiment they showed the same set of five faces, one at a time, for several trials. Most neurons showed rather stable responses. Then the experimenters introduced a new face into the series. After one or two presentations the response pattern to the familiar faces changed. This finding suggests that learning caused a "rewiring" of the neural circuits.

All of the experiments I have discussed so far support the hypothesis that visual long-term mem-

ories involve the establishment of new circuits in the inferior temporal cortex by means of synaptic changes. Visual short-term memory—that is, memory of a visual stimulus that has just been perceived—is stored in the form of activity of these circuits of neurons. But under some conditions the information can be transferred out of the visual association cortex. The studies I described that involved short-term memory all required animals to remember a *stimulus* during the delay interval. For example, until the matching stimuli are presented, they will not know whether they will have to push the right-hand button or the left-hand button. But some tasks permit the subject to remember a *response,* instead. For example, if someone shows you a written word, you can remember what the word looks like, what it sounds like, or what you would do to pronounce it. We might predict, then, that seeing a word would first activate neurons in the visual association cortex; but after that, neurons in the auditory association cortex or motor association cortex would become active. As we shall see, this is exactly what happens. Later in this chapter I will describe an experiment demonstrating the transfer of short-term memory to the frontal lobes in the monkey brain; and in Chapter 16 I will describe research on recognition and short-term memory for verbal information.

Auditory Learning

Although visual learning has received more attention than other forms of perceptual learning, it is clear that learning to recognize stimuli presented to the other sense modalities involves changes in neural networks located in other areas of sensory association cortex. I will discuss one other example of perceptual learning: recognition of an auditory stimulus that evokes a conditioned emotional response.

A series of experiments by Weinberger and his colleagues showed that an auditory learning task modifies the response characteristics of neurons in various parts of the auditory system (Bakin and Weinberger, 1990; Edeline and Weinberger, 1991a; 1991b; 1992). The researchers established a classically conditioned emotional response in guinea pigs by pairing a tone of a particular frequency with a brief foot shock. As we saw in Chapter 11, after these stimuli are paired, the tone becomes a CS; it elicits a range of behavioral, autonomic, and hormonal responses, such as freezing, increased blood pressure, secretion of adrenal stress hormones, and so on. Before the training the researchers implanted microelectrodes in various parts of the auditory system. They presented the animals with a series of tones of different frequencies and recorded the rate of neural firing to each frequency. Most neurons in the auditory system are frequency-sensitive; they are activated more by some frequencies than by others.

After determining the cells' responses to tones of different frequencies, the experimenters presented the animals with the tone-shock pairs and then recorded the cells' responses again. They found that the training changed the pattern of many of the neurons' responses. Figure 14.12a shows the record obtained from one such cell, located in the primary auditory cortex. The pretraining response is shown in black, and the posttraining response (obtained 1 hour after training) is shown in color. As you can

see, before the training the cell responded best to a 9.5-Hz tone. After the training the cell responded best to the 9-Hz training tone and reduced its response to the 9.5-Hz tone. Figure 14.12b shows the difference between the two curves. (See *Figure 14.12.*)

Weinberger and his colleagues studied the effects of training on neurons in the auditory cortex and the three major divisions of the medial geniculate nucleus—the thalamic nucleus that relays auditory information to the auditory cortex. As we just saw, the training changed the response characteristics of neurons in the primary auditory cortex. Most of these changes were still present 24 hours later. In addition, two of the three regions of the medial geniculate nucleus showed changes: the dorsal division and the medial division. The ventral division, which provides the major input to the primary auditory cortex, showed the least change. As we saw in Chapter 11, the medial division (the MGM) plays an important role in classically conditioned emotional responses. It receives information from both the auditory system and the somatosensory system, which detects the US—the foot shock. It is directly connected with the central nucleus of the amygdala, which in turn has direct connections with other brain regions that are responsible for the various components of the conditioned emotional response.

Weinberger and his colleagues believe that the MGM is largely responsible for initiating the changes in the responses of neurons in the primary auditory cortex. They suggest that when the MGM is stimulated by the simultaneous presence of an auditory stimulus and a painful somatosensory stimulus, it activates the central nucleus of the amygdala. Besides organizing an emotional response, the central nucleus activates the **nucleus basalis,** a nucleus that contains acetylcholinergic neurons that innervate most of the cerebral cortex. The acetylcholinergic input to the auditory cortex tells the cells to pay particular attention to the input they are currently receiving from the ventral division of the medial geniculate nucleus and to become more sensitive to that input. The results are changes in the response characteristics of the auditory cortex neurons.

I suspect that the list of names may be confusing—ventral and medial divisions of the medial

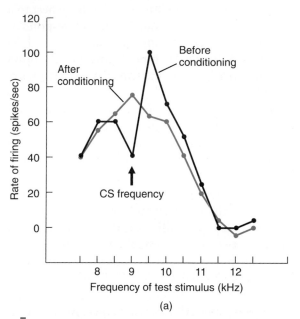
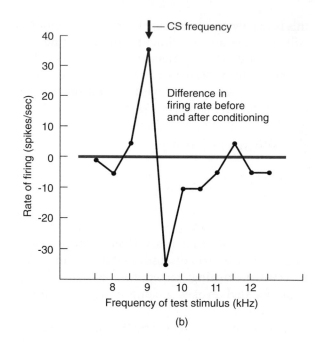

FIGURE 14.12

Rate of firing of a single neuron in the primary auditory cortex to tones of various frequencies.
(a) Responses before (black) and after (color) classical conditioning. The CS was a tone of 9 kHz
(arrow). (b) Changes in responses caused by conditioning.

(Adapted from Bakin, J.S., and Weinberger, N.M. *Brain Research*, 1990, *536*, 271–286.)

geniculate nucleus, central nucleus, and so on—so I have prepared a figure that illustrates Weinberger's hypothesis. (See ***Figure 14.13.***)

Weinberger and his colleagues (Metherate, Ashe, and Weinberger, 1990; Metherate and Weinberger, 1990) obtained evidence that the release of acetylcholine in the primary auditory cortex stimulates neurons there to become more sensitive to the auditory information they are currently receiving—that is, to the CS. They recorded from single cortical neurons and determined their responses to tones of various frequencies. Then they simultaneously presented a tone and injected acetylcholine into the vicinity of the neuron whose activity they were recording. The pairing made most of the neurons become more responsive to the tone.

The results of these experiments indicate that perceptual learning is an important component of classical conditioning; animals are more likely to learn to recognize stimuli that are important to them. As we shall see in the next major section of this chapter, recent research is beginning to discover just how experience can change the strength of synaptic connections and establish both perceptual and stimulus-response learning.

Modeling the Brain's Ability to Learn: Neural Networks

So far I have been talking in rather vague terms about "neural circuits" that are responsible for recognizing particular stimuli. The experiments I have described clearly indicate that experience changes the response characteristics of single neurons, which must mean that the synaptic connections between them and other neurons must have changed. Experience changes the synaptic connections, and these changes represent what is learned. But what is the relation between synaptic changes and the operations of neural circuits?

A possible answer comes from a recent approach to modeling the function of neural circuits, called

neural networks. Investigators have discovered that when they construct a network of simple elements, interconnected in certain ways, the network does some surprising things. (The authors of neural networks use computers to model them; they do not construct actual networks with electrical components.) The elements are given properties like those of neurons. They are connected to each other through junctions similar to synapses. Like synapses, these junctions can have either excitatory or inhibitory effects. When an element receives a critical amount of excitation, it sends a message to the elements with which it communicates, and so on. Some of the elements of a network have input lines that can receive signals from the "outside," which could represent a sensory organ or the information received from another network. Other elements have output lines, which communicate with other networks or control muscles, producing behavior. Thus, particular patterns of input can represent particular stimuli, and particular patterns of output can represent responses. (See *Figure 14.14.*)

Neural networks can be taught to recognize particular stimuli. For example, the authors of a neural network can specify that the connections between

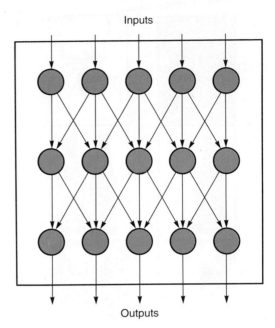

Inputs

Outputs

FIGURE 14.14

A very simple neural network, used as a model of brain function. The connections (arrows) can be excitatory or inhibitory, depending on the particular model.

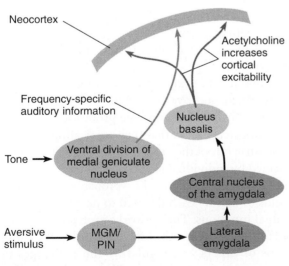

FIGURE 14.13

Weinberger's hypothetical explanation for the changes in frequency responses of neurons in the primary auditory cortex that occur after a tone is paired with an aversive stimulus.

elements are strengthened by an unconditional stimulus or by a reinforcement system. Or they can use other techniques to teach a network to recognize a particular stimulus. In this case the networks receive only one input pattern (there is no "reinforcing stimulus"), but inhibitory elements within the circuit refine the response the network makes to a particular input. Networks such as these are "shown" a particular stimulus by being presented with a particular pattern of activity on the input lines, and their output is monitored. The first time a particular stimulus is presented, the output elements respond weakly and nonspecifically; but after it is presented several times, a strong and reliable output pattern emerges. The network can be shown more and more stimuli, producing unique output patterns for each of them.

The characteristics of neural networks are similar to many of those exhibited by real nervous systems, which is what makes them exciting to scientists interested in the neural basis of learning. For example, neural networks show generalization,

(a)   (b)

FIGURE 14.15

Responses of a neural network that had "learned" seven different images. (a) Degraded or incomplete images presented to the network. (b) Responses of the network to the inputs.

(Adapted by permission from Hertz, J., Krogh, A., and Palmer, R.G. *Introduction to the Theory of Neural Computation.* Redwood City, Calif.: Addison-Wesley, 1991.)

discrimination, and graceful degradation. *Generalization* refers to the ability to recognize similarities between stimuli. Suppose that a network has learned to recognize a few very different stimuli. If we then show it a stimulus that resembles one it knows—such as a part of the original stimulus—the circuit will act as if it saw the entire stimulus. (See *Figure 14.15.*) *Discrimination* refers to the ability to recognize differences between stimuli. If we show a network several similar stimuli, it will learn to distinguish among them, producing very different output patterns to each of them. Finally, *graceful degradation* refers to the fact that random damage to

elements of a neural network or to their connections ("synapses") does not bring the network to a crashing halt. Instead, the performance of the network deteriorates, at a level proportional to the amount of damage. These three phenomena, generalization, discrimination, and graceful degradation, also characterize the way that our brains work.

Obviously, because the brain is made of networks of neurons, learning occurs in neural networks. The question is whether the neural networks that scientists construct work the same way that the brain does, and the only way to find that out is to learn the detailed anatomy of real neural circuits and the physiological characteristics of individual neurons and synaptic connections. As more is learned about these subjects, more realistic models of neural networks can be constructed. The reason that neural networks have captured the imagination of neuroscientists is that even though investigators have been working with them for only a few years, and thus the state of the art is still relatively primitive, the resemblance of these model networks to the workings of the nervous system is uncanny. In just a few years investigators have constructed many models, including those that recognize patterns, learn names of objects, control the finger movements used by a typist, read words, and learn the past tenses of English verbs (Rumelhart et al., 1986). Of course, with only a few years of experience with this new approach we cannot be sure that it will live up to its promise. In my decision to describe the approach to you, I am obviously betting that it will; I expect to be writing about neural networks for some years to come.

Investigators studying the properties of neural networks emphasize that they are dealing with the *microstructure* of the brain—with the functions performed by individual modules. The brain contains a large number of networks—probably many thousands of them—each devoted to performing individual functions. The networks probably exist in a sort of hierarchy, with some controlling the functions of others and regulating the exchanges of information between them. Thus, understanding the operations of individual neural networks will never reveal all we need to know about the functions of the brain. We will also need to know the organization of the brain—the relations between the individual networks of which it is constructed. We will need to know the *macrostructure* of the brain as well as its microstructure.

||||| INTERIM SUMMARY

Perceptual learning occurs as a result of changes in synaptic connections within the sensory association cortex. Damage to a monkey's inferior temporal cortex—the highest level of visual association cortex—disrupts visual discriminations. Electrical-recording studies have shown that some neurons in the inferior temporal cortex encode the information presented during the sample period of a delayed matching-to-sample task and continue to fire during the delay interval. Electrical stimulation of the inferior temporal cortex during the delay interval of this task disrupts performance, as if the memory of the stimulus had been erased. Recording studies suggest that pairing of visual stimuli causes connections to be made in the neural circuits responsible for their recognition. Other recording studies have shown that some neurons respond preferentially to particular complex stimuli, including faces. When new stimuli are presented, the response patterns of some neurons in the inferior temporal cortex change, which suggests that "rewiring" may be taking place.

A series of studies using auditory stimuli suggest that when a tone is paired with an aversive stimulus, changes can be seen in the responses of neurons in the auditory cortex when that stimulus is presented again. The change appears to be triggered by the activation of the central nucleus of the amygdala (via the medial division of the medial geniculate nucleus), which plays an important role in emotional responses. The central nucleus activates the nucleus basalis, which results in the release of acetylcholine in the cortex. The changes in the response characteristics of the cortical neurons is triggered by this neurotransmitter.

Recently, investigators have begun to construct models of neural networks, in which interconnected elements that have some of the known properties of neurons are presented with "stimuli" encoded by particular patterns of inputs to the network.

Although these networks are very simple, they have been found to be capable of simulating many characteristics of the brain, including perceptual and stimulus-response learning.

MECHANISMS OF SYNAPTIC PLASTICITY

THE HEBB RULE STATES THAT IF A SYNAPSE IS active at about the same time that the postsynaptic neuron is active, that synapse will be strengthened. Research on a phenomenon originally discovered in the hippocampal formation has found at least one way that the Hebb rule may operate.

Induction of Long-Term Potentiation

Electrical stimulation of circuits within the hippocampal formation can lead to long-term physiological changes that seem to be among those responsible for learning. Lømo (1966) discovered that intense electrical stimulation of axons leading from the entorhinal cortex to the dentate gyrus caused a long-term increase in the magnitude of excitatory postsynaptic potentials in the postsynaptic cells; this increase has come to be called **long-term potentiation.** (The word *potentiate* means "to strengthen, to make more potent.")

First, let us review some anatomy. The **hippocampal formation** is a specialized region of the limbic cortex located in the temporal lobe. Because the hippocampal formation is folded in one dimension and then curved in another, it has a complex, three-dimensional shape. Thus, it is difficult to show what it looks like with a diagram on a two-dimensional sheet of paper. I must confess that I looked at diagrams of the hippocampus for many years without ever really being able to picture its structure in three dimensions. Finally, I read an article on the anatomy of the hippocampal formation that presented a set of drawings that showed its embryonic development, and the picture became clearer. I have based my illustrations on that article (Swanson, Köhler, and Björklund, 1987). The next few para-

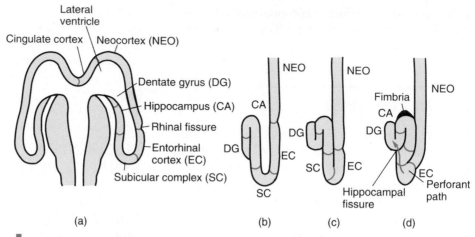

FIGURE 14.16

Development of the hippocampal formation. (a) Horizontal section of the developing brain. (b) Ammon's horn folding back on itself. (c) Dentate gyrus folding forward. (d) Formation of the perforant path and the fimbria.

(Adapted from Swanson, L.W., Köhler, C., and Björklund, A., in *Handbook of Chemical Neuroanatomy. Vol. 5: Integrated Systems of the CNS, Part I.* Amsterdam: Elsevier Science Publishers, 1987. Reprinted with permission.)

graphs give many details about neuroanatomy; in fact, this is probably the most concentrated dose you will receive in this book outside of Chapter 4. Let me assure you that learning this information is worthwhile; you will use some of it in this chapter, and the rest will come up again in Chapter 15.

Figure 14.16 shows the development of the hippocampal formation, which includes the **entorhinal cortex,** the **subicular complex,** the hippocampus itself, and the **dentate gyrus.** The drawings illustrate a rat brain, but the development of a human brain is very similar. The hippocampus is also called "Ammon's horn," or, in Latin, *cornu ammonis.* That fact may seem like a piece of trivia, but it explains why its two major divisions are called **CA1** and **CA3.** (CA2 and CA4 exist, too, but we will not need to talk about them.) Figure 14.16a shows a horizontal section of the developing brain that you may remember from Chapter 4. In the temporal lobe the *rhinal fissure* marks the border between the neocortex and the hippocampal formation, which is composed of limbic cortex. Going medially from the rhinal fissure, we encounter the entorhinal cortex, the subicular complex, the hippocampus (Ammon's horn), and the dentate gyrus. (See *Figure 14.16a.*)

Figures 14.16b, 14.16c, and 14.16d show the further development of the hippocampal formation. First, Ammon's horn folds back on itself, then the dentate gyrus folds forward. Axons of neurons in the entorhinal cortex grow toward the dentate gyrus, forming the **perforant path** (which *perforates* the hippocampal fissure). The **fimbria** forms on the rostral fold of Ammon's horn. This structure consists of a bundle of axons that becomes the *fornix* after it detaches itself from the hippocampal formation. It connects the hippocampal formation with the basal forebrain, diencephalon, and brain stem. (See *Figures 14.16b–14.16d.*)

Figure 14.17 shows a photomicrograph of a horizontal section through the hippocampal formation of a rat brain and an accompanying drawing that shows its intrinsic connections. The major neocortical inputs and outputs of the hippocampal formation are channeled through the entorhinal cortex. Neurons in the entorhinal cortex relay incoming information through the perforant path to the *granule cells* of the dentate gyrus. These neurons then send axons known as *mossy fibers* to field CA3, where they form synapses with dendritic spines of the *pyramidal cells.* The axons of CA3 pyramidal cells branch in two directions. Axons in one branch, known as the *Schaffer Collateral system,* project to the adjacent field CA1, where they form synapses with other pyramidal cells. Axons in the other branch, project to the septum and the mammillary bodies, via the fornix. CA1 pyramidal cells also receive input from the contralateral hippocampus, through axons of the *Schaffer commisural system.* CA1 pyramidal cells send axons to neurons in the subicular complex. The axons of these neurons project out of the hippocampal formation via the entorhinal cortex and also through the fimbria. (See *Figure 14.17.*)

Figure 14.18 shows a typical procedure for producing long-term potentiation. A stimulating electrode is placed in the perforant path, and a recording electrode is placed in the dentate gyrus, near the granule cells. (See *Figure 14.18.*) First, a single pulse of electrical stimulation is delivered to the perforant path, and then the resulting popula-

tion EPSP is recorded in the dentate gyrus. The **population EPSP** is an extracellular measurement of the excitatory postsynaptic potentials (EPSP) produced by the synapses of the perforant path axons with the dentate granule cells. The size of the first population EPSP indicates the strength of the synaptic connections before long-term potentiation has taken place. Long-term potentiation can be induced by stimulating the axons in the perforant path with a burst of approximately one hundred pulses of electrical stimulation, delivered within a few seconds. Evidence that long-term potentiation has occurred is obtained by periodically delivering single pulses to the perforant path and recording the response in the dentate gyrus. (See *Figure 14.19.*)

Long-term potentiation can be produced in other regions of the hippocampal formation and, as we shall see, in other places in the brain. It can last for several months (Bliss and Lømo, 1973). It can be produced in isolated slices of the hippocampal

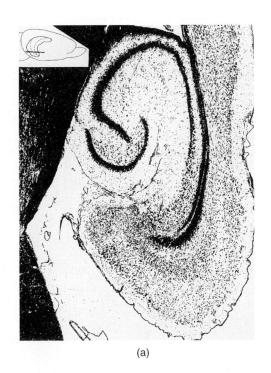

(a)

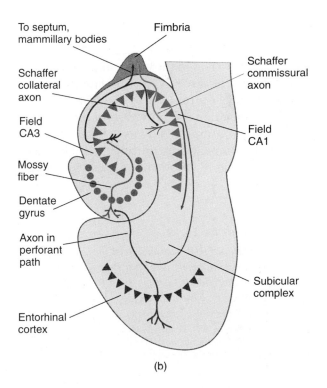

(b)

FIGURE 14.17

Connections of the components of the hippocampal formation.

(Photograph from Swanson, L.W., Köhler, C., and Björklund, A., in *Handbook of Chemical Neuroanatomy. Vol. 5: Integrated Systems of the CNS, Part I.* Amsterdam: Elsevier Science Publishers, 1987.)

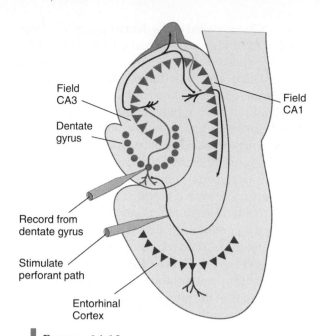

FIGURE 14.18

The procedure for producing long-term potentiation.

Field CA3

Dentate gyrus

Record from dentate gyrus

Stimulate perforant path

Entorhinal Cortex

Field CA1

formation as well as in the brains of living animals, which allows researchers to stimulate and record from individual neurons and to analyze biochemical changes. The brain is removed from the skull, the hippocampal complex is dissected, and slices are placed in a temperature-controlled chamber filled with liquid that resembles interstitial fluid. Figure

14.20 shows a 400-micrometer slice of hippocampal formation being maintained in a tissue chamber. Under optimal conditions a slice remains alive for up to 40 hours. (See *Figure 14.20.*)

Many experiments have demonstrated that long-term potentiation in hippocampal slices can follow the Hebb rule. That is, when weak and strong synapses to a single neuron are stimulated at approximately the same time, the weak synapse becomes strengthened. This phenomenon is called **associative long-term potentiation,** because it is produced by the association (in time) between the activity of the two sets of synapses. Kelso and Brown (1986) stimulated two different weak inputs (W1 and W2) and one strong input (S) to pyramidal cells in the CA1 field. (See *Figure 14.21.*) In some cases they paired W1 with S; in others they paired W2 with S. They found that only the synapses stimulated at the same time as the strong input were strengthened. (See *Figure 14.22.*) These results are particularly important because they indicate that the pairing did not simply make the CA1 pyramidal cells become more sensitive to *all* its inputs. Thus, the strengthening occurs in *specific synapses.*

Role of NMDA Receptors

Long-term potentiation requires some sort of additive effect. That is, a series of pulses delivered at a high rate all in one burst will produce long-term potentiation, but the same number of pulses given at

FIGURE 14.19

Population EPSPs recorded from the dentate gyrus before and after electrical stimulation that led to long-term potentiation. Note that the tops of some of the waves are missing.

(From Berger, T.W. *Science,* 1984, *224,* 627–630. Copyright 1984 by the American Association for the Advancement of Science.)

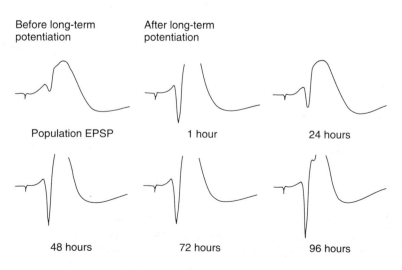

Before long-term potentiation

After long-term potentiation

Population EPSP

1 hour

24 hours

48 hours

72 hours

96 hours

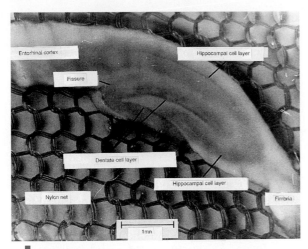

FIGURE 14.20

A photograph of a hippocampal slice in a tissue chamber.
(From Teyler, T.J. *Brain Research Bulletin,* 1980, *5,* 391–403.
Reprinted with permission.)

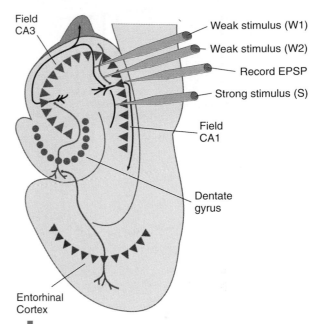

FIGURE 14.21

The procedure used by Kelso and Brown (1986) to demonstrate associative long-term potentiation.

a slow rate will not. (In fact, as we shall see, low-frequency stimulation can lead to the opposite phenomenon: long-term *depression.*) The most likely explanation for this difference is that each pulse produces an aftereffect that dissipates with time. If the next pulse comes before the aftereffect fades away, its own effect will be amplified. Thus, each pulse "primes" the following one. In addition, long-term potentiation can be produced in an initially weak synapse by the simultaneous stimulation of a strong synapse. In this case the effects produced by the activity of one synapse facilitate ("prime") the effects of the activity at another.

There is good evidence that the priming explanation is correct. Although earlier studies investigating the nature of long-term potentiation used bursts of approximately one hundred pulses, later studies discovered that if the interval between pulses is chosen carefully, much less stimulation is required. In fact, Diamond, Dunwiddie, and Rose (1988) were able to produce long-term potentiation with as few as five pulses of electrical stimulation: a priming pulse followed 170 milliseconds later by a burst of four pulses. (See *Figure 14.23.*)

Experiments have made it clear that the priming effect consists of a depolarization of the postsynaptic membrane. If the postsynaptic membrane is already depolarized (by a priming pulse or by the activation of adjacent excitatory synapses), then synaptic activity causes strengthening of the synaptic connection. Kelso, Ganong, and Brown (1986) found that if they artificially depolarized CA1 neurons and then stimulated the axons that formed

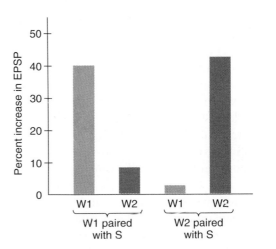

FIGURE 14.22

Differential associative long-term potentiation.
(Data from Kelso, S.R., and Brown, T.H. *Science,* 1986, *232,* 85–87.)

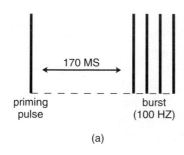

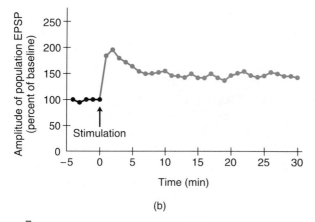

FIGURE 14.23

Long-term potentiation produced by four pulses of stimulation presented 170 msec after a priming pulse. (a) Pattern of the electrical stimulation. (b) Population EPSP.
(Adapted from Diamond, D.M., Dunwiddie, T.V., and Rose, G.M. *Journal of Neuroscience*, 1988, 8, 4079–4088.)

synapses with them, the synapses became stronger. However, if the stimulation of the synapses and the depolarization of the neuron occurred at different times, no effect was seen; thus, the two events had to occur together. And Malinow and Miller (1986) found that when they prevented depolarization of the postsynaptic membrane by hyperpolarizing the pyramidal cell with an intracellular electrode, high-frequency stimulation of inputs to that cell did *not* result in long-term potentiation.

Experiments such as the ones I just described indicate that long-term potentiation requires two events: activation of synapses and depolarization of the postsynaptic neuron. The explanation for this phenomenon, at least in some parts of the hippocampal formation, lies in the characteristics of a very special receptor. One of the most important excitatory neurotransmitters in the brain is glutamic acid (usually referred to as *glutamate*). As you have

already learned, many neurotransmitters are detected by more than one type of receptor. For example, there are two major types of acetylcholine receptors—nicotinic and muscarinic, named for the agonists that best stimulate them. Similarly, there are several different types of glutamate receptors, also named for their agonists. One of them, the NMDA receptor (short for *N*-methyl-D-aspartate), plays a critical role in long-term potentiation.

The **NMDA receptor** has some unusual properties (see Cotman, Monaghan, and Ganong, 1988, for a review). It is found in the hippocampal formation, especially in field CA1. The NMDA receptor controls a calcium ion channel. However, this channel is normally blocked by a magnesium ion (Mg^{2+}), which prevents calcium ions from entering the cell, even when the receptor is stimulated by glutamate. But if the postsynaptic membrane is depolarized, the Mg^{2+} is ejected from the ion channel, and the channel is free to admit Ca^{2+} ions. Thus, calcium ions enter the cells through the channels controlled by NMDA receptors only when glutamate is present *and* when the postsynaptic membrane is already depolarized. That means that the ion channel controlled by the NMDA receptor is a neurotransmitter-*and* voltage-dependent channel. (See *Figure 14.24*.)

The strongest evidence implicating NMDA receptors in long-term potentiation comes from research with drugs that block NMDA receptors, such as AP5 (2-amino-5-phosphonopentanoate). AP5 prevents the establishment of long-term potentiation in field CA1 and the dentate gyrus. However, it has no effect on long-term potentiation that has already been established (Brown et al., 1989). Thus, although the activation of NMDA receptors is necessary for long-term potentiation, transmission in the potentiated synapses involves *non*-NMDA receptors

Cell biologists have discovered that the calcium ion is used by many cells as a second messenger. For example, as we saw in Chapter 3, the entry of calcium ions into terminal buttons triggers the release of the transmitter substance. The entry of calcium ions through the ion channels controlled by NMDA receptors is an essential step in long-term potentiation. Lynch et al. (1984) demonstrated this fact by injecting EGTA directly into hippocampal pyrami-

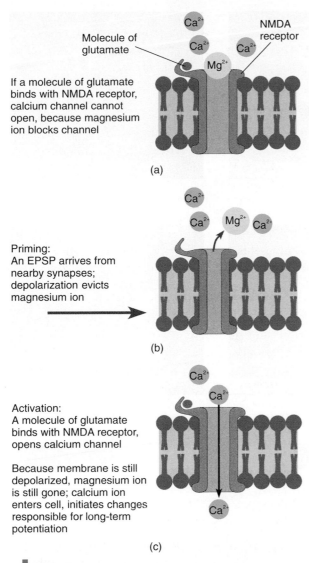

If a molecule of glutamate binds with NMDA receptor, calcium channel cannot open, because magnesium ion blocks channel

(a)

Priming:
An EPSP arrives from nearby synapses; depolarization evicts magnesium ion

(b)

Activation:
A molecule of glutamate binds with NMDA receptor, opens calcium channel

Because membrane is still depolarized, magnesium ion is still gone; calcium ion enters cell, initiates changes responsible for long-term potentiation

(c)

FIGURE 14.24

The NMDA receptor. (a) Before priming. (b) Priming. Depolarization from nearby non-NMDA glutamate receptors evicts the magnesium ion. (c) Activation. When glutamate attaches to the binding site, the ion channel opens, allowing calcium ions to enter the dendritic spine.

dal cells. This chemical binds with calcium and makes it insoluble, destroying its biological activity. The EGTA blocked the establishment of long-term potentiation in the injected cells; their excitability was not increased by high-frequency stimulation of axons that formed synapses with them. However, neighboring cells, which were not injected with EGTA, showed long-term potentiation.

Malenka et al. (1988) demonstrated that not only is calcium *necessary* for long-term potentiation, but it is *sufficient.* They injected a chemical called nitr-5 into CA1 pyramidal cells and then exposed them to ultraviolet light. Nitr-5 is a special calcium chelator. When it is exposed to ultraviolet light, it releases its hold on calcium ions; thus, when the cells were exposed to ultraviolet light, their intracellular concentration of free calcium ions suddenly increased. This increase produced a large enhancement of synaptic transmission between these cells and their inputs. (See **Figure 14.25.**)

Lerea et al. (1992) removed individual neurons from the dentate gyrus, placed them in a liquid similar to that used for hippocampal slices, and then injected them with a special dye called fura-2. This dye is sensitive to the presence of calcium ions; when they are present, it will fluoresce when exposed to ultraviolet light. **Figure 14.26** shows computer-generated images of some of these cells before and after

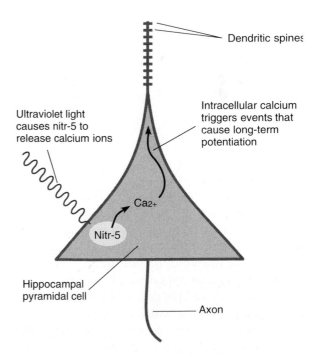

FIGURE 14.25

An explanation of the experiment by Malenka et al. (1988), which demonstrated that increased intracellular calcium in CA1 pyramidal cells produced long-term potentiation.

FIGURE 14.26

Individual neurons of the dentate gyrus, maintained in a tissue culture and injected with fura-2, a calcium-sensitive dye. (a) Basal levels of calcium. (b) Increased intracellular calcium after the application of NMDA to the culture medium. (c) Restoration of basal levels of calcium after the NMDA was rinsed away. (d) Failure of NMDA to increase intracellular calcium levels in the absence of calcium in the culture medium.

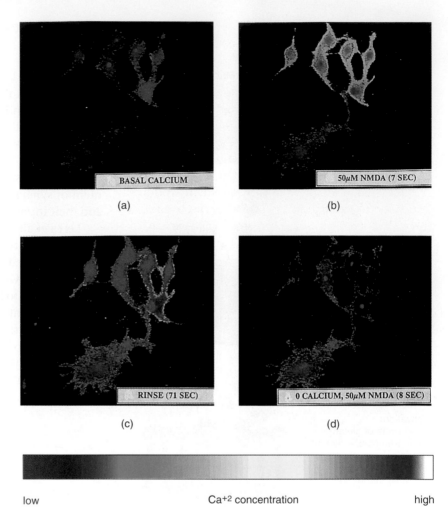

(a) (b)

(c) (d)

low   Ca^{+2} concentration   high

NMDA was added to the liquid bathing them. (The liquid did not contain magnesium; thus, the calcium channels were not blocked with magnesium ions.) Within 7 seconds the intracellular levels of calcium increased by approximately 600 percent. This effect did not occur when they bathed the cells with a liquid that did not contain calcium ions; thus, the calcium clearly entered the cells through the calcium channels controlled by NMDA receptors.

I think that considering what you already know about associative long-term potentiation, you can anticipate the role that NMDA receptors play in this phenomenon. If weak synapses are active by themselves, nothing happens, because the membrane of the dendritic spine does not depolarize sufficiently for the calcium channels controlled by the NMDA receptors to open. (Remember that in order for these channels to open, the postsynaptic membrane must depolarize and displace the Mg^{2+} ions that normally block them.) However, if strong synapses on the same dendrite are active at the same time, then the postsynaptic membrane will become depolarized enough for calcium to enter the ion channels controlled by the NMDA receptors. Thus, the special properties of NMDA receptors account not only for the existence of long-term potentiation but also for its associative nature. (See *Figure 14.27*.)

Mechanism of Synaptic Strengthening

What is responsible for the increases in synaptic strength that occur during long-term potentiation?

These increases could be caused by several different means. They could be produced presynaptically, through increased release of transmitter substance; or they could be produced postsynaptically, through an increased number of receptors, an increased ability of the receptors to activate changes in the permeability of the postsynaptic membrane, or increased communication between the region of the postsynaptic membrane and the rest of the neuron. (See *Figure 14.28.*) They could also be produced by an increased number of synapses, which would involve both presynaptic and postsynaptic changes. As we shall see, *each* of these possibilities has at least some supporting evidence.

Several studies have found that NMDA-mediated long-term potentiation either increases the sensitivity of postsynaptic glutamate receptors or produces more of them. Although the induction of long-term potentiation involves NMDA receptors, it is the *non-NMDA* receptors that become more sensitive (or more numerous). For example, Muller, Joly, and Lynch (1988) investigated the effects of two drugs on the expression of long-term potentiation in CA1: AP5 (an NMDA receptor blocker) and DNQX (a non-NMDA receptor blocker). They measured the size of the population EPSP in the presence of one drug or the other after long-term potentiation had been established. They found that the depolarization produced by activation of non-NMDA receptors was augmented by long-term potentiation, but that the depolarization produced by activation of NMDA receptors was not. (See *Figure 14.29.*)

Using a different procedure, Tocco et al. (1992) obtained results that support those of Muller and his colleagues. They established long-term potentiation in the dentate gyrus in intact animals by stimulating the perforant path. One hour later, they removed and sliced the brains, incubated alternate slices with radioactive ligands for NMDA and non-NMDA receptors, and looked at the density and distribution of these receptors by means of autoradiography. They found evidence for increased sensitivity (or numbers) of non-NMDA receptors. However, the long-term potentiation had no effect on binding of the ligand for NMDA receptors.

Obviously, the study by Tocco et al. supports the hypothesis that long-term potentiation is a postsynaptic event, but it leaves open the possibility that the terminal buttons could also be releasing more glutamate. But if more glutamate were being

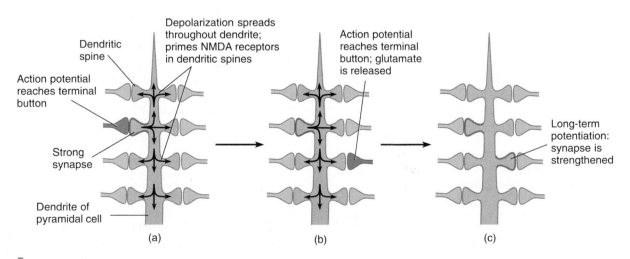

FIGURE 14.27

Associative long-term potentiation. (a) Activity of a strong synapse depolarizes dendritic membrane, primes NMDA receptors in dendritic spines. (b) Activity of a weak synapse releases glutamate, opens NMDA receptors. (c) The opening of NMDA receptors and the subsequent entry of calcium ions strengthens the weak sysnapse.

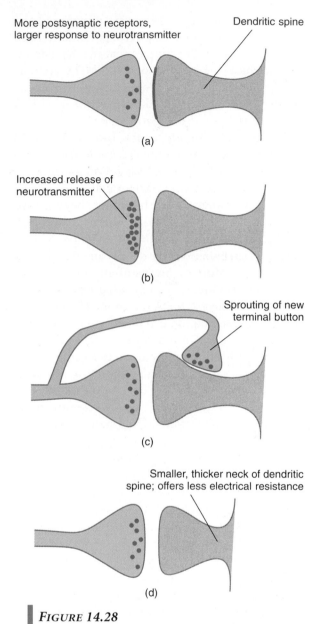

More postsynaptic receptors, larger response to neurotransmitter

Dendritic spine

(a)

Increased release of neurotransmitter

(b)

Sprouting of new terminal button

(c)

Smaller, thicker neck of dendritic spine; offers less electrical resistance

(d)

▌ FIGURE 14.28

Hypothetical changes that could account for the synaptic strengthening produced by long-term potentiation.

released, then we would expect that depolarizations produced by NMDA receptors would be augmented by long-term potentiation; and as Muller, Joly, and Lynch found, they were not. Nevertheless, several studies using a different approach to the problem have suggested that long-term potentiation may, after all, cause terminal buttons to release more transmitter substance (Malinow and Tsien, 1990).

These studies involve complex analyses of the post-synaptic responses to the quantal release of gluta-mate—that is, to the amount released by individual synaptic vesicles. Conclusive evidence is still lacking, but it is certainly possible that long-term potentiation involves both postsynaptic and presynaptic changes.

In any event, researchers agree that long-term potentiation produced through by the activation of NMDA receptors is initiated postsynaptically, by the entry of calcium ions. Most also agree that the entry of calcium activates some **calcium-dependent enzymes**—those that are inactive until a calcium ion binds with them. But which enzymes are involved, and what do these enzymes do? Evidence suggests that at least three enzymes may be involved, but exactly how they strengthen the transmission at particular synapses is still not known.

The three calcium-dependent enzymes that have received the most attention in the past few years are all *protein kinases*—enzymes that add phosphate groups (PO_4) to protein molecules, which causes some part of the protein to move, changing its prop-erties. These three enzymes are protein kinase C, type II calcium-calmodulin kinase, and tyrosine kinase.

The first of these enzymes, protein kinase C (best known as **PKC**), is normally present in the cyto-plasm and then moves to the cell membrane when it is activated by calcium ions, where it produces some poorly understood effects that potentiate synaptic transmission (Linden and Routtenberg, 1989; Muller et al., 1991). Hu et al. (1987) found that injection of activated PKC into CA1 pyramidal cells produced long-term potentiation. Malinow, Schulman, and Tsien (1989) found that injection of a PKC inhibitor into CA1 pyramidal cells prevented the induction of long-term potentiation. However, the drug had no effect on long-term potentiation that had previously been established; thus, PKC appears to play a role in the *induction* of synaptic strengthening but not in its maintenance.

The second enzyme, type II calcium-calmodulin kinase (best known as **CaM-KII**), is present in espe-cially high concentrations in the postsynaptic thick-ening of neurons in the hippocampal formation. CaM-KII has an unusual property: When it is acti-vated by calcium, it switches states, so that even if

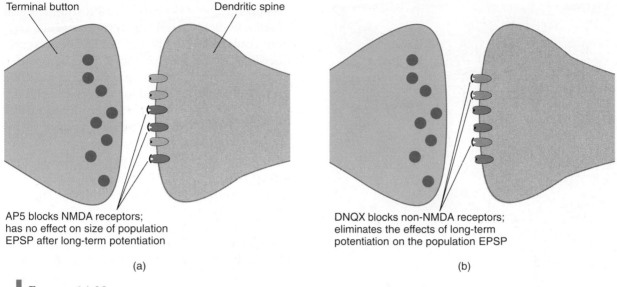

Terminal button

Dendritic spine

AP5 blocks NMDA receptors; has no effect on size of population EPSP after long-term potentiation

(a)

DNQX blocks non-NMDA receptors; eliminates the effects of long-term potentiation on the population EPSP

(b)

FIGURE 14.29

The experiment by Muller, Joly, and Lynch (1988). Long-term potentiation is established by activation of NMDA receptors, but it is expressed by activation of non-NMDA receptors.

the intracellular level of calcium falls again, it remains active until a specific enzyme puts it back into the inactive state (Hall, 1992). Thus, the brief entry of calcium ions into the cell could activate CaM-KII for a relatively long time, permitting it to participate in the establishment of long-term potentiation. Molecular biologists have found that CaM-KII is involved in many different types of chemical reactions; just what role it may play in the induction of long-term potentiation is not yet known.

A recent study provides very strong evidence that CaM-KII does, indeed, play an important role. Silva et al. (1992a) produced a mutation in mice using newly developed genetic engineering techniques that permit investigators to "knock out" a particular gene—in this case, the gene responsible for the production of CaM-KII. The mice had no obvious neuroanatomical defects, and the responses of NMDA receptors were normal. However, the investigators were unable to produce long-term potentiation in field CA1 of hippocampal slices taken from these animals.

A similar investigation indicates that the third calcium-dependent protein kinase, **tyrosine kinase,** also plays a role in long-term potentiation. Tyro-

sine kinases (there are several of them) alter proteins by phosphorylating parts of them that contain tyrosine, an amino acid. Grant et al. (1992) found that knocking out the gene responsible for the production of a particular tyrosine kinase (*fyn*) interfered with the production of long-term potentiation in CA1 pyramidal neurons. Long-term potentiation could still be produced, but the stimulus had to be much greater than normal.

So normal long-term potentiation involves the activation of at least three enzymes by the entry of calcium ions through the ion channels controlled by NMDA receptors. But what do these enzymes do that strengthens synaptic transmission? Perhaps they somehow increase the sensitivity of non-NMDA glutamate receptors or stimulate their production. Perhaps they change the physical characteristics of the dendritic spine so that EPSPs are more effectively transmitted to the dendrite. Perhaps they increase the size of the dendritic spine, which induces a corresponding increase in the number of glutamate receptors. In fact, Geinisman, de Toledo-Morrell, and Morrell (1991) found that long-term potentiation in the dentate gyrus increased the number of "perforated synapses"—

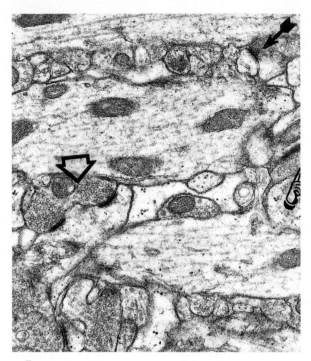

FIGURE 14.30

Photomicrograph of the dentate gyrus after stimulation that led to long-term potentiation. A perforated synapse is indicated by the open arrow.

(From Geinisman, Y., DeToledo-Morrell, L., and Morrell, F. *Brain Research,* 1991, *566,* 77–88. Reprinted with permission.)

synapses with more than one active zone, and more than one region containing a postsynaptic thickening. Whether this change represents an increase in synaptic strength is not yet known. (See *Figure 14.30.*)

What about the possibility of presynaptic changes? How could a process that occurs postsynaptically, in the dendritic spines, cause presynaptic changes? A possible answer comes from the recent discovery that a simple molecule, nitric oxide, can communicate messages from one cell to another. As we saw in Chapter 3, nitric oxide is a soluble gas produced by the activity of an enzyme known as **nitric oxide synthase.** Researchers have found that nitric oxide (NO) is used as a messenger in many parts of the body; for example, it is involved in the control of the muscles in the wall of the intestines, it dilates blood vessels in regions of the brain that

become metabolically active, and it stimulates the changes in blood vessels that produce penile erections (Culotta and Koshland, 1992). Once it is produced, NO lasts only a short time before it is destroyed. Thus, if it were produced in dendritic spines in the hippocampal formation, it could diffuse only as far as the nearby terminal buttons, where it might produce changes related to the induction of long-term potentiation.

Several experiments suggest that NO may, indeed, be a retrograde messenger involved in long-term potentiation. (*Retrograde* means "moving backward"; in this context it refers to messages sent from the dendritic spine back to the terminal button.) Bredt, Hwang, and Snyder (1990) found that nitric oxide synthase is found in neurons in various parts of the brain, including the hippocampus. East and Garthwaite (1991) found that when hippocampal slices were exposed to NMDA, levels of cyclic GMP increased. This increase did not occur when the investigators administered a drug that prevents the synthesis of nitric oxide, so the activation of NMDA must have resulted in the production of NO. Soon after these studies appeared, four laboratories reported that drugs that block nitric oxide synthase prevented the establishment of long-term potentiation in hippocampal slices (O'Dell et al., 1991; Schuman and Madison, 1991; Bon et al., 1992; Haley, Wilcox, and Chapman, 1992). They also found that long-term potentiation was blocked by a chemical that destroys NO that is present in the interstitial fluid—presumably on its way between the dendritic spine and the presynaptic terminal buttons.

Figure 14.31 summarizes the biochemistry discussed in this subsection. I suspect that you may feel overwhelmed by all the new terms I have introduced here, and I hope that the figure will help clarify things. The evidence we have seen so far indicates that the entry of calcium ions through channels controlled by NMDA receptors activates several calcium-dependent protein kinases, including CaM-KII, PKC, and tyrosine kinase. One or more of these enzymes may produce postsynaptic changes that increase the sensitivity of the non-NMDA glutamate receptors in the postsynaptic membrane. (See *Figure 14.31.*) In addition, these enzymes all activate NO synthase, and the newly produced NO

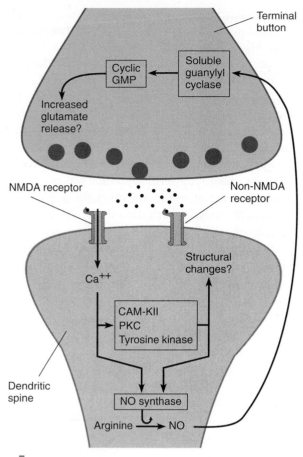

FIGURE 14.31

A summary of the chemical reactions triggered by the entry of an adequate amount of calcium into the dendritic spine.

then presumably diffuses out of the dendritic spine, back to the terminal button. There, it activates soluble guanylyl cyclase, an enzyme found in the cytoplasm that triggers the synthesis of cyclic GMP. The cyclic GMP then catalyzes unknown chemical reactions that increase the release of glutamate. (See *Figure 14.31*.)

We have seen that there is strong evidence in favor of the postsynaptic changes outlined in Figure 14.31. The evidence that long-term potentiation requires the synthesis of NO is also good, except for one fact: So far, although NO synthase is found in the hippocampal formation, researchers have failed to find it in hippocampal pyramidal cells (Bredt,

Hwang, and Snyder, 1990). Some investigators believe that these cells may contain a different form of NO synthase—one that is not detected by the method of analysis that is presently available. But until that missing link is found, we must consider the role of NO in long-term potentiation to be an open question.

Modulation of Long-Term Potentiation

So far in this section, I have discussed only one neurotransmitter, glutamate. But research indicates that long-term potentiation is modulated by other neurotransmitters. The hippocampal formation receives input from serotonergic, dopaminergic, noradrenergic, and acetylcholinergic neurons, all of which enter through the fornix. A study by Buzsáki and Gage (1988) indicates that at least some of these inputs are essential for the establishment of long-term potentiation. They cut the fornix of rats and then several months later implanted electrodes in the perforant path and dentate gyrus. They found that stimulation of the perforant path led to long-term potentiation in the dentate gyrus of control animals but not in those with fornix transections.

Which of the inputs to the hippocampal formation are important? Although all of the inputs may be important, the strongest case can be made for the involvement of norepinephrine and acetylcholine. Several studies have shown that norepinephrine or ß-adrenergic agonists facilitate long-term potentiation in the dentate gyrus and in field CA3 and that ß-adrenergic antagonists block its development (Johnston, Hopkins, and Gray, 1989; Dahl and Sarvey 1989, 1990). Robinson and Racine (1982) found that stimulation of the medial septum (which contains the cell bodies of acetylcholine-secreting axons that terminate in the hippocampal formation) facilitated the formation of long-term potentiation in the dentate gyrus. Studies with hippocampal slices have confirmed these results and have shown that acetylcholine facilitates long-term potentiation in field CA1, as well (Burgard and Sarvey, 1990; Markram and Segal, 1990).

The hippocampal formation also contains inhibitory interneurons that secrete GABA and the endogenous opioids. Endogenous opioids have inhibitory effects on long-term potentiation in synapses between mossy fibers and CA3 neurons but not between commissural/associational fibers and CA3 neurons. Benzodiazepines, antianxiety drugs that act on the GABA_A receptor, inhibit long-term potentiation in field CA1 (del Cerro, Jung, and Lynch, 1992). This effect may explain the fact that benzodiazepines interfere with memory .

I mentioned earlier that low-frequency stimulation of the synaptic inputs to a cell can *decrease* rather than increase their strength. This phenomenon, known as **long-term depression,** probably also plays a role in learning. After all, although the number of synapses in the brain is very large, it is still finite, and animals can continue to learn throughout their lives. Thus, it seems unlikely that once a synapse is strengthened, it must remain that way forever. Dudek and Bear (1992) stimulated Schaffer collateral inputs to CA1 neurons in hippocampal slices with 900 pulses of electrical current, delivered at rates ranging from 1 to 50 Hz. They found that frequencies above 10 Hz caused long-

term potentiation, whereas those below 10 Hz caused long-term depression. Both of these effects were blocked by application of AP5, the NMDA receptor blocker; thus, both effects require the activation of NMDA receptors. (See *Figure 14.32.*)

Stanton and Sejnowski (1989) demonstrated *associative* long-term depression in field CA1. They found that when a weak input was paired with a strong input, long-term potentiation was produced. However, when the two inputs were stimulated at different times, long-term *depression* was produced. Thus, at least at some synapses the Hebb rule appears to work in both directions: Weak inputs correlated with strong inputs are strengthened, whereas weak inputs *not* correlated with strong inputs are further weakened. This mechanism could conceivably allow for the reversal of previously established synaptic changes when the contingencies in the environment change.

Other Forms of Long-Term Potentiation

Long-term potentiation was discovered in the hippocampal formation and has been studied more in this region than in others, but it also occurs elsewhere in the brain. So far, it has been demonstrated in the prefrontal cortex, piriform cortex, entorhinal cortex, motor cortex, visual cortex, thalamus, and amygdala (Gerren and Weinberger, 1983; Clugnet and LeDoux, 1990; Aroniadou and Teyler, 1991; Baranyi, Szente, and Woody, 1991; Lynch et al., 1991). NMDA receptors are probably involved in the potentiation that takes place in the piriform and entorhinal cortex and in the amygdala, but research on the role of these receptors in the other regions has not yet been reported. At least one form of long-term potentiation that takes place in the visual cortex does not involve NMDA receptors (Aroniadou and Teyler, 1991).

In the hippocampal formation NMDA receptors are present in highest concentrations in field CA1 and in the dentate gyrus. However, very few NMDA receptors are found in the region of field CA3 that receives mossy fiber input from the dentate gyrus (Monaghan and Cotman, 1985). High-frequency stimulation of the mossy fibers produces a long-lasting potentiation that gradually decays

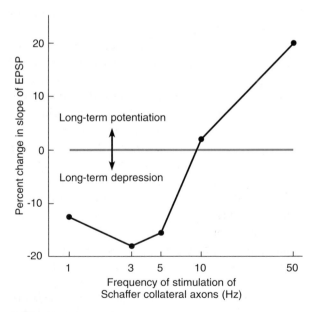

FIGURE 14.32

Changes in the sensitivity of synapses of Schaffer collateral axons with CA1 pyramidal cells after electrical stimulation at various frequencies.

(Adapted from Dudek, S.M., and Bear, M.F. *Proceedings of the National Academy of Sciences,* 1992, *89,* 4363–4367.)

over a period of several hours (Lynch et al., 1991). AP5, the drug that blocks NMDA receptors and prevents the establishment of long-term potentiation in CA1 neurons, has no effect on long-lasting potentiation in field CA3. The mechanism responsible for this phenomenon is not yet known, but electrophysiological studies suggest that it takes place presynaptically.

In recent years the phenomenon of long-term potentiation has received a considerable amount of attention from scientists interested in the cellular basis of learning, and their interest appears to be justified. The fact that long-term potentiation can be produced in several regions besides the hippocampal formation suggests that the mechanisms that underlie this phenomenon may be widespread in the brain. (We will examine evidence that supports this suggestion later in this chapter.) The discovery of the functions of the NMDA receptor provides solid evidence for at least one mechanism that produces the type of synapse that Hebb predicted over forty years ago. However, other mechanisms of synaptic plasticity also exist, and little is known about them. The progress that has been made during the last few years in research on the cellular basis of learning suggests that someday we really may come to understand it.

Role of Long-Term Potentiation in Learning

If the synaptic changes that constitute learning are accomplished by long-term potentiation, then we should suspect that disruption of long-term potentiation should also disrupt learning; and it does. The injection of AP5 into the hippocampal formation, which disrupts NMDA-mediated long-term potentiation, interferes with learning. In addition, certain learning experiences produce synaptic changes in the hippocampal formation. Because the role of the hippocampus in learning is complex, research on this topic is discussed in Chapter 15, which deals with relational learning.

Several studies have investigated the relation between long-term potentiation elsewhere in the brain and the acquisition of a classically conditioned emotional response; these studies are discussed in the next section of this chapter.

||||| INTERIM SUMMARY

The study of long-term potentiation in the hippocampal formation has suggested a mechanism that might be responsible for at least some of the synaptic changes that occur during learning. A circuit of neurons passes through the hippocampal formation, from the entorhinal cortex to the dentate gyrus to field CA3 to field CA1 to the subiculum. High-frequency stimulation of the axons in this circuit strengthens synapses; it leads to an increase in the size of the EPSPs in the dendritic spines of the postsynaptic neurons. Associative long-term potentiation can also occur, in which weak synapses are strengthened by the action of strong ones. In fact, the only requirement for long-term potentiation is that the postsynaptic membrane be depolarized at the same time that the synapses are active.

In field CA1 and in the dentate gyrus NMDA receptors play a special role in long-term potentiation. These receptors, sensitive to glutamate, control calcium channels but can open them only if the membrane is already depolarized. Thus, the combination of membrane depolarization (from a priming pulse or from the activity of a strong synapse nearby) and activation of an NMDA receptor causes the entry of calcium ions. The increase in calcium activates several calcium-dependent enzymes, including PKC, CaM-KII, and tyrosine kinase. Inhibition of these enzymes disrupts long-term potentiation; presumably, they catalyze changes in the sensitivity of the dendritic spine to the release of glutamate by the presynaptic terminal button. The enzymes may also produce presynaptic changes, through the activation of NO synthase, an enzyme responsible for the production of nitric oxide. This soluble gas may diffuse into nearby terminal buttons where it triggers the synthesis of cyclic GMP. This second messenger (actually, it is about the fourth or fifth messenger by now) may facilitate the release of glutamate.

Norepinephrine and acetylcholine also appear to play a role in long-term potentiation. The stimulation of ß receptors facilitates long-term potentiation in field CA3, and drugs that block these receptors prevent its formation. Stimulation of the medial septum, which causes the release of acetylcholine in the hippocampal formation, facilitates the formation of long-term potentiation in the hippocampal formation. If long-term potentiation occurred only in the hippocampal formation, it would be an important finding, but the fact that it also occurs in several other regions of the brain suggests that it may play an important role in many forms of learning.

S-R LEARNING: CLASSICAL CONDITIONING

NEUROSCIENTISTS HAVE STUDIED THE ANATOMY and physiology of classical conditioning using many models, such as the gill withdrawal reflex in *Aplysia* (a marine invertebrate) or the eyeblink reflex in the rabbit (Carew, 1989; Lavond, Kim, and Thompson, 1993). I have chosen to describe a simple mammalian model of classical conditioning—the conditioned emotional response—to illustrate the results of such investigations.

The central nucleus of the amygdala plays an important role in organizing a pattern of emotional responses that are provoked by aversive stimuli, both learned and unlearned. As we saw in Chapter 11, when this nucleus is activated, its efferent connections with other regions of the brain trigger several behavioral, autonomic, and endocrine responses that are elicited by aversive stimuli. Most stimuli that cause an aversive emotional response are not intrinsically aversive; we have to *learn* to fear them. The central nucleus of the amygdala is part of an important system involved in a particular form of stimulus-response (S-R) learning: the classically conditioned emotional responses.

As we saw earlier in this chapter, one of the things that the central nucleus of the amygdala does when it is activated is stimulate the release of acetylcholine in the cerebral cortex. This release sensitizes cortical neurons and facilitates the establishment of neural circuits sensitive to the CS. Presumably, the rewiring of these circuits is accomplished by means of long-term potentiation.

What about classical conditioning itself? A conditioned emotional response to a very simple auditory stimulus can occur in the absence of auditory

cortex (LeDoux et al., 1984), so I will confine my discussion to the subcortical components of this process. Information about the CS (the tone) reaches the MGM/PIN (the medial division of the medial geniculate nucleus and the posterior intralaminar nucleus of the thalamus). Information about the US (the foot shock) reaches both the MGM/PIN and the basolateral amygdala. Thus, there is convergence of information about the CS and the US in two regions: the MGM/PIN and the basolateral amygdala. Synaptic changes responsible for learning could take place in either (or both) of these locations.

A hypothetical neural circuit is shown in Figure 14.33. When a rat encounters a painful stimulus, strong synapses in the MGM/PIN and the basolateral amygdala are activated; as a result, neurons in the central nucleus begin firing, evoking an unlearned (unconditioned) emotional response. If a tone is paired with the painful stimulus, the weak synapses in the MGM/PIN and the basolateral amygdala are strengthened, through the action of the Hebb rule. (See *Figure 14.33.*)

We have already seen that good evidence supports this hypothesis: Lesions of the MGM/PIN, basolateral amygdala, or central nucleus disrupt conditioned emotional responses (Iwata et al., 1986; LeDoux et al., 1986, 1990; Sananes and Davis, 1992). In addition, electrical stimulation of the MGM/PIN can serve as a US, just as foot shock can (Cruikshank, Edeline, and Weinberger, 1992). By them-

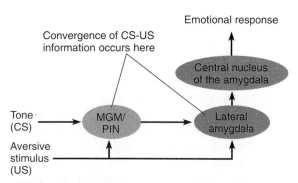

FIGURE 14.33

The probable location of the changes in synaptic strength produced by the classically conditioned emotional response that results from pairing a tone with a foot shock.

selves, these studies do not prove that learning actually takes place in these nuclei, but other studies suggest that it probably does.

A single-unit-recording study by Weinberger and his colleagues (reported by Weinberger, 1982) showed that neurons in the MGM/PIN increased their responsiveness to the auditory CS after this stimulus was paired with an aversive US. Figure 14.34 shows the responses of a single neuron in this nucleus during ten trials of a control procedure and ten trials of conditioning (two trials per graph). During the control procedure (*left column*) the tone (CS) and the shock (US) were presented at random intervals and were not paired. During conditioning (*right column*) the tone and the shock were paired. The data show that during the control procedure the neuron initially responded to the tone (indicated by the color horizontal line), but this response soon habituated. However, once conditioning trials began, the neuron quickly began responding during the tone. (See *Figure 14.34.*)

Applegate et al. (1982) found that the responsiveness of neurons in the central nucleus also changes during classical conditioning. (See *Figure 14.35.*) It seems likely that these changes are a result of learning that has taken place either in the MGM/PIN or in the basolateral amygdala—or perhaps in both locations.

Seeing that it is likely that the synaptic changes responsible for classically conditioned emotional responses take place in two particular locations, we can ask whether these changes may be produced by a phenomenon we already know something about: long-term potentiation. Indeed, studies have shown that long-term potentiation can take place in the synaptic connections in the MGM/PIN and the basolateral amygdala. Gerren and Weinberger (1983) found that high-frequency stimulation of the axons that bring auditory information into the MGM produced long-term potentiation in this nucleus. Clugnet and LeDoux (1990) found that stimulation of the medial geniculate nucleus produced long-term potentiation in the lateral amygdala. Using the brain slice technique, Chapman et al. (1990) found that stimulation of the axons from the cerebral cortex to the lateral amygdala also produced long-term potentiation. Obviously, animals can learn classically conditioned emotional responses

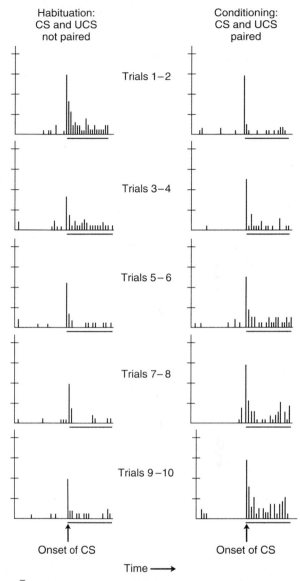

FIGURE 14.34

Responses of a single neuron in the magnocellular medial geniculate nucleus during aversive classical conditioning.
(From Weinberger, N.M., in *Conditioning: Representation of Involved Neural Functions*, edited by C.D. Woody. New York: Plenum Press, 1982. Drawn with permission.)

to complex stimuli that can be analyzed only by the cerebral cortex. The finding that long-term potentiation can be established in the synapses that convey cortical input to the amygdala suggests that plasticity in these synapses may be responsible for this learning, too.

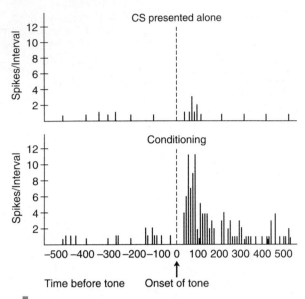

FIGURE 14.35

Multiple-unit activity in the central nucleus of the amygdala during habituation of the orienting response and during conditioning and extinction of the bradycardia response.

(Adapted from Kapp, B.S., Gallagher, M., Applegate, C.D., and Frysinger, R.C., in *Conditioning: Representation of Involved Neural Functions,* edited by C.D. Woody. New York: Plenum Press, 1982. Reprinted with permission.)

As we saw, long-term potentiation in at least some parts of the brain is accomplished through the activation of NMDA receptors. An experiment by Campeau, Miserendino, and Davis (1992) suggests that these receptors also participate in the synaptic plasticity that occurs in the amygdala. Campeau, Miserendino, and Davis (1992) found that when they injected AP5 (a drug that blocks NMDA receptors) directly into the basolateral amygdala, rats no longer learned a conditioned emotional response. However, if the investigators established a classically conditioned emotional response *before* they injected the AP5, the drug had no effect. Also, Melia, Falls, and Davis (1992) found that pertussis toxin, a drug that prevents long-term potentiation by deactivating certain forms of G protein, had similar effects. Thus, it seems that by preventing synaptic plasticity in the basolateral amygdala, these drugs disrupt the establishment of learning but do not affect the synaptic changes that have already been produced.

A recent study found that NMDA-dependent long-term potentiation may also play a role in *extinction* of a classically conditioned emotional response. Classical conditioning is not always forever. If, after classical conditioning has been established by pairing a CS and a US, the CS is presented repeatedly by itself, the conditioned response will eventually disappear—a process known as **extinction.** Falls, Miserendino, and Davis (1992) found that thirty presentations of the CS alone were sufficient to extinguish a classically conditioned emotional response. However, if they injected AP5 into the amygdala just before these thirty extinction trials, the response did *not* extinguish. Thus, NMDA-mediated synaptic plasticity seems to be necessary for both learning and extinction. It would be interesting to know whether there is a relation between these results and the fact that uncorrelated stimulation of two inputs to cells in field CA1 of the hippocampal formation weaken synaptic connections—that is, produce long-term depression (Stanton and Sejnowski, 1989).

When I was a graduate student, I doubted that within my lifetime we would be able to figure out the physiological nature of learning. The progress that has been made in our understanding of the nature of synaptic plasticity and its application to learning proves that I was too pessimistic.

INTERIM SUMMARY

You have already encountered the conditioned emotional response in Chapter 11 and earlier in this chapter, where I discussed perceptual learning. When an auditory stimulus (CS) is paired with a foot shock (US), the two types of information converge in the medial division of the medial geniculate nucleus/posterior intralaminar nucleus (MGM/PIN) and again in the lateral amygdala. The lateral amygdala is connected with the central nucleus, which is responsible for the various components of the emotional response. Lesions of any of these regions disrupt the response.

Recordings of single neurons in both the MGM/PIN and the central amygdala indicate that classical conditioning changes the response of neurons to the CS. The mechanism of synaptic plasticity in this system appears to be NMDA-mediated long-term potentiation. High-frequency electrical stimulation of the inputs to both the MGM/PIN and of the lateral amygdala produce long-term potentiation, and the infusion of NMDA into the lateral amygdala prevents classical conditioning from taking place but has no effect on conditioning that was established earlier. It also prevents the *extinction* of a conditioned emotional response.

S-R LEARNING: INSTRUMENTAL CONDITIONING

AS WE SAW EARLIER IN THIS CHAPTER, INSTRU-mental (operant) conditioning involves strengthening of the connection between neural circuits that detect a particular stimulus and neural circuits that produce a particular response. This strengthening occurs only when the response is followed by a reinforcing stimulus, such as a morsel of food or a sip of water—and it is controlled by a reinforcement mechanism. The discovery of this mechanism, one of the most interesting discoveries in the history of neuroscience, was made by accident.

Discovery of Reinforcing Brain Stimulation

In 1954 James Olds was trying to determine whether electrical stimulation of the reticular formation might increase arousal and thus facilitate learning. He was assisted in this project by Peter Milner, who was a graduate student at the time. Olds had heard a talk by Neal Miller that described the aversive effects of electrical stimulation of the brain. Therefore, he decided to make sure that stimulation of the reticular formation was not aversive—if it were, the effects of this stimulation on the speed of learning would be difficult to assess. Fortunately for the investigators, one of the electrodes missed its target; the tip wound up some millimeters away, probably in the hypothalamus. (Unfortunately, the brain of the animal was lost, so histological verification could not be obtained.) If all of the electrodes had reached

their intended target, Olds and Milner would not have discovered what they did.

Here is Olds's description of what happened when he tested this animal to see whether the brain stimulation was aversive:

> I applied a brief train of 60-cycle sine-wave electrical current whenever the animal entered one corner of the enclosure. The animal did not stay away from the corner, but rather came back quickly after a brief sortie which followed the first stimulation and came back even more quickly after a briefer sortie which followed the second stimulation. By the time the third electrical stimulus had been applied the animal seemed indubitably to be "coming back for more." (Olds, 1973, p. 81)

Olds and Milner were intrigued and excited by this result. They implanted electrodes in the brains of a group of rats and allowed the animals to administer their own stimulation by pressing a lever-operated switch in an operant chamber. (See *Figure 14.36.*) The animals readily pressed the lever; in their initial study Olds and Milner (1954) reported response rates of over seven hundred per hour. (The self-administration of electrical brain stimulation is usually referred to as **self-stimulation.**) In subsequent studies rates of many thousands of responses per hour have been obtained. Clearly, electrical stimulation of the brain can be a very potent reinforcer.

Mechanisms of Reinforcing Brain Stimulation

An animal's behavior can be reinforced by electrical stimulation of many parts of the brain, including the olfactory bulb, prefrontal cortex, nucleus accumbens, caudate nucleus, putamen, various thalamic nuclei, reticular formation, amygdala, ventral tegmental area, substantia nigra, and locus coeruleus (Olds and Fobes, 1981). But the best and most reliable location is the **medial forebrain bundle** (MFB), a bundle of axons that travel in a rostral-caudal axis from the midbrain to the rostral basal forebrain. The MFB passes through the lateral hypothalamus, and it is in this region that most investigators place the tips of their electrodes. The MFB contains long ascending and descending axons

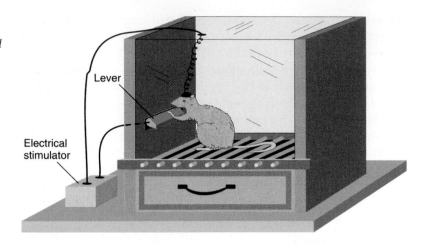

Figure 14.36

An operant chamber with a lever, used in studies of the effects of reinforcing brain stimulation.

Lever

Electrical stimulator

that interconnect forebrain and midbrain structures, and short axons that connect adjacent regions. It also contains ascending dopaminergic, noradrenergic, and serotonergic axons on their way from the brain stem to their projection areas in the forebrain. As we will see, the activity of a particular subset of these fibers is responsible for the reinforcing effects of electrical stimulation of the MFB.

In the past several years investigators have made considerable progress in identifying the neural systems that mediate reinforcement. We now know that dopaminergic neurons play a critical role and that electrical stimulation of the MFB activates axons that descend to a nucleus in the midbrain that contains the cell bodies of these neurons. It is likely that other systems of neurons, which do not contain dopaminergic axons, also mediate reinforcing effects; but I shall restrict my discussion to the dopaminergic system, because it has received the most attention from researchers.

Anatomy of Dopaminergic Pathways

As we saw in Chapter 5, the development of special staining methods has permitted investigators to trace the pathways of neurons that secrete particular transmitter substances. Investigators soon discovered that the distribution of reinforcing electrode sites nicely coincided with the distribution of catecholaminergic neurons—those that secrete norepinephrine and dopamine. That is, brain stimulation through electrodes whose tips were placed in fiber bundles that contained catecholaminergic axons or in structures that received

catecholaminergic projections generally had reinforcing effects. This finding suggested that perhaps one or both of the catecholamines were involved in reinforcement. In fact, one of them is: dopamine.

There are several systems of neurons whose terminal buttons secrete dopamine. The major pathways begin in two regions of the midbrain: the substantia nigra and the ventral tegmental area (Lindvall, 1979; Fallon, 1988). Although the cell bodies of these neurons are gathered together in compact clusters, their axons divide extensively; each axon can give rise to several hundred thousand terminal buttons. Thus, the activity of a small number of cell bodies can affect an enormous number of neurons in widespread areas of the brain. Most investigators believe that dopamine serves as a neuromodulator rather than a neurotransmitter—that the activation of postsynaptic dopamine receptors affects the sensitivity of *other* types of receptors.

The *nigrostriatal system* starts in the *pars compacta* of the substantia nigra and projects to the *neostriatum*—the caudate nucleus and putamen. As we saw in Chapters 4 and 8, this system is important in the control of movement; its degeneration results in Parkinson's disease. The **mesolimbic system** begins in the ventral tegmental area (located in the midbrain—mesencephalon—just adjacent to the substantia nigra) and projects through the medial forebrain bundle to the amygdala, the lateral septum, the bed nucleus of the stria terminalis, the hippocampus, and the nucleus accumbens. Much of the research on the physiology of reinforcement has focused on the last of these structures. The

nucleus accumbens is a region of the *paleostriatum,* located in the basal forebrain rostral to the preoptic area and immediately adjacent to the septum. (In fact, the full name of this region is the *nucleus accumbens septi,* or "nucleus leaning against the septum.") (See *Figure 14.37.*)

The third major system of dopaminergic axons, the **mesocortical system,** also begins in the ventral tegmental area. In rats this system projects to the prefrontal neocortex, limbic cortex (entorhinal, suprarhinal, and anterior cingulate cortex), and hippocampus. In primates the mesocortical projections are much more widespread; in addition to the regions just listed, all of the frontal lobes and all regions of association cortex in the parietal and temporal lobes receive dopaminergic innervation (Berger, Gaspar, and Verney, 1991).

Effects of Dopamine Antagonists

Studies using drugs that block dopamine receptors clearly indicate that dopamine is involved in reinforcement—provided not only by electrical stimulation of the brain but also by natural reinforcing stimuli.

Many studies have shown that drugs that block dopamine receptors also block the process of reinforcement. For example, Rolls et al. (1974) trained rats to press a lever for several different types of reinforcement (including brain stimulation, food, and water) and then administered a drug that blocks

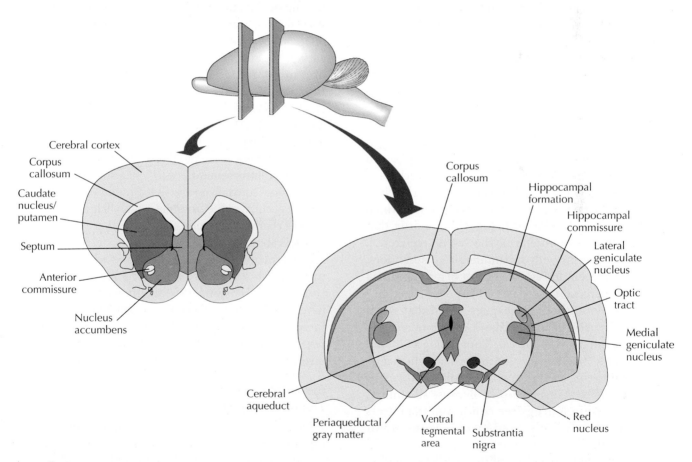

FIGURE 14.37

A section through a rat brain showing the location of the ventral tegmental area and the nucleus accumbens.

(Adapted from Paxinos, G., and Watson, C. *The Rat Brain in Stereotaxic Coordinates.* Sydney: Academic Press, 1982.)

dopamine receptors (spiroperidol). They found that the drug suppressed the animals' instrumental responding. However, we cannot determine from studies such as this one whether the animals stopped responding because the food, water, or electrical stimulation was no longer reinforcing, or whether they stopped because the drug interfered with motor systems that controlled their behavior. The drug could have simply made it difficult for the animal to move.

Subsequent studies have shown that the drugs do block reinforcement and do not simply produce side effects that interfere with movement. For example, if an animal receives food (or another reinforcer) in a particular location, it will return to that location later. In other words, when an animal encounters a reinforcing stimulus in a particular place, it develops a **conditioned place preference.** Spyraki, Fibiger, and Phillips (1982a) trained two groups of hungry rats in a conditioned place preference task. On alternate days the rats were placed in each of two chambers. They received food in one chamber but not the other. After eight days of training the animals were permitted to choose between the two chambers. Rats in the control group, which received an injection of saline just before each day's training, chose the chamber where they had received food. Rats in the experimental group, which received an injection of haloperidol, a drug that blocks dopamine receptors, showed no preference. Thus, interfering with dopaminergic synapses does, indeed, prevent the establishment of a conditioned place preference.

Spyraki and her colleagues noted that when food was present in the chamber, the rats in the experimental group *did* eat. Thus, haloperidol did not simply block the response normally elicited by the reinforcing stimulus; it blocked the *reinforcing consequences* of this response. Because all animals were tested in a drug-free condition, the effects were obviously not caused by changes in motor performance.

Drugs that block dopamine receptors interfere with excitatory effects of appetitive stimuli as well as their reinforcing effects. For example, Falk (1972) discovered that when a very hungry rat receives small pieces of food at infrequent intervals—say, every 2 minutes—the animal becomes very active,

engaging in a variety of species-typical behaviors. If water is present, the animal will drink copiously, sometimes consuming an amount equal to 30 percent of its body weight during a 3-hour session. The behaviors are not limited to ingestive ones: If a block of wood is present, the rat will gnaw on it; if another male is present, the rat will attack it; and so on. Behaviors elicited by these means are called **adjunctive behaviors,** because they occur as an adjunct (auxiliary feature) of intermittent reinforcement.

Several studies indicate that these excitatory effects of reinforcing stimuli involve the release of dopamine in the nucleus accumbens. For example, Salamone (1988) found that an injection of haloperidol blocked these excitatory effects of reinforcing stimuli; the drug abolished adjunctive activity when rats were given small pieces of food every 30 to 360 seconds. The drug did not interfere with eating; the animals simply stayed next to the food dish and ate the food when it was delivered. In addition, Robbins and Koob (1980) and Mittleman et al. (1990) found that destruction of the dopaminergic input to the nucleus accumbens disrupted adjunctive behaviors.

Not all reinforcement involves appetitive stimuli. **Negative reinforcement** occurs when something the animal does turns off an aversive stimulus or prevents it from occurring. For example, a rat will learn to run out of a chamber when a buzzer warns that an electric shock is about to be applied to the floor. (Negative reinforcement should not be confused with punishment, which *suppresses* a response.) Several studies (for example, Posluns, 1962; Beninger et al., 1980) have shown that drugs that block dopamine receptors interfere with negatively reinforced avoidance responses. Thus, dopaminergic neurons appear to be involved in negative reinforcement, too.

Systemic Administration of Dopamine Agonists

If dopamine antagonists interfere with the effects of reinforcing stimuli, then we might expect that dopamine agonists would enhance them. Indeed, they do—and when these drugs are given by themselves, they produce their own reinforcing effect. For example, Gallistel and Karras (1984) found that injections of amphetamine, a dopaminergic agonist, increase the rate at which a rat will press a lever to obtain reinforcing brain stimulation. Spyraki, Fibiger, and Phillips (1982b) found that rats would learn a conditioned place preference if they were given an injection of amphetamine just before being put in a particular chamber. (They did not receive any food—only the drug.)

Probably the most dramatic effect of dopamine agonists is seen in experiments in which animals administer the drugs themselves. In such **self-administration** studies animals are able to press a lever that turns on a pump that injects the drug directly into their veins, by means of a flexible plastic tube. Members of a variety of species, including rats, monkeys, and humans, will eagerly and vigorously inject themselves with dopamine agonists such as amphetamine and cocaine (Koob and Bloom, 1988). (I am sure you realize that the evidence concerning humans did not require laboratory experiments.)

Studies have shown that animals will self-administer all drugs that are potentially addictive in humans—drugs such as opiates, THC (the active ingredient in marijuana), nicotine, and caffeine. In addition, these drugs trigger the release of dopamine in the nucleus accumbens. The physiology of addiction is discussed in more detail in Chapter 18.

Intracranial Administration of Drugs

A large body of experimental evidence indicates that the mesolimbic pathway—particularly the branch that terminates in the nucleus accumbens—is the pathway responsible for the reinforcing effects of electrical stimulation of the medial forebrain bundle. It also plays an important role in the reinforcing effects of amphetamine and cocaine and in those of many natural appetitive stimuli. Treatments that stimulate dopamine receptors in the nucleus accumbens will reinforce behaviors; thus, animals will press a lever that causes electrical stimulation of the ventral tegmental area, medial forebrain bundle, or nucleus accumbens itself (Routtenberg and Malsbury, 1969; Crow, 1972; Olds and Fobes, 1981). They will also press a lever that delivers direct injections of very small amounts of dopamine or amphetamine directly into the nucleus accumbens (Hoebel et al., 1983; Guerin et al., 1984).

Several electrophysiological studies have shown that electrical stimulation of the MFB does not directly activate dopaminergic axons; instead, it acti-

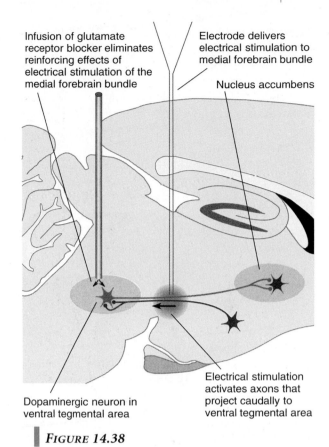

Labels in figure:
- Infusion of glutamate receptor blocker eliminates reinforcing effects of electrical stimulation of the medial forebrain bundle
- Electrode delivers electrical stimulation to medial forebrain bundle
- Nucleus accumbens
- Dopaminergic neuron in ventral tegmental area
- Electrical stimulation activates axons that project caudally to ventral tegmental area

FIGURE 14.38

The experiment by Herberg and Rose (1990). Blocking glutamate receptors in the ventral tegmental area abolishes the reinforcing effects of electrical stimulation of the medial forebrain bundle.

vates axons that originate in the lateral hypothalamus and basal forebrain and terminate in the ventral tegmental area (Yeomans, 1975; Bielajew and Shizgal, 1986). Dopaminergic axons are small and unmyelinated and, as such, are not easily depolarized by electrical stimulation. The descending axons are larger and are myelinated. More recently, these electrophysiological studies have been confirmed by pharmacological experiments. For example, Herberg and Rose (1990) found that when they injected drugs that blocked glutamate receptors into the ventral tegmental area, rats would no longer press a lever that delivered electrical stimulation of the medial forebrain bundle. This drug apparently prevented the descending axons from activating the dopaminergic neurons. (See **Figure 14.38.**)

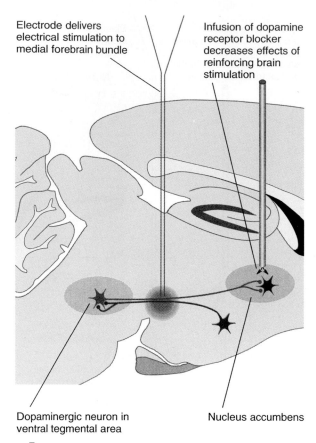

Electrode delivers electrical stimulation to medial forebrain bundle

Infusion of dopamine receptor blocker decreases effects of reinforcing brain stimulation

Dopaminergic neuron in ventral tegmental area

Nucleus accumbens

FIGURE 14.39

The experiment by Stellar, Kelley, and Corbett (1983). Blocking dopamine receptors in the nucleus accumbens reduces the reinforcing effects of electrical stimulation of the medial forbrain bundle.

If the activation of dopamine receptors in the nucleus accumbens is necessary for reinforcement to occur, then we would expect that the injection of drugs that block these receptors would interfere with reinforcement. And it does. Stellar, Kelley, and Corbett (1983) trained rats to travel through a runway in order to receive electrical stimulation of the medial forebrain bundle. They found that when they injected a dopamine receptor blocker into the nucleus accumbens, they had to turn up the current level of the stimulator in order to get the animals to run. That is, the drug reduced the reinforcing value of the electrical brain stimulation. (See *Figure 14.39.*)

Dopaminergic neurons can be selectively killed by the drug 6-HD (6-hydroxydopamine). When injected into the brain, the drug is taken up by the cell bodies, axons, or terminals of these cells, collects inside them, and kills them. (The drug will also kill noradrenergic neurons; but if it is administered along with imipramine, a drug that blocks the reuptake mechanism in these cells, they will be spared.) You will probably not be surprised to learn that 6-HD lesions of the ventral tegmental area, medial forebrain bundle, or nucleus accumbens disrupt the reinforcing effects of electrical brain stimulation (Fibiger et al., 1987).

Several types of studies indicate that dopamine agonists such as amphetamine exert their reinforcing effects in the nucleus accumbens, which contains the terminal buttons of the neurons of the tegmentostriatal pathway. An interesting approach employs the **drug discrimination procedure.** This procedure uses the physiological effects of drugs as discriminative stimuli in order to learn something about the nature of these effects (Schuster and Balster, 1977). An animal is given a drug and then is trained to press one of two levers to receive food. The next day, it receives an injection of saline and is trained to press the other lever. Each day thereafter, it receives either the drug or the saline, and it receives food only if it presses the appropriate lever. Obviously, the presence or absence of internal sensations produced by the drug tells the animal which lever to press. Then on test days the animal is given another drug. If the animal presses the "drug" lever, we can conclude that the internal sensations feel similar to the first drug; if it presses the "saline" lever, we can conclude that they do not.

Nielsen and Scheel-Kruger (1986) trained rats to discriminate between the effects of injections of amphetamine and saline and then administered amphetamine directly into the brain on test days. During test days they injected the drug into the nucleus accumbens. They found that the rats pressed the "amphetamine" lever only when they had received the drug in the nucleus accumbens; when they received the drug in the caudate nucleus, they pressed the "saline" lever. They also pressed the "saline" lever when they received an injection of amphetamine mixed with a drug that blocks dopamine receptors. Thus, to the rats, the effects of an injection of amphetamine in the nucleus accumbens felt like the effects of a injection into a vein—but not when the dopamine receptors in the nucleus accumbens were blocked.

Microdialysis Studies

Chapter 5 described a research technique called *microdialysis* that is being adopted by an increasing number of laboratories. As we saw in Chapter 13, microdialysis has been used to measure the relation between hunger and satiety and the release of norepinephrine and serotonin in the hypothalamus. Researchers using this method have shown that reinforcing electrical stimulation of the medial forebrain bundle or the ventral tegmental area or the administration of cocaine or amphetamine cause the release of dopamine in the nucleus accumbens (Moghaddam and Bunney, 1989; Nakahara et al., 1989; Phillips et al., 1992). (See ***Figure 14.40.***)

You will recall that adjunctive behaviors—nonspecific behaviors produced by the activating effects of reinforcing stimuli—are disrupted by dopamine antagonists or the destruction of the dopaminergic input to the nucleus accumbens. In a study using microdialysis, McCullough and Salamone (1992) found that these adjunctive behaviors were accompanied by the release of dopamine in the nucleus accumbens.

Microdialysis studies have also found that aversive stimuli, as well as reinforcing stimuli, can cause the release of dopamine in various parts of the brain—including the nucleus accumbens (Salamone, 1992). Thus, it is clear that reinforcement is not the sole function of dopaminergic neurons; these neurons appear to be involved in stress as well as reinforcement.

Functions of the Reinforcement System

What does reinforcing brain stimulation tell us about the brain mechanisms involved in instrumental conditioning? Almost all investigators believe that electrical stimulation of the medial forebrain bundle is reinforcing because it activates the same system that is activated by natural reinforcers, such as food, water, or sexual contact. The reinforcement

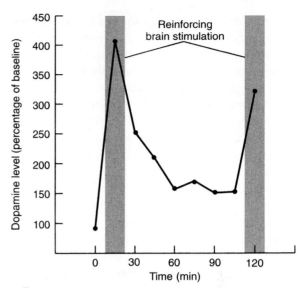

FIGURE 14.40

Release of dopamine in the nucleus accumbens, measured by microdialysis, produced when a rat pressed a lever that delivered electrical stimulation to the ventral tegmental area.

(Adapted from Phillips, A.G., Coury, A., Fiorino, D., LePiane, F.G., Brown, E., and Fibiger, H.C. *Annals of the New York Academy of Sciences,* 1992, *654,* 199–206.)

system must perform two functions: detect the presence of a reinforcing stimulus and strengthen the connections between the neurons that detect the discriminative stimulus (such as the sight of a lever) and the neurons that produce the instrumental response (a lever press).

Assuming that this proposed mechanism is correct, we can ask three major questions: (1) What activates the dopaminergic neurons in the ventral tegmental area, causing their terminal buttons to release dopamine? (2) What role does the release of dopamine play in strengthening synaptic connections? (3) Where do these synaptic changes take place? Research that suggests some preliminary answers to these three questions is discussed in the rest of this section.

Detecting Reinforcing Stimuli

Reinforcement occurs when neural circuits detect a reinforcing stimulus and cause the activation of dopaminergic neurons in the ventral tegmental area.

Detection of a reinforcing stimulus is not a simple matter; a stimulus that serves as a reinforcer on one occasion may fail to do so on another. For example, the presence of food will reinforce the behavior of a hungry organism but not one that has just eaten. Thus, the reinforcement system is not automatically activated when particular stimuli are present; its activation also depends on the state of the organism.

In general, if a stimulus causes the animal to engage in an appetitive behavior (that is, if it approaches the stimulus rather than runs away from it), the reinforcement mechanism is activated, and the link between the discriminative stimulus and the instrumental response is strengthened. If, on the other hand, a stimulus elicits a defensive behavior, such as freezing or running away, then the stimulus will do just the opposite: It will *punish* the response.

Electrical stimulation of some parts of the brain causes aversive effects, not reinforcing ones. If an animal presses a lever that elicits a defensive behavior such as attack or attempt to escape, it will avoid pressing it again. In other words, the lever pressing will be punished. (I described these behaviors in Chapter 11, "Emotion and Stress.") It will also learn to make a response that turns off such stimulation or prevents it from happening. Thus, activation of neural circuits that produce escape or avoidance behaviors is aversive.

The ventral tegmental area seems to be a focal point in the process of reinforcement; reinforcing stimuli cause the release of dopamine in the mesolimbic and mesocortical systems by activating neurons in this region. For example, Ljungberg, Apicella, and Schultz (1992) operated on monkeys and implanted microelectrodes so that they could record the electrical activity of dopaminergic neurons in the ventral tegmental area when the animals were awake and alert. They put the animals in a chair facing a panel that contained a small door with a sliding panel. During pretraining they opened the door from time to time. The first few times the door opened, the animals looked at it (the door made a noise as it slid open), and the activity of many of the dopaminergic neurons briefly increased. After a few times, the animals stopped looking at the door, and the neurons stopped responding.

Then the experimenters began placing a small piece of apple behind the door from time to time. As you might expect, the animals began looking at the door again—and the dopaminergic neurons began firing again, too. Now that the sound and sight of the door opening was paired with an occasional piece of apple (which the monkeys reached for and ate), this stimulus became capable of triggering the release of dopamine. On those trials in which food was present, the response was even stronger. Thus, a stimulus that previously had no effect on the activity of dopaminergic neurons began to excite them once it was paired with an appetitive stimulus.

This experiment indicates that dopaminergic neurons in the ventral tegmental area are activated not only by primary reinforcing stimuli such as food but also by conditioned reinforcers. When a neutral stimulus is paired several times with a reinforcing stimulus, it acquires the ability to serve as a reinforcing stimulus itself—it becomes a **conditioned reinforcer.** The process of classical conditioning is responsible for this phenomenon: The response an animal makes to the primary reinforcer becomes attached to the conditioned reinforcer. Similarly, when a neutral stimulus is paired with an aversive stimulus, it becomes a **conditioned punisher.** Our behavior can be reinforced by an enormous variety of conditioned reinforcers, including money, good grades, and words of praise. It can also be punished by conditioned punishers such as fines, bad grades, and signs of disapproval.

What neural circuits are responsible for detecting the presence of a reinforcing stimulus (primary or conditioned) and then activating dopaminergic neurons in the ventral tegmental area? The ventral tegmental area receives inputs from many regions of the brain: the raphe nuclei, the locus coeruleus, the globus pallidus, the medial and lateral preoptic areas, the lateral hypothalamus, the bed nucleus of the stria terminalis, the septum, the lateral habenula, the central amygdala, the nucleus accumbens, and the prefrontal cortex. Although we still know very little about how reinforcing stimuli are detected, the evidence we have so far points to three of these inputs: the amygdala, the lateral hypothalamus, and the prefrontal cortex.

As we saw in Chapter 11 and again in this chapter, the amygdala is involved in classically conditioned emotional responses. Several studies suggest that it is also involved in reinforcement. For example, destruction of the amygdala or its disconnection from the visual system has no effect on monkeys' ability to recognize particular visual stimuli by sight, but it does disrupt their ability to remember which of them has been paired with food (Spiegler and Mishkin, 1981; Gaffan, Gaffan, and Harrison, 1988). In addition, Cador, Robbins, and Everitt (1989) and Everitt, Cador, and Robbins (1989) found that neurotoxic lesions of the basolateral amygdala reduced the reinforcing value of stimuli that had been paired with natural reinforcers: water (in thirsty rats) and sexual contact. The experimenters paired the reinforcing stimuli with a flashing light and found that later, the animals would press a lever that turned on the flashing light. Thus, the flashing light had become a conditioned reinforcer. The lesions of the amygdala severely depressed the animals' rate of responding for the flashing light, without otherwise affecting their motor performance.

The amygdala communicates with the ventral tegmental area directly and through the lateral hypothalamus. Some evidence suggests that the connection through the lateral hypothalamus is particularly important. As we saw in Chapter 13, studies by Rolls and his colleagues found that neurons in the lateral hypothalamus of the monkey become active when an animal sees food, but only when it is hungry. These neurons even show sensory-specific satiety. That is, once a monkey has had all it wants of a particular food, the neurons stop responding to the sight of that food but continue to respond to the sight of foods that the animal is still willing to eat. Thus, the activity of these neurons is clearly related to the presence of reinforcing stimuli.

The prefrontal cortex provides an important input to the ventral tegmental area. The terminal buttons of the axons connecting these two areas secrete glutamate, an excitatory transmitter substance, and the activity of these synapses makes dopaminergic neurons in the ventral tegmental area fire in a bursting pattern, which greatly increases the amount of dopamine they secrete in the nucleus accumbens (Gariano and Groves, 1988). The prefrontal cortex is generally involved in devising strategies, making plans, evaluating progress made toward goals, judging the appropriateness of one's own behavior, and so on (Mesulam, 1986). Perhaps the prefrontal cortex turns on the reinforcement mechanism when it determines that the ongoing behavior is bringing the organism nearer to its goals—that the present strategy is working.

Even private behaviors such as thinking and planning may be subject to reinforcement. For example, recall the last time you were thinking about a problem and suddenly had an idea that might help you solve it. Did you suddenly feel excited and happy? It would be interesting if we could record the activity of the axons leading from your frontal cortex to your ventral tegmental area at times like that.

Strengthening Neural Connections: Dopamine and Neural Plasticity

Like classical conditioning, instrumental conditioning involves strengthening of synapses located on neurons that have just been active. For example, let us consider a hungry rat learning to press a lever and obtain food. As we saw, the neural circuit responsible for this response consists of strengthened connections between neurons in the visual system that detect the presence of the lever and those that control the muscular movements required to press the lever. The reinforcing stimulus (the food) turns on the reinforcing mechanism, which strengthens the synapses between terminal buttons that have just been active and motor neurons that have just fired.

There is an important difference between classical conditioning and instrumental conditioning: Instrumental conditioning requires a reinforcement system. As we saw in a previous section, NMDA receptors appear to be responsible for the interaction between the strong and weak synapses activated by the CS and the US, although other mechanisms may also exist. But classical conditioning involves only two elements, a CS and a US, whereas instrumental conditioning involves three elements: a discriminative stimulus, a response, and a reinforcing stimulus. How are the neural manifestations of these three elements combined?

As in classical conditioning, one element (the discriminative stimulus) activates a weak synapse. The second element—the particular circumstance that happened to induce the animal to press the lever—activates a strong synapse, making the neuron fire. The third element comes into play only if the response is followed by a reinforcing stimulus.

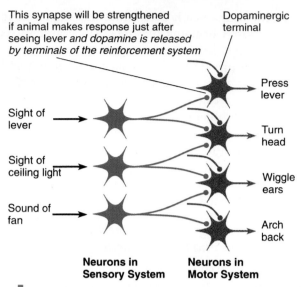

This synapse will be strengthened if animal makes response just after seeing lever *and dopamine is released by terminals of the reinforcement system*

Dopaminergic terminal

Press lever

Sight of lever

Turn head

Sight of ceiling light

Wiggle ears

Sound of fan

Arch back

Neurons in Sensory System   **Neurons in Motor System**

FIGURE 14.41

A hypothetical explanation for the reinforcing effects of dopamine on associative long-term potentiation.

If it is, the reinforcement mechanism triggers the secretion of a neurotransmitter or neuromodulator throughout the region in which the synaptic changes take place. This neuromodulator is the third element; only if it is present can weak synapses be strengthened. Dopamine appears to serve such a role, but other neurotransmitters may do so as well. (See *Figure 14.41*.)

Stein and Belluzzi (1989) obtained evidence that dopamine can facilitate synaptic strengthening. They prepared slices of the hippocampus, and they recorded from single pyramidal neurons in field CA1, which are known to contain dopamine receptors. They attempted to reinforce bursts of neural activity by infusing dopamine or dopamine agonists onto the neuron through a micropipette. Whenever the neuron spontaneously produced a burst of action potentials lasting at least 0.5 second, they applied the dopamine. Figure 14.42 shows the results of administering dopamine, cocaine, or saline. *Baseline* refers to periods during which they simply recorded the number of bursts of action potentials. During *reinforcement* periods they followed each burst with the infusion. During *noncontingent* periods they administered infusions that were not paired with the bursts. As you can see, both

dopamine and cocaine increased the rate of the bursts, but only when they were applied contingently. (See *Figure 14.42*.)

These findings indicate that if dopamine is administered at the time that cells are already firing in bursts, their firing rate will increase. Although Stein and Belluzzi did not record the activity of the inputs to the pyramidal neurons, it seems likely that the bursts occur when excitatory synaptic inputs to these neurons become active. Perhaps the dopamine acts by increasing the strength of the "successful" synapses—those that are firing at the same time that the pyramidal cell is bursting. The effect of this strengthening would be to increase the rate of firing of the pyramidal cell.

The Location of Synaptic Changes

Clearly, reinforcement strengthens synaptic connections somewhere in the brain—but where? As we saw, reinforcing brain stimulation increases the secretion of dopamine in the nucleus accumbens, which suggests that at least some of the synaptic changes may take place there.

Nucleus Accumbens.   Microdialysis studies show that natural reinforcers, as well as electrical stimulation of the medial forebrain bundle, triggers the release of dopamine in the nucleus accumbens: drinking, induced by dehydration or by an injection of angiotensin; salt intake, induced by sodium depletion; or eating, induced by food deprivation (Blander et al., 1988; Chang et al., 1988; Hernandez and Hoebel, 1988).

Sexual behavior, too, causes the release of dopamine in the nucleus accumbens (Pfaus et al., 1990; Damsma et al., 1992). Figure 14.44 shows the effects of sexual contact on the level of dopamine in the nucleus accumbens of a male rat. When the rat was placed in the test chamber (where he had copulated before), the dopamine level increased. Next, a female rat was introduced behind a wire screen; the dopamine level increased further. Finally, the screen was removed and the rats were permitted to copulate; the dopamine level increased still further. After copulation, the female was removed and the dopamine level declined. (See *Figure 14.43*.)

As I mentioned earlier in this chapter, when a stimulus is paired with a reinforcing or punishing

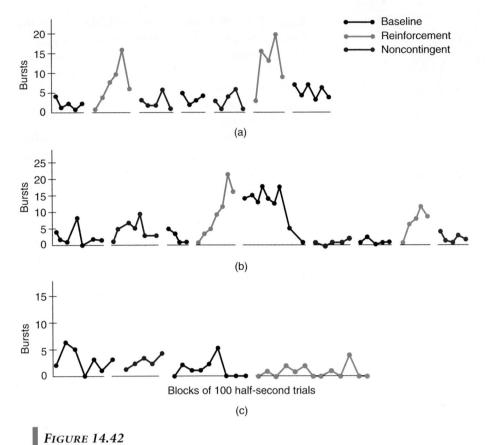

	Baseline
	Reinforcement
	Noncontingent

(a)

(b)

Blocks of 100 half-second trials

(c)

FIGURE 14.42

Instrumental conditioning of single neurons in the CA1 field of the hippocampal formation.
(a) Dopamine infusion. (b) Cocaine infusion. (c) Saline infusion.

(From Stein, L., and Belluzzi, J.D., in *Brain Reward Systems and Abuse*, edited by J. Engel and L. Oreland. New York: Raven Press, 1987.)

stimulus, its acquires the reinforcing (or punishing) properties of the second stimulus. As we saw in Chapter 13, a conditioned flavor aversion can be established by pairing a particular flavor with treatments that produce illness, such as an injection of lithium chloride. Mark et al. (1989) found that although the taste of saccharin normally caused an increase in dopamine release in the nucleus accumbens of naive animals, it caused a *decrease* in dopamine release if the flavor had previously been paired with an injection of lithium chloride. Thus, the same stimulus can have very different effects on the activity of dopaminergic neurons, depending on the animal's prior experience with this stimulus.

Scott and his colleagues have performed a series of experiments indicating that in rats the coding of gustatory information in the brain stem is changed by the physiological condition of the animal and by its prior experience with particular foods. For example, Jacobs, Mark, and Scott (1988) have shown that a conditioned aversion to saccharin changes the response pattern of neurons in the nucleus of the solitary tract (a region that receives taste information from the tongue) to the taste of saccharin; the pattern resembles the response made to quinine, a substance that rats avoid. On the other hand, inducing a salt appetite by depleting the animals of sodium changed the pattern produced by a salty

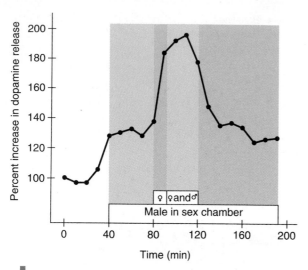

FIGURE 14.43

Levels of extracellular dopamine in the nucleus accumbens of a male rat before, during, and after engaging in sexual behavior, measured by microdialysis. ♀ = *female,* ♂ = *male.*

(Adapted with permission from Pfaus, J.G., Damsma, G., Nomikos, G.G., Wenkstern, D.G., Blaha, C.D., Phillips, A.G., and Fibiger, H.C. *Brain Research,* 1990, *530,* 345–348.)

taste so that it resembled the one produced by the taste of sucrose. Thus, there were two patterns, "good" and "bad." Perhaps the presence of the "good" pattern stimulates the activity of neurons involved in reinforcement, whereas the presence of the "bad" pattern does not—or may even *decrease* this activity. In fact, the nucleus of the solitary tract is connected to the ventral tegmental area (Scheel-Krüger and Willner, 1991), so this hypothesis may have some merit.

As we saw earlier in this section, destruction of dopaminergic synapses in the nucleus accumbens or the injection of dopamine antagonists into this region block the reinforcing effect of electrical stimulation of the medial forebrain bundle. Several studies have shown that disruption of dopaminergic transmission in the nucleus accumbens also impairs the expression of behaviors that are reinforced by natural stimuli. For example, Salamone et al. (1991) trained rats to press a lever in order to obtain some highly preferred food. When the animals were placed in the operant chamber, they pressed the lever to obtain this food, ignoring some less pre-ferred food that was freely available. When the investigators injected a dopamine receptor blocker in the nucleus accumbens, the rats stopped pressing a lever. But the drug did not affect the animals' hunger; they began eating the less preferred food that they could obtain without making the instrumental response.

If some instrumental conditioning involves synaptic changes in the nucleus accumbens, how are these changes translated into behavior? Neurons in the nucleus accumbens send axons to several regions of the brain involved in movement, including the globus pallidus and the mesencephalic locomotor region of the pedunculopontine nucleus. In turn, axons in the globus pallidus project to the prefrontal cortex (via the dorsomedial nucleus of the thalamus) and to the premotor cortex. Thus, the direct or indirect outputs of the nucleus accumbens include the two major motor systems of the brain: the basal ganglia and the motor areas of the frontal cortex (Scheel-Krüger and Willner, 1991).

Some evidence indicates that the nucleus accumbens can indeed affect behavior through its connections with the globus pallidus. For example, lesions of this nucleus block the behavioral excitation produced by injections of dopaminergic agonists directly into the nucleus accumbens, and they also decrease the reinforcing effects of cocaine (Hubner and Koob, 1990).

Motor Systems. Even if some of the synapses modified by instrumental conditioning are located in the nucleus accumbens, this nucleus certainly does not contain *all* of the synaptic changes. Both classical conditioning and instrumental conditioning involve the strengthening of connections between neurons that detect the presence of particular stimuli and those that control particular behaviors. Unfortunately, investigators have not yet identified specific neural circuits that are responsible for instrumentally conditioned responses, as they have for the classically conditioned emotional response. We would expect that the circuits responsible for instrumental conditioning would include neurons that receive input from several perceptual systems and are able to activate motor mechanisms responsible for behaviors. We might predict that the basal ganglia and frontal cortex contain neurons that play this role.

Lesions of the basal ganglia in both humans and laboratory animals do disrupt behaviors learned through instrumental conditioning—especially those that involve well practiced, automatic responses (Heindel, Butters, and Salmon, 1988; Saint-Cyr, Taylor, and Lang, 1988; Reading, Dunnett, and Robbins, 1991). The basal ganglia receive dopaminergic innervation from the substantia nigra. This innervation certainly plays an important role in motor performance; Parkinson's disease is caused by its degeneration. Whether this innervation also plays a role in synaptic plasticity in the basal ganglia is not yet known.

The prefrontal cortex, like the nucleus accumbens, receives dopaminergic input. Because much of the control of movement is funneled via the prefrontal and premotor cortex to the primary motor cortex, it seems likely that many of the synapses modified by instrumental conditioning are located in the frontal cortex. Several studies have shown that damage to the prefrontal or premotor cortex in humans or laboratory animals disrupts the learning of complex instrumentally conditioned responses (Petrides, 1985a, 1985b; Passingham, 1988, 1989). In addition, Deiber et al. (1991) measured cerebral blood flow with a PET scanner while human subjects were learning to make an instrumental response. After subtracting out the activity produced simply by making motor movements, they found that metabolic activity went up in the left parietal cortex, premotor cortex, and supplementary motor cortex. (The task was learned using the right hand.) The region of parietal cortex whose activity increased receives information from all regions of the sensory association cortex and serves as an important input to the frontal lobe; it would not be surprising to find that it, too, plays a role in learning.

As we saw earlier, the prefrontal cortex may activate the reinforcement system when it detects that the animal's behavior is resulting in progress toward a goal. But the prefrontal cortex is a *target* of dopaminergic neurons as well as a source of their control. The dopaminergic system of this region certainly seems to be involved in reinforcement. For example, Stein and Belluzzi (1989) found that rats will press a lever that produces an injection of a dopamine agonist into this region.

Duvauchelle and Ettenberg (1991) found that electrical stimulation of the prefrontal cortex will produce a conditioned place preference—an effect that is blocked by injections of a drug that blocks dopamine receptors. And in a microdialysis study Hernandez and Hoebel (1990) found that when rats were performing a food-reinforced lever-pressing task, the levels of dopamine in the prefrontal cortex increased. Further research will undoubtedly tell us more about the role of the frontal cortex in instrumental conditioning.

INTERIM SUMMARY

When our actions have favorable consequences, we tend to repeat them. The process responsible for this fact—reinforcement—is what enables us to profit from experience. Olds and Milner discovered that rats would perform a response that caused electrical current to be delivered through an electrode placed in their brain; thus, the stimulation was reinforcing. Subsequent studies found that stimulation of many locations had reinforcing effects but that the medial forebrain bundle produced the strongest and most reliable ones.

Although several neurotransmitters may play a role in reinforcement, one is particularly important: dopamine. The cell bodies of the most important system of dopaminergic neurons are located in the ventral tegmental area, and their axons project to the nucleus accumbens, prefrontal cortex, and amygdala. Electrical stimulation of this nucleus is reinforcing, and its deactivation with a glutamate receptor blocker abolishes the reinforcing effects of electrical stimulation of the MFB.

Systemic injections of dopamine agonists are reinforcing, and systemic injections of dopamine antagonists will block the reinforcing effects of natural stimuli or electrical stimulation of the medial forebrain bundle. Infusions of dopamine antagonists directly into the nucleus accumbens have the same effects as systemic injections. Laboratory animals (and humans) will self-administer dopamine agonists such as amphetamine or cocaine; laboratory animals will press a lever to have amphetamine injected directly into the nucleus accumbens. Microdialysis studies have also shown that natural and artificial reinforcers stimulate the release of dopamine in the nucleus accumbens. The system of neurons that activate the dopaminergic neurons in the mesolimbic and mesocortical systems probably involves the amygdala and lateral hypothalamus; these neurons fire in response to food-related stimuli capable of reinforcing an animal's behavior. The frontal cortex may play a role in reinforcement that occurs when our own behavior brings us nearer to a goal.

Dopamine (and, almost certainly, other neurotransmitters such as acetylcholine and norepinephrine) induces synaptic plasticity by facilitating associative long-term potentiation. Direct evidence for this phenomenon was seen in a study with hippocampal slices. An increase in the spontaneous response rate of CA1 neurons can be increased by contingent infusions of dopamine; thus, single neurons can be instrumentally conditioned.

The location of synaptic changes responsible for instrumental conditioning may be the nucleus accumbens, basal ganglia, and frontal cortex. Studies show that damage to the basal ganglia and the frontal cortex disrupt instrumental responses; and the metabolic activity of the premotor and supplementary motor cortex increases while humans learn instrumental responses. Microdialysis studies suggest that the release of dopamine in the prefrontal cortex may also be important.

New Terms

The Nature of Learning

classical conditioning p. 433

unconditional stimulus p. 433

unconditional response p. 433

conditional stimulus p. 433

conditional response p. 433

Hebb rule p. 434

instrumental conditioning p. 435

reinforcing stimulus p. 435

punishing stimulus p. 435

Perceptual Learning

delayed matching-to-sample task p. 438

nucleus basalis p. 443

neural network p. 445

Mechanisms of Synaptic Plasticity

long-term potentiation p. 447

hippocampal formation p. 447

entorhinal cortex *(en toe RY nul)* p. 448

subicular complex p. 448

dentate gyrus p. 448

CA1 p. 448

CA3 p. 448

perforant path p. 448

fimbria p. 448

population EPSP p. 449

associative long-term potentiation p. 450

NMDA receptor p. 452

calcium-dependent enzyme p. 456

PKC p. 456

CaM-KII p. 456

tyrosine kinase p. 457

nitric oxide synthase p. 458

long-term depression p. 460

S-R Learning: Classical Conditioning

extinction p. 464

S-R Learning: Instrumental Conditioning

self-stimulation p. 465

medial forebrain bundle p. 465

mesolimbic system *(mee zo LIM bik)* p. 466

nucleus accumbens p. 467

mesocortical system p. 467

conditioned place preference p. 468

adjunctive behavior p. 468

negative reinforcement p. 468

self-administration p. 469

drug discrimination procedure p. 470

conditioned reinforcer p. 472

conditioned punisher p. 472

Suggested Readings

Byrne, J.H., and Berry, W.O. *Neural Models of Plasticity: Experimental and Theoretical Approaches.* San Diego: Academic Press, 1989.

Gazzaniga, M.S. *Perspectives in Memory Research.* Cambridge, Mass.: MIT Press, 1988.

Graf, P., and Masson, M.E.J. *Implicit Memory: New Directions in Cognition, Development, and Neuropsychology.* Hillsdale, N.J.: Erlbaum Associates, 1993.

Ono, T. *Brain Mechanisms of Perception and Memory: From Neuron to Behavior.* New York: Oxford University Press, 1992.

Squire, L.R., Weinberger, N.M., Lynch, G., and McGaugh, J.L. *Memory: Organization and Locus of Change.* New York: Oxford University Press, 1991.

Squire, L.R., and Butters, N. *Neuropsychology of Memory.* New York: Guilford Press, 1992.

Thompson, R.F. Mammalian brain substrates of aversive classical conditioning. *Annual Review of Psychology,* 1993, *43,* 317–342.

CHAPTER 15

Relational Learning and Amnesia

Human Anterograde Amnesia
- Basic Description
- Spared Learning Abilities
- Declarative and Nondeclarative Memories
- Anterograde Amnesia: Failure of Relational Learning
- Anatomy of Anterograde Amnesia
  Interim Summary

Relational Learning in Laboratory Animals
- Working Memory: Remembering Places Visited
- Spatial Perception and Learning
- Place Cells in the Hippocampal Formation
- Other Functions of the Hippocampal Formation
- Role of Long-Term Potentiation in Hippocampal Functioning
- Modulation of Hippocampal Functions by Acetylcholinergic Neurons
- A Theory of Hippocampal Functioning
  Interim Summary

Chapter 14 discussed relatively simple forms of learning, which can be understood as changes in neural networks that detect the presence of particular stimuli or as strengthened connections between neurons that convey sensory information and those that produce responses. But most forms of learning are more complex; most memories of real objects and events are related to other memories. Seeing a photograph of an old friend may remind you of the sound of the person's name and of the movements you have to make to pronounce it. You may also be reminded of things you have done with your friend: places you have visited, conversations you have had, experiences you have shared. Each of these memories can contain a series of events, complete with sights and sounds, which you will be able to recall in the proper sequence. Obviously, the neural circuits in the inferior temporal cortex that recognize your friend's face are connected to circuits in many other parts of the brain, and these circuits are connected to many others. This chapter discusses research on relational learning, which includes the establishment and retrieval of memories of events and episodes.

HUMAN ANTEROGRADE AMNESIA

ONE OF THE MOST DRAMATIC AND INTRIGUING phenomena caused by brain damage is *anterograde amnesia,* which, at first glance, appears to be the inability to learn new information. However, when we examine the phenomenon more carefully, we find that the basic abilities of perceptual learning, sensory-response learning, and motor learning are intact, but that complex relational learning, of the type I just described, is gone. This section discusses the nature of anterograde amnesia in humans and its anatomical basis. The section that follows discusses related research in laboratory animals.

The term **anterograde amnesia** refers to difficulty in learning new information. A person with pure anterograde amnesia can remember events that occurred in the past, during the time before the brain damage occurred, but cannot retain information he or she encountered *after* the damage. In contrast, **retrograde amnesia** refers to inability to remember events that happened *before* the brain damage occurred. (See *Figure 15.1.*) As we shall see, pure anterograde amnesia is rare; usually, there is also a retrograde amnesia for events that occurred for a period of time before the brain damage occurred.

In 1889 Sergei Korsakoff, a Russian physician, first described a severe memory impairment caused by brain damage, and the disorder was given his name. The most profound symptom of **Korsakoff's syndrome** is a severe anterograde amnesia: The patients appear to be unable to form new memories, although they can still remember old ones. They can converse normally and can remember events that happened long before their brain damage occurred, but they cannot remember events that happened afterward.

Korsakoff's syndrome is usually (but not always) a result of chronic alcoholism. The disorder actually results from a thiamine (vitamin B_1) deficiency caused by the alcoholism (Adams, 1969; Haas, 1988). Because alcoholics receive a substantial number of calories from the alcohol they ingest, they usually eat a poor diet, so their vitamin intake is consequently low. Furthermore, alcohol interferes with intestinal absorption of thiamine. The ensuing deficiency produces brain damage. Thiamine is an essential for a step in metabolism: the carboxylation of pyruvate, an intermediate product in the breakdown of carbohydrates, fats, and amino acids. Korsakoff's syndrome sometimes occurs in people who have been severely malnourished and have then received intravenous infusions of glucose; the sudden availability of glucose to the cells of the brain without adequate thiamine with which to metabolize it damages them, probably because the cells accumulate pyruvate. Hence, standard medical practice is to administer thiamine along with intravenous glucose to severely malnourished patients. I will discuss the location of the brain damage that causes Korsakoff's syndrome later in this section.

Anterograde amnesia can also be caused by damage to the temporal lobes. Scoville and Milner (1957) reported that bilateral removal of the medial temporal lobe produced a memory impairment in

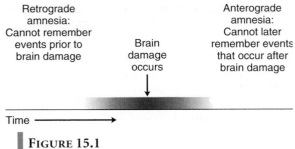

FIGURE 15.1

A schematic definition of retrograde amnesia and antero-grade amnesia.

humans that was apparently identical to that seen in Korsakoff's syndrome. Thirty operations had been performed on psychotic patients in an attempt to alleviate their mental disorder, but it was not until this operation was performed on patient H.M. that the anterograde amnesia was discovered. The psychotic patients' behaviors were already so disturbed that amnesia was not detected. However, patient H.M. was reasonably intelligent and was not psychotic; therefore, his postoperative deficit was discovered immediately. He received the surgery in an attempt to treat his very severe epilepsy, which could not be controlled even by high doses of anticonvulsant medication.

The surgery successfully treated H.M.'s seizure disorder, but it became apparent that he suffered a serious memory impairment. Subsequently, Scoville and Milner (1957) examined eight of the psychotic patients who were able to cooperate with them. Careful testing revealed that some of these patients also had anterograde amnesia; the deficit appeared to occur only when the hippocampus was removed. Thus, they concluded that the hippocampus was the critical structure destroyed by the surgery. Later in this chapter, I will say more about the anatomical basis of anterograde amnesia caused by temporal lobe damage.

Once it was discovered that bilateral medial temporal lobectomy causes anterograde amnesia, neurosurgeons stopped performing them and now are careful to operate on only one temporal lobe. (Unilateral temporal lobectomy may cause minor memory problems, but nothing like what occurs after bilateral operations.) In a few cases surgeons were

surprised to find that unilateral removal of the medial temporal lobe produced anterograde amnesia. When the patients eventually died and their brains were examined, the investigators discovered that the hippocampus on the other side of the brain had been damaged, too—probably very early in life (Penfield and Milner, 1958; Warrington and Duchen, 1992). Thus, the operation on the undamaged temporal lobe left the patients without a functioning hippocampal system. To prevent such cases physicians now administer a *Wada test* (Wada and Rasmussen, 1960). Before a patient receives a unilateral temporal lobectomy, a short-acting anesthetic is injected into the carotid artery that serves the hemisphere that is to be operated on. If the patient is able to learn and remember items that are presented while that hemisphere is anesthetized, we can conclude that the other hemisphere contains a functioning hippocampal system, and the one in the anesthetized hemisphere can safely be removed. The Wada test has detected unexpected damage to the hippocampal system and has thus prevented new cases of anterograde amnesia.

Basic Description

In order for you to understand more fully the nature of anterograde amnesia, I will discuss the case of patient H.M. in more detail (Milner, Corkin, and Teuber, 1968; Milner, 1970; Corkin et al., 1981). Patient H.M. has been extensively studied because his amnesia is relatively pure. His intellectual ability and his immediate verbal memory appear to be normal. He can repeat seven numbers forward and five numbers backward; and he can carry on conversations, rephrase sentences, and perform mental arithmetic. He has a retrograde amnesia for events that occurred during several years preceding the operation, but he can recall older memories very well. He showed no personality change after the operation, and he appears to be generally polite and well-mannered.

However, since the operation, H.M. has been unable to learn anything new. He cannot identify by name people he met since the operation (performed in 1953, when he was twenty-seven years old), nor can he find his way back home if he leaves his house. (His family moved to a new house after his operation, and he never learned how to get around in the new neighborhood. He now lives in a facility where he can be cared for.) He is aware of his disorder and often says something like this:

> Every day is alone in itself, whatever enjoyment I've had, and whatever sorrow I've had . . . . Right now, I'm wondering. Have I done or said anything amiss? You see, at this moment everything looks clear to me, but what happened just before? That's what worries me. It's like waking from a dream; I just don't remember. (Milner, 1970, p. 37)

H.M. is capable of remembering a small amount of verbal information as long as he is not distracted; constant rehearsal can keep information in his immediate memory for a long time. However, rehearsal does not appear to have any long-term effects; if he is distracted for a moment, he will completely forget whatever he had been rehearsing. He works very well at repetitive tasks. Indeed, because he so quickly forgets what previously happened, he does not easily become bored. He can endlessly reread the same magazine or laugh at the same jokes, finding them fresh and new each time. His time is typically spent solving crossword puzzles and watching television.

From these findings Milner and her colleagues made the following conclusions:

1. *The hippocampus is not the location of long-term memories; nor is it necessary for the retrieval of long-term memories.* If it were, H.M. would not have been able to remember events from early in his life, he would not know how to talk, he would not know how to dress himself, and so on.

2. *The hippocampus is not the location of immediate (short-term) memories.* If it were, H.M. would not be able to carry on a conversation, because he would not remember what the other person said long enough to think of a reply.

3. *The hippocampus is involved in converting immediate (short-term) memories into long-term memories.* This conclusion is based on a particular hypothesis of memory function: that our immediate memory of an event is retained by neural activity, and that long-term memories consist of relatively permanent biochemical or structural changes in neurons. The conclusion seems a rea-

sonable explanation for the fact that when presented with new information, H.M. seems to understand it and remember it as long as he thinks about it, but that a permanent record of the information is just never made.

As we will see, these three conclusions are too simple. Subsequent research on patients with anterograde amnesia indicates that the facts are more complicated—and more interesting—than they first appeared to be. But in order to appreciate the significance of the findings of more recent research, we must understand these three conclusions and remember the facts that led to them.

Many psychologists believe that learning consists of at least two stages: short-term memory and long-term memory. They conceive of short-term memory as a means of storing a limited amount of information temporarily and long-term memory as a means of storing an unlimited amount (or at least an enormously large amount) of information permanently. **Short-term memory** is an immediate memory for stimuli that have just been perceived. We can remember a new item of information (such as a telephone number) as long as we want to by engaging in a particular behavior: rehearsal. However, once we stop rehearsing the information, we may or may not be able to remember it later. That is, the information may or may not get stored in **long-term memory.**

Short-term memory can hold only a limited amount of information. To demonstrate this fact, read the following numbers to yourself just once, and then close your eyes and recite them back.

1 4 9 2 3 0 7

You probably had no trouble remembering them. Now, try the following set of numbers, and go through them *only once* before you close your eyes.

7 2 5 2 3 9 1 6 5 8 4

Very few people can repeat eleven numbers; in fact, you may not have even bothered to try, once you saw how many numbers there were. Thus, short-term memory has definite limits. But of course, if you wanted to, you could recite the numbers again and again until you had memorized them; that is, you could rehearse the information in short-term memory until it was eventually stored

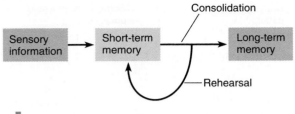

FIGURE 15.2

A simple model of the learning process.

in long-term memory. Long-term memory has no known limits; and as its name suggests, it is relatively durable. Presumably, it is a result of changes in synaptic strength, such as the ones responsible for long-term potentiation. If we stop thinking about something we have just perceived (that is, something contained in short-term memory), we may or may not remember the information later. However, information in long-term memory need not be continuously rehearsed; once we have learned something, we can stop thinking about it until we need the information at a future time.

The most simple model of the memory process says that sensory information enters short-term memory, rehearsal keeps it there, and eventually, the information makes its way into long-term memory, where it is permanently stored. The conversion of short-term memories into long-term memories has been called **consolidation,** because the memories are "made solid," so to speak. (See *Figure 15.2.*)

Now you can understand the original conclusions of Milner and her colleagues: If H.M.'s short-term memory is intact and if he can remember events from before his operation, then the problem must be that consolidation does not take place. Thus, the role of the hippocampal formation in memory is consolidation—converting short-term memories to long-term memories.

Spared Learning Abilities

H.M.'s memory deficit is striking and dramatic. However, when he and other patients with anterograde amnesia are more carefully studied, it becomes apparent that the amnesia does not represent a total failure in learning ability. When the patients are appropriately trained and tested, we find that they are capable of three of the four major types of learning: perceptual learning, sensory-response learning, and motor learning.

First, let us consider perceptual learning. Figure 15.3 shows two sample items from a test of the ability to recognize broken drawings; note how the drawings are successively more complete. (See *Figure 15.3.*) Subjects are first shown the least complete set (set I) of each of twenty different drawings. If they do not recognize a figure (and most people do not recognize set I), they are shown more complete sets until they identify it. One hour later, the subjects are tested again for retention, starting with set I. H.M. was given this test and, when retested an hour later, showed considerable improvement (Milner, 1970). When he was retested four months later, he *still* showed this improvement. His performance was not as good as that of normal control subjects, but he showed unmistakable evidence of long-term retention.

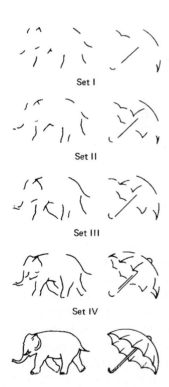

FIGURE 15.3

Examples of broken drawings.

(Reproduced with permission of author and publisher from Gollin, E.S. Developmental studies of visual recognition of incomplete objects. *Perceptual and Motor Skills,* 1960, *11,* 289-298. © Southern Universities Press.)

The incomplete drawing task is known as a **priming task.** *Priming* refers to the fact that when people perceive a particular stimulus, it becomes easier for them to perceive it again. As we will see, researchers have used several different types of priming tasks to investigate the nature of anterograde amnesia. Priming need not involve familiar objects, as the broken-drawings study did. For example, Gabrieli et al. (1990) presented H.M. and nonamnesic control subjects with a series of patterns of five dots connected by straight lines. (These patterns were referred to as the *targets.*) They asked the subjects to copy the lines on sheets of paper that contained identical dot patterns. (See *Figure 15.4.*) Later, they gave the subjects fresh sheets of papers with the dot patterns and asked them to connect the dots with whatever pattern of straight lines they chose. And all the subjects—H.M. as well as the nonamnesic controls—showed a priming effect, drawing significantly more target patterns than would be expected by chance.

Johnson, Kim, and Risse (1985) found that patients with anterograde amnesia could learn to recognize faces and melodies. They played unfamiliar melodies from Korean songs to amnesic patients and found that when they were tested later, the patients preferred these melodies to ones they had not heard before. The experimenters also presented photographs of two men along with stories of their lives: One man was dishonest, mean, and vicious, and the other was nice enough to invite home to dinner. Twenty days later, the amnesic patients said they liked the picture of the "nice" man better than the "nasty" one.

Investigators have also succeeded in demonstrating stimulus-response learning by H.M. and other amnesic subjects. For example, Weiskrantz and Warrington (1979) found that subjects with anterograde amnesia could acquire a classically conditioned eyeblink response. Sidman, Stoddard, and Mohr (1968) successfully trained patient H.M. on an instrumental conditioning task—a visual discrimination task in which pennies were given for correct responses.

Finally, Milner (1965) demonstrated motor learning. She and her colleagues presented H.M. with a mirror-drawing task. This procedure requires the subject to trace the outline of a figure (in this

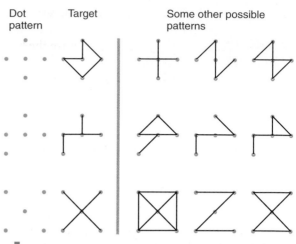

| Figure 15.4

Stimuli used in the priming experiment by Gabrieli et al. (1990). The subjects copied the straight lines of the targets onto the dot patterns, which were printed on sheets of paper. Examples of some other possible patterns of lines are shown in the right-hand column.

(Adapted from Gabrieli, J.D.E., Milberg, W., Keane, M.M., and Corkin, S. *Neuropsychologia,* 1990, *28,* 417-427.)

case, a star) with a pencil while looking at the figure in a mirror. (See *Figure 15.5.*) The task may seem simple, but it is actually rather difficult and requires some practice to perform well. With practice H.M. became proficient at mirror drawing; his errors were reduced considerably during the first session, and his improvement was retained on subsequent days of testing. He also learned a pursuit rotor task, which required him to try to keep a pointer placed above a spot of light moving in a circular path. Thus, several different forms of long-term memory can certainly be established in patients with anterograde amnesia.

Declarative and Nondeclarative Memories

If amnesic patients can learn tasks like these, you might ask, why do we call them *amnesic?* The answer is this: Although the patients can learn to perform these tasks, they do not remember anything about having learned them. They do not remember the experimenters, the room in which the training took place, the apparatus that was used, or any events that occurred during the training. Thus, although H.M. learned to recognize the broken drawings, he denied that he had ever seen them before. Although he drew many of the patterns of lines he had seen in the pattern-priming task (the one with the dots), he did not remember having seen them before. And although the amnesic patients in the study by Johnson, Kim, and Risse learned to like some melodies better, they did not recognize that they had heard them before; nor did they remember having seen the pictures of the two young men. Similarly, in the experiment by Sidman, Stoddard, and Mohr, although H.M. learned to make the correct response (press a panel with a picture of a circle on it), he was unable to recall having done so. In fact, once H.M. had learned the task, the experimenters interrupted him, had him count his pennies (to distract him for a little while), and then asked him to say what he was supposed to do. He seemed puzzled by the question; he had absolutely no idea. But when they turned on the stimuli again, he immediately made the correct response.

The distinction between what people with anterograde amnesia can and cannot learn is obviously important, because it reflects the basic organization of the learning process. Clearly, there are at least two major categories of memories. Psychologists have given them several different names. For example, some investigators (Eichenbaum, Otto, and Cohen, 1992; Squire, 1992) suggest that patients with anterograde amnesia are unable to form **declarative memories,** which have been defined as those that are "explicitly available to conscious recollection as facts, events, or specific stimuli" (Squire, Shimamura, and Amaral, 1989, p. 218). The term *declarative* obviously comes from *declare,* which means "to proclaim; to announce." The term reflects the fact that patients with anterograde amnesia cannot talk about experiences that they have had since the time of their brain damage. And note that the definition refers specifically to *stimuli.* Thus, according to Squire and his colleagues, declarative memory is a form of perceptual memory that we can think and talk about.

The other type of memories, often called **nondeclarative memories,** includes instances of perceptual, stimulus-response, and motor learning that we are not conscious of. (Some psychologists refer to these two categories as *explicit* and *implicit* memories.) Nondeclarative memories appear to operate automatically. They do not require deliberate attempts on the part of the learner to memorize something. They do not seem to include facts; instead, they control behaviors. If someone asks us a question about a fact or about something we have experienced, the question evokes images in the declarative (or explicit) memory system that we can then describe in words. For example, suppose that someone asks you how many windows your house has. If you have never answered that question before, you will probably do so by taking a "mental tour" of your house, going from room to room and counting the windows you see there. The question evokes the image (that is, gets you to call up a memory), which you then examine.

In contrast, nondeclarative (implicit) memories are not something we answer questions about. Suppose we learn to ride a bicycle. We do so quite consciously and develop declarative memories about our attempts: who helped us learn, where we rode, how we felt, how many times we fell, and so on. But we also form nondeclarative stimulus-response and

FIGURE 15.5

The mirror-drawing task.

motor memories; *we learn to ride.* We learn to make automatic adjustments with our hands and bodies that keep our center of gravity above the wheels. Most of us cannot describe the rules that govern our behavior. For example, what do you think you must do if you start falling to the right while riding a bicycle? Many cyclists would say that they compensate by leaning to the left. But they are wrong; what they really do is turn the handlebars to the right. Leaning to the left would actually make them fall faster, because it would force the bicycle even farther to the right. The point is that although they have learned to make the appropriate movements (which involve stimulus-response and motor learning), they cannot necessarily describe in words what these movements are.

Graf, Squire, and Mandler (1984) demonstrated a priming effect for verbal stimuli in subjects with anterograde amnesia. They showed lists of six-letter words to amnesic and nonamnesic subjects and asked them to study each one carefully and rate how much they liked them. The purpose of the rating was to make sure that the subjects spent some time thinking about each word. The investigators then administered two types of memory tests. In the *explicit memory* (declarative memory) condition they simply asked the subjects to recall the words they had seen. In the *implicit memory* (nondeclarative memory) condition they presented cards containing the first three letters of the words. For example, if one of the words had been DEFINE, they would have been shown a card on which DEF was printed. Several different six-letter words besides *define* begin with the letters DEF, such as *deface, defame, defeat, defect, defend, defied,* and *deform,* so there are several possible responses. The investigators asked the subjects simply to say the first word that started with those letters that came into their minds. As Figure 15.6 shows, the amnesic subjects explicitly remembered less than half as many words as the control subjects, but both groups performed equally well on the implicit memory task. (See *Figure 15.6.*)

A particularly interesting experiment by Squire et al. (1992) showed that the priming task that I just described does not involve the hippocampus but that a test of declarative memory does. Normal subjects were given lists of words to study. Then they

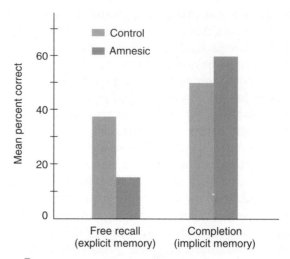

FIGURE 15.6

Explicit and implicit memory of amnesic patients and control subjects. The performance of amnesic patients was impaired when they were instructed to try to recall the words they had previously seen but not when they were asked to say the first word that came into their minds.
(Based on data from Graf, Squire, and Mandler, 1984.)

were placed in a PET scanner and were given an injection of radioactive water so that their regional cerebral blood flow (an index of regional brain activation) could be measured. They were shown the first three letters of the words and were asked either to say the first word that came to mind (*priming task*) or to use the letter sequences as cues and try to remember the words they saw on the list (*memory task*). Note that the stimuli were the same in both cases; only the instructions were different.

When the subjects performed the memory task, increased activity was seen in the right hippocampus and right prefrontal cortex. When they performed the priming task, changes were seen in a region of the visual association cortex; no changes were seen in the hippocampus. (See *Figure 15.7.*)

Anterograde Amnesia: Failure of Relational Learning

As we have seen, anterograde amnesia appears to be a loss of the ability to establish new declarative memories; the ability to establish new nondeclarative memories (perceptual, stimulus-response, or

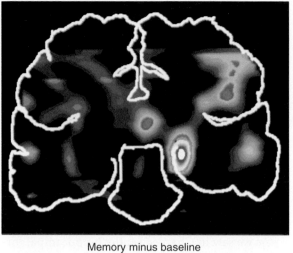

Memory minus baseline

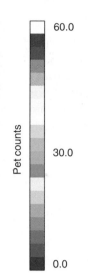

Pet counts

60.0

30.0

0.0

FIGURE 15.7

PET scan of regional cerebral blood flow. The image represents the difference between blood flow during the baseline condition and during performance of the memory task, averaged across fourteen normal subjects. The peak activity (white center ringed by red, yellow, green, and blue) is located in the region of the hippocampal formation and parahippocampal gyrus.

(From Squire, L.R., Ojemann, J.G., Miezin, F.M., Petersen, S.E., Videen, T.O., and Raichle, M.E. *Proceedings of the National Academy of Sciences,* 1992, *89,* 1837-1841. Reprinted with permission.)

motor learning) is intact. What, exactly, are declarative memories? Are they *verbal* memories? Is it simply that people with anterograde amnesia cannot learn new verbal information?

Clearly, verbal learning *is* disrupted in anterograde amnesia. Gabrieli, Cohen, and Corkin (1988) found that patient H.M. does not seem to have learned any words that have been introduced into the English language since his surgery. For example, he defined *biodegradable* as "two grades," *flower child* as "a young person who grows flowers," and *soul food* as "forgiveness." As the authors noted, for H.M. modern-day English is partly a foreign language. But declarative memories are not necessarily *verbal* memories; they are retelling of things or events we have previously experienced.

Let us consider the most complex forms of declarative memories: memories of particular episodes. Episodic memories consist of collections of perceptions of events organized in time and identified by a particular context. For example, consider my memory of this morning's breakfast. I put on my robe and slippers, walked downstairs, filled the coffee maker with ten cups of water, put the coffee grinder on the counter and plugged it in, went to the cupboard and took out the container of coffee beans . . . well, you probably are not interested in all the details. The point is that the memory contains many events, organized in time. I could go into much greater detail, putting into words my mem-

ory of the episode. But would we say that my memory is a *verbal* memory? Clearly not; what I remember about my experience this morning is perceptions of a series of *events,* not a series of *words.* I remember not words but perceptions: the sight of the snow falling outside, the feel of the cold floor replaced by the comfortable warmth of my slippers, the smell of the coffee beans as I opened the container, the irritating rasping sound made by the coffee grinder, and so on.

What started my reminiscence about this morning's breakfast? In this case it was prompted by my thinking about how to explain a particular concept to you. But suppose that you had asked me to tell you about my breakfast. Your words would bring to mind memories of what happened, and I would then describe these memories to you. That sounds simple enough, but in fact, what happens must be extraordinarily complex. The phrase *this morning's breakfast* makes me think of a particular episode. My memory contains many details about many breakfasts, and if I wanted to, I could describe a good number of them. The distinguishing feature among them is the context: today's breakfast, yesterday's breakfast, the first breakfast in a hotel room in Paris, and so on. How do I keep them straight and tell you about the right one?

Obviously, memories must be organized. When you ask me about this morning's breakfast, your words bring to mind a *set* of perceptual memories—

memories of events that occurred at a particular time and place. What does the hippocampal formation have to do with that ability? The most likely explanation is that during the original experience it somehow ties together a series of perceptions in such a way that their memories, too, are linked. The hippocampal formation enables us to learn the *relation* between the stimuli that were present at the time and the sequence of events that occurred during the episode. As we saw, people with anterograde amnesia can form perceptual memories. As the priming studies have shown, once they see something, they are more likely to recognize it later. But their perceptual memories are isolated; the memories of individual objects and events are not tied together. Thus, seeing a particular person does not remind them of other times they have seen that person or of the things they have done together. Anterograde amnesia appears to be a loss of the ability to learn about the relations among stimuli, including the order of their occurrence in time.

Why have I introduced the term *relational learning?* Why not simply use the term *declarative?* If we consider only humans, there probably would be no reason to introduce a new term. But as we shall see later in this chapter, nonverbal animals can have anterograde amnesia, too. And obviously, the term *declarative* cannot apply to animals that cannot talk. Therefore, we must look beyond a verbal-nonverbal distinction to understand what functions have been disrupted. And that is exactly what we will do when we consider research with laboratory animals later in this chapter. I will develop the idea of relational learning more fully there, in the section devoted to a theory of hippocampal functioning.

▎Anatomy of Anterograde Amnesia

The phenomenon of anterograde amnesia—and its implications for the nature of relational learning—has led investigators to study this phenomenon in laboratory animals. But before I review this research (which has provided some very interesting results), we should examine the brain damage that produces anterograde amnesia. One fact is clear: Damage to the hippocampus, or to regions that supply its inputs and receive its outputs, causes anterograde amnesia. As you will recall, Scoville and Milner

(1957) studied patients who had received temporal lobectomies and concluded that anterograde amnesia occurred only when the hippocampus was bilaterally damaged. After many years of controversy researchers have finally concluded that they were right.

Connections of the Hippocampal Formation with the Rest of the Brain

I will spare you the controversy and present the most conclusive evidence that is available from anatomical studies with both humans and laboratory animals. But first let us examine some relevant anatomy.

As we saw in Chapter 14, the hippocampal formation consists of the dentate gyrus, the CA fields, and the subiculum. The most important input to the hippocampal formation is the entorhinal cortex; neurons there have axons that terminate in the dentate gyrus, CA3, and CA1. The entorhinal cortex receives its inputs from the cingulate cortex and all regions of the association cortex, either directly or via two adjacent regions of limbic cortex: the **perirhinal** and **parahippocampal** cortex. (See *Figure 15.8.*) The outputs of the hippocampal system come primarily from the subiculum, and these outputs are relayed back through the entorhinal, perirhinal, and parahippocampal to the same regions that provide inputs: the cingulate cortex and all regions of the association cortex.

The hippocampal formation also receives input from subcortical regions via the fornix. As far as we know, these inputs select and modulate the functions of the hippocampal formation but do not supply it with specific information. (An analogy may make this distinction clearer. An antenna supplies a radio with information that is being broadcast, whereas the on-off switch, the volume control, and the station selector control the radio's functions.) The hippocampal formation receives dopaminergic input from the ventral tegmental area, noradrenergic input from the locus coeruleus, serotonergic input from the raphe nuclei, and acetylcholinergic input from the medial septum. The release of these neurotransmitters modulates hippocampal functions. The hippocampal formation also sends a set of efferent fibers through the fornix to nuclei contained in the mammillary bodies, located at the cau-

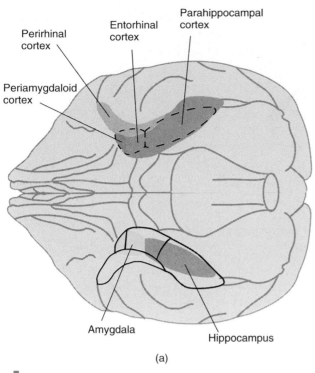

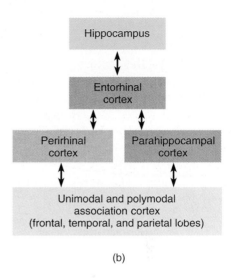

(a)

FIGURE 15.8

The major connections of the hippocampal formation with the rest of the brain.
(Adapted from Squire, L.R. *Psychological Review,* 1992, 99, 195-231.)

dal end of the hypothalamus. The mammillary bodies send axons to the anterior thalamus, which in turn sends axons to the cingulate cortex. (See *Figure 15.9.*) The hippocampal formation also receives information from the amygdala, via the entorhinal cortex.

Evidence That Hippocampal Damage Causes Anterograde Amnesia

The clearest evidence that damage to the hippocampal formation produces anterograde amnesia comes from a case studied by Zola-Morgan, Squire, and Amaral (1986). Patient R.B., a 52-year-old man with a history of heart trouble, sustained a cardiac arrest. Although his heart was successfully restarted, the period of anoxia caused by the temporary halt in blood flow resulted in brain damage. The primary symptom of this brain damage was a permanent anterograde amnesia, which Zola-Morgan and his colleagues carefully documented. Five years after the onset of the amnesia, R.B. died of heart failure. His

family gave permission for histological examination of his brain.

The investigators discovered that field CA1 of the hippocampal formation was gone; its neurons had completely degenerated. Figure 15.10 shows two photomicrographs, one of a section through a normal hippocampus and one of a section through that of patient R.B. Although the sections were taken at slightly different angles, you will have no difficulty seeing the difference in the appearance of field CA1 in the two brains. (See *Figure 15.10.*)

Another group of investigators has found another case of CA1 damage and anterograde amnesia caused by anoxia (Victor and Agamonolis, 1990). In addition, several studies have found that a period of anoxia causes damage to field CA1 in monkeys and in rats and that the damage causes anterograde amnesia in these species, too (Auer, Jensen, and Whishaw, 1989; Zola-Morgan et al., 1992).

Why is field CA1 of the hippocampal formation so sensitive to anoxia? The answer appears to lie in

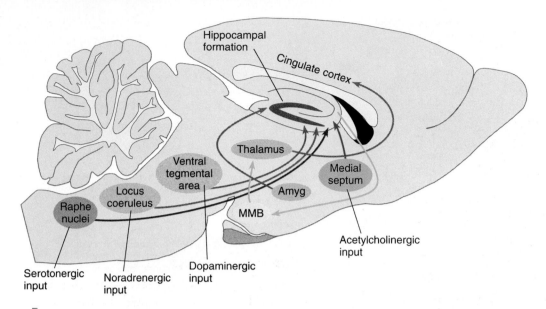

FIGURE 15.9

The major subcortical connections of the hippocampal formation. (Amyg = amygdala, MMB = mamillary bodies.)

the fact that this region is especially rich in NMDA receptors. For some reason, metabolic disturbances of various kinds, including seizures, anoxia, or hypoglycemia, cause glutamergic terminal buttons to release glutamate at abnormally high levels. The effect of this glutamate release is to stimulate NMDA receptors, which permit the entry of calcium. Within a few minutes excessive amounts of intracellular calcium begins to destroy the neurons. If animals are pretreated with drugs that block NMDA receptors, a period of anoxia is much less likely to produce brain damage. (See Rothman and Olney, 1987, for a review.) CA1 neurons contain many NMDA receptors, and so long-term potentiation can quickly become established there. This flexibility undoubtedly contributes to our ability to learn as quickly as we do. But it also renders these neurons particularly susceptible to damage by metabolic disturbances.

Although the evidence I have discussed in this section indicates that hippocampal damage can cause anterograde amnesia, it does not rule out the possibility that other structures are also involved. In fact, the amnesia produced by damage limited to CA1 is not as severe as that caused by medial tem-poral lobectomy, which destroys other parts of the hippocampal formation, the amygdala, and the sur-rounding cortex. In studies with monkeys Mishkin (1978, 1982) found evidence that combined damage to the hippocampus and the amygdala produced a more severe deficit than damage to either structure alone. Thus, he hypothesized that human antero-grade amnesia is caused by damage to both of these structures.

Several studies suggest that the amygdala does not play an important role in relational learning. Zola-Morgan, Squire, and Amaral (1989a) pointed out that when amygdala lesions are produced in a monkey's brain, the surgeon invariably damages the cortex surrounding the entorhinal cortex. As we saw in the review of the anatomy of the hippocampal formation, most connections between the neocortex and the hippocampal formation pass through this region of cortex. Thus, these connections are dis-rupted in the course of surgically destroying the amygdala. The amygdala lesions, besides destroying the amygdala, cause further damage to the hip-pocampal complex.

Zola-Morgan and his colleagues tested several groups of monkeys on a memory task. They found

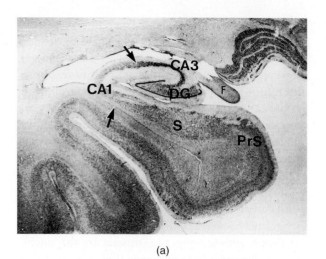

(a)

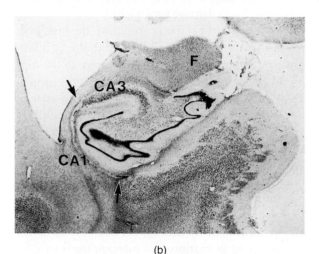

(b)

| FIGURE 15.10

Damage to field CA1 caused by anoxia. (a) Section through a normal hippocampus. (b) Section through the hippocampus of patient R.B. The pyramidal cells of field CA1 (between the two arrowheads) have degenerated. (DG = dentate gyrus, PrS = presubiculum, S = subiculum, F = fornix.)

(From Squire, L.R., in *Molecules to Models: Advances in Neurosciences,* edited by K.L Kelner and D.E. Koshland. Washington, D.C.: American Association for the Advancement of Science, 1989. Reprinted with permission.)

that stereotaxic lesions of the amygdala, which did not damage the adjacent cortex, had no effect on tests of anterograde amnesia and did not worsen an animal's performance when they were combined

with hippocampal lesions. And in follow-up studies (Zola-Morgan et al., 1989b, 1993) the investigators found that damage to the perirhinal and parahippocampal cortex surrounding the entorhinal cortex would produce anterograde amnesia or contribute to the severity of amnesia produced by hippocampal damage. When the major inputs and outputs of the hippocampus are damaged, it obviously cannot function normally. Although the amygdala certainly plays a role in emotional learning (as we saw in Chapter 14), its destruction does not appear to contribute to anterograde amnesia.

Evidence for Involvement of Other Brain Structures

We can conclude that bilateral lesions of the medial temporal lobes cause anterograde amnesia because they damage the hippocampal formation and the region of cortex that surrounds it, but what about Korsakoff's syndrome? You will recall that I promised earlier to discuss the anatomy of this disorder. Postmortem examination of the brains of patients with Korsakoff's syndrome almost always reveal severe degeneration of the mammillary bodies. As we saw, most of the efferent axons of the fornix columns, which originate in the subiculum, terminate in the mammillary bodies. Thus, it would appear that this pathway plays a role in relational learning. (See *Figure 15.11.*)

Not all investigators agree that Korsakoff's syndrome is caused by damage to the mammillary bodies. Victor, Adams, and Collins (1971) studied the autopsies of patients with Korsakoff's syndrome and concluded that amnesia was even more reliably associated with damage to the dorsomedial thalamus. However, Cole et al. (1992) report that even large, bilateral thalamic lesions (caused by strokes) do not necessarily produce anterograde amnesia. Malamut et al. (1992) studied a patient with a bilateral thalamic lesion who *did* have anterograde amnesia, but the lesion (also caused by a stroke) severed the mammillothalamic tract—the fiber bundle that connects the mammillary bodies with the anterior thalamus. So perhaps the *anterior* thalamus, not the dorsomedial thalamus, is involved in relational learning. If so, the facts are consistent: Damage to the hippocampal system or its major inputs and out-

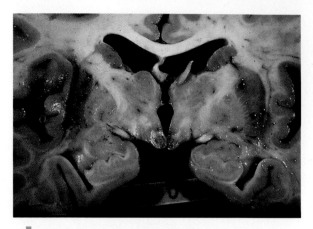

FIGURE 15.11

Degeneration of the mammillary bodies in a patient with Korsakoff's syndrome.

(Courtesy of A. D'Agostino, Good Samaritan Hospital, Portland, Oregon.)

puts causes anterograde amnesia. But we do not yet have enough evidence to be sure that this conclusion is correct.

Experimenters have examined the effects of lesions of the dorsomedial thalamic nucleus, the fornix, or the mammillary bodies in monkeys. These lesions do produce memory deficits, but they are not as severe as those seen in humans with Korsakoff's syndrome (Zola-Morgan and Squire, 1985a; Murray, et al., 1989; Zola-Morgan, Squire, and Amaral, 1989b). Thus, the anatomy of Korsakoff's syndrome remains uncertain; more research is needed to settle the issue definitively.

‖‖‖ *INTERIM SUMMARY*

Brain damage can produce anterograde amnesia, which consists of the inability to remember events that happen after the damage occurs, even though short-term memory (such as that needed to carry on a conversation) is largely intact. The patients also have a retrograde amnesia of several years' duration but can remember information from the distant past. Anterograde amnesia can be caused by the thiamine deficiency that sometimes accompanies chronic alcoholism, or it can be produced by bilateral removal of the medial temporal lobes.

The first explanation for anterograde amnesia was that the ability of the brain to consolidate short-term memories into long-term memories was damaged. However, ordinary perceptual, stimulus-response, and motor learning do not appear to be impaired; people can learn to recognize new stimuli, they are capable of instrumental and classical conditioning, and they can acquire motor memories. But they are not capable of *declarative learning*—of describing events that happen to them. The amnesia has also been called a deficit in explicit memory. An even more descriptive term—one that applies to laboratory animals as well as to humans—is *relational learning*. People with anterograde amnesia are also unable to learn the meanings of words they did not know before the brain damage took place.

Although other structures may be involved, researchers are now confident that the primary cause of anterograde amnesia is damage to the hippocampal formation or to its inputs and outputs. Temporary anoxia damages field CA1 (because of the high concentration of NMDA receptors there) and produces anterograde amnesia. The entorhinal cortex receives information from all regions of the association cortex, directly and through its connections with the cortex of the perirhinal and parahippocampal that surrounds it. The outputs of the hippocampal formation are relayed through these same regions. Subcortical inputs and outputs to the hippocampal formation pass through the fornix.

Korsakoff's syndrome is apparently caused by damage to the mammillary bodies (which receive input from the hippocampal formation via the fornix), but some investigators suspect that damage to the dorsomedial or anterior thalamus may also be involved.

RELATIONAL LEARNING IN LABORATORY ANIMALS

THE DISCOVERY THAT HIPPOCAMPAL LESIONS produced anterograde amnesia in humans stimulated interest in the exact role that this structure plays in the learning process. To pursue this interest, many investigators turned to studies with laboratory animals. After the discovery that lesions of the hippocampus caused anterograde amnesia, experimenters began making lesions of the hippocampus in animals and testing their learning ability. They quickly found that the animals remained capable of learning most tasks. At the time they were surprised, and some even thought that the hippocampus had different functions in humans than it had in other animals. We now realize that most of the learning tasks that the animals were given tested simple sensory-response learning, and as we saw in the previous section, even humans with anterograde amnesia can do well on such tasks. Researchers have developed other tasks that require relational learning, and on such tasks laboratory animals with hippocampal lesions show memory deficits, just as humans do.

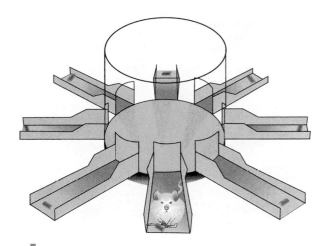

FIGURE 15.12

An eight-arm radial maze.

Working Memory: Remembering Places Visited

Olton and Samuelson (1976) devised a task that requires rats to remember where they have just been and discovered that hippocampal lesions severely impaired the animals' performance. The investigators placed the rats on a circular platform located at the junction of eight arms, which radiated away from the center like the spokes of a wheel. (See *Figure 15.12.*) The entire maze was elevated high enough above the ground so that the rats would not jump to the floor. Before placing the rats on the platform in the center, the experimenters put a piece of food at the end of each of the arms. The rats (who were hungry, of course) were permitted to explore the maze and eat the food. The animals soon learned to retrieve the food efficiently, entering each arm once. After twenty trials most animals did not enter an arm from which they had already obtained food during that session. A later study (Olton, Collison, and Werz, 1977) showed that rats could perform well even when they were prevented from following a fixed sequence of visits to the arms; thus, they had to remember where they had been, not simply follow the same pattern of responses each time. Control procedures in several studies ruled out the possibility that the rats simply smelled their own odor in arms they had previously visited.

The radial-arm-maze task uses a behavioral capacity that is well developed in rats. Rats are scavengers and often find food in different locations each day. Thus, they must be able to find their way around the environment efficiently, not getting lost and not revisiting too soon a place where they previously found food. Of course, they must also learn which places in the environment are likely to contain food and visit them occasionally. Although these two abilities might appear to require the same brain functions, they do not. Let us consider the ability to avoid revisiting a place where food was just found. Olton and his colleagues (reviewed by Olton, 1983) found that lesions of the hippocampus, fornix, or entorhinal cortex severely disrupted the ability of rats to visit the arms of a radial maze efficiently. In fact, their postoperative performance reached chance levels; they acted as if they had no memory of which arms they had previously entered. They eventually obtained all the food, but only after entering many of the arms repeatedly.

The problem was not that the rats could not distinguish among the eight arms of the maze; indeed, they could. Rats with hippocampal lesions can learn that particular locations sometimes contain food or never do. This type of learning is a form of stimulus-response learning; thus, it is analogous to nondeclarative (implicit) learning. Olton and Papas (1979) demonstrated the distinction between explicit and implicit learning in a single experiment. They trained rats in a seventeen-arm radial maze. Before each session eight of the arms were baited

Eight arms always contained food; rats with hippocampal lesions entered them aimlessly, visiting ones from which they had already received food.

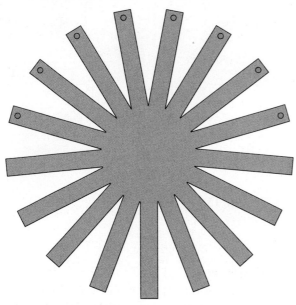

Nine arms never contained food; rats with hippocampal lesions learned not to enter them.

FIGURE 15.13

An explanation of the experiment by Olton and Papas (1979).

with food; the other nine *never* were. Although rats with lesions of the fornix visited the baited arms randomly, failing to avoid visiting the ones in which they had just eaten, they learned to stay away from the nine arms that never contained food. They apparently could not remember where they had just been, but they could learn which locations regularly contained food. (See *Figure 15.13.*)

On the basis of such results, Olton (1983) has suggested that lesions of the hippocampus or its connections impair working memory but leave reference memory relatively intact. **Working memory** consists of information about things that have just happened, information that is useful in the immediate future but may change from day to day. Thus, it is "erasable" memory that is replaced on a regular basis. **Reference memory** is permanent, long-term memory, produced by consistent conditions.

Although these results can be explained by the concepts of working memory and reference memory, they can also be explained in terms of relational memory. Each set of trials can be seen as a separate episode, during which the animal enters the arms in a particular order. The study with the seventeen-arm maze proves that rats with hippocampal lesions have no trouble learning the association between a particular arm and the presence or absence of food. But the task in the eight-arm maze is more complicated than that: The animal must remember where it has been *that day.* Somehow, the memory of today's explorations must be kept separate from the memory of yesterday's explorations, and those of the day before, and so on. If we think of each day's trials as separate episodes, we can see the similarity to the ability of humans to remember today's breakfast without confusing it with yesterday's or that of the day before. Of course, the rats are not telling us about what they remember, but their performance suggests that without a functioning hippocampal system they cannot keep the episodes straight. In this case all episodes take place in the same location, so the nature of the contextual stimulus is *time.*

Spatial Perception and Learning

Hippocampal lesions disrupt the ability to keep track of and remember spatial locations. As we saw, H.M. never learned to find his way home when his parents moved after his surgery. Laboratory animals show similar problems in navigation. Morris et al. (1982) developed a task that has been adopted by other researchers as a standard test of rodents' spatial abilities. The task requires rats to find a particular location in space solely by means of visual cues external to the apparatus. The "maze" consists of a circular pool, 1.3 meters in diameter, filled with a mixture of water and powdered milk. The milk hides the location of a small platform, situated just beneath the surface of the liquid. The experimenters put the rats into the milky water and let them swim until they encountered the hidden platform and climbed onto it. They released the rats from a new position on each trial. After a few trials normal rats learned to swim directly to the hidden platform from wherever they were released. However, rats with hippocampal lesions swam in what appeared to be an aimless fashion until they encountered the platform. Figure 15.14 shows the performance of

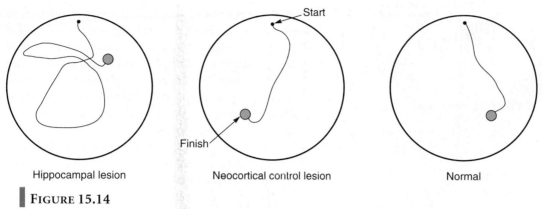

FIGURE 15.14

Effects of hippocampal lesions and neocortical control lesions on performance in the circular "milk maze." The small circle marks the location of the submerged platform.

(Reprinted by permission from Morris, R.G.M., Garrud, P., Rawlins, J.N.P., and O'Keefe, J. *Nature*, 1982, *297*, 681-683. Copyright © 1982, Macmillan Journals Limited.)

three rats: a normal rat, one with a neocortical lesion (to control for the fact that removal of the hippocampus entails damage to the overlying neocortex), and one with a hippocampal lesion. The results speak for themselves. (See *Figure 15.14.*)

The Morris milk maze requires relational learning; to navigate around the maze, the animals get their bearings from the relative locations of stimuli located outside the maze. But the maze can be used for nonrelational, stimulus-response learning, too. If the platform is elevated just above the surface of the water so that the rats can see it, even those with hippocampal lesions quickly learn to swim directly toward it. Similarly, if the animals are always released at the same place, they learn to head in a particular direction—say, toward a particular landmark they can see above the wall of the maze (Eichenbaum, Stewart, and Morris, 1990). I will say more later about why spatial learning is an example of relational learning.

Many different types of studies have confirmed the importance of the hippocampus in spatial learning. For example, Bingman and Mench (1990) found that hippocampal lesions disrupted navigation in homing pigeons. The lesions did not seem to disrupt the birds' ability to get their initial bearing toward the home roost. Instead, the lesions disrupted their ability to keep track of where they were when they got near the end of their flight—at a time during which the birds begin to use familiar land-marks to determine where they are. In addition, Rehkämper, Haase, and Frahm (1988) found that homing pigeons have larger hippocampal formations than breeds of pigeons that do not have such good navigational ability. In a review of the literature Sherry, Jacobs, and Gaulin (1992) reported that the hippocampal formation of species of birds and rodents that normally store seeds in hidden caches and later retrieve them (and that thus have excellent memories for spatial locations) is larger than that of animals without this ability. The size of the hippocampal formation is even sexually dimorphic in some species. In one species of voles (small rodents) the male is polygamous and ranges over a territory up to seven times larger than that of the females of his species; his hippocampus is also larger. In contrast, the size of the hippocampal formation is the same in males and females of monogamous voles, whose territories are similar in size.

Place Cells in the Hippocampal Formation

One of the most intriguing discoveries about the hippocampal formation was made by O'Keefe and Dostrovsky (1971), who recorded the activity of individual pyramidal cells in the hippocampus as an animal moved around the environment. The experimenters found that some neurons fired at a high rate only when the rat was in a particular loca-

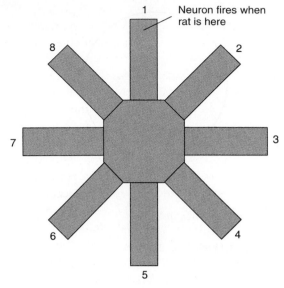

1

Neuron fires when
rat is here

Before Rotation

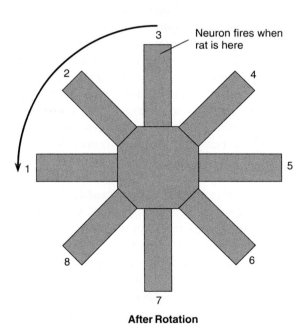

3

Neuron fires when
rat is here

After Rotation

FIGURE 15.15

Response of place cells to environmental cues. If the maze is rotated 90 degrees, place cells maintain their locations relative to objects located outside the maze.

tion. Different neurons had different *spatial receptive fields;* that is, they responded in different locations. For obvious reasons these neurons were named **place cells.** When, for example, a rat is exploring a radial-arm maze, place cells in its hip-

pocampus respond to places defined in relation to objects in the environment outside the maze (for example, lighting fixtures, cabinets, and racks of cages). If a particular place cell is active when the rat is at the end of the arm that points north, it will continue to fire in the end of the northern arm, even after the maze is rotated so that a different arm points north. (See *Figure 15.15.*)

When a rat is placed in a symmetrical chamber, where there are few cues to distinguish one part of the apparatus from another, the animal must keep track of its location from objects it sees (or hears or smells) in the environment outside the maze. Changes in these items affect the firing of the rats' place cells as well as their navigational ability. When experimenters move the stimuli as a group, maintaining their relative positions, the animals simply reorient their responses accordingly. However, when the experimenters interchange the stimuli so that they are arranged in a new order, the animals' performance (and the firing of their place cells) is disrupted. (Imagine how disoriented you might be if you entered a familiar room and found that the windows, doors, and furniture were in new positions.)

Hippocampal place cells are obviously guided by visual stimuli, because their receptive fields change when objects outside an environment are moved. They also receive internally generated stimuli. Hill and Best (1981) deafened and blindfolded rats and found that the spatial receptive fields of most of their place cells remained constant—even when they rotated the maze. At first the experimenters were surprised and puzzled by the results, but then it occurred to them that the animals may have been keeping track of where they were by feedback from proprioceptive cues. The rats may have been keeping track of their starting point, left and right turns, and so on, which kept resetting their "mental map." To test this hypothesis, Hill and Best wrapped their deafened and blindfolded rats in a towel, spun them around, and then placed them in the maze. (If you have ever played blindman's bluff or pin-the-tail-on-the-donkey, you will understand how disorienting this treatment is.) The experimenters' hypothesis was correct; after the rats had been spun, the receptive fields of their place cells were disrupted.

Other investigators have confirmed these results, using somewhat different procedures. McNaughton,

Leonard, and Chen (1989) let rats become familiar with an eight-arm radial maze and then found single neurons in the hippocampus that had spatial receptive fields. Next, they introduced the rats into the maze in complete darkness, using different starting points on each trial. Because the animals could no longer see the cues outside the maze, they could not tell which way the arms of the maze were oriented with respect to the room. Indeed, the receptive fields of the place cells were disrupted. Then the experimenters turned on the lights briefly, showing the rats the environmental cues that surrounded the maze. The receptive fields now reoriented themselves, and they continued to respond appropriately even when the lights were turned off again. O'Keefe and Speakman (1987) found that if they placed rats in a familiar environment and then removed the external cues one by one, the animals' place cells would continue to fire in their customary locations.

How does a rat keep track of its location in the dark, when it cannot see any landmarks outside the chamber? McNaughton and his colleagues obtained evidence that the parietal cortex provides the information that the hippocampal formation needs. They recorded from single neurons in the parietal cortex and found that their responses encoded various types of spatial information provided by movements that the rat made. For example, some responded when the rat turned left or right, some when it moved toward the center or toward the outside of the maze, and so on. Presumably, the hippocampus makes use of this information to keep track of its location in the maze when the external cues are not visible.

The hippocampus appears to receive its spatial information through the entorhinal cortex. Quirk et al. (1992) found that neurons in the entorhinal cortex have spatial receptive fields, although these fields are not nearly as clear-cut as those of hippocampal pyramidal cells. These results corroborated those of Rose (1983), who had found that single granule cells in the dentate gyrus also had spatial receptive fields. (As you know, neurons in the dentate gyrus receive input from those in the entorhinal cortex.) Damage to the entorhinal cortex impairs animals' ability to navigate in spatial tasks, and it also disrupts the spatial receptive fields of place cells in the hippocampus (Miller and Best, 1980).

The fact that neurons in the hippocampal formation have spatial receptive fields does not mean that each neuron encodes a particular location. Instead, this information is undoubtedly represented by particular *patterns* of activity in neural networks within the hippocampal formation. Muller and Kubie (1987) examined the spatial receptive fields of hippocampal place cells in different environments. They found that if environments differed only in size, the receptive fields would be found in the same relative locations. However, if the environments differed in shape, the locations of the receptive fields would be located in places that the investigators could not have predicted. Receptive fields also adapted themselves to changes in the environment. For example, if the experimenters placed a barrier in the middle of a neuron's receptive field, the shape of the field would change; but if the barrier was outside the field, no change would occur.

Most investigators believe that when animals encounter new environments, they learn their layout and establish "maps" in their hippocampus, in the form of neural networks. (Presumably, these maps are formed through the process of synaptic strengthening that is responsible for long-term potentiation.) An animal's location within each environment (the animal's place on the map) is encoded by the pattern of firing of these neurons. Obviously, a useful map must remain stable over time. Indeed, Thompson and Best (1990) obtained evidence that the hippocampal maps *are* stable; they found that the receptive fields of hippocampal neurons remained unchanged for as long as they were able to record from them—up to 153 days in one case.

Other Functions of the Hippocampal Formation

As we saw in the discussion of human anterograde amnesia, although people with hippocampal damage also have difficulty finding their way around, anterograde amnesia in both humans and laboratory animals includes many deficits not related to space. For example, monkeys with lesions of the hippocampal formation and humans with anterograde amnesia perform similarly on a variety of memory tasks (Zola-Morgan and Squire, 1985b; Squire, Zola-Morgan, and Chen, 1988; Zola-Morgan and

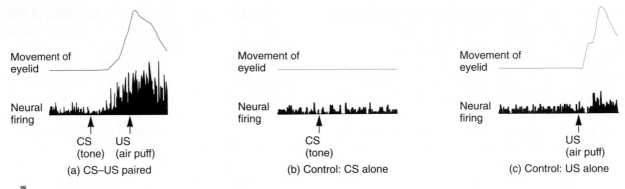

FIGURE 15.16

Pattern of firing of single neurons in the rabbit hippocampus along with a record of the movement of the eyelid. (a) Conditional responses of a trained rabbit. Note that the response and neural firing begin before the unconditional stimulus. (b) Lack of response from a rabbit presented with the tone alone. (c) Unconditional response of a rabbit presented with the puff of air alone. Note that the activity of the hippocampal neurons does not increase with the unconditional response.

(From Berger, T.W., Rinaldi, P.C., Weisz, D.J., and Thompson, R.F. *Journal of Neurophysiology,* 1983, *50,* 1197-1219. Reprinted with permission.)

Squire, 1990). In particular, the hippocampal lesions disrupted the monkeys' ability to remember for more than a few seconds a three-dimensional stimulus they had just seen.

Several studies by Berger and his colleagues (reviewed by Berger, Berry, and Thompson, 1986) have shown that neurons in the hippocampus respond not only to an animal's location in the environment but also to the animal's classically conditioned response. Berger and his colleagues recorded from single neurons in the hippocampus while they trained the animals to make a classically conditioned eyeblink response. (The CS was a tone; the US was a puff of air that elicited an eyeblink.) They discovered that the pattern of unit activity recorded from these neurons was closely correlated with the movement of the eyelid during a conditioned response. The neurons did *not* respond during an unconditioned response elicited by the puff of air alone.

Figure 15.16 shows the pattern of firing (series of vertical bars) of a single hippocampal neuron, along with a graph of the movement of the eyelid. (Actually, the experimenters recorded the movement of the *nictitating membrane,* located beneath the outer eyelids of several species of animals.) The record in Figure 15.16a is from a rabbit that had learned to make a conditioned response to the tone; the fact that the eyelid began to move before the puff of air was presented indicates that the response was a learned one, not one elicited by the air. Note the good correspondence between the firing pattern of the neuron and the movement of the eyelid. The response of the neuron precedes the movement by approximately 40 milliseconds. (See *Figure 15.16a.*) The other two records are from a rabbit that was presented with a tone (CS) or a puff of air (US), but not both. Note that under these conditions the hippocampal neuron does not alter its rate of firing. (See *Figures 15.16b* and *15.16c.*)

Although the hippocampus is *informed* about the execution of a conditioned response, it does not appear to play a direct role in learning that response. Solomon and Moore (1975) found that rabbits with bilateral hippocampal lesions learned a conditioned eyeblink response as rapidly as nonlesioned animals. However, Weisz, Solomon, and Thompson (1980) found that when a delay is imposed between the CS and the US (the tone and the air puff), hippocampal lesions prevented the learning of a conditioned response. This disruption occurs with delays as short as 0.5 second (Moyer, Deyo, and Disterhoft, 1990). Perhaps the hippocampal formation helps the animal remember the CS during the delay interval. In addition, Berger and Orr (1983) found that hippocampal lesions disrupted the reversal of a differential classical conditioning task. In this task the rabbits were presented tones of two different frequencies, only one of which (CS⁺) was followed by the puff of air (US). The CS⁻ was presented by itself, alone. Berger and Orr found that the hippocampal lesions had no effect on learning the discrimination; but when they reversed the significance of the two stimuli, changing the old CS⁺ to a CS⁻ and vice versa, the lesioned animals took over three times as long to change their response pattern. (See *Figure 15.17.*) These results suggest that the hippocampus may also play a role in learning *not* to make a response to one stimulus and to make it to another instead. I will suggest an explanation for this phenomenon later.

Role of Long-Term Potentiation in Hippocampal Functioning

In Chapter 14 we saw how synaptic connections could be quickly modified in the hippocampal formation, leading to long-term potentiation or long-term depression. How are these changes in synaptic strength related to the role the hippocampus plays in learning?

As you just learned, pyramidal cells in the hippocampal formation become active when the animal is present in particular locations. The sensory information reaches the dentate gyrus from the entorhinal cortex by means of the perforant path. Does this increased activity cause changes in the excitability of neurons in the hippocampal formation? The answer is clearly yes. Sharp, McNaughton, and Barnes (1983) measured the population EPSP in the dentate gyrus in response to a single shock delivered to the perforant path. Next, they placed the rats in an enriched environment filled with boxes, ramps, and other objects. This experience would be expected to cause an increased firing rate in the cells in the hippocampal formation as the animal explored the new environment, which might produce long-term potentiation. Indeed, the investigators found that it did; the experience increased the population EPSP by 48 percent. In a more recent study Van der Zee et al. (1992) found that when mice were trained on a spatial learning task, the level

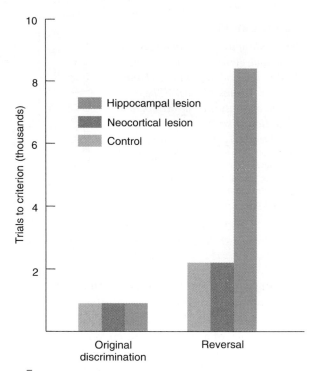

■ FIGURE 15.17

Effects of hippocampal lesions on acquisition of a differential classical conditioning task and its reversal.
(Adapted from Berger, T.W., and Orr, W.B. *Behavioural Brain Research*, 1983, *8*, 49-68.)

of activated PKC (protein kinase C) increased in the dendrites and cell bodies of neurons in the hippocampal formation. (As you will recall from Chapter 14, levels of activated PKC are increased by long-term potentiation.) Thus, when an animal participates in spatial learning tasks, changes in synaptic strength occur in the hippocampal formation.

We also saw that cells in the hippocampus are activated when an animal makes a classically conditioned response. Thus, it is not surprising that classical conditioning, too, affects synaptic strength in the hippocampal formation. Weisz et al. (1982) found that the amplitude of the population EPSP in the dentate gyrus doubled during the course of classical conditioning of an eyeblink response. (See *Figure 15.18.*) In addition, LoTurco, Coulter, and Alkon (1988) found similar effects in field CA1.

If the kinds of neural changes seen in long-term potentiation are really those that take place during

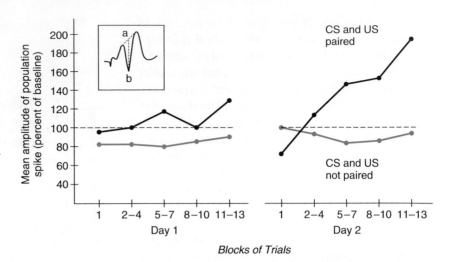

FIGURE 15.18

Amplitude of the population EPSP in the dentate gyrus of a rabbit during classical conditioning of the eyeblink response. The inset indicates the method of measuring the extracellular population spike.

(From Weisz, D.J., Clark, G.A., Yank, B., Thompson, R.F., and Solomon, P.R., in *Conditioning: Representation of Involved Neural Functions,* edited by C.D. Woody. New York: Plenum Press, 1982. Reprinted with permission.)

learning, then treatments that interfere with long-term potentiation should also interfere with learning. And they do. Morris et al. (1986) found that performance of a spatially guided task (the Morris milk maze) was disrupted by chronic infusion of AP5 (a drug that blocks NMDA receptors) into the lateral ventricles. Figure 15.19 shows the effects of AP5 and a control injection of saline on two rats' performances in the maze. For this test the pedestal was removed after eight days of training, and the rats were placed in the maze and permitted to swim for 60 minutes. The control animals concentrated their search in the quadrant of the pool that previously contained the platform, whereas the rats that had been infused with AP5 appeared to search the maze in a random fashion. (See *Figure 15.19.*)

Davis, Butcher, and Morris (1992) administered varying doses of AP5 to rats and determined the minimum amount needed to disrupt spatial learning. (They used a microdialysis probe to measure the precise level of the drug that reached the hippocampus.) They found that if a level of the drug was sufficient to disrupt spatial learning, it would also disrupt long-term potentiation in hippocampal slices.

In Chapter 14 we saw that researchers use genetic engineering methods to "knock out" specific genes in inbred strains of mice. These mutations (which block the production of two different enzymes) suppressed long-term potentiation. They also produced impairments in the animals' ability to learn the

Morris milk maze (Grant et al., 1992; Silva et al., 1992b).

Several studies have shown that long-term potentiation itself can impair learning. For example, McNaughton et al. (1986) found that high-frequency stimulation of the perforant path disrupted the learning of a spatially guided task. The authors suggest the reason for the deficit was that the artificial stimulation produced changes in a large number of synapses in the hippocampal formation, leaving very few synapses available for encoding the new information. These results emphasize the fact that information is stored in the form of a *pattern* of synaptic changes. Almost certainly, the changes that occur in any one task involve only a small proportion of the synapses in the hippocampal formation.

Modulation of Hippocampal Functions by Acetylcholinergic Neurons

I mentioned in Chapter 14 that long-term potentiation can most easily be established when the pattern of stimulation matches a rhythm normally found in the hippocampal formation. Green and Arduini (1954) discovered that the hippocampus produces a regular rhythmical pattern of electrical activity called **theta activity**—medium-amplitude, medium-frequency (5-8 hertz) waves. As we saw in Chapter 14, long-term potentiation can most easily be established in the hippocampal formation if a

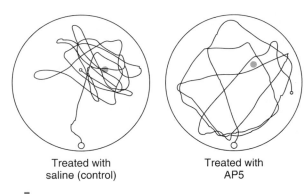

Treated with
saline (control)

Treated with
AP5

FIGURE 15.19

Performance of rats treated with saline or AP5 (a drug that blocks NMDA receptors) on the Morris milk maze.
(Adapted from Morris, R.G.M., Anderson, E., Lynch, G., and Baudry, M. *Nature*, 1986, *319*, 774-776.)

priming pulse of electrical stimulation is followed 170 milliseconds later by a burst of several pulses. The interval between the priming pulse and the burst of stimulation is equal to the interval between two waves of theta activity. In addition, Pavlides et al. (1988) found that when bursts of electrical stimulation coincided with the peaks of the theta waves, long-term potentiation was more easily established. In other words, theta activity consists of waxing and waning excitability of the hippocampal formation.

Hippocampal theta activity is controlled by acetylcholinergic neurons in the medial septum that send axons to the hippocampal formation via the fornix (Stewart and Fox, 1990). As we saw in Chapter 14, acetylcholine facilitates the establishment of long-term potentiation in the hippocampus. And as we saw earlier in this chapter, lesions of the fornix disrupt relational learning. One reason for the memory deficit appears to be the loss of acetylcholinergic input to the hippocampal formation.

Several studies have found that drugs that block muscarinic acetylcholine receptors abolish hippocampal theta activity and also impair relational learning (Deutsch, 1983). In addition, injection of a muscarinic receptor blocker directly into the medial septal nucleus of rats blocks theta activity and the release of acetylcholine in the hippocampus—and disrupts a relational learning task (Givens and Olton, 1990).

Several studies have shown that transplantation of acetylcholine-secreting cells from the medial septum into the hippocampus can partially reverse the effects of damage to its cholinergic input. For example, such transplants can restore theta activity or spatial receptive fields that are lost by cutting the fornix in rats (Buzsáki, Gage, and Czopf, 1987; Shapiro et al., 1989). These transplants can also reduce deficits in performance on the Morris milk maze task caused by fornix lesions (Nilsson et al., 1987). Similar results were obtained in monkeys (Ridley et al., 1991, 1992). In all cases histological examination of the tissue after the experiment was over showed that the transplants took and that they began secreting acetylcholine.

One of the effects of aging is a loss of acetylcholinergic neurons. Studies have shown that manipulations that increase the release of acetylcholine in the hippocampal formation can reduce the deficit in relational memory that occurs in older animals. For example, Gage et al. (1984) found that transplanting fetal medial septal tissue into the hippocampus of aged rats significantly improved their performance on the Morris milk maze. Olton et al. (1991) found that the performance of old rats (but not young ones) on a test of relational learning was improved by an injection of an acetylcholinergic agonist into the medial septum. The drug stimulated the neurons there to release more acetylcholine in the hippocampal formation.

Vanderwolf and his colleagues (Vanderwolf, 1969; Vanderwolf et al., 1975) observed that hippocampal theta activity is closely related to the type of behavior the animal is performing. In rats, *theta behaviors* are associated with exploration or investigation; they include such behaviors as walking, running, rearing up on the hind legs, sniffing, and manipulating objects with the forepaws. They also occur during REM sleep (when the animal is dreaming?). *Nontheta behaviors* are not involved with exploration; they include alert immobility ("freezing"), drinking, and various self-directed behaviors.

Many investigators believe that the presence of theta is correlated with the acquisition of sensory information by the hippocampal formation. When a rat investigates odors in the environment, its rate of sniffing is synchronized with the waves of its hippocampal theta rhythm (Wiener, Paul, and Eichenbaum, 1989). And as we saw, when pulses of electrical stimulation are delivered to the perforant pathway in synchrony with the peaks of the theta waves, long-term potentiation can be established more easily. Buzsáki (1989) suggests that during theta rhythms information is sampled by the dentate gyrus and CA3 field. Then after the bout of exploration is over, the cessation of the theta rhythms permits the information to be transferred to the CA1 field and, ultimately, to the rest of the brain. These waves are reminiscent of the cycles of a computer; whether they actually function this way will have to be resolved by future research.

A Theory of Hippocampal Functioning

As we saw earlier, people with anterograde amnesia can learn to recognize new stimuli, can learn new responses, and can learn to make a particular response when a particular stimulus is presented. What they cannot do is to talk about what they have learned. Anterograde amnesia appears to be a loss of the ability to learn about complex relations between many stimuli, including the order of their occurrence in time. How does research with laboratory animals help us understand this process?

Many investigators have come to the conclusion that the deficit in spatial learning produced by hippocampal lesions is caused by a failure to learn complex relations. For example, according to Wiener, Paul, and Eichenbaum (1989), "An emerging consensus . . . has indicated that the hippocampus is critical to learning and memory over a large range of information modalities that share a common demand for representing relationships among multiple independent precepts, but not for acquiring independent stimulus-reinforcement associations" (p. 2761). Sutherland and Rudy (1989) present a "configurational association theory," which suggests that the hippocampal system "combines the representations of elementary stimulus events to construct unique representations and allows for the formation of associations between these configural representations and other elementary representations" (p. 129).

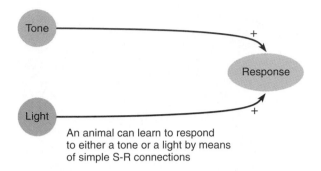

An animal can learn to respond to either a tone or a light by means of simple S-R connections

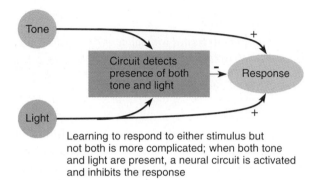

Learning to respond to either stimulus but not both is more complicated; when both tone and light are present, a neural circuit is activated and inhibits the response

Figure 15.20

Contextual learning. A simple auditory or visual discrimination can be accomplished through stimulus-response learning. Learning not to respond to the joint presence of two stimuli requires more complicated neural circuitry, which appears to involve the hippocampus.

I think it is likely that the original function of the hippocampus was to help the animal learn to navigate in the environment. Later, the process of evolution gave the hippocampus the ability to detect other types of contexts, also. Let us consider the spatial functions. Suppose you are standing in an environment similar to the circular milk maze I described earlier: a large field covered with grass, surrounded by distinctive objects, such as trees and buildings. You are familiar with the environment, having walked across it and played games on it many times. If someone blindfolds you and then picks you up and drops you somewhere on the field, you will recognize your location as soon as you remove the blindfold. Your location is defined by the *configuration* of objects you see—the *relation* they have with respect to each other. You will get a different view of these objects from each position on the field. Of course, if there are distinctive objects present on the field itself (trees, garbage cans, drinking fountains), the task will be even easier, because you can judge your position relative to nearby objects as well as distant ones.

Many experiments have shown that hippocampal lesions disrupt the performance of tasks that require the animal to remember relations among stimuli, rather than individual stimuli. For example, Rudy and Sutherland (1989) trained rats on a *conditional discrimination task*. A conditional discrimination is one in which a response to a particular stimulus is reinforced under one condition but not under another. Thus, a response depends on the *relation* between stimuli. They trained rats to press a lever when a light was present *or* when a tone was present, but not when both were present at the same time. This task cannot be learned simply by establishing connections between the visual system and the motor system, and between the auditory system and the motor system. Instead, some circuits must detect the occurrence of particular patterns of activity in both the visual system and the motor system and *inhibit* a response. (See *Figure 15.20.*)

As you have undoubtedly guessed, Rudy and Sutherland found that rats with hippocampal lesions were unable to learn this task. That is, they readily learned to respond when either the light or the tone was present, but they failed to learn *not to respond* when both stimuli were present at the same time.

In the experiment by Rudy and Sutherland the contextual stimulus was the joint presence of a light and a tone. Another contextual stimulus is *time*. Several experiments have shown that the hippocampal formation is involved in an animal's ability to distinguish between situations that differ only in terms of time. For example, Aggleton, Hunt, and Rawlins (1986) constructed a Y-shaped maze with fifty different interchangeable arms that could be attached to the stem. Training consisted of fifty trials. The animal was placed in the stem of the maze and was permitted to enter one of the arms, where it received a piece of food. The rat was then removed from the maze, and the experimenters prepared for the next trial by removing the nonreinforced arm

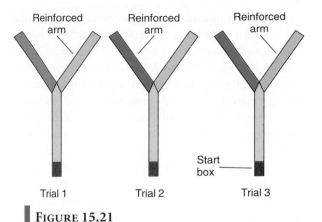

FIGURE 15.21

The procedure of the experiment by Aggleton, Hunt, and Rawlins (1986). The animal receives a piece of food if it enters the arm different from the one in which it received food on the previous trial.

and attaching a new one from the set of fifty. Thus, the maze contained a familiar arm in which the rat had just received food and an unfamiliar one. The position of the arms was varied randomly from trial to trial, so that the animals could not simply learn to enter the left or the right arm. Hence the task was to enter the arm they had not entered before. (See *Figure 15.21.*) Rats with hippocampal lesions had no difficulty learning this problem; they could easily distinguish between an arm they had previously visited and one that they had never visited before.

The task used by Aggleton and his colleagues does not require the animals to learn relations; it only requires them to distinguish old from new—familiar from unfamiliar. Raffaele and Olton (1988) trained rats in a task that differed in one important way: The same two arms were used on all trials. Thus, the animals had to remember which arm they had found food in *on the previous trial*. They had already entered each of the arms on many occasions, so their choice had to be based on a contextual stimulus: time. Damage to the hippocampal complex prevented animals from learning the task.

How can we put all the information about the hippocampal complex together? As you will recall, the hippocampal complex receives information from all regions of the sensory association cortex and from the motor association cortex of the frontal lobe. It also receives information from the amygdala concerning odors and dangerous stimuli and from neural circuits involved in classical conditioning. Thus, the hippocampal complex knows what is going on in the environment, where the animal is located, and what responses it has just made. It probably also knows about the animal's emotional state: whether the animal is hungry, sexually aroused, frightened, and so on. Thus, when something happens, the hippocampal system has all the information necessary to put that event into the proper context.

Several experiments indicate that hippocampal damage does, indeed, disrupt an animal's ability to distinguish particular contexts. Penick and Solomon (1991) trained normal rabbits, rabbits with hippocampal lesions, and rabbits with neocortical control lesions on a classically conditioned eyeblink task. All animals readily learned the conditioned response. Then half of the animals in each group were placed in a novel chamber, which looked and smelled different and was of a different size. The control animals that were placed in the new environment showed an immediate decrease in their rate of responding; the change in the context disrupted their performance. The performance of the animals with the hippocampal lesions was *not* disrupted; they acted as if they did not recognize that a change had taken place. It was as if the rabbits had learned the task but not the episodic information that was present at the same time—just like people with hippocampal lesions. (See *Figure 15.22.*)

Another study, using a different behavioral task, supports these findings. Phillips and LeDoux (1992) placed normal rats, rats with amygdala lesions, rats with hippocampal lesions, and rats with control lesions of the neocortex in a distinctive chamber and then established a conditioned emotional response (freezing) by presenting a tone paired with a foot shock several times. The following day, the experimenters placed the animals in the same chamber, watched them for a while, and then presented the tone (without the shock) several times. The normal animals showed signs of conditioned fear as soon as they entered the chamber; they froze, indicating that they recognized the environment as one in which they had received shocks. As expected, the amyg-

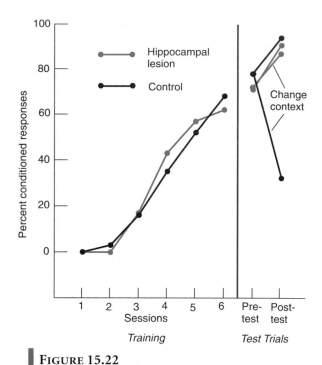

FIGURE 15.22

Effects of context: Acquisition of a classically conditioned eyeblink response in one chamber and subsequent performance in a different chamber.

(Adapted from Penick, S., and Solomon, P.R. *Behavioral Neuroscience*, 1991, *105*, 611-617.)

dala lesions disrupted all signs of conditioned fear—both to the context and to the tones. The hippocampal lesions had no effect on fear that was conditioned to the tone, but the animals showed very few signs of fear to the context. Like the rabbits in the study by Penick and Solomon, they did not seem to form a memory of the episode. (See *Figure 15.23.*)

Let us work through two learning tasks for which the hippocampal system is needed. First, let us consider Rudy and Sutherland's conditional discrimination experiment. The animals learn to press the lever when either the light or the tone is present; the hippocampus is not needed for this task. But then the experimenters introduce some trials in which the light and the tone are present simultaneously and do *not* give the animals food if they make a response. The hippocampal formation detects the joint presence of the light and the tone—something that has never occurred before. Through connections that go back to the neocortex, the hippocampus informs the rest of the brain that a new situation has just occurred. Because the animal never receives food when it responds in this situation, the information received from the hippocampal formation begins to modify connections in the neocortex. Eventually, the animal learns not to respond to the compound stimulus of light plus tone.

For the second example we will return to anterograde amnesia in humans. Consider a normal person learning to press a panel with a picture of a circle on it, as patient H.M. did in the experiment by Sidman, Stoddard, and Mohr. While the person is seated in front of the apparatus, his or her hippocampal formation receives information about the context in which the learning is taking place: the room, the other people present, the person's mood, and so on. These pieces of information are collected and are somehow attached to the patterns of activity in the association cortex in several different regions of the brain. Later, when the person is asked about the task, the question reactivates the pattern of activity in the hippocampus, which causes the retrieval of the memory of the episode, pieces of which are stored all over the brain. Patient H.M., lacking a functioning hippocampal system, is unable to accomplish this act.

Rolls (1989) presents a hypothetical model of the role of the hippocampal formation in learning and memory that may prove to be useful. He suggests that the hippocampal system is a neural network that functions as an *autoassociator.* Each part of the hippocampal system—dentate gyrus, field CA3, field CA1, and the three parts of the subicular complex—successively analyzes information and passes the results of its analysis on to the next part. An autoassociative network quickly and efficiently learns to recognize a particular pattern of inputs and produces a unique output for each pattern. Then if a similar pattern is presented later—or if parts of the pattern are presented—the network produces the appropriate output.

As you will recall from Chapter 14, neural networks such as these are capable of *pattern completion:* When they are presented with a fuzzy version of the original pattern or simply a fragment of it, they supply the complete pattern in their output. (Refer to *Figure 14.15.*) This morning when I got

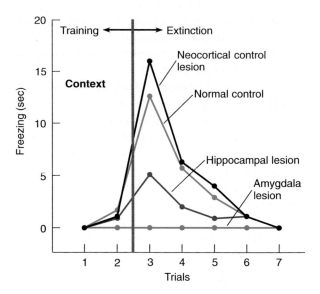

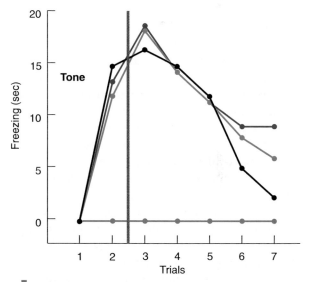

FIGURE 15.23

Effects of context: Conditioned emotional responses (freezing) during five days of extinction produced by the context (the experimental chamber) and by the CS (a tone).
(Adapted from Phillips, R.G., and LeDoux, J.E. *Behavioral Neuroscience,* 1992, *106,* 274-285.)

up, put on my slippers and robe, and went downstairs to have breakfast, my hippocampus kept track of where I was, about what time it was, how I was feeling, and so on. That is, it registered the context of that situation. As I went about preparing my breakfast, the memories of what was happening were being recorded in the form of synaptic changes in various regions of my sensory association cortex. The hippocampus communicated with these regions, somehow tying together these memories as they were being formed.

When you asked me about what I had for breakfast this morning, the words were recognized and understood by language mechanisms in my left temporal and parietal lobes (more about that in Chapter 16). Information about this recognition provided enough information for my hippocampal formation to recognize the context—to *complete the pattern*. The pattern was broadcast through outputs of the hippocampal formation to the locations in my neocortex that contain the individual components of the memory of the episode, and I told you about my breakfast.

This analysis is certainly speculative, but I think it is consistent with the experimental data I have presented in this chapter. Of course, it is vague about many parts of the process. For example, just how does asking someone a question activate the pattern of activity in the hippocampus? And how, exactly, are memories "tied together"? How are pieces of information collected and attached to sets of neural circuits? Obviously, we need to think about these questions, design clever experiments to obtain useful information, think about the questions in light of the new information, design more clever experiments . . . .

I left a puzzle for the end of this discussion: that of retrograde amnesia. I already told you that people with anterograde amnesia inevitably have some retrograde amnesia. For example, Squire, Haist, and Shimamura (1989) found that the period of retrograde amnesia in patients with anterograde amnesia (including some known to have hippocampal damage) lasted approximately fifteen years. That is, the patients are unable to remember events for several years before the time of their brain damage but can remember events from the remote past. This finding means that the hippocampal system is involved in the retrieval of relatively young declarative memories but is not needed for the retrieval of old ones. What happens over the course of several years that makes declarative memories accessible without the use of the hippocampal complex? Is it simply a matter of practice? Does the act of remembering something again and again, over a period of years, somehow reinforce that memory so that it can be more easily retrieved later? When we can answer this question, we will really know something about the memory process.

INTERIM SUMMARY

Studies with laboratory animals indicate that damage to the hippocampal formation disrupts the ability to learn spatial relations and to distinguish events that have just occurred from those that have occurred at another time. For example, rats with hippocampal damage cannot remember the arms of a radial maze that they have just visited, but they can learn to visit only those arms that contain food. Also, they cannot learn the Morris milk maze unless they can see the platform or they are always released from the same place in the maze. The basic deficit appears to be an inability to distinguish among different contexts, which includes locations in space and in time. Although the animals can learn simple discrimination tasks, they cannot learn conditional discrimination tasks, in which a stimulus has different meanings in different contexts.

The hippocampal formation contains neurons that respond when the animal is in a particular location, which implies that the hippocampus contains neural networks that keep track of the relations among stimuli in the environment that define the animal's location. Much of this information is received from the parietal cortex, via the entorhinal cortex. The hippocampal formation is also informed about learned responses that the animal is about to make; electrical activity there is closely correlated with the movement of the classically conditioned eyeblink response. Perhaps this information helps the animal determine the context in which it is performing the behavior; hippocampal lesions disrupt reversal of a differential classical conditioning task but not its original acquisition.

Long-term potentiation appears to be related to learning. When rats are exposed to novel, complex environments, or when rabbits are trained with a classical conditioning procedure, the extracellular EPSP in the dentate gyrus increases, just as it does when the entorhinal cortex is subjected to high-frequency stimulation. In addition, drugs that block long-term potentiation produce effects on learning similar to those of hippocampal lesions.

Hippocampal theta activity, controlled by acetylcholinergic neurons in the medial septum, appears to be a time during which the hippocampus receives and stores sensory input. In addition, the establishment of long-term potentiation is modulated by the presence of theta waves. The memory deficits produced by fornix lesions, which appear to be caused by loss of acetylcholinergic neurons that send axons to the hippocampal formation, can be ameliorated by hippocampal transplants of fetal brain tissue rich in ACh-secreting neurons. The performance of aged rats can also be improved by these transplants.

The original role of the hippocampal formation may well have been to provide animals with the ability to orient in space, keeping track of the multiple stimuli that define spatial location; but it is clear that its role has expanded to learning relations among nonspatial stimuli and situations, as well. Presumably, people with anterograde amnesia can no longer learn about episodes in their lives because their inability to distinguish one context from another prevents the elements that make up an episode from being tied together.

New Terms

Human Anterograde Amnesia

anterograde amnesia *(ANN ter o grade)* p. 482

retrograde amnesia p. 482

Korsakoff's syndrome p. 482

short-term memory p. 484

long-term memory p. 484

consolidation p. 485

priming task p. 486

declarative memory p. 487

nondeclarative memory p. 487

perirhinal *(pair ee RYE nul)* p. 490

parahippocampal p. 490

Relational Learning in Laboratory Animals

working memory p. 496

reference memory p. 496

place cell p. 498

theta activity p. 502

Suggested Readings

Byrne, J.H., and Berry, W.O. *Neural Models of Plasticity: Experimental and Theoretical Approaches.* San Diego: Academic Press, 1989.

Gazzaniga, M.S. *Perspectives in Memory Research.* Cambridge, Mass.: MIT Press, 1988.

Graf, P., and Masson, M.E.J. *Implicit Memory: New Directions in Cognition, Development, and Neuropsychology.* Hillsdale, N.J.: Erlbaum Associates, 1993.

Ono, T. *Brain Mechanisms of Perception and Memory: From Neuron to Behavior.* New York: Oxford University Press, 1992.

Squire, L.R., Weinberger, N.M., Lynch, G., and McGaugh, J.L. *Memory: Organization and Locus of Change.* New York: Oxford University Press, 1991.

Squire, L.R., and Butters, N. *Neuropsychology of Memory.* New York: Guilford Press, 1992.

Thompson, R.F. Mammalian brain substrates of aversive classical conditioning. *Annual Review of Psychology,* 1993, *43,* 317-342.

CHAPTER 16

Human Communication

Speech Production and Comprehension: Brain Mechanisms
- Lateralization
- Speech Production
- Speech Comprehension
- Prosody: Rhythm, Tone, and Emphasis in Speech
  Interim Summary

Reading and Writing Disorders
- Relation to Aphasia
- Pure Alexia
- Toward an Understanding of Reading
- Toward an Understanding of Writing
- Developmental Dyslexias
  Interim Summary

VERBAL BEHAVIORS CONSTITUTE ONE OF the most important classes of human social behavior. Our cultural evolution has been possible because we can talk and listen, write and read. Language enables our discoveries to be cumulative; knowledge gained by one generation can be passed on to the next.

The basic function of verbal communication is seen in its effects on other people. When we talk to someone, we almost always expect our speech to induce the person to engage in some sort of behavior. Sometimes, the behavior is of obvious advantage to us, as when we ask for an object or for help performing a task. At other times, we are simply asking for a social exchange. Even "idle" conversation is not idle, because it causes another person to look at us and say something in return.

This chapter discusses the neural basis of verbal behavior: talking, understanding speech, reading, and writing.

SPEECH PRODUCTION AND COMPREHENSION: BRAIN MECHANISMS

OUR KNOWLEDGE OF THE PHYSIOLOGY OF LANguage has been obtained primarily by observing the effects of brain lesions on people's verbal behavior. Although investigators have studied people who have undergone brain surgery or who have sustained head injuries, brain tumors, or infections, most of the observations have been made on people who have suffered strokes, or **cerebrovascular accidents.** The most common type of cerebrovascular accident is caused by obstruction of a blood vessel. The interruption in blood flow deprives a region of the brain of its blood supply, which causes cells in that region to die. Figure 16.1 shows a CT scan from a person with a stroke that caused Broca's aphasia (described later). The lesion is the dark region indicated by the arrow. (See *Figure 16.1.*)

The most important category of speech disorders is **aphasia,** a primary disturbance in the comprehension or production of speech, caused by brain damage. Not all speech disturbances are aphasias; a patient must have difficulty comprehending, repeating, or producing meaningful speech, and this difficulty must not be caused by simple sensory or motor deficits or by lack of motivation. For example, inability to speak caused by deafness or paralysis of the speech muscles is not considered to be aphasia. In addition, the deficit must be relatively isolated; that is, the patient must appear to be aware of what is happening in his or her environment and to comprehend that others are attempting to communicate.

Lateralization

Verbal behavior is a *lateralized* function; most language disturbances occur after damage to the left side of the brain. The best way to determine which side of the brain is dominant for speech is to perform a *Wada test,* named after its inventor. (As we saw in Chapter 15, this test is also used to assess memory functions.) A patient who is about to undergo surgery that might encroach on a speech area receives a short-acting anesthetic in one carotid artery and then, when the effects have worn off, in the other. This procedure anesthetizes first one cerebral hemisphere and then the other; thus, in a few minutes the involvement of each hemisphere in speech functions can be assessed. In over 95 percent of right-handed people the left hemisphere is dominant for speech. That is, when the left hemisphere is anesthetized, the person loses the ability to speak. However, when the right hemisphere is anesthetized, the person can still talk and carry on a conversation. The figure is somewhat lower in left-handed people: approximately 70 percent. Therefore, unless I say otherwise, you can assume that the brain damage described in this chapter is located in the left (speech-dominant) hemisphere.

Why is one hemisphere specialized for speech? The perceptual functions of the left hemisphere are more specialized for the analysis of sequences of stimuli, occurring one after the other. The perceptual functions of the right hemisphere are more specialized for the analysis of space and geometrical shapes and forms, the elements of which are all present at the same time. Speech is certainly sequential; it consists of sequences of words, which are composed of sequences of sounds. Thus, it makes

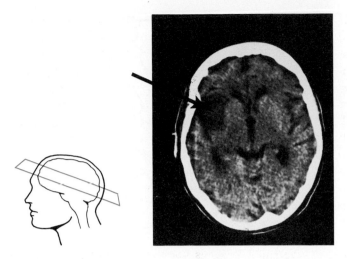

FIGURE 16.1

A CT scan from a patient with Broca's aphasia. The lesion, located in the left frontal lobe, is indicated by the arrow.
(Scans courtesy of Brian Chiango and Jean Dempster, Brigham and Women's Hospital, Boston, Massachusetts.)

sense for the left hemisphere to have become specialized at perceiving speech. In addition, as we saw in Chapter 8, the left hemisphere is involved in the control of sequences of voluntary movements. Perhaps this fact accounts for the localization of neural circuits involved in speech production, as well as speech perception, in the left hemisphere.

Although the circuits *primarily* involved in speech comprehension and production are located in the left hemisphere, it would be a mistake to conclude that the right hemisphere plays no role in speech. Speech is not simply a matter of talking—it is also having something to say. Similarly, listening is not simply hearing and recognizing words—it is understanding the meaning of what has been said. When we hear and understand words, and when we talk about or think about our own perceptions or memories, we are using neural circuits besides those directly involved in speech. Thus, these circuits, too, play a role in verbal behavior. For example, damage to the right hemisphere makes it difficult for a person to read maps, perceive spatial relations, and recognize complex geometrical forms. People with such damage will also have trouble talking about things like maps and complex geometrical forms or understanding what other people have to say about them. The right hemisphere also appears to be involved in organizing a narrative—selecting and assembling the elements of what we want to say (Gardner et al., 1983). As we saw in Chapter 11, the right hemisphere is involved in the expression and recognition of emotion in the tone of voice. And as

we shall see in this chapter, it is also involved in control of *prosody*—the normal rhythm and stress found in speech. Therefore, both hemispheres of the brain have a contribution to make to our language abilities.

Speech Production

Being able to talk—that is, to produce meaningful speech—requires several abilities. First, the person must have something to talk about. Let us consider what this means. We can talk about something that is presently happening or something that happened in the past. In the first case we are talking about our perceptions: of things we are seeing, hearing, feeling, smelling, and so on. In the second case we are talking about our memories of what happened in the past. Both perceptions of current events and memories of events that occurred in the past involve brain mechanisms in the posterior part of the cerebral hemispheres (the occipital, temporal, and parietal lobes). Thus, this region is largely responsible for our having something to say.

Of course, we can also talk about something that *did not* happen. That is, we can use our imagination to make up a story (or tell a lie). We know little about the neural mechanisms responsible for imagination, but it seems likely that they involve the mechanisms responsible for perceptions and memories; after all, when we make up a story, we must base it on knowledge that we originally acquired through perception and have retained in our memory.

Given that a person has something to say, actually doing so requires some additional brain functions. As we shall see in this section, the conversion of perceptions, memories, and thoughts into speech makes use of neural mechanisms located in the frontal lobes.

Damage to a region of the inferior left frontal lobe (Broca's area) disrupts the ability to speak: It causes **Broca's aphasia.** This disorder is characterized by slow, laborious, and nonfluent speech. When trying to talk with patients who have Broca's aphasia, most people find it hard to resist supplying the words they are obviously groping for. But although they often mispronounce words, the ones they manage to come out with are meaningful. The posterior part of the cerebral hemispheres has something to say, but the damage to the frontal lobe makes it difficult for the patients to express these thoughts.

People with Broca's aphasia find it easier to say some types of words than others. They have great difficulty saying the little words with grammatical meaning, such as *a, the, some, in,* or *about.* These words are called **function words,** because they have important grammatical functions. The words that they do manage to say are almost entirely **content words**—words that convey meaning, including nouns, verbs, adjectives, and adverbs, such as *apple, house, throw,* or *heavy.* Here is a sample of speech from a man with Broca's aphasia, who is telling the examiner why he has come to the hospital. As you will see, his words are meaningful, but what he says is certainly not grammatical. The dots indicate long pauses.

> Ah . . . Monday . . . ah Dad and Paul [patient's name] . . . and Dad . . . hospital. Two . . . ah doctors . . . , and ah . . . thirty minutes . . . and yes . . . ah . . . hospital. And, er Wednesday . . . nine o'clock. And er Thursday, ten o' clock . . . doctors. Two doctors . . . and ah . . . teeth. Yeah, . . . , fine. (Goodglass, 1976, p. 278)

People with Broca's aphasia can comprehend speech much better than they can produce it. In fact, some observers have said that their comprehension is unimpaired, but as we will see, this is not quite true. Broca (1861) suggested that this form of aphasia is produced by a lesion of the frontal association cortex, just anterior to the face region of the primary

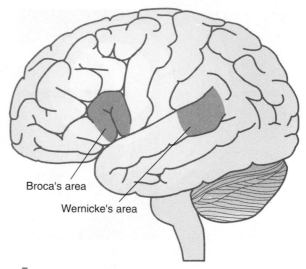

FIGURE 16.2

The location of the primary speech areas of the brain. (Wernicke's area will be described later.)

motor cortex. Subsequent research proved him to be essentially correct, and we now call the region **Broca's area.** (See *Figure 16.2.*)

Lesions that produce Broca's aphasia are certainly centered in the vicinity of Broca's area. However, damage restricted to the cortex of Broca's area does not appear to produce Broca's aphasia; the damage must extend to surrounding regions of the frontal lobe and to the underlying subcortical white matter (H. Damasio, 1989; Naeser et al., 1989). In addition, there is evidence that lesions of the basal ganglia—especially the head of the caudate nucleus—can also produce a Broca-like aphasia (Damasio, Eslinger, and Adams, 1984). Figure 16.3 shows the averaged plot of PET scans of regional blood flow from a group of subjects who were reading words aloud (Leblanc et al., 1992). As you can see, the task activated subcortical regions under Broca's area (including the head of the caudate nucleus) as well as the neocortex. (See *Figure 16.3.*)

Recent studies using PET scanners have shown that a *functional* lesion can often be much more extensive than the area of primary tissue damage. For example, Metter (1991) notes that small lesions in the basal ganglia and in the adjacent subcortical white matter can cause decreased metabolism of a fairly large region of the frontal cortex—even when

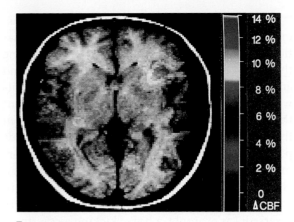

FIGURE 16.3

An averaged plot of PET scans of regional cerebral blood flow, superimposed on an MRI scan, taken while the subjects were reading words aloud. Note that the region of activation includes subcortical regions as well as the cerebral cortex of Broca's area.

(From Leblanc, R., Meyer, E., Bub, D., Zatorre, R.J., and Evans, A.C. *Neurosurgery*, 1992, *31*, 369–373. Reprinted with permission.)

autopsy shows no loss of neurons in the cortex. In addition, lesions in the frontal lobe can often cause decreased metabolism in the temporal and parietal lobes, presumably because the lesions disrupt connections between these areas. Thus, the full extent of a lesion will often be underestimated by examining CT or MRI scans alone.

Wernicke (1874) suggested that Broca's area contains motor memories—in particular, *memories of the sequences of muscular movements that are needed to articulate words.* Talking involves rapid movements of the tongue, lips, and jaw, and these movements must be coordinated with each other and with those of the vocal cords; thus, talking requires some very sophisticated motor control mechanisms. Obviously, circuits of neurons somewhere in our brain will, when properly activated, cause these sequences of movements to be executed. Because damage to the inferior caudal left frontal lobe (including Broca's area) disrupts the ability to articulate words, this region is the most likely candidate for the location of these "programs." The fact that this region is located just in front of the part of the primary motor cortex that controls the muscles used for speech certainly supports this conclusion.

But the speech functions of the left frontal lobe include more than programming the movements used to speak. Broca's aphasia is much more than a deficit in pronouncing words. In general, three major speech deficits are produced by lesions in and around Broca's area: *agrammatism, anomia,* and *articulation difficulties.* Although most patients with Broca's aphasia will have all of these deficits to some degree, their severity can vary considerably from person to person—presumably, because their brain lesions differ.

Agrammatism refers to a patient's difficulty in using grammatical constructions. This disorder can appear all by itself, without any difficulty in pronouncing words (Nadeau, 1988). As we saw, people with Broca's aphasia rarely use function words. In addition, they rarely use grammatical markers such as *-ed* or auxiliaries such as *have* (as in *I have gone*). For some reason, they *do* often use *-ing,* perhaps because this ending converts a verb into a noun. A study by Saffran, Schwartz, and Marin (1980) illustrates this difficulty. The following quotations are from agrammatic patients attempting to describe pictures:

Picture of a boy being hit in the head by a baseball
The boy is catch . . . the boy is hitch . . . the boy is hit the ball. (Saffran, Schwartz, and Marin, 1980, p. 229)

Picture of a girl giving flowers to her teacher
Girl . . . wants to . . . flowers . . . flowers and wants to . . . . The woman . . . wants to . . . . The girl wants to . . . the flowers and the woman. (Saffran, Schwartz, and Marin, 1980, p. 234)

The second major speech deficit seen in Broca's aphasia is **anomia** ("without name"). Anomia refers to a word-finding difficulty; and because all aphasics omit words or use inappropriate ones, anomia is actually a primary symptom of *all* forms of aphasia. However, because the speech of Broca's aphasics lacks fluency, their anomia is especially apparent; their facial expression and frequent use of sounds like "uh" make it obvious that they are groping for the correct words.

The third major characteristic of Broca's aphasia is *difficulty with articulation.* Patients mispronounce words, often altering the sequence of sounds. For example, *lipstick* might be pronounced

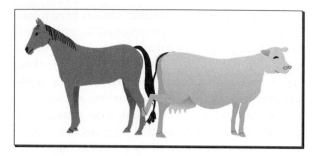

FIGURE 16.4

An example of the stimuli used in the experiment by Schwartz, Saffran, and Marin (1980).

"likstip." People with Broca's aphasia recognize that their pronunciation is erroneous, and they usually try to correct it.

As I said, these three deficits are seen in various combinations in different patients, depending on the exact location of the lesion and, to a certain extent, on their stage of recovery. Although the anatomical correlates are not yet worked out, we can characterize these deficits hierarchically. On the lowest, most elementary level is control of the sequence of movements of the muscles of speech; damage to this ability leads to articulation difficulties. The next higher level is selection of the particular "programs" for individual words; damage to this ability leads to anomia. Finally, the highest level is selection of grammatical structure, including word order, use of function words, and word endings; damage to this ability leads to agrammatism. Presumably, the control of articulation involves the face area of the primary motor cortex and portions of the basal ganglia; the selection of words, word order, and grammatical markers involves Broca's area and adjacent regions of the frontal association cortex.

So far, I have described Broca's aphasia as a disorder in speech *production.* In an ordinary conversation Broca's aphasics seem to understand everything that is said to them. They appear to be irritated and annoyed by their inability to express their thoughts well, and they often make gestures to supplement their scanty speech. The striking disparity between their speech and their comprehension often leads people to assume that their comprehension is normal. But it is not. Schwartz, Saffran, and Marin (1980) showed Broca's aphasics pairs of pictures in which agents and objects of the action were reversed: for example, a horse kicking a cow and a cow kicking a horse, a truck pulling a car and a car pulling a truck, and a dancer applauding a clown and a clown applauding a dancer. As they showed each pair of pictures, they read the subject a sentence, for example, *The horse kicks the cow.* The subjects' task was to point to the appropriate picture, indicating whether they understood the grammatical construction of the sentence. (See **Figure 16.4.**) They performed very poorly.

The correct picture in the study by Schwartz and her colleagues was specified by a particular aspect of grammar: word order. The agrammatism that accompanies Broca's aphasia appears to disrupt patients' ability to use grammatical information, including word order, to decode the meaning of a sentence. Thus, their deficit in comprehension parallels their deficit in production. If they heard the sentence *The man swats the mosquito,* they would understand that it concerns a man and a mosquito and the action of swatting. They would have no trouble figuring out who is doing what to whom. But the sentence *The horse kicks the cow* does not provide any extra cues; if the grammar is not understood, neither is the meaning of the sentence.

Other experiments have shown that people with Broca's aphasia have difficulty carrying out a sequence of commands, such as "Pick up the red circle and touch the green square with it" (Boller and Dennis, 1979). This finding, along with the other symptoms I have described in this section, suggests that an important function of the left frontal lobe is sequencing—of movements of the muscles of speech (producing words) and of words (comprehending and producing grammatical speech).

Speech Comprehension

Comprehension of speech obviously begins in the auditory system, which is needed to detect and analyze sounds. But *recognizing* words is one thing; *comprehending* them is another. Recognizing a spoken word is a complex perceptual task that relies on memories of sequences of sounds. This task appears to be accomplished by neural circuits in the middle and posterior portion of the superior temporal gyrus of the left hemisphere—a region that has come to be known as **Wernicke's area.** (Refer to *Figure 16.2.*)

Wernicke's Aphasia: Description

The primary characteristics of **Wernicke's aphasia** are poor speech comprehension and production of meaningless speech. Unlike Broca's aphasia, Wernicke's aphasia is fluent and unlabored; the person does not strain to articulate words and does not appear to be searching for them. The patient maintains a melodic line, with the voice rising and falling normally. When you listen to the speech of a person with Wernicke's aphasia, it appears to be grammatical. That is, the person uses function words such as *the* and *but* and employs complex verb tenses and subordinate clauses. However, the person uses few content words, and the words that he or she strings together just do not make sense. In the extreme, speech deteriorates into a meaningless jumble, illustrated by the following quotation.

EXAMINER: What kind of work did you do before you came into the hospital?

PATIENT: Never, now mista oyge I wanna tell you this happened when happened when he rent. His—his kell come down here and is—he got ren something. It happened. In thesse ropiers were with him for hi—is friend—like was. And it just happened so I don't know, he did not bring around anything. And he did not pay it. And he roden all o these arranjen from the pedis on from iss pescid. In these floors now and so. He hadn't had em round here. (Kertesz, 1981, p. 73)

Because of the speech deficit of people with Wernicke's aphasia, when we try to assess their ability to comprehend speech, we must ask them to use nonverbal responses. That is, we cannot assume that they do not understand what other people say to them just because they do not give the proper answer. A commonly used test of comprehension assesses their ability to understand questions by pointing to objects on a table in front of them. For example, they are asked to "Point to the one with ink." If they point to an object other than the pen, they have not understood the request. When tested this way, people with severe Wernicke's aphasia do indeed show poor comprehension.

A remarkable fact about people with Wernicke's aphasia is that they often seem unaware of their deficit. That is, they do not appear to recognize that their speech is faulty, nor do they recognize that they cannot understand the speech of others. They do not look puzzled when someone tells them something, even though they obviously cannot understand what they hear. Perhaps their comprehension deficit prevents them from realizing that what they say and hear makes no sense. They still follow social conventions, taking turns in conversation with the examiner, even though they do not understand what the examiner says—and what they say in return makes little sense. They remain sensitive to the other person's facial expression and tone of voice and begin talking when he or she asks a question and pauses for an answer. One patient with Wernicke's aphasia made the following responses when asked to name ten common objects.

toothbrush → "stoktery"
cigarette → "cigarette"
pen → "tankt"
knife → "nike"
fork → "fahk"
quarter → "minkt"
pen → "spentee"
matches → "senktr"
key → "seek"
comb → "sahk"

He acted sure of himself and gave no indication that he recognized that most of his responses were meaningless. The responses he made were not simply new words that he had invented; he was asked several times to name the objects and gave different responses each time (except for cigarette, which he always named correctly).

Even when patients recognize that something is wrong, they appear unsure of what the problem is. The following quotation illustrates this puzzlement.

EXAMINER: Can you tell me a little bit about why you're here?

PATIENT: I don't know whata wasa down here for me, I just don't know why I wasn't with up here, at all you, it was neva, had it been walked me today ta died.

EXAMINER: Uh huh. Okay.

PATIENT: Sine just don't know why, what is really wrong, I don't know, cause I can eaten treffren eatly an everythin like that I'm all right at home. (Kertesz, 1980)

The patient appears to recognize that she has a problem of some kind, but she is also saying (I think) that at home she can prepare her own meals and otherwise take care of herself.

Wernicke's Aphasia: Analysis

Because the superior temporal gyrus is a region of auditory association cortex, and because a comprehension deficit is so prominent in Wernicke's aphasia, this disorder has been characterized as a *receptive* aphasia. Wernicke suggested that the region that now bears his name is the location of *memories of the sequences of sounds that constitute words.* This hypothesis is reasonable; it suggests that the auditory association cortex of the superior temporal gyrus recognizes the sounds of words, just as the visual association cortex of the inferior temporal gyrus recognizes the sight of objects.

Evidence obtained from studies of patients using CT and MRI scans suggests that this conclusion is correct (Kertesz, 1979; Damasio, 1981). In addition, PET studies show that listening to words increases the metabolic activity of this region (Petersen et al., 1989; Price et al., 1992). But why should damage to an area responsible for the ability to recognize spoken words disrupt people's ability to speak? In fact, it does not; Wernicke's aphasia, like Broca's aphasia, actually appears to consist of several deficits. The

abilities that are disrupted include *recognition of spoken words, comprehension of the meaning of words,* and the *ability to convert thoughts into words.* Let us consider each of these abilities in turn.

Recognition: Pure Word Deafness. As I said in the introduction to this section, *recognizing* a word is not the same as *comprehending* it. If you hear a foreign word several times, you will learn to recognize it; but unless someone tells you what it means, you will not comprehend it. Recognition is a perceptual task; comprehension involves retrieval of additional information from memory.

Damage to the left temporal lobe can produce a disorder of auditory word recognition, uncontaminated by other problems. This syndrome is called **pure word deafness.** Although people with pure word deafness are not deaf, they cannot understand speech. As one patient put it, "I can hear you talking, I just can't understand what you're saying." Another said, "It's as if there were a bypass somewhere, and my ears were not connected to my voice" (Saffran, Marin, and Yeni-Komshian, 1976, p. 211). These patients can recognize nonspeech sounds such as the barking of a dog, the sound of a doorbell, the chirping of a bird, and so on. Often, they can recognize the emotion expressed by the intonation of speech even though they cannot understand what is being said. More significantly, their own speech is excellent. They can often understand what other people are saying by reading their lips. They can also read and write, and sometimes, they ask people to communicate with them in writing. Clearly, pure word deafness is not an inability to comprehend the meaning of words; if it were, people with this disorder would not be able to read people's lips or read words written on paper.

Exactly what do we mean when we say that the auditory system of the left hemisphere is specialized for the analysis of speech sounds? First, the specialization is only for the discrimination of the sounds that distinguish one word from another, not the sounds related to the prosodic aspects of speech—the changes in rhythm and pitch that convey emphasis or emotional state. In general, the sounds that distinguish between words are very brief, whereas those that convey prosody are of longer duration. Perhaps the auditory system of the left hemisphere

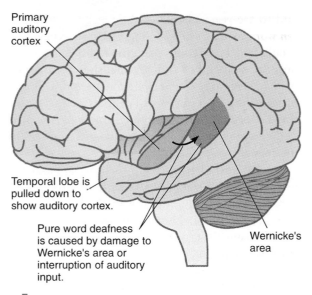

Primary
auditory
cortex

Temporal lobe is
pulled down to
show auditory cortex.

Pure word deafness
is caused by damage to
Wernicke's area or
interruption of auditory
input.

Wernicke's
area

FIGURE 16.5

The brain damage that causes pure word deafness.

is simply specialized for the recognition of acoustical events of short duration.

In a review of the literature Phillips and Farmer (1990) suggest precisely this hypothesis. They note that careful studies of patients with pure word deafness have shown that the patients can distinguish between different vowels but not between different consonants—especially between different stop consonants, such as /t/, /d/, /k/, or /p/. (Linguists represent speech sounds by putting letters or special phonetic symbols between pairs of slashes.) Patients with pure word deafness *can* generally recognize consonants with a long duration, such as /s/, /z/, or /f/. (Say these consonants to yourself and you will see how different they sound.)

Phillips and Farmer note that the important acoustical events in speech sounds fall within a time range of a few milliseconds to a few tens of milliseconds. Speech sounds are made by rapidly moving lips, tongue, and soft palate, which produce acoustical events that can be distinguished only by a fine-grained analysis. In contrast, most environmental sounds do not contain such a fine temporal structure. The authors also note that "pure" word deafness is not absolutely pure. That is, when people with this disorder are tested carefully with recordings of a variety of environmental sounds, they have

difficulty recognizing at least some of them. Although *most* environmental sounds do not contain a fine temporal structure, some do—and patients have difficulty recognizing them. For example, one patient with pure word deafness could no longer understand messages in Morse code but could still *send* messages that way.

Apparently, two types of brain injury can cause pure word deafness: disruption of auditory input to Wernicke's area or damage to Wernicke's area itself. Disruption of auditory input can be produced by bilateral damage to the primary auditory cortex, or it can be caused by damage to the white matter in the left temporal lobes that cuts axons bringing auditory information from the primary auditory cortex to Wernicke's area. (See *Figure 16.5.*) Either type of damage—disruption of auditory input or damage to Wernicke's area—disrupts the analysis of the sounds of words and, hence, prevents people from recognizing other people's speech.

Comprehension: Transcortical Sensory Aphasia.
The other symptoms of Wernicke's aphasia—failure to comprehend the meaning of words and inability to express thoughts in meaningful speech—appear to be produced by damage that extends beyond Wernicke's area into the region just caudal to Wernicke's area, near the junction of the temporal, occipital, and parietal lobes. For want of a better term, I will refer to this region as the *posterior language area*. (See *Figure 16.6.*) The posterior language area appears to serve as a place for interchanging information between the auditory representation of words and the meanings of these words, stored as memories in the rest of the sensory association cortex.

Damage to the posterior language area alone produces a disorder known as **transcortical sensory aphasia**. (See *Figure 16.6.*) The difference between transcortical sensory aphasia and Wernicke's aphasia is that patients with this disorder *can repeat what other people say to them*; thus, they can recognize words. However, *they cannot comprehend the meaning of what they hear and repeat; nor can they produce meaningful speech of their own.* How can these people repeat what they hear? Because the posterior language area is damaged, repetition does not involve this part of the brain. Obviously, there must be a

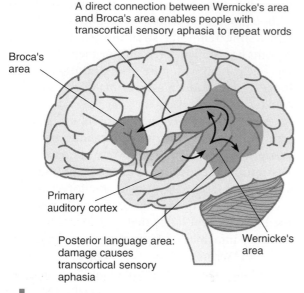

A direct connection between Wernicke's area and Broca's area enables people with transcortical sensory aphasia to repeat words

Broca's area

Primary auditory cortex

Posterior language area: damage causes transcortical sensory aphasia

Wernicke's area

FIGURE 16.6

The location and interconnections of the posterior language area.

direct connection between Wernicke's area and Broca's area that bypasses the posterior language area. (See *Figure 16.6.*)

The fact that recognition and comprehension of speech require separate brain functions is illustrated dramatically by a case reported by Geschwind, Quadfasel, and Segarra (1968). The patient sustained extensive brain damage from carbon monoxide produced by a faulty water heater. (The damage included considerably more brain tissue than occurs in most cases of transcortical sensory aphasia, but it illustrates the distinction between the recognition and comprehension of speech.) The patient spent several years in the hospital before she died, without ever saying anything meaningful on her own. She did not follow verbal commands or otherwise give signs of understanding them. However, she often repeated what was said to her. The repetition was not parrotlike; she did not imitate accents different from her own, and if someone made a grammatical error while saying something to her, she sometimes repeated correctly, without the error. She could also recite poems if someone started them. For example, when an examiner said "Roses are red, violets are blue," she continued with "Sugar is sweet and so are you." She could sing and would do so when someone started singing a song she knew. She even learned new songs from the radio while in the hospital. Remember, though, that she gave *no signs of understanding anything she heard or said.* This disorder, along with pure word deafness, clearly confirms the conclusion that *recognizing* spoken words and *comprehending* them involve different brain mechanisms.

In conclusion, transcortical sensory aphasia can be seen as Wernicke's aphasia without a repetition deficit. Or to put it another way, the symptoms of Wernicke's aphasia consist of those of pure word deafness plus those of transcortical sensory aphasia. (See *Figure 16.6.*)

What Is Meaning? As we have seen, Wernicke's area is involved in the analysis of speech sounds and, thus, in the recognition of words. Damage to the posterior language area does not disrupt people's ability to recognize words, but it does disrupt their ability to understand them or to produce meaningful speech of their own. But what, exactly, do we mean by the word *meaning?* And what types of brain mechanisms are involved?

Words refer to objects, actions, or relations in the world. Thus, the meaning of a word is defined by particular memories associated with it. For example, knowing the meaning of the word *tree* means being able to imagine the physical characteristics of trees: what they look like, what the wind sounds like blowing through their leaves, what the bark feels like, and so on. It also means knowing facts about trees: about their roots, buds, flowers, nuts, wood, and the chlorophyll in their leaves. These memories are not stored in the primary speech areas but in other parts of the brain, especially regions of the association cortex. Different categories of memories may be stored in particular regions of the brain, but they are somehow tied together, so that hearing the word *tree* activates all of them. (As we saw in Chapter 15, the hippocampal formation is involved in this process of tying related memories together.)

In thinking about the brain's verbal mechanisms involved in recognizing words and comprehending their meaning, I find that the concept of a dictionary serves as a useful analogy. Dictionaries contain entries (the words) and definitions (the meanings of the words). In the brain we have at least two types of entries: auditory and visual. That is, we can look up a word according to how it sounds or looks (in writing). Let us just consider just one type of entry: the sound of a word. (I will discuss reading and writing later in this chapter.) We hear a familiar word and understand its meaning. How do we do so?

First, we must recognize the sequence of sounds that constitute the word—we find the auditory entry for the word in our "dictionary." As we saw, this entry appears in Wernicke's area. Next, the memories that constitute the meaning of the word must be activated. Presumably, Wernicke's area is connected—through the posterior language area—with the neural circuits that contain these memories. (See *Figure 16.7.*)

The process works in reverse when we describe our thoughts or perceptions in words. Suppose we want to tell someone about a tree that we just planted in our lawn. Thoughts about the tree (for example, a visual image of it) occur in our association cortex—the visual association cortex, in this example. Information about the activity of these circuits is sent first to the posterior language area and then to Broca's area, which causes the words to be set into a grammatical sentence and pronounced. (See *Figure 16.7.*)

What evidence do we have that meanings of words are represented by neural circuits in various regions of association cortex? The best evidence comes from the fact that damage to particular regions of the sensory association cortex can damage particular kinds of information and thus abolish particular kinds of meanings. For example, I met a patient who had recently had a stroke that damaged a part of her right parietal lobe that played a role in spatial perception. She was alert and intelligent and showed no signs of aphasia. However, she was confused about directions and other spatial relations. When asked to, she could point to the ceiling and the floor, but she could not say which was *over* the other. Her perception of other people appeared to be entirely normal, but she could not say whether a person's head was at the *top* or *bottom* of the body.

I wrote a set of multiple-choice questions to test her ability to use words denoting spatial relations. The results of the test indicated that she did not know the meaning of words such as *up, down,* or

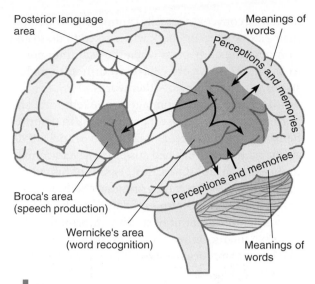

FIGURE 16.7

The "dictionary" in the brain. Wernicke's area contains the auditory entries of words; the meanings are contained as memories in the sensory association areas. Black arrows represent comprehension of words; color arrows represent translation of thoughts or perceptions into words.

under when they referred to spatial relations, but she could use these words normally when they referred to nonspatial relations. For example, here are some of her incorrect responses when the words referred to spatial relations:

A tree's branches are *under* its roots.

The sky is *down.*

The ceiling is *under* the floor.

She made only ten correct responses on the sixteen-item test. In contrast, she got all eight items correct when the words referred to nonspatial relations like the following:

After exchanging pleasantries, they got *down* to business.

He got sick and threw *up.*

Damage to part of the association cortex of the *left* parietal lobe can produce an inability to name the body parts. The disorder is called **autotopagnosia,** or "poor knowledge of one's own topography." (A better name would have been *autotopanomia,* "poor naming of one's own topography.") People who can otherwise converse normally cannot reliably point to their elbow, knee, or cheek when asked to do so and cannot name body parts when the examiner points to them. However, they have no difficulty understanding the meaning of other words.

More widespread damage to the temporal and parietal lobes can cause a general loss in comprehension. For example, Damasio and Tranel (1990) studied a patient who had sustained severe damage to the cortical and subcortical regions of his temporal lobes. Besides becoming amnesic (his hippocampal formation was destroyed bilaterally), he had lost a considerable amount of specific information. For example, he recognized that a raccoon was an animal but had no idea of where it lived, what it ate, or what its name was. Hodges et al. (1992) reported several similar cases, caused by progressive degeneration of the temporal lobes. One patient was asked, "Have you been to America?" She replied, "What's America?" When she was asked, "What is your favorite food?" she said, "Food, food, I wish I knew what that was" (p. 1786). Another patient was frightened when he found a snail in his garden and thought that a goat was a strange creature. Hodges and his colleagues suggest the term *semantic aphasia* to refer to this syndrome.

Students often ask me whether people with severe communication deficits, such as patients with Wernicke's aphasia or transcortical sensory aphasia, are still able to think. I usually say that their ability to think in words is undoubtedly as severely disrupted as their ability to talk, but that it is difficult to imagine what nonverbal thinking would be like. A study by Anderson et al. (1992) suggests that at least some aphasic patients with severe communication deficits do indeed have something to communicate. Anderson and his colleagues tried to teach sign language to three patients with severe Wernicke's aphasia. Fluent users of sign language taught the patients signs for individual words, letters, and numbers. They paired these signs with spoken words, words printed on cards, objects, pictures of objects, and gestures. All three subjects learned at least eighty signs, and two of them used sequences of signs to communicate with other people in and out of the laboratory. One subject, who had severe damage to the cortex of the temporal lobes, learned to make individual signs but not sequences of signs, and he did not use them to

communicate. This study suggests that alternative methods of communication might be available to at least some patients with severe aphasia.

Repetition: Conduction Aphasia. As we saw earlier in this section, the fact that people with transcortical sensory aphasia can repeat what they hear suggests that there is a direct connection between Wernicke's area and Broca's area—and there is, the **arcuate fasciculus** ("arch-shaped bundle"). This bundle of axons appears to convey information about the *sounds* of words but not their *meanings*. The best evidence for this conclusion comes from a syndrome known as conduction aphasia, which is produced by damage to the inferior parietal lobe that extends into the subcortical white matter and damages the arcuate fasciculus (Damasio and Damasio, 1980).

Conduction aphasia is characterized by meaningful, fluent speech; relatively good comprehension; but very poor repetition. For example, the spontaneous speech of patient L.B. (observed by Margolin and Walker, 1981) was excellent; he made very few errors and had no difficulty naming objects. But let us see how patient L.B. performed when he was asked to repeat words.

EXAMINER: bicycle
   PATIENT: bicycle
EXAMINER: hippopotamus
   PATIENT: hippopotamus
EXAMINER: blaynge
   PATIENT: I didn't get it.
EXAMINER: Okay, some of these won't be real words, they'll just be sounds. Blaynge.
   PATIENT: I'm not . . .
EXAMINER: blanch
   PATIENT: blanch
EXAMINER: north
   PATIENT: north
EXAMINER: rilld
   PATIENT: Nope, I can't say.

You will notice that the patient can repeat individual words (all nouns, in this case) but utterly fails to repeat nonwords. People with conduction aphasia can repeat speech sounds they hear *only if these sounds have meaning.*

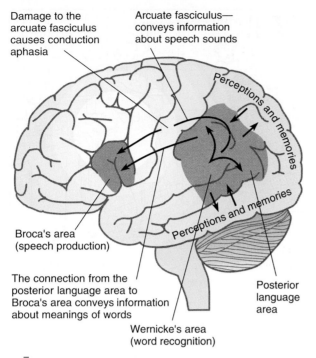

Damage to the arcuate fasciculus causes conduction aphasia

Arcuate fasciculus—conveys information about speech sounds

Perceptions and memories

Perceptions and memories

Broca's area (speech production)

The connection from the posterior language area to Broca's area conveys information about meanings of words

Wernicke's area (word recognition)

Posterior language area

FIGURE 16.8

A hypothetical explanation of conduction aphasia. A lesion that damages the arcuate fasciculus disrupts transmission of auditory information, but not information related to meaning, to the frontal lobe. The black arrows represent the flow of information as a patient hears a sentence, understands it, and then says it back, in his or her own words.

Sometimes, when a person with conduction aphasia is asked to repeat a word, he or she says a word with the same meaning—or at least, one that is related. For example, if the examiner says *house,* the patient may say *home.* If the examiner says *chair,* the patient may say *sit.* One patient made the following response when asked to repeat an entire sentence.

EXAMINER: The auto's leaking gas tank soiled the roadway.
PATIENT: The car's tank leaked and made a mess on the street.

The symptoms seen in transcortical sensory aphasia and conduction aphasia lead to the conclusion that there are pathways connecting the speech mechanisms of the temporal lobe with those of the frontal lobe. The direct pathway through the arcuate fasciculus simply conveys speech sounds to the

frontal lobes. We use this pathway to repeat unfamiliar words—for example, when we are learning a foreign language or trying to repeat a nonword such as *blaynge.* The second pathway is indirect and is based on the *meaning* of words, not the sounds they make. When patients with conduction aphasia hear a word or a sentence, the meaning of what they hear evokes some sort of image related to that meaning. (The patient in the second example presumably imagined the sight of an automobile leaking fuel onto the pavement.) They are then able to describe that image, just as they would put their own thoughts into words. Of course, the words they choose may not be the same ones used by the person who spoke to them. (See *Figure 16.8.*)

Memory of Words: Anomic Aphasia

As I already noted, anomia, in one form or other, is a hallmark of aphasia. However, one category of aphasia consists of almost pure anomia, the other symptoms being inconsequential. Speech of patients with anomic aphasia is fluent and grammatical, and their comprehension is excellent, but they have difficulty finding the appropriate words. They often employ **circumlocutions** (literally, "to speak in a roundabout way") to get around missing words. Anomic aphasia is different from Wernicke's aphasia. People with anomic aphasia can understand what other people say, and what they say makes perfect sense, even if they often choose roundabout ways to say it.

The following quotation is from a patient that some colleagues and I studied (Margolin, Marcel, and Carlson, 1985). We asked her to describe the picture shown in *Figure 16.9.* Her pauses, which are marked with three dots, indicate word-finding difficulties. In some cases, when she could not find a word, she supplied a definition instead (a form of circumlocution) or went off on a new track. I have added the words in brackets that I think she intended to use.

EXAMINER: Tell us about that picture.
PATIENT: It's a woman who has two children, a son and a daughter, and her son is to get into the . . . cupboard in the kitchen to get out [*take*] some . . . cookies out of the [*cookie jar*] . . . that she possibly had

made, and consequently he's slipping [*falling*] . . . the wrong direction [*backward*] . . . on the . . . what he's standing on [*stool*], heading to the . . . the cupboard [*floor*] and if he falls backwards he could have some problems [*get hurt*], because that [*the stool*] is off balance.

The patient's anomia was most obvious when we asked her to name pictures of common objects. When a person talks spontaneously, he or she has more flexibility in choosing words. If the person has difficulty finding a word to express a particular thought, he or she can either find a circumlocution or change the subject. But when confronted with a picture, the person must find a particular word, and failure to do so is obvious. On one occasion the patient correctly named only fourteen from a list of fifty pictures. Here is her attempt to name a picture of a carpenter's saw. Note that she tried to remember the word by starting sentences that would use it. She almost, but not quite, got the word. Clearly, she knew what the object is, so her deficit was not one of perception or comprehension. She recognized the object and understood what one did with it. She did not have visual agnosia or a loss of comprehension—only a deficit in the ability to name object.

PATIENT: I know what it is. I can't tell you—maybe I can. If I was to carry the wood and cut it in half with that . . . you know, if I had to cut the wood down and bring it in . . .

EXAMINER: You'd use one of these?

PATIENT: It's called a . . . I have 'em in the garage. They are your . . . You cut the wood with them . . . it . . . sah! . . . ah . . . Ss . . . sahbing . . . sah . . . I can't say it. I know what it is and I can cut the wood with it and it's in my garage. . . .

Anomia has been described as a partial amnesia for words. It can be produced by lesions in either the anterior or posterior regions of the brain, but only posterior lesions produce a *fluent* anomia. Little is known about the precise location of lesions that produce anomia without the other symptoms of aphasia, such as comprehension deficits, agrammatism, or difficulties in articulation, except that they generally occur in the left temporal or parietal lobe, usually sparing Wernicke's area. In the case of the woman described above, the damage included the middle and inferior temporal gyri, which includes an important region of the visual association cortex. (See **Figure 16.10.**)

When my colleagues and I were studying the anomic patient, I was struck by the fact that she seemed to have more difficulty finding nouns than other types of words. I informally tested her ability to name actions by asking her what people shown in a series of pictures were doing. She made almost no errors finding verbs. For example, although she could not say what a boy was holding in his hand, she had no trouble saying that he was *throwing* it. Similarly, she knew that a girl was *climbing* something but could not tell me the name of what she was climbing (a fence). In addition, she had no trouble finding nonvisual adjectives; for example, she could say that lemons tasted *sour,* that ice was *cold,* and that a cat's fur felt *soft.*

For several years I thought that our patient was unique. But more recently, similar patterns of deficits have been reported in the literature. For example, Manning and Campbell (1992) described a patient who had difficulty naming objects but not actions. Some patients have even more specific deficits; Semenze and Zettin (1989) described a patient who had great difficulty with proper nouns (names of people and places). Damasio et al. (1992) studied several patients with similar deficits and concluded that anomia for proper nouns is caused by damage to the temporal pole, whereas anomia for common nouns is caused by damage to the inferior temporal cortex. Damage to both regions causes anomia for both types of nouns. They suggest that the important distinction between the two types of words is that proper nouns are specific to particular individuals (people or places) whereas common nouns apply to *categories.* Presumably, the cortex of

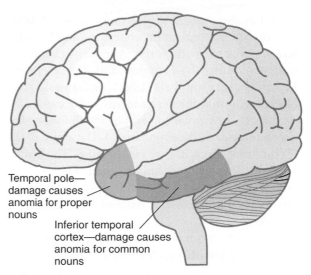

Temporal pole—damage causes anomia for proper nouns

Inferior temporal cortex—damage causes anomia for common nouns

▌ FIGURE 16.11

The location of brain damage that causes anomia for proper or common nouns, according to Damasio et al. (1992).

the temporal pole is specifically involved with recognition of individuals. (See **Figure 16.11.**)

Other investigators have reported verbal deficits that include disruption of particular categories of meaning. For example, McCarthy and Warrington (1988) reported the case of a man with left temporal lobe damage (patient T.B.) who was unable to explain the meaning of words that denoted living things. For example, when he was asked to define the word *rhinoceros,* he said, "Animal, can't give you any functions." However, when he was shown a *picture* of a rhinoceros, he said, "Enormous, weighs over one ton, lives in Africa." Similarly, when asked what a *dolphin* was, he said, "a fish or a bird"; but he responded to a *picture* of a dolphin by saying, "Dolphin lives in water . . . they are trained to jump up and come out . . . In America during the war years they started to get this particular animal to go through to look into ships." Clearly, patient T.B. does not have a semantic aphasia; he has not lost his knowledge of specific animals but only the ability to name them. In addition, when he was asked to define the meanings of words that denoted inanimate objects (such as *lighthouse* or *wheelbarrow*), he had no trouble at all.

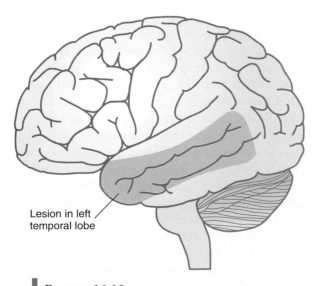

Lesion in left temporal lobe

▌ FIGURE 16.10

The location of the brain damage of patient R.F.

What about the ability to name actions? As we saw, the anomic patient my colleagues and I studied had no trouble with verbs. And neither did the patients studied by Semenze and Zettin (1989), Manning and Campbell (1992), or Damasio et al. (1992). Anomia for verbs seems to be caused by damage to the frontal cortex; poor verb finding is a characteristic of Broca's aphasia (A. Damasio, 1992). If you think about it, that makes sense. The frontal lobes are devoted to planning, organizing, and executing actions, so it should not surprise us that they are involved in the task of remembering the names of actions.

The picture I have drawn so far suggests that comprehension of speech includes a flow of information from Wernicke's area to the posterior language area to the sensory association cortex. Production of spontaneous speech involves the flow of information concerning perceptions and memories from the posterior language area to Broca's area. This model is certainly an oversimplification, but it is a useful starting point in conceptualizing basic mental processes. For example, thinking in words probably involves two-way communication between the speech areas and surrounding association cortex (and subcortical regions such as the hippocampus, of course).

Prosody: Rhythm, Tone, and Emphasis in Speech

When we speak, we do not merely utter words. Our speech has a regular rhythm and cadence; we give some words stress (that is, pronounce them louder), and we vary the pitch of our voice to indicate phrasing and to distinguish between assertions and questions. In addition, we can impart information about our emotional state through the rhythm, emphasis, and tone of our speech. These rhythmic, emphatic, and melodic aspects of speech are referred to as **prosody.** The importance of these aspects of speech is illustrated by our use of punctuation symbols to indicate some elements of prosody when we write. For example, a comma indicates a short pause; a period indicates a longer one with an accompanying fall in the pitch of the voice; a question mark indicates a pause and a rise in the pitch of the voice; an

exclamation mark indicates that the words are articulated with special emphasis; and so on.

The prosody of people with fluent aphasias, caused by posterior lesions, sounds normal. Their speech is rhythmical, pausing after phrases and sentences, and has a melodic line. Even when the speech of a person with severe Wernicke's aphasia makes no sense, the prosody sounds normal. As Goodglass and Kaplan (1972) note, a person with Wernicke's aphasia may "sound like a normal speaker at a distance, because of his fluency and normal melodic contour of his speech." (Up close, of course, we hear the speech clearly enough to realize that it is meaningless.) In contrast, just as the lesions that produce Broca's aphasia destroy grammar, they also severely disrupt prosody. In patients with Broca's aphasia articulation is so labored and words are uttered so slowly that there is little opportunity for the patient to demonstrate any rhythmic elements; and because of the relative lack of function words, there is little variation in stress or pitch of voice.

Evidence from studies of normal people and patients with brain lesions suggests that prosody is a special function of the right hemisphere. This function is undoubtedly related to the more general role of this hemisphere in musical skills and the expression and recognition of emotions: Production of prosody is rather like singing, and prosody often serves as a vehicle for conveying emotion.

Weintraub, Mesulam, and Kramer (1981) tested the ability of patients with right-hemisphere damage to recognize and express prosodic elements of speech. In one experiment they showed their subjects two pictures, named one of them, and asked them to point to the appropriate one. For example, they showed them a picture of a greenhouse and a house that was painted green. In speech we distinguish between *greenhouse* and *green house* by stress: *GREEN house* means the former and *GREEN HOUSE* (syllables equally stressed) means the latter. In a second experiment Weintraub and her colleagues tested the subjects' ability simply to detect differences in prosody. They presented pairs of sentences and asked the subjects whether they were the same or different. The pairs of sentences either were identical or differed in terms of intonation (for example, *Margo plays the piano?* and *Margo plays the piano*) or location of stress (for example, *STEVE drives the car* and *Steve drives the CAR*). The patients with right-hemisphere lesions (but not control subjects) performed poorly on both of these tasks. Thus, they showed a deficit in prosodic comprehension.

To test production, the investigators presented two written sentences and asked a question about them. For example, they presented the following pair:

The man walked to the grocery store.
The woman rode to the shoe store.

The subjects were instructed to answer questions by reading one of the sentences. Try this one yourself. Read the question below and then read aloud the sentence (above) that answers it.

Who walked to the grocery store, the man or the woman?

The question asserts that someone walked to the grocery store but asks who that person was. When answering a question like this, people normally stress the requested item of information—in this case they say, "The *man* walked to the grocery store." However, Weintraub and her colleagues found that although patients with right-hemisphere brain damage chose the correct sentence, they either failed to stress a word or stressed the wrong one. Thus, the right hemisphere plays a role in production as well as perception of prosody.

▏▏▏▏▏ INTERIM SUMMARY

Two regions of the brain are especially important in understanding and producing speech. Broca's area, in the frontal lobe just rostral to the region of the primary motor cortex that controls the muscles of speech, is involved with speech production. This region contains memories of the sequences of muscular movements that produce words, each of which is connected with its auditory counterpart in the posterior part of the brain. Broca's aphasia—which is caused by damage to Broca's area, adjacent regions of the frontal cortex, and underlying white matter—consists of varying degrees of agrammatism, anomia, and articulation difficulties.

Wernicke's area, in the posterior superior temporal lobe, is involved with speech perception. The region just adjacent to Wernicke's area, which I have called the posterior language area, is necessary for speech comprehension and the translation of thoughts into words. Presumably, Wernicke's area contains memories of the sounds of words, each of which is connected through the posterior language area with memories about the properties of the things the words denote. Damage restricted to Wernicke's area causes pure word deafness—loss of the ability to understand speech but intact speech production, reading, and writing. Wernicke's aphasia, caused by damage to Wernicke's area and the posterior language area, consists of poor speech comprehension, poor repetition, and production of fluent, meaningless speech. Transcortical sensory aphasia, caused by damage to the posterior speech area, consists of poor speech comprehension and production, but the patients can repeat what they hear. The fact that people with transcortical sensory aphasia can repeat words they cannot understand suggests that there is a direct connection between Wernicke's area and Broca's area. Indeed, there is—the arcuate fasciculus—and damage to this bundle of axons produces conduction aphasia.

The meanings of words are our memories of objects, actions, and other concepts associated with them. These meanings are memories and are stored in the association cortex, not in the speech areas themselves. Pure anomia, caused by damage to the temporal or parietal lobes, consists of difficulty in word finding—particularly in naming objects. Some patients have a specific difficulty with proper nouns, while others have difficulty with common nouns; most patients have little difficulty with verbs. Brain damage can also disrupt the "definitions" as well as the "entries" in the mental dictionary; damage to specific regions of the association cortex effectively erases some categories of the *meanings* of words.

Prosody includes changes in intonation, rhythm, and stress that add meaning, especially emotional meaning, to the sentences that we speak. The neural mechanisms that control the prosodic elements of speech appear to be in the right hemisphere.

TABLE 16.1

Aphasic Syndromes Produced by Brain Damage

Disorder	Areas of lesion	Spontaneous speech	Comprehension	Repetition	Naming
Wernicke's aphasia	Posterior portion of superior temporal gyrus (Wernicke's area) and posterior language area	Fluent	Poor	Poor	Poor
Pure word deafness	Wernicke's area or its connestion with primary auditory cortex	Fluent	Poor	Poor	Good
Broca's aphasia	Frontal cortex rostral to base of primary motor cortex (Braca's area)	Nonfluent	Good	Poor[a]	Good
Conduction aphasia	White matter beneath parietal lobe superior to lateral fissure (arcuate fasciculus)	Fluent	Good	Poor	Good
Anomic aphasia	Variuos parts of parietal and temporal lobes	Fluent	Good	Good	Poor
Transcortical sensory aphasia	Posterior language area	Fluent	Poor	Good	Poor

[a]May be better than spontaneous speech.

Because so many terms and symptoms were described in this section, I have provided a table that summarizes them. (See *Table 16.1.*)

READING AND WRITING DISORDERS

READING AND WRITING ARE CLOSELY RELATED TO listening and talking; thus, oral and written language abilities have many brain mechanisms in common. This section discusses the neural basis of reading and writing disorders. As you will see, the study of these disorders has provided us with some useful and interesting information.

Relation to Aphasia

The reading and writing skills of people with aphasia almost always resemble their speaking and comprehending abilities. For example, patients with Wernicke's aphasia have as much difficulty reading and writing as they do speaking and understanding speech. Patients with Broca's aphasia comprehend what they read about as well as they can understand speech, but their reading aloud is poor, of course. If their speech is agrammatical, so is their writing; and to the extent that they fail to comprehend grammar when listening to speech, they fail to do so when reading. Patients with conduction aphasia generally have some difficulty reading; and when they read aloud, they often make semantic paraphasias (saying synonyms for some of the words they read), just as they do when attempting to repeat what they hear. Depending on the location of the lesion, some patients with transcortical sensory aphasia may read aloud accurately but fail to comprehend what they read.

There are a few exceptions to this general rule. For example, Semenza, Cipolotti, and Denes (1992) studied a patient with a severe fluent aphasia. Although she could not understand the speech of others, she could read. She clearly understood what she was reading, because she could follow written instructions. And although her spontaneous speech was meaningless and she could not say the names of objects, she could write their names, and she could read aloud. Clearly, her comprehension and production of oral language was very different from that of written language. Although cases like this one are rare, they do indicate that our verbal abilities make use of a large number of individual neural modules. Reading and writing undoubtedly share many modules with oral comprehension and production, but some modules are devoted to particular methods of communication.

Pure Alexia

Dejerine (1892) described a remarkable syndrome, which we now call **pure alexia,** or sometimes *pure word blindness* or *alexia without agraphia.* His patient had a lesion in the visual cortex of the left occipital lobe and the posterior end of the corpus callosum. The patient could still write, although he had lost the ability to read. In fact, even if he was shown some of his own writing, he could not read it.

Several years ago, some colleagues and I studied a man with pure alexia who discovered his ability to write in an interesting way. A few months after sustaining a head injury that caused his brain damage, he and his wife were watching a service person repair their washing machine. The patient wanted to say something privately to his wife, so he picked up a pad of paper and jotted a note. As he was handing it to her, they suddenly realized with amazement that although he could not read, he was able to write. His wife brought the note to their neurologist, who asked the patient to read it. Although he remembered the gist of the message, he could not read the words. (See *Figure 16.12.*)

Although patients with pure alexia cannot read, they can recognize words that are spelled aloud to them; thus, they have not lost their memories of the spellings of words. Pure alexia is obviously a perceptual disorder; it is similar to pure word deafness, except that the patient has difficulty with visual input, not auditory input. The disorder is caused by lesions that prevent visual information from reaching the extrastriate cortex of the left hemisphere (Damasio and Damasio, 1983, 1986). Figure 16.13 explains why Dejerine's original patient could not read. The first diagram shows the pathway that visual information would take if a person had damage *only to the left primary visual cortex.* In this case the person's right visual field would be blind; he or she would see nothing to the right of the fixation point. But people with this disorder can read. Their only problem is that they must look to the right of each word so that they can see all of it, which means that they read somewhat more slowly than someone with full vision.

Let us trace the flow of visual information for a person with this brain damage. Information from the left side of the visual field is transmitted to the right striate cortex (primary visual cortex) and then to the lingual and fusiform gyri—a region of extrastriate cortex involved in the recognition of written text. From there, the information crosses the posterior corpus callosum and is transmitted to the left extrastriate cortex and then to speech mechanisms located in left frontal lobe. Thus, the person can read the words aloud. (See *Figure 16.13a.*)

The second diagram shows Dejerine's patient. Notice how the additional lesion of the corpus callosum prevents visual information, concerning written text from reaching the posterior left hemisphere. Without this information the patient cannot read. (See *Figure 16.13b.*)

If this model presented in Figure 16.13 is correct, we would predict that a lesion restricted to the posterior corpus callosum should cause a left *hemialexia*—an inability to read words presented entirely in the left visual field. In fact, Binder et al. (1992) studied a patient who had precisely that lesion and precisely that deficit. Their patient, a thirty-year-old woman, was operated on to remove a vascular malformation in her brain. While removing the malformation, the surgeons were obliged to damage the posterior end of the corpus callosum. When Binder and his colleagues tested the woman later, they found that she often made errors in reading that involved the left side of words. For example, she read *car* as *ear* and *seat* as *heat*. In addition, she could not read simple three-letter words presented to her left visual field. (See *Figure 16.13c.*)

I must note that the diagrams shown in Figure 16.10 are as simple and schematic as possible. They only illustrate the pathway involved in seeing a word and pronouncing it, and they ignore neural structures that would be involved in understanding its

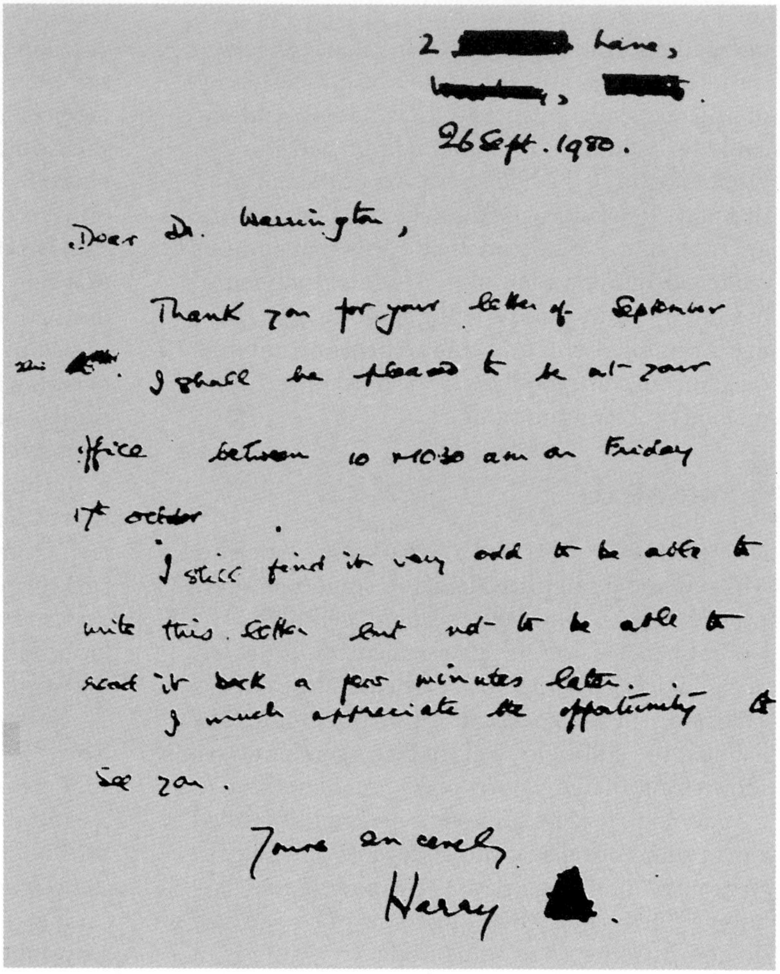

FIGURE 16.12

A letter written to Dr. Elizabeth Warrington by a patient with pure alexia. The letter reads as follows: "Dear Dr. Warrington, Thank you for your letter of September 16th. I shall be pleased to be at your office between 10–10:30 am on Friday 17th october. I still find it very odd to be able to write this letter but not to be able to read it back a few minutes later. I much appreciate the opportunity to see you. Yours sincerely, Harry X."

(From McCarthy, R.A., and Warrington, E.K. *Cognitive Neuropsychology: A Clinical Introduction.* San Diego: Academic Press, 1990. Reprinted with permission.)

meaning. As we will see later in this chapter, evidence from patients with brain lesions indicates that seeing and pronouncing words can take place independently of understanding them. Thus, although the diagrams are simplified, they are not unreasonable given what we know about the neural components of the reading process.

You will recall from Chapter 6 that visual agnosia is a perceptual deficit in which people with bilateral damage to the visual association cortex cannot recognize objects by sight. Patients with pure alexia do *not* have visual agnosia; they can recognize objects and supply their names. Similarly, people with visual agnosia can still read. Thus, the perceptual analysis of objects and words requires different mechanisms.

I find this fact both interesting and puzzling. Certainly, the ability to read cannot have had an effect on the evolution of the human brain, because the invention of writing is only a few thousand years old, and until very recently, the vast majority of the world's population was illiterate. Thus, reading and object recognition use brain mechanisms that undoubtedly existed even before the invention of writing. What is the nature of these mechanisms? What features of the world around us require analysis similar to the analysis we use to recognize objects versus words?

Although these questions have not yet been answered, a region of the extrastriate cortex essential for visual analysis of written text has been identified.

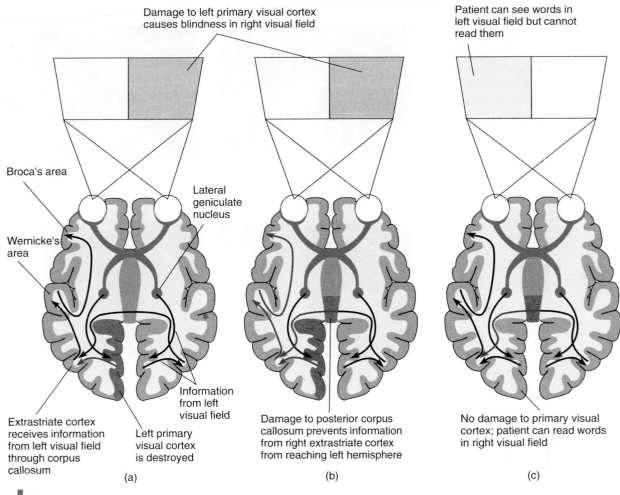

Damage to left primary visual cortex causes blindness in right visual field

Patient can see words in left visual field but cannot read them

Broca's area

Lateral geniculate nucleus

Wernicke's area

Extrastriate cortex receives information from left visual field through corpus callosum

Left primary visual cortex is destroyed

Information from left visual field

Damage to posterior corpus callosum prevents information from right extrastriate cortex from reaching left hemisphere

No damage to primary visual cortex; patient can read words in right visual field

(a)

(b)

(c)

FIGURE 16.13

Pure alexia. (a) The route followed by information as a person with damage to the left primary visual cortex reads aloud. (b) Additional damage to the posterior corpus callosum interrupts the flow of information and produces pure alexia. (c) Damage to the posterior corpus callosum alone produces left hemialexia: an inability to read words presented in the left visual field.

Petersen et al. (1990) used a PET scanner to measure regional cerebral blood flow while presenting subjects with four types of visual stimuli: unfamiliar letterlike forms, strings of consonants, pronounceable nonwords, and real words. They found that one region of the extrastriate cortex was activated only by pronounceable nonwords or real words. Their finding suggests that this region, which includes the fusiform and lingual gyri, plays a role in recognition of familiar combinations of letters. (See *Figure 16.14.*)

Toward an Understanding of Reading

Most investigators believe that reading involves at least two different processes: direct recognition of the word as a whole, and sounding it out letter by letter. When we see a familiar word, we normally recognize it by its shape and pronounce it—a process known as **whole-word reading.** (With very long words we might instead perceive segments of several letters each.) The second method, which we use for

FIGURE 16.14

PET scans of the medial surface of the brains of subjects who read letterlike forms (a), strings of consonants (b), pronounceable nonwords (c), or real words (d).

(From Petersen, S.E., Fox, P.T., Snyder, A.Z., and Raichle, M.E. *Science,* 1990, *249,* 1041–1044. Reprinted with permission.)

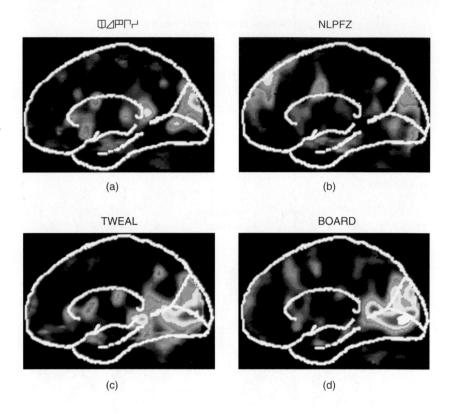

(a)   (b)

(c)   (d)

unfamiliar words, requires recognition of individual letters and knowledge of the sounds they make. This process is known as **phonetic reading.**

Evidence for our ability to sound out words is easy to obtain. In fact, you can prove to yourself that phonetic reading exists by trying to read the following words:

glab   trisk   chint

Well, as you could see, they are not really words, but I doubt that you had trouble pronouncing them. Obviously, you did not *recognize* them, because you probably never saw them before. Therefore, you had to use what you know about the sounds that are represented by particular letters (or groups of letters, such as *ch*) to figure out how to pronounce the words.

The best evidence that proves that people can read words without sounding them out, using the whole-word method, comes from studies of patients with acquired dyslexias. *Dyslexia* means "faulty reading." *Acquired* dyslexias are those caused by

damage to the brains of people who already know how to read. In contrast, *developmental* dyslexias refer to reading difficulties that become apparent when children are learning to read. Developmental dyslexias may involve anomalies in brain circuitry, and they are discussed in a later section.

Figure 16.15 illustrates some elements of the reading processes. The diagram is an oversimplification of a very complex process, but it helps organize some of the facts that investigators have obtained. It only considers reading and pronouncing single words, not understanding the meaning of text. When we see a familiar word, we normally recognize it as a whole and pronounce it. If we see an unfamiliar word or a pronounceable nonword, we must try to read it phonetically. (See *Figure 16.15.*)

Although investigators have reported several types of acquired dyslexias, I will mention five of them here. **Surface dyslexia** is a deficit in whole-word reading (Marshall and Newcombe, 1973; McCarthy and Warrington, 1990). The term *surface* reflects the fact that people with this disorder make errors related to the visual appearance of the words and to pronunciation rules, not to the meaning of the words, which is metaphorically "deeper" than the appearance. Because patients with surface dyslexia have difficulty recognizing words as a whole, they are obliged to sound them out. Thus, they can easily read words with regular spelling, such as *hand, table,* or *chin*. However, they have difficulty reading words with irregular spelling, such as *sew, pint,* and *yacht*. In fact, they may read these words as *sue, pinnt,* and *yatchet*. They have no difficulty reading pronounceable nonwords, such as *glab, trisk,* and *chint*. (See *Figure 16.16.*)

Patients with **phonological dyslexia** have the opposite problem; they can read by the whole-word method but cannot sound words out. Thus, they can read words that they are already familiar with but have great difficulty figuring out how to read unfamiliar words or pronounceable nonwords (Beauvois and Dérouesné, 1979; Dérouesné and Beauvois, 1979). (*Phonology*—loosely translated as "laws of sound"—refers to the relation between letters and

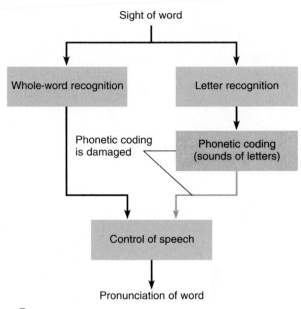

FIGURE 16.16

A hypothetical explanation of surface dyslexia. Only whole-word reading remains.

the sounds they represent.) People with phonological dyslexia may be excellent readers if they had already acquired a good reading vocabulary before their brain damage occurred.

Phonological dyslexia provides further evidence that whole-word reading and phonological reading involve different brain mechanisms. Phonological reading, which is the only way we can read nonwords or words we have not yet learned, entails some sort of letter-to-sound decoding. Obviously, phonological reading of English requires more than decoding of the sounds produced by single letters, because, for example, some sounds are transcribed as two-letter sequences (such as *th* or *sh*) and the addition of the letter *e* to the end of a word lengthens an internal vowel (*can* becomes *cane*). (See *Figure 16.17.*)

The Japanese language provides a particularly interesting distinction between phonetic and whole-word reading. The Japanese language makes use of two kinds of written symbols. *Kanji* symbols are pictographs, adopted from the Chinese language (although they are pronounced as Japanese words). Thus, they represent concepts by means of visual

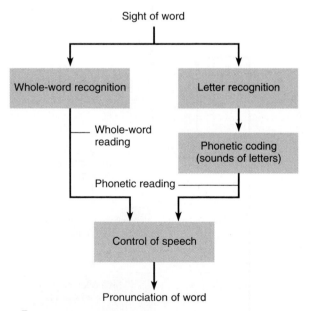

FIGURE 16.15

A simplified model of the reading process, showing whole-word and phonetic reading. Whole-word reading is used for most familiar words; phonetic reading is used for unfamiliar words and for nonwords such as glab, trisk, *or* chint.

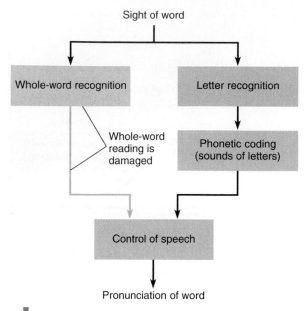

FIGURE 16.17

A hypothetical explanation of phonological dyslexia. Only phonetic reading remains.

symbols but do not provide a guide to their pronunciation. Reading words expressed in kanji symbols is analogous, then, to whole-word reading. *Kana* symbols are phonetic representations of syllables; thus, they encode acoustical information. Reading words expressed in kana symbols is obviously phonetic.

Studies of Japanese people with localized brain damage have shown that the reading of kana and kanji symbols involves different brain mechanisms (Iwata, 1984). In general, damage to the posterior parietal lobe produces dyslexia for kanji symbols, and damage to the posterior temporal lobe produces dyslexia for kana symbols. Difficulty reading kanji symbols is analogous to surface dyslexia, whereas difficulty reading kana symbols is analogous to phonological dyslexia.

What would happen if individuals sustained brain damage that did not make them blind but destroyed their ability to read words either by the whole-word or phonetic methods. Would they be *completely* unable to read? The answer is no—not quite. They would have a disorder known as **word-form dyslexia** or **spelling dyslexia** (Warrington and Shallice, 1980). Although patients with word-form dyslexia cannot either recognize words as a whole

or sound them out phonetically, they can still recognize individual letters and can read the words if they are permitted to name the letters, one at a time. Thus, they read very slowly, taking more time with longer words. As you might expect, they can identify words that someone else spells aloud, just as they can recognize their own oral spelling. Sometimes, the deficit is so severe that patients have difficulty identifying individual letters, in which case they make mistakes in spelling that prevent them from reading test words. For example, a patient studied by Patterson and Kay (1980) was shown the word *men* and said, "h, e, n, hen." (See **Figure 16.18**.)

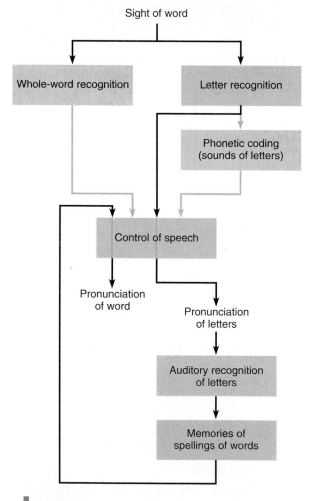

FIGURE 16.18

A hypothetical explanation of spelling dyslexia. The patient pronounces the letters, recognizes the words, and then says them.

As we saw earlier in this chapter, recognizing a spoken word is different from understanding it. For example, patients with transcortical sensory aphasia can repeat what is said to them even though they show no signs of understanding what they hear or say. The same is true for reading. **Direct dyslexia** resembles transcortical sensory aphasia, except that the words in question are written, not spoken (Schwartz, Marin, and Saffran, 1979; Lytton and Brust, 1989). Patients with direct dyslexia are able to read aloud *even though they cannot understand the words they are saying*. After sustaining a stroke that damaged his left frontal and temporal lobes, Lytton and Brust's patient lost the ability to communicate verbally; his speech was meaningless and he was unable to comprehend what other people said to him. However, he could read words with which he was already familiar. He could *not* read pronounceable nonwords; thus, he had lost the ability to read phonetically. His comprehension deficit seemed complete; when the investigators presented him with a word and several pictures, one of which corresponded to the word, he read the word correctly but had no idea what picture went with it.

Several investigators have reported a deficit opposite to that of direct dyslexia. People with this unnamed disorder (we could call it *comprehension without reading*) show some comprehension of words that they cannot read (Margolin, Marcel, and Carlson, 1985). Our patient, R.F., sustained a head injury in an automobile accident that destroyed much of her left temporal lobe and part of the anterior occipital lobe. She had a classic case of anomic aphasia—in fact, I quoted her in the section on that topic earlier in this chapter. Although her speech was fluent and she could repeat whatever we said to her, she could not name most common objects, nor could she read most words. Nevertheless, she could match pictures of *objects she could not name* with *words she could not read*. For example, when we showed her the picture and words that appear in Figure 16.19, she immediately pointed to the correct word, *flag*, even though she could not name the object or read any of the words. (See **Figure 16.19**.)

Patient R.F. was utterly unable to read words phonetically. However, the fact that she could match words with pictures indicates that she could still *perceive* them by the whole-word method. This fact was

FIGURE 16.19

An item from a task given to patient R.F. Although she could not read, she could choose the word that went with the picture.

made especially apparent one day when she was trying (without success) to read some words that I had typed. Suddenly, she said, "Hey! You spelled this one wrong." I looked at the word and realized that she was right; I had. But even though she saw that the word was misspelled, she still could not say what it was, even when she tried very hard to sound it out. That evening I made up a list of eighty pairs of words, one spelled correctly and the other incorrectly. The next day she was able to go through the list quickly and easily, correctly identifying 95 percent of the misspelled words. She was able to *read* only five of them.

Toward an Understanding of Writing

Writing depends on knowledge of the words that are to be used, along with the proper grammatical structure of the sentences they are to form. Thus, if a patient is unable to express himself or herself by speech, we should not be surprised to see a writing disturbance as well.

One type of writing disorder involves difficulties in motor control—in directing the movements of a pen or pencil to form letters and words. Investigators have reported surprisingly specific types of writing disorders that fall under this category. For example, some patients can write numbers but not letters, some can write uppercase letters but not lowercase letters, some can write consonants but not vowels, and others can write letters normally but have difficulty placing them in an orderly fashion on the page (Cubelli, 1991; Alexander et al., 1992; Margolin and Goodman-Schulman, 1992).

The second type of writing disorder involves problems in spelling, as opposed to problems with making accurate movements with the fingers. I will devote the rest of this section to this type of disorder. Like reading, writing (or more specifically, spelling) involves more than one method. The first is related to audition. When children acquire language skills, they first learn the sounds of words, then learn to say them, then learn to read, and then learn to write. Undoubtedly, reading and writing depend heavily on the skills that are learned earlier. For example, in order to write most words, we must be able to "sound them out in our heads," that is, to hear them and to articulate them subvocally. If you want to demonstrate this to yourself, try to write a long word such as *antidisestablishmentarianism* from memory and see whether you can do it without saying the word to yourself. If you recite a poem or sing a song to yourself under your breath at the same time, you will see that the writing comes to a halt.

A second way of writing involves transcribing an image of what a particular word looks like—copying a visual mental image. Have you ever looked off into the distance to picture a word so that you can remember how to spell it? Some people are not very good at phonological spelling and have to write some words down to see whether they look correct. This method obviously involves *visual* memories, not acoustical ones.

Neurological evidence supports these speculations. Brain damage can sometimes impair people's ability to write phonetically, a deficit called **phono-**

logical dysgraphia (Shallice, 1981). (*Dysgraphia* refers to a writing deficit just as *dyslexia* refers to a reading deficit.) People with this disorder are unable to sound out words and write them phonetically. Thus, they cannot write unfamiliar words or pronounceable nonwords, such as the ones I presented in the section on reading. They can, however, visually imagine familiar words and then write them. **Orthographic dysgraphia** is just the opposite—a disorder of visually based writing. People with orthographic dysgraphia can *only* sound words out; thus, they can spell regular words such as *care* or *tree* and they can write pronounceable nonsense words. However, they have difficulty spelling irregular words such as *half* or *busy* (Beauvois and Dérouesné, 1981); they may write *haff* or *bizzy*. In general, phonological dysgraphia (impaired phonological writing) is caused by damage to the superior temporal lobe, whereas orthographic dysgraphia (impaired visual, whole-word writing) is caused by damage to the inferior parietal lobe (Benson and Geschwind, 1985).

Japanese patients show writing deficits similar to those of patients whose languages use the Roman alphabet; some patients have difficulty writing kana symbols, whereas others have difficulty with kanji symbols (Iwata, 1984; Yokota et al., 1990). Kawamura, Hirayama, and Yamamoto (1989) reported a particularly interesting case of a man with damage to the middle part of the corpus callosum who could write kana symbols with both hands and could write kanji symbols with the right hand but not the left. He could *copy* kanji symbols with his left hand; he just could not write them down when the investigators dictated them to him. (See *Figure 16.20.*) These results have interesting implications. Writing appears to be organized in the left hemisphere; that is, the information needed to specify the shape of the symbols is provided by circuits in this hemisphere. When a person uses his or her left hand to write these symbols, the information must be sent across the corpus callosum to the motor cortex of the right hemisphere, which controls the left hand. Apparently, information about the two forms of Japanese symbols is transmitted through different parts of the corpus callosum; the man's brain damage disrupted one of these pathways but not the other. (See *Figure 16.21.*)

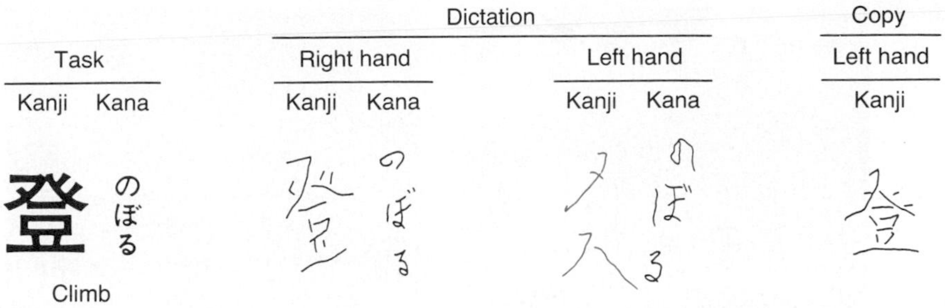

		Dictation				Copy
Task		Right hand		Left hand		Left hand
Kanji	Kana	Kanji	Kana	Kanji	Kana	Kanji

登 のぼる

Climb

FIGURE 16.20

The writing of a Japanese patient with damage to the middle part of the corpus callosum. He could write both kanji and kana characters with his right hand, but he could not write kanji characters with his left hand (color). He could, however, copy kanji characters with his left hand if he was given a model to look at.

(From Kawamura, M., Hirayama, K., and Yamamoto, H. *Brain*, 1989, *112*, 1011–1018. Reprinted by permission of Oxford University Press.)

As we saw in the section on reading, some patients (those with direct dyslexia) can read aloud without being able to understand what they are reading. Similarly, some patients can write words that are dictated to them even though they cannot understand these words (Roeltgen, Rothi, and Heilman, 1986; Lesser, 1989). Some of these patients can even spell pronounceable nonwords, which indicates that their ability to spell phonetically is intact. Roeltgen referred to this disorder as *semantic agraphia,* but perhaps the term *direct dysgraphia* would be more appropriate, because of the parallel with direct dyslexia.

Developmental Dyslexias

Some children have great difficulty learning to read and never become fluent readers, even though they are otherwise intelligent. Specific language learning disorders, called **developmental dyslexias,** tend to occur in families, which suggests a genetic (and hence biological) component (Pennington et al., 1991). The reading difficulties shown by most people with developmental dyslexia resemble those of phonological dyslexia—that is, a deficit in sounding out words, rather than in reading them by the whole-word method (Rumsey et al., 1992).

Several studies (Galaburda et al., 1985; Galaburda, 1988; Humphreys, Kaufmann, and Gal-

aburda, 1990) have found evidence that brain abnormalities may be responsible for at least some cases of developmental dyslexia. The investigators obtained the brains of deceased people with histories of developmental dyslexia. In all cases they found abnormalities in the **planum temporale,** a part of Wernicke's area. Figure 16.22 shows a section through the left planum temporale of a normal person (a) and of a dyslexic accident victim (b). Notice

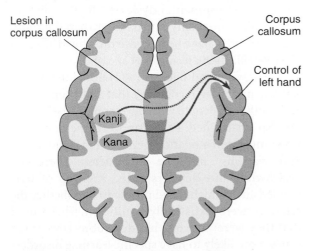

FIGURE 16.21

The role of the corpus callosum in Japanese writing. Information about kana and kanji characters apparently crosses different parts of the callosum.

FIGURE 16.22

Photomicrographs of the left planum temporale (a portion of Wernicke's area). (a) Of a normal person. (b) Of a person with developmental dyslexia. Nissl stain.

(Photographs courtesy of A. Galaburda.)

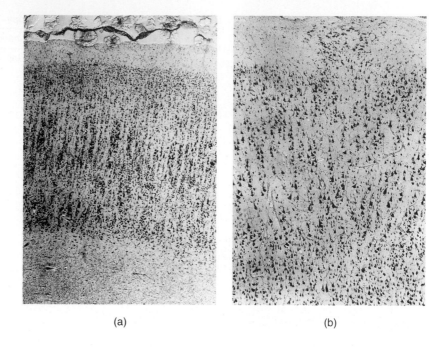

(a)   (b)

the regular columnar arrangement of cells in the normal brain but not in the brain of the dyslexic accident victim. (See **Figure 16.22.**) The investigators attributed these microscopic abnormalities to problems in prenatal development of the brain. In addition, the right and left planum temporale were approximately the same size. In the brains of people without developmental dyslexia, the left planum temporale is normally much larger than the right. These findings have been confirmed by MRI scans (Hynd et al., 1990; Jernigan et al., 1991).

Geschwind and Behan (1984) noted that investigators have long recognized that a disproportionate number of people with developmental dyslexias are also left-handed. Furthermore, clinical observations suggested a relation between left-handedness and various immune disorders. Therefore, Geschwind and Behan studied a group of left-handed and right-handed people to see whether the relations were statistically significant. They found that they were: The left-handed subjects were ten times more likely to have specific learning disorders (10 percent versus 1 percent) and two and one-half times more likely to have immune disorders (8 percent versus 3 percent). The immune disorders included various thyroid and bowel diseases, dia-

betes, and rheumatoid arthritis. Of course, although the relation was statistically significant, it was not perfect. After all, most left-handed people are healthy and are good readers.

Geschwind and Behan suggest that left-handedness, developmental dyslexia, and immune disorders are causally related. They note that although the superior temporal gyrus develops one to two weeks earlier on the right, the left superior temporal gyrus ultimately becomes larger (Chi, Dooling, and Gilles, 1977). In fact, slowing the rate of development may be the mechanism that causes the left language area to become larger than the corresponding region of the right hemisphere; by growing more slowly, it ultimately achieves a larger size. Perhaps dyslexia occurs when the development of the left hemisphere is suppressed so much that it fails to develop normally.

Humphreys, Kaufmann, and Galaburda (1990) propose a specific mechanism to explain the microscopic brain abnormalities. They suggest that pregnant women who belong to families with a genetic predisposition to developmental dyslexia may produce antibodies against the cells that make up capillaries and small arteries in the cerebral cortex. These antibodies attack these cells during a

TABLE 16.2

Reading and Writing Disorders Produced by Brain Damage

Reading Disorders	Whole-word reading	Phonetic reading	Remarks
Pure alexia	Poor	Poor	Can write
Surface dyslexia	Poor	Good	
Phonological dyslexis	Good	Poor	
Spelling dyslexia	Poor	Poor	Can read words letter-by-letter
Direct dyslexia	Good	Good	Cannot comprehend words
Comprehension without reading	Poor	Poor	Shows some comprehension of words
Writing Disorders	**Whole-word writing**	**Phonetic writing**	
Phonological dysgraphia	Good	Poor	
Orthographic dysgraphia	Poor	Good	

critical stage of prenatal development and cause the abnormalities. These hypothesis are interesting, but much research has yet to be done to test them experimentally.

||||| INTERIM SUMMARY

Brain damage can produce reading and writing disorders. With few exceptions, aphasias are accompanied by writing deficits that parallel the speech production deficits and by reading deficits that parallel the speech comprehension deficits. Pure alexia is caused by lesions that produce blindness in the right visual field and that destroy fibers of the posterior corpus callosum. Damage restricted to the posterior corpus callosum produces alexia only in the left visual field.

Research in the past few decades has discovered that acquired reading disorders (dyslexias) can fall into one of several categories, and the study of these disorders has provided neuropsychologists and cognitive psychologists with thought-provoking information that has helped them understand how normal people read. Surface dyslexia is a loss of whole-word reading ability. Phonological dyslexia is loss of the ability to read phonetically. Word-form (spelling) dyslexia is caused by a deficit in both phonetic and whole-word reading; patients can still recognize individual letters and can read slowly by pronouncing each letter. Direct dyslexia is analogous to transcortical sensory aphasia; the patients can read words aloud but cannot understand what they are reading. Some dyslexia patients can at least partially comprehend written words without being able to pronounce them; they can match corresponding words and pictures and recognize misspelled words they cannot read.

Brain damage can disrupt writing ability by impairing people's ability to form letters—or even specific types of letters, such as uppercase or lowercase letters, or vowels. Other deficits involve the ability to spell words. At least two different types of dysgraphia—phonological and orthographic—have been observed, which indicates that several different brain mechanisms are involved in the process of writing. In addition, some patients have a deficit parallel to direct dyslexia; they can write words they cannot understand. Developmental dyslexia appears to involve abnormal development of parts of the brain that play a role in language, perhaps because of a hereditary condition that affects the immune system. A better understanding of the components of reading and writing may help us develop effective teaching methods that will permit people with dyslexia to take advantage of the abilities that they do have.

Table 16.2 summarizes the disorders described in this section.

 New Terms

Speech Production and Comprehension: Brain Mechanisms

cerebrovascular accident p. 512

aphasia p. 512

Broca's aphasia p. 514

function word p. 514

content word p. 514

Broca's area p. 514

agrammatism p. 515

anomia p. 515

Wernicke's area p. 517

Wernicke's aphasia p. 517

pure word deafness p. 518

transcortical sensory aphasia p. 519

autotopagnosia p. 521

arcuate fasciculus *(ARE kew ett fa SIK yew luss)* p. 522

conduction aphasia p. 522

circumlocution *(sir kum low KEW shun)* p. 523

prosody *(PROSS a dee)* p. 526

Reading and Writitng Disorders

pure alexia *(ay LEX ee uh)* p. 529

whole-word reading p. 531

phonetic reading p. 532

surface dyslexia p. 532

phonological dyslexia p. 533

word-form dyslexia p. 534

spelling dyslexia p. 534

direct dyslexia p. 535

phonological dysgraphia p. 536

orthographic dysgraphia p. 536

developmental dyslexia p. 537

planum temporale *(PLAN um tem pa RAHL ee)* p. 537

Suggested Readings

Caplan, D. *Neurolinguistics and Linguistic Aphasiology.* Cambridge, England: Cambridge University Press, 1987.

Coltheart, M., Patterson, K., and Marshall, J.C. *Deep Dyslexia,* 2nd ed. London: Routledge and Kegan Paul, 1987.

Kolb, B., and Whishaw, I.Q. *Fundamentals of Human Neuropsychology,* 3rd ed. New York: W.H. Freeman, 1990.

Margolin, D.I. *Cognitive Neuropsychology in Clinical Practice.* New York: Oxford University Press, 1992

McCarthy, R.A., and Warrington, E.K. *Cognitive Neuropsychology: A Clinical Introduction.* San Diego: Academic Press, 1990.

Plum, F. *Language, Communication, and the Brain.* New York: Raven Press, 1988.

CHAPTER 17

Mental Disorders: Schizophrenia and the Affective Disorders

Schizophrenia
- Description
- Heritability
- Pharmacology of Schizophrenia: The Dopamine Hypothesis
- Schizophrenia as a Neurological Disorder
  Interim Summary

Major Affective Disorders
- Description
- Heritability
- Physiological Treatments
- Role of Monoamines
- Evidence for Brain Abnormalities
- Role of Circadian Rhythms
  Interim Summary

MOST OF THE DISCUSSION IN THIS BOOK has concentrated on the physiology of normal, adaptive behavior. This chapter summarizes research on the nature and physiology of mental disorders—of syndromes characterized by maladaptive behavior. The symptoms of mental disorders include deficient or inappropriate social behaviors; illogical, incoherent, or obsessional thoughts; inappropriate emotional responses, including depression, mania, or anxiety; and delusions and hallucinations. Research in recent years indicates that many of these symptoms are caused by abnormalities in the brain, both structural and biochemical.

The most serious mental disorders are called **psychoses.** This chapter discusses the two most important psychoses, schizophrenia and the major affective disorders, which can disrupt people's behavior so severely that they cannot survive without the care of others. Chapter 18 discusses some of the most important nonpsychotic mental disorders: anxiety disorders, substance abuse disorders, and autism.

SCHIZOPHRENIA

Description

Schizophrenia is the most common psychosis, afflicting approximately 1 percent of the world's population. Descriptions of symptoms in ancient writings indicate that the disorder has been around for thousands of years (Jeste et al., 1985). *Schizophrenia* is probably the most misused psychological term in existence. The word literally means "split mind," but it does *not* imply a split or multiple personality. People often say that they "feel schizophrenic" about an issue when they really mean that they have mixed feelings about it. A person who sometimes wants to build a cabin in Alaska and live off the land and at other times wants to take over the family insurance business may be undecided, but he or she is not schizophrenic. The man who invented the term, Eugen Bleuler, intended it to refer to a break with reality, caused by disorganiza-

tion of the various functions of the mind, so that thoughts and feelings no longer worked together normally.

Schizophrenia is characterized by two categories of symptoms, positive and negative. **Positive symptoms** make themselves known by their presence. They include thought disorders, hallucinations, and delusions. A **thought disorder**—disorganized, irrational thinking—is probably the most important symptom of schizophrenia. Schizophrenics have great difficulty arranging their thoughts logically and sorting out plausible conclusions from absurd ones. In conversation they jump from one topic to another, as new associations come up. Sometimes, they utter meaningless words or choose words for their rhyme rather than for their meaning. **Delusions** are beliefs that are obviously contrary to fact. Delusions of *persecution* are false beliefs that others are plotting and conspiring against oneself. Delusions of *grandeur* are false beliefs in one's power and importance, such as a conviction that one has godlike powers or has special knowledge that no one else possesses. Delusions of *control* are related to delusions of persecution; the person believes (for example) that he or she is being controlled by others through such means as radar or tiny radio receivers implanted in his or her brain.

The third positive symptom of schizophrenia is **hallucinations,** which are perceptions of stimuli that are not actually present. The most common schizophrenic hallucinations are auditory, but they can also involve any of the other senses. The typical schizophrenic hallucination consists of voices talking to the person. Sometimes, they order the person to do something; sometimes, they scold the person for his or her unworthiness; sometimes, they just utter meaningless phrases. Olfactory hallucinations are also fairly common; often they contribute to the delusion that others are trying to kill the person with poison gas.

In contrast to the positive symptoms, the **negative symptoms** of schizophrenia are known by the absence of normal behaviors: flattened emotional response, poverty of speech, lack of initiative and persistence, inability to experience pleasure, and social withdrawal (Crow, 1980; Andreasen and Olsen, 1982). Negative symptoms are not specific to schizophrenia; they are seen in many neurological disorders that involve brain damage, especially to the frontal lobes. As we will see later in this chapter, evidence suggests that these two sets of symptoms result from different physiological disorders: Positive symptoms appear to involve excessive activity in some neural circuits that include dopamine as a neurotransmitter, and negative symptoms appear to be caused by brain damage. Many researchers believe that these two sets of symptoms involve a common set of underlying causes.

Heritability

One of the strongest pieces of evidence that schizophrenia is a biological disorder is that it appears to be heritable. Two approaches have established a linkage between schizophrenia and genes: adoption studies and twin studies.

Kety et al. (1968) performed one of the earliest and best-known adoption studies. Kety and his colleagues identified a group of schizophrenic people who had been adopted when they were children. They found that the incidence of schizophrenia in the adopted families of the patients was exactly what would be expected in the general population. Thus, it did not appear that the patients became schizophrenic because they were raised in a family of schizophrenics. However, the investigators did find an unusually high incidence of schizophrenia in the patients' *biological* relatives (parents and siblings), even though they were not raised by and with them—and probably, in most cases, did not even know them. The results clearly favor the conclusion that a tendency to develop schizophrenia is heritable.

Twin studies have produced similar results. These studies take advantage of the fact that monozygotic twins have identical genotypes, whereas the genetic similarity between dizygotic twins is, on the average, 50 percent. Investigators study records to identify pairs of twins in which at least one member has received a diagnosis of schizophrenia or perhaps of a related but milder condition, such as schizotypal personality disorder. If both twins have been diagnosed as having schizophrenia, then they are said to be *concordant*. If only one has received this diagnosis, the twins are said to be *discordant*. Thus, if a disorder has a genetic basis, the percentage of monozygotic twins concordant for the diagnosis will be higher than that for dizygotic twins. As many studies have shown, this is exactly what occurs (Gottesman and Shields, 1982; Tsuang, Gilbertson, and Faraone, 1991). According to these studies, the concordance rate for monozygotic twins is at least four times higher than the concordance rate for dizygotic twins, which provides strong evidence that schizophrenia is a heritable trait.

If schizophrenia were a simple trait produced by a single gene, we would expect to see this disorder in at least 50 percent of the children of two schizophrenic parents if the gene were dominant. If it were recessive, *all* children of two schizophrenic parents should become schizophrenic. However, the actual incidence is less than 50 percent, which means either that several genes are involved or that having a "schizophrenia gene" imparts a *susceptibility* to develop schizophrenia, the disease itself being triggered by other factors. Perhaps, in certain kinds of environments, the susceptible individual develops schizophrenia. As we will see, evidence suggests that one of the inherited traits may include defects in the immune system that directly cause brain damage or that render a person susceptible to brain-damaging effects of viral illnesses.

If the susceptibility hypothesis is true, then we would expect that some people carry a "schizophrenia gene" but do not express it; that is, their environment is such that schizophrenia is never triggered. One such person would be the nonschizophrenic member of a pair of monozygotic twins discordant for schizophrenia. The logical way to test this hypothesis is to examine the children of both members of discordant pairs. Gottesman and Bertelsen (1989) found that the percentage of schizophrenic children was identical for both members of such pairs: 16.8% for the schizophrenic parents and 17.4% for the nonschizophrenic parents. For the dizygotic twins the percentages were 17.4% and 2.1%, respectively. These results provide strong evidence for heritability of schizophrenia and also support the conclusion that carrying a "schizophre-

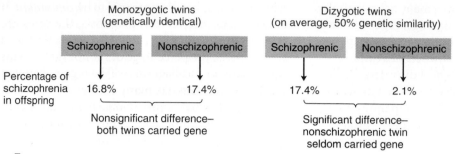

FIGURE 17.1

An explanation for evidence that people can have an unexpressed "schizophrenia gene."

nia gene" does not mean that a person will necessarily become schizophrenic. (See **Figure 17.1.**)

Studies have suggested two possible locations for a "schizophrenia gene": chromosome 5 and a special region of the X chromosome. Bassett et al. (1988) found a schizophrenic man with a schizophrenic maternal uncle, both of whom had an abnormality of the long arm of chromosome 5; they had three copies of this arm rather than two. The abnormality suggested that this region might be a worthwhile place to look for a defective gene. Sherrington et al. (1988) used DNA markers to study five families in Iceland and two in England that had some schizophrenic members, and they found evidence that implicated this location. However, other studies (Kennedy et al., 1988; St. Clair et al., 1989) failed to confirm the results. Thus, unless the correlation in the first study was accidental, we must conclude that there is more than one gene that can produce a susceptibility to schizophrenia.

A second candidate is found on the X chromosome. Normally, if a dominant gene is found on the X chromosome, the trait associated with it will occur with equal frequency in both males and females. However, there is a special location on the short arm of the X chromosome that normally exchanges genetic material with the short arm of the Y chromosome during sperm production in males, through a process that geneticists call *crossing-over*. This region is called the *pseudoautosomal segment* because genes there act as if they were on an autosome (that is, nonsex chromosome). (See **Figure 17.2.**)

The exact location of the point at which the chromosomes cross over is variable; thus, depending on the exact location of a particular gene found here, it will sometimes cross over to the Y chromosome and sometimes remain on the X chromosome; thus, it will sometimes be found on the X chromosome in a man's sperms and sometimes on the Y chromosome. If the "schizophrenia gene" ends up on the Y chromosome, a father will give it to his sons; if it ends up on the X chromosome, he will give it to his daughters.

Several studies (Crow, DeLisi, and Johnstone, 1989; Gorwood et al. 1992) have found that when a family contains more than one schizophrenic child, the children are more likely to be of the same sex when the history of schizophrenia is on the father's side rather than the mother's. This difference suggests that the "schizophrenia gene" is found on the pseudoautosomal region.

As we shall see, the positive symptoms of schizophrenia are diminished by drugs that block dopamine receptors. This fact has led some investigators to suggest that the hypothetical "schizophrenia gene" may actually be involved in the production of these receptors; for example, it could produce abnormally sensitive postsynaptic receptors or abnormally insensitive presynaptic receptors. So far, researchers have cloned five different dopamine receptors and have determined the location of the genes that produce them. But as Coon et al. (1993) report, studies of nine different multigenerational families have found no evidence that schizophrenia is linked to any of these genes.

Several studies have obtained evidence that schizophrenia can sometimes be caused by non-genetic factors. These studies have found that if a schizophrenic person does not have relatives with a

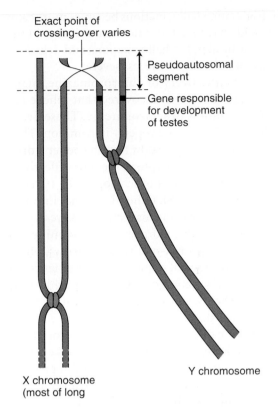

Exact point of
crossing-over varies

Pseudoautosomal
segment

Gene responsible
for development
of testes

X chromosome
(most of long

Y chromosome

FIGURE 17.2

Crossing-over between an X chromosome and a Y chromosome in the pseudoautosomal segment during sperm production.

(Adapted from Crow, T.J., DeLisi, L.E., and Johnstone, E.C. *British Journal of Psychiatry*, 1989, *155*, 92-97.)

schizophrenic disorder, the person is more likely to have had a history of complications at or around the time of childbirth—and the person is more likely to develop the schizophrenic symptoms at an earlier age (Schwarzkopf et al., 1989; O'Callaghan, 1990; O'Callaghan et al., 1992). Sometimes, brain damage received during adulthood can produce the symptoms of schizophrenia. Buckley et al. (1993) found three such cases and reported that MRI scans revealed damage in the left temporal lobe. Thus, brain damage *not related to heredity* may also be a cause of schizophrenia.

Some investigators have attempted to find other traits that correlate with schizophrenia, traits that may make it possible to detect the presence of even an unexpressed "schizophrenia gene" (that is, a "schizophrenia gene" in a person without the disorder). For example, many studies have found that difficulty in tracking a smoothly moving object with the eyes is highly correlated with schizophrenia. Up to 85 percent of all schizophrenics show abnormal tracking, as compared with under 10 percent in nonschizophrenics. Approximately half of the first-degree relatives (children, parents, and siblings) of schizophrenic people show this abnormality, even if they themselves are not schizophrenic (Holzman et al., 1974; Rea et al., 1989; Abel, Levin, and Holzman, 1992). The evidence suggests that a single gene may be responsible for both schizophrenia and abnormal eye tracking; presumably, a brain abnormality is responsible for the two conditions.

Pharmacology of Schizophrenia: The Dopamine Hypothesis

Pharmacological evidence suggests that the positive symptoms of schizophrenia are caused by a biochemical disorder. The explanation that has accrued the most evidence is the *dopamine hypothesis*, which suggests that schizophrenia is caused by overactivity of dopaminergic neurons, probably those of the mesolimbic system, which projects from the ventral tegmental area to the nucleus accumbens and amygdala.

Effects of Dopamine Agonists and Antagonists

The treatments for most physiological disorders are developed after we understand their causes. For example, once it was discovered that diabetes was caused by the lack of a hormone produced by the pancreas, researchers were able to extract a substance from pancreatic tissue (insulin) that would alleviate the symptoms of this disease. However, in some cases treatments are discovered before the causes of the disease. For example, natives of tropical regions discovered that tea made from the bark of the cinchona tree would prevent death from malaria many years before scientists discovered that this disease is caused by microscopic parasites that are transmitted in the saliva of a certain species of mosquito. (The bark of the cinchona tree contains quinine, now used to treat malaria.)

In the case of schizophrenia a treatment was discovered before its causes were understood. (In fact, its causes are *still* not completely understood.) The discovery was accidental (Snyder, 1974). Antihistamine drugs were discovered in the early 1940s and were found to be useful in the treatment of allergic reactions. Because one of the effects of histamine release is a lowering of blood pressure, a French surgeon named Henri Laborit began to study the effects of antihistamine drugs on the sometimes-fatal low blood pressure that can be produced by surgical shock. He found that one of the drugs, promethazine, had an interesting effect: It reduced anxiety in his presurgical patients without causing mental confusion.

Laborit's findings spurred drug companies to examine other antihistamine drugs for sedative effects. Paul Charpentier, a chemist with a French drug company, developed **chlorpromazine,** which appeared to be promising from tests with animals. Laborit tried the drug in humans and found that it had profound calming effects but did not seem to decrease the patient's alertness. This drug produced "not any loss in consciousness, nor any change in the patients' mentality but a slight tendency to sleep and above all 'disinterest' for all that goes on around him" (Laborit, 1950, quoted by Snyder, 1974). Chlorpromazine was tried on patients with a variety of mental disorders: mania, depression, anxiety, neuroses, and schizophrenia (Delay and Deniker, 1952a, 1952b). The drug was not very effective in treating neuroses or affective psychoses, but it had dramatic effects on schizophrenia.

The discovery of the antipsychotic effects of chlorpromazine profoundly altered the way in which physicians treated schizophrenic patients and made prolonged hospital stays unnecessary for many of them (the patients, that is). The efficacy of antipsychotic drugs has been established in many double-blind studies (Baldessarini, 1977). They actually eliminate, or at least diminish, the patients' symptoms; they do not simply mask them by tranquilizing the patients. Although some antipsychotic drugs do have tranquilizing effects, these effects are not related to the amount of relief the patients receive from their psychotic symptoms. Moreover, antipsychotic drugs can have either activating or calming effects, depending upon the patient's symptoms. An immobile patient becomes more active, whereas a furiously active patient who is suffering

from frightening hallucinations becomes more calm and placid. The results are not just a change in the patient's attitudes; the hallucinations and delusions go away, or at least become less severe.

Since the discovery of chlorpromazine, many other drugs have been discovered that relieve the positive symptoms of schizophrenia. These drugs were found to have one property in common: They block dopamine receptors. In fact, the better a drug blocks D_2 dopamine receptors, the more effectively it reduces the symptoms of schizophrenia (Creese, Burt, and Snyder, 1976). Other drugs that interfere with dopaminergic transmission, such as reserpine (which prevents the storage of monoamines in synaptic vesicles) or α-methyl *p*-tyrosine (which blocks the synthesis of dopamine), either facilitate the antipsychotic action of drugs such as chlorpromazine or themselves exert antipsychotic effects (Tamminga et al., 1988).

Another category of drugs has the opposite effect, namely, the production of the positive symptoms of schizophrenia. The drugs that can produce these symptoms have one known pharmacological effect in common: They act as dopamine agonists. These drugs include amphetamine, cocaine, and methylphenidate (which block the reuptake of dopamine) and L-DOPA (which stimulates the synthesis of dopamine). The symptoms that these drugs produce can be alleviated with antipsychotic drugs, which further strengthens the argument that these drugs exert their therapeutic effects by blocking dopamine receptors.

An example of the psychosis-inducing effect of amphetamine was demonstrated by Griffith, Cavanaugh, Held, and Oates (1972). The investigators recruited a group of people who had a history of amphetamine use and gave them large doses (10 milligrams) of dextroamphetamine every hour for up to five days. (Experimentally, it would have been better to study nonusers. Ethically, it was better not to introduce this drug to people who did not normally use it.) None of the subjects had prior histories of psychotic behavior. All seven volunteers became psychotic within two to five days. They became suspicious and began to believe that the experimenters were trying to poison them. One developed a delusion that an electric dynamo was controlling his thoughts. Most had auditory hallucinations. Similar symptoms—the classic positive symptoms of schizophrenia—are seen today in many people who abuse cocaine.

The Search for Abnormalities in Dopamine Transmission in the Brains of Schizophrenic Patients

The dopamine hypothesis suggests that schizophrenia is caused by the overactivity of dopaminergic synapses. There is little evidence to suggest that the production and release of dopamine in the brains of schizophrenic patients is abnormal (Wyatt, Kirch, and DeLisi, 1988; Pickar et al., 1990). In fact, some studies have found *decreased* levels of the principal breakdown product of dopamine (homovanillic acid) in the cerebrospinal fluid. However, as we shall see later in this chapter, the ventricles of patients with schizophrenia tend to be larger than those of nonschizophrenics; thus, the substance could simply be diluted in a larger pool of CSF (Reynolds, 1989). In any event, most investigators have studied the possibility that too many dopamine receptors are present on the postsynaptic membrane at dopaminergic synapses. This overabundance of dopamine receptors would increase the size of the postsynaptic potentials at dopaminergic synapses. Two types of analyses have been made: postmortem measurements in the brains of deceased schizophrenic patients and PET scans after treatment with radioactive ligands for dopamine receptors.

Postmortem measurements of dopamine receptors are performed by removing the regions of the brain that contain dopaminergic terminals, homogenizing the tissue, extracting the cell membranes, and incubating them with a radioactive ligand of dopamine receptors. The degree of radioactivity of the tissue reveals the relative number of dopamine receptors. Jaskiw and Kleinman (1988) reviewed twelve such studies published between 1978 and 1987 and found that ten of them observed an increase in the number of D_2 dopamine receptors present in the neostriatum (caudate nucleus and putamen).

Measurements of levels of D_2 receptors in the brains of living schizophrenic patients have yielded mixed results. Wong et al. (1986) administered a radioactive ligand for D_2 receptors and used a PET scanner to measure the radioactivity in the caudate

nucleus. Their results suggested that the number of D_2 receptors was 30 to 100 percent higher in the brains of schizophrenic patients. However, Farde et al. (1990) and Martinot et al. (1990), using even more specific ligands for D_2 receptors, found no differences between the level of these receptors in schizophrenic and normal brains.

What conclusion can we make? Farde and his colleagues studied young patients who had just been diagnosed as being schizophrenic. The patients had not yet been given an antipsychotic medication, so the results of the study were not contaminated by possible effects of the medication. Many—perhaps most—of the schizophrenic patients used in previous studies (including the postmortem studies) had received antipsychotic drugs. This issue is important; several studies have shown that the administration of an antipsychotic medication for several days increases the number of D_2 receptors in the neostriatum of laboratory animals (Burt, Creese, and Snyder, 1977). Indeed, Farde and his colleagues found that the level of D_2 receptors in a patient who had been receiving an antipsychotic medication was elevated. Thus, it would seem premature to conclude that schizophrenia is caused by increased numbers of D_2 dopamine receptors.

The failure to obtain solid, unambiguous evidence that dopaminergic synapses are hyperactive in schizophrenic patients does not mean that the dopamine hypothesis should be abandoned. For one thing, investigators may have been looking in the wrong part of the brain. The neostriatum contains many dopamine receptors, which makes this region the easiest one in which to study their concentration. If schizophrenia were caused by a genetic defect that created an overproduction of dopamine receptors, then we would expect to find more of the receptors in the neostriatum. But what we know about the functions of the dopaminergic pathways in the brain would not make us suspect that the neostriatum would be involved in schizophrenia. The neostriatum is involved in motor control. A deficiency in the release of dopamine in the neostriatum causes Parkinson's disease; thus, we would expect that excessive dopaminergic activity there would cause excessive movement, not schizophrenia.

Most investigators believe that the nucleus accumbens, which also receives input from dopaminergic neurons, is a much better candidate than the neostriatum. Probably the best evidence that the nucleus accumbens, not the neostriatum, is involved in schizophrenia is the fact that one of the most effective antipsychotic drugs, clozapine, inhibits the activity of dopaminergic synapses in the nucleus accumbens but not in the neostriatum (Davis et al., 1991).

Why might overactivity of dopaminergic synapses in the nucleus accumbens produce the symptoms of schizophrenia? As we saw in Chapter 14, the activity of these synapses appears to be a vital link in the process of reinforcement. Drugs that act as agonists at these synapses (such as cocaine and amphetamine) strongly reinforce behavior; and if taken in large doses, they also produce the positive symptoms of schizophrenia. Perhaps the two effects of the drugs are related. If reinforcement mechanisms were activated at inappropriate times, then inappropriate behaviors—including delusional thoughts—might be reinforced. At one time or other, all of us have had some irrational thoughts, which we normally brush aside and forget. But if neural mechanisms of reinforcement became active while these thoughts were occurring, we would tend to take them more seriously. In time, full-fledged delusions might develop.

As Snyder (1974) notes, schizophrenics often report feelings of elation and euphoria at the beginning of a schizophrenic episode, when their symptoms flare up. Presumably, this euphoria is caused by hyperactivity of dopaminergic neurons involved in reinforcement. But the positive symptoms of schizophrenia also include disordered thinking and unpleasant, often terrifying delusions. The disordered thinking may be caused by disorganized attentional processes; the indiscriminate activity of the dopaminergic synapses in the nucleus accumbens makes it difficult for the patients to follow an orderly, rational thought sequence. Fibiger (1991) suggests that paranoid delusions may be caused by increased activity of the dopaminergic input to the amygdala. As we saw in Chapter 11, the central nucleus of the amygdala is involved with conditioned emotional responses elicited by aversive stimuli. The central nucleus receives a strong projection from the mesolimbic dopaminergic system, so Fibiger's suggestion is certainly plausible.

Even if dopaminergic neurons are directly involved in the production of the symptoms of schizophrenia, it is possible that nothing is wrong with dopaminergic neurons or dopamine receptors; the abnormality could lie elsewhere. For example, overactivity of neurons that excite dopaminergic neurons or underactivity of neurons that inhibit them would both result in dopaminergic activation. I will discuss some specific hypotheses later in this chapter.

Drug Treatment of Schizophrenia

The discovery of drugs that reduce or eliminate the symptoms of schizophrenia has had a revolutionary effect on the treatment of this disorder. Prior to this discovery, many schizophrenics spent much of their lives in psychiatric hospitals. Now many of these people receive antipsychotic medication on an outpatient basis and are able to live normal lives. But not everyone is helped; the symptoms of up to one-third of all schizophrenic patients are not substantially reduced by antipsychotic drugs. One possible explanation is that individual differences in the permeability of the blood-brain barrier to these drugs or in metabolic processes that deactivate them could be responsible for the differences in their effectiveness. However, PET scan studies (Wolkin et al., 1989; Seeman, 1992) have found that antipsychotic drugs produce equal levels of D_2 dopamine receptor blockade in the brains of schizophrenics, regardless of whether the patients respond to the drug.

Another problem with antipsychotic drugs is that they sometimes produce serious side effects. As you know, the nigrostriatal dopamine system is involved in movement; degeneration of the neurons of this system causes Parkinson's disease. Until recently, all the drugs commonly used to treat schizophrenia caused at least some symptoms resembling those of Parkinson's disease: slowness in movement, lack of facial expression, and general weakness. For most patients these symptoms are temporary, but for some they are so severe that the patients cannot tolerate a dose of the drug strong enough to alleviate their schizophrenic symptoms.

Antipsychotic drugs also appear to be responsible for another motor problem: **tardive dyskinesia.** *Tardus* means "slow" and *dyskinesia* means "faulty movement"; thus, tardive dyskinesia is a late-developing movement disorder. This syndrome includes peculiar facial tics and gestures, including tongue protrusion, cheek puffing, and pursing of the lips. In some cases speech is affected. Sometimes, writhing movements of the hands and trunk are also seen. Tardive dyskinesia is seen in approximately 10 percent of the patients who receive antipsyotic drugs.

The symptoms of tardive dyskinesia are the opposite of those of Parkinson's disease. (Indeed, dyskinesia commonly occurs when patients with Parkinson's disease receive too much L DOPA.) In schizophrenic patients tardive dyskinesia is made *worse* by discontinuing the antipsychotic drug and is improved by increasing the dose. The symptoms are also intensified by dopamine agonists such as L-DOPA or amphetamine (Baldessarini and Tarsy, 1980). Therefore, the disorder appears to be produced by an *overstimulation* of dopamine receptors of the neostriatum. If it is, why should it be caused by antipsychotic drugs, which are dopamine antagonists?

The answer appears to be provided by a phenomenon called **supersensitivity.** If the afferent axons to a neuron or muscle are cut or the release of neurotransmitter is prevented with a drug, the postsynaptic membrane often develops an increased sensitivity to the neurotransmitter. This phenomenon is usually caused by an increase in the number of postsynaptic receptors. Thus, supersensitivity is a compensatory mechanism in response to decreased synaptic activity (Baldessarini and Tarsy, 1980). In the case of tardive dyskinesia, blocking dopamine receptors in the caudate nucleus causes a compensatory supersensitivity to dopamine. This supersensitivity results in dyskinesia when the drug is withdrawn. In cases in which the antipsychotic medication continues for a long time, the supersensitivity becomes so great that it *overcompensates* for the effects of the drug, causing the tardive dyskinesia to occur even while the drug is still being administered.

In recent years an "atypical" antipsychotic drug has become one of the most popular treatments for schizophrenia. This drug, *clozapine,* has only 10 percent as much affinity for the dopamine D_2 receptor as traditional antipsychotic drugs (hence the term *atypical*), but it is at least as effective in reducing schizophrenic symptoms (Davis et al., 1991). In fact, it often helps patients whose symptoms are not reduced by the more traditional medications (Meltzer, 1992). Because the drug is much less likely to produce parkinsonian side effects, it can be given to patients who cannot tolerate other antipsychotic drugs.

The primary effect of clozapine appears to be its ability to block dopamine D_4 receptors (Seeman, 1992). Apparently, these receptors regulate dopaminergic activity in the nucleus accumbens but not in the neostriatum; thus, the drug reduces the symptoms of schizophrenia without producing parkinsonian side effects. Most investigators therefore believe that long-term use of the drug will not cause tardive dyskinesia.

Schizophrenia as a Neurological Disorder

So far, I have been discussing the physiology of the positive symptoms of schizophrenia—principally, hallucinations, delusions, and thought disorders. These symptoms are plausibly related to one of the known functions of dopaminergic neurons: reinforcement. But the negative symptoms of schizophrenia—social withdrawal, flattened emotional reaction, and poverty of thought and speech—are very different. Whereas the positive symptoms are unique to schizophrenia (and to amphetamine or cocaine psychosis), the negative symptoms are similar to those produced by brain damage caused by several different means. Many pieces of evidence suggest that the negative symptoms of schizophrenia are indeed a result of brain damage.

Evidence for Brain Damage in Schizophrenia

Although schizophrenia has been traditionally labeled as a psychiatric disorder, most patients with schizophrenia exhibit neurological symptoms that suggest the presence of brain damage. These symptoms include catatonia; facial dyskinesias; unusually high or low rates of blinking; staring and avoidance of eye contact; absent blink reflex in response to a tap on the forehead; episodes of deviation of the eyes (especially to the right), accompanied by speech arrest; paroxysmal bursts of jerky eye movements; very poor visual pursuit of a smoothly moving object; inability to move the eyes without

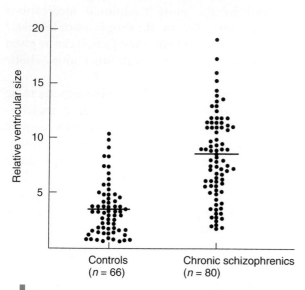

FIGURE 17.3

Relative ventricular size in chronic schizophrenics and controls.

(From Weinberger, D.R., and Wyatt, R.J., in *Schizophrenia as a Brain Disease*, edited by F.A. Henn and H.A. Nasrallah. New York: Oxford University Press, 1982. Reprinted with permission.)

moving the head; poor pupillary light reactions; and continuous elevation of the brows, causing characteristic horizontal creasing of the forehead (Stevens, 1982). Although these symptoms can be caused by a variety of neuropathological conditions and are hence not unique to schizophrenia, their presence suggests that schizophrenia may be associated with brain damage of some kind.

Many studies have found evidence of brain damage from CT and MRI scans of schizophrenic patients. In one study Weinberger and Wyatt (1982) obtained CT scans of eighty chronic schizophrenics and sixty-six normal controls of the same mean age (twenty-nine). Without knowledge of the patients' diagnoses they measured the area of the lateral ventricles in the scan that cut through them at their largest extent, and they expressed this area relative to the area of brain tissue in the same scan. The relative ventricle size of the schizophrenic patients was more than twice as great as that of normal control subjects. (See **Figure 17.3.**) The most likely cause of the enlarged ventricles is loss of brain tissue; thus, the CT scans provide evidence that chronic schizophrenia is associated with brain damage.

Subsequent studies have found evidence for degeneration (or developmental abnormalities) in several parts of the brain. Abnormalities are commonly seen in the medial temporal lobe (Breier et al., 1992; Degreef et al., 1992; Bogerts et al., 1993), in the frontal lobes (Klausner et al., 1992; Raine et al., 1992), and in the medial diencephalon (Bornstein et al., 1992; D'Amato et al., 1992). In several of these studies the severity of the brain abnormalities were correlated with the severity of the patients' negative symptoms.

Causes of the Brain Damage

As we saw earlier, schizophrenia is a heritable disease, but its heritability is less than perfect. Why do fewer than half the children of parents with chronic schizophrenia become schizophrenic? A possible answer is that what is inherited is a defect in the immune system that renders a person susceptible to brain-damaging effects of viral illnesses.

No direct evidence for virally induced schizophrenia exists, but evidence reveals similarities between schizophrenia and known viral disorders. There is no doubt that viruses can cause brain damage. One example is the herpes simplex virus, which normally hides in the trigeminal nerve ganglion. From time to time the virus emerges from its hiding place, following branches of the trigeminal nerve to the region around the mouth, where it produces harmless cold sores. In rare instances the virus goes the other way and enters the brain, where it damages neurons in the limbic cortex that borders the frontal and temporal lobes. In addition, the virus that caused the 1918 influenza epidemic caused brain damage in many patients and produced illnesses that resembled schizophrenia (Menninger, 1926).

Stevens (1988) notes some interesting similarities between schizophrenia and a known neuropathological condition, multiple sclerosis. Multiple sclerosis is an autoimmune disease—probably triggered by a virus—in which the patient's own immune system attacks myelin. The natural histories of multiple sclerosis and schizophrenia are similar in several ways. Both diseases show a *latitude effect*—they are more prevalent and more malignant in people who spent their childhood in latitudes far from the equator. And both diseases are character-

ized by one of three general courses: (1) attacks followed by remissions, many of which produce no
residual deficits; (2) recurrent attacks with only partial remissions, causing an increasingly major
deficit; or (3) an insidious onset with a steady and
relentless progression, leading to permanent and
severe deficits. These similarities suggest that
schizophrenia, like multiple sclerosis, could be a
virally induced autoimmune disease.

Of course, it is possible that viral illnesses could
cause the brain damage associated with schizophrenia directly. Torrey (1991) suggests that a virus
might enter an infant's brain via the trigeminal
nerve and remain dormant in the medial temporal
region, ready to be activated by the hormonal
changes that accompany puberty. In this case genetic
susceptibility to schizophrenia may reside in deficiencies in the patient's immune system that impair
its ability to fight the virus, or even in the shape of
the skull and brain that permit easy access to the
virus.

Most investigators appear to favor another
hypothesis—that the brain anomalies occur during
prenatal development and that if a viral infection is
responsible, it is probably the mother who contracts
it. One interesting fact about schizophrenia supports
this suggestion: the *seasonality effect.* Several studies
have shown that people born during the late winter
and early spring are more likely to develop
schizophrenia. For example, Kendell and Adams
(1991) studied the month of birth of over thirteen
thousand schizophrenic patients born in Scotland
between 1914 and 1960. They found that dispropor-
tionately more patients were born in February,
March, April, and May. (See *Figure 17.4.*) The investigators also found that the relative number of
schizophrenic births was especially high during
these months if the temperature was lower than normal during the previous autumn.

What might cause the seasonality effect? One
obvious possibility is that pregnant women may be
more likely to contract a viral illness during a critical
phase of their infant's development. The brain
development of their fetuses may be adversely
affected either by a toxin produced by the virus or by
the mother's antibodies against the virus. Several
studies have found a relation between influenza epidemics and the birth of babies that later develop

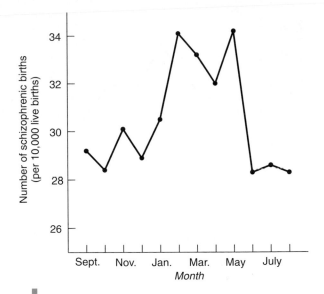

FIGURE 17.4

*The seasonality effect. The graph shows the number of
schizophrenic births per 10,000 live births.*
(Based on data from Kendell, R.E., and Adams, W. *British Journal
of Psychiatry,* 1991, *158,* 758-763.)

schizophrenia. For example, a study of the offspring
of women who were pregnant during an epidemic of
type A2 influenza in Finland during 1957 showed an
elevated incidence of schizophrenia (Mednick,
Machon, and Huttunen, 1990). The increased incidence was seen only in the children of women who
were in the second trimester of their pregnancy
when the epidemic occurred. Another study (Sham
et al., 1992) confirmed these findings in a study of
infants born to mothers who were pregnant during
several influenza epidemics in England and Wales
between 1939 and 1960. As Figure 17.5 shows, the
peak number of schizophrenic births occurred five
months after the start of the epidemic, which means
that the greatest susceptibility appears to occur during the second trimester of pregnancy. (See *Figure
17.5.*)

Another prenatal effect was discovered by Susser
and Lin (1992), who studied the offspring of women
who were pregnant during the *Hungerwinter*—a
severe food shortage that occurred in The Nether-
lands during World War II. The investigators found
that the daughters (but not the sons) of these
women were more likely to become schizophrenic.
In this case the vulnerable period came during the

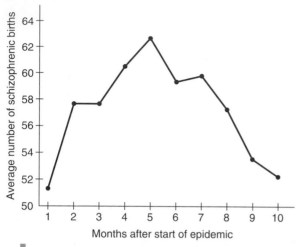

FIGURE 17.5

Average number of schizophrenic births in each of the ten months following an influenza epidemic in England and Wales between 1939 and 1960.

(Adapted from Sham, P.C., O'Callaghan, E., Takei, N., Murray, G.K., Hare, E.H., and Murray, R.M. *British Journal of Psychiatry,* 1992, *160,* 461-466.)

first trimester. To date, we have no explanation for the fact that only females were affected.

So far, the evidence that I have cited concerning developmental factors in schizophrenia is epidemiological, having come from studies of populations, not individuals. Is there any direct evidence that abnormal prenatal development is associated with schizophrenia? The answer is yes. During prenatal development of the brain a particular population of neurons migrates from one location to another in the neocortex. The neurons contain an enzyme known as *NADPH-d* (nicotinamide-adenine dinucleotide phosphate-diaphorase, if you really want to know). Akbarian et al. (1993a, 1993b) studied the brains of five deceased schizophrenics and found that the distribution of neurons containing NADPH-d in the various layers of the cerebral cortex of the frontal and temporal lobes was abnormal. The results strongly suggest that something had interfered with normal prenatal brain development.

As I mentioned earlier, some monozygotic twins are discordant for schizophrenia; that is, one of them develops schizophrenic and the other does not. Suddath et al. (1990) obtained evidence that differences in the structure of the brain may account for the discordance. The investigators examined MRI scans of monozygotic twins discordant for schizophrenia and found that in almost every case the twin with schizophrenia had larger lateral and third ventricles. In addition, the anterior hippocampus was smaller in the schizophrenic twins, and the total volume of the gray matter in the left temporal lobe was reduced. Figure 17.6 shows a set of MRI scans from a pair of twins; as you can see, the lateral ventricles are larger in the brain of the twin with schizophrenia. (See *Figure 17.6.*)

Of course, we cannot be sure when the brain abnormalities occurred; they could have been caused during development, at the time of birth, or later in life. Bracha et al. (1992) obtained evidence that sug-

FIGURE 17.6

MRI scans of the brains of twins discordant for schizophrenia. The arrows point to the lateral ventricles. (a) Normal twin. (b) Twin with schizophrenia.

(Courtesy of D.R. Weinberger, National Institute of Mental Health, Saint Elizabeth's Hospital, Washington, D.C.)

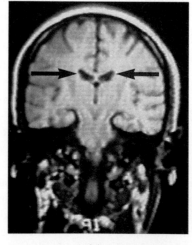

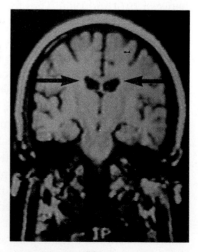

(a)   (b)

gests that at least some cases of discordance may occur during development. The investigators examined the fingerprints of fifty-three pairs of monozygotic twins, twenty-three of whom were discordant for schizophrenia. The migration of neurons to the cerebral cortex takes place during the second trimester of prenatal development. During this period cells in the skin of the fingertips also migrate, forming the ridges that give us our fingerprints. Bracha and his colleagues reasoned that if something were interfering with the brain development of one of the twins, it might show itself in the development of that individual's fingerprints, too. And they found exactly that. The fingerprints of the twins who were concordant for schizophrenia were nearly identical, whereas the fingerprints of many of the discordant twins showed distinctive differences.

As you can see, the evidence that prenatal factors play a role in the development of schizophrenia is strong. But not all cases of schizophrenia are caused this way, which means that other factors must be important, too. We already saw that some cases of schizophrenia can be caused by obstetric complications. In addition, several studies have shown that only schizophrenia that has a gradual onset and a long, unremitting course shows a seasonality effect (O'Callaghan et al., 1991; Franzek et al., 1992). Also, only this form of schizophrenia is related to the occurrence of infectious diseases during pregnancy (Stöber, Franzek, and Beckman, 1992). Neither a seasonality effect nor the effect of maternal infection is associated with schizophrenia characterized by an abrupt onset of symptoms and frequent remissions.

Relation Between Brain Damage and Positive and Negative Symptoms

The evidence reviewed in the previous two subsections indicates that schizophrenia is associated with brain damage, which may occur prenatally, during childbirth, or postnatally. Even if the brain damage associated with schizophrenia can be caused by several different means, we would at least expect some similarity in the location of the damage.

As we have seen, CT and MRI scans have found that schizophrenia is associated with damage to the frontal lobes, medial temporal lobes, and diencephalon. Weinberger (1988) suggests that the negative symptoms of schizophrenia are caused

FIGURE 17.7

Examples of the type of cards used in the Wisconsin Card Sort Test (WCST).

primarily by damage to the frontal lobes—in particular, the dorsolateral prefrontal cortex. One of the most reliable tests of the functions of the dorsolateral prefrontal cortex is the Wisconsin Card Sort Test (WCST). In this test subjects are presented with a deck of cards that contain patterns that differ in number, shape, and color. The cards contain between one and four objects having one of four shapes and one of four different colors. (See *Figure 17.7*.) The subjects are instructed to pick up the cards, one at a time, and place each of them in one of four piles, according to the card's number, shape, or color. The experimenter does not tell the subjects what the criterion is; he or she simply says "right" or "wrong" after each response. Once the subjects learn to respond appropriately (which usually does not take very long), the experimenter changes the criterion without warning. For example, if the first criterion was number, the second one might be color. People with damage to the dorsolateral prefrontal cortex learn the first task as rapidly as normal subjects do, but they have great difficulty switching their strategy when the criterion changes; they persist with the outmoded strategy. Thus, one of the functions of the dorsolateral prefrontal cortex is related to behavioral flexibility.

Weinberger, Berman, and Zec (1986) tested schizophrenic patients and normal control subjects on a computerized version of the WCST, in which patterns were presented on a color video screen and subjects had to respond by pressing one of four switches. While the subjects were performing the task, the investigators measured their regional cerebral blood flow.

The investigators found that the schizophrenic patients performed poorly on the task, just as subjects with lesions of the dorsolateral prefrontal cor-

FIGURE 17.8

Maps of regional cerebral blood flow. The upper two scans are averages from a group of normal subjects, and the lower two scans are averages from a group of schizophrenic subjects. During the scan the subjects were attempting to solve two different problems ("Number" and "WCS"). The schizophrenic subjects fail to show an increased rate of blood flow in the dorsolateral prefrontal cortex during the "WCS" task.

(From Weinberger, D.R., Berman, K.F., and Zec, R.F. *Archives of General Psychiatry,* 1986, *43,* 113-124. Reprinted by permission.)

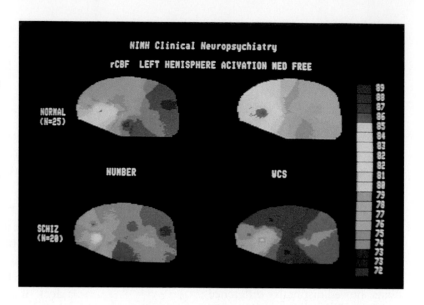

tex do. In addition, whereas the lateral prefrontal cortex of the normal subjects showed an increased blood flow during the card-sorting task, the cortex of the schizophrenic subjects did not. The results are shown in Figure 17.8. The two scans on the left were made while the subjects were performing a simple number-matching task that is not impaired by lesions of the dorsolateral prefrontal cortex; as you can see, the blood flow is similar for both groups. The two scans on the right were made during the sorting task; in this case only the normal subjects showed signs of increased activation of the lateral prefrontal cortex. (See *Figure 17.8.*)

These results have been confirmed by other investigators. For example, Rubin et al. (1991) found poor performance on the WCST and decreased blood flow in the prefrontal cortex in patients who had just been diagnosed as having schizophrenia, and Buchsbaum et al. (1991) found evidence for decreased glucose metabolism in this region.

What might cause the "hypofrontality" that so many studies have observed? Weinberger and his colleagues suggest that the primary cause may be subcortical lesions or abnormalities that reduce the dopaminergic input to the prefrontal cortex. Dopamine does indeed play an important role in the normal functioning of the prefrontal cortex; studies with monkeys indicate that destruction of the dopaminergic input to the prefrontal cortex lowers its metabolic rate and leads to cognitive dys-

functions (Brozowski et al., 1979; Schwartzman et al., 1987). In addition, Daniel et al. (1991) found that when they administered amphetamine to schizophrenic patients, the blood flow in their dorsolateral prefrontal cortex increased—and their performance on the WCST improved.

Weinberger et al. (1992) studied a group of monozygotic twins discordant for schizophrenia. Each schizophrenic subject, then, had a genetically identical control with which comparisons could be made. The investigators took MRI scans and PET scans of the subjects' brains in order to measure structural brain abnormalities and differences in regional cerebral blood flow. They found that, relative to their nonschizophrenic siblings, the schizophrenic subjects had smaller hippocampal formations and showed lower metabolic activity in the dorsolateral prefrontal cortex while performing the WCST. In addition, the decreased volume of the hippocampal formation was strongly correlated with the hypofrontality. Studies in laboratory animals have shown that the hippocampal formation sends efferent axons to the ventral tegmental area, the source of the dopaminergic input to the prefrontal cortex. Perhaps the abnormality in the hippocampal formation results in decreased activity of the dopaminergic projection to the prefrontal cortex, which accounts for the hypofrontality.

What relation does hypoactivity of the prefrontal cortex have to the positive symptoms of schizophrenia, which appear to be produced by *hyperactivity* of dopaminergic synapses in the nucleus accumbens? Weinberger, Berman, and Zec (1986) suggest that the hypoactivity of the prefrontal cortex causes an excitation of the mesolimbic dopamine system. In fact, several studies with rats have found that destruction of the dopaminergic input to the prefrontal cortex by injection of 6-HD *increases* the activity of dopaminergic terminals in the nucleus accumbens and the neostriatum (Pycock, Kerwin, and Carter, 1980; Haroutunian, Knott, and Davis, 1988).

Grace (1991) suggests a specific hypothesis for the link between hypofrontality and the increased activity in the nucleus accumbens. The prefrontal cortex communicates with the nucleus accumbens by means of axons that secrete glutamate. Hypofrontality results in a low rate of activity of these axons, which, along with dopaminergic terminals, form synapses on dendritic spines in the nucleus accumbens. Grace hypothesizes that the low activity of the glutamergic terminals results in a low tonic release of dopamine, which causes a compensatory increase in the sensitivity of postsynaptic dopamine receptors. Then when the dopaminergic neurons in the mesolimbic pathway are activated by environmental events, the neurons in the nucleus accumbens overreact—and lead to the occurrence of the positive symptoms of schizophrenia. (See *Figure 17.9.*)

A study by Kimura, Nomikos, and Svensson (1993) supports Grace's hypothesis. These investigators implanted microdialysis probes in the brains of rats to measure the release of dopamine in the nucleus accumbens. They found that administering an atypical antipsychotic drug, amperozide, increased the tonic release of dopamine in the nucleus accumbens of rats. However, when they subsequently gave the rats an injection of potent dopamine agonists (amphetamine or cocaine), the animals showed much smaller behavioral responses than control animals that were not pretreated with amperozide. Thus, increased *tonic* secretion of dopamine in the nucleus accumbens does appear to decrease the behavioral effectiveness of *phasic* secretion of dopamine in this region.

In the interest of clarity and brevity, I have been selective in my review of research on schizophrenia.

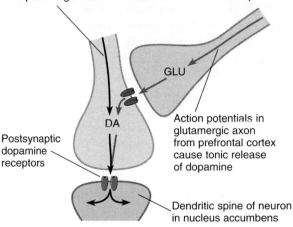

Activating or reinforcing events produce action potentials in dopaminergic axon and cause tonic release of dopamine

GLU

DA

Action potentials in glutamergic axon from prefrontal cortex cause tonic release of dopamine

Postsynaptic dopamine receptors

Dendritic spine of neuron in nucleus accumbens

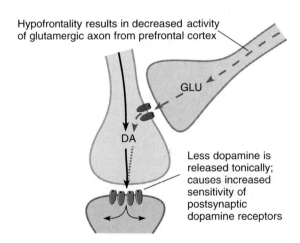

Hypofrontality results in decreased activity of glutamergic axon from prefrontal cortex

GLU

DA

Less dopamine is released tonically; causes increased sensitivity of postsynaptic dopamine receptors

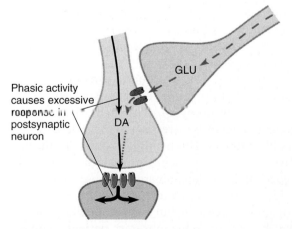

GLU

Phasic activity causes excessive response in postsynaptic neuron

DA

FIGURE 17.9

A hypothetical explanation for the relation between hypofrontality and the positive symptoms of schizophrenia.

This puzzling and serious disorder has stimulated many ingenious hypotheses and much research. Some hypotheses have been proved wrong; others have not yet been adequately tested. Possibly, future research will find that all of these hypotheses (including the ones I have discussed) are incorrect, or one that I have not mentioned is correct. However, I am impressed with recent research, and I believe that we have real hope of finding the causes of schizophrenia in the near future. With the discovery of the causes we can hope for the discovery of methods of prevention.

INTERIM SUMMARY

Researchers have made considerable progress in the past few years in their study of the physiology of mental disorders, but many puzzles still remain. Schizophrenia consists of positive and negative symptoms, the former involving the presence of an unusual behavior and the latter involving the absence of a normal behavior. Because schizophrenia is at least somewhat heritable, it appears to have a biological basis. But evidence indicates that not all cases are caused by heredity, and some people who appear to carry a "schizophrenia gene" do not become schizophrenic. The location of this gene (if, indeed, a single gene exists) may be at the end of the X chromosome, in the pseudoautosomal segment. Deficits in the ability to track smoothly moving objects with the eyes may be a genetic marker for schizophrenia. Schizophrenia also has nongenetic causes, such as obstetrical complications that produce brain damage.

The dopamine hypothesis—inspired by the findings that dopamine antagonists alleviate the positive symptoms of schizophrenia and that dopamine agonists increase or even produce them—is still dominant. This hypothesis states that the positive symptoms of schizophrenia are caused by hyperactivity of dopaminergic synapses. There is no evidence that an abnormally large amount of dopamine is released, but some studies indicate that the brains of schizophrenic patients contain increased numbers of D_2 dopamine receptors in the neostriatum. However, some investigators have suggested that the increase is caused by the administration of antipsychotic drugs. It is still possible that an abnormality exists in the dopaminergic systems that project to the nucleus accumbens. The involvement of dopamine in reinforcement could plausibly explain the positive effects of schizophrenia; inappropriately reinforced thoughts could persist and become delusions. Paranoid thoughts may be caused by dopaminergic activation of the central nucleus of the amygdala, a region involved in negative emotional responses.

That some patients are not helped by antipsychotic drugs poses an unsolved problem for the dopamine hypothesis. In addition, these drugs cause parkinsonian side effects (usually temporary) and, in some cases, tardive dyskinesia. An atypical antipsychotic drug, clozapine, binds with dopamine D_4 receptors and decreases dopaminergic activity in the nucleus accumbens and not in the neostriatum. Thus, this drug does not produce parkinsonian side effects and, one hopes, will not produce tardive dyskinesia. In addition, the drug reduces the symptoms of some patients who are not helped by traditional antipsychotic medication.

CT and MRI scans indicate that brain damage—especially in the frontal lobes, medial temporal lobes, and diencephalon—is associated with the negative symptoms of schizophrenia. Studies of the epidemiology of schizophrenia suggest that, as in multiple sclerosis, one of the causes may be an autoimmune process produced by an infection in people who are genetically vulnerable. In addition, the disorder may be caused by obstetrical problems or by toxins (such as those produced by viral infections) that are present during pregnancy. The seasonality effect and the increased incidence of schizophrenic births after influenza epidemics provides evidence for problems with prenatal development. A study of NADPH-d, an enzyme found in some neurons, provides direct evidence of developmental abnormalities in the brains of schizophrenics. Further evidence is provided by comparisons of the fingerprints of twins concordant and discordant for schizophrenia.

Some evidence suggests that the hypofrontality responsible for at least some of the negative symptoms of schizophrenia may be caused by decreased dopaminergic activity in the prefrontal cortex. Abnormalities in the hippocampal formation may be responsible for this decreased dopaminergic activity. And the hypofrontality may cause increased dopaminergic activity in the nucleus accumbens, thus producing positive symptoms. The mechanism for this increase may be decreased tonic release of dopamine, which causes a compensatory increase in reactivity to dopamine when it is phasically released.

MAJOR AFFECTIVE DISORDERS

AFFECT, AS A NOUN, REFERS TO FEELINGS OR emotions. Just as the primary symptom of schizophrenia is disordered thoughts, the **major affective disorders** (also called *mood disorders*) are characterized by disordered feelings.

Description

Feelings and emotions are essential parts of human existence; they represent our evaluation of the events in our lives. In a very real sense, feelings and emotions are what human life is all about. The emotional state of most of us reflects what is happening to us: Our feelings are tied to events in the real world, and they are usually the result of reasonable assessments of the importance these events have for our lives. But for some people, affect becomes divorced from reality. These people have feelings of extreme elation (*mania*) or despair (*depression*) that are not justified by events in their lives. For example, depression that accompanies the loss of a loved one is normal, but depression that becomes a way of life—and will not respond to the sympathetic effort of friends and relatives or even to psychotherapy—is pathological.

Almost everyone experiences some depression from time to time, mostly caused by events that sadden us. This form of depression is called **reactive depression** because it occurs as a reaction to events in the world. The form of depression seen in the major affective disorders is quite different. It seems to be an intrinsic characteristic of the person rather than a reaction to the environment; thus, it is referred to as **endogenous depression.**

There are two principal types of major affective disorders. The first type is characterized by alternating periods of mania and depression—a condition called **bipolar disorder.** This disorder afflicts men and women in approximately equal numbers. Episodes of mania can last a few days or several months, but they usually take a few weeks to run their course. The episodes of depression that follow generally last three times as long as the mania. The second type is **unipolar depression,** or depression without mania. This depression may be continuous and unremitting or, more typically, may come in episodes. Unipolar depression strikes women two to three times more often than men. Mania without periods of depression sometimes occurs, but it is rare.

Severely depressed people usually feel extremely unworthy and have strong feelings of guilt. The affective disorders are dangerous; a person who suffers from endogenous depression runs a considerable risk of death by suicide. Depressed people have very little energy, and they move and talk slowly, sometimes becoming almost torpid. At other times they may pace around restlessly and aimlessly. They may cry a lot. They are unable to experience pleasure; they lose their appetite for food and sex. Their sleep is disturbed; they usually fall asleep readily but awaken early and find it difficult to get to sleep again. (In contrast, people with reactive depression usually have trouble falling asleep and do not awaken early.) Even their body functions become depressed; they often become constipated, and secretion of saliva decreases.

Episodes of mania are characterized by a sense of euphoria that does not seem to be justified by circumstances. The diagnosis of mania is partly a matter of degree—one would not call exuberance and a zest for life pathological. People with mania usually exhibit nonstop speech and motor activity. They flit from topic to topic and often have delusions, but they lack the severe disorganization that is seen in schizophrenia. They are usually full of their own importance and often become angry or defensive if they are contradicted. Frequently, they go for long periods without sleep, working furiously on projects that are often unrealistic. (Sometimes, their work is fruitful; George Frideric Handel wrote *The Messiah*, one of the masterpieces of choral music, during one of his periods of mania.)

Heritability

The tendency to develop an affective disorder appears to be heritable. (See Moldin, Reich, and Rice, 1991, for a review.) For example, Rosenthal (1971) found that close relatives of people who suffer from affective psychoses are ten times more likely to develop these disorders than people without afflicted relatives. Of course, this study does not prove that genetic mechanisms are operating; relatives have similar environments as well as similar genes. However, Gershon et al. (1976) found that if one member of a set of monozygotic twins was afflicted with an affective disorder, the likelihood that the other twin was similarly afflicted was 69 percent. In contrast, the concordance rate for dizygotic twins was only 13 percent. Furthermore, the concordance rate for monozygotic twins appears to be the same whether the twins were raised together or apart (Price, 1968). The heritability of the affective disorders implies that they have a physiological basis.

For a while, it looked as if the locus of a gene responsible for bipolar disorder had been found. Egeland et al. (1987) studied a large Amish family that contained several members with bipolar disorder. They correlated the presence or absence of the disorder with the presence or absence of various proteins in the blood that are controlled by genes with known locations. They concluded that the gene appeared to be located at the tip of the short arm of chromosome 11. However, several other studies failed to confirm their results in other families (Byerley et al., 1989); and finally, after having found more family members and reanalyzing the data, Kelsoe et al. (1989) concluded that the earlier study was mistaken.

Physiological Treatments

There are four effective biological treatments for endogenous depression: monoamine oxidase (MAO) inhibitors, drugs that inhibit reuptake of norepinephrine and serotonin, electroconvulsive therapy (ECT), and sleep deprivation. (Sleep deprivation is discussed in a later section.) Bipolar disorder is effectively be treated by lithium salts. The response of these disorders to medical treatment provides additional evidence that they have a physi-

ological basis. Furthermore, the fact that lithium is very effective in treating bipolar affective disorders but not unipolar depression suggests that there is a fundamental difference between these two illnesses.

Prior to the 1950s there was no effective drug treatment for depression. In the late 1940s clinicians noticed that some drugs used for treating tuberculosis seemed to elevate the patient's mood. Researchers subsequently found that a derivative of these drugs, iproniazid, reduced symptoms of psychotic depression (Crane, 1957). Iproniazid inhibits the activity of MAO, which destroys excess monoamine transmitter substances within terminal buttons. Thus, the drug increases the release of dopamine, norepinephrine, and serotonin. Other MAO inhibitors were soon discovered. Unfortunately, MAO inhibitors can have harmful side effects. The most common problem is the *cheese effect*. Many foods (for example, cheese, yogurt, wine, yeast breads, chocolate, and various fruits and nuts) contain *pressor amines*—substances similar to catecholamines. Normally, these amines are deactivated by MAO, which is present in the blood and in other tissues of the body. But a person who is being treated with an MAO inhibitor may suffer a serious sympathetic reaction after eating food containing pressor amines. The pressor amines simulate the effects of increased activity of the sympathetic nervous system, increasing blood pressure and heart rate. The reaction can raise blood pressure enough to produce intracranial bleeding or cardiovascular collapse.

Fortunately, another class of antidepressant drugs was soon discovered that did not produce a cheese effect: the **tricyclic antidepressants.** These drugs were found to inhibit the reuptake of 5-HT and norepinephrine by terminal buttons. By retarding reuptake, the drugs keep the neurotransmitter in contact with the postsynaptic receptors, thus prolonging the postsynaptic potentials. Thus, both the MAO inhibitors and the tricyclic antidepressant drugs are monoaminergic agonists. Since the discovery of the tricyclic antidepressants, other drugs have been discovered that have similar effects.

The third biological treatment for depression has an interesting history. Earlier in this century, a physician named von Meduna noted that psychotic patients who were also subject to epileptic seizures showed improvement immediately after each attack.

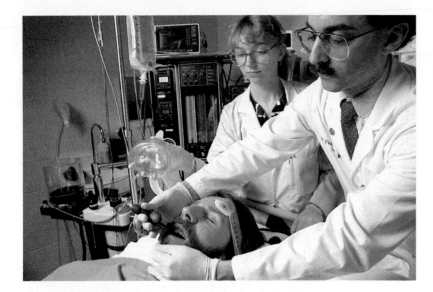

FIGURE 17.10

A patient being prepared for electro-convulsive therapy.
(McIntyre/Photo Researchers, Inc.)

He reasoned that the violent storm of neural activity in the brain that constitutes an epileptic seizure somehow improved the patients' mental condition. He developed a way to produce seizures by administering a drug, but the procedure was dangerous to the patient. In 1937 Ugo Cerletti, an Italian psychiatrist, developed a less dangerous method for producing seizures. He had previously learned that the local slaughterhouse applied a jolt of electricity to animals' heads to stun them before killing them. The electricity appeared to produce a seizure that resembled an epileptic attack. He decided to attempt to use electricity to induce a seizure more safely.

Cerletti tried the procedure on dogs and found that an electrical shock to the skull did produce a seizure and that the animals recovered with no apparent ill effects. He then used the procedure on humans and found it to be safer than the chemical treatment previously used. As a result, **electroconvulsive therapy** (ECT) became a common treatment for mental illness. Although it was originally used for a variety of disorders, including schizophrenia, we now know that its usefulness is limited to depression. (See *Figure 17.10.*)

A depressed patient does not respond immediately to treatment with antidepressant drugs; improvement in symptoms is not usually seen before two to three weeks of drug treatment. In contrast, the effects of ECT are more rapid. A few seizures induced by ECT can often snap a person out of a deep depression within a few days. Although prolonged and excessive use of ECT causes brain damage, resulting in long-lasting impairments in memory (Squire, 1974), the judicious use of ECT during the interim period before antidepressant drugs become effective has undoubtedly saved the lives of some suicidal patients (Baldessarini, 1977). In addition, some severely depressed people are not helped by drug therapy; for them, occasional ECT is the only effective treatment.

The therapeutic effect of **lithium,** the drug used to treat bipolar affective disorders, is very rapid. This drug, which is administered in the form of lithium carbonate, is most effective in treating the manic phase of a bipolar affective disorder; once the mania is eliminated, depression usually does not follow (Gerbino, Oleshansky, and Gershon, 1978). Many clinicians and investigators have referred to lithium as psychiatry's wonder drug: It does not suppress normal feelings of emotions, but it leaves patients able to feel and express joy and sadness to events in their lives. Similarly, it does not impair intellectual processes; many patients have received the drug continuously for years without any apparent ill effects (Fieve, 1979). Reifman and Wyatt (1980) calculated that during a ten-year period in the United States lithium treatment saved at least $4 billion in treatment costs and lost productivity.

One of the most serious difficulties in treating bipolar disorder is compliance with the prescribed treatment. After taking lithium for a while, some patients find that they miss the intense pleasure they felt during their manic periods. Some of them apparently tell themselves that now that they are "cured," they can stop taking their medication—and when they do, their cycling begins again. Then the pain of the depression usually motivates them to start taking the drug again. Several studies suggest that strong efforts should be made to convince patients with bipolar disorder not to discontinue their medication, because occasionally the drug is no longer effective after a relapse (Suppes et al., 1991; Post et al., 1992).

Investigators have not yet discovered the pharmacological effects of lithium that are responsible for its ability to eliminate mania. Some suggest that the drug stabilizes the population of certain classes of neurotransmitter receptors in the brain, thus preventing wide shifts in neural sensitivity. A later section will describe research with other drugs that suggests the relevance of receptor sensitivity to the treatment of the affective disorders.

Role of Monoamines

The fact that depression can be treated effectively with MAO inhibitors and drugs that inhibit the reuptake of norepinephrine suggested the **monoamine hypothesis:** Depression is caused by insufficient activity of monoaminergic neurons. Because the symptoms of depression do not respond to potent dopamine agonists such as amphetamine or cocaine, most investigators have focused their research efforts on the other two monoamines: norepinephrine and serotonin.

The Monoamine Hypothesis

As we saw, the dopamine hypothesis of schizophrenia receives support from the fact that dopamine agonists can produce the symptoms of schizophrenia. Similarly, the monoamine hypothesis of depression receives support from the fact that depression can be caused by monoamine antagonists. Many hundreds of years ago, an alkaloid extract from *Rauwolfia serpentina,* a shrub of Southeast Asia, was found to be useful for treating snakebite, circulatory disorders, and insanity. Modern research has confirmed that the alkaloid, now called reserpine,

has both an antipsychotic effect and a hypotensive effect (that is, it lowers blood pressure). The effect on blood pressure precludes its use in treating schizophrenia, but the drug is still occasionally used to treat patients with high blood pressure.

Reserpine has a serious side effect: It can cause depression. In fact, in the early years of its use as a hypotensive agent, up to 15 percent of the people who received it became depressed (Sachar and Baron, 1979). Reserpine acts on the membrane of synaptic vesicles in the terminal buttons of monoaminergic neurons, making the membranes "leaky," so that the neurotransmitters are lost from the vesicles and are destroyed by MAO. Thus, the drug serves as a potent norepinephrine, dopamine, and serotonin antagonist. The pharmacological and behavioral effects of reserpine complement the pharmacological and behavioral effects of the drugs used to treat depression—MAO inhibitors and drugs that block the reuptake of norepinephrine and serotonin. That is, a monoamine antagonist produces depression, whereas monoamine agonists alleviate it.

Several studies have found that suicidal depression is related to decreased CSF levels of **5-HIAA** (5-hydroxyindoleacetic acid), a metabolite of serotonin that is produced when serotonin is destroyed by MAO. A decreased level of 5-HIAA implies that less 5-HT (serotonin) is being produced and released in the brain. Träskmann et al. (1981) found that CSF levels of 5-HIAA in people who had attempted suicide were significantly lower than those of controls. In a follow-up study of depressed and potentially suicidal patients, 20 percent of those with levels of 5-HIAA below the median subsequently killed themselves, whereas none of those with levels above the median committed suicide. More recent studies have confirmed these results (Roy, De Jong, and Linnoila, 1989).

Sedvall et al. (1980) analyzed the CSF of healthy, nondepressed volunteers. The families of subjects with unusually low levels of 5-HIAA were more likely to include people with depression. The results suggest that serotonin metabolism or release is genetically controlled and is linked to depression. Thus, these findings clearly support the monoamine hypothesis.

As we saw in Chapter 11, the activity of serotonergic neurons appears to inhibit aggression. Some investigators have suggested that this role is consistent with the findings of Sedvall et al. Suicide can be seen as a form of aggression—self-directed aggression (Siever et al., 1991); thus, the decreased CSF levels of 5-HIAA may simply indicate a lower level of impulse control. Of course, the fact that serotonin is involved in aggression does not rule out the possibility that low levels of serotonin are for depressed mood, as well.

Delgado et al. (1990) used a different approach to study the role of serotonin in depression. They observed depressed patients who were receiving antidepressant medication and were currently feeling well. For one day, they had the patients follow a low-tryptophan diet (for example, salad, corn, cream cheese, and a gelatin dessert). Then the next day, the patients drank an amino acid "cocktail" that contained no tryptophan. The uptake of amino acids through the blood-brain barrier is accomplished by amino acid transporters. Because the patients' blood level of tryptophan was very low and that of the other amino acids was high, very little tryptophan found its way into the brain, and the level of tryptophan in the brain fell drastically. As you will recall, tryptophan is the precursor of 5-HT, or serotonin. Thus, the treatment lowered the level of serotonin in the brain.

Delgado and his colleagues found that the tryptophan depletion caused most of the patients to relapse back into depression. Then when they began eating a normal diet again, they recovered. These results strongly suggest that the therapeutic effect of at least some antidepressant drugs depends on the availability of serotonin in the brain.

Long-Term Changes in Receptor Sensitivity

Although researchers have known for a long time that depression does not respond immediately to antidepressant medication, most studies of their pharmacological effects in laboratory animals have investigated the acute, immediate effects of these drugs. But perhaps the *acute* effects of the drugs are not the ones that relieve the symptoms of depression. Instead, the relevant effects may take two to three weeks to develop, because the delay in symptom reduction takes this long.

Sulser and Sanders-Bush (1989) reviewed research that suggests that the long-term effect of most, if not all, biological treatments for depression causes a **subsensitivity** of postsynaptic noradrenergic ß receptors.

The subsensitivity, which is just the opposite of supersensitivity, appears to be caused by a decreased number of ß receptors. Table 17.1 illustrates some of the drugs and other biological treatments that are effective in reducing the symptoms of depression and that also reduce the sensitivity of ß receptors. To be effective, these treatments must be applied chronically, over many days; subsensitivity is not produced by short-term treatment. (See *Table 17.1.*)

As you can see, a wide variety of antidepressant treatments—drugs that block the reuptake of 5-HT

TABLE 17.1

Antidepressant Treatments That Produce Subsensitivity of Noradranergic β Receptors

Antidepressant drugs that block reuptake of 5-HT and norepinephrine (NE)

Chlorimipramine	Amitriptyline
Imipramine	

Antidepressant drugs that predominantly block reuptake of NE

Desipramine
Nisoxetine

Antidepressant drugs that predominantly block reuptake of 5-HT

Fluvoxamine	Fluoxetine
Sertraline	

Antidepressant drugs that block MAO

Pargyline	Tranylcypromine
Nialamide	Moclobemide

Antidepressant drugs that act as GABA agonists

Fengabine
Bupropion

Antidepressant drugs that act as phosphodiesterase inhibitors

Rolipram

Electroconvulsive therapy

REM sleep deprivation

Source: Adapted from Sulser, F., in *Typical and Atypical Antidepressants: Molecular Mechanisms,* edited by E. Costa and G. Racagni. New York: Raven Press, 1982; and Sulser, F., and Sanders-Bush, E., in *Tribute to B.B. Brodie,* Raven Press, 1989.

or norepinephrine, MAO inhibitors, GABA agonists, a phosphodiesterase inhibitor, ECT, and sleep deprivation—affect the sensitivity of noradrenergic ß receptors. (I will discuss the significance of sleep deprivation later.) The change in sensitivity of the noradrenergic ß receptors takes about as much time as the therapeutic response does. Electroconvulsive therapy, the treatment that produces the quickest therapeutic effects, also produces the fastest change in sensitivity of ß receptors. (The mechanism by which ECT affects these receptors is not known.) In addition, reserpine, which can produce symptoms of depression, makes ß receptors *super*sensitive (Leonard, 1982).

Little can be said about the physiological relevance of the subsensitivity of ß receptors. For example, desipramine acts acutely as a noradrenergic agonist, but its chronic effect would appear to classify it as a noradrenergic antagonist. What, then, is the net effect of this drug on the noradrenergic synapses? Are antidepressant treatments correcting overactivity or underactivity of noradrenergic synapses? We still do not have enough information to answer these questions.

As we saw in the previous subsection, serotonin appears to play an important role in depression. In fact, there is evidence for an important link between serotonergic and noradrenergic neurons. Sulser and Sanders-Bush (1989) note that several studies have shown that destruction of 5-HT neurons or the blocking of 5-HT synthesis with injections of PCPA prevents antidepressant drugs from making noradrenergic ß receptors become less sensitive. Thus, the therapeutic effects of antidepressant treatment appear to require the participation of serotonergic neurons.

There is some evidence that long-term treatment for depression may cause increases in the sensitivity of 5-HT receptors as well as decreases in the sensitivity of noradrenergic ß receptors. Chaput et al. (1991) administered ECT every other day for fourteen days to one group of rats and gave other groups of rats various antidepressant drugs or a placebo for twenty-one days. They used various electrophysiological procedures (including iontophoretic application of serotonin) to test the sensitivity of presynaptic and postsynaptic 5-HT receptors. They found that tricyclic antidepressants (which block the reuptake of both norepinephrine and serotonin)

and ECT treatment both increased the sensitivity of postsynaptic 5-HT$_{1A}$ receptors, whereas selective blockers of serotonin increased serotonergic activity by reducing the sensitivity of inhibitory 5-HT autoreceptors in the terminal buttons.

As you learned in Chapter 14, reinforcement involves the release of dopamine in the nucleus accumbens. Because inability to experience pleasure is one of the most important symptoms of depression, we might expect to find some involvement of dopaminergic neurons in this disorder. However, dopaminergic agonists such as cocaine and amphetamine do not relieve depression; they simply make depressed patients become agitated. In addition, Reynecke et al. (1989) found that chronic treatment with an antidepressant drug had no effect on the sensitivity of D$_1$ or D$_2$ dopamine receptors in the nucleus accumbens; nor did it affect the release of dopamine by electrical stimulation. Therefore, although we do not yet have enough evidence to rule out a role for dopamine in depression, only serotonin and norepinephrine have been shown to play a role.

Evidence for Brain Abnormalities

As we saw earlier in this chapter, many studies have found structural and biochemical abnormalities in the brains of schizophrenic patients. A few studies have reported abnormalities in patients with affective disorders, but the evidence is still inconclusive. Andreasen et al. (1990) note that four out of nine studies of depressed patients found evidence for increased ventricular size, and three out of six studies of patients with bipolar disorder found similar effects. Their own study found no differences in depressed patients and found increased ventricular size in male patients with bipolar disorder but not in female patients. Thus, if affective disorders are associated with brain damage, the effect does not appear to be a large one.

Two recent studies with PET scanners have found evidence for increased regional metabolic activity in depressed patients; Drevets et al. (1992) found an increase in the prefrontal cortex and the amygdala, and Wu et al. (1992) found an increase in the anterior cingulate cortex. Further studies will be needed to determine whether these findings can be replicated.

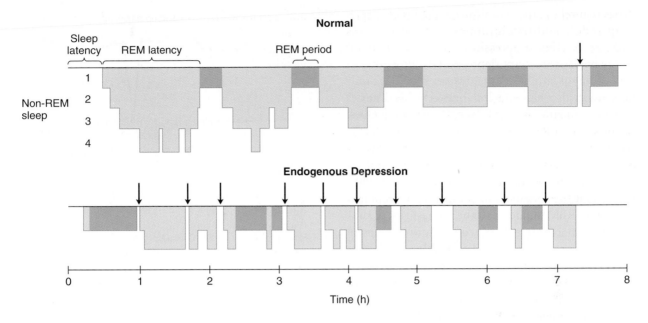

FIGURE 17.11

Patterns of the stages of sleep of a normal subject and of a patient with endogenous depression.
Note the reduced sleep latency, reduced REM latency, reduction in slow-wave sleep (stages 3 and
4), and general fragmentation of sleep (arrows) in the depressed patient.

(From Gillin, J.C., and Borbély, A.A. *Trends in Neurosciences*, 1985, *8*, 537–542. Reprinted with permission.)

Role of Circadian Rhythms

One of the most prominent symptoms of depression is disordered sleep. The sleep of people with endogenous depression tends to be shallow; slow-wave delta sleep (stages 3 and 4) is reduced and stage 1 is increased. Sleep is fragmented; people tend to waken frequently, especially toward the morning. In addition, REM sleep occurs earlier, the first half of the night contains a higher proportion of REM periods, and REM sleep contains an increased number of rapid eye movements (Kupfer, 1976; Vogel et al., 1980). (See *Figure 17.11.*)

REM Sleep Deprivation

One of the most effective antidepressant treatments is sleep deprivation, either total or selective. Selective deprivation of REM sleep, accomplished by monitoring people's EEG and awakening them whenever they show signs of REM sleep, alleviates depression (Vogel et al., 1975; Vogel et al., 1990). The thera-

peutic effect, like that of the antidepressant medications, occurs slowly, over the course of several weeks. Some patients show long-term improvement even after the deprivation is discontinued; thus, it is a practical as well as an effective treatment. In addition, regardless of their specific pharmacological effects, other treatments for depression suppress REM sleep, delaying its onset and decreasing its duration. These facts suggest that REM sleep and mood might somehow be causally related.

Scherschlicht et al. (1982) examined the effects of twenty antidepressant drugs on the sleep cycles of cats and found that all of them profoundly reduced REM sleep and most of them increased slow-wave sleep. In an extensive review of the literature Vogel et al. (1990) found that all drugs that suppressed REM sleep (and produced a rebound effect when their administration was discontinued) acted as antidepressants. These results suggest that the primary effect of antidepressant medication may be to suppress REM sleep, and the changes in mood may be a result of this suppression. However, some drugs that relieve the symptoms of depression (such as iprindole and trimipramine) do not suppress REM sleep. Thus, suppression of REM sleep cannot be the *only* way that antidepressant drugs work.

Studies of families with a history of endogenous depression also suggest a link between this disorder and abnormalities in REM sleep. For example, Giles, Roffwarg, and Rush (1987) found that first-degree relatives of people with depression are likely to show a short REM sleep latency, even if they have not yet had an episode of depression. Giles et al. (1988) found that the members of these families who had the lowest REM latency had the highest risk of subsequently becoming depressed. Abnormalities in REM sleep are seen early in life; Coble et al. (1988) found that newborn infants of mothers with a history of endogenous depression showed patterns of REM sleep that were different from those of the infants of mothers without such a history.

Vogel et al. (1990) have developed what they believe to be an animal model of depression, which may be useful in studying the physiological basis of this disorder. They gave young rats injections of clomipramine (an antidepressant drug that blocks the reuptake of 5-HT) twice a day from age eight days to twenty-one days. This early treatment appears to have affected the development of the brain; perhaps, the authors suggest, it permanently decreased the sensitivity of postsynaptic serotonin receptors. Later, when the rats reached maturity, they showed many of the symptoms of endogenous depression: decreased sexual behavior, increased irritability, and decreased pleasure-seeking behavior (specifically, decreased willingness to work for reinforcing brain stimulation or for a taste of sucrose). The animals' sleep was also altered; the latency to the first bout of REM sleep was shorter, and the proportion of REM sleep was higher. The animals even responded to antidepressant treatment; imipramine and REM sleep deprivation both increased sexual behavior.

Total Sleep Deprivation

Total sleep deprivation also has an antidepressant effect. Unlike specific deprivation of REM sleep, which takes several weeks to reduce depression, total sleep deprivation produces immediate effects (Wu and Bunney, 1990). Figure 17.12 shows the mood

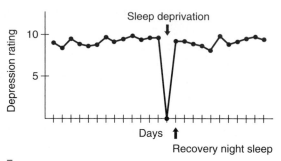

FIGURE 17.12

Changes in the depression rating of a depressed patient produced by a single night's total sleep deprivation.
(From Wu, J.C., and Bunney, W.E. *American Journal of Psychiatry,* Vol. 147, pp. 14-21, 1990. Copyright 1990, the American Psychiatric Association. Reprinted by permission.)

rating of a patient who stayed awake one night; as you can see, the depression was lifted by the sleep deprivation but returned the next day, after a normal night's sleep. (See **Figure 17.12.**)

Wu and Bunney suggest that during sleep a substance is produced that has a *depressogenic* effect. That is, the substance produces depression in a susceptible person. Presumably, this substance is produced in the brain and acts as a neuromodulator. During waking this substance is gradually metabolized and hence inactivated. Some of the evidence for this hypothesis is presented in Figure 17.13. The data are taken from eight different studies (cited by Wu and Bunney, 1990) and show self-ratings of depression of people who did and did not respond to sleep deprivation. (Total sleep deprivation improves the mood of patients with endogenous depression approximately two-thirds of the time.) (See **Figure 17.13.**)

Why do only some people profit from sleep deprivation? This question has not yet been answered, but several studies have shown that it is possible to predict who will profit and who will not (Reinink et al., 1990; Haug, 1992; Riemann et al., 1992). In general, depressed patients whose mood remains stable throughout the day will probably not benefit from sleep depression, whereas those whose mood fluctuates probably will. The patients most likely to respond are those who feel depressed in the morning but then gradually feel better as the day progresses. In these people sleep deprivation appears to prevent the depressogenic effects of sleep from taking place and simply permits the trend to continue. If you examine Figure 17.13, you can see that the responders were already feeling better by the end of the day. This improvement continued through the sleepless night and during the following day. The next night they were permitted to sleep normally, and their depression was back the next morning. As Wu and Bunney note, these data are consistent with the hypothesis that sleep produces a substance with a depressogenic effect. (See *Figure 17.13.*)

An alternative interpretation of the results we just saw is that waking might produce a substance with *antidepressant* effects, which is destroyed during sleep. However, Wu and Bunney point out that several studies have found that for some subjects a short nap reinstates the depression that had been reduced by sleep deprivation. In some cases a nap as short as 90 seconds (timed by EEG monitoring) can eliminate the beneficial effects of sleep depression. They conclude that the simplest hypotheses is that a nap produces a sudden secretion of a substance that causes depression. It seems less likely that a nap could be responsible for the sudden *destruction* of a substance with an antidepressant effect.

The antidepressant effects of REM sleep deprivation and that of total sleep deprivation appear to be different; one is slow and long-lasting, whereas the other is fast and short-lived. In addition, total sleep deprivation can even trigger an episode of mania in patients with bipolar disorder (Wehr, 1992). (Even nondepressed people often report feeling "high" after spending a night without sleep.) The fact that a person's mood can so quickly be altered suggests that it would be worthwhile to look for physiological changes before and after sleep deprivation to try to identify those that may play a role in the control of mood.

Although total sleep deprivation is not a practical method for treating depression (it is impossible to keep people awake indefinitely), several studies suggest that *partial* sleep deprivation can hasten the beneficial effects of antidepressant drugs (Szuba, Baxter, and Fairbanks, 1991; Leibenluft and Wehr, 1992) According to Szuba et al., the best method is to awaken patients at 2:00 A.M. and keep them awake until 9:00 P.M. Some investigators have found that *intermittent* total sleep deprivation (say, twice a week for four weeks) can have beneficial results (Papadimitriou et al., 1993).

Role of Zeitgebers

Yet another phenomenon relates depression to sleep and waking—or, more specifically, to the mechanisms responsible for circadian rhythms. Some people become depressed during the winter season, when days are short and nights are long. The symptoms of this form of depression, called **seasonal affective disorder,** are somewhat different from those of major depression; both forms include lethargy and sleep disturbances, but seasonal depression includes a craving for carbohydrate and an accompanying weight gain. (As you will recall, people with major depression tend to lose their appetite.)

Seasonal affective disorder—but not nonseasonal depression—can be treated by **phototherapy:** exposing people to bright light for several hours a day (Rosenthal et al., 1985; Stinson and Thompson, 1990). As you will recall, circadian rhythms of sleep and wakefulness are controlled by the activity of the suprachiasmatic nucleus of the hypothalamus. Light serves as a *zeitgeber;* that is, it synchronizes the activity of the biological clock to the day/night cycle. It is possible that people with seasonal affective disorder require a stronger-than-normal zeitgeber to reset their biological clock.

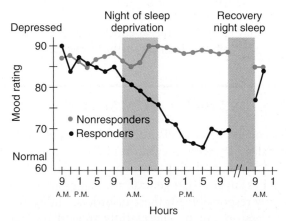

FIGURE 17.13

Mean mood rating of responding and nonresponding patients deprived of one night's sleep as a function of the time of day.

(From Wu, J.C., and Bunney, W.E. *American Journal of Psychiatry,* Vol. 147, pp. 14-21, 1990. Copyright 1990, the American Psychiatric Association. Reprinted by permission.)

Many people are sensitive to seasonal changes in the hours of sunlight and darkness. Ninety-two percent of the respondents to a survey by Kasper et al. (1989a) said that they noticed seasonal changes in their mood, 27 percent reported that these changes caused problems, and 4 percent reported problems severe enough to qualify as a seasonal affective disorder. Kasper et al. (1989b) recruited people with "winter blahs" through newspaper advertisements. They excluded people with evidence of a true seasonal affective disorder and exposed the others to bright light each day. They found that the exposure to bright light improved the mood of the subjects with the "blahs," whereas the mood of normal subjects was not changed. Of course, a placebo effect may have affected the results, but it is difficult to imagine how one could design a double-blind study in which subjects would spend a few hours each day under a bright light without noticing it. In any case, the study suggests that we should consider increasing the level of illumination in the home or workplace. The only negative aspect of the change would seem to be a higher electric bill.

It is possible that all the phenomena discussed in this section are related in a fundamental way. Goodwin, Wirz-Justice, and Wehr (1982) have suggested that all affective disorders are caused by a disturbance in circadian rhythms. As we saw in Chapter 9, several hormonal and biochemical systems (such as the secretion of growth hormone) are linked to various stages of sleep. In a depressed person some of these systems may become uncoupled from the normal control mechanisms, so that specific components of interrelated systems occur at the wrong times. One of the consequences of this uncoupling could be the production of a depressogenic substance during sleep.

Although most people who suffer from seasonal affective disorder become depressed in the winter, some people become depressed in the summer. Even though both disorders are seasonal, they are fundamentally different (Wehr et al., 1991). Whereas patients with winter depression sleep more and show an increased appetite and weight gain, patients with summer depression have insomnia and show a decreased appetite. Furthermore, phototherapy has no effect for summer depression.

Ehlers, Frank, and Kupfer (1988) have proposed an intriguing hypothesis that integrates behavioral and biological evidence. They suggest that some cases of depression may be triggered by the loss of social zeitgebers. They note that in humans social interactions, as well as light, may serve as zeitgebers. For example, people tend to synchronize their daily rhythms to those of their spouses. After loss of a spouse people's daily schedules are usually disrupted, and, of course, many of them become depressed.

Ehlers and her colleagues (1988) suggest that some people may be especially susceptible to the disruptive effects of changes in social contacts and regular daily routines. This susceptibility could represent one of the genetic contributions toward developing mood disorders. Almost everyone becomes depressed, at least for a period of time, after the loss of a loved one. Other events that change a person's daily routine, such as the birth of an infant or the loss of a job, can also precipitate a period of depression. Perhaps people who "spontaneously" become depressed may be reacting to minor changes in their daily routine that disrupt their biological rhythms. Szuba et al. (1992) suggest that depressed patients who "spontaneously" get better as soon as they are admitted to a psychiatric ward—even before therapy begins—may actually be responding to social zeitgebers. The structured daily schedule imposed on the patients by the hospital staff may in itself be therapeutic. Clearly, this interesting hypothesis deserves further research.

‖‖‖‖ INTERIM SUMMARY

The major affective disorders include bipolar affective disorder, with its cyclical episodes of mania and depression, and unipolar depression. Heritability studies suggest that genetic anomalies are at least partly responsible for these disorders. Endogenous depression can be successfully treated by MAO inhibitors, drugs that block the reuptake of norepinephrine and serotonin, electroconvulsive therapy, and sleep deprivation. Bipolar disorder can be successfully treated by lithium salts.

Several lines of evidence suggest that depression is caused by abnormalities in monoamine metabolism, release, or transmission. Low levels of 5-HIAA (a serotonin metabolite) in the cerebrospinal fluid correlate with attempts at suicide. It is possible that these results are related to the effects of serotonin on (self-directed) aggression. Depletion of tryptophan (the precursor of 5-HT) in the brain reverses the therapeutic effects of antidepressant medication, which lends further support to the conclusion that 5-HT plays a role in mood.

Early studies on the physiological effects of antidepressant drugs focused on their acute effects. However, because the effects of antidepressant treatment are delayed, more recent investigations have studied the chronic effects, some of which are quite different. Research indicates that effective treatments for depression reduce the number or sensitivity of postsynaptic noradrenergic ß receptors. This effect occurs only if the system of serotonergic neurons is intact. In addition, long-term treatment for depression may alter the sensitivity of presynaptic or postsynaptic 5-HT receptors.

A few studies have looked for abnormalities in the brains of depressed patients, but the results have been variable. Depression may be associated with increased metabolic activity in the prefrontal cortex, amygdala, and anterior cingulate cortex.

Sleep disturbances are characteristic of affective disorders. In fact, total sleep deprivation rapidly (but temporarily) reduces depression in many people, and selective deprivation of REM sleep does so slowly (but more lastingly). In addition, almost all effective antidepressant treatments suppress REM sleep. Finally, a specific form of depression, seasonal affective disorder, can be treated by exposure to bright light, the zeitgeber that resets the biological clock. Clearly, the mood disorders are somehow linked to biological rhythms, perhaps through their regulatory effects on receptors or neuromodulators. Social zeitgebers may play a particularly important role in human circadian rhythms, and their disruption may precipitate an episode of depression.

New Terms

psychosis p. 542

Schizophrenia

schizophrenia (*SKITS o FREE nee ah*) p. 542

positive symptom p. 542

thought disorder p. 542

delusion p. 542

hallucination p. 542

negative symptom p. 542

chlorpromazine (*klor PROAM a zeen*) p. 546

tardive dyskinesia (*TAR dive diss kin EE zha*) p. 548

supersensitivity p. 549

Major Affective Disorders

major affective disorder p. 557

reactive depression p. 557

endogenous depression p. 557

bipolar disorder p. 557

unipolar depression p. 557

tricyclic antidepressant p. 558

electroconvulsive therapy p. 559

lithium p. 559

monoamine hypothesis p. 560

5-HIAA p. 560

subsensitivity p. 561

seasonal affective disorder p. 565

phototherapy p. 565

Suggested Readings

Depue, R.A., and Iacono, W.G. Neurobehavioral aspects of affective disorders. *Annual Review of Psychology,* 1989, *40,* 457-492.

Goodwin, D.W., and Guze, S.B. *Psychiatric Diagnosis,* 5th ed. New York: Oxford University Press, 1989.

Mednick, S.A. *Fetal Neural Development and Adult Schizophrenia.* New York: Cambridge University Press, 1991.

Miller, R. Schizophrenia as a progressive disorder: Relations to EEG, CT, neuropathological and other evidence. *Progress in Neurobiology,* 1989, *33,* 17-44.

Strange, P.G. *Brain Biochemistry and Brain Disorders.* Oxford: Oxford University Press, 1992.

CHAPTER 18

Mental Disorders: Anxiety Disorders, Autism, and Addiction

Anxiety Disorders
- Panic Disorder
- Obsessive Compulsive Disorder
  Interim Summary

Autistic Disorder
- Description
- Possible Causes
  Interim Summary

Addiction
- Characteristics of Addictive Substances
- Genetics of Addiction
  Interim Summary
  Concluding Remarks

Not too many years ago, the topics contained in this chapter would not be discussed in a book that is concerned with the physiology of behavior. The anxiety disorders and autism were believed to be learned, primarily from parents who did a bad job raising their children. Although there was always at least some support for the suggestion that serious psychoses such as schizophrenia had a biological basis, other mental disorders were almost universally believed to be psychogenic in origin—that is, produced by "psychological" factors. And addiction was seen as a failure of will, caused by hopeless circumstances, a permissive society, and (of course) one's parents.

The tide has turned (or the pendulum has swung back, if you prefer that metaphor). Certainly, a person's family environment, social class, economic status, and similar factors affect the likelihood that he or she will develop a mental disorder and may help or hinder recovery. But physiological factors, including inherited ones and those that adversely affect development or damage the brain, play an important role, too. This chapter is devoted to research on these physiological factors.

ANXIETY DISORDERS

As we have just seen, the affective disorders are characterized by unrealistic extremes of emotion: depression or elation (mania). The **anxiety disorders** are characterized by unrealistic, unfounded fear and anxiety. This section describes two of the anxiety disorders that appear to have biological causes: panic disorder and obsessive compulsive disorder.

Panic Disorder

Description

People with **panic disorder** suffer from episodic attacks of acute anxiety—periods of acute and unremitting terror that grips them for variable lengths of time, from a few seconds to a few hours.

The estimated incidence of panic disorder is between 1 and 2 percent of the population (Robbins et al., 1984). Women are approximately twice as likely as men to suffer from panic disorder. The disorder usually has its onset in young adulthood; it rarely begins after age thirty-five (Woodruff, Guze, and Clayton, 1972).

Panic attacks include many physical symptoms, such as shortness of breath, clammy sweat, irregularities in heartbeat, dizziness, faintness, and feelings of unreality. The victim of a panic attack often feels that he or she is going to die. Anxiety is a normal reaction to many stresses of life, and none of us is completely free from it. In fact, anxiety is undoubtedly useful in causing us to be more alert and to take important things seriously. However, the anxiety we all feel from time to time is obviously different from the intense fear and terror experienced by a person gripped by a panic attack.

Between panic attacks many people with panic disorder suffer from **anticipatory anxiety**—the fear that another panic attack will strike them. This anticipatory anxiety often leads to the development of a serious phobic disorder: **agoraphobia** (*agora* means "open space"). According to the American Psychiatric Association's official *Diagnostic and Statistical Manual III-R*, agoraphobia associated with panic attacks is a fear of "being in places or situations from which escape might be difficult (or embarrassing) or in which help might not be available in the event of a panic attack. . . . As a result of this fear, the person either restricts travel or needs a companion when away from home." Agoraphobia can be severely disabling; some people with this disorder have stayed inside their houses or apartments for years, afraid to venture outside.

Possible Causes

Because the physical symptoms of panic attacks are so overwhelming, many patients reject the suggestion that they have a mental disorder, insisting that their problem is medical. In fact, they may be correct: A considerable amount of evidence suggests that panic disorder may have biological origins. First, the disorder appears to be hereditary; there is a higher concordance rate for the disorder between monozygotic twins than between dizygotic twins

(Slater and Shields, 1969), and almost 30 percent of the first-degree relatives of a person with panic disorder also have panic disorder (Crowe et al., 1983). The pattern of panic disorder within a family tree suggests that the disorder is caused by a single, dominant gene (Crowe et al., 1987).

Panic attacks can be triggered in people with a history of panic disorder by giving them injections of lactic acid (a by-product of muscular activity) or by having them breathe air containing an elevated amount of carbon dioxide (Gaffney et al., 1988; Woods et al., 1988). Cowley and Arana (1990) report that between 40 and 60 percent of people with such a history will react to an injection on a particular occasion. An injection of lactic acid (or one of its salts, sodium lactate) appears to produce physiological arousal, especially in people with panic disorder. Koenigsberg et al. (1992) gave intravenous injections of sodium lactate to subjects while they were sleeping (through catheters that had been inserted earlier). They found that the injection awakened significantly more subjects with panic disorder than normal control subjects.

Some investigators have suggested that people with panic attacks simply have more reactive autonomic nervous systems. That is, a stressful event produces a stronger reaction in the sympathetic branch of the ANS, resulting in an emotional response that the patient interprets as a medical crisis. However, Roth et al. (1992) found no evidence for increased autonomic reactivity. The investigators had normal subjects and subjects with panic disorder breathe air containing 5 percent carbon dioxide. Forty-six percent of the subjects with panic disorder reported having a panic attack; none of the normal subjects did. However, physiological measures of autonomic arousal showed no differences in reactivity between the two groups. These measures did show, though, that even before breathing the carbon dioxide, the subjects with panic disorder showed a higher level of arousal; thus, they appeared to be chronically fearful.

Susceptibility to lactate-induced panic attacks appears to be at least partly heritable. Balon et al. (1989) infused forty-five normal subjects with sodium lactate and found that ten of them had panic attacks. The investigators obtained the family history of their subjects, using an interviewer who did not know which subjects had had panic attacks. They found that over 24 percent of the relatives of the subjects with the panic attacks themselves had a history of anxiety disorders, compared with less than 8 percent in the nonresponders.

Several studies have measured cerebral blood flow by means of PET scans during panic attacks triggered by an injection of lactate. Reiman et al. (1986) found that the activity of the parahippocampal gyrus rose just before the panic attack occurred, and that the activity of the anterior ends of the temporal lobes was elevated during the attack itself. Reiman et al. (1989) produced anticipatory anxiety in normal subjects by leading them to believe that they were about to receive an intensely painful electric shock. (The subjects received a mild shock at the beginning of the experiment to make them believe what the experimenters said, but they did not actually receive a strong shock.) The PET scan showed that in normal subjects, too, anxiety produces increased activity of the temporal poles. (See *Figure 18.1.*)

Reiman and his colleagues note that studies with laboratory animals also suggest that the temporal poles are involved in anxiety reactions. For example, stimulation of this region in monkeys produces autonomic responses and facial expressions indicating fear, and humans with epilepsy caused by a focus in the anterior temporal lobes often report feelings of anxiety and fear just before their seizures occur. Of course, even if the anterior temporal cortex is involved in an anxiety reaction, we have no reason to suspect that panic disorder is caused by an abnormality in this region; the reaction could be provoked by an abnormality elsewhere in the brain. As we saw in Chapter 11, the anterior temporal lobes supply the amygdala with information concerning stimuli with emotional significance—including dangerous ones. Although imaging studies with humans have not yet implicated the amygdala in panic disorder, it is difficult to imagine that it is not involved, given the importance of this structure in negative emotional responses.

Anxiety disorders are usually treated by a combination of behavior therapy and a benzodiazepine. As we saw in Chapter 3, benzodiazepines have

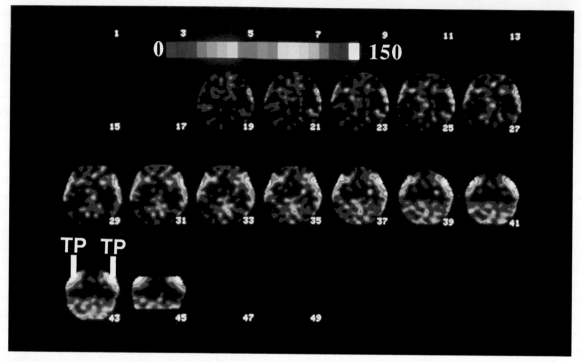

FIGURE 18.1

PET scans of regional blood flow during anticipatory anxiety in normal patients awaiting a painful shock (which was not delivered). The scans are sequential horizontal sections, with rostral toward the top. The increased activity of the anterior temporal lobes is marked with the lines labeled TP (temporal pole).

(From Reiman, E.M., Fusselman, M.J., Fox, P.T., and Raichle, M.E. *Science,* 1989, *243,* 1071–1074. Copyright [c] 1989 by the American Association for the Advancement of Science. Reprinted with permission.)

strong *anxiolytic* ("anxiety dissolving") effects. The brain possesses benzodiazepine receptors, which are part of the GABA receptor complex. When a benzodiazepine agonist binds with its receptor, it increases the sensitivity of the GABA binding site and produces an anxiolytic effect. On the other hand, when a benzodiazepine *inverse agonist* occupies the receptor site, it reduces the sensitivity of the GABA binding site and *increases* anxiety. Anxiety disorders, then, might be caused by a diminished number of benzodiazepine receptors or by the secretion of a neuromodulator that acts as an inverse agonist at benzodiazepine receptors.

As we saw in Chapter 17, rats that receive an antidepressant medication (clomipramine) early in life later develop the symptoms of depression, which can be reduced by an antidepressant drug or by REM sleep deprivation. Similarly, fearfulness can be produced in cats by prenatal administration of a benzodiazepine tranquilizer. Marczynski and Urbancic (1988) gave pregnant cats injections of diazepam (Valium) and assessed the fearfulness of the offspring of these cats when they were one year old. They found that the animals showed restlessness and anxiety in novel situations. This fearfulness could be reduced with an injection of diazepam. Afterward, they measured the level of benzodiazepine receptors in the animals' brains and found a decrease in the hypothalamus, frontal cortex, anterior parietal cortex, and midline thalamus. Thus, fearfulness appears to be associated with a decreased number of benzodiazepine receptors and, presumably, lower sensitivity to the endogenous benzodiazepine agonist, whatever that may be.

Two other substances have been implicated in panic disorder: cholecystokinin and serotonin. As we saw in Chapter 13, cholecystokinin (CCK) may play a role in satiety. This peptide is produced by cells in the duodenum and also by neurons in the brain, where it is co-released with neurotransmitters such as dopamine. In a review of the literature Bradwejn et al. (1992) conclude that there is good evidence that CCK may be involved in anxiety. In a double-blind study Bradwejn, Koszycki, and Meterissian (1990) found that an injection of CCK-4 (a form of CCK that crosses the blood-brain barrier) triggered panic attacks in subjects with panic disorder but not in normal controls. A study with rats found that injection of CCK directly into the amygdala causes an anxiety reaction that can be blocked by injection of a benzodiazepine (Csonka et al., 1988).

As we saw earlier in this chapter, serotonin appears to play a role in depression. Evidence suggests that serotonin may play a role in anxiety disorders, too. Even though the symptoms of panic disorder and obsessive compulsive disorder (described in the next section) are different, drugs that serve as serotonin agonists have been successfully used to treat both disorders (Coplan, Gorman, and Klein, 1992). Thus, benzodiazepines, CCK, and serotonin all appear to play a role in anxiety. What this role is and how these chemicals interact are not yet known.

Obsessive Compulsive Disorder

Description

As the name implies, people with an **obsessive compulsive disorder** suffer from **obsessions**—thoughts that will not leave them—and **compulsions**—behaviors that they cannot keep from performing. Obsessions are seen in a variety of mental disorders, including schizophrenia. However, unlike schizophrenics, people with obsessive compulsive disorder recognize that their thoughts and behaviors are senseless and desperately wish that they would go away. Compulsions often become more and more demanding, until they interfere with people's careers and daily lives.

The incidence of obsessive compulsive disorder is 1–2 percent. Females are slightly more likely than males to have this diagnosis. Like panic disorder, obsessive compulsive disorder most commonly begins in young adulthood (Robbins et al., 1984). Cross-cultural studies find that the symptoms of this disorder are similar in various racial and ethnic groups (Akhtar et al., 1975; Khanna and Channabasavanna, 1987; Hinjo et al., 1989). People with this disorder are unlikely to marry, perhaps because of the common obsessional fear of dirt and contamination or because of the shame associated with the rituals they are compelled to perform, which causes them to avoid social contacts (Turner, Beidel, and Nathan, 1985).

Most compulsions fall into one of four categories: *counting, checking, cleaning,* and *avoidance.* For example, people might repeatedly check burners on the stove to see that they are off and windows and locks to be sure that they are locked. Davison and Neale (1974) reported the case of a woman who washed her hands more than five hundred times a day because she feared being contaminated by germs. The hand washing persisted even when her hands became covered with painful sores. Other people meticulously clean their apartment or endlessly wash, dry, and fold their clothes. Some become afraid to leave home because they fear contamination, and they refuse to touch other members of their family. If they do accidentally become "contaminated," they usually have lengthy purification rituals. (See *Table 18.1.*)

Some investigators believe that the compulsive behaviors seen in obsessive compulsive disorder are forms of species-typical behaviors—for example, grooming, cleaning, and attention toward sources of potential danger—that are released from normal control mechanisms by a brain dysfunction (Wise and Rapoport, 1988).

Possible Causes

Evidence is beginning to accumulate suggesting that obsessive compulsive disorder may have a genetic origin. Family studies have found that this disorder is associated with a neurological disorder that appears during childhood (Pauls and Leckman, 1986; Pauls et al., 1986). This disorder, **Tourette's**

Table 18.1	
Reported Obsessions and Compulsions of Child and Adolescent Patients	
Major Presenting Symptoms	**Percent Reporting Symptom at Initial Interview**
Obsession	
Concern or Disgust with bodily wastes or secretions (urine, stool, saliva), dirt, germs, environmental toxins, etc.	43
Fear something terrible might happen (fire, death/illness of loved one, self, or others)	24
Concern or need for symmetry, order, or exactness	17
Scrupulosity (excessive praying or religious concerns out of keeping with patient's background	13
Lucky/unlucky numbers	18
Forbidden or perverse sexual thoughts, images, or impulses	14
Intrusive nonsense sounds, words, or music	11
Compulsion	
Excessive or ritualized hand washing, showering, bathing, toothbrushing, or grooming	85
Reapeating rituals (going in/out of door, up/down from chair, etc.)	51
Checking doors, locks, stove, appliances, car brakes, etc.	46
Cleaning and other rituals to remave contact with contaminants	23
Touching	20
Ordering/arranging	17
Measures to prevent harm to self or others (e.g., hanging clothes a certain way)	16
Counting	18
Hoarding/collecting	11
Miscellaneous rituals (e.g., licking, spitting, special dress pattern)	26

Source: From Rapoport, J. L. *Journal of the American Medical Association,* 1988, *260,* 2888–2890.

syndrome, is characterized by muscular and vocal tics: facial grimaces, squatting, pacing, twirling, barking, sniffing, coughing, grunting, or repeating specific words (especially vulgarities). Leonard et al. (1992a, 1992b) found that many patients with obsessive compulsive disorder had tics and that many patients with Tourette's syndrome showed obsessions and compulsions. Both groups of investigators believe that the two disorders are produced by the same underlying causes, which may be the result of a single, dominant gene. It is not clear why some people with the faulty gene develop Tourette's syndrome early in childhood and others develop obsessive compulsive disorder later in life.

As with schizophrenia, not all cases of obsessive compulsive disorder have a genetic origin; the disorder sometimes occurs after brain damage caused by various means, such as birth trauma, encephalitis, and head trauma (Hollander et al., 1990). In particular, the symptoms appear to be associated with damage to or dysfunction of the basal ganglia, cingulate gyrus, and prefrontal cortex. Several investigators have found that obsessive compulsive disorder sometimes accompanies Huntington's chorea and Sydenham's chorea, both of which involve degeneration of the basal ganglia (Swedo et al., 1989b; Cummings and Cunningham, 1992). Laplane et al. (1989) found that damage to the basal ganglia (caused by anoxia or toxic substances) sometimes leads to obsessive and compulsive symptoms.

Several studies using PET scans have found evidence of increased activity in the frontal lobes and cingulate gyrus (Baxter et al., 1987, 1989; Swedo et al., 1989c; Rubin et al., 1992). Some studies have found evidence of decreased activity in the basal ganglia (consistent with the lesion studies I just cited), while others have reported an *increase*. As we saw in Chapter 11, the prefrontal cortex (particularly the orbitofrontal cortex) and the cingulate cortex are involved in emotional reactions, so it is not surprising to learn that they might be implicated in obsessive compulsive disorder. In fact, some patients with severe obsessive compulsive disorder have been successfully treated with surgical destruction of the cingulum bundle, a group of axons that connects the prefrontal and cingulate cortex with the limbic cortex of the temporal lobe (Ballantine et al., 1987). Obviously, because a brain lesion cannot be undone, these operations are performed only in severe cases, after behavior therapy and drug therapy have been found to be ineffective.

Swedo et al. (1992) used a PET scanner to measure regional cerebral blood flow in patients with obsessive compulsive disorder before they had received drug treatment and again one year later. They found that improvement in a patient's symptoms was correlated with a reduction in the activity of the orbitofrontal cortex. These results provide especially strong evidence that the prefrontal cortex plays an important role in this disorder.

By far, the most effective treatment of obsessive compulsive disorder is drug therapy. To date, three effective drugs have been found: clomipramine, fluoxetine, and fluvoxamine. Although these drugs are also effective antidepressants, their antidepressant action does not seem to be related to their ability to relieve the symptoms of obsessive compulsive dis-

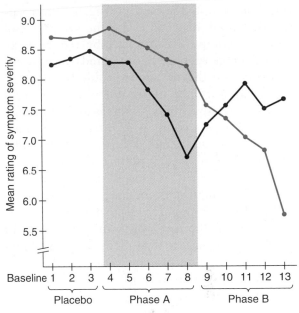

FIGURE 18.2

Mean rating of symptom severity of patients with obsessive compulsive disorder treated with desipramine (DMI) or clomipramine (CMI).

(From Leonard, H.L., Swedo, S.E., Rapoport, J.L., Koby, E.V., Lenane, M.C., Cheslow, D.L., and Hamburger, S.D. *Archives of General Psychiatry*, 1989, 46, 1088–1092. Reprinted with permission.)

order. For example, Leonard et al. (1989) compared the effects of clomipramine and desipramine (an antidepressant drug) on the symptoms of children and adolescents with severe obsessive compulsive disorder. For three weeks all patients received a placebo. Then for five weeks half of them received clomipramine (CMI) and the other half received desipramine (DMI), on a double-blind basis. At the end of that time the drugs were switched. As Figure 18.2 shows, CMI was a much more effective drug; in fact, when the patients were switched from CMI to DMI, their symptoms got worse. (See **Figure 18.2**.)

All of the effective antiobsessional drugs are specific blockers of 5-HT reuptake; thus, they are specific serotonergic agonists. When patients are given a serotonin *antagonist*, their symptoms get worse (Hollander et al., 1992). In general, serotonin has an inhibitory effect on species-typical behaviors, which has tempted several investigators to speculate that these drugs alleviate the symptoms of obsessive compulsive disorder by reducing the strength of the washing, cleaning, and danger avoidance behaviors that may underlie this disorder.

The importance of serotonergic activity in inhibiting compulsive behaviors is underscored by three interesting compulsions: trichotillomania, onychophagia, and acral lick dermatitis. *Trichotillomania* is compulsive hair pulling. People with this disorder (almost always females) often spend hours each night pulling hairs out one by one, sometimes eating them (Rapoport, 1991). *Onychophagia* is compulsive nail biting, which in its extreme can cause severe damage to the ends of the fingers. (Toenail biting is not uncommon.) Double-blind studies have shown that both of these disorders can successfully be treated by clomipramine, the drug of choice for obsessive compulsive disorder (Swedo et al., 1989b; Leonard et al., 1992).

Acral lick dermatitis is a disease of dogs, not humans. Some dogs will continuously lick at a part of their body, especially their wrist or ankle (called the *carpus* and the *hock*). The licking removes the hair and often erodes away the skin as well. The disorder seems to be genetic; it is seen almost exclusively in large breeds such as Great Danes, Labrador retrievers, and German shepherds, and it runs in families. A double-blind study found that clomipramine reduces this compulsive behavior (Rapoport, Ryland, and Kriete, 1992). At first, when I read the term "double-blind" in the report by Rapoport and her colleagues, I was amused to think that the investigators were careful not to let the dogs learn whether they were receiving the clomipramine or a placebo. Then I realized that, of course, it was the dogs' owners who had to be kept in the dark.

‖‖‖ INTERIM SUMMARY

The anxiety disorders severely disrupt some people's lives. People with panic disorder periodically have panic attacks, during which they experience intense symptoms of autonomic activity and often feel as if they were going to die. Frequently, panic attacks lead to the development of agoraphobia, an avoidance

of being away from a safe place, such as home. Panic disorder is at least partly heritable, which suggests that it has biological causes.

Panic attacks can be triggered in many susceptible people by inhalation of air containing an elevated amount of carbon dioxide or by giving them an injection of lactic acid or a lactate salt. During a panic attack people show increased activity of the anterior ends of the temporal lobes.

Panic attacks can be alleviated by the administration of a benzodiazepine, which suggests that the disorder may involve decreased numbers of benzodiazepine receptors or an inadequate secretion of an endogenous benzodiazepine agonist. Cats given a benzodiazepine prenatally will become especially fearful when they reach adulthood, and the treatment decreases the number of benzodiazepine receptors in parts of their brain. Cholecystokinin (CCK) increases the likelihood of panic attacks, and serotonin decreases it.

Obsessive compulsive disorder is characterized by obsessions—unwanted thoughts—and compulsions—uncontrollable behaviors, especially those involving cleanliness and attention to danger. Some investigators believe that these behaviors represent overactivity of species-typical behavioral tendencies.

Obsessive compulsive disorder has a heritable basis and is related to Tourette's syndrome, a neurological disorder characterized by tics and strange verbalizations. It can also be caused by brain damage at birth, encephalitis, and head injuries, especially when the basal ganglia are involved. PET scans indicate that people with obsessive compulsive disorder tend to show increased glucose metabolism in the frontal lobes and cingulate gyrus, structures that are probably involved in emotional reactions. The destruction of the cingulum bundle, which links them with the anterior temporal lobe, reduces the symptoms, as do drugs such as clomipramine, which specifically block the reuptake of serotonin. Some investigators believe that clomipramine and related drugs alleviate the symptoms of obsessive compulsive disorder by increasing the activity of serotonergic pathways that play an inhibitory role on species-typical behaviors. Three other compulsions, hair pulling, nail biting, and (in dogs) acral lick syndrome, are also suppressed by clomipramine.

AUTISTIC DISORDER

Description

When a child is born, the parents normally expect to love and cherish it, and to be loved and cherished in return. Unfortunately, approximately four in every ten thousand infants are born with a disorder that impairs their ability to return their parents' affection. The symptoms of **autistic disorder** include a failure to develop normal social relations with other people, impaired development of communicative ability, and lack of imaginative ability. The syndrome was named and characterized by Kanner (1943), who chose the term (*auto*, "self," -*ism*, "condition") to refer to the child's apparent self-absorption. The disorder afflicts boys more often than girls.

Infants with autistic disorder do not seem to care if they are held, or they may arch their backs when picked up, as if they do not want to be held. They do not look or smile at their caregivers. If they are ill, hurt, or tired, they will not look to someone else for comfort. As they get older, they do not enter into social relationships with other children and avoid eye contact with them. Their language development is abnormal or even nonexistent. They often echo what is said to them, and they may refer to themselves as others do—in the second or third person. For example, they may say, "You want some milk?" to mean "I want some milk." They may learn words and phrases by rote, but they fail to use them productively and creatively. Those who do acquire reasonably good language skills talk about their own preoccupations, without regard for other people's interests. They usually interpret other people's speech literally. For example, when an autistic person is asked, "Can you pass the salt?" he may simply say "Yes"—and not because he is trying to be funny or sarcastic.

Autistic people generally show abnormal interests and behaviors. For example, they may show stereotyped movements, such as flapping their hand back and forth or rocking back and forth. They may become obsessed with investigating objects, sniffing them, feeling their texture, or moving them back and forth. They may become attached to a particular object and insist on carrying it around with them. They may become preoccupied in lining up objects or in forming patterns with them, oblivious to everything else that is going on about them. They often insist on following precise routines and may become violently upset when they are hindered from doing so. They show no make-believe play and are uninterested in stories that involve fantasy. Although many autistic people are mentally retarded, not all are; and unlike most retarded people, they may be physically adept and graceful. Some have isolated skills, such as the ability to multiply two four-digit numbers very quickly, without apparent effort.

As you can see, autistic disorder includes affective, cognitive, and behavioral abnormalities. Frith, Morton, and Leslie (1991) suggest that the impaired socialization, communicative ability, and imagination that characterize autism stem from abnormalities in the brain that prevent the person from forming a "theory of mind." That is, the person is unable "to predict and explain the behavior of other humans in terms of their mental states" (p. 434). He or she just cannot see things from another person's point of view. As one autistic man complained, "Other people seem to have a special sense by which they can read other people's thoughts" (Rutter, 1983).

Frith and her colleagues cite an experiment of Baron-Cohen, Leslie, and Frith (1985), who administered the following test: Children were presented with a puppet show in which Sally put a marble in a basket and then left the room. The other puppet, Anne, took the marble out of the basket and put it in a box. When Sally returned, she wanted to play with the marble. Where will she look for it? (See *Figure 18.3.*) A normal four-year-old child will say, "In the basket," because he or she realizes that Sally does not know that Anne has moved it into the box. So will a retarded child with a mental age of five or six years. However, sixteen of twenty autistic children with a mean mental age of nine years said that Sally would look in the box. Apparently, they were unable to understand that people can hold beliefs different from their own.

Of course, this explanation does not account for all the symptoms of autism. For example, it does not explain why autistic children engage in stereotyped

FIGURE 18.3

A test of the ability of children to understand what another person might be thinking. Sally has a marble and puts it in a basket and leaves the room. Anne takes it out of the basket and puts it into the box. Sally returns and wants to play with her marble. Where will she look for it? Autistic children were more likely to say "in the box."

(Adapted from Frith, U., Morton, J., and Leslie, A.M. *Trends in Neuroscience,* 1991, *14,* 433–438.)

behaviors and seem to have a need for sameness in their environment. But it does suggest that a careful analysis of the syndrome may yield some hints about the underlying brain functions that are disrupted.

Possible Causes

When Kanner first described autism, he suggested that it was of biological origin; but not long after-

ward, influential clinicians argued that autism was learned. More precisely, it was taught—by cold, insensitive, distant, demanding, introverted parents. Bettelheim (1967) believed that autism was similar to the apathetic, withdrawn, and hopeless behavior seen in some of the survivors of the German concentration camps of World War II. You can imagine the guilt felt by parents who were told by a mental health professional that they were to blame for their child's pitiful condition. Some professionals saw the existence of autism as evidence for child abuse and advocated that autistic children be removed from their families and placed with foster parents.

Nowadays, researchers and mental health professionals almost universally believe that autism is caused by biological factors and that parents should be given help and sympathy, not blame. Careful studies have shown that the parents of autistic children are just as warm, sociable, and responsive as other parents (Cox et al., 1975). In addition, parents with one autistic child often raise one or more normal children. If the parents were at fault, we should expect *all* of their offspring to be autistic.

Heritability

Like all the mental disorders I have described so far, at least some forms of autism appear to be heritable. As we shall see, there appear to be *several* hereditary causes, as well as some nonhereditary ones. Between 2 and 3 percent of the siblings of people with autism are themselves autistic (Folstein and Piven, 1991; Bailey, 1993). That figure may seem low, but it is between 50 and 100 times the expected frequency of autism in the general population (3–5 cases per 10,000 people). As Jones and Szatmari (1988) note, many parents stop having children after an autistic child is born for fear of having another one with the same disorder; if they did not, the percentage of autistic siblings would be even larger.

The best evidence for genetic factors in autism comes from twin studies. These studies indicate that the concordance rate for monozygotic twins is as high as 96 percent, while the rate for dizygotic twins appears to be no higher than that for normal siblings (Folstein and Piven, 1991). This difference is extremely large and indicates that autism is highly heritable. Folstein and Piven also report that in the relatively few cases of monozygotic twins discordant for autism, the affected member was likely to have had a history of obstetric complications. This finding suggests that like schizophrenia and obsessive compulsive disorder, autism can be caused by both hereditary and nonhereditary factors.

Investigators have suggested that autism is associated with some specific genetic disorders, such as phenylketonuria, Tourette's syndrome, and fragile X syndrome. **Phenylketonuria** (PKU) is caused by an inherited lack of an enzyme that converts phenylalanine (an amino acid) into tyrosine (another amino acid). Excessive amounts of phenylalanine in the blood interfere with the myelinization of neurons in the central nervous system, much of which takes place after birth. When PKU is diagnosed soon after birth, it can be treated by putting the infant on a low-phenylalanine diet. The diet keeps the blood level of phenylalanine low, and myelinization of the central nervous system takes place normally. However, if PKU is not diagnosed and an infant born with this disorder receives foods containing phenylalanine, the amino acid accumulates and the brain fails to develop normally. The result is a severe mental retardation—and, in some cases, autism (Lowe et al., 1980; Folstein and Rutter, 1988).

As we saw earlier in this chapter, obsessive compulsive disorder and Tourette's syndrome appear to be linked genetically. The same may be true for autism. As several investigators have noted, children with autism show obsessive interest in particular inanimate objects and engage in compulsive, stereotyped behaviors and rituals; thus, there is some similarity between the symptoms of these three disorders. Comings and Comings (1991) note that autistic patients and patients with Tourette's syndrome have the following symptoms in common: "attention deficits, babbling, echolalia, palilalia, echopraxia, facial grimacing, hand flicking, hyperactivity, inappropriate anger, obsessive-compulsive behaviors, onset in childhood, panic at minor environmental change, perseveration, poor control of speech volume, sniffing and smelling of objects, [and] stereotyped movements" (p. 180). (*Palilalia* is incessant repetition of words and phrases, and *echopraxia* is imitation of motions made by other people.) Comings and Comings also note that previous studies reported forty-one cases of autistic patients who subsequently developed Tourette's syn-

drome and described sixteen more such patients. Sverd (1991) reported ten additional patients with symptoms of both autism and Tourette's syndrome whose families contained relatives with Tourette's syndrome and related disorders. Two of these cases are listed in *Table 18.2.*

Another disorder, **fragile X syndrome,** is currently the leading hereditary cause of mental retardation. (As we shall see, alcoholism is the leading nonhereditary cause). This syndrome, caused (as you might expect) by a faulty gene on the X chromosome, results in mental retardation and, sometimes, the symptoms of autism (Reiss and Freund, 1992). However, it seems likely that autistic symptoms are not specific to the fragile X syndrome but are simply an occasional consequence of mental retardation. Fisch (1992) analyzed previously published data and found that 5.4 percent of 1006 autistic males tested positive for the fragile X compared with 5.5 percent of 5601 mentally retarded males. Not surprisingly, these percentages were not statistically different.

Brain Pathology

The fact that autism is highly heritable is presumptive evidence that the disorder is a result of structural or biochemical abnormalities in the brain. In addition, a variety of nongenetic pathological conditions can produce the symptoms of autism. For example, women who have contracted an infectious disease such as rubella (German measles) during pregnancy sometimes give birth to an autistic child (Chess, Fernandez, and Korn, 1971). Fernell, Gillberg, and Von Wendt (1991) found that 23 percent of children with infantile hydrocephalus showed autistic symptoms and that the severity of the hydrocephalus was correlated with the severity of the symptoms. Of course, hydrocephalus causes widespread brain damage, so this finding does not help us decide what part of the brain might be involved in autism.

Ritvo et al. (1990) found the presence of twelve rare diseases in 26 of 233 autistic individuals studied in an epidemiological survey. The authors estimate the probability of finding twelve such rare and diverse diseases in 11 percent of a random sample of the population at 16 in 100 million. Thus, we can safely conclude that the occurrence of these diseases

TABLE 18.2

Symptoms and Family Histories of Two Patients with Autistic Disorder and Tourette's Syndrome

Patient	Autistic symptoms	Tourette's symptoms	Family history
Case 6 Anna 4 years old	Poor eye contact. Disregarded people and ran into them as if they did not exist. Sometimes too attached to mother. Inconsistent response to verbal stimuli. Preferred solitary play. Echolalic, pronominal reversal. Unable to initiate and engage in conversation. Lined up toys. Flicks light switch on and off. Hand flapping. Covers ears when upset. Acute episode of agitation and aggressivity.	Onset age 3—eye blinking, facial tics, repetitive face touching and pushing hair from face, growling noises.	Father—eye blinking. Uncle—head tics. Grandfather—mouth stretches, eye twitches, delusional episode. Great Aunt—facial grimaces. Delusions she is a world class musician. Great uncle—claimed he controlled weather with a machine. Maternal uncle—socially awkward as adult, socially isolated as school boy. Uncle—fidgety, tapped fingers. Grandfather—socially awkward.
Case 7 Ronald 8 years old	Ignored people. Ran over children as if they did not exist. Poor eye contact. "Doesn't know how to address children and get into their circle." Brings up irrelevant topics, "out of blue." No imaginative play. Used single words until age 3. Echolalic. Lined up toys. Markedly restricted interests and activities. Hyperactive.	Onset age 6—eye blinking, head jerks, shoulder shrugs. hand clapping, finger snapping, throat clearing, clucking noises.	Father—head jerks, shoulder shrugs, eye blinking. Doesn't work. Paternal uncle—throat clearing, head jerks, doesn't work. Paternal grandfather—strange, impulsive, fidgety.

Source: Adapted from Sverd, J. *American Journal of Medical Genetics,* 1991, *39,* 173–179.

is *not* due to chance, and that the diseases are probably related to the development of the disorder. Besides providing further evidence that autism is caused by biological factors, this finding suggests that autism is not a single-disease entity, but that its symptoms can be produced by several means.

Researchers have found evidence for both structural and biochemical abnormalities in the brains of autistics, but so far we cannot point to any single abnormality as the cause of the disorder. MRI scans and histological examination of the brains of deceased autistic patients have found evidence for abnormalities in the medial temporal lobe, including the hippocampus (DeLong, 1992). Studies of electrical responses evoked by auditory stimulation indicate the presence of abnormalities in the brain stem (Thivierge et al., 1990). However, evidence for

structural abnormalities in the brain stem is mixed. An MRI study by Hashimoto et al. (1992) found that the width of the pons and midbrain was smaller in the brains of autistics, but a study by Holttum et al. (1992), which carefully matched autistic subjects with controls, found no difference.

Several studies have suggested that the development of the cerebellum may be abnormal in people with autism. In a review of the literature Courchesne (1991) concluded that the vermis of the cerebellum is less developed in cases of autism. In support of this conclusion Holroyd, Reiss, and Bryan (1991) reported that *Joubert syndrome,* a genetic disorder that results in lack of development of the cerebellar vermis, produced symptoms of autism. Figure 18.4 shows midsagittal MRI scans of a normal subject and two patients with Joubert syndrome. As you can

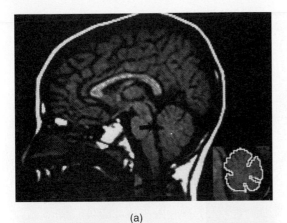

(a)

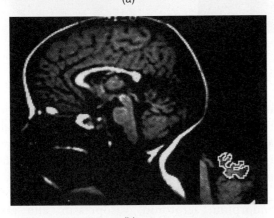

(b)

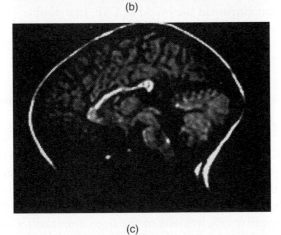

(c)

FIGURE 18.4

Midsagittal MRI scans. The cerebellar vermis is shown in the lower right corner of each panel, outlined in white. (a) From a normal child. (b) and (c) From two children with Joubert syndrome, who also showed symptoms of autism. The vermis is completely lacking in (c).

(From Holroyd, S., Reiss, A., and Bryan, R.N. *Biological Psychiatry,* 1991, *29,* 287–294. Reprinted with permission.)

see, the vermis is absent or severely underdeveloped in the Joubert patients. (See *Figure 18.4.*)

Although Joubert syndrome may indeed be one cause of autism, more recent studies cast some doubt on the conclusion that the cerebellum is abnormal in most cases of autism. Several MRI studies that were published after Courchesne's review found no differences between autistic patients and control subjects (Garber and Ritvo, 1992; Holttum et al., 1992; Piven et al., 1992). Thus, it seems too early to conclude that cerebellar malformations are an important cause of autism.

An MRI study by Piven et al. (1990) suggests that at least some cases of autism may involve abnormalities in prenatal brain development. They studied thirteen high-functioning adult male autistic subjects and thirteen nonautistic control subjects, matched on the basis of age and nonverbal IQ. Seven of the autistic subjects (53.8 percent) had evidence of abnormal development of the cerebral cortex, but none of the normal subjects had such abnormalities. The most common finding was *polymicrogyria,* a condition in which multiple, abnormally small cerebral gyri develop in the place of one or more larger ones. Such developmental malformations occur during the first six months of gestation and may be caused by an episode of anoxia, by a viral infection of the mother, or by a genetic defect. (See *Figure 18.5.*)

Several studies have found evidence of biochemical or metabolic abnormalities in patients with autism. A consistent finding seems to be elevated levels of serotonin, ß-endorphin (an endogenous opiate), vasopressin, and norepinephrine (Cook, 1990; Leboyer et al., 1992). In fact, two double-blind studies (Scifo et al., 1990; Leboyer et al., 1992) found that injections of naltrexone, a drug that blocks opiate receptors, alleviated the patients' autistic symptoms. Clearly, these promising findings deserve to be followed up.

A PET study of regional cerebral blood flow (George et al., 1992) found evidence for decreased total cerebral blood flow and, beyond that, specific decreases in the frontal lobes and left lateral temporal lobe. However, because the control subjects were not matched with the autistic subjects on the basis of IQ, we cannot be sure that the differences are directly related to the autistic symptoms.

FIGURE 18.5

MRI scans from two patients with autism showing polymicrogyria, caused by faulty prenatal development of the cerebral cortex.

(From Piven, J., Berthier, M.L., Starkstein, S.E., Nehme, E., Pearlson, G., and Folstein, S. *American Journal of Psychiatry,* 1990, *147,* 734–739. Reprinted with permission.)

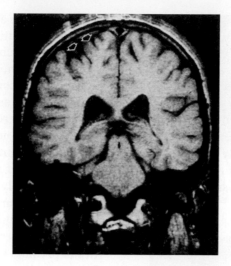

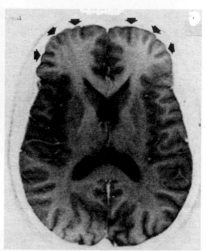

INTERIM SUMMARY

Autistic disorder occurs in 3–5 out of 10,000 infants. It is characterized by poor or absent social relations, communicative abilities, and imaginative abilities and the presence of repetitive, purposeless movements. Although autistics are often, but not always, retarded, they may have a particular, isolated talent. Some investigators believe that the most important cognitive deficit is the inability to imagine what others know or think about something and how they feel.

In the past clinicians blamed parents for autism, but now it is generally accepted as a disorder with biological roots. Twin studies have shown that autism is highly heritable. It is often associated with Tourette's syndrome (like obsessive compulsive disorder) and can be caused by untreated phenylketonuria. Some investigators have suggested a link with fragile X syndrome, the leading genetic cause of mental retardation, but more recent research suggests that the two disorders are independent. Autism can also be caused by maternal infection with rubella during pregnancy, with hydrocephalus, and with a wide variety of rare diseases.

MRI studies suggest that autism is associated with abnormalities in the medial temporal lobe. Although autism can be caused by Joubert syndrome, a hereditary disorder that results in the lack of development of the cerebellar vermis, suggestions that autism is regularly associated with cerebellar abnormalities have not been supported by more recent MRI studies. Some evidence indicates abnormal prenatal development of the cerebral cortex.

Autistic patients often have elevated levels of ß-endorphin, serotonin, vasopressin, and norepinephrine in the blood or CSF. Two double-blind studies found that treatment with naltrexone, an opiate receptor blocker, has beneficial effects.

ADDICTION

DRUG ADDICTION IS ONE OF THE MOST SERIOUS problems that our species presently faces. Consider the disastrous effects caused by the abuse of our oldest drug, alcohol: automobile accidents, fetal alcohol syndrome, cirrhosis of the liver, Korsakoff's syndrome, increased rate of heart disease, and increased rate of intracerebral hemorrhage. Smoking (nicotine addiction) greatly increases the chances of dying of lung cancer, heart attack, and stroke; and women who smoke give birth to smaller, less healthy babies. Cocaine addiction often causes psychosis, brain damage, and death from overdose; it produces babies born with severe brain damage and consequent psychological problems; and competition for lucrative markets terrorizes neighborhoods, subverts political and judicial systems, and causes many deaths. The use of "designer drugs" exposes users to unknown dangers of untested and often contaminated products, as several young people discovered when they acquired Parkinson's disease. Addicts who take their drugs intravenously run a serious risk of contracting AIDS. Why do people use these drugs and subject themselves to these dangers?

The answer, as you may have predicted from what you have learned about the physiology of reinforcement in Chapter 14, is that all of these substances stimulate the release of dopamine in the nucleus accumbens; thus, they reinforce the behaviors responsible for their delivery to the body: swallowing, smoking, sniffing, or injecting. The immediate consequences of these drugs are more powerful than the realization that in the long term bad things will happen.

Characteristics of Addictive Substances

Most substances to which people can become addicted produce an excitatory effect, although some, like opiates and alcohol, produce both excitation and inhibition. Most investigators believe that the excitatory effects are the most important in producing addiction.

Opiates

Opium, derived from a sticky resin produced by the opium poppy, has been eaten and smoked for centuries. Morphine, one of the naturally occurring ingredients of opium, is sometimes used as a painkiller but has largely been supplanted by synthetic opiates. Heroin, a compound produced from morphine, is the most commonly abused opiate.

Opiate addiction has several high personal and social costs. First, because heroin is an illegal drug, an addict becomes, by definition, a criminal. Second, the behavioral response to opiates declines with continued use, which means that a person must take increasing amounts of the drug to achieve a "high." The habit thus becomes more and more expensive, and the person often turns to crime to obtain enough money to support his or her habit. (If the addict is a pregnant woman, her infant will also become dependent on the drug, which easily crosses the placental barrier. The infant must be given opiates right after being born and then be given gradually decreasing doses.) Third, an opiate addict often uses unsanitary needles; at present, a substantial percentage of people who inject illicit drugs have been exposed in this way to the AIDS virus. Fourth, the uncertainty about the strength of a given batch of heroin makes it possible for a user to receive an unusually large dose of the drug, with possibly fatal consequences. In addition, dealers typically dilute pure heroin with various adulterants such as milk sugar, quinine, or talcum powder; and dealers are not known for taking scrupulous care with the quality and sterility of the substances they use. Some heroin-induced deaths have actually been reactions to the adulterants mixed with the drugs.

Tolerance and Withdrawal Symptoms. Many people—including many health care professionals—think of heroin as the prototype for addiction. People who habitually take heroin (or other opiates) become physically dependent on the drug. Eddy et al. (1965) define *physical dependence* as "an adaptive state that manifests itself by intense physical disturbances when the administration of a drug is suspended" (p. 723). In contrast, they define *psychic dependence* as a condition in which a drug produces "a feeling of satisfaction and a psychic drive that requires periodic or continuous administration of the drug to produce pleasure or to avoid discomfort" (p. 723). In fact, the distinction between "physical" and "psychic" dependence reflects a misunderstanding of the process of addiction.

Tolerance is the decreased sensitivity to a drug that comes from its continued use; the drug user must take larger and larger amounts of the drug in order for it to be effective. Once a person has taken an opiate regularly enough to develop tolerance, that person will suffer **withdrawal symptoms** if he or she stops taking the drug. Withdrawal symptoms are primarily the opposite of the effects of the drug itself. That is, heroin produces euphoria; withdrawal from it produces *dysphoria*—a feeling of anxious misery. (*Euphoria* and *dysphoria* mean "easy to bear" and "hard to bear," respectively.) Heroin produces constipation; withdrawal from it produces nausea and cramping. Heroin produces relaxation; withdrawal from it produces agitation.

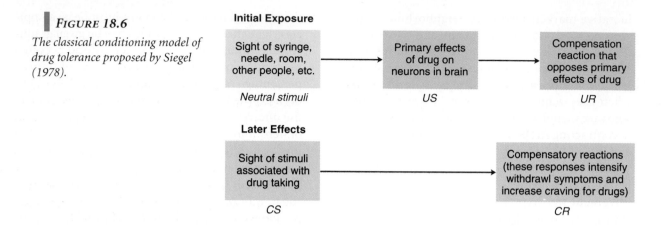

FIGURE 18.6

The classical conditioning model of drug tolerance proposed by Siegel (1978).

Most investigators believe that the withdrawal symptoms are produced by the body's attempt to compensate for the unusual condition of heroin intoxication. That is, most systems of the body, including those controlled by the brain, are regulated so that they stay at an optimal value. When a drug artificially changes these systems for a prolonged time, homeostatic mechanisms begin to produce the opposite reaction, thus partially compensating for the disturbance from the optimal value. These compensatory mechanisms account for the fact that more and more heroin must be taken in order to achieve the effects that were produced when the person first started taking the drug (tolerance). They also account for the symptoms of withdrawal: When the person stops taking the drug, the compensatory mechanisms make themselves felt, unopposed by the action of the drug.

Research suggests that there are basically two types of compensatory mechanisms. The first mechanism involves a decrease in the effectiveness of opiates as a neuromodulator. Either opiate receptors become less sensitive or the mechanisms that couple them to ion channels in the membrane become less effective; or both effects occur. A second effect, described by Siegel (1978), involves classical conditioning. When a person takes heroin, the drug produces its primary effects, which in turn activate the homeostatic compensatory mechanisms. The activation of these compensatory mechanisms can become classically conditioned to environmental stimuli present at the time. The stimuli associated with taking the drug—including the paraphernalia involved in preparing the solution of the drug, the syringe, the needle, the feel of the needle in a vein, and even the room in which the drug is taken— serve as conditional stimuli. The homeostatic compensatory responses provoked by the effects of the drug serve as the unconditional response, which becomes conditioned to the environmental stimuli. Thus, once classical conditioning has taken place, the compensatory mechanisms are activated not only by the primary effects of the drug but also *by the stimuli associated with taking the drug.* (See **Figure 18.6.**)

Heroin addiction has provided such a striking example of drug dependence that some authorities have concluded that "real" addiction does not occur unless a drug causes tolerance and withdrawal. Without doubt, withdrawal symptoms make it difficult for a person to stop taking heroin—they keep the person hooked, so to speak. However, withdrawal symptoms do not explain why a person *becomes* a heroin addict, nor do they explain why people continue taking the drug. Certainly, people do not start taking heroin so that they will become physically dependent on it and feel miserable when they go without it. In fact, when the cost of a habit gets too high, some addicts stop taking heroin "cold turkey." Doing so is not as painful as most people believe; withdrawal symptoms have been described as similar to a bad case of the flu. After a week or two, when their nervous system adapts to the absence of the drug, they recommence their habit. If their only reason for taking the drug was to avoid unpleasant withdrawal symptoms, they would never be capable of following this strategy. The reason that people take—and continue to take—drugs such as heroin is that the drugs give them a pleasurable "rush"; in other words, the drugs have a reinforcing effect on their behavior.

There are two kinds of evidence that contradict the belief that drug addiction is caused by physical dependence. First, some very potent drugs—including cocaine—do not produce physical dependence. That is, people who take the drug do not show tolerance, and if they stop, they do not show any withdrawal symptoms. And yet the people show just as strong an addiction as heroin addicts. Second, some drugs produce physical dependence (tolerance and withdrawal symptoms) but are not abused (Jaffe, 1985). The reason they are not abused is that they do not have reinforcing effects on behavior.

Effects on Dopaminergic Neurons. Laboratory animals, like humans, will self-administer opiates. As you learned in Chapters 3 and 7, opiates act by stimulating specialized receptors on the membranes of neurons located in various parts of the nervous system. When an opiate is administered systemically, it stimulates all of these receptors and produces a variety of effects, including analgesia, hypothermia (lowering of body temperature), sedation, and reinforcement. Opiate receptors in the periaqueductal gray matter are responsible for the analgesia, those in the preoptic area are responsible for the hypothermia, those in the mesencephalic reticular formation are responsible for the sedation, and those in the ventral tegmental area and the nucleus accumbens are responsible for the reinforcement.

Several different kinds of experimental evidence indicate that opiates exert their reinforcing effects by activating dopaminergic neurons. Laboratory animals will work for opiates to be injected into two regions of the brain known to be involved in the effects of dopamine on reinforcement: the ventral tegmental area and the nucleus accumbens (Bozarth and Wise, 1984; Goeders, Lane, and Smith, 1984). Injection of morphine into the ventral tegmental area increases the activity of dopaminergic neurons located there (Matthews and German, 1984). In addition, after the dopaminergic neurons of the mesolimbic system or the terminals of these neurons in the nucleus accumbens have been destroyed with

6-HD, rats will not press a lever that administers intravenous heroin (Zito, Vickers, and Roberts, 1985; Bozarth and Wise, 1986). Finally, if a drug that blocks opiate receptors is injected into either the ventral tegmental area or the nucleus accumbens, the reinforcing effect of intravenous heroin is decreased (Vaccarino, Bloom, and Koob, 1985; Maldonado et al., 1993).

Several studies have investigated the neural systems responsible for the withdrawal effects of opiates. Bozarth and Wise (1984) found that repeated injections of morphine into the periaqueductal gray matter produce withdrawal symptoms when the injections are stopped, even though the injections are not reinforcing. Baumeister et al. (1989) gave rats increasing doses of morphine for several days in order to produce tolerance. Then they injected naloxone, a drug that blocks opiate receptors, into various regions of the ventral midbrain, including the substantia nigra and the ventral tegmental area. They found that the injections produced the symptoms of withdrawal. Stinus, Le Moal, and Koob (1990) found that injections of an opiate antagonist into the nucleus accumbens, amygdala, and periaqueductal gray matter in morphine-dependent rats all produced signs of withdrawal. The results of these studies suggest that withdrawal symptoms are produced by several different neural mechanisms.

As we saw in Chapter 14, microdialysis studies have shown that reinforcing brain stimulation and many natural stimuli that reinforce behaviors cause dopamine to be released in the nucleus accumbens. Using the microdialysis procedure, Di Chiara and Imperato (1987) found that injections of opiates, too, produced this effect.

Cocaine and Amphetamine

Cocaine and amphetamine have similar behavioral effects, because both act as dopamine agonists by blocking its reuptake after it is released by the terminal buttons. In addition, amphetamine directly stimulates the release of dopamine. "Crack," a particularly potent form of cocaine, is smoked and thus enters the blood supply of the lungs and reaches the brain very quickly. Because its effects are so potent and so rapid, it is probably the most effective reinforcer of all available drugs.

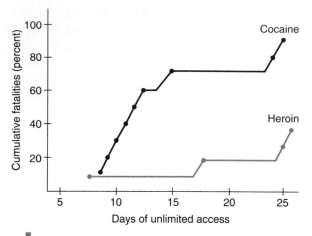

FIGURE 18.7

Cumulative fatalities in groups of rats self-administering cocaine or heroin.

(Modified from Bozarth, M.A., and Wise, R.A. *Journal of the American Medical Association*, 1985, *254*, 81–83. Copyright 1985 American Medical Association.)

When people take cocaine, they become euphoric, active, and talkative. They say that they feel powerful and alert. Some of them become addicted to the drug, and obtaining it becomes an obsession to which they devote more and more time and money. Laboratory animals, who will quickly learn to self-administer cocaine intravenously, also act excited and show intense exploratory activity. After receiving the drug for a day or two, rats start showing stereotyped movements, such as grooming, head bobbing, and persistent locomotion (Geary, 1987). If rats or monkeys are given continuous access to a lever that permits them to self-administer cocaine, they often self-inject so much cocaine that they die. In fact, Bozarth and Wise (1985) found that rats that self-administered cocaine were almost three times more likely to die than rats that self-administered heroin. (See *Figure 18.7.*)

One of the alarming effects of cocaine and amphetamine seen in people who abuse these drugs regularly is psychotic behavior: hallucinations, delusions of persecution, mood disturbances, and repetitive behaviors. These symptoms so closely resemble those of paranoid schizophrenia that even a trained mental health professional cannot distinguish them unless he or she knows about the person's history of drug abuse. As we saw in Chapter 17, the fact that these symptoms are provoked by dopamine agonists and reduced by drugs that block dopamine receptors suggests that overactivity of dopaminergic synapses is one of the causes of schizophrenia.

Usually, a psychotic reaction caused by use of cocaine or amphetamine will subside once the person stops taking the drug. However, the exposure to the drug appears to produce long-term changes in the brain that make the person more likely to display psychotic symptoms if he or she takes the drug later—even months or years later (Sato et al., 1983; Sato, 1986). A study with rats suggests that this effect is produced by long-term changes in the nucleus accumbens. Robinson et al. (1988) administered escalating daily doses of amphetamine to rats over a period of five weeks, in a pattern designed to mimic that of people who abuse the drug and become psychotic. Two to three weeks later, the investigators administered a single dose of amphetamine and observed the animals' behavior and measured the release of dopamine in the nucleus accumbens by means of microdialysis. As **Figure 18.8** shows, the rates of head and limb movements, sniffing, and dopamine release were much higher in animals that had previously received the amphetamine.

Nicotine and Caffeine

Stimulant drugs such as nicotine and caffeine may seem rather tame after a discussion of opiates, cocaine, and amphetamine. Nevertheless, these drugs, too, have addictive potential. Fortunately, caffeine is relatively innocuous; most people do not take enough to impair their health or produce serious behavioral effects. Nicotine is a different story. The combination of nicotine and other substances in tobacco smoke is carcinogenic and leads to cancer of the lungs, mouth, throat, and esophagus. Although nicotine is less potent than the "hard" drugs, many more people who try it go on to become addicts. The addictive potential of nicotine should not be underestimated; many people continue to smoke even when doing so causes serious health problems. For example, Sigmund Freud, whose theory of psychoanalysis stressed the importance of insight in changing one's behavior, was unable to stop smoking even after most of his jaw had been removed because of the cancer that this habit had caused (Brecher, 1972). His cancer finally killed him.

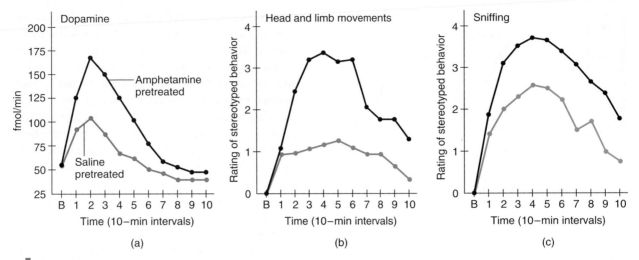

FIGURE 18.8

Sensitization to the effects of amphetamine in rats that had been pretreated for five weeks with amphetamine or saline. (a) Effects of amphetamine on the release of dopamine in the nucleus accumbens. (b) and (c) Effects of amphetamine or stereotyped behaviors.

(Adapted from Robinson, T.E., Jurson, P.A., Bennett, J.A., and Bentgen, K.M. *Brain Research*, 1988, *462*, 211–222.)

As we saw in Chapter 3, many transmitter substances exert their effects on the postsynaptic membrane through the production of a second messenger, such as cyclic AMP. Caffeine prevents the destruction of the second messenger by inactivating phosphodiesterase, the enzyme that normally destroys cyclic nucleotides; thus, caffeine acts as an agonist at many synapses. Cyclic AMP and related substances have many other functions as well, so the effects of caffeine are not at all specific. Nevertheless, there is some evidence that caffeine activates dopaminergic neurons (Wise, 1988).

Ours is not the only species willing to self-administer nicotine; so will laboratory animals (Henningfield and Goldberg, 1983). Nicotine stimulates acetylcholine receptors, of course. It also increases the activity level of dopaminergic neurons, which contain these receptors (Svensson, Grenhoff, and Aston-Jones, 1986), and causes dopamine to be released in the nucleus accumbens (Damsma, Day, and Fibiger, 1989). Figure 18.9 shows the effects of two injections of nicotine or saline on the extracellular dopamine level of the nucleus accumbens, measured by microdialysis probes. (See **Figure 18.9**.)

Wise (1988) notes that because nicotine stimulates the tegmentostriatal dopaminergic system, smoking could potentially make it more difficult for a cocaine or heroin addict to stop taking the drug. As several studies with laboratory animals have shown, if self-administration of cocaine or heroin is extinguished through nonreinforcement, an injection of drugs that stimulate dopaminergic neurons can reinstate the responding. A similar "cross-priming" effect from cigarette smoking could potentially contribute to a relapse in people who are trying to abstain. (As we shall see, alcohol also stimulates dopaminergic neurons, so drinking could present the same problem.)

Marijuana

Another drug that people regularly self-administer—almost exclusively by smoking—is THC, the active ingredient in marijuana. As you learned in Chapter 3, THC receptors have been discovered, and their distribution in the brain has been mapped. However, we still do not know what types of neurons contain these receptors, and we still do not know the physiological effects of THC. The fact that the brain contains THC receptors implies that the

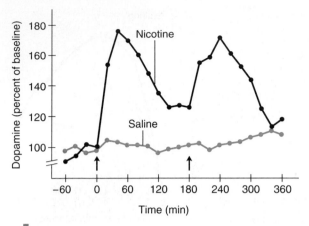

FIGURE 18.9

Release of dopamine in the nucleus accumbens caused by injections of nicotine or saline. The arrows indicate the time of the injections.

(From Damsma, G., Day, J., and Fibiger, H.C. *European Journal of Pharmacology*, 1989, *168*, 363–368. Reprinted with permission.)

brain produces an endogenous ligand for them. What this chemical is and what functions it serves are yet to be discovered.

One thing we do now know about THC is that it, like other drugs with abuse potential, has an effect on dopaminergic neurons. Chen et al. (1990) injected rats with low doses of THC and measured the release of dopamine in the nucleus accumbens by means of microdialysis. Sure enough, they found that the injections caused the release of dopamine. (See *Figure 18.10*.) As we saw in Chapter 3, the hippocampus contains a large concentration of THC receptors. Since the hippocampus is involved in learning, perhaps it is ultimately responsible for stimulating the release of dopamine in the nucleus accumbens. Marijuana is known to affect people's short-term memory; specifically, it impairs their ability to keep track of a particular topic—they frequently lose the thread of a conversation. Perhaps the drug does so by disrupting the normal functions of the hippocampus.

Alcohol and Barbiturates

Alcohol has greater costs to society than any other drug. A large percentage of deaths and injuries caused by motor vehicle accidents are related to

alcohol use, and alcohol contributes to violence and aggression. Chronic alcoholics often lose their jobs, their homes, and their families; and many die of cirrhosis of the liver, exposure, or diseases caused by poor living conditions and abuse of their body. Women who drink during pregnancy run the risk of giving birth to babies with the fetal alcohol syndrome, which includes malformation of the head and the brain. Figure 18.11 compares a child and a rat pup with fetal alcohol syndrome; as you can see, similar malformations are seen in the face and head in both species. More serious, of course, are the malformations in the brain. (See *Figure 18.11*.) The leading cause of mental retardation in the Western world today is alcohol consumption by pregnant women (Abel and Sokol, 1986). Thus, understanding the physiological and behavioral effects of this drug is an important issue.

At low doses alcohol produces mild euphoria and has an *anxiolytic* effect—that is, it reduces the discomfort of anxiety. At higher doses it produces incoordination and sedation. In studies with laboratory animals the anxiolytic effects manifest themselves as a release from the punishing effects of aversive stimuli. For example, if an animal is given electric shocks whenever it makes a particular response (say, one that obtains food or water), it will stop doing so. However, if it is then given some

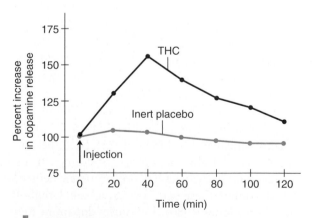

FIGURE 18.10

Release of dopamine in the nucleus accumbens caused by injections of THC or an inert placebo.

(From Chen, J., Paredes, W., Li, J., Smith, D., Lowinson, J., and Gardner, E.L. *Psychopharmacology*, 1990, *102*, 156–162. Reprinted with permission.)

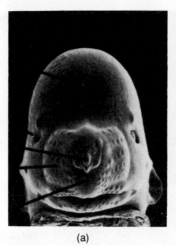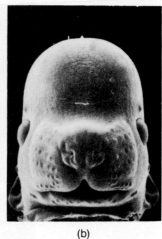

Narrow forehead

Short palpebral
fissures

Small nose

Long upper lip
with deficient
philtrum

(a)   (b)

FIGURE 18.11

*A child with fetal alcohol syndrome, along with magnified views of rat fetuses. (a) Fetus whose
mother received alcohol during pregnancy. (b) Normal rat fetus.*

(Photograph courtesy of Katherine K. Sulik.)

alcohol, it will begin making the response again
(Koob et al., 1984). This phenomenon explains why
people often do things they normally would not
when they have had too much to drink; the alcohol
removes the inhibitory effect of social controls on
their behavior.

Alcohol probably produces both positive and negative reinforcement. *Positive* reinforcement is reinforcement caused by the presence of an appetitive
stimulus, which, as we have seen, is related to the
release of dopamine by neurons of the tegmentostriatal system. *Negative* reinforcement is reinforcement
caused by the termination of an aversive stimulus. For
example, an animal can be trained to press a lever if
doing so turns off a loud noise. Similarly, if we find a
medication that makes a painful headache go away,
we will quickly turn to that medication the next time
we have a headache. Negative reinforcement is provided by the anxiolytic effect of alcohol. If a person
feels anxious and uncomfortable, then a drug that
relieves this discomfort provides at least a temporary
escape from an unpleasant situation.

The negative reinforcement provided by the anxiolytic effect of alcohol is probably not enough to
explain the drug's addictive potential. Other drugs,
such as the benzodiazepines (tranquilizers such as
Valium), are even more potent anxiolytics than alcohol, and yet such drugs are rarely abused. It is prob-

ably the unique combination of stimulating and
anxiolytic effects—of positive and negative reinforcement—that makes alcohol so difficult for some
people to resist.

In low doses alcohol appears to act on the nervous system by stimulating the GABA-benzodiazepine receptor complex (described in Chapter 3).
Suzdak et al. (1986) found that alcohol makes GABA
receptors become more sensitive. In fact, they discovered a drug (Ro15-4513) that reverses alcohol
intoxication, presumably by blocking one of the
receptor sites on the GABA-benzodiazepine receptor
complex. Figure 18.12 shows two rats who received
injections of enough alcohol to make them pass out.
The one facing us also received an injection of the
alcohol antagonist and appears completely sober.
(See *Figure 18.12.*)

This wonder drug is not likely to reach the market soon, if ever. Although the behavioral effects of
alcohol may be mediated by benzodiazepine receptors, alcohol has other, potentially fatal effects on
all cells of the body. Alcohol destabilizes the membrane of cells, interfering with their functions. Thus,
a person who takes some of the alcohol antagonist
could then go on to drink himself or herself to
death, without becoming drunk in the process. Drug
companies naturally fear possible liability suits
stemming from such occurrences.

FIGURE 18.12

Effects of Ro15-4513, an alcohol antagonist. Both rats received an injection of alcohol, but the one facing us also received an injection of the alcohol antagonist. (Photograph courtesy of Steven M. Paul, National Institute of Mental Health, Bethesda, Md.)

The site (or sites) of action of alcohol in the brain is not yet known. However, the positive reinforcement produced by the drug apparently involves the release of dopamine. Alcohol increases the firing rate of dopaminergic neurons in the ventral tegmental area, both in vitro (Brodie, Shefner, and Dunwiddie, 1990) and in vivo (Gessa et al., 1985). It also causes the release of dopamine in the nucleus accumbens, as measured by microdialysis (Imperato and Di Chiara, 1986). It remains to be seen just how alcohol activates dopaminergic neurons and causes this dopamine release.

Barbiturates have effects very similar to those of alcohol. In fact, both drugs appear to act on the GABA-benzodiazepine receptor complex (Maksay and Ticku, 1985). Proctor et al. (1992) used the microiontophoresis technique to record the activity of single neurons in the cerebral cortex of slices of rat brains. They found that the presence of alcohol significantly increased the postsynaptic response produced by the action of GABA at the $GABA_A$ receptor complex. However, the binding sites for alcohol and barbiturates appear to be different; Ro15-4513, the alcohol antagonist, does not reverse the intoxicating effects of barbiturates (Suzdak et al., 1986). The effects of alcohol and barbiturates are additive; if a person takes a moderate dose of alcohol and a moderate dose of a barbiturate, the effect can be fatal. Barbiturates do *not* appear to affect dopaminergic neurons (Wood, 1982).

Although the effects of heroin withdrawal have been exaggerated, those produced by barbiturate or alcohol withdrawal are serious and can even be fatal (Julien, 1981). Convulsions caused by alcohol withdrawal are considered to be a medical emergency and are usually treated with benzodiazepines or barbiturates.

Genetics of Addiction

Not everyone is equally likely to become addicted to a drug. Many people manage to drink alcohol moderately, and even many users of potent drugs such as cocaine and heroin use them "recreationally," without becoming dependent on them. There are only two possible sources of individual differences in any characteristic: heredity and environment. Because this book considers the *physiology* of behavior, I will not discuss the role that environment plays in a person's susceptibility to the addicting effects of drugs. Obviously, environmental effects are important; people raised in a squalid environment without any real hope for a better life are more likely than other people to turn to drugs for some temporary euphoria and removal from the unpleasant world that surrounds them. But even in a given environment, poor or privileged, some people become addicts and some do not—and some of these behavioral differences are a result of genetic differences, as we will see.

Research on Human Heredity

Most of the research on the effects of heredity on addiction have been devoted to alcoholism. One of the most important reasons for this focus—aside from the importance of the problems caused by alcohol—is that almost everyone is exposed to alcohol. Most people drink alcohol sometime in their lives and thus receive firsthand experience with its reinforcing effects. The same is not true for cocaine, heroin, and other drugs that have even more potent effects. In most countries alcohol is freely and legally available in local shops, whereas cocaine and heroin must often be purchased in dangerous neighborhoods from unsavory dealers. From what we now know about the effects of addictive drugs on the nervous system, it seems likely that the results of studies on the heredity of alcoholism will apply to other types of drug addiction as well.

Alcohol consumption is not distributed equally across the population; in the United States 10 percent of the people drink 50 percent of the alcohol (Heckler, 1983). The best evidence for an effect of heredity on susceptibility to alcoholism comes from two main sources: twin studies and cross-fostering studies. As you know, there are two types of twins. Monozygotic twins come from a single fertilized ovum, which splits apart early in development, becoming two independent individuals with identical heredity. Dizygotic twins come from two different ova, fertilized by two different sperms. Thus, they share (on the average) 50 percent of their chromosomes, just like any two siblings. If a trait is influenced by heredity, then we would expect that, with respect to this trait, monozygotic twins would resemble each other more than dizygotic twins. Monozygotic twins (identical twins) have the same body shape, facial characteristics, and hair and eye color, because these traits certainly are influenced by heredity. Many of their personality characteristics

are also similar, which tells us that these traits, too, are influenced by heredity. Alcoholism is one of those traits; monozygotic twins are more likely to resemble each other with respect to alcohol abuse than dizygotic twins (Goodwin, 1979).

The second type of heritability study uses children who were adopted by nonrelatives when they were young. A study like this permits the investigator to estimate the effects of family environment as well as genetics. That is, one can examine the effects of being raised by an alcoholic parent, or having a biological parent who is an alcoholic, or both, on the probability of becoming alcoholic. Such a study was carried out in Sweden by Cloninger et al. (1985). Briefly, the study found that heredity was much more important than family environment. But the story is not quite that simple.

In a review of the literature on alcohol abuse Cloninger (1987) notes that many investigators have concluded that there are two principal types of alcoholics: those who cannot abstain but drink consistently, and those who are able to go without drinking for long periods of time but are unable to control themselves once they start. (For convenience, I will refer to these two groups as "steady drinkers" and "bingers.") Steady drinking is associated with antisocial personality disorder, which includes a lifelong history of impulsiveness, fighting, lying, and lack of remorse for antisocial acts. Binge drinking is associated with emotional dependence, behavioral rigidity, perfectionism, introversion, and guilt feelings about one's drinking behavior. Steady drinkers usually begin their alcohol consumption early in life, whereas binge drinkers begin much later. (See *Table 18.3*.)

Steady drinking is strongly influenced by heredity. The Swedish adoption study found that men with fathers who were steady drinkers were almost seven times more likely to become steady drinkers themselves than men whose fathers did not abuse alcohol. Family environment had no measurable effect; the boys began drinking whether or not the members of their adoptive family themselves drank heavily. Very few women become steady drinkers; the daughters of steady-drinking fathers instead tend to develop *somatization disorder*. People with this disorder chronically complain of symptoms for which no physiological cause can be found, leading

TABLE 18.3

Characteristic Features of Two Types of Alcoholism

Feature	Type of Alcoholism	
	Steady	Binge
Usual age of onset (years)	Before 25	After 25
Spontaneous alcohol seeking (inability to abstain)	Frequent	Infrequent
Fighting and arrests when drinking	Frequent	Infrequent
Psychological dependence (loss of control)	Infrequent	Frequent
Guilt and fear about alcohol dependence	Infrequent	Frequent
Novelty seeking	High	Low
Harm avoidance	Low	High
Reward dependence	Low	High

Source: From Cloninger, C. R. *Science*, 1987, *236*, 410–416. Copyright 1987 by the American Association for the Advancement of Science.

them to seek medical care almost continuously. Thus, the genes that predispose a man to become a steady-drinking alcoholic (antisocial type) predispose a woman to develop somatization disorder. The reason for this interaction with gender is not known.

Binge drinking is influenced both by heredity and by environment. The Swedish adoption study found that having a biological parent who was a binge drinker had little effect on the development of binge drinking unless the child was exposed to a family environment in which there was heavy drinking. The effect was seen in both males and females.

Possible Mechanisms

When we find an effect of heredity on behavior, we have good reason to suspect the existence of a biological difference. That is, genes affect behavior only by affecting the body. A susceptibility to alcoholism could conceivably be caused by differences in the ability to digest or metabolize alcohol or by differences in the structure or biochemistry of the brain.

Most investigators believe that differences in brain physiology are more likely to play a role. Cloninger (1987) notes that many studies have shown that people with antisocial tendencies, which includes the group of steady drinkers, show a strong tendency to seek novelty and excitement. These people are disorderly and distractible (many have a history of hyperactivity as children) and show little restraint in their behavior. They tend not to fear dangerous situations or social disapproval. They are easily bored. On the other hand, binge drinkers tend to be anxious, emotionally dependent, sentimental, sensitive to social cues, cautious and apprehensive, fearful of novelty or change, rigid, and attentive to details. Their EEGs show little slow alpha activity, which is characteristic of a relaxed state (Propping, Kruger, and Mark, 1981). When they take alcohol, they report a pleasant relief of tension (Propping, Kruger, and Janah, 1980). Perhaps, as Cloninger suggests, these personality differences are a result of differences in the sensitivity of neural mechanisms involved in reinforcement, exploration, and punishment.

For example, steady drinkers may have an undersensitive punishment mechanism, which makes them unresponsive to danger and to social disapproval. They may also have an undersensitive reinforcement system, which leads them to seek more intense thrills (including those provided by alcohol) in order to experience pleasurable sensations. Thus, they seek the excitatory (dopamine-stimulating) effect of alcohol. Binge drinkers may have oversensitive punishment systems. Normally, they avoid drinking because of the guilt they experience afterward; but once they begin, and once the sedative effect begins, the alcohol-induced suppression of the punishment system makes it impossible for them to stop.

Recently, investigators have focused on the possibility that susceptibility to addiction may involve differences in dopaminergic mechanisms—for reasons you will understand, having read this chapter. Blum et al. (1990) reported that severe alcoholism was related to the presence of the A1 allele of the gene responsible for the production of the D2 dopamine receptor, which is found on chromosome 11. (An *allele* is a particular form of a gene.) The idea that susceptibility to addiction is related to genetic differences in receptors known to be involved in the physiology of reinforcement is an intriguing one, and the report of the research was greeted with considerable interest from clinicians and other researchers. Although one subsequent study (Bolos et al., 1990) failed to find such a difference, other subsequent studies did. Noble (1993) reviewed the literature on the subject and reported that nine studies compared a total of 491 alcoholics with a total of 495 controls, finding the A1 allele in 43 percent of the alcoholics and 25.7 of the control subjects. When only severe alcoholics are considered, the frequency rises to 56.3 percent. In addition, Noble reports that some preliminary evidence suggests that the prevalence of the A1 allele is higher in other chronic drug abusers.

Another approach to the study of the physiology of addiction is through the use of animal models. Several different strains of alcohol-preferring rats have been developed through selective breeding, and studies have shown that these animals differ in interesting ways. Alcohol-preferring rats do just what their name implies: If given a drinking tube containing a solution of alcohol along with their water and food, they become heavy drinkers. The alcohol-nonpreferring rats abstain (Li, Lumeng, and Doolittle, 1993). Figure 18.13 shows the amount of alcohol consumed by subsequent generations of rats selected for high and low preference for alcohol. (See *Figure 18.13.*)

Alcohol-preferring rats and alcohol-nonpreferring rats show interesting behavioral and physiological differences. If they are given small doses of alcohol, the alcohol-preferring rats show more behavioral activation. They also are more tolerant of the aversive effects of high doses, and they have lower brain levels of serotonin and dopamine (Gongwer et al., 1989; McBride et al., 1991). Li, Lumeng, and Doolittle (1993) suggest that the mesolimbic dopaminergic system in alcohol-preferring rats may be more sensitive to the effects of alcohol, but so far the evidence is inconclusive.

As we have seen, serotonin agonists have proved themselves useful in treatment of panic disorder and obsessive compulsive disorder (and related disorders such as hair pulling and nail biting). These drugs also appear to be useful in treating alcoholism; several double-blind studies have found that 5-HT

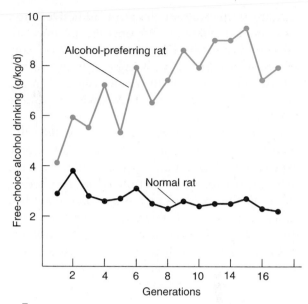

FIGURE 18.13

Alcohol intake of successive generations of rats selected for alcohol preference and nonpreference.

(Adapted from Li, T.-.K., Lumeng, L., and Doolittle, D.P. *Behavioral Genetics,* 1993, *23,* 163–170.)

reuptake blockers make it easier for alcoholics to abstain. For example, Naranjo et al. (1992) found that citalopram (a serotonin agonist) "decreased interest, desire, craving, and liking for alcohol" in alcoholics who were receiving treatment for their addiction. It appeared to do so by decreasing the reinforcing effects of alcohol.

The hypotheses concerning the physiology of addiction are speculative; we should view them as suggestions for further research rather than explanations. But even if these particular hypotheses are wrong, they do give us hope that research with humans and laboratory animals may some day help us understand the causes of addictive behaviors.

INTERIM SUMMARY

Research on the physiology of reinforcement has led to considerable progress in understanding the physiology of drug addiction, which is one of the most serious problems our society faces today. Apparently, all substances that produce addiction have an excitatory effect, although several addictive drugs, such as alcohol and the opiates, produce an inhibitory effect as well. The excitatory effect, correlated with reinforcement, appears to involve the release of dopamine in the nucleus accumbens, as microdialysis studies and studies with dopamine antagonists have shown.

Opiates produce tolerance and withdrawal symptoms, which certainly makes the habit become expensive and makes quitting more difficult, but the primary reason for addiction is the reinforcing effect, not the unpleasant symptoms produced when an addict tries to quit. Tolerance appears to be produced by homeostatic mechanisms, one involving mechanisms coupled to opiate receptors and another involving classical conditioning of compensatory responses to the environmental stimuli associated with taking the drug. Both the ventral tegmental area and the nucleus accumbens contain opiate receptors that are involved in the reinforcing effects of opiates. Withdrawal symptoms appear to involve opiate receptors on neurons in several parts of the brain, including the periaqueductal gray matter, the nucleus accumbens, the amygdala, and the ventral tegmentum.

Cocaine and amphetamine are potent dopamine agonists and thus serve as potent reinforcers—and substances with a high addictive potential. Nicotine and caffeine also increase the release of dopamine in the nucleus accumbens. THC, the active ingredient in marijuana, causes its behavioral effects by binding with THC receptors, which are found throughout the brain. THC, too, causes the release of dopamine in the nucleus accumbens.

Alcohol has both excitatory and antianxiety effects and thus is able to produce both positive and negative reinforcement. Its sedative effects are initiated by its binding with a particular site on the $GABA_A$ receptor complex. Its reinforcing effects involve the release of dopamine in the nucleus accumbens, but how this is accomplished is not known.

Most people who are exposed to addictive drugs—even drugs with a high abuse potential—do not become addicts. Evidence suggests that the likelihood of addiction, especially to alcohol, is strongly affected by heredity. There may be two types of alcoholism, one related to an antisocial, pleasure-seeking personality (steady drinkers), and another related to a repressed, anxiety-ridden personality (binge drinkers). Alcoholism may be related to the presence of the A1 allele of the D2 dopamine receptor. Some investigators believe that a better understanding of the physiological basis of reinforcement and punishment will help us understand the effects of heredity on susceptibility to addiction. In fact, animal studies have shown that it is possible to selectively breed animals who do or do not prefer alcohol, and physiological studies have found that the level of dopamine and serotonin release is lower in alcohol-preferring rats. The low level of serotonin may play an important role in alcoholism; double-blind studies have found that serotonin agonists make it easier for alcoholics to abstain.

CONCLUDING REMARKS

THE DISORDERS DESCRIBED IN THE LAST TWO chapters of this book are serious problems for the afflicted individuals and for their friends and family. In addition, the rest of society helps pay for treatment or confinement of people with these disorders and suffers from lost productivity and the antisocial behaviors that some of these people commit. Early in this century most psychiatrists believed that the psychoses, at least, were caused by brain abnormalities, but with the ascendancy of psychotherapy, this belief fell into disrepute. More recently, with the discovery of the hereditary basis of these disorders and the efficacy of drug treatment, most researchers and clinicians again believe that the serious mental disorders reflect abnormalities in brain structure or biochemistry. We have seen some of the more important hypotheses being investigated by researchers today and some of the progress that has been made in understanding and treating the disorders. The future offers hope to people who suffer from the major mental disorders and to their families and friends.

A personal note: You are now at the end of the book (as you well know), and you have spent a considerable amount of time reading my words. While working on this book, I have tried to imagine myself talking to someone who is interested in learning something about the physiology of behavior. As I mentioned in the preface, writing is often a lonely activity, and the imaginary audience helped keep me company. If you would like to turn this communication into a two-way conversation, write to me—my address is given at the end of the preface.

New Terms

Anxiety Disorders

anxiety disorder p. 570

panic disorder p. 570

anticipatory anxiety p. 570

agoraphobia p. 570

obsessive compulsive
    disorder p. 573

obsession p. 573

compulsion p. 573

Tourette's syndrome p. 573

Autistic Disorder

autistic disorder p. 577

phenylketonuria p. 579

fragile X syndrome p. 579

Addiction

tolerance p. 583

withdrawal symptom p. 583

Suggested Readings

Bauman, M.L., and Kemper, T.L. *The Neurobiology of Autism.* Baltimore: Johns Hopkins University Press, 1994.

Bozarth, M.A. *Methods of Assessing the Reinforcing Properties of Abused Drugs.* New York: Springer-Verlag, 1987.

Gershon, E.S., and Cloninger, C.R. *New Genetic Approaches to Mental Disorders.* Washington, D.C.: American Psychiatric Press, 1994.

Goodwin, D.W., and Guze, S.B. *Psychiatric Diagnosis,* 5th ed. New York: Oxford University Press, 1989.

Hollander, E. *Obsessive-Compulsive Related Disorders.* Washington, D.C.: American Psychiatric Press, 1993.

Spitz, H.I., and Rosecan, J.S. *Cocaine Abuse: New Directions in Treatment and Research.* New York: Brunner/Mazel, 1987.

GLOSSARY

Absorptive phase. The phase of metabolism during which nutrients are absorbed from the digestive system. Glucose and amino acids constitute the principal source of energy for cells during this phase. Stores of glycogen are increased, and excess nutrients are stored in adipose tissue in the form of triglycerides.

Accessory olfactory bulb. A neural structure located in the main olfactory bulb. It receives information from the vomeronasal organ.

Accommodation. Changes in the thickness of the lens of the eye, accomplished by the ciliary muscles, that focus images of near or distant objects on the retina.

Acetylcholine (ACh). A neurotransmitter found in the brain, spinal cord, ganglia of the autonomic nervous system, and postganglionic terminal buttons of the parasympathetic division of the autonomic nervous system.

Acetylcholinesterase (AChE). The enzyme that destroys acetylcholine soon after it is liberated by the terminal buttons, thus terminating the postsynaptic potential.

Acetyl CoA. A cofactor that supplies acetate for the synthesis of acetylcholine.

Achromatopsia. An inability to discriminate among different hues; caused by damage to the visual association cortex.

Acquired dyslexia. A reading deficit in someone who could previously read; caused by brain damage.

ACTH. See *adrenocorticotrophic hormone (ACTH)*.

Actin. Actin and myosin are the proteins that provide the physical basis for muscular contraction.

Action potential. The brief electrical impulse that provides the basis for conduction of information along an axon. The action potential results from brief changes in membrane permeability to sodium and potassium ions.

Activational effects. See under *hormone*.

Adaptation. Decreasing sensitivity to a stimulus that is applied continuously.

Adenohypophysis. See under *pituitary gland*.

Adenosine triphosphate (ATP). A molecule of prime importance to cellular energy metabolism. The conversion of ATP to adenosine diphosphate (ADP) liberates energy. ATP can also be converted to cyclic AMP, which serves as an intermediate messenger in the production of postsynaptic potentials by some neurotransmitters and in the mediation of the effects of peptide hormones.

Adipose tissue. Fat tissue, composed of cells that can absorb nutrients from the blood and store them in the form of lipids during the absorptive phase or release them in the form of fatty acids and ketones during the fasting phase.

Adipsia. The complete lack of drinking. It can be produced by lesions of the lateral hypothalamus or the region around the anteroventral tip of the third ventricle.

Adjunctive behavior. A species-typical behavior such as drinking that occurs when a very hungry animal receives small pieces of food intermittently.

Ad libitum. Literally, "to the desire." More generally, "as much as is wanted."

Adrenal gland. An endocrine gland located atop the kidney. The *adrenal cortex* produces steroid hormones such as corticosterone, androstenedione, and aldosterone. The *adrenal medulla*, controlled by sympathetic nerve fibers, secretes epinephrine and norepinephrine.

Adrenalin. See *epinephrine*.

Adrenocorticotropic hormone (ACTH). A hormone produced and liberated by the anterior pituitary gland in response to corticotropin-releasing hormone, produced by the hypothalamus. ACTH stimulates the adrenal cortex to produce various steroid hormones.

Adrenogenital syndrome.   A condition characterized by hypersecretion of androgens by the adrenal cortex. The result, in females, is masculinization of the external genitalia.

Affect.   An emotional state of strong feelings, either positive or negative.

Afferent.   Toward a structure. All neurons afferent to the central nervous system convey sensory information.

Agonist.   Literally, a contestant, or one who takes part in the contest. An agonistic drug facilitates the effects of a particular neurotransmitter on the postsynaptic cell. An agonistic muscle produces or facilitates a particular movement. Antonym: antagonist.

Agoraphobia.   A fear of being away from home or other protected places. See *panic attack.*

Agrammatism.   One of the usual symptoms of Broca's aphasia; a difficulty in comprehending or properly employing grammatical devices, such as verb endings and word order.

Agraphia.   An inability to write; caused by brain damage.

Akinesia.   A motor disorder characterized by a relative lack of movement. Unlike paralysis, with akinesia, movement is possible if the patient is adequately stimulated.

Akinetic mutism.   A motor disorder characterized by a relative lack of movement and lack of speech.

Aldosterone.   A hormone of the adrenal cortex that causes the retention of sodium by the kidneys.

Alexia.   An inability to read; caused by brain damage.

All-or-none law.   States that once an action potential is triggered in an axon, it is propagated, without decrement, to the end of the fiber.

Alpha activity.   Smooth electrical activity of 8–12 Hz recorded from the brain. Alpha activity is generally associated with a state of relaxation.

Alpha motor neuron.   A neuron whose cell body is located in the ventral horn of the spinal cord or in one of the motor nuclei of the cranial nerves. Stimulation of an alpha motor neuron results in contraction of the extrafusal muscle fibers upon which its terminal buttons synapse.

Alzheimer's disease.   A degenerative brain disorder of unknown origin; causes progressive memory loss, motor deficits, and eventual death. Acetylcholine-secreting neurons are the first to be affected.

Amacrine cell.   A neuron in the retina that interconnects adjacent ganglion cells and the inner arborizations of the bipolar cells.

Amino acid.   A molecule that contains both an amino group and a carboxyl group. Amino acids are linked together by peptide bonds and serve as the constituents of proteins.

Amino group. NH_2; two atoms of hydrogen attached to an atom of nitrogen.

Amitriptyline.   A monoamine agonist; retards reuptake by the terminal buttons.

Ammon's horn.   The hippocampus proper; part of the hippocampal formation; consists of fields CA1–CA4 (for *cornu Ammonis*).

Amphetamine.   A catecholamine agonist: facilitates neurotransmitter release, stimulates postsynaptic receptors (slightly), and retards reuptake by the terminal buttons.

AMPT.   See α *methyl-p-tyrosine (AMPT).*

Ampulla.   An enlargement in a semicircular canal; contains the cupula and the crista.

Amygdala.   The term commonly used for the *amygdaloid complex;* a set of nuclei located in the base of the temporal lobe. The amygdala is a part of the limbic system.

Analgesia.   A lack of sensitivity to pain.

Androgen.   A male sex steroid hormone. Testosterone is the principal mammalian androgen.

Androgen insensitivity syndrome.   A condition, also called *testicular feminization,* caused by a congenital lack of functioning androgen receptors. Because androgens cannot exert their effects, a person with XY sex chromosomes develops as a female, with female external genitalia. Because the fetal testes produce Müllerian-inhibiting hormone, neither the Wolffian nor the Müllerian systems develop into internal sex organs.

Androgenization.   The process initiated by exposure of the cells of a developing animal to androgens. Exposure to androgens causes embryonic sex organs to develop as male and produces certain changes in the brain. See also *hormone.*

Androstenedione.   An androgen secreted by the adrenal cortex of both males and females.

Angiotensin.   See under *renin.*

Angiotensinogen.   See under *renin.*

Animism.   A primitive belief that all animals, or even all moving objects, possessed spirits providing their motive force.

Anion.   See under *ion*.

Anomia.   Difficulty in finding (remembering) the appropriate word to describe an object, action, or attribute; one of the symptoms of aphasia.

Anorexia nervosa.   A disorder that most frequently afflicts young women; exaggerated concern with overweight that leads to excessive dieting and often compulsive exercising; can lead to starvation.

ANS.   See *autonomic nervous system (ANS)*.

Antagonist.   An antagonistic muscle produces a movement contrary or opposite to the one being described. An antagonistic drug opposes or inhibits the effects of a particular neurotransmitter on the postsynaptic cell. Antonym: agonist.

Anterior.   See Figure 4.1.

Anterior nuclei (of thalamus).   A group of three nuclei of the thalamus (anterodorsal, anteromedial, and anteroventral); part of the limbic system; receive input from the hippocampus (via the fornix columns) and mammillary bodies of the hypothalamus; send axons to the cingulate gyrus.

Anterior pituitary gland.   See under *pituitary gland*.

Anterograde amnesia.   An amnesia for events that occur after some disturbance to the brain, such as head injury, electroconvulsive shock, or certain degenerative brain diseases.

Anterograde labeling method.   A histological method that labels the axons and terminal buttons of neurons whose cell bodies are located in a particular region.

Antibody.   A protein produced by a cell of the immune system that recognizes antigens present on invading microorganisms.

Anticipatory anxiety.   A fear of having a panic attack. It may lead to the development of agoraphobia.

Antigen.   A protein present on a microorganism that permits the immune system to recognize it as an invader.

Antipsychotic drug.   A drug that reduces or eliminates the symptoms of psychosis. Antischizophrenic drugs appear to exert their effect by antagonizing dopaminergic synapses.

Anxiety disorder.   A psychological disorder characterized by tension, overactivity of the autonomic nervous system, expectation of an impending disaster, and continuous vigilance for danger.

Aphagia.   A complete lack of eating; can be produced by lesions of the lateral hypothalamus.

Aphasia.   Difficulty in producing or comprehending speech not produced by deafness or a simple motor deficit; caused by brain damage.

Apomorphine.   A drug that blocks dopamine autoreceptors when administered at low doses. At higher doses it blocks postsynaptic receptors as well.

Apperceptive visual agnosia.   See under *visual agnosia*.

Apraxia.   Difficulty in carrying out purposeful movements, in the absence of paralysis or muscular weakness.

Aprosodia.   Difficulty in producing or comprehending those aspects of speech that are conveyed by changes in intonation or emphasis; apparently related to difficulties in the communication or perception of emotions.

Arachnoid membrane.   The middle layer of the meninges, between the outer dura mater and inner pia mater. The subarachnoid space beneath the arachnoid membrane is filled with cerebrospinal fluid, which cushions the brain.

Arcuate fasciculus.   A bundle of axons that connects Wernicke's area with Broca's area; damage causes conduction aphasia.

Arcuate nucleus.   The hypothalamic nucleus that contains the cell bodies of the neurosecretory cells that produce the hypothalamic hormones.

Area postrema.   A region of the medulla where the blood-brain barrier is weak. Systemic poisons can be detected there and can initiate vomiting.

Aromatization.   A form of chemical conversion catalyzed by an aromatase; the process by which testosterone is transformed into estradiol.

Association cortex.   Those regions of cortex that receive information from the sensory areas (sensory association cortex) or that project to the primary motor cortex (motor association cortex). It plays an important role in perception, learning, and planning.

Associative long-term potentiation.   A long-term potentiation in which concurrent stimulation of weak and strong synapses to a given neuron strengthens the weak ones.

Associative visual agnosia.   See under *visual agnosia*.

Astrocyte (astroglia).   A glial cell that provides support for neurons of the central nervous system. Astrocytes also participate in the formation of scar tissue after injury to the brain or spinal cord.

ATP.   See *adenosine triphosphate (ATP)*.

Atrial natriuretic peptide (ANP).   A peptide secreted by the atria of the heart when blood volume is higher than normal. It increases water and sodium excretion; inhibits renin, vasopressin, and aldosterone secretion; and inhibits sodium appetite.

Atropine.   A drug that blocks muscarinic acetylcholine receptors.

Auditory nerve. The auditory nerve has two principal branches. The *cochlear nerve* transmits auditory information, and the *vestibular nerve* transmits information related to balance.

Auditory tuning curve. A graph that indicates the minimal loudness of auditory stimuli of various frequencies that can produce a response in a particular neuron.

Autistic disorder. A chronic disorder that begins in infancy. Symptoms include failure to develop normal social relations with other people, impaired development of communicative ability, lack of imaginative ability, and repetitive, stereotyped movements.

Autoimmune disease. A disease in which the immune system attacks and damages some of the body's own tissue. Examples include multiple sclerosis, diabetes mellitus, and rheumatoid arthritis.

Autonomic ganglion. See under *ganglion*.

Autonomic nervous system (ANS). The portion of the peripheral nervous system that controls the body's vegetative function. The *sympathetic division* mediates functions that accompany arousal; the *parasympathetic division* mediates functions that occur during a relaxed state.

Autoradiography. A procedure that locates radioactive substances in body tissue, usually in the brain or spinal cord. The tissue is sliced, mounted on a microscope slide, and covered with a photographic emulsion or piece of film. The radiation exposes the emulsion, which is subsequently developed.

Autoreceptor. A receptor molecule located on a neuron that responds to the neurotransmitter or neuromodulator that the neuron itself secretes. Some autoreceptors are located on the presynaptic membrane; they participate in the regulation of the amount of neurotransmitter that is synthesized and released.

Autotopagnosia. An inability to name body parts or to identify body parts that another person names.

Axoaxonic synapse. The synapse of a terminal button upon the axon of another neuron, near its terminal buttons. These synapses mediate presynaptic inhibition.

Axodendritic synapse. The synapse of a terminal button of the axon of one neuron upon the dendrite of another neuron.

Axon. A thin, elongated process of a neuron that can transmit action potentials toward its terminal buttons, which synapse upon other neurons, gland cells, or muscle cells.

Axonal varicosity. Enlarged regions along the length of an axon that contain and release synaptic vesicles.

Axon hillock. The initial part of the axon, at the junction of the axon and soma. It is capable of producing an action potential and generally has a slightly lower threshold of excitation than the rest of the axon.

Axoplasmic transport. An active mechanism involving proteins similar to actin and myosin that propel substances down the axons from the soma to the terminal buttons. A slower form of axoplasmic transport carries substances in the opposite direction.

Axosomatic synapse. The synapse of a terminal button of the axon of one neuron upon the membrane of the soma of another neuron.

Balint's syndrome. A syndrome caused by bilateral damage to the parieto-occipital region. It includes *optic ataxia* (difficulty in reaching for objects under visual guidance), *ocular apraxia* (difficulty in visual scanning), and *simultanagnosia* (difficulty in perceiving more than one object at a time).

Baroreceptor. A special receptor that transduces changes in barometric pressure (chiefly within the heart or blood vessels) into neural activity.

Basal forebrain region. The region at the base of the forebrain rostral to the hypothalamus.

Basal ganglia. Caudate nucleus, globus pallidus, putamen, and amygdala. The first three are important parts of the motor system.

Basic rest-activity cycle (BRAC). A 90-min. cycle (in humans) of waxing and waning alertness, controlled by a biological clock in the caudal brain stem. During sleep, it controls cycles of REM sleep and slow-wave sleep.

Basilar artery. An artery found at the base of the brain, connecting the blood supplies of the vertebral and carotid arteries.

Basilar membrane. A membrane in the cochlea of the inner ear; contains the organ of Corti, the receptor organ for hearing.

Basolateral group. The phylogenetically newer portion of the amygdaloid complex.

Benzodiazepine. A class of drug with anxiolytic ("tranquilizing") effects. It works by activating benzodiazepine receptors coupled to GABA receptors on neurons, making the latter more sensitive to the neurotransmitter.

Beta activity. Irregular electrical activity of 13–30 Hz recorded from the brain. Beta activity is generally associated with a state of arousal.

Bilateral. On both sides of the midline of the body.

Binding site. The location on a receptor protein to which a ligand binds. For example, acetylcholine binds to the binding site of a nicotinic receptor and opens the associated neurotransmitter-dependent ion channel.

Bipolar disorder. A psychosis characterized by cyclical periods of mania and depression; effectively treated with lithium carbonate.

Bipolar neuron. A neuron with only two processes—a dendritic process at one end and an axonal process at the other end. *Bipolar cells* constitute the middle layer of the retina, conveying information from the receptor cells to the ganglion cells, whose axons give rise to the optic nerves.

Blindsight. The ability of a person to reach for objects located in his or her "blind" field. It occurs after damage restricted to the primary visual cortex.

Blob. The central region of a module of the primary visual cortex, revealed by a stain for cytochrome oxidase; contains wavelength-sensitive neurons; part of the parvocellular system.

Blood-brain barrier. A barrier produced by the astrocytes and cells in the walls of the capillaries in the brain. This barrier permits passage of only certain substances.

B-lymphocyte. A white blood cell that originates in the bone marrow; part of the immune system.

Botulinum toxin. An acetylcholine antagonist: prevents release by terminal buttons.

BRAC. See *basic rest-activity cycle (BRAC)*.

Brain stem. The "stem" of the brain, from the medulla to the midbrain, excluding the cerebellum.

Bregma. The junction of the sagittal and coronal sutures of the skull. It is often used as a reference point for stereotaxic brain surgery.

Broca's aphasia. See under *Broca's area*.

Broca's area. A region of frontal cortex, located just rostral to the base of the left primary motor cortex, that is necessary for normal speech production. Damage to this region results in *Broca's aphasia*, characterized by agrammatism and extreme difficulty in speech articulation.

Brown adipose tissue. Fat cells densely packed with mitochondria, which can generate heat. It is important in hibernating animals and is thought to play an important role in converting excessive calories of nutrients into heat rather than increased size of fat deposits.

Bruce effect. Termination of pregnancy caused by the odor of a pheromone in the urine of a male other than the one that impregnated the female; first identified in mice.

Bulimia. Bouts of excessive hunger and eating; often seen in people with anorexia nervosa.

CA1, CA3. See under *Ammon's horn*.

Cable properties. The passive conduction of electrical current, in a decremental fashion, down the length of an axon, similar to the way in which electrical current traverses a submarine cable.

Caffeine. An alkaloid drug found in coffee, chocolate, and other commonly ingested substances. It blocks the activity of phosphodiesterase, an enzyme that destroys cyclic nucleotides, the second messengers in the response of many cells to neurotransmitters, neuromodulators, or peptide hormones.

Calcarine fissure. A horizontal fissure on the inner surface of the posterior cerebral cortex; the location of the primary visual cortex.

Calcium-dependent enzyme. An enzyme that is inactive unless calcium ions bind with it.

Callosal apraxia. An apraxia of the left hand caused by damage to the anterior corpus callosum.

Calpain. A proteolytic (protein-cleaving) enzyme. It is thought to cause some of the cellular changes responsible for long-term potentiation by cleaving spectrin, a protein found immediately inside the neural membrane.

CaM-KII. Type II calcium-calmodulin kinase; an enzyme that must be activated by calcium. When activated, it remains so until deactivated by another enzyme.

Cannula. A small tube that may be inserted into the body to permit introduction of chemicals or removal of fluid for analysis.

Capsaicin. An ingredient in hot peppers that can destroy small, unmyelinated axons of the peripheral nervous system.

Carboxyl group. COOH; two atoms of oxygen and one atom of hydrogen bound to a single atom of carbon.

Cardiac muscle. The muscle responsible for the contraction of the heart.

Carotid artery. An artery, the branches of which serve the rostral portions of the brain.

Cataplexy. A symptom of narcolepsy; complete paralysis that occurs during waking. It is thought to be related to REM sleep mechanisms.

Catecholamine. A class of biologically active amines that includes the neurotransmitters dopamine, norepinephrine, and epinephrine.

Cation. See under *ion.*

Cauda equina. A bundle of spinal roots located caudal to the end of the spinal cord.

Caudal. See Figure 4.1.

Caudal block. The anesthesia and paralysis of the lower part of the body produced by injection of a local anesthetic into the cerebrospinal fluid surrounding the cauda equina.

Caudate nucleus. A telencephalic nucleus, one of the basal ganglia. The caudate nucleus is principally involved with inhibitory control of movement.

CCK. See *cholecystokinin (CCK).*

Central canal. The narrow tube, filled with cerebrospinal fluid, that runs through the length of the spinal cord.

Central nervous system (CNS). The brain and spinal cord.

Central nucleus. A nucleus of the amygdala that is involved in organizing the behavioral, autonomic, and endocrine components of conditioned emotional responses.

Central sulcus. The sulcus that separates the frontal lobe from the parietal lobe.

Central tegmental tract. An alternative name for the ventral noradrenergic bundle, which carries fibers of noradrenergic neurons from regions of the medulla and from the locus coeruleus and the subcoerulear area of the pons to the hypothalamus.

Cerebellar peduncle. One of three bundles of axons that attach each cerebellar hemisphere to the dorsal pons.

Cerebellum. A major part of the brain, situated dorsal to the pons, containing the two cerebellar hemispheres, covered with the cerebellar cortex. It is an important component of the motor system, involved in integrating, sequencing, and smoothing movements.

Cerebral aqueduct. A narrow tube interconnecting the third and fourth ventricles of the brain.

Cerebral cortex. The outermost layer of gray matter of the cerebral hemispheres.

Cerebral hemisphere. The two major portions of the forebrain, covered by the cerebral cortex.

Cerebrospinal fluid (CSF). A clear fluid, similar to blood plasma, that fills the ventricular system of the brain and the subarachnoid space surrounding the brain and spinal cord.

Chemoreceptor. A receptor that responds, by means of receptor potentials or neural impulses, to the presence of a particular chemical.

Chlorpromazine. A dopamine antagonist: blocks postsynaptic receptors. It is the most commonly prescribed antischizophrenic drug.

Cholecystokinin (CCK). A hormone secreted by the duodenum that regulates gastric motility and causes the gallbladder (cholecyst) to contract, expelling bile into the digestive system. It is also found in neurons in the brain, where it may serve as a neurotransmitter or neuromodulator.

Choline acetyltransferase. The enzyme that transfers the acetate ion from acetyl coenzyme A to choline, producing the neurotransmitter acetylcholine.

Chorda tympani. A branch of the facial nerve (seventh cranial nerve) that passes beneath the eardrum. It conveys taste information from the anterior part of the tongue and controls the secretion of some salivary glands.

Chorea. A movement disorder characterized by uncontrollable jerky movements.

Choroid plexus. The highly vascular tissue that protrudes into the ventricles and produces cerebrospinal fluid.

Chromosome. A strand of DNA, with associated proteins, found in the nucleus; carries genetic information.

Ciliary muscles. The muscles arranged around the lens of the eye. They control the shape of the eye to focus images of near or distant objects on the retina.

Cilium. A hairlike appendage of a cell; involved in movement or in transducing sensory information. Cilia are found on the receptors in the auditory and vestibular system.

Cingulate gyrus. A strip of limbic cortex lying along the lateral walls of the groove separating the cerebral hemispheres, just above the corpus callosum.

Circadian rhythm. A daily rhythmical change in behavior or physiological process.

Circumlocution. A strategy by which a person with anomia finds alternate ways to say something when he or she is unable to think of the most appropriate word.

Cisterna. A part of the Golgi apparatus. Through the process of pinocytosis, it receives portions of the presynaptic membrane and recycles them into synaptic vesicles.

Citric acid cycle. See *Krebs cycle.*

Clasp-knife reflex. A reflex that occurs when force is applied to flex or extend the limb of an animal showing decerebrate rigidity. Resistance occurs at first, replaced by sudden relaxation caused by activation of the Golgi tendon organs.

Classical conditioning. A learning procedure. When a stimulus that initially produces no more than an orienting response is followed several times by an *unconditional stimulus* that produces a defensive or appetitive response (the *unconditional response*), e first stimulus (now called a *conditional stimulus*) itself evokes the response (now called a *conditional response*).

CNS. Central nervous system; the brain and spinal cord.

CoA. See *coenzyme A (CoA)*.

Cocaine. A drug that retards the reuptake of the catecholamines, especially dopamine; a potent dopamine agonist.

Cochlea. The snail-shaped structure of the inner ear that contains the auditory transducing mechanisms.

Cochlear microphonics. The electrical activity recorded from the cochlear nerve that corresponds to the sound vibrations received at the oval window.

Cochlear nerve. See under *auditory nerve*.

Cochlear nuclei. A group of nuclei in the medulla that receive auditory information from the cochlea.

Coenzyme A (CoA). A chemical that, along with the enzyme choline acetyltransferase, participates in the synthesis of acetylcholine.

Color constancy. The relatively constant appearance of the colors of objects viewed under varying lighting conditions.

Commissure. A fiber bundle that interconnects corresponding regions on each side of the brain.

Complex cell. A neuron in the visual cortex that responds to the presence of a line segment with a particular orientation located within its receptive field, especially when the line moves perpendicularly to its orientation. Complex cells are distinguished from *simple cells* by their larger receptive fields and their response to movement.

Compulsion. The feeling that one is obliged to perform a behavior, even if one prefers not to do so.

Computerized tomography. See *CT scanner*.

Conditional response (CR). See under *classical conditioning*.

Conditional stimulus (CS). See under *classical conditioning*.

Conditioned emotional response. A classically conditioned response that occurs when a neutral stimulus is followed by an aversive stimulus; usually includes autonomic, behavioral, and endocrine components such as changes in heart rate, freezing, and secretion of stress-related hormones.

Conditioned flavor aversion. The avoidance of a relatively unfamiliar flavor that previously caused (or was followed by) illness.

Conditioned place preference. The learned preference for a location in which an organism encountered a reinforcing stimulus, such as food or a reinforcing drug.

Conditioned punisher. A previously neutral stimulus that has been followed by an aversive stimulus, which then becomes capable, through classical conditioning, of punishing a response.

Conditioned reinforcer. A previously neutral stimulus that has been paired with an appetitive stimulus, which then becomes capable, through classical conditioning, of reinforcing a response.

Conduction aphasia. Caused by damage to the connections between Wernicke's area and Broca's area; results in the inability to repeat words that are heard, although they can usually be understood and responded to appropriately.

Cone. See under *photoreceptor*.

Consolidation. The process by which short-term memories are converted into long-term memories.

Constructional apraxia. Difficulty in drawing pictures or diagrams or in making geometrical constructions of elements such as building blocks or sticks; caused by brain damage, especially to the right parietal lobe.

Content word. A noun, verb, adjective, or adverb that conveys meaning. (See also *function word*.)

Contralateral. Residing in the side of the body opposite to the reference point.

Converging operations. The use of different research methods to investigate a particular problem. If the methods all give the same answer, we can be more confident that the answer is correct.

Coolidge effect. The restorative effect of introducing a new female sex partner to a male that has apparently become "exhausted" by sexual activity.

Coping response. A response through which an organism can avoid, escape from, or minimize an aversive stimulus. The opportunity to make a coping response minimizes the stressful effects of an aversive stimulus.

Cornea. The transparent outer surface of the eye, in front of the iris and pupil.

Corpus callosum. The largest commissure of the brain, interconnecting the areas of neocortex on each side of the brain.

Corpus luteum. After ovulation, the ovarian follicle develops into a corpus luteum and secretes estradiol and progesterone.

Correctional mechanism. In a regulatory process, the mechanism that is capable of changing the value of the system variable.

Corticobulbar pathway. A bundle of axons from the neocortex (principally the primary motor cortex) to the nuclei of the fifth, seventh, and twelfth cranial nerves in the medulla, which control movements of the face and tongue.

Corticomedial group. The phylogenetically older portion of the amygdaloid complex.

Corticotropin-releasing factor (CRF). A hypothalamic hormone that stimulates the anterior pituitary gland to secrete ACTH (adrenocorticotrophic hormone).

Corticospinal pathway. The system of axons that originates in the cortex (especially the primary motor cortex) and terminates in the ventral gray matter of the spinal cord. Axons of the *lateral corticospinal tract* cross the midline in the medulla and synapse on spinal motor neurons and interneurons that control the arms and hands. Axons of the *ventral corticospinal tract* cross the midline near their site of termination in the spinal cord and primarily control movements of the trunk muscles.

CR. Conditional response. See under *classical conditioning.*

Cranial nerve. One of a set of twelve pairs of nerves that exit from the base of the brain.

Cranial nerve ganglion. See under *ganglion.*

Cross section. See Figure 4.2.

CS. Conditional stimulus. See under *classical conditioning.*

CSF. See *cerebrospinal fluid (CSF).*

CT scanner. A device that uses a computer to analyze data obtained by a scanning beam of X-rays to produce a two-dimensional picture of a "slice" through the body.

Cupula. A gelatinous mass found in the ampulla of the semicircular canals; moves in response to the flow of the fluid in the canals.

Curare. A drug that blocks nicotinic acetylcholine receptors.

Cutaneous sense. One of the somatosenses; includes sensitivity to stimuli that involve the skin.

Cyclic adenosine monophosphate (cyclic AMP). An intermediate messenger in the production of postsynaptic potentials by some neurotransmitters and in the mediation of the effects of peptide hormones.

Cyclic guanosine monophosphate (cyclic GMP). Similar in form and function to cyclic adenosine monophosphate, except that guanosine substitutes for adenosine. (See also *cyclic adenosine monophosphate.*)

Cyclic nucleotide. A compound such as cyclic AMP or cyclic GMP, important in mediating the intracellular effects of many neurotransmitters and peptide hormones.

Cytokine. A category of chemicals released by certain white blood cells when they detect the presence of an invading microorganism. It causes other white blood cells to proliferate and mount an attack against the invader.

Cytoplasm. The viscous, semiliquid substance contained in the interior of a cell.

DA. See *dopamine (DA).*

Decerebrate. Describes an animal whose brain stem has been transected.

Decerebrate rigidity. Simultaneous contraction of agonistic and antagonistic muscles; usually caused by damage to the reticular formation.

Declarative memory. Memory that can be verbally expressed, such as memory for events in a person's past. The ability to form new declarative memories is disrupted by lesions of the hippocampal formation or related structures.

Decremental conduction. Conduction of a subthreshold stimulus along an axon, according to its cable properties.

Decussation. The crossing of a fiber to the other side of the brain.

Deep cerebellar nucleus. One of several nuclei within the cerebellar hemispheres. These nuclei receive input from the Purkinje neurons of the cerebellar cortex and transmit information out of the cerebellum.

Defeminizing effect. The effect of a hormone present early in development. It reduces or prevents the later development of anatomical or behavioral characteristics typical of females. (See also *masculinizing effect.*)

Defensive behavior. A species-typical behavior by which an animal defends itself against the threat of another animal.

2–DG. See *2-deoxyglucose (2–DG).*

Deiters's cell. A supporting cell found in the organ of Corti; sustains the auditory hair cells.

Delayed conditioning. A classical conditioning procedure in which the unconditional stimulus is presented just before the conditional stimulus is turned off (both stimuli are turned off at the same time).

Delayed matching-to-sample task. A task that requires an animal to indicate which of several stimuli has just been seen.

Delta activity. Regular, synchronous electrical activity of approximately 1–4 Hz recorded from the brain. Delta activity is generally associated with slow-wave sleep.

Delusion. A belief that is clearly in contradiction to reality.

Dementia. A loss of cognitive abilities such as memory, perception, verbal ability, and judgment. Its common causes are multiple strokes or Alzheimer's disease.

Dendrite. A treelike process attached to the soma of a neuron, which receives messages from the terminal buttons of other neurons.

Dendritic spine. Small buds on the surface of a dendrite, upon which terminal buttons from other neurons synapse.

Dendrodendritic synapse. The synaptic connection between dendrites of adjacent neurons.

Denervation supersensitivity. The increased sensitivity of the neural postsynaptic membrane or motor endplate to the neurotransmitter; caused by damage to the afferent axons or long-term blockage of neurotransmitter release.

Dentate gyrus. Part of the hippocampal formation. It receives inputs from the entorhinal cortex via the perforant path and projects to the CA3 field of the hippocampus proper (Ammon's horn).

Dentate nucleus. A deep cerebellar nucleus; involved in the control of rapid, skilled movements by the corticospinal and rubrospinal systems.

2–Deoxyglucose (2-DG). A sugar that interferes with the metabolism of glucose.

Deoxyribonucleic acid (DNA). A long, complex macromolecule consisting of two interconnected helical strands. Strands of DNA, along with their associated proteins, constitute the chromosomes, which contain the genetic information of the animal.

Depolarization. Reduction (toward zero) of the membrane potential of a cell from its normal resting potential of approximately -70 mV.

Desynchrony. Irregular electrical activity recorded from the brain, generally associated with periods of arousal. (See also *beta activity*.)

Detector. In a regulatory process, a mechanism that signals when the system variable deviates from its set point.

Deuteranopia. An inherited form of defective color vision in which red and green hues are confused. "Green" cones appear to be filled with "red" cone opsin.

Developmental dyslexia. A reading difficulty in a person of normal intelligence and perceptual ability; of genetic origin or caused by prenatal or perinatal factors.

Diabetes insipidus. The loss of excessive amounts of water through the kidneys; caused by lack of secretion of vasopressin.

Diabetes mellitus. A disease that results from insufficient production of insulin, thus causing, in an untreated state, a high level of blood glucose.

Diencephalon. See Table 4.1.

Diffusion. Movement of molecules from regions of high concentration to regions of low concentration.

Dihydrotestosterone. An androgen, produced from testosterone through the action of the enzyme 5-α reductase.

DiI. A dye that can be used to trace neural pathways in the brains of deceased organisms.

Direct dyslexia. A language disorder caused by brain damage in which the person can read words aloud without understanding them.

Discriminative stimulus. A stimulus that signifies that a particular response will be followed by a particular event. In an instrumental conditioning task, a discriminative stimulus indicates that a response will be reinforced.

DNA. See *deoxyribonucleic acid (DNA)*.

Doctrine of specific nerve energies. Müller's observation that different nerve fibers convey different information, but that the basic nature of the message (later found to be the action potential) is the same.

DOPA decarboxylase. The enzyme that converts the L-DOPA to the neurotransmitter dopamine.

Dopamine (DA). A neurotransmitter; one of the catecholamines.

Dopamine ß-hydroxylase. The enzyme that converts dopamine to the neurotransmitter norepinephrine. The conversion occurs within synaptic vesicles.

Dorsal. See Figure 4.1.

Dorsal columns.   Vertically oriented bundles of axons in the dorsal spinal cord; convey somatosensory information to the brain.

Dorsal lateral geniculate nucleus.   See under *lateral geniculate nucleus.*

Dorsal motor nuclei of the vagus.   Nuclei of the tenth cranial nerve; control parasympathetic functions of the vagus nerve, such as the secretion of insulin.

Dorsal root.   See under *spinal root.*

Dorsal root ganglion.   See under *ganglion.*

Dorsal tegmental bundle.   An alternative name for the dorsal noradrenergic bundle, which carries fibers of noradrenergic neurons from the locus coeruleus to various forebrain structures.

Dorsolateral column.   A fiber bundle in the spinal cord that contains serotonergic axons that mediate opiate-induced analgesia.

Dorsolateral pathway.   The system of axons that travel from the brain stem to the spinal cord, primarily those of the *rubrospinal tract*, which controls muscles that move the forelimbs.

Double labeling.   Labeling neurons in a particular region by two different means; for example, by using an anterograde tracer and a label for a particular enzyme.

Drive reduction hypothesis.   The hypothesis that reinforcement occurs when a drive (presumed to be aversive) is reduced; for example, when hunger is reduced by eating.

Drug dependency insomnia.   An insomnia caused by the side effects of ever-increasing doses of sleeping medications.

Drug discrimination procedure.   An experimental procedure in which an animal shows, through instrumental conditioning, whether the perceived effects of two drugs are similar.

Dualism.   The philosophical position that the universe is divided into two realms: the physical and the nonphysical (spiritual). Thus, people have physical bodies and nonphysical minds or souls.

Duodenum.   The portion of the small intestine immediately adjacent to the stomach.

Dura mater.   The outermost layer of the three meninges.

Dynorphin.   See under *endogenous opiate.*

Dyslexia.   A term that refers to a variety of reading disorders.

EEG.   See *electroencephalogram (EEG).*

Efferent.   Away from a structure. Efferent axons of the central nervous system control the muscles and glands.

Electroconvulsive shock (ECS).   A brief electrical shock, applied to the head, that results in electrical seizure and convulsions. It is used therapeutically to alleviate severe depression and experimentally (in animals) to study the consolidation process.

Electroconvulsive therapy.   See *electroconvulsive shock.*

Electrode.   A conductive medium (generally made of metal) that can be used to apply electrical stimulation or to record electrical potentials.

Electroencephalogram (EEG).   An electrical brain potential recorded by placing electrodes on or in the scalp or on the surface of the brain.

Electrolyte.   An aqueous solution of a material that ionizes—namely, a soluble acid, base, or salt.

Electromyogram (EMG).   An electrical potential recorded from an electrode placed on or in a muscle.

Electro-oculogram (EOG).   An electrical potential from the eyes, recorded by means of electrodes placed on the skin around them; detects eye movements.

Electrostatic pressure.   The attractive force between atomic particles charged with opposite signs, or the repulsive force between atomic particles charged with the same sign.

Embolus.   A piece of matter (such as a blood clot, fat, or bacterial debris) that dislodges from its site of origin and occludes an artery. In the brain, an embolus can lead to a stroke.

Endocrine gland.   A gland that liberates its secretions into the extracellular fluid around capillaries and hence into the bloodstream.

Endogenous depression.   A depression that appears to have no environmental cause and is thus apparently of biological origin.

Endogenous opioid.   A class of peptides secreted by the brain or pituitary gland that act as opiates; includes the *endorphins, dynorphins,* and *enkephalins.*

Endoplasmic reticulum.   Parallel layers of mem-brane found within the cytoplasm of a cell. Rough endoplasmic reticulum contains ribosomes and is involved with production of proteins that are secreted by the cell. Smooth endoplasmic reticulum is concerned with the segregation and transport of substances within the cell.

ß-Endorphin.   An endogenous opioid secreted by cells in the brain and by the anterior pituitary gland.

Endplate potential. The postsynaptic potential that occurs on the membranes of muscle fibers in response to release of acetylcholine by terminal buttons.

Enkephalin. See under *endogenous opioid*.

Entorhinal cortex. A region of the limbic cortex that provides the major source of input to the hippocampal formation.

Enzymatic deactivation. The destruction of a transmitter substance by an enzyme after its release. The destruction of acetylcholine by acetylcholinesterase is the most common example.

Enzyme. A protein that facilitates a biochemical reaction without itself becoming part of the end product.

EOG. See *electro-oculogram (EOG)*.

Ependyma. The layer of tissue around blood vessels and on the interior walls of the ventricular system of the brain.

Epinephrine. A hormone, secreted by the adrenal medulla, that produces physiological effects characteristic of the sympathetic division of the autonomic nervous system.

EPSP. See under *postsynaptic potential*.

Equilibrium. A balance of forces, during which the system is not changing.

Esophageal fistula. A diversion of the esophagus so that when an animal eats or drinks, the substance does not reach the stomach.

Estradiol. The principal estrogen of many mammals, including humans.

Estrogen. A class of sex hormones that cause maturation of the female genitalia, growth of breast tissue, and development of other physical features characteristic of females. Estrogens are also necessary for normal sexual behavior of most mammals other than primates.

Estrous cycle. A cyclic change in the hormonal level and sexual receptivity of subprimate mammals.

Estrus. That portion of the estrous cycle during which a female is sexually receptive.

Evoked potential. A regular series of alterations in the slow electrical activity recorded from the central nervous system, produced by a sensory stimulus or an electrical shock to some part of the nervous system.

Excitatory postsynaptic potential (EPSP). See under *postsynaptic potential*.

Exocrine gland. A gland that liberates its secretions into a duct.

Exocytosis. The secretion of a substance by a cell through means of vesicles; the process by which neurotransmitters are secreted.

Experimental ablation. The removal or destruction of a portion of the brain of an experimental animal for the purpose of studying the functions of that region. Presumably, the functions that can no longer be performed are the ones the region previously controlled.

Extension. A movement of a limb that tends to straighten its joints; the opposite of flexion. The muscles that support the weight of a four-legged animal are those that produce extension.

Extinction. The reduction or elimination of a behavior caused by ceasing the presentation of the reinforcing stimulus.

Extracellular fluid. All body fluids outside cells: interstitial fluid, blood plasma, and cerebrospinal fluid.

Extrafusal muscle fiber. One of the muscle fibers that are responsible for the force exerted by a muscular contraction.

Extrastriate cortex. A region of visual association cortex. It receives fibers from the striate cortex and from the superior colliculi and projects (in primates) to the inferior temporal cortex.

Fastigial nucleus. A deep cerebellar nucleus; involved in the control of movement by the reticulospinal and vestibulospinal tracts.

Fasting phase. The phase of metabolism during which nutrients are not available from the digestive system. Glucose, amino acids, fatty acids, and ketones are derived from glycogen, protein, and adipose tissue during this phase.

Fatty acid. A substance of importance to metabolism during the fasting phase. Fats can be broken down to fatty acids and glycerol. Fatty acids can be metabolized by most cells of the body. Their basic structure is an alkyl group (CH) attached to a carboxyl group (COOH).

Feature detector. A neuron whose synaptic connections with afferent neurons cause it to respond when particular classes of stimuli, with characteristic features, are detected.

Fight-or-flight response. A species-typical response preparatory to fighting or fleeing; thought to be responsible for some of the deleterious effects of stressful situations on health.

Fimbria. A fiber bundle that runs along the lateral surface of the hippocampal complex, connecting this structure with other regions of the forebrain. The fibers of the fimbria become the *fornix* as they course rostrally from the hippocampal formation. The *precommissural fornix* conveys axons from the medial septum to the hippocampus and from the hippocampus to the lateral septum. The *fornix columns* convey axons from the subiculum to the anterior thalamic nuclei and to the mammillary bodies of the hypothalamus.

Fissure. A major groove in the surface of the brain. A smaller groove is called a sulcus.

Fixative. A chemical (for example, formalin) used to prepare and preserve body tissue.

Flexion. A movement of a limb that tends to bend its joints; opposite of extension.

Flocculonodular lobe. A region of the cerebellum; involved in control of postural reflexes.

Fluorogold. A dye that serves as a retrograde label. It is taken up by terminal buttons and carried back to the cell bodies.

Focal epilepsy. A condition in which recurrent seizures are produced by hyperirritability of a localized region of the brain, especially the medial temporal lobe or orbital frontal lobe.

Follicle. A small secretory cavity. The *ovarian follicle* consists of epithelial cells surrounding an oocyte, which develops into an ovum.

Follicle-stimulating hormone (FSH). The hormone of the anterior pituitary gland that causes development of an ovarian follicle and the maturation of its oocyte into an ovum.

Foramen. A normal passage that allows communication between two cavities of the body. The *intervertebral foramen* permits passage of the spinal nerves through the vertebral column. The *foramens of Magendie and Luschka* permit the passage of cerebrospinal fluid out of the fourth ventricle and into the subarachnoid space. The *foramen of Monro* interconnects the lateral and third ventricles.

Forebrain. See Table 4.1.

Formalin. The aqueous solution of formaldehyde gas; the most commonly used tissue fixative.

Fornix. See under *fimbria*.

Fornix columns. See under *fimbria*.

Fos. A protein produced in the nucleus of a neuron in response to synaptic stimulation.

Fourth ventricle. See under *ventricle*.

Fovea. The region of the retina that mediates the most acute vision of birds and higher mammals. Color-sensi-

tive cones constitute the only type of photoreceptor found in the fovea.

Fragile X syndrome. A genetic disorder caused by a faulty gene on the X chromosome; the leading genetic cause of mental retardation.

Frontal lobe. The front portion of the cerebral cortex, including Broca's speech area and the motorcortex. Damage to the frontal lobe impairs movement, planning, and flexibility in behavioral strategies.

Frontal section. See Figure 4.2.

FSH. See *follicle-stimulating hormone (FSH)*.

Functionalism. The strategy of understanding a species' structural or behavioral features by attempting to establish their usefulness with respect to survival or reproductive success.

Function word. A preposition, article, or other word that conveys little of the meaning of a sentence but is important in specifying its grammatical structure. (See also *content word*.)

Fundamental frequency. The lowest, and usually most intense, frequency of a complex sound; most often perceived as the sound's basic pitch.

GAD. See *glutamic acid decarboxylase (GAD)*.

Galanin. A neuropeptide that may increase an animal's appetite for lipids.

Gamete. A mature reproductive cell; a sperm or ovum.

Gamma-aminobutyric acid (GABA). An important inhibitory transmitter substance.

Gamma motor neuron. A lower motor neuron whose terminal buttons synapse upon intrafusal muscle fibers.

Ganglion. A collection of neural cell bodies, covered with connective tissue, located outside the central nervous system. *Autonomic ganglia* contain the cell bodies of postganglionic neurons of the sympathetic and parasympathetic branches of the autonomic nervous system. *Dorsal root ganglia (spinal nerve ganglia)* contain cell bodies of afferent spinal nerve neurons. *Cranial nerve ganglia* contain cell bodies of afferent cranial nerve neurons. The *basal ganglia* include the amygdala, caudate nucleus, globus pallidus, and putamen; in this case the term *ganglion* is a misnomer, since the basal ganglia are actually brain nuclei.

Ganglion cells. Neurons located in the retina that receive visual information from bipolar cells. Their axons give rise to the optic nerve.

Gap junction. A special junction between cells that permits direct communication by means of electrical coupling.

Gene. The functional unit of the chromosome, which directs synthesis of one or more proteins.

Generalization. Along with reduction, one of the forms of explanation in science; describing a phenomenon in general terms that permits one to explain similar phenomena.

Gestagen. A group of hormones that promote and support pregnancy. Progesterone is the principal mammalian gestagen.

GH. See *growth hormone (GH)*.

Glabrous skin. Skin that does not contain hair; found on the palms and soles of the feet.

Glia (glial cells). The supportive cells of the central nervous system—the astroglia, oligodendroglia, and microglia.

Globus pallidus. One of the basal ganglia; an excitatory structure of the extrapyramidal motor system.

Glucagon. A pancreatic hormone that promotes the conversion of liver glycogen into glucose.

Glucocorticoid. One of a group of hormones of the adrenal cortex that are important in protein and carbohydrate metabolism, secreted especially in times of stress.

Glucoprivation. A dramatic fall in the blood level of glucose.

Glucose. A simple sugar, of great importance in metabolism. Glucose and ketones constitute the major sources of energy for the brain.

Glucostatic hypothesis. A hypothesis that states that the level or availability of glucose in the interstitial fluid determines whether an organism is hungry or satiated.

Glutamic acid (glutamate). An amino acid; an important excitatory transmitter substance.

Glutamic acid decarboxylase (GAD). The enzyme that converts glutamic acid into GABA, an important inhibitory transmitter substance.

Glycerol (glycerin). A trihydric alcohol. The breakdown of triglycerides (fats stored in adipose tissue) yields fatty acids and glycerol. Glycerol can be converted by the liver into glucose.

Glycine. An amino acid; an important inhibitory transmitter substance.

Glycogen. A polysaccharide often referred to as *animal starch*. The hormone glucagon causes conversion of liver glycogen into glucose.

Golgi apparatus. A complex of parallel membranes in the cytoplasm that wraps the products of a secretory cell.

Golgi-Cox stain. A stain that colors the cell membrane.

Golgi tendon organ. The receptor organ at the junction of the tendon and muscle that is sensitive to stretch.

Gonad. The ovaries or testes.

Gonadotropic hormone. A hormone of the anterior pituitary gland that has a stimulating effect on cells of the gonads. See *follicle-stimulating hormone (FSH)* and *luteinizing hormone (LH)*.

Gonadotropin-releasing hormone. A hypothalamic hormone that stimulates the anterior pituitary gland to secrete gonadotropic hormone.

G protein. A protein that binds with guanosine diphosphate and guanosine triphosphate; when activated, modifies the activity of particular enzymes.

Granule cell. A small, granular cell. The granule cells of the dentate gyrus are part of the trisynaptic circuit; they send axons to the CA3 field of Ammon's horn.

Growth hormone (GH). A hormone necessary for the normal growth of the body before adulthood; also called *somatotropic hormone (STH)*.

Gyrus. A convolution of the cortex of the cerebral hemispheres, separated by sulci or fissures.

Hair cell. The receptive cell of the auditory or vestibular apparatus.

6–HD. See *6-hydroxydopamine (6–HD)*.

Hebb rule. The hypothesis proposed by David Hebb that the cellular basis of learning involves strengthening of a synapse that is repeatedly active at the time when the postsynaptic neuron fires.

Hepatic portal system. The system of blood vessels that drain the capillaries of the digestive system, travel to the liver, and divide again into capillaries.

Hertz (Hz). A cycle per second; a measure of frequency of vibration.

5-HIAA. See *5-hydroxyindoleacetic acid (5-HIAA)*.

Hindbrain. See Table 4.1.

Hippocampal formation. A forebrain structure of the temporal lobe, constituting an important part of the limbic system; includes the hippocampus proper (Ammon's horn), dentate gyrus, and subiculum.

Histology. The microscopic study of tissues of the body.

Homeostasis. The process by which the body's substances and characteristics (such as temperature and glucose level) are maintained at their optimal level.

Homoiothermous. A "warm-blooded" animal, which regulates its body temperature by altering its metabolic activity.

Horizontal cell. A neuron in the retina that interconnects adjacent photoreceptors and the outer arborizations of the bipolar cells.

Horizontal section. See Figure 4.2.

Hormone. A chemical substance liberated by an endocrine gland that has effects on target cells in other organs. *Organizational effects* of a hormone affect tissue differentiation and development; for example, androgens cause prenatal development of male genitalia. *Activational effects* of a hormone are those that occur in the fully developed organism; many of them depend upon the organism's prior exposure to the organizational effects of hormones.

Horseradish peroxidase (HRP). An enzyme extracted from the horseradish root that can be made visible by special histological techniques. Since it is taken up by terminal buttons or by severed axons and is carried by axoplasmic transport, it is useful in anatomical studies.

5-HTP decarboxylase. The enzyme that converts 5-hydroxytryptophan (5-HTP) to the neurotransmitter 5-hydroxytryptamine (5-HT, or serotonin).

Huntington's chorea. An inherited disorder that causes degeneration of the basal ganglia. It is characterized by progressively more severe uncontrollable jerking movements, writhing movements, dementia, and, finally, death.

Hydrocephalus. A condition in which all or some of the brain's ventricles are enlarged. *Obstructive hydrocephalus* occurs when the normal flow of cerebrospinal fluid is impeded, increasing the intraventricular pressure. *Hydrocephalus ex vacuo* occurs when brain tissue degenerates and the ventricles expand to take up the space the tissue formerly occupied.

6–Hydroxydopamine (6–HD). A chemical that is selectively taken up by axons and terminal buttons of noradrenergic or dopaminergic neurons and that acts as a poison, damaging or killing them.

5-Hydroxyindoleacetic acid (5-HIAA). A breakdown product of the neurotransmitter serotonin.

5-Hydroxytryptamine (5-HT). An indolamine transmitter substance; also called *serotonin*.

5-Hydroxytryptophan (5-HTP). Derived from the amino acid tryptophan; converted to the neurotransmitter 5-hydroxytryptamine (5-HT) by the enzyme 5-HTP decarboxylase.

Hyperpolarization. An increase in the membrane potential of a cell, relative to the normal resting potential. Inhibitory postsynaptic potentials (IPSPs) are hyperpolarizations.

Hypertonic. The characteristic of a solution that contains enough solute that it will draw water out of a cell placed in it, through the process of osmosis.

Hypnagogic hallucinations. A symptom of narcolepsy; vivid dreams that occur just before a person falls asleep; accompanied by sleep paralysis.

Hypoglycemia. A low level of blood glucose.

Hypothalamic hormone. A hormone produced by cells of the hypothalamus that affects the secretion and production of hormones of the anterior pituitary gland. The effects are excitatory in the case of releasing hormones and inhibitory in the case of inhibitory hormones.

Hypothalamic-hypophyseal portal system. A system of blood vessels that connect capillaries of the hypothalamus with capillaries of the anterior pituitary gland. Hypothalamic hormones travel to the anterior pituitary gland by means of this system.

Hypothalamus. The part of the diencephalon situated beneath the thalamus. It is involved in regulation of the autonomic nervous system, control of the anterior and posterior pituitary glands, and integration of species-typical behaviors.

Hypotonic. The characteristic of a solution that contains so little solute that a cell placed in it will absorb water, through the process of osmosis.

Hypovolemia. See under *volumetric thirst*.

Hz. See *hertz (Hz)*.

Imipramine. A noradrenergic agonist; retards reuptake of norepinephrine by terminal buttons. It is one of the most commonly used tricyclic antidepressants.

Immune system. The system by which the body protects itself from foreign proteins. In response to an infection, the white blood cells produce antibodies that attack and destroy the foreign antigen.

Immunocytochemical method. A histological method that uses radioactive antibodies or antibodies bound with a dye molecule to indicate the presence of particular proteins of peptides.

Immunoglobulin. An antibody released by B-lymphocytes that bind with antigens and help destroy invading microorganisms.

Incus. One of the bones of the middle ear, shaped somewhat like an anvil.

Inferior colliculi. Protrusions on top of the midbrain that relay auditory information to the medial geniculate nucleus.

Inferior temporal cortex. In monkeys, the highest level of visual association cortex, located on the inferior surface of the temporal lobe.

Ingestive behavior. Eating or drinking.

Inhibitory postsynaptic potential (IPSP). See under *postsynaptic potential.*

In situ hybridization. The production of DNA complementary to a particular messenger RNA in order to detect the presence of the RNA.

Instrumental conditioning. A learning procedure whereby the effects of a particular behavior in a particular situation increase (reinforce) or decrease (punish) the probability of the behavior; also called *operant conditioning.*

Insulin. A pancreatic hormone that facilitates entry of glucose and amino acids into the cell, facilitates conversion of glucose into glycogen, and facilitates transport of fats into adipose tissue.

Internal carotid artery. Along with the vertebral artery, the major source of blood to the brain.

Interposed nuclei. A set of deep cerebellar nuclei. They are involved in the control of the rubrospinal system.

Interstitial fluid. The fluid that bathes the cells, filling the space between the cells of the body (the "interstices").

Intervertebral foramen. See under *foramen.*

Intracellular fluid. The fluid contained within cells.

Intrafusal muscle fiber. A muscle fiber that functions as a stretch receptor, arranged parallel to the extrafusal muscle fibers, thus detecting muscle length; also called *muscle spindle.*

Intraperitoneal (IP). Pertaining to the peritoneal cavity, the space surrounding the abdominal organs.

Intravascular fluid. The fluid found within the blood vessels.

Intromission. The insertion of one part into another, especially of a penis into a vagina.

Ion. A charged molecule. *Cations* are positively charged, and *anions* are negatively charged.

Ion channel. A specialized protein molecule that permits specific ions to enter or leave cells. *Voltage-dependent ion channels* open or close according to the value of the membrane potential. *Neurotransmitter-dependent ion channels* open when they detect molecules of the appropriate neurotransmitter or molecules of a cyclic nucleotide that serves as a second messenger.

Ionotropic receptor. A receptor that contains a binding site for a neurotransmitter and an ion channel. When a molecule of the neurotransmitter binds with the receptor, the ion channel opens. (See also *metabotropic receptor.*)

IP. See *intraperitoneal (IP).*

Iproniazid. A monoamine agonist; deactivates monoamine oxidase and thus prevents destruction of extravesicular monoamines in the terminal buttons.

Ipsilateral. Located on the same side of the body as the point of reference.

IPSP. See under *postsynaptic potential.*

Isotonic. Equal in osmotic pressure to the contents of a cell. A cell placed in an isotonic solution neither gains nor loses water.

James-Lange theory. A theory of emotion that suggests that behaviors and physiological responses are directly elicited by situations, and that feelings of emotions are produced by feedback from these behaviors and responses.

Kainic acid. A molecule similar to glutamic acid that destroys neurons with which it comes in contact, apparently by causing continuous excitation. It is used to produce brain lesions that spare axons that pass through the area containing the cells targeted for destruction.

Kindling. The establishment of a seizure focus by daily administration of a small amount of localized electrical brain stimulation; used to produce animal models of focal epilepsy.

Kinesthesia. Perception of the body's own movements.

Korsakoff's syndrome. A permanent anterograde amnesia (inability to learn new information) caused by brain damage resulting from chronic alcoholism or malnutrition.

Krebs cycle (citric acid cycle, tricarboxylic acid cycle). A series of chemical reactions that involve oxidation of pyruvate. The Krebs cycle takes place on the cristae of the mitochondria and supplies the principal source of energy to the cell.

Lamella. A layer of membrane containing photopigments; found in rods and cones of the retina.

Lateral.   See Figure 4.1.

Lateral-basomedial group.   A group of nuclei in the amygdala that receive auditory, somatosensory, and visual information.

Lateral corticospinal tract.   See under *corticospinal pathway.*

Lateral fissure.   The fissure that separates the temporal lobe from the overlying frontal and parietal lobes.

Lateral geniculate nucleus.   A group of cell bodies within the lateral geniculate body of the thalamus. The *dorsal lateral geniculate nucleus* receives fibers from the retina and projects fibers to the primary visual cortex.

Lateral hypothalamus.   A region of the hypothalamus that contains cell bodies and diffuse fiber systems. Destruction of the lateral hypothalamus produces a relative lack of spontaneous movement, adipsia, aphagia, and weight loss, from which the animal at least partially recovers.

Lateral lemniscus.   A band of fibers running rostrally through the medulla and pons; carries fibers of the auditory system.

Lateral preoptic area.   See under *preoptic area.*

Lateral ventricle.   See under *ventricle.*

L-Dihydroxyphenylalanine.   See *L-DOPA.*

L-DOPA.   The levorotatory isomeric form of dihydroxyphenylalanine; the precursor of the catecholamines dopamine, norepinephrine, and epinephrine. It is often used to treat Parkinson's disease because of its effect as a dopamine agonist.

Lee-Boot effect.   The increased incidence of false pregnancies seen in female animals that are housed together; caused by a pheromone in the animals' urine; first observed in mice.

Left parietal apraxia.   An apraxia caused by damage to the left parietal lobe. It is characterized by difficulty in producing sequences of movements by verbal request or in imitation of movements made by someone else.

Lemniscal system.   The somatosensory fibers of the lateral or trigeminal lemniscus, as contrasted with the extralemniscal system, a polysynaptic pathway that ascends through the reticular formation.

LH.   See *luteinizing hormone (LH).*

Ligand.   A chemical that binds with the binding site of a receptor.

Limbic cortex.   Phylogenetically old cortex, located at the edge ("limbus") of the cerebral hemispheres; part of the limbic system.

Limbic system.   A group of brain regions including the anterior thalamic nuclei, amygdala, hippocampus, limbic cortex, and parts of the hypothalamus, as well as their interconnecting fiber bundles.

Lipoprivation.   A dramatic fall in the blood level of fatty acids.

Lithium.   An element. Lithium carbonate is used to treat bipolar disorder.

Locus coeruleus.   A dark-colored group of noradrenergic cell bodies located in the pons near the rostral end of the floor of the fourth ventricle.

Long-term depression.   A long-term decrease in the excitability of a neuron to a particular synaptic input caused by repeated low-frequency activity of that input.

Long-term memory.   Relatively stable memory, as opposed to short-term memory.

Long-term potentiation.   A long-term increase in the excitability of a neuron to a particular synaptic input caused by repeated high-frequency activity of that input.

Lordosis.   A spinal sexual reflex seen in many four-legged female mammals; arching of the back in response to approach of a male or to touching the flanks, which elevates the hindquarters.

Lower motor neuron.   A neuron located in the intermediate horn or ventral horn of the gray matter of the spinal cord or in one of the motor nuclei of the cranial nerves, the axon of which synapses on muscle fibers.

Luteinizing hormone (LH).   A hormone of the anterior pituitary gland that causes ovulation and development of the ovarian follicle into a corpus luteum.

Lysosome.   An organelle surrounded by membrane. It contains enzymes that break down waste products.

Macroelectrode.   An electrode used to record the electrical activity of large numbers of neurons in a particular region of the brain. It is much larger than a microelectrode.

Magnetic resonance imaging (MRI).   A technique whereby the interior of the living body (particularly the brain) can be accurately imaged; involves the interaction between radio waves and a strong magnetic field.

Magnocellular nucleus.   A nucleus in the medulla; involved in the atonia (muscular paralysis) that accompanies REM sleep.

Magnocellular system.   The phylogenetically older portion of the visual system, named after the magnocellular layers of the lateral geniculate nucleus. It is responsible for the perception of form, movement, depth, and small differences in brightness.

Major affective disorder. A serious mood disorder; includes unipolar depression and bipolar disorder.

Malleus. One of the bones of the middle ear, shaped somewhat like a hammer.

Mammillary body. A protrusion of the bottom of the brain at the posterior end of the hypothalamus, containing the medial and lateral mammillary nuclei.

MAO. See *monoamine oxidase (MAO)*.

Masculinizing effect. The effect of a hormone present early in development. It promotes the later development of anatomical or behavioral characteristics typical of males. (See also *defeminizing effect*.)

Massa intermedia. A bridge of tissue across the third ventricle that connects the right and left portions of the thalamus.

Medial. See Figure 4.1.

Medial forebrain bundle (MFB). A fiber bundle that runs in a rostral-caudal direction through the basal forebrain and lateral hypothalamus.

Medial geniculate nucleus. A group of cell bodies within the medial geniculate body of the thalamus; part of the auditory system.

Medial lemniscus. A fiber bundle that ascends rostrally through the medulla and pons, carrying fibers of the somatosensory system.

Medial nucleus of the amygdala. A nucleus that receives olfactory information from the olfactory bulb and accessory olfactory bulb. It is involved in the effects of odors and pheromones on reproductive behavior.

Medial preoptic area. See *preoptic area*.

Median preoptic nucleus. A small nucleus situated around the decussation of the anterior commissure. It plays a role in thirst stimulated by angiotensin II.

Medulla oblongata (usually medulla). The most caudal portion of the brain, immediately rostral to the spinal cord.

Meiosis. The process by which a cell divides to form gametes (sperms or ova).

Meissner's corpuscle. The touch-sensitive end organs located in the papillae, small elevations of the dermis that project up into the epidermis.

Melatonin. A hormone secreted during the night by the pineal body. It plays a role in circadian and seasonal rhythms.

Membrane. A structure consisting principally of lipid molecules that defines the outer boundaries of a cell and also constitutes many of the cell organelles, such as the Golgi apparatus.

Membrane potential. The electrical charge across a cell membrane; the difference in electrical potential inside and outside the cell. It is expressed as inside voltage relative to outside voltage (for example, -70 mV signifies that the inside is 70 mV negative to the outside).

Meninges (singular: **meninx**). The three layers of tissue that encase the central nervous system: the dura mater, arachnoid membrane, and pia mater.

Merkel's disk. The touch-sensitive end organs found at the base of the epidermis, adjacent to sweat ducts.

Mesencephalic locomotor region. A region of the reticular formation of the midbrain. Stimulation of this region causes alternating movements of the limbs normally seen during locomotion.

Mesencephalon. See Table 4.1.

Mesocortical system. A system of dopaminergic neurons whose cell bodies are located in the ventral tegmental area and whose terminal buttons are located in the cerebral cortex—primarily the prefrontal, limbic, and hippocampal cortex.

Mesolimbic system. A system of dopaminergic neurons whose cell bodies are located in the ventral tegmental area and whose terminal buttons are located in the nucleus accumbens, amygdala, lateral septum, hippocampus, and bed nucleus of the stria terminalis.

Messenger ribonucleic acid (mRNA). See under *ribonucleic acid*.

Metabolism. The sum of all physical and chemical changes that take place in an organism, including all reactions that liberate energy. (See also *absorptive phase* and *fasting phase*.)

Metabotropic receptor. A receptor that, when activated by a molecule of the appropriate neurotransmitter, activates an enzyme that begins a series of events that opens an ion channel elsewhere in the membrane of the cell. (See also *ionotropic receptor*.)

Metencephalon. See Table 4.1.

α-Methyl-*p*-tyrosine (AMPT). A substance that interferes with the activity of tyrosine hydroxylase and thus prevents the synthesis of dopamine and norepinephrine.

MFB. See *medial forebrain bundle (MFB)*.

Microdialysis. A procedure for analyzing chemicals present in the interstitial fluid. A small piece of tubing made of a semipermeable membrane is implanted in the brain, and fluid circulating within it receives substances from the brain through the process of diffusion.

Microelectrode. A very fine electrode, generally used to record activity of individual neurons.

Microglia. Small glial cells that serve as phagocytes.

Microiontophoresis. A procedure that uses electricity to eject a chemical from a micropipette in order to determine the effects of the chemical on the electrical activity of a cell.

Micrometer (μm). A unit of measurement; one-millionth of a meter, or one-thousandth of a millimeter.

Microtome. An instrument that produces very thin slices of body tissues.

Microtubule. An organelle consisting of long protein filaments. It is involved in maintaining the structure of a cell and in transporting substances from place to place within the cell.

Midbrain. See Table 4.1.

Midsagittal plane. The plane that divides the body in two symmetrical halves through the midline.

Mitochondrion. A cell organelle in which the chemical reactions of the Krebs cycle take place.

Mitosis. Duplication and division of a somatic cell into a pair of daughter cells.

Mitral cell. A neuron located in the olfactory bulb. It receives information from olfactory receptors; axons of mitral cells bring information to the rest of the brain.

Monism. The philosophical position that all aspects of the universe are subject to physical laws, and that nothing exists besides matter and energy; thus, the mind is part of the body.

Monoamine. A class of amines that includes indolamines (such as serotonin) and catecholamines (such as dopamine and norepinephrine).

Monoamine hypothesis. A hypothesis that states that depression is caused by a low level of one or more of the monoamines in the brain and could involve underactivity of monoaminergic neurons or underresponsiveness of postsynaptic monoaminergic receptors.

Monoamine oxidase (MAO). A class of enzymes that destroy the monoamines: dopamine, norepinephrine, and serotonin.

Monosynaptic stretch reflex. A reflex consisting of the afferent axon of the intrafusal muscle fiber synapsing upon an alpha motor neuron, and the efferent axon of the alpha motor neuron synapsing on the extrafusal muscle fibers in the same muscle. When a muscle is quickly stretched, the monosynaptic stretch reflex causes it to contract.

Morphology. Physical shape and structure.

Motor endplate. The region of the membrane of a muscle fiber upon which the terminal buttons of the efferent axon synapse.

Motor neuron (motoneuron). A neuron whose stimulation results in contractions of muscle fibers.

Motor unit. A motor neuron and its associated muscle fibers.

mRNA. See under *ribonucleic acid (RNA)*.

Müllerian-inhibiting hormone. A peptide secreted by the fetal testes that inhibits the development of the Müllerian system, which would otherwise become the female internal sex organs.

Müllerian system. The embryonic precursors of the female internal sex organs.

Multibarreled micropipette. A group of micropipettes attached together. It can be used to infuse several different substances by means of iontophoresis.

Multipolar neuron. A neuron with a single axon and numerous dendritic processes originating from the somatic membrane.

Muscarinic receptor. One of the two major types of acetylcholine (ACh) receptors; stimulated by muscarine and blocked by atropine.

Muscle spindle. See *intrafusal muscle fiber*.

Myelencephalon. See Table 4.1.

Myelin. A complex, fatlike substance produced by the oligodendroglia in the central nervous system and by the Schwann cells in the peripheral nervous system, which surrounds and insulates myelinated axons.

Myofibril. An element of muscle fibers that consists of overlapping strands of actin and myosin. It is responsible for muscular contractions.

Myosin. Actin and myosin are the proteins that provide the physical basis for muscular contraction.

Naloxone. A drug that blocks opiate receptors and thus blocks the effects of endogenous and exogenous opiates. It is used in treating opiate overdoses and in experimental investigations.

Narcolepsy. A sleep disorder characterized by periods of irresistible sleep, attacks of cataplexy, sleep paralysis, and hypnagogic hallucinations.

Natural killer cell. A white blood cell that destroys cells infected by viruses.

NE. See *norepinephrine (NE)*.

Negative feedback. A process whereby the effect produced by an action serves to diminish or terminate that action. Regulatory systems are characterized by negative feedback loops.

Negative reinforcement. The removal or reduction of an aversive stimulus that is contingent on a particular response, with an attendant increase in the frequency of that response; the effect of an escape response.

Negative symptom. A symptom of schizophrenia characterized by the absence of behaviors that are normally present; examples are social withdrawal, lack of affect, and reduced motivation.

Neocortex. The phylogenetically newest cortex, including the primary sensory cortex, primary motor cortex, and association cortex.

Neostriatum. The caudate nucleus and putamen.

Nephron. A functional unit of the kidney. It extracts fluid from the blood and carries the fluid, through collecting ducts, to the ureter.

Neural integration. The process by which inhibitory and excitatory postsynaptic potentials summate and control the rate of firing of a neuron.

Neural network. A model of the nervous system based on interconnected networks of elements that have some of the properties of neurons.

Neuraxis. An imaginary line drawn through the center of the length of the central nervous system, from the bottom of the spinal cord to the front of the forebrain.

Neurofilament. A long protein fiber located just under the membrane of a neuron. It gives neurons their particular shape and controls the location of proteins embedded in the membrane.

Neuroglia. The formal name for *glia*.

Neurohypophysis. See under *pituitary gland*.

Neuromodulator. A naturally secreted substance that acts like a neurotransmitter except that it is not restricted to the synaptic cleft but diffuses through the interstitial fluid. Presumably, it activates receptors on neurons that are not located at synapses.

Neuromuscular junction. The synapse between the terminal buttons of an axon and a muscle fiber.

Neuropeptide Y. A biologically active peptide secreted by a neuron or a neurosecretory cell.

Neurosecretory cell. A neuron that secretes a hormone or hormonelike substance into the interstitial fluid.

Neurotransmitter. See under *transmitter substance*.

Neurotransmitter-dependent ion channel. See under *ion channel*.

Nicotinic receptor. One of the two major types of acetylcholine (ACh) receptors; stimulated by nicotine

and blocked by curare. It is found on skeletal muscle fibers and in the central nervous system.

Nigrostriatal bundle. A bundle of axons originating in the substantia nigra and terminating in the neostriatum (caudate nucleus and putamen).

Nissl substance. A cytoplasmic material dyed by cell-body stains (Nissl stains).

Nitric oxide synthase. An enzyme responsible for the production of nitric oxide.

NMDA receptor. A specialized glutamate receptor that controls a calcium channel that is normally blocked by Mg^{2+} ions. It is involved in long-term potentiation, seizures, brain damage produced by anoxia, and learning.

Node of Ranvier. A naked portion of a myelinated axon, between adjacent oligodendroglia or Schwann cells.

Nondeclarative memory. Memory whose formation does not depend on the hippocampal formation; a collective term for perceptual, stimulus-response, and motor memory.

Non-REM sleep. All stages of sleep except REM sleep.

Nonshivering thermogenesis. Heat production by means of cell metabolism that does not involve muscular movement.

Noradrenalin. See *norepinephrine*.

Norepinephrine (NE). A neurotransmitter found in the brain and in the terminal buttons of postganglionic fibers of the sympathetic division of the autonomic nervous system.

Nucleolus. An organelle within the nucleus of a cell that produces the ribosomes.

Nucleus. 1. The central portion of an atom. 2. A spherical structure, enclosed by a membrane, located in the cytoplasm of most cells and containing the chromosomes. 3. A histologically identifiable group of neural cell bodies in the central nervous system.

Nucleus accumbens. A nucleus of the basal forebrain near the septum. It receives dopamine-secreting terminal buttons from neurons of the ventral tegmental area and is thought to be involved in reinforcement and attention.

Nucleus basalis. A nucleus of the basal forebrain that contains most of the acetylcholine-secreting neurons that send axons to the neocortex; degenerates in patients with Alzheimer's disease.

Nucleus of the solitary tract. A nucleus of the medulla that receives information from visceral organs and from the gustatory system; appears to play a role in sleep.

Nucleus raphe magnus. One of the nuclei of the raphe. It contains serotonin-secreting neurons that project to the dorsal gray matter of the spinal cord via the dorsolateral columns and is involved in analgesia produced by opiates.

Obsessive compulsive disorder. A neurotic disorder characterized by obsessions and compulsions.

Occipital lobe. The rearmost portion of the cerebral cortex; contains the primary visual cortex.

Ocular apraxia. See under *Balint's syndrome*.

Offensive behavior. A species-typical behavior in which an animal approaches another animal and threatens or attacks it.

Olfactory bulb. The protrusion at the end of the olfactory nerve; receives input from the olfactory receptors.

Olfactory epithelium. The epithelial tissue of the nasal sinus that covers the cribriform plate; contains the cilia of the olfactory receptors.

Olfactory glomerulus. A bundle of dendrites of mitral cells and the associated terminal buttons of the axons of olfactory receptors.

Oligodendroglia. A type of glial cell in the central nervous system that forms myelin sheaths.

Olivocochlear bundle. A bundle of efferent axons that travel from the olivary complex of the medulla to the auditory hair cells on the cochlea.

Operant conditioning. See *instrumental conditioning*.

Opioid. A neuropeptide whose actions are mimicked by the opiates, such as morphine and heroin.

Opsin. A class of protein that, together with retinal, constitutes the photopigments that are responsible for the transduction of visual information in the eye.

Optic ataxia. See under *Balint's syndrome*.

Optic chiasm. A cross-shaped connection between the optic nerves, located below the base of the brain, just anterior to the pituitary gland.

Optic disk. See under *optic nerve*.

Optic nerve. The second cranial nerve, carrying visual information from the retina to the brain. The *optic disk* is formed at the exit point from the retina of the fibers of the ganglion cells that form the optic nerve.

Optic radiation. The band of axons that project from the dorsal lateral geniculate nuclei of the thalamus to the primary visual cortex.

Orbitofrontal cortex. The region of the prefrontal cortex at the base of the anterior frontal lobes.

Organic sense. A sense modality that arises from receptors located within the inner organs of the body.

Organizational effects. See under *hormone*.

Organ of Corti. The sensory organ on the basilar membrane that contains the auditory hair cells.

Orthographic dysgraphia. A writing disorder in which the person can spell regularly spelled words but not irregularly spelled ones.

Oscilloscope. A laboratory instrument capable of displaying a graph of voltage as a function of time on the face of a cathode ray tube.

Osmometric thirst. Thirst produced by an increase in the osmotic pressure of the interstitial fluid relative to the intracellular fluid, thus producing cellular dehydration.

Osmoreceptor. A neuron that detects changes in the solute concentration of the interstitial fluid that surrounds it.

Osmosis. Movement of ions through a semipermeable membrane, down their concentration gradient.

Ossicles. The three smallest bones in the body, located within the middle ear and transmitting sound waves from the eardrum to the cochlea: the malleus (hammer), incus (anvil), and stapes (stirrup).

Outer plexiform layer. The layer of the retina that contains synapses between the arborizations of bipolar cells, horizontal cells, and photoreceptors.

Oval window. An opening in the bone surrounding the cochlea. The baseplate of the stapes presses against a membrane exposed by the oval window and transmits sound vibrations into the fluid within the cochlea.

Ovarian follicle. See under *follicle*.

Overtone. The frequency of complex tones that occurs at multiples of the fundamental frequency.

OVLT (organum vasculosum of the lamina terminalis). A circumventricular organ located anterior to the anteroventral portion of the third ventricle. It is served by fenestrated capillaries and thus lacks a blood-brain barrier.

Oxytocin. A hormone secreted by the posterior pituitary gland. It causes contraction of the smooth muscle of the milk ducts, the uterus, and the male ejaculatory system.

Pacinian corpuscle. A specialized, encapsulated somatosensory nerve ending, which detects mechanical stimuli, especially vibrations.

Paleostriatum. The globus pallidus.

Panic attack. Episodic periods of symptoms such as shortness of breath, irregularities in heartbeat, and other autonomic symptoms, accompanied by intense fear. Fear of having a panic attack is called *anticipatory anxiety;* it often leads to agoraphobia.

Parabrachial nucleus. A nucleus of the pons. It relays gustatory information from the nucleus of the solitary tract of the medulla to the thalamic taste area.

Parachlorophenylalanine (PCPA). A substance that blocks the action of the enzyme tryptophan hydroxylase and hence prevents synthesis of serotonin (5-HT).

Paradoxical sleep. See *REM sleep.*

Parahippocampal gyrus. A region of limbic cortex adjacent to the hippocampal formation. With the perirhinal cortex, it relays information between the hippocampus and other regions of the brain.

Parasympathetic division. See under *autonomic nervous system (ANS).*

Paraventricular nucleus. A hypothalamic nucleus that contains cell bodies of neurons that produce antidiuretic hormone and oxytocin and transport them through their axons to the posterior pituitary gland.

Parietal lobe. The region of the cerebral cortex behind the frontal lobe and above the temporal lobe; contains the somatosensory cortex. It is involved in spatial perception and memory for and planning of the execution of motor sequences.

Parkinson's disease. A neurological disease that is characterized by fine tremor, rigidity, and difficulty in movement. It is caused by degeneration of the nigrostriatal bundle.

Parvocellular system. The phylogenetically newer portion of the visual system, named after the parvocellular layers of the lateral geniculate nucleus; responsible for perception of color and fine details.

Patch clamp. A method by which an investigator can record from isolated regions of the membrane of cells.

PCPA. See *parachlorophenylalanine (PCPA).*

Peptide. A chain of amino acids joined together by peptide bonds. Many peptides produced by cells of the brain serve as neurotransmitters, neuromodulators, or hormones. Proteins are long peptides.

Perforant path. The system of axons that travel from cells in the entorhinal cortex to the dentate gyrus of the hippocampal formation.

Perfusion. The process by which an animal's blood is replaced by a fluid such as a saline solution or a fixative such as formalin, in preparation of the brain for histological examination.

Periaqueductal gray matter. The region of the midbrain that surrounds the cerebral aqueduct. It contains neural circuits that control aggressive behavior and female sexual behavior and opiate-sensitive cells that mediate analgesia.

Peripheral nervous system (PNS). The cranial nerves, spinal nerves, and peripheral ganglia.

Perirhinal cortex. A region of limbic cortex adjacent to the hippocampal formation. With the cortex of the parahippocampal gyrus, it relays information between the hippocampus and other regions of the brain.

Permeability. The degree to which a membrane permits passage of a particular substance.

PGO waves. Bursts of phasic electrical activity originating in the pons, followed by activity in the lateral geniculate nucleus and visual cortex; a characteristic of REM sleep.

Phagocytosis. The process by which cells engulf and digest other cells or debris caused by cellular degeneration. The cells that perform this function are *phagocytes.*

PHA-L. Phaseolus vulgaris leukoagglutinin; a protein derived from lima beans used as an anterograde tracer.

Phantom limb. Sensations that appear to originate in a limb that has been amputated.

Phase difference. The difference in arrival times of sound waves at each of the eardrums.

Phenylketonuria (PKU). A hereditary disorder caused by the absence of an enzyme that converts the amino acid phenylalanine to tyrosine. The accumulation of phenylalanine causes brain damage unless a special diet is implemented soon after birth.

Pheromone. A chemical released by one animal that affects the behavior or physiology of another animal; usually smelled or tasted.

Phonetic reading. Reading by decoding the phonetic significance of letter strings, or "sound reading," as opposed to whole-word reading, or "sight reading." Brain injury can abolish one method without affecting the other.

Phonological dysgraphia. A writing disorder in which the person cannot sound out words and write them phonetically.

Phonological dyslexia. A reading disorder in which a person can read familiar words but has difficulty reading unfamiliar words or pronounceable nonwords; caused by brain damage.

Phosphodiesterase. A class of enzymes that deactivate cyclic nucleotides.

Photopigment. A protein dye bonded to a substance derived from vitamin A. When struck by light, it bleaches and stimulates the membrane of the photoreceptor in which it resides.

Photoreceptor. The receptor cell of the retina, which transduces photic energy into electrical potentials. *Cones* are maximally sensitive to one of three different wavelengths of light and hence encode color vision, whereas all *rods* are maximally sensitive to light of the same wavelength and hence do not encode color vision.

Phototherapy. Treatment of seasonal affective disorder by daily exposure to bright light.

Physostigmine. An acetylcholine agonist; inactivates acetylcholinesterase.

Pia mater. The layer of the meninges adjacent to the surface of the brain.

Pineal gland. A gland attached to the dorsal tectum; produces melatonin and plays a role in circadian and seasonal rhythms.

Pinocytosis. The pinching off of a bud of cell membrane, which travels to the interior of the cell. It is used to incorporate substances present in the interstitial fluid and to recycle pieces of the membrane used for producing synaptic vesicles.

Pituitary gland. The "master endocrine gland" of the body, attached to the base of the brain. The *anterior pituitary gland* (adenohypophysis) secretes hormones in response to the hypothalamic hormones. The *posterior pituitary gland* (neurohypophysis) secretes oxytocin or antidiuretic hormone in response to stimulation from its neural input.

PKC. Protein kinase C; an enzyme involved in the production of long-term potentiation.

Placebo. An inert substance given to an organism in lieu of a physiologically active drug. It is used experimentally to control for the effects of mere administration of a drug.

Place cell. A neuron of the hippocampus that becomes active when the animal is in a particular location in the environment.

Place code. With respect to audition, the system by which information about different frequencies is coded by different locations on the basilar membrane.

Planum temporale. A region of the superior temporal lobe; normally larger in the left hemisphere. It shows abnormalities in the brains of some people with developmental dyslexia.

Platelet. A cell fragment that is necessary for the formation of blood clots.

Plexus. A network formed by the junction of several adjacent nerves.

PNS. The peripheral nervous system: the cranial nerves, spinal nerves, and peripheral ganglia.

Poikilothermous. Not capable of regulating body temperature by producing heat endogenously. Most poikilothermous animals regulate their body temperature but must approach or avoid sources of heat to do so.

Pons. The region of the brain rostral to the medulla and caudal to the midbrain.

Pontine nucleus. A large nucleus in the pons that serves as an important source of input to the cerebellum.

Population EPSP. An evoked potential recorded from portions of the trisynaptic circuit of the hippocampal formation that represents the EPSPs of a population of neurons. Long-term potentiation is detected by recording the population EPSP.

Positive symptom. A symptom of schizophrenia; delusions, hallucinations, or thought disorders.

Posterior. See Figure 4.1.

Posterior pituitary gland. See under *pituitary gland*.

Postganglionic neurons. Neurons of the autonomic nervous system that synapse directly upon their target organ.

Postsynaptic membrane. The cell membrane opposite the terminal button in a synapse; the membrane of the cell that receives the message.

Postsynaptic potential. Alterations in the membrane potential of a postsynaptic neuron, produced by liberation of transmitter substance at the synapse. *Excitatory postsynaptic potentials (EPSPs)* are depolarizations and increase the probability of firing of the postsynaptic neuron. *Inhibitory postsynaptic potentials (IPSPs)* are hyperpolarizations and decrease the probability of neural firing.

Postsynaptic receptor. A receptor molecule in the postsynaptic membrane of a synapse that detects the presence of a neurotransmitter and controls neurotransmitter-dependent ion channels, thus producing excitatory or inhibitory postsynaptic potentials.

Precommissural fornix. See under *fimbria*.

Predation. Attack of one animal directed at an individual of another species, on which the attacking animal normally preys.

Preganglionic neuron. The efferent neuron of the autonomic nervous system whose cell body is located in a cranial nerve nucleus or in the intermediate horn of the spinal gray matter and whose terminal buttons synapse upon postganglionic neurons in the autonomic ganglia.

Preoptic area. An area of cell bodies (usually divided into the *lateral preoptic area* and *medial preoptic area*) just rostral to the hypothalamus. Some investigators refer to the preoptic area as a part of the hypothalamus, although embryologically they are derived from different tissue.

Presynaptic facilitation. The action of a presynaptic terminal button in an axoaxonic synapse; enhances the effects of the postsynaptic terminal button on the neuron with which it forms a synapse.

Presynaptic inhibition. The action of a presynaptic terminal button in an axoaxonic synapse; diminishes the effects of the postsynaptic terminal button on the neuron with which it forms a synapse.

Presynaptic membrane. The membrane of a terminal button that lies parallel to the postsynaptic membrane.

Primary motor cortex. The precentral gyrus, which contains neurons that control movements of skeletal muscles.

Primary sensory cortex. Regions of cortex whose primary input is from one of the sensory systems.

Priming. A phenomenon in which exposure to a particular stimulus automatically facilitates perception of that stimulus or related stimuli.

Primordial. In embryology, refers to the undeveloped early form of an organ.

Progesterone. A steroid hormone produced by the ovary. It maintains the endometrial lining of the uterus during the later part of the menstrual cycle and during pregnancy; along with estradiol, it promotes receptivity in female mammals with estrous cycles.

Projection. The efferent connection between neurons in one specific region of the brain and those in another region.

Prolactin. A hormone of the anterior pituitary gland, necessary for production of milk and (in some subprimate mammals) development of a corpus luteum; occasionally called luteotropic hormone.

Propranolol. A noradrenergic antagonist; blocks postsynaptic ß-noradrenergic receptors.

Prosody. The use of changes in intonation and emphasis to convey meaning in speech besides that specified by the particular words; an important means of communication of emotion.

Prosopagnosia. The inability to recognize people by the sight of their faces.

Prostaglandin. A member of a family of fatty acid derivatives that serve as hormones; first discovered in the prostate gland; involved in many physiological processes, including pain perception.

Prosthesis. A device used to substitute for a missing or damaged part of the body.

Protanopia. An inherited form of defective color vision in which red and green hues are confused. "Red" cones appear to be filled with "green" cone opsin.

Protein. A long peptide that can serve in a structural capacity or as an enzyme.

Protein kinase. An enzyme that attaches a phosphate (PO_4) to a protein and thereby causes it to change its shape. Protein kinases are activated by cyclic nucleotides and open ion channels by phosphorylating membrane proteins.

Pseudobulbar palsy. A paralysis of the face caused by forebrain damage to the corticobulbar system; the ability remains to make automatic facial movements such as coughing, sneezing, or expressions of emotion.

Psychoneuroimmunology. The branch of neuroscience involved with interactions between environmental stimuli, the nervous system, and the immune system.

Psychosis. A serious mental disorder, such as schizophrenia, major depression, or bipolar disorder.

Psychosurgery. The destruction of brain tissue to treat behavioral disorders in the absence of verified brain damage.

Pulvinar. A large thalamic nucleus. It projects to the visual association cortex and may play a role in compensating for eye and head movements.

Punishing stimulus. An aversive stimulus that follows a particular behavior and thus makes the behavior become less frequent.

Pure alexia. The loss of the ability to read without the loss of the ability to write; produced by brain damage.

Pure word deafness. The ability to hear, to speak, and (usually) to write, without being able to comprehend the meaning of speech; caused by bilateral temporal lobe damage.

Pursuit movement. The movement that the eyes make to maintain an image upon the fovea.

Putamen. One of the nuclei that constitute the basal ganglia. The putamen and caudate nucleus compose the neostriatum.

Pylorus. The ring of smooth muscle at the junction of the stomach and duodenum that controls the release of the stomach contents.

Pyramidal cell. A category of large neurons with a pyramid shape; found in the cerebral cortex and Ammon's horn of the hippocampal formation.

Pyramidal tract. A fiber bundle that contains axons of the lateral and ventral corticospinal tracts.

Raphe. A group of nuclei located in the reticular formation of the medulla, pons, and midbrain, situated along the midline.

Rate code. With respect to audition, the system by which information about different frequencies is coded by the rate of firing of neurons in the auditory system.

Rate law. States that variations in the intensity of a stimulus or other information being transmitted in an axon are represented by variations in the rate of "firing," that is, the number of action potentials per unit of time.

Reactive depression. A depression caused by events in a person's life.

Rebound phenomenon. The increased frequency or intensity of a phenomenon after it has been temporarily suppressed; for example, the increase in REM sleep seen after a period of REM sleep deprivation.

Receptive field. That portion of the visual field in which the presentation of visual stimuli will produce an alteration in the firing rate of a particular neuron.

Receptor blocker. A drug that attaches to postsynaptic receptors without stimulating them, thus preventing the neurotransmitter from acting on them.

Receptor cell. A specialized type of cell that transduces physical stimuli into slow, graded receptor potentials.

Receptor molecule. A protein molecule situated in the membrane of a cell that is sensitive to a particular chemical, such as a neurotransmitter or hormone. When the appropriate chemical stimulates a receptor site, changes take place in the membrane or within the cell.

Receptor potential. A slow, graded electrical potential produced by a receptor cell in response to a physical stimulus. Receptor potentials alter the firing rate of neurons upon which the receptor cells synapse.

Red nucleus. A large nucleus of the midbrain that receives inputs from the cerebellum and motor cortex and sends axons to the spinal cord via the rubrospinal tract and to various subcortical motor nuclei.

Reduction. Along with generalization, one of the forms of explanation in science; describing a phenomenon in terms of more elementary processes; for example, describing behavioral phenomena in terms of physiological events.

Reference memory. A form of long-term memory of stable conditions and contingencies in the environment. Perceptual memory and stimulus-response memory are examples of reference memory.

Reflex. A stereotyped glandular secretion or movement produced as the direct result of a stimulus.

Refractory period. A period of time after a particular action (for example, an action potential or an ejaculation by a male) during which that action cannot occur again.

Reinforcing stimulus. An appetitive stimulus that follows a particular behavior and thus makes the behavior become more frequent.

Release zone. A region of the interior of the postsynaptic membrane of a synapse to which synaptic vesicles attach. The release of transmitter substance takes place here.

REM sleep. A period of desynchronized EEG activity during sleep, at which time dreaming, rapid eye movements, and muscular paralysis occur; also called *paradoxical sleep.*

REM without atonia. A neurological disorder in which the person does not become paralyzed during REM sleep and thus acts out dreams.

Renin. A hormone that causes the conversion of *angiotensinogen* in the blood into *angiotensin*. Sympathetic stimulation of the kidney, or reduction of its blood flow, results in the liberation of renin. Angiotensin produces thirst, constricts blood vessels (thus raising blood pressure), and stimulates the adrenal cortex to produce aldosterone, a hormone that stimulates the kidney to retain sodium.

Reserpine. A monoamine antagonist; makes synaptic vesicles leaky, so that the neurotransmitter (dopamine, norepinephrine, or serotonin) cannot be kept inside.

Resting potential. The membrane potential of a neuron when it is not being altered by excitatory or inhibitory postsynaptic potentials; approximately -70 mV.

Reticular formation. A large network of neural tissue located in the central region of the brain stem, from the medulla to the diencephalon.

Reticulospinal tract. A bundle of axons that travel from the reticular formation to the gray matter of the spinal cord; controls the muscles responsible for postural movements.

Retina. The neural tissue and photoreceptive cells located on the inner surface of the posterior portion of the eye.

Retinal. A chemical synthesized from vitamin A; joins with an opsin to form a photopigment.

Retinal disparity. The fact that points on objects located at different distances from the observer will fall on slightly different locations on the two retinas. It provides the basis for stereopsis, one of the forms of depth perception.

Retrograde amnesia. Amnesia for events that preceded some disturbance to the brain, such as a head injury or electroconvulsive shock.

Retrograde labeling method. A histological method that labels cell bodies that give rise to the terminal buttons that form synapses with cells in a particular region.

Reuptake. The reentry of a transmitter substance just liberated by a terminal button back through its membrane, thus terminating the postsynaptic potential that is induced in the postsynaptic neuron.

Rhodopsin. A particular opsin found in rods.

Ribonucleic acid (RNA). A complex macromolecule composed of a sequence of nucleotide bases attached to a sugar-phosphate backbone. *Messenger RNA (mRNA)* delivers genetic information from a portion of a chromosome to a ribosome, where the appropriate amino acids are assembled to produce the polypeptide coded for by the active portion of the chromosome.

Ribosome. A cytoplasmic structure, made of protein, that serves as the site of production of proteins translated from mRNA.

RNA. See *ribonucleic acid (RNA)*.

Rod. See under *photoreceptor*.

Rostral. See Figure 4.1.

Round window. An opening in the bone surrounding the cochlea of the inner ear that permits vibrations to be transmitted, via the oval window, through the fluids and receptive tissue contained within the cochlea.

Rubrospinal tract. See under *dorsolateral pathway*.

Ruffini corpuscle. A vibration-sensitive organ located in hairy skin.

Saccadic movement. The rapid movement of the eyes that is used in scanning a visual scene, as opposed to the smooth pursuit movements used to follow a moving object.

Saccule. With the utricle, one of the vestibular sacs; detects the angle of tilt of the head and provides a signal to help produce eye movements to compensate for sudden head movements.

Sagittal section. See Figure 4.2.

Saltatory conduction. Conduction of action potentials by myelinated axons. The action potential "jumps" from one node of Ranvier to the next.

Saralasin. A drug that blocks angiotensin receptors.

Satellite cell. A cell that serves to support neurons of the peripheral nervous system, such as the Schwann cells that provide the myelin sheath.

Satiety. Cessation of hunger, produced by adequate and available supplies of nutrients.

Scanning electron microscope. A microscope that provides three-dimensional information about the shape of the surface of a small object.

Schizophrenia. A serious mental disorder (psychosis) characterized by disordered thoughts, delusions, hallucinations, and often bizarre behaviors.

Schwann cell. A cell in the peripheral nervous system that is wrapped around a myelinated axon, providing one segment of its myelin sheath.

SCN. See *suprachiasmatic nucleus (SCN)*.

Scotoma. A region of blindness within an otherwise normal visual field, produced by localized damage somewhere in the visual system.

Seasonal affective disorder. A mood disorder characterized by depression, lethargy, sleep disturbances, and craving for carbohydrates. It occurs during the winter season and can be treated by daily exposure to bright lights.

Second messenger. A chemical produced in the cytoplasm of the postsynaptic cell when a neurotransmitter binds with a metabotropic receptor; carries a signal that results in the opening of the ion channel.

Semicircular canal. One of the three ringlike structures of the vestibular apparatus that transduce changes in head rotation into neural activity.

Sensory coding. Representation of sensory events in the form of neural activity.

Sensory modality. A particular form of sensory input, such as vision, audition, or olfaction.

Sensory-specific satiety. Satiety for a specific food that has been ingested recently in the absence of general satiety for all foods.

Sensory transduction. The process by which sensory stimuli are transduced into slow, graded receptor potentials.

Septum. A portion of the limbic system, lying between the walls of the anterior portions of the lateral ventricles.

Serotonin. An alternative name for the neurotransmitter 5-hydroxytryptamine (5-HT); named because of its constricting effect on blood vessels.

Set point. The optimal value of the system variable in a regulatory mechanism. The set point for human body temperature, recorded orally, is approximately 37°C.

Sex chromosomes. The X and Y chromosomes, which determine an organism's gender. Normally, XX individuals are female, and XY individuals are male.

Sexually dimorphic behavior. A behavior that has different forms or that occurs with different probabilities or under different circumstances in males and females.

Sexually dimorphic nucleus. A nucleus in the preoptic area that is much larger in males than in females; first observed in rats.

SFO. See *subfornical organ (SFO)*.

Sham feeding. Feeding behavior of an animal with a gastric or esophageal fistula. Food does not remain in the stomach.

Short-term memory. Immediate memory for sensory events that may or may not be consolidated into long-term memory.

Simultanagnosia. See under *Balint's syndrome*.

Sine-wave grating. A series of straight parallel bands varying continuously in brightness according to a sine-wave function, along a line perpendicular to their lengths.

Single unit. An individual neuron.

Single-unit recording. Recording of the electrical activity of a single neuron.

Sleep apnea. Failure to breathe while asleep. Periods of sleep apnea occur in normal people, but when they are especially frequent, they substantially disturb sleep and pose a risk to life in infants and old or debilitated people.

Sleep attack. A symptom of narcolepsy; an irresistible urge to sleep during the day, after which the person awakes feeling refreshed.

Sleep paralysis. A symptom of narcolepsy; paralysis occurring just before a person falls asleep.

Slow-wave sleep. Non-REM sleep, characterized by synchronized EEG activity during its deeper stages.

Smooth muscle. Nonstriated muscle innervated by the autonomic nervous system, found in the walls of blood vessels, in sphincters, within the eye, in the digestive system, and around hair follicles.

Sodium-potassium transporter. A protein found in the membrane of all cells that extrudes sodium ions from and transports potassium ions into the cell.

Solitary nucleus. See *nucleus of the solitary tract*.

Soma. A cell body or, more generally, the body.

Somatic nervous system. The part of the peripheral nervous system that controls the movement of skeletal muscles or transmits somatosensory information to the central nervous system. (See also *autonomic nervous system*.)

Somatosenses. Bodily sensation; sensitivity to such stimuli as touch, pain, and temperature.

Somatosensory cortex. The gyrus caudal to the central sulcus, which receives many projection fibers from the somatosensory system.

Somatotropic hormone (STH). See *growth hormone (GH)*.

Spatial frequency. The relative width of the bands in a sine-wave grating, measured in cycles per degree of visual angle.

Species-typical behavior. A behavior that is typical of all or most members of a species of animal, especially a behavior that does not appear to have to be learned.

Spectrin. A protein that lies just inside the neural membrane; thought to be involved in the structural changes that accompany long-term potentiation. (See also *calpain*.)

Spelling dyslexia. A disorder in which a person can read a word only after spelling out the individual letters; caused by brain damage.

Spinal nucleus of the bulbocavernosus. A nucleus located in the lower spinal cord. In laboratory rodents the nucleus has been found to be sexually dimorphic, being present only in males.

Spinal root. A bundle of axons surrounded by connective tissue that occurs in pairs, which fuse and form a spinal nerve. The *dorsal root* contains afferent fibers, whereas the *ventral root* contains efferent fibers.

Spinal sympathetic ganglia. Sympathetic ganglia either adjacent to the spinal cord in the sympathetic chain or located in the abdominal cavity.

Split-brain operation. A surgical procedure in which the corpus callosum is severed; performed to treat a seizure disorder.

Stapes. One of the bones of the inner ear, shaped somewhat like a stirrup.

Stereotaxic apparatus. A device that permits the experimenter to place an object such as an electrode or cannula into a specific part of the brain.

Stereotaxic atlas. A book containing photographs or drawings of sections of the brain of a particular animal; contains measurements that permit a surgeon to reach a particular part of an animal's brain with a stereotaxic apparatus.

Steroid hormone. A hormone of low molecular weight, derived from cholesterol. Steroid hormones affect their target cells by attaching to receptors found within the cell.

STH. See *growth hormone (GH)*.

Stress. A general, imprecise term that can refer either to a stress response or to a stressor (stressful situation).

Stressor. A stimulus (or situation) that produces a stress response.

Stress response. A physiological reaction caused by the perception of aversive or threatening situations.

Striate cortex. Primary visual cortex.

Striated muscle. Skeletal muscle; muscle that contains striations.

Stria terminalis. A long fiber bundle that connects portions of the amygdala with the hypothalamus.

Subarachnoid space. The fluid-filled space between the arachnoid membrane and the pia mater.

Subcoerulear nucleus. A group of neurons adjacent to the locus coeruleus; involved in the muscular paralysis (atonia) that accompanies REM sleep.

Subcortical region. The region located within the brain, beneath the cortical surface.

Subfornical organ (SFO). A small organ located in the confluence of the lateral ventricles, attached to the underside of the fornix. It contains neurons that detect the presence of angiotensin in the blood and excite neural circuits that initiate drinking.

Subiculum. Part of the hippocampal formation. See under *fimbria*.

Submissive behavior. A stereotyped behavior shown by an animal in response to threat behavior by another animal; serves to prevent an attack.

Subsensitivity. Decreased sensitivity of neurotransmitter receptors; a compensatory response to their prolonged stimulation.

Substantia nigra. A darkly stained region of the tegmentum, which communicates with the neostriatum via the nigrostriatal bundle.

Sulcus. A groove in the surface of the cerebral hemisphere, smaller than a fissure.

Superior cerebellar peduncle. One of the three pairs of bands of white matter connecting the cerebellum and brain stem.

Superior colliculi. Protrusions on top of the midbrain; part of the visual system.

Superior olivary complex. A group of nuclei in the medulla; involved with auditory functions, including localization of the source of sounds.

Supersensitivity. Increased sensitivity of neurotransmitter receptors; a compensatory response to a lack of stimulation caused by lack of presynaptic activity or the presence of drugs that block the receptors.

Suprachiasmatic nucleus (SCN). A nucleus situated atop the optic chiasm. It contains a biological clock responsible for organizing many of the body's circadian rhythms.

Supraoptic nucleus. A hypothalamic nucleus that contains cell bodies of neurons that produce antidiuretic hormone and transport it through their axons to the posterior pituitary gland.

Surface dyslexia. A reading disorder in which a person can read words phonetically but has difficulty reading irregularly spelled words by the whole-word method; caused by brain damage.

Sympathetic apraxia. A movement disorder of the left hand caused by damage to the left frontal lobe; similar to callosal apraxia.

Sympathetic chain. One of a pair of groups of sympathetic ganglia that lie ventrolateral to the vertebral column.

Sympathetic division. See under *autonomic nervous system (ANS)*.

Synapse. A junction between the terminal button of an axon and the membrane of another neuron.

Synaptic cleft. The space between the presynaptic membrane and the postsynaptic membrane.

Synaptic vesicle. A small, hollow, beadlike structure found in terminal buttons. Synaptic vesicles contain transmitter substance.

Synchrony. High-voltage, low-frequency EEG activity, characteristic of slow-wave sleep or coma. During synchrony, neurons are presumably firing together in a regular fashion.

System variable. A variable that is controlled by a regulatory mechanism; for example, temperature in a heating system.

Tardive dyskinesia. A movement disorder that occasionally occurs after prolonged treatment with antischizophrenic medication, characterized by involuntary movements of the face and neck, sometimes interfering with speech.

Target cell. The type of cell that is directly affected by a hormone or nerve fiber.

Tectorial membrane. A membrane located above the basilar membrane; serves as a shelf against which the cilia of the auditory hair cells move.

Tectospinal tract. A bundle of axons that travel from the tectum to the spinal cord. It coordinates head and trunk movements with eye movements.

Tectum. The roof of the midbrain, comprising the inferior and the superior colliculi.

Tegmentum. The portion of the midbrain beneath the tectum, containing the red nucleus and nuclei of various cranial nerves.

Telencephalon. See Table 4.1.

Temporal lobe. The portion of the cerebral cortex below the frontal and parietal lobes and containing the auditory cortex. Damage produces deficits in audition, speech perception and production, sexual behavior, visual perception, and/or social behaviors.

Terminal button. The rounded swelling at the end of an axonal process that synapses upon another neuron, muscle fiber, or gland cell.

Testicular feminization. See *androgen insensitivity syndrome.*

Testosterone. The principle androgen found in males.

Thalamus. The largest portion of the diencephalon, located above the hypothalamus. It contains nuclei that project information to specific regions of the cerebral cortex and receive information from it.

Theta activity. EEG activity of 5-8 Hz. Theta activity of the hippocampus is an important indication of its physiological state.

Third ventricle. See under *ventricle.*

Thought disorder. Disorganized, irrational thinking; one of the primary symptoms of schizophrenia.

Threat behavior. A stereotyped species-typical behavior that warns another animal that it may be attacked if it does not flee or show a submissive behavior.

Threshold of excitation. The value of the membrane potential that must be reached in order to produce an action potential.

Timbre. A perceptual dimension of sound, determined by the complexity of the sound, as shown, for example, by a mathematical analysis of the sound wave.

T-lymphocyte. A white blood cell that originates in the thymus gland; part of the immune system.

Tolerance. The fact that increasingly large doses of drugs must be taken to achieve a particular effect. It is presumably caused by compensatory mechanisms that oppose the effect of the drug.

Tourette's syndrome. A neurological disorder characterized by tics and involuntary vocalizations and sometimes by compulsive uttering of obscenities and repetition of the utterances of others.

Trace conditioning. A classical conditioning procedure in which the unconditional stimulus follows the conditional stimulus by a short interval of time.

Transcortical sensory aphasia. A speech disorder in which a person has difficulty comprehending speech and producing meaningful spontaneous speech but can repeat speech; caused by damage to the region of the brain posterior to Wernicke's area.

Transmitter substance. A chemical that is liberated by the terminal buttons of an axon and produces an EPSP or an IPSP in the membrane of the postsynaptic cell; also called *neurotransmitter.*

Transverse section. See Figure 4.2.

Tricarboxylic acid cycle. See *Krebs cycle.*

Tricyclic antidepressant. A class of drugs used to treat depression; named for their molecular structure.

Trigeminal lemniscus. A bundle of fibers running parallel to the medial lemniscus; conveys afferent fibers from the trigeminal nerve to the thalamus.

Triglyceride. The form of fat storage in adipose cells. It consists of a molecule of glycerol joined with the three fatty acids: stearic acid, oleic acid, and palmitic acid.

Trisynaptic circuit. The recurrent circuit formed by connections between the entorhinal cortex, dentate gyrus, and CA1 and CA3 fields of Ammon's horn. Repeated stimulation of this circuit leads to long-term potentiation of the extracellular population spike.

Tritanopia. An inherited form of defective color vision in which hues with short wavelengths are confused. "Blue" cones are either lacking or faulty.

Tryptophan. An amino acid; the precursor for 5-HT (serotonin).

Tryptophan hydroxylase. The enzyme that converts tryptophan to 5-hydroxytryptophan (5-HTP).

Turner's syndrome. The presence of only one sex chromosome (an X chromosome); characterized by lack of ovaries but otherwise normal female sex organs and genitalia.

Tympanic membrane. The eardrum.

Type A pattern. A behavior pattern characterized by competitive drive, impatience, hostility, fast movements, and rapid speech; said to be related to a higher incidence of cardiovascular disease.

Type B pattern. behavior pattern characterized by a less competitive, less hostile, more patient, and more easygoing and tolerant nature than a type A pattern; said to be related to a lower incidence of cardiovascular disease.

Tyrosine. An amino acid; the precursor of the catecholamines: dopamine, norepinephrine, and epinephrine.

Tyrosine hydroxylase. The enzyme that converts tyrosine to L-DOPA, the immediate precursor of dopamine.

Tyrosine kinase. type of protein kinase that may play a role in the establishment of long-term potentiation.

Umami. The taste sensation produced by amino acids.

Unconditional response (UR). See under *classical conditioning.*

Unconditional stimulus (US). See under *classical conditioning.*

Unipolar depression. A psychosis; unremitting depression or periods of depression that do not alternate with periods of mania.

Unipolar neuron. A neuron with a long, continuous fiber that has dendritic processes on one end and axonal processes and terminal buttons on the other. The fiber connects with the soma of the neuron by means of a single, short process.

Ureter. One of two tubes that carries urine from the kidneys to the bladder.

Utricle. With the saccule, one of the vestibular sacs. It detects the angle of tilt of the head and provides a signal to help produce eye movements to compensate for sudden head movements.

Vagus nerve. he largest of the cranial nerves, conveying efferent fibers of the parasympathetic division of the autonomic nervous system to organs of the thoracic and abdominal cavities. The vagus nerve also carries nonpainful sensory fibers from these organs to the brain.

Vandenbergh effect. The earlier onset of puberty seen in female animals that are housed with males; caused by a pheromone in the male's urine; first observed in mice.

Vasopressin. A hormone secreted by the posterior pituitary gland that causes the kidneys to excrete a more concentrated urine, thus retaining water in the body.

Ventral. See Figure 4.1.

Ventral corticospinal tract. See under *corticospinal pathway.*

Ventral horn (of gray matter of spinal cord). Location of the cell bodies of alpha and gamma motor neurons of the spinal cord.

Ventral posterior nucleus (of thalamus). The thalamic nucleus that projects to the primary somatosensory cortex.

Ventral root. See under *spinal root.*

Ventral tegmental area. A nucleus in the ventral tegmentum that contains dopamine-secreting neurons whose axons project to the forebrain, especially to the cortex and nucleus accumbens; thought to be important in arousal and reinforcement.

Ventricle. One of the hollow spaces within the brain, filled with cerebrospinal fluid, including the *lateral, third,* and *fourth ventricles.*

Ventrolateral nucleus (of the thalamus). A nucleus that receives inputs from the cerebellum and sends axons to the primary motor cortex.

Ventromedial nucleus (of the hypothalamus; VMH). A large nucleus of the hypothalamus located near the walls of the third ventricle; important in controlling female sexual behavior.

Ventromedial pathways. The vestibulospinal, tectospinal, and reticulospinal tracts.

Vergence movement. The cooperative movement of the eyes, which ensures that the image of an object falls on identical portions of both retinas.

Vermis. The portion of the cerebellum located at the midline. It receives somatosensory information and helps control the vestibulospinal and reticulospinal tracts, through its connections with the fastigial nucleus.

Vertebral artery. An artery whose branches serve the posterior region of the brain.

Vestibular ganglion. A nodule on the vestibular nerve that contains the cell bodies of the bipolar neurons that convey vestibular information to the brain.

Vestibular nerve. See under *auditory nerve.*

Vestibular sac. One of a set of two receptor organs in each inner ear that detect changes in the tilt of the head.

Vestibulospinal tract. A bundle of axons from the vestibular nuclei of the brain stem to the gray matter of the spinal cord; controls postural movements in response to information from the vestibular system.

Visual agnosia. Deficits in visual perception in the absence of blindness; caused by brain damage. *Apperceptive visual agnosia* is a failure to perceive objects, even though detection of individual components is relatively normal. *Associative visual agnosia* is the inability to name objects that are perceived visually, even though the form of the perceived object can be matched with similar objects.

VMH. See *ventromedial nucleus (of the hypothalamus; VMH)*.

Voltage-dependent ion channel. See under *ion channel*.

Volumetric thirst. Thirst produced by *hypovolemia*, or reduction in the amount of extracellular fluid. Volumetric thirst is produced by baroreceptors in the right atrium of the heart and by reduced blood flow from the kidneys.

Vomeronasal organ. A sensory organ in some species that detects the presence of certain chemicals, especially when a liquid is actively sniffed; mediates the effects of some pheromones.

Wernicke's aphasia. See under *Wernicke's area*.

Wernicke's area. A region of auditory association cortex on the left temporal lobe of humans, which is important in the comprehension of words and the production of meaningful speech. *Wernicke's aphasia*, which occurs as a result of damage to this area, results in fluent but meaningless speech.

White noise. Noise that contains all frequencies of audible sounds; analogous to white light, which contains all wavelengths of visible light.

Whitten effect. The synchronization of the menstrual or estrous cycles of a group of females, which occurs only when a male (or his pheromone) is present.

Whole-word reading. Reading by means of recognition of a word as a whole, or "sight reading," as opposed to phonetic reading, or "sound reading." Brain injury can abolish one method without affecting the other.

Withdrawal symptom. The appearance of symptoms opposite to those produced by a drug when the drug is suddenly no longer taken; presumably caused by the presence of compensatory mechanisms. (See also *tolerance*.)

Wolffian system. The embryonic precursors of the male internal sex organs.

Word-form dyslexia. A disorder in which a person can read a word only after spelling out the individual letters; caused by brain damage.

Working memory. Memory of what has just been perceived and what is currently being thought about. It consists of new information and related information that has recently been "retrieved" from long-term memory.

X chromosome. See under *sex chromosomes*.

Y chromosome. See under *sex chromosomes*.

Zeitgeber. A stimulus (usually the light of dawn) that resets the biological clock responsible for circadian rhythms. (See also *suprachiasmatic nucleus*.)

Zona incerta. An oblong extension of the midbrain reticular formation, extending from the midbrain to the medial diencephalon.

REFERENCES

Abe, H., Rusak, B., and Robertson, H.A. Photic induction of Fos protein in the suprachiasmatic nucleus is inhibited by the NMDA receptor antagonist MK-801. *Neuroscience Letters*, 1991, *127*, 9–12.

Abel, E.L., and Sokol, R.J. Fetal alcohol syndrome is now a leading cause of mental retardation. *Lancet*, 1986, *2*, 1222.

Abel, L.A., Levin, S., and Holzman, P.S. Abnormalities of smooth pursuit and saccadic control in schizophrenia and affective disorders. *Vision Research*, 1992, *32*, 1009–1014.

Adamec, R.E. Individual differences in temporal lobe sensory processing of threatening stimuli in the cat. *Physiology and Behavior*, 1991, *49*, 455–464.

Adams, D.B., Boudreau, W., Cowan, C. W., Kokonowski, C., Oberteuffer, K., and Yohay, K. Offense produced by chemical stimulation of the anterior hypothalamus of the rat. *Physiology and Behavior*, 1993, in press.

Adams, D.B. Ventromedial tegmental lesions abolish offense without disturbing predation or defense. *Physiology and Behavior*, 1986, *38*, 165–168.

Adams, D.B., Gold, A.R., and Burt, A.D. Rise in female-initiated sexual activity at ovulation and its suppression by oral contraceptives. *New England Journal of Medicine*, 1978, *299*, 1145–1150.

Adams, R.D. The anatomy of memory mechanisms in the human brain. In *The Pathology of Memory*, edited by G.A. Talland and N.C. Waugh. New York: Academic Press, 1969.

Adams, R.D., and Victor, M. *Principles of Neurology*. New York: McGraw-Hill, 1989.

Adey, W.R., Bors, E., and Porter, R.W. EEG sleep patterns after high cervical lesions in man. *Archives of Neurology*, 1968, *19*, 377–383.

Adieh, H.B., Mayer, A.D., and Rosenblatt, J.S. Effects of brain antiestrogen implants on maternal behavior and on postpartum estrus in pregnant rats. *Neuroendocrinology*, 1987, *46*, 522–531.

Adolph, E.F. Measurements of water drinking in dogs. *American Journal of Physiology*, 1939, *125*, 75–86.

Aggleton, J.P., Hunt, P.R., and Rawlins, J.N.P. The effects of hippocampal lesions upon spatial and non-spatial tests of working memory. *Behavioural Brain Research*, 1986, *19*, 133–146.

Akabas, M.H., Dodd, J., and Al-Awqati, Q. A bitter substance induces a rise in intracellular calcium in a sub-population of rat taste cells. *Science*, 1988, *242*, 1047–1050.

Akbarian, S., Bunney, W.E., Potkin, S.G., Wigal, S.B., Hagman, J.O., Sandman, C.A., and Jones, E.G. Altered distribution of nicotinamide-adenine dinucleotide phosphate-diaphorase cells in frontal lobe of schizophrenics implies disturbances of cortical development. *Archives of General Psychiatry*, 1993, *50*, 169–177.

Akbarian, S., Vinuela, A., Kim, J.J., Potkin, S.G., Bunney, W.E., and Jones, E.G. Distorted distribution of nicotinamide-adenine dinucleotide phosphate-diaphorase neurons in temporal lobe of schizophrenics implies anomalous cortical development. *Archives of General Psychiatry*, 1993, *50*, 178–187.

Akhtar, S., Wig, N., Pershad, D., and Varma, S. A phenomenological analysis of symptoms in obsessive compulsive disorder. *British Journal of Psychiatry*, 1975, *127*, 342–348.

Akil, H., Mayer, D., and Liebeskind, J.C. Antagonism of stimulation-produced analgesia by Naloxone, a narcotic antagonist. *Science*, 1976, *191*, 961–962.

Akil, H., Watson, S.J., Young, E., Lewis, M.E., Khachaturian, H., and Walker, J.M. Endogenous opioids: Biology and function. *Annual Review of Neuroscience*, 1984, *7*, 223–255.

Albers, H.E., and Ferris, C.F. Neuropeptide Y: Role in light-dark cycle entrainment of hamster circadian rhythms. *Neuroscience Letters*, 1984, *50*, 163–168.

Albrecht, D.G. *Analysis of visual form*. Doctoral dissertation, University of California, Berkeley, 1978.

Albright, T.D., Desimone, R., and Gross, C.G. Columnar organization of directionally selective cells in visual area MT of the macaque. *Journal of Neurophysiology*, 1984, *51*, 16–31.

Aldrich, M.S. Current concepts: Narcolepsy. *New England Journal of Medicine*, 1990, *323*, 389–394.

Alexander, G.M., Sherwin, B.B., Bancroft, J., and Davidson, D.W. Testosterone and sexual behavior in oral contraceptive users and nonusers: A prospective study. *Hormones and Behavior*, 1990, *24*, 388–402.

Alexander, M.P., and Albert, M.L. The anatomical basis of visual agnosia. In *Localization in Neuropsychology,* edited by A. Kertesz. New York: Academic Press, 1983.

Alexander, M.P., Fischer, R.S., and Friedman, R. Lesion localization in apractic agraphia. *Archives of Neurology*, 1992, *49*, 246–251.

Allen, L.S., and Gorski, R.A. Sexual orientation and the size of the anterior commissure in the human brain. *Proceedings of the National Academy of Sciences*, 1992, *89*, 7199–7202.

Almers, W. Exocytosis. *Annual Review of Physiology*, 1990, *52*, 607–624.

Amir, S. Intra-ventromedial hypothalamic injection of glutamate stimulates brown adipose tissue thermogenesis in the rat. *Brain Research*, 1990a, *511*, 341–344.

Amir, S. Stimulation of the paraventricular nucleus with glutamate activates interscapular brown adipose tissue thermogenesis in rats. *Brain Research*, 1990b, *508*, 152–155.

Amyes, E.W., and Nielsen, J.M. Clinicopathologic study of vascular lesions of the anterior cingulate region. *Bulletin of the Los Angeles Neurological Societies*, 1955, *20*, 112–130.

Anand, B.K., and Brobeck, J.R. Hypothalamic control of food intake in rats and cats. *Yale Journal of Biology and Medicine*, 1951, *24*, 123–140.

Anderson, R.H., Fleming, D.E., Rhees, R.W., and Kinghorn, E. Relationships between sexual activity, plasma testosterone, and the volume of the sexually dimorphic nucleus of the preoptic area in prenatally stressed and non-stressed rats. *Brain Research*, 1986, *370*, 1–10.

Anderson, S.W., Damasio, H., Damasio, A.R., Klima, E., Bellugi, U., and Brandt, J.P. Acquisition of signs from American Sign Language in hearing individuals following left hemisphere damage and aphasia. *Neuropsychologia*, 1992, *30*, 329–340.

Andersson, B. The effect of injections of hypertonic NaCl solutions in different parts of the hypothalamus of goats. *Acta Physiologica Scandinavica*, 1953, *28*, 188–201.

Andreasen, N.C., and Olsen, S.A. Negative vs positive schizophrenia: Definition and validation. *Archives of General Psychiatry*, 1982, *39*, 789–794.

Andreasen, N.C., Swayze V, I.I., Flaum, M., Alliger, R., and Cohen, G. Ventricular abnormalities in affective disorder: Clinical and demographic correlates. *American Journal of Psychiatry*, 1990, *147*, 893–900.

Andrews, K.M., McGowan, M.K., Gallitano, A., and Grossman, S.P. Water intake during chronic preoptic infusions of osmotically active or inert solutions. *Physiology and Behavior*, 1992, *52*, 241–245.

Anonymous. Effects of sexual activity on beard growth in man. *Nature*, 1970, *226*, 867–870.

Applegate, C.D., Frysinger, R.C., Kapp, B.S., and Gallagher, M. Multiple unit activity recorded from the amygdala central nucleus during Pavlovian heart rate conditioning in the rabbit. *Brain Research*, 1982, *238*, 457–462.

Argiolas, A., and Gessa, G.L. Central functions of oxytocin. *Neuroscience and Biobehavioral Reviews*, 1991, *15*, 217–231.

Arletti, R., Benelli, A., and Bertolini, A. Oxytocin involvement in male and female sexual behavior. *Annals of the New York Academy of Sciences*, 1992, *652*, 180–193.

Arnold, A.P., and Jordan, C.L. Hormonal organization of neural circuits. In *Frontiers in Neuroendocrinology*, Vol. 10, edited by L. Martini and W.F. Ganong. New York: Raven Press, 1988.

Aroniadou, V.A., and Teyler, T.J. The role of NMDA receptors in long-term potentiation (LTP) and depression (LTD) in rat visual cortex. *Brain Research*, 1991, *562*, 136–143.

Artmann, H., Grau, H., Adelman, M., and Schleiffer, R. Reversible and non-reversible enlargement of cerebrospinal fluid spaces in anorexia nervosa. *Neuroradiology*, 1985, *27*, 103–112.

Asanuma, H., and Rosén, I. Topographical organization of cortical efferent zones projecting to distal forelimb muscles in monkeys. *Experimental Brain Research*, 1972, *13*, 243–256.

Aschoff, J. Circadian rhythms: General features and endocrinological aspects. In *Endocrine Rhythms*, edited by D.T. Krieger. New York: Raven Press, 1979.

Aston-Jones, G., and Bloom, F.E. Activity of norepinephrine-containing locus coeruleus neurons in behaving rats anticipates fluctuations in the sleep-waking cycle. *Journal of Neuroscience*, 1981a, *1*, 876–886.

Aston-Jones, G., and Bloom, F.E. Norepinephrine-containing locus coeruleus neurons in behaving rats exhibit pronounced responses to non-noxious environmental stimuli. *Journal of Neuroscience*, 1981b, *1*, 887–900.

Aston-Jones, G., Ennis, M., Pieribone, V.A., Nickell, W.T., and Shipley, M.T. The brain nucleus locus coeruleus: Restricted afferent control of a broad efferent network. *Science*, 1986, *234*, 734–737.

Auer, R.N., Jensen, M.L., and Whishaw, I.Q. Neurobehavioral deficit due to ischemic brain damage limited to half of the CA1 section of the hippocampus. *Journal of Neuroscience*, 1989, *9*, 1641–1647.

Avenet, P., Hoffman, F., and Lindemann, B. Transduction in taste receptor cells requires cAMP-dependent protein kinase. *Nature*, 1988, *331*, 351–354.

Avenet, P., and Lindemann, B. Perspectives of taste reception. *Journal of Membrane Biology*, 1989, *112*, 1–8.

Bailey, A.J. The biology of autism. *Psychological Medicine*, 1993, *23*, 7–11.

Bailey, J.M., and Pillard, R.C. A genetic study of male sexual orientation. *Archives of General Psychiatry*, 1991, *48*, 1089–1096.

Baizer, J.S., Ungerleider, L.G., and Desimone, R. Organization of visual inputs to the inferior temporal and posterior parietal cortex in macaques. *Journal of Neuroscience*, 1991, *11*, 168–190.

Bakalyar, H.A., and Reed, R.R. The second messenger cascade in olfactory receptor neurons. *Current Opinion in Neurobiology*, 1991, *1*, 204–208.

Bakin, J.S., and Weinberger, N.M. Classical conditioning induces CS-specific receptive field plasticity in the auditory cortex of the guinea pig. *Brain Research*, 1990, *536*, 271–286.

Baldessarini, R.J. *Chemotherapy in Psychiatry*. Cambridge, Mass.: Harvard University Press, 1977.

Baldessarini, R.J., and Tarsy, D. Dopamine and the pathophysiology of dyskinesias induced by antipsychotic drugs. *Annual Review of Neuroscience*, 1980, *3*, 23–42.

Balint, R. Seelenlahmung des "Schauens", optische Ataxie, raumliche Storung der Aufmerksamkeit. *Monatsschr. Psychiat. Neurol.*, 1909, *25*, 51–81.

Ballantine, H.T., Bouckoms, A.J., Thomas, E.K., and Giriunas, I.E. Treatment of psychiatric illness by stereotactic cingulotomy. *Biological Psychiatry*, 1987, *22*, 807–819.

Balon, R., Jordan, M., Pohl, R., and Yeragani, V.K. Family history of anxiety disorders in control subjects with lactate-induced panic attacks. *American Journal of Psychiatry*, 1989, *146*, 1304–1306.

Baranyi, A., Szente, M.B., and Woody, C.D. Properties of associative long-lasting potentiation induced by cellular conditioning in the motor cortex of conscious cats. *Neuroscience*, 1991, *42*, 321–334.

Barclay, C.D., Cutting, J.E., and Kozlowski, L.T. Temporal and spatial factors in gait perception that influence gender recognition. *Perception and Psychophysics*, 1978, *23*, 145–152.

Baron-Cohen, S., Leslie, A.M., and Frith, U. Does the autistic child have a "theory of mind"? *Cognition*, 1985, *21*, 37–46.

Basbaum, A.I., and Fields, H.L. Endogenous pain control mechanisms: Review and hypothesis. *Annals of Neurology*, 1978, *4*, 451–462.

Basbaum, A.I., and Fields, H.L. Endogenous pain control systems: Brainstem spinal pathways and endorphin circuitry. *Annual Review of Neuroscience*, 1984, *7*, 309–338.

Bassett, A.S., McGillivray, B.C., Jones, B., and Pantzar, J.T. Partial trisomy chromosome 5 cosegregating with schizophrenia. *Lancet*, 1988, *1*, 799–801.

Baumeister, A.A., Anticich, T.G., Hebert, G., Hawkins, M.F., and Nagy, M. Evidence that physical dependence on morphine is mediated by the ventral midbrain. *Neuropharmacology*, 1989, *28*, 1151–1157.

Baxter, L.R., Phelps, M.E., Mazziotta, J.C., Guze, B.H., Schwartz, J.M., and Selin, C.E. Local cerebral glucose metabolic rates in obsessive-compulsive disorder. *Archives of General Psychiatry*, 1987, *44*, 211–218.

Baxter, L.R., Schwartz, J.M., Mazziotta, J.C., Phelps, M.E., Pahl, J.J., and Guze, B.H. Cerebral glucose metabolic rates in non-depressed obsessive compulsives. *American Journal of Psychiatry*, 1989, *145*, 1560–1563.

Baylis, G.C., Rolls, E.T., and Leonard, C.M. Selectivity between faces in the responses of a population of neurons in the cortex in the superior temporal sulcus of the monkey. *Brain Research*, 1985, *342*, 91–102.

Bazett, H.C., McGlone, B., Williams, R.G., and Lufkin, H.M. Sensation. I. Depth, distribution, and probable identification in the prepuce of sensory end-organs concerned in sensations of temperature and touch: Thermometric conductivity. *Archives of Neurology and Psychiatry* (Chicago), 1932, *27*, 489–517.

Beach, F.A. Cerebral and hormonal control of reflexive mechanisms involved in copulatory behavior. *Physiological Review*, 1967, *47*, 289–316.

Bean, N.J., and Conner, R. Central hormonal replacement and home-cage dominance in castrated rats. *Hormones and Behavior*, 1978, *11*, 100–109.

Beauvois, M.F., and Dérouesné, J. Phonological alexia: Three dissociations. *Journal of Neurology, Neurosurgery and Psychiatry*, 1979, *42*, 1115–1124.

Beauvois, M.F., and Dérouesné, J. Lexical or orthographic dysgraphia. *Brain*, 1981, *104*, 21–45.

Beck, B., Burlet, A., Bazin, R., Nicolas, J.P., and Burlet, C. Coexistence of increase in neuropeptide Y (NPY) with the beginning of hyperphagia in the obese Zucker rat. *Society for Neuroscience Abstracts*, 1991, *17*, 193.

Beck, B., Burlet, A., Nicolas, J.P., and Burlet, C. Hyperphagia in obesity is associated with a central peptide dysregulation in rats. *Journal of Nutrition*, 1990, *120*, 806–811.

Beckstead, R.M., Morse, J.R., and Norgren, R. The nucleus of the solitary tract in the monkey: Projections to the thalamus and brainstem nuclei. *Journal of Comparative Neurology*, 1980, *190*, 259–282.

Beecher, H.K. *Measurement of Subjective Responses: Quantitative Effects of Drugs*. New York: Oxford University Press, 1959.

Beeman, E.A. The effect of male hormone on aggressive behavior in mice. *Physiological Zoology*, 1947, *20*, 373–405.

Beidler, L.M. Physiological properties of mammalian taste receptors. In *Taste and Smell in Vertebrates*, edited by G.E.W. Wolstenholme. London: J.&A. Churchill, 1970.

Beitz, A.J. The organization of afferent projections to the midbrain periaqueductal gray of the rat. *Neuroscience*, 1982, *7*, 133–159.

Bell, A.P., Weinberg, M.S., and Hammersmith, S.K. *Sexual Preference: Its Development in Men and Women*. Bloomington: Indiana University Press, 1981.

Bender, J. Characterization of cholecystokinin, bombesin, fenfluramine and an endogenous factor from fed pig plasma according to criteria of satiety. Paper presented at the Conference of the Society for the Study of Ingestive Behavior, Princeton, N.J., June 1992.

Benedek, G., Obal, F., Lelkes, Z., and Obal, F. Thermal and chemical stimulation of the hypothalamus heat detectors: The effects on the EEG. *Acta Physiologica Hungaria*, 1982, *60*, 27–35.

Beninger, R.J., Mason, S.T., Phillips, A.G., and Fibiger, H.C. Use of conditioned suppression to evaluate the nature of neuroleptic-induced avoidance deficits. *Journal of Pharmacology and Experimental Therapeutics*, 1980, *213*, 623–627.

Benson, D.F., and Geschwind, N. The alexias. In *Handbook of Clinical Neurology*, Vol. 4, edited by P. Vinken and G. Bruyn. Amsterdam: North-Holland, 1969.

Benson, D.F., and Geschwind, N. Aphasia and related disorders: A clinical approach. In *Principles of Behavioral Neurology*, edited by M.-M. Mesulam. Philadelphia: F.A. Davis, 1985.

Berger, B., Gaspar, P., and Verney, C. Dopaminergic innervation of the cerebral cortex: Unexpected differences between rodents and primates. *Trends in Neuroscience*, 1991, *14*, 21–27.

Berger, T.W., Berry, S.D., and Thompson, R.F. Role of the hippocampus in classical conditioning of aversive and appetitive behaviors. In *The Hippocampus*, Vol. 4, edited by R.L. Isaacson and K.H. Pribram. New York: Plenum Press, 1986.

Berger, T.W., and Orr, W.B. Hippocampectomy selectively disrupts discrimination reversal conditioning of the rabbit nictitating membrane response. *Behavioural Brain Research*, 1983, *8*, 49–68.

Bermant, G., and Davidson, J.M. *Biological Bases of Sexual Behavior*. New York: Harper & Row, 1974.

Bernard, C. *Leçons de Physiologie Expérimentale Appliquée à la Médicine Faites au Collège de France*, Vol. 2. Paris: Bailliere, 1856.

Bernstein, I.L. Learned taste aversion in children receiving chemotherapy. *Science*, 1978, *200*, 1302–1303.

Bernstein, I.L. Meal patterns in "free running humans." *Physiology and Behavior*, 1981, *27*, 621–624.

Bernstein, I.L., Lotter, E.C., Kulkosky, P.J., Porte, D., and Woods, S.C. Effect of force-feeding upon basal insulin levels of rats. *Proceedings of the Society for Experimental Biology and Medicine*, 1975, *150*, 546–548.

Besson, J.M., Guilbaud, G., Abdelmoumene, M., and Chaouch, A. Physiologie de la nociception. *Journal of Physiology* (Paris), 1982, *78*, 7–107.

Bettelheim, B. *The Empty Fortress*. New York: Free Press, 1967.

Bielajew, C., and Shizgal, P. Evidence implicating descending fibers in self-stimulation of the medial forebrain bundle. *Journal of Neuroscience*, 1986, *6*, 919–929.

Binder, J.R., Lazar, R.M., Tatemichi, T.K., Mohr, J.P., Desmond, D.W., and Ciecierski, K.A. Left hemiparalexia. *Neurology*, 1992, *42*, 562–569.

Bingman, V.P., and Mench, J.A. Homing behavior of hippocampus and parahippocampus lesioned pigeons following short-distance releases. *Behavioural Brain Research*, 1990, *40*, 227–238.

Birch, L.L., McPhee, L., Shoba, B.C., Steinberg, L., and Krehbiel, R. "Clean up your plate": Effects of child feeding practices on the conditioning of meal size. *Learning and Motivation*, 1987, *18*, 301–317.

Birch, L.L., McPhee, L., Sullivan, S., and Johnson, S. Conditioned meal initiation in young children. *Appetite*, 1989, *13*, 105–113.

Bitran, D., and Hull, E.M. Pharmacological analysis of male rat sexual behavior. *Neuroscience and Biobehavioral Reviews*, 1987, *11*, 365–389.

Blanchard, R.J., Weiss, S., Agullana, R., Flores, T., and Blanchard, D.C. Antipredator ultrasounds: Sex differences and drug effects. *Society for Neuroscience Abstracts*, 1991, *17*, 878.

Blander, D.S., Mark, G.P., Hernandez, L., and Hoebel, B.G. Angiotensin and drinking induce dopamine release in the nucleus accumbens. *Neuroscience Abstracts*, 1988, *14*, 527.

Blasdel, G.G. Differential imaging of ocular dominance and orientation selectivity in monkey striate cortex. *Journal of Neuroscience*, 1992a, *12*, 3115–3138.

Blasdel, G.G. Orientation selectivity, preference, and continuity in monkey striate cortex. *Journal of Neuroscience*, 1992b, *12*, 3139–3161.

Blass, E.M., and Epstein, A.N. A lateral preoptic osmosensitive zone for thirst. *Journal of Comparative and Physiological Psychology*, 1971, *76*, 378–394.

Blaustein, J.D., and Feder, H.H. Cytoplasmic progestin receptors in guinea pig brain: Characteristics and relationship to the induction of sexual behavior. *Brain Research*, 1979, *169*, 481–497.

Blaustein, J.D., and Olster, D.H. Gonadal steroid hormone receptors and social behaviors. In *Advances in Comparative and Environmental Physiology*, Vol. 3., edited by J. Balthazart. Berlin: Springer-Verlag, 1989.

Blaza, S. Brown adipose tissue in man: A review. *Journal of the Royal Society of Medicine*, 1983, *76*, 213–216.

Blest, A.D. The function of eyespot patterns in insects. *Behaviour*, 1957, *11*, 209–256.

Bliss, T.V.P., and Lømo, T. Long-lasting potentiation of synaptic transmission in the dentate area of the anaesthetized rabbit following stimulation of the perforant path. *Journal of Physiology* (London), 1973, *232*, 331–356.

Bloch, V., Hennevin, E., and Leconte, P. Interaction between post-trial reticular stimulation and subsequent paradoxical sleep in memory consolidation processes. In *Neurobiology of Sleep and Memory*, edited by R.R. Drucker-Colín, and J.L. McGaugh. New York: Academic Press, 1977.

Blonder, L.X., Bowers, D., and Heilman, K.M. The role of the right hemisphere in emotional communication. *Brain*, 1991, *114*, 1115–1127.

Blum, K., Noble, E.P., Sheridan, P.J., Montgomery, A., Ritchie, T., Jagadeeswaran, P., Nogami, H., Briggs, A.H., and Cohn, J.B. Allelic association of human dopamine D_2 receptor gene in alcoholism. *Journal of the American Medical Association*, 1990, *263*, 2055–2060.

Blumer, D., and Walker, A.E. The neural basis of sexual behavior. In *Psychiatric Aspects of Neurologic Disease*, edited by

D.F. Benson and D. Blumer. New York: Grune & Stratton, 1975.

Bogerts, B., Lieberman, J.A., Ashtari, M., Bilder, R.M., Degreef, G., Lerner, G., Johns, C., and Masiar, S. Hippocampus-amygdala volumes and psychopathology in chronic schizophrenia. *Biological Psychiatry*, 1993, *33*, 236–246.

Boller, F., and Dennis, M. (eds.). *Auditory Comprehension: Clinical and Experimental Studies with the Token Test*. New York: Academic Press, 1979.

Bolos, A.M., Dean, M., Lucas-Derse, S., Ramsburg, M., Brown, G.L., and Goldman, D. Population and pedigree studies reveal a lack of association between the dopamine D2 receptor gene and alcoholism. *Journal of the American Medical Association*, 1990, *264*, 3156–3160.

Bon, C., Böhme, G.A., Doble, A., Stutzmann, J.-.M., and Blanchard, J.-.C. A role for nitric oxide in long-term potentiation. *European Journal of Neuroscience*, 1992, *4*, 420–424.

Bonsall, R.W., Clancy, A.N., and Michael, R.P. Effects of the nonsteroidal aromatase inhibitor, Fadrozole, on sexual behavior in male rats. *Hormones and Behavior*, 1992, *26*, 240–254.

Borbély, A.A., and Tobler, I. Endogenous sleep-promoting substances and sleep regulation. *Physiological Reviews*, 1989, *69*, 605–670.

Bordi, F., and LeDoux, J. Sensory tuning beyond the sensory system: An initial analysis of auditory response properties of neurons in the lateral amygdaloid nucleus and overlying areas of the striatum. *Journal of Neuroscience*, 1992, *12*, 2493–2503.

Born, R.T., and Tootell, R.B.H. Spatial frequency tuning of single units in macaque supragranular striate cortex. *Proceedings of the National Academy of Sciences*, 1991, *88*, 7066–7070.

Bornstein, B., Stroka, H., and Munitz, H. Prosopagnosia with animal face agnosia. *Cortex*, 1969, *5*, 164–169.

Bornstein, R.A., Schwarzkopf, S.B., Olson, S.C., and Nasrallah, H.A. Third-ventricle enlargement and neuropsychological deficit in schizophrenia. *Biological Psychiatry*, 1992, *31*, 954–961.

Bos, N.P.A., and Mirmiran, M. Circadian rhythms in spontaneous neuronal discharges of the cultured suprachiasmatic nucleus. *Brain Research*, 1990, *511*, 158–162.

Bouchard, C. Genetic factors in obesity. *Medical Clinics of North America*, 1989, *73*, 67–81.

Bouchard, C. Heredity and the path to overweight and obesity. *Medicine and Science of Sports Exercise*, 1991, *23*, 285–291.

Boulos, Z., Rosenwasser, A.M., and Terman, M. Feeding schedules and the circadian organization of behavior in the rat. *Behavioural Brain Research*, 1980, *1*, 39–65.

Boussaoud, D., Desimone, R., and Ungerleider, L.G. Visual topography of area TEO in the macaque. *Journal of Comparative Neurology*, 1991, *306*, 554–575.

Bowers, D., Blonder, L.X., Feinberg, T., and Heilman, K.M. Differential impact of right and left hemisphere lesions on facial emotion and object imagery. *Brain*, 1991, *114*, 2593–2609.

Bowers, D., and Heilman, K.M. A dissociation between the processing of affective and nonaffective faces. Paper presented at the meeting of the International Neuropsychological Society, Atlanta, 1981.

Bowers, R.L., Herzog, C.D., Stone, E.H., and Dionne, T.J. Defensive burying following injections of cholecystokinin, bombesin, and LiCl in rats. *Physiology and Behavior*, 1992, *51*, 969–972.

Bowersox, S.S., Kaitin, K.I., and Dement, W.C. EEG spindle activity as a function of age: Relationship to sleep continuity. *Brain Research*, 1985, *63*, 526–539.

Boynton, R.M. *Human Color Vision*. New York: Holt, Rinehart and Winston, 1979.

Bozarth, M.A., and Wise, R.A. Anatomically distinct opiate receptor fields mediate reward and physical dependence. *Science*, 1984, *224*, 516–517.

Bozarth, M.A., and Wise, R.A. Toxicity associated with long-term intravenous heroin and cocaine self-administration in the rat. *Journal of the American Medical Association*, 1985, *254*, 81–83.

Bracha, H.S., Torrey, E.F., Gottesman, I.I., Bigelow, L.B., and Cunniff, C. Second-trimester markers of fetal size in schizophrenia: A study of monozygotic twins. *American Journal of Psychiatry*, 1992, *149*, 1355–1361.

Brackett, N.L., and Edwards, D.A. Medial preoptic connections with the midbrain tegmentum are essential for male sexual behavior. *Physiology and Behavior*, 1984, *32*, 79–84.

Bradbury, M.W.B. *The Concept of a Blood-Brain Barrier*. New York: John Wiley & Sons, 1979.

Bradwejn, J., Koszycki, D., Coeuetoux du Tertre, A., Bourin, M., Palmour, R., and Ervin, F. The cholecystokinin hypothesis of panic and anxiety disorders: A review. *Journal of Psychopharmacology*, 1992, 6, 345–351.

Bradwejn, J., Koszycki, D., and Meterissian, G. Cholecystokinin-tetrapeptide induced panic attacks in patients with panic disorder. *Canadian Journal of Psychiatry*, 1990, *35*, 83–85.

Brand, T., Kroonen, J., Mos, J., and Slob, A.K. Adult partner preference and sexual behavior of male rats affected by perinatal endocrine manipulations. *Hormones and Behavior*, 1991, *25*, 323–341.

Bray, G.A. Drug treatment of obesity. *American Journal of Clinical Nutrition*, 1992, *55*, 538S-544S.

Brecher, E.M. *Licit and Illicit Drugs*. Boston: Little, Brown & Co., 1972.

Bredt, D.S., Hwang, P.H., and Snyder, S.H. Localization of nitric oxide synthase indicating a neural role for nitric oxide. *Nature*, 1990, *347*, 768–770.

Breedlove, S.M. Sexual differentiation of the brain and behavior. In *Behavioral Endocrinology*, edited by J.B. Becker, S.M. Breedlove, and D. Crews. Cambridge, Mass.: MIT Press, 1992.

Breedlove, S.M., and Arnold, A. Hormone accumulation in a sexually dimorphic motor nucleus of the rat spinal cord. *Science*, 1980, *210*, 564–566.

Breedlove, S.M., and Arnold, A. Sex differences in the pattern of steroid accumulation by motorneurons of the rat lumbar spinal cord. *Journal of Comparative Neurology*, 1983, *215*, 211–216.

Breedlove, S.M., Jacobson, C.D., Gorski, R., and Arnold, A.P. Masculinization of the female rat spinal cord following a single neonatal injection of testosterone propionate but not estradiol benzoate. *Brain Research*, 1982, *237*, 173–181.

Breger, L., Hunter, I., and Lane, R.W. The effects of stress on dreams. *Physiological Issues Monograph Number 27*. New York: International University Press, 1971.

Breier, A., Buchanan, R.W., Elkashef, A., Munson, R.C., Kirkpatrick, B., and Gellad, F. Brain morphology and schizophrenia: A magnetic resonance imaging study of limbic, prefrontal cortex, and caudate structures. *Archives of General Psychiatry*, 1992, *49*, 921–926.

Breisch, S.T., Zemlan, F.P., and Hoebel, B.G. Hyperphagia and obesity following serotonin depletion by intraventricular *p*-chlorphenylalanine. *Science*, 1976, *192*, 382–384.

Brickner, R.M. *The Intellectual Functions of the Frontal Lobe. A Study Based Upon Observations of a Man After Partial Frontal Lobectomy*. New York: Macmillan, 1936.

Bridges, R.S. A quantitative analysis of the roles of dosage, sequence and duration of estradiol and progesterone exposure in the regulation of maternal behavior in the rat. *Endocrinology*, 1984, *114*, 930–940.

Bridges, R.S., and Ronsheim, P.M. Prolactin (PRL) regulation of maternal behavior in rats: Bromocriptine treatment delays and PRL promotes the rapid onset of behavior. *Endocrinology*, 1990, *126*, 837–848.

Broberg, D.J., and Bernstein, I.L. Cephalic insulin release in anorexic women. *Physiology and Behavior*, 1989, *45*, 871–874.

Broca, P. Remarques sur le siège de la faculté du langage articulé, suivies d'une observation d'aphemie (perte de la parole). *Bulletin de la Société Anatomique* (Paris), 1861, *36*, 330–357.

Brodie, M.S., Shefner, S.A., and Dunwiddie, T.V. Ethanol increases the firing rate of dopamine neurons of the rat ventral tegmental area in vitro. *Brain Research*, 1990, *508*, 65–69.

Brown, T.H., Ganong, A.H., Kairiss, E.W., Keenan, C.L., and Kelso, S.R. Long-term potentiation in two synaptic systems of the hippocampal brain slice. In *Neural Models of Plasticity: Experimental and Theoretical Approaches*, edited by J.H. Byrne and W.O. Berry. San Diego: Academic Press, 1989.

Brownell, K.D., Greenwood, M.R.C., Stellar, E., and Shrager, E.E. The effects of repeated cycles of weight loss and regain in rats. *Physiology and Behavior*, 1986, *38*, 459–464.

Brownell, W.E., Bader, C.R., Bertrand, D., and de-Ribaupierre, Y. Evoked mechanical responses of isolated cochlear outer hair cells. *Science*, 1985, *227*, 194–196.

Brozowski, T.J., Brown, R.M., Rosvold, H.E., and Goldman, P.S. Cognitive deficit caused by regional depletion of dopamine in prefrontal cortex of rhesus monkey. *Science*, 1979, *205*, 929–932.

Bruce, H.M. A block to pregnancy in the mouse caused by proximity of strange males. *Journal of Reproduction and Fertility*, 1960a, *1*, 96–103.

Bruce, H.M. Further observations of pregnancy block in mice caused by proximity of strange males. *Journal of Reproduction and Fertility*, 1960b, *2*, 311–312.

Bryden, M.P., and Ley, R.G. Right-hemispheric involvement in the perception and expression of emotion in normal humans. In *Neuropsychology of Human Emotion*, edited by K.M. Heilman and P. Satz. New York: Guilford Press, 1983.

Buchsbaum, M.S., Gillin, J.C., Wu, J., Hazlett, E., Sicotte, N., Dupont, R.M., and Bunney, W.E. Regional cerebral glucose metabolic rate in human sleep assessed by positron emission tomography. *Life Sciences*, 1989, *45*, 1349–1356.

Buchsbaum, M.S., Hershey, T.G., Hazlett, E., Sicotte, N., and Johnson, J.C. PET in generalized anxiety disorder. *Biological Psychiatry*, 1991, *29*, 1181–1199.

Buck, L., and Axel, R. A novel multigene family may encode odorant receptors: A molecular basis for odor recognition. *Cell*, 1991, *65*, 175–187.

Buck, R., and Duffy, R.J. Nonverbal communication of affect in brain damaged patients. *Cortex*, 1980, *16*, 351–362.

Buckley, P., Stack, J.P., Madigan, C., O'Callaghan, E., Larkin, C., Redmond, O., Ennis, J.T., and Waddington, J.L. Magnetic resonance imaging of schizophrenia-like psychoses associated with cerebral trauma: Clinicopathological correlates. *American Journal of Psychiatry*, 1993, *150*, 146–148.

Buggy, J., Hoffman, W.E., Phillips, M.I., Fisher, A.E., and Johnson, A.K. Osmosensitivity of rat third ventricle and interactions with angiotensin. *American Journal of Physiology*, 1979, *236*, R75–R82.

Burgard, E.C., and Sarvey, J.M. Muscarinic receptor activation facilitates the induction of long-term potentiation (LTP) in the rat dentate gyrus. *Neuroscience Letters*, 1990, *116*, 34–39.

Burt, D.R., Creese, I., and Snyder, S.H. Antischizophrenic drugs: Chronic treatment elevated dopamine receptor binding in brain. *Science*, 1977, *196*, 326–328.

Burton, M.J., Rolls, E.T., and Mora, F. Effects of hunger on the responses of neurons in the lateral hypothalamus to the sight and taste of food. *Experimental Neurology*, 1976, *51*, 668–677.

Buzsáki, G. Two-stage model of memory trace formation: A role for "noisy" brain states. *Neuroscience*, 1989, *31*, 551–570.

Buzsáki, G., and Gage, F.H. Mechanisms of action of neural grafts in the limbic system. *Canadian Journal of Neurological Sciences*, 1988, *15*, 99–105.

Buzsáki, G., Gage, F.H., Czopf, J., and Björklund, A. Restoration of rhythmic slow activity (theta) in the subcortically denervated hippocampus by fetal CNS transplants. *Brain Research*, 1987, *400*, 334–347.

Byerley, W., Mellon, C., O'Connell, P., Lalouel, J.-M., Nakamura, Y., Leppert, M., and White, R. Mapping genes for manic-depression and schizophrenia with DNA markers. *Trends in Neurosciences*, 1989, *12*, 46–48.

Cabanac, M., and Lafrance, L. Facial consummatory responses in rats support the ponderostat hypothesis. *Physiology and Behavior*, 1991, *50*, 179–183.

Cador, M., Robbins, T.W., and Everitt, B.J. Involvement of the amygdala in stimulus-reward associations: Interaction with the ventral striatum. *Neuroscience*, 1989, *30*, 77–86.

Cain, W.S. Olfaction. In *Stevens' Handbook of Experimental Psychology. Vol. 1. Perception and Motivation*, edited by R.C. Atkinson, R.J. Herrnstein, G. Lindzey, and R.D. Luce. New York: John Wiley & Sons, 1988.

Callaway, C.W., Lydic, R., Baghdoyan, H.A., and Hobson, J.A. Pontogeniculoocipital waves: Spontaneous visual system activity during rapid eye movement sleep. *Cellular and Molecular Neurobiology*, 1987, *2*, 105–149.

Calles-Escandon, J., and Horton, E.S. The thermogenic role of exercise in the treatment of morbid obesity: A critical evaluation. *American Journal of Clinical Nutrition*, 1992, *55*, 533S–537S.

Campbell, R., Heywood, C.A., Cower, A., Regard, M., and Landis, T. Sensitivity to eye gaze in prosopagnosic patients and monkeys with superior temporal sulcus ablation. *Neuropsychologia*, 1990, *28*, 1123–1142.

Campeau, S., Hayward, M.D., Hope, B.T., Rosen, J.B., Nestler, E.J., and Davis, M. Induction of the c-fos proto-oncogene in rat amygdala during unconditioned and conditioned fear. *Brain Research*, 1991, *565*, 349–352.

Campeau, S., Miserendino, M.J.D., and Davis, M. Intra-amygdala infusion of the N-methyl-D-aspartate receptor antagonist AP5 blocks acquisition but not expression of fear-potentiated startle to an auditory conditioned stimulus. *Behavioral Neuroscience*, 1992, *106*, 569–574.

Campfield, L.A., and Smith, F.J. Systemic factors in the control of food intake: Evidence for patterns as signals. In *Handbook of Behavioral Neurobiology. Vol. 10. Neurobiology of Food and Fluid Intake*, edited by E.M. Stricker. New York: Plenum Press, 1990.

Card, J.P., and Moore, R.Y. Ventral lateral geniculate nucleus efferents to the rat suprachiasmatic nucleus exhibit avian pancreatic polypeptide-like immunoreactivity. *Journal of Comparative Neurology*, 1982, *206*, 390–396.

Card, J.P., Riley, J.N., and Moore, R.Y. The suprachiasmatic hypothalamic nucleus: Ultrastructure of relations to optic chiasm. *Neuroscience Abstracts*, 1980, *6*, 758.

Carpenter, C.R. Sexual behavior of free ranging rhesus monkeys (*Macaca mulatta*). I. Specimens, procedures and behavioral characteristics of estrus. *Journal of Comparative Psychology*, 1942, *33*, 113–142.

Carr, C.E., and Konishi, M. Axonal delay lines for time measurement in the owl's brainstem. *Proceedings of the National Academy of Sciences, USA*, 1989, *85*, 8311–8315.

Carr, C.E., and Konishi, M. A circuit for detection of interaural time differences in the brain stem of the barn owl. *Journal of Neuroscience*, 1990, *10*, 3227–3246.

Carter, C.S. Hormonal influences on human sexual behavior. In *Behavioral Endocrinology*, edited by J.B. Becker, S.M. Breedlove, and D. Crews. Cambridge, Mass.: MIT Press, 1992a.

Carter, C.S. Neuroendocrinology of sexual behavior in the female. In *Behavioral Endocrinology*, edited by J.B. Becker, S.M. Breedlove, and D. Crews. Cambridge, Mass.: MIT Press, 1992b.

Cavada, C., and Goldman-Rakic, P.S. Posterior parietal cortex in rhesus monkey: II. Evidence for segregated cortico-cortical networks linking sensory and limbic areas with the frontal lobe. *Journal of Comparative Neurology*, 1989, *287*, 422–445

Cenci, M.A., Kalen, P., Mandel, R.J., and Bjoerklund, A. Regional differences in the regulation of dopamine and noradrenaline release in medial frontal cortex, nucleus accumbens and caudate-putamen: A microdialysis study in the rat. *Brain Research*, 1992, *581*, 217–228.

Chang, V.C., Mark, G.P., Hernandez, L., and Hoebel, B.G. Extracellular dopamine increases in the nucleus accumbens following rehydration or sodium repletion. *Society for Neuroscience Abstracts*, 1988, *14*, 527.

Chapman, P.F., Kairiss, E.W., Keenan, C.L., and Brown, T.H. Long-term synaptic potentiation in the amygdala. *Synapse*, 1990, *6*, 271–278.

Chaput, Y., De Montigny, C., and Blier, P. Presynaptic and postsynaptic modifications of the serotonin system by long-term administration of antidepressant treatments. An in vivo electrophysiologic study in the rat. *Neuropsychopharmacology*, 1991, *5*, 219–229.

Chen, J., Paredes, W., Li, J., Smith, D., Lowinson, J., and Gardner, E.L. Delta[9]–tetrahydrocannabinol produces naloxone-blockable enhancement of presynaptic basal dopamine efflux in nucleus accumbens of conscious, freely-moving rats as measured by intracerebral microdialysis. *Psychopharmacology*, 1990, *102*, 156–162.

Chess, S., Fernandez, F., and Korn, S.J. *Psychiatric Disorders of Children with Congenital Rubella*. New York: Brunner-Mazel, 1971.

Chi, J.G., Dooling, E.C., and Gilles, F.H. Gyral development of the human brain. *Annals of Neurology*, 1977, *1*, 86–93.

Chung, S.K., McVary, K.T., and McKenna, K.E. Sexual reflexes in male and female rats. *Neuroscience Letters*, 1988, *94*, 343–348.

Clark, J.R., Kalra, P.S., and Kalra, S.P. Neuropeptide Y stimulates feeding but inhibits sexual behavior in rats. *Endocrinology*, 1985, *117*, 2435–2442.

Clark, J.T., Gist, R.S., Kalra, S.P., and Kalra, P.S. α_2-adrenoreceptor blockade attenuates feeding behavior induced by neuropeptide Y and epinephrine. *Physiology and Behavior*, 1988, *42*, 417–422.

Clark, J.T., Kalra, P.S., Crowley, W.R., and Kalra, S.P. Neuropeptide Y and human pancreatic polypeptide stimulates feeding behavior in rats. *Endocrinology*, 1984, *115*, 427–429.

Cloninger, C.R. Neurogenetic adaptive mechanisms in alcoholism. *Science*, 1987, *236*, 410–416.

Cloninger, C.R., Bohmann, M., Sigvardsson, S., and von Knorring, A.-L. Psychopathology in adopted-out children of alcoholics. The Stockholm Adoption Study. *Recent Developments in Alcoholism*, 1985, *3*, 37–51.

Clugnet, M.-C., and LeDoux, J.E. Synaptic plasticity in fear conditioning circuits: Induction of LTP in the lateral nucleus of the amygdala by stimulation of the medial geniculate body. *Journal of Neuroscience*, 1990, *10*, 2818–2824.

Cobb, S., and Rose, R.M. Hypertension, peptic ulcer, and diabetes in air traffic controllers. *Journal of the American Medical Association*, 1973, *224*, 489–492.

Coble, P.A., Scher, M.S., Reynolds, C.F., Day, N.L., and Kupfer, D.J. Preliminary findings on the neonatal sleep of offspring of women with and without a prior history of affective disorder. *Sleep Research*, 1988, *16*, 120.

Coburn, P.C., and Stricker, E.M. Osmoregulatory thirst in rats after lateral preoptic lesions. *Journal of Comparative and Physiological Psychology*, 1978, *92*, 350–361.

Cohen, E.A. *Human Behavior in the Concentration Camp.* New York: W.W. Norton, 1953.

Cohen, S., Tyrrell, D.A.J., and Smith, A.P. Psychological stress and susceptibility to the common cold. *New England Journal of Medicine*, 1991, *325*, 606–612.

Coirini, H., Magarinos, A.M., DeNicola, A.F., Rainbow, T.C., and McEwen, B.S. Further studies of brain aldosterone binding sites employing new mineralocorticoid and glucocorticoid receptor markers in vitro. *Brain Research*, 1985, *12*, 212–216.

Cole, M., Winkelman, M.D., Morris, J.C., Simon, J.E., and Boyd, T.A. Thalamic amnesia: Korsakoff syndrome due to left thalamic infarction. *Journal of Neurological Sciences*, 1992, *110*, 62–67.

Comarr, A.E. Sexual function among patients with spinal cord injury. *Urologia Internationalis*, 1970, *25*, 134–168.

Comings, D.E., and Comings, B.G. Clinical and genetic relationships between autism-pervasive developmental disorder and Tourette syndrome: A study of 19 cases. *American Journal of Medical Genetics*, 1991, *39*, 180–191.

Cook, E.H. Autism: Review of neurochemical investigation. *Synapse*, 1990, *6*, 292–308.

Coon, H., Byerley, W., Holik, J., Hoff, M., Myles-Worsley, M., Lannfelt, L., Sokoloff, P., Schwartz, J.-C., Waldo, M., Freedman, R., and Plaetke, R. Linkage analysis of schizophrenia with five dopamine receptor genes in nine pedigrees. *American Journal of Human Genetics*, 1993, *52*, 327–334.

Cooper, J.R., Bloom, F.E., and Roth, R.H. *The Biochemical Basis of Neuropharmacology*, 5th ed. New York: Oxford University Press, 1987.

Coover, G.D., Murison, R., and Jellestad, F.K. Subtotal lesions of the amygdala: The rostral central nucleus in passive avoidance and ulceration. *Physiology and Behavior*, 1992, *51*, 795–803.

Coplan, J.D., Gorman, J.M., and Klein, D.F. Serotonin related functions in panic-anxiety: A critical overview. *Neuropsychopharmacology*, 1992, *6*, 189–200.

Corbetta, M., Miezin, F.M., Doobmeyer, S., Shulman, G.L., and Petersen, S.E. Attentional modulation of neural processing of shape, color, and velocity in humans. *Science*, 1990, *248*, 1556–1559.

Corbetta, M., Miezin, F.M., Doobmeyer, S., Shulman, G.L., and Petersen, S.E. Selective and divided attention during visual discriminations of shape, color, and speed: Functional anatomy by positron emission tomography. *Journal of Neuroscience*, 1991, *11*, 2383–2402.

Corkin, S., Sullivan, E.V., Twitchell, T.E., and Grove, E. The amnesic patient H.M.: Clinical observations and test performance 28 years after operation. *Society for Neuroscience Abstracts*, 1981, *7*, 235.

Cornwall, J., Cooper, J.D., and Phillpison, O.T. Afferent and efferent connections of the laterodorsal tegmental nucleus in the rat. *Brain Research* Bulletin, 1990, *25*, 271–284.

Corwin, J.T., and Warchol, M.E. Auditory hair cells: Structure, function, development, and regeneration. *Annual Review of Neuroscience*, 1991, *14*, 301–333.

Cotman, C.W., Monaghan, D.T., and Ganong, A.H. Excitatory amino acid neurotransmission: NMDA receptors and Hebb-type synaptic plasticity. *Annual Review of Neuroscience*, 1988, *11*, 61–80.

Courchesne, E. Neuroanatomic imaging in autism. *Pediatrics*, 1991, *87*, 781–790.

Cowey, A., and Stoerig, P. The neurobiology of blindsight. *Trends in Neuroscience*, 1991, *14*, 140–145.

Cowley, D.S., and Arana, G.W. The diagnostic utility of lactate sensitivity in panic disorder. *Archives of General Psychiatry*, 1990, *47*, 277–284.

Cowley, J.J., and Brooksbank, B.W.L. Human exposure to putative pheromones and changes in aspects of social behaviour. *Journal of Steroid Biochemistry and Molecular Biololgy*, 1991, *39*, 647–659.

Cox, A., Rutter, M., Newman, S., and Bartak, L. A comparative study of infantile autism and specific developmental language disorders. I. Parental characteristics. *British Journal of Psychiatry*, 1975, *126*, 146–159.

Crane, G.E. Iproniazid (Marsilid) phosphate, a therapeutic agent for mental disorders and debilitating diseases. *Psychiatry Research Reports*, 1957, *8*, 142–152.

Creese, I., Burt, D.R., and Snyder, S.H. Dopamine receptor binding predicts clinical and pharmacological potencies of antischizophrenic drugs. *Science*, 1976, *192*, 481–483.

Crick, F., and Mitchison, G. The function of dream sleep. *Nature*, 1983, *304*, 111–114.

Criswell, H.E., and Rogers, F.B. Narcotic analgesia: Changes in neural activity recorded from periaqueductal gray matter of rat brain. *Society for Neuroscience Abstracts*, 1978, *4*, 458.

Crow, T.J. A map of the rat mesencephalon for electrical self-stimulation. *Brain Research*, 1972, *36*, 265–273.

Crow, T.J. Molecular pathology of schizophrenia: More than one disease process? *British Medical Journal of Clinical Research*, 1980, *280*, 66–68.

Crow, T.J., DeLisi, L.E., and Johnstone, E.C. Concordance by sex in sibling pairs with schizophrenia is paternally inherited. *British Journal of Psychiatry*, 1989, *155*, 92–97.

Crowe, R.R., Noyes, R., Pauls, D.L., and Slymen, D. A family study of panic disorder. *Archives of General Psychiatry*, 1983, *40*, 1065–1069.

Crowe, R.R., Noyes, R., Wilson, A.F., Elston, R.C., and Ward, L.J. A linkage study of panic disorder. *Archives of General Psychiatry*, 1987, *44*, 933–937.

Crowley, W.R., Nock, B., and Feder, H.H. Facilitation of lordosis behavior by clinidine in female guinea pigs. *Pharmacology, Biochemistry, and Behavior*, 1978, *8*, 207–209.

Crowley, W.R., Rodriguez-Sierra, J.F., and Komisaruk, B.R. Monoaminergic mediation of the antinociceptive effect of vaginal stimulation in rats. *Brain Research*, 1977, *137*, 67–84.

Cruikshank, S.J., Edeline, J.-M., and Weinberger, N.M. Stimulation at a site of auditory-somatosensory convergence in the medial geniculate nucleus is an effective unconditioned stimulus for fear conditioning. *Behavioral Neuroscience*, 1992, *106*, 471–483.

Csonka, E., Fekete, M., Nagy, G., Sxanto-Fekete, M., Feledgy, G., Penke, B., and Kovaks, K. Anxiogenic effect of cholecystokinin in rats. In *Peptides*, edited by B. Penke and A. Torok. New York: Walter de Gruyter & Co., 1988.

Cubelli, R. A selective deficit for writing vowels in acquired dysgraphia. *Nature*, 1991, *353*, 258–260.

Culebras, A., and Moore, J.T. Magnetic resonance findings in REM sleep behavior disorder. *Neurology*, 1989, *39*, 1519–1523.

Culotta, E., and Koshland, D.E. NO news is good news. *Science*, 1992, *258*, 1862–1865.

Cummings, J.L., and Cunningham, K. Obsessive-compulsive disorder in Huntington's disease. *Biological Psychiatry*, 1992, *31*, 263–270.

Cunningham, J.T., Beltz, T., Johnson, R.F., and Johnson, A.K. The effects of ibotenate lesions of the median preoptic nucleus on experimentally-induced and circadian drinking behavior in rats. *Brain Research*, 1992, *580*, 325–330.

Czech, D.A., and Stein, E.A. Effect of drinking on angiotensin-II-induced shifts in regional cerebral blood flow in the rat. *Brain Research Bulletin*, 1992, *28*, 529–535.

Czeisler, C.A., Kronauer, R.E., Allan, J.S., Duffy, J.F., Jewett, M.E., Brown, E.N., and Ronda, J.M. Bright light induction of strong (type 0) resetting of the human circadian pacemaker. *Science*, 1989, *244*, 1328–1332.

Czeisler, C.A., Weitzman, E.D., Moore-Ede, M.C., Zimmerman, J.C., and Knauer, R.S. Human sleep: Its duration and organization depend on its circadian phase. *Science*, 1980, *210*, 1264–1267.

Dabbs, J.M., Frady, R.L., Carr, T.S., and Besch, N.F. Saliva testosterone and criminal violence in young adult prison inmates. *Psychosomatic Medicine*, 1987, *49*, 174–182.

Dabbs, J.M., Ruback, J.M., Frady, R.L., and Hopper, C.H. Saliva testosterone and criminal violence among women. *Personality and Individual Differences*, 1988, *9*, 269–275.

Dahl, D., and Sarvey, J.M. Norepinephrine induces pathway-specific long-lasting potentiation and depression in the hippocampal dentate gyrus. *Proceedings of the National Academy of Sciences, USA*, 1989, *86*, 4776–4780.

Dahl, D., and Sarvey, J.M. Beta-Adrenergic agonist-induced long-lasting synaptic modifications in hippocampal dentate gyrus require activation of NMDA receptors, but not electrical activation of afferents. *Brain Research*, 1990, *526*, 347–350.

Damasio, A. Aphasia. *New England Journal of Medicine*, 1992, *326*, 531–539.

Damasio, A.R. Disorders of complex visual processing: Agnosias, achromatopsia, Balint's syndrome, and related difficulties of orientation and construction. In *Principles of Behavioral Neurology*, edited by M.-M. Mesulam. Philadelphia: F.A. Davis, 1985.

Damasio, A.R., Brandt, J.P., Tranel, D., and Damasio, H. Name dropping: Retrieval of proper or common noun depends on different systems in left temporal cortex. *Society for Neuroscience Abstracts*, 1991, *17*, 4.

Damasio, A.R., and Damasio, H. The anatomic basis of pure alexia. *Neurology*, 1983, *33*, 1573–1583.

Damasio, A.R., and Damasio, H. Hemianopia, hemiachromatopsia, and the mechanisms of alexia. *Cortex*, 1986, *22*, 161–169.

Damasio, A.R., Damasio, H., and Van Hoesen, G.W. Prosopagnosia: Anatomic basis and behavioral mechanisms. *Neurology*, 1982, *32*, 331–341.

Damasio, A.R., and Tranel, D. Knowing that "Colorado" goes with "Denver" does not imply knowledge that "Denver" is in "Colorado." *Behavioural Brain Research*, 1990, *40*, 193–200.

Damasio, A.R., Yamada, T., Damasio, H., Corbett, J., and McKee, J. Central achromatopsia: Behavioral, anatomic, and physiologic aspects. *Neurology*, 1980, *30*, 1064–1071.

Damasio, H. Cerebral localization of the aphasias. In *Acquired Aphasia*, edited by M.T. Sarno. New York: Academic Press, 1981.

Damasio, H. Neuroimaging contributions to the understanding of aphasia. In *Handbook of Neuropsychology*, Vol. 2, edited by F. Boller and J. Grafman. Amsterdam: Elsevier, 1989.

Damasio, H., and Damasio, A.R. The anatomical basis of conduction aphasia. *Brain*, 1980, *103*, 337–350.

Damasio, H., Eslinger, P., and Adams, H.P. Aphasia following basal ganglia lesions: New evidence. *Seminars in Neurology*, 1984, *4*, 151–161.

D'Amato, T., Rochet, T., Dalery, J., Laurent, A., Chauchat, J.-H., Terra, J.-L., and Marie-Cardine, M. Relationship between symptoms rated with the Positive and Negative Syndrome Scale and brain measures in schizophrenia. *Psychiatry Research*, 1992, *44*, 55–62.

Damsma, G., Day, J., and Fibiger, H.C. Lack of tolerance to nicotine-induced dopamine release in the nucleus accumbens. *European Journal of Pharmacology*, 1989, *168*, 363–368.

Damsma, G., Pfaus, J.G., Wenkstern, D., Phillips, A.G., and Fibiger, H.C. Sexual behavior increases dopamine transmission in the nucleus accumbens and striatum of male rats: Comparison with novelty and locomotion. *Behavioral Neuroscience*, 1992, *106*, 181–191.

Daniel, D.G., Weinberger, D.R., Jones, D.W., Zigon, J.R., Cippola, R., Handel, S., Bigelow, L.B., Goldberg, T.E., Berman, K.F., and Kleinman, J.E. The effect of amphetamine on regional cerebral blood flow during cognitive activation in schizophrenia. *Journal of Neuroscience*, 1991, *11*, 1907–1917.

Darwin, C. *The Expression of the Emotions in Man and Animals*. Chicago: University of Chicago Press, 1872/1965.

Davidson, J.M. Hormones and sexual behavior in the male. In *Neuroendocrinology*, edited by D.T. Krieger and J.C. Hughes. Sunderland, Mass.: Sinauer Associates, 1980.

Davis, J.D., and Campbell, C.S. Peripheral control of meal size in the rat: Effect of sham feeding on meal size and drinking rate. *Journal of Comparative and Physiological Psychology*, 1973, *83*, 379–387.

Davis, J.D., Campbell, C.S., Gallagher, R.J., and Zukarov, M.A. Disappearance of a humoral satiety factor during food deprivation. *Journal of Comparative and Physiological Psychology*, 1971, *75*, 476–482.

Davis, J.D., Gallagher, R.J., Ladove, R.F., and Turausky, A.J. Inhibition of food intake by a humoral factor. *Journal of Comparative and Physiological Psychology*, 1969, *67*, 407–414.

Davis, K.L., Kahn, R.S., Ko, G., and Davidson, M. Dopamine in schizophrenia: A review and reconceptualization. *American Journal of Psychiatry*, 1991, *148*, 1474–1486.

Davis, M. The role of the amygdala in fear and anxiety. *Annual Review of Neuroscience*, 1992a, *15*, 353–375.

Davis, M. The role of the amygdala in fear-potentiated startle: Implications for animal models of anxiety. *Trends in Pharmacological Sciences*, 1992b, *13*, 35–41.

Davis, S., Butcher, S.P., and Morris, R.G.M. The NMDA receptor antagonist D-2–amino-5–phosphonopentanoate (D-AP5) impairs spatial learning and LTP in vivo at intracerebral concentrations comparable to those that block LTP in vitro. *Journal of Neuroscience*, 1992, *12*, 21–34.

Davison, G.C., and Neale, J.M. *Abnormal Psychology: An Experimental Clinical Approach*. New York: John Wiley & Sons, 1974.

Daw, N.W. Colour-coded ganglion cells in the goldfish retina: Extension of their receptive fields by means of new stimuli. *Journal of Physiology* (London), 1968, *197*, 567–592.

Day, J., Damsma, G., and Fibiger, H.C. Cholinergic activity in the rat hippocampus, cortex and striatum correlates with

locomotor activity: An in vivo microdialysis study. *Pharmacology, Biochemistry, and Behavior*, 1991, *38*, 723–729.

Dean, P. Visual behavior in monkeys with inferotemporal lesions. In *Analysis of Visual Behavior*, edited by D.J. Ingle, M.A. Goodale, and R.J.W. Mansfield. Cambridge, Mass.: MIT Press, 1982.

De Andres, I., Gutierrez-Rivas, E., Nava, E., and Reinoso-Suarez, F. Independence of sleep-wakefulness cycle in an implanted head "encéphale isolé." *Neuroscience Letters*, 1976, *2*, 13–18.

De Bold, A.J. Atrial natriuretic factor: A hormone produced by the heart. *Science*, 1985, *230*, 767–770.

De Bold, A.J., Borenstein, H.B., Veres, A.T., and Sonnenberg, H. A rapid and potent natriuretic response to intravenous injection of atrial myocardial extracts in rats. *Life Science*, 1981, *28*, 89–94.

de Castro, J.M. A microregulatory analysis of spontaneous fluid intake by humans: Evidence that the amount of liquid ingested and its timing is mainly governed by feeding. *Physiology and Behavior*, 1988, *43*, 705–714.

de Castro, J.M., and de Castro, E.S. Spontaneous meal patterns of humans: Influence of the presence of other people. *American Journal of Clinical Nutrition*, 1989, *50*, 237–247.

de Castro, J.M., McCormick, J., Pedersen, M., and Kreitzman, S.N. Spontaneous human meal patterns are related to preprandial factors regardless of natural environmental constraints. *Physiology and Behavior*, 1986, *38*, 25–29.

Degreef, G., Ashtari, M., Bogerts, B., Bilder, R.M., Jody, D.N., Alvir, J.M.J., and Lieberman, J.A. Volumes of ventricular system subdivisions measured from magnetic resonance images in first-episode schizophrenic patients. *Archives of General Psychiatry*, 1992, *49*, 531–537.

Deiber, M.P., Passingham, R.E., Colebatch, J.G., and Friston, K.J. Cortical areas and the selection of movement: A study with positron emission tomography. *Experimental Brain Research*, 1991, *84*, 393–402.

Dejerine, J. Contribution à l'étude anatomo-pathologique et clinique des différentes variétés de cécité verbale. *Comptes Rendus des Séances de la Société de Biologie et de Ses Filiales*, 1892, *4*, 61–90.

De Jonge, F.H., Louwerse, A.L., Ooms, M.P., Evers, P., Endert, E., and van de Poll, N.E. Lesions of the SDN-POA inhibit sexual behavior of male Wistar rats. *Brain Research Bulletin*, 1989, *23*, 483–492.

De Jonge, F.H., Oldenburger, W.P., Louwerse, A.L., and Van de Poll, N.E. Changes in male copulatory behavior after sexual exciting stimuli: Effects of medial amygdala lesions. *Physiology and Behavior*, 1992, *52*, 327–332.

DeKosky, S., Heilman, K.M., Bowers, D., and Valenstein, E. Recognition and discrimination of emotional faces and pictures. *Brain and Language*, 1980, *9*, 206–214.

Delay, J., and Deniker, P. Le traitement des psychoses par une methode neurolytique derivée d'hibernothéraphie; le 4560 RP utilisée seul une cure prolongée et continuée. *Comptes Rendus Congrès des Médecins Aliénistes et Neurolo-*

gistes de France et des Pays de Langue Française, 1952a, *50*, 497–502.

Delay, J., and Deniker, P. 38 cas des psychoses traitées par la cure prolongée et continuée de 4560 RP. *Comptes Rendus Congrès des Médecins Aliénistes et Neurologistes de France et des Pays de Langue Française*, 1952b, *50*, 503–513.

del Cerro, S., Jung, M., and Lynch, G. Benzodiazepines block long-term potentiation in slices of hippocampus and piriform cortex. *Neuroscience*, 1992, *49*, 1–6.

Delgado, P.L., Charney, D.S., Price, L.H., Aghajanian, G.K., Landis, H., and Heninger, G.R. Serotonin function and the mechanism of antidepressant action: Reversal of antidepressant induced remission by rapid depletion of plasma tryptophan. *Archives of General Psychiatry*, 1990, *47*, 411–418.

DeLong, G.R. Autism, amnesia, hippocampus, and learning. *Neuroscience and Biobehavioral Reviews*, 1992, *16*, 63–70.

DeLong, M. Motor functions of the basal ganglia: Single-unit activity during movement. In *The Neurosciences: Third Study Program*, edited by F.O. Schmitt and F.G. Worden. Cambridge, Mass.: MIT Press, 1974.

Dement, W.C. The effect of dream deprivation. *Science*, 1960, *131*, 1705–1707.

Denlinger, S.L., Patarca, R., and Hobson, J.A. Differential enhancement of rapid eye movement sleep signs in the cat: A comparison of microinjection of the cholinergic agonist carbachol and the ß-adrenergic antagonist propranolol on pontogeniculo-occipital wave clusters. *Brain Research*, 1988, *473*, 116–126.

Deol, M.S., and Gluecksohn-Waelsch, S. The role of inner hair cells in hearing. *Nature*, 1979, *278*, 250–252.

Dérousné, J., and Beauvois, M.-F. Phonological processing in reading: Data from alexia. *Journal of Neurology, Neurosurgery, and Psychiatry*, 1979, *42*, 1125–1132.

Desimone, R., Albright, T.D., Gross, C.G., and Bruce, D. Stimulus-selective properties of inferior temporal neurons in the macaque. *Journal of Neuroscience*, 1984, *8*, 2051–2062.

Deutsch, J.A. The cholinergic synapse and the site of memory. In *The Physiological Basis of Memory*, edited by J.A. Deutsch. New York: Academic Press, 1983.

Deutsch, J.A., and Gonzalez, M.F. Gastric nutrient content signals satiety. *Behavioral and Neural Biology*, 1980, *30*, 113–116.

Deutsch, J.A., and Hardy, W.T. Cholecystokinin produces bait shyness in rats. *Nature*, 1977, *266*, 196.

De Valois, R.L., Albrecht, D.G., and Thorell, L. Cortical cells: Bar detectors or spatial frequency filters? In *Frontiers in Visual Science*, edited by S.J. Cool and E.L. Smith. Berlin: Springer-Verlag, 1978.

De Valois, R.L., and De Valois, K.K. *Spatial Vision*. New York: Oxford University Press, 1988.

Devane, W.A., Hanus, L., Breuer, A., Pertwee, R.G., Stevenson, L.A., Griffin, G., Gibson, D., Mandelbaum, A., Etinger, A., and Mechoulam, R. Isolation and structure of a brain constituent that binds to the cannabinoid receptor. *Science*, 1992, *258*, 1946–1949.

DeVries, G.J. Sex differences in neurotransmitter systems. *Journal of Neuroendocrinology*, 1990, *2*, 1–13.

Diamond, D.M., Dunwiddie, T.V., and Rose, G.M. Characteristics of hippocampal primed burst potentiation in vitro and in the awake rat. *Journal of Neuroscience*, 1988, *8*, 4079–4088.

Di Chiara, G., and Imperato, A. Preferential simulation of dopamine release in the nucleus accumbens by opiates, alcohol, and barbiturates: Studies with transcerebral dialysis in freely moving rats. *Annals of the New York Academy of Sciences*, 1987, *473*, 367–381.

Dimsdale, J.E. A perspective on type A behavior and coronary disease. *The New England Journal of Medicine*, 1988, *318*, 110–112.

Doherty, P.C., Baum, M.J., and Todd, R.B. Effects of chronic hyperprolactinemia on sexual arousal and erectile function in male rats. *Neuroendocrinology*, 1986, *42*, 368–375.

Dolan, R.P., and Schiller, P.H. Evidence for only depolarizing rod bipolar cells in the primate retina. *Visual Neuroscience*, 1989, *2*, 421–424.

Doty, R.L., Ford, M., Preti, G., and Huggins, G.R. Changes in the intensity and pleasantness of human vaginal odors during the menstrual cycle. *Science*, 1975, *190*, 1316.

Downer, J.L. deC. Changes in visual gnostic functions and emotional behaviour following unilateral temporal pole damage in the "split-brain" monkey. *Nature*, 1961, *191*, 50–51.

Dray, A. The physiology and pharmacology of mammalian basal ganglia. *Progress in Neurobiology*, 1980, *14*, 221–335.

Drevets, W.C., Videen, T.O., Price, J.L., Preskorn, S.H., Carmichael, S.T., and Raichle, M.E. A functional anatomical study of unipolar depression. *Journal of Neuroscience*, 1992, *12*, 3628–3641.

Dudek, S.M., and Bear, M.F. Homosynaptic long-term depression in area CA1 of hippocampus and effects of N-methyl-D-aspartate receptor blockade. *Proceedings of the National Academy of Sciences*, 1992, *89*, 4363–4367.

Dujardin, K., Guerrien, A., and Leconte, P. Sleep, brain activation and cognition. *Physiology and Behavior*, 1990, *47*, 1271–1278.

Dunn, A., and Berridge, C.W. Physiological and behavioral responses to corticotropin-releasing factor administration: Is CRF a mediator of anxiety or stress responses? *Brain Research Reviews*, 1990, *15*, 71–100.

Dunnett, S.B., Lane, D.M., and Winn, P. Ibotenic acid lesions of the lateral hypothalamus: Comparison with 6–hydroxydopamine-induced sensorimotor deficits. *Neuroscience*, 1985, *14*, 509–518.

Durie, D.J. Sleep in animals. In *Psychopharmacology of Sleep*, edited by D. Wheatley. New York: Raven Press, 1981.

Duvauchelle, C.L., and Ettenberg, A. Haloperidol attenuates conditioned place preferences produced by electrical stimulation of the medial prefrontal cortex. *Pharmacology, Biochemistry, and Behavior*, 1991, *38*, 645–650.

Dykes, R.W. Parallel processing of somatosensory information: A theory. *Brain Research Reviews*, 1983, *6*, 47–115.

East, S.J., and Garthwaite, J. NMDA receptor activation in rat hippocampus induces cyclic GMP formation through the L-arginine-nitric oxide pathway. *Neuroscience Letters*, 1991, *123*, 17–19.

Eddy, N.B., Halbach, H., Isbell, H., and Seevers, M.H. Drug dependence: Its significance and characteristics. *Bulletin of the World Health Organization*, 1965, *32*, 721–733.

Edeline, J.-M., and Weinberger, N.M. Subcortical adaptive filtering in the auditory system: Associative receptive field plasticity in the dorsal medial geniculate body. *Behavioral Neuroscience*, 1991a, *105*, 154–175.

Edeline, J.-M., and Weinberger, N.M. Thalamic short-term plasticity in the auditory system: Associative retuning of receptive fields in the ventral medial geniculate body. *Behavioral Neuroscience*, 1991b, *105*, 618–639.

Edeline, J.-M., and Weinberger, N.M. Associative retuning in the thalamic source of input to the amygdala and auditory cortex: Receptive field plasticity in the medial division of the medial geniculate body. *Behavioral Neuroscience*, 1992, *106*, 81–105.

Egawa, M., Yoshimatsu, H., and Bray, G.A. Neuropeptide Y (NPY) suppresses sympathetic activity to interscapular brown adipose tissue in rats. *American Journal of Physiology*, 1991, *260*, R328–R334.

Egeland, J.A., Gerhard, D.S., Pauls, D.L., Sussex, J.N., Kidd, K.K., Allen, C.R., Hostetter, A.M., and Housman, D.E. Bipolar affective disorders linked to DNA markers on chromosome 11. *Nature*, 1987, *325*, 783–787.

Ehlers, C.L., Frank, E., and Kupfer, D.J. Social zeitgebers and biological rhythms. *Archives of General Psychiatry*, 1988, *45*, 948–952.

Ehrhardt, A.A., and Meyer-Bahlburg, H.F.L. Effects of prenatal sex hormones on gender-related behavior. *Science*, 1981, *211*, 1312–1318.

Ehrlich, K.J., and Fitts, D.A. Atrial natriuretic peptide in the subfornical organ reduces drinking induced by angiotensin or in response to water deprivation. *Behavioral Neuroscience*, 1990, *104*, 365–372.

Eichenbaum, H., Otto, T., and Cohen, N.J. The hippocampus—What does it do? *Behavioral and Neural Biology*, 1992, *57*, 2–36.

Eichenbaum, H., Steward, C., and Morris, R.G.M. Hippocampal representation in spatial learning. *Journal of Neuroscience*, 1990, *10*, 331–339.

Eilam, R., Malach, R., Bergmann, F., and Segal, M. Hypertension induced by hypothalamic transplantation from genetically hypertensive to normotensive rats. *Journal of Neuroscience*, 1991, *11*, 401–411.

Ekman, P. *The Face of Man: Expressions of Universal Emotions in a New Guinea Village*. New York: Garland STPM Press, 1980.

Ekman, P., and Friesen, W.V. Constants across cultures in the face and emotion. *Journal of Personality and Social Psychology*, 1971, *17*, 124–129.

Ekman, P., Levenson, R.W., and Friesen, W.V. Autonomic nervous system activity distinguished between emotions. *Science*, 1983, *221*, 1208–1210.

Elias, M. Serum cortisol, testosterone and testosterone binding globulin responses to competitive fighting in human males. *Aggressive Behavior*, 1981, *7*, 215–224.

El Mansari, M., Sakai, K., and Jouvet, M. Unitary characteristics of presumptive cholinergic tegmental neurons during the sleep-waking cycle in freely moving cats. *Experimental Brain Research*, 1989, *76*, 519–529.

Engen, T. Method and theory in the study of odor preferences. In *Human Responses to Environmental Odors*, edited by A. Turk, J.W. Johnston, and D.G. Moulton. New York: Academic Press, 1974.

Engen, T. *The Perception of Odors*. New York: Academic Press, 1982.

Ennis, M., and Aston-Jones, G. Potent excitatory input to the nucleus locus coeruleus from the ventrolateral medulla. *Neuroscience Letters*, 1986, *71*, 299–305.

Ennis, M., and Aston-Jones, G. Excitatory synaptic transmission from paragigantocellularis to locus coeruleus: A new amino acid pathway in the brain. *Journal of Neuroscience*, 1988, *8*, 3644–3657.

Epstein, A.N. Epilogue: Retrospect and prognosis. In *The Neuropsychology of Thirst: New Findings and Advances in Concepts*, edited by A.N. Epstein, H.R. Kissileff, and E. Stellar. New York: John Wiley & Sons, 1973.

Ernulf, K.E., Innala, S.M., and Whitam, F.L. Biological explanation, psychological explanation, and tolerance of homosexuals: A cross-national analysis of beliefs and attitudes. *Psychological Reports*, 1989, *248*, 183–188.

Eslinger, P.J., and Damasio, A.R. Severe disturbance of higher cognition after bilateral frontal lobe ablation: Patient EVR. *Neurology*, 1985, *35*, 1731–1741.

Evans, E.F. Auditory processing of complex sounds: An overview. *Philosophical Transactions of the Royal Society of London [B]*, 1992, *336*, 295–306.

Evarts, E.V. Sensorimotor cortex activity associated with movements triggered by visual as compared to somesthetic inputs. In *The Neurosciences: Third Study Program*, edited by F.O. Schmitt and F.G. Worden. Cambridge, Mass.: MIT Press, 1974.

Everitt, B.J., Cador, M., and Robbins, T.W. Interactions between the amygdala and ventral striatum in stimulus-reward associations: Studies using a second-order schedule of sexual reinforcement. *Neuroscience*, 1989, *30*, 63–75.

Everitt, B.J., Herbert, J., and Hamer, J.D. Sexual receptivity of bilaterally adrenalectomised female rhesus monkeys. *Physiology and Behavior*, 1972, *8*, 409–415.

Falk, J.L. The nature and determinants of adjunctive behavior. In *Schedule Effects: Drugs, Drinking, and Aggression*, edited by R.M. Gilbert and J.D. Keehn. Toronto: University of Toronto Press, 1972.

Fallon, J.H. Topographic organization of ascending dopaminergic projections. *Annals of the New York Academy of Sciences*, 1988, *537*, 1–9.

Falls, W.A., Miserendino, M.J.D., and Davis, M. Extinction of fear-potentiated startle: Blockade by infusion of an NMDA antagonist into the amygdala. *Journal of Neuroscience*, 1992, *12*, 854–863.

Fang, F.G., Moreau, J.O., and Fields, H.L. Dose-dependent antinociceptive action of neurotensin microinjected into the rostroventromedial medulla of the rat. *Brain Research*, 1987, *426*, 171–174.

Fanselow, M.S. Naloxone attenuates rat's preference for signaled shock. *Physiological Psychology*, 1979, *7*, 70–74.

Farde, L., Wiesel, F.-A., Stone-Elander, S., Halldin, C., Nördstrom, A.-L., Hall, H., and Sedvall, G. D$_2$ dopamine receptors in neuroleptic-naive schizophrenic patients: A positron emission tomography study with [^{11}C]raclopride. *Archives of General Psychiatry*, 1990, *47*, 213–219.

Fava, M., Copeland, P.M., Schweiger, U., and Herzog, M.D. Neurochemical abnormalities of anorexia nervosa and bulimia nervosa. *American Journal of Psychiatry*, 1989, *146*, 963–971.

Feder, H.H. Estrous cyclicity in mammals. In *Neuroendocrinology of Reproduction*, edited by N.T. Adler. New York: Plenum Press, 1981.

Feigenbaum, S.L., Masi, A.T., and Kaplan, S.B. Prognosis in rheumatoid arthritis: A longitudinal study of newly diagnosed younger adult patients. *American Journal of Medicine*, 1979, *66*, 377–384.

Feigin, M.B., Sclafani, A., and Sunday, S.R. Species differences in polysaccharide and sugar taste preferences. *Neuroscience and Biobehavioral Reviews*, 1987, *11*, 231–240.

Ferguson, N.B.L., and Keesey, R.E. Effect of a quinine-adulterated diet upon body weight maintenance in male rats with ventromedial hypothalamic lesions. *Journal of Comparative and Physiological Psychology*, 1975, *89*, 478–488.

Fernandez-Guasti, A., Larsson, K., and Beyer, C. Potentiative action of α- and ß-adrenergic receptor stimulation in inducing lordosis behavior. *Pharmacology, Biochemistry, and Behavior*, 1985, *22*, 613–617.

Fernell, E., Gillberg, C., and Von Wendt, L. Autistic symptoms in children with infantile hydrocephalus. *Acta Paediatr Scand*, 1991, *80*, 451–457.

Ferris, C.F., Gold, L., DeVries, G.J., and Potegal, M. Evidence for a functional and anatomical relationship between the lateral septum and the hypothalamus in the control of flank marking behavior in golden hamsters. *Journal of Comparative Neurology*, 1990, *293*, 476–485.

Fibiger, H.C. The dopamine hypothesis of schizophrenia and mood disorders: Contradictions and speculations. In *The Mesolimbic Dopamine System: From Motivation to Action*, edited by P. Willner and J. Scheel-Krüger. Chichester, England: John Wiley & Sons, 1991.

Fibiger, H.C., Le Piane, F.G., Jakubovic, A., and Phillips, A.G. The role of dopamine in intracranial self-stimulation of the ventral tegmental area. *Journal of Neuroscience*, 1987, *7*, 3888–3896.

Field, T., Woodson, R., Greenberg, R., and Cohen, D. Discrimination and imitation of facial expressions in neonates. *Science*, 1982, *218*, 179–181.

Fieve, R.R. The clinical effects of lithium treatment. *Trends in Neurosciences*, 1979, *2*, 66–68.

Firestein, S., Zufall, F., and Shepherd, G.M. Single odor-sensitive channels in olfactory receptor neurons are also gated by cyclic nucleotides. *Journal of Neuroscience*, 1991, *11*, 3565–3572.

Fish, B., Marcus, J., Hans, S.L., Auerbach, J.G., and Perdue, S. Infants at risk for schizophrenia: Sequelae of a genetic neurointegrati e defect: A review and replication analysis of pandysmaturation in the Jerusalem Infant Development Study. *Archives of General Psychiatry*, 1992, *49*, 221–235.

Fisher, C., Byrne, J., Edwards, A., and Kahn, E. A psychophysiological study of nightmares. *Journal of the American Psychoanalytic Association*, 1970, *18*, 747–782.

Fisher, C., Gross, J., and Zuch, J. Cycle of penile erection synchronous with dreaming (REM) sleep: Preliminary report. *Archives of General Psychiatry*, 1965, *12*, 29–45.

Fitts, D.A., and Masson, D.B. Preoptic angiotensin and salt appetite. *Behavioral Neuroscience*, 1990, *104*, 643–650.

Fitzpatrick, D., Itoh, K., and Diamond, I.T. The laminar organization of the lateral geniculate body and the striate cortex in the squirrel monkey (*Saimiri sciureus*). *Journal of Neuroscience*, 1983, *3*, 673–702.

Fitzsimons, J.T. Drinking by rats depleted of body fluid without increase in osmotic pressure. *Journal of Physiology (London)*, 1961, *159*, 297–309.

Fitzsimons, J.T. Thirst. *Physiological Reviews*, 1972, *52*, 468–561.

Fitzsimons, J.T., and Le Magnen, J. Eating as a regulatory control of drinking in the rat. *Journal of Comparative and Physiological Psychology*, 1969, *3*, 273–283.

Fitzsimons, J.T., and Moore-Gillon, M.J. Drinking and antidiuresis in response to reductions in venous return in the dog: Neural and endocrine mechanisms. *Journal of Physiology (London)*, 1980, *308*, 403–416.

Fleming, A., and Rosenblatt, J.S. Olfactory regulation of maternal behavior in rats. II. Effects of peripherally induced anosmia and lesions of the lateral olfactory tract in pup-induced virgins. *Journal of Comparative and Physiological Psychology*, 1974, *86*, 233–246.

Fleming, A., Vaccarino, F., and Luebke, C. Amygdaloid inhibition of maternal behavior in the nulliparous female rat. *Physiology and Behavior*, 1980, *25*, 731–745.

Fleming, A., Vaccarino, F., Tambosso, L., and Chee, P. Vomeronasal and olfactory system modulation of maternal behavior in the rat. *Science*, 1979, *203*, 372–374.

Fleming, A.S., Cheung, U., Myhal, N., and Kessler, Z. Effects of maternal hormones on "timidity" and attraction to pup-related odors in female rats. *Physiology and Behavior*, 1989, *46*, 449–453.

Fleming, A.S., and Sarker, J. Experience-hormone interactions and maternal behavior in rats. *Physiology and Behavior*, 1990, *47*, 1165–1173.

Flock, A. Physiological properties of sensory hairs in the ear. In *Psychophysics and Physiology of Hearing*, edited by E.F. Evans and J.P. Wilson. London: Academic Press, 1977.

Flood, J.F., and Morley, J.E. Increased food intake by neuropeptide Y is due to an increased motivation to eat. *Peptides*, 1991, *12*, 1329–1332.

Floody, O.R. Hormones and aggression in female mammals. In *Hormones and Aggressive Behavior*, edited by B.B. Svare. New York: Plenum Press, 1983.

Flynn, J., Vanegas, H., Foote, W., and Edwards, S. Neural mechanisms involved in a cat's attack on a rat. In *The Neural Control of Behavior*, edited by R.F. Whalen, M. Thompson, M. Verzeano, and N. Weinberger. New York: Academic Press, 1970.

Folstein, S.E., and Piven, J. Etiology of autism: Genetic influences. *Pediatrics*, 1991, *87*, 767–773.

Folstein, S.E., and Rutter, M.L. Autism: Familiar aggregation and genetic implications. *Journal of Autism and Developmental Disorders*, 1988, *18*, 3–30.

Foltin, R.W., Fischman, M.W., Moran, T.H., Rolls, B.J., and Kelly, T.H. Caloric compensation for lunches varying in fat and carbohydrate content by humans in a residential laboratory. *American Journal of Clinical Nutrition*, 1990, *52*, 969–980.

Fort, P., Luppi, P.-H., Wenthold, R., and Jouvet, M. Neurones immunoréactifs à la glycine dans le bulbe rachidien du chat. *Comptes Rendus de l'Académie des Sciences* (Paris), 1990, *311*, 205–212.

Freeman, P.H., and Wellman, P.J. Brown adipose tissue thermogenesis induced by low level electrical stimulation of hypothalamus in rats. *Brain Research Bulletin*, 1987, *18*, 7–11.

Friedman, D.I., Johnson, J.K., Chorsky, R.L., and Stopa, E.G. Labeling of human retinohypothalamic tract with the carbocyanine dye, DiI. *Brain Research*, 1991, *560*, 297–302.

Friedman, M., and Rosenman, R.H. Association of specific overt behavior patterns with blood and cardiovascular findings—Blood cholesterol level, blood clotting time, incidence of arcus senilis, and clinical coronary artery disease. *Journal of the American Medical Association*, 1959, *162*, 1286–1296.

Friedman, M.I., and Bruno, J.P. Exchange of water during lactation. *Science*, 1976, *191*, 409–410.

Friedman, M.I., Tordoff, M.G., and Ramirez, I. Integrated metabolic control of food intake. *Brain Research Bulletin*, 1986, *17*, 855–859.

Frith, U., Morton, J., and Leslie, A.M. The cognitive basis of a biological disorder: Autism. *Trends in Neuroscience*, 1991, *14*, 433–438.

Fulton, J.F. *Functional Localization in Relation to Frontal Lobotomy*. New York: Oxford University Press, 1949.

Fulton, J.F., and Bailey, P. Tumors in the region of the third ventricle: Their diagnosis and relation to pathological sleep. *Journal of Nervous and Mental Disorders*, 1929, *69*, 1–25, 145–164, 261–277.

Fuster, J.M. Inferotemporal units in selective visual attention and short-term memory. *Journal of Neurophysiology*, 1990, *64*, 681–697.

Fuster, J.M., and Jervey, J.P. Inferotemporal neurons distinguish and retain behaviorally relevant features of visual stimuli. *Science*, 1981, *212*, 952–955.

Gabrieli, J.D.E., Cohen, N.J., and Corkin, S. The impaired learning of semantic knowledge following bilateral medial temporal-lobe resection. *Brain and Cognition*, 1988, *7*, 157–177.

Gabrieli, J.D.E., Milberg, W., Keane, M.M., and Corkin, S. Intact priming of patterns despite impaired memory. *Neuropsychologia*, 1990, *28*, 417–427.

Gaffan, D., Gaffan, E.A., and Harrison, S. Disconnection of the amygdala from visual association cortex impairs visual reward-association learning in monkeys. *Journal of Neuroscience*, 1988, *9*, 3144–3150.

Gaffney, F.A., Fenton, B.J., Lane, L.D., and Lake, C.R. Hemodynamic, ventilatory, and biochemical responses of panic patients and normal controls with sodium lactate infusion and spontaneous panic attacks. *Archives of General Psychiatry*, 1988, *45*, 53–60.

Gage, F.H., Björklund, A., Stenevi, U., Dunnett, S.B., and Kelly, P.A.T. Intrahippocampal septal grafts ameliorate learning impairments in aged rats. *Science*, 1984, *225*, 533–536.

Galaburda, A.M. The pathogenesis of childhood dyslexia. In *Language, Communication, and the Brain*, edited by F. Plum. New York: Raven Press, 1988.

Galaburda, A.M., Sherman, G.F., Rosen, G.D., Aboitiz, F., and Geschwind, N. Developmental dyslexia: Four consecutive patients with cortical anomalies. *Annals of Neurology*, 1985, *18*, 222–233.

Gallistel, C.R., and Karras, D. Pimozide and amphetamine have opposing effects on the reward summation function. *Pharmacology, Biochemistry, and Behavior*, 1984, *20*, 73–77.

Garber, H.J., and Ritvo, E.R. Magnetic resonance imaging of the posterior fossa in autistic adults. *American Journal of Psychiatry*, 1992, *149*, 245–247.

Garcia, J., and Koelling, R.A. Relation of cue to consequence in avoidance learning. *Psychonomic Science*, 1966, *4*, 123–124.

Garcia-Velasco, J., and Mondragon, M. The incidence of the vomeronasal organ in 1000 human subjects and its possible clinical significance. *Journal of Steroid Biochemistry and Molecular Biololgy*, 1991, *39*, 561–563.

Gardner, H., Brownell, H.H., Wapner, W., and Michelow, D. Missing the point: The role of the right hemisphere in the processing of complex linguistic materials. In *Cognitive Processing in the Right Hemisphere*, edited by E. Pericman. New York: Academic Press, 1983.

Gariano, R.F., and Groves, P.M. Burst firing induced in midbrain dopamine neurons by stimulation of the medial prefrontal and anterior cingulate cortices. *Brain Research,* 1988, *462,* 194–198.

Gatchel, R.J., Baum, A., and Krantz, D.S. *An Introduction to Health Psychology,* 2nd ed. New York: Newbery Award Records, 1989.

Gaw, A.C., Chang, L.W., and Shaw, L.-C. Efficacy of acupuncture on osteoarthritic pain. *New England Journal of Medicine,* 1975, *293,* 375–378.

Gazzaniga, M.S. *The Bisected Brain.* New York: Appleton-Century-Crofts, 1970.

Gazzaniga, M.S., and LeDoux, J.E. *The Integrated Mind.* New York: Plenum Press, 1978.

Geary, N. Cocaine: Animal research studies. In *Cocaine Abuse: New Directions in Treatment and Research,* edited by H.I. Spitz and J.S. Rosecan. New York: Brunner-Mazel, 1987.

Gebhardt, G.F. Opiate and opioid peptide effects on brain stem neurons: Relevance to nociception and antinociceptive mechanisms. *Pain,* 1982, *12,* 93–140.

Geinisman, Y., DeToledo-Morrell, L., and Morrell, F. Induction of long-term potentiation is associated with an increase in the number of axospinous synapses with segmented postsynaptic densities. *Brain Research,* 1991, *566,* 77–88.

Gentil, C.G., Mogenson, G., and Stevenson, J.A.F. Electrical stimulation of septum, hypothalamus and amygdala and saline preference. *American Journal of Physiology,* 1971, *220,* 1172–1177.

Gentilucci, M., and Rizzolatti, G. In *Vision and Action: The Control of Grasping,* edited by M.A. Goodale. Norwood, N.J.: Ablex, 1990.

George, M.S., Costa, D.C., Kouris, K., Ring, H.A., and Ell, P.J. Cerebral blood flow abnormalities in adults with infantile autism. *Journal of Nervous and Mental Disorders,* 1992, *180,* 413–417.

Gerbino, L., Oleshansky, M., and Gershon, S. Clinical use and mode of action of lithium. In *Psychopharmacology: A Generation of Progress,* edited by M.A. Lipton, A. DiMascio, and K.F. Killam. New York: Raven Press, 1978.

Gerren, R., and Weinberger, N.M. Long term potentiation in the magnocellular medial geniculate nucleus of the anesthetized cat. *Brain Research,* 1983, *265,* 138–142.

Gershon, E.S., Bunney, W.E., Leckman, J., Van Eerdewegh, M., and DeBauche, B. The inheritance of affective disorders: A review of data and hypotheses. *Behavior Genetics,* 1976, *6,* 227–261.

Geschwind, N., Quadfasel, F.A., and Segarra, J.M. Isolation of the speech area. *Neuropsychologia,* 1968, *6,* 327–340.

Geschwind, N.A., and Behan, P.O. Laterality, hormones, and immunity. In *Cerebral Dominance: The Biological Foundations,* edited by N. Geschwind and A.M. Galaburda. Cambridge, Mass.: Harvard University Press, 1984.

Gessa, G.L., Muntoni, F., Collu, M., Vargiu, L., and Mereu, G. Low doses of ethanol activate dopaminergic neurons in the ventral tegmental area. *Brain Research,* 1985, *348,* 201–204.

Gibbs, J., Young, R.C., and Smith, G.P. Cholecystokinin decreases food intake in rats. *Journal of Comparative and Physiological Psychology,* 1973, *84,* 488–495.

Giles, D.E., Biggs, M.M., Rush, A.J., and Roffwarg, H.P. Risk factors in families of unipolar depression. I. Psychiatric illness and reduced REM latency. *Journal of Affective Disorders,* 1988, *14,* 51–59.

Giles, D.E., Roffwarg, H.P., and Rush, A.J. REM latency concordance in depressed family members. *Biological Psychiatry,* 1987, *22,* 910–924.

Giordano, A.L., Siegel, H.I., and Rosenblatt, J.S. Nuclear estrogen receptor binding in the preoptic area and hypothalamus of pregnancy-terminated rats: Correlation with the onset of maternal behavior. *Neuroendocrinology,* 1989, *50,* 248–258.

Givens, B.S., and Olton, D.S. Cholinergic and GABAergic modulation of medial septal area: Effect on working memory. *Behavioral Neuroscience,* 1990, *104,* 849–855.

Giza, B.K., Scott, T.R., and Vanderweele, D.A. Administration of satiety factors and gustatory responsiveness in the nucleus tractus solitarius of the rat. *Brain Research Bulletin,* 1992, *28,* 637–639.

Glaser, R., Rice, J., Sheridan, J., Post, A., Fertel, R., Stout, J., Speicher, C.E., Kotur, M., and Kiecolt-Glaser, J.K. Stress-related immune suppression: Health implications. *Brain, Behavior, and Immunity,* 1987, *1,* 7–20.

Glavin, G.B., Murison, R., Overmier, J.B., Pare, W.P., Bakke, H.K., Henke, P.G., and Hernandez, D.E. The neurobiology of stress ulcers. *Brain Research Reviews,* 1991, *16,* 301–343.

Glick, Z., Teague, R.J., and Bray, G.A. Brown adipose tissue: Thermic response increased by a single low protein, high carbohydrate meal. *Science,* 1981, *213,* 1125–1127.

Goeders, N.E., Lane, J.D., and Smith, J.E. Self-administration of methionine enkephalin into the nucleus accumbens. *Pharmacology, Biochemistry, and Behavior,* 1984, *20,* 451–455.

Golgi, C. *Opera Omnia, Vols. I and II.* Milan: Hoepli, 1903.

Gongwer, M.A., Murphy, J.M., McBride, W.J., Lumeng, L., and Li, R.-K. Regional brain contents of serotonin, dopamine and their metabolites in the selectively bred high- and low-alcohol drinking lines of rats. *Alcohol,* 1989, *6,* 317–320.

Gonzalez, M.F., and Deutsch, J.A. Vagotomy abolishes cues of satiety produced by gastric distension. *Science,* 1981, *212,* 1283–1284.

Goodale, M.A., and Milner, A.D. Separate visual pathways for perception and action. *Trends in Neuroscience,* 1992, *15,* 20–25.

Goodglass, H. Agrammatism. In *Studies of Neurolinguistics,* edited by H. Whitaker and H.A. Whitaker. New York: Academic Press, 1976.

Goodglass, H., and Kaplan, E. *Assessment of Aphasia and Related Disorders.* Philadelphia: Lea & Febiger, 1972.

Goodwin, D.W. Alcoholism and heredity: A review and hypothesis. *Archives of General Psychiatry,* 1979, *36,* 57–61.

Goodwin, F.K., Wirz-Justice, A., and Wehr, T.A. Evidence that the pathophysiology of depression and the mechanisms of action of antidepressant drugs both involve alterations in circadian rhythms. In *Typical and Atypical Antidepressants: Clinical Practice*, edited by E. Costa and G. Racagni. New York: Raven Press, 1982.

Gorski, R.A., Gordon, J.H., Shryne, J.E., and Southam, A.M. Evidence for a morphological sex difference within the medial preoptic area of the rat brain. *Brain Research*, 1978, *148*, 333–346.

Gorwood, P., Leboyer, M., D'Amato, T., Jay, M., Campion, D., Hillaire, D., Mallet, J., and Feingold, J. Evidence for a pseudoautosomal locus for schizophrenia. I. A replication study using phenotype analysis. *British Journal of Psychiatry*, 1992, *161*, 55–58.

Gorzalka, B.B., Mendelson, S.D., and Watson, N.V. Serotonin receptor subtypes and sexual behavior. *Annals of the New York Academy of Sciences*, 1990, *600*, 435–446.

Gottesman, I.I., and Bertelsen, A. Confirming unexpressed genotypes for schizophrenia. *Archives of General Psychiatry*, 1989, *46*, 867–872.

Gottesman, I.I., and Shields, J. *Schizophrenia: The Epigenetic Puzzle*. New York: Cambridge University Press, 1982.

Gouras, P. Identification of cone mechanisms in monkey ganglion cells. *Journal of Physiology (London)*, 1968, *199*, 533–538.

Goy, R.W., Bercovitch, F.B., and McBrair, M.C. Behavioral masculinization is independent of genital masculinization in prenatally androgenized female rhesus macaques. *Hormones and Behavior*, 1988, *22*, 552–571.

Grace, A.A. Phasic versus tonic dopamine release and the modulation of dopamine system responsivity: A hypothesis for the etiology of schizophrenia. *Neuroscience*, 1991, *41*, 1–24.

Graf, P., Squire, L.R., and Mandler, G. The information that amnesic patients do not forget. *Journal of Experimental Psychology: Learning, Memory, and Cognition*, 1984, *10*, 164–178.

Grant, S.G.N., O'Dell, T.J., Karl, K.A., Stein, P.L., Soriano, P., and Kandel, E.R. Impaired long-term potentiation, spatial learning, and hippocampal development in *fyn* mutant mice. *Science*, 1992, *258*, 1903–1910.

Gray, C., Freeman, W.J., and Skinner, J.E. Chemical dependencies of learning in the rabbit olfactory bulb: Acquisition of the transient and spatial pattern change depends on norepinephrine. *Behavioral Neuroscience*, 1986, *100*, 585–596.

Green, J.D., and Arduini, A.A. Hippocampal electrical activity in arousal. *Journal of Neurophysiology*, 1954, *17*, 533–557.

Greenberg, D., Kava, R., Lewis, D.R., and Greenwood, M.R.C. Satiation following intraduodenal Intralipid preceded appearance of [^{14}C]-Intralipid in hepatic portal blood. *FASEB Journal*, 1991, *5*, A1451.

Greenberg, D., Smith, G.P., and Gibbs, J. Intraduodenal infusions of fats elicit satiety in the sham feeding rat. *American Journal of Physiology*, 1990, *259*, R110–R118.

Greenberg, R., and Pearlman, C.A. Cutting the REM nerve: An approach to the adaptive role of REM sleep. *Perspectives in Biology and Medicine*, 1974, *17*, 513–521.

Greenberg, R., Pillard, R., and Pearlman, C. The effect of dream (stage REM) deprivation on adaptation to stress. *Psychosomatic Medicine*, 1972, *34*, 257–262.

Griffith, J.D., Cavanaugh, J., Held, N.N., and Oates, J.A. Dextroamphetamine: Evaluation of psychotomimetic properties in man. *Archives of General Psychiatry*, 1972, *26*, 97–100.

Grijalva, C.V., Levin, E.D., Morgan, M., Roland, B., and Martin, F.C. Contrasting effects of centromedial and basolateral amygdaloid lesions on stress-related responses in the rat. *Physiology and Behavior*, 1990, *48*, 495–500.

Grill, H.J., and Kaplan, J.M. Caudal brainstem participates in the distributed neural control of feeding. In *Handbook of Behavioral Neurobiology. Vol. 10. Neurobiology of Food and Fluid Intake*, edited by E. Stricker. New York: Plenum Press, 1990.

Gross, C.G. Visual functions of inferotemporal cortex. In *Handbook of Sensory Physiology, Vol. 7: Central Processing of Visual Information*, edited by R. Jung. Berlin: Springer-Verlag, 1973.

Grossman, S.P., and Grossman, L. Parametric study of the regulatory capabilities of rats with rostromedial zona incerta lesions: Responsiveness to hypertonic saline and polyethylene glycol. *Physiology and Behavior*, 1978, *21*, 431–440.

Guerin, G.F., Goeders, N.E., Dworkin, S.I., and Smith, J.E. Intracranial self-administration of dopamine into the nucleus accumbens. *Society for Neuroscience Abstracts*, 1984, *10*, 1072.

Gulevich, G., Dement, W.C., and Johnson, L. Psychiatric and EEG observations on a case of prolonged (264 hours) wakefulness. *Archives of General Psychiatry*, 1966, *15*, 29–35.

Haas, R.H. Thiamin and the brain. *Annual Review of Nutrition*, 1988, *8*, 483–515.

Hackney, C.M., Furness, D.N., Benos, D.J., Woodley, J.F., and Barratt, J. Putative immunolocalization of the mechanoelectrical transduction channels in mammalian cochlear hair cells. *Proceedings of the Royal Society of London [B]*, 1992, *248*, 215–221.

Halasz, P., Pal, I., and Rajna, P. K-complex formation of the EEG in sleep. A survey and new examinations. *Acta Physiologica Hungarica*, 1985, *65*, 3–35.

Haley, J.E., Wilcox, G.L., and Chapman, P.F. The role of nitric oxide in hippocampal long-term potentiation. *Neuron*, 1992, *8*, 211–216.

Hall, W.G. A remote stomach clamp to evaluate oral and gastric controls of drinking in the rat. *Physiology and Behavior*, 1973, *11*, 897–901.

Hall, W.G., and Blass, E.M. Orogastric determinants of drinking in rats: Interaction between absorptive and peripheral controls. *Journal of Comparative and Physiological Psychology*, 1977, *91*, 365–373.

Hall, Z. *An Introduction to Molecular Neurobiology.* Sunderland, Mass.: Sinauer Associates, 1992.

Halmi, K.A. Anorexia nervosa: Recent investigations. *Annual Review of Medicine*, 1978, *29*, 137–148.

Halmi, K.A., Eckert, E., LaDu, T.J., and Cohen, J. Anorexia nervosa: Treatment efficacy of cyproheptadine and amitriptyline. *Archives of General Psychiatry*, 1986, *43*, 177–181.

Halpern, M. The organization and function of the vomeronasal system. *Annual Review of Neuroscience*, 1987, *10*, 325–362.

Hansen, S., and Ross, S.B. Role of descending monoaminergic neurons in the control of sexual behavior: Effects of intrathecal infusion of 6–hydroxydopamine and 5,7–dihydroxytryptamine. *Brain Research*, 1983, *268*, 285–290.

Hansen, S., Stanfield, E.J., and Everitt, B.J. The role of ventral bundle noradrenergic neurons in sensory components of sexual behaviours and coitus-induced pseudopregnancy. *Nature*, 1980, *286*, 152–154.

Harmon, L.D., and Julesz, B. Masking in visual recognition: Effects of two-dimensional filtered noise. *Science*, 1973, *180*, 1194–1197.

Haroutunian, V., Knott, P., and Davis, K.L. Effects of mesocortical dopaminergic lesions upon subcortical dopaminergic function. *Psychopharmacology Bulletin*, 1988, *24*, 341–344.

Harries, M.H., and Perrett, D.I. Visual processing of faces in the temporal cortex: Physiological evidence for a modular organization and possible anatomical correlates. *Journal of Cognitive Science*, 1991, *3*, 9–24.

Harrington, M.E., and Rusak, B. Lesions of the thalamic intergeniculate leaflet alter hamster circadian rhythms. *Journal of Biological Rhythms*, 1986, *1*, 309–325.

Harris, G.W., and Jacobsohn, D. Functional grafts of the anterior pituitary gland. *Proceedings of the Royal Society of London [B]*, 1951–1952, *139*, 263–267.

Hart, B. Sexual reflexes and mating behavior in the male dog. *Journal of Comparative and Physiological Psychology*, 1967, *66*, 388–399.

Hart, B. Gonadal hormones and sexual reflexes in the female rat. *Hormones and Behavior*, 1969, *1*, 65–71.

Hart, B.L. Hormones, spinal reflexes, and sexual behaviour. In *Determinants of Sexual Behaviour*, edited by J.B. Hutchinson. Chichester, England: John Wiley & Sons, 1978.

Hartline, H.K. The response of single optic nerve fibers of the vertebrate eye to illumination of the retina. *American Journal of Physiology*, 1938, *121*, 400–415.

Hashimoto, T., Tayama, M., Miyazaki, M., Sakurama, N., Yoshimoto, T., Murakawa, K., and Kuroda, Y. Reduced brainstem size in children with autism. *Brain Development*, 1992, *14*, 94–97.

Haug, H.-J. Prediction of sleep deprivation outcome by diurnal variation of mood. *Biological Psychiatry*, 1992, *31*, 271–278.

Hawke, C. Castration and sex crimes. *American Journal of Mental Deficiency*, 1951, *55*, 220–226.

Hayaishi, O. Sleep-wake regulation by prostaglandins D2 and E2. *Journal of Biological Chemistry*, 1988, *263*, 14593–14596.

Hebb, D.O. *The Organization of Behaviour.* New York: Wiley-Interscience, 1949.

Heckler, M.M. *Fifth Special Report to the U.S. Congress on Alcohol and Health.* Washington, D.C.: U.S. Government Printing Office, 1983.

Heffner, H.E., and Heffner, R.S. Role of primate auditory cortex in hearing. In *Comparative Perception. Vol. II. Complex Signals*, edited by W.C. Stebbins and M.A. Berkley. New York: John Wiley & Sons, 1990.

Heilman, K.M., Rothi, L., and Kertesz, A. Localization of apraxia-producing lesions. In *Localization in Neuropsychology*, edited by A. Kertesz. New York: Academic Press, 1983.

Heilman, K.M., Scholes, R., and Watson, R.T. Auditory affective agnosia: Disturbed comprehension of affective speech. *Journal of Neurology, Neurosurgery, and Psychiatry*, 1975, *38*, 69–72.

Heilman, K.M., Watson, R.T., and Bowers, D. Affective disorders associated with hemispheric disease. In *Neuropsychology of Human Emotion*, edited by K.M. Heilman and P. Satz. New York: Guilford Press, 1983.

Heimer, L., and Larsson, K. Impairment of mating behavior in male rats following lesions in the preoptic-anterior hypothalamic continuum. *Brain Research*, 1966/1967, *3*, 248–263.

Heindel, W.C., Butters, N., and Salmon, D.P. Impaired learning of a motor skill in patients with Huntington's disease. *Behavioral Neuroscience*, 1988, *102*, 141–147.

Hellhammer, D.H., Hubert, W., and Schurmeyer, T. Changes in saliva testosterone after psychological stimulation in men. *Psychoneuroendocrinology*, 1985, *10*, 77–81.

Helmer, D.C., Ragland, D.R., and Syme, S.L. Hostility and coronary artery disease. *American Journal of Epidemiology*, 1991, *133*, 112–122.

Hendrickson, A.E., Wagoner, N., and Cowan, W.M. Autoradiographic and electron microscopic study of retino-hypothalamic connections. *Zeitschrift für Zellforschung und Mikroskopische Anatomie*, 1972, *125*, 1–26.

Hendrie, C.A. The calls of murine predators activate endogenous analgesia mechanisms in laboratory mice. *Physiology and Behavior*, 1991, *49*, 569–573.

Henke, P.G. The telencephalic limbic system and experimental gastric pathology: A review. *Neuroscience and Biobehavioral Reviews*, 1982, *6*, 381–390.

Hennessey, A.C., Camak, L., Gordon, F., and Edwards, D.A. Connections between the pontine central gray and the ventromedial hypothalamus are essential for lordosis in female rats. *Behavioral Neuroscience*, 1990, *104*, 477–488.

Henningfield, J.E., and Goldberg, S.R. Nicotine as a reinforcer in human subjects and laboratory animals. *Pharmacology, Biochemistry, and Behavior*, 1983, *19*, 989–992.

Herberg, L.J., and Rose, I.C. Excitatory amino acid pathways in brain-stimulation reward. *Behavioural Brain Research*, 1990, *39*, 230–239.

Hering, E. *Outlines of a Theory of the Light Sense*, 1905. Translated by L.M. Hurvich and D. Jameson. Cambridge, Mass.: Harvard University Press, 1965.

Hernandez, L., and Hoebel, B.G. Food reward and cocaine increase extracellular dopamine in the nucleus accumbens as measured by microdialysis. *Life Sciences*, 1988, *42*, 1705–1712.

Hernandez, L., and Hoebel, B.G. Feeding can enhance dopamine turnover in the prefrontal cortex. *Brain Research Bulletin*, 1990, *25*, 975–979.

Herz, A., Albus, K., Metys, J., Schubert, P., and Teschemacher, H. On the central sites for the antinociceptive action of morphine and fentanyl. *Neuropharmacology*, 1970, *9*, 539–551.

Hetherington, A.W., and Ranson, S.W. Hypothalamic lesions and adiposity in the rat. *Anatomical Record*, 1942, *78*, 149–172.

Heuser, J.E. Synaptic vesicle exocytosis revealed in quick-frozen frog neuromuscular junctions treated with 4–aminopyridine and given a single electrical shock. In *Society for Neuroscience Symposia, Vol. II*, edited by W.M. Cowan and J.A. Ferrendelli. Bethesda, Md.: Society for Neuroscience, 1977.

Heuser, J.E., and Reese, T.S. Evidence for recycling of synaptic vesicle membrane during transmitter release at the frog neuromuscular function. *Journal of Cell Biology*, 1973, *57*, 315–344.

Heuser, J.E., Reese, T.S., Dennis, M.J., Jan, Y., Jan, L., and Evans, L. Synaptic vesicle exocytosis captured by quick freezing and correlated with quantal transmitter release. *Journal of Cell Biology*, 1979, *81*, 275–300.

Heywood, C.A., and Cowey, A. The role of the "face-cell" area in the discrimination and recognition of faces by monkeys. *Philosophical Transactions of the Royal Society of London [B]*, 1992, *335*, 31–38.

Hill, A.J., and Best, P.J. Effects of deafness and blindness on the spatial correlates of hippocampal unit activity in the rat. *Experimental Neurology*, 1981, *74*, 204–217.

Himmi, T., Boyer, A., and Orsini, J.C. Changes in lateral hypothalamic neuronal activity accompanying hyper- and hypoglycemias. *Physiology and Behavior*, 1988, *44*, 347–354.

Himms-Hagen, J. Current status of nonshivering thermogenesis. In *Assessment of Energy Metabolism in Health and Disease*, edited by J.W. Kinney. Columbus, Ohio: Ross Laboratories, 1980.

Hines, M., Allen, L.S., and Gorski, R.A. Sex differences in subregions of the medial nucleus of the amygdala and the

bed nucleus of the stria terminalis of the rat. *Brain Research*, 1992, *579*, 321–326.

Hinjo, S., Hirano, C., Murase, S., Kaneko, T., Sugiyama, T., Ohtaka, K., Aoyama, T., Takei, Y., Inoko, K., and Wakbayshai, S. Obsessive-compulsive symptoms in childhood and adolescence. *Acta Psychiatrica Scandanivica*, 1989, *80*, 83–91.

Hitchcock, J., and Davis, M. Lesions of the amygdala, but not of the cerebellum or red nucleus, block conditioned fear as measured with the potentiated startle paradigm. *Behavioral Neuroscience*, 1986, *100*, 11–22.

Hobson, J.A. *The Dreaming Brain*. New York: Basic Books, 1988.

Hodges, J.R., Patterson, K., Oxbury, S., and Funnell, E. Semantic dementia. Progressive fluent aphasia with temporal lobe atrophy. *Brain*, 1992, *115*, 1783–1806.

Hoebel, B.G., Monaco, A.P., Hernandez, L., Aulisi, E.F., Stanley, B.G., and Lenard, L. Self-injection of amphetamine directly into the brain. *Psychopharmacology*, 1983, *81*, 158–163.

Hoebel, B.G., and Teitelbaum, P. Weight regulation in normal and hypothalamic hyperphagic rats. *Journal of Comparative and Physiological Psychology*, 1966, *61*, 189–193.

Hogan, S., Himms-Hagen, J., and Coscina, D.V. Lack of diet-induced thermogenesis in brown adipose tissue of obese medial hypothalamic-lesioned rats. *Physiology and Behavior*, 1985, *35*, 287–294.

Hohman, G.W. Some effects of spinal cord lesions on experienced emotional feelings. *Psychophysiology*, 1966, *3*, 143–156.

Hollander, E., DeCaria, C.M., Nitescu, A., Gully, R., Suckow, R.F., Cooper, T.B., Gorman, J.M., Klein, D.F., and Liebowitz, M.R. Serotonergic function in obsessive-compulsive disorder: Behavioral and neuroendocrine responses to oral m-chlorophenylpiperazine and fenfluramine in patients and healthy volunteers. *Archives of General Psychiatry*, 1992, *49*, 21–28.

Hollander, E., Schiffman, E., Cohen, B., Rivera-Stein, M.A., Rosen, W., Gorman, J.M., Fyer, A.J., Papp, L., and Liebowitz, M.R. Signs of central nervous system dysfunction in obsessive-compulsive disorder. *Archives of General Psychiatry*, 1990, *47*, 27–32.

Holmes, G. The cerebellum of man. *Brain*, 1939, *62*, 21–30.

Holroyd, S., Reiss, A.L., and Bryan, R.N. Autistic features in Joubert syndrome: A genetic disorder with agenesis of the cerebellar vermis. *Biological Psychiatry*, 1991, *29*, 287–294.

Holton, T., and Hudspeth, A.J. The transduction channel of hair cells from the bullfrog characterized by noise analysis. *Journal of Physiology* (*London*), 1986, *375*, 195–227.

Holttum, J.R., Minshew, N.J., Sanders, R.S., and Phillips, N.E. Magnetic resonance imaging of the posterior fossa in autism. *Biological Psychiatry*, 1992, *32*, 1091–1101.

Holzman, P.S., Proctor, L.R., Levy, D.L., Yasillo, N.J., Meltzer, H.Y., and Hurt, S.W. Eye tracking dysfunction in schizophrenic patients and their relatives. *Archives of General Psychiatry*, 1974, *31*, 143–151.

Horne, J.A. A review of the biological effects of total sleep deprivation in man. *Biological Psychology*, 1978, *7*, 55–102.

Horne, J.A. The effects of exercise on sleep. *Biological Psychology*, 1981, *12*, 241–291.

Horne, J.A. *Why We Sleep: The Functions of Sleep in Humans and Other Mammals*. Oxford, England: Oxford University Press, 1988.

Horne, J.A., and Harley, L.J. Human SWS following selective head heating during wakefulness. In *Sleep '88*, edited by J. Horne. New York: Gustav Fischer Verlag, 1989.

Horne, J.A., and Minard, A. Sleep and sleepiness following a behaviourally "active" day. *Ergonomics*, 1985, *28*, 567–575.

Horne, J.A., and Moore, V.J. Sleep effects of exercise with and without additional body cooling. *Electroencephalography and Clinical Neurophysiology*, 1985, *60*, 347–353.

Horowitz, R.M., and Gentili, B. Dihydrochalcone sweeteners. In *Symposium: Sweeteners*, edited by G.E. Inglett. Westport, Conn.: Avi Publishing, 1974.

Horton, J.C., and Hubel, D.H. Cytochrome oxidase stain preferentially labels intersection of ocular dominance and vertical orientation columns in macaque striate cortex. *Society for Neuroscience Abstracts*, 1980, *6*, 315.

Howard, J., and Hudspeth, A.J. Compliance of the hair bundle associated with gating of mechanoelectrical transduction channels in the bull-frog's saccular hair cell. *Neuron*, 1988, *1*, 189–199.

Howard, J.H., Cunningham, D.A., and Rechnitzer, P.A. Health patterns associated with type A behavior: A managerial population. *Journal of Human Stress*, 1976, *2*, 24–31.

Hu, G.Y., Hvalby, O., Walaas, S.I., and Albert, K.A. Protein kinase C injection into hippocampal pyramidal cells elicits features of long term potentiation. *Nature*, 1987, *328*, 426–429.

Huang, Y.H., and Mogenson, G.J. Neural pathways mediating drinking and feeding in rats. *Experimental Neurology*, 1972, *37*, 269–286.

Hubel, D.H., and Wiesel, T.N. Functional architecture of macaque monkey visual cortex. *Proceedings of the Royal Society of London*, 1977, *198*, 1–59.

Hubel, D.H., and Wiesel, T.N. Brain mechanisms of vision. *Scientific American*, 1979, *241*, 150–162.

Hubner, C.B., and Koob, G.F. The ventral pallidum plays a role in mediating cocaine and heroin self-administration in the rat. *Brain Research*, 1990, *508*, 20–29.

Hudspeth, A.J. Mechanoelectrical transduction by hair cells in the acousticolateralis sensory system. *Annual Review of Neuroscience*, 1983, *6*, 187–215.

Hughes, J., Smith, T.W., Kosterlitz, H.W., Fothergill, L.A., Morgan, B.A., and Moris, H.R. Identification of two related pentapeptides from the brain with potent opiate agonist activity. *Nature*, 1975, *258*, 577–579.

Hulsey, M.G., and Martin, R.J. An anorectic agent from adipose tissue of overfed rats: Effects on feeding behavior. *Physiology and Behavior*, 1992, *52*, 1141–1149.

Humphrey, A.L., and Hendrickson, A.E. Radial zones of high metabolic activity in squirrel monkey striate cortex. *Society for Neuroscience Abstracts*, 1980, *6*, 315.

Humphreys, P., Kaufmann, W.E., and Galaburda, A.M. Developmental dyslexia in women: Neuropathological findings in three patients. *Annals of Neurology*, 1990, *28*, 727–738.

Hwang, P.M., Verma, A., Bredt, D.S., and Snyder, S.H. Localization of phosphatidylinositol signaling components in rat taste cells: Role in bitter taste transduction. *Proceedings of the National Academy of Sciences, USA*, 1990, *87*, 7395–7399.

Hynd, G.W., Semrud-Clikeman, M., Lorys, A.R., Novey, E.S., and Eliopulos, D. Brain morphology in developmental dyslexia and attention deficit disorder/hyperactivity. *Archives of Neurology*, 1990, *47*, 919–926.

Ibuka, N., and Kawamura, H. Loss of circadian rhythm in sleep-wakefulness cycle in the rat by suprachiasmatic nucleus lesions. *Brain Research*, 1975, *96*, 76–81.

Iggo, A., and Andres, K.H. Morphology of cutaneous receptors. *Annual Review of Neuroscience*, 1982, *5*, 1–32.

Imaki, T., Shibasaki, T., Hotta, M., and Demura, H. Early induction of c-fos precedes increased expression of corticotropin-releasing factor messenger ribonucleic acid in the paraventricular nucleus after immobilization stress. *Endocrinology*, 1992, *131*, 240–246.

Imperato, A., and Di Chiara, G. Preferential stimulation of dopamine-release in the accumbens of freely moving rats by ethanol. *Journal of Pharmacology and Experimental Therapeutics*, 1986, *239*, 219–228.

Ingelfinger, F.J. The late effects of total and subtotal gastrectomy. *New England Journal of Medicine*, 1944, *231*, 321–327.

Institute of Medicine. *Sleeping Pills, Insomnia, and Medical Practice*. Washington, D.C.: National Academy of Sciences, 1979.

Irvine, J., Garner, D.M., Craig, H.M., and Logan, A.G. Prevalence of type A behavior in untreated hypertensive individuals. *Hypertension*, 1991, *18*, 72–78.

Iwai, E., and Mishkin, M. Further evidence of the locus of the visual area in the temporal lobe of the monkey. *Experimental Neurology*, 1969, *25*, 585–594.

Iwai, E., Osawa, Y., and Umitsu, Y. Elevated visual pattern discrimination limen in monkeys with total removal of inferotemporal cortex. *Japanese Journal of Physiology*, 1979, *29*, 749–765.

Iwata, J., LeDoux, J.E., Meeley, M.P., Arneric, S., and Reis, D.J. Intrinsic neurons in the amygdaloid field projected to by the medial geniculate body mediate emotional responses conditioned to acoustic stimuli. *Brain Research*, 1986, *383*, 195–214.

Iwata, M. Kanji versus Kana: Neuropsychological correlates of the Japanese writing system. *Trends in Neurosciences*, 1984, *7*, 290–293.

Jacobs, B.L., Asher, R., and Dement, W.C. Electrophysiological and behavioral effects of electrical stimulation of the raphe nuclei in cats. *Physiology and Behavior*, 1973, *11*, 489–496.

Jacobs, B.L., and McGinty, D.J. Participation of the amygdala in complex stimulus recognition and behavioral inhibition: Evidence from unit studies. *Brain Research*, 1972, *36*, 431–436.

Jacobs, B.L., Wilkinson, L.O., and Fornal, C.A. The role of brain serotonin: A neurophysiologic perspective. *Neuropsychopharmacology*, 1990, *3*, 473–479.

Jacobs, K.M., Mark, G.P., and Scott, T.R. Taste responses in the nucleus tractus solitarius of sodium-deprived rats. *Journal of Physiology (London)*, 1988, *406*, 393–410.

Jacobsen, C.F., Wolfe, J.B., and Jackson, T.A. An experimental analysis of the functions of the frontal association areas in primates. *Journal of Nervous and Mental Disorders*, 1935, *82*, 1–14.

Jaffe, J.H. Drug addiction and drug abuse. In *The Pharmacological Basis of Therapeutics, Vol. 7*, edited by L.S. Goodman and A. Gilman. New York: Macmillan, 1985.

Jakobson, L.S., Archibald, Y.M., Carey, D., and Goodale, M.A. A kinematic analysis of reaching and grasping movements in a patient recovering from optic ataxia. *Neuropsychologia*, 1991, *29*, 803–809.

James, W. What is an emotion? *Mind*, 1884, *9*, 188–205.

James, W.P.T., and Trayhurn, P. Thermogenesis and obesity. *British Medical Bulletin*, 1981, *27*, 43–48.

Jaskiw, G., and Kleinman, J. Postmortem neurochemistry studies in schizophrenia. In *Schizophrenia: A Scientific Focus*, edited by S.C. Schulz and C.A. Tamminga. New York: Oxford University Press, 1988.

Jasper, J.H., and Tessier, J. Acetylcholine liberation from cerebral cortex during paradoxical (REM) sleep. *Science*, 1969, *172*, 601–602.

Jeffcoate, W.J., Lincoln, N.B., Selby, C., and Herbert, M. Correlations between anxiety and serum prolactin in humans. *Journal of Psychosomatic Research*, 1986, *30*, 217–222.

Jeffress, L.A. A place theory of sound localization. *Journal of Comparative and Physiological Psychology*, 1948, *41*, 35–39.

Jensen, T., Genefke, I., and Hyldebrandt, N. Cerebral atrophy in young torture victims. *New England Journal of Medicine*, 1982, *307*, 1341.

Jernigan, T.L., Hesselink, J.R., Sowell, E., and Tallal, P.A. Cerebral structure on magnetic resonance imaging in language- and learning-impaired children. *Archives of Neurology*, 1991, *48*, 539–545.

Jeste, D.V., Del Carmen, R., Lohr, J.B., and Wyatt, R.J. Did schizophrenia exist before the eighteenth century? *Comprehensive Psychiatry*, 1985, *26*, 493–503.

Jewett, D.C., Cleary, J., Levine, A.S., Schaal, D.W., and Thompson, T. Effects of neuropeptide Y on food-reinforced behavior in satiated rats. *Pharmacology, Biochemistry, and Behavior*, 1992, *42*, 207–212.

Jiang, C.L., and Hunt, J.N. The relation between freely chosen meals and body habitus. *American Journal of Clinical Nutrition*, 1983, *38*, 32–40.

Johansson, G. Visual perception of biological motion and a model for its analysis. *Perception and Psychophysics*, 1973, *14*, 201–211.

Johnson, A.K., and Cunningham, J.T. Brain mechanisms and drinking: The role of lamina terminalis-associated systems in extracellular thirst. *Kidney International*, 1987, *32*, S35–S42.

Johnson, A.K., and Edwards, G.L. The neuroendocrinology of thirst: Afferent signaling and mechanisms of central integration. *Current Topics in Neuroendocrinology*, 1990, *10*, 149–190.

Johnson, M.K., Kim, J.K., and Risse, G. Do alcoholic Korsakoff's syndrome patients acquire affective reactions? *Journal of Experimental Psychology: Learning, Memory, and Cognition*, 1985, *11*, 22–36.

Johnston, D., Hopkins, W.F., and Gray, R. The role of norepinephrine in long-term potentiation at mossy-fiber synapses in the hippocampus. In *Neural Models of Plasticity: Experimental and Theoretical Approaches*, edited by J.H. Byrne and W.O. Berry. San Diego: Academic Press, 1989.

Jones, B.E. Influence of the brainstem reticular formation, including intrinsic monoaminergic and cholinergic neurons, on forebrain mechanisms of sleep and waking. In *The Diencephalon and Sleep*, edited by M. Mancia and G. Marini. New York: Raven Press, 1990.

Jones, B.E., and Beaudet, A. Distribution of acetylcholine and catecholamine neurons in the cat brain stem studied by choline acetyltransferase and tyrosine hydroxylase immunohistochemistry. *Journal of Comparative Neurology*, 1987, *261*, 15–32.

Jones, D.T., and Reed, R.R. G_{olf}: An olfactory neuron specific-G protein involved in odorant signal transduction. *Science*, 1989, *244*, 790–795.

Jones, M.B., and Szatmari, P. Stoppage rules and genetic studies of autism. *Journal of Autism and Developmental Disorders*, 1988, *18*, 31–40.

Jones, S.S., Collins, K., and Hong, H.-W. An audience effect on smile production in 10–month old infants. *Psychological Science*, 1991, *2*, 45–49.

Josso, N., Boussin, L., Knebelmann, B., Nihoul-Fekete, C., and Picard, J.-Y. Anti-Muellerian hormone and intersex states. *Trends in Endocrinology and Metabolism*, 1991, *2*, 227–233.

Jouvet, M. The role of monoamines and acetylcholine-containing neurons in the regulation of the sleep-waking cycle. *Ergebnisse der Physiologie*, 1972, *64*, 166–307.

Jouvet, M. Paradoxical sleep and the nature-nurture controversy. *Progress in Brain Research*, 1980, *53*, 331–346.

Juji, T.M., Satake, Y., Honda, Y., and Doi, Y. HLA antigens in Japanese patients with narcolepsy: All the patients were CR2 positive. *Tissue Antigens*, 1984, *24*, 316–319.

Julien, R.M. *A Primer of Drug Action*. San Francisco: W.H. Freeman, 1981.

Kadekaro, M., Cohen, S., Terrell, M.L., Lekan, H., Gary, H., and Eisenberg, H.M. Independent activation of subfornical organ and hypothalamo-neurohypophysial system during administration of angiotensin II. *Peptides*, 1989, *10*, 423–429.

Kales, A., Scharf, M.B., Kales, J.D., and Soldatos, C.R. Rebound insomnia: A potential hazard following withdrawal of certain benzodiazepines. *Journal of the American Medical Association*, 1979, *241*, 1692–1695.

Kales, A., Tan, T.-L., Kollar, E.J., Naitoh, P., Preston, T.A., and Malmstrom, E.J. Sleep patterns following 205 hours of sleep deprivation. *Psychosomatic Medicine*, 1970, *32*, 189–200.

Kanamori, N., Sakai, K., and Jouvet, M. Neuronal activity specific to paradoxical sleep in the ventromedial medullary reticular formation of unrestrained cats. *Brain Research*, 1980, *189*, 251–255.

Kanner, L. Autistic disturbances of affective contact. *The Nervous Child*, 1943, *2*, 217–250.

Karacan, I., Salis, P.J., and Williams, R.L. The role of the sleep laboratory in diagnosis and treatment of impotence. In *Sleep Disorders: Diagnosis and Treatment*, edited by R.J. Williams and I. Karacan. New York: John Wiley & Sons, 1978.

Karacan, I., Williams, R.L., Finley, W.W., and Hursch, C.J. The effects of naps on nocturnal sleep: Influence on the need for stage 1 REM and stage 4 sleep. *Biological Psychiatry*, 1970, *2*, 391–399.

Karlson, P., and Luscher, M. "Pheromones": A new term for a class of biologically active substances. *Nature*, 1959, *183*, 55–56.

Kasper, S., Rogers, S.L.B., Yancey, A., Schulz, P.M., Skwerer, R.G., and Rosenthal, N.E. Phototherapy in individuals with and without subsyndromal seasonal affective disorder. *Archives of General Psychiatry*, 1989a, *46*, 837–844.

Kasper, S., Wehr, T.A., Bartko, J.J., Gaist, P.A., and Rosenthal, N.E. Epidemiological findings of seasonal changes in mood and behavior: A telephone survey of Montgomery County, Maryland. *Archives of General Psychiatry*, 1989b, *46*, 823–833.

Katayama, Y., DeWitt, D.S., Becker, D.P., and Hayes, R.L. Behavioral evidence for cholinoceptive pontine inhibitory area: Descending control of spinal motor output and sensory input. *Brain Research*, 1986, *296*, 241–262.

Katsuki, Y. In *Sensory Communication*, edited by W.A. Rosenblith. Cambridge, Mass.: MIT Press, 1961.

Kauer, J.S. Real-time imaging of evoked activity in local circuits of the salamander olfactory bulb. *Nature*, 1988, *331*, 166–168.

Kaupp, U.B. The cyclic nucleotide-gated channels of vertebrate photoreceptors and olfactory epithelium. *Trends in Neuroscience*, 1991, *14*, 150–157.

Kavaliers, M. Brief exposure to a natural predator, the short-tailed weasel, induces benzodiazepine-sensitive analgesia in white-footed mice. *Physiology and Behavior*, 1985, *43*, 187–193.

Kawamura, M., Hirayama, K., and Yamamoto, H. Different interhemispheric transfer of kanji and kana writing evidenced by a case with left unilateral agraphia without apraxia. *Brain*, 1989, *112*, 1011–1018.

Kayama, Y., Ohta, M., and Jodo, E. Firing of "possibly" cholinergic neurons in the rat laterodorsal tegmental nucleus during sleep and wakefulness. *Brain Research*, 1992, 569, 210–220.

Kaye, W.H., Berrettini, W., Gwirtsman, H., and George, D.T. Altered cerebrospinal fluid neuropeptide Y and peptide YY immunoreactivity in anorexia and bulimia nervosa. *Archives of General Psychiatry*, 1990, *47*, 548–556.

Keithley, E.M., and Schreiber, R.C. Frequency map of the spiral ganglion in the cat. *Journal of the Acoustical Society of America*, 1987, *81*, 1036–1042.

Keller, S.E., Weiss, J.M., Schleifer, S.J., Miller, N.E., and Stein, M. Stress-induced suppression of immunity in adrenalectomized rats. *Science*, 1983, *221*, 1301–1304.

Kelly, D.H., Walker, A.M., Cahen, L.A., and Shannon, D.C. Periodic breathing in siblings of SIDS victims. *Pediatric Research*, 1980, *14*, 645–650.

Kelso, S.R., and Brown, T.H. Differential conditioning of associative synaptic enhancement in hippocampal brain slices. *Science*, 1986, *232*, 85–87.

Kelsoe, J.R., Ginns, E.I., Egeland, J.A., Gerhard, D.S., Goldstein, A.M., Bale, S.J., Pauls, D.L., Long, R.T., Kidd, K.K., Conte, G., Housman, D.E., and Paul, S.M. Re-evaluation of the linkage relationship between chromosome 11p loci and the gene for bipolar affective disorder in the Old Order Amish. *Nature*, 1989, *342*, 238–243.

Kemp, D.T. Stimulated acoustic emissions from within the human auditory system. *Journal of the Acoustical Society of America*, 1978, *64*, 1386–1391.

Kendell, R.E., and Adams, W. Unexplained fluctuations in the risk for schizophrenia by month and year of birth. *British Journal of Psychiatry*, 1991, *158*, 758–763.

Kennedy, J.L., Giuffra, L.A., Moises, H.W., Cavalli-Sforza, L.L., Pakstis, A.J., Kidd, J.R., Castiglione, C.M., Sjögren, B., Wetterberg, L., and Kidd, K.K. Evidence against linkage of schizophrenia to markers on chromosome 5 in a northern Swedish pedigree. *Nature*, 1988, *336*, 167–170.

Kennedy, S.H., and Goldbloom, D.S. Current perspectives on drug therapies for anorexia nervosa and bulimia nervosa. *Drugs*, 1991, *41*, 367–377.

Kertesz, A. *Aphasia and Associated Disorders: Taxonomy, Localization, and Recovery*. New York: Grune & Stratton, 1979.

Kertesz, A. Personal communication, 1980.

Kertesz, A. Anatomy of jargon. In *Jargonaphasia*, edited by J. Brown. New York: Academic Press, 1981.

Kessler, S., Guilleminault, C., and Dement, W.C. A family study of 50 REM narcoleptics. *Acta Neurologica Scandinavica*, 1974, *50*, 503–512.

Kety, S.S., Rosenthal, D., Wender, P.H., and Schulsinger, K.F. The types and prevalence of mental illness in the biological and adoptive families of adopted schizophrenics. In *The Transmission of Schizophrenia*, edited by D. Rosenthal and S.S. Kety. New York: Pergamon Press, 1968.

Keverne, E.B., and de la Riva, C. Pheromones in mice: Reciprocal interactions between the nose and brain. *Nature*, 1982, *296*, 148–150.

Khanna, S., and Channabasavanna, S. Toward a classification of compulsions in obsessive compulsive neurosis. *Psychopathology*, 1987, *20*, 23–28.

Kiang, N.Y.-S. *Discharge Patterns of Single Fibers in the Cat's Auditory Nerve*. Cambridge, Mass.: MIT Press, 1965.

Kiecolt-Glaser, J.K., Glaser, R., Shuttleworth, E.C., Dyer, C.S., Ogrocki, P., and Speicher, C.E. Chronic stress and immunity in family caregivers of Alzheimer's disease victims. *Psychosomatic Medicine*, 1987, *49*, 523–535.

Kimura, K., Nomikos, G.G., and Svensson, T.H. Effects of amperozide on psychostimulant-induced hyperlocomotion and dopamine release in the nucleus accumbens. *Pharmacology, Biochemistry, and Behavior*, 1993, *44*, 27–36.

King, B.M., and Frohman, L.A. Hypothalamic obesity: Comparison of ratio-frequency and electrolytic lesions in male and female rats. *Brain Research Bulletin*, 1986, *17*, 409–413.

Kinnamon, J.C., and Roper, S.D. Evidence for a role of voltage-sensitive apical K^+ channels in sour and salt taste transduction. *Chemical Senses*, 1988, *13*, 115–121.

Kinnamon, S.C., and Cummings, T.A. Chemosensory transduction mechanisms in taste. *Annual Review of Physiology*, 1992, *54*, 715–731.

Kinsey, A.C., Pomeroy, W.B., Martin, C.E., and Gebhard, P.H. *Sexual Behavior in the Human Female*. Philadelphia: Saunders, 1943.

Kirchgessner, A.L., and Sclafani, A. PVN-hindbrain pathway involved in the hypothalamic hyperphagia-obesity syndrome. *Physiology and Behavior*, 1988, *42*, 517–528.

Klausner, J.D., Sweeney, J.A., Deck, M.D.F., Haas, G.L., and Kelly, A.B. Clinical correlates of cerebral ventricular enlargement in schizophrenia. Further evidence for frontal lobe disease. *Journal of Nervous and Mental Disorders*, 1992, *180*, 407–412.

Kleitman, N. The nature of dreaming. In *The Nature of Sleep*, edited by G.E.W. Wolstenholme and M. O'Connor. London: J.&A. Churchill, 1961.

Kleitman, N. Basic rest-activity cycle—22 years later. *Sleep*, 1982, *4*, 311–317.

Knapp, P.H., Levy, E.M., Giorgi, R.G., Black, P.H., Fox, B.H., and Heeren, T.C. Short-term immunological effects of induced emotion. *Psychosomatic Medicine*, 1992, *54*, 133–148.

Knebelmann, B., Boussin, L., Guerrier, D., Legeai, L., Kahn, A., Josso, N., and Picard, J.-Y. Anti-Müellerian hormone Bruxelles: A nonsense mutation associated with the persistent Müellerian duct syndrome. *Proceedings of the National Academy of Sciences, USA*, 1991, *88*, 3767–3771.

Kobashi, M., and Adachi, A. Effect of hepatic portal infusion of water on water intake by water-deprived rats. *Physiology and Behavior*, 1992, *52*, 885–888.

Koenigsberg, H.W., Pollak, C.P., Fine, J., and Kakuma, T. Lactate sensitivity in sleeping panic disorder patients and healthy controls. *Biological Psychiatry*, 1992, *32*, 539–542.

Kolvalzon, V.M., and Mukhametov, L.M. Temperature fluctuations of the dolphin brain corresponding to unihemispheric slow-wave sleep. *Journal of Evolutionary Biochemistry and Physiology*, 1982, *18*, 307–309.

Komisaruk, B.R., and Larsson, K. Suppression of a spinal and a cranial nerve reflex by vaginal or rectal probing in rats. *Brain Research*, 1971, *35*, 231–235.

Komisaruk, B.R., and Steinman, J.L. Genital stimulation as a trigger for neuroendocrine and behavioral control of reproduction. *Annals of the New York Academy of Sciences*, 1987, *474*, 64–75.

Koob, G.F., and Bloom, F.E. Cellular and molecular mechanisms of drug dependence. *Science*, 1988, *242*, 715–723.

Koob, G.F., Thatcher-Britton, K., Britton, D., Roberts, D.C.S., and Bloom, F.E. Destruction of the locus coeruleus or the dorsal NE bundle does not alter the release of punished responding by ethanol and chlordiazepoxide. *Physiology and Behavior*, 1984, *33*, 479–485.

Koolhaas, J.M., Van den Brink, T.H.C., Roozendaal, B., and Boorsma, F. Medial amygdala and aggressive behavior: Interaction between testosterone and vasopressin. *Aggressive Behavior*, 1990, *16*, 223–229.

Koopman, P., Gubbay, J., Vivian, N., Goodfellow, P.N., and Lovell-Badge, R. Male development of chromosomally female mice transgenic for Sry. *Nature*, 1991, *351*, 117–121.

Koopmans, H.S. Internal signals cause large changes in food intake in one-way crossed intestines of rats. *Brain Research Bulletin*, 1985, *14*, 595–603.

Kornhuber, H.H. Cerebral cortex, cerebellum, and basal ganglia: An introduction to their motor functions. In *The Neurosciences: Third Study Program*, edited by F.O. Schmitt and F.G. Worden. Cambridge, Mass.: MIT Press, 1974.

Kovner, R., and Stamm, J.S. Disruption of short-term visual memory by electrical stimulation of inferotemporal cortex in the monkey. *Journal of Comparative and Physiological Psychology*, 1972, *81*, 163–172.

Kozlowski, L.T., and Cutting, J.E. Recognizing the sex of a walker from a dynamic point-light display. *Perception and Psychophysics*, 1977, *21*, 575–580.

Kozlowski, S., and Drzewiecki, K. The role of osmoreception in portal circulation in control of water intake in dogs. *Acta Physiologica Polonica*, 1973, *24*, 325–330.

Kral, J.G. Surgical treatment of obesity. *Medical Clinics of North America*, 1989, *73*, 251–264.

Kraly, F.S. Histamine plays a part in induction of drinking by food intake. *Nature*, 1983, *301*, 65–66.

Kraly, F.S. Drinking elicited by eating. In *Progress in Psychobiology and Physiological Psychology, Vol. 14*, edited by A.N. Epstein and A. Morrison. New York: Academic Press, 1990.

Kraly, F.S., and Corneilson, R. Angiotensin II mediates drinking elicited by eating in the rat. *American Journal of Physiology*, 1990, *258*, R436–R442.

Kraly, F.S., and Specht, S.M. Histamine plays a major role for drinking elicited by spontaneous eating in rats. *Physiology and Behavior*, 1984, *33*, 611–614.

Kramer, F.M., Jeffery, R.W., Forster, J.L., and Snell, M.K. Long-term follow-up of behavioral treatment for obesity: Patterns of weight regain among men and women. *International Journal of Obesity*, 1989, *13*, 123–136.

Kraut, R.E., and Johnston, R. Social and emotional messages of smiling: An ethological approach. *Journal of Personality and Social Psychology*, 1979, *37*, 1539–1553.

Kruk, M.R. Ethology and pharmacology of hypothalamic aggression in the rat. *Neuroscience and Biobehavioral Reviews*, 1991, *15*, 527–538.

Kuczmarski, R.J. Prevalence of overweight and weight gain in the United States. *American Journal of Clinical Nutrition*, 1992, *55*, 495S-502S.

Kuffler, S.W. Neurons in the retina: Organization, inhibition and excitation problems. *Cold Spring Harbor Symposium on Quantitative Biology*, 1952, *17*, 281–292.

Kuffler, S.W. Discharge patterns and functional organization of mammalian retina. *Journal of Neurophysiology*, 1953, *16*, 37–68.

Kumar, K., Wyant, G.M., and Nath, R. Deep brain stimulation for control of intractable pain in humans, present and future: A ten-year follow-up. *Neurosurgery*, 1990, *26*, 774–782.

Kupfer, D.J. REM latency: A psychobiologic marker for primary depressive disease. *Biological Psychiatry*, 1976, *11*, 159–174.

Kurihara, K. Recent progress in taste receptor mechanisms. In *Umami: A Basic Taste*, edited by Y. Kawamura and M.R. Kare. New York: Dekker, 1987.

Laborit, H. La thérapeutique neuro-végétate du choc et de la maladie post-traumatique. *Presse Medicale*, 1950, *58*, 138–140. Cited by Snyder, 1974.

Land, E.H. The retinex theory of colour vision. *Proceedings of the Royal Institute of Great Britain*, 1974, *47*, 23–57.

Lange, C.G. *Über Gemüthsbewegungen*. Leipzig, East Germany: T. Thomas, 1887.

Langston, J.W., Ballard, P., Tetrud, J., and Irwin, I. Chronic parkinsonism in humans due to a product of meperidine-analog synthesis. *Science*, 1983, *219*, 979–980.

Langston, J.W., Irwin, I., Langston, E.B., and Forno, L.S. Pargyline prevents MPTP-induced parkinsonism in primates. *Science*, 1984, *225*, 1480–1482.

Lankenau, H., Swigar, M.E., Bhimani, S., Luchins, S., and Quinlon, D.M. Cranial CT scans in eating disorder patients and controls. *Comprehensive Psychiatry*, 1985, *26*, 136–147.

Laplane, D., Levasseur, M., Pillon, B., Dubois, B., Baulac, M., Mazoyer, B., Tran Din, S., Sette, G., Danze, F., and Baron, J. Obsessive-compulsive and other behavioural changes with bilateral basal ganglia lesions. A neuropsycho-

logical, magnetic resonance imaging and positron tomography study. *Brain*, 1989, *112*, 699–725.

Laschet, U. Antiandrogen in the treatment of sex offenders: Mode of action and therapeutic outcome. In *Contemporary Sexual Behavior: Critical Issues in the 1970's*, edited by J. Zubin and J. Money. Baltimore: Johns Hopkins University Press, 1973.

Lavie, P., Pratt, H., Scharf, B., Peled, R., and Brown, J. Localized pontine lesion: Nearly total absence of REM sleep. *Neurology*, 1984, *34*, 1118–1120.

Lawrence, D.G., and Kuypers, G.J.M. The functional organization of the motor system in the monkey. I. The effects of bilateral pyramidal lesions. *Brain*, 1968a, *91*, 1–14.

Lawrence, D.G., and Kuypers, G.J.M. The functional organization of the motor system in the monkey. II. The effects of lesions of the descending brain-stem pathways. *Brain*, 1968b, *91*, 15–36.

LeBlanc, J., and Cabanac, M. Cephalic postprandial thermogenesis in human subjects. *Physiology and Behavior*, 1989, *46*, 479–482.

Leblanc, R., Meyer, E., Bub, D., Zatorre, R.J., and Evans, A.C. Language localization with activation positron emission tomography scanning. *Neurosurgery*, 1992, *31*, 369–373.

Leboyer, M., Bouvard, M.P., Lauday, J.-M., Tabuteau, F., Waller, D., Dugas, M., Kerdelhue, B., Lensing, P., and Panksepp, J. Brief report: A double-blind study of naltrexone in infantile autism. *Journal of Autism and Developmental Disorders*, 1992, *22*, 309–319.

LeDoux, J.E. Brain mechanisms of emotion and emotional learning. *Current Opinion in Neurobiology*, 1992, *2*, 191–197.

LeDoux, J.E., Iwata, J., Cicchetti, P., and Reis, D.J. Different projections of the central amygdaloid nucleus mediate autonomic and behavioral correlates of conditioned fear. *Journal of Neuroscience*, 1988, *8*, 2517–2529.

LeDoux, J.E., Iwata, J., Pearl, D., and Reis, D.J. Disruption of auditory but not visual learning by destruction of intrinsic neurons in the rat medial geniculate body. *Brain Research*, 1986, *371*, 395–399.

LeDoux, J.E., Sakaguchi, A., and Reis, D.J. Subcortical efferent projections of the medial geniculate nucleus mediate emotional responses conditioned to acoustic stimuli. *Journal of Neuroscience*, 1984, *4*, 683–698.

Lee, J.-H., and Beitz, A.J. Electroacupuncture modifies the expression of c-fos in the spinal cord induced by noxious stimulation. *Brain Research*, 1992, *577*, 80–91.

Lehman, C.D., Rodin, J., McEwen, B., and Brinton, R. Impact of environmental stress on the expression of insulin-dependent diabetes mellitus. *Behavioral Neuroscience*, 1991, *105*, 241–245.

Lehman, M.N., Silver, R., Gladstone, W.R., Kahn, R.M., Gibson, M., and Bittman, E.L. Circadian rhythmicity restored by neural transplant: Immunocytochemical characterization with the host brain. *Journal of Neuroscience*, 1987, *7*, 1626–1638.

Lehman, M.N., and Winans, S.S. Vomeronasal and olfactory pathways to the amygdala controlling male hamster sexual behavior: Autoradiographic and behavioral analyses. *Brain Research*, 1982, *240*, 27–41.

Leibenluft, E., and Wehr, T.A. Is sleep deprivation useful in the treatment of depression? *American Journal of Psychiatry*, 1992, *149*, 159–168.

Leibowitz, S.F., Weiss, G.F., and Shor-Posner, G. Hypothalamic serotonin: Pharmacological, biochemical and behavioral analyses of its feeding-suppressive action. *Clinical Neuropharmacology*, 1988, *11*, 551–571.

Leibowitz, S.F., Weiss, G.F., and Suh, J.S. Medial hypothalamic nuclei mediate serotonin's inhibitory effect on feeding behavior. *Pharmacology, Biochemistry, and Behavior*, 1990, *37*, 735–742.

Leibowitz, S.F., Weiss, G.F., Yee, F., and Tretter, J.B. Noradrenergic innervation of the paraventricular nucleus: Specific role in control of carbohydrate ingestions. *Brain Research Bulletin*, 1985, *14*, 561–567.

Le Magnen, J. Hyperphagie provoquée chez le rat blanc par l'altération du méchanisme de satiéte périphérique. *Comptes Rendus de la Société de Biologie*, 1956, *147*, 1753–1757.

Le Magnen, J., and Tallon, S. Enregistrement et analyse préliminaire de la "périodicité alimentaire spontanée" chez le rat blanc. *Journal of Physiology* (Paris), 1963, *55*, 286–297.

Le Magnen, J., and Tallon, S. La périodicité spontanée de la prise d'aliments *ad libitum* du rat blanc. *Journal of Physiology* (Paris), 1966, *58*, 323–349.

Leon, M. Plasticity of olfactory output circuits related to early olfactory learning. *Trends in Neurosciences*, 1987, *10*, 434–438.

Leonard, B.E. On the mode of action of mianserin. In *Typical and Atypical Antidepressants: Molecular Mechanisms*, edited by E. Costa and G. Racagni. New York: Raven Press, 1982.

Leonard, C.M., Rolls, E.T., Wilson, F.A.W., and Baylis, G.C. Neurons in the amygdala of the monkey with responses selective for faces. *Behavioral Brain Research*, 1985, *15*, 159–176.

Leonard, H.L., Lenane, M.C., Swedo, S.E., Rettew, D.C., Gershon, E.S., and Rapoport, J.L. Tics and Tourette's disorder: A 2- to 7-year follow-up of 54 obsessive-compulsive children. *American Journal of Psychiatry*, 1992, *149*, 1244–1251.

Leonard, H.L., Lenane, M.C., Swedo, S.E., Rettew, D.C., and Rapoport, J.L. A double-blind comparison of clomipramine and desipramine treatment of severe onychophagia (nail biting). *Archives of General Psychiatry*, 1992, *48*, 821–827.

Leonard, H.L., Swedo, S.E., Rapoport, J.L., Koby, E.V., Lenane, M.C., Cheslow, D.L., and Hamburger, S.D. Treatment of obsessive-compulsive disorder with clomipramine and desipramine in children and adolescents: A double-blind crossover comparison. *Archives of General Psychiatry*, 1989, *46*, 1088–1092.

Leonard, H.L., Swedo, S.E., Rapoport, J.L., Rickler, K.C., Topol, D., Lee, S., and Rettew, D. Tourette syndrome and obsessive-compulsive disorder. *Advances in Neurology*, 1992, *58*, 83–93.

Lepkovsky, S., Lyman, R., Fleming, D., Nagumo, M., and Dimick, M. Gastrointestinal regulation of water and its effect on food intake and rate of digestion. *American Journal of Physiology*, 1957, *188*, 327–331.

Lerea, L.S., Butler, L.S., and McNamara, J.O. NMDA and non-NMDA receptor-mediated increase of c-fos mRNA in dentate gyrus neurons involves calcium influx via different routes. *Journal of Neuroscience*, 1992, *12*, 2973–2981.

Lesser, R. Selective preservation of oral spelling without semantics in a case of multi-infarct dementia. *Cortex*, 1989, *25*, 239–250.

Lester, L.S., and Fanselow, M.S. Exposure to a cat produces opioid analgesia in rats. *Behavioral Neuroscience*, 1985, *99*, 756–759.

LeVay, S. A difference in hypothalamic structure between heterosexual and homosexual men. *Science*, 1991, *253*, 1034–1037.

Levenson, R.W., Ekman, P., and Friesen, W.V. Voluntary facial action generates emotion-specific autonomic nervous system activity. *Psychophysiology*, 1990, *27*, 363–384.

Levine, J.D., Gordon, N.C., and Fields, H.L. The role of endorphins in placebo analgesia. In *Advances in Pain Research and Therapy, Vol. 3*, edited by J.J. Bonica, J.C. Liebeskind, and D. Albe-Fessard. New York: Raven Press, 1979.

Ley, R.G., and Bryden, M.P. Hemispheric differences in recognizing faces and emotions. *Brain and Language*, 1979, *7*, 127–138.

Ley, R.G., and Bryden, M.P. A dissociation of right and left hemispheric effects for recognizing emotional tone and verbal content. *Brain and Cognition*, 1982, *1*, 3–9.

Li, T.-K., Lumeng, L., and Doolittle, D.P. Selective breeding for alcohol preference and associated responses. *Behavioral Genetics*, 1993, *23*, 163–170.

Liang, K.C., Melia, K.R., Miserendino, M.J.D., Falls, W.A., Campeau, S., and Davis, M. Corticotropin-releasing factor: Long-lasting facilitation of the acoustic startle reflex. *Journal of Neuroscience*, 1992, *12*, 2303–2312.

Lichtman, S.W., Pisarska, K., Berman, E.R., Pestone, M., Dowling, H., Offenbacher, E., Weisel, H., Heshka, S., Matthews, D.E., and Heymsfield, S.B. Discrepancy between self-reported and actual caloric intake and exercise in obese subjects. *New England Journal of Medicine*, 1992, *327*, 1893–1898.

Lind, R.W., and Johnson, A.K. Central and peripheral mechanisms mediating angiotensin-induced thirst. In *The Renin Angiotensin System in the Brain*, edited by D. Ganten, M. Printz, M.I. Phillips, and B.A. Schölkens. Berlin: Springer-Verlag, 1982.

Lind, R.W., Thunhorst, R.L., and Johnson, A.K. The subfornical organ and the integration of multiple factors in thirst. *Physiology and Behavior*, 1984, *32*, 69–74.

Linden, D.J., and Routtenberg, A. The role of protein kinase C in long-term potentiation: A testable model. *Brain Research*, 1989, *14*, 279–296.

Lindvall, O. Dopamine pathways in the rat brain. In *The Neurobiology of Dopamine*, edited by A.S. Horn, J. Korb, and B.H.C. Westerink. New York: Academic Press, 1979.

Lisk, R.D., Pretlow, R.A., and Friedman, S. Hormonal stimulation necessary for elicitation of maternal nest-building in the mouse (*Mus musculus*). *Animal Behaviour*, 1969, *17*, 730–737.

Liuzzi, F.J., and Lasek, R.J. Astrocytes block axonal regeneration in mammals by activating the physiological stop pathway. *Science*, 1987, *237*, 642–645.

Livingstone, M.S., and Hubel, D. Segregation of form, color, movement, and depth: Anatomy, physiology, and perception. *Science*, 1988, *240*, 740–749.

Livingstone, M.S., and Hubel, D.H. Thalamic inputs to cytochrome oxidase-rich regions in monkey visual cortex. *Proceedings of the National Academy of Sciences, USA*, 1982, *79*, 6098–6101.

Livingstone, M.S., and Hubel, D.H. Psychophysical evidence for separate channels for the perception of form, color, movement, and depth. *Journal of Neuroscience*, 1987, *7*, 3416–3468.

Ljungberg, T., Apicella, P., and Schultz, W. Responses of monkey dopamine neurons during learning of behavioral reactions. *Journal of Neurophysiology*, 1992, *67*, 145–163.

Loewenstein, W.R., and Mendelson, M. Components of receptor adaptation in a Pacinian corpuscle. *Journal of Physiology (London)*, 1965, *177*, 377–397.

Lombardo, R., and Carreno, L. Relationship of type A behavior pattern in smokers to carbon monoxide exposure and smoking topography. *Health Psychology*, 1987, *6*, 445–452.

Lømo, T. Frequency potentiation of excitatory synaptic activity in the dentate area of the hippocampal formation. *Acta Physiologica Scandinavica*, 1966, *68* (Suppl. 227), 128.

LoTurco, J.J., Coulter, D.A., and Alkon, D.L. Enhancement of synaptic potentials in rabbit CA1 pyramidal neurons following classical conditioning. *Proceedings of the National Academy of Sciences, USA*, 1988, *85*, 1672–1676.

Louis-Sylvestre, J., and Le Magnen, J. A fall in blood glucose level precedes meal onset in free-feeding rats. *Neuroscience and Biobehavioral Reviews*, 1980, *4*, 13–16.

Lowe, T.L., Tanaka, K., Seashore, M.R., Young, J.G., and Cohen, D.J. Detection of phenylketonuria in autistic and psychotic children. *Journal of the American Medical Association*, 1980, *243*, 126–128.

Lu, C.-L., Shaikh, M.B., and Siegel, A. Role of NMDA receptors in hypothalamic facilitation of feline defensive rage elicited from the midbrain periaqueductal gray. *Brain Research*, 1992, *581*, 123–132.

Lydic, R., Baghdoyan, H.A., Hibbard, L., Bonyak, E.V., De-Joseph, M.R., and Hawkins, R.A. Regional brain glucose metabolism is altered during rapid eye movement sleep in the cat: A preliminary study. *Journal of Comparative Neurology*, 1991, *304*, 517–529.

Lydic, R., McCarley, R.W., and Hobson, J.A. The time-course of dorsal raphe discharge, PGO waves and muscle tone averaged across multiple sleep cycles. *Brain Research*, 1983, *274*, 365–370.

Lydic, R., Schoene, W.C., Czeisler, C.A., and Moore-Ede, M.C. Suprachiasmatic region of the human hypothalamus: Homolog to the primate circadian pacemaker? *Sleep*, 1980, *2*, 355–361.

Lynch, G., Larson, J., Kelso, S., Barrionuevo, G., and Schottler, F. Intracellular injections of EGTA block induction of long-term potentiation. *Nature*, 1984, *305*, 719–721.

Lynch, G., Larson, J., Staubli, U., and Granger, R. Variants of synaptic potentiation and different types of memory operations in hippocampus and related structures. In *Memory: Organization and Locus of Change*, edited by L.R. Squire, N.M. Weinberger, G. Lynch, and J.L. McGaugh. New York: Oxford University Press, 1991.

Lytton, W.W., and Brust, J.C.M. Direct dyslexia: Preserved oral reading of real words in Wernicke's aphasia. *Brain*, 1989, *112*, 583–594.

MacLean, P.D. Psychosomatic disease and the "visceral brain": Recent developments bearing on the Papez theory of emotion. *Psychosomatic Medicine*, 1949, *11*, 338–353.

Madsen, P.L., Holm, S., Vorstrup, S., Friberg, L., Lassen, N.A., and Wildschiodtz, G. Human regional cerebral blood flow during rapid-eye-movement sleep. *Journal of Cerebral Blood Flow and Metabolism*, 1991, *11*, 502–507.

Maier, S.F., Drugan, R.C., and Grau, J.W. Controllability, coping behavior, and stress-induced analgesia in the rat. *Pain*, 1982, *12*, 47–56.

Maksay, G., and Ticku, M.K. Dissociation of [^{35}S]t-butylbicyclophosphorothionate binding differentiates convulsant and depressant drugs that modulate GABAergic transmission. *Journal of Neurochemistry*, 1985, *44*, 480–486.

Malamut, B.L., Graff-Radford, N., Chawluk, J., Grossman, R.I., and Gur, R.C. Memory in a case of bilateral thalamic infarction. *Neurology*, 1992, *42*, 163–169.

Maldonado, R., Robledo, P., Chover, A.J., Caine, S.B., and Koob, G.F. D1 dopamine receptors in the nucleus accumbens modulate cocaine self-administration in the rat. *Pharmacology, Biochemistry, and Behavior*, 1993, *45*, 239–242.

Malenka, R.C., Kauer, J.A., Zucker, R.S., and Nicoll, R.A. Postsynaptic calcium is sufficient for potentiation of hippocampal synaptic transmission. *Science*, 1988, *242*, 81–84.

Malinow, R., and Miller, J.P. Postsynaptic hyperpolarization during conditioning reversibly blocks induction of long-term potentiation. *Nature*, 1986, *321*, 175–177.

Malinow, R., Schulman, H., and Tsien, R.W. Inhibition of postsynaptic PKC or CaMKII blocks induction but not expression of LTP. *Science*, 1989, *245*, 862–866.

Malinow, R., and Tsien, R.W. Presynaptic enhancement shown by whole-cell recordings of long-term potentiation in hippocampal slices. *Nature*, 1990, *346*, 177–180.

Mallick, B.N., Siegel, J.M., and Fahringer, H. Changes in pontine unit activity with REM sleep deprivation. *Brain Research*, 1989, *515*, 94–98.

Mallow, G.K. The relationship between aggression and cycle stage in adult female rhesus monkeys (*Macaca mulatta*). *Dissertation Abstracts*, 1979, *39*, 3194.

Malsbury, C.W. Facilitation of male rat copulatory behavior by electrical stimulation of the medial preoptic area. *Physiology and Behavior*, 1971, *7*, 797–805.

Mann, F., Bowsher, D., Mumford, J., Lipton, S., and Miles, J. Treatment of intractable pain by acupuncture. *Lancet*, 1973, *2*, 57–60.

Manning, L., and Campbell, R. Optic aphasia with spared action naming: A description and possible loci of impairment. *Neuropsychologia*, 1992, *30*, 587–592.

Mantyh, P.W. Connections of midbrain periaqueductal gray in the monkey. II. Descending efferent projections. *Journal of Neurophysiology*, 1983, *49*, 582–594.

Manuck, S.B., Kaplan, J.R., and Clarkson, T.B. Behaviorally-induced heart rate reactivity and atherosclerosis in cynomolgous monkeys. *Psychosomatic Medicine*, 1983, *45*, 95–108.

Manuck, S.B., Kaplan, J.R., and Matthews, K.A. Behavioral antecedents of coronary heart disease and atherosclerosis. *Arteriosclerosis*, 1986, *6*, 1–14.

Maquet, P., Dive, D., Salmon, E., Sadzot, B., Franco, G., Poirrier, R., Von Frenckell, R., and Franck, G. Cerebral glucose utilization during sleep-wake cycle in man determined by positron emission tomography and [18F]2-fluoro-2-deoxy-D-glucose method. *Brain Research*, 1990, *513*, 136–143.

Marczynski, T.J., and Urbancic, M. Animal models of chronic anxiety and "fearlessness." *Brain Research Bulletin*, 1988, *21*, 483–490.

Margolin, D.I., and Goodman-Schulman, R. Oral and written spelling impairments. In *Cognitive Neuropsychology in Clinical Practice*, edited by D.I. Margolin. New York: Oxford University Press, 1992.

Margolin, D.I., Marcel, A.J., and Carlson, N.R. Common mechanisms in dysnomia and post-semantic surface dyslexia: Processing deficits and selective attention. In *Surface Dyslexia: Neuropsychological and Cognitive Studies of Phonological Reading*, edited by M. Coltheart. London: Lawrence Erlbaum Associates, 1985.

Margolin, D.I., and Walker, J.A. Personal communication, 1981.

Mark, G.P., Blander, D.S., Hernandez, L., and Hoebel, B.G. Effects of salt intake, rehydration and conditioned taste aversion (CTA) development on dopamine output in the rat nucleus accumbens. *Appetite*, 1989, *12*, 224.

Mark, V.H., Ervin, F.R., and Yakovlev, P.I. The treatment of pain by stereotaxic methods. *Confina Neurologica*, 1962, *22*, 238–245.

Markram, H., and Segal, M. Acetylcholine potentiates responses to N-methyl-D-aspartate in the rat hippocampus. *Neuroscience Letters*, 1990, *113*, 62–65.

Marshall, J.C., and Newcombe, F. Patterns of paralexia: A psycholinguistic approach. *Journal of Psycholinguistic Research*, 1973, *2*, 175–199.

Martinot, J.-L., Peron-Magnan, P., Huret, J.-D., Mazoyer, B., Baron, J.-C., Boulenger, J.P., Loc'h, C., Maziere, B., Caillard, V., Loo, H., and Syrota, A. Striatal D_2 dopaminergic receptors assessed with positron emission tomography and [^{76}Br]bromospiperone in untreated schizophrenic patients. *American Journal of Psychiatry*, 1990, *147*, 44–50.

Mather, P., Nicolaïdis, S., and Booth, D.A. Compensatory and conditioned feeding responses to scheduled glucose infusions in the rat. *Nature*, 1978, *273*, 461–463.

Matsuda, L.A., Lolait, S.J., Brownstein, M.J., Young, A.C., and Bonner, T.I. Structure of a cannabinoid receptor and functional expression of the cloned cDNA. *Nature*, 1990, *346*, 561–564.

Matteo, S., and Rissman, E.F. Increased sexual activity during the midcycle portion of the human menstrual cycle. *Hormones and Behavior*, 1984, *18*, 249–255.

Matthews, R.T., and German, D.C. Electrophysiological evidence for excitation of rat ventral tegmental area dopaminergic neurons by morphine. *Neuroscience*, 1984, *11*, 617–626.

Maunsell, J.H.R. Functional visual streams. *Current Opinion in Neurobiology*, 1992, *2*, 506–510.

Mawson, A.R. Anorexia nervosa and the regulation of intake: A review. *Psychological Medicine*, 1974, *4*, 289–308.

Mayer, D.J., and Liebeskind, J.C. Pain reduction by focal electrical stimulation of the brain: An anatomical and behavioral analysis. *Brain Research*, 1974, *68*, 73–93.

Mayer, D.J., Price, D.D., Rafii, A., and Barber, J. Acupuncture hypalgesia: Evidence for activation of a central control system as a mechanism of action. In *Advances in Pain Research and Therapy, Vol. 1*, edited by J.J. Bonica, and D. Albe-Fessard. New York: Raven Press, 1976.

Mayer, J. Regulation of energy intake and the body weight: The glucostatic theory and the lipostatic hypothesis. *Annals of the New York Academy of Science*, 1955, *63*, 15–43.

Mazur, A. Hormones, aggression, and dominance in humans. In *Hormones and Aggressive Behavior*, edited by B.B. Svare. New York: Plenum Press, 1983.

Mazur, A., and Lamb, T. Testosterone, status, and mood in human males. *Hormones and Behavior*, 1980, *14*, 236–246.

McBride, W.J., Murphy, J.M., Gatto, G.J., Levy, A.D., Lumeng, L., and Li, T.-K. Serotonin and dopamine systems regulating alcohol self-administration. *Alcohol and Alcoholism (Suppl.)*, 1991, *1*, 411–416.

McCann, M.J., Verbalis, J.G., and Stricker, E.M. LiCl and CCK inhibit gastric emptying and feeding and stimulate OT secretion in rats. *American Journal of Physiology*, 1989, *256*, R463–R468.

McCarley, R.W., and Hobson, J.A. The form of dreams and the biology of sleep. In *Handbook of Dreams: Research, Theory, and Applications*, edited by B. Wolman. New York: Van Nostrand Reinhold, 1979.

McCarthy, R.A., and Warrington, E.K. Evidence for modality-specific meaning systems in the brain. *Nature*, 1988, *334*, 428–435.

McCarthy, R.A., and Warrington, E.K. *Cognitive Neuropsychology: A Clinical Introduction.* San Diego: Academic Press, 1990.

McClintock, M.K. Menstrual synchrony and suppression. *Nature*, 1971, *229*, 244–245.

McClintock, M.K., and Adler, N.T. The role of the female during copulation in wild and domestic Norway rats (*Rattus norvegicus*). *Behaviour*, 1978, *67*, 67–96.

McCullough, L.D., and Salamone, J.D. Involvement of nucleus accumbens dopamine in the motor activity induced by periodic food presentation: A microdialysis and behavioral study. *Brain Research*, 1992, *592*, 29–36.

McGinty, D., and Szymusiak, R. Keeping cool: A hypothesis about the mechanisms and functions of slow-wave sleep. *Trends in Neuroscience*, 1990, *13*, 480–487.

McGinty, D.J., and Sterman, M.B. Sleep suppression after basal forebrain lesions in the cat. *Science*, 1968, *160*, 1253–1255.

McGowan, M.K., Andrews, K.M., and Grossman, S.P. Chronic intrahypothalamic infusions of insulin or insulin antibodies alter body weight and food intake in the rat. *Physiology and Behavior*, 1992, *51*, 753–766.

McGrath, M.J., and Cohen, D.B. REM sleep facilitation of adaptive waking behavior: A review of the literature. *Psychological Bulletin*, 1978, *85*, 24–57.

McIver, B., Connacher, A., Whittle, I., Baylis, P., and Thompson, C. Adipsic hypothalamic diabetes insipidus after clipping of anterior communicating artery aneurysm. *British Medical Journal*, 1991, *303*, 1465–1467.

McKenna, T.M., Weinberger, N.M., and Diamond, D.M. Responses of single auditory cortical neurons to tone sequences. *Brain Research*, 1989, *481*, 142–153.

McNaughton, B.L., Barnes, C.A., Rao, G., Baldwin, J., and Rasmussen, M. Long-term enhancement of hippocampal synaptic transmission and the acquisition of spatial information. *Journal of Neuroscience*, 1986, *6*, 565–571.

McNaughton, B.L., Leonard, B., and Chen, L. Cortical-hippocampal interactions and cognitive mapping: A hypothesis based on reintegration of the parietal and inferotemporal pathways for visual processing. *Psychobiology*, 1989, *17*, 230–235.

Meddis, R., Pearson, A., and Langford, G. An extreme case of healthy insomnia. *Electroencephalography and Clinical Neurophysiology*, 1973, *35*, 213–214.

Mednick, S.A., Machon, R.A., and Huttunen, M.O. An update on the Helsinki influenza project. *Archives of General Psychiatry*, 1990, *47*, 292.

Meijer, J.H., and Rietveld, W.J. Neurophysiology of the suprachiasmatic circadian pacemaker in rodents. *Physiological Reviews*, 1989, *69*, 671–707.

Meijer, J.H., van der Zee, E.A., and Dietz, M. Glutamate phase shifts circadian activity rhythms in hamsters. *Neuroscience Letters*, 1988, *86*, 177–183.

Melander, T., Fuxe, K., Harfstrand, A., Eneroth, P., and Hökfelt, T. Effects of intraventricular injections of galanin on neuroendocrine functions in the male rat: Possible involvement of hypothalamic catecholamine neuronal systems. *Acta Physiologica Scandanavica*, 1987, *131*, 25–32.

Melges, F.T. *Time and the Inner Future: A Temporal Approach to Psychiatric Disorders.* New York: John Wiley & Sons, 1982.

Melia, K.R., Falls, W.A., and Davis, M. Involvement of pertussis toxin sensitive G-proteins in conditioned fear-potentiated startle: Possible involvement of the amygdala. *Brain Research*, 1992, *584*, 141–148.

Meltzer, H.Y. Treatment of the neuroleptic-nonresponsive schizophrenic patient. *Schizophrenia Bulletin*, 1992, *18*, 515–542.

Melzak, R. Phantom limbs. *Scientific American*, 1992, *266*(4), 120–126.

Menco, B.P.M., Bruch, R.C., Dau, B., and Danho, W. Ultrastructural localization of olfactory transduction components: The G protein subunit $G_{olf\alpha}$ and type III adenylyl cyclase. *Neuron*, 1992, *8*, 441–453.

Menninger, K.A. Influenza and schizophrenia. An analysis of post-influenzal "dementia praecox" as of 1918 and five years later. *American Journal of Psychiatry*, 1926, *5*, 469–529.

Meredith, M. Chronic electrophysiological recordings of vomeronasal pump activation in awake animals. *Chemical Senses*, 1987, *12*, 683.

Meredith, M., and O'Connell, R.J. Efferent control of stimulus access to the hamster vomeronasal organ. *Journal of Physiology*, 1979, *286*, 301–316.

Mesulam, M.-M. Frontal cortex and behavior. *Annals of Neurology*, 1986, *19*, 320–325.

Metherate, B., Ashe, J.H., and Weinberger, N.M. Acetylcholine modifies neuronal acoustic rate-level functions in guinea pig auditory cortex by an action at muscarinic receptors. *Synapse*, 1990, *6*, 364–368.

Metherate, R., and Weinberger, N.M. Cholinergic modulation of responses to single tones produces tone-specific receptive field alterations in cat auditory cortex. *Synapse*, 1990, *6*, 133–145.

Metter, E.J. Brain-behavior relationships in aphasia studied by positron emission tomography. *Annals of the New York Academy of Sciences*, 1991, *620*, 153–164.

Meyer-Bahlburg, H.F.L. Psychoendocrine research on sexual orientation. Current status and future options. *Progress in Brain Research*, 1984, *63*, 375–398.

Miller, G.A., and Taylor, W.G. The perception of repeated bursts of noise. *Journal of the Acoustical Society of America*, 1948, *20*, 171–182.

Miller, J.D., Faull, K.F., Bowersox, F.S., and Dement, W.C. CNS monoamines and their metabolites in canine narcolepsy: A replication study. *Brain Research*, 1990, *509*, 169–171.

Miller, N.E. Understanding the use of animals in behavioral research: Some critical issues. *Annals of the New York Academy of Sciences*, 1983, *406*, 113–118.

Miller, N.E., Sampliner, R.I., and Woodrow, P. Thirst reducing effects of water by stomach fistula versus water by mouth, measured by both a consummatory and an instrumental response. *Journal of Comparative and Physiological Psychology*, 1957, *50*, 1–5.

Miller, V.M., and Best, P.J. Spatial correlates of hippocampal unit activity are altered by lesions of the fornix and entorhinal cortex. *Brain Research*, 1980, *194*, 311–323.

Milner, A.D., Perrett, D.I., Johnston, R.S., and Benson, P.J. Perception and action in "visual form agnosia." *Brain*, 1991, *114*, 405–428.

Milner, B. Memory disturbance after bilateral hippocampal lesions. In *Cognitive Processes and the Brain*, edited by P. Milner and S. Glickman. Princeton, N.J.: Van Nostrand, 1965.

Milner, B. Memory and the temporal regions of the brain. In *Biology of Memory*, edited by K.H. Pribram and D.E. Broadbent. New York: Academic Press, 1970.

Milner, B., Corkin, S., and Teuber, H.-L. Further analysis of the hippocampal amnesic syndrome: 14-year follow-up study of H.M. *Neuropsychologia*, 1968, *6*, 317–338.

Miselis, R.R., Weiss, M.L., and Shapiro, R.E. Modulation of the visceral neuraxis. In *Circumventricular Organs and Body Fluids*, edited by P.M. Gross. Boca Raton, Fla.: CRC Press, 1987.

Mishkin, M. Visual mechanisms beyond the striate cortex. In *Frontiers in Physiological Psychology*, edited by R.W. Russell. New York: Academic Press, 1966.

Mishkin, M. Memory in monkeys severely impaired by combined but not by separate removal of amygdala and hippocampus. *Nature*, 1978, *273*, 297–298.

Mishkin, M. A memory system in the monkey. *Philosophical Transactions of the Royal Society of London*, 1982, *298*, 85–95.

Mishkin, M., Ungerleider, L.G., and Macko, K. Object vision and spatial vision: Two cortical pathways. *Trends in Neuroscience*, 1983, *6*, 414–417.

Mitchell, J.E. Psychopharmacology of eating disorders. *Annals of the New York Academy of Sciences*, 1989, *575*, 41–49.

Mittleman, G., Whishaw, I.Q., Jones, G.H., Koch, M., and Robbins, T.W. Cortical, hippocampal, and striatal mediation of schedule-induced behaviors. *Behavioral Neuroscience*, 1990, *104*, 399–409.

Miyauchi, S., Takino, R., and Azakami, M. Evoked potentials during REM sleep reflect dreaming. *Electroencephalography and Clinical Neurophysiology*, 1990, *76*, 19–28.

Moghaddam, B., and Bunney, B.S. Differential effect of cocaine on extracellular dopamine levels in rat medial prefrontal cortex and nucleus accumbens: Comparison to amphetamine. *Synapse*, 1989, *4*, 156–161.

Mok, D., and Mogenson, G.J. Contribution of zona incerta to osmotically induced drinking in rats. *American Journal of Physiology*, 1986, *251*, R823–R832.

Moldin, S.O., Reich, T., and Rice, J.P. Current perspectives on the genetics of unipolar depression. *Behavioral Genetics*, 1991, *21*, 211–242.

Mollon, J.D. "Tho' she kneel'd in that place where they grew. . ." The uses and origins of primate colour vision. *Journal of Experimental Biology*, 1989, *146*, 21–38.

Moltz, H., Lubin, M., Leon, M., and Numan, M. Hormonal induction of maternal behavior in the ovariectomized nulliparous rat. *Physiology and Behavior*, 1970, *5*, 1373–1377.

Monaghan, D.T., and Cotman, C.W. Distribution of NMDA-sensitive L-^{3}H-glutamate binding sites in rat brain as determined by quantitative autoradiography. *Journal of Neuroscience*, 1985, *5*, 2909–2919.

Money, J. Components of eroticism in man: Cognitional rehearsals. In *Recent Advances in Biological Psychiatry*, edited by J. Wortis. New York: Grune & Stratton, 1960.

Money, J., and Ehrhardt, A. *Man & Woman, Boy & Girl*. Baltimore: Johns Hopkins University Press, 1972.

Money, J., Schwartz, M., and Lewis, V.G. Adult erotosexual status and fetal hormonal masculinization and demasculinization: 46,XX congenital virilizing adrenal hyperplasia and 46,XY androgen-insensitivity syndrome compared. *Psychoneuroendocrinology*, 1984, *9*, 405–414.

Montero, S., Fuentes, J.A., and Fernandez-Tome, P. Lesions of the ventral noradrenergic bundle prevent the rise in blood pressure induced by social deprivation stress in the rat. *Cellular and Molecular Neurobiology*, 1990, *10*, 497–505.

Mook, D. Some determinants of preference and aversion in the rat. *Annals of the New York Academy of Sciences*, 1969, *157*, 1158–1170.

Moore, B.O., and Deutsch, J.A. An antiemetic is antidotal to the satiety effects of cholecystokinin. *Nature*, 1985, *315*, 321–322.

Moore, C.L. Interaction of species-typical environmental and hormonal factors in sexual differentiation of behavior. *Annals of the New York Academy of Sciences*, 1986, *474*, 108–119.

Moore, C.L., Dou, H., and Juraska, J.M. Maternal stimulation affects the number of motor neurons in a sexually dimorphic nucleus of the lumbar spinal cord. *Brain Research*, 1992, *572*, 52–56.

Moore, R.Y., and Bernstein, M.E. Synaptogenesis in the rat suprachiasmatic nucleus demonstrated by electron microscopy and synapsin I immunoreactivity. *Journal of Neuroscience*, 1989, *9*, 2161–2162.

Moore, R.Y., Card, J.P., and Riley, J.N. The suprachiasmatic hypothalamic nucleus: Neuronal ultrastructure. *Neuroscience Abstracts*, 1980, *6*, 758.

Moore, R.Y., and Eichler, V.B. Loss of a circadian adrenal corticosterone rhythm following suprachiasmatic lesions in the rat. *Brain Research*, 1972, *42*, 201–206.

Moore-Gillon, M.J., and Fitzsimons, J.T. Pulmonary vein-atrial junction stretch receptors and the inhibition of drinking. *American Journal of Physiology*, 1982, *242*, R452–R457.

Morales, F.R., Boxer, P.A., and Chase, M.H. Behavioral state-specific inhibitory postsynaptic potentials impinge on cat lumbar motoneurons during active sleep. *Experimental Neurology*, 1987, *98*, 418–435.

Moran, T.H., Shnayder, L., Hostetler, A.M., and McHugh, P.R. Pylorectomy reduces the satiety action of cholecystokinin. *American Journal of Physiology*, 1989, *255*, R1059–R1063.

Morin, L.P., Blanchard, J., and Moore, R.Y. Intergeniculate leaflet and suprachiasmatic nucleus organization and connections in the golden hamster. *Visual Neuroscience*, 1992, *8*, 219–230.

Morrell, M.J. Sexual dysfunction in epilepsy. *Epilepsia*, 1991, *32*, S38–S45.

Morris, G.O., Williams, H.L., and Lubin, A. Misperception and disorientation during sleep deprivation. *Archives of General Psychiatry*, 1960, *2*, 247–254.

Morris, N.M., Udry, J.R., Khan-Dawood, F., and Dawood, M.Y. Marital sex frequency and midcycle female testosterone. *Archives of Sexual Behavior*, 1987, *16*, 27–37.

Morris, R.G.M., Anderson, E., Lynch, G., and Baudry, M. Selective impairment of learning and blockade of long-term potentiation by an *N*-methyl-D-aspartate receptor antagonist, AP5. *Nature*, 1986, *319*, 774–776.

Morris, R.G.M., Garrud, P., Rawlins, J.N.P., and O'Keefe, J. Place navigation impaired in rats with hippocampal lesions. *Nature*, 1982, *297*, 681–683.

Moscovitch, M., and Olds, J. Asymmetries in emotional facial expressions and their possible relation to hemispheric specialization. *Neuropsychologia*, 1982, *20*, 71–81.

Mountcastle, V.B. Modality and topographic properties of single neurons of cat's somatic sensory cortex. *Journal of Neurophysiology*, 1957, *20*, 408–434.

Mountcastle, V.B., Lynch, J.C., Georgopoulos, A., Sakata, H., and Acuna, C. Posterior parietal association cortex: Command functions for operations within extra-personal space. *Journal of Neurophysiology*, 1975, *38*, 871–908.

Moyer, J.R., Deyo, R.A., and Disterhoft, J.F. Hippocampectomy disrupts trace eye-blink conditioning in rabbits. *Behavioral Neuroscience*, 1990, *104*, 243–252.

Mukhametov, L.M. Sleep in marine mammals. In *Sleep Mechanisms*, edited by A.A. Borbély and J.L. Valatx. Munich: Springer-Verlag, 1984.

Muller, D., Buchs, P.-A., Stoppini, L., and Boddeke, H. Long-term potentiation, protein kinase C, and glutamate receptors. *Molecular Neurobiology*, 1991, *5*, 277–288.

Muller, D., Joly, M., and Lynch, G. Contributions of quisqualate and NMDA receptors to the induction and expression of LTP. *Science*, 1988, *242*, 1694–1697.

Muller, R.U., and Kubie, J.L. The effects of changes in the environment on the spatial firing of hippocampal complex-spike cells. *Journal of Neuroscience*, 1987, *7*, 1935–1950.

Munro, J.F., Stewart, I.C., Seidelin, P.H., Mackenzie, H.S., and Dewhurst, N.E. Mechanical treatment for obesity. *Annals of the New York Academy of Sciences*, 1987, *499*, 305–312.

Murray, E.A., Davidson, M., Gaffan, D., Olton, D.S., and Suomi, S. Effects of fornix transection and cingulate cortical ablation on spatial memory in rhesus monkeys. *Experimental Brain Research*, 1989, *74*, 173–186.

Nadeau, S.E. Impaired grammar with normal fluency and phonology. *Brain*, 1988, *111*, 1111–1137.

Naeser, M.A., Palumbo, C.L., Helm-Estabrooks, N., Stiassny-Eder, D., and Albert, M.L. Severe nonfluency in aphasia: Role of the medial subcallosal fasciculus and other white matter pathways in recovery of spontaneous speech. *Brain*, 1989, *112*, 1–38.

Nafe, J.P., and Wagoner, K.S. The nature of pressure adaptation. *Journal of General Psychology*, 1941, *25*, 323–351.

Naito, K., Osama, H., Ueno, R., Hayaishi, O., Honda, K., and Inoue, S. Suppression of sleep by prostaglandin synthesis inhibitors in unrestrained rats. *Brain Research*, 1988, *453*, 329–336.

Nakahara, D., Ozaki, N., Miura, Y., Miura, H., and Nagatsu, T. Increased dopamine and serotonin metabolism in rat nucleus accumbens produced by intracranial self-stimulation of medial forebrain bundle as measured by in vivo microdialysis. *Brain Research*, 1989, *495*, 178–181.

Naranjo, C.A., Poulos, C.X., Bremner, K.E., and Lanctot, K.L. Citalopram decreases desirability, liking, and consumption of alcohol in alcohol-dependent drinkers. *Clinical Pharmacology and Therapeutics*, 1992, *51*, 729–739.

Nathans, J., Piantanida, T.P., Eddy, R.L., Shows, T.B., and Hogness, D.S. Molecular genetics of inherited variation in human color vision. *Science*, 1986, *232*, 203–210.

Nauta, W.J.H. Hypothalamic regulation of sleep in rats: Experimental study. *Journal of Neurophysiology*, 1946, *9*, 285–316.

Nauta, W.J.H. Some efferent connections of the prefrontal cortex in the monkey. In *The Frontal Granular Cortex and Behavior*, edited by J.M. Warren and K. Akert. New York: McGraw-Hill, 1964.

Nelson, D.O., and Johnson, A.K. Subfornical organ projections to nucleus medianus: Electrophysiological evidence for angiotensin II synapses. *Federation Proceedings*, 1985, *44*, 1010.

Nermo-Lindquist, E., Kadekaro, M., Terrell, M.L., Nassar, J., Lekan, H., and Freeman, S. Atriopeptin prevents angiotensin II-stimulated glucose utilization in the subfornical organ. *Peptides*, 1990, *11*, 837–842.

Newman, E.A., and Evans, C.R. Human dream processes as analogous to computer programme clearance. *Nature*, 1965, *206*, 54.

Nicholl, C.S., and Russell, R.M. Analysis of animal rights literature reveals the underlying motives of the movement: Ammunition for counter offensive by scientists. *Endocrinology*, 1990, *127*, 985–989.

Nichols, D.G. Brown adipose tissue mitochondria. *Biochimica et Biophysica Acta*, 1979, *549*, 1–29.

Nichols, D.S., Thorn, B.E., and Berntson, G.G. Opiate and serotonergic mechanisms of stimulation-produced analgesia within the periaqueductal gray. *Brain Research Bulletin*, 1989, *22*, 717–724.

Nicolaïdis, S. Short-term and long-term regulation of energy balance. *Proceedings of the International Congress of Physiological Sciences*, 1974, *10*, 122–123.

Nicolaïdis, S. What determines food intake? The ischymetric theory. *NIPS*, 1987, *2*, 104–107.

Nicoll, R.A., Alger, B.E., and Nicoll, R.A. Enkephalin blocks inhibitory pathways in the vertebrate CNS. *Nature*, 1980, *287*, 22–25.

Niijima, A. Afferent impulse discharge from glucoreceptors in the liver of the guinea pig. *Annals of the New York Academy of Sciences*, 1969, *157*, 690–700.

Niijima, A. Glucose-sensitive afferent nerve fibers in the hepatic branch of the vagus nerve in the guinea pig. *Journal of Physiology*, 1982, *332*, 315–323.

Nilsson, O.G., Shapiro, M.L., Gage, F.H., Olton, D.S., and Björklund, A. Spatial learning and memory following fimbria-fornix transection and grafting of fetal septal neurons to the hippocampus. *Experimental Brain Research*, 1987, *67*, 195–215.

Nishino, S., Arrigoni, J., Valtier, D., Miller, J.D., Guilleminjault, C., Dement, W.C., and Mignot, E. Dopamine D_2 mechanisms in canine narcolepsy. *Journal of Neuroscience*, 1991, *11*, 2666–2671.

Noble, E.P. The D2 dopamine receptor gene: A review of association studies in alcoholism. *Behavioral Genetics*, 1993, *23*, 119–129.

Noirot, E. Selective priming of maternal responses by auditory and olfactory cues from mouse pups. *Developmental Psychobiology*, 1972, *5*, 371–387.

Norgren, R., and Grill, H. Brain-stem control of ingestive behavior. In *The Physiological Mechanisms of Motivation*, edited by D.W. Pfaff. New York: Springer-Verlag, 1982.

Nose, H., Morita, M., Yawata, T., and Morimoto, T. Continuous determination of blood volume on conscious rats during water and food intake. *Japanese Journal of Physiology*, 1986, *36*, 215–218.

Novin, D., Robinson, B.A., Culbreth, L.A., and Tordoff, M.G. Is there a role for the liver in the control of food intake? *American Journal of Clinical Nutrition*, 1983, *9*, 233–246.

Novin, D., VanderWeele, D.A., and Rezek, M. Hepatic-portal 2-deoxy-D-glucose infusion causes eating: Evidence for peripheral glucoreceptors. *Science*, 1973, *181*, 858–860.

Nowlis, G.H., and Frank, M. Qualities in hamster taste: Behavioral and neural evidence. In *Olfaction and Taste, Vol. 6*, edited by J. LeMagnen and P. MacLeod. Washington, D.C.: Information Retrieval, 1977.

Numan, M. Medial preoptic area and maternal behavior in the female rat. *Journal of Comparative and Physiological Psychology*, 1974, *87*, 746–759.

Numan, M., and Numan, M.J. Preoptic-brainstem connections and maternal behavior in rats. *Behavioral Neuroscience*, 1991, *105*, 1013–1029.

Numan, M., Rosenblatt, J.S., and Komisaruk, B.R. Medial preoptic area and onset of maternal behavior in the rat. *Journal of Comparative and Physiological Psychology*, 1977, *91*, 146–164.

Numan, M., and Smith, H.G. Maternal behavior in rats: Evidence for the involvement of preoptic projections to the ventral tegmental area. *Behavioral Neuroscience*, 1984, *98*, 712–727.

Oaknin, S., Rodriguez del Castillo, A., Guerra, M., Battaner, E., and Mas, M. Change in forebrain Na,K-ATPase activity and serum hormone levels during sexual behavior in male rats. *Physiology and Behavior*, 1989, *45*, 407–410.

Obál, F., Payne, L., Kapas, L., Opp, M., and Krueger, J.M. Inhibition of growth hormone-releasing factor suppresses both sleep and growth hormone secretion in the rat. *Brain Research*, 1991, *557*, 149–153.

O'Callaghan, E. Obstetric complications, the putative familial-sporadic distinction, and tardive dyskinesia in schizophrenia. *British Journal of Psychiatry*, 1990, *157*, 578–584.

O'Callaghan, E., Gibson, R., Colohan, H.A., Walshe, D., Buckley, P., Larkin, C., and Waddington, J.L. Season of birth in schizophrenia. Evidence for confinement of an excess of winter births to patients without a family history of mental disorder. *British Journal of Psychiatry*, 1991, *158*, 764–769.

O'Callaghan, E., Gibson, T., Colohan, H.A., Buckley, P., Walshe, D.G., Larkin, C., and Waddington, J.L. Risk of schizophrenia in adults born after obstetric complications and their association with early onset of illness: A controlled study. *British Medical Journal*, 1992, *305*, 1256–1259.

O'Dell, T.J., Hawkins, R.D., Kandel, E.R., and Arancio, O. Tests of the roles of two diffusible substances in long-term potentiation: Evidence for nitric oxide as a possible early retrograde messenger. *Proceedings of the National Academy of Sciences, USA*, 1991, *88*, 11285–11289.

O'Keefe, J., and Bouma, H. Complex sensory properties of certain amygdala units in the freely moving cat. *Experimental Neurology*, 1969, *23*, 384–398.

O'Keefe, J., and Dostrovsky, T. The hippocampus as a spatial map: Preliminary evidence from unit activity in the freely moving rat. *Brain Research*, 1971, *34*, 171–175.

O'Keefe, J., and Speakman, A. Single unit activity in the rat hippocampus during a spatial memory task. *Experimental Brain Research*, 1987, *68*, 1–27.

Olds, J. Commentary. In *Brain Stimulation and Motivation*, edited by E.S. Valenstein. Glenview, Ill.: Scott, Foresman, 1973.

Olds, J., and Milner, P. Positive reinforcement produced by electrical stimulation of septal area and other regions of rat brain. *Journal of Comparative and Physiological Psychology*, 1954, *47*, 419–427.

Olds, M.E., and Fobes, J.L. The central basis of motivation: Intracranial self-stimulation studies. *Annual Review of Psychology*, 1981, *32*, 523–574.

Olton, D.S. Memory functions and the hippocampus. In *Neurobiology of the Hippocampus*, edited by W. Siefert. New York: Academic Press, 1983.

Olton, D.S., Collison, C., and Werz, M.A. Spatial memory and radial arm maze performance in rats. *Learning and Motivation*, 1977, *8*, 289–314.

Olton, D.S., Givens, B.S., Markowska, A.L., Shapiro, M., and Golski, S. Mnemonic functions of the cholinergic septohippocampal system. In *Memory: Organization and Locus of Change*, edited by L.R. Squire, N.M. Weinberger, G. Lynch, and J.L. McGaugh. New York: Oxford University Press, 1991.

Olton, D.S., and Papas, B.C. Spatial memory and hippocampal function. *Neuropsychologia*, 1979, *17*, 669–682.

Olton, D.S., and Samuelson, R.J. Remembrance of places past: Spatial memory in rats. *Journal of Experimental Psychology: Animal Behavior Processes*, 1976, *2*, 97–116.

Oomura, Y. Significance of glucose, insulin and free fatty acid on the hypothalamic feeding and satiety neurons. In *Hunger: Basic Mechanisms and Clinical Implications*, edited by D. Novin, W. Wyrwicka, and G. Bray. New York: Raven Press, 1976.

Panksepp, J. Aggression elicited by electrical stimulation of the hypothalamus in albino rats. *Physiology and Behavior*, 1971, *6*, 321–329.

Panksepp, J. Oxytocin effects on emotional processes: Separation distress, social bonding, and relationships to psychiatric disorders. *Annals of the New York Academy of Sciences*, 1992, *652*, 243–252.

Papadimitriou, G.N., Christodoulou, G.N., Katsouyanni, K., and Stefanis, C.N. Therapy and prevention of affective illness by total sleep deprivation. *Journal of the Affective Disorders*, 1993, *27*, 107–116.

Papez, J.W. A proposed mechanism of emotion. *Archives of Neurology and Psychiatry*, 1937, *38*, 725–744.

Park, C.R., Johnson, L.H., Wright, J.H., and Bastel, H. Effect of insulin on transport of several hexoses and pentoses into cells of muscle and brain. *American Journal of Physiology*, 1957, *191*, 13–18.

Passingham, R.E. Premotor cortex and preparation for movement. *Experimental Brain Research*, 1988, *70*, 590–596.

Patterson, K., and Kay, J.A. How word-form dyslexics form words. Paper presented at the meeting of the British Psychological Society Conference on Reading, Exeter, England, 1980.

Pauls, D.L., and Leckman, J.F. The inheritance of Gilles de la Tourette's syndrome and associated behaviors. *New England Journal of Medicine*, 1986, *315*, 993–997.

Pavlides, C., Greenstein, Y.J., Grudman, M., and Winson, J. Long-term potentiation in the dentate gyrus is induced preferentially on the positive phase of theta rhythms. *Brain Research*, 1988, *439*, 383–387.

Peck, B.K., and Vanderwolf, C.H. Effects of raphe stimulation on hippocampal and neocortical activity and behaviour. *Brain Research*, 1991, *568*, 244–252.

Peck, J.W., and Blass, E.M. Localization of thirst and antidiuretic osmoreceptors by intracranial injections in rats. *American Journal of Physiology*, 1975, *5*, 1501–1509.

Penfield, W., and Jasper, H. *Epilepsy and the Functional Anatomy of the Human Brain*. Boston: Little, Brown & Co., 1954.

Penfield, W., and Milner, B. Memory deficit produced by bilateral lesions in the hippocampal zone. *American Medical Association Archives of Neurological Psychiatry*, 1958, *79*, 475–497.

Penfield, W., and Rasmussen, T. *The Cerebral Cortex of Man: A Clinical Study of Localization*. Boston: Little, Brown & Co., 1950.

Penick, S., and Solomon, P.R. Hippocampus, context, and conditioning. *Behavioral Neuroscience*, 1991, *105*, 611–617.

Pennington, B.F., Gilger, J.W., Pauls, D., Smith, S.A., Smith, S.D., and DeFries, J.C. Evidence for major gene transmission of developmental dyslexia. *Journal of the American Medical Association*, 1991, *266*, 1527–1534.

Perrett, D.I., Hietanen, J.K., Oram, M.W., and Benson, P.J. Organization and functions of cells responsive to faces in the temporal cortex. *Philosophical Transactions of the Royal Society of London [B]*, 1992, *335*, 23–30.

Perrett, D.I., Mistlin, A.J., Chitty, A.J., Harries, M.H., Newcombe, F., and de Haan, E. Neuronal mechanisms of face perception and their pathology. In *Physiological Aspects of Clinical Neuro-opthalmology*, edited by C. Kennard and F. Clifford Rose. London: Chapman and Hall, 1988.

Persky, H. Reproductive hormones, moods, and the menstrual cycle. In *Sex Differences in Behavior*, edited by R.C. Friedman, R.M. Richart, and R.L. Vande Wiele. New York: John Wiley & Sons, 1974.

Persky, H., Lief, H.I., Strauss, D., Miller, W.R., and O'Brien, C.P. Plasma testosterone level and sexual behavior of couples. *Archives of Sexual Behavior*, 1978, *7*, 157–173.

Pert, C.B, Snowman, A.M., and Snyder, S.H. Localization of opiate receptor binding in presynaptic membranes of rat brain. *Brain Research*, 1974, *70*, 184–188.

Petersen, S.E., Fox, P.T., Posner, M.I., Mintun, M., and Raichle, M.E. Positron emission tomographic studies of the processing of single words. *Journal of Cognitive Neuroscience*, 1989, *1*, 153–170.

Petersen, S.E., Fox, P.T., Snyder, A.Z., and Raichle, M.E. Activation of extrastriate and frontal cortical areas by visual words and word-like stimuli. *Science*, 1990, *249*, 1041–1044.

Petrides, M. Deficits in non-spatial conditional associative learning after periarcuate lesions in the monkey. *Behavioural Brain Research*, 1985a, *16*, 95–101.

Petrides, M. Deficits on conditional associative-learning tasks after frontal- and temporal-lobe lesions in man. *Neuropsychologia*, 1985b, *23*, 601–614.

Pfaff, D.W., and Keiner, M. Atlas of estradiol-concentrating cells in the central nervous system of the female rat. *Journal of Comparative Neurology*, 1973, *151*, 121–158.

Pfaff, D.W., and Sakuma, Y. Deficit in the lordosis reflex of female rats caused by lesions in the ventromedial nucleus of the hypothalamus. *Journal of Physiology*, 1979, *288*, 203–210.

Pfaus, J.G., Damsma, G., Nomikos, G.G., Wenkstern, D.G., Blaha, C.D., Phillips, A.G., and Fibiger, H.C. Sexual behavior enhances central dopamine transmission in the male rat. *Brain Research*, 1990, *530*, 345–348.

Phillips, D.P., and Farmer, M.E. Acquired word deafness, and the temporal grain of sound representation in the primary auditory cortex. *Behavioural Brain Research*, 1990, *40*, 85–94.

Phillips, M.I., and Felix, D. Specific angiotensin II receptive neurons in the cat subfornical organ. *Brain Research*, 1976, *109*, 531–540.

Phillips, R.G., and LeDoux, J.E. Differential contribution of amygdala and hippocampus to cued and contextual fear conditioning. *Behavioral Neuroscience*, 1992, *106*, 274–285.

Pickar, D., Breier, A., Hsiao, J.K., Doran, A.R., Wolkowitz, O.M., Pato, C.N., Konicki, P.E., and Potter, W.Z. Cerebrospinal fluid and plasma monoamine metabolites and their relation to psychosis: Implications for regional brain dysfunction in schziophrenia. *Archives of General Psychiatry*, 1990, *47*, 641–648.

Pilleri, G. The blind Indus dolphin, *Platanista indi. Endeavours*, 1979, *3*, 48–56.

Piven, J., Berthier, M.L., Starkstein, S.E., Nehme, E., Pearlson, G., and Folstein, S. Magnetic resonance imaging evidence for a defect of cerebral cortical development in autism. *American Journal of Psychiatry*, 1990, *147*, 734–739.

Piven, J., Nehme, E., Simon, J., Barta, P., Pearlson, G., and Folstein, S.E. Magnetic resonance imaging in autism: Measurement of the cerebellum, pons, and fourth ventricle. *Biological Psychiatry*, 1992, *31*, 491–504.

Pleim, E.T., and Barfield, R.J. Progesterone versus estrogen facilitation of female sexual behavior by intracranial administration to female rats. *Hormones and Behavior*, 1988, *22*, 150–159.

Poggio, G.F., and Poggio, T. The analysis of stereopsis. *Annual Review of Neuroscience*, 1984, *7*, 379–412.

Posluns, D. An analysis of chlorpromazine-induced suppression of the avoidance response. *Psychopharmacology*, 1962, *3*, 361–373.

Post, R.M., Leverich, G.S., Altshuler, L., and Mikalauskas, K. Lithium-discontinuation-induced refractoriness: Preliminary observations. *American Journal of Psychiatry*, 1992, *149*, 1727–1729.

Powers, J.B., and Winans, S.S. Vomeronasal organ: Critical role in mediating sexual behavior of the male hamster. *Science*, 1975, *187*, 961–963.

Price, C., Wise, R., Ramsay, S., Friston, K., Howard, D., Patterson, K., and Frackowiak, R. Regional response differences within the human auditory cortex when listening to words. *Neuroscience Letters*, 1992, *146*, 179–182.

Price, J. The genetics of depressive behavior. *British Journal of Psychiatry*, 1968, *2*, 37–45.

Price, R.A., and Gottesman, I.I. Body fat in identical twins reared apart: Roles for genes and environment. *Behavioral Genetics*, 1991, *21*, 1–7.

Pritchard, T.C., Hamilton, R.B., Morse, J.R., and Norgren, R. Projections of thalamic gustatory and lingual areas in the monkey, *Macaca fascicularis. Journal of Comparative Neurology*, 1986, *244*, 213–228.

Proctor, W.R., Soldo, B.L., Allan, A.M., and Dunwiddie, T.V. Ethanol enhances synaptically evoked GABAA receptor-mediated responses in cerebral cortical neurons in rat brain slices. *Brain Research*, 1992, *595*, 220–227.

Propping, P., Kruger, J., and Janah, A. Effect of alcohol on genetically determined variants of the normal electroencephalogram. *Psychiatry Research*, 1980, *2*, 85–98.

Propping, P., Kruger, J., and Mark, N. Genetic disposition to alcoholism: An EEG study in alcoholics and their relatives. *Human Genetics*, 1981, *59*, 51–59.

Prosser, R.A., and Gillette, M.U. Cyclic changes in cAMP concentration and phosphodiesterase activity in a mammalian circadian clock studied in vitro. *Brain Research*, 1991, *568*, 185–192.

Pucilowski, O., Plaznik, A., and Kostowski, W. Aggressive behavior inhibition by serotonin and quipazine injected into the amygdala in the rat. *Behavioural and Neural Biology*, 1985, *43*, 58–68.

Pycock, C.J., Kerwin, R.W., and Carter, C.J. Effects of lesion of cortical dopamine terminals on subcortical dopamine in rats. *Nature*, 1980, *286*, 74–77.

Quillen, E.W., Keil, L.C., and Reid, I.A. Effects of baroreceptor denervation on endocrine and drinking responses to caval constriction in dogs. *American Journal of Physiology*, 1990, *259*, R618–R626.

Quirion, R. Receptor sites for atrial natriuretic factors in brain and associated structures: An overview. *Cellular and Molecular Neurobiology*, 1989, *9*, 45–55.

Quirion, R., Dalpe, M., De Lean, A., Gutkowska, J., Cantin, M., and Genest, J. Atrial natriuretic factor (ANF) binding sites in brain and related structures. *Peptides*, 1984, *5*, 1167–1172.

Quirk, G.J., Muller, R.U., Kubie, J.L., and Ranck, J.B. The positional firing properties of medial entorhinal neurons: Description and comparison with hippocampal place cells. *Journal of Neuroscience*, 1992, *12*, 1945–1963.

Radke, K.J., Willis, L.R., Zimmerman, G.W., Weinberger, M.H., and Selkurt, E.E. Effects of histamine-receptor antagonists on histamine-stimulated renin secretion. *European Journal of Pharmacology*, 1986, *123*, 421–426.

Raffaele, K.C., and Olton, D.S. Hippocampal and amygdala involvement in working memory for nonspatial stimuli. *Behavioral Neuroscience*, 1988, *102*, 349–355.

Ragland, D.R., and Brand, R.J. Type A behavior and mortality from coronary heart disease. *New England Journal of Medicine*, 1988, *318*, 65–69.

Raine, A., Lencz, T., Reynolds, G.P., Harrison, G., Sheard, C., Medley, I., Reynolds, L.M., and Cooper, J.E. An evaluation of structural and functional prefrontal deficits in schizophrenia: MRI and neuropsychological measures. *Psychiatry Res Neuroimaging*, 1992, *45*, 123–137.

Rajendren, G., Dudley, C.A., and Moss, R.L. Role of the vomeronasal organ in the male-induced enhancement of sexual receptivity in female rats. *Neuroendocrinology*, 1990, *52*, 368–372.

Raleigh, M.J., McGuire, M.T., Brammer, G.L., Pollack, D.B., and Yuwiler, A. Serotonergic mechanisms promote dominance acquisition in adult male vervet monkeys. *Brain Research*, 1991, *559*, 181–190.

Ralph, M.R., Foster, R.G., Davis, F.C., and Menaker, M. Transplanted suprachiasmatic nucleus determines circadian period. *Science*, 1990, *247*, 975–978.

Ralph, M.R., and Lehman, M.N. Transplantation: A new tool in the analysis of the mammalian hypothalamic circadian pacemaker. *Trends in Neuroscience*, 1991, *14*, 362–366.

Ramirez, I. Why do sugars taste good? *Neuroscience and Biobehavioral Reviews*, 1990, *14*, 125–134.

Ramm, P., and Smith, C.T. Rates of cerebral protein synthesis are linked to slow wave sleep in the rat. *Physiology and Behavior*, 1990, *48*, 749–753.

Rampin, C., Cespuglio, R., Chastrette, N., and Jouvet, M. Immobilisation stress induces a paradoxical sleep rebound in rat. *Neuroscience Letters*, 1991, *126*, 113–118.

Ramsay, D.J., Rolls, B.J., and Wood, R.J. Thirst following water deprivation in dogs. *American Journal of Physiology*, 1977, *232*, R93–R100.

Rapoport, J.L. Recent advances in obsessive-compulsive disorder. *Neuropsychopharmacology*, 1991, *5*, 1–10.

Rapoport, J.L., Ryland, D.H., and Kriete, M. Drug treatment of canine acral lick: An animal model of obsessive-compulsive disorder. *Archives of General Psychiatry*, 1992, *49*, 517–521.

Ratcliff, G., and Newcombe, F. Object recognition: Some deductions from the clinical evidence. In *Normality and Pathology in Cognitive Functions*, edited by A.W. Ellis. London: Academic Press, 1982.

Ratnasuriya, R.H., Eisler, I., Szmukler, G.I., and Russell, G.F.M. Anorexia nervosa: Outcome and prognostic factors after 20 years. *British Journal of Psychiatry*, 1991, *158*, 495–502.

Rawson, N.E., Blum, H., Osbakken, M.D., and Friedman, M.I. Hepatic phosphate trapping, decreased ATP and increased feeding after 2,5-anhydro-D-mannitol. *American Journal of Physiology*, 1993, in press.

Rawson, N.E., Ulrich, P., and Friedman, M.I. The methionine analogue, L-ethionine, elicits feeding in rats. Paper presented at the Conference of the Society for the Study of Ingestive Behavior, Princeton, N.J., June 1992.

Raybin, J.B., and Detre, T.P. Sleep disorder and symptomatology among medical and nursing students. *Comprehensive Psychiatry*, 1969, *10*, 452–467.

Rea, M.M., Sweeney, J.A., Solomon, C.M., Walsh, V., and Frances, A. Changes in eye tracking during clinical stabilization in schizophrenia. *Psychiatry Research*, 1989, *28*, 31–39.

Reading, P.J., Dunnett, S.B., and Robbins, T.W. Dissociable roles of the ventral, medial and lateral striatum on the acquisition and performance of a complex visual stimulus-response habit. *Behavioural Brain Research*, 1991, *45*, 147–161.

Rechtschaffen, A., Bergmann, B.M., Everson, C.A., Kushida, C.A., and Gilliland, M.A. Sleep deprivation in the rat: X. Integration and discussion of the findings. *Sleep*, 1989, *12*, 68–87.

Rechtschaffen, A., Gilliland, M.A., Bergmann, B.M., and Winter, J.B. Physiological correlates of prolonged sleep deprivation in rats. *Science*, 1983, *221*, 182–184.

Rechtschaffen, A., Wolpert, E.A., Dement, W.C., Mitchell, S.A., and Fisher, C. Nocturnal sleep of narcoleptics. *Electroencephalography and Clinical Neurophysiology*, 1963, *15*, 599–609.

Rehkämper, G., Haase, E., and Frahm, H.D. Allometric comparison of brain weight and brain structure volumes in different breeds of the domestic pigeon, *Columbia livia f.d.* (fantails, homing pigeons, strassers). *Brain, Behavior and Evolution*, 1988, *31*, 141–149.

Reich, P., Geyer, S.J., and Karnovsky, M.L. Metabolism of brain during sleep and wakefulness. *Journal of Neurochemistry*, 1972, *19*, 487–497.

Reifman, A., and Wyatt, R.J. Lithium: A brake in the rising cost of mental illness. *Archives of General Psychiatry*, 1980, *37*, 385–388.

Reiman, E.M., Fusselman, M.J., Fox, P.T., and Raichle, M.E. Neuroanatomical correlates of anticipatory anxiety. *Science*, 1989, *243*, 1071–1074.

Reiman, E.M., Raichle, M., Robins, E., Butler, F.K., Herscovitch, P., Fox, P., and Perlmutter, J. The application of positron emission tomography to the study of panic disorder. *American Journal of Psychiatry*, 1986, *143*, 469–477.

Reinink, E., Bouhuys, N., Wirz-Justice, A., and van den Hoofdakker, R. Prediction of the antidepressant response to total sleep deprivation by diurnal variation of mood. *Psychiatry Research*, 1990, *32*, 113–124.

Reiss, A.L., and Freund, L. Behavioral phenotype of fragile X syndrome: DSM-III-R autistic behavior in male children. *American Journal of Medical Genetics*, 1992, *43*, 35–46.

Reppert, S.M., and Schwartz, W.J. The suprachiasmatic nuclei of the fetal rat: Characterization of a functional circadian clock using ^{14}C-labeled deoxyglucose. *Journal of Neuroscience*, 1984, *4*, 1677–1682.

Review Panel. Coronary-prone behavior and coronary heart disease: A critical review. *Circulation*, 1981, *673*, 1199–1215.

Reynecke, L., Allin, R., Russell, V.A., and Taljaard, J.J.F. Lack of effect of chronic desipramine treatment on dopaminergic activity in the nucleus accumbens of the rat. *Neurochemical Research*, 1989, *14*, 661–665.

Reynolds, D.V. Surgery in the rat during electrical analgesia induced by focal brain stimulation. *Science*, 1969, *164*, 444–445.

Reynolds, G.P. Beyond the dopamine hypothesis: The neurochemical pathology of schizophrenia. *British Journal of Psychiatry*, 1989, *155*, 315–316.

Rhees, R.W., Shryne, J.E., and Gorski, R.A. Termination of the hormone-sensitive period for differentiation of the sexually dimorphic nucleus of the preoptic area in male and female rats. *Developmental Brain Research*, 1990, *52*, 17–23.

Ricardo, J.A. Efferent connections of the subthalamic region in the rat. II. The zona incerta. *Brain Research*, 1981, *214*, 43–60.

Richmond, G., and Clemens, L. Ventromedial hypothalamic lesions and cholinergic control of female sexual behavior. *Physiology and Behavior*, 1988, *42*, 179–182.

Ridley, R.M., Thornley, H.D., Baker, H.F., and Fine, A. Cholinergic neural transplants into hippocampus restore learning ability in monkeys with fornix transections. *Experimental Brain Research*, 1991, *83*, 533–538.

Ris-Stalpers, C., Kuiper, G.G.J.M., Faber, P.W., Schweikert, H.U., Van Rooij, H.C.J., Zegers, N.D., Hodgins, M.B., Degenhart, H.J., Trapman, J., and Brinkmann, A.O. Aberrant splicing of androgen receptor mRNA results in synthesis of a nonfunctional receptor protein in a patient with androgen insensitivity. *Proceedings of the National Academy of Sciences*, 1990, *87*, 7866–7870.

Ritter, R.C., Brenner, L., and Yox, D.P. Participation of vagal sensory neurons in putative satiety signals from the upper gastrointestinal tract. In *Neuroanatomy and Physiology of Abdominal Vagal Afferents*, edited by S. Ritter, R.C. Ritter, and C.D. Barnes. Boca Raton, Fla.: CRC Press, 1992.

Ritter, R.C., Slusser, P.G., and Stone, S. Glucoreceptors controlling feeding and blood glucose: Location in the hindbrain. *Science*, 1981, *213*, 451–453.

Ritter, S., Calingasan, N.Y., Hutton, B., and Dinh, T.T. Cooperation of vagal and central neural systems in monitoring metabolic events controlling feeding behavior. In *Neuroanatomy and Physiology of Abdominal Vagal Afferents*, edited by S. Ritter, R.C. Ritter, and C.D. Barnes. Boca Raton, Fla.: CRC Press, 1992.

Ritter, S., and Taylor, J.S. Capsaicin abolishes lipoprivic but not glucoprivic feeding in rats. *American Journal of Physiology*, 1989, *256*, R1232–R1239.

Ritter, S., and Taylor, J.S. Vagal sensory neurons are required for lipoprivic but not glucoprivic feeding in rats. *American Journal of Physiology*, 1990, *258*, R1395–R1401.

Ritvo, E.R., Mason-Brothers, A., Freeman, B.J., Pingree, C., Jenson, W.R., McMahon, W.M., Petersen, P.B., and Jorde, L.B. The UCLA-University of Utah epidemiologic survey of autism: The etiologic role of rare diseases. *American Journal of Psychiatry*, 1990, *147*, 1614–1621.

Rizzo, M., and Robin, D.A. Simultanagnosia: A defect of sustained attention yields insights on visual information processing. *Neurology*, 1990, *40*, 447–455.

Robbins, L.N., Helzer, J.E., Weissman, M.M., Orvaschel, H., Gruenberg, E., Burke, J.D., and Regier, D.A. Lifetime prevalence of specific psychiatric disorders in three sites. *Archives of General Psychiatry*, 1984, *41*, 949–958.

Robbins, T.W., and Koob, G.F. Selective disruption of displacement behaviour by lesions of the mesolimbic dopamine system. *Nature*, 1980, *285*, 409–412.

Roberts, W.W., and Robinson, T.C.L. Relaxation and sleep induced by warming of preoptic region and anterior hypothalamus in cats. *Experimental Neurology*, 1969, *25*, 282–294.

Robertson, G.S., Pfaus, J.G., Atkinson, L.J., Matsumura, H., Phillips, A.G., and Fibiger, H.C. Sexual behavior increases c-fos expression in the forebrain of the male rat. *Brain Research*, 1991, *564*, 352–357.

Robinson, D.L., McClurkin, J.W., Kurtzman, C., and Petersen, S.E. Visual responses of pulvinar and collicular neurons during eye movements of awake, trained macaques. *Journal of Neurophysiology*, 1991, *66*, 485–496.

Robinson, D.L., and Petersen, S.E. The pulvinar and visual salience. *Trends in Neuroscience*, 1992, *15*, 127–132.

Robinson, G.B., and Racine, R.J. Heterosynaptic interactions between septal and entorhinal inputs to the dentate gyrus: Long-term potentiation effects. *Brain Research*, 1982, *249*, 162–166.

Robinson, T.E., Jurson, P.A., Bennett, J.A., and Bentgen, K.M. Persistent sensitization of dopamine neurotransmission in ventral striatum (nucleus accumbens) produced by prior experience with (+)-amphetamine: A microdialysis study in freely moving rats. *Brain Research*, 1988, *462*, 211–222.

Rodin, J., Schank, D., and Striegel-Moore, R. Psychological features of obesity. *Medical Clinics of North America*, 1989, *73*, 47–66.

Rodman, H.R., Gross, C.G., and Albright, T.D. Afferent basis of visual response properties in area MT of the macaque. I. Effects of striate cortex removal. *Journal of Neuroscience*, 1989, *9*, 2033–2050.

Rodman, H.R., Gross, C.G., and Albright, T.D. Afferent basis of visual response properties in area MT of the macaque. II. Effects of superior colliculus removal. *Journal of Neuroscience*, 1990, *10*, 1154–1164.

Roeltgen, D.P., Rothi, L.H., and Heilman, K.M. Linguistic semantic apraphia: A dissociation of the lexical spelling system from semantics. *Brain and Language*, 1986, *27*, 257–280.

Roffwarg, H.P., Dement, W.C., Muzio, J.N., and Fisher, C. Dream imagery: Relation to rapid eye movements of sleep. *Archives of General Psychiatry*, 1962, *7*, 235–258.

Roffwarg, H.P., Muzio, J.N., and Dement, W.C. Ontogenetic development of human sleep-dream cycle. *Science*, 1966, *152*, 604–619.

Rogers, M.P., Trentham, D.E., McCune, W.J., Ginsberg, B.I., Rennke, H.G., Reike, P., and David, J.R. Effect of psychological stress on the induction of arthritis in rats. *Arthritis and Rheumatology*, 1980, *23*, 1337–1342.

Roland, P.E. Metabolic measurements of the working frontal cortex in man. *Trends in Neurosciences*, 1984, *7*, 430–435.

Rolls, B.J., Rowe, E.A., Rolls, E.T., Kingston, B., Megson, A., and Gunary, R. Variety in a meal enhances food intake in man. *Physiology and Behavior*, 1981, *26*, 215–221.

Rolls, E.T. Feeding and reward. In *The Neural Basis of Feeding and Reward*, edited by B.G. Hobel and D. Novin. Brunswick, Maine: Haer Institute, 1982.

Rolls, E.T. Neuronal activity related to the control of feeding. In *Neural and Humoral Controls of Food Intake*, edited by R. Ritter and S. Ritter. New York: Academic Press, 1986.

Rolls, E.T. Functions of the primate hippocampus in spatial processing and memory. In *Neurobiology of Comparative Cognition*, edited by D.S. Olton and R.P. Kesner. Hillsdale, N.J.: Lawrence Erlbaum Associates, 1989.

Rolls, E.T., and Baylis, G.C. Size and contrast have only small effects on the responses to faces of neurons in the cortex of the superior temporal sulcus of the monkey. *Experimental Brain Research*, 1986, *65*, 38–48.

Rolls, E.T., Baylis, G.C., Hasselmo, M.E., and Nalwa, V. The effect of learning on the face selective responses of neurons in the cortex in the superior temporal sulcus of the monkey. *Experimental Brain Research*, 1989, *76*, 153–164.

Rolls, E.T., Rolls, B.J., Kelly, P.H., Shaw, S.G., Wood, R.J., and Dale, R. The relative attenuation of self-stimulation, eating and drinking produced by dopamine-receptor blockade. *Psychopharmacologia*, 1974, *38*, 219–230.

Romero, P.R., Beltramino, C.A., and Carrer, H.F. Participation of the olfactory system in the control of approach behavior of the female rat to the male. *Physiology and Behavior*, 1990, *47*, 685–690.

Rose, G. Physiological and behavioral characteristics of dentate granule cells. In *Neurobiology of the Hippocampus*, edited by W. Seifert. London: Academic Press, 1983.

Rose, G.A., and Williams, R.T. Metabolic studies of large and small eaters. *British Journal of Nutrition*, 1961, *15*, 1–9.

Rose, J.D. Changes in hypothalamic neuronal function related to hormonal induction of lordosis in behaving hamsters. *Physiology and Behavior*, 1990, *47*, 1201–1212.

Roselli, C.E., Handa, R.J., and Resko, J.A. Quantitative distribution of nuclear androgen receptors in microdissected areas of the rat brain. *Neuroendocrinology*, 1989, *49*, 449–453.

Rosén, I., and Asanuma, H. Peripheral inputs to the forelimb area of the monkey motor cortex: Input-output relations. *Experimental Brain Research*, 1972, *14*, 257–273.

Rosen, J.B., et al. Unpublished results cited by Davis, M. The role of the amygdala in fear-potentiated startle: Implications for animal models of anxiety. *Trends in Pharmacological Sciences*, 1992, *13*, 35–41.

Rosenblatt, J.S., and Aronson, L.R. The decline of sexual behavior in male cats after castration with special reference to the role of prior sexual experience. *Behaviour*, 1958a, *12*, 285–338.

Rosenblatt, J.S., and Aronson, L.R. The influence of experience on the behavioural effects of androgen in prepuberally castrated male cats. *Animal Behaviour*, 1958b, *6*, 171–182.

Rosenman, R.H., Brand, R.J., Jenkins, C.D., Friedman, M., Straus, R., and Wurm, M. Coronary heart disease in the Western Collaborative Group Study: Final follow-up experience of 8 $1/2$ years. *Journal of the American Medical Association*, 1975, *233*, 872–877.

Rosenthal, D. A program of research on heredity in schizophrenia. *Behavioral Science*, 1971, *16*, 191–201.

Rosenthal, N.E., Sack, D.A., James, S.P., Parry, B.L., Mendelson, W.B., Tamarkin, L., and Wehr, T.A. Seasonal affective disorder and phototherapy. *Annals of the New York Academy of Sciences*, 1985, *453*, 260–269.

Rosser, A.E., and Keverne, E.B. The importance of central noradrenergic neurons in the formation of an olfactory memory in the prevention of pregnancy block. *Neuroscience*, 1985, *16*, 1141–1147.

Roth, W.T., Margraf, J., Ehlers, A., Taylor, C.B., Maddock, R.J., Davies, S., and Agras, W.S. Stress test reactivity in panic disorder. *Archives of General Psychiatry*, 1992, *49*, 301–310.

Rothman, S.M., and Olney, J.W. Excitotoxicity and the NMDA receptor. *Trends in Neurosciences*, 1987, *10*, 299–302.

Rothwell, N.J., and Stock, M.J. A role for brown adipose tissue in diet-induced thermogenesis. *Nature*, 1979, *281*, 31–35.

Routtenberg, A. "Self-starvation" of rats living in activity wheels: Adaptation effects. *Journal of Comparative Psychology*, 1968, *66*, 234–238.

Routtenberg, A., and Malsbury, C. Brainstem pathways of reward. *Journal of Comparative and Physiological Psychology*, 1969, *68*, 22–30.

Roy, A., De Jong, J., and Linnoila, M. Cerebrospinal fluid monoamine metabolites and suicidal behavior in depressed patients. *Archives of General Psychiatry*, 1989, *46*, 609–612.

Rozin, P., and Kalat, J.W. Specific hungers and poison avoidance as adaptive specializations of learning. *Psychological Review*, 1971, *78*, 459–486.

Rubin, B.S., and Barfield, R.J. Priming of estrous responsiveness by implants of 17B-estradiol in the ventromedial hypothalamic nucleus of female rats. *Endocrinology*, 1980, *106*, 504–509.

Rubin, P., Holm, S., Friberg, L., Videbech, P., Andersen, H.S., Bendsen, B.B., Stromso, N., Larsen, J.K., Lassen, N.A., and Hemmingsen, R. Altered modulation of prefrontal and subcortical brain activity in newly diagnosed schizophrenia and schizophreniform disorder: A regional cerebral blood flow study. *Archives of General Psychiatry*, 1991, *48*, 987–995.

Rubin, R.T., Villanueva-Meyer, J., Ananth, J., Trajmar, P.G., and Mena, I. Regional xenon 133 cerebral blood flow and cerebral technetium 99m HMPAO uptake in unmedicated patients with obsessive-compulsive disorder and matched normal control subjects: Determination by high-resolution single-photon emission computed tomography. *Archives of General Psychiatry*, 1992, *49*, 695–702.

Rudy, J.W., and Sutherland, R.J. The hippocampal formation is necessary for rats to learn and remember configural discriminations. *Behavioural Brain Research*, 1989, *34*, 97–109.

Ruggero, M.A. Responses to sound of the basilar membrane of the mammalian cochlea. *Current Opinion in Neurobiology*, 1992, *2*, 449–456.

Rumelhart, D.E., McClelland, J.L., and the PDP Research Group. *Parallel Distributed Processing: Explorations in the Microstructure of Cognition*. Cambridge, Mass.: MIT Press, 1986.

Rumsey, J.M., Andreason, P., Zametkin, A.J., Aquino, T., King, A.C., Hamburger, S.D., Pikus, A., Rapoport, J.L., and Cohen, R.M. Failure to activate the left temporoparietal cortex in dyslexia: An oxygen 15 positron emission tomographic study. *Archives of Neurology*, 1992, *49*, 527–534.

Rusak, B., and Groos, G. Suprachiasmatic stimulation phase shifts rodent circadian rhythms. *Science*, 1982, *215*, 1407–1409.

Rusak, B., McNaughton, L., Robertson, H.A., and Hunt, S.P. Circadian variation in photic regulation of immediate-early gene mRNAs in rat suprachiasmatic nucleus cells. *Molecular Brain Research*, 1992, *14*, 124–130.

Rusak, B., Meijer, J.H., and Harrington, M.E. Hamster circadian rhythms are phase-shifted by electrical stimulation of the geniculohypothalamic tract. *Brain Research*, 1989, *493*, 283–291.

Rusak, B., and Morin, L.P. Testicular responses to photoperiod are blocked by lesions of the suprachiasmatic nuclei in golden hamsters. *Biology of Reproduction*, 1976, *15*, 366–374.

Rusak, B., Robertson, H.A., Wisden, W., and Hunt, S.P. Light pulses that shift rhythms induce gene expression in the suprachiasmatic nucleus. *Science*, 1990, *248*, 1237–1240.

Russchen, F.T., Amaral, D.G., and Price, J.L. The afferent connections of the substantia innominata in the monkey, *Macaca fascicularis*. *Journal of Comparative Neurology*, 1986, *242*, 1–27.

Russek, M. Hepatic receptors and the neurophysiological mechanisms controlling feeding behavior. In *Neurosciences Research, Vol. 4*, edited by S. Ehrenpreis. New York: Academic Press, 1971.

Russell, G.F.M., and Treasure, J. The modern history of anorexia nervosa: An interpretation of why the illness has changed. *Annals of the New York Academy of Sciences*, 1989, *575*, 13–30.

Russell, M.J. Human olfactory communication. *Nature*, 1976, *260*, 520–522.

Russell, M.J., Switz, G.M., and Thompson, K. Olfactory influences on the human menstrual cycle. Paper presented at the meeting of the American Association for the Advancement of Science, San Francisco, June 1977.

Rutter, M. Cognitive deficits in the pathogenesis of autism. *Journal of Child Psychology and Psychiatry*, 1983, *24*, 513–531.

Ryback, R.S., and Lewis, O.F. Effects of prolonged bed rest on EEG sleep patterns in young, healthy volunteers. *Electroencephalography and Clinical Neurophysiology*, 1971, *31*, 395–399.

Saayman, G.S. Aggressive behaviour in free-ranging chacma baboons (*Papio ursinus*). *Journal of Behavioral Science*, 1971, *1*, 77–83.

Sachar, E.J., and Baron, M. The biology of affective disorders. *Annual Review of Neuroscience*, 1979, *2*, 505–518.

Sackheim, H.A., and Gur, R.C. Lateral asymmetry in intensity of emotional expression. *Neuropsychologia*, 1978, *16*, 473–482.

Saffran, E.M., Marin, O.S.M., and Yeni-Komshian, G.H. An analysis of speech perception in word deafness. *Brain and Language*, 1976, *3*, 209–228.

Saffran, E.M., Schwartz, M.F., and Marin, O.S.M. Evidence from aphasia: Isolating the components of a production model. In *Language Production*, edited by B. Butterworth. London: Academic Press, 1980.

Sahu, A., Kalra, P.S., and Kalra, S.P. Food deprivation and ingestion induce reciprocal changes in neuropeptide Y concentrations in the paraventricular nucleus. *Peptides*, 1988, *9*, 83–86.

Saint-Cyr, J.A., Taylor, A.E., and Lang, A.E. Procedural learning and neostriatal dysfunction in man. *Brain*, 1988, *111*, 941–959.

Saitoh, K., Maruyama, N., and Kudoh, M. Sustained response of auditory cortex units in the cat. In *Brain Mechanisms of Sensation*, edited by Y. Katsuki, R. Norgren, and M. Sato. New York: John Wiley & Sons, 1981.

Sakai, F., Meyer, J.S., Karacan, I., Derman, S., and Yamamoto, M. Normal human sleep: Regional cerebral haemodynamics. *Annals of Neurology*, 1979, *7*, 471–478.

Sakai, K. Some anatomical and physiological properties of pontomesencephalic tegmental neurons with special reference to the PGO waves and postural atonia during paradoxical sleep in the cat. In *The Reticular Formation Revisited*, edited by J.A. Hobson and M.A. Brazier. New York: Raven Press, 1980.

Sakai, K. Anatomical and physiological basis of paradoxical sleep. In *Brain Mechanisms of Sleep*, edited by D. McGinty, A. Morrison, R.R. Drucker-Colín, and P.L. Parmeggiani. New York: Spectrum, 1985.

Sakai, K., and Jouvet, M. Brain stem PGO-on cells projecting directly to the cat dorsal lateral geniculate nucleus. *Brain Research*, 1980, *194*, 500–505.

Sakai, K., and Miyashita, Y. Neural organization for the long-term memory of paired associates. *Nature*, 1991, *354*, 152–155.

Sakai, R.R., Chow, S.Y., Epstein, A.N. Peripheral angiotensin II is not the cause of sodium appetite in the rat. *Appetite*, 1990 *15*, 161–170.

Sakuma, Y., and Pfaff, D.W. Facilitation of female reproductive behavior from mesencephalic central grey in the rat. *American Journal of Physiology*, 1979a, *237*, R278–R284.

Sakuma, Y., and Pfaff, D.W. Mesencephalic mechanisms for integration of female reproductive behavior in the rat. *American Journal of Physiology*, 1979b, *237*, R285–R290.

Sakuma, Y., and Pfaff, D.W. Convergent effects of lordosis-relevant somatosensory and hypothalamic influences on central gray cells in the rat mesencephalon. *Experimental Neurology*, 1980a, *70*, 269–281.

Sakuma, Y., and Pfaff, D.W. Excitability of female rat central gray cells with medullary projections: Changes produced by hypothalamic stimulation and estrogen treatment. *Journal of Neurophysiology*, 1980b, *44*, 1012–1023.

Salamone, J.D. Dopaminergic involvement in activational aspects of motivation: Effects of haloperidol on schedule-induced activity, feeding, and foraging in rats. *Psychobiology*, 1988, *16*, 196–206.

Salamone, J.D., Steinpreis, R.E., McCullough, L.D., Smith, P., Grebel, D., and Mahan, K. Haloperidol and nucleus accumbens dopamine depletion suppress lever pressing for food but increase free food consumption in a novel food choice procedure. *Psychopharmacology* (*Berlin*), 1991, *104*, 515–521.

Saller, C.F., and Stricker, E.M. Hyperphagia and increased growth in rats after intraventricular injection of 5,7-dihydroxytryptamine. *Science*, 1976, *192*, 385–387.

Salzman, C.D., Murasugi, C.M., Britten, K.H., and Newsome, W.T. Microstimulation in visual area MT: Effects on direction discrimination performance. *Journal of Neuroscience*, 1992, *12*, 2331–2355.

Sanacora, G., Finkelstein, J.A., and White, J.D. Developmental aspect of differences in hypothalamic preproneuropeptide Y messenger ribonucleic acid content in lean and genetically obese Zucker rats. *Journal of Neuroendocrinology*, 1992, *4*, 353–357.

Sananes, C.B., and Campbell, B.A. Role of the central nucleus of the amygdala in olfactory heart rate conditioning. *Behavioral Neuroscience*, 1989, *103*, 519–525.

Sananes, C.B., and Davis, M. N-methyl-D-aspartate lesions of the lateral and basolateral nuclei of the amygdala block fear-potentiated startle and shock sensitization of startle. *Behavioral Neuroscience*, 1992, *106*, 72–80.

Sapolsky, R. Glucocorticoid toxicity in the hippocampus: Reversal by supplementation with brain fuels. *Journal of Neuroscience*, 1986, *6*, 2240–2244.

Sapolsky, R.M. Neuroendocrinology of the stress-response. In *Behavioral Endocrinology*, edited by J.B. Becker, S.M. Breedlove, and D. Crews. Cambridge, Mass.: MIT Press, 1992.

Sapolsky, R.M., Krey, L.C., and McEwen, B.S. The neuroendocrinology of stress and aging: The glucocorticoid cascade hypothesis. *Endocrine Reviews*, 1986, *7*, 284–301.

Sassenrath, E.N., Powell, T.E., and Hendrickx, A.G. Perimenstrual aggression in groups of female rhesus monkeys. *Journal of Reproduction and Fertility*, 1973, *34*, 509–511.

Sato, M. Acute exacerbation of methamphetamine psychosis and lasting dopaminergic supersensitivity—a clinical survey. *Psychopharmacology Bulletin*, 1986, *22*, 751–756.

Sato, M., Chen, C.-C., Akiyama, K., and Otsuki, S. Acute exacerbation of paranoid psychotic state after long-term abstinence in patients with previous methamphetamine psychosis. *Biological Psychiatry*, 1983, *18*, 429–440.

Sawchenko, P.E., Gold, R.M., and Leibowitz, S.F. Evidence for vagal involvement in the eating elicited by adrenergic stimulation of the paraventricular nucleus. *Brain Research*, 1981, *225*, 249–269.

Sawchenko, P.E., Swanson, L.W., Grzanna, R., Howe, P.R.C., Bloom, S.R., and Polak, J.M. Colocalization of neuropeptide Y immunoreactivity in brain stem catecholaminergic neurons that project to the paraventricular nucleus of the hypothalamus. *Journal of Comparative Neurology*, 1985, *241*, 138–153.

Scheel-Krüger, J., and Willner, P. The mesolimbic system: Principles of operation. In *The Mesolimbic Dopamine System: From Motivation to Action*, edited by P. Willner and J. Scheel-Krüger. Chichester, England: John Wiley & Sons, 1991.

Schein, S.J., and Desimone, R. Spectral properties of V4 neurons in the macaque. *Journal of Neuroscience*, 1990, *10*, 3369–3389.

Schenck, C.H., Bundlie, S.R., Ettinger, M.G., and Mahowald, M.W. Chronic behavioral disorders of human REM sleep: A new category of parasomnia. *Sleep*, 1986, *9*, 293–308.

Schenck, C.H., and Mahowald, M.W. Motor dyscontrol in narcolepsy: Rapid-eye-movement (REM) sleep without atonia and REM sleep behavior disorder. *Annals of Neurology*, 1992, *32*, 3–10.

Schenkel, E., and Siegel, J.M. REM sleep without atonia after lesions of the medial medulla. *Neuroscience Letters*, 1989, *98*, 159–165.

Scherschlicht, R., Polc, P., Schneeberger, J., Steiner, M., and Haefely, W. Selective suppression of rapid eye movement sleep (REMS) in cats by typical and atypical antidepressants. In *Typical and Atypical Antidepressants: Molecular Mechanisms*, edited by E. Costa and G. Racagni. New York: Raven Press, 1982.

Schiffman, P.L., Westlake, R.E., Santiago, T.V., and Edelman, N.H. Ventilatory control in parents of victims of the sudden infant death syndrome. *New England Journal of Medicine*, 1980, *302*, 486–491.

Schiffman, S.S., Lockhead, E., and Maes, F.W. Amiloride reduces the taste intensity of Na^+ and Li^+ salts and sweeteners. *Proceedings of the National Academy of Sciences, USA*, 1983, *80*, 6136–6140.

Schiller, P.H. The ON and OFF channels of the visual system. *Trends in Neuroscience*, 1992, *15*, 86–92.

Schiller, P.H., and Malpeli, J.G. Properties and tectal projections of monkey retinal ganglion cells. *Journal of Neurophysiology*, 1977, *40*, 428–445.

Schiller, P.H., Sandell, J.H., and Maunsell, J.H.R. Functions of the ON and OFF channels of the visual system. *Nature*, 1986, *322*, 824–825.

Schleifer, S.J., Keller, S.E., Camerino, M., Thornton, J.C., and Stein, M. Suppression of lymphocyte stimulation following bereavement. *Journal of the American Medical Association*, 1983, *15*, 374–377.

Schulkin, J., Marini, J., and Epstein, A.N. A role for the medial region of the amygdala in mineralocorticoid-induced salt hunger. *Behavioral Neuroscience*, 1989, *103*, 178–185.

Schumacher, M., Coirini, H., Frankfurt, M., and McEwen, B.S. Localized actions of progesterone in hypothalamus involve oxytocin. *Proceedings of the National Academy of Sciences, USA*, 1989, *86*, 6798–6801.

Schumacher, M., Coirini, H., Pfaff, D.W., and McEwen, B.S. Behavioral effects of progesterone associated with rapid modulation of oxytocin receptors. *Science*, 1990, *250*, 691–694.

Schuman, E.R., and Madison, D.V. A requirement for the intercellular messenger nitric oxide in long-term potentiation. *Science*, 1991, *254*, 1503–1506.

Schuster, C.R., and Balster, R.L. The discriminative stimulus properties of drugs. *Advances in Behavioral Pharmacology*, 1977, *1*, 85–138.

Schwartz, D.H., Hernandez, L., and Hoebel, B.G. Serotonin release in lateral and medial hypothalamus during feeding and its anticipation. *Brain Research Bulletin*, 1990, *25*, 797–802.

Schwartz, M.F., Marin, O.S.M., and Saffran, E.M. Dissociations of language function in dementia: A case study. *Brain and Language*, 1979, *7*, 277–306.

Schwartz, M.F., Saffran, E.M., and Marin, O.S.M. The word order problem in agrammatism. I. Comprehension. *Brain and Language*, 1980, *10*, 249–262.

Schwartz, W.J., and Gainer H. Suprachiasmatic nucleus: Use of ^{14}C-labelled deoxyglucose uptake as a functional marker. *Science*, 1977, *197*, 1089–1091.

Schwartz, W.J., Gross, R.A., and Morton, M.T. The suprachiasmatic nuclei contain a tetrodotoxin-resistant circadian pacemaker. *Proceedings of the National Academy of Sciences, USA*, 1987, *84*, 1694–1698.

Schwartz, W.J., Reppert, S.M., Eagan, S.M., and Moore-Ede, M.C. In vivo metabolic activity of the suprachiasmatic nuclei: A comparative study. *Brain Research*, 1983, *274*, 184–187.

Schwarzkopf, S.B., Nasrallah, H.A., Olson, S.C., Coffman, J.A., and McLaughlin, J.A. Perinatal complications and genetic loading in schizophrenia: Preliminary findings. *Psychiatry Research*, 1989, *27*, 233–239.

Schwartzman, R.J., Alexander, G.M., Grothusen, J.R., and Stahl, S. CNS glucose metabolic changes in the stages of the MPTP primate model of Parkinson's disease. *Neurology*, 1987, *37*, 338.

Scifo, R., Batticane, N., Quattropani, M.C., Spoto, G., and Marchetti, B. A double-blind trial with naltrexone in autism. *Brain Dysfunctions*, 1991, *4*, 301–307.

Sclafani, A., and Aravich, P.F. Macronutrient self-selection in three forms of hypothalamic obesity. *American Journal of Physiology*, 1983, *244*, R686–R694.

Sclafani, A., and Nissenbaum, J.W. Robust conditioned flavor preference produced by intragastric starch infusions in rats. *American Journal of Physiology*, 1988, *255*, R672–R675.

Scott, T.R., and Plata-Salaman, C.R. Coding of taste quality. In *Smell and Taste in Health and Disease*, edited by T.N. Getchell. New York: Raven Press, 1991.

Scott, T.R., Yaxley, S., Sienkiewicz, Z.J., and Rolls, E.T. Gustatory responses in the nucleus tractus solitarius of the alert cynomolgus monkey. *Journal of Neurophysiology*, 1986, *55*, 182–200.

Scoville, W.B., and Milner, B. Loss of recent memory after bilateral hippocampal lesions. *Journal of Neurology, Neurosurgery and Psychiatry*, 1957, *20*, 11–21.

Seagraves, M.A., Goldberg, M.E., Deny, S., Bruce, C.J., Ungerleider, L.G., and Mishkin, M. The role of striate cortex in the guidance of eye movements in the monkey. *The Journal of Neuroscience*, 1987, *7*, 3040–3058.

Sedvall, G., Fyrö, B., Gullberg, B., Nybäck, H., Wiesel, F.-A., and Wode-Helgodt, B. Relationship in healthy volunteers between concentrations of monoamine metabolites in cerebrospinal fluid and family history of psychiatric morbidity. *British Journal of Psychiatry*, 1980, *136*, 366–374.

Seeman, P. Dopamine receptor sequences. Therapeutic levels of neuroleptics occupy D2 receptors, clozapine occupies D4. *Neuropsychopharmacology*, 1992, *7*, 261–284.

Segal, K.R., and Pi-Sunyer, F.X. Exercise and obesity. *Medical Clinics of North America*, 1989, *73*, 217–236.

Selye, H. *The Stress of Life*. New York: McGraw-Hill, 1976.

Selye, H., and Tuchweber, B. Stress in relation to aging and disease. In *Hypothalamus, Pituitary and Aging*, edited by A. Everitt and J. Burgess. Springfield, Ill.: Charles C. Thomas, 1976.

Semenza, C., Cipolotti, L., and Denes, G. Reading aloud in jargonaphasia: An unusual dissociation in speech output. *Journal of Neurology, Neurosurgery, and Psychiatry*, 1992, *55*, 205–208.

Semenza, C., and Zettin, M. Evidence from aphasia for the role of proper names as pure referring expressions. *Nature*, 1989, *342*, 678–679.

Sergent, J., Ohta, S., and MacDonald, B. Functional neuroanatomy of face and object processing. A positron emission tomography study. *Brain*, 1992, *115*, 15–36.

Sergent, J., and Signoret, J.-L. Functional and anatomical decomposition of face processing: Evidence from prosopagnosia and PET study of normal subjects. *Philosophical Transactions of the Royal Society of London* [B], 1992, *335*, 55–62.

Sergent, J., and Villemure, J.-G. Prosopagnosia in a right hemispherectomized patient. *Brain*, 1989, *112*, 975–995.

Shaikh, M.B., Barrett, J.A., and Siegel, A. The pathways mediating affective defense and quiet biting attack from the midbrain central gray of the cat: An autoradiographic study. *Brain Research*, 1987, *437*, 9–25.

Shallice, T. Phonological agraphia and the lexical route in writing. *Brain*, 1981, *104*, 413–429.

Sham, P.C., O'Callaghan, E., Takei, N., Murray, G.K., Hare, E.H., and Murray, R.M. Schizophrenia following pre-natal exposure to influenza epidemics between 1939 and 1960. *British Journal of Psychiatry*, 1992, *160*, 461–466.

Shapiro, M.L., Simon, D.K., Olton, D.S., Gage, F.H., Nilsson, O., and Björklund, A. Intrahippocampal grafts of fetal basal forebrain tissue alter place fields in the hippocampus of rats with fimbria-fornix lesions. *Neuroscience*, 1989, *32*, 1–18.

Sharp, F.R., Sagar, S.M., Hicks, K., Lowenstein, D., and Hisanaga, K. C-fos mRNA, Fos, and Fos-related antigen induction by hypertonic saline and stress. *Journal of Neuroscience*, 1991, *11*, 2321–2331.

Sharp, P.E., McNaughton, B.L., and Barnes, C.A. Spontaneous synaptic enhancement in hippocampi of rats exposed to a spatially complex environment. *Society for Neuroscience Abstracts*, 1983, *9*, 647.

Shavit, Y., Depaulis, A., Martin, F.C., Terman, G.W., Pechnick, R.N., Zane, C.J., Gale, P.P., and Liebeskind, J.C. Involvement of brain opiate receptors in the immune-suppressive effect of morphine. *Proceedings of the National Academy of Sciences, USA*, 1986, *83*, 7114–7117.

Shavit, Y., Lewis, J.W., Terman, G.W., Gale, R.P., and Liebeskind, J.C. Opioid peptides mediate the suppressive effect of stress on natural killer cell cytotoxicity. *Science*, 1984, *223*, 188–190.

Sher, A.E. Surgery for obstructive sleep apnea. *Progress in Clinical Biology Research*, 1990, *345*, 407–415.

Sherrington, R., Brynjolfsson, J., Petursson, H., Potter, M., Dudleston, K., Barraclough, B., Wasmuth, J., Dobbs, M., and Gurling, H. Localization of a susceptibility locus for schizophrenia on chromosome 5. *Nature*, 1988, *336*, 164–167.

Sherry, D.F., Jacobs, L.F., and Gaulin, S.J.C. Spatial memory and adaptive specialization of the hippocampus. *Trends in Neuroscience*, 1992, *15*, 298–303.

Shik, M.L., and Orlovsky, G.N. Neurophysiology of locomotor automatism. *Physiological Review*, 1976, *56*, 465–501.

Shimura, T., and Shimokochi, M. Involvement of the lateral mesencephalic tegmentum in copulatory behavior of male rats: Neuron activity in freely moving animals. *Neuroscience Research*, 1990, *9*, 173–183.

Shock, N. Systems integration. In *Handbook of the Biology of Aging*, edited by C. Finch and L. Hayflick. New York: Van Nostrand Reinhold, 1977.

Shor-Posner, G., Azar, A.P., Jhanwar-Uniyal, M., Filart, R., and Leibowitz, S.F. Destruction of noradrenergic innervation to the paraventricular nucleus: Deficits in food intake, macronutrient selection, and compensatory eating after food deprivation. *Pharmacology, Biochemistry, and Behavior*, 1986, *25*, 381–392.

Shouse, M.N., and Siegel, J.M. Pontine regulation of REM sleep components in cats: Integrity of the pedunculopontine tegmentum (PPT) is important for phasic events but unnecessary for atonia during REM sleep. *Brain Research*, 1992, *571*, 50–63.

Sidman, M., Stoddard, L.T., and Mohr, J.P. Some additional quantitative observations of immediate memory in a patient with bilateral hippocampal lesions. *Neuropsychologia*, 1968, *6*, 245–254.

Siegel, J.M., and McGinty, D.J. Pontine reticular formation neurons: Relationship of discharge to motor activity. *Science*, 1977, *196*, 678–680.

Siegel, R.M., and Andersen, R.A. Motion perceptual deficits following ibotenic acid lesions of the middle temporal area (MT) in the behaving monkey. *Society for Neuroscience Abstracts*, 1986, *12*, 1183.

Siegel, S. A Pavlovian conditioning analysis of morphine tolerance. In *Behavioral Tolerance: Research and Treatment Implications*, edited by N.A. Krasnegor. Washington, D.C.: NIDA Research Monographs, 1978.

Siever, L.J., Kahn, R.S., Lawlor, B.A., Trestman, R.L., Lawrence, T.L., and Coccaro, E.F. Critical issues in defining the role of serotonin in psychiatric disorders. *Pharmacological Reviews*, 1991, *43*, 509–526.

Silva, A.J., Stevens, C.F., Tonegawa, S., and Wang, Y. Deficient hippocampal long-term potentiation in α-calcium-calmodulin kinase II mutant mice. *Science*, 1992, *257*, 201–206.

Silverman, M.S., Grosof, D.G., De Valois, R.L., and Elfar, S.D. Spatial-frequency organization in primate striate cortex. *Proceedings of the National Academy of Sciences, USA*, 1989, *86*, 711–715.

Silverstein, L.D., and Levy, C.M. The stability of the sigma sleep spindle. *Electroencephalography and Clinical Neurophysiology*, 1976, *40*, 666–670.

Simpson, J.B., Epstein, A.N., and Camardo, J.S. The localization of dipsogenic receptors for angiotensin II in the subfornical organ. *Journal of Comparative and Physiological Psychology*, 1978, *92*, 581–608.

Sims, E.A.H., and Horton, E.S. Endocrine metabolic adaptation to obesity and starvation. *American Journal of Clinical Nutrition*, 1968, *21*, 1455–1470.

Sinclair, D. *Mechanisms of Cutaneous Sensation*. Oxford, England: Oxford University Press, 1981.

Singer, A.G. A chemistry of mammalian pheromones. *Journal of Steroid Biochemistry and Molecular Biology*, 1991, *39*, 627–632.

Singer, A.G., Macrides, F., Clancy, A.N., and Agosta, W.C. Purification and analysis of a proteinaceous aphrodisiac pheromone from hamster vaginal discharge. *Journal of Biological Chemistry*, 1986, *261*, 13323–13326.

Singer, F., and Zumoff, B. Subnormal serum testosterone levels in male internal medicine residents. *Steroids*, 1992, *57*, 86–89.

Sirigu, A., Duhamel, J.-R., and Poncet, M. The role of sensorimotor experience in object recognition. A case of multimodal agnosia. *Brain*, 1991, *114*, 2555–2573.

Sitaram, N., Moore, A.M., and Gillin, J.C. Experimental acceleration and slowing of REM ultradian rhythm by cholinergic agonist and antagonist. *Nature*, 1978, *274*, 490–492.

Slater, B., and Shields, J. Genetical aspects of anxiety. In *British Journal of Psychiatry Special Publication No. 3: Studies of Anxiety*. Ashford, Kent: Headley Bros., 1969.

Slimp, J.C., Hart, B.L., and Goy, R.W. Heterosexual, autosexual, and social behavior of adult male rhesus monkeys with medial preoptic-anterior hypothalamic lesions. *Brain Research*, 1975, *142*, 105–122.

Smith, C. Sleep states and learning: A review of the animal literature. *Neuroscience and Biobehavioral Reviews*, 1985, *9*, 157–168.

Smith, C., and Lapp, L. Increased number of REMs following an intensive learning experience in college students. *Sleep Research*, 1991, *14*, 325–330.

Smith, D.J., Perotti, J.M., Crisp, T., Cabral, M.E.Y., Long, J.T., and Scalzitti, J.M. The μ opiate receptor is responsible for descending pain inhibition originating in the periaqueductal gray region of the rat brain. *European Journal of Pharmacology*, 1988, *156*, 47–54.

Smith, G.P., Gibbs, J., and Kulkosky, P.J. Relationships between brain-gut peptides and neurons in the control of food intake. In *The Neural Basis of Feeding and Reward*, edited by B.G. Hoebel and D. Novin. Brunswick, Maine: Haer Institute, 1982.

Smith, G.P., and Jerome, C. Effects of total and selective abdominal vagotomies on water intake in rats. *Journal of the Autonomic Nervous System*, 1983, *9*, 259–271.

Smith-Swintosky, V.L., Plata-Salaman, C.R., and Scott, T.R. Gustatory neural coding in the monkey cortex: Stimulus quality. *Journal of Neurophysiology*, 1991, *66*, 1156–1165.

Snyder, F. Towards an evolutionary theory of dreaming. *American Journal of Psychiatry*, 1966, *123*, 121–136.

Snyder, S.H. *Madness and the Brain*. New York: McGraw-Hill, 1974.

Solomon, P.R., and Moore, J.W. Latent inhibition and stimulus generalization of the classically conditioned nictitating membrane response in rabbits (*Oryctolagus cuniculus*) following dorsal hippocampal ablation. *Journal of Comparative and Physiological Psychology*, 1975, *89*, 1192–1203.

Solyom, L., Turnbull, I.M., and Wilensky, M. A case of self-inflicted leucotomy. *British Journal of Psychiatry*, 1987, *151*, 855–857.

Sperry, R.W. Brain bisection and consciousness. In *Brain and Conscious Experience*, edited by J. Eccles. New York: Springer-Verlag, 1966.

Spiegler, B.J., and Mishkin, M. Evidence for the sequential participation of inferior temporal cortex and amygdala in the acquisition of stimulus-reward associations. *Behavioural Brain Research*, 1981, *3*, 303–317.

Spoendlin, H. The innervation of the cochlear receptor. In *Basic Mechanisms in Hearing*, edited by A.R. Møeller. New York: Academic Press, 1973.

Spyraki, C., Fibiger, H.C., and Phillips, A.G. Attenuation by haloperidol of place preference conditioning using food reinforcement. *Psychopharmacology*, 1982, *77*, 379–382.

Squire, L.R. Stable impairment in remote memory following electroconvulsive therapy. *Neuropsychologia*, 1974, *13*, 51–58.

Squire, L.R. Memory and the hippocampus: A synthesis from findings with rats, monkeys, and humans. *Psychological Review*, 1992, *99*, 195–231.

Squire, L.R., Haist, F., and Shimamura, A.P. The neurology of memory: Quantitative assessment of retrograde amnesia in two groups of amnesia patients. *Journal of Neuroscience*, 1989, *9*, 828–839.

Squire, L.R., Ojemann, J.G., Miezin, F.M., Petersen, S.E., Videen, T.O., and Raichle, M.E. Activation of the hippocampus in normal humans: A functional anatomical study of memory. *Proceedings of the National Academy of Sciences, USA*, 1992, *89*, 1837–1841.

Squire, L.R., Shimamura, A.P., and Amaral, D.G. Memory and the hippocampus. In *Neural Models of Plasticity: Experimental and Theoretical Approaches*, edited by J.H. Byrne and W.O. Berry. San Diego: Academic Press, 1989.

Squire, L.R., Zola-Morgan, S., and Chen, K.S. Human amnesia and animal models of amnesia: Performance of amnesia patients on tests designed for the monkey. *Behavioral Neuroscience*, 1988, *102*, 210–221.

Sørensen, T.I.A., Price, R.A., Stunkard, A.J., and Schulsinger, F. Genetics of obesity in adult adoptees and their biological siblings. *British Medical Journal*, 1989, *298*, 87–90.

Stallone, D., and Nicolaïdis, S. Increased food intake and carbohydrate preference in the rat following treatment with the serotonin antagonist metergoline. *Neuroscience Letters*, 1989, *102*, 319–324.

Stanley, B.G., Magdalin, W., and Leibowitz, S.F. A critical site for neuropeptide Y–induced eating lies in the caudolateral paraventricular/perifornical region of the hypothalamus. *Society for Neuroscience Abstracts*, 1989, *15*, 894.

Stanley, B.G., Magdalin, W., Seirafi, A., Nguyen, M.M., and Leibowitz, S.F. Evidence for neuropeptide Y mediation of eating produced by food deprivation and for a variant of the Y1 receptor mediating this peptide's effect. *Peptides*, 1992, *13*, 581–587.

Stanley, B.G., Magdalin, W., Seirafi, A., Thomas, W.J., and Leibowitz, S.F. The perifornical area: The major focus of (a) patchily distributed hypothalamic neuropeptide Y–sensitive feeding system(s). *Brain Research*, 1993, *604*, 304–317.

Stanton, P.K., and Sejnowski, T.J. Associative long-term depression in the hippocampus induced by Hebbian covariance. *Nature*, 1989, *339*, 215–218.

Stöber, G., Franzek, E., and Beckmann, H. The role of maternal infectious diseases during pregnancy in the etiology of schizophrenia in offspring. *European Psychiatry*, 1992, *7*, 147–152.

St. Clair, D.M., Blackwood, D., Muir, W., Baillie, D., Hubbard, A., Wright, A., and Evans, H.J. No linkage of chromosome 5q11–q13 markers to schizophrenia in Scottish families. *Nature*, 1989, *339*, 305–309.

Stebbins, W.C., Miller, J.M., Johnsson, L.-G., and Hawkins, J.E. Ototoxic hearing loss and cochlear pathology in the monkey. *Annals of Otology, Rhinology and Laryngology*, 1969, *78*, 1007–1026.

Steen, S.N., Oppliger, R.A., and Brownell, K.D. Metabolic effects of repeated weight loss and regain in adolescent wrestlers. *Journal of the American Medical Association*, 1988, *260*, 47–50.

Steffens, A.B. Influence of reversible obesity on eating behavior, blood glucose and insulin in the rat. *American Journal of Physiology*, 1975, *228*, 1738–1744.

Stein, L., and Belluzzi, J.D. Cellular investigations of behavioral reinforcement. *Neuroscience and Biobehavioral Reviews*, 1989, *13*, 69–80.

Stellar, J.R., Kelley, A.E., and Corbett, D. Effects of peripheral and central dopamine blockade on lateral hypothalamic self-stimulation: Evidence for both reward and motor deficits. *Pharmacology, Biochemistry, and Behavior*, 1983, *18*, 433–442.

Stephan, F.K., and Nuñez, A.A. Elimination of circadian rhythms in drinking activity, sleep, and temperature by isolation of the suprachiasmatic nuclei. *Behavioral Biology*, 1977, *20*, 1–16.

Stephan, F.K., and Zucker, I. Circadian rhythms in drinking behavior and locomotor activity of rats are eliminated by hypothalamic lesion. *Proceedings of the National Academy of Sciences, USA*, 1972, *69*, 1583–1586.

Steriade, M., Paré, D., Datta, S., Oakson, G., and Curró Dossi, R. Different cellular types in mesopontine cholinergic nuclei related to ponto-geniculo-occipital waves. *Journal of Neuroscience*, 1990, *10*, 2560–2579.

Sterman, M.B., and Clemente, C.D. Forebrain inhibitory mechanisms: Cortical synchronization induced by basal forebrain stimulation. *Experimental Neurology*, 1962a, *6*, 91–102.

Sterman, M.B., and Clemente, C.D. Forebrain inhibitory mechanisms: Sleep patterns induced by basal forebrain stimulation in the behaving cat. *Experimental Neurology*, 1962b, *6*, 103–117.

Stern, J.M. A revised view of the multisensory control of maternal behaviour in rats: Critical role of tactile inputs. *Ethoexperimental Approaches to the Study of Behavior*, edited by R.J. Blanchard, D.C. Blanchard, S. Parmigiani, and P.F. Brain. The Hague: Nijhoff Publishing Co., 1989a.

Stern, J.M. Maternal behavior: Sensory, hormonal, and neural determinants. In *Psychoendocrinology*, edited by S. Levine and F.R. Brush. New York: Academic Press, 1989b.

Sternbach, R.A. *Pain: A Psychophysiological Analysis*. New York: Academic Press, 1968.

Stevens, J.R. Neurology and neuropathology of schizophrenia. In *Schizophrenia As a Brain Disease*, edited by F.A. Henn and H.A. Nasrallah. New York: Oxford University Press, 1982.

Stevens, J.R. Schizophrenia and multiple sclerosis. *Schizophrenia Bulletin*, 1988, *14*, 231–241.

Stevens, S.S., and Newman, E.B. Localization of actual sources of sound. *American Journal of Psychology*, 1936, *48*, 297–306.

Stewart, M., and Fox, S.E. Do septal neurons pace the hippocampal theta rhythm? *Trends in Neuroscience*, 1990, *13*, 163–168.

Stinson, D., and Thompson, C. Clinical experience with phototherapy. *Journal of the Affective Disorders*, 1990, *18*, 129–135.

Stinus, L., Le Moal, M., and Koob, G.F. Nucleus accumbens and amygdala are possible substrates for the aversive stimulus effects of opiate withdrawal. *Neuroscience*, 1990, *37*, 767–773.

Stone, A.A., Reed, B.R., and Neale, J.M. Changes in daily event frequency precede episodes of physical symptoms. *Journal of Human Stress*, 1987, *13*, 70–74.

Stoyva, J., and Metcalf, D. Sleep patterns following chronic exposure to cholinesterase-inhibiting organophosphate compounds. *Psychophysiology*, 1968, *5*, 206.

Stricker, E.M., and Verbalis, J.G. Caloric and noncaloric controls of food intake. *Brain Research Bulletin*, 1991, *27*, 299–303.

Stricker, E.M., and Zigmond, M.J. Recovery of function after damage to central catecholamine-containing neurons: A neurochemical model for the lateral hypothalamic syndrome. *Progress in Psychobiology and Physiological Psychology*, 1976, *6*, 121–188.

Striem, B.J., Pace, U., Zehavi, U., Naim, M., and Lancet, D. Sweet tastants stimulate adenylate cyclase coupled to GTP-binding protein in rat tongue membranes. *Biochemical Journal*, 1989, *260*, 121–126.

Stunkard, A.J., Sørensen, T.I.A., Harris, C., Teasdale, T.W., Chakraborty, R., Schull, W.J., and Schulsinger, F. An adoption study of human obesity. *New England Journal of Medicine*, 1986, *314*, 193–198.

Sturup, G.K. Correctional treatment and the criminal sexual offender. *Canadian Journal of Correction*, 1961, *3*, 250–265.

Suddath, R.L., Christison, G.W., Torrey, E.F., Casanova, M.F., and Weinberger, D.R. Anatomical abnormalities in the brains of monozygotic twins discordant for schizophrenia. *The New England Journal of Medicine*, 1990, *322*, 789–794.

Sulser, F., and Sanders-Bush, E. From neurochemical to molecular pharmacology of antidepressants. In *Tribute to B.B. Brodie*, edited by E. Costa. New York: Raven Press, 1989.

Sunderland, G.S., and Sclafani, A. Taste preferences of squirrel monkeys and bonnet macaques for polycose, maltose, and sucrose. *Physiology and Behavior*, 1988, *43*, 685–690.

Suppes, T., Baldessarini, R.J., Faedda, G.L., and Tohen, M. Risk of recurrence following discontinuation of lithium treatment in bipolar disorder. *Archives of General Psychiatry*, 1991, *48*, 1082–1088.

Susser, E.S., and Lin, S.P. Schizophrenia after prenatal exposure to the Dutch Hunger Winter of 1944–1945. *Archives of General Psychiatry*, 1992, *49*, 983–988.

Sutherland, R.J., and Rudy, J.W. Configural association theory: The role of the hippocampal formation in learning, memory, and amnesia. *Psychobiology*, 1989, *17*, 129–144.

Sutter, M.I., and Schreiner, C.E. Physiology and topography of neurons with multipeaked tuning curves in cat primary auditory cortex. *Journal of Neurophysiology*, 1991, *65*, 1207–1226.

Suzdak, P.D., Glowa, J.R., Crawley, J.N., Schwartz, R.D., Skolnick, P., and Paul, S.M. A selective imidazobenzodiazepine antagonist of ethanol in the rat. *Science*, 1986, *234*, 1243–1247.

Svensson, T.H., Grenhoff, J., and Aston-Jones, G. Midbrain dopamine neurons: Nicotinic control of firing patterns. *Society for Neuroscience Abstracts*, 1986, *12*, 1154.

Sverd, J. Tourette syndrome and autistic disorder: A significant relationship. *American Journal of Medical Genetics*, 1991, *39*, 173–179.

Swaab, D.F., and Hofman, M.A. An enlarged suprachiasmatic nucleus in homosexual men. *Brain Research*, 1990, *537*, 141–148.

Swanson, L.W., Köhler, C., and Björklund, A. The limbic region. I. The septohippocampal system. In *Handbook of Chemical Neuroanatomy. Vol. 5. Integrated Systems of the CNS, Part I*, edited by A. Björklund, T. Hökfelt, and L.W. Swanson. Amsterdam: Elsevier, 1987.

Swedo, S., Rapoport, J., Cheslow, D., Leonard, H., Ayoub, E., Hosier, D., and Wald, E. High prevalence of obsessive compulsive symptoms in patients with Sydenham's chorea. *American Journal of Psychiatry*, 1989a, *146*, 246–249.

Swedo, S.E., Pietrini, P., Leonard, H.L., Schapiro, M.B., Rettew, D.C., Goldberger, E.L., Rapoport, S.I., Rapoport, J.L., and Grady, C.L. Cerebral glucose metabolism in childhood-onset obsessive-compulsive disorder: Revisualization during pharmacotherapy. *Archives of General Psychiatry*, 1992, *49*, 690–694.

Swedo, S.E., Schapiro, M.B., Grady, C.L., Cheslow, D.L., Leonard, H.L., Kumarn, A., Friedland, R., Rapoport, S.I., and Rapoport, J.L. Cerebral glucose metabolism in childhood-onset obsessive-compulsive disorder. *Archives of General Psychiatry*, 1989b, *46*, 518–523.

Sweeney, M.E., Hill, J.O., Heller, P.A., Baney, R., and Di-Girolamo, M. Severe vs. moderate energy restriction with and without exercise in the treatment of obesity: Efficiency of weight loss. *American Journal of Clinical Nutrition*, 1993, *57*, 127–134.

Szuba, M.P., Baxter, L.R., and Fairbanks, L.A. Effects of partial sleep deprivation on the diurnal variation of mood and motor activity in major depression. *Biological Psychiatry*, 1991, *30*, 817–829.

Szuba, M.P., Yager, A., Guze, B.H., Allen, E.M., and Baxter L.R. Disruption of social circadian rhythms in major depression: A preliminary report. *Psychiatry Research*, 1992, *42*, 221–230.

Szymusiak, R., and McGinty, D. Sleep-related neuronal discharge in the basal forebrain of cats. *Brain Research*, 1986a, *370*, 82–92.

Szymusiak, R., and McGinty, D. Sleep suppression following kainic acid-induced lesions of the basal forebrain. *Experimental Neurology*, 1986b, *94*, 598–614.

Szymusiak, R.S., and McGinty, D.J. State-dependent neurophysiology of the basal forebrain: Relationship to sleep, arousal, and thermoregulatory function. In *The Diencephalon and Sleep*, edited by M. Mancia and G. Marini. New York: Raven Press, 1990.

Takahashi, L.K. Hormonal regulation of sociosexual behavior in female mammals. *Neuroscience and Biobehavioral Reviews*, 1990, *14*, 403–413.

Takahashi, L.K., Turner, J.G., and Kalin, N.H. Prenatal stress alters brain catecholaminergic activity and potentiates stress-induced behavior in adult rats. *Brain Research*, 1992, *574*, 131–137.

Takahashi, Y. Growth hormone secretion related to the sleep waking rhythm. In *The Functions of Sleep*, edited by R. Drucker-Colín, M. Shkurovich, and M.B. Sterman. New York: Academic Press, 1979.

Talairach, J., Bancaud, J., Geier, S., Bordas-Ferrer, M., Bonis, Z., Szikla, G., and Rusu, M. The cingulate gyrus and human behaviour. *Electroencephalography and Clinical Neurophysiology*, 1973, *34*, 45–52.

Talbot, J.D., Marrett, S., Evans, A.C., Meyer, E., Bushnell, M.C., and Duncan, G.H. Multiple representations of pain in human cerebral cortex. *Science*, 1991, *251*, 355–358.

Tamminga, C.A., Burrows, G.H., Chase, T.N., Alphs, L.D., and Thaker, G.K. Dopamine neuronal tracts in schizophrenia: Their pharmacology and *in vivo* glucose metabolism. *Annals of the New York Academy of Sciences*, 1988, *537*, 443–450.

Tanabe, T., Iino, M., Ooshima, Y., and Takagi, S.F. An olfactory area in the prefrontal lobe. *Brain Research*, 1974, *80*, 127–130.

Tanabe, T., Iino, M., and Takagi, S.G. Discrimination of odors in olfactory bulb, pyriform-amygdaloid areas, and orbitofrontal cortex of the monkey. *Journal of Neurophysiology*, 1975, *38*, 1284–1296.

Tanaka, K. Inferotemporal cortex and higher visual functions. *Current Opinion in Neurobiology*, 1992, *2*, 502–505.

Tarjan, E., Denton, D.A., and Weisinger, R.S. Atrial natriuretic peptide inhibits water and sodium intake in rabbits. *Regulatory Peptides*, 1988, *23*, 63–75.

Teitelbaum, P., and Epstein, A.N. The lateral hypothalamic syndrome: Recovery of feeding and drinking after lateral hypothalamic lesions. *Psychological Review*, 1962, *69*, 74–90.

Teitelbaum, P., and Stellar, E. Recovery from the failure to eat produced by hypothalamic lesions. *Science*, 1954, *120*, 894–895.

Tempel, D.L., Leibowitz, K.J., and Leibowitz, S.F. Effects of PVN galanin on macronutrient selection. *Peptides*, 1988, *9*, 309–314.

Tempel, D.L., and Leibowitz, S.F. Galanin inhibits insulin and corticosterone release after injection into the PVN. *Brain Research*, 1990, *536*, 353–357.

Terenius, L., and Wahlström, A. Morphine-like ligand for opiate receptors in human CSF. *Life Sciences*, 1975, *16*, 1759–1764.

Tetrud, J.W., and Langston, J.W. The effect of deprenyl (Selegiline) on the natural history of Parkinson's disease. *Science*, 1989, *245*, 519–522.

Thach, W.T. Correlation of neural discharge with pattern and force of muscular activity, joint position, and direction of intended movement in motor cortex and cerebellum. *Journal of Neurophysiology*, 1978, *41*, 654–676.

Theorell, T., Leymann, H., Jodko, M., Konarski, K., Norbeck, H.E., and Eneroth, P. "Person under train" incidents: Medical consequences for subway drivers. *Psychosomatic Medicine*, 1992, *54*, 480–488.

Thivierge, J., Bedard, C., Cote, R., and Maziade, M. Brainstem auditory evoked response and subcortical abnormalities in autism. *American Journal of Psychiatry*, 1990, *147*, 1609–1613.

Thompson, L.T., and Best, P.J. Long-term stability of the place-field activity of single units recorded from the dorsal hippocampus of freely behaving rats. *Brain Research*, 1990, *509*, 299–308.

Thornton, S.N., de Beaurepaire, R., and Nicolaïdis, S. Electrophysiological investigation of cells in the region of the anterior hypothalamus firing in relation to blood pressure and volaemic changes. *Brain Research*, 1984, *299*, 1–7.

Thrasher, T.N. Role of forebrain circumventricular organs in body fluid balance. *Acta Physiologica Scandanavica*, 1989, *136 (Suppl. 583)*, 141–150.

Thrasher, T.N., and Keil, L.C. Regulation of drinking and vasopressin secretion: Role of organum vasculosum laminae terminalis. *American Journal of Physiology*, 1987, *253*, R108–R120.

Tocco, G., Maren, S., Shors, T.J., Baudry, M., and Thompson, R.F. Long-term potentiation is associated with increased [^{3}H]AMPA binding in rat hippocampus. *Brain Research*, 1992, *573*, 228–234.

Tordoff, M.G., and Friedman, M.I. Hepatic portal glucose infusions decrease food intake and increase food preference. *American Journal of Physiology*, 1986, *251*, R192–R196.

Tordoff, M.G., and Friedman, M.I. Hepatic control of feeding: Effect of glucose, fructose, and mannitol. *American Journal of Physiology*, 1988, *254*, R969–R976.

Tordoff, M.G., Hopfenbeck, J., and Novin, D. Hepatic vagotomy (partial hepatic denervation) does not alter ingestive responses to metabolic challenges. *Physiology and Behavior*, 1982, *28*, 417–424.

Tordoff, M.G., Rawson, N., and Friedman, M.I. 2,5-Anhydro-D-mannitol acts in liver to initiate feeding. *American Journal of Physiology*, 1991, *261*, R283–R288.

Tordoff, M.G., Schulkin, J., and Friedman, M.I. Further evidence for hepatic control of salt intake in rats. *American Journal of Physiology*, 1987, *253*, R444–R449.

Torrey, E.F. A viral-anatomical explanation of schizophrenia. *Schizophrenia Bulletin*, 1991, *17*, 15–18.

Triandafillou, J., and Himms-Hagen, J. Brown adipose tissue in genetically obese (*fa/fa*) rats: Response to cold and diet. *American Journal of Physiology*, 1983, *244*, E145–E150.

Träskmann, L., Åsberg, M., Bertilsson, L., and Sjöstrand, L. Monoamine metabolites in CSF and suicidal behavior. *Archives of General Psychiatry*, 1981, *38*, 631–636.

Trulson, M.E., and Jacobs, B.L. Raphe unit activity in freely moving cats: Correlation with level of behavioral arousal. *Brain Research*, 1979, *163*, 135–150.

Tsou, K., and Jang, C.S. Studies on the site of analgesia action of morphine by intracerebral microinjection. *Scientia Sinica*, 1964, *13*, 1099–1109.

Tsuang, M.T., Gilbertson, M.W., and Faraone, S.V. The genetics of schizophrenia. Current knowledge and future directions. *Schizophrenia Research*, 1991, *4*, 157–171.

Turner, A.M., and Greenough, W.T. Differential rearing effects on rat visual cortex synapses. I. Synaptic and neuronal density and synapses per neuron. *Brain Research*, 1985, *329*, 195–203.

Turner, B.H., and Herkenham, M. Thalamoamygdaloid projections in the rat: A test of the amygdala's role in sensory processing. *Journal of Comparative Neurology*, 1991, *313*, 295–325.

Tyrell, J.B., and Baxter, J.D. Glucocorticoid therapy. In *Endocrinology and Metabolism*, edited by P. Felig, J.D. Baxter, A.E. Broadus, and L.A. Frohman. New York: McGraw-Hill, 1981.

Ungerleider, L.G., and Mishkin, M. Two cortical visual systems. In *Analysis of Visual Behavior*, edited by D.J. Ingle, M.A. Goodale, and R.J.W. Mansfield. Cambridge, Mass.: MIT Press, 1982.

Uno, H., Tarara, R., Else, J.G., Suleman, M.A., and Sapolsky, R.M. Hippocampal damage associated with prolonged and fatal stress in primates. *Journal of Neuroscience*, 1989, *9*, 1705–1711.

Urca, G., and Nahin, R.L. Morphine-induced multiple unit changes in analgesic and rewarding brain sites. *Pain Abstracts*, 1978, *1*, 261.

Vaccarino, F.J., Bloom, F.E., and Koob, G.F. Blockade of nucleus accumbens opiate receptors attenuates intravenous heroin reward in the rat. *Psychopharmacology*, 1985, *86*, 37–42.

Valenstein, E.S. *Great and Desperate Cures: The Rise and Decline of Psychosurgery and Other Radical Treatments for Mental Illness*. New York: Basic Books, 1986.

Vandenbergh, J.G., Witsett, J.M., and Lombardi, J.R. Partial isolation of a pheromone accelerating puberty in female mice. *Journal of Reproductive Fertility*, 1975, *43*, 515–523.

Van den Berghe, G. Metabolic effects of fructose in the liver. In *Current Topics in Cellular Regulation*, edited by B.L.

Horecker and E.R. Stadtman. New York: Academic Press, 1978.

van de Poll, N.E., Taminiau, M.S., Endert, E., and Louwerse, A.L. Gonadal steroid influence upon sexual and aggressive behavior of female rats. *International Journal of Neuroscience*, 1988, *41*, 271–286.

van der Lee, S., and Boot, L.M. Spontaneous pseudopregnancy in mice. *Acta Physiologica et Pharmacologica Néerlandica*, 1955, *4*, 442–444.

Vanderwolf, C.H. Hippocampal electrical activity and voluntary movement in the rat. *Electroencephalography and Clinical Neurophysiology*, 1969, *26*, 407–418.

Vanderwolf, C.H. The electrocorticogram in relation to physiology and behavior: A new analysis. *Electroencephalography and Clinical Neurophysiology*, 1992, *82*, 165–175.

Vanderwolf, C.H., Kramis, R., Gillespie, L.A., and Bland, B.G. Hippocampal rhythmical slow activity and neocortical low voltage fast activity: Relations to behavior. In *The Hippocampus. Vol. 2. Neurophysiology and Behavior*, edited by R.L. Isaacson and K.H. Pribram. New York: Plenum Press, 1975.

Van der Zee, E.A., Compaan, J.C., De Boer, M., and Luiten, P.G.M. Changes in PKC-gamma immunoreactivity in mouse hippocampus induced by spatial discrimination learning. *Journal of Neuroscience*, 1992, *12*, 4808–4815.

Van Eekelen, J.A.M., and Phillips, M.I. Plasma angiotensin II levels at moment of drinking during angiotensin II intravenous infusion. *American Journal of Physiology*, 1988, *255*, R500–R506.

Van Essen, D.C., Anderson, C.H., and Felleman, D.J. Information processing in the primate visual system: An integrated systems perspective. *Science*, 1992, *255*, 419–423.

Vathy, I.U., and Etgen, A.M. Hormonal activation of female sexual behavior is accompanied by hypothalamic norepinephrine release. *Journal of Neuroendocrinology*, 1989, *1*, 383–388.

Vergnes, M., Depaulis, A., Boehrer, A., and Kempf, E. Selective increase of offensive behavior in the rat following intrahypothalamic 5,7-DHT-induced serotonin depletion. *Brain Research*, 1988, *29*, 85–91.

Verney, E.B. The antidiuretic hormone and the factors which determine its release. *Proceedings of the Royal Society of London [B]*, 1947, *135*, 25–106.

Victor, M., Adams, R.D., and Collins, G.H. *The Wernicke-Korsakoff Syndrome*. Philadelphia: F.A. Davis, 1971.

Victor, M., and Agamanolis, J. Amnesia due to lesions confined to the hippocampus: A clinical-pathological study. *Journal of Cognitive Neuroscience*, 1990, *2*, 246–257.

Vindlacheruvu, R.R., Ebling, F.J.P., Maywood, E.S., and Hastings, M.H. Blockade of glutamatergic neurotransmission in the suprachiasmatic nucleus prevents cellular and behavioural responses of the circadian system to light. *European Journal of Neuroscience*, 1992, *4*, 673–679.

Voci, V.E., and Carlson, N.R. Enhancement of maternal behavior and nest behavior following systemic and dien-

cephalic administration of prolactin and progesterone in the mouse. *Journal of Comparative and Physiological Psychology*, 1973, *83*, 388–393.

Vogel, G.W., Buffenstein, A., Minter, K., and Hennessey, A. Drug effects on REM sleep and on endogenous depression. *Neuroscience and Biobehavioral Reviews*, 1990, *14*, 49–63.

Vogel, G.W., Thurmond, A., Gibbons, P., Sloan, K., Boyd, M., and Walker, M. REM sleep reduction effects on depression syndromes. *Archives of General Psychiatry*, 1975, *32*, 765–777.

Vogel, G.W., Vogel, F., McAbee, R.S., and Thurmond, A.J. Improvement of depression by REM sleep deprivation: New findings and a theory. *Archives of General Psychiatry*, 1980, *37*, 247–253.

vom Saal, F.S., and Bronson, F.H. *In utero* proximity of female mouse fetuses to males: Effect on reproductive performance during later life. *Biology of Reproduction*, 1980, *22*, 777–780.

von Békésy, G. *Experiments in Hearing*. New York: McGraw-Hill, 1960.

von der Heydt, R., Peterhans, E., and Duersteler, M.R. Periodic-pattern-selective cells in monkey visual cortex. *Journal of Neuroscience*, 1992, *12*, 1416–1434.

Wada, J. and Rasmussen, T. Intracarotid injection of sodium Amytal for the lateralization of cerebral speech dominance. *Journal of Neurosurgery*, 1960, *17*, 266–282.

Wade, G.N., and Schneider, J.E. Metabolic fuels and reproduction in female mammals. *Neuroscience and Biobehavioral Reviews*, 1992, *16*, 235–272.

Waldbillig, R.J. Offense, defense, submission, and attack: Problems of logic and lexicon. *The Behavioral and Brain Sciences*, 1979, *2*, 227–228.

Wallace, D.M., Magnuson, D.J., and Gray, T.S. Organization of amygdaloid projections to brainstem dopaminergic, noradrenergic, and adrenergic cell groups in the rat. *Brain Research Bulletin*, 1992, *28*, 447–454.

Wallen, K. Desire and ability: Hormones and the regulation of female sexual behavior. *Neuroscience and Biobehavioral Reviews*, 1990, *14*, 233–241.

Wallen, K., Mann, D.R., Davis-DaSilva, M., Gaventa, S., Lovejoy, J.C., and Collins, D.C. Chronic gonadotropin-releasing hormone agonist treatment suppresses ovulation and sexual behavior in group-living female rhesus monkeys (*macaca mulatta*). *Animal Behaviour*, 1986, *36*, 369–375.

Walsh, L.L., and Grossman, S.P. Dissociation of responses to extracellular thirst stimuli following zona incerta lesions. *Pharmacology, Biochemistry, and Behavior*, 1978, *8*, 409–415.

Ward, I. Prenatal stress feminizes and demasculinizes the behavior of males. *Science*, 1972, *175*, 82–84.

Ward, I.L., and Stehm, K.E. Prenatal stress feminizes juvenile play patterns in male rats. *Physiology and Behavior*, 1991, *50*, 601–605.

Warner, R.K., Thompson, J.T., Markowski, V.P., Loucks, J.A., Bazzett, T.J., Eaton, R.C., and Hull, E.M. Microinjection of the dopamine antagonist cis-flupenthixol into the MPOA impairs copulation, penile reflexes and sexual motivation in male rats. *Brain Research*, 1991, *540*, 177–182.

Warrington, E.K., and Duchen, L.W. A re-appraisal of a case of persistent global amnesia following right temporal lobectomy: A clinico-pathological study. *Neuropsychologia*, 1992, *30*, 437–450.

Warrington, E.K., and James, M. Visual apperceptive agnosia: A clinico-anatomical study of three cases. *Cortex*, 1988, *24*, 1–32.

Warrington, E.K., and Shallice, T. Word-form dyslexia. *Brain*, 1980, *103*, 99–112.

Watson, N.V., and Gorzalka, B.B. Relation of spontaneous wet dog shakes and copulatory behavior in male rats. *Pharmacology, Biochemistry, and Behavior*, 1990, *37*, 825–829.

Webb, W.B. *Sleep: The Gentle Tyrant*. Englewood Cliffs, N.J.: Prentice-Hall, 1975.

Webb, W.B. Some theories about sleep and their clinical implications. *Psychiatric Annals*, 1982, *11*, 415–422.

Webster, H.H., and Jones, B.E. Neurotoxic lesions of the dorsolateral pontomesencephalic tegmentum-cholinergic cell area in the cat. II. Effects upon sleep-waking states. *Brain Research*, 1988, *458*, 285–302.

Wehr, T.A. Improvement of depression and triggering of mania by sleep deprivation. *Journal of the American Medical Association*, 1992, *267*, 548–551.

Wehr, T.A., Giesen, H.A., Schulz, P.M., Anderson, J.L., Joseph-Vanderpool, J.R., Kelly, K., Kasper, S., and Rosenthal, N.E. Contrasts between symptoms of summer depression and winter depression. *Journal of the Affective Disorders*, 1991, *23*, 173–183.

Weidner, G., Sexton, G., McLellarn, R., Connor, S.L., and Matarazzo, J.D. The role of type A behavior and hostility in an elevation of plasma lipids in adult women and men. *Psychosomatic Medicine*, 1987, *49*, 136–145.

Weinberger, D.R. Schizophrenia and the frontal lobe. *Trends in Neurosciences*, 1988, *11*, 367–370.

Weinberger, D.R., Berman, K.F., Suddath, R., and Torrey, E.F. Evidence of dysfunction of a prefrontal-limbic network in schizophrenia: A magnetic resonance imaging and regional cerebral blood flow study of discordant monozygotic twins. *American Journal of Psychiatry*, 1992, *149*, 890–897.

Weinberger, D.R., Berman, K.F., and Zec, R.F. Physiologic dysfunction of dorsolateral prefrontal cortex in schizophrenia. I. Regional cerebral blood flow evidence. *Archives of General Psychiatry*, 1986, *43*, 114–124.

Weinberger, D.R., and Wyatt, R.J. Brain morphology in schizophrenia: *In vivo* studies. In *Schizophrenia as a Brain Disease*, edited by F.A. Henn and H.A. Nasrallah. New York: Oxford University Press, 1982.

Weinberger, N.M. Sensory plasticity and learning: The magnocellular medial geniculate nucleus of the auditory system. In *Conditioning: Representation of Involved Neural Functions*, edited by C.D. Woody. New York: Plenum Press, 1982.

Weingarten, H.P. Conditioned cues elicit feeding in sated rats: A role for learning in meal initiation. *Science*, 1983, *220*, 431–432.

Weingarten, J.P., Chang, P.K., and McDonald, T.J. Comparison of the metabolic and behavioral disturbances following paraventricular- and ventromedial-hypothalamic lesions. *Brain Research Bulletin*, 1985, *14*, 551–559.

Weintraub, S., Mesulam, M.-M., and Kramer, L. Disturbances in prosody: A right-hemisphere contribution to language. *Archives of Neurology*, 1981, *38*, 742–744.

Weiskrantz, L. Residual vision in a scotoma: A follow-up study of "form" discrimination. *Brain*, 1987, *110*, 77–92.

Weiskrantz, L., and Warrington, E.K. Conditioning in amnesia patients. *Neuropsychologia*, 1979, *17*, 187–194.

Weiskrantz, L., Warrington, E.K., Sanders, M.D., and Marshall, J. Visual capacity in the hemianopic field following a restricted occipital ablation. *Brain*, 1974, *97*, 709–728.

Weiss, G.F., Rogacki, N., Fueg, A., Buchen, D., Suh, J.S., Wong, D.T., and Leibowitz, S.F. Effect of hypothalamic and peripheral fluoxetine injection on natural patterns of macronutrient intake in the rat. *Psychopharmacology (Berlin)*, 1991, *105*, 467–476.

Weiss, J.M. Effects of coping response on stress. *Journal of Comparative and Physiological Psychology*, 1968, *65*, 251–260.

Weisz, D.J., Clark, G.A., Yank, B., Thompson, R.F., and Solomon, P.R. Activity of dentate gyrus during NM conditioning in rabbit. In *Conditioning: Representation of Involved Neural Functions*, edited by C.D. Woody. New York: Plenum Press, 1982.

Weisz, D.W., Solomon, P.R., and Thompson, R.F. The hippocampus appears necessary for trace conditioning. *Bulletin of the Psychonomic Society*, 1980, *16* (Abstract).

Weitzman, E.D. Sleep and its disorders. *Annual Review of Neuroscience*, 1981, *4*, 381–418.

Welle, S.L., Nair, K.S., and Campbell, R.G. Failure of chronic ß-adrenergic blockade to inhibit overfeeding-induced thermogenesis in humans. *American Journal of Physiology*, 1989, *256*, R653–R658.

Weltzin, T.E., Hsu, L.K.G., Pollice, C., and Kaye, W.H. Feeding patterns in bulimia nervosa. *Biological Psychiatry*, 1991, *30*, 1093–1110.

Wernicke, C. *Der Aphasische Symptomenkomplex*. Breslau, Poland: Cohn & Weigert, 1874.

Westbrook, P.R. Treatment of sleep disordered breathing: Nasal continuous positive airway pressure (CPAP). *Progress in Clinical Biology Research*, 1990, *345*, 387–394.

Whipple, B., and Komisaruk, B.R. Analgesia produced in women by genital self-stimulation. *Journal of Sex Research*, 1988, *24*, 130–140.

White, J.C., and Sweet, W.H. *Pain and the Neurosurgeon: A Forty-Year Experience*. Springfield, Ill.: Charles C. Thomas, 1969.

Whitehead, R.G., Rowland, M.G.M., Hutton, M., Prentice, A.M., Müller, E., and Paul, A. Factors influencing lactation performance in rural Gambian mothers. *Lancet*, 1978, *2*, 178–181.

Whitfield, I.C., and Evans, E.F. Responses of auditory cortical neurons to stimuli of changing frequency. *Journal of Neurophysiology*, 1965, *28*, 655–672.

Whitten, W.K. Occurrence of anestrus in mice caged in groups. *Journal of Endocrinology*, 1959, *18*, 102–107.

Wiener, S.I., Paul, C.A., and Eichenbaum, H. Spatial and behavioral correlates of hippocampal neuronal activity. *Journal of Neuroscience*, 1989, *9*, 2737–2763.

Wiesner, B.P., and Sheard, N. *Maternal Behaviour in the Rat.* London: Oliver and Brody, 1933.

Wilckens, T., Schweiger, U., and Pirke, K.M. Activation of 5-HT1C-receptors suppresses excessive wheel running induced by semi-starvation in the rat. *Psychopharmacology (Berlin)*, 1992, *109*, 77–84.

Williams, R.B., Hanel, T.L., Lee, K.L., and Kong, Y.H. Type A behavior, hostility, and coronary atherosclerosis. *Psychosomatic Medicine*, 1980, *42*, 539–549.

Wilska, A. Eine Methode zur Bestimmung der Horschwellenamplituden der Tromenfells bei verscheideden Frequenzen. *Skandinavisches Archiv für Physiologie*, 1935, *72*, 161–165.

Winans, S.S., and Powers, J.B. Olfactory and vomeronasal deafferentation of male hamsters: Histological and behavioral analyses. *Brain Research*, 1977, *126*, 325–344.

Winn, P., Tarbuck, A., and Dunnett, S.B. Ibotenic acid lesions of the lateral hypothalamus: Comparison with electrolytic lesion syndrome. *Neuroscience*, 1984, *12*, 225–240.

Winslow, J.T., Ellingoe, J., and Miczek, J.A. Effects of alcohol on aggressive behavior in squirrel monkeys: Influence of testosterone and social context. *Psychopharmacology*, 1988, *95*, 356–363.

Winslow, J.T., and Miczek, J.A. Social status as determinants of alcohol effects on aggressive behavior in squirrel monkeys (*Saimiri sciureus*). *Psychopharmacology*, 1985, *85*, 167–172.

Winter, P., and Funkenstein. H. The auditory cortex of the squirrel monkey: Neuronal discharge patterns to auditory stimuli. *Proceedings of the 3rd Congress of Primatology, Zurich*, 1971, *2*, 24–28.

Wise, R.A. Psychomotor stimulant properties of addictive drugs. *Annals of the New York Academy of Sciences*, 1988, *537*, 228–234.

Witt, D.M., and Insel, T.R. A selective oxytocin antagonist attenuates progesterone facilitation of female sexual behavior. *Endocrinology*, 1991, *128*, 3269–3276.

Wolf, G., Schulkin, J., and Simson, P.E. Multiple factors in the satiation of salt appetite. *Behavioral Neuroscience*, 1984, *98*, 661–673.

Wolkin, A., Barouche, F., Wolf, A.P., Rotrosen, J., Fowler, J.S., Shiue, C.-Y., Cooper, T.B., and Brodie, J.D. Dopamine blockade and clinical response: Evidence for two biological subgroups of schizophrenia. *American Journal of Psychiatry*, 1989, *146*, 905–908.

Wong, D.F., Wagner, H.N., Tune, L.E., Dannals, R.F., Pearlson, G.D., Links, J.M., Tamminga, C.A., Broussolle, E.P., Ravert, H.T., Wilson, A.A., Toung, J.K.T., Malat, J., Williams, J.A., O'Tuama, L.A., Snyder, S.H., Kuhar, M.J., and Gjedde, A. Positron emission tomography reveals elevated D_2 dopamine receptors in drug-naive schizophrenics. *Science*, 1986, *234*, 1558–1563.

Wong-Riley, M. Personal communication, 1978. Cited by Livingstone and Hubel, 1982.

Wood, D.L., Sheps, S.G., Elveback, L.R., and Schirder, A. Cold pressor test as a predictor of hypertension. *Hypertension*, 1984, *6*, 301–306.

Wood, P.L. Actions of GABAergic agents on dopamine metabolism in the nigrostriatal pathway of the rat. *Pharmacology and Experimental Therapeutics*, 1982, *222*, 674–679.

Woodruff, R.A., Guze, S.B., and Clayton, P.J. Anxiety neurosis among psychiatric outpatients. *Comprehensive Psychiatry*, 1972, *13*, 165–170.

Woods, S.C., Decke, E., and Vasselli, J.R. Metabolic hormones and regulation of body weight. *Psychological Review*, 1974, *81*, 26–43.

Woods, S.C., Porte, D., Bobbioni, E., Ionescu, E., Sauter, J.-F., Rohner-Jeanrenaud, F., and Jeanrenaud, B. Insulin: Its relationship to the central nervous system and to the control of food intake and body weight. *American Journal of Clinical Nutrition*, 1985, *42*, 1063–1071.

Woods, S.W., Charney, D.S., Goodman, W.K., and Heninger, G.R. Carbon dioxide-induced anxiety. *Archives of General Psychiatry*, 1988, *45*, 43–52.

Wu, J.C., and Bunney, W.E. The biological basis of an antidepressant response to sleep deprivation and relapse: Review and hypothesis. *American Journal of Psychiatry*, 1990, *147*, 14–21.

Wu, J.C., Gillin, J.C., Buchsbaum, M.S., Hershey, T., Johnson, J.C., and Bunney, W.E. Effect of sleep deprivation on brain metabolism of depressed patients. *American Journal of Psychiatry*, 1992, *149*, 538–543.

Wyatt, R.J., Kirch, D.G., and DeLisi, L.E. Biochemical, endocrine, and immunologic studies of schizophrenia. In *Comprehensive Textbook of Psychiatry*, 5th ed., edited by H.I. Kaplan and B.J. Sadock. Baltimore: Williams and Wilkins, 1988.

Wysocki, C.J. Neurobehavioral evidence for the involvement of the vomeronasal system in mammalian reproduction. *Neuroscience and Biobehavioral Reviews*, 1979, *3*, 301–341.

Wysocki, C.J., Katz, Y., and Bernhard, R. The male vomeronasal organ mediates female-induced testosterone surges. *Biology of Reproduction*, 1983, *28*, 917–922.

Yadin, E., Thomas, E., Strickland, C.E., and Grishkat, H.L. Anxiolytic effects of benzodiazepines in amygdala-lesioned rats. *Psychopharmacology*, 1991, *103*, 473–479.

Yates, W.R., Perry, P., and Murray, S. Aggression and hostility in anabolic steroid users. *Biological Psychiatry*, 1992, *31*, 1232–1234.

Ye, Q., Heck, G.L., and DeSimone, J.A. The anion paradox in sodium taste reception: Resolution by voltage-clamp studies. *Science*, 1991, *254*, 724–726.

Yee, F., MacLow, C., Chan, I.N., and Leibowitz, S.F. Effects of chronic paraventricular nucleus infusion of clonidine and α-methyl-*para*-tyrosine on macronutrient intake. *Appetite*, 1987, *9*, 127–138.

Yeomans, J.S. Quantitative measurement of neural post-stimulation excitability with behavioral methods. *Physiology and Behavior*, 1975, *15*, 593–602.

Yeung, J.C., and Rudy, T. Sites of antinociceptive action of systemically injected morphine: Involvement of supraspinal loci as revealed by intracerebroventricular injection of naloxone. *Journal of Pharmacology and Experimental Therapeutics*, 1980, *215*, 626–632.

Yokoo, H., Tanaka, M., Yoshida, M., Tsuda, A., Tanaka, T., and Mizoguchi, K. Direct evidence of conditioned fear-elicited enhancement of noradrenaline release in the rat hypothalamus assessed by intracranial microdialysis. *Brain Research*, 1990, *536*, 305–308.

Yokota, T., Ishiai, S., Furukawa, T., and Tsukagoshi, H. Pure agraphia of kanji due to thrombosis of the Labbe vein. *Journal of Neurology, Neurosurgery, and Psychiatry*, 1990, *53*, 335–338.

Yoshii, K., Yokouchi, C., and Kurihara, K. Synergistic effects of 5'-nucleotides on rat taste responses to various amino acids. *Brain Research*, 1986, *367*, 45–51.

Yost, W.A. Auditory image perception and analysis: The basis for hearing. *Hearing Research*, 1991, *56*, 8–18.

Young, G.B., Barr, H.W.K., and Blume, W.T. Painful epileptic seizures involving the second sensory area. *Annals of Neurology*, 1986, *19*, 412.

Zeki, S. The visual image in mind and brain. *Scientific American*, 1992, *267*(3), 69–76.

Zeki, S., and Shipp, S. The functional logic of cortical connections. *Nature*, 1988, *335*, 311–317.

Zeki, S., Watson, J.D.G., Lueck, C.J., Friston, K.J., Kennard, C., and Frackowiak, R.S. A direct demonstration of functional specialization in human visual cortex. *Journal of Neuroscience*, 1991, *11*, 641–649.

Zeki, S.M. The representation of colours in the cerebral cortex. *Nature*, 1980, *284*, 412–418.

Zenner, H.-P., Zimmermann, U., and Schmitt, U. Reversible contraction of isolated mammalian cochlear hair cells. *Hearing Research*, 1985, *18*, 127–133.

Zhang, S.P., Bandler, R., and Carrive, P. Flight and immobility evoked by excitatory amino acid microinjection within distinct parts of the subtentorial midbrain periaqueductal gray of the cat. *Brain Research*, 1990, *520*, 73–82.

Zihl, J., Von Cramon, D., Mai, N., and Schmid, C. Disturbance of movement vision after bilateral posterior brain damage. Further evidence and follow up observations. *Brain*, 1991, *114*, 2235–2252.

Zito, K.A., Vickers, G., and Roberts, D.C.S. Disruption of cocaine and heroin self-administration following kainic acid lesions of the nucleus accumbens. *Pharmacology, Biochemistry, and Behavior*, 1985, *23*, 1029–1036.

Zola-Morgan, S., and Squire, L.R. Amnesia in monkeys following lesions of the mediodorsal nucleus of the thalamus. *Annals of Neurology*, 1985a, *17*, 558–564.

Zola-Morgan, S., and Squire, L.R. Medial temporal lesions in monkeys impair memory in a variety of tasks sensitive to human amnesia. *Behavioral Neuroscience*, 1985b, *99*, 22–34.

Zola-Morgan, S., Squire, L.R., and Amaral, D.G. Human amnesia and the medial temporal region: Enduring memory impairment following a bilateral lesion limited to field CA1 of the hippocampus. *Journal of Neuroscience*, 1986, *6*, 2950–2967.

Zola-Morgan, S., Squire, L.R., and Amaral, D.G. Lesions of the amygdala that spare adjacent cortical regions do not impair memory or exacerbate the impairment following lesions of the hippocampal formation. *Journal of Neuroscience*, 1989a, *9*, 1922–1936.

Zola-Morgan, S., Squire, L.R., and Amaral, D.G. Lesions of the hippocampal formation but not lesions of the fornix or the mammillary nuclei produce long-lasting memory impairment in monkeys. *Journal of Neuroscience*, 1989b, *9*, 898–913.

Zola-Morgan, S., Squire, L.R., Amaral, D.G., and Suzuki, W.A. Lesions of perirhinal and parahippocampal cortex that spare the amygdala and hippocampal formation produce severe memory impairment. *Journal of Neuroscience*, 1989, *9*, 4355–4370.

Abe, H., 273
Abel, E.L., 588
Abel, L.A., 545
Adachi, A., 391
Adamec, R.E., 354
Adams, D., 353
Adams, D.B., 310, 352–353
Adams, H.P., 514
Adams, R.D., 206, 482, 493
Adams, W., 551
Adey, W.R., 263
Adieh, H.B., 328
Adler, N.T., 301
Adolph, E.F., 389
Agamanolis, J., 491
Aggleton, J.P., 505
Akabas, M.H., 217
Akbarian, S., 552
Akhtar, S., 573
Akil, H., 208, 210
Al-Awqati, Q., 217
Albers, H.E., 274
Albert, M.L., 172
Albrecht, D.G., 158–159
Albright, T.D., 175
Aldrich, M.S., 269
Alexander, G.M., 310
Alexander, M.P., 172, 536
Alger, B.E., 209
Alkon, D.L., 501
Allen, L.S., 312, 319
Almers, W., 051
Amaral, D.G., 217, 487, 491–492, 494
Amir, S., 424
Amyes, E.W., 343
Anand, B.K., 415
Andersen, R.A., 175
Anderson, C.H., 166
Anderson, R.H., 313, 318
Anderson, S.W., 522
Andersson, B., 379

Andreasen, N.C., 542, 562
Andres, K.H., 202
Andrews, K.M., 380, 413
Apicella, P., 472
Applegate, C.D., 463
Arana, G.W., 571
Aravich, P.F., 415
Arduini, A.A., 502
Argiolas, A., 319
Arletti, R., 319
Arnold, A.P., 315–316
Aroniadou, V.A., 460
Aronson, L.R., 311
Artmann, H., 428
Asanuma, H., 237
Aschoff, J., 272
Ashe, J.H., 444
Asher, R., 288
Aston-Jones, G., 279–280, 587
Auer, R.N., 491
Avenet, P., 214, 216
Axel, R., 221
Azakami, M., 257

Bailey, A.J., 578
Bailey, J.M., 313
Bailey, P., 275
Baizer, J.S., 166
Bakalyar, H.A., 221
Bakin, J.S., 443
Baldessarini, R.J., 546, 549, 559
Balint, R., 177
Ballantine, H.T., 575
Balon, R., 571
Balster, R.L., 470
Bancroft, J., 357
Bandler, R., 354
Baranyi, A., 460
Barber, J., 211
Barclay, C.D., 177
Barfield, R.J., 320

Barnes, C.A., 501
Baron, M., 560
Baron-Cohen, S., 577
Barr, H.W.K., 206
Barrett, J.A., 354
Basbaum, A.I., 209–210
Bassett, A.S., 544
Baum, A., 363
Baum, M.J., 301
Baumeister, A.A., 585
Baxter, J.D., 361
Baxter, L.R., 565, 575
Baylis, G.C., 171, 441
Bazett, H.C., 204
Beach, F.A., 315
Beam, K.G., 216
Bean, N.J., 355
Bear, M.F., 460
Beaudet, A., 285
Beauvois, M.F., 533, 536
Beck, B., 423
Beckman, H., 553
Beckstead, R.M., 217–218
Beecher, H.K., 206
Beeman, E.A., 354
Behan, P.O., 538
Beidel, D.C., 573
Beidler, L.M., 214
Beitz, A.J., 209–211
Bell, A.P., 312
Belluzzi, J.D., 474, 477
Bender, J., 412
Benedek, G., 282
Benelli, A., 319
Beninger, R.J., 468
Benson, D.F., 536
Bercovitch, F.B., 308
Berger, B., 467
Berger, T.W., 500–501
Berman, K.F., 553, 555
Bermant, G., 300

Bernard, C., 390
Bernhard, R., 305
Bernstein, I.L., 401, 403, 412, 427
Bernstein, M.E., 276
Berntson, G.G., 210
Berridge, C.W., 361
Berry, S.D., 500
Bertelsen, A., 543
Bertolini, A., 319
Besson, J.M., 205
Best, P.J., 498–499
Bettelheim, B., 578
Beyer, C., 322
Bielajew, C., 469
Binder, J.R., 529
Bingman, V.P., 497
Birch, L.L., 400, 421
Bitran, D., 320
Björklund, A., 447
Blanchard, J., 273
Blanchard, R.J., 339
Blander, D.S., 474
Blasdel, G.G., 165
Blass, E.M., 379, 390
Blaustein, J.D., 302, 320
Blaza, S., 425
Blest, A.D., 008
Bliss, T.V.P., 449
Bloch, V., 265
Blonder, L.X., 349
Bloom, F.E., 208, 279–280, 469
Bloom, R.E., 585
Blum, K., 592
Blume, W.T., 206
Blumer, D., 319
Bogerts, B., 550
Boller, F., 516
Bolos, A.M., 593
Bon, C., 458
Bonsall, R.W., 300
Boot, L.M., 303
Booth, D.A., 408
Borbély, A.A., 278
Born, R.T., 169
Bornstein, B., 173
Bornstein, R.A., 550
Bors, E., 263
Bos, N.P.A., 276
Bouchard, C., 423
Boulos, Z., 276
Bouma, H., 333
Boussaoud, D., 169
Bowers, D., 348–349
Bowers, R.L., 410
Bowersox, S.S., 256
Boxer, P.A., 287
Boyer, A., 419

Boynton, R.M., 154
Bozarth, M.A., 585–586
Bracha, H.S., 552
Brackett, N.L., 318
Bradbury, M.W.B., 029
Bradwejn, J., 573
Brand, R.J., 364
Brand, T., 303
Bray, G.A., 419, 424, 426
Brecher, E.M., 586
Bredt, D.S., 458–459
Breedlove, S.M., 302–303, 315
Breger, L., 266
Breier, A., 550
Breisch, S.T., 417
Brickner, R.M., 341
Bridges, R.S., 327
Brobeck, J.R., 415
Broberg, D.J., 427
Broca, P., 514
Brodie, M.S., 590
Bronson, F.H., 356
Brooksbank, B.W.L., 307
Brown, T.H., 450–452
Brownell, K.D., 423
Brownell, W.E., 192
Brozowski, T.J., 554
Bruce, H.M., 303
Bruno, J.P., 325
Brust, J.C.M., 535
Bryan, R.N., 580
Bryden, M.P., 346–347
Buchsbaum, M.S., 262, 554
Buck, L., 221
Buck, R., 349
Buckley, P., 545
Buggy, J., 380
Bunney, B.S., 471
Bunney, W.E., 564
Burgard, E.C., 459
Burt, A.D., 310
Burt, D.R., 546–547
Burton, M.J., 419
Butcher, S.P., 502
Butters, N., 477
Buzsáki, G., 459, 503–504
Byerley, W., 558

Cabanac, M., 412, 424
Cador, M., 473
Cain, W.S., 221
Callaway, C.W., 285
Calles-Escandon, J., 422
Camardo, J.S., 384
Campbell, B.A., 335
Campbell, C.S., 408
Campbell, R., 171, 173, 525–526

Campbell, R.G., 424
Campeau, S., 333, 464
Campfield, L.A., 404
Card, J.P., 273
Carew, T.J., 462
Carlson, N.R., 327, 523, 535
Carpenter, C.R., 356
Carr, C.E., 195
Carreno, L., 364
Carrive, P., 354
Carter, C.J., 555
Carter, C.S., 301–302, 311
Cavada, C., 178
Cavanaugh, J., 546
Cenci, M.A., 360
Chang, L.W., 211
Chang, P.K., 415
Chang, V.C., 474
Channabasavanna, S., 573
Chapman, P.F., 458, 463
Chaput, Y., 562
Chase, M.H., 287
Chen, J., 588
Chen, K.S., 499
Chen, L., 499
Chess, S., 579
Chi, J.G., 538
Chow, S.Y., 388
Chung, S.K., 315
Cipolotti, L., 528
Clancy, A.N., 300
Clark, J.R., 419
Clark, J.T., 418–419
Clayton, P.J., 570
Clemens, L., 320
Clemente, C.D., 282
Cloninger, C.R., 591–592
Clugnet, M.-C., 460, 463
Cobb, S., 359
Coble, P.A., 564
Coburn, P.C., 380
Cohen, D.B., 265
Cohen, E.A., 359
Cohen, N.J., 487, 489
Cohen, S., 368
Coirini, H., 388
Cole, M., 493
Collins, G.H., 493
Collison, C., 495
Comarr, A.E., 315
Comings, B.G., 579
Comings, D.E., 579
Conner, R., 355
Cook, E.H., 581
Coon, H., 545
Cooper, J.D., 285
Cooper, J.R., 208

Coover, G.D., 333
Coplan, J.D., 573
Corbett, D., 470
Corbetta, M., 172, 177
Corkin, S., 483, 489
Corneilson, R., 383
Cornwall, J., 285
Corwin, J.T., 188, 193
Coscina, D.V., 424
Cotman, C.W., 452, 460
Coulter, D.A., 501
Courchesne, E., 580
Cowan, W.M., 273
Cowey, A., 169, 171
Cowley, D.S., 307, 571
Cox, A., 578
Crane, G.E., 558
Creese, I., 546–547
Crick, F., 265
Criswell, H.E., 209
Crow, T.J., 469, 542, 545
Crowe, R.R., 571
Crowley, W.R., 322
Cruikshank, S.J., 462
Csonka, E., 573
Cubelli, R., 536
Culebras, A., 270
Culotta, E., 069, 458
Cummings, J.L., 575
Cummings, T.A., 214, 217
Cunningham, D.A., 364
Cunningham, J.T., 386–387
Cunningham, K., 575
Cutting, J.E., 177
Czech, D.A., 388
Czeisler, C.A., 275, 283
Czopf, J., 503

Dabbs, J.M., 357
Dahl, D., 459
Damasio, A.R., 168, 172, 177, 343,
    522–526, 529
Damasio, H., 172, 514, 518, 529
D'Amato, T., 550
Damsma, G., 281, 474, 587
Daniel, D.G., 554
Dark, J., 277
Darwin, C., 345
Davidson, J.M., 300, 317
Davis, J.D., 408, 412
Davis, K.L., 548–549, 555
Davis, M., 333, 335–336, 462
Davis, S., 502
Davison, G.C., 573
Daw, N.W., 155
Day, J., 281, 587
Dean, P., 169

De Andres, I., 278
de Beaurepaire, R., 384
De Bold, A.J., 392
de Castro, E.S., 401
de Castro, J.M., 382, 400–401
Decke, E., 412
Degreef, G., 550
Deiber, M.P., 477
Dejerine, J., 529
De Jong, J., 560
De Jonge, F.H., 318–319
DeKosky, S., 348
de la Riva, C., 304
del Cerro, S., 460
DeLisi, L.E., 545, 547
DeLong, G.R., 580
DeLong, M., 245
Delay, J., 546
Delgado, P.L., 561
Dement, W.C., 256, 261, 265, 269, 288
Denes, G., 528
Deniker, P., 546
Denlinger, S.L., 288
Dennis, M., 516
Denton, D.A., 392
Deol, M.S., 188
Dérouesné, J., 533, 536
DeSimone, J.A., 214
Desimone, R., 166, 168–170, 175
DeToledo-Morrell, L., 458
Detre, T.P., 267
Deutsch, J.A., 408–410, 503
De Valois, K.K., 159, 165
De Valois, R.L., 158–159, 165
Devane, W.A., 069
DeVries, G.J., 319
Deyo, R.A., 500
Diamond, D.M., 197, 451
Diamond, I.T., 162
Di Chiara, G., 585, 590
Dietz, M., 273
Dimsdale, J.E., 364
Dionne, T.J., 216
Disterhoft, J.F., 500
Dodd, J., 217
Doherty, P.C., 301
Dolan, R.P., 152
Dooling, E.C., 538
Doolittle, D.P., 593
Dostrovsky, T., 497
Doty, R.L., 306
Dou, H., 317
Downer, J.L., 339
Dray, A., 244
Drevets, W.C., 562
Drugan, R.C., 210
Drzewiecki, K., 390

Duchen, L.W., 483
Dudek, S.M., 460
Dudley, C.A., 306
Duffy, R.J., 349
Duhamel, J.-R., 178
Dujardin, K., 266
Dunn, A., 361
Dunnett, S.B., 418, 477
Dunwiddie, T.V., 451, 590
Durie, D.J., 259
Dürstler, M.R., 160
Duvauchelle, C.L., 477
Dykes, R.W., 206

East, S.J., 458
Eddy, N.B., 583
Edeline, J.-M., 443, 462
Edwards, D.A., 318
Edwards, G.L., 380, 384
Egawa, M., 419
Egeland, J.A., 558
Ehlers, C.L., 566
Ehrhardt, A.A., 309, 311–312, 318
Ehrlich, K.J., 392
Eichenbaum, H., 487, 497, 504
Eichler, V.B., 272
Eilam, R., 363
Ekman, P., 345, 351
Elias, M., 357
Ellingoe, J., 358
El Mansari, M., 286
Engen, T., 402
Ennis, M., 280
Epstein, A.N., 377, 379, 384, 387–388
Ernulf, K.E., 313
Ervin, F.R., 206
Eslinger, P.J., 514, 343
Etgen, A.M., 322
Ettenberg, A., 477
Evans, C.R., 265
Evans, E.F., 192, 197
Evarts, E.V., 237
Everitt, B.J., 311, 322, 473

Fahringer, H., 287
Fairbanks, L.A., 565
Falk, J.L., 468
Fallon, J.H., 466
Falls, W.A., 464
Fang, F.G., 209
Fanselow, M.S., 211
Faraone, S.V., 543
Farde, L., 547
Farmer, M.E., 519
Fava, M., 428
Feder, H.H., 301, 320, 322
Feigenbaum, S.L., 368

Feigin, M.B., 217
Felix, D., 384
Felleman, D.J., 166
Ferguson, N.B.L., 415
Fernandez, F., 579
Fernandez-Guasti, A., 322
Fernandez-Tome, P., 360
Fernell, E., 579
Ferris, C.F., 274, 353
Fibiger, H.C., 281, 468–470, 548
Field, T., 351
Fields, H.L., 209–211
Fieve, R.R., 559
Finkelstein, J.A., 423
Firestein, S., 221
Fisch, B., 579
Fisher, C., 257–258
Fitts, D.A., 389, 392
Fitzpatrick, D., 162
Fitzsimons, J.T., 377, 379, 381–382
Fleming, A.S., 326–327
Flock, A., 186
Flood, J.F., 419
Floody, O.R., 356
Flynn, J., 354
Fobes, J.L., 465, 469
Folstein, S.E., 578–579
Foltin, R.W., 399
Fornal, C.A., 281
Fort, P., 287
Fox, S.E., 503
Frahm, H.D., 497
Frank, E., 566
Frank, M., 218
Franzek, E., 553
Freeman, P.H., 424
Freeman, W.J., 305
Freund, L., 579
Friedman, D.I., 275
Friedman, M.I., 325, 363, 391,
    405–406, 411–412
Friedman, S., 327
Friesen, W.V., 345, 351
Frith, U., 577
Frohman, L.A., 126
Fuentes, J.A., 360
Fulton, J.F., 275, 341
Funkenstein, H., 197
Fuster, J.M., 438

Gabrieli, J.D.E., 486, 489
Gaffan, D., 473
Gaffan, E.A., 473
Gaffney, F.A., 571
Gage, F.H., 459, 503
Gainer, H., 275
Galaburda, A.M., 537–538

Gallistel, C.R., 468
Ganong, A.H., 451–452
Garber, H.J., 581
Garcia, J., 402
Garcia-Velasco, J., 306
Gardner, H., 513
Gariano, R.F., 473
Garthwaite, J., 458
Gaspar, P., 467
Gatchel, R.J., 363
Gaulin, S.J.C., 497
Gaw, A.C., 211
Gazzaniga, M.S., 012
Geary, N., 586
Gebhardt, G.F., 210
Geinisman, Y., 458
Genefke, I., 362
Gentil, C.G., 389
Gentili, B., 216
Gentilucci, M., 178
George, M.S., 581
Gerbino, L., 559
German, D.C., 585
Gerren, R., 460, 463
Gershon, E.S., 558–559
Geschwind, N.A., 520, 536, 538
Gessa, G.L., 319, 590
Geyer, S.J., 264
Gibbs, J., 410–411
Gilbertson, M.W., 543
Giles, D.E., 564
Gillberg, C., 579
Gilles, F.H., 538
Gillette, M.U., 276
Gillin, J.C., 285
Giordano, A.L., 328
Givens, B.S., 503
Giza, B.K., 414
Glaser, R., 368
Glavin, G.B., 363
Glick, Z., 424
Gluecksohn-Waelsch, S., 188
Goeders, N.E., 585
Gold, A.R., 310
Gold, R.M., 416
Goldberg, S.R., 587
Goldbloom, D.S., 428
Goldman-Rakic, P.S., 178
Golgi, C., 026
Gonzalez, M.F., 408–409
Goodale, M.A., 178
Goodglass, H., 514, 526
Goodman-Schulman, R., 536
Goodwin, D.W., 591
Goodwin, F.K., 566
Gordon, N.C., 211
Gorman, J.M., 573

Gorski, R.A., 312, 317, 319
Gorwood, P., 545
Gorzalka, B.B., 320
Gottesman, I.I., 423, 543
Gouras, P., 155
Goy, R.W., 308, 318
Grace, A.A., 555
Graf, P., 488
Grant, S.G.N., 457, 502
Grau, J.W., 210
Gray, C., 305
Gray, R., 459
Gray, T.S., 360
Green, J.D., 502
Greenberg, D., 411
Greenberg, R., 265–266
Grenhoff, J., 587
Griffith, J.D., 546
Grijalva, C.V., 335
Grill, H.J., 414
Groos, G., 273
Gross, C.G., 169, 175
Gross, J., 257
Gross, R.A., 276
Grossman, L., 389
Grossman, S.P., 388–389, 413
Groves, P.M., 473
Guerin, G.F., 469
Guerrien, A., 266
Guilleminault, C., 269
Gulevich, G., 261
Gur, R.C., 347
Guze, S.B., 570

Haas, R.H., 482
Haase, E., 497
Hackney, C.M., 188
Haist, F., 508
Halasz, P., 256
Haley, J.E., 458
Hall, W.G., 390
Hall, Z., 457
Halmi, K.A., 427–428
Halpern, M., 304
Hamer, J.D., 311
Hammersmith, S.K., 312
Handa, R.J., 317
Hansen, S., 322
Hardy, W.T., 410
Harley, L.J., 263
Harmon, L.D., 160
Haroutunian, V., 555
Harries, M.H., 171
Harrington, M.E., 274
Harris, G.W., 296
Harrison, S., 473
Hart, B.L., 315, 318

Hartline, H.K., 150
Hashimoto, T., 580
Haug, H.-J., 564
Hawke, C., 357
Hayaishi, O., 283
Hebb, D.O., 434
Heck, G.L., 214
Heckler, M.M., 591
Heffner, H.E., 196–197
Heffner, R.S., 196–197
Heilman, K.M., 240–241, 348–349, 537
Heimer, L., 317
Heindel, W.C., 477
Held, N.N., 546
Hellhammer, D.H., 312
Helmer, D.C., 364
Hendrickson, A.E., 162, 273
Hendrickx, A.G., 356
Hendrie, C.A., 211
Henke, P.G., 333
Hennessey, A.C., 321
Hennevin, E., 265
Henningfield, J.E., 587
Herberg, L.J., 469
Herbert, J., 311
Hering, E., 153
Herkenham, M., 333
Hernandez, L., 417, 474, 477
Herz, A., 208
Hetherington, A.W., 415
Heuser, J.E., 050, 052
Heywood, C.A., 171
Hill, A.J., 498
Himmi, T., 419
Himms-Hagen, J., 424–425
Hines, M., 319
Hinjo, S., 573
Hirayama, K., 536
Hitchcock, J., 335
Hobson, J.A., 258, 270, 288
Hodges, J.R., 522
Hoebel, B.G., 399, 417, 469, 474, 477
Hoffman, F., 216
Hofman, M.A., 312
Hogan, S., 424
Hohman, G.W., 350–351
Hollander, E., 574–575
Holmes, G., 249
Holroyd, S., 580
Holton, T., 187
Holttum, J.R., 580–581
Holzman, P.S., 545
Hopfenbeck, J., 407
Hopkins, W.F., 459
Horne, J.A., 261–264
Horowitz, R.M., 216

Horton, E.S., 422
Horton, J.C., 162
Howard, J., 187
Howard, J.H., 364
Hu, G.Y., 456
Huang, Y.H., 388
Hubel, D.H., 157, 162, 165–166
Hubert, W., 312
Hubner, C.B., 476
Hudspeth, A.J., 187, 193
Hughes, J., 67, 208
Hull, E.M., 320
Hulsey, M.G., 412
Humphrey, A.L., 162
Humphreys, P., 537–538
Hunt, J.N., 400
Hunt, P.R., 505
Hunter, I., 266
Huttunen, M.O., 551
Hwang, P.H., 458–459
Hwang, P.M., 217
Hyldebrandt, N., 362
Hynd, G.W., 538

Ibuka, N., 272
Iggo, A., 202
Iino, M., 221
Imaki, T., 367
Imperato, A., 585, 590
Ingelfinger, F.J., 408
Innala, S.M., 313
Insel, T.R., 322
Irvine, J., 364
Itoh, K., 162
Iwai, E., 169–170
Iwata, J., 338, 462
Iwata, M., 534, 536

Jackson, T.A., 341
Jacobs, B.L., 281, 288, 333
Jacobs, K.M., 475
Jacobs, L.F., 497
Jacobsen, C.F., 341
Jacobsohn, D., 296
Jaffe, J.H., 585
Jakobson, L.S., 178
James, M., 172
James, W., 350
James, W.P.T., 423
Janah, A., 592
Jang, C.S., 208
Jaskiw, G., 547
Jasper, H., 137
Jasper, J.H., 285
Jeffcoate, W.J., 357
Jeffress, L.A., 195
Jellestad, F.K., 333

Jensen, M.L., 491
Jensen, T., 362
Jernigan, T.L., 538
Jerome, C., 391
Jervey, J.P., 438
Jeste, D.V., 542
Jewett, D.C., 419
Jiang, C.L., 400
Jodo, E., 286
Johansson, G., 177
Johnson, A.K., 380, 384–386
Johnson, L., 261
Johnson, M.K., 486
Johnston, D., 459
Johnston, R., 345
Johnstone, E.C., 545
Joly, M., 455
Jones, B.E., 279, 281, 285–287
Jones, D.T., 221
Jones, M.B., 578
Jones, S.S., 345
Jordan, C.L., 316
Josso, N., 295
Jouvet, M., 265, 286–288
Juji, T.M., 269
Julesz, B., 160
Julien, R.M., 590
Jung, M., 460
Juraska, J.M., 317

Kadekaro, M., 384
Kaitin, K.I., 256
Kalat, J.W., 403
Kales, A., 262, 268
Kalin, N.H., 362
Kalra, P.S., 419
Kalra, S.P., 419
Kanamori, N., 287
Kanner, L., 577
Kaplan, E., 526
Kaplan, J.M., 414
Kaplan, S.B., 368
Kapp, B.S., 333
Karacan, I., 257, 278
Karlson, P., 303
Karnovsky, M.L., 264
Karras, D., 468
Kasper, S., 566
Katayama, Y., 285
Katsuki, Y., 191
Katz, Y., 305
Kauer, J.S., 221
Kaufmann, W.E., 537–538
Kaupp, U.B., 221
Kavaliers, M., 211
Kawamura, H., 272
Kawamura, M., 536

Kay, J.A., 534
Kayama, Y., 286
Kaye, W.H., 428
Keesey, R.E., 415
Keil, L.C., 380, 382
Keiner, M., 328
Keithley, E.M., 188
Keller, S.E., 367
Kelley, A.E., 470
Kelly, D.H., 268
Kelso, S.R., 450–451
Kelsoe, J.R., 558
Kemp, D.T., 192
Kendell, R.E., 551
Kennedy, J.L., 544
Kennedy, S.H., 428
Kertesz, A., 240–241, 517–518
Kerwin, R.W., 555
Kessler, S., 269
Kety, S.S., 543
Keverne, E.B., 304–305
Khanna, S., 573
Kiang, N.Y.-S., 192
Kiecolt-Glaser, J.K., 366
Kim, J.K., 486
Kimura, K., 555
King, B.M., 126
Kinnamon, J.C., 216
Kinnamon, S.C., 214, 217
Kinsey, A.C., 308
Kirch, D.G., 547
Kirchgessner, A.L., 415
Klausner, J.D., 550
Klein, D.F., 573
Kleinman, J., 547
Kleitman, N., 257
Knapp, P.H., 367
Knebelmann, B., 294
Knott, P., 555
Kobashi, M., 391
Koelling, R.A., 402
Koenigsberg, H.W., 571
Köhler, C., 447
Kolvalzon, V.M., 283
Komisaruk, B.R., 211, 322, 328
Konishi, M., 195
Koob, G.F., 468–469, 476, , 589
Koolhaas, J.M., 353
Koopman, P., 293
Koopmans, H.S., 412
Korn, S.J., 579
Kornhuber, H.H., 245, 249
Koshland, D.E., 069, 458
Kostowski, W., 354
Koszycki, D., 573
Kovner, R., 439
Kozlowski, L.T., 177

Kozlowski, S., 390
Kral, J.G., 426
Kraly, F.S., 382–383
Kramer, F.M., 422
Kramer, L., 526
Krantz, D.S., 363
Kraut, R.E., 345
Krey, L.C., 361
Kriete, M., 576
Kruger, J., 592
Kruk, M.R., 354
Kubie, J.L., 499
Kuczmarski, R.J., 421
Kudoh, M., 197
Kuffler, S.W., 151
Kulkosky, P.J., 410
Kumar, K., 209
Kupfer, D.J., 563, 566
Kurihara, K., 217
Kuypers, G.J.M., 238–240

Laborit, H., 546
Lafrance, L., 412
Lamb, T., 357
Land, E.H., 167
Lane, D.M., 418
Lane, J.D., 585
Lane, R.W., 266
Lang, A.E., 477
Lange, C., 350
Langford, G., 267
Langston, J.W., 244
Lankenau, H., 428
Laplane, D., 575
Lapp, L., 266
Larsson, K., 211, 317, 322
Laschet, U., 357
Lasek, R.J., 028
Lavie, P., 267
Lavond, D.G., 462
Lawrence, D.G., 238–240
LeBlanc, J., 424
Leblanc, R., 514
Leboyer, M., 581
Leckman, J.F., 573
Leconte, P., 265–266
LeDoux, J.E., 012, 333, 335, 338–339, 460, 463, 506
Lee, J.-.H., 211
Lehman, C.D., 368
Lehman, M.N., 274, 277, 305
Leibenluft, E., 565
Leibowitz, K.J., 418
Leibowitz, S.F., 415–418
Le Magnen, J., 382, 401–402, 404
Le Moal, M., 585
Leon, M., 305, 327

Leonard, B., 499
Leonard, B.E., 562
Leonard, C.M., 333, 441
Leonard, H.L., 574–576
Lepkovsky, S., 382
Lerea, L.S., 453
Leslie, A.M., 577
Lesser, R., 537
Lester, L.S., 211
LeVay, S., 312
Levenson, R.W., 351
Levin, S., 545
Levine, J.D., 211
Levy, C.M., 256
Lewis, O.F., 263
Lewis, V.G., 308
Ley, R.G., 346–347
Li, T.-.K., 593
Liang, K.C., 361
Lichtman, S.W., 422
Liebeskind, J.C., 208, 210
Lin, S.P., 551
Lind, R.W., 385–386
Lindemann, B., 214, 216
Linden, D.J., 456
Lindvall, O., 466
Linnoila, M., 560
Lisk, R.D., 327
Liuzzi, F.J., 028
Livingstone, M.S., 162, 165–166
Ljungberg, T., 472
Lockhead, E., 214
Loewenstein, W.R., 203
Lombardi, J.., 303
Lombardo, R., 364
Lømo, T., 447, 449
LoTurco, J.J., 501
Louis-Sylvestre, J., 404
Lowe, T.L., 579
Lu, C.-.L., 354
Lubin, A., 261
Lubin, M., 327
Luebke, C., 326
Lumeng, L., 593
Luscher, M., 303
Lydic, R., 275, 285, 288
Lynch, G., 452, 455, 460–461
Lytton, W.W., 535

MacDonald, B., 173
MacLean, P.D., 091
Machon, R.A., 551
Macko, K., 170
Madison, D.V., 458
Madsen, P.L., 258
Maes, F.W., 214
Magnuson, D.J., 360

Mahowald, M.W., 270
Maier, S.F., 210
Maksay, G., 590
Malamut, B.L., 493
Maldonado, R., 585
Malenka, R.C., 453
Malinow, R., 452, 456
Mallick, B.N., 287
Mallow, G.K., 356
Malpeli, J.G., 151
Malsbury, C.W., 317, 469
Mandler, G., 488
Mann, F., 211
Manning, L., 525–526
Mantyh, P.W., 210
Manuck, S.B., 363
Maquet, P., 283
Marcel, A.J., 523, 535
Marczynski, T.J., 572
Margolin, D.I., 522–523, 535–536
Marin, O.S.M., 515–516, 518
Marini, J., 388
Mark, G.P., 475
Mark, N., 592
Mark, V.H., 206
Markram, H., 459
Marshall, J.C., 532
Martin, R.J., 412
Martinot, J.-L., 547
Maruyama, N., 197
Masi, A.T., 368
Masson, D.B., 389
Mather, P., 408
Matsuda, L.A., 068
Matteo, S., 310
Matthews, R.T., 585
Maunsell, J.H.R., 152, 166
Mawson, A.R., 427
Mayer, A.D., 328
Mayer, D.J., 208, 210–211
Mayer, J., 404
Mazur, A., 356–357
McBrair, M.C., 308
McBride, W.J., 593
McCann, M.J., 410
McCarley, R.W., 270, 288
McCarthy, R.A., 525, 532
McClintock, M.K., 301, 306
McCullough, L.D., 471
McDonald, T.J., 415
McEwen, B.S., 361
McGinty, D.J., 249, 282–283, 333
McGowan, M.K., 413
McGrath, M.J., 265
McIver, B., 384
McKenna, K.E., 315
McKenna, T.M., 197

McNaughton, B.L., 498, 501–502
McVary, K.T., 315
Meddis, R., 267
Mednick, S.A., 551
Meijer, J.H., 273–274
Melander, T., 418
Melges, F.T., 258
Melia, K.R., 464
Meltzer, H.Y., 549
Melzak, R., 207
Mench, J.A., 497
Menco, B.P.M., 221
Mendelson, M., 203
Mendelson, S.D., 320
Menninger, K.A., 550
Meredith, M., 304
Mesulam, M.-M., 473, 526
Metcalf, D., 285
Meterissian, G., 573
Metherate, B., 444
Metter, E.J., 514
Meyer-Bahlburg, H.F.L., 312
Michael, R.P., 300
Miczek, J.A., 358
Miller, G.A., 192
Miller, J.D., 269
Miller, J.P., 452
Miller, N.E., 013, 389
Miller, V.M., 499
Milner, A.D., 178
Milner, B., 482–486, 490
Milner, P., 465
Minard, A., 264
Mirmiran, M., 276
Miselis, R.R., 384
Miserendino, M.J.D., 464
Mishkin, M., 166, 169–170, 177–178,
    438–439, 473
Mitchell, J.E., 428
Mitchison, G., 265
Mittleman, G., 468
Miyashita, Y., 440
Miyauchi, S., 257
Mogenson, G.J., 388–389
Moghaddam, B., 471
Mohr, J.P., 486
Mok, D., 388
Moldin, S.O., 558
Mollon, J.D., 153
Moltz, H., 327
Monaghan, D.T., 452, 460
Mondragon, M., 306
Money, J., 308–309, 311, 318
Montero, S., 360
Mook, D., 391
Moore, A.M., 285
Moore, B.O., 410

Moore, C.L., 303, 317
Moore, J.T., 270
Moore, J.W., 500
Moore, R.Y., 272–273, 276
Moore, V.J., 263
Moore-Gillon, M.J., 382
Mora, F., 419
Morales, F.R., 287
Moran, T.H., 410
Moreau, J.O., 209
Morin, L.P., 273, 277
Morita, M., 382
Morley, J.E., 419
Morrell, F., 458
Morrell, M.J., 319
Morris, G.O., 261
Morris, N.M., 310
Morris, R.G.M., 496–497, 502
Morse, J.R., 217–218
Morton, J., 577
Morton, M.T., 276
Moscovitch, M., 348
Moss, R.L., 306
Mountcastle, V.B., 205, 242
Moyer, J.R., 500
Mukhametov, L.M., 260, 278, 283
Muller, D., 455–456
Muller, R.U., 499
Munitz, H., 173
Munro, J.F., 425
Murison, R., 333
Murray, E.A., 494
Murray, S., 357
Muzio, J.N., 265

Nadeau, S.E., 515
Naeser, M.A., 514
Nafe, J.P., 203
Nahin, R.L., 209
Nair, K.S., 424
Naito, K., 283
Nakahara, D., 471
Nath, R., 209
Nathan, J., 573
Nathans, J., 154
Nauta, W.J.H., 217, 281
Neale, J.M., 368, 573
Nelson, D.O., 386
Nermo-Lindquist, E., 392
Newcombe, F., 174, 532
Newman, E.A., 265
Newman, E.B., 194
Nicholl, C.S., 014
Nichols, D.G., 424
Nichols, D.S., 210
Nicolaïdis, S., 384, 407–408, 417
Nicoll, R.A., 209

Nielsen, J.M., 470, 343
Niijima, A., 406
Nilsson, O.G., 503
Nishino, S., 269
Nissenbaum, J.W., 402, 412
Noble, E.P., 593
Nock, B., 322
Noirot, E., 326
Nomikos, G.G., 555
Norgren, R., 217–218, 414
Norimoto, T., 382
Nose, H., 382
Novin, D., 406–407, 411
Nowlis, G.H., 218
Nuñez, A.A., 272
Numan, M.J., 327–328

Oaknin, S., 301, 317
Oates, J.A., 546
Obál, F., 264
O'Callaghan, E., 545, 553
O'Connell, R.J., 304
O'Dell, T.J., 458
Ohta, M., 286
Ohta, S., 173
O'Keefe, J., 333, 497, 499
Olds, J., 348, 465
Olds, M.E., 465, 469
Oleshansky, M., 559
Olney, J.W., 492
Olsen, S.A., 542
Olster, D.H., 302
Olton, D.S., 495–496, 503
Oomura, Y., 419
Oppliger, R.A., 423
Orlovsky, G.N., 249
Orr, W.B., 501
Orsini, J.C., 419
Osawa, Y., 170
Otto, T., 487

Pal, I., 256
Panksepp, J., 068, 354
Papadimitriou, G.N., 565
Papas, B.C., 495
Papez, J.W., 091
Park, C.R., 411
Pascoe, J.P., 333
Passingham, R.E., 477
Patarca, R., 288
Patterson, K., 534
Paul, C.A., 504
Pauls, D.L., 573
Pavlides, C., 503
Pearlman, C.A., 265–266
Pearson, A., 267
Peck, B.K., 281

Peck, J.W., 379
Penfield, W., 137, 235, 483
Penick, S., 506
Pennington, B.F., 537
Perrett, D.I., 171, 174
Perry, P., 357
Persky, H., 310, 356
Pert, C.B., 067, 208
Peterhans, E., 160
Petersen, S.E., 176, 518, 531
Petrides, M., 477
Pfaff, D.W., 320–321, 328
Pfaus, J.G., 474
Phillips, A.G., 468–469
Phillips, M.I., 382, 384
Phillips, R.G., 339, 471, 506
Phillipson, O.T., 285
Pi-Sunyer, F.X., 422
Pickar, D., 547
Pillard, R.C., 266, 313
Pilleri, G., 260
Pirke, K.M., 427
Piven, J., 578, 581
Plata-Salaman, C.R., 217–218
Plaznik, A., 354
Pleim, E.T., 320
Poggio, G.F., 162
Poggio, T., 162
Poncet, M., 178
Porter, R.W., 263
Posluns, D., 468
Post, R.M., 560
Powell, T.E., 356
Powers, J.B., 305
Pretlow, R.A., 327
Price, C., 518
Price, D.D., 211
Price, J., 558
Price, J.L., 217
Price, R.A., 423
Pritchard, T.C., 217
Proctor, W.R., 590
Propping, P., 592
Prosser, R.A., 276
Pucilowski, O., 354
Pycock, C.J., 555

Quadfasel, F.A., 520
Quillen, E.W., 382
Quirion, R., 392
Quirk, G.J., 499

Racine, R.J., 459
Radke, K.J., 383
Raffaele, K.C., 505
Rafii, A., 211
Ragland, D.R., 364

Raine, A., 550
Rajendren, G., 306
Rajna, P., 256
Raleigh, M.J., 353
Ralph, M.R., 274, 277
Ramirez, I., 213, 405
Ramm, P., 264
Rampin, C., 266
Ramsay, D.J., 389
Ranson, S.W., 415
Rapoport, J.L., 573, 576
Rasmussen, T., 235, 483
Ratcliff, G., 174
Ratnasuriya, R.H., 427
Rawlins, J.N.P., 505
Rawson, N.E., 406–407
Raybin, J.B., 267
Rea, M.M., 545
Reading, P.J., 477
Rechnitzer, P.A., 364
Rechtschaffen, A., 262, 269
Reed, B.R., 368
Reed, R.R., 221
Reese, T.S., 052
Rehkämper, G., 497
Reich, P., 264
Reich, T., 558
Reid, I.A., 382
Reifman, A., 559
Reiman, E.M., 564, 571
Reinink, E., 564
Reis, D.J., 338
Reiss, A.L., 579–580
Reppert, S.M., 276
Resko, J.A., 317
Reynecke, L., 562
Reynolds, D.V., 208
Reynolds, G.P., 547
Rezek, M., 406
Rhees, R.W., 317
Ricardo, J.A., 388
Rice, J.P., 558
Richmond, G., 320
Ridley, R.M., 503
Rietveld, W.J., 273–274
Riley, J.N., 273
Ris-Stalpers, C., 309
Risse, G., 486
Rissman, E.F., 310
Ritter, R.C., 406–407, 411
Ritter, S., 406, 414
Ritvo, E.R., 579, 581
Rizzo, M., 178
Rizzolatti, G., 178
Robbins, L.N., 570, 573
Robbins, T.W., 468, 473, 477
Roberts, D.C.S., 585

Roberts, W.W., 282
Robertson, G.S., 317
Robertson, H.A., 273
Robin, D.A., 178
Robinson, D.L., 176
Robinson, G.B., 459
Robinson, T.C.L., 282
Robinson, T.E., 586
Rodin, J., 422
Rodman, H.R., 175
Rodriguez-Sierra, J.F., 322
Roeltgen, D.P., 537
Roffwarg, H.P., 257, 265, 564
Rogers, F.B., 209
Rogers, M.P., 368
Roland, P.E., 264
Rolls, B.J., 389, 402
Rolls, E.T., 171, 218, 333, 419,
    441–442, 467
Romero, P.R., 306
Rose, G., 499
Rose, G.A., 422
Rose, G.M., 451
Rose, I.C., 469
Rose, J.D., 320
Rose, R.M., 359
Roselli, C.E., 317
Rosén, I., 237
Rosen, J.B., 339
Rosenblatt, J.S., 311, 326, 328
Rosenman, R.H., 363–364
Rosenthal, D., 558
Rosenthal, N.E., 565
Rosenwasser, A.M., 276
Ross, S.B., 322
Rosser, A.E., 305
Roth, R.H., 208
Roth, W.T., 571
Rothi, L.H., 240–241, 537
Rothman, S.M., 492
Rothwell, N.J., 424
Routtenberg, A., 427, 456, 469
Roy, A., 560
Rozin, P., 403
Rubin, B.S., 320
Rubin, P., 554
Rubin, R.T., 575
Rudy, J.W., 504–505
Rudy, T., 209
Ruggero, M.A., 192
Rumelhart, D.E., 446
Rumsey, J.M., 537
Rusak, B., 273–274, 277
Rush, A.J., 564
Russchen, F.T., 217
Russek, M., 411
Russell, G.F.M., 428

Russell, M.J., 306–307
Russell, R.M., 014
Rutter, M.L., 577, 579
Ryback, R.S., 263
Ryland, D.H., 576

Saayman, G.S., 356
Sachar, E.J., 560
Sackheim, H.A., 347
Saffran, E.M., 515–516, 518
Sahu, A., 419
St. Clair, D.M., 544
Saint-Cyr, J.A., 477
Saitoh, K., 197
Sakaguchi, A., 338
Sakai, F., 262
Sakai, K., 286–288, 440
Sakai, R.R., 388
Sakuma, Y., 320–321
Salamone, J.D., 468, 471, 476
Salis, P.J., 257
Saller, C.F., 417
Salmon, D.P., 477
Salzman, C.D., 175
Sampliner, R.I., 389
Samuelson, R.J., 495
Sanacora, G., 423
Sananes, C.B., 335, 462
Sandell, J.H., 152
Sanders-Bush, E., 561–562
Sapolsky, R.M., 361, 366
Sarker, J., 327
Sarvey, J.M., 459
Sassenrath, E.N., 356
Sato, M., 586
Sawchenko, P.E., 416, 419
Schank, D., 422
Scheel-Krüger, J., 470, 476
Schein, S.J., 168
Schenck, C.H., 269–270
Schenkel, E., 287
Scherschlicht, R., 563
Schiffman, P.L., 268
Schiffman, S.S., 214
Schiller, P.H., 151–152
Schleifer, S.J., 367
Schmitt, U., 192
Schneider, J.E., 419
Scholes, R., 348
Schreiber, R.C., 188
Schreiner, C.E., 197
Schulkin, J., 388, 391
Schulman, H., 456
Schultz, W., 472
Schumacher, M., 322
Schuman, E.R., 458
Schurmeyer, T., 312

Schuster, C.R., 470
Schwartz, D.H., 417
Schwartz, M., 308
Schwartz, M.F., 515–516, 535
Schwartz, W.J., 275–276
Schwartzman, R.J., 554
Schwarzkopf, S.B., 545
Schweiger, U., 427
Scifo, R., 581
Sclafani, A., 217, 402, 412, 415
Scott, T.R., 217–218, 414
Scoville, W.B., 482–483, 490
Seagraves, M.A., 175
Sedvall, G., 560
Seeman, P., 548–549
Segal, K.R., 422
Segal, M., 459
Segarra, J.M., 520
Sejnowski, T.J., 460, 464
Selye, H., 361
Semenza, C., 528
Semenze, C., 525–526
Sergent, J., 173–174
Shaikh, M.B., 354
Shallice, T., 534, 536
Sham, P.C., 551
Shapiro, M.L., 503
Shapiro, R.E., 384
Sharp, F.R., 367
Sharp, P.E., 501
Shavit, Y., 367
Shaw, L.-C., 211
Sheard, N., 326
Shefner, S.A., 590
Shepherd, G.M., 221
Sher, A.E., 268
Sherrington, R., 544
Sherry, D.F., 497
Shields, J., 543, 571
Shik, M.L., 249
Shimamura, A.P., 487, 508
Shimokochi, M., 318
Shimura, T., 318
Shipp, S., 166
Shizgal, P., 469
Shock, N., 361
Shor-Posner, G., 415–416
Shouse, M.N., 287
Shryne, J.E., 317
Sidman, M., 486
Siegel, A., 354
Siegel, J.M., 249, 287
Siegel, R.M., 175
Siegel, S., 584
Siever, L.J., 561
Signoret, J.-L., 173–174
Silva, A.J., 457, 502

Silverman, M.S., 169
Silverstein, L.D., 256
Simpson, J.B., 384
Sims, E.A.H., 422
Simson, P.E., 391
Sinclair, D., 204
Singer, A.G., 306
Singer, F., 360
Sirigu, A., 178
Sitaram, N., 285
Skinner, J.E., 305
Slater, B., 571
Slimp, J.C., 318
Slusser, P.G., 406, 415
Smith, A.P., 368
Smith, C.T., 264–266
Smith, D.J., 209
Smith, F.J., 404
Smith, G.P., 391, 410–411
Smith, H.G., 328
Smith, J.E., 585
Smith-Swintosky, V.L., 218
Snowman, A.M., 067, 208
Snyder, F., 265
Snyder, S.H., 067, 208, 458–459,
    546–548
Sokol, R.J., 588
Solomon, P.R., 500, 506
Solyom, L., 343
Sørensen, T.I.A., 423
Speakman, A., 499
Specht, S.M., 383
Sperry, R.W., 012
Spiegler, B.J., 473
Spoendlin, H., 188
Spyraki, C., 468–469
Squire, L.R., 487–488, 491–492, 494,
    500, 508
Stallone, D., 417
Stamm, J.S., 439
Stanfield, E.J., 322
Stanley, B.G., 416, 419
Stanton, P.K., 460, 464
Stebbins, W.C., 191
Steen, S.N., 423
Steffens, A.B., 399
Stehm, K.E., 313
Stein, E.A., 388
Stein, L., 474, 477
Steinman, J.L., 211
Stellar, E., 415
Stellar, J.R., 470
Stephan, F.K., 272
Steriade, M., 286
Sterman, M.B., 282
Stern, J.M., 326
Sternbach, R.A., 206

Stevens, J.R., 550
Stevens, S.S., 194
Stevenson, J.A.F., 389
Stewart, C., 497
Stewart, M., 503
Stinson, D., 565
Stinus, L., 585
Stöber, G., 553
Stock, M.J., 424
Stoddard, L.T., 486
Stoerig, P., 169
Stone, A.A., 368
Stone, S., 406, 415
Stoyva, J., 285
Stricker, E.M., 380, 410, 417–418
Striegel-Moore, R., 422
Striem, B.J., 216
Stroka, H., 173
Stunkard, A.J., 423
Sturup, G.K., 357
Suddath, R.L., 552
Suh, J.S., 417
Sulser, F., 561–562
Sunday, S.R., 217
Sunderland, G.S., 217
Suppes, T., 560
Susser, E.S., 551
Sutherland, R.J., 504–505
Sutter, M.I., 197
Suzdak, P.D., 589–590
Svensson, T.H., 555, 587
Sverd, J., 579
Swaab, D.F., 312
Swanson, L.W., 447
Swedo, S.E., 575–576
Sweeney, M.E., 422
Sweet, W.H., 206
Switz, G.M., 306
Syme, S.L., 364
Szatmari, P., 578
Szente, M.B., 460
Szuba, M.P., 565–566
Szymusiak, R., 282–283

Takagi, S.G., 221
Takahashi, L.K., 301, 362
Takahashi, Y., 264
Takino, R., 257
Talairach, J., 343
Talbot, J.D., 206
Tallon, S., 401
Tamminga, C.A., 546
Tanabe, T., 221
Tanaka, K., 170
Tarbuck, A., 418
Tarjan, E., 392
Tarsy, D., 549

Taylor, A.E., 477
Taylor, J.S., 406, 414
Taylor, W.G., 192
Teague, R.J., 424
Teitelbaum, P., 387, 399, 415
Tempel, D.L., 418
Terenius, L., 067, 208
Terman, M., 276
Tessier, J., 285
Tetrud, J.W., 244
Teuber, H.-L., 483
Teyler, T.J., 460
Thach, W.T., 249
Theorell, T., 359
Thivierge, J., 580
Thompson, C., 565
Thompson, K., 306
Thompson, L.T., 499
Thompson, R.F., 462, 500
Thorell, L., 158
Thorell, L.G., 159
Thorn, B.E., 210
Thornton, S.N., 384
Thrasher, T.N., 380, 386
Thunhorst, R.L., 385
Ticku, M.K., 590
Tobler, I., 278
Tocco, G., 455
Todd, R.B., 301
Tootell, R.B.H., 169
Tordoff, M.G., 391, 405–407, 411–412
Torrey, E.F., 551
Träskmann, L., 560
Tranel, D., 522
Trayhurn, P., 423
Treasure, J., 428
Triandafillou, J., 424
Trulson, M.E., 281
Tsien, R.W., 456
Tsou, K., 208
Tsuang, M.T., 543
Tuchweber, B., 361
Turnbull, I.M., 343
Turner, B.H., 333
Turner, J.G., 362
Tyrell, J.B., 361
Tyrrell, D.A.J., 368

Umitsu, Y., 170
Ungerleider, L.G., 166, 169–170,
    177–178
Uno, H., 361
Urbancic, M., 572
Urca, G., 209

Vaccarino, F.J., 326, 585
Valenstein, E.S., 342

Vandenbergh, J.G., 303
van den Berghe, G., 411
van de Poll, N.E., 355
van der Lee, S., 303
VanderWeele, D.A., 406, 414
Vanderwolf, C.H., 281, 503
van der Zee, E.A., 273, 501
Van Eekelen, J.A.M., 382
Van Essen, D.C., 166
Van Hoesen, G.W., 172
Vasselli, J.R., 412
Vathy, I.U., 322
Verbalis, J.G., 410
Vergnes, M., 353
Verney, C., 467
Verney, E.B., 377
Vickers, G., 585
Victor, M., 206, 491, 493
Villemure, J.-G., 173
Vindlacheruvu, R.R., 273
Voci, V.E., 327
Vogel, G.W., 563–564
vom Saal, F.S., 356
von Békésy, G., 184
von der Heydt, R., 160
Von Wendt, L., 579

Wada, J., 483
Wade, G.N., 419
Wagoner, K.S., 203
Wagoner, N., 273
Wahlström, A., 067, 208
Waldbillig, R.J., 354
Walker, A.E., 319
Walker, J.A., 522
Wallace, D.M., 360
Wallen, K., 310
Walsh, L.L., 388
Warchol, M.E., 188, 193
Ward, I.L., 313
Warner, R.K., 320
Warrington, E.K., 172, 483, 486, 525, 532, 534
Watson, N.V., 320
Watson, R.T., 348
Webb, W.B., 260
Webster, H.H., 286–287
Wehr, T.A., 565–566
Weidner, G., 364
Weinberg, M.S., 312

Weinberger, D.R., 550, 553–555
Weinberger, J.H., 444
Weinberger, N.M., 197, 443–444, 460, 463
Weingarten, H.P., 400
Weingarten, J.P., 415
Weintraub, S., 526
Weisinger, R.S., 392
Weiskrantz, L., 169, 486
Weiss, G.F., 415, 417
Weiss, J.M., 363
Weiss, M.L., 384
Weisz, D.J., 501
Weisz, D.W., 500
Weitzman, E.D., 268
Welle, S.L., 424
Wellman, P.J., 424
Weltzin, T.E., 427
Wernicke, C., 515
Werz, M.A., 495
Westbrook, P.R., 268
Whipple, B., 211
Whishaw, I.Q., 491
Whitam, F.L., 313
White, J.C., 206
White, J.D., 423
Whitehead, R.G., 423
Whitfield, I.C., 197
Whitsett, J.M., 303
Whitten, W.K., 303
Wiener, S.I., 504
Wiesel, T.N., 157
Wiesner, B.P., 326
Wilckens, T., 427
Wilcox, G.L., 458
Wilensky, M., 343
Wilkinson, L.O., 281
Williams, H.L., 261
Williams, R.B., 364
Williams, R.L., 257
Williams, R.T., 422
Willner, P., 476
Wilska, A., 192
Winans, S.S., 305
Winn, P., 418
Winslow, J.T., 358
Winter, P., 197
Wirz-Justice, A., 566
Wise, R.A., 573, 585–587
Witt, D.M., 322

Wolf, G., 391
Wolf, J.B., 341
Wolkin, A., 548
Wong, D.F., 547
Wong-Riley, M., 162
Wood, D.L., 363
Wood, R.J., 389
Woodrow, P., 389
Woodruff, R.A., 570
Woods, S.C., 412
Woods, S.W., 571
Woody, C.D., 460
Wu, J.C., 562, 564
Wyant, G.M., 209
Wyatt, R.J., 547, 550, 559
Wysocki, C.J., 304–305

Yadin, E., 336
Yakovlev, P.I., 206
Yamamoto, H., 536
Yates, W.R., 357
Yawata, T., 382
Ye, Q., 214
Yee, F., 416
Yeni-Komshian, G.H., 518
Yeomans, J.S., 469
Yeung, J.C., 209
Yokoo, H., 360
Yokota, T., 536
Yokouchi, C., 217
Yoshii, K., 217
Yoshimatsu, H., 419
Yost, W.A., 196
Young, G.B., 206
Young, R.C., 410

Zec, R.F., 553, 555
Zeki, S.M., 166, 167, 169, 177
Zemlan, F.P., 417
Zenner, H.-P., 192
Zhang, S.P., 354
Zigmond, M.J., 418
Zihl, J., 176
Zimmermann, U., 192
Zito, K.A., 585
Zola-Morgan, S., 491–494, 499
Zuch, J., 257
Zucker, I., 272
Zufall, F., 221
Zumoff, B., 360

SUBJECT INDEX

Ablation, experimental, 6, 124–130
Absorptive phase, of metabolism, 398
Accessory olfactory bulb, 304
Accommodation, 144
Acetate, 61
Acetylcholine (ACh), 54, 68
    in REM sleep, 285–288
    termination of postsynaptic potentials for, 57
    as transmitter substance, 61–62
Acetylcholinesterase (AChE), 57, 62, 73
Acetyl coenzyme A (acetyl CoA), 61–62
Achromatopsia, 168–169
Acquired dyslexias, 532
Acral lick dermatitis, 576
ACTH (adrenocorticotropic hormone), 360–361
Actin, 226, 228
Action potential, 20–21, 32, 35–39, 133
Activational effects of sex hormones, 316
    on females, 310–311, 355
    on males, 311–312
    on sexual orientation, 312–313
Acuity, visual, 144
Acupuncture, 211
Adaption, sleep as, 259–260
Addiction, 582–594
    alcohol and, 588–593
    amphetamine and, 585–586, 587
    barbiturates and, 590
    caffeine and, 586–587
    cocaine and, 585–586
    genetics of, 590–594
    marijuana and, 587–588
    nicotine and, 586–587, 588

opiates and, 583–585
    tolerance and, 583, 584
    withdrawal symptoms and, 583–585, 590
Adenosine monophosphate (AMP), cyclic, 54, 587
Adenosine triphosphate (ATP), 23, 54
Adipose satiety factor, 412
Adipose tissue, 397, 398–399
    brown, 424–425
    white, 424
Adjunctive behaviors, 468
Adrenalectomy, 367, 368
Adrenalin, 64–65
Adrenal medulla, 103
Adrenocorticotropic hormone (ACTH), 360–361
Adrenogenital syndrome, 308
Affective disorders. *See* Major affective disorders
Afferent axons, 100, 112–113
Aggressive behavior, 352–359
    androgens and, 355, 356–358
    in females, 355–356
    hormonal control of, 48, 354–359
    in males, 354–355
    nature and functions of, 352–353
    neural control of, 353–354
Agnosia
    auditory, 197
    visual, 171–175
Agonist(s), 70, 73
    dopamine, 468–469, 545–547
    inverse, 572
    serotonin, 573
Agonist muscles, 234, 235
Agoraphobia, 570
Agrammatism, 515
Agraphia

apraxic, 240
    semantic, 537
AIDS, 583
Akinesia, 245
Akinetic mutism, 343
Albumin, 109
Alcohol
    addiction to, 588–593
    aggressive behavior and, 358
    heredity and, 590–593
    Korsakoff's syndrome and, 482–483
    reinforcement and, 589
Alcohol antagonist, 589, 590
Aldosterone, 360, 375, 383, 388
Alexia, pure, 529–531, 539
Alkaloids, 72, 213
All-or-none law, 37
Alpha activity, 255
Alpha motor neurons, 226
Amacrine cells, 145, 146
Amino acid transmitter substances, 66–67
2–amino–5–phosphonapentanoate (AP5), 502, 503
Amnesia
    anterograde, 482–494
    retrograde, 482, 508
AMP (adenosine monophosphate), cyclic, 54, 587
Amphetamine
    addiction to, 585–586, 587
    psychosis-inducing effect of, 546–547
    reinforcement and, 470–471
AMPT (α-methyl-p-tyrosine), 416
Ampulla, 199
Amygdala (amygdaloid complex), 91, 92, 93, 217
    aggressive behavior and, 354

basolateral group of, 333, 463
central nucleus of, 333–335, 336, 548
classical conditioning and, 462–464
emotional responses and, 332–337
major divisions of, 333
medial nucleus of, 304
reinforcement and, 472–473
relational learning and, 492–493
schizophrenia and, 548
Anabolic steroids, 357–358
Analgesia, 205, 207–211
Anandamide, 69
Androgen(s), 293
aggressive behavior and, 355, 356–358
in female sexual behavior, 302–303, 308–310
in male sexual behavior, 302–303
organizational effects of, 302–303, 307–310, 355
in sexual development, 293, 295, 297
Androgen insensitivity syndrome, 309–310
Androgenization
failure of, 309–310
prenatal, 307–310, 313, 356–357
Androstenedione, 297
Androstenol, 307
Angiotensin, 381–382, 383, 384–387, 388–389
Angiotensinogen, 381
Animal research, 12–15
Animism, 2
Anion, 32
Anion effect, 214–215, 216
Anomia, 515, 525
Anomic aphasia, 523–526, 528
Anorexia nervosa, 427–428
Anosmia, 213
ANP (atrial natriuretic peptide), 392
ANS (autonomic nervous system), 102–103, 104
Antagonist(s), 70–72
alcohol, 589, 590
dopamine, 467–468, 545–547
serotonin, 575–576
Antagonist muscles, 234, 235
Anterior, 78, 79
Anterograde amnesia, 482–494
anatomy of, 490–494
description of, 483–485
hippocampus and, 484, 490–493
relational learning and, 488–490

Anterograde labeling methods, 111, 113
Antibodies, 111, 365
Anticipatory anxiety, 570, 572
Anticipatory drinking, 382
Antidepressant drugs, 558, 560–562
Antidepressant effects, 565
Antidiuretic hormone, 376
Antigens, 111–112, 365
Antigravity muscles, 226
Antihistamine drugs, 546
Antiobsessional drugs, 575–576
Antipsychotic drugs, 548–549
Anxiety, anticipatory, 570, 572
Anxiety disorders, 336, 570–576
causes of, 570–576
obsessive compulsive disorder, 343, 573–576
panic disorder, 570–573
treatment of, 573, 575–576
Anxiety-reducing drugs, 336
Anxiolytic effects, 572, 588–589
AP5 (2–amino-5–phosphonapen-tanoate), 502, 503
Aphasia, 512
anomic, 523–526, 528
Broca's, 513, 514–516, 528
conduction, 522–523, 528
reading and writing skills and, 528–529
transcortical sensory, 519–520, 528
Wernicke's, 517–526, 528
Aphrodisin, 306
Apomorphine, 72
Apperceptive visual agnosia, 172–174
Apraxia, 240–243
callosal, 241–242
constructional, 240, 242–243
left parietal, 242, 243
limb, 240, 241–242, 243
ocular, 177–178
oral, 240
sympathetic, 242
Apraxic agraphia, 240
Arachnoid membrane, 81, 82
Arcuate fasciculus, 522, 523
Area postrema, 29
Aromatic compound, 300
Aromatization, 300
Arousal, neural control of, 279–281
Articulation difficulties, 515–516
Association cortex, 90–91
auditory, 91
frontal, 235, 236
somatosensory, 91, 339–340

visual, 91, 166–179
Associative long-term potentiation, 450, 451, 455
Associative visual agnosia, 174–175
Astrocytes (astroglia), 25, 26
Ataxia, optic, 177, 178
ATP (adenosine triphosphate), 23, 54
Atrial baroreceptors, 382, 388, 389
Atrial natriuretic peptide (ANP), 392
Atropine, 72
Audition, 182–201
anatomy of ear and, 183–186
behavioral functions in, 196–197
feature detection in, 193–196
hair cells in, 184, 186–188, 189, 190, 192, 199, 201
loudness detection in, 192–193
pathway of, 188–190
pitch detection in, 191–192
stimulus in, 182–183
timbre detection in, 193
transduction in, 186–188, 189
Auditory agnosia, 197
Auditory association cortex, 91
Auditory canal, 183
Auditory cortex, primary, 90, 190, 197, 443–444, 445
Auditory information, coding of, 191–192
Auditory learning, 443–444
Auditory nerve, 183
Auditory pathway, 188–190
Auditory tuning curves, 191, 192
Autistic disorder, 577–582
brain pathology of, 579–582
heritability of, 578–579
possible causes of, 578–582
symptoms of, 577–578, 580
Autoassociator, 507
Autoimmune diseases, 366
Autolytic enzymes, 108
Autonomic nervous system (ANS), 102–103, 104
Autonomic response, 332
Autoradiography, 115, 116, 117
Autoreceptors, 57
Autotopagnosia, 521–522
Aversive emotional learning, 333–334
Axoaxonic synapse, 58
Axodendritic synapse, 58
Axon(s), 20–21
action potential of, 20–21, 32, 35–39, 133
afferent, 100, 112–113
cable properties of, 38

Axons (*continued*)
efferent, 101, 110–112
electrical potential of, 30–32
membrane potential of, 31–35
myelinated vs. unmyelinated, 26–27
staining by DiI, 113, 114
Axonal varicosities, 64
Axoplasmic transport, 25
Axosomatic synapse, 58

Balint's syndrome, 177, 178
Ballistic movements, 248
Barbiturates, 590
Baroreceptors, 382, 388, 389
Basal forebrain region, 281–282
Basal ganglia, 92, 93
in movement control, 243–245, 246
in stimulus-response learning, 477
Basic rest-activity cycle (BRAC), 257, 271
Basilar membrane, 184, 186, 187, 190
Basolateral group of amygdala, 333, 463
Bed nucleus of the stria terminalis (BNST), 112, 113
Bedwetting, 270–271
Behavior
adjunctive, 468
brain stimulation and, 136–137
defensive, 353
hearing and, 196–197
nest-building, 11, 324–327
offensive, 353
physiological basis of, 7–8, 10–11
physiological model of, 3–4
submissive, 353
threat, 353
type A and type B patterns of, 363–364
Behavioral response, 332
Belladonna alkaloids, 72
Benzodiazepines, 67, 336, 571–572, 589
Bereavement, and immune system, 367
Bernard, Claude, 372
Beta activity, 255
Binding site, 48
Biological clocks, 271–278, 563–566
Bipolar cells, 145, 146, 147
Bipolar disorder, 557, 558, 559–560
Bipolar neurons, 21, 22
Bisexual organs, 293
Bitterness, 213, 215, 216–217, 218
Blindsight, 165

Blind spot, 145
Blobs, 162
Blood-brain barrier, 29
Blood pressure, high, 359, 360, 363, 364
Blood supply, to brain, 79–81
B-lymphocytes, 365, 367
BNST (bed nucleus of the stria terminalis), 112, 113
Body fat, 397, 398–399
Bony labyrinths, 198
Botulinum toxin, 71
BRAC (basic rest-activity cycle), 257, 271
Brain
autistic disorder and, 579–582
blood supply to, 79–81
Broca's area of, 6, 7, 514
cerebrospinal fluid production in, 82–83
connection with eye, 147–149
control of movement by, 235–250
control of sexual behavior by, 317–322
development of, 85–87
eating and, 414–421
fixation of, 108
forebrain structures of, 86, 88–95
hemispheres of. *See* Hemispheres, of brain
hindbrain structures of, 86, 97–99
homosexuality and, 312–313
inhibition of, 134–137, 138
lesions in. *See* Lesions
living, study of, 117–122
macrostructure of, 447
messages received by, 6–7
microstructure of, 446–447
midbrain structures of, 85, 86, 95–97
recording electrical activity of, 130–134
REM sleep and, 265
salt appetite and, 388–389
of schizophrenic patients, 547–556
sectioning, 108–109
sleep control by, 272–289
sleep deprivation and, 261–262
speech and, 512–528
stimulation of, 134–137, 138, 208–209, 210, 451–454, 465–471
thirst and, 383–389
tracing connections in, 113, 114
Wernicke's area of, 514, 517, 521, 537, 538

Brain-blood barrier, 29
Brain damage
anomia and, 525
behavioral effects of, 125
causes of, 550–553
expression of emotion and, 349
recognition of emotion and, 348–349
relational learning and, 492–493, 496–497
in schizophrenia, 549–556
stress and, 362
visual agnosia and, 172–173
Brain stem, 95, 97, 414–415
Bregma, 128
Brightness, 143
Broca, Paul, 6
Broca's aphasia, 513, 514–516, 528
Broca's area, 6, 7, 514
Brood nest, 324
Bruce effect, 303–304
Bulimia nervosa, 427–428

CA1 fields, 448–450, 455, 456, 459, 460, 474, 475, 491–492, 493
Ca²⁺. *See* Calcium ions
CA3 fields, 448, 449, 459–460
Cable properties, of axon, 38
Caffeine, 586–587
Calcarine fissure, 148
Calcium-calmodulin kinase, type II (CaM-KII), 456–457
Calcium-dependent enzymes, 456
Calcium ions (Ca²⁺)
in long-term potentiation, 452–454
in migration of synaptic vesicles, 51
in postsynaptic potentials, 55, 56
Callosal apraxia, 241–242
CaM-KII (type II calcium-calmodulin kinase), 456–457
Cannula, 134, 135
Capsaicin, 406
Capsule, of muscle fiber, 226
Carbohydrates, taste of, 217
Cardiac muscles, 230
Cardiovascular disease, and stress, 363–364
Carotid artery, 80, 81
Castration, 302, 311, 354, 355, 357
Cataplexy, 269, 270
Catecholamines, 63–65, 126
Cations, 32
Cauda equina, 98, 100
Caudal, 78, 79
Caudal block, 79

Caudate nucleus, 244, 245, 246, 466, 470
CCK (cholecystokinin), 410, 412, 573
Cell(s)
  bipolar, 145, 146, 147
  complex, 158
  Deiters's, 184
  horizontal, 145, 146
  natural killer, 365, 367–368
  nerve. *See* Neurons
  place, 497–499
  Schwann, 27–28, 38–39
  simple, 158
  structure of, 20–25
  supporting, 25–29
Cell body, 20, 21
Cell-body stains, 109–110
Cell-mediated immune reactions, 365–366
Cell membrane, 22, 24
Central auditory system, 189–190
Central nervous system (CNS), 78, 84–100
  blood-brain barrier in, 29
  development of, 84–87
  forebrain in. *See* Forebrain
  hindbrain in, 86, 97–99
  midbrain in, 85, 86, 95–97
  neural communication in, 30–45, 48–74
  neurons in, 20–25
  spinal cord in, 98–99
  supporting cells in, 25–29
  See also Brain
Central nucleus of amygdala, 333–335, 336, 548
Central sulcus, 88
Cerebellar cortex, 97
Cerebellar nuclei, deep, 97
Cerebellar peduncles, 97
Cerebellum, 97, 245–249
Cerebral aqueduct, 82, 83
Cerebral cortex, 6–7, 88–91, 206–207
Cerebral hemispheres. *See* Hemispheres, of brain
Cerebral ventricles, 3
Cerebrospinal fluid (CSF), 81, 82–83, 412–413
Cerebrovascular accidents (strokes), 14, 512
Cerletti, Ugo, 559
Cheese effect, 558
Chemical control, of sleep, 278–279
Chemically mediated immune reactions, 365–366

Chemical stimulation, 134–136
Children
  autistic disorder in, 577–582
  sleep problems of, 270–271
  sudden death of, 268
Chloride ion (Cl⁻)
  in membrane potential, 33–35
  in postsynaptic potentials, 54, 56
Chlorpromazine, 67, 546
Cholecystokinin (CCK), 410, 412, 573
Choline, 61
Choline acetyltransferase, 61
Chorda tympani, 217, 218
Choroid plexus, 82
Chromosomes, 8, 22, 292–293, 294
  fragile X syndrome, 579
  schizophrenia and, 544–545
  sex, 292–293, 294, 544–545, 579
  See also Heredity
Cilia
  on hair cells, 186–187, 188, 190, 192, 199, 201
  on tongue, 213, 214
Cingulate gyrus, 88, 90, 343
Circadian rhythms
  major affective disorders and, 563–566
  in sleep, 271–272, 273, 275–277
Circumlocutions, 523
Circumvallate papillae, 213
Circumventricular organ, 380, 384–387
Cisternae, 50
Clasp-knife reflex, 233
Classical conditioning, 334–336, 433–435, 462–464
  of eating, 400, 401
  extinction and, 464
  Hebb rule and, 434–435
  model of drug tolerance, 584
  neural model of, 434
Clomipramine (CMI), 572, 575
Clonidine, 416
Clozapine, 548, 549
CMI (clomipramine), 572, 575
CNS. *See* Central nervous system
Cocaine, 73, 585–586
Cochlea, 183–184, 185, 192
Cochlear nerve, 188–189, 192
Cochlear nerve ganglion, 188
Cochlear nucleus, 189, 336
Coding
  of auditory information, 191–192
  of color, 152–156
  of gustatory information, 218

opponent-process, 155–156
  of visual information, 150–157
Cold pressor test, 363
Colliculi
  inferior, 95, 97, 189–190
  superior, 95, 97
Colloid, 380–381
Color, coding of, 152–156
Color blindness, 145
Color constancy, 168
Color mixing, 153–154
Color vision
  genetic defects in, 154–155
  photoreceptors and, 144–145, 154–155
  role of visual association cortex in, 167–169
  striate cortex and, 162–163
Commissural/associational system, 449
Commissure, 88
Communication, 512–540
  of emotions, 344–349
  reading, 528–535
  speech comprehension, 512–513, 517–528
  speech production, 513–516
  writing, 528–529, 535–539
  See also Neural communication
Communication disorders
  acquired dyslexias, 532
  agrammatism, 515
  anomia, 515, 525
  anomic aphasia, 523–526, 528
  articulation difficulties, 515–516
  Broca's aphasia, 513, 514–516, 528
  conduction aphasia, 522–523, 528
  developmental dyslexias, 532, 537–539
  direct dysgraphia, 537
  direct dyslexia, 535, 539
  orthographic dysgraphia, 536, 537, 539
  phonological dysgraphia, 536, 539
  phonological dyslexia, 533–534, 539
  pure alexia, 529–531, 539
  pure word deafness, 348, 518–519, 528
  semantic agraphia, 537
  surface dyslexia, 532–533, 539
  transcortical sensory aphasia, 519–520, 528
  Wernicke's aphasia, 517–526, 528

Communication disorders (*continued*)
word-form (spelling) dyslexia, 534, 539
Complex cells, 158
Complex stimulus, 339–343
Compulsions, 573–576
Computer, as output device, 134, 135
Computerized tomography (CT scan), 117–118, 119
Concordant twins, 313, 543
Conditional discrimination task, 505
Conditional response (CR), 433
Conditional stimulus (CS), 433
Conditioned emotional response, 334–336
Conditioned flavor aversion, 402–403
Conditioned place preference, 468
Conditioned punisher, 435, 472
Conditioned reinforcer, 435, 472
Conditioning. *See* Classical conditioning; Instrumental conditioning
Conduction aphasia, 522–523, 528
Cones, of eye, 144–145, 155–156
Conjunctiva, 143
Consolidation, 485
Constructional apraxia, 240, 242–243
Content words, 514
Contralateral, 78
Converging operations, 108, 138
Coolidge effect, 300
Coping response, 334, 362–363
Corpus callosum, 11, 88, 90, 536, 537
Corpus luteum, 299
Correctional mechanism, 372
Corticobulbar pathway, 238, 239, 241
Corticomedial group of amygdala, 333
Corticospinal pathway, 237, 239, 241
Corticotropin-releasing factor (CRF), 360–361
Cortisol, 360–361
Crack, 585
Cranial nerves, 101–102
Craniosacral system, 103
CRF (corticotropin-releasing factor), 360–361
Cribriform plate, 219–220
Cristae, of mitochondria, 23
Crossing-over, 544–545
Cross sections, 78
Cryode, 127, 128
CSF (cerebrospinal fluid), 81, 82–83, 412–413
CT (computerized tomography) scan, 117–118, 119
Cupula, 199

Curare, 72
Cutaneous senses, 201
anatomy of skin in, 202–203
neural pathways in, 205–206
pain perception by, 204–205, 206–211
stimuli of, 201–202
transduction from, 203
Cyclic adenosine monophosphate (cyclic AMP), 54, 587
Cytokines, 366
Cytoplasm, 23, 24

DA. *See* Dopamine
Darwin, Charles, 7, 345
Decerebrate, 233
Decerebrate rigidity, 233
Declarative memories, 487, 488
Decomposition of movement, 248
Decremental conduction, 38
Deep cerebellar nuclei, 97
Defeminizing effect, 293, 296, 302–303
Defensive behaviors, 353
Degradation, graceful, 446
Deiters's cells, 184
Delayed matching-to-sample task, 438, 439
Delta activity, 256, 264
Delusions, 542
Dendrites, 20, 21
Dendrodendritic synapse, 58
Dentate gyrus, 448–449, 453–454, 455, 458
Dentate nucleus, 248
2–deoxyglucose (2–DG), 116–117
Deoxyribonucleic acid (DNA), 22
Depolarization, 31, 32, 41–43, 146, 147
Depression
endogenous, 557
long-term, 451, 460, 557–567
low-frequency stimulation and, 451
reactive, 557
REM sleep and, 266–267, 563–564
unipolar, 557
Depressogenic effect, 564
Dermatitis, acral lick, 576
Dermis, 202
Descartes, René, 3–4, 5
Desipramine (DMI), 575
Desynchrony, 255
Detectors, 372
feature, 193–196
of muscle length, 228–229

Determinism, 4–5
Deuteranopia, 154–155
Developmental dyslexias, 532, 537–539
2–DG (2–deoxyglucose), 116–117
Diabetes insipidus, 376
Dialysis, 122, 471
Diazepam, 67, 572
Diencephalon, 85, 86, 92–95
Diet, and eating, 401–403
Diffusion, 32–35
Digestion, 396–397, 408–412
Dihydrotestosterone, 293, 297
DiI, 113, 114
Direct dysgraphia, 537
Direct dyslexia, 535, 539
Discordant twins, 313, 543, 552
Discrimination, 446, 505
Diseases
autoimmune, 366
cardiovascular, 363–364
immune system and, 365–369
infectious, 368–369
Disgust, 337
DMI (desipramine), 575
DNA (deoxyribonucleic acid), 22
Doctrine of specific nerve energies, 6
L-DOPA (L–3,4–dihydroxyphenylalanine), 62–63, 549
DOPA decarboxylase, 63
Dopamine (DA), 63–64, 68
agonists for, 468–469, 545–547
antagonists for, 467–468, 545–547
in Parkinson's disease, 63
receptors for, 64
in reinforcement, 466–469, 473–474
Dopamine hypothesis, 63–64, 545–549
Dopaminergic neurons, and opiates, 585
Dopaminergic pathways, in reinforcement, 466–467
Dorsal, 78, 79
Dorsal column, 205
Dorsal lateral geniculate nucleus, 147, 148
Dorsal root, 99
Dorsal root ganglia, 100
Dorsolateral columns, 210
Double labeling, 116
Drinking, 372–392
anticipatory, 382
fluid balance in, 373–377, 378
food-related, 382–383

neural control of, 384–389
osmometric thirst in, 377–380, 382, 383–384
regulatory mechanisms in, 372–373
salt appetite and, 377–383, 388–389, 391–392
satiety in, 372–373, 389–392
volumetric thirst in, 377, 380–382
Drug(s)
addiction to, 582–594
antidepressant, 558, 560–562
antihistamine, 546
antipsychotic, 548–549
anxiety-reducing, 336
intracranial administration of, 469–471
for obsessive compulsive disorder, 575–576
Parkinson's disease and, 120, 121
physical dependence on, 583–585
psychic dependence on, 583
reinforcement and, 467–471
self-administration of, 469
serotonergic, 353–354
sleep and, 268
synaptic activity and, 70–73
tolerance for, 583, 584
in treatment of major affective disorders, 558, 560–562
in treatment of obesity, 426
in treatment of schizophrenia, 548–549
withdrawal symptoms and, 583–585, 590
See also specific drugs
Drug dependency insomnia, 268
Drug discrimination procedure, 470
Dualism, 2–4
Duodenum, 390
Dura mater, 81, 82
Dynorphins, 208
Dysgraphia
direct, 537
orthographic, 536, 537, 539
phonological, 536, 539
Dyslexia, 532
acquired, 532
developmental, 532, 537–539
direct, 535, 539
phonological, 533–534, 539
surface, 532–533, 539
word-form (spelling), 534, 539
Dysphoria, 583

Ear, 183–186
Eardrum, 183, 193
Eating, 396–429
body fat regulation and, 398–399
brain mechanisms and, 414–421
classical conditioning of, 400, 401
dietary selection and, 401–403
digestive process and, 396–397, 408–412
disorders of, 421–429
drinking and, 382–383
fasting and, 398
initiation of, 400–408
metabolism and, 396–400
neural control of, 414–421
recognition of food and, 408
sleep and, 264
social and environmental factors in, 400–401
storage and utilization of nutrients in, 396–398, 399, 403–407
termination of, 408–414
weight regulation and, 398–399
Echopraxia, 579
ECT (electroconvulsive shock), 558, 559, 562
EEG (electroencephalogram), 133–134, 254–256, 257
Efferent axons, 101, 110–112
EGTA, 451
Ejaculation, 299
Electrical activity, of brain, 130–134
Electrical stimulation, 134–137, 138
learning and, 465–471
NMDA receptors and, 451–454
pain and, 208–209, 210
seizures and, 137
Electroconvulsive shock (ECT), 558, 559, 562
Electrodes, 30
macroelectrodes, 132
microelectrodes, 31, 131–132
Electroencephalogram (EEG), 133–134, 254–256, 257
Electrolytes, 32
Electromyogram (EMG), 254, 256
Electron microscopy, 123
Electro-oculogram (EOG), 254, 256
Electrostatic pressure, 32–35
Embedding, of brain tissue, 109
EMG (electromyogram), 254, 256
Emotion(s), 332–359
aggression and, 352–359
expression of, 344–349
feelings of, 349–352

James-Lange theory of, 350–351
neural control of, 332–337
perception of stimuli and, 337–343
recognition of, 346–347, 348–349
stress and, 359–370
types of responses, 332
Endocrine glands, 48
Endogenous depression, 557
Endogenous opiates, 67, 207–208
Endolymph, 199
Endoplasmic reticulum, 23, 24
β-endorphin, 208
Endplate potential, 227
Enkephalins, 67, 208
Entorhinal cortex, 448
Enuresis, nocturnal, 270–271
Enzymatic deactivation, 57
Enzymes, 22–23
autolytic, 108
calcium-dependent, 456
localization of, 114–115
EOG (electro-oculogram), 254, 256
Epidermis, 202
Epididymis, 293
Epilepsy, 66–67
electrical stimulation and, 137
scanning brain for seizures, 120–122
split-brain operation and, 11–12, 13
Epinephrine, 64–65, 68, 360
Episodic learning, 436
EPSPs. *See* Excitatory postsynaptic potentials
Esophageal fistula, 390
Estradiol, 296–297, 301, 302, 323, 327, 328, 329
Estrogens, 296
Estrous cycles, 298
L-ethionine, 407
Evoked potentials, 133
Evolution, 7–10
Excitation, threshold of, 32
Excitatory postsynaptic potentials (EPSPs), 43, 449, 450, 501, 502
Excitatory synapses, 42
Excitotoxicity, 135
Exercise effects on sleep, 262–264
Exocytosis, 25
Experimental ablation, 6, 124–130
Experimental physiology, 5–7
Explicit memories, 487, 488
Expression, of emotions, 344–349
Extension, 226
External auditory canal, 183

External genitalia, 294–295
Extinction, 464
Extracellular fluid, 33–35, 373
Extrafusal muscle fibers, 226
Extraocular muscles, 143
Extrastriate cortex, 166
Eye
    connection with brain, 147–149
    movements of, 144
    photoreceptors in, 144, 146–147,
        154–155
    structure of, 143–145

Faces, recognition of, 172–174
Facial expression of emotions, 345,
    346
Fallopian tubes, 293
Fastigial nucleus, 246
Fasting phase, of metabolism, 398
Fat, 397–399
Fatty acids, 397, 398, 405
Fear, 334–336
Feature detection, in auditory system,
    193–196
Feedback
    from muscles, 228–229
    negative, 372
    from simulated emotions, 351, 352
Feelings, 349–352. See also
        Emotion(s)
Fenestration, 185
Fenfluramine, 417, 426
Fertilization, 292
Fight-or-flight response, 359
Fimbria, 293, 448
Finger spelling, 175
Fissures, 88, 89, 148, 448
Fixative, 108
Flavor aversion, 402–403
Flexion, 226
Flocculonodular lobe, 246, 247
Flourens, Pierre, 6
Fluid(s)
    cerebrospinal, 81, 82–83, 412–
        413
    extracellular, 33–35, 373
    hypertonic, 373
    hypotonic, 373
    interstitial, 122–123, 373
    intracellular, 33–35, 373
    isotonic, 373
Fluid balance, 373–377, 378
Fluorogold, 112, 113
Focal-seizure disorders, 137
Foliate papillae, 213

Follicle-stimulating hormone (FSH),
    295, 297, 298
Food. See Eating
Force
    of diffusion, 32–35
    of electrostatic pressure, 32–35
Forebrain, 86, 88–95
    basal region of, 281–282
    gustation and, 217
    medial forebrain bundle, 465–466,
        469
Form, perception of, 169–175
Formalin, 108
Fos, 117
Fourth ventricle, 82, 83
Fovea, 144
Foveal vision, 144–145
Fragile X syndrome, 579
Free will, 4–5
Freezing, of brain tissue, 109
Freezing response, 334, 335
Frequency
    fundamental, 193
    spatial, 158–160, 161
Freud, Sigmund, 586
Fritsch, Gustav, 6
Frontal association cortex, 235, 236
Frontal lobes, 88, 89, 90
Frontal sections, 78
FSH (follicle-stimulating hormone),
    295, 297, 298
Functionalism, 7–10
Function words, 514
Fundamental frequency, 193
Fungiform papillae, 213
Fusion pore, 52

GABA (gamma-aminobutyric acid),
    66–67, 68
GABA-benzodiazepine receptor com-
    plex, 67, 589, 590
Gage, Phineas, 341
Galanin, 418, 421
Galvani, Luigi, 5, 6
Gametes, 292
Gamma-aminobutyric acid. See
        GABA
Gamma motor neurons, 226, 232
Gap junction, 58, 59
Gases, soluble, 69–70
Gastric factors, in eating, 408–409
Gastroplasty, 425
Gene(s), 22, 293, 543–545. See also
        Heredity
Generalization, 10, 445–446

Genitalia, 294–295
Gestagens, 297
Glabrous skin, 202
Glia (glial cells), 25–27
Glossopharyngeal nerve, 217, 218
Glucagon, 397, 398
Glucocorticoids, 360–361, 367
Glucoprivation, 405
Glucose, 396–398, 403–405
Glucose transporters, 397–398
Glucostat, 404
Glucostatic hypothesis, 403–405
Glutamate, 66, 217, 452
Glutamate receptors, 66
Glutamic acid (glutamate), 66, 217,
    452
Glycerol, 397, 398
Glycine, 67
Glycogen, 396, 398
Golgi, Camillo, 26
Golgi apparatus, 24, 25
Golgi-Cox stain, 110, 111
Golgi tendon organ (GTO), 228–229,
    233, 234
Gonad(s), 292–293
Gonadotropic hormones (go-
    nadotropins), 95, 295, 296, 297
Gonadotropin-releasing hormones
    (GnRH), 295, 297
G protein, 54
Graceful degradation, 446
Granule cells of dentate gyrus,
    448–449
Gray matter, 88, 89, 96, 97. See also
        Periaqueductal gray matter
Growth hormone, 264
GTO (Golgi tendon organ), 228–229,
    233, 234
Gustation, 213–219
    anatomy of taste buds in, 213–214
    coding for, 218
    pathway for, 217–218
    stimuli in, 213
    transduction for, 214–217
Gustatory cells, 213–214
Gustatory pathway, 217–218
Gyri, 88, 89

Hair cells
    in audition, 184, 186–188, 189, 190,
        192, 199, 201
    vestibular, 199, 201
Hair pulling, compulsive, 576
Hairy skin, 202
Hallucinations, 269, 542, 546–547

6–HD (6–hydroxydopamine), 126
Head factors, in eating, 408
Hearing. *See* Audition
Heart disease, and stress, 363–364
Heart muscles, 230
Hebb rule, 434–435, 447
Helmholtz, Hermann von, 7
Hemispheres, of brain, 11–12, 13
    in expression and recognition of
        emotion, 346–348
    speech and, 512–513
    visual agnosia and, 173
Hepatic portal system, 390, 391
Heredity
    addiction and, 590–594
    alcohol and, 590–593
    anorexia nervosa and, 428
    autistic disorder and, 578–579
    color vision and, 154–155
    major affective disorders and, 558
    obesity and, 423
    panic disorder and, 570–571
    schizophrenia and, 543–545
Hering, Ewald, 153
Heroin, 583, 584–585
Hertz, Heinrich, 182
Hertz (Hz), 182
5–HIAA (5–hydroxyindoleacetic
    acid), 560
High blood pressure, 359, 360, 363,
    364
High-precision liquid chromatogra-
    phy (HPLC), 122
Hindbrain, 86, 97–99
Hippocampus (hippocampal forma-
    tion), 91, 92, 447
    anatomy of, 490–491
    anterograde amnesia and, 484,
        490–493
    connections of components of,
        448–449
    development of, 448
    EEG activity from, 133–134
    emotional response and, 339–340
    learning and, 448–450, 485, 496,
        497–508
    long-term potentiation and,
        501–502
    place cells in, 497–499
    in relational learning, 485, 496,
        497–508
    spatial perception and, 496–497
    stress and, 361, 362
    theory of function of, 504–508
    theta activity of, 502–504

Histamine, 205, 546
Histological procedures, 108–110
Hitzig, Eduard, 6
Homeostasis, 372, 584
Homosexuality, 312–313
Horizontal cells, 145, 146
Horizontal sections, 78, 80
Hormonal control
    of aggressive behavior, 48, 354–359
    of female reproductive cycles,
        298–299
    of human sexual behavior, 298–315
    of kidneys, 375–376, 378
    of maternal behavior, 327–328
    of sexual behavior in laboratory an-
        imals, 299–307
    of sexual development, 293–295
    of sexual maturation, 295–297
    of sexual orientation, 312–313
Hormonal response, 332
Hormones, 48, 59, 95, 264. *See also*
    Sex hormones; *specific hormones*
Horseradish peroxidase (HRP), 52–53
HPLC (high-precision liquid chro-
    matography), 122
Hubel, David, 157–158
Hue, 143
Hunger, 400–408. *See also* Eating
Huntington's chorea, 244, 246, 575
Hydrocephalus, 83
6–hydroxydopamine (6–HD), 126
5–hydroxyindoleacetic acid
    (5–HIAA), 560
Hyperpolarization, 32, 41–43, 146
Hypertension, 359, 360, 363, 364
Hypertonic fluid, 373
Hypnagogic hallucinations, 269
Hypothalamic hormones, 297
Hypothalamus, 93–95, 217–218, 335
    aggressive behavior and, 354
    eating and, 415–420
    kidney control and, 376
    lateral, 387, 418–420
    medial, 415–418
    paraventricular nucleus of. *See* Par-
        aventricular nucleus of the hy-
        pothalamus
    ventromedial (VMH), 320–322,
        415
Hypotonic fluid, 373
Hypovolemia, 373–374, 383

Ibotenic acid, 126, 127
Immune reactions, 365–366
Immune system, 365–366

neural control of, 366–368
    stress and, 368–369
Immunocytochemical methods, 111,
    114–115
Immunoglobulins, 365, 368
Implicit memories, 487–488
Incus, 183
Infants, sudden death of, 268
Infectious diseases, 368–369
Inferior colliculi, 95, 97, 189–190
Inferior temporal cortex, 169–171
Inflammatory reaction, 365
Ingestive behavior, 372. *See also*
    Drinking; Eating
Inhibition, of brain, 134–137, 138
Inhibitory postsynaptic potentials
    (IPSPs), 43
Inhibitory synapses, 42
Ink-writing oscillograph, 133–134
Inner ear, 183–185, 198
In situ hybridization, 115, 116, 117
Insomnia, 267–268
Instrumental conditioning, 435–436,
    465–478
    functions of reinforcement system
        in, 471–477
    negative reinforcement in, 468
    neural model of, 435
    reinforcing brain stimulation in,
        465–471
Insulin, 396, 398, 412–413, 423
Intensity differences, 195–196
Interferon, 365
Intergeniculate leaflet, 273, 274
Interleukin-1, 366
Interleukin-2, 366
Internal carotid arteries, 80, 81
Interneurons, 44
Interposed nuclei, 246
Interstitial fluid, 122–123, 373
Intestinal bypass surgery, 425
Intestinal factors, in eating, 409–411
Intracellular fluid, 33–35, 373
Intrafusal muscle fibers, 201, 226
Intralipid, 411
Intraperitoneal (IP) injections, 411
Intromission, 299
Inverse agonist, 572
Ion(s), 32–37. *See also specific ions*
Ion channels, 35, 36, 53
Ionotropic receptor, 53–54, 58, 62
Iproniazid, 73
Ipsilateral, 78
IPSPs (inhibitory postsynaptic poten-
    tials), 43

Ischymetric hypothesis of hunger, 407
Isotonic fluid, 373

James-Lange theory, 350–351
Joubert syndrome, 580–581

Kainic acid, 126, 135
K complex, 256
Kidneys
    fluid balance and, 375–376, 378
    renin production by, 381
Killer cells, natural, 365, 367–368
Kinesthesia, 201
Kinsey report, 308
Korsakoff's syndrome, 482–483,
    493–494

Labeling
    anterograde, 111, 113
    double, 116
    retrograde, 112, 113
Labyrinths, bony, 198
Lactation, 327–328
Lactic acid, 571
Lamellae, 146
Lateral, 78, 79
Lateral-basomedial group of amyg-
    dala, 333
Lateral corticospinal tract, 237, 241
Lateral fissure, 88
Lateral geniculate nucleus, 93, 94, 147,
    148, 273
Lateral hypothalamus, 387, 418–420
Lateralization, 512–513. See also
    Hemispheres, of brain
Lateral lemniscus, 189–190, 336
Lateral reticulospinal tract, 241
Lateral ventricles, 82, 83
Laterodorsal tegmental nucleus
    (LDT), 285, 286
Latitude effect, 550–551
Learning
    auditory, 443–444
    consolidation in, 485
    declarative, 487, 488
    emotional responses and, 333–336
    episodic, 436
    hippocampus and, 448–450, 485,
        496, 497–508
    long-term potentiation and,
        459–462
    motor, 435–436, 486, 487
    nature of, 432–437
    neural communication in, 434–435,
        444–447

NMDA receptors in, 450–458, 460,
    461
nondeclarative, 487–488
observational, 436
perceptual, 432, 437–447, 485–
    486
relational, 436, 482–509
REM sleep and, 265–266
spatial, 436
spatial perception and, 496–497
stimulus-response, 432–435,
    462–478, 486
verbal, 487–488
visual, 437–443
See also Amnesia; Classical condi-
    tioning; Memory; Reinforcement
Lectins, 111
Lee-Boot effect, 303
Left parietal apraxia, 242, 243
Lemniscus
    lateral, 189–190, 336
    medial, 205
Lesions
    eating and, 414, 415
    motor deficits and, 236, 241–242
    neurotoxic, 126, 127
    producing in brain, 125–127
    relational learning and, 492–493,
        496–497
    sexual behavior and, 319
    speech production and, 513,
        514–515
    subcortical, 126
    visual agnosia and, 173
Leucine, 208
Leu-enkephalin, 208
LH (luteinizing hormone), 295, 297,
    299, 360
Librium, 67
Ligand, 48
Light
    biological clock and, 272, 273
    perception of, 150–152
    properties of, 142–143
Limb
    flexing of, 226
    phantom, 207
Limb apraxia, 240, 241–242, 243
Limbic cortex, 88
Limbic system, 91–92
Lipids, 68–69
Lipoprivation, 405
Lithium, 558, 559–560
Liver
    in initiation of eating, 396–397

in termination of drinking, 390,
    391
in termination of eating, 411–412
Lobotomy, prefrontal, 341–343
Localization
    of neurochemicals, 114–116
    of receptors, 116, 117
    of sound, 194–196
Location, perception of, 177–179
Locus coeruleus, 279, 280
Long-term depression, 451, 460,
    557–567
Long-term memory, 484–485
Long-term potentiation, 459–462
    associative, 450, 451, 455
    in hippocampal functioning,
        501–502
    induction of, 447–450
    learning and, 459–462
    modulation of, 459–460
    other forms of, 460–461
Lordosis, 301
Loudness, 182
    detection of, 192–193
    localization by, 193–196
Luteinizing hormone (LH), 295, 297,
    299, 360
Lymphocytes, 365–366, 367, 368
Lysosomes, 24, 25

MA (mercaptoacetate), 405
Macroelectrodes, 132
Magnetic resonance imaging (MRI),
    118–119, 120
Magnocellular layers, 148, 166
Magnocellular nucleus, 287
Major affective disorders, 557–567
    brain abnormalities and, 562
    circadian rhythms and, 563–566
    drug treatment of, 558, 560–562
    ECT treatment of, 558, 559, 562
    heritability of, 558
    monoamine hypothesis of, 560–561
    physiological treatments of,
        558–560
    REM sleep deprivation and,
        563–564
    symptoms of, 557
    total sleep deprivation and,
        564–565
    types of, 557
    zeitgebers and, 565–566
Malleus, 183
Mania, 557
MAO (monoamine oxidase), 63

MAO inhibitors, 73, 244, 558, 560, 561
Marijuana, 587–588
Masculinizing effect, 293, 296, 302–303
Massa intermedia, 82, 83, 92, 93
Maternal behavior, 324–329
    hormonal control of, 327–328
    neural control of, 328–329
    in rodents, 324–325
    stimuli for, 325–327
Meals
    dietary selection in, 401–403
    initiation of, 400–408
    termination of, 408–414
    See also Eating
Medial, 78, 79
Medial forebrain bundle (MFB), 465–466, 469
Medial geniculate nucleus (MGM), 93, 94, 190, 338, 443, 462, 463
Medial hypothalamus, 415–418
Medial lemniscus, 205
Medial nucleus of the amygdala, 304
Medial preoptic area (MPA), 317, 318, 319, 328, 355
Medial reticulospinal tract, 241
Median preoptic nucleus, 386
Medulla (medulla oblongata), 97–98, 208–209
Meissner's corpuscles, 203
Melatonin, 277
Membrane
    of cell, 22, 24
    postsynaptic, 42
    presynaptic, 42
Membrane potential, 31–35, 146
Membrane stains, 110
Memory, 432
    in anterograde amnesia, 482–494
    declarative, 487, 488
    explicit, 487, 488
    hippocampus in, 484, 485, 490–493, 497–508
    implicit, 487–488
    long-term, 484–485
    nondeclarative, 487–488
    reference, 496
    short-term, 484, 485
    working, 495–496
Memory task, 488, 489, 492–493
Meninges, 81–83
Menstrual cycles, 298–299, 306–307, 310, 356

Mental disorders, 542–594
    addiction, 582–594
    anxiety disorders, 570–576
    autistic disorder, 577–582
    major affective disorders, 557–567
    obsessive compulsive disorder, 343, 573–576
    panic disorder, 570–573
    psychoses, 542, 586
    schizophrenia, 542–557
    symptoms of, 542–543
    See also specific disorders
Mercaptoacetate (MA), 405
Merkel's disks, 203
Mesencephalic locomotor region, 249
Mesencephalon, 85, 86, 95–97, 466
Mesocortical system, 467
Mesolimbic system, 466
Messenger ribonucleic acid (mRNA), 22, 114–116, 117
Metabolism, 396–400
    absorptive phase of, 398
    fasting phase of, 398
    fatty acid, 397, 398, 405
    glucose, 396–398, 403–405
    measuring, 116–117
    in obesity, 422–424
Metabotropic receptors, 54, 59, 62
Metencephalon, 85, 86, 97
Met-enkephalin, 208
Methionine, 208
Methyl palmoxirate (MP), 405
α-methyl-p-tyrosine (AMPT), 416
MFB (medial forebrain bundle), 465–466, 469
MGM (medial geniculate nucleus), 93, 94, 190, 338, 443, 462, 463
Microdialysis, 122, 471
Microelectrode, 31, 131–132
Microelectrode puller, 131
Microiontophoresis, 136
Micrometer, 26
Micropipette, multi-barreled, 136
Microscopy, electron, 123
Microtome, 108–109
Microtubules, 24, 25
Midbrain, 85, 86, 95–97
Middle ear, 183, 185
Mind-body question, 2, 4
Mineralocorticoid, 360
Mirror-drawing task, 486, 487
Mitochondria, 23, 24
Mitral cells, 220
Modules, in striate cortex, 163–165
Monism, 4–5

Monoamine, 62–66
Monoamine hypothesis, 560–561
Monoamine oxidase (MAO), 63
Monoamine oxidase inhibitors, 73, 244, 558, 560, 561
Monosodium glutamate (MSG), 66, 217
Monosynaptic stretch reflex, 230–232, 233
Mood disorders. See Major affective disorders
Morphine, 209, 583, 585
Morphinelike factor, 208
Mossy fibers, 449
Motor cortex, primary, 6–7, 90, 235–240
    control of movement by, 237–240
    organization of, 235–237
Motor endplates, 227
Motor homunculus, 235, 236
Motor learning, 435–436, 486, 487
Motor neurons, 20, 226, 227, 232
    alpha, 226
    gamma, 226, 232
Motor unit, 226
Movement
    ballistic, 248
    decomposition of, 248
    of eye, 144
    perception of, 158, 175–177
    sequence of, 249
Movement control, 226–250
    basal ganglia in, 243–245, 246
    by brain, 235–250
    cerebellum in, 245–249
    deficits in, 240–243, 248–249
    motor cortex in, 235–240
    muscles in, 226–230
    by reflexes, 230–234, 235
    reticular formation in, 249
MP (methyl palmoxirate), 405
MPA (medial preoptic area), 317, 318, 319, 328, 355
MRI (magnetic resonance imaging), 118–119, 120
MSG (monosodium glutamate), 66, 217
Müller, Johannes, 5–6, 7
Müllerian-inhibiting hormone, 293, 294, 309
Müllerian system, 293, 294
Multi-barreled micropipette, 136
Multipolar neurons, 21, 24
Multiunit smooth muscles, 230
Muscarinic receptors, 62

Muscle(s)
  agonist, 234, 235
  antagonist, 234, 235
  antigravity, 226
  cardiac, 230
  contraction of, 226, 227–228
  control of, by brain, 235–250
  deficits in control of, 240–243
  extraocular, 143
  of eye, 143
  feedback from, 228–229
  kinesthesia for, 201
  reflex control of, 230–234, 235
  skeletal, 226–229
  smooth, 230
  striated, 226
Muscle fibers
  extrafusal, 226
  intrafusal, 201, 226
Muscle length detectors, 228–229
Muscle spindles, 226, 232
Mutations, 8–9
Mutism, 245, 343
Myasthenia gravis, 73
Myelencephalon, 85, 86, 97–98
Myelin sheath, 20, 21, 26
Myelin stains, 110
Myofibrils, 226
Myosin, 226, 228
Myosin cross bridges, 226, 227–228

Na⁺. See Sodium ions
Nail-biting, compulsive, 576
Naloxone
  opiate receptors and, 585
  in pain perception, 208, 209, 210, 211
Narcolepsy, 269
Natural killer cells, 365, 367–368
Natural selection, 7–10
NE. See Norepinephrine
Negative feedback, 372
Negative reinforcement, 468, 589
Negative symptoms, 542–543
Neocortex, 88, 90–91
Neostriatum, 243, 466, 547, 548
Nephrons, 375
Nerve cells. See Neurons
Nervous system
  autonomic, 102–103, 104
  basic features of, 78–84
  blood-brain barrier in, 29
  blood supply of, 79–81
  meninges of, 81–83

neural communication in. See Neural communication
  neurons in, 20–25
  parasympathetic, 103, 104
  peripheral, 20, 27–28, 78, 81, 100–104
  somatic, 102
  structure of, 84–104
  supporting cells in, 25–29
  sympathetic, 102–103, 104
  See also Brain; Central nervous system
Nest-building behavior, 11, 324–325, 327
Neural communication, 30–45, 48–74
  action potential in, 20–21, 32, 35–39, 133
  axoaxonic synapses in, 58
  dendrodendritic synapses in, 58
  in learning, 434–435, 444–447
  membrane potential in, 31–35
  neural integration in, 41–43
  within neuron, 30–45
  between neurons, 48–74
  nonsynaptic, 58–59
  overview of, 40–45
  pharmacology of synapses in, 70–74
  synaptic transmission in, 48–58
  transmitter substances in, 61–70
Neural conduction, speed of, 39
Neural connections
  between eye and brain, 147–149
  strengthening, 473–474
  study of, 110–113
Neural control
  of aggressive behavior, 353–354
  of arousal, 279–281
  of drinking, 384–389
  of eating, 414–421
  of emotional response patterns, 332–337
  of immune system, 366–368
  of maternal behavior, 328–329
  of REM sleep, 279, 283–288
  of reproductive behavior, 315–323, 328–329
  of sexual behavior, 315–323
  of sleep, 279–288
  of slow-wave sleep, 281–283
Neural integration, 41–43
Neural networks, 444–447
Neural plasticity
  dopamine and, 473–474

mechanisms of, 447–462
Neuraxis, 78, 79
Neuroanatomical and neurochemical research procedures, 108–124
Neurochemicals, localization of, 114–116
Neurofilaments, 25
Neuroglia, 25–27
Neuromas, 207
Neuromodulators, 48
Neuromuscular junction, 227
Neurons
  bipolar, 21, 22
  communications of. See Neural communication
  glia and, 25–27
  motor, 20, 226, 227, 232
  multipolar, 21, 24
  postganglionic, 103, 104
  preganglionic, 103, 104
  sensory, 20
  structure of, 20–25
  unipolar, 21, 22
Neuropeptide Y, 273–274, 418–419, 421, 423, 428
Neurosecretory cells, 95, 96
Neurotensin, 209–210
Neurotoxic lesions, 126, 127
Neurotransmitter. See Transmitter substances
Neurotransmitter-dependent ion channels, 53
New Guinea tribe, 345, 346
Nicotine, 72, 586–587, 588
Nicotinic receptors, 62
Nictitating membrane, 500
Nightmare, 258–259
Night terrors, 270–271
Night vision, 145
Nigrostriatal system, 244, 466–467
Nimiety, 425
Nissl stains, 110
Nissl substance, 109
Nitric oxide, 69–70
Nitric oxide synthase, 458
NMDA (N-methyl-D-aspartate), 87
NMDA receptors, 87, 450–458, 460, 461, 492, 502, 503
Nocturnal enuresis, 270–271
Node of Ranvier, 26, 27, 38, 39
Nondeclarative memories, 487–488
Non-REM sleep, 256, 257
Nonshivering thermogenesis, 424
Nonspecific immune reaction, 365
Nontheta behaviors, 503

Noradrenergic neurons, 65
Noradrenergic receptors, 65
Norepinephrine (NE), 64–65, 68
    eating and, 415–417, 421, 428
    localization of, 114
    reproductive behavior and, 323
    sleep and, 288
    stress response and, 360
Nose. See Olfaction
NST (nucleus of the solitary tract),
    217, 384, 414
Nucleolus, 22, 24
Nucleus
    of cell, 22, 24
    of thalamus, 93
Nucleus accumbens, 467, 471,
    474–476, 548, 555
Nucleus basalis, 443
Nucleus of the solitary tract (NST),
    217, 384, 414
Nucleus raphe magnus, 209–210
Nucleus reticularis pontis caudalis,
    336
Nutrients
    depletion of, 403–407
    storage and utilization of, 396–398,
    399, 403–407
Nystagmus, 198

Obesity, 421–426
    possible causes of, 421–425
    treatment of, 422, 425–426
Object recognition, 174–175
Observational learning, 436
Obsessions, 573, 574
Obsessive compulsive disorder, 343,
    573–576
Occipital lobes, 88, 89
Ocular apraxia, 177–178
Odor. See Olfaction
Offensive behaviors, 353
Olfaction, 219–222
    anatomy of receptors in, 219–221
    brain hemispheres and, 12
    responses in, 221
    stimuli in, 219
    transduction in, 221
Olfactory bulbs, 102, 220, 222, 304
Olfactory epithelium, 219, 220
Olfactory glomeruli, 220
Olfactory system, 220, 304
Oligodendroglia, 25, 26–27, 38
Olivary complex, superior, 189, 196
Olivocochlear bundle, 189
Omnivores, 401

ON/OFF ganglion cells, 150–152
Onychophagia, 576
Operant conditioning. See Instrumen-
    tal conditioning
Opiate(s)
    addiction to, 583–585
    central nucleus and, 336
    dopaminergic neurons and, 585
    endogenous, 67, 207–208
Opiate-induced analgesia, 208–211
Opiatelike peptides, 208
Opiate receptors, 208
Opioids, 208, 428. See also Opiate(s)
Opium, 583
Opponent-process coding, 155–156
Opsin, 146
Optic ataxia, 177, 178
Optic chiasm, 93, 95, 148
Optic disk, 145
Oral apraxia, 240
Orbitofrontal cortex, 340–343
Organic senses, 201, 202
Organizational effects of sex hor-
    mones, 293
    androgens, 302–303, 307–310, 355
    prenatal androgens, 307–310
    on sexual development, 293
    on sexual orientation, 312–313
    testosterone, 355
Organ of Corti, 184, 185, 186, 192
Organum vasculosum of the lamina
    terminalis (OVLT), 380, 384, 387
Orientation, and vision, 158
Orthographic dysgraphia, 536, 537,
    539
Oscillograph, ink-writing, 133–134
Oscilloscope, 31, 32, 132–133
Osmometric thirst, 377–380, 382,
    383–384
Osmoreceptors, 377–380
Osmosis, 377
Ossicles, 183
Otoconia, 199
Output devices, 132–134
    computers, 134, 135
    ink-writing oscillograph, 133–134
    oscilloscope, 31, 32, 132–133
Oval window, 183, 185
Ovarian follicles, 298
Ovarian hormones, 310–311
Ovaries, 294, 296
Overcompensation, 549
Overtones, 193
OVLT (organum vasculosum of the
    lamina terminalis), 380, 384, 387

Ovulation, 299, 356
Oxytocin, 68, 297, 300–301, 311

Pacemaker, 230
Pacemaker potentials, 230
Pacinian corpuscles, 202–203
PAG. See Periaqueductal gray matter
Pain
    acupuncture and, 211
    cerebral cortex and, 206–207
    perception of, 204–205, 206–
    211
    reduction of, 207–211
Paleostriatum, 467
Palilalia, 579
Panic disorder, 570–573
Papillae, 213
Parachlorophenylalanine (PCPA), 70,
    210, 281, 562
Paradoxical sleep, 256
Paraffin, 109
Parahippocampal cortex, 490, 493
Paranoid schizophrenia, 586
Parasympathetic division of ANS,
    103, 104
Paraventricular nucleus (PVN) of the
    hypothalamus, 277
    drinking and, 376, 386
    eating and, 415–418
    stress and, 360
Parietal apraxia, left, 242, 243
Parietal lobes, 88, 89
Parkinson's disease, 63
    basal ganglia and, 243–244
    drug abuse and, 120, 121
    symptoms of, vs. schizophrenic
    symptoms, 548, 549
Parturition, 324
Parvocellular layers, 148, 166
Patch clamp, 54
Pavor nocturnus, 270–271
PCPA (parachlorophenylalanine), 70,
    210, 281, 562
Pedunculopontine nucleus, 243
Pedunculopontine tegmental nucleus
    (PPT), 285, 286
Pelvic thrusting, 299
Peptide(s), 59, 67–68
    localization of, 114–116
    opiatelike, 208
Peptide bonds, 59
Perceptual learning, 432, 437–447,
    485–486
Perforant path, 448
Perfusion, of brain tissue, 108

Periaqueductal gray matter (PAG), 96, 97
  aggressive behavior and, 354
  emotional responses and, 335
  perception of pain and, 208–210
  sexual behavior and, 321
Perilymph, 199
Peripheral nervous system (PNS), 20, 27–28, 78, 100–104
  autonomic nervous system of, 102–103, 104
  cranial nerves of, 101–102
  meninges covering, 81
  spinal nerves of, 100–101
Perirhinal cortex, 490, 493
Permeability, selective, 29
Persistence, in oscilloscope screens, 132
PET (positron emission tomography) scan, 119–120, 121
PGO waves, 283–284, 285, 286, 287
Phagocytosis, 26
PHA-L (*phaseolus vulgaris leukoagglutinin*), 111–112, 113
Phantom limb, 207
Phase differences, 194–195
Phenylketonuria (PKU), 579
Pheromones, 49, 303–307
Phonetic reading, 532, 533
Phonological dysgraphia, 536, 539
Phonological dyslexia, 533–534, 539
Photopigments, 146
Photoreceptors, 144–147
  in color vision, 144–145, 154–155
  membrane potential of, 146
  structure and function of, 146–147
  trichromatic coding and, 154–155
Phototherapy, 565
Physiological mechanisms
  of regulation of drinking, 372–373
  of sleep, 278–289
  of waking, 278–281
Physiological psychology
  biological roots of, 5–10
  contributions of modern psychology to, 10–15
  philosophical roots of, 2–5
  research methods of, 5–10, 108–139
Physiology, experimental, 5–7
Physostigmine, 73
Pia mater, 81, 82
Picogram (pg), 382
Picrotoxin, 353
Pigment mixing, vs. color mixing, 153
Piloerection, 230

PIN (posterior intralaminar nucleus of the thalamus), 338, 462, 463
Pineal body, 3, 4
Pineal gland, 277
Pinna, 183
Pinocytosis, 52, 53
Pitch, 182, 191–192
Pituitary gland, 93, 95, 96
PKC (protein kinase C), 456
PKU (phenylketonuria), 579
Placebo, 211
Place cells, in hippocampal formation, 497–499
Place code, 191–192
Place preference, conditioned, 468
Planum temporale, 537–538
PMS (premenstrual syndrome), 356
PNS. *See* Peripheral nervous system
Polyethylene glycol, 381
Polysynaptic reflexes, 232–234
Pons, 97
Pontine nucleus, 248
Population EPSP, 449, 450, 501, 502
Positive reinforcement, 589
Positive symptoms, 542
Positron emission tomography (PET), 119–120, 121
Posterior intralaminar nucleus (PIN) of the thalamus, 338, 462, 463
Posterior lobes, 90
Posterior pituitary gland, 95, 96
Postganglionic neurons, 103, 104
Postsynaptic membrane, 42
Postsynaptic potentials, 42–43, 54–57
  excitatory, 43, 449, 450, 501, 502
  inhibitory, 43
Postsynaptic receptors, 53–54
Posture, monosynaptic stretch reflex in, 232, 233
Potassium ion (K^+)
  in action potential, 35–37
  in membrane potential, 33–35
  in postsynaptic potentials, 54, 55
Potential
  action, 20–21, 32, 35–39, 133
  endplate, 227
  evoked, 133
  excitatory postsynaptic, 43, 449, 450, 501, 502
  inhibitory postsynaptic, 43
  membrane, 31–35, 146
  pacemaker, 230
  postsynaptic, 42–43, 54–57, 449, 450, 501, 502

receptor, 146
  resting, 31
Potentiation. *See* Long-term potentiation
PPT (pedunculopontine tegmental nucleus), 285, 286
Predation, 353, 354
Prefrontal cortex, 473, 477, 554–555
Prefrontal lobotomies, 341–343
Preganglionic neurons, 103, 104
Premenstrual syndrome (PMS), 356
Prenatal androgenization, 307–310, 313, 356–357
Preoptic area, 282, 317, 318, 319, 328, 355
Pressor amines, 558
Pressure sensation, 201, 203
Presynaptic facilitation, 58
Presynaptic inhibition, 58
Presynaptic membrane, 42
Primary auditory cortex, 90, 190, 197, 443–444, 445
Primary motor cortex, 6–7, 90, 235–240
Primary somatosensory cortex, 90, 205–206, 236–237
Primary visual cortex, 90
  anatomy of, 162–163
  pure alexia and, 529, 531
Primary visual pathway, 147–149
Priming task, 486, 488
Pro-dynorphin, 208
Pro-enkephalin, 208
Progesterone, 297, 299, 301, 302, 322, 323, 327, 328
Projection fibers, 92–93
Prolactin, 297, 301, 327, 328
Pro-opiomelanocortin, 208
Prosody, 526–527
Prosopagnosia, 172–173
Prostaglandins, 205, 283
Prostate, 293
Protanopia, 154
Protein kinase(s), 456
Protein kinase C (PKC), 456
Pseudoautosomal segment, 544, 545
Pseudobulbar palsy, 348
Pseudopodia, 26
Psychic dependence, 583
Psychoneuroimmunology, 365–369
Psychoses, 542, 586. *See also* Major affective disorders; Schizophrenia
Psychosurgery, 341–343
Puberty, 295–297, 356–357

Pulvinar, 176
Punishers, 435, 472
Punishing stimulus, 435
Pure alexia, 529–531, 539
Pure word deafness, 348, 518–519, 528
Pursuit movement, 144
Putamen, 244, 245, 466
PVN. *See* Paraventricular nucleus of the hypothalamus
Pylorus, 390
Pyramidal cells, 449
Pyramidal tracts, 237, 238

Radio frequency lesions, 126
Raphe nuclei, 209–210, 281, 282, 288
Rate code, 192
Rate law, 40–41
Rate of firing, 41
Rauwolfia serpentina, 560
Reactive depression, 557
Reading
    phonetic, 532, 533
    whole-word, 531, 533
Reading disorders, 528–535
    aphasia and, 528–529
    direct dyslexia, 535, 539
    phonological dyslexia, 533–534, 539
    pure alexia, 529–531, 539
    surface dyslexia, 532–533, 539
    word-form dyslexia, 534, 539
Rebound phenomenon, 265
Receptive fields, in vision, 150, 155
Receptor(s)
    activation of, 53–54
    autoreceptors, 57
    baroreceptors, 382, 388, 389
    dopamine, 64
    drug effects on, 72
    GABA, 67, 589, 590
    glutamate, 66
    ionotropic, 53–54, 58, 62
    localization of, 116, 117
    long-term changes in sensitivity of, 561–562
    metabotropic, 54, 59, 62
    muscarinic, 62
    nicotinic, 62
    NMDA, 87, 450–458, 460, 461, 492, 502, 503
    noradrenergic, 65
    olfactory, 219–221
    opiate, 208
    osmoreceptors, 377–380

photoreceptors, 144–147, 154–155
    postsynaptic, 53–54
    stretch, 228
    thermal, 204
Receptor blockers, 72
Receptor cells, of vestibular system, 199, 201
Receptor potential, 146
Recording
    of brain's electrical activity, 130–134
    single-unit, 131
Red nucleus, 96, 97
Reduction, 10
Reference memory, 496
Reflexes
    clasp-knife, 233
    in control of movement, 230–234, 235
    monosynaptic stretch, 230–232, 233
    polysynaptic, 232–234
    secondary, 235
    simple, 43–45
    spinal, 315–317
    vestibulo-ocular, 200
Refractory period, 299
Regulatory mechanisms, 372–373
Reinforcement, 435, 465–477
    alcohol and, 589
    anatomy of, 466–478
    by brain stimulation, 465–471
    dopamine and, 473–474
    dopamine agonists in, 468–469
    dopamine antagonists in, 467–468
    dopaminergic pathways in, 466–467
    drugs and, 467–471
    medial forebrain bundle in, 465–466, 469
    microdialysis studies and, 471
    negative, 468, 589
    neural circuitry of, 465–471, 473–477
    neurochemistry of, 466–477
    nucleus accumbens in, 467, 471, 474–476
    positive, 589
    self-stimulation and, 465
Reinforcers, 435, 472
Reinforcing stimulus, 435, 471–473
Relation, 490
Relational learning, 436, 482–509
    anterograde amnesia and, 488–490
    failure of, 488–490

hippocampus and, 485, 496, 497–508
    in laboratory animals, 494–509
    spatial perception and, 496–497
    working memory and, 495–496
Release zone, 50
REM sleep, 256–258, 260, 261–262, 263, 278
    without atonia, 269–270, 287
    characteristics of, 258
    depression and, 266–267, 563–564
    deprivation of, 266, 563–564
    disorders of, 269–270
    functions of, 265–267
    learning and, 265–266
    major affective disorders and, 563–564
    mental activity in, 258
    neural control of, 279, 283–288
    paralysis in, 257, 269, 287
    stress and, 266
Renin, 381, 383
Reproductive behavior, 292–329
    hormonal control of, 298–315, 327–328
    human, 307–313, 315–323
    in laboratory animals, 299–307, 315–329
    maternal behavior and, 324–329
    menstrual cycles and, 298–299, 306–307, 310
    neural control of, 315–323, 328–329
    pheromones in, 303–307
    sexual development and, 292–298
Research
    on analysis of form, 169–175
    animal, 12–15
    goals of, 10–11
    on perception of color, 167–169
    on perception of movement, 175–177
Research techniques, 108–139
    analyzing chemicals in interstitial fluid, 122–123
    electron microscopy, 123
    evaluation of behavioral effects of brain damage, 125
    experimental ablation, 6, 124–130
    histological procedures, 108–110
    lesion production, 125–127
    localization of neurochemicals, 114–116
    localization of receptors, 116, 117

Research techniques (*continued*)
measurement of metabolic activity, 116–117
microiontophoresis, 136
neuroanatomical and neurochemical procedures, 108–124
stereotaxic surgery, 127–130
stimulation or inhibition of brain, 134–138
in study of living brain, 117–122
tracing of neural connections, 110–113
Reserpine, 71, 560
Responses
adaptive, 259–260
autonomic, 332
behavioral, 332
conditional, 433
coping, 334, 362–363
emotional, 332–343
fight-or-flight, 359
freezing, 334, 335
hormonal, 332
startle, 335–336, 337
in stimulus-response learning, 432–435, 462–478, 486
stress, 359–362
unconditional, 433
Rest-activity cycle, 257, 271
Resting potential, 31
Restorative function of sleep, 260–265
Reticular formation, 95–96, 249
Reticular membrane, 184
Reticulospinal tracts, 239–240, 241, 246, 247
Retina, 144
anatomy of, 144–145
coding of visual information in, 150–157
neural circuitry in, 147
photoreceptors in, 144–147, 154–155
Retinal, 146
Retinal disparity, 161–162
Retinal ganglion cells, 145, 150–152, 155–156
Retrograde amnesia, 482, 508
Retrograde labeling methods, 112, 113
Reuptake, 56, 72–73
Rhinal fissure, 448
Rhodopsin, 146
Ribonucleic acid (RNA), 22, 114–116, 117
Ribosomes, 22, 24

Rigidity, decerebrate, 233
RNA (ribonucleic acid), 22, 114–116, 117
Rods, of eye, 144–145
Rostral, 78, 79
Rostroventral medulla, 208–209
Rough endoplasmic reticulum, 23, 24
Round window, 184, 185
Rubrospinal tract, 238–239, 241
Ruffini corpuscles, 202

Saccadic movements, 144
Saccule, 198, 199, 200
Sagittal sections, 78, 80
Salt appetite, 377–383, 388–389, 391–392
Saltatory conduction, 39
Saltiness, 213, 214–215, 216, 218
Saralasin, 382
Satiety factors, in eating, 412–413
Satiety mechanisms, 372
in drinking, 372–373, 389–392
in eating, 401–402
Saturation, 143
Scala media, 184
Scala tympani, 184
Scala vestibuli, 184
Scanning electron microscope, 123
Schaffer collateral system, 449
Schizophrenia, 542–557
biochemical abnormalities in, 547–548
brain damage in, 549–556
dopamine hypothesis of, 63–64, 545–549
drug treatment of, 548–549
heritability of, 543–545
as neurological disorder, 549–556
nongenetic factors for, 545
paranoid, 586
symptoms of, 542–543, 546–547, 553–556
viral cause of, 550–551
Schizophrenic gene, 543–545
Schwann cells, 27–28, 38–39
SCN (suprachiasmatic nucleus), 272–275, 277, 417
SDN (sexually dimorphic nucleus), 317–318
Seasonal affective disorder, 565
Seasonality effect, 551
Secondary reflex, 235
Second messengers, 54
Sectioning, of brain tissue, 108–109
Seizures, 66–67, 206

electrical stimulation and, 137
scanning brain for, 120–122
split-brain operation and, 11–12, 13
Selective advantage, 8–9
Selective permeability, 29
Self-administration, of drugs, 469
Self-awareness, 4, 11–12
Self-stimulation, 465
Semantic agraphia, 537
Semicircular canals, 198–199
Seminal vesicles, 293
Sensory neurons, 20
Sensory-specific satiety, 401–402
Serotonergic drugs, 353–354
Serotonergic neurons, 283, 560–561
Serotonin (5–HT), 65–66, 68, 210
depression and, 560–561, 562
eating and, 418, 421, 426, 428
panic disorder and, 573
sleep and, 288
Serotonin agonist, 573
Serotonin antagonist, 575–576
Set point, 372
Sex, determination of, 292–295
Sex attractant pheromones, 305–307
Sex characteristics, 295–297
Sex chromosomes, 292–293, 294, 544–545, 579
Sex hormones
activational effects of. *See* Activational effects of sex hormones
aggression and, 48, 354–359
in development of sex organs, 293–295
in female reproductive cycle, 298–299
in human sexual behavior, 298–315
in laboratory animals, 299–307
in maternal behavior, 327–328
organizational effects of. *See* Organizational effects of sex hormones
in sexual maturation, 295–297
Sex organs, 292–295
Sexual behavior
female, 298–299, 301, 310–311, 320–322
hormonal control of, 298–315
human, 307–315, 317–322
of laboratory animals, 299–307, 315–329
male, 299–301, 311–312, 315–320
neural control of, 315–323
orientation in, 312–313
pheromones in, 303–307

Sexual development, 292–298
Sexual dimorphism, 292–298
Sexually dimorphic behaviors, 292
Sexually dimorphic nucleus (SDN), 317–318
Sexual maturation, 295–297
Sexual orientation, 312–313
SFO (subfornical organ), 384, 385, 386, 387
Sham feeding, 411
Shock treatment, 558, 559, 562
Short-term memory, 484, 485
SIDS (sudden infant death syndrome), 268
Simple cells, 158
Simple reflex, 43–45
Simple stimulus, 337–339
Simultanagnosia, 178
Sine-wave grating, 158–159
Single-unit recording, 131
Single-unit smooth muscles, 230
Skeletal muscles, 226–229
Skin
    anatomy of, 202–203
    glabrous, 202
    hairy, 202
Skin senses. *See* Cutaneous senses
Sleep
    as adaptive response, 259–260
    biological clocks and, 271–278
    brain mechanisms of, 272–289
    chemical control of, 278–279
    circadian rhythms in, 271–272, 273, 275–277
    deprivation of, 260–262, 263, 563–565
    disorders of, 267–271
    eating and, 264
    EEG during, 254–256, 257
    exercise and, 262–264
    functions of, 265–267
    mental activity and, 258–259, 264
    neural control of, 279–288
    non-REM, 256, 257
    paradoxical, 256
    physiological mechanisms of, 278–289
    reasons for, 259–267
    as restorative process, 260–265
    stages of, 254–258
    suprachiasmatic nucleus role in, 272–275, 277
    wakefulness vs., 279–281
    See also REM sleep; Slow-wave sleep

Sleep apnea, 268
Sleep attack, 269
Sleep deprivation
    effects of, 260–262, 263, 563–565
    major affective disorders and, 563–565
    of REM sleep, 266, 563–564
    of slow-wave sleep, 262
Sleep laboratory, 254
Sleep paralysis, 257, 269, 287
Sleep spindles, 255–256
Sleepwalking, 270, 271
Slow-wave sleep, 256
    characteristics of, 258
    deprivation of, 262
    disorders of, 270–271
    exercise and, 263
    mental activity in, 258–259, 264
    neural control of, 281–283
    physiological mechanisms in, 264–265
Smell. *See* Olfaction
Smoking, 586–587, 588
Smooth endoplasmic reticulum, 23, 24
Smooth muscle, 230
SNB (spinal nucleus of the bulbocavernosus), 315–317
Social situations, emotional responses to, 340–343
Sodium balance, 375–376, 378
Sodium chloride, 213, 214–215, 216, 218. *See also* Salt appetite
Sodium ions (Na+)
    in action potential, 35–37
    in membrane potential, 33–35
    in postsynaptic potential, 54, 55
Sodium-potassium pump, 35
Sodium-potassium transporters, 34
Solitary tract, nucleus of, 217, 384, 414
Soluble gases, 69–70
Soma, 20, 21
Somatic nervous system, 102
Somatosensation, 142
Somatosenses, 201–212
    anatomy of skin in, 202–203
    pain perception and, 204–205, 206–211
    pathways of, 205–206
    stimuli of, 201–202, 203–205
    temperature perception and, 204
    transduction by, 203
    types of, 201

Somatosensory association cortex, 91, 339–340
Somatosensory cortex, primary, 90, 205–206, 236–237
Somatosensory pathways, 205–206
Somnambulism, 270, 271
Sound, localization of, 194–196
Sound waves, 182, 194
Sourness, 213, 215–216, 218
Spatial frequency, 158–160, 161
Spatial learning, 436
Spatial perception, 496–497
Specific immune reaction, 365
Speech
    comprehension of, 512–513, 517–528
    lateralization and, 512–513
    physiological basis of, 6
    production of, 513–516
    prosody in, 526–527
Speech disorders
    agrammatism, 515
    anomia, 515
    anomic aphasia, 523–526, 528
    articulation difficulties, 515–516
    Broca's aphasia, 513, 514–516, 528
    conduction aphasia, 522–523, 528
    pure word deafness, 348, 518–519, 528
    transcortical sensory aphasia, 519–520, 528
    Wernicke's aphasia, 517–526, 528
Spelling dyslexia, 534, 539
Spinal cord, 98–99
Spinal foramens, 98
Spinal nerves, 100–101
Spinal nucleus of the bulbocavernosus (SNB), 315–317
Spinal reflexes, in sexual behavior, 315–317
Spinal roots, 98, 99
Spinal sympathetic ganglia, 103, 104
Spinothalamic tract, 205
Spiral ganglion, 188
Split-brain operation, 11–12, 13
Staining, 109–110, 111, 113, 114
Stapes, 183, 184
Startle response, 335–336, 337
Stereopsis, 162
Stereotaxic apparatus, 129–130
Stereotaxic atlas, 128–129
Stereotaxic surgery, 127–130
Stereotaxis, 128
Steroids, 59
    anabolic, 357–358

stress and, 360–361
Stimulation, of brain, 134–137, 138, 208–209, 210, 451–454, 465–471
Stimulus
  complex, 339–343
  conditional, 433
  with emotional significance, 337–343
  punishing, 435
  reinforcing, 435, 471–473
  sensory association cortex and, 339–340
  simple, 337–339
  thalamus and, 337–339
  unconditional, 433
Stimulus-response learning, 432–435, 462–478, 486
Stomach
  in termination of drinking, 390
  in termination of eating, 408–409, 425–426
Stress, 359–370
  cardiovascular disease and, 363–364
  coping response and, 362–363
  health and, 359
  physiology of, 359–362
  psychoneuroimmunology and, 365–369
  REM sleep and, 266
Stressors, 359
Stress response, 359–362
Stretch receptors, in skeletal muscles, 228
Stretch reflex, monosynaptic, 230–232, 233
Striate cortex, 148, 157–166
  anatomy of, 157–158
  color vision and, 162–163
  modular organization of, 163–165
  role in vision, 157–166
Striated muscle, 226
Stria terminalis, 326
Strokes, 14, 512
Subarachnoid space, 81, 82
Subcoerulear nucleus, 287
Subcortical brain lesions, 126
Subcortical regions, 88
Subcutaneous tissue, 202
Subfornical organ (SFO), 384, 385, 386, 387
Subicular complex, 448
Submissive behaviors, 353
Subsensitivity, 561
Substantia nigra, 63, 96, 97

Sudden infant death syndrome (SIDS), 268
Suicide, 560–561
Sulci, 88
Superior colliculi, 95, 97
Superior olivary complex, 189, 196
Supersensitivity, 549
Supporting cells, 25–29
Suprachiasmatic nucleus (SCN), 272–275, 277, 417
Supraoptic nucleus of the hypothalamus, 376, 386
Surface dyslexia, 532–533, 539
Surgery
  for obesity, 425
  psychosurgery, 341–343
  removing epileptic focus, 137
  stereotaxic, 127–130
Sweetness, 213, 215, 216, 218
Sydenham's chorea, 575
Sympathetic apraxia, 242
Sympathetic chain, 103, 104
Sympathetic division of ANS, 102–103, 104
Synapses, 20
  axoaxonic, 58
  axodendritic, 58
  axosomatic, 58
  dendrodendritic, 58
  excitatory, 42
  increases in strength of, 454–459
  inhibitory, 42
  location of, 20, 23
  in neural communication, 48–58
  pharmacology of, 70–74
  structure of, 49–50
Synaptic changes, location of, 474–477
Synaptic cleft, 49
Synaptic plasticity, mechanisms of, 447–462
Synaptic vesicles, 49–53
Synchrony, 255
System variable, 372

Tachistoscope, 346
Tardive dyskinesia, 548–549
Taste
  eating and, 402–403
  neural coding of, 218
  qualities of, 213, 214–217, 218
  See also Gustation
Taste buds, 213–214
Tectorial membrane, 184, 186, 192
Tectospinal tract, 239, 240, 241

Tectum, 95
Tegmentum, 95–96, 97
Telencephalon, 85, 86, 88–92
Temperature
  brown adipose tissue and, 424–425
  perception of, 204
  REM sleep and, 287–288
Temporal cortex, inferior, 169–171
Temporal lobes, 88, 89, 339
Tendons, 226
Terminal buttons, 21–22, 51–52
Testis-determining factor, 293
Testosterone, 293, 296–297
  activational effects of, 311–312, 355
  aggressive behavior and, 48, 354, 355, 356–357, 358
  organizational effects, 355
Tetrodotoxin (TTX), 276
Texture, perception of, 160–161, 162
Thalamus, 92–99, 147, 190, 206
  nuclei of, 93
  posterior intralaminar nucleus of, 338, 462, 463
  stimulus and, 337–339
THC (tetrahydrocannibinal), 68–69, 587–588
Thermal receptors, 204
Thermogenesis, nonshivering, 424
Theta activity, 255, 502–504
Theta behaviors, 503
Third ventricle, 82, 83
Thirst. *See* Drinking
Thoracolumbar system, 103
Thought disorder, 542
Threat behaviors, 353
Threshold of excitation, 32
Timbre, 182, 193
Time differences, 195
T-lymphocytes, 365, 367
Tolerance, 583, 584
Tomography
  computerized, 117–118, 119
  positron emission, 119–120, 121
Tongue, 213, 214
Tonotopic representation, 190
Touch, 142, 202–203. *See also* Cutaneous senses
Tourette's syndrome, 573–574, 579, 580
Tracing methods, 110–113
  anterograde, 111, 113
  retrograde, 112, 113
Transcortical sensory aphasia, 519–520, 528
Transduction

auditory, 186–188, 189
gustatory, 214–217
olfactory, 221
sensory, 203
visual, 146, 147
Transmitter substances, 21, 48–49, 386
effects of drugs on, 70–74
in neural communication, 61–70
release of, 48–49, 50–53, 71–72
reuptake of, 72–73
types of, 61–70
Transorbital leucotome, 342
Trichotillomania, 576
Trichromatic coding, 154–155
Trichromatic theory, 153
Tricyclic antidepressants, 558
Triglycerides, 397, 398
Tritanopia, 155
Tryptophan, 66, 561
Tryptophan hydroxylase, 66, 70
TTX (tetrodotoxin), 276
Tuning curves, auditory, 191, 192
Turner's syndrome, 294, 295
Twin studies
of autistic disorder, 578–579
of major affective disorders, 558
of panic disorder, 570–571
of schizophrenia, 543, 552
of sexual orientation, 313
Tympanic membrane, 183
Type A pattern of behavior, 363–364
Type B pattern of behavior, 363–364
Tyrosine kinase, 457

Umami, 217
Unconditional response (UR), 433
Unconditional stimulus (US), 433
Unipolar depression, 557
Unipolar neurons, 21, 22
Ureter, 375
Uterus, 293
Utricle, 198, 199, 200

Vagina, 293
Vagus nerve, 101
Valium, 67, 572, 589
Vandenbergh effect, 303
Vas deferens, 293
Vasoactive intestinal peptide (VIP), 68
Vasopressin, 68, 319, 320, 375–376, 378
Ventral, 78, 79
Ventral cochlear nucleus, 336

Ventral corticospinal tract, 237–238, 241
Ventral lateral geniculate nucleus, 273
Ventral nucleus of the lateral lemniscus, 336
Ventral roots, 99
Ventral tegmental area (VTA), 328, 353, 466, 467, 473
Ventricles, 3, 82, 83
Ventricular system, 82–83
Ventrolateral nucleus, 93, 94
Ventromedial nucleus of the hypothalamus (VMH), 320–322, 415
Ventromedial pathways, 238, 239–240, 241
Verbal learning, 487–488
Vergence movements, 144
Vermis, 246
Vertebral arteries, 80, 81
Vestibular apparatus, 198–199
Vestibular ganglion, 200
Vestibular hair cells, 199, 201
Vestibular nerve, 200
Vestibular pathway, 199–200
Vestibular sacs, 198, 199
Vestibular system, 198–201
Vestibule, 183
Vestibulo-ocular reflex, 200
Vestibulospinal tract, 239, 240, 241, 246, 247
Vibration, sensation of, 201, 203
Vigilance, and REM sleep, 265
VIP (vasoactive intestinal peptide), 68
Viruses, and schizophrenia, 550–551
Vision, 142–180
anatomy of, 143–150, 157–158
blindsight, 165
blind spot in, 145
color, 144–145, 152–156, 162–163, 167–169
extrastriate cortex in, 166
eye, 143–149
eye-brain connections in, 147–149
form and, 169–175
foveal, 144–145
inferior temporal cortex in, 169–171
light and, 142–143, 150–152
location and, 177–179
movement and, 158, 175–177
night, 145
orientation and, 158
photoreceptors in, 144, 146–147, 154–155

primary visual cortex in, 90, 162–163, 529, 531
receptive fields in, 150, 155
retinal coding of information and, 150–157
retinal disparity and, 161–162
retinal ganglion cells and, 145, 150–152, 155–156
spatial frequency and, 158–160, 161
stimulus in, 142–143
striate cortex and, 148, 157–166
texture and, 160–161, 162
transduction in, 146, 147
visual association cortex in, 91, 166–179
Visual acuity, 144
Visual agnosia, 171–175
apperceptive, 172–174
associative, 174–175
Visual association cortex, 91
analysis of form and, 169–175
perception of color and, 167–169
perception of movement and, 175–176
role of, 166–179
visual analysis and, 166–167
Visual cortex, primary. See Primary visual cortex
Visual information
analysis of, 157–179
coding of, 150–157
Visual learning, 437–443
Visual pathway, primary, 147–149
VMH (ventromedial nucleus of the hypothalamus), 320–322, 415
VMH syndrome, 415
Voice, tone of, 346–347. See also Speech
Volta, Alessandro, 5
Voltage-dependent ion channels, 36
Volumetric thirst, 377, 380–382
Vomeronasal organ, 221, 304
Von Békésy, Georg, 184, 191, 192
VTA (ventral tegmental area), 328, 353, 466, 467, 473

Wada test, 483, 512
Wakefulness
biological clocks in, 271–278
neural control of, 279–281
WCST (Wisconsin Card Sort Test), 553, 554
Weight, regulation of, 398–399
Wernicke's aphasia, 517–526, 528

Wernicke's area, 514, 517, 521, 537, 538
White blood cells, 365–366, 367, 368
White matter, 88, 89
White noise, 192
Whitten effect, 303
Whole-word reading, 531, 533
Wiesel, Torsten, 157–158
Wisconsin Card Sort Test (WCST), 553, 554
Withdrawal symptoms, 583–585, 590
Wolffian system, 293
Word(s)
    comprehension of, 517–526
    content, 514
    function, 514
    meaning of, 520–522
Word blindness, pure, 529–531, 539
Word deafness, pure, 348, 518–519, 528
Word-form dyslexia, 534, 539
Working memory, 495–496
Writing disorders, 528–529, 535–539
    acquired dyslexias, 532
    aphasia and, 528–529
    developmental dyslexias, 532, 537–539
    direct dysgraphia, 537
    orthographic dysgraphia, 536, 537, 539
    phonological dysgraphia, 536, 539
    semantic agraphia, 537

X chromosome, 292–293, 294
    fragile X syndrome and, 579
    schizophrenia and, 544–545

Y chromosome, 292–293, 294, 544–545
Yoked-control procedure, 262
Young, Thomas, 153

Zeitgeber, 272, 273, 565–566
Zona incerta, 387–388